OXFORD PAPERBACK REFERENCE

THE OXFORD COMPANION TO CLASSICAL LITERATURE

THE OXFORD COMPANION TO CLASSICAL LITERATURE

Compiled by

PAUL HARVEY

Oxford   New York

OXFORD UNIVERSITY PRESS

Oxford University Press, Walton Street, Oxford OX2 6DP

Oxford New York Toronto
Delhi Bombay Calcutta Madras Karachi
Kuala Lumpur Singapore Hong Kong Tokyo
Nairobi Dar es Salaam Cape Town
Melbourne Auckland
and associated companies in
Beirut Berlin Ibadan Nicosia

Oxford is a trade mark of Oxford University Press

First published October 1937
Reprinted with corrections 1940, 1946, 1951, 1955
1959, 1962, 1966, 1969, 1974, 1980, 1984
First issued as an Oxford University Press paperback 1984
Reprinted 1984
Paperback and hardback reprinted 1986

British Library Cataloguing in Publication Data
Harvey, Paul, 1869–1948
The Oxford companion to classical literature.
—(Oxford paperbacks)
1. Classical literature—Dictionaries
I. Title
880'.03'21   PA31
ISBN 0–19–281490–7 pbk
ISBN 0–19–866103–7

Library of Congress Cataloging in Publication Data
Harvey, Paul, 1869–1948.
The Oxford companion to classical literature.
(Oxford paperbacks)
1. Classical dictionaries.   I. Title.
DE5.H3 1984   880'.03   84–871
ISBN 0–19–281490–7 (pbk.)
ISBN 0–19–866103–7

Printed in Great Britain by
Richard Clay (The Chaucer Press) Ltd.
Bungay, Suffolk

PREFACE

THE aim of this book, as designed by the publishers, is to present, in convenient form, information which the ordinary reader, not only of the literatures of Greece and Rome, but also of that large proportion of modern European literature which teems with classical allusions, may find useful. It endeavours to do two things: in the first place to bring together what he may wish to know about the evolution of classical literature, the principal authors, and their chief works; in the second place, to depict so much of the historical, political, social, and religious background as may help to make the classics understood. Accordingly, for the first of the above purposes, articles in alphabetical arrangement (1) explain the various elements of classical literature—epic, tragedy, comedy, metre, &c; (2) give an account of the principal authors; and (3) describe the subjects or contents of their works, either under the name of the author, or, where more convenient, under the title of the work itself. Interesting points of connexion between the classics and medieval and modern English literature are noticed. In general the book confines itself to the classical period, but some authors of the decline, such as Plutarch and Lucian, Jerome and Ausonius, are included, because of their exceptional interest or importance.

In addition, to effect the second of the above purposes, articles are added:

(1) on the principal phases of the history of Greece (more particularly Athens) and Rome, down to the end of the period of their classical literatures, and on their political institutions and economic conditions; outstanding historical characters, inseparable from literature, such as Pericles and Pompey, are separately mentioned;

(2) on Greek and Roman religion and religious institutions, and the principal schools of philosophy;

(3) on various aspects of the social conditions, under such

headings as *Houses*, *Women* (*Position of*), *Slavery*, *Education*, *Food*, *Clothing*, and *Games*; the art, industry, commerce, and agriculture of the Greek and Roman periods are also noticed;

(4) on the more important myths and mythological characters, as an essential element in Greek and Roman literature;

(5) on geographical names of importance in a literary connexion, as the birthplaces of authors, or as the scene of events frequently alluded to; something is said of the topography of Athens and Rome, and further geographical information is furnished by maps and plans;

(6) on the manner in which ancient books were written, and the texts transmitted and studied through the ages;

(7) on such things as Roman camps, roads, and aqueducts, ancient ships and chariot-races, horses and elephants in antiquity, and domestic pets.

It should be remembered, nevertheless, that this work does not include articles on antiquities as such, but only those antiquities which concern the study of classical literature.

The compiler of a book such as this is necessarily under a heavy debt to previous writers. It would be impossible, within the limits of a preface, to enumerate the works, whether editions of and commentaries on ancient authors, or treatises on various aspects of antiquity, which have been consulted in the course of its preparation. Of such works I may specially mention, rather as an illustrative sample than as giving any indication of the extent of my obligations, the works of Werner Jaeger on Aristotle, of Prof. Gilbert Murray on Aristophanes, of C. M. Bowra on Homer, of Sir J. C. Sandys on Epigraphy and on the History of Scholarship, of A. W. Pickard-Cambridge on the evolution of the Greek drama, of F. G. Kenyon and F. W. Hall on ancient books, of W. W. Tarn on Hellenistic Civilization, of R. C. Jebb on the Attic Orators, and of R. G. Collingwood on Roman Britain. Apart from this general acknowledgement of my indebtedness, I must confine myself to naming a few

works from which I have more especially and more frequently
sought guidance, viz.: in the matter of *Greek Literature*, the
histories of the subject by A. and M. Croiset, Prof. Gilbert
Murray, and Prof. Rose; *Latin Literature*, the works of J. W.
Mackail, R. Pichon, J. Wight Duff, and Prof. Rose; *Greek
mythology and religion*, Prof. Rose's 'Handbook of Greek
Mythology' and M. P. Nilsson's 'History of Greek Religion';
Roman religion, the works of W. Warde Fowler and Cyril Bailey
and Sir J. G. Frazer's commentary on Ovid's 'Fasti'; *Greek
and Roman History*, the works of G. Glotz, M. Cary, J. B. Bury,
M. Rostovtzeff, G. Ferrero, and the Cambridge Ancient History.
On antiquities in general I have obtained much assistance from
the Cambridge Companions to Greek and Latin Studies, from
the dictionaries of Daremberg and Saglio and of Seyffert
(Sandys and Nettleship), and from Stuart Jones's 'Companion
to Roman History'; on points of biography from Lübker's
'Reallexikon'; and on certain matters from the 'Real-Encyclopädie' of Pauly-Wissowa.

I must also acknowledge the helpful suggestions which I have
received from several people who were concerned with this book
in its various stages: from Dr. Cyril Bailey; Mr. J. B. Poynton
of Winchester College; Mr. W. H. Walsh of Merton College,
Oxford; Mr. A. H. M. Jones of All Souls College, Oxford; Mr.
H. A. Murray of King's College, Aberdeen; Mr. J. M. Wyllie;
Mr. S. H. Steadman; and Miss C. M. M. Leask of Aberdeen;
also from the staff of the Clarendon Press. Such value as the
book may have is largely due to them.   H.P.H.

September, 1937.

LIST OF PLATES AND MAPS

PLATES

1. Greek and Roman Houses.
2. Roman Villas and Roman Camp.
3. Greek Armour.
4. Roman Armour.
5. Greek and Roman Theatres.
6. Greek and Roman Temples.

MAPS

7. Asia Minor and the East: Routes of Xerxes, Cyrus, Alexander, and the March of the Ten Thousand.
8. Greece and Asia Minor.
9. Roman Empire.
10. Italy.
11. Gaul.
12. Roman Britain.
13 (a). Athens. (b). Piraeus.
14 (a). Rome under the Republic.
   (b). Centre of Rome under the Early Empire.

GENERAL ARTICLES

THE following selected list indicates the headings under which information on general subjects can be found.

Administration, Public (*Athens*, § 9; *Rome*, § 12).
Agriculture.
Alphabet.
Aqueducts.
Architecture, Greek (for Roman Architecture, see *Art*).
Army.
Art, Roman (for Greek Art see *Architecture, Painting, Sculpture, Toreutic Art*).
Augury and Auspices.
Augustan Age.
Baths.
Birthplaces of Greek and Roman authors.
Books, Ancient.
Burial and Cremation.
Byzantine Age of Greek Literature.
Calendar.
Castra.
Chariot races.
Ciceronian Age.
Classic.
Clothing and Toilet.
Colonization.
Comedy.
Corn Supply.
Dancing.
Dictionaries.
Didactic poetry.
Divination.
Dogs.
Economic Conditions (*Athens*, § 10; *Rome*, § 13).
Editions of Collections of the Classics.
Education.
Elegy.
Elephants.
Epic.
Epigraphy.
Epitaphs.
Festivals.
Finances (*Athens*, § 11; *Rome*, § 14).
Food and Wine.
Games.
Gladiators.
Glass.
Guilds.
Hellenistic Age.
Historians, Ancient, and Modern.
Homeric Age.
Horses.
Houses and Furniture.
Hunting.
Judicial Procedure.
Law, Roman.
Libraries.
Ludi.
Lyric Poetry.
Magic.
Maps.
Metre.
Migrations and Dialects, Greek.
Mines.
Money and Coins.
Monsters.
Museums.
Music.
Mysteries.
Mythology.
Names.
Novel.
Omens.
Oracles.
Oratory.
Ostraca.
Painting, Greek (for Roman Painting see *Art*).
Papyri, Discoveries of.
Pets.
Philosophy.
Pottery.
Priests.
Prose.
Provinces, Roman.
Religion.
Roads.
Roman Age of Greek Literature.
Sacrifice.
Satire.
Satyric Drama.
Sculpture, Greek (for Roman Sculpture see *Art*).
Ships.
Slavery.
Temples.
Texts and Studies.
Theatre.
Tragedy.
Vase-painting.
Weights and Measures.
Women, Position of.

A date chart of Greek and Latin authors and of events contemporary with them is given on pages 455–62.

ABBREVIATIONS

ad fin.: ad finem, at or near the end.
b.: born.
c.: century.
cc.: centuries.
c.: circa, about.
cf.: *confer,* compare.
d.: died.
dr.: daughter.
et seq.: *et sequentes,* and following.
fl.: floruit, flourished.

gen.: genitive.
Gk.: Greek.
L. or Lat.: Latin.
m.: married.
O.T.: Old Testament.
q.v.: *quod vide,* which see.
qq.v.: *quae vide,* both which, or all which, see.
sc.: *scilicet,* understand or supply.

The abbreviated names of authors and works, such as 'Hom. Il.', 'Virg. Aen.', appearing in this book are for the most part sufficiently familiar to need no explanation; but the following may be noted:

Apoph. Reg.: Apophthegmata Regum.
Ep.: Epistulae (Epistles).
Epod.: Epodes.
Nub.: Nubes (Clouds).
Phaed.: Phaedo.

Phaedr.: Phaedrus.
Ran.: Ranae (Frogs).
Sep. c. Th.: Septem contra Thebas (Seven against Thebes).
Vesp.: Vespae (Wasps).

PRELIMINARY NOTE

HEAD-WORDS

PROPER names are entered as head-words in the form in which they are most familiar to ordinary readers, e.g. Ā'jax, A'ristotle, Menelā'us, Phī'dias, Te'rence. The Greek υ appears as *y*, κ as *c*, and final -ος as -*us* where these are the more familiar forms. The correct transliteration of Greek names and the full Latin names are added in brackets where required: e.g. Ā'jax (*Aiās*), A'ristotle (*Aristotelēs*), Menelā'us (*Menelāos*), Phī'dias (*Pheidiās*), Te'rence (*Publius Terentius Āfer*). (Less familiar names, not head-words, such as Āsōpichos, Pherenīkos, are given in transliterated form.)

Latin proper names appear under the person's *nomen* unless he is generally known by his *cognomen*; e.g. Cicero appears under that name, not under 'Tullius'. In a few cases the names are given under the *praenomen*, e.g. Appius Claudius, where this is the customary designation.

QUANTITIES AND PRONUNCIATION

The ordinary English pronunciation of names is shown, by stress and quantity marks, in **head-words** *only* (i.e. in the words printed in **heavy black type** at the beginning of each article). Where the quantities in the English pronunciation differ from those in Greek or Latin, the name is repeated in brackets with the Greek or Latin quantities. The quantities shown in all names and common nouns *other than head-words* are their quantities as Greek or Latin words, and are not necessarily an indication of their accepted pronunciation in English. For instance

(1) **Catu'llus**, GĀĬUS VALĔRIUS,

(2) **Clau'dius** (*Tibĕrius Claudius Nĕrō Germānicus*),

(3) a river in Pamphȳlia,

where **Catu'llus** and **Clau'dius** represent the ordinary English pronunciation, while GĀĬUS, VALĔRIUS, *Tibĕrius*, *Nĕrō*, *Germānicus*, Pamphȳlia, show the quantities of the Latin or Greek names.

In general only the long vowels are marked, and vowels are to be taken as short unless marked as long; but

(1) a syllable in which the vowel is long (or common) by position,

under the ordinary rules of Greek and Latin prosody, as being followed by two consonants, is usually not marked; e.g. the first syllables in Thersītēs, Petrōnius;

(2) the vowels of Latin case-endings which are long by the ordinary rules of Latin prosody, for instance -o, -a, -is of the ablative, -i, -orum, -arum of the genitive, are not marked; e.g. De Amīcitia.

(3) short vowels are occasionally marked with the short sign, e.g. for emphasis, as where a vowel which is short in Greek or Latin is usually pronounced long in English; e.g. Sō'lon (Sŏlōn), Tī'tus (Titus).

Where a vowel is common (sometimes short, sometimes long) otherwise than under (1) above, this is indicated by the sign ⌣; e.g. Dĭāna. Where, in a name of some importance, a quantity is unknown or uncertain, the fact is stated.

The groups of letters AE, AI, AU, EI, EU, OU, are to be taken as diphthongs unless it is indicated that the letters are to be pronounced separately, e.g. Alphē'us, Anti'nŏus.

Where a name which appears as a head-word occurs also elsewhere in the course of an article, the quantities are not always again indicated there. For instance, where 'Socrates' occurs in the article on Plato, it is printed without indication of the quantities. The great majority of the names of persons and places mentioned in the course of articles are given also as head-words, if only for purpose of cross-reference; and this applies also to Greek and Latin common nouns such as ecclesia, venationes. Accordingly a reader who desires to know the quantities of the syllables of such a name or noun should first look for it among the head-words. If it does not appear there and no quantities are marked where it is found in an article, it may be inferred that its syllables are short.

COMPANION TO
CLASSICAL LITERATURE

A

Abbreviations denoting certain editions of the Classics, etc.

ALG. *Anthologia Lyrica Graeca.*

Budé. *Collection des Universités de France, publiée sous le patronage de l'Assoc. Guillaume Budé.*

CAF. *Comicorum Atticorum Fragmenta.*

CAH. *Cambridge Ancient History.*

CGF. *Comicorum Graecorum Fragmenta.*

CIE. *Corpus Inscriptionum Etruscarum.*

CIG. *Corpus Inscriptionum Graecarum.*

CIL. *Corpus Inscriptionum Latinarum.*

CLA. *Codices Latini Antiquiores.*

Cl. Qu. *Classical Quarterly.*

Cl. Rev. *Classical Review.*

CPL. *Corpus Poetarum Latinorum.*

CRF. *Comicorum Romanorum Fragmenta.*

FdV. *Fragmente der Vorsokratiker.*

FHG. *Fragmenta Historicorum Graecorum.*

HRR. *Historicorum Romanorum Reliquiae.*

IG. *Inscriptiones Graecae* (Berlin, 1873–).

IGA. *Inscriptiones Graecae Antiquissimae* (Berlin, 1882).

JHS. *Journal of Hellenic Studies.*

OCT. *Oxford Classical Texts.*

PLG. *Poetae Lyrici Graeci.*

RE. *Pauly-Wissowa, Real-Encyclopädie.*

Rev. Arc. *Revue Archéologique.*

SEG. *Supplementum Epigraphicum Graecum.*

SVF. *Stoicorum Veterum Fragmenta.*

Teubner or **BT.** *Bibliotheca scriptorum Graec. et Lat. Teubneriana.*

Thes. L. L. *Thesaurus Linguae Latinae.*

Abdē′ra (τὰ Ἄβδηρα), a Greek city on the coast of Thrace, founded in the 7th c. and refounded in the 6th by Ionians (of Teŏs in Asia Minor), the birthplace of Protagoras and Democritus (qq.v.); nevertheless proverbial for the stupidity of its inhabitants.

Absy′rtus (*Apsurtos*), brother of Medea; see *Argonauts.*

Aby′dos (*Abŭdos*), see *Colonization*, § 2, and *Leander.*

Acadē′mica, a dialogue by Cicero on the philosophical theories of knowledge, composed in 45 B.C. In its first form the treatise consisted of two books, and the interlocutors were L. Licinius Lucullus (q.v.), Q. Lutătius Catulus, an aristocratic leader (consul in 78 B.C.), Q. Hortensius (q.v.), and Cicero. The two books of this first edition were called 'Catulus' and 'Lucullus' after the chief interlocutors. Cicero then came to the conclusion that these interlocutors could not agree, and as Varro had asked that a work should be dedicated to him, Cicero altered his plan and dedicated a new edition to him. He rearranged the work in four books, and made the interlocutors Varro, Atticus, and Cicero. We have the first book (i.e. the first quarter) of the second edition (sometimes known as 'Academica Posteriora'), and the second book (i.e. the second half, 'Lucullus') of the first edition (sometimes known as 'Academica Priora'). The scene of the conversations is laid at various villas on the shores of the Gulf of Naples. The date of the conversations, in the first edition, was supposed to be before 60 B.C.; in the second, near the time of composition.

In Book I of the second edition Varro expounds the evolution of the doctrines of the Academy (q.v.), from the dogmatism of the old school to the scepticism of Arcesilas and Carneades. In Book II of the first edition Lucullus attacks the position of the sceptics. Cicero defends the sceptic view and Carneades' doctrine of probability.

Acadē′mus, see *Academy.*

Academy (*Akadēmeia*), a grove of olive-trees near Athens, adjoining the Cēphĭsus, sacred to the hero Acadēmus (see *Dioscuri*), and containing a gymnasium (q.v.). It was in this grove that Plato and his successors taught, and his school of philosophy was in consequence known as the Academy,

the olive grove of Academe,

Plato's retirement, where the Attic bird
Trills her thick-warbl'd notes the summer
    long. (Milton, P.R. iv. 244 et seq.).

Sulla cut down the trees during his siege of Athens, but they must have grown again, for Horace, who studied at Athens, refers to the 'woods of Academus' (Ep. II. ii. 45). Plato was buried near the grove.

His immediate successors as leaders of the school were Speusippus, Xenocrates, Polemo, and Crates, and the Academy under these leaders was known as the Old Academy. A brief account of the general character of the Platonic teaching will be found under *Plato*, § 3. Arcesilas of Pitanē (c. 315–240 B.C.), who introduced the doctrines of Pyrrhonian scepticism (see *Sceptics*) into the teaching of the school and engaged in controversy with the Stoics on the question of the certitude of knowledge, was the founder of what is known as the Second or Middle Academy. This sceptical attitude was further developed by Carneades (q.v.) in the 2nd c. B.C. Antiochus of Ascalon in the 1st c. B.C. effected a reconciliation with the Stoic school and claimed to restore the Old Academy. See also *Neoplatonism*.

Aca′stus (*Akastos*), son of Pelias (see *Argonauts*) and father of Laodameia (see *Protesilaus*). See also *Peleus*.

Acca Lāre′ntia or LAURE′NTIA, probably originally an Italian goddess of the earth to whom the seed was entrusted. She was worshipped at the *Lārentālia* on Dec. 23. In legend she was the wife of the herdsman Faustulus and the nurse of Romulus and Remus. For a discussion of her possible connexion with the Lares (q.v.) see Frazer on Ov. Fast. iii. 55.

Accents, GREEK, were invented by Aristophanes of Byzantium (q.v.), about the beginning of the 2nd c. B.C., with a view to preserving the correct pronunciation, which in the Hellenistic Age was being corrupted by the extension of the Greek language to many new countries. The accents indicated not stress but variations in the pitch of the voice. The grave accent signified the ordinary tone, the acute a rise in the voice, the circumflex a rise followed by a fall. In the period of papyrus rolls (see *Books*) accents are as a rule only occasionally indicated. The use of them became generalized about the 3rd c. A.D. The most important work on accentuation was that of Herodian (q.v.). H. W. Chandler's *Greek Accentuation* (2nd ed. 1881, Clarendon Press) is a standard treatise on this subject.

A′ccius or A′TTIUS, LŪCIUS (170–c.86 B.C.), a Latin poet, probably of Pisaurum in Umbria, of a humble family. He was a younger contemporary of Pacuvius (q.v.), whom he rivalled as a great Roman tragedian. Cicero records that he conversed with him. We have the titles of some 45 of his tragedies, which dealt with Greek themes such as Andromeda, Medea, Philoctetes. He also wrote two *praetextae* (q.v.) (on Decius Mus and Brutus the liberator) and works on literature ('Didascalica', a short history of Greek and Latin poetry, perhaps in verse and prose, thus anticipating the 'Menippean Satires' of Varro), agriculture (in verse), and history (annals, of rather a mythological and theological character, in verse). He was the first great Latin grammarian of whom tradition tells. His tragedies were marked by dignity of style and by the faculty of depicting terror, pathos, and fortitude. He is perhaps the first Latin poet to show some appreciation of the beauty of nature. His 'Atreus' contained the tyrant's phrase 'Oderint dum metuant', said by Suetonius to have been frequently in Caligula's mouth.

Ace′stēs, in the 'Aeneid', son of the Sicilian river-god Crīmīsus and a Trojan woman (Egesta or Segesta). He entertains Aeneas and his comrades in Sicily.

Achae′a, Achae′ans (*Achaia, Achaioi*). 'Achaeans', according to a view widely held by modern students, was the name by which the first Hellenic invaders of Greece were called (see *Migrations and Dialects*), and Achaea was the name of two territories in Greece, the region where they first settled in the north (the name was subsequently restricted to the mountains of Phthīā), and a strip along the southern shore of the Corinthian Gulf, which they occupied later. But it is pointed out that there is no evidence of any tradition that the Achaeans were invaders, and that Herodotus and Pausanias speak of them as autochthonous. Homer uses the term in two senses: in a narrower sense of a people inhabiting the kingdom of Achilles near the Sperchēus in Thessaly, and in a wider sense of the Greek army besieging Troy and of the Greeks generally, no doubt because the Achaeans were a prominent tribe among them.

The Achaeans of the Peloponnese were the founders, probably in the 8th c. B.C., of the important group of colonies at the southern extremity of Italy (including Sybaris and Croton) which formed the greater part of what was known as Magna Graecia. Much later, Peloponnesian Achaea became important in the history of the 3rd c. B.C. as the centre of the Achaean League (q.v.). In a later age again Achāia was the name given by the Romans to the province, comprising the greater part of Greece, formed by Augustus.

Achaean League, a league of cities of Achaea in the Peloponnese which had detached themselves from the rule of Antigonus Gonātas (see *Macedonia*, § 3) in 275 B.C. Its constitution is interesting because the affairs of the League were administered by a Council composed of delegations from the cities in proportion to their population; each delegation was chosen by its city, but we do not know by what method. It was the nearest approach to representative government which we find in Greece. The power and influence of the League increased under the leadership of Arātus of Sicyōn, who from 245 was for thirty years the director of the League's policy, and in alternate years its general (he wrote his 'Memoirs', now lost, and there is a life of him by Plutarch, including a vivid description of his capture of Corinth). He made the League the leading power in the Peloponnese, with Corinth as its chief stronghold. On the military side the League subsequently derived great strength from the ability of Philopoemen (q.v.), and was finally (in 188) able to overcome Sparta herself. But its high-handed policy brought it into conflict with Rome. After the defeat of the Macedonians at Pydna (168), Rome, as a measure of future security, deported to Italy a thousand Achaeans suspected of hostility to her cause; among these was Polybius (q.v.). In 148, when the surviving exiles (other than Polybius) had returned to Greece, there was again trouble between the League and Sparta. Rome intervened and imposed harsh terms on the League. The League rebelled and declared war, but after a short struggle was completely defeated by Mummius in 146 and dissolved.

Achaeme′nidae, the first royal house of Persia, so named from the hero Achaemenēs (Pers. *Hakhāmanis*), founder of the family. To this family belonged Cyrus, Cambyses, and Darius (see *Persian Wars*).

Acha′rnians (*Acharnēs*), a comedy by Aristophanes, produced at the Lenaea in 425 B.C., his first surviving play.

The Athenians had for six years been suffering the horrors of the Peloponnesian War, the devastation of their territory, plague in the overcrowded city, and shortage of food, but their spirit was unbroken. The Acharnians (inhabitants of an Attic deme lying NW. of Athens near the foot of Mt. Parnes), of whom the chorus of this play is composed, had been among the chief sufferers, for their territory had been repeatedly ravaged. The comedy, which is a plea for peace as the only rational solution, was produced, not in the name of Aristophanes, who was still a youth, but in that of Callistratus, probably also a comic poet. It won the first prize, in spite of the unpopularity of the theme.

Dikaiopolis, an Athenian farmer, sits awaiting the meeting of the Assembly, sighing for the good times of peace. A Demigod appears, sent by the gods to arrange peace with Sparta, but unfortunately lacking the necessary travelling-money. This Dikaiopolis provides, but the treaty with Sparta is to be a private one for himself alone. The Demigod presently brings the treaty, narrowly escaping from the chorus of infuriated Acharnians. Dikaiopolis celebrates his peace with a procession consisting of his daughter and servants, and this leads to a dispute between Dikaiopolis and the chorus on the question of peace or war, in which Lamachus (q.v.), the typical general, takes part. Dikaiopolis is allowed to make a speech before being executed as a traitor; and to render this more pathetic borrows from Euripides some of the stage properties that make his tragedies so moving. As a result the chorus are won over to the view of Dikaiopolis. After the parabasis, in which the poet defends his position, there is a succession of amusing scenes illustrative of the benefits of peace. A Megarian (Athens had been trying to starve out Megara by a blockade) comes to Dikaiopolis to buy food, offering in exchange his little daughters disguised as pigs in sacks. A Boeotian brings eels and other good things, and wants in return local produce of Attica; he is given an Informer tied up in a sack. A yeoman wants peace-salve for his eyes, which he has cried out for the loss of his oxen; and so forth. Finally Lamachus has to march off through the snow against the Boeotians, and returns wounded by a vine-stake on which he has impaled himself, while Dikaiopolis makes merry with the priest of Bacchus.

Achā′tēs, in the 'Aeneid', the faithful friend and squire of Aeneas, frequently referred to as 'fidus Achates'.

A′cheron (*Acherōn*), in Greek mythology, one of the rivers of the lower world (see *Hades*). The name was that of a river in southern Epirus, which, issuing from a deep and gloomy gorge, traversed the Acherūsian swamps, and after receiving the waters of the tributary Cōcȳtus fell into the Thesprotian Gulf.

Achillē′id (*Achillēis*), an epic poem in hexameters by Statius (q.v.) on the story of Achilles (q.v.), of which only one book and part of a second were written. The poem describes how Thetis, anxious that her son shall not take part in the Trojan War (from which she knows he will not return), removes him from the care of the centaur Chiron (q.v.) to Scyros. It relates his adventures there in the disguise of a girl, his discovery by Ulysses, and departure for Troy. The work was begun in A.D. 95 and was probably cut short by the writer's death.

Achi'llēs (*Achil(l)eūs*), son of Peleus and Thetis (qq.v.), the chief hero on the Greek side in the Trojan War (q.v.). When an infant, he was plunged by his mother in the Styx, and rendered invulnerable except in the heel by which she held him. She later hid him, disguised as a girl, at the court of Lycomēdēs, King of Scȳros, in order that he should not take part in the Trojan War; but he was discovered by Odysseus (q.v.), who set arms before him, for Achilles betrayed himself by the fondness with which he handled them. (There is a play by Robert Bridges, 'Achilles in Scyros'). By Dēidamīa, daughter of Lycomedes, Achilles had a son, Neoptolemus (q.v.). At the siege of Troy, Achilles was leader of the Myrmidons (see *Aeacus*). He is represented as a man of fierce and implacable temper. When he sulked in his tent in consequence of his quarrel with Agamemnon, as related in the 'Iliad', the Greeks were driven back to their ships and almost overwhelmed. Then followed the intervention of his friend Patroclus (q.v.) in the battle, the death of the latter, and the terrible grief of Achilles. After he had been reconciled with Agamemnon, he slew Hector, and later Penthesilēa, queen of the Amazons, who was fighting on the Trojan side. Mourning her for her beauty, he was mocked by Thersites (q.v.) and killed him in a rage. Soon afterwards he was shot in the heel by Paris (q.v.), or by Apollo, and killed. Odysseus saw him in Hades (Od. xi), but it was said later that he lived immortal in an island in the Euxine (see under *Colonization*, § 2, for his worship there). After the fall of Troy his ghost claimed Polyxena, daughter of Priam, as his prize, and she was slain on his tomb. Landor has an 'Imaginary Conversation' between Achilles and Helen on Mt. Ida. The 'heel of Achilles' is proverbial for a vulnerable spot.

Achi'llēs Ta'tius, see *Novel*.

Ā'cis (*Ākis*), see *Galatea*.

A'cragas (*Akragās*), see *Agrigentum*.

Acri'sius (*Akrisios*), see *Danae*.

Acro'polis ('Upper Town'), the citadel, standing on high ground, of a Greek town. The Acropolis of Athens is a rocky plateau, about 200 ft. high and about 300 yds. long by 150 yds. wide. It was surrounded by walls, which, with the buildings within them, were destroyed by the Persians in 480 B.C.; the walls were rebuilt by Themistocles and Cimon (qq.v.). In the centre stood a colossal statue of Athene Promachos ('the Champion') whose golden spear-point could be seen by mariners from the sea. On the N. side stood the Erecthēum, the original temple of the tutelary deities of Athens, Athene, Poseidon, and Erechthēūs (qq.v.), burnt by the Persians and rebuilt in the latter part of the 5th c. in the Ionic style, with Caryatides (q.v.) supporting its southern porch. In the age of Pericles were added the Parthenon and Propylaea (qq.v.). There also was erected after the peace of 421 B.C. (see *Peloponnesian War*) the beautiful little temple of Athene Nīkē ('Victory'), which survives reconstructed. It stood on a bastion adjoining the Propylaea and was demolished by the Turks about 1685 to make place for a battery. Other sanctuaries, such as that of Artemis (q.v.) Brauronia, and many statues and altars, stood on various parts of the rock. There were also a large number of marble slabs and columns, with inscriptions of decrees, memorials, casualty-lists, treaties and alliances, public accounts, inventories, etc. Many of these inscriptions, more or less mutilated, have survived.

Actae'on (*Actaiōn*), in Greek mythology, son of Aristaeus (q.v.) and Autonoē, daughter of Cadmus (q.v.). For some offence, either because he boasted that he was a better hunter than Artemis or because he came upon her bathing, the goddess changed him into a stag, and he was torn to pieces by his own hounds.

A'ctium, a promontory in the south of Ēpirus, at the mouth of the Ambracian Gulf, off which Octavian defeated the fleets of Antony and Cleopatra in 31 B.C. (see *Rome*, § 7). This battle marked the end of the Roman republic and introduced the Roman empire. Early in 31 Octavian had landed an army in Epirus in the hope of surprising Antony's fleet in the Ambracian Gulf. In this hope he had been disappointed, for Antony had succeeded in bringing up his army for the defence of the fleet and establishing it at Actium. For several months the armies and fleets of the two generals confronted each other. At last, late in August, Antony decided to fight a battle at sea; but what precisely were his plans is uncertain. The fight began at dawn on 2 September. At first the heavier ships of Antony appeared to be prevailing; but presently the sixty Egyptian ships forming the contingent of Cleopatra were seen to set sail and make off southwards. Antony himself followed her in a swift quinquereme. Antony's fleet was destroyed, and his army shortly went over to Octavian.

Ad Here'nnium, *Rhetorica*, see *Rhetorica*.

Ade'lphoe (or *Adelphi*, 'The Brothers'), a comedy by Terence, adapted from Menander and Diphilus (see *Comedy*, § 4), produced in 160 B.C.

The two sons of Dēmea, Aeschinus and Ctēsiphō, are brought up, the former by his uncle Micio in the town, the latter by his father in the country, and the theme of the comedy is the contrast between their methods of education. Demea makes himself hated and distrusted by his harshness and frugality; Micio makes himself loved and trusted by his indulgence and open-handedness. Aeschinus has seduced an Athenian lady of small means, loves her dearly, and wishes to marry her. Ctesipho, whom his father believes a model of virtue, has fallen in love with a music-girl. Aeschinus, to help his brother, carries off the girl from the slave-dealer to whom she belongs and brings her to Micio's house. He thereby incurs the suspicion of carrying on an intrigue with this girl at the very moment when the lady whom he has seduced has most need of his sympathy and support. The truth becomes known. Aeschinus is forgiven by Micio and his marriage arranged. Demea is confounded at discovering the profligacy of Ctesipho. Finding that his boasted method of education has earned him only hatred, he suddenly changes his attitude and makes an amusing display of geniality—forcing his old bachelor brother into a reluctant marriage with the bride's mother, endowing her relative with a farm at Micio's expense, and obliging the latter to free his slave and start him in life—showing that even geniality can be overdone.

The 'Adelphoe' was played at the funeral games of Aemilius Paullus (q.v.).

Admē'tus (*Admētos*), in Greek mythology, son of Pherēs and king of Pherae in Thessaly. When Zeus killed Asclepius (q.v.) for restoring Hippolytus to life, Apollo, the father of Asclepius, furious at this treatment of his son, took vengeance on the Cyclopes (q.v.) who had forged Zeus's thunderbolt, and slew them. To expiate this crime he was made for a year the serf of Admetus, who treated him kindly. Apollo, having learnt from the Fates that Admetus was destined to an early death, from gratitude to him cajoled the Fates (with the help of wine) into granting Admetus longer life, provided that at the appointed hour of his death he could persuade some one else

to die for him. The father and mother of Admetus having refused, his wife Alcestis consented, and accordingly died. Just after this, Heracles, on his way to one of his labours, visited the castle of Admetus. The latter, in obedience to the laws of hospitality, concealed the death of his wife, and welcomed the hero. Heracles presently discovered the truth, went out to intercept Thanatos, the messenger from Hades, set upon him and took from him Alcestis, whom he restored to her husband.

For Euripides' treatment of the story see *Alcestis*.

Administration, PUBLIC, see *Athens*, § 9, *Rome*, § 12.

Adō'niasū'sae, see *Theocritus*.

Adō'nic, see *Metre*, § 3.

Adō'nis, in Greek mythology, a beautiful youth sprung from the unnatural love of Myrrha (or Smyrna) for her father Cinyras (q.v.), king of Cyprus, with which she had been smitten by Aphrodite for refusing to honour the goddess. When Cinyras, discovering the crime, sought to kill Myrrha, she was changed into a myrtle, from which Adonis was born. Aphrodite (q.v.) fell in love with him and, when he was killed by a boar while hunting, caused the rose or the anemone to spring from his blood (or the anemone sprang from the tears that Aphrodite shed for Adonis). Both Aphrodite and Persephone (q.v.) then claimed him, and Zeus decided that he should spend part of the year with each. The name Adonis is probably the Semitic word *Adon*, lord, and the myth is symbolical of the course of vegetation. His death and survival were widely celebrated (in the East under the name of his Syrian equivalent, *Thamuz*; cf. Milton, P.L. i. 446–52). As a feature of his worship, the image of Adonis was surrounded with beds of rapidly withering plants, 'Gardens of Adonis'. These are referred to in Shakespeare's '1 Henry VI', I. vi, and, though the similarity there is only in the name, in Spenser, F.Q. III. vi. 29, and in Milton, P.L. ix. 440. The story of the love of Venus for Adonis is the subject of Shakespeare's poem 'Venus and Adonis'.

Adra'stus (*Adrastos*), legendary king of Argos at the time of the conflict of Polynices and Eteocles for the kingdom of Thebes (see *Oedipus*). Polynices married his daughter Argēlā, Tydeus married her sister Dēipylē; and Adrastus collected and led the army of the 'Seven against Thebes'. When the expedition was defeated, Adrastus escaped, thanks to the swiftness of his horse Arīon, the offspring of Poseidon and Demeter. In his old age he led the second expedition against Thebes, that of the *Epigoni* (q.v.) and died on his way home, after its successful conclusion, from grief for the loss of his son, who alone had fallen in the attack.

Ae'a (*Aia*), in the story of the Argonauts (q.v.), the realm of Aeetes (q.v.), later identified with Colchis.

Ae'acus (*Aiakos*), in Greek mythology, son of Zeus and the nymph Aegina. He was the father of Telamon (father of the greater Ajax) and of Peleus (father of Achilles) (qq.v.). He was a man of great piety, and when the inhabitants of his island, Aegina, were destroyed by a plague, Zeus, to reward him, created human beings out of ants (*murmēkes*) to repeople it, and these were called Myrmidons, the name by which the subjects of Peleus and Achilles are known in Homer. See also *Minos, Rhadamanthus, and Aeacus.*

Aeäe'a (*Aiaiē*), in the 'Odyssey', the island of Circe, situated in the stream Oceanus (q.v.).

Ae'diles (*Aedīlēs*) **of the plebs,** at Rome, originally two plebeian magistrates (named 'aediles' from the *aedes* or temple of Ceres, where they preserved the decrees of the people), who had the charge of temples, buildings, markets, and games. To them were later added two *Curule Aediles* representing the whole people. The aediles were charged with the corn-supply of the metropolis until this was entrusted to special officers (see *Annona*).

Ăē'dŏn, in Greek mythology, daughter of Pandareōs and wife of Zēthus king of Thebes. She was envious of Niobe (q.v.) her sister-in-law (wife of Amphion brother of Zethus) because she had many children, and plotted to kill them. By mistake she slew her own child, Itylus (or Itys), and mourned for him so bitterly that the gods changed her into a nightingale. Swinburne has a poem 'Itylus' on this legend. Cf. the story of Procne (see *Philomela*).

Aeë'tēs (*Aiētēs*), in Greek mythology, son of Helios (q.v.), king of Colchis, brother of Circe (q.v.), and father of Medea. See *Athamas* and *Argonauts.*

Aegā'tēs I'nsulae, islands off Lilybaeum in Sicily, near which was fought in 242 B.C. the naval battle in which Q. Lutātius Catulus, the Roman admiral, defeated the Punic fleet, thereby terminating the First Punic War (see *Punic Wars*).

Aegean Sea (*Aigaios Pontos*), the part of the Mediterranean between Greece and Asia Minor. The etymology of the name is unknown.

Ae'gēus (*Aigeūs*), see *Theseus* and *Medea* (Euripides' tragedy).

Aegī'na (*Aigīna*), (1) a nymph, the mother of Aeacus (q.v.). (2) An island in the Saronic Gulf which was occupied by the Dorians (see *Migrations*). In the 6th c. it was a strong naval power and at enmity with Athens. When Persia threatened Greece early in the 5th c., it was feared that the Aeginē'tans would support the invaders. By the intervention of Sparta Aegina was forced to give Athens hostages for her good conduct, and an indecisive war between Aegina and Athens followed, beginning probably in 488. Aegina, as a matter of fact, fought bravely on the Greek side at Salamis. After the Persian Wars she opposed the imperial policy of Athens and was subdued in 457–6. During the Peloponnesian War the inhabitants were expelled and the island was colonized (c. 429) by Athenian cleruchs (q.v.). The island was an important centre of Greek sculpture and contained a famous temple of Aphaia (see *Britomartis*), of which the fine pediments survive (at Munich). In mythology Aegina was the realm of Aeacus (q.v.)

Aegi'sthus (*Aigisthos*), see *Pelops.*

Aegospo'tami (*Aigospotamoi*, 'Goat's Rivers'), a small river in the Thracian Chersonese, off the mouth of which Athens suffered her final naval defeat in the Peloponnesian War (q.v.) in 405 B.C.

Aegy'ptus (*Aiguptos*), (1) see *Danaus*; (2) see *Egypt.*

Ae'lian (*Claudius Aeliānus*) (*fl. c.* A.D. 200), author of fourteen books (in Greek) of 'Historical Miscellanies' (*Poikilē Historiā*), showing wide but uncritical learning about political and literary celebrities; and of a work 'On the Characteristics of Animals' in seventeen books. Both works (the former partly in epitomized form) survive.

Ae'lius Aristī'dēs, see *Aristides.*

Ae'lius Lamprī'dius, see *Historia Augusta.*

Ae'lius Spartiā'nus, see *Historia Augusta.*

Aemi'lius Paullus, LŪCIUS (d. 160 B.C.), son of the Aemilius Paullus who fell at Cannae (q.v.), was consul for the second time in 168 B.C., when the Macedonian War, owing to the incompetence of the Roman generals and the indiscipline of the army, was going ill for Rome. He restored discipline and in a single campaign brought the war to a successful end by his victory at Pydna. He formed, with the books that had belonged to the Macedonian king (Perseus), the first private library at Rome. The proceeds of the booty gained at Pydna were enormous, and were scrupulously paid into the Roman treasury. He combined old Roman virtue with Greek enlightenment. He was father of Scipio Aemilianus (q.v.). There is a life of him by Plutarch.

Aenē′as (Gk. *Ainaiās*), son of Anchises and Aphrodite (qq.v.) and a member of the younger branch of the royal family of Troy (see genealogy under *Troy*). In the 'Iliad' he is represented as under the disfavour of Priam and is a secondary figure. But it is there stated (xx. 307) that 'his might shall reign among the Trojans, and his children's children, who shall be born in the aftertime'. There was an early tradition that he escaped when Troy fell, and went to some place in Italy. Timaeus (q.v.) appears to have been the first to make him the originator of the future Roman State. The tale of Aeneas's wanderings to Italy was perhaps told by Stesichorus (q.v.), and we have it in its fully developed form in the 'Aeneid' (q.v.) of Virgil. That the legend was officially recognized in the 3rd c. B.C. is shown by the fact that after the 1st Punic War the Acarnanians requested the help of Rome against the Aetolians on the ground that their ancestors alone of all the Greeks had not taken part in the expedition against Troy. The legend was adopted by Fabius Pictor in his history, and by the poets Naevius and Ennius. See also *Tabula Iliaca*. For the reconciliation of the legend with the story of the founding of Rome by Romulus see *Rome*, § 2.

Ae′neid (*Aenēis*), an epic poem in twelve books of hexameters by Virgil, composed in seclusion in Campania during the last eleven years of his life, 30–19 B.C. (that is to say, after the battle of Actium had finally established the principate of Augustus). The poem was left unfinished and Virgil is said, when dying, to have ordered it to be destroyed. He had read portions of the work to Augustus and his family in 23 B.C.

The poem is a national epic, designed to celebrate the origin and growth of the Roman Empire, The groundwork is the legend that Aeneas (q.v.), after the fall of Troy and long wanderings, founded a Trojan settlement in Latium, the source of the Roman race (see *Rome*, § 2). This afforded scope for the mythical and supernatural element found in Homeric epic, for recalling the ancient beliefs and practices of magic and religion, for glorifying the Roman people and their chief

families by representing their ancestors in the heroic age, and for recounting, by the device of prophecy, the historical triumphs of Rome and of Augustus. The striking feature of the poem is the conception of Italy as a single nation, and of Roman history as a continuous whole from the founding of the city to the full expansion of the Empire. The greatness of the theme made a profound impression on the Roman people; the dignity with which it is set forth is enhanced by the poet's tender contemplative spirit, his sympathy with suffering humanity, and his feeling for nature. The poem has been criticized in certain respects. Its mythology is stiff and conventional; the Homeric Olympus was discredited in Virgil's day (for the poet's treatment of religion see under *Virgil*). Many of the characters are said to lack force and distinctness. The episode of Aeneas and Dido has been the subject of the most frequent censure. It is out of harmony with our ideas of right and wrong that Dido, deserted by Aeneas, should perish, while Aeneas goes shabbily away scot-free. It is unlikely that Virgil's contemporaries would have taken this view. A marriage with Dido, a foreign woman, is not one of which they would have approved; Dido's passion had entangled Aeneas, but the will of the gods, they would have said, must prevail over human passion; and the incident has many parallels in Greek mythology (Theseus and Ariadne, Jason and Medea, &c.). It is perhaps unintentionally that the poet so powerfully enlists our sympathy for Dido. Conington says that Virgil in this episode 'struck the chord of modern passions, and it vibrated more powerfully than the minstrel himself expected'.

Virgil, in composing the Aeneid, drew on many sources; primarily on the 'Iliad' and the 'Odyssey', combining in his poem the travel-adventures of the latter with the warfare of the former, and modelling on Homer many episodes (e.g. the funeral games in Bk. V, the visit to the nether world in Bk. VI, the description of the shield in Bk. VIII). Virgil also drew on the Homeric Hymns and Cyclic poets, the 'Argonautica' of Apollonius Rhodius, the Greek tragedians, and on his own immediate predecessors, Ennius, Lucretius, and others. His picture of the lower world appears to be a poetic treatment of the various opinions about it, popular and philosophical, prevalent in his day. The contents of the work may be briefly summarized as follows:

Book I. Aeneas, who for seven years

since the fall of Troy has been pursuing his way to Latium, has just left Sicily. Juno, knowing that a race of Trojan origin will in future ages threaten her beloved city Carthage, incites Aeolus to let loose a storm on the Trojan fleet. Some of the ships are wrecked, and the fleet scattered; but Neptune pacifies the sea and Aeneas reaches the Libyan coast. The remaining ships also arrive and the Trojans are kindly received by Dido, queen of the newly founded Carthage and widow of Sychaeus. She has fled from Tyre, where her husband had been killed by his brother Pygmalion, king of the land. Venus, though Jupiter has revealed to her the future destiny of Aeneas and his race, dreading the hate of Juno and the wiles of the Tyrians, designs that Dido shall be smitten with love for Aeneas.

Book II. At Dido's request, Aeneas relates the fall of Troy and the subsequent events: the building of the Trojan Horse, the guile of Sinon, the death of Laocoon (qq.v.), the firing of the city, the desperate resistance of Aeneas himself and his comrades, the death of Priam, and his own final flight by the order of Venus; how he carries off Anchises his father on his shoulders and takes his son Iūlus (Ascanius) by the hand; his wife Creūsa follows but is lost. Her ghost tells him the destiny that awaits him.

Book III. (Aeneas continues his narrative.) He and his companions build a fleet and set out. They touch at Thrace (where Aeneas hears the voice of his murdered kinsman Polydorus from his grave) and Delos. The Delian oracle bids them seek the land that first bore the Trojan race. This is wrongly interpreted to mean Crete, from which they are driven by a pestilence. Aeneas now learns that Italy is meant. On their way the Trojans land on the island of the Harpies (q.v.) and attack them. The Harpy Celaeno prophesies that they shall found no city till hunger compels them to eat the tables at which they feed. At Būthrōtum in Chāonia they find Helenus the seer (son of Priam) and Andromache, and the former instructs Aeneas in the route he must follow, visiting the Cumaean Sibyl and founding his city where by a secluded stream he shall find a white sow with a litter of thirty young. Aeneas pursues his way and visits the country of the Cyclops (q.v.) in Sicily; his father dies at Drepanum. Thence he reaches Libya.

Book IV. Dido, though bound by a vow to her dead husband, confesses to her sister Anna her passion for Aeneas. A hunting expedition is interrupted by a storm; Dido and Aeneas take refuge in a cave and are united by the design of Juno and Venus. The rumour of their love reaches the neighbouring Iarbas, who has been rejected by Dido and who now appeals to Jupiter. Jupiter orders Aeneas to leave Carthage. Dido discovers Aeneas's preparations for departure and makes a piteous plea. Her lover's sorry excuses for his desertion call down on him Dido's withering rejoinder. But Aeneas is steadfast. Dido, distraught by anguish and fearful visions, makes a last entreaty for delay, and when this is unavailing prepares for death. When she sees the Trojan fleet sailing away, she takes her own life, heaping in her frenzy curses on Aeneas and his race.

Book V. The Trojans return to Sicily, landing in the territory of their compatriot Acestes (q.v.). The anniversary of the death of Anchises is celebrated with sacrifices and games. First, a race between four ships. Gyās in 'Chimaera' is leading; he heaves his pilot overboard for not hugging close enough the turning point; he is passed by Cloanthus in 'Scylla'. Sergestus in 'Centaur' runs aground. Mnestheus in 'Pristis' presses hard on Cloanthus, but the latter wins. Then a foot-race, in which Nisus, leading, slips and falls and deliberately trips Salius so as to give the victory to his friend Euryalus. A boxing match follows between Darēs of Troy and Entellus of Sicily; the former is worsted and Aeneas stops the fight. Finally a shooting-match, and a riding display by thirty-six youths led by Ascanius (see *Ludus Troiae*). Meanwhile the Trojan women, incited by Juno and weary of their long wanderings, fire the ships; four are destroyed, but a rainstorm quells the fire. When the Trojans sail away, Palinūrus the helmsman, overcome by sleep, falls into the sea and is lost.

Book VI. Aeneas visits the Cumaean Sibyl, who foretells his wars in Latium. After plucking by her direction the Golden Bough (see *Diana*) he descends with her, through the cave of Avernus, to the nether world. They reach the Styx and on the hither side see the ghosts of the unburied dead; among them Palinurus (q.v.), who recounts his fate and begs for burial. The Golden Bough gains for Aeneas permission from Charon to cross the Styx. Cerberus (q.v.) is pacified with a drugged honey cake. Various groups of dead are seen: infants, those unjustly condemned, those who have died from love (among whom Dido receives in silence the renewed excuses of Aeneas), and those who have fallen in war. They approach the entrance to Tartarus, where the worst criminals suffer torments; but turn aside to Elysium, where the blest enjoy a care-free life. Here Aeneas finds and vainly seeks to embrace Anchises. He sees ghosts drinking at the river Lethe (q.v.) and Anchises expounds to him the reincarnation of souls after a long purgation (a Pythagorean doctrine drawn by Virgil perhaps from the Orphic and Eleusinian traditions). Among these souls he points out to his son those of men who are in the future to be illustrious in Roman history, from Romulus and the early kings to the great generals of later days, Augustus himself, and his nephew Marcellus (q.v.), to whose brief life the poet makes touching allusion. Aeneas and the Sibyl then leave the lower world through the Ivory Gate, through which false dreams are sent to mortals (perhaps a hint that what the poet has described is no more than a dream). This book contains the memorable lines (851–3) on the destiny of Rome, the central thought of the whole poem:

Tu regere imperio populos, Romane, memento;

Hae tibi erunt artes: pacisque imponere morem,

Parcere subjectis, et debellare superbos.

Book VII. The Trojans reach the mouth of the Tiber; here the Harpy's prophecy (see Bk. III above) is fulfilled, for the Trojans eat cakes of bread which they have used as platters. Of this land, Latium, Latīnus is the king. His daughter is Lāvīnia. The goodliest of her wooers is Turnus, king of the Rutuli; but her father has been divinely warned to marry her to a stranger who shall come. The embassy sent by Aeneas is welcomed by Latinus, who offers alliance and the hand of his daughter. Juno calls out the Fury Allecto, who stirs Amāta (the mother of Lavinia) and Turnus to fierce hostility against the Trojans. The wounding of a stag from the royal herds by Ascanius causes an affray; Latinus is overborne, and the Italian tribes gather to expel the Trojans. Virgil enumerates these and their leaders; notable among them besides Turnus are Mēzentius 'scorner of the gods', a tyrant hated by his people, Messāpus, Virbius (son of Hippolytus, q.v.), and the Volscian warrior-maid, Camilla (q.v.).

Book VIII. Aeneas faces war reluctantly, but is encouraged by the god of the river Tiber, who sends him to seek the alliance of the Arcadian Evander (q.v.), the founder of the city on the Palatine hill, part of the future Rome. On the bank of the Tiber Aeneas sees a white sow with her litter, as foretold by Helenus. Evander promises support and urges alliance with the Etruscans. He leads Aeneas through the city and explains the origin of various Roman sites and names. Vulcan, at the request of Venus, forges armour for Aeneas. The shield is described, on which are depicted various events in the future history of Rome, down to the battle of Actium.

Book IX. While Aeneas is thus absent, Turnus blockades the Trojan camp. He sets the Trojan ships on fire, but Neptune turns them into sea-nymphs. Nisus and Euryalus pass through the enemy lines at night to summon Aeneas. They slay some of the enemy in their drunken sleep, but fall in with a hostile column and are killed, Nisus gallantly striving to save his friend. The Rutulians assault the camp; Ascanius performs his first exploit; Turnus is cut off within the rampart, but escapes by plunging into the river.

Book X. The gods debate in Olympus, and Aeneas secures the alliance of Tarchon, king of the Etruscans, and returns to the seat of war, accompanied by Pallas (son of Evander) and Tarchon. Turnus opposes them on the shore, to prevent the junction of the Trojan forces. In the battle Turnus kills Pallas; he pursues a phantom of Aeneas contrived by Juno and is borne away to his city. Aeneas wounds Mezentius, whose son Lausus tries to save him; Aeneas reluctantly kills the lad. Mezentius addresses his gallant horse, Rhaebus, and again faces Aeneas; horse and man are killed.

Book XI. Aeneas celebrates the Trojan victory and laments Pallas. A truce with the Latins is arranged. The Italian chiefs debate. Drancēs proposes that the issue shall be settled by single combat between Turnus and Aeneas, and Turnus accepts. The debate is interrupted by a report that Aeneas and his army are moving against the city. A cavalry engagement follows in which Camilla takes the lead. Tarchon plucks Venulus from his horse and carries him off before him on his saddle-bow. Camilla is killed by Arruns and is avenged by Ōpis, messenger of Diana.

Book XII. The Latins are discouraged, and Turnus decides to meet Aeneas alone. Latinus and Amata try in vain to dissuade him. A compact is made for the single combat. But Juturna, sister of Turnus, stirs up the Rutulians, and the general fighting is resumed. Aeneas is wounded by an unknown hand, but healed by Venus. The Trojans, seeing the city of Latinus left unguarded, attack and fire it. Amata takes her life. Turnus returns from his pursuit of Trojan stragglers and the opposing forces suspend their struggle while he and Aeneas fight. Aeneas wounds Turnus. Even now he would spare him; but he sees on his body the spoils of Pallas and in fierce anger buries his sword in his enemy's body.

The 'Aeneid' was edited after Virgil's death by his friends Varius Rufus (q.v.) and Plōtius Tucca. For famous editions and translations see under *Virgil*. It may be of interest to recall that the two passages of the 'Aeneid' which Dr. Johnson picked out for their wonderful quality were the descriptions of the tomb of Polydorus dripping blood (iii. 19 et seq.), and of the Trojan ships turned to sea-nymphs (ix. 77 et seq.).

Aeŏ'lians (*Aiŏleis*), see *Migrations and Dialects*.

Ae'olis, the northern portion of the coast of Asia Minor, from the Troad to the river Hermus, which was occupied by Aeolian Greeks (see *Migrations*).

Ae'olus (*Aiolos*), (1) described in the 'Odyssey' as the son of Hippotēs and friend of the gods, who lives an agreeable life in the floating island Aeolia. He gave Odysseus a leather bag in which were secured the winds adverse to the latter's voyage, and thus he later came to be regarded as the god of the winds. Virgil (Aen. i. 50–9) depicts him as keeping the winds imprisoned in a cave. (2) A son of Hellēn (see *Hellenes* and *Deucalion*) and the legendary ancestor of the Aeolian race (see *Migrations*) and father of Sisyphus, Athamas, Salmoneus, Alcyone (qq.v.), Calycē (mother of Endymion, q.v.), and other children.

Ae'pytus (*Aiputos*), see *Merope*.

Aerā'rium, the treasury of the Roman republic. It was maintained under the empire, but distinguished from the *fiscus* (q.v.) or imperial treasury. Its chief source of income in imperial times was the revenue of the senatorial provinces, and it appears to have borne the cost of maintenance of public buildings, of the construction of roads, and of State religion; it issued the copper coinage. Though nominally under the management of the Senate, the control of the emperors over it increased with time, till the two treasuries were in practice almost indistinguishable. The *aerarium* was housed in the temple of Saturn beside the Capitol. See *Rome*, § 14.

The *aerarium mīlitāre* was a pension fund for disabled soldiers instituted by Augustus in A.D. 6.

Ae'schinēs (*Aischinēs*), a famous Athenian orator, was born about 390 B.C. and was thus a few years older than his great rival Demosthenes. His parents were in modest circumstances (his father Atromētus was a schoolmaster). As a young man he won some distinction in military service and then became a tragic actor and a public clerk. He first appears in political life in 348 as an envoy sent by Eubulus (q.v.) to the Peloponnese to organize Hellenic resistance to Philip. But, with Eubulus, he soon abandoned this policy and became an advocate of peace with Macedonia. He formed part of the embassies sent to Philip for the negotiation of the Peace of Philocrates and in 343 was impeached by Demosthenes (q.v.) for his conduct on these occasions. His defence (which we possess) was successful and he was acquitted. Demosthenes was to have been associated with one Timarchus in the accusation of Aeschines, but Aeschines had retorted by bringing a charge against Timarchus of immoral life. His speech against Timarchus (345), which was successful, is the first of the three speeches of Aeschines that have survived. He next came into prominence in 340, when, at a session of the Amphictyonic (q.v.) council, the Locrians of Amphissa, at the instigation of Thebes, were to bring an accusation of sacrilege against Athens. To forestall this, Aeschines accused the Locrians themselves of sacrilege (see *Sacred Wars*). A Sacred War was decreed against Amphissa, and it was this war which provided the pretext for the invasion of Philip of Macedon (q.v.) that culminated in the battle of Chaeronea (q.v.). The action of Aeschines on this occasion was made the ground of part of Demosthenes' denunciation of Aeschines in his speech 'On the Crown'. The rivalry between the two statesmen finally manifested itself when Ctēsiphōn in 336 proposed that Demosthenes should be publicly crowned for his services to the state. Aeschines indicted Ctesiphon for the alleged illegality of this proposal, and in his speech six years later, which survives, attacked the whole career of Demosthenes as injurious to Athens. The jury by an overwhelming majority acquitted Ctesiphon. Aeschines retired into exile and died there.

The speeches of Aeschines reveal his inferiority to his great rival. He was excessively vain, and deficient in nobility of character and political sagacity, but there is no proof of the corruption of which Demosthenes accused him. His speeches are in a lighter, livelier style than those of Demosthenes; he had had no special rhetorical training, but his stage experience had given him a good delivery and a wide acquaintance with literature.

Among Landor's 'Imaginary Conversations' is one between Aeschines and Phocion (q.v.).

Ae'schylus (*Aischulos*) (525–456 B.C.), a great Greek tragic poet, born at Eleusis, near Athens, of a noble family. He took part in the Persian Wars; his epitaph (composed, it is said, by himself) represents him as fighting at Marathon, and his description of Salamis in the 'Persians' suggests that he was present at that battle also. He visited Syracuse at the invitation of Hieron I (see *Syracuse*, § 1) more than once and died at Gela in Sicily; an anecdote relates that an eagle dropped a tortoise on his bald head and killed him. He appears at some time in his life to have been prosecuted on the charge of divulging the Eleusinian mysteries, but to have exculpated himself. Pericles was his choregus (see *Chorus*) at some uncertain date; perhaps in the production of the 'Persians' in 472, or possibly later. Aeschylus was honoured as a classic soon after his death and special privileges were decreed for his plays. He had a son, Euphorion, like himself a tragic poet.

Aeschylus wrote some ninety plays (including satyric dramas), of which seven have come down to us: 'Suppliants', 'Persians', 'Seven against Thebes', 'Prometheus Vinctus' (qq.v.); and 'Agamemnon', 'Choephoroe', and 'Eumenides', forming the Oresteia (q.v.) trilogy. He also wrote paeans, elegies, and epigrams, of which very scanty fragments survive. He was the rival in his early days of Pratinas, Phrynichus (qq.v.), and Choerilus (of Athens, *fl.* 482), and in later life of Sophocles. He won his first prize in 484, was successful again with the 'Persians' in 472, was defeated by Sophocles in 468, and won his last victory with the 'Oresteia' in 458.

Aeschylus is generally regarded as the real founder of Greek tragedy: by the introduction of a second actor he made true dialogue and dramatic action possible. Though Aristotle says that Sophocles introduced scenery, Aeschylus must have used some primitive spectacular devices, e.g. in the 'Prometheus'. He also developed the use of stage dress. His plays show rapid progress in dramatic technique: the 'Suppliants', an early play, is simple, lacks action, and has no individual characters; the 'Oresteia' has outstanding individual characters and a well developed plot. Aeschylus chose themes of the utmost grandeur, often superhuman and terrible, generally from mythology (the 'Persians' is an exception), and delighted in picturesque, sonor-

ous language and bold metaphors. His lyrics, which play a more important part in his tragedies than in those of his successors, reached the highest point in that branch of poetic art. His plays are permeated with the religious spirit; he accepts the traditional mythology without criticizing it in the manner of Euripides, but tries to reconcile it with morality. Among the ideas prominent in his plays are those of destiny or fatality, working through the divine will and human passion; of the heredity of crime, both in the sense that crime provokes vengeance in the next generation, and in the sense of the inheritance of a criminal taint; and of the vengeance of the gods on overweening pride (*hubris*). His principal characters are drawn without complexity or elaboration, governed by a single dominating idea, such as vengeance (e.g. Clytemnestra in the 'Agamemnon'). For Aristophanes' estimate of Aeschylus, see *Frogs*.

Quintilian, while commending the sublimity, dignity, and eloquence of Aeschylus, thought him at times uncouth and lacking in harmony.

Aescula'pius, the Latin form of the Greek name Asclepius (q.v.). The first temple to him was founded at Rome in 293 B.C., in consequence of a severe pestilence. The temple, with a sanatorium, stood on the island of the Tiber.

Ae'son (*Aisōn*), see *Argonauts*.

Ae'sop (*Aisōpos*), the traditional composer of Greek fables about animals, is said by Herodotus to have lived in the reign of Amasis of Egypt (middle of the 6th c. B.C.), and to have been a slave of Iadmon, a Thracian. Many stories about animals, adapted to moral or satirical ends, circulated under his name, and we are told that Socrates, when in prison, put some of these into verse. A collection of them was turned into choliambic verse by Babrius (q.v.), and five books of Latin fables after Aesop were published by Phaedrus (q.v.). An apocryphal life of Aesop was written by Maximus Planudēs, a 14th c. Byzantine monk. Landor has two 'Imaginary Conversations' between Aesop and his fellow-slave Rhodope (q.v.).

Aesō'pus, CLAUDIUS, a celebrated Roman tragic actor in the 1st c. B.C. Horace places him on an equality with Roscius (q.v.), the great comic actor. He was a friend of Cicero, and during the latter's exile contributed to move popular feeling in his favour by allusions to him on the stage. Cicero says that he had great power of facial expression and gesture.

Aethio′pica (*Aithiopika*), see *Novel.*

Ae′thiopis (*Aithiopis*), a lost poem of the Epic Cycle (q.v.), ascribed to Arctinus of Miletus, a sequel to the Iliad. It contained the story of the coming to Troy of Penthesilēa, queen of the Amazons, and her slaying by Achilles. It told also of the coming of the Ethiopian Memnon (whence the name of the poem), who likewise was killed by Achilles; and of the death of Achilles himself.

Ae′thra (*Aithrā*), the mother of Theseus (q.v.).

Ae′tna, a Latin didactic poem in 644 hexameters attributed by its MS. and doubtfully by Donatus to Virgil, but probably not by him. It was perhaps by Lucilius, the friend to whom Seneca the Philosopher addressed his 'Letters'. It describes and purports to explain the eruptions of Mt. Etna. These are due, not to Vulcan or Enceladus (see *Giants*), but to the action of wind in cavities of the earth on subterranean fires (substantially the same explanation as that of Lucretius, vi. 680 et seq.). The poem closes with an illustration of the moral character of the forces of nature. On the occasion of a sudden eruption the inhabitants of a neighbouring town hastily fled, each carrying the property he thought most precious. But they were overwhelmed. A certain Amphinomus and his brother, however, who carried away nothing but their aged father and mother and their household gods, were spared by the flames.

Aetōlian League, a confederacy of cities or districts of Aetolia, developed after the death of Alexander. It was governed at first by an Assembly of all free Aetolian citizens (including the citizens of federated cities adjoining Aetolian territory); at the head of it was a general elected annually. There was also a Council, possessing little power, composed of delegations from the League cities proportionate to their military contingents. When, with the expansion of the League, administration by the Assembly became impossible, a small committee of the Council was formed which, with the general, became the real government of the League; the Assembly, however, retained the decision of peace and war. From about 290 the League occupied Delphi, and it gradually extended its territory till by 220 it controlled the whole of central Greece outside Attica, and became the chief rival of Macedonia in the peninsula. But the Aetolians were a predatory people and the League was not a source of Hellenic unity and strength. It joined

Antiochus III in his war with Rome (see *Seleucids*); and his defeat in 190 brought about the League's virtual extinction.

Afrā′nius, Lūcius (b. *c.* 150 B.C.), a writer of Roman comedies (*togatae*, q.v.), of which only fragments survive. He appears to have desired to found a national comedy, and his plays depicted Italian life and characters. He had a long popularity, and Horace in Ep. II. i. 57 says that admirers compared him to Menander ('Dicitur Afrani toga convenisse Menandro'). Afranius acknowledges his indebtedness to Menander, but the extent of this is unknown.

Agamē′dēs, see *Trophonius.*

Agame′mnon (*Agamemnōn*), in Greek mythology, son of Atreus, brother of Menelaus, husband of Clytemnestra (qq.v.), king of Mycenae, and leader of the Greek host in the Trojan War (q.v.). He is represented in the 'Iliad' as a valiant fighter, a proud and passionate man, but vacillating in purpose and easily discouraged.

When the Greek expedition against Troy had assembled at Aulis occurred the incident of the sacrifice of Agamemnon's daughter Iphigenia (q.v.). During the siege the most famous event in which Agamemnon was involved was his disastrous quarrel with Achilles (see *Iliad*). When Troy at last was captured, Agamemnon returned safely home with his captive, Cassandra (q.v.). But now the curse of the house of Pelops (q.v.) overtook him. Clytemnestra had never forgiven the sacrifice of her daughter Iphigenia, and during Agamemnon's absence Aegisthus had become her paramour (see *Pelops*). She now received Agamemnon with a show of welcome, and then, with Aegisthus, murdered him and Cassandra. It was to revenge his death that his children, Orestes and Electra, later killed Clytemnestra and Aegisthus (see *Oresteia, Orestes, Electra*).

Agamemnon, (1) a tragedy by Aeschylus; see *Oresteia.* (2) A tragedy by Seneca the Philosopher, perhaps based on the 'Agamemnon' of Aeschylus, or more probably on some later play. It is far inferior to the tragedy of Aeschylus and shows variations of detail. The ghost of Thyestes is introduced urging Aegisthus to the crime, and Aegisthus confirms a weaker Clytemnestra in her purpose. Cassandra is not murdered with Agamemnon, but later. Electra appears and effects the escape of her brother Orestes.

Agani′ppē, a spring sacred to the Muses on Mt. Helicon (q.v.). Cf. *Hippocrene.*

Aga'thoclēs (*Agathoklēs*), see *Syracuse*, § 3.

A'gathon (*Agathōn*), an Athenian tragic poet, the most important of the successors of the three great tragedians. His first victory was gained in 416 B.C. It is the banquet held at his house to celebrate this victory that forms the setting of Plato's 'Symposium' (q.v.). Later he went to the court of Archelaus of Macedonia and died there (*c.* 400). Only fragments of his work survive. Agathon was an innovator: he was the first to construct a tragedy on an imaginary subject with imaginary characters; he made the songs of the chorus mere interludes (*embolima*) without reference to the subject of the play, thus preparing the way for the division of the tragedy into acts; and he also introduced some changes in the character of the music. His lyrics are satirically described by Aristophanes in the 'Thesmophoriazusae' as like the walking of ants. Aristophanes also makes fun of Agathon's effeminate appearance.

Agā'vē (*Agauē*), the mother of Pentheus (see *Bacchae*). Statius is thought, from a passage in Juvenal (vii, 82 et seq.), to have written a libretto 'Agave' for the pantomimic dancer, Paris.

Agē'nōr, in Greek mythology, king of Tyre, and father of Cadmus and Europa (qq.v.).

Ager publicus, land acquired by confiscation from States conquered by Rome. In theory it belonged to the Roman People, in actual practice it was looked after by the Senate and magistrates—consul, censor, quaestor. There were two chief types of tenure. (1) It might be held on lease at a yearly rental, e.g. the fertile Ager Campānus; the censors were responsible for this rental. (2) It might be held by squatters (*possessōrēs*) against a rental, but not on lease. They were therefore at liberty to go when they liked or liable to be expelled at the State's pleasure. This rental was collected by the local governments and paid to the censors. There was a tendency after the Punic Wars for such squatters to absorb large tracts of waste land and in time to regard it as their own, despite the Licinian (q.v.) laws, which limited the amount of land which could be held. Hence arose the evictions and disputes in connexion with the legislation of the Gracchi, who desired to resume the public land in order to create settlements for distressed citizens. Stability was restored by a law of 111 (for which see E. G. Hardy's 'Roman Laws and Charters'), but the question of public land came up again after Marius's army reforms. The creation of a professional army meant that some sort of a pension system had to be devised, and until Augustus pensions took the form of grants of public land. Hence the land legislation of Saturninus, Sulla, and Julius Caesar (in his first consulship). The proposed agrarian law of Rullus (63) had a different object, because it was really an attempt by Crassus and Caesar to strengthen their position against Pompey. There seems to have been no serious problem in connexion with the *ager publicus* in the early empire.

Ager Rōmā'nus, see *Rome*, § 4.

Agesilā'us (*Agēsilāos*) (*c.* 444–361 B.C.), king of Sparta from about 398. He was chosen king in place of his nephew, who was the direct heir, by the influence of Lysander (q.v.). He was lame, and his opponents drew attention to the warning of an ancient oracle against a 'lame reign' at Sparta. But he was a man of great energy and intelligence. His successful campaigns against the Persians in 396–5 and his victory over the Thebans at Coronea are related by his friend Xenophon in his 'Hellenica'. He was less successful in the wars of Sparta with Thebes 379–362. Sparta needed money, and in order to earn a subsidy for her, Agesilaus conducted an expedition in aid of an Egyptian prince against Persia in 361. In this he met his death. There is a life of him by Nepos, and see below.

Agesilaus, one of the minor works of Xenophon, an encomium on his friend Agesilaus (see above). Its authenticity as a work by Xenophon has been questioned, but is generally accepted. Xenophon relates in some detail the campaign of Agesilaus against Tissaphernēs in 395 and the march back to Greece through Macedonia and Thessaly, and gives a full description of the battle of Coronea, where Xenophon may have fought under Agesilaus against his own countrymen. The remaining events of his reign are touched on more briefly. The author then passes from his deeds to his virtues, and illustrates his piety, justice, wisdom, and patriotism.

A'gōn ('contest'), (1) in Greece and later at Rome, an athletic, dramatic, or musical contest forming part of public games (see *Festivals* and *Ludi*, § 2); (2) see *Comedy*, § 2.

A'gora (*Agora*), in Greece, an assembly of the people, as opposed to the Council (*Boule*, q.v.). In the constitution of Cleisthenes (q.v.) the name was applied to the assembly of the people in each tribe and deme. It was also the name of the place of assembly, which might serve besides as a market-place. This place was adorned with temples and statues and planted with trees. In the Athenian agora stood the famous Stoa (q.v.) Poikilē and the Stoa Basilikē, the Council-house of the Five Hundred, statues of various heroes, certain temples, and a row of Hermae (q.v.), including a statue of Hermes Agoraios ('of the Market-place'). Here in the open space the peasants sold their produce, fishmongers and bakers had their stalls, and bankers and money-changers their tables. It was a general place of meeting and conversation. Cf. *Forum.*

Agri'cola, a laudatory monograph by Tacitus on the life of his father-in-law, Cn. Jūlius Agricola, published about A.D. 98; Agricola had died in A.D. 93.

Tacitus recounts Agricola's distinguished ancestry and early military service in Britain in the troubled times when Suētōnius Paulīnus was governor (the days of Boadicea), his advancement to the quaestorship and the praetorship, to the command of the 20th Legion in Britain, to the governorship of Aquitānia (A.D. 74–6), to the consulate, and finally to the governorship of Britain (A.D. 77 or 78). Then follows an account of Britain and its tribes, the continual rain and cloud, the long days and short nights of summer. Tacitus is very hazy about its geography, and even seems to regard the earth as flat. He briefly narrates the history of the successive stages of the conquest of Britain by the Romans, culminating in the achievements of Agricola, who in 80 or 81 secures the country as far north as the line Clota-Bodotria (the Clyde and the Forth). In 82 or 83 he passes beyond this line and invades Caledonia, winning in 83 or 84 the decisive battle of Mt. Graupius, the site of which remains uncertain. Readers of Scott's 'The Antiquary' will remember that Monkbarns claimed to have found the scene of the battle on his land in Forfarshire. It is in the speech of a chieftain before the battle that Tacitus places the well-known saying 'omne ignotum pro magnifico'. The narrative passes to Agricola's return to Rome and to the prudent conduct by which he disarmed Domitian's jealousy. It ends with his death and an eloquent apostrophe to a great Roman. See *Britain.*

Agriculture.

§ 1. *In Greece*

The territory of Greece was in large part mountainous and sterile, and fertile plains were few. Where possible the hillsides were terraced, but only about one-fifth of the total area of the country was cultivable, and this in part explains the constant search of the Greeks for more fertile lands to colonize. The deficiency of rainfall, aggravated by the destruction of the forests that at one time clothed the Greek mountains, was made good by great attention to irrigation, and the misappropriation of water was punished by ancient laws. Agriculture was regarded as an honourable occupation for freemen (except at Sparta) from Homeric times, when old Laertes busied himself in his garden, to those of Philopoemen, who used to work along with his vine-dressers and ploughmen. Xenophon in the 'Oeconomicus' praises agriculture as the most honoured and the most beneficent of the arts. It retained its prestige at Athens even when that city had become a rich commercial and industrial centre, partly, no doubt, because foreigners were excluded from it as being incapable of owning land.

In certain aristocratic States, such as Thessaly, the system of large estates tilled by serfs prevailed. In democratic States land was held in smaller lots. Attica was a country of small estates, of which the average size tended to diminish with the breaking up of properties on inheritance. In order to be a *Zeugites* (see *Athens*, § 2) an Athenian had to own some 50 acres of corn-land (assuming that it yielded the moderate amount of eight bushels the acre and was fallowed alternate years) or a much smaller acreage of vineyard. Seventy-five acres of corn-land would provide the qualification of a knight, while 125 acres would bring the owner into the richest class. The son of Aristides received as a grant from the State a property of 45 acres; Demosthenes thought this a relatively large area. The average value of eight properties referred to in speeches of Attic orators in the 4th c. is under 7,230 drs. (Glotz) or say £250. The process of subdivision of estates till each lot was too small to support the owner led to the indebtedness of the peasantry, and facilitated in turn a process of concentration of land in the hands of wealthy purchasers, who lived in the city and had overseers to manage their property.

Agriculture gradually became more scientific during the 5th and 4th c., and a three-year rotation of crops on corn land was adopted. The vine, the fig, and the olive were especially suited to the stony soil, and Athens paid great attention to the production of a good quality of olive oil. The destruction of vines and olive-trees by the Spartans in the Peloponnesian War was a severe blow to Attica. Vegetables and even flowers (which were in demand for religious ceremonies) were cultivated in the neighbourhood of Athens. Oxen were scarce, but pigs were plentiful. The sheep of Attica produced an exceptionally fine wool.

For the system of land tenure at Sparta see *Sparta*, § 2.

§ 2. *Italy*

Agriculture in Roman territory was at first domestic and elementary, carried on by the family of the landowner on a small scale and by primitive methods, and devoted mainly to the production of grain. It was the only respectable vocation for a Roman citizen. When the Volscian and Sabine hills were brought into the Roman territory in the 4th c., they provided summer pasture during the months when the grass was dried up in the plains. Sheep- and cattle-breeding then became profitable, at least for the rich farmer possessed of capital. The Punic Wars brought contact with the more scientific agriculture of Carthage and introduced the age of great farms and slave gangs working under overseers. The small peasant-proprietors tended to disappear; many were ruined by compulsory service in the frequent wars and sold their farms, and many emigrated. They survived, however, in reduced numbers in most parts of Italy. On the other hand slaves were abundant, and there were wealthy capitalists willing to take up large areas and work them with slave labour. Another tendency was to substitute, in suitable districts of Italy, the more remunerative culture of the vine and olive for the production of grain. The latter could be obtained cheaply from Sicily and, after the destruction of Carthage, from Africa. Ranches for cattle and sheep became very common in S. Italy. Frequent attempts were made to restore the small cultivator, but without success. The Gracchi failed to solve the problem; the settlement of Sulla did more harm than good owing to the confiscations it involved. In imperial times cultivation by slave labour gradually gave place to the system of *colŏni*, tenants who paid part of their produce as rent. This was perhaps because slave labour was found not to be economical, or because it needed closer supervision and was more troublesome. But the *coloni* sank into mere serfs, and this system proved little more satisfactory than that of cultivation by slaves.

Nevertheless, agriculture was of capital importance in the economic life of the early empire. 'It is no exaggeration to say that most of the provinces were al-

most exclusively agricultural countries' (Rostovtzeff). Moreover agriculture was extended in regions where it had previously hardly existed. The tendency towards the concentration of land in the hands of absentee proprietors and of the State was general throughout the empire. The tillage of corn land was improved, and attention was increasingly given to the vine and the olive, vegetables and fruit, stock-breeding and poultry.

The importance attached to agriculture in the early Roman community is attested by the large number of religious festivals connected with it, such as the Cerealia (see *Ceres*), the Vinalia, the Fordicidia, the Robigalia (qq 7.). That it continued in high estimation is shown by the treatises devoted to the subject, from the 'De Agri Cultura' of Cato, to Varro's 'De Re Rustica', Virgil's 'Georgics', and the works of Columella and Palladius (qq.v.).

Agrige'ntum, the Roman name of *Acragas* (modern Girgenti, recently changed to Agrigento), a city on the S. coast of Sicily founded by Gela (a Rhodian and Cretan colony, also in the S. of Sicily) about 580 B.C. It attained great wealth and splendour under Theron (q.v.). Its prosperity was cut short by the Carthaginians, who sacked it in 406; and although it was refounded by Timoleon (see *Syracuse*, § 3), it never regained the position it held in the 5th c. The ruins of several beautiful temples are still to be seen there. Acragas was the birthplace of Empedocles (q.v.).

Agri'ppa, *Marcus Jūlius*. See *Herod* (2).

Agri'ppa, MARCUS VIPSĀNIUS (*c.* 62–12 B.C.), a friend of Octavian in his youth, and the holder of important military commands under him in the Civil War. He was one of Octavian's principal advisers, especially in military matters, when the latter reached the principate. He carried out some notable public works at Rome and in the provinces (see also *Maps*). By his first marriage, with Pompōnia, daughter of Atticus (q v.), he had a daughter Vipsānia Agrippīna, whom Tiberius married. Among the children of his third marriage, with Julia, daughter of Augustus, were the elder Agrippīna (q.v.), wife of Germanicus, and Gaius and Lucius Caesar, who were adopted by Augustus but died young. See the genealogy under *Julio-Claudian Family*. He wrote an autobiography which is lost.

Agri'ppa, POSTUMUS (12 B.C.- A.D. 14), son of Marcus Vipsanius Agrippa (see above) and Julia. He was passed over by Augustus for the throne because of his boorish ways, and put to death, possibly by order of Tiberius, soon after the old emperor's death in 14.

Agrippi′na. (1) VIPSĂNIA AGRIPPINA, daughter of Agrippa (q.v.) and Pomponia, and wife of Tiberius. (2) AGRIPPINA THE ELDER, daughter of Agrippa (q.v.) and Julia, and wife of Germanicus (see *Germanicus Julius Caesar*). She was present at his death-bed in Syria and brought back his ashes to Rome. Tacitus has a moving description of the arrival at Brundisium and the general grief (Ann. iii. 1–2). The bitter nostility to Tiberius that she subsequently showed led to her exile and her death by starvation, A.D. 29. She was mother of the emperor Caligula. (3) AGRIPPINA THE YOUNGER, daughter of (2), wife first of Cn. Domitius Ahenobarbus, by whom she was mother of Nero, secondly of the emperor Claudius, who adopted Nero. She is said to have poisoned Claudius, but this is improbable. She was a haughty, imperious woman and opposed her son's inclination first for the freedwoman Actê, then for Poppaea Sabina, whom Nero proposed to marry by divorcing Octavia. To remove this opposition Nero had Agrippina murdered. An attempt to scuttle the ship in which she was returning from a visit to Nero having failed (for she swam ashore), she was killed by assassins in the villa where she had taken refuge (A.D. 59). The memoirs that she left were used by Tacitus as a source for his 'Annals.'

For all the above, see the genealogy under *Julio-Claudian Family*.

Ahênoba′rbus (later AENOBARBUS), 'red-beard', the name of a distinguished Roman family of the Domitian gens. Legend related that the Dioscuri (q.v.) had announced to an early member of the family the victory of Lake Regillus (496 B.C.), and to prove their supernatural powers had stroked his black beard, which had immediately turned red. Cn. Domitius Ahenobarbus, after fighting against Caesar at Pharsalus (48) and being subsequently pardoned by him, was one of the republican leaders after Caesar's death. He was later reconciled to Antony, accompanied him in his expedition against the Parthians, and was with him in Egypt. He finally joined the cause of Octavian. He figures in Shakespeare's 'Antony and Cleopatra'.

Another Cn. Domitius Ahenobarbus, consul in A.D. 32, married Agrippina (q.v. (3)), daughter of Germanicus, and was father of the emperor Nero (see *Julio-Claudian Family*).

Aidēs, Aïdō′neūs, variant forms of Hades (q.v.).

A′jax (*Aiãs*), TELAMŌNIAN, sometimes called 'the Greater Ajax', son of Telamōn (q.v.) and leader of the Salaminians at the siege of Troy, depicted by Homer as a man obstinate in his bravery to the point of stupidity. After the death of Achilles, Ajax and Odysseus contended for the hero's arms. When these were awarded to Odysseus, Ajax, maddened with resentment, slaughtered a flock of sheep in the belief that they were his enemies, and afterwards from shame took his own life.

A′jax (*Aiãs*), son of Oïleūs, and captain of the Locrians at the siege of Troy, a man, according to Homer, 'far less' than Telamonian Ajax (q.v.). He was shipwrecked on his way home, but swimming ashore with Poseidon's help, boasted that he had escaped in spite of the gods. Whereupon Poseidon threw down the rock on which he stood, and Ajax was drowned. (See also *Cassandra*).

A′jax (*Aiãs*), a tragedy by Sophocles, of uncertain date, perhaps the first of his surviving plays.

Ajax, the son of Telamōn (see above), demented by resentment because the arms of Achilles have been awarded to Odysseus, has vented his wrath by slaughtering a flock of sheep, taking them for his enemies. He is first seen in his madness, then after his recovery, stricken with grief and shame, while his slave, Tecmessa, and the chorus of Salaminian sailors try to soothe him. He calls for his son Eurysacès, gives him his shield, and leaves his last injunctions for his brother Teucer. He then takes his sword, to bury it, as he says, and goes to purge himself of his guilt by the sea. Teucer has now returned from a foray and has learnt from the seer Calchas that, to avert calamity, Ajax, who has angered the gods by his arrogance, must be kept within his tent for that day. But it is too late. Ajax is found transfixed by his own sword. Menelaus forbids his burial, as an enemy to the Greeks, and Agamemnon confirms the edict, but is persuaded by Odysseus to relent, and Ajax is carried to his grave.

A Latin version of this tragedy was played at Cambridge before Queen Elizabeth in 1564.

Albinovā′nus Pēdō, a Roman poet of the time of Augustus and Tiberius, and a friend of Ovid. Seneca the Rhetorician has preserved a passage from what appears to be an epic by him on the Roman wars against the Germans, describing a storm which the Roman fleet encountered in the North Sea. The majority of German authorities are of opinion that the epic dealt with the expeditions into

Germany of Germanicus (A 2 in the article *Germanicus and Drusus*) to whom Albinovanus Pedo was *praefectus equitum* in A.D. 15. Some authorities regard the extant fragment as referring to the first naval expedition in the North Sea, commanded by Drusus the Elder (A 1 in the above-mentioned article). An epic on the son's achievements would not preclude mention of similar exploits by the father. Tacitus (Ann. ii. 23) has described a storm which shattered the fleet of the son. Albinovanus also wrote a 'Thēsēid', epigrams, and elegies, which have not survived.

Alcāē′us (*Alkaios*), (1) a lyric poet of the 7th–6th c. B.C., born at Mytilēnē in Lesbos, a contemporary of Sappho. He took an active part in the war with Athens which followed the seizure by the latter of the Lesbian fortress of Sigēum at the entrance of the Hellespont, and in the local struggles against tyrants. When Pittacus was given dictatorial power, he went into exile. His poems, of which only fragments remain, dealt vividly with political as well as personal themes, wine, love, his sufferings and hatreds. Where public affairs are concerned he shows a passionate energy. One of his odes, of which the opening survives, was addressed to Sappho. We also possess a fragment of what may be her reply. He also wrote hymns to various gods. His name is especially associated with the Alcaic stanza (see *Metre*, § 3), which he invented or adopted and frequently used. Horace (Od. IV. ix. 7–8) speaks of his 'minaces Camenae', and uses his metre more frequently than any other.

(2) In Greek mythology, a son of Perseus and father of Amphitryon (qq.v.). See also *Alcides*.

Alcā′ic, see *Metre*, §§ 3 and 5.

Alce′stis (*Alkēstis*), a drama oy Euripides. It was the fourth play in a tetralogy produced in 438 B.C. and accordingly contains a certain burlesque element (see *Satyric drama*), provided by the character of the genial Heracles and by Euripides' general treatment of the subject.

For the story which forms the subject of the play, see *Admetus*. Admetus, the husband of Alcestis, is presented at first as an ingenuous egoist, fond of his wife, deeply grieved to lose her, and indignant with his father for refusing to make the required sacrifice in her place. But Admetus returns from his wife's burial completely changed, having 'learnt his lesson'. Alcestis is a simple, unromantic woman, devoted to her husband, and accepting as natural the duty of dying for him, but

perhaps even more concerned, in a practical way, for the future of her children. Heracles is an attractive character, relaxing between the labours that form the main business of his life, to revel a little and do a good turn for a friend.

This is the play that Balaustion recites, in R. Browning's 'Balaustion's Adventure'.

Alcibī′adēs (*Alkibiadēs*), an Athenian of noble family, born shortly before 450 B.C., a man of remarkable beauty and talent, but arrogant, unscrupulous, and dissolute. He was educated by Pericles, and was a friend of Socrates. He became a dexterous politician and joined the democratic party. His experience in the army at Potidaea and Dēlium led to his election as strategus in 420. His influence contributed to the renewal of the Peloponnesian War (q.v.) after the Peace of Nicias, and to the launching of the Sicilian Expedition, of which he was appointed one of the three leaders. The mutilation of the Hermae (q.v.) just before its departure was laid at the door of Alcibiades and his accomplices. It was nevertheless decided that he should embark and be tried later. When summoned back to Athens for this purpose, he escaped, and was condemned to death in his absence and his property confiscated. Alcibiades went to Sparta, where he urged vigorous measures against the Athenians, the sending of a Spartan general to aid the Syracusans, and the occupation of Decelea in Attica as a permanent threat to Athens. In 412 he went to Ionia and with a Spartan squadron supported the Ionian revolt against Athens, but an intrigue with the wife of the Spartan king Agis and his dealings with Tissaphernes, the Persian satrap, made him suspect at Sparta. In 407 the restored democracy at Athens recalled Alcibiades, hoping to find in him a capable commander and a means of alliance with the Persians, but the defeat of Notium (407) lost him his prestige. He retired to the Chersonese, where the good advice he gave to the Athenian commanders before Aegospotami was disregarded. He was finally assassinated by Persian order in Phrygia (404).

The chief authority for the career of Alcibiades is Thucydides. Alcibiades figures in the dialogue of Plato (q.v.) that bears his name and also in his 'Symposium' (q.v.), and there are lives of him by Nepos and Plutarch. There is an interesting reference to him in Aristophanes' 'Frogs' (1009 et seq.): Euripides condemns the man who is slow to help and quick to injure his country, while

Aeschylus thinks it wiser not to rear a lion's whelp, but if you do, you must accept its ways. Two speeches of Lysias and one of Isocrates (against the son of Alcibiades) refer to the father's career.

Alcibiades, a dialogue by Plato (q.v., § 2).

Alci'dēs (*Alkeidēs*), (1) in Greek mythology, meaning 'descendant of Alcaeus', a name used to designate Heracles, whose stepfather, Amphitryon (q.v.), was son of Alcaeus. (2) A Spartan admiral in the early part of the Peloponnesian War.

Alci'noüs (*Alkinoos*), in the 'Odyssey' (q.v.), the king of the Phaeacians.

A'lciphron (*Alkiphrōn*) (c. A.D. 200), a Greek writer, author of fictitious letters (of which we have about a hundred) purporting to be by Athenians of various classes of society, depicting Athenian life in the 4th c. B.C.

Alcmae'on or A'lcmeon (*Alkmaiōn* or *Alkmeōn*), in Greek mythology, son of Amphiaraus (q.v.). In accordance with his father's command he took part in the expedition of the Epigoni (q.v.) against Thebes. On his return, in further execution of his father's commands, he avenged him by slaying his own mother Eriphȳlē. For this murder he was (like Orestes) pursued from place to place by the Furies. At Psōphis in Arcadia he received partial purification from Phēgeūs, and married his daughter Arsinoe. To her he gave the necklace of Harmonia (see *Cadmus* (1)). But the crops of the country began to fail, and Alcmaeon set out again to discover a land on which the sun had not shone when he murdered his mother. This he found in an island newly thrown up at the mouth of the river Achelōus (between Acarnania and Aetolia). Here he married Callirhoe, a daughter of Oeneūs (see *Meleager*) king of Calydon. She in turn begged for the necklace of Harmonia, and Alcmaeon obtained it from Phegeus on a false pretence. When Phegeus discovered that he had been cheated, he caused his sons to waylay Alcmaeon and kill him. The sons of Alcmaeon, Acarnān and Amphoteros, avenged their father by killing Phegeus and his sons; and the fatal necklace was dedicated to Apollo at Delphi. A later story tells that it was stolen by a Phocian at the time of the war with Philip of Macedon, and brought ill luck on the thief.

Alcmaeo'nidae (*Alkmeōnidai*), a noble family at Athens, which came into prominence in 632 B.C. when Megaclēs, an Alcmaeonid, was archon. A young aristocrat, Cylon, with a band of supporters, seized the Acropolis with a view to making himself tyrant He was besieged by Megacles, but escaped, with his brother, to Megara. His associates took refuge at the altar of Athene Poliās. They were lured away on promise of their lives, and slaughtered. The Megarians, urged by Cylon, made war on Athens, occupied Salamis and devastated Attica This reverse was attributed to the sacrilege committed against A᷈henē, and the Alcmaeonids were banished. They returned under Solon (q.v.), withdrew again during the tyranny of Pisistratus (q.v.), and returned once more after the fall of Hippias. Among famous Alcmaeonids were Cleisthenes the law-giver, and Pericles and Alcibiades, who both through their mothers belonged to the family. At the beginning of the Peloponnesian War, Sparta called upon Athens to expel the Alcmaeonids, having Pericles particularly in view. For their reconstruction of the temple of Apollo at Delphi, see *Delphi*.

A'lcman (*Alkmān*), a Greek lyric poet of the second half of the 7th c. B.C., born at Sardis, who came to Sparta and there composed choral lyrics for the festivals. Of these his *parthenia* (q.v.) were especially celebrated. He was an innovator in metre, generally abandoning the hexameter for various systems of a lighter, tripping character. Only fragments of his work survive, one of them part of a *parthenion*.

Alcmē'na (*Alkmēnē*), see *Amphitryon*.

A'lcuin, see *Texts and Studies*, § 6.

Alcy'onē (*Alkuonē*), in Greek mythology, (1) a daughter of Aeolus (q.v. (2)) and wife of Cēyx (*Kēux*), son of the Morning Star. They were changed into birds, she into the halcyon (kingfisher), he into the bird of his name (perhaps a tern or gannet), either because he was drowned at sea and her despair was so great that the gods reunited them, or because of their impiety. *Halcyon days* were fourteen days of calm weather supposed by the ancients to occur about the winter solstice when the halcyon was brooding.

(2) One of the Pleiades (q.v.).

Aldine Classics, see *Editions*.

Āle'cto, see *Allecto*.

Alexa'nder of Aphrodi'sias (*fl. c.* A.D. 200), the most important of the early commentators on Aristotle. Of his commentaries (in Greek) a few survive, and his works are largely quoted by later writers.

Alexander of Phe'rae, nephew of Jason (q.v.) of Pherae and tyrant of Pherae in Thessaly from 369 B.C. He allied himself with Athens to oppose Theban expansion, and when Pelopidas (q.v.) visited him on one of his expeditions, detained him as a hostage until he was rescued by a Theban expedition in 368. In 364 Pelopidas marched against him and defeated him at Cynoscephalae, but was himself killed. Later, Alexander became the ally of the Thebans, defeated the Athenians at sea and raided the Piraeus (362). It was this humiliation that caused the Athenians to sentence Callistratus (q.v.) to death. Alexander was assassinated in 358.

Alexander (*Alexandros*) **the Great**, Alexander III of Macedon (356–323 B.C.), son of Philip II and Olympias.

§ 1. *Education, accession, and campaigns in Europe*

Alexander had Aristotle for instructor, and learnt military science in his father's school, being present at the age of eighteen at the battle of Chaeronea, where he commanded the cavalry. He was an enthusiastic admirer of Homer's 'Iliad', of which he carried a copy on his campaigns in a casket taken from the spoils of Darius. His father's marriage with Cleopatra (see *Philip*, § 3) imperilled his own succession, and his position on his father's death (336) was full of dangers. But Cleopatra, her child, and her father were before long murdered, the first two by Olympias, the last by Alexander's order. The numerous attempts at revolt among the peoples whom his father had subjugated were promptly crushed. Alexander first dealt with Greece and rapidly brought it to order. The Congress at Corinth appointed him, though without enthusiasm, to his father's place as leader of the Greek federation. (It was while he was at Corinth that Alexander, according to an anecdote, saw Diogenes lying in the sun. Alexander asked what he could do for him. 'Don't keep the sun off me', was the reply. 'If I were not Alexander, I should wish to be Diogenes', Alexander remarked.) Alexander next turned to the north and with amazing speed subdued the tribes that were threatening his N. and NW. frontiers. On a report that Alexander had been killed in Thrace, Thebes revolted and blockaded the Macedonian garrison in its citadel. With the same astonishing rapidity Alexander was upon the insurgents and captured their city. The Congress at Corinth decided that Thebes should be razed to the ground (the house of Pindar being spared by Alexander's order). From Athens, which had given Thebes some support, Alexander required the surrender of Demosthenes and of others who had been obstinate in their hostility to Macedonia, but did not persist in his demand.

The whole of the above campaigns had occupied little more than a year (336–5).

§ 2. *Invasion of Asia: the Granicus* (334)

Alexander now devoted himself to the conquest of Persia (See Pl. 7), ruled at that time by Darius Codomānus, a mild, amiable prince, unequal to the struggle before him. Though overwhelmingly stronger than Alexander in men, ships, and wealth, his forces lacked efficient leadership and military science. In 334 Alexander crossed to the Troad, where the Macedonian general Parmeniŏ, had maintained a footing. By his victory on the Grānicus Alexander first showed the superiority of the Macedonian over the Persian army. He next subdued Sardis and such Greek cities of the coast as did not open their gates to him. After the siege and destruction of Halicarnassus, he subdued Lycia, and marching north through Pamphȳlia and Pisidia, reached Gordium, the capital of Phrygia. It was here that he is said to have cut the 'Gordian knot' (q.v.) and applied the legend about it to himself; but the story is poorly attested.

§ 3. *Campaign of 333: battle of Issus*

In the spring of 333 Alexander marched south through Cappadocia to the Cilician Gates and reached Tarsus. The King of Persia was now advancing to meet him, but Alexander, before facing him, subdued Western Cilicia. Darius attributed the delay of Alexander to fear, and instead of awaiting him in the broad expanses of Syria, which would have favoured his larger army, crossed Mt. Amānus and was brought to battle (333) in the narrow plain of Issus. While the event was still undecided, the flight of Darius himself started a panic and caused the rout of the Persian host. The mother, wife, and children of Darius were captured and humanely treated.

§ 4. *Conquest of Syria and Egypt* (332–331)

Before undertaking the final destruction of the Persian king, Alexander proceeded to the conquest of Syria and Egypt, so as not to leave these Persian territories, and particularly the bases of the Phoenician fleet, unsubdued in his rear. Tyre, an apparently impregnable fortress on an island half a mile from the shore, offered a prolonged resistance, and its capture called for all the ingenuity and perseverance of Alexander. A mole was constructed across to the island and the stronghold fell, after a six months' siege, in the summer of 332. After its capture and that of Gaza, the occupation of Egypt was an easy matter. Its most notable incident was the foundation (331) of the city of Alexandria (q.v.). The new city was designed to be a Greek, as distinct from a Phoenician, commercial centre in the eastern Mediterranean. While in Egypt, Alexander visited the temple of Ammon (q.v.). There he was recognized by the oracle as son of Ammon. (Among Landor's 'Imaginary Conversations' is one between Alexander and the priest of Ammon.) It may have been before this that Darius sent an embassy to Alexander offering as a basis of peace to surrender all his territory west of the Euphrātēs, to give him his daughter for wife, and to pay a great ransom for the members of his family. Parmenio, the story goes, said that if he were Alexander he would accept the terms. 'So should I, if I were Parmenio', Alexander replied.

§ 5. *Victory of Gaugamela (331) and death of Darius (330)*

In 331 Alexander started for the heart of the Persian empire. He crossed the Euphrates and the Tigris high up, at Thapsacus and Bezabde, and turned south towards Babylon. Darius, with an even larger host than at Issus, met him at Gaugamēla (near Arbēla, from which the battle is sometimes named). Once more Darius fled, and the Persian army was routed. Darius escaped N. to Ecbatana in Media, but Alexander pursued his way to Babylon and Susa, and in the palaces of the Persian kings at Persepolis found an immense treasure. During his sojourn there it is said that after a carouse, at the suggestion of the Greek courtesan Thāïs, he set on fire and destroyed the palace of Xerxes. In the late spring of 330 he resumed his pursuit of Darius to Ecbatana and eastwards, but when Darius wished to stand, his followers turned against him. Bessus, his kinsman and satrap of Bactria, with other conspirators seized and bound him, and when Alexander drew near, stabbed the king and made off. Alexander found Darius dead.

§ 6. *Campaigns of 330–327. Alexander's policy*

The campaigns of the years 330–327 resulted in the submission of the vast regions of Hyrcānia, Arcia, Drangiāna, Bactria, and Sogdiāna, and the capture and execution of Bessus. Candahar is perhaps a corruption of Alexandria, the capital that Alexander founded in Arachōsia. He reached Maracanda (Samarcand), and on the Jaxartēs founded Alexandria Ultima (Eschatē), Khodjend. On his way he crossed in early spring the Hindu-Kush mountains, a feat com-

parable to Hannibal's crossing of the Alps.

Meanwhile a change had come about in the policy and position of Alexander himself. He had set out to subjugate the barbarians to the Greeks. But although he had from the first shown tolerance to the religions and institutions of the former, he had before long gone farther, and begun to treat his European and Asiatic subjects on a more equal footing, had received Persian noblemen into his confidence, and had adopted the dress and customs of an Oriental court. (Alexander recognized the importance of the co-operation of the Iranian element in the organization of his empire. The failure to secure this later on contributed to the empire's dissolution). This change of attitude had caused deep dissatisfaction among his Macedonians, and the smouldering resentment broke out in 327, when at a banquet Cleitus, one of his friends and the brother of his foster-mother, taunted Alexander, and the latter killed him with a spear. Deep remorse followed the drunken act. Before this, Philōtas, son of Parmenio, had been executed for conspiracy against Alexander, and Parmenio himself, by a questionable act of authority, had been put to death. In 327 there were further executions of noble Macedonians for plotting against the king's life; and also of Callisthenes (nephew of Aristotle), who was following the campaigns as their historian, as being privy to the plot. In the same year also Alexander married Roxana, daughter of Oxyartēs, a Sogdian chief.

§ 7. *The conquest of India and the return (327–325)*

Alexander now undertook the invasion of India, a country of whose configuration and extent little was known. His followers saw in the adventure a repetition of the legendary conquest of India by Dionysus (q.v.). He again crossed the Hindu-Kush in the late summer of 327, and while Hephaestion with part of the army took the Khyber Pass, he himself entered the rugged country to the N. and engaged the fierce tribes of the hills. His greatest achievement in this advance was the capture of the rock of Aornus on the right bank of the Indus, above the junction with the Cabul river. In 326 '·e crossed the Indus and reached the Hydaspēs (Jhelum). There by skilful dispositions he defeated Porus, king of the land between the Hydaspes and the Acesīnēs (Chenab), a courageous ruler at the head of a large army, rendered more formidable by a contingent of elephants. His advance through the remainder of the Punjab was a comparatively easy matter; but when he arrived at the Hyphasis (Beas) and contemplated proceeding to the Ganges and thus reaching what he conceived to be the extremity of the earth, his weary Macedonians at last turned against him and refused to go farther. Alexander was forced to yield and abandon his hope of bringing the whole earth from the western to the eastern ocean under his sway. The Macedonians, setting their faces westward, descended the Hydaspes in a fleet of transports commanded by Nearchus, while Onēsicritus, who wrote an account of the expedition, had charge of Alexander's ship. Having reached Patala at the head of the delta of the Indus at midsummer 325, Alexander started on a land-march homewards, leaving Nearchus to explore the sea-route up the Persian Gulf.

§ 8. *Alexander's last measures and his death* (*325–323*)

At Susa, where the army arrived in the winter of 325–4 after suffering terrible hardships in the deserts of Gedrōsia, Alexander set about punishing the many satraps and other officers who had failed in their duty. Harpalus, his treasurer, had appropriated a large sum and withdrawn to Tarsus. He now fled to Greece, where his intrigues involved Demosthenes (q.v.) in a discreditable affair. Alexander also extended his policy of fusing the European and Asiatic portions of his empire, by colonization, by mixed marriages (he himself married Statira, daughter of Darius, and his friend Hephaestion married her sister), and by unification of the military services. (This policy of equalizing the Greek and Eastern races, it may be noted, was censured by Aristotle). He also cherished schemes for the development of a commercial sea-route between the Indus, the Euphrates and Tigris, and the Gulf of Suez. As Nearchus was about to set out on a voyage of exploration to further this scheme, Alexander, who had been saddened by the death of his intimate comrade, Hephaestion, in 324, himself died of fever at Babylon in the summer of 323. He was only 32 years old.

§ 9. *Alexander's achievement*

We owe to Alexander, a man of genius at the head of a military monarchy, what no Greek city-state would have been able to achieve, the extension of Greek civilization over the East. As a result of his conquests the character of that civilization itself was changed. Greece sank into a secondary position; her city-states lost

their independence, and with it the special atmosphere in which their literary masterpieces had been produced. Hellenic civilization, as it extended to new regions, became exposed to new influences, and the Hellenistic Age (q.v.) came into being.

§ 10. *The literature concerning Alexander*

The principal authority for the history of Alexander's campaigns is Arrian (q.v.), who drew on the narratives of Aristobūlus and Ptolemy, companions of Alexander. Authentic materials were also available in Alexander's official journals, on which Ptolemy drew. There was also the history of Callisthenes (see above, § 6). A fabulous element was introduced by another writer, Cleitarchus (probably *c.* 300 B.C.), and many further legends grew up in the East round the name of the conqueror. These crystallized, probably in the 3rd c. A.D., in a Greek narrative falsely attributed to Callisthenes. There were also later Armenian, Syriac, Ethiopic, and Arabic versions (the Syrians made Alexander a Christian). Of the narrative attributed to Callisthenes several Latin versions were made, and the legends thence passed into the French poetry of the 11th and 12th cc. (see *Julius Valerius*). One of these French poems, written in twelve-syllabled lines, perhaps gave its name to the *Alexandrine*, the French heroic verse of six feet. There are also two Old English works of the 11th c. based on the Latin legend, a 'Letter from Alexander to Aristotle' and 'The Wonders of the East'. From the French poems the Alexander-saga passed into the English metrical romances of the Middle English period (1200–1500), notably the alliterative poem 'King Alisaunder', and to them may be traced the frequency of the Christian name 'Alexander' ('Sandy') in Scotland. It may be noted that Fluellen, the Welsh officer in Shakespeare's ' Henry V,' is represented as having a fairly detailed knowledge of the history of Alexander. See also *Curtius Rufus*. There is a succinct and striking summary of the reign of Alexander and of the struggles of his successors over his inheritance, written from the Jewish standpoint, in the first nine verses of the First Book of the Maccabees.

Alexa'ndra, see *Lycophron* (2).

Alexa'ndria (*Alexandreia*, L. *Alexandrēa* or *Alexandria*), a city on the N. coast of Egypt, near the Canōpic or western mouth of the Nile, founded by Alexander the Great in 331 B.C., the capital of the Ptolemies and famous as one of the chief intellectual centres of the Hellenistic world. It was laid out on the sandy neck of land that runs E. and W., separating Lake

Mareotis from the sea. A broad street ran E. and W. through the centre of it and was crossed by another running N. and S. On the island of Pharos, which Alexander connected with the mainland by a mole nearly a mile long, Ptolemy II erected a lighthouse, said to be the first of its kind, to guide mariners to the greater of the two sea-harbours, that lying on the eastern side of the mole. Another harbour on Lake Mareotis received the traffic from the Nile. Near the eastern sea-harbour lay the quarter known as Brucheion in which stood the royal palace, the Museum and the great Library, and the spendid tomb to which Alexander's body was brought from Asia by Ptolemy II. To the SW. of this, in the quarter called Rhakōtis and near what is to-day known as 'Pompey's Pillar', stood the Serāpēum (the great temple of Serāpis). Here, and extending beyond the walls, was the native quarter. A canal brought fresh water from the Nile. By 200 B.C. Alexandria was the largest city in the world (later it was surpassed by Rome). The population, apart from the native Egyptians, was divided into *politeumata* or corporations based on nationality, of which the Greek was the most important; and the whole city was under Ptolemy's governor. Intermarriage between Greeks and Egyptians began in the 2nd c. B.C. and the mixed population (with the exception of the Jews and some of the Greeks) gradually blended into a more or less homogeneous whole. See *Alexandrian Library, Museum, Hellenistic Age, Ptolemies.*

Alexandrian or HELLENISTIC AGE of Greek literature; see *Hellenistic Age.*

Alexandrian Library, THE, was founded by Ptolemy I (see *Ptolemies*) and greatly increased by Ptolemy II. It was housed in a building in the Brucheion or royal quarter, supplemented by a subsidiary building near the Serapeum (see *Alexandria*). In the time of Callimachus (q.v.) the larger library is said to have contained 400,000 volumes, and in the 1st c. 700,000. It is said that Ptolemy II purchased the library that Aristotle had formed; and (by Galen) that Ptolemy III (Euergetes) appropriated the official copy of the text of Aeschylus, Sophocles, and Euripides (see *Lycurgus*), forfeiting the large deposit he had paid when borrowing i' from the Athenians. Galen also states that vessels entering the harbour of Alexandria were required to surrender any manusc. that they had on board. There was keen rivalry between the kings of Alexandria and Pergamum in the enlargement of their respective libraries (see *Books*, § 5). In

47 B.C. when Caesar was in Alexandria, some 40,000 volumes which were stored near the Arsenal, perhaps with a view to their shipment to Rome, were accidentally burnt. It is improbable that the library itself was destroyed. The story that it was finally burnt in A.D. 642 by Amrou, general of the Caliph Omar, is now discredited.

The first great librarians of Alexandria were Zenodotus (*fl. c.* 285 B.C.), Eratosthenes (*fl. c.* 234), Aristophanes of Byzantium (*fl. c.* 195), and Aristarchus (*fl. c.* 180) (qq.v.). Callimachus and Apollonius Rhodius (qq.v.) are sometimes mentioned as among the librarians, but there are chronological difficulties in the way of admitting them.

Alexandrianism or ALEXANDRINISM, a term used of the influence of the Alexandrian school of Greek poets (see *Hellenistic Age*) on Roman poetry. The chief features of the school were artificiality, an excessive display of mythological learning, and beauty and elaboration of form. The influence is seen, for instance, in some of the poems of Catullus (e.g. 'Attis', 'Peleus and Thetis', 'Coma Berenices'), in Propertius, and, in a less degree, in Virgil and Ovid.

Alexipha'rmaca, see *Nicander.*

Ale'xis, see *Comedy,* § 4.

Al(l)e'cto (Gk. *Allēktō*), see *Furies.*

Allegory, the presentation of a subject (in narrative or other form) under the guise of another suggestively similar; e.g. Horace's Ode I. xiv (O navis, referent in mare te novi fluctus), where the Roman State is presented under the guise of a storm-tossed ship.

A'llia, a small tributary of the Tiber, near which the Romans suffered a memorable defeat by the Gauls in 390 B.C.

Alliteration, the beginning with the same letter of two or more words in close connexion. It was a constant device in Saturnian (q.v.) verse, and was adopted thence by later Roman poets including Ennius and Virgil; as where Ennius writes:

Fraxinu' frangitur atque abies consternitur alta.

Pinus proceras pervortunt.

It is carried to grotesque excess by Ennius in the line,

O Tite tute Tati tibi tanta tiranne tulisti.

A'lmagest. see *Ptolemy.*

Alōi'dae (*Alōeidai*), see *Otus.*

Alphabet, (1) GREEK. The Greek alphabet was probably derived from some form of the Phoenician alphabet, with additions such as distinctive symbols for the vowel sounds, and certain letters such as ϕ, χ, ψ from other sources (perhaps the Cretan script). (*Alpha* is the equivalent of the Phoenician *aleph*, meaning 'ox', the name of one of the Phoenician 'breaths'.) At first there was no single alphabet common to all the Greek States; the local varities had elements in common but differed in certain respects. Finally, about the end of the 5th c B.C. the Ionic type prevailed and was generally adopted. See also *Digamma*.

(2) LATIN. The Italian alphabet was probably derived from that of the Greek inhabitants of Italy and Sicily, with certain modifications, such as the rejection of the symbols for ϕ, χ, ψ, and the early abandonment of the symbol for ζ. C, one of the forms of the Greek gamma, was employed for the sounds of both G and K, and when intended to represent the sound of gamma was modified into G. The old spelling of the abbreviations C. and Cn. for Gaius and Gnaeus was retained when this new form G was introduced. The letters Y and Z were not adopted until the last century of the Roman republic, when they were required for the transcription of Greek words such as 'Zephyrus'.

As to the direction in which letters were written, from right to left or left to right, etc., see *Epigraphy*, § 2.

Alphe′us (*Alpheios*), one of the largest rivers in Greece, rising in Arcadia, and after receiving many tributaries (including the Erymanthus and the Ladon), flowing through Elis. The plain of Olympia (q.v.) is situated by the side of it. See also *Arethusa*. It is referred to by Milton in 'Lycidas': 'Return, Alpheus; the dread voice is past That shrunk thy streams.'

Althae′a (*Althaia*), in Greek mythology, mother of Meleager (q.v.).

Amalthe′a (*Amaltheia*), in Greek mythology, the goat that suckled the infant Zeus (q.v.) in Crete; or a nymph (according to one version the daughter of Melissus, king of Crete) who fed Zeus with the milk of a goat. Zeus gave her the horn of the goat; it had the power of producing whatever its possessor wished, and was known (in Latin) as the *cornucopiae* (horn of plenty).

Ama′ta, in the 'Aeneid', the wife of Latinus and mother of Lavinia (qq.v.).

A′mazons (*Amāzones*), a legendary nation of women-warriors, supposed to have lived in heroic times in the neighbourhood of the Euxine. The name means 'breastless', and it was said that they removed their right breasts in order the better to handle the bow. They were allies of the Trojans

in the Trojan War, and their queen, Penthesilēa, was killed by Achilles. One of the Labours of Heracles (q.v.) was to secure the girdle of Hippolytē, queen of the Amazons. According to Athenian legend, Attica once suffered an invasion of Amazons, which Theseus (q.v.) repelled, capturing the Amazon queen, Hippolyte (or Antiopē).

Ambarvā′lia, at Rome, a solemn annual purification of the fields by the several farmers, while a purification of the boundaries of the State was performed by special priests, the Arval (q.v.) Brethren. The ceremony included the leading of victims round the boundaries of the fields that were to be purified; hence the name. The victims sacrificed were the principal agricultural animals, pig, sheep, and ox (*suovetaurīlia*). In the ancient hymn of the Arval priests, Mars is invoked as an agricultural deity. In later republican days the deity concerned is Ceres, and in imperial times the earth deity, Dea Dia. The celebration of the Ambarvalia is depicted in the first chapter of Pater's 'Marius the Epicurean'.

A′mbiorix, leader of the Gaulish tribe of the Eburōnēs in their revolt against the Romans in 54–53 B.C. See *Commentaries* ('Gallic War', Bks. V and VI).

Ambrose, ST., (*Aurēlius Ambrōsius*) (c. A.D. 340–397) was born of a Christian Roman family; his father was Prefect of Gallia Narbonensis. He was educated at Rome and entered on an official career, and at an early age was made governor of Milan with the title of consul. On the death of Auxentius, the Arian bishop of Milan, Ambrose was chosen to replace him by popular acclamation, and actually received baptism and the priesthood after his appointment. He had a high conception of the importance of his new functions, and showed himself not only a patriotic Roman, but a wise and resolute, if kindly, ecclesiastic. His greatest achievements were in the practical field, notably in the affair of the Altar of Victory (see *Symmachus*) in which his advocacy of the Christian cause (Ep. xvii and xviii) was one of the final blows to the pagan religion. Ambrose did not shrink from reproving the emperor Theodosius in church, and even from imposing penance on him (after a punitive massacre ordered by Theodosius at Thessalonica). Among his important writings is a treatise on the duties of priests ('De Officiis Ministrorum') modelled on the 'De Officiis' of Cicero. He also published explanatory commentaries on many parts of the scriptures, dogmatic treatises ('De Fide', 'De Spiritu

Sancto'), and minor treatises on the ascetic life. Many of his works had first taken the form of sermons and show an oratorical style. We also have a large number of his letters, mostly on church matters. The influence of his Roman education is evident in many quotations from, and reminiscences of, the great Roman and Greek authors. Of the hymns attributed to him, a few are certainly authentic, but he was not the author of the *Te Deum*, as tradition relates. The Ambrosian Library at Milan (founded in 1609) is named after him.

Ammiā'nus Marcelli'nus, born at Antioch about A.D. 330, wrote in Latin at Rome about A.D. 390 a continuation of the history of Tacitus, in 31 books, of which we possess Bks. xiv–xxxi. These cover the period A.D. 353–378, from Constantius to the death of Valens. Ammianus was a patriotic Roman and a philosophic historian, with a high conception of the role of history, and he aimed at truthfulness and accuracy. He himself served under Julian against the Persians and his experience lends vividness to some of the campaigns he describes. There are interesting digressions on a variety of subjects, such as the Egyptian obelisks and their hieroglyphics, earthquakes, lions in Mesopotamia, the artillery of his time; and impartial judgements on the various nations dealt with, on the Christians (he was a pagan but opposed to the persecution of Christians), and on the emperors themselves. Latin was not his native tongue, and his style is marred by clumsiness, Graecisms, and bombast.

A'mmon (*Ammŏn* or *Hammŏn*), an Egyptian god, represented sometimes as a ram, sometimes as a man with ram's head and curved horns. He had a famous oracle in an oasis (Siwah) in the Libyan desert, which was visited by Alexander the Great (q.v., § 4). The Greeks identified Ammon with Zeus.

Amoebe'an verses (*amoibaia melē*, from Gk. *amoibē*, 'change'), verses sung alternately by two persons in competition, a form of contest in use among Sicilian shepherds in antiquity. It was developed by Theocritus (q.v.) in some of his Idylls, and by Virgil in some of his Eclogues.

Amō'res, love poems by Ovid in elegiacs, some of them being among his earliest works. There were two editions of the 'Amores', the first in five books, the second in three; it is the second that has survived.

The poems, for the most part, are studies or sketches of love in different moods, from that of the simple, constant lover to that of Don Juan. They are artificial, literary, the product of fancy rather than of passion. 'Corinna' is a prominent figure in them, but if she had real existence, she was probably one of many loves. Some of the poems throw an interesting light on contemporary life—a scene at the Circus, or a festival of Juno; one of them (III. ix) is a beautiful lament for the death of Tibullus.

A'mphiarā'us (*Amphiardos*), in Greek mythology, an Argive hero and seer, who took part in the Calydonian boar-hunt (see *Meleager*) and the expedition of the Argonauts (q.v.). He married Eriphȳlē, whom Polynices bribed, by the gift of the fatal necklace of his ancestress Harmonia (see *Cadmus* (1)), to persuade Amphiaraus to take part in the expedition of the Seven against Thebes (see *Oedipus*), though the seer knew that none of the Seven except Adrastus would return from it alive. He set out reluctantly, but before starting laid on his children the charge that they should avenge his death by killing their mother, and by making a second expedition against Thebes. Amphiaraus perished, as he foresaw, at Thebes (he was swallowed up in the earth as he retreated), and was in due course avenged by his son Alcmaeon (q.v.). A shrine was erected to him near Orōpus, where oracles were given by means of dreams. The fee for consulting the oracle was nine obols (say, one shilling). Sulla, in fulfilment of a vow made during his campaign in Greece, consecrated to the god Amphiaraus the revenues derived from Oropus by the Romans. But later the Roman tax-gatherers contested this diversion of the revenue, on the ground that Amphiaraus was no god. The question was tried before the consuls in 73 B.C. (Cicero was one of their assessors) and the ordinance of Sulla was upheld.

Amphi'ctyon (*Amphiktuŏn*), see *Amphictyony*.

Amphi'ctyony (*Amphiktuoneia*), a religious association of Greeks worshipping at the shrine of the same god (from *amphictiones*, 'dwellers around'). The most important Amphictyony was that of Delphi, whose sanctuaries were the temples of Apollo at Delphi and of Demeter at Thermopylae. Many of the principal peoples of Greece, including Thessalians, Dorians, and Ionians, belonged to it. The assemblies of this Amphictyonic League met twice a year, alternately at Delphi and Thermopylae. Though it might have been a source of union among Greek States, it exercised little influence in this direction;

but see *Sacred Wars*. Both Jason of Pherae and Philip of Macedon (qq.v.) attached importance to it as a means of advancing their schemes of Greek hegemony. The foundation of the Amphictyony was attributed to one Amphictyon, a legendary person, son of Deucalion (q.v.) and brother of Hellēn (the ancestor of the Greeks).

Amphi'on (*Amphiōn*), see *Antiope*.

Amphitheatre, a circular or elliptical theatre, in which the seats of the spectators completely surrounded the arena. The earliest built at Rome were wooden structures; a stone amphitheatre was erected in 29 B.C. but was destroyed in the fire of Rome during Nero's reign. The great Flavian Amphitheatre, known as the Colossēum, whose enormous ruins survive, was built by Vespasian and his successors to take its place. It stood at the foot of the Esquiline Hill, east of the Forum (see Pl. 14). Displays of wild beasts and gladiatorial shows were held there; and the arena could be flooded for mimic sea-fights (*naumachiae*, q.v.).

Amphitri'tē, a Nereid (see *Nereus*), wife of Poseidon (q.v.).

Amphi'truō, a comedy by Plautus, perhaps an adaptation of a play by Philemon (see *Comedy*, § 4), on the legend of Zeus taking the appearance of Amphitryon to visit the latter's wife, Alcmena (see *Amphitryon*). Plautus designates the play a *tragico-comoedia* because of the unusual blend of contrasting elements, the character of the chaste and dignified Alcmena on the one hand, and the burlesque situation on the other. The gross and irreverent presentation of Jupiter and Mercury is noteworthy. Molière and Dryden followed Plautus's play in their comedies on the same subject.

Amphi'tryon (*Amphitruōn*), in Greek mythology, son of Alcaeus and grandson of Perseus (q.v.), and nephew of Electryon, king of Mycenae, to whose daughter, Alcmene, he was betrothed. Having had the misfortune to kill Electryon by accident, Amphitryon took refuge at Thebes, where he was followed by Alcmene. By her wish he set out to war with the Teleboans, in order to avenge her brothers, who had been killed in a quarrel with them. On the night of his return, Zeus, who had been captivated by the charms of Alcmene, introduced himself to her disguised as the victorious Amphitryon, and was shortly followed by Amphitryon himself. Alcmene gave birth to twin children, Iphicles who was regarded as Amphitryon's son, and Heracles (q.v.)

who was held to be the son of Zeus. The legend has been made the subject of amusing plays by Plautus, Molière, and Dryden. Amphitryon's association with gastronomy is purely modern and arises from a line in Molière's play. The servant of Amphitryon, perplexed by the resemblance of the two who both claim to be his master, hears Zeus invite some friends to dinner, and is thereby convinced he is the genuine Amphitryon—'Le véritable Amphitryon est l'Amphitryon où l'on dîne.'

Amū'lius, see *Rome*, § 2.

A'mycus (*Amukos*), in Greek mythology, a son of Poseidon and king of the Bebrўces (a people of Bithȳnia), a mighty boxer. When the Argonauts came to his country, Pollux accepted his challenge and knocked him out. The Bebryces broke into the ring to avenge their king, but were routed by the Argonauts. The episode is treated by Apollonius Rhodius and by Theocritus (xxiii).

Amȳmō'nē (*Amūmōnē*), in Greek mythology, one of the fifty daughters of Danaus (q.v.), rescued from a satyr by Poseidon and loved by him. Milton (P.R. ii. 185 et seq.) includes her among the heroines of legend thus loved by the gods:

to waylay
Some beauty rare, Calisto, Clymene,
Daphne or Semele, Antiopa,
Or Amymone, Syrinx, many more . . .

Ana'basis (*Kūrou Anabasis*), a prose narrative in seven books, by Xenophon, of the expedition (lit. 'going up' from the sea-coast to the interior) of the younger Cȳrus, son of Dārius II, against his brother Artaxerxēs II, king of Persia. The work was published as by Themistogenēs of Syracuse, for motives which can only be conjectured.

Cyrus, who was satrap of Lydia, was disappointed that he was not chosen to succeed his father, partly as the favourite son, partly as having been born after his father's accession to the throne. His resentment against his brother was increased, according to Xenophon, by the fact that shortly after his accession Artaxerxes arrested him on a false accusation of conspiracy. Cyrus thereafter made careful preparations to attack Artaxerxes, recruiting an auxiliary force of ten thousand Greeks for the purpose. Xenophon describes the long march of the expeditionary force in 401 B.C. from Sardis to the neighbourhood of Babylon; he accompanied it in a private capacity at the invitation of his friend Proxenus, one of the Greek generals. The march was interrupted by the reluctance of some of the troops to proceed when the true object of the expedition, which had been concealed from them, became known. However, the great bulk of the force was induced to go on, and was present at the battle of Cūnaxa near Babylon, where Cyrus himself was killed, and his Asiatic troops took flight.

This disaster reduced the Greeks to great perplexity and distress, but there was no yielding to the attempts of Artaxerxes to induce them to surrender. The perplexity increased when Tissaphernes, who had been conducting the negotiations on the Persian side, lured the Greek generals into his quarters, where they were seized and beheaded. At this point Xenophon came forward, induced the remaining officers to reorganize the force and take the measures necessary for its safe retreat. Thereafter Cheirisophus commanded the van and Xenophon the rear, the most dangerous post. By his advice on the choice of route, by his resourcefulness, and by the example of his courage, he enabled the Greek army, after great hardships and severe fighting in the mountains of Armenia, to reach the Euxine. His description of the scene when the Greeks, climbing Mt. Thēchēs, at last beheld the sea and cried 'Thalassa, thalassa!' is famous (iv. 7. 20–6). They now reached Trapezus (Trebizond), a Greek colony on the coast, and were comparatively safe; but difficulties had still to be surmounted, and grave dissensions arose among the troops before they reached Byzantium. After a winter spent in the service of the treacherous Seuthēs, a Thracian, Xenophon handed over the remnant of the Ten Thousand to the Spartan Thimbrōn, for the war against Persia. Xenophon's piety is a noticeable feature in the narrative; he takes no important decision without sacrificing to the gods and being guided by the omens.

Anacha'rsis, a Scythian sage, who, according to Herodotus, visited many countries in the 6th c. B.C. to study their customs, and endeavoured to introduce these into Scythia, but was put to death by the Scythian king. According to Plutarch, he made at Athens the acquaintance of Solon, and Lucian has a dialogue ('Anacharsis') between the two. He is said to have invented, among other things, the potter's wheel and the true anchor with arms.

Anacolū'thon (Gk. 'not following'), a change of construction in the course of a sentence, e.g. 'Utile videbatur Ulixi, ut

quidem poetae prodiderunt (nam apud Homerum . . . talis de Ulixe nulla suspicio est), sed insimulant eum tragoediae simulatione insaniae militiam subterfugere voluisse' (Cicero, De Off. iii. 26. 97).

Ana'creon (*Anakreōn*) (6th c. B.C.), a lyric poet born at Teōs in Ionia, whence he migrated to the Teian colony of Abdēra; but he spent most of his life elsewhere, first at the court of Polycrates (q.v.) of Samos, and later at Athens under Hipparchus. There are grounds for thinking he ended his days in Thessaly, but the date and place of his death are unknown. His poems, of which we have only short fragments, were chiefly light and playful songs of love and wine, without depth of passion; some of them were mocking and satirical. They are written with perfect clearness of expression and rhythm, in various metres, but he avoids the alcaic and the sapphic. Anacreon also wrote iambics, elegies, and epigrams. He was much imitated in all periods, and we possess a collection of some sixty of these imitations, known as 'Anacreontēa'.

Among Landor's 'Imaginary Conversations' is one between Anacreon and Polycrates.

Anacrū'sis, see *Metre*, §§ 2 and 3.

Anagnō'risis, see *Tragedy*, § 3.

Analy'tica Priōra and **Posteriōra**, treatises on logic by Aristotle (q.v., § 3).

A'napaest, see *Metre*, § 1.

Ana'phora, the repetition of a word or phrase in several successive clauses; a rhetorical device frequent in oratory, e.g. 'Verres calumniatores apponebat, Verres adesse jubebat, Verres cognoscebat . . .' (Cicero, Verr. ii. 2, 10.) The rhetorician Demetrius quotes as an example of anaphora the beautiful lines of Sappho:

Ἔσπερε πάντα φέρων ὅσα φαίνολις ἐσκέδασ᾽ Αὔως,
φέρεις ὄιν, φέρεις αἶγα, φέρεις ἄπυ μάτερι παῖδα.

Anaxa'goras (*Anaxagorās*) of Clazomenae in Ionia, a Greek philosopher born about 500 B.C. He went to Athens about the year 460, spent some thirty years there, and became the friend of Pericles (q.v.). Fragments survive of his book 'On Nature', written in the Ionian dialect, and in a simple, sober style. According to his explanation of the universe, the permanent elements of which it is constituted are unlimited in number, and are combined in bodies in changing proportions, as the result of a system of circulation (περιχώρησις) directed by Spirit or Intelligence (Νοῦς), a supreme independent force. This last was a conception destined to revolutionize Greek philosophy. It is the ultimate origin of what is now known as dualism, the doctrine that mind and matter exist as two distinct entities. Anaxagoras was also a scientist; he was the first to explain solar eclipses.

Anaximan'der (*Anaximandros*) of Miletus, a practical scientist and philosopher of the early part of the 6th c. B.C., contemporary of Thales (q.v.). He is said to have constructed a sun-dial and a map of the world. He sought the basis of the universe in an indefinite, unlimited substance other than the forms of matter usually recognized, but capable of being transformed into them. He left a written account of his philosophical opinions, which has perished. He is said to have been the first Greek author to write in prose.

Anaxi'menēs of Miletus, a philosopher of the 6th c. B.C., later than Anaximander (q.v.). He found in air the primary basis of the universe; and thought that this, by condensation and rarefaction, gave rise to other forms of matter.

Anchi'sēs, a member of the royal house of Troy (see genealogy under *Troy*), with whom Aphrodite fell in love. The child of their union was Aeneas (q.v.). Anchises boasted of the goddess's favour and was struck blind or paralysed by the thunderbolt of Zeus. We are told in the Aeneid that he was carried out of burning Troy on his son's shoulders, and accompanied him in his wanderings, dying in Sicily, where he was buried on Mt. Eryx.

Anci'lia. A shield (*ancile*) was said to have fallen from heaven at Rome in the reign of Numa, and an oracle declared that the seat of empire would lie wherever that shield should be. Thereupon Numa caused eleven other shields to be made like it, so that, if a traitor should wish to remove it, the genuine shield could not be distinguished. These shields were preserved in the Temple of Mars in the custody of the Salii (q.v.), and were carried round the city yearly in solemn procession in the month of March. On a declaration of war, the Roman general moved the shields, with the words, 'Awake, Mars!'

Ancus Ma'rcius, one of the legendary kings of Rome (see *Rome*, § 2).

Ancȳrā'num Monumentum, see *Monumentum Ancyranum*.

Ando'cidēs (*Andokidēs*) (b. c. 440 B.C.), a member of a distinguished Athenian family, and one of the earlier Attic orators. He was implicated in the affair of the mutilation of the Hermae (see *Peloponnesian War*), and having with his father and several of his relatives been denounced and imprisoned, he was persuaded to tell all he knew in order to save these and other innocent victims. He acknowledged his own guilt (but subsequently repudiated the confession) and named certain other participants in the outrage. A decree of *atimia* (disgrace), virtually equivalent to banishment, was passed on him. We possess three of his speeches, the first, 'On his Return', delivered in the Ecclesia, probably in 410, when he unsuccessfully sought permission to return to Athens; the second, 'On the Mysteries', made in 399 when, having been readmitted in 403 to his city, he was accused of impiety (for having contrary to the decree of *atimia* attended the Mysteries); the third, a political discourse urging peace with Sparta in 390, the fourth year of the Corinthian War. The date of his death is unknown. Andocides was not, like the other orators, a trained or professional rhetorician, but a man of ability and shrewdness, who excelled rather in a natural and persuasive eloquence than in style, clearness, or fire.

A'ndria ('The Woman of Andros'), a comedy by Terence, the earliest of his plays, produced in 166 B.C., adapted from two plays by Menander.

Pamphilus, a young gentleman of Athens, has seduced Glycerium, supposed to be the sister of a courtesan from Andros, and is devoted to her. His father, Simō, has arranged a match for him with the daughter of his friend Chremēs. But Chremes has heard of the relations of Pamphilus and Glycerium and withdraws his consent to the match. Simo conceals this, pretends to go on with the preparations for an immediate marriage, and hopes by this means to put an end to the amour. Pamphilus, learning from his cunning slave, Dăvus, that the intended marriage is a pretence, temporizes and offers no objection. Simo now persuades Chremes to withdraw his objection; and Pamphilus is reduced to despair. At this stage Glycerium bears a son to Pamphilus, and Davus arranges that the fact shall become known to Chremes, who now finally breaks off the match. An acquaintance just arrived from Andros reveals to Chremes that Glycerium as a child was shipwrecked at Andros in circumstances which show that she is a daughter of Chremes. Chremes and Simo consent to the marriage of Pamphilus and Glycerium, and all ends happily.

The play contains the often-quoted

phrases, 'hinc illae lacrimae' and 'amantium irae amoris integratiost'. It was translated into English and printed early in the 16th c. Steele's 'The Conscious Lovers' is largely based on it.

Andro'machē, in Greek mythology, daughter of Ēëtiŏn (king of Thēbē in Cilicia), wife of Hector (q.v.), and mother of Astyanax. In the 'Iliad' she is the type of the true wife and mother, noble in misfortune, smiling in her tears. After the capture of Troy she fell to the lot of Neoptolemus (q.v.). Her separation from her child, whom the Greeks ordered to be killed, forms the most tragic incident in the 'Trojan Women' (q.v.) of Euripides. Later she married the Trojan seer Helenus, a son of Priam.

Andromache, a tragedy by Euripides, probably produced about the beginning of the Peloponnesian War (431 B.C.).

The play deals with that period in the life of Andromache (see previous article) when she was living as the thrall of Neoptolemus in Thessaly. She had borne him a son, Molossus, and after ten years Neoptolemus had married Hermione, daughter of Menelaus. Hermione remained childless, and suspected as the cause of this the arts of her hated rival, Andromache. Aided by the contemptible Menelaus, Hermione takes advantage of the absence of Neoptolemus on a journey to Delphi to draw Andromache, by the threat of the murder of Molossus, from the shrine of Thetis where she has taken refuge, in order to kill both mother and child. They are saved by the intervention of the aged Peleus, the grandfather of Neoptolemus. Orestes (q.v.), who has contrived the murder of Neoptolemus at Delphi and who arrives unexpectedly, carries off Hermione, to whom, before her marriage to Neoptolemus, he was betrothed. The death of Neoptolemus is announced. Thetis appears and arranges matters. The odious character which the poet attributes to Menelaus is in accord with the feeling against Sparta that prevailed at this time at Athens.

Andro'meda (*Andromedē*), see *Perseus.*

Androni'cus, Lūcius Līvius, see *Livius Andronicus.*

Andro'tion (*Androtiōn*), *Against*, a speech in a public prosecution by Demosthenes. See *Demosthenes* (2), § 3 (a).

Ane'cdŏta see *Procopius.*

Animā'lium, *Historia*, a treatise by Aristotle (q.v., § 3).

A'nna, sister of Dido (q.v.). According to Ovid, Anna, after Aeneas had established himself in Italy, came there, and was entrusted by him to Lavinia. But Lavinia was jealous of her, and Anna fled to the river Numicius and was taken by the river-god into his care.

Anna Comnē'na (b. 1083), daughter of the Byzantine emperor Alexius I Comnenus, a learned and ambitious woman. She married Nicēphorus Bryennius, and after her father's death conspired to place him on the throne in place of her brother. The conspiracy was defeated and she was banished. In her exile she wrote a life of her father, the 'Alexiad', in fifteen books, the first Greek historical work written by a woman. It includes an account of the First Crusade (1095–9).

Anna Pere'nna, an ancient Roman deity of the year, whose festival was celebrated on the Ides of March. This was a feast at the full moon in what was then the first month of the year. She was probably a moon-goddess, but her attributes are not clear. Of the six explanations of her given by Ovid, 'quia mensibus impleat annum' (Fast. iii. 657) is regarded as the most probable, and it is thought likely that she was 'Anna ac Perenna', she who begins and ends the year.

Annā'lēs. The *Annales Pontificum* or *Annales Maximi* were records of important events kept by the Pontifex Maximus, who displayed annually a white table on which these and the names of the magistrates for the year were set out. The early records are said to have been destroyed in the fire of 390 B.C. Mucius Scaevola (consul in 133 and Pontifex Maximus in 130) collected such of the *Annales Pontificum* as were available and published them in 130 B.C., according to Servius in eighty books.

Early Roman historians, sometimes spoken of as annalists, include Fabius Pictor (q.v.) who wrote in Greek, M. Porcius Cato (q.v.), L. Calpurnius Pisō Frūgī (consul 133 B.C.), L. Caelius Antipater (late 2nd c. B.C.), Q. Claudius Quadrīgārius (1st c. B.C.), and C. Licinius Macer (q.v.).

Annales, (1) of Ennius, see *Ennius*; (2) of Tacitus, see *Annals*; (3) of Fenestella, see *Fenestella.*

Annals (*Annālēs* or *Ab Excessu Divi Augusti*), a history of the reigns of Tiberius, Caligula, Claudius, and Nero, by Tacitus, written after the 'Histories' (q.v.). There is evidence that Tacitus was writing the work c. A.D. 115–17. The surviving portions are Books I–IV, parts of V and VI, and XI–XVI (incomplete at the beginning and end). The work is notable for its style, concise to the point of obscurity (in strong contrast to the Ciceronian amplitude), its sustained dignity and vividness, its epigrammatic sayings memorable for their irony or melancholy. The record of these reigns is in the main a gloomy and depressing one, and although Tacitus bears witness here and there to the efficient civil administration of the empire, the emphasis seems to be rather on the crimes, the sycophancy, the delations, and the oppression, that marked this period at Rome. Though Tacitus claims to write without partiality and prejudice, to aim at saving worthy actions from oblivion while holding up evil deeds to the reprobation of posterity (iii. 65), he is in fact influenced by a republican bias. It is generally recognized that the impression he gives of Tiberius is unduly dark, and that in particular the life of debauchery imputed to him in his last years at Capri is inherently improbable. The matters of most interest or importance in the several books are as follows:

Bk. I (A.D. 14–15), after a rapid review of the reign of Augustus, passes to the reign of Tiberius, relating the suppression by Germanicus of the mutiny of the legions in Pannonia and Germany (A.D. 14), and his first two campaigns (14–15) against the Germans. There is a notable description of the visit of the Roman army to the scene of the disaster of Varus.

Bk. II (A.D. 16–19). The third campaign of Germanicus (16), in which he defeats Arminius. His expedition to the East with Cn. Pīsō (17), and his death (19), suspected to have been due to Piso.

Bk. III (A.D. 20–22). The return of Agrippina, the widow of Germanicus, to Italy, and the trial (20) and suicide of Piso. The growth of luxury and sycophancy at Rome.

Bk. IV (A.D. 23–28). Sejanus, his character and career. In league with Livia, the wife of Drusus (son of Tiberius), he causes Drusus to be poisoned (23), and plots against the children of Germanicus. The proposal of his marriage with Livia is put aside by Tiberius. Tiberius withdraws to Capri (26). The increase in the activity of informers and in judicial murders: the case, for instance, of Cremūtius Cordus, accused of having in a history praised Brutus and Cassius.

Bk. V (A.D. 29). The death of Julia Augusta or Livia (29), mother of Tiberius. The story of the conspiracy and fall of Sejanus (31), which formed part of this book, is lost.

Bk. VI (A.D. 31–37). Tiberius at Capri, his vicious life, anguish of soul, and ferocity. The death of Drusus (son of Germanicus) by starvation in prison, and of Agrippina his mother (33). The ceaseless bloodshed at Rome, by executions and suicides. The death of Tiberius (37), and a summary of his life.

Bk. XI (A.D. 47–49), resumes the narrative after the hiatus, in the seventh year of Claudius (A.D. 47). The principal subjects of the book are the excesses of Messalina, her marriage with Silius, the perturbation of the emperor, and the execution (48) of Silius and Messalina at the instance of the freedman Narcissus.

Bk. XII (A.D. 49–54). Claudius marries (49) his niece, Agrippina (daughter of Germanicus). Through her influence her son (the future emperor Nero) is adopted by Claudius, preferred to his own son, Britannicus, and married to Octavia (daughter of Claudius). Silānus, to whom Octavia had been betrothed, is brought to ruin and death (49) by Agrippina. Seneca is recalled from exile to be Nero's tutor. The insurrection in Britain and the defeat (50) of Carātacus, king of the Silurēs, who is brought to Rome and pardoned. Claudius is poisoned by Agrippina. Accession of Nero (54).

Bk. XIII (A.D. 55–58). The promising beginning of the reign of Nero, who is restrained by Seneca and Burrus (prefect of the praetorians). Cn. Domitius Corbulō is sent to the East to resist Parthian aggression (54). Agrippina, whose influence is weakened, takes up the cause of Britannicus. Nero has Britannicus poisoned 55) and Agrippina removed from the palace. Nero in love with Poppaea Sabina.

Bk. XIV (A.D. 59–62). The attempted destruction of Agrippina by scuttling her ship, followed by her brutal murder (61). The great rising (61) in Britain under Boudicca (Boadicea), and its suppression. London is mentioned as much frequented by merchants and trading vessels. Armenia is recovered from the Parthians by the Romans under Corbulo. The death of Burrus (62) and retirement of Seneca. Nero marries Poppaea; his former wife, the virtuous Octavia, is banished to Pandātāria and there murdered.

Bk. XV (A.D. 62–65). Ignominious defeat of Caesennius Paetus in Armenia, followed by the reduction of the country by a Roman army under Corbulo to a dependency of the empire (63). The great fire of Rome (64) which devastated ten out of its fourteen districts; the rebuilding of the city on an improved plan. The persecution of the Christians, to whom Nero attributes the fire. The conspiracy of C. Calpurnius Pīsō and putting to death of Seneca and Lucan (65).

Bk. XVI (A.D. 65–66). The extravagances of Nero, who appears in public as a singer. The death of Poppaea (65). The suicide of the Stoic Thrasea and the banishment of his son-in-law, Helvidius (66). In one of the last surviving chapters of the book (16) Tacitus laments the melancholy and monotony of the record of bloodshed. The portion of the 'Annals' relating to the last two years of Nero's reign is lost.

Anno'na, at Rome, the corn supply, always a source of solicitude to the authorities owing to the fluctuation of prices and the danger of famine from the failure of crops and the uncertainty of communications. From the 5th c. B.C. the government appears to have occupied itself with procuring supplies of wheat from overseas and selling it to the people, the aediles of the plebs being charged with this duty. The details of the legislation on the subject at various later dates are still a vexed question, and the following statements only indicate the more recent views on the subject. C. Gracchus caused a certain quantity of corn to be sold at a moderate price, probably to each adult citizen who applied for it; the price appears to have been 6⅓ asses per modius (nearly two gallons), but what relation this bore to the open-market price we do not know. This special price may have been reduced by the law of Saturninus (q.v.) of 100 B.C. Sulla seems to have abolished corn distributions, but immediately after his death Lepidus reintroduced them, at the rate of five modii a month gratis. By the *lex Terentia Cassia* of 73 B.C. corn was supplied to a restricted number—40,000—gratis. In 63 B.C. the Gracchan law was revised and some charge was again made. Clodius (q.v.) in 58 B.C. gave corn free of charge to the proletariat. Julius Caesar appointed two *Aediles Ceriāles* specially to look after the distribution; the recipients, greatly reduced in number, were entered on a register. Between A.D. 6 and 14 Augustus appointed a *praefectus annonae* who regulated the price and distribution. He had in 22 B.C. taken over the *cūra annonae*, and from that date it was under imperial control. The expense, which was considerable, had hitherto been met by the *aerarium* or State treasury. It was now met by the imperial revenues, but the *aerarium* may also have contributed. The harbour built at Ostia by Claudius was to enable the corn ships to have direct communication with Rome instead of unloading at Puteoli, whence the corn had to be conveyed overland a distance of 138 miles. Further harbour improvements were carried out by Trajan.

Antae'us (*Antaios*), son of Poseidon and Ge (qq.v.), a giant with whom Heracles (q.v.) wrestled. Whenever he was thrown, he arose stronger than before from contact with his mother Earth. Heracles, perceiving this, lifted him in the air and crushed him to death.

Antei'a, see *Bellerophon*.

Antē'nōr, one of the elders of Troy during the siege. He was in favour of restoring Helen to the Greeks, since she had been taken by treachery. It was said that the Greeks, recognizing his fairness, spared him and his family when the city was captured. Later legend made him out a traitor to the Trojans.

Anthestē'ria, see *Festivals*, § 4.

Anthologies.

§ 1. *Greek Anthologies*

The ancient Greek anthologies were collections of Greek 'Epigrams', i.e. short elegiac poems, of from one to four distichs on various subjects and by various authors. Meleager of Gadara (1st c. B.C.) compiled such an anthology from the works of forty-six poets. It is now lost, but served, with other similar compilations, as the basis of the famous collection of Constantinus Cephalās (c. A.D. 917). This is known as the Palatine Anthology, because it was discovered (by the great French scholar Salmasius at the age of 19) in the Palatine Library of Heidelberg in the 17th c. It includes poems by 320 authors. The *Anthologia Planūdēa* was made by the monk Maximus Planūdēs in the 14th c.; it was an abridgement (with a few additions) of the anthology of Cephalas. The modern 'Greek Anthology' is composed of the 'Palatine Anthology', with the additional poems supplied by that of Planudes, and further epigrams found in other Greek authors or in inscriptions. It contains over six thousand epigrams, many of them poems of great charm, ranging in time over seventeen centuries, from the 7th c. B.C. to the 10th c. A.D., and over a great variety of subjects. There are epitaphs (including the famous epitaphs attributed to Simonides), dedications, reflections on life and death and fate, poems on love, on family life, on great poets and artists and their works, and on the beauties of nature. A certain proportion are humorous or satirical, making fun of doctors, rhetoricians, athletes, &c., or of personal peculiarities, such as Nicon's long nose.

The dedicatory poems form perhaps the group that throws most light on ancient Greek life: there are dedications not only of arms, but of many kinds of implements of daily use. A maiden about to wed offers up her dolls and toys, a traveller his old hat, 'a small gift, but given in piety'.

§ 2. *The Anthologia Latina*

The Anthologia Latina is a collection of some 380 short Latin poems, most of them of very late date, compiled in the Vandal kingdom of Africa in the first half of the 6th c. A.D. It includes the 'Pervigilium Veneris' (q.v.) and some poems by Seneca the Philosopher.

Anticlē'a (*Antikleia*), in Greek mythology, the wife of Laertes and mother of Odysseus (q.v.).

Anticlimax, see *Climax*.

Anti'dosis. A wealthy Athenian was required to undertake certain public services (see *Liturgy*). To avoid one of these, he might challenge some other citizen, whose means he thought greater than his own, either to undertake the service or to make an exchange (*antidosis*) of properties. This might lead to a lawsuit, if the other citizen refused.

Antidosis, On the, see *Isocrates*.

Anti'gonē (*Antigonē*), see *Oedipus*.

Antigone, a tragedy by Sophocles, of unknown date, probably an early work.

Creon, ruler of Thebes, has forbidden on pain of death the burial of the body of Polynices (see *Oedipus*). Antigone resolves to defy the outrageous edict and perform the funeral rites for her brother. She is caught doing this and brought before the infuriated king. She justifies her act as in accordance with the overriding laws of the gods. Creon, unrelenting, condemns her to be immured alive in a cave. Her sister, Ismene, who has refused to share in her defiant act, now claims a share in her guilt and in her penalty, but is treated by Creon as demented. Haemon, Creon's son, betrothed to Antigone, pleads in vain with Creon. He goes out, warning his father that he will die with her. The seer Tiresias threatens Creon with the fearful consequences of his defiance of the divine laws. Creon, at last moved, sets out hurriedly for the cave where Antigone has been immured. He finds Haemon clasping her dead body, for Antigone has hanged herself. Haemon thrusts at Creon with his sword, but misses him, and then kills himself. Creon returns to the palace, to find that Eurydice, his wife, in despair has taken her own life.

Anti'gonus and Anti'gonids, see *Macedonia*, §§ 2 and 3.

Anti'machus (*Antimachos*) of Colophōn, see *Epic*, § 1. He also wrote short love poems in elegiacs, collected under the title *Lŷdē*, which were to some extent the forerunners of poems of the Alexandrian school.

Anti'nŏus (Gk. *Antinoos*), (1) in the 'Odyssey' (q.v.), the most arrogant of the wooers of Penelope. He is the first of these that Odysseus kills. (2) A Bithynian youth of great beauty and a favourite of the emperor Hadrian. He drowned himself in the Nile in A.D. 130. Hadrian founded the city of Antinoopolis on the Nile and erected temples in his memory. Antinous was frequently represented in sculpture, and some of these representations survive.

A'ntioch (*Antiocheia*), on the Orontes, the capital of Syria, founded by Seleucus I (see *Seleucids*) about 300 B.C., and named after his father. Antiochus the Great (223–187 B.C.) adorned it with works of art, a theatre, and a library. It was a trade centre and a pleasure city, never a centre of learning, though Aratus of Soli lived for a time at the court of Antiochus I, and Euphorion was appointed librarian of the public library. Antiochus IV Epiphanes, an ardent Hellenist, made Antioch for a time a centre of Greek art. Many other cities, besides the capital, founded by the Seleucids bore the name Antioch.

Anti'ochus (*Antiochos*), (1) the name of several of the Seleucid kings of Asia; see *Seleucids*. (2) of Ascalon, see *Academy*, *ad fin.*

Anti'opē (*Antiopē*) (1) in Greek mythology, daughter of Nyctēus, son of Chthonios, one of the Spartoi (see *Cadmus*) of Thebes. Antiope was loved by Zeus and became the mother of the twin brothers, Amphīōn and Zēthus. To avoid her father's anger she fled to Sicyōn. Nycteus in despair killed himself, but first charged his brother, Lycus, who was king of Thebes during the minority of Laïus (q.v.), to punish Antiope. Lycus captured Sicyon and imprisoned Antiope; her treatment was made more cruel by the jealousy of Dirce, the wife of Lycus. At last Antiope escaped and joined her sons, now grown to maturity. These revenged her by tying Dirce to the horns of a bull, so that she was dragged to death; and they killed or deposed Lycus. Amphion and Zethus now became rulers of Thebes and built its walls. Amphion was a harper of such skill that the stones were drawn into their places by his music. He married Niobe (q.v.). Zethus married the nymph Thēbē, whence was derived the name of Thebes.

(2) See *Hippolyte*.

Anti'pater (*Antipatros*), a Macedonian general, left by Alexander the Great (q.v.) as regent of Macedonia during his eastern campaigns. See under *Macedonia*, § 2, and also *Athens*, § 7.

Anti'pater (*Antipatros*) **of Sidon** (*fl. c.* 100 B.C.), a Greek writer of elegiac poetry, some of which is preserved in the Palatine Anthology (q.v.).

Anti'phanēs, see *Comedy*, § 4.

A'ntiphōn (*c.* 480–411), the first of the Attic orators whose speeches in part survive, a representative of the older and more austere form of pleading. He was the first professional writer of speeches to be spoken by the actual litigants (*logographos*, in the second sense of the word, q.v.). He was also a teacher of rhetoric, and Thucydides is said to have been his pupil. Though living in obscurity, he was the soul of the oligarchic conspiracy which in 411 established the rule of the Four Hundred (see *Athens*, § 5). When these were overthrown, Antiphon was tried, found guilty of treason, and put to death, in spite of a plea for his life which Thucydides declares unequalled down to his time. Antiphon is said to have been unpopular owing to 'a repute for cleverness'. He excelled as a pleader in cases of homicide, and his dignified style was better suited to the Areopagus than to the Ecclesia. We have three of his speeches for murder trials, and also three Tetralogies, exercises in which the author gives two speeches for the accuser and two for the defendant in imaginary cases of homicide; one, for instance, where a boy practising with the javelin kills another boy who runs between him and the target.

Antiquitā'tēs Rērum Humāna'rum et Divīna'rum, see *Varro* (*M. T.*).

Anti'sthenēs, see *Cynic*.

Anti'stius La'beō, MARCUS, see *Labeo*.

Anti'thesis ('placing opposite'), such choice or arrangement of words as emphasizes a contrast; e.g. 'Dominetur in contionibus, jaceat in judiciis' (Cic., Pro Cluent. 2, 5).

Antōni'nus Pius (*Titus Aurēlius Fulvus Boiōnius Arrius Antoninus*, after adoption *Titus Aelius Hādriānus Antoninus*) (A.D. 86–161), Roman emperor A.D. 138–161 in succession to Hadrian, by whom he had been adopted as heir. He belonged to a Roman family which had settled in Gaul; his father had been *consul suffectus*. Antoninus maintained good relations with the Senate and his reign was peaceful and orderly, without striking incident. He was diligent, tolerant, frugal, 'a good

Italian bourgeois of the senatorial class, who had no intellectual tendencies, but a sound common sense, and a gift of humour' (Rostovtzeff). He was father of Faustina (q.v.). It was in his reign (in 142) that the wall of turf known as the Wall of Antoninus was built by his lieutenant Lollius Urbicus between the Forth and the Clyde (see *Britain*, § 2).

Antō'nius, MARCUS, (1) (143–87 B.C.), one of the greatest orators of his day, consul in 99, a member of the party of Sulla, and put to death by the Marians. He was grandfather of Antony the triumvir. He is one of the chief interlocutors in Cicero's 'De Oratore' (q.v.). (2) See *Antony*.

Antonoma'siā, a rhetorical figure, in which a descriptive term or phrase is substituted for a proper name, e.g. 'Tȳdidēs' for Diomedes, or 'Dīvum pater' for Jupiter. Cf. *Metonymy*.

Antony, MARK (*Marcus Antōnius*) (c. 82–30 B.C.), grandson of M. Antonius (q.v.) the orator. After serving under Gabinius in the East and under Caesar in Gaul, he was one of the tribunes in 49, when he supported Caesar's cause, joined him before the crossing of the Rubicon, and held a command in the ensuing campaigns in Italy and Epirus. After Pharsalus (48) he remained in Italy as Caesar's Master of the Horse and held the chief power there during the lawless period of Caesar's absence. He was consul at the time of Caesar's assassination and his eloquence won over the populace to his side and made him ruler of Rome. Civil war broke out. It was at this time that Cicero delivered his 'Philippics' against Antony, and powerfully contributed to raise the republican opposition to him. Antony was defeated at the battle of Mutina (43). Octavian had attached himself to the republican party, but after Mutina the differences between him and Antony were composed, and Octavian, Antony, and Lepidus formed the Triumvirate. Proscriptions followed, in which Cicero and his brother were sacrificed to Antony's desire for vengeance. After Philippi (42), where Antony shared the command with Octavian, a division of the Roman world was made, in which the East was assigned to Antony. But hostilities soon broke out between him and Octavian, temporarily composed by the treaty of Brundisium in 40, and the marriage of Antony with Octavian's sister Octavia (Antony's first wife Fulvia, q.v., had died in 40). Antony now fell under the influence of Cleopatra (q.v.), queen of Egypt, whom he had met when he visited Cilicia in 41. Both stood to profit by close alliance; Antony would have at his disposal the resources of Egypt to further his scheme of obtaining complete power over the East; Cleopatra would be confirmed in her rule over Egypt, which was none too secure. But the campaign which Antony undertook against the Parthians in 36 was unsuccessful. After subduing Armenia in 34 he returned to Alexandria, where he lived like an oriental ruler. He made donations of large parts of the Eastern provinces to form kingdoms for Cleopatra, Caesarion (q.v.), and his three children by Cleopatra. In 32 he divorced Octavia, and war broke out once more between Octavian on the one side and Antony and Cleopatra on the other, and was decided by Octavian's victory at Actium (31), when Cleopatra's sixty ships sailed away, followed by Antony himself. In 30 Octavian invaded Egypt, and Antony, after defeat, took his own life. Antony's fatal entanglement with Cleopatra is the subject of Shakespeare's historical play 'Antony and Cleopatra'. (This play is based on Plutarch's life of Antony, which may give a romantic and distorted view of the facts.)

Anū'bis, in Egyptian religion, the dog-headed god who conducted the souls of the dead to the region of immortal life; identified by the Greeks with Hermes.

Āo'nia. The Aonians were, according to legend, ancient inhabitants of Boeotia, whom Cadmus (q.v.) allowed to remain in the country along with the immigrant Phoenicians. Aonia is sometimes used by learned poets for Boeotia, and Aonian for Boeotian (a name which carried with it a shade of contempt).

Apatū'ria (*Apatouria*), see *Phratriai*.

Ape'lla (*Apellā*), the assembly of the people at Sparta (q.v., § 2).

Ape'llēs, the greatest painter of antiquity, born at Colophōn in Ionia in the first half of the 4th c. B.C. He studied under the Ephesian painter Ephorus and the Sicyonian Pamphilus, and later worked at Corinth, Athens, and at the Macedonian court. The distinctive quality of his work was grace and charm, coupled with ease of execution. He painted mainly portraits, but his most famous picture was that of Aphrodite Anadyomenē, wringing from her hair the water of the sea from which she has just risen. This picture Augustus acquired for 100 talents. Apelles was the favourite painter of Alexander the Great, of whom he painted several portraits, generally in some allegorical situation, e.g. wielding a thunderbolt, or riding in triumph, with War a captive behind

him. See *Painting*. To Apelles is attributed by Pliny a saying which has become proverbial. A cobbler had criticized the drawing of a sandal in a picture by Apelles; Apelles altered the sandal as desired. Next day the cobbler went further and criticized the drawing of the leg. To this Apelles replied, 'ne sutor supra crepidam', the origin of our 'a cobbler should stick to his last'.

Apelles figures in Lyly's 'Alexander and Campaspe' (1584).

Aphai'a, see *Britomartis.*

A'phobus (*Aphobos*), *Against*, speeches by Demosthenes against his fraudulent guardian. See *Demosthenes* (2), § 2.

Aphrodi'tē, the Greek goddess of love, identified by the Romans with Venus (q.v.). Homer makes her the daughter of Zeus and Dione (q.v.). According to Hesiod she sprang from the foam (*aphros*) of the sea that gathered about the severed member of Uranus when Cronos (q.v.) mutilated him. Her name *Cypris* (the Cyprian, see *Cyprus*) and many of her attributes indicate her partially oriental origin and her kinship to the Asian goddess Astartē. This is borne out by the legend that she first landed either at Paphos in Cyprus or at Cythēra (an island off the Laconian coast), whence her title 'Cytherean'. She was the wife of Hephaestus (q.v.), but was unfaithful to him; her amorous intrigue with Ares (q.v.) was discovered, and the pair were caught in a net by Hephaestus and exposed to the ridicule of the assembled gods. In later literature she is the mother of Eros (q.v.). For other legends about her see *Adonis, Anchises, Paris* (*Judgement of*). She was worshipped in Greece both as Aphrodite Ūrania, 'goddess of the sky', and as Aphrodite Pandēmos, 'goddess of all the people' (a goddess of marriage and family life). Later the distinction acquired a new meaning: Aphrodite Urania became the goddess of higher, purer love; Aphrodite Pandemos the goddess of sensual lust. Aphrodite had a famous sanctuary on Mt. Eryx on the NW. coast of Sicily. This the Romans especially honoured, because Aphrodite, as the mother of Aeneas (see *Anchises*), passed for their ancestress. The title of Venus Erycīna, who had a temple at Rome outside the Colline Gate, was derived from the sanctuary on Mt. Eryx.

Api'cius (*Apicius*), QUINTUS (?) GĀVIUS, a gourmet of the reign of Tiberius. His receipts were written down; but the work on cookery which bears the name of Caelius Apicius is thought to be a compilation of a much later date. It is sometimes entitled ' De opsōniis et condimentis sive de re culināria libri decem'. Perhaps the name Apicius was added to ensure a ready sale.

Apocolocyntō'sis, a work bearing in the MSS. the title *Ludus de Morte Claudii*, ascribed traditionally to Seneca the Philosopher, who according to Dio Cassius wrote an *apocolocyntosis* or 'pumpkinification' (a parody of 'Apotheosis') of Claudius after his death. It is a tasteless if amusing lampoon, in the form of a Menippean satire (a medley of verse and prose), on the recently deceased emperor Claudius, describing the proceedings in heaven on his death; his arrival there, the difficulty of ascertaining who he is owing to his inarticulate speech, the debate whether he shall be made a god, and Augustus's motion that he shall be deported from heaven for the murders he has committed. Claudius is haled off to the lower regions, where he meets his victims, and is brought before Aeacus for trial. Aeacus (following Claudius's own system) hears the case against him, but refuses to hear the other side, and sentences him. Claudius is finally made lawclerk to one of his own freedmen.

Apollinā'ris Sidō'nius, see *Sidonius*.

Apo'llō (Gk. *Apollōn*).

§ 1. *In Greek Mythology*

Apollo was the son of Zeus and Leto (q.v.), and brother of Artemis; the god of medicine, music (especially the lyre), archery, and prophecy; the god also of light (whence his epithet Phoebus, 'the bright') and youth; sometimes identified with the sun. He was also associated with the care of flocks and herds, whence the epithet *nomios* ('of the pastures'). The sense of the frequent title Lyceius (*lukeios*) is disputed; it may mean Lycian, or have some reference to wolves. Apollo *Smintheus*, referred to in Hom. Il. i. 39, was so called either from the name of a place in the Troad where he was worshipped, or from *sminthos*, a mouse, as the 'Mousekiller', the god who protected farmers against mice.

Apollo's first feat was the seizure of Delphi (q.v.) for his abode, and the destruction of its guardian, the dragon Python, personifying the dark forces of the underworld; an act which Apollo had to expiate by exile and purification. This myth was celebrated in pantomime at the Delphic festival of the Steptēria, and explains his title 'Pythian'. For other legends of Apollo see *Admetus, Aristaeus, Asclepius, Cassandra, Daphne, Hyacinthus,* *Marpessa, Marsyas, Niobe, Pan, Sibyl, Tityus.*

Apollo, though a younger immigrant among the Greek gods, held a prominent place among them and was widely worshipped. The chief centres of his cult were Delphi, the island of Delos, and, for the Greeks of Asia, Didyma near Miletus. He was regarded as a type of moral excellence, and his influence, as propagated from Delphi (see *Delphic Oracle*), was a beneficent and elevating one; for it prescribed purification and penance for the expiation of crime, and discouraged vengeance (it is, e.g., Apollo who defends Orestes against the Furies). The Homeric Hymns to the Delian and the Pythian Apollo relate the story of his birth and of the founding of his Pythian temple. In modern literature see Shelley's *Hymn of Apollo*. See also *Paean.*

§ 2. *In Roman religion*

Apollo, or Phoebus Apollo, was adopted among the Roman gods from Greek sources, according to tradition by Servius Tullius, or at any rate at a very early date. He was known to the Etrurians, and the Romans had early dealings with Delphi. He was first introduced as a god of healing, but soon became prominent as a god of oracles and prophecy. In Virgil he figures in both these characters, but especially as the giver of oracles; the Cumaean Sibyl was his priestess. In the 'Eclogues' Apollo appears also as the patron of poetry and music. The oldest temple to him in Rome was erected in 432 B.C. Games (*Ludi Apollinares*) were instituted in his honour in 212 B.C. after Hannibal's capture of Tarentum, and later were made annual on 13 July in consequence of a pestilence. His cult was further developed by Augustus, who took him as his special patron and erected to him a great temple on the Palatine.

Apollodō'rus (*Apollodōros*) of Athens (c. 140 B.C.) was author of a long treatise in Greek prose 'On the Gods', and of a 'Chronicle' (*Chronikē Suntaxis*), a chronological work of some importance, written in iambic trimeters, covering the period from the fall of Troy. Only fragments of these survive. The 'Bibliothēkē', a valuable extant compilation of myths, wrongly attributed to him, dates probably from the time of the Roman Empire.

Apollō'nius (*Apollōnios*) **Dy'scolus** (*Duskolos*, 'crabbed') (2nd c. A.D.) was the author of Greek treatises which first placed Greek grammar on a scientific basis. He lived in poverty at Alexandria and wrote numerous works, most of which are lost, on the parts of speech and on syntax. His writings were much used by Priscian (q.v.). He was father of Aelius Herodianus (q.v.), who wrote on Greek accents.

Apollō'nius of Tyā'na in Cappadocia (b. *c.* 4 B.C.), a wandering Pythagorean philosopher and mystic who attained so great a fame by his pretended wonder-working powers that div¹ne honours were paid to him. He wrote a life of Pythagoras and other works, of which hardly anything has survived. His own life was written by Philostratus (q.v.).

Apollō'nius of Tyre, see *Novel*.

Apollō'nius Rhō'dius (*Rhŏdius*) (*c.* 295–215 B.C.), a native of Alexandria who spent part of his life at Rhodes, is said by Suidas to have succeeded Eratosthenes as head of the Alexandrian Library; but this presents chronological difficulties. He wrote 'Argonautica' in four books, a Greek epic on the story of Jason and the Argonauts, which survives. It lacks the epic fire, but contains a beautiful description of the love of Jason and Medea (imitated by Virgil in the story of Dido in the 4th Aeneid) and some other good episodes. Those of the loss of Hylas and the fight of Pollux with Amycus (q.v.) were rehandled by Theocritus as short, separate poems. For the quarrel between Apollonius and Callimachus, see under *Callimachus*.

Apology (*Apologiā*) of Socrates, the speech made by Socrates, as related by Plato, in answer to the charge of impiety that was brought against him. How far it represents the words actually used by Socrates is unknown. (Plato, it appears, was present at the trial.)

Socrates distinguishes between the old, vague accusations (that he speculated about physical questions and made the worse cause appear the better) and the specific charge of impiety now brought by Melētus, and, answering the former first, explains that he is neither a sophist nor a natural philosopher; his only wisdom consists in knowing that he knows nothing. Instigated by an oracle, he has sought constantly to find a wiser man than himself, but has found none. He has gone to those who had a reputation for wisdom, and finding they had none, he has tried to convince them of this, thereby provoking their enmity and giving rise to these vague charges. He next turns to Meletus and cross-examines him on his accusations, using a sophistical form of argument which seems to us unsatisfactory. He then addresses the judges and declares himself unrepentant. He will persist in the practices complained of, for he must remain at his post and continue,

in obedience to the divine voice, to preach the necessity of virtue. If they kill him, they will be injuring themselves, for he is the gadfly sent by the god to stir Athens to life.

Socrates is convicted and the death penalty is proposed. His speech assumes a more lofty tone. Why should he propose an alternative penalty? As a benefactor of Athens he ought to be rewarded. Imprisonment, exile, a fine, would be certain evils, whereas of death he does not know whether it is an evil or a good. However, he suggests a fine of thirty minae, for which his friends will offer surety, for he himself has no money. He is sentenced to death. In his final words he prophesies that many will arise after his death to condemn his judges. He comforts his friends with regard to his own fate, for death is either a dreamless sleep or a journey to a place of true justice, where, moreover, he will be able to converse with Hesiod and Homer and the heroes of old. Nothing evil can happen to a good man; if he is to die, it is because it is better for him. He forgives his accusers and judges.

Apology (*Apologiā Sōkratous*), an account by Xenophon of Socrates' defence in his trial on the charge of impiety. Xenophon at the time was taking part in the expedition of Cyrus (see *Anabasis*) and he relies on the authority of Hermogenēs, a friend of Socrates, mentioned in Plato's 'Phaedo' as present at the execution. It is designed to bring out especially that Socrates was willing to die, not for the spiritual reasons given in Plato's 'Apology', but in order to escape the disabilities of old age. His pleas are stated with less elaboration than by Plato.

Aposiōpē'sis, a rhetorical artifice, in which the speaker comes to a sudden halt in the middle of a sentence, as if unable or unwilling to proceed. The best-known instance is Virgil, Aen. i. 133–5:

Iam caelum terramque meo sine numine,
  Venti,
Miscere et tantas audetis tollere moles?
Quos ego —! Sed motos praestat componere fluctus.

Apo'strophe (Gk. *apostrophē*, 'turning away'), a rhetorical figure by which the speaker interrupts the thread of his discourse to address pointedly some person present, or supposed to be present; e.g.
[Extulit] haec Decios, Marios, magnosque
  Camillos,
Scipiadas duros bello, et te, maxime
  Caesar.   (Virg. Georg. ii. 169–70)

A'ppian (*Appiānos*) of Alexandria (*fl. c.* A.D. 160), who practised as a lawyer in

Rome, was a compiler of narratives in Greek of the various Roman wars from the earliest times to the accession of Vespasian, in 24 books. Of these, 10 books and portions of others survive, including those dealing with the Punic Wars and the Civil Wars (from Marius and Sulla to 34 B.C.).

A'ppius Clau'dius, consul in 451 B.C. and one of the decemvirs appointed at Rome in that year to draw up a code of laws. The decemvirs, led by Appius Claudius, appear, when reappointed for a second year, to have become oppressive. The attempted outrage by Appius on Virginia (q.v.) is said to have led to their overthrow (Livy iii. c. 33).

A'ppius Clau'dius Cae'cus, a famous Roman censor (312–308 B.C.), a man of original and broad views, proud and obstinate, who endeavoured to renovate the governing class by admitting rich plebeians and even freedmen to the Senate. As censor, while war with the Samnites was in progress, he built the first of the great Roman roads, the Via Appia; also the first of the aqueducts bringing water to Rome. In his old age, when blind, he resolutely opposed the proposals of Pyrrhus (q.v.) for peace (280 B.C.). He composed aphorisms in Saturnian (q.v.) verse, of which a few have been preserved. Cicero says that he was a notable orator, and that even in his day some of Appius's funeral orations were extant.

Apulē'ius (*Āpulēius*: the quantity of the second syllable appears to be doubtful), LŪCIUS (*fl. c.* A.D. 155), was born at Madaura, on the borders of Numidia and Gaetūlia. On a journey to Alexandria, when a young man, he fell ill, was nursed by a rich widow named Aemilia Pudentilla, and married her. Her relatives brought an action against him on the charge of having won her by the use of magic. His 'Apologia' or speech for the defence survives. From this we learn that he had inherited a considerable fortune but had wasted it, that he was deeply interested in natural science, and that the accusation of magic was founded on trivial grounds. That Apuleius was in fact much interested in magic appears from many passages of his 'Metamorphoses' (see below). He subsequently settled at Carthage and travelled among the African towns, lecturing in Latin on philosophy. We possess a collection made by himself of purple passages from these lectures, under the name 'Flōrida'; also a treatise on the philosophy of Plato ('De Platone et ejus dogmate') and one on the

Platonic doctrine of God and the daemons ('De Deo Socratis'); a free translation ('De Mundo') of the Περὶ κόσμου attributed falsely to Aristotle; and a certain number of verses. His philosophical writings show a bent to religious mysticism.

But the work for which he is famous is his 'Metamorphōsēs' or 'Golden Ass', a Latin romance in eleven books. Th plot was based on an extant Greek work, Λούκιος ἢ ὄνος doubtfully attributed to Lucian, or an earlier lost work which was the common basis of both. This original was remodelled by Apuleius and enlarged by many incidental tales.

The romance takes the form of a narrative by one Lucius, a Greek, of his adventures, beginning with a visit to Thessaly, the reputed home of sorceries and enchantments. There, while staying at the house of one Milo, he sees the wife of his host, a sorceress, turn herself by means of an ointment into an owl, and, desirous of imitating her, induces the maid to procure him the ointment. But the maid gives him the wrong ointment, and Lucius is turned by it into an ass, falls into the hands of robbers, and becomes an unwilling and much beaten partaker in their exploits. Some of the robber stories are excellent, as that of the robber chief Lamachus, who, thrusting his hand through a hole in the door of a house he is going to rob, has it seized and nailed to the doorpost by the house-owner, so that his companions have to cut off his arm to secure his escape; and the romantic tale of the young man Tlēpolemus, who, pretending to be the renowned thief Haemus the Thracian, gets himself made captain of the robber band in order to rescue his betrothed, whom the bandits have carried off. But the most beautiful and famous of the tales recounted is the fairy story of Cupid and Psyche (see *Psyche*). After many vicissitudes, in the course of which he serves one of the strange bands of wandering priests of Cybele, and becomes a famous performing ass, Lucius is transformed back into human shape by the favour of the goddess Isis, and appears to become Apuleius the author himself. The last portion of the work refers to his initiation into the mysteries of Isis and Osiris and bears witness to his interest in oriental religions, at this time the object of popular favour. In the whole story some see an allegory of human life (the sensual abasement of the soul and its recovery), and in the fable of Cupid and Psyche an allegory of the soul in relation to love. The style of Apuleius is lively, picturesque, and highly polished. The many realistic details that he gives vividly illuminate the popular life of his time.

The 'Golden Ass' was translated into English in the 16th c. by W. Adlington. For translations of the fable of Cupid and Psyche, see *Psyche*.

Aquā'rius, 'the Water-bearer', in Greek *Hydrochoos*, one of the signs of the zodiac, variously thought by the ancients to have been Ganymede transported to the sky, or Deucalion. The sun entered Aquarius in January ('Simul inversum contristat Aquarius annum', Hor. Sat. I. i. 36).

Aqueducts (*Aquae*). The aqueducts of Rome were among the most important of the State's public works. For our knowledge of their history we are chiefly indebted to Frontinus (q.v.); in a less degree to notices in other authors, to inscriptions, and to modern archaeological research. They supplied Rome with water, whose purity was praised by Galen (q.v.), by means of conduits in some cases as much as 60 miles in length, hewn in the rock or carried over arches. The total supply provided by the aqueducts under the early empire cannot be stated with any certainty, but it has been deduced from the figures of Frontinus that the system was capable of delivering no less than 222 million gallons in 24 hours (Ashby, 'The Aqueducts of Ancient Rome', Clarendon Press, 1935). At the present time a supply of 40 million gallons a day would be considered sufficient for a city of a million inhabitants.

The first of the aqueducts was the APPIA, built in 312 B.C., during the Samnite Wars, by the censor Appius Claudius Caecus (q.v.). Its source is stated by Frontinus to have been near the Via Praenestina between the seventh and eighth milestones, but it has not been identified. The conduit was almost entirely underground, was eleven miles long, and terminated near the Porta Trigemina (between the Aventine and the Tiber).

Forty years later, in 272–269 B.C., the ANIO (or as it was later known, the ANIO VETUS) was constructed by the censors out of the booty captured from Pyrrhus. The source was the river Anio above Tibur (Tivoli), and its conduit was 43 miles long, almost entirely underground. This and the Appia were low-level aqueducts.

A larger water-supply having become necessary, a new aqueduct, the MARCIA, was built in 144–143 B.C. by the praetor, Q. Marcius Rex. This was a high-level aqueduct. It had its source in springs in the Anio valley and a length of over 60 miles, of which some 7 miles were above ground. It crossed a valley by the

fine bridge of Ponte Lupo, and for the last 6½ miles of its course to the city was carried on arches, the ruins of which are still visible. It entered the city at the Porta Praenestina (now the Porta Maggiore) and terminated near the Viminal, with branches thence in various directions. In spite of a warning in the Sibylline Books, Marcius carried a branch to the Capitol, probably by means of a siphon. The water of the Marcia was exceptionally cold and sparkling. This aqueduct and the Anio Vetus each had the large capacity, as calculated from the figures of Frontinus, of some 40 million gallons in 24 hours.

Agrippa (q.v.), probably in 40 B.C., constructed the aqueduct called JULIA, having its source in the Alban Hills near the Via Latina, and a length of 15½ miles, 6½ of which were on the same arches as the Marcia. Agrippa also, in 19 B.C., built the AQUA VIRGO, drawing on springs at the eighth milestone of the Via Collātina. It had a length of 12 miles, mostly underground. It was called Virgo, Frontinus states, because a little girl pointed out the springs to soldiers seeking water. The aqueduct supplied the baths of Agrippa in the Campus Martius. Ovid in his exile recalls with regret the view of the green Campus with the Aqua Virgo (Ex Pont. I. viii. 33–8).

Augustus built the ALSIETĪNA (also called AUGUSTA) to supply his Naumachia (q.v.) on the right bank of the Tiber. Its water, drawn from the Lacus Alsietīnus (Lake Martignano), 20 miles from Rome, was unwholesome and not intended for private consumers. This was the lowest of the aqueducts and its course has never been determined.

Gaius (Caligula) began two further aqueducts, which were completed by Claudius, the CLAUDIA and the ANIO NOVUS. The former drew its supply from springs near the source of the Marcia, and had a course of 46 miles. For a distance of 9 miles it was carried on fine arches, great stretches of which survive. It entered the city near the modern Porta Maggiore (where there is an inscription of Claudius recording its construction and that of the Anio Novus) and had its distributing station close by.

The Anio Novus had its source originally in the Anio at Subiaco; later, as the result of an improvement carried out by Trajan, its water was drawn from a lake above Subiaco formed by a dam across the Anio built by Nero near his villa. It was 59 miles long, being carried in the latter part of its course on the same arches as the Claudia, but above it. These two had the highest level of all the aqueducts, and their capacity, on the basis of the figures of Frontinus, has been calculated at over 40 million gallons a day each.

Further aqueducts were built at Rome by Trajan, Caracalla, and Alexander Severus. There were also important aqueducts in the provinces. The most striking survival of these is that known as the Pont du Gard, near Nîmes in southern France.

The channel (*specus*) of a Roman aqueduct, where it ran underground, was tunnelled by means of shafts (*putei*) sunk at short intervals. Above ground it was built of stone slabs keyed together, or of concrete faced in brick or stone, and was lined with fine cement; it was roofed against rain and sun. The normal arrangement was that the channels terminated in main reservoirs (*castella*), whence the supply was carried in part to public fountains and public baths, in part to secondary reservoirs. From these secondary reservoirs water was distributed in pipes to private consumers, who paid a water rental.

Under the republic the maintenance of the aqueducts was let out by the censors to contractors and supervised by the censors, and when there were no censors, by the aediles. These magistrates also had control of the distribution of the water. After the death of Agrippa, who had personally looked after the public works, a new organization was adopted (11 B.C.). A board was appointed consisting of a *cūrātŏr* of consular rank and two assistants of senatorial rank, to have charge of the water supply. These were unlikely to have technical knowledge. Under Claudius a *procurator aquarum* of equestrian rank was established, who probably did most of the real work. The post of curator was one of great importance and authority. The board had under them a permanent staff, composed at first of 240 skilled slaves bequeathed to Augustus by Agrippa, and maintained by the *aerarium* or State treasury. To these Claudius added a further 460 slaves, at the charge of the *fiscus* (q.v.). This permanent staff carried out the minor jobs, important work being let out to contractors. The aqueducts were in constant need of repair, for leaks, especially in the stone-built channels, were caused by excessive heat or frost. The arches near the city also gave a great deal of trouble. Frontinus, who was appointed *curator aquarum* in A.D. 97, brought to light many abuses in connexion with the system, notably the tapping of the channels by unauthorized persons to secure a supply of water for

their land. Pliny the Elder (N.H. 31. 42) also tells of the Roman aqueducts, giving much praise to the Marcia water, and deploring the loss of the Marcia and Virgo to the city, because private persons had diverted the supplies to their villas and suburban residences.

A'quilo, the north wind (Gk. *Boreās*).

Aqui'nas, THOMAS, see *Texts and Studies*, § 8.

Āra Ma'xima, the altar of Hercules (q.v.) at Rome, stood in the Forum Boarium (q.v.). It was here that, as related by Virgil (Aen. viii. 102 et seq.), Aeneas found Evander sacrificing. The spot was connected with the legend of Hercules and Cacus (q.v.). Tithes of booty, of commercial profits, &c., were offered at this altar.

Āra Pācis, 'Altar of Peace', in Rome, was dedicated by order of the Senate in 9 B.C. in honour of the peace restored by Augustus. It was erected in the Campus Martius. The walls of the small court surrounding the altar were covered with beautiful sculptures in relief, of which fragments survive in the museums of Rome, Florence, and Paris.

Ara'chnē, in Greek mythology, a woman of Lydia, who challenged Athene (q.v.) to a contest in weaving. She depicted in her web the amours of the gods, and Athene, angered at her presumption and choice of subject, tore the web to pieces and beat the weaver. Arachne in despair hanged herself, but Athene turned her into a spider.

Arā'tus (*Arātos*), (1) a Greek of Soli in Cilicia (b. c. 315 B.C.), who came to Athens and became acquainted with Callimachus, and subsequently spent part of his life at the court of Antigonus Gonātās, king of Macedonia, where he wrote hymns for the marriage of the king. He was the author of an extant poem entitled 'Phainomena' (in 1154 hexameters) describing the stellar regions (the relative positions, that is, of the chief stars and constellations, their risings and settings, with little mythological allusion), based on an earlier astronomical work by Eudoxus. The last 400 lines of the poem, dealing with signs of the weather, were sometimes given the separate title of 'Diosēmiai' The poem was translated into Latin by Cicero in his youth, and the latter part of it also by Germanicus and Avienus (qq.v.) (see also *Hipparchus* (2)). Cicero's translation is thought to have had considerable influence on the style of Lucretius. Other poems, which have not survived, were ascribed to him. He has sometimes been thought identical with the 'Aratus' of Idyll vii of Theocritus; but this has now been disproved by inscriptions. (2) Of Sicyŏn, see *Achaean League*.

Arbē'la, a town in Assyria; near it was fought in 331 B.C. the battle of Gaugamēla (sometimes called battle of Arbela) in which Alexander the Great (q.v., § 5) finally overthrew Darius.

Arcā'dia (*Arkădiă*), a region in the centre of the Peloponnese, very mountainous, especially in the north, where Cyllēnē, Erimanthus, and Aroanius towered to nearly 8,000 feet. The largest plains were in the southern part, about Mantinea and Megalopolis. Its inhabitants claimed to be the oldest people in Greece and resisted the Dorian invasion (see *Migrations*) and later Spartan aggressions; they retained a dialect which may have represented the original Achaean language. Arcadia has many associations with Greek mythology. According to one account Zeus was born there, on Mt. Lycaeus. Hermes and Pan were originally Arcadian deities. Through Evander (q.v.), said to have been an Arcadian, Arcadia is connected with the origins of Rome. Lake Stymphalus lay among the lofty mountains of northern Arcadia, and Styx was the name of a little river falling down a tremendous cliff on Mt. Aroanius (the modern Mt. Chelmos). Arcadia also contains the famous temple to Apollo at Bassae near Phigalia, in a lonely and impressive situation which heightens the effect of the beautiful ruins. The frieze of the cella, representing the battle of the Centaurs and the Lapithae and the battle of the Greeks and the Amazons, discovered in 1812, is now in the British Museum. The Arcadians derived their name from a legendary Arcas, son of Zeus and Callisto (q.v.).

Arce'silas (*Arkesilăs*) or ARCESILĀ'US (*Arkesilăos*), of Pitanē in Asia Minor, see *Academy*.

Arcesilā'us (*Arkesilăos*), the name of four of the kings of Cyrene (q.v.) between the end of the 7th c. and the middle of the 5th c. B.C.

Archelā'us (*Archelăos*), see *Macedonia*, § 1.

Archetype, see *Texts and Studies*, § 11.

Archidā'mus, see *Isocrates*.

Archi'lochus (*Archilochos*), a celebrated Greek poet, probably of the 7th c. B.C., member of a distinguished family of Paros, but himself the son, it is said, of a slave woman. Poverty drove him to migrate to Thasos, and he was at one time a mercenary soldier. He fell in love with Neobūlē, daughter of Lycambēs, but her father forbade the marriage, and Archilochus avenged himself with such biting satires that father and daughter, according to tradition, hanged themselves. He is said to have perished in a battle between Parians and Naxians.

He is chiefly famous for his iambic poetry (q.v.), but he also wrote elegies and hymns and is said to be the author of various metrical inventions. His iambic poems show a great variety of talent, mockery, enthusiasm, melancholy, and a mordant wit. Some of them celebrate Neobule. Eustathius spoke of him as 'scorpion-tongued'. Only fragments of his work survive. See also *Epode*.

Archimē'dēs (*c.* 287–212 B.C.), born at Syracuse, one of the greatest mathematicians of antiquity, an astronomer, and an inventor in physics and mechanics. He probably studied at Alexandria and subsequently lived at the court of Hieron II of Syracuse, where he was killed at the capture of the city by Marcellus, a capture which his devices had helped to postpone for two years. He left a number of treatises on statics and hydrostatics, on the circle, and on the 'Sphere and Cylinder', which are still extant. He invented the compound pulley and the 'Screw of Archimedes', a contrivance for raising irrigation water which may still be seen in use on the canals of Egypt. 'Give me a place to stand, and I will move the earth', is a saying attributed to him. 'Eurēka' ('I have found it') is said to have been his exclamation when he discovered, by observing in his bath the water displaced by his body, the means of testing (by specific gravity) whether base metal had been introduced into Hieron's crown. There is a good deal about Archimedes in Plutarch's life of Marcellus.

Cicero, who was quaestor in Sicily in 75 B.C., discovered the tomb of Archimedes near one of the gates of Syracuse, overgrown with brambles and forgotten. It had on it a column on which was represented a sphere inscribed in a cylinder, recalling his discovery of the relation between their volumes (Tusc. Disp. v. 23. 64–6).

Architecture.

§ 1. *Greek architecture*

The earliest remains of Greek architecture known to us are the so-called *Cyclopean* walls of Tiryns and Mycenae, built of huge polygonal blocks fitted together. This form of building gradually gave place to squared blocks, of which primitive specimens are also seen at Mycenae. In the same ancient town may still be seen the wonderful 'beehive' tombs of the early princes, circular chambers built of horizontal courses of stone which gradually approach till they form a vault. The later development of Greek architecture is best studied in the Greek temples (see *Temples*). See also *Houses*. Among famous Greek architects were Mnésiclês, architect of the Propylaea, and Ictinus and Callicratês, architects of the Parthenon.

§ 2. *Orders of Architecture*

There were three orders of Greek architecture, based on the form of the column. (1) In the *Doric* order, the most ancient, the column, starting without base direct from the floor, rose to a height about 5½ times its diameter at the foot, tapering slightly from about a quarter of the way up. It had wide, shallow flutings, and was surmounted by a capital consisting of a basin-shaped circular moulding and plain, square slab. On this rested the architrave, a quadrangular beam of stone stretching from pillar to pillar. Above the architrave was the frieze, divided into metopes (square spaces adorned with sculpture) by the triglyphs, surfaces cut in vertical grooves (see *Temples*, § 1). Above this again was a projecting cornice. (2) In the *Ionic* order the column was taller, being in height about nine times its diameter at the foot, and the fluting was narrower and deeper. The column stood on a base and was surmounted by a capital characterized by lateral volutes (like ram's horns). The frieze was continuous, not interrupted by triglyphs. (3) In the *Corinthian* order the column was similar to that of the Ionic order, but the capital was of an inverted bell shape, adorned with rows of acanthus leaves, giving rise to graceful volutes.

For ROMAN ARCHITECTURE, see *Art*.

Architheō'riā, see *Liturgy*.

A'rchon (*Archōn*), see *Athens*, § 2.

Archȳ'tas (*Archūtās*) of Tarentum, a Pythagorean philosopher and geometrician who flourished about 400 B.C. (and thus a contemporary of Plato). He was also a military commander and repeatedly led the forces of his city in successful campaigns. He is said to have invented the screw and the pulley, and to have solved (by geometry) the problem of the proportion between the sides of two cubes, one of which has double the content of the other. He was also said to have been drowned at sea, a tradition perhaps founded on Horace, Od. I. xxviii.

Arcti'nus (*Arktinos*), see *Epic Cycle*.

Arctū'rus (*Arktouros*, 'guardian of *Arktos*', the Bear), a bright star in the constellation Arctophylax (which likewise means 'guardian of the Bear'), situated in the heavens near the Great Bear. The name Arcturus is sometimes wrongly applied to the whole constellation, of which it is one star. The Great Bear is also known as the Wain, in which case Arctophylax becomes Boötês, 'the Waggoner'. The morning rising of Arcturus, in September, was regarded as the time of the vintage and as the time when the cattle left the upland pastures. See the prologue to the 'Rudens' of Plautus, which is spoken by the star Arcturus. For the myth of the origin of Arcturus, see *Callisto*.

Areopagī'ticus, see *Isocrates*.

Areo'pagus (*Areios Pagos*), the Hill of Ares at Athens, to the W. of the Acropolis and separated from it by a depression (See Pl. 13a). According to legend, it was so called because it was there that Ares was tried for the murder of Halirrhothios son of Poseidon, the lover of Ares' daughter. According to legend again, as set forth in the 'Eumenides' of Aeschylus (see *Oresteia*), it was there that Orestes was tried for the murder of Clytemnestra, Athena referring the case to a tribunal of Athenian citizens. After the synoecism (see *Athens*, § 2), it was on the Areopagus that the Boule or Council of State held its sittings. Later, under the constitutions of Draco and Solon (qq.v.), the name was applied to the body which, sitting on this hill, judged cases of murder, malicious wounding, arson, and poisoning. These definite powers were never withdrawn from the Court of Areopagus, but it had also certain indefinite powers, which were abolished by Ephialtes (q.v.), viz. a general supervision of the magistrates, guardianship of the laws, control of education, and censorship of morals; and the competence to assume, in great emergencies, a dictatorial authority. It was composed of the men who had discharged without reproach one of the archonships, and these remained members of the Areopagus for life.

Ā'rēs (*Ărēs*), in Greek mythology, the son of Zeus and Hera (qq.v.), the god of war, or rather of warlike frenzy. He is not a personage of great importance in mythology, and plays no very glorious part in the stories in which he appears. He is a stirrer of strife, unchivalrous, and does not always have the advantage in encounters with mortals (see, e.g., under *Otus* and *Ephialtes*). For his intrigue with Aphrodite, see under her name. The Romans identified him with Mars (q.v.), a god of greater dignity.

Arē′tē (*Árētē*), in the 'Odyssey', the wife of Alcinous, king of the Phaeacians.

A′rethās, see *Byzantine Age* and *Texts and Studies*, § 4.

Arethū′sa (*Arethousa*), (1) one of the Hesperides (q.v.). (2) A fountain in Ortygia (the island in the harbour of Syracuse). Legend relates that the river-god Alpheus (q.v.) fell in love with the nymph Arethusa when she bathed in his stream. She fled from him to Ortygia where Artemis transformed her into a fountain. But Alpheus, flowing under the sea, was united with the fountain. It was believed in antiquity that there was a real connexion between the river and the spring. The myth is the subject of Shelley's poem 'Arethusa', and Milton refers to it in 'Arcades',

    Divine Alpheus, who, by secret sluice,
    Stole under seas to meet his Arethuse.

Argē′i, bundles of rushes, resembling men bound hand and foot, which on the 14th May (according to Ovid) of each year were carried to the Tiber by *pontifices* (q.v.) and thrown into the river from the Pons Sublicius by the Vestal Virgins. The meaning of the rite is disputed. The Argei may have been scapegoats in a rite of purification, or offerings to the river-god to pacify him and induce him to tolerate the bridge across his stream (the *pontifices* were said to have built the Pons Sublicius, the oldest in Rome). The rite, again, is thought by some to have been a rain-spell. There were twenty-seven shrines of these *argei* throughout the city, and probably twenty-seven *argei* connected with the shrines (the lucky number twenty-seven, thrice nine, is frequently met with both in Greek and Roman ritual).

A′rgēs, see *Cyclopes*.

Argilē′tum, at Rome, a district NE. of the Forum, between the Esquiline and the Quirinal (see Pl. 14). It was occupied by artisans and shopkeepers, notably booksellers and shoemakers.

Arginū′sae (*Arginousai*), islets S. of Lesbos, off which in 406 B.C. the Athenian fleet heavily defeated that of Sparta, capturing or destroying seventy Spartan ships. The Athenians lost twenty-five ships, and, owing to bad weather, their crews were not rescued. It was thought at Athens that insufficient efforts had been made to save them, and the blame was laid on the eight generals who had been present. These were condemned to death by the Assembly, and six were executed, including Pericles, son of the great statesman, and Thrasyllus (see *Thrasybulus*). See also *Socrates*.

Argonau′tica, see *Apollonius Rhodius*, *Valerius Flaccus*, and *Varro Atacinus*.

A′rgonauts (*Argonautai*), in Greek mythology, the men who sailed in the ship *Argo* with Jason, son of Aeson, to Colchis (q.v.) to recover the golden fleece of the ram that had carried away Phrixus and Helle (see *Athamas*). The story was probably built up from various sources, owing to the desire of many families to claim an Argonautic ancestor, and in different lands, for its geography centres both in Thessaly and about the Black Sea, where Miletus had settlements at an early date. Pelias (see *Tyro*) had usurped the throne of Iolcos in Thessaly, which properly belonged to his half-brother Aeson, and after the latter's death to Jason. Jason had been sent for safety and education to the Centaur Chiron (q.v.). When Jason reached maturity he returned to Iolcos. Pelias, warned by an oracle to beware of a one-sandalled lad (and Jason had arrived with only one sandal), promised, in order to get rid of him, to restore the throne if he would first recover the golden fleece. Jason undertook the adventure and embarked in the *Argo* at Pagasae with some fifty of the chief heroes of Greece (among them the Dioscuri, Orpheus, and, for part of the way, Heracles, qq.v.), and after many adventures (see *Hylas, Hypsipyle, Phineus, Symplegades*) reached Colchis. Aeētēs, king of Colchis, consented to surrender the fleece (probably regarded as possessing valuable magic properties) if Jason would perform certain apparently impossible tasks. These included the sowing of a dragon's teeth, from which armed men would arise, whose fury would be turned against Jason. With the help of the magic arts of Medea (q.v.), the king's daughter, who fell in love with Jason, the tasks were successfully accomplished, and Jason and Medea and the other Argonauts returned to Iolcos with the golden fleece. Medea, in their flight from Colchis, according to one version of the story, murdered and cut in pieces her young brother Absyrtus and scattered the fragments, that her father, seeking for them, might be delayed in his pursuit. At Iolcos Medea took vengeance on Pelias for the wrong done by him to Jason's family. First she restored Aeson to youth by boiling him in a cauldron with magic herbs, and then persuaded the daughters of Pelias to submit their father to the same process.

But on this occasion the right herbs were omitted, and the experiment resulted in Pelias's death. Acastus, his son, thereupon drove Jason and Medea from Iolcos, and they took refuge at Corinth. For Jason's abandonment of Medea in favour of Glaucē, daughter of Creön, king of Corinth, and its tragic consequences, see *Medea* (Euripides' tragedy). Jason himself died at Corinth, killed, according to one story, as he sat under the old *Argo*, by the falling o' a piece of her woodwork. For the subsequent adventures of Medea see *Theseus*.

The story of the Argonauts is the subject of Pindar's Fourth Pythian Ode, of the 'Argonautica' of Apollonius Rhodius, Valerius Flaccus, and Varro Atacinus (qq.v.), and in modern English literature of W. Morris's 'Life and Death of Jason'. The 'Golden Fleece' was the name of a famous order of chivalry instituted by Philip the Good, duke of Burgundy, in 1429.

A'rgos, a word meaning 'the plain', in the Homeric poems designated the whole of the plain of Argolis, roughly a triangle flanked on the NE. and NW. by mountains and on the S. by the sea, with Mycenae near the apex and nine miles from the sea, and Tiryns nearer the sea on the east (see Pl. 8). This was the country of Agamemnon, which had Mycenae (q.v.) for its capital; and the word Argives was also extended to include all the Achaeans who recognized him as their leader. After the Dorian invasion (see *Migrations and Dialects*), Argos was the name of the new capital of the conquerors of the region. They subdued Mycenae, Tiryns, and Nauplia, and the name Argos covered the whole of their territory. The city of Argos itself stood on the western side of the plain, four miles from the sea, at the foot of a steep mountain which formed its acropolis. In the first half of the 7th c. B.C., under king Pheidōn, Argos was the most important State in the Peloponnese, and the system of weights and measures that he introduced was adopted by the Peloponnesians. But the power of Argos sank as that of Sparta (q.v.) rose, and thereafter, largely under the influence of jealousy of Sparta, she played a secondary and not very glorious role in the history of Greece. At the time of the Persian Wars (q.v.) she concealed her unfaithfulness to the Greek cause under a mask of neutrality. A democratic government was introduced and Argos allied herself with Athens against Sparta in 461. In the first part of the Peloponnesian War (q.v.) she remained neutral. After the Peace of

Nicias, as a result of the efforts of Alcibiades, she in 420 joined Athens and shared her defeat at Mantinea in 418. This led to a fierce conflict between her aristocratic and democratic parties, which sided respectively with Sparta and Athens, and the decadence of the State increased in the course of this struggle; thereafter Argos exerted no considerable influence on the course of events.

A'rgus (*Argos*), (1) the herdsman that Hera set to watch Io (q.v.); he was called Argos Panoptēs, having eyes all over his body. When Hermes killed him, Hera placed his eyes in the peacock's tail; (2) the craftsman who built the ship *Argo* (see *Argonauts*); (3), in the 'Odyssey' (xvii. 292), the dog of Odysseus, which recognizes him on his return and then dies.

Aria'dne (*Ariadnē*), see *Theseus*.

Ari'cia (*Aricia*), a town in a hollow of the Alban Hills. In a grove near it was the famous seat of the worship of Diana Nemorensis (see *Diana*).

Ari'on (*Ar(e)iōn*), (1) a semi-mythical poet of uncertain date, born according to legend at Methymna in Lesbos. He is said to have been a pupil of Alcman (q.v.), to have spent the greater part of his life at the court of Periander, tyrant of Corinth, and also to have visited Italy, where he amassed much wealth. On his return he was thrown overboard by the sailors, who desired to acquire his treasure. But a dolphin, charmed by the song he had been allowed to sing before his death, carried him to land. To Arion was attributed the creation of the dithyramb (q.v.) as a literary composition. He is also said to have been the inventor of the τραγικὸς τρόπος, probably meaning the tragic mode in music, the musical mode afterwards adopted in tragedy.

(2) The name of a legendary horse, the offspring of Poseidon (q.v.) and Demeter. It belonged to Adrastus (q.v.) and its swiftness enabled him to escape after the failure of his expedition against Thebes.

Aristae'us (*Aristaios*), in Greek mythology, son of the nymph Cyrēnē, whom Apollo loved and carried off to the region in Africa that bears her name. Aristaeus was a god of various kinds of husbandry, including bee-keeping, and of hunting. He fell in love with Eurydice (q.v.) and she, in trying to escape from him, trod on a serpent, from whose bite she died. The Dryads avenged her by killing all the bees of Aristaeus. In this calamity, according to Virgil (Georg. iv. 315 et seq.) Aristaeus on the advice of his mother consulted Proteus, appeased the nymphs, and obtained new swarms from the carcases of bulls. Aristaeus married Autonoë daughter of Cadmus, and became father of Actaeon (q.v.). See also *Etesian Winds*.

Arista′gorās, tyrant of Miletus, the instigator of the Ionian revolt against Persia of 499 B.C. See *Persian Wars*.

Arista′rchus (*Aristarchos*) of Samos (b. c. 320 B.C.), an astronomer (not to be confused with Aristarchus of Samothrace, see below), who first put forward the view that the sun was the centre of the planetary system. It was on this hypothesis that Copernicus founded his researches. As, however, Aristarchus supposed that the planets revolved in circles (instead of ellipses), this theory could not be reconciled with the observations, and was abandoned by his immediate successors, such as Hipparchus.

Aristarchus of Samothrace, head of the Alexandrian Library (q.v.) from c. 180 to c. 145 B.C. and 'the founder of scientific scholarship' (Sandys). He produced editions of Homer, Hesiod, Alcaeus, Anacreon, and Pindar, and a great number of volumes of commentaries and treatises on literary and grammatical subjects. His critical notes on Homer are in part preserved in the *scholia* of one of the Venetian MSS. See *Texts and Studies*, § 2.

Aristi′dēs (*Aristeidēs*) (d. c. 468 B.C.), known as 'The Just', son of Lysimachus, and one of the democratic leaders at Athens, famous for his rectitude, patriotism, and moderation. He was one of the strategi at Marathon, and subsequently archon. He came into conflict with Themistocles (q.v.) when the latter rose to power, and as a consequence he was ostracized in 482. According to Plutarch, who has a life of Aristides, an illiterate citizen requested Aristides to record his vote in favour of the ostracism. Being asked whether Aristides had ever injured him, he replied 'No, but it vexes me to hear him everywhere called the Just'. Aristides returned from exile when the expedition of Xerxes was threatening, held a command at Salamis, and led the Athenian contingent at Plataea. His greatest achievement was in the organization of the Delian confederacy (see *Delos*), when he apportioned the tribute to the various confederate States, a task entrusted to him on account of his rectitude and discretion. He served Athens faithfully to the end and died about 468. We have a life of him also by Nepos.

Aristi′dēs (*Aristeidēs*), AELIUS (d. A.D. 189), a Greek rhetorician who wrote speeches, letters, and a kind of prose

hymns, in a good imitation of the Attic style. Fifty-five of his compositions are extant.

Aristi′dēs of Miletus, see *Milesian Tales*.

Aristi′ppus (*Aristippos*), of Cyrene, a pupil of Socrates (q.v.) and founder of the Cyrenaic school of philosophy. He regarded pleasure as the only absolute good in life, but he distinguished between pleasures, for some are a source of pain. Man must therefore select his pleasures, and this implies both intelligence and self-control. Aristippus was thus a predecessor of Epicurus (q.v.). His works are entirely lost.

Aristo′cratēs, *Against*, a speech in a public prosecution by Demosthenes. See *Demosthenes* (2), § 3 (c).

Aristogi′ton (*Aristogeitōn*), see *Harmodius*.

Aristo′phanēs (c. 448–c. 380 B.C.), the great Athenian comic poet. His family belonged to the deme Kūdathēnaion in the city of Athens, but his father Philippos had a small property in the island of Aegina, to which the family moved when Aristophanes was still a boy. The purity of his Athenian descent appears to have been questioned. His first comedy, now lost, 'Daitaleis' (people of the imaginary deme of 'the Banqueters'), a satire on the product of a city education as compared with the old-fashioned country training, won the second prize in 427. The 'Babylonians' (also lost) appeared in 426, soon after the reduction of the rebellious Mytilene and its bare escape from the massacre of its male inhabitants desired by Cleon (see *Lesbos*). The play, which included a chorus of Babylonian slaves working in a mill, representing the Athenian allies, was a vigorous attack on the policy of Cleon. Aristophanes was in consequence prosecuted by Cleon, on a charge, it appears, of alien birth and high treason. None the less, at the Lenaea of the following year, 425, appeared the 'Acharnians' (q.v.), the first of his surviving comedies, a plea for the termination of the war, with indications of continued hostility to Cleon. This won the first prize. The above plays had not been produced in Aristophanes' own name, why is not known; but in his next play, the 'Knights' (q.v.), 424, the author comes forward undisguised. With astonishing courage he heaps invective and ridicule on Cleon (then at the height of his power) and satirizes the defects of democracy. This play again won the first prize. The 'Clouds' (q.v.) followed in 423, the 'Wasps' (q.v.) in 422, the 'Peace' (q.v.) in 421. The plays that he produced during the next six years are lost. In 414 appeared the 'Birds' (q.v.), in 411 'Lysitrata' (q.v.), in 411 or 410 the 'Thesmophoriazusae' (q.v.), about 392 the 'Ecclesiazusae' (q.v.), and in 388 'Plutus' (q.v.). He wrote two comedies after this, which he gave to his son Araros to produce, but which are now lost. One of these, the 'Kōkalus', we are told, started the type of the New Comedy, introducing romantic features which are characteristic of the plays of Menander. The life-work of Aristophanes, therefore, shows him as the chief representative of the Old Comedy (see *Comedy*), developing and intellectualizing it, then gradually transforming it in the direction of a new form of art. His dialogue is vivid and natural; his lyrics contain passages of much beauty; his indecency is coarse and outspoken but not prurient or morbid.

The political plays of Aristophanes show him a supporter of the country party, the farmers and landowners, and a vigorous opponent of the war policy from which these were the chief sufferers. But he jibes at all the leaders in turn, from Pericles to Cleophōn. He brings out, by caricaturing them, the ridiculous or evil sides of the opinions or customs of the moment, and no doubt the jokes and sarcasms that he levels at individuals and at institutions human and divine were taken good-humouredly and not too literally by his audience. Plato in his 'Symposium' (q.v.) represents Aristophanes as an agreeable and convivial companion who gives an amusing turn to a serious discussion, and this is perhaps the light in which to regard much of his work. It does not appear in fact to have affected the course of events.

Aristophanes had a direct influence on English literature, notably on Ben Jonson, Middleton, and Fielding. John Hookham Frere, one of the contributors to the 'Anti-Jacobin', translated several of his plays. R. Browning, in his 'Aristophanes' Apology' (1875), presents Aristophanes discussing with Balaustion, the former defending comedy as the representation of real life, and attacking the unnatural and ascetic Euripides, while Balaustion maintains the superiority of the tragic poet. The 'Plutus' and the 'Peace' were acted at Cambridge in 1536 and 1546 respectively. For an appreciation of Aristophanes' character and work, see Gilbert Murray, 'Aristophanes' (Oxford, 1933).

Aristo'phanēs of Byzantium, head of the Alexandrian Library (q.v.) *c.* 195 B.C. For his critical work in this capacity see *Texts and Studies*, § 2. He is said to have invented or regularized Greek accents; and he devised a set of critical signs indicating passages in manuscripts suspected of being interpolations or otherwise noteworthy.

A'ristotle (*Aristotelēs*) (384–322 B.C.), a great Greek philosopher.

§ 1. *Biography*

Aristotle was born at Stageira in Chalcidice, the son of Nicomachus, physician to Amyntas II, king of Macedonia. In 367 he came to Athens, and was a pupil of Plato until the latter's death in 347, that is to say for twenty years. He then left Athens. Stageira was destroyed in the same year by Philip of Macedon, and Aristotle settled at Assos in the Troad, where there was a sort of small colony of philosophers of the Athenian Academy, favoured by Hermeiās, the enlightened prince of the neighbouring city of Atarneus. There Aristotle remained for three years, probably lecturing and writing. He then went to Mytilene, teaching there till 343/2. In that year he was invited by Philip of Macedon (q.v.) to be tutor to his son Alexander the Great (q.v.). To explain Aristotle's acceptance of this post it has been suggested that the appointment was perhaps made in connexion with some kind of diplomatic mission from Hermeias, who was negotiating with Philip against his Persian overlord. Hermeias, whose niece Aristotle married, presently came under Persian suspicion, was carried off to Susa, and there crucified. Aristotle wrote an epigram for his cenotaph at Delphi and a beautiful commemorative hymn. In 335, when Alexander started on his expedition to Asia, Aristotle returned to Athens, and opened there a school of philosophy which came to be known as the Peripatetic school from his habit of walking up and down (περιπατεῖν), while conversing with his pupils, in the paths of the Lyceum (a grove sacred to Apollo Lyceius, where there was a gymnasium). He collected manuscripts and formed the first considerable library; also a museum of natural objects, in the assembling of which he is said to have been aided by Alexander. He enjoyed the friendship and protection of Antipater, whom Alexander had left as governor of Macedon and Greece. After the death of Alexander in 323 the anti-Macedonian party at Athens regained the ascendant (Antipater had been summoned to Asia), and Aristotle quitted Athens. He died the following year at Chalcis. His will, preserved by Diogenes Laertius (q.v.), shows him to have been of a kindly and affectionate disposition, and he appears to have instilled in his school a spirit of familiarity and friendship.

§ 2. *General character of his work*

Aristotle left a vast number of works on a great variety of subjects; some four hundred were attributed to him. But he was primarily a teacher whose influence was exerted on his pupils by the spoken word, not a literary author. It was his practice to treat more difficult subjects with his pupils in the morning, and to give lectures to larger audiences in the afternoon. The former lessons came to be known as *acroamatic* (i.e. oral) or *esoteric*, the latter as *exoteric*. But Aristotle himself did not use the word 'esoteric'; and it seems probable that he applied the word 'exoteric' to his early published writings (intended for the cultivated public outside his school), as opposed to his lectures. Among these published writings were dialogues on philosophical and other subjects, lucid, eloquent, grave, less poetical than those of Plato, many of them probably composed when he was still a member of Plato's Academy or was teaching at Assos. We possess fragments of fourteen of these, notably of a 'Protrepticus' or 'exhortation to philosophy'. To a late period of his life probably belong another class of writings, collections of data obtained by systematic research, in pursuance of his final system (see below) of basing philosophical speculation on a wide ascertainment of facts. To this class belonged the great collection of the constitutions of 158 cities, and the 'Didascaliae' (q.v.) or records of dramatic performances at Athens. These likewise are lost, with the exception of the 'Polity of the Athenians', discovered in an Egyptian papyrus in 1890, the first of the collected constitutions.

The treatises, which form the bulk of Aristotle's surviving work, consist mainly of notes or summaries of his oral lectures, written either by himself or some of his pupils, and put together by later editors, sometimes without regard to the fact that various passages belong to different periods of his philosophical development and do not harmonize together. They disappeared not long after his death and were not brought to light until the 1st c. B.C. There is a story, recorded by Strabo, that they were disinterred in a cellar belonging to the descendants of Neleus, an important Aristotelian of the group at Assos. The story has been doubted, but is not improbable.

A study of the surviving treatises and fragments of Aristotle's writings shows that their author went through a process of philosophical evolution: from being a disciple of Plato in sympathy with much of his teaching, he passed into a critic of some of the leading Platonic doctrines (e.g. that of Ideas), and finally adopted a wholly independent position and philosophical method. Of this the principal features were the careful analysis of current philosophical conceptions, e.g. the analysing of a given object (τόδε τι) in terms of matter and form; and the revolutionary view that speculation must be based on experience of reality and systematic research, converting Ethics and Politics, for instance, from abstract theoretical sciences into practical sciences based on careful observation of life. He thus extended philosophy to cover universal science.

§ 3. *Aristotle's extant works*

The surviving treatises may be classified as follows:

1. On Logic, the *Organon* ('instrument'), as this group came to be called much later, consisting of six treatises known as: *Categoriae* (a theory of terms and predicates), *De interpretatione*, *Analytica priora* and *posteriora*, *Topica*, and *De sophisticis elenchis*. In these Aristotle was the first to explore the science of reasoning, both formal (in the Prior Analytics) and scientific (in the Posterior Analytics), basing himself on the syllogism, which he discovered. Later logicians have added little to his conclusions on the syllogism. The Schoolmen of the Middle Ages summarized his teaching on this subject in the famous mnemonic lines 'Barbara, Celarent, Darii, Ferioque prioris . . .', in which the vowels of the words Barbara–Ferio, etc. indicate the nature of the major and minor premisses and conclusion of the various moods of the syllogism, A a universal affirmative, E a universal negative, I a particular affirmative, O a particular negative.

2. On Metaphysics, a group of treatises known as *Metaphysica*, a name not due to Aristotle (who uses the term πρώτη φιλοσοφία), but to the editors who placed the writings on this subject after the Physics (μετὰ τὰ φυσικά). In these Aristotle explores the nature of the real, the essential substance of the universe. At the base of his doctrine is the distinction between matter and form. He finds in the universe a hierarchy of existences, each of which is the 'matter' of that next above it, and imparts form and change to that next below. At the lower end of the scale is primary formless matter, which has no real but only logical existence. At the

upper end is the 'prime unmoved mover,' an eternal activity of thought, free from matter, giving motion to the universe through an attraction akin to love; this prime mover he identifies with God. The Aristotelian 'form', the intelligible nature of a thing, differs from the Platonic 'idea' (at least as Aristotle conceived it) in being immanent in the thing and not existing apart from it. The 'Metaphysica', as we have it, is a medley of materials from detached writings or lectures of different periods, and is not self-consistent.

3. ON NATURAL PHILOSOPHY (Physics, Biology, Psychology), treatises known as (a) *Physica*, an examination of the constituent elements of things that exist by 'nature' ('nature' being 'an innate impulse to movement'), and a discussion of such notions as matter and form, time, space, and movement, with an exposition of the Four Causes, the Material Cause (that out of which a thing comes to be), the Formal Cause (the intelligible nature of a thing, that in virtue of which it is what it is), the Moving Cause (from which immediately originates the change), the Final Cause (the end or aim of the change); (b) *De caelo*, on the movement of celestial and terrestrial bodies. Aristotle knew that the earth is a sphere, but thought it was situated at the centre of the universe; his view that the distance between Spain and India by a westerly voyage might not be very great influenced Columbus; (c) *De generatione et corruptione*, on coming into being and passing away; (d) *Meteorologica*, principally on weather phenomena. The group of works on biology includes the *Historia Animalium*, an introductory collection of facts regarding animal life, showing in some respects a surprising degree of observation (Aristotle knew, for instance, that whales are mammals); and a series of treatises in which he deals with the classification of animals, their reproduction, and the adaptation and evolution of their organs; for he lays stress on final causes in the problems of organic life. The group is closed by a treatise in three books—*De anima*, that is to say on the internal principle of movement and sensibility which holds bodies together and gives them life. This vital principle or 'soul' does not survive the death of the body, though the intelligent soul of man possesses a portion of 'active reason', which is immortal, and is perhaps to be identified with God. To the same group belong a monograph 'On the interpretation of dreams', and the *Parva Naturalia* on the general physiological conditions of life.

4. ON ETHICS AND POLITICS. Aristotle regards ethics as a branch of politics in the wider sense, for the individual is essentially a member of society. His ethical treatises are known as the *Nicomachean* and *Eudemian Ethics*. These cover much the same ground, though with certain important differences of view. The relation between the two works is not certain; they are probably editions by Aristotle's son Nicomachus and his disciple Eudemus of two courses of his lectures on Ethics, the Eudemian earlier than the Nicomachean and representing an earlier stage in the development of Aristotle's moral theory, when the Platonic influence was still strong. The Nicomachean Ethics is generally regarded as the more valuable work. It is in the main a study of the end to which conduct should be directed —the Good. Aristotle accepts happiness (εὐδαιμονία) as this end, but rejects pleasure, honour, and wealth as the basis of happiness. He finds the highest happiness in a life of contemplation, as being the activity peculiar to man, in accord with the virtue of the best part of him (the rational principle), and manifested not for short periods but in a complete life. By contemplation he means contemplation of philosophic truth. But such a life is beyond the reach of the ordinary man, whose happiness is to be sought in moral virtue and practical wisdom. Aristotle, distinguishing between the moral and intellectual virtues, discusses the nature of moral virtue, and defines it as a disposition, developed by a proper exercise of the capacity, to choose a certain mean, as determined by a man of practical wisdom, between two opposite extremes of conduct; a mean, for instance, between asceticism and the yielding to uncontrolled impulses. Aristotle lays stress on the notion of moral intention; virtue of character becomes pre-eminent instead of virtue of intellect (cf. *Socrates*).

In the eight books of the *Politica*, Aristotle discusses the science of politics from the point of view of the city-state, which he assumes to be that most conducive to the fullest life of the citizen. He thinks the State was developed naturally by the grouping of families in villages, and of villages in a State, for the purpose of securing to the citizens a good and self-sufficing life. Since this moral end, and not material purposes, is the essential characteristic of the State, it is necessary that the power should rest, not with the wealthy or the whole body of free citizens, but with the good. He discusses citizenship, the classification of actual constitutions, and the various types of these, their diseases and the remedies; he recognizes the advantages of democracy, but finds the highest type in the monarchy of the perfect ruler if such a ruler is available, and failing this in an aristocracy of men of virtue and enlightenment. But this, too, is difficult, and on the whole he regards a limited democracy as the constitution best suited to the practical conditions of Greece of his day. He regards slavery as a natural institution, so far as based on the inferiority of nature of the slave (not on right of conquest). But the master must not abuse his authority, and slaves must have the hope of emancipation. It is 'improbable that the treatise as we have it was ever planned as a whole or sprung from a single creative act of the mind' (Jaeger). Books VII and VIII containing the discussion of the ideal State belong to an early text in which the purely constructive method of Plato is followed. Books IV–VI, dealing with actual historical States and containing an allusion to the death of King Philip, must have been written later, when Aristotle had at his disposal the collection of the 158 constitutions. Aristotle's treatise on the *Polity of the Athenians* has already been referred to. It traces the development of the Athenian constitution from the earliest times (the first chapters are missing) down to the fall of the Thirty, and then describes the matured democracy of Aristotle's day. The discovery of the treatise has thrown a new light on a number of historical points.

5. On Rhetoric and Poetry. Aristotle's *Rhetoric* deals with the methods of persuasion, divided into those by which the speaker produces on his audience a favourable view of his own character, those by which he produces emotion, and thirdly argument, whether by means of example or of enthymeme (the rhetorical form of the syllogism). It then discusses style (of which the leading characteristics should be clearness and appropriateness) and arrangement. The whole subject was one that deeply interested the Greeks, and the treatise had for long a much greater authority than it has to-day.

For Aristotle's *Poetics*, see that word.

§ 4. *The influence of Aristotle*

The influence that Aristotle exerted on later generations of philosophers and scientists was immense, by the stimulus he gave, by the instrument of investigation he forged, and by his actual contributions to knowledge. In the Middle Ages this influence, after having been seen in Boethius and the great French teacher Abélard, became especially prominent in the works of the Schoolmen. The writings of Aristotle reached them mainly in Latin translations of

Arabic versions (see *Texts and Studies*, § 8), and were used in support of Christian theology, notably in the lectures and *Summa* of Thomas Aquinas. The recognition in Britain of his importance is especially seen in the writings of John of Salisbury (d. 1180, *Polycraticus* and *Metalogicus*); Michael Scot the astrologer (1175 ?–1234 ?), who translated an Arabic summary of the 'Historia Animalium'; Bishop Grosseteste (d. 1253), himself a powerful influence on subsequent English thought; Roger Bacon (1214?–94), Duns Scotus (1265?–1308?), though he was partly a Platonist; and William of Ockham (d. 1349 ?). Aristotle's philosophy was one of the principal subjects of study in our medieval universities. At a later date we see his influence on Francis Bacon (1561–1626), who, though contemptuous of the ancient philosophers in general, adopts Aristotle's division of the Four Causes, and entitles part of his work the *Novum Organum*. In the sphere of literature, Aristotle's 'Poetics' was regarded as an authority from Elizabethan days onward, and we find references to it in the writings of Sidney, Ben Jonson, and Milton; and other traces of his fame occur in Marlowe, Spenser, and Shakespeare. Landor has an 'Imaginary Conversation' between Aristotle and Callisthenes (q.v.) in which the author represents Aristotle as an enemy to Alexander the conqueror and despot.

Arminius, see *Varus*.

Army.

§ 1. *Greek Army*

In Homeric times the warrior, armed with spear and sword and protected by helmet, cuirass, greaves, and an ox-hide shield strengthened with bronze, rode out to battle in a chariot. From this he dismounted to encounter some opposing champion. He used his spear as a missile, or thrust with it as a pike, and sometimes supplemented it by hurling a boulder. Bows and arrows were also used. But there was no cavalry. The common folk, who were lightly armed, played a minor part in the battles. In later times all this was changed. The armies were drawn up in well-ordered lines of armoured hoplites (see below) and rushed against each other, each endeavouring to hurl back, outflank, or break the opposite line. As time went on this simple manœuvre was elaborated. More use was made of light-armed archers and slingers and of cavalry. Epaminondas (q.v.) introduced real tactics; and Philip of Macedon developed the phalanx (q.v.).

At Athens in the 5th and 4th cc. B.C. military service was obligatory on all citizens, and from the age of 18 to 20 they underwent military training as recruits (see also *Ephebi*). The cavalry, service in which entailed heavy expense, was formed mainly from the *hippeis* (see *Athens*, § 2); the *hoplites* or heavy infantry, who made up the bulk of the army, were drawn from the *zeugitai* and the richer metics. The *thêtes* served as light infantry or in the fleet. From 20 to 49 years of age an Athenian formed part of the active army. From 50 to 60 he was included, with the recruits and the remaining metics, in a territorial militia. In 431 at the beginning of the Peloponnesian War, Athens had a field army of 13,000 and a territorial army of 16,000 men. There were also some foreign mercenaries, light-armed archers. The cavalry (1,000 in number after 446) were organized in ten squadrons, the hoplites in ten regiments (*taxeis*), based on the ten tribes. Each regiment numbered about 1,300 men, was divided into battalions (*lochoi*), and was commanded by a taxiarch. The hoplite wore a helmet, cuirass, and greaves of metal, carried a shield of leather with a metal rim, and was armed with a lance six feet long (very different from the Macedonian *sarissa* of 13 feet), and a short sword. He received, on service, pay at two (afterwards three) obols a day, and subsistence allowance at the same rate (in the cavalry the allowance was 1 drachma). Military officers, strategi (q.v.), taxiarchs, etc., were elected (not chosen by lot) annually, but unlike most of the civil officials might be re-elected indefinitely (see also *Polemarch*). See Pl. 3a.

At Sparta (q.v.), where the whole life of the male citizens was organized with a view to the military efficiency of the State, liability to foreign military service extended from 20 to 60 years of age, and a high degree of mobility and dexterity in the use of weapons was attained by constant exercises. It was from Sparta that the institution of armoured spearmen fighting on foot in serried ranks (hoplites) spread through Greece. Our knowledge of the organization of the Spartan army is not very certain, and the details given by Thucydides and Xenophon, respectively, are not easy to reconcile. Moreover the Spartans deliberately kept the strength of their army secret. At Mantinea in 418 B.C. it consisted, according to Thucydides, of seven *lochoi* of 512 spears, subdivided down to 16 platoons (*enômotiai*) of 32, each with its commanding officer thus securing rapidity of movement and flexibility. It seems probable that before the end of the Peloponnesian War the organization was modified, and a formation called a *môra* introduced, numbering

about 600 men, subdivided as before down to platoons. Four such *morai* fought under Cleombrotus at Leuctra, but the number of Spartiatae included in them was only about 700. With the dwindling number of Spartan citizens, the ranks were increasingly filled with *perioeci* (see *Sparta*, § 2), supplemented in great emergencies by helots. Cavalry appears to have played a subordinate part in the Spartan army. This army was unique not only in its tactical organization (which caused Xenophon amazement) but in having a uniform and military flute-players. In all Greek armies the men had to supply their own arms and fend for themselves in provisions.

In the early part of the 4th c. the increasing use of mercenary troops, drawn especially from the wilder parts of Greece, became of importance. These professional troops, known as *peltasts* (from *peltê*, a small, light, leather shield), were armed with a javelin and light shield, and were more mobile than the hoplites (see Pl. 3b). In the Corinthian War (see *Corinth*) of this period, a force of peltasts, with improved weapons, was organized by the Athenian Iphicrates, and was used with great success against the Spartans. Mercenary service grew in importance during the 4th and later centuries, and Greek mercenaries were largely employed by the Persian kings and their satraps (Xenophon and the 10,000 afford a conspicuous example). Demosthenes frequently protests against it. For the later development of Greek military tactics see *Epaminondas* and *Phalanx*. Alexander's military successes were principally due to his skilful use of cavalry (who were more numerous in his than in earlier Greek armies and were trained to charge home). These delivered flank attacks, while the phalanx attacked the enemy front. In the narrative of Alexander's battles we constantly find him commanding in person the best of the cavalry and delivering the decisive blow. The successors of Alexander relied largely on great masses of inferior oriental troops, doubling the depth of the phalanx and thus further diminishing its mobility. Pyrrhus appears to have tried to remedy this defect in his wars with Rome by breaking up the phalanx into a number of columns with bodies of Italian troops placed between them; but he failed to overcome the Roman resistance. The later eastern adversaries of Rome, such as Philip V, Perseus, and Antiochus III, were even less successful.

§ 2. *Greek siege-craft*

Siege-craft made no considerable progress before the 5th c. B.C. In earlier days

Greek citadels on rocky hills, or walled towns such as Thebes, were impregnable, and had to be reduced by blockade, unless treachery opened a way to the besiegers. In the 5th c. we first hear of siege engines (chiefly rams, scaling-ladders, and screens for the protection of the attacking force). But the defence still had the advantage, as may be seen from the account given by Thucydides (II. lxxv et seq.) of the successful resistance offered by the Plataeans in 429 B.C. to the engines of the besiegers. A great advance in siege-craft was made when, at the beginning of the 4th c., Dionysius I of Syracuse introduced the use of the catapult. From a large cross-bow of increased range and power, this was developed into an engine capable of discharging heavy missiles against fortifications. During this century sieges began to be conducted more scientifically, with regular covered approaches, mines, movable towers, and various types of catapults. The methods of the defence were likewise improved. Countermines were sunk to upset movable towers, catapults were extensively used against the engines of the besiegers, and fire-arrows and similar devices were employed to set them on fire. Among the most notable sieges of this century were the siege of Tyre by Alexander the Great (q.v., § 4) and the unsuccessful siege of Rhodes by Demetrius Poliorcētēs (see *Macedonia*, § 2, and *Rhodes*).

§ 3. *Roman Army*

The earliest Roman army is said by tradition to have been an exclusively patrician body (the *legio*) consisting of three regiments of 1,000 infantry each, with three 'centuries' of cavalry. This force was reorganized and enlarged by Servius Tullius on the basis of his classification of the community (see *Rome*, § 2). It was raised to four legions, each of about 3,000 infantry, drawn in certain proportions from the various classes of the census but with a minimum property qualification of 11,000 *asses* (12,500 according to some authorities). These were required to equip themselves and serve without pay. The legionaries were armed with shield, sword, and long spear (*hasta*); there were certain differences of equipment according to class. The legion fought in mass formation, six ranks deep, with a front of 500. There were also eighteen 'centuries' of cavalry. Pay was introduced, according to tradition, in 406 during the siege of Veii, owing to the prolonged character of the service. The legion was reorganized at some date before the 2nd c. B.C. on the basis of the 'maniple'

of two centuries, designed to give the formation greater flexibility. It was further divided between heavy-armed and light-armed troops (*velites*); and the heavy-armed in turn into *hastāti*, *principēs*, and *triārii*, according to their age and military experience, the *hastati* being the youngest soldiers, the *triarii* the veterans. The *hastati* and *principes*, occupying the front ranks, had two javelins (*pila*) for throwing; the *triarii*, used as a reserve, retained the *hasta*. The heavy-armed troops had a bronze helmet, the light-armed a leather helmet; all had a shield and a sword, a short cut-and-thrust weapon, worn, unlike the modern sword, on the right side. See Pl. 4.

The Roman cavalry, which originally were merely mounted infantry, were under the Servian organization drawn from the richest class. *Equites equo publico* received their horses from the State; *equites equo privato* provided their own. Roman cavalry disappeared after 146 B.C., and Italians did not serve in the cavalry after the 1st c. B.C. Thereafter the cavalry formed part of the auxiliary troops. Before the enfranchisement of Italy the Roman army proper was assisted by contingents from the Latin and Italian allies (nominally equal, in practice often more numerous). Foreign mercenaries were freely employed for cavalry (Numidians, Gauls, Spaniards) and special arms (Balearic slingers).

The original Roman army was a militia of Roman citizens in which service was compulsory. But the shrinkage in the number of available citizens, in spite of the lowering of the census standard from 11,000 *asses* to 4,000, led Marius to effect a reorganization. There had been a gradual transition before his time; owing to the almost continuous wars a professional type of soldier was growing up. Marius abolished the property qualification and abandoned conscription. The cohort (of three maniples) became the military unit; there were ten cohorts in the legion; the legion was raised (nominally) to 6,000 men (in practice it sometimes fell to half this strength), and equipment became uniform. The *hasta* was abandoned, and all carried the *pilum*. The eagle was adopted as the standard of the legion, and was carried by the first maniple of the first cohort. Enlistment was normally for twenty years; pay was 120 *dēnārii* a year (increased under Caesar to 225 *denarii*); the cost of rations was deducted from the pay. The command of each legion was exercised by one of six tribunes (*tribūni mīlitum*), commanding in turn (in Caesar's army and under the empire each legion had one commanding officer, the *lēgātus*; the tribunes were retained with subordinate duties). Under these were sixty centurions, each commanding a century.

Professional armies of this description, owing their allegiance to their generals, to whom they looked for rewards and chances of booty, were at the root of the civil wars of the 1st c. B.C. Great military commanders, relying on their legions, were able to dominate the State, and their conflicting ambitions brought about the terrible struggles of that period.

The number of legions varied with the requirements of the time. Augustus was the first to create a standing army, which at his death included 25 legions, permanently existing, with fixed stations and definite members and names. Three legions, XVII, XVIII, and XIX, had been destroyed in the Varus (q.v.) disaster and these numbers were never used again. Two legions were added by Claudius, and three more before the accession of Vespasian; and this total of 30 legions was retained in the reign of Trajan. The origin of the practice of giving names as well as numbers to certain legions appears to be the retention by Augustus of some of the legions of Antony as well as his own; those bearing the same number in their original armies kept them, with a distinguishing name in addition, e.g. II Adjutrix and II Augusta. The military establishment of the empire consisted of: (A) Legions, recruited nominally from Roman citizens, but actually often from provincials; from Hadrian's time, if not earlier, local recruitment became the rule. The term of service in the legions was 16 years (soon raised to 20). Pay was at the rate of 225 *denarii* a year (with a free ration of corn), raised to 300 by Domitian, with a lump sum on discharge of 3,000 *denarii*. The legionaries were not allowed to marry during their service, but the unions they formed during their service were legalized on their discharge. (B) Auxiliary cohorts (under *tribuni*) and *ālae* (under prefects of equestrian rank), infantry and cavalry respectively, recruited from provincials; they had a longer period of service and lower pay, and acquired Roman citizenship on discharge. They were originally recruited from special races, after which they are normally called. They also for the most part came to be recruited locally and Roman citizens often entered them. There were also some cohorts of Roman citizens. Some of the auxiliary infantry retained their national weapons and were called *sagittārii* (archers), *funditōrēs* (slingers), etc. Auxiliary cohorts were attached to the several legions, or were used for the

garrisons of the less important provinces. A contingent of auxiliary cavalry (four *alae* of 30 men each in Hadrian's time) was attached to each legion. Pay in the auxiliary forces was at the rate of 70 *denarii* a year. (C) Special corps, (*a*) Praetorians (q.v. and see also *Praefectus Praetorio*), nominally Italians till Septimius Severus; (*b*) four *cohortes urbanae* for police duties in the capital, recruited from freedmen; they served under the Prefect of the City, ranked after the Praetorians, and received higher pay than the legions; (*c*) *Vigilum cohortes*, the fire-brigade, also recruited from freedmen.

The army of the empire was stationed almost entirely on the frontiers. These were defended by forts (*castella*), and, where the frontier was not protected by a river, by methods which varied at different periods. Under Domitian a series of small earth forts were erected, with larger stone forts at greater intervals in the rear; under Trajan and his successors the defence consisted of a wall of stone or earth with a ditch in front of it and forts at intervals. For Hadrian's Wall from the Solway to the Tyne, see *Britain*, § 2. For the Roman camps, see under *Castra*. See also *Elephants*.

§ 4. *Roman siege-craft*

Siege-craft developed in the Roman army in much the same way as in the Greek armies (see above, § 2). Blockade was increasingly supplemented or replaced by assault, as the devices of Greek engineers came to the knowledge of the Romans and were developed by them. The *testūdō* was a Roman device by which interlocked shields formed a screen under which a scaling party could approach the walls; and there were other protective devices of the same kind, such as the *musculus* (a long gallery on wheels with sloping roof), used by Caesar at the siege of Massilia. The lines of the besieging force were protected by trenches and pits against sallies of the enemy, and when threatened by a relieving army (as at Alesia in 52 B.C.), by an external rampart and palisade. A causeway (*agger*) might be built up to the walls and a huge movable tower brought along it into a position from which the assailants could drive the defenders from the wall and cross to it by drawbridges. The chief battering engine was the ram (*ariēs*), a beam tipped with iron, sometimes of great weight and swung on ropes, in the more developed type on a wheeled frame. The catapult and *ballista* (discharging respectively large arrows and heavier missiles) were a sort of giant crossbow to which the propulsive force was given by the torsion of ropes; the *onager* was a large mechanical sling. These engines were used especially for the defence.

Arnold, THOMAS, see *Historians* (*Modern*).

Arpi'num, a town in Latium, the birth-place of Marius and Cicero.

A'rria, (1) wife of Caecina Paetus, who, when her husband was ordered to death under the emperor Claudius, 'taught her husband how to die', stabbing herself and handing him the dagger, with the words 'Paete, non dolet'. (2) The daughter of the above, wife of Thrasea, a Stoic philo-sopher who was put to death by Nero.

A'rrian (*Flāvius Arriānus*) (*c.* A.D. 95–175), a Greek of Nicomēdīa in Bĭthȳnia, a successful officer in the Roman army, who became consul and legate in Cappa-docia. He was author of various extant works in Greek: a valuable *Anabasis* of Alexander the Great, in seven books, narrating his campaigns, with an eighth book descriptive of India and Indian customs and relating the voyage of Nearchus in the Persian Gulf; an *Encheiri-dion* or manual of the philosophy of his master Epictetus (q.v.), and a record of the 'Lectures' (*Diatribai*) of the same philosopher, four books of which out of the original eight survive; a *Periplous* or geographical description of the Euxine Sea; a *Kunēgetikos* (on Hunting) purport-ing to supplement the treatise attributed to Xenophon; and other minor works.

Ars Amātō'ria, a poem in three books of elegiacs by Ovid, written shortly before the beginning of the Christian era. The term 'ars' was applied to a technical treatise, and is playfully applied to a treatise on the devices of love. The first two books consist of instructions to men on the wooing of women of easy virtue; the third, of instructions to women on the seduction of men. The work is full of humour and charm, and contains interesting glimpses of Roman life and manners—the circus, the theatre, the ban-quet. It was very popular, and quotations from it have been found on the walls of Pompeii. It was perhaps partly on account of its immorality that Augustus banished the poet to Tomi.

Ars Poē'tica, the title (it was not the author's) by which the 'Epistle to the Pisos' of Horace is generally known. It is addressed to a father and two sons of the name of Pīsō, whose identity depends on the date to be assigned to the work (see *Horace*); the elder was perhaps the son of the Piso who was Caesar's father-in-law. It is a rather haphazard letter of advice on the pursuit of literature, and appears to consist largely (and this agrees with a statement by an early commenta-tor) of maxims extracted from a Greek manual by Neoptolemus of Parium, a Hellenistic writer of uncertain date, each followed by the comments of Horace himself. But the poet's charm pervades the whole, which is rendered more inter-esting by apt illustrations and by shrewd criticisms on authors of the day. After dealing with technical points on the composition of a drama (such as pro-portion, subject, metre, language) and a short passage on the epic, Horace passes to advice on poetic composition in general. He insists on the seriousness of the poetic art: study life and human rela-tions; avoid the corrupting influences of gain and flattery; do not write unless inspired by the Muse; submit your work to a competent judge; keep it by you for nine years. The work exercised a great influence in later ages on European litera-ture, notably on French drama through Boileau's translation. It was translated into English by Ben Jonson. Many liter-ary phrases, such as the 'purple patch', the 'ridiculus mus' of bathos, the refer-ence to 'Homer nodding', the 'labour of the file', the abrupt entry on a subject ('in medias res'), have their origins in it.

Arsi'noë, (1) see *Alcmaeon*. (2) The name of several Macedonian princesses. The most important was Arsinoe II Phila-delphus, the daughter of Ptolemy I and the wife successively of Lysimachus, Ptolemy Ceraunus, and her brother Ptolemy II. She was a woman of great vigour and ability, successful both in war and peace, and 'the years till her death in 270 were Egypt's golden age' (Tarn). She was deified before her death. (3) For the Egyptian town of that name see *Fayoum*.

Art. (1) GREEK, see *Architecture, Paint-ing, Sculpture, Toreutic Art.* (2) ROMAN. Whether or not there existed an indigen-ous Italian or Romano-Etruscan art before the invasion of Hellenism is a matter of discussion. But such remains as can be claimed for it are of no high merit. Greek art on the other hand, whose inspiration had become exhausted and whose expres-sion had become conventional, found re-newed youth and fresh themes on Roman soil and in Roman history. Roman *sculp-ture* reached its highest excellence in the 1st–2nd c. A.D., and is seen at its best in portrait busts, where it showed great power of expressing character, and in bas-reliefs, the subjects of which are largely

historical. Fine examples of them are seen
in the sculptures of the Ara Pacis (q.v.)
of the Augustan Age, and, at later stages
of development, of the Arch of Titus
and the frieze and column of Trajan; but
breadth and grandeur of treatment are
sometimes marred by excessive crowding
of figures and meticulous attention to
detail. There are also many examples of
decoration of altars and columns with
convolutions and festoons of foliage and
flowers. Though the artists may, at least
in the first period, have been mainly
Greeks, the art was a new one.

Painting was used by the Romans
chiefly to decorate the inner walls of
houses. The subjects of these frescoes,
of which many examples have been found
in Herculaneum and Pompeii, were principally scenes from Greek myth, or single
figures such as Orpheus or a Centaur, less
frequently landscapes, still life, or contemporary scenes. Many of them show much
beauty of colour, line, and expression.

Roman *architecture* was even more distinctive, being marked especially by the
development of the arch, the vault, and
the dome. It evolved the plans of great
public buildings, on which our modern
conceptions have been based; these buildings were remarkable for unity of design,
solidity of construction, and grandeur of
decoration (though the latter was sometimes tasteless). The masonry took the
form of either ashlar, concrete, or brick.
The architecture is seen at its best in
such buildings as the Pantheon built by
Agrippa in 27 B.C. (which survives much
altered), the mighty Colosseum, and in
the plan of the Baths of Caracalla; also
in the great aqueducts, bridges, theatres,
&c., of which the remains are still to be
seen in all parts of the Roman Empire.

Mention must also be made of the art
of *gem-engraving* which became popular
at Rome in the last century of the republic
and was further developed under the
empire, both in the form of the *intaglio*
where the design is sunk, and in the *cameo*
where it is engraved in relief. Engraved
gems were used for signet-rings, and the
surviving examples include portraits of
Caesar, Pompey, Cicero, and Tiberius.
Larger examples are the splendid portrait
of Augustus in the British Museum; the
Gemma Augustēa at Vienna representing
Augustus, Tiberius, Germanicus, and a
group of deities, with a military scene
below; and the *grand camée* in Paris representing Tiberius, Livia, and Germanicus,
with various symbolical figures. The
gem-cutters were probably Greeks or
artists from the Hellenistic East; the most
famous of them was named Dioscoridēs.

Artemidō′rus (*Artemidōros*) of Daldis,
see *Divination* (*ad fin.*).

A′rtemis (identified by the Romans with
Diana, q.v.), in Greek mythology the
daughter of Zeus and Leto (q.v.), and
sister of Apollo. For the legend of her
birth see *Apollo*. She was a goddess of
wild life, a virgin huntress, attended by
a train of nymphs, and also a goddess of
childbirth and of all very young things.
She was also identified with the moon.
A famous centre of her cult was Ephesus
(q.v.), where her maternal character was
prominent, and where she may have been
in origin the Asiatic goddess of fertility,
identified by the Ionians with the Greek
Artemis; the high priest of the temple at
Ephesus was known as the Megabȳzus.
At Braurōn in Attica there was an ancient
shrine of the moon-goddess, supposed
to contain the image of the goddess
brought from Tauris by Iphigenia (q.v.).
It was so highly venerated that a sanctuary
was dedicated on the Acropolis of Athens
to Artemis Braurōniā. Artemis had a
special association with the bear (she
turned Callisto, q.v., into a bear) and the
little girls who were her temple-servants
at Athens were called 'bears'. She is
treated with scanty respect in the 'Iliad'
(xxi. 489 et seq.), where Homer represents
her as beaten by Hera with her own bow,
and sent away weeping. See also *Hecate*.
Artemis is involved in the myths of
Callisto, Hippolytus, and Orion (qq.v.).
See also *Britomartis*.

Artemi′sia (*Artemisiā*). (1) daughter of
Lygdamis king of Halicarnassus and after
his death regent of his kingdom. With
five ships she accompanied Xerxes in his
invasion of Greece, and is said to have
shown bravery and resource at Salamis.
(2) The wife of Mausolus (q.v.).

Arundel Marbles, see *Marmor Parium*.

Arval Priests (*Frātrēs Arvālēs*), a college
of twelve priests charged in ancient times
with the observance of the annual ceremony (*Ambarvalia*, q.v.) designed to propitiate the gods of agriculture. The text
of an Arval hymn survives, one of the
earliest fragments of Latin literature. It
is an invocation of the Lares and Mars (in
his early character of an agricultural god)
to protect the fields. The college of the
Arval priests was revived by Augustus.
As we know from inscriptions that have
been recovered, they worshipped in a
grove on the Via Campānia, five miles
from Rome. They carried on the cult of
the Dea Dia, an earth goddess, and on
solemn occasions offered sacrifices for the

imperial house. Hence the inscriptions recording their sacrifices are of historical importance.

Arx, at Rome, the NE. summit of the Capitoline Hill, the citadel proper. Here was the temple of Juno (q.v.) Monēta.

Asca'laphus (*Askalaphos*), see *Persephone.*

Asca'nius or IŪLUS, the son of Aeneas, and according to legend the ancestor of the *gens Julia* (q.v.). See *Aeneid.*

Asclē'piadē'an, see *Metre,* § 3.

Asclēpi'adēs of Samos (*c.* 290 B.C.), a famous Greek writer of epigrams, of the Hellenistic Age, a contemporary of Philitas and Theocritus (qq.v.). Eighteen of his poems are included in the Palatine Anthology (q.v.) and show great elegance and finish. He probably gave his name to the Asclepiadean metre (see *Metre,* § 3) employed by Horace.

Asclē'pius (*Asklēpiós,* Lat. *Aesculāpius*), in Greek mythology, son of Apollo (q.v.), and god of medicine. Apollo loved Corōnis, daughter of Phlegyās, but she was unfaithful to him, and he slew her. Afterwards he was sorry, and turned the crow which had told him of her infidelity from a white bird into a black. He saved the child of Coronis (Asclepius) and entrusted him to the wise Centaur Chiron (q.v.). From him Asclepius learnt the art of medicine. At the prayer of Artemis he restored her favourite Hippolytus to life. Zeus, angered at his interference, slew Asclepius with a thunderbolt. Apollo, in turn, was wroth at the death of his son, and in revenge killed the Cyclopes (q.v.) who had made the thunderbolt. To expiate this murder he became for a year the slave of Admetus (q.v.). Homer represents Asclepius as the father of Machāōn and Podaleirius, the surgeons of the Greek host before Troy; and he came to be worshipped as the god of healing, the most famous seat of his cult being Epidaurus. Here patients coming to be cured slept in his temple, and the cure was effected in the night, or the means of it communicated by dreams. The sanctuary of Asclepius at Athens stood under the S. cliff of the Acropolis, adjoining the Theatre of Dionysus (q.v.). It was here that Plutus (q.v.) in Aristophanes' play was cured of his blindness. The attribute of Asclepius was the snake, a symbol of rejuvenescence (because the snake sloughing his skin was thought to renew his youth), and sacred serpents were kept in the temples of Asclepius; these were believed to heal the sick by licking them. The yellow snakes referred to by Pausanias

as kept in the sanctuary of Epidaurus, a harmless variety, are said still to be found in the neighbourhood. Sacred dogs were also kept in this sanctuary, and Asclepius is represented on coins with a dog under his chair. According to some authorities Asclepius after his death was turned into the constellation Ophiūchus, the snake-holder. See also *Aesculapius.*

Asia Minor, GREEK CITIES 'OF. Greek cities and States (Aeolian, Ionian, and Dorian) extended along the W. coast of Asia Minor and the adjoining islands from the Troad in the N. to Halicarnassus and Rhodes in the S. (see *Migrations and Dialects* and Pl. 8). In the early stages of their history these Greek States were in contact with the neighbouring kingdom of Lydia and the more distant Phrygia, and Greeks and Asiatics influenced one another. The Phrygians and Lydians adopted the alphabet of the Greeks, and the Phrygian king, Midas, dedicated a throne at Delphi. The Greeks adopted the Asiatic modes of music, introduced Eastern myths into their religion, took from Lydia the invention of coinage, and were affected by Asia in their art, science, and technical skill. They came in the 6th c. under the dominion of Croesus of Lydia, and a little later under that of the Persian Cyrus. But the Persians did not interfere much with their trade or internal life. The Greek cities had been independent States, jealous of each other, torn by aristocratic and democratic factions, and strategically weak against attack from the interior. The Persians favoured the establishment of tyrannies, which became common. These States were wealthy and prosperous communities. Their soil was more fertile than that of Greece and they had good harbours. They grew corn, raised stock, and cultivated the olive and (especially in the islands) the vine. They were important industrial centres, for they had raw materials, metals, wood, wool, leather, and dyes, and produced textiles, furniture, gems, and pottery. Their trade became active, and was facilitated by their inclusion in the Persian Empire. Prosperity developed their social and political life and led them to send out fresh colonies, especially to places from which they could obtain corn and salt fish (see *Colonization,* § 2). Prosperity also encouraged a great intellectual development, of which we see the proof in the large number of philosophers and poets born in Ionia at a time when Greece itself was still comparatively benighted (see *Birthplaces*). With the coming of the 5th c. the history of Greek Asia Minor becomes bound up with that of Greece proper. See *Persian Wars*, *Athens*, § 4, and the names of the principal Greek cities in Asia such as *Ephesus* and *Miletus*.

Asianism, see *Oratory*, § 1, ad *fin*.

Asinā'ria, a farcical comedy by Plautus adapted from the 'Onāgos' of the Greek comedian Dēmophilus.

Dēmaenētus, an indulgent father, wishes to help his son Argyrippus to redeem the courtesan Philaenium from an old procuress; but he is tyrannized over by his wife Artemōna, who keeps a tight control of the purse-strings. By a trick of one of his slaves he gets possession of twenty minae which were to be paid to Artemona's steward for some asses which have been sold (whence the name of the play), and father and son spend the evening banqueting with Philaenium. But a rival for the girl's favours, furious at finding himself anticipated, warns Artemona, who descends on the party, and with dire threats carries off her guilty husband.

The saying 'homo homini lupus' is derived from this play (l. 495).

Asi'nius Po'lliō, see *Pollio*.

Aspā'sia (*Aspāsiā*), see *Pericles*.

Assa'racus, the great-grandfather of Aeneas (see genealogy under *Troy*). Virgil refers to the Lar (see *Lares*) of Assaracus (Aen. ix. 259), and Aeneas finds Assaracus among his Trojan ancestors in Elysium.

Aste'ropē, one of the Pleiades (q.v.).

Astrae'a (*Astraia*), the 'Starry Maid', the constellation Virgo, identified with Dikē (Justice) by Aratus (q.v.). In the Golden Age (q.v.) she lived among men, but in the later ages, owing to the wickedness of men, she withdrew to the sky.

Astrology, the art of predicting the future from signs given by the stars, was introduced into Rome from the East. It came into some repute in the later days of the republic, and still more under the empire. Attempts to repress it were repeatedly made by the emperors, and astrologers were banished under, e.g., Tiberius, Claudius, Vitellius, and Vespasian, not from disbelief in the genuineness of the art, but probably from fear of it as likely to favour conspiracies. The emperors themselves kept their own astrologers and caused horoscopes to be cast. In spite of repression, astrology continued to be generally practised, as appears from Juvenal, Sat. vi. 535 et seq.

Astrono'mica, see *Manilius*.

Asty'anax (*Astūanax*), known also as SKAMANDRIOS, the son of Hector and Andromache (qq.v.), born during the siege of Troy, and thrown from its battlements by the victorious Greeks after the capture of the city. See *Trojan Women*.

Asty'nomi (*Astunomoi*), see *Athens*, § 9.

Asy'ndeton ('not bound together'), a figure of speech in which words or clauses which in ordinary speech would be connected by conjunctions, are left unconnected; e.g. 'Quaero ab inimicis, sintne haec investigata, comperta, patefacta, sublata, deleta, extincta per me' (quoted by Quintilian, probably from a lost passage of Cicero).

Atala'nta (*Atalantē*), in Greek mythology, daughter either of Īasos an Arcadian, and Clymene (q.v.), or of Schoinēūs, a Boeotian. She was a great huntress and her part in the hunt of the Calydonian boar is told under *Meleager*. She refused to marry any man who could not defeat her in a foot-race; and any suitor whom she defeated was put to death. Hippomenēs (or Meilaniōn) took up the challenge, and by the advice of Aphrodite carried with him three apples of the Hesperides (q.v.). He dropped these at intervals, and as Atalanta could not resist the temptation to stop and pick them up, he won the race. The story of Atalanta and Meleager is the subject of Swinburne's beautiful drama 'Atalanta in Calydon' (1865).

Ā'tē (from *âσθαι* 'to be blinded'), in early Greek mythology the personification of blind folly or the agency which causes it. The *Litai* (prayers) follow after her, undoing the evil she has done. In the tragedians, Ate is a bane or curse avenging unrighteousness.

Atē'ius Ca'pitō, GĀIUS, see *Capito*.

Ate'llan Farces (*Fābulae Ātellānae*), named from the town of Ātella in Campania, appear to have been (for the subject is obscure) ancient comic dramatic performances, representing scenes in the life of country towns. Certain stock characters, Maccus the fool, Dossennus the hunchback, Mandūcus the glutton, Pappus the greybeard, &c., were probably introduced in ridiculous situations. Some of the later titles suggest burlesques of mythology. Atellan plays became popular at Rome probably in the 3rd c. B.C. and were acted by amateurs. They were revived in more literary form, with the same stock characters and with a written verse plot, by Pompōnius of Bonōnia and Novius, who probably flourished early in the 1st c. B.C. These farces were acted by professional comedians, and continued intermittently until the end of the 1st c.

A.D. In this later form the Atellan farce was played after a tragic performance.

A'thamas (*Athamâs*) in Greek mythology, son of Aeolus (q.v. (2)) and king of Thebes. By his first wife Nephelê ('the Cloud') he had two children, Phrixus and Helle. Ino (q.v.), his second wife, conceived a bitter hatred of her step-children. They escaped from the death that menaced them on a winged and golden-fleeced ram, which carried them away across the sea. Helle became giddy and fell off into the part of the sea called, in consequence, the Hellespont. Phrixus arrived safely in Colchis, where the king Aeêtês received him hospitably. The ram was sacrificed to Zeus and its golden fleece hung up in Colchis and guarded by a dragon. For the continuation of this myth see *Argonauts*; and for the fate of Athamas, Ino, and her two sons see *Dionysus*.

Athenae'us (*Athênaios*) (*fl. c.* A.D. 200) of Naucratis, a Greek writer, author of the *Deipnosophistai* ('Sophists at Dinner' or more correctly 'Connoisseurs in Dining') in fifteen books, in which twenty-three learned men (some of whom have the names of real persons, such as Galen and Ulpian) are represented meeting at dinner in Rome on several occasions, and conversing on food in all its aspects and on a wide range of other subjects. In reality Athenaeus was an industrious collector of excerpts and anecdotes, which he reproduces in the form of conversation. The work is the source of much information on the literature and usages of ancient Greece; it survives with the exception of the first two books and part of the third, which we have only in a later epitome.

Athē'nē or **Athē'na** (in Homer *Athênê*, from the 4th c. commonly *Athênâ*) or PALLAS ATHĒNĒ, in Greek mythology the daughter of Zeus and of his first wife Metis (qq.v.). Zeus swallowed Metis for fear that she should give birth to a son stronger than himself. Thereafter Athene sprang from the head of her father, which Hephaestus (or Prometheus) had opened with an axe. Athene was probably a pre-Hellenic goddess, and this curious legend may be the outcome of an attempt to reconcile her cult with that of the chief god of the invading Greeks. She was the patron goddess of Athens (for her conflict with Poseidon for Attica, see *Athens*, § 2) and of Greek cities in general, and in this capacity had a dual aspect, as *Athene Promachos* or *Poliás*, the protector and champion of the city, and secondly as the patroness of urban arts and handicrafts, especially spinning and weaving (in this connexion see *Arachne*). She was also

the inventor of the flute (see *Marsyas*). She is generally represented as a woman of severe beauty, in armour, with the Gorgon's (q.v.) head on her shield. She is frequently referred to as *glaukôpis*, which probably meant blue-eyed, and Pausanias remarks on the blue eyes of a statue of Athene which he saw. No certain explanation of her title 'Pallas' is known, nor of the epithet Tritogeneia applied to her by Homer. For her great temple on the Acropolis see *Parthenon*, and for the temple there of *Athene Nîkê* or 'Victory Athene' see *Acropolis*. See also *Pallas*. The Romans identified Athene with their goddess Minerva (q.v.).

Athenians, *Polity* or *Constitution of, The* (*Athênaiôn Polîteia*), see *Aristotle*, §§ 2 and 3.

A'thens (*Athênai*, L. *Athênae*), the capital of Attica (q.v.).

§ 1. General topography in the 5th and 4th centuries B.C.

The city, standing about three miles from the sea at its nearest point, included within its walls (built or rebuilt on the advice of Themistocles after Plataea, see *Persian Wars*) three principal eminences: the Acropolis (its fortress) roughly in the centre, the Areopagus to the W. of this, and the Pnyx to the SW. of the Areopagus. N. and NW. of the Acropolis and Areopagus was the district known as the Ceramicus. This contained the Agora or market-place, on which abutted the *Stoa Poikilê* or Painted Colonnade and the *Stoa Basileios* or Royal Colonnade. The Outer Ceramicus outside the walls was a cemetery. The Acropolis was approached at its western extremity by the splendid gateway of the Propylaea. At the foot of the southern slope of the Acropolis was the great theatre of Dionysus. To the SE. of the Acropolis stood the partially built Olympieum or sanctuary of Olympian Zeus. The principal gate in the walls was the Dipylon, on the NW. side of the city. From this, roads led to Colonus and the grove of Academus. From the adjoining Sacred Gate the Sacred Way led to Eleusis. Other gates led to the Piraeus, to Phalerum, to Sunium, &c. An aqueduct dating probably from the 6th c. B.C., perhaps built by Pisistratus, brought water to the centre of the city, perhaps from the upper course of the Ilissus. The houses of the citizens were grouped in narrow, winding streets about the Acropolis, and must have presented a mean appearance, especially as the walls of the houses, built of sun-dried bricks, were usually blank on the street side. W. of the city flowed the Cēphīsus; the bed of the Ilissus, generally dry, lay close to the city on the SE. and S. The Stadium or racecourse was outside the walls, on the left bank of the Ilissus. For the places, rivers, and buildings above mentioned, see under their names. See also *Long Walls, Parthenon, Metroum, Cynosarges,* and see Pl. 13.

§ 2. *Origins and primitive constitution*

The Athenians claimed to be autochthonous (original inhabitants of the land), but in fact there had been a pre-Hellenic population (see *Migrations and Dialects*) to which the Mycenean (q.v.) civilization had extended. To this population the migrations added successive Hellenic elements, especially Ionian, but, it is thought, without any violent conquest. Attica, by its position, lay outside the stream of the Dorian invasion. Its population in later times was further modified by the gradual infiltration of foreigners from many lands, attracted to it by the commercial importance of its capital. The country was not at first a single political whole, but was divided into small communities. At some moment, not later than the 8th c., a union (synoecism) of these communities was effected, associated by the ancients with the name of Theseus (q.v.). The precipitous hill known later as the Acropolis, which had long been occupied, was taken as the capital of the new State. It had at some early date been held sacred to the owl, later to the serpent-god Cecrops (q.v.), the legendary ancestor of the Cecropes, probably the first Greek occupants of the citadel. Some later change in the dominating race appears to underlie the myth of the defeat of Poseidon by the goddess Athene. There was a contest between Athene and Poseidon for the land of Attica, and the gods promised the preference to whichever gave the more useful present to the inhabitants. Poseidon struck the ground with his trident and a horse sprang up (according to another version a salt spring on the Acropolis); Athene produced the olive-tree and was adjudged the victor. From her Athens took its name. The State was at first governed by kings, said to be descendants of Erechtheus (q.v.); the population was grouped in families (*genē*), *phratriai* (q.v.), and in four tribes (*phŭlai*). The monarchical power gradually succumbed to the attacks of the old aristocratic families (*eupatridai,* q.v.), and it was replaced by the rule of three archons, elected at first for ten years and later annually, and a council (*Boulē,* q.v.). The three archons

were, (1) the King Archon, the king reduced in powers and made elective, the religious representative of the State; (2) the Eponymous Archon, the real head of the State, especially the supreme judge; he gave his name to the year (an event was said to have occurred in the archonship of So-and-so); (3) the Polemarch (q.v.), who commanded the military forces and saw to the safety of the State. Later the demand of the lower classes for the publication of the laws, hitherto unwritten, led to the appointment of six additional archons, *thesmothetai,* codifiers and guardians of the law (later these had important functions connected with judicial procedure, q.v. § 1). The Boule supervised the magistrates and was the judicial tribunal. It was composed of the men who had previously occupied one of the archonships. It held its meetings on the Areopagus (q.v.). Each of the four tribes was divided into twelve *naukrariai,* and each of these was required to furnish a ship for the State's navy. The presidents of the *naukrariai* appear to have formed an important administrative council. The population was further divided into *eupatridai* (the nobles), *geōrgoi* (peasants), and *dēmiourgoi* (artisans), and later according to wealth into *pentakosiomedimnoi* (those whose land yielded five hundred measures of corn or oil), *hippeis* (knights, those whose property yielded three hundred such measures, and who could therefore keep a horse), *zeugitai* (those whose property yielded two hundred measures, and who could keep a team of oxen), and *thētes* (small peasants and labourers). (For the area of land represented by the above qualifications, see *Agriculture,* § 1.) The definition of the three upper classes was later established on a monetary basis: the *pentakosiomedimnoi* were those who had an income of 500 drachmas, the *hippeis* of 300, and the *zeugitai* of 200. The magistrates were chosen from the wealthy aristocracy.

§ 3. *Seventh and Sixth centuries B.C.*

The accumulation of land and wealth in comparatively few hands, the increasing indebtedness of the peasantry and their consequent reduction to the position of serfs bound to the soil, provoked a social crisis about the middle of the 7th c. In the troublous period that ensued occurred the affair of Cylon and the Alcmaeonidae (q.v.), followed by the legislation of Draco (q.v.), and at the beginning of the 6th c. by the legislation of Solon (q.v.). But the reforms introduced by the latter had only a limited success, and the strife of parties continued. They were now difterently grouped, into the 'men of the plain' (*pediakoi*), consisting of the nobles and well-to-do farmers whose interests lay in the land, and the 'men of the shore' (*paralioi*), the sailors, fishermen, and artisans whose interests were commercial. Later Pisistratus gathered about himself a third group, the 'men of the hills' (*diakrioi*), the herdsmen and poor peasants who had no share in either agricultural or commercial prosperity, and these he organized as a frankly revolutionary faction; he seized the supreme power in 561. For the period of his tyranny and that of his sons, the 'men of the hills' (*diakrioi*), the herdsmen and poor peasants *stratus*. Their fall was succeeded by a struggle between the partisans of oligarchy and of democracy, headed respectively by Isagoras and Cleisthenes (q.v.). The latter won the day and introduced the changes that were to transform Athens into a truly democratic State, and in which Herodotus rightly saw one of the chief sources of her future greatness. The new democracy was attacked by jealous neighbours (Sparta, Boeotia, and Chalcis), but was able to drive them back (506) and consolidate its position.

It is in this period that the literary and artistic history of Athens may be said to begin. Although she did not as yet produce native poets and artists of importance (except Solon and the shadowy Thespis), Pisistratus and his sons were zealous patrons of literature and art, attracting Simonides and Anacreon to Athens, decorating the city with the works of foreign sculptors, and establishing musical and poetic contests at the festival of the Panathenaea. See also under *Homer*. Attic sculpture, still somewhat primitive, but graceful and sincere, was developing, and also the art of vasepainting.

§ 4. *Growth of the Athenian Empire: Fifth century to the Thirty Years Peace (446)*

At the beginning of the 5th c. Athens already figures as a powerful State, but exposed to the menace of Persia, where the exiled Hippias was intriguing to get himself restored. The Persian attack was delayed for six years by the revolt of the Greek cities of Ionia (see *Persian Wars*), to which Athens, in contrast to the selfish policy of Sparta, lent her assistance. The first Persian invasion was defeated at Marathon (490). When the second invasion came, ten years later, Athens had, under the influence of Themistocles (q.v.), built a strong navy, and she emerged from the struggle (briefly described under *Persian Wars*) with her city in ruins and her

territory ravaged, but with her fleet intact, her prestige increased, and her position as leader of all the Ionian Greeks acknowledged. She had become, moreover, since the days of Pisistratus, a great commercial and industrial centre, needing foodstuffs for her population and raw materials for her industries; the control of the sea was therefore of great importance to her. She alone possessed a fleet capable of protecting Greece and the islands of the Aegean against Persian attack. The Greek cities which had rebelled against Persia accepted the leadership of Athens, and this was the origin of the Delian Confederacy (see *Delos*). As head of this confederacy and by means of her colonies and cleruchs (q.v.) on the shores of the Aegean and Euxine, Athens under the guidance of Cimon and Pericles (qq.v.) became an imperial power. She obtained complete control of the allied forces by a series of administrative and political measures, and only three of her allies, Samos, Chios, and Mytilene, remained autonomous. By the constitutional reforms of Ephialtes (q.v.) and Pericles democracy reached its fullest development—the government of the people by themselves, offices open to all, and payment of the citizens for exercising their political rights, so that even the poorest could afford to take their share of the public duties. But the empire of Athens offended Greek political sentiment, which was essentially in favour of the independence of each city-state; and her commercial expansion brought her into competition with the great trading city of Corinth. The uneasiness of the latter was increased by the Athenian occupation of Naupactus at the mouth of the Gulf of Corinth (c. 459), and by the Athenian control over Megara, both of which threatened the freedom of Corinthian commerce. By 459 Athens was at war with Corinth, and soon after with Aegina and Sparta. But Athens, by also undertaking an attack on the Persian power in Egypt, attempted too much. The expeditionary force was blockaded and had to capitulate, and a relief squadron was almost entirely destroyed in 454; and although Aegina had fallen after a long blockade in 457–456, and Boeotia had been subdued in 457 (battle of Oenophyta), Athens met with reverses in various directions, including a severe defeat by the Boeotians at Coronea in 447. She was therefore glad to make a thirty years' peace with Sparta in 446, thus ending what is sometimes known as the First Peloponnesian War. Some important constitutional changes fall in this period, notably the creation of ten generals (see *Strategus*) from 501, and from 487 the choosing of the archons by lot. The archonship was in effect thrown open to all citizens from about 458/7.

The fifty years that followed the close of the Persian War saw the beginning of the great poetical and creative age of Athens, and were rendered illustrious by the names of Aeschylus, Sophocles, Euripides, Phidias, and Polygnotus. The position of Athens as saviour of Hellas from the barbarian, her sense of independence and political freedom, her newly acquired maritime empire, brought about an exaltation favourable to the production of great intellectual works. She was now moreover one of the chief commercial centres of the eastern Mediterranean, a point of attraction to visitors from all parts of the Greek world, where ideas and information could be freely interchanged, and wits were sharpened in the process. See *Pentecontaetia*.

§ 5. *The great struggle with Sparta to the Peace of Antalcidas (387)*

The peace with Sparta was destined to last only fifteen years, and in 431 began the decisive struggle between Athens and Sparta for the hegemony of Greece, and at the same time between Athens and Corinth for the control of the trade routes to the West (see *Peloponnesian War*). The failure of the Sicilian Expedition, the culminating incident of this war, was the signal for the revolt of many of the subject-allies of Athens, which she made vigorous and partially successful efforts to suppress. The latter part of the war was marked also by the co-operation against her of Sparta and Persia, furthered by the intrigues of the exiled Alcibiades (q.v.). An oligarchical revolution broke out in the city itself. A council of Four Hundred was established in 411, nominally supplemented by an assembly of Five Thousand, which was in fact never summoned. But the Athenian fleet at Samos remained democratic in sentiment, led by Alcibiades whom it had recalled. The revolt of Euboea at this time caused deep alarm at Athens, and the Four Hundred were overthrown by the end of the same year. In this oligarchic movement and also in its overthrow Theramenes (q.v.) took an important part. A constitution devised by him, the rule of the Five Thousand, was now set up. It was a mixture of oligarchy and democracy praised by Thucydides and Aristotle. This was displaced after the victory of the Athenian fleet at Cyzicus (410) and democracy was restored, largely under the influence of the demagogue Cleophon;

democratic rule endured until the surrender of Athens to Sparta in 404. Athens emerged from the Peloponnesian War crippled, impoverished, and at the mercy of the Spartan Lysander (q.v.). This gave an opportunity to the oligarchs, and under the menace of Lysander, a body known as the Thirty, of which Critias (q.v.) was the leading spirit, was nominated to frame a constitution and meanwhile to rule the State. A council of Five Hundred, supporters of the oligarchy, was appointed, and a reign of terror followed. But dissensions arose among the oligarchs and civil war broke out, the democrats being led by Thrasybulus (q.v.). It was ended by the intervention of the Spartan king Pausanias, and the old democracy was restored (403). In 395 Athens joined Thebes, Argos, and Corinth in their attempt to overthrow the Spartan supremacy (see *Thebes*), an attempt that failed in its object and was terminated by the inglorious peace of Antalcidas (387), dictated by the king of Persia, who recovered the Ionian cities of Asia Minor and remained master of the Aegean.

During this period, although the age of the great tragedians was drawing to a close (Euripides died in 406), the wonderful intellectual productiveness of Athens continued, illustrated by the names of Socrates, Plato, Thucydides, and Aristophanes.

§ 6. *The Fourth century to the rise of the Macedonian Empire*

The political interest now passes to the struggle of Sparta and Thebes (q.v.), in which Athens played only a secondary part. A wanton raid by a Spartan force under Sphodriās on the Piraeus in 378 led to the alliance of Athens with Thebes, to war with Sparta, and to the development of a second Athenian Confederacy, composed of various islands and cities of the Aegean, Corcyra, and other States, professedly directed against Sparta. Athens retained her commercial supremacy and recovered a good deal of her maritime power, for the loss of her empire had not deprived her of her sources of prosperity, and her successes in the war with Sparta, which was terminated by the peace of Calliās in 371, did much to restore her prestige. The most prominent Athenian statesman of this period was Callistratus (q.v.), whose general policy was based on harmony with Sparta and hostility to Thebes. The latter State, under the leadership of Epaminondas (q.v.), was now rising to the hegemony of Greece, and Athens was more influenced by jealousy of her neighbour than by her old rivalry with Sparta. In the ensuing struggle between Sparta and Thebes we find Athens in alliance with Sparta (369), and an Athenian contingent was present at the battle of Mantinea (362). Meanwhile Athens was reviving her old empire in the Aegean (see *Timotheus* (2)) and causing discontent and uneasiness among her allies. A revolt of these broke out in 357, and the attempts of Athens to suppress it were ineffectual. What is known as the 'Social War' ended in the peace of 354, by which the independence of the principal members of the Confederacy was recognized; in accordance with the policy urged by Isocrates (q.v.), Athens renounced her attempt at naval empire. Her attention was shortly required in another direction, for Macedonia (q.v.) was rising to importance and threatening the Athenian position in the northern Aegean.

§ 7. *The struggle with Macedonia and the subjugation of Athens*

For the growth of Macedonian ascendancy, see *Philip of Macedon*. In the face of this development Athens had to choose between two policies: an attempt to recover her hegemony, or accommodation with Philip. Her course of action was the outcome of the conflict of two parties, a peace party directed by Eubulus, an able financier and a cautious statesman, the orator Aeschines, the honest and sensible soldier Phocion, and Philocrates (qq.v.); and a war party, determined on hostility to Philip, led by Demosthenes, Lycurgus, and Hyperides (qq.v.). The passionate eloquence of Demosthenes prevailed, the attempts made by Philip to conciliate Athens failed, and Philip was driven to assert his supremacy by force of arms at Chaeronea (338). Athens was obliged to accept the lenient peace-terms imposed by Philip and to join the Hellenic confederacy organized by him. Whether the opposite policy might have proved more advantageous depends on whether Philip and Alexander would in any event have left Athens really independent. If not, the policy of Demosthenes was the only one that offered her a chance of freedom. After the abortive risings that followed the accession of Alexander the Great, and the destruction of Thebes which ended them, a period of tranquillity ensued at Athens. During this the most notable incidents are the attack on Demosthenes by Aeschines and the affair of Harpalus (see *Demosthenes*, § 1). The death of Alexander in 323 appeared to give an opportunity for the recovery of freedom, and Athens with

various States of northern Greece revolted against Macedonia. Under the Athenian general Leōsthenēs the Greeks were for a time successful, and besieged Antipater, the regent of Macedonia, in Lámia (a Thessalian town). But in 322, after Leosthenes had been killed, the Lamian War ended with the battle of Crannōn, in which the Macedonians had the advantage. The Macedonian fleet had played an important part in the war, and put an end for ever to the sea-power of Athens. Antipater imposed on Athens a change of her democratic constitution, and the franchise was restricted to citizens possessed of more than 2,000 drachmas. He placed a Macedonian garrison at Munychia. He also demanded the surrender of Demosthenes and the other anti-Macedonian agitators. Demosthenes took poison to avoid capture; the others were put to death. The democrats were reinstated at Athens under the brief rule of Polyperchon (the immediate successor of Antipater), but Cassander (Antipater's son) restored in the main his father's constitution and appointed (317) as his viceroy at Athens a distinguished Athenian citizen, Demetrius (q.v.) of Phalerum, a learned man and a friend of Aristotle. His ten years of virtual rule were a period of peace and prosperity for the city. None the less, when Demetrius Poliorcetes, son of Antigonus (see *Macedonia*, § 2), captured the city from Cassander in 307, he was looked upon by the Athenians as a liberator and was granted divine honours.

The 4th c. shows the last phase of the literary and artistic pre-eminence of Athens. The character of her intellectual activity had somewhat changed: it had become less creative, more analytical and critical, more concerned with facts and their reasons. It was the age of Aristotle, the age also of the great orators, and of the New Comedy. Art became less simple and more realistic; it sought to render youth and grace rather than to interpret the old religious ideas. Praxiteles was the great sculptor of this period.

§ 8. *The Period of Decadence*

The 3rd c. B.C. saw the end of the political importance of Athens. The Chremonidean War (266–262 B.C.) is notable as the last occasion when Athens took the lead against Macedon. Supported by Sparta and Ptolemy II, she revolted against Antigonus Gonātas (see *Macedonia*, § 3), was besieged, and finally yielded to famine. The war derives its name from the Athenian Chremōnidēs, who organized the alliance. In 229, on the death of Demetrius II, son of Gonatas, Athens recovered her freedom. Philip V, grandson of Gonatas, once attacked her, but otherwise she had a peaceful existence until 88. After the defeat of the Achaean League by Mummius in 146, Greece became a Roman protectorate, not yet a province. Some cities were taxed by Rome; others, including Athens and Sparta, were not. There was a revival of material prosperity and of religion. The great quadrennial festival of Athens at Delos, for instance, was restored. But this prosperous period came to an end with the Mithridatic War of 88–86, when Athens, which had espoused the cause of Mithridates, was sacked and in part destroyed by Sulla. Greece suffered severely both from Sulla's exactions and depredations and from the barbarian allies of Mithridates, who sacked Delphi. Even greater ruin followed from the Roman civil wars, and endured until Augustus made Greece a Roman province in 27 B.C. But in spite of her political decline, Athens retained much of her intellectual prestige and continued to be frequented as a centre of philosophic study (see *Hellenistic Age*, § 2). She was patronized in the 2nd c. B.C. by the Attalids (q.v.) of Pergamum, who adorned her with colonnades and sculptures. Apollodorus (q.v.) composed there his works on chronology and mythology; Timaeus (q.v.) spent many years there. It became fashionable for Romans to pass some time in study at Athens. Atticus (q.v.) lived there for many years; Cicero and Cicero's son and Horace were among those who studied in the city. Horace, and in a later age Lucian, rejoiced in the peaceful charm of Athens as compared with the turmoil of Rome. Athens enjoyed some revival of her lustre under Hadrian and the Antonines, and Julian the Apostate was a lover of the city. The end of her period of intellectual eminence came in A.D. 529, when Justinian ordered the closing of her schools of philosophy.

§ 9. *General administration in the Fifth and Fourth centuries*

A striking feature of the Athenian democratic system is the power wielded by orators who held no official position. We have instances of this in Alcibiades, Cleon, and Demosthenes, who as private citizens exerted at times a dominating influence on the course of events. The actual administration in the 5th and 4th cc. was carried on by a large number of officials of various grades. Except where experience or technical knowledge was required, officials were as a rule chosen by lot, for one year, and as a rule in

boards of ten, one from each tribe. Though this method may appear strange to us, its results seem to have been on the whole satisfactory. It must be remembered that the lots were drawn only among candidates who offered themselves, that the successful candidate had to pass the ordeal of the *dokimasia* (examination as to worthiness by the Boule or Heliaea) before entering on office, that he was liable to account for his actions while in office, and that the system of boards tended to yield an average of ability. The chief administrative officials were the archons (but their functions were largely ceremonial and judicial) and the *strategi* (see *Strategus*). Next in order of importance were perhaps the numerous treasurers, who had charge of the public moneys assigned to various funds (see § 11 below). Chief among these were the ten Treasurers (*tamiai*) of Athene. There were also (besides the receivers-general referred to in § 11 below) ten *pōlētai*, who sold confiscated property, farmed out taxes, &c.; ten *praktores*, who collected judicial fines; and ten *logistai*, who audited the accounts of outgoing magistrates. The policing and care of the city were in the charge of ten *astunomoi* (five for Athens and five for the Piraeus), while street repairs were looked after by five *hodopoioi*. There were also boards of market-inspectors, inspectors of weights and measures, &c. All the above were chosen by lot. The *hellēnotamiai* or treasurers of the federal tribute were probably elected, as were also such technical officials as the surveyor of the water-supply, and the specially appointed commissioners of public works (when such works were undertaken). The policing of the city was carried out by a body of 300 Scythian archers (public slaves), and there was a board known as *the Eleven*, under whom were the executioner, the gaolers, and the officials who arrested malefactors (all these subordinates were public slaves). Public slaves were also employed in many clerical functions, some of them important, such as the care of archives. See also *Boule, Ecclesia*, and *Judicial Procedure*, § 1.

§ 10. *Economic Conditions*

(a) *The Archaic period*. The archaic period (7th–6th cc. B.C.) which succeeded the Homeric Age (q.v.) witnessed a transformation of the Homeric patriarchal economy. The power of the head of the family weakened, the State became more powerful, the individual freer. Population increased and the soil became insufficient to support it. Land was converted largely from pasture to arable. A great part of it was held by the aristocracy and worked for them by tenants. Below the aristocracy, a middle class included the owners of smaller estates sufficient for their support and the artisans and traders who were profiting by the development of industry and commerce. The lowest class included the peasants, owners of an inadequate plot or tenants of the great landowners. They were heavily in debt and in general were in a miserable condition. The legislation of Solon (q.v.) at the beginning of the 6th c. had at least this measure of success, that in freeing the person of the debtor it prevented the Athenian peasant from becoming permanently a serf like the helot of Sparta.

(b) *The 5th and 4th centuries.* The population of Attica in the 5th and 4th cc. is unknown and has been very variously estimated. One of the latest estimates (Glotz, 'Histoire grecque') is based on the number of Athenian hoplites at the beginning of the Peloponnesian War, as stated by Thucydides: according to this calculation there were then some 40,000 adult Athenian citizens of all classes, making with their families some 140,000 souls. The metics (q.v.) may have numbered (both sexes and all ages) some 70,000. The number of slaves is likewise a matter of conjecture, but was probably between 150,000 and 400,000 at this time. The census taken by Demetrius of Phalerum at the end of the 4th c. is said to have shown 21,000 citizens, 10,000 metics, and 400,000 slaves. The soil of Attica was unable to feed the population, and Athens imported large quantities of wheat, dried fish, salt meat, and cattle; also raw materials, such as copper, wood, ivory, wool, flax, papyrus, and also some manufactured articles such as furniture. She exported wine and oil, silver, marble, pottery, arms, books. She also derived large profits from her position as a commercial centre and from her carrying trade. Her ships plied to many parts of the Mediterranean—Thrace and Chalcidice, Asia Minor, Phoenicia, Egypt, Italy (and later Sicily); and especially to the Euxine, the principal source of the Athenian corn supply. The annual value of the total trade of the Piraeus at the beginning of the 4th c., that is to say at a moment of extreme depression, has been estimated, on the basis of the yield of the import and export dues, at a sum varying between 1,875 and 2,400 talents (equivalent in bullion value to about £375,000–£480,000, but of much greater purchasing power); it was doubtless much greater at a time of Athenian prosperity (Glotz,

'Le travail dans la Grèce ancienne', on which the present section is in part founded). Athens had merchant ships of 10,000 talents (say 250 tons displacement) which could go five knots, could cross the open sea (instead of hugging the coast), and could sail at night. Traffic by land, on the other hand, was hampered by the scarcity and defective condition of the roads. The cost of transporting goods by land was extremely high. Some idea of the cost of living may be formed from the following data. The price of the medimnus (1·4 bushels) of wheat appears to have risen during the 5th c. with fluctuations from 1 to 3 or 4 drachmas; in Demosthenes' time it normally averaged 5 dr. A day's allowance of wheat for a man (his staple food) was 1 choenix, $\frac{1}{48}$th part of a medimnus, about 1$\frac{1}{3}$ lb.; at 3 dr. the medimnus this would cost 22$\frac{1}{2}$ dr. a year. Adding about the same amount for *opsōnion* (relish, i.e. meat, fish, vegetables, fruit), it has been estimated that a single man could feed himself for 60 dr. a year, and could live in comfort for 120 dr. A family of four could live for about 280 dr. In the 4th c., with wheat at 5 dr., the cost of living for a single man and for a family may be put at 180 dr. and 450 dr. respectively. In the latter part of the 5th c. the normal rate of pay for skilled and unskilled labour was 1 dr. a day; but to arrive at a man's annual earnings allowance must be made for the sixty holidays in the year and for varying periods of unemployment. He would probably find it difficult to earn 300 dr. in the year. With this may be compared the remuneration of the architect of the Erechtheum in 409–408: he was paid, as a public official, at the rate of 1 dr. for every day in the year. In the 4th c. the wages of skilled labour rose to 2 or 2$\frac{1}{2}$ dr., the wages of unskilled labour remaining at 1 dr. or rising a little above it. The remuneration of the architect at Eleusis in the latter part of the 4th c. was at the rate of 2 dr. a day for every day in the year. At the same period public slaves at Athens received for their subsistence 180 dr. a year, besides their clothing. The poorer classes were supported at first by the great works of fortification and embellishment of the city; later in part by the *misthos* or payment for the discharge of public duties, while the Theoric Fund (q.v.) provided for their amusement. In times of war or distress the State came to the aid of the needy by means of the *diōbelia* or daily grant of two obols. Further, to provide land for the poor, thousands were established as cleruchs (q.v.) in territories across the sea. The accounts of the construction of the Erechtheum in 409–408 suggest that citizens were then taking only a small part in industry, leaving manual occupations to metics (q.v.) and slaves. These seem likewise to have taken the chief part in commerce.

The annual rent of land and houses in the 4th c. was normally equal to about 8 per cent. of their capital value. The rate of interest on loans on mortgage was normally 12 per cent. For commercial loans it was generally 16–18 per cent.; but for loans on marine ventures it was much higher. For the full navigation season of seven months it might be 30 per cent.; it might even be more for voyages involving special risks. Banking was highly organized by the end of the 5th c.; banks lent on mortgage, on cargoes, or on personal security, and issued letters of credit on correspondents abroad. The bank founded by Antisthenēs and Archestratos at the end of the 5th c. and carried on in the 4th c. by the famous Pasiōn, had large foreign transactions, especially with Byzantium; when Pasion retired it had a capital of 50 talents (£10,000).

Urban industries (pottery, metal-working, &c.) were conducted on a comparatively small scale. The largest factory we know of was that of Cephalus, the father of Lysias, which employed 120 slaves on the manufacture of shields. The two factories of the father of Demosthenes employed respectively 33 on the manufacture of arms and 20 on the manufacture of beds. The shoemaker in the mime of Herodas had 13 assistants. Even ship-building appears to have been carried on in a large number of small yards. Many industries were purely family affairs in the hands of an artisan and his wife. The return from industry appears to have been normally 30 per cent. a year on the capital value of the slaves employed, but allowance has to be made in this for amortization.

There is occasional mention of large fortunes at Athens, but they do not appear to have been numerous. Callias, cousin of Aristides and son-in-law of Cimon, was reputed the richest man in Greece; he is said to have had 200 talents (say £40,000). Nicias had 100 talents. Both these fortunes were derived from mining enterprises.

See also *Agriculture*, § 1, *Slavery*, § 1, *Colonization*, § 1, *Hellenistic Age*, § 1.

§ 11. *Finances in the Fifth and Fourth centuries*

The public revenue of Athens in the 5th and 4th cc. consisted principally of the following items (talent = about £200, drachma = about 8d.).

(a) The produce of the silver mines at Laurium. These were leased to contractors, who extracted the ore by slave labour. The annual revenue was probably 50–100 talents.

(b) The *metoikion*, a direct tax on the resident aliens, 12 drachmas on each head of a family. The yield was probably 20 talents or more.

(c) Customs duty on goods imported and exported at the Piraeus, 2 per cent. *ad valorem*, yielding 30–40 talents. There were also minor taxes, such as octroi and market dues.

(d) Judicial fees and fines. In addition to the judicial fees payable by litigants, a considerable revenue accrued to the State from penalties in public suits (see *Judicial Procedure*, § 1), which took largely the form of fines, and occasionally of confiscation of property. Moreover the accuser in a public suit who failed to secure one-fifth of the votes paid a fine of 1,000 drachmas. The revenue from these sources (which went to supply the fund from which the jurymen were paid) must have varied considerably and cannot be estimated.

(e) In war time the *eisphora*, an extraordinary tax on the estimated capital of each citizen owning property worth more than 1,000 drachmas, at the rate of 2 or 3 per cent. Metics were subject to the tax at a higher rate. In 428 B.C., when it was perhaps first imposed, it yielded 200 talents.

(f) From the middle of the 5th c. and until the break-up of the Athenian Empire, the *phoros* or tribute of the allies, an amount that varied, at first about 400 talents (actually received), later much more, perhaps 1,000 talents.

(g) The budget was helped out by the system of liturgies (q.v.) or public services discharged by the wealthier citizens.

The total revenue amounted in 431, according to Xenophon, to not less than 1,000 talents.

The public expenditure varied greatly, especially as between periods of peace and war. At certain moments, for instance after the Persian Wars, and in the time of Pericles, heavy expenditure was incurred for public works and the building of temples (see the figures under *Parthenon*). The provision of the fleet and the pay of the crews absorbed the greater part of the tribute of the allies. Even in time of peace part of the fleet was kept in commission. A trireme with its crew of 200 men receiving 2–3 obols a day would cost for pay alone 2,000 to 3,000 drachmas a month. At the beginning of the Peloponnesian War Athens had 300 triremes, later increased to 400. The initial cost of a ship in the 5th c. is unknown, but it was more than one talent. The peace expenditure on the army (pay of 1,500 recruits constantly in training, equipment and forage allowance of cavalry, pay of mercenaries) is estimated at 40–50 talents. In war time each hoplite received 1–2 drachmas a day.

The normal peace-time expenditure included these further items:

(a) The members of the Boule each received (in Aristotle's day) 5 obols, and those of the Prytany 1 drachma for each day's sitting. The citizens attending meetings of the Ecclesia received in the first half of the 4th c. 3 obols a day (afterwards raised to 1 drachma). The archons received only 4 obols a day, but there were a considerable number of subordinate officials to be paid. The total cost rose perhaps from 15 talents to 40 talents or more.

(b) The total cost of the pay of the heliasts or jurymen must have depended on the number employed and the number of days of employment. If 2,000 on the average were employed on 300 days, with pay at 3 obols (from 425 B.C.), the charge would be 50 talents.

(c) Miscellaneous expenditure on festivals, embassies, reception of foreign missions, public relief to the poor and disabled, &c.

There was no single budget, but the Ecclesia distributed the revenues over a number of separate funds, administered and accounted for by various magistrates and their treasurers. The revenues were all paid to ten *apodektai* or receivers-general, chosen by lot from the ten tribes, who handed them over to the magistrates as directed. The goddess Athena (and the other gods) played an important part in the financial system. From 454 B.C. Athena received 1/60th of the tribute of the allies; she and the other gods, moreover, had revenues from sacred lands, offerings, and miscellaneous receipts. The temples consequently became extremely wealthy, and from their treasures loans were made at interest to the State as required. The distribution between these sacred funds and the public funds was in fact nominal, and the sacred treasuries were much impoverished by the failure to repay the large loans made during the Peloponnesian War. In the 4th c. there was a tendency to the simplification and unification both of funds and accounts. Moreover the advantage of centralized control was discovered; this was first

realized in the person of Eubulus, the president of the Theoric Fund (q.v.), who was in fact from 354 to 339 a general minister of finance; and after him in Lycurgus, who discharged the same functions from 338 to 326, with the actual title of Treasurer-general (ταμίας τῆς διοικήσεως).

Atla'ntids, the daughters of Atlas (q.v.).

Atla'ntis, see *Timaeus* (Plato's dialogue).

A'tlas (*Atlas*), in Greek mythology, according to Hesiod a son of the Titan Iapetus and Clymenē, daughter of Oceanus (qq.v.). As punishment for his part in the revolt of the Titans (q.v.), he was employed to support the heavens with his head and hands, somewhere in the extreme west of the earth. He was father of the Pleiades and the Hyades (qq.v.) and (in Homer) of Calypso; also, in later writers, of the Hesperides (q.v.). Perseus (q.v.), being inhospitably received by him, turned him into a mountain by means of the Medusa's head. See also *Heracles.*

Atossa, mother of Darius I (q.v.).

A'treūs, in Greek mythology, one of the sons of Pelops; he was king of Mycenae, brother of Thyestes, and father of Agamemnon and Menelaus. For the story of his house, see *Pelops.*

Atreus appears to represent a real person, if, as there is reason to suppose, he is the Attarisayas, ruler of the Ahhiyava (Achaeans?), whose bands, according to the Hittite archives, attacked the Hittite coasts in the latter part of the 13th c. B.C.

A'trium Libertā'tis, at Rome; see *Libraries.* The censors had their office there, and it was in this ' Hall of Liberty ' that, in Cicero's time, the judicial examination of slaves by torture was carried out (Pro Mil. 59); also their manumission.

A'trium Ve'stae, or Hall of Vesta, was the residence at Rome of the Vestal Virgins, in which they lived as in a convent. It stood near the Temple of Vesta, in the Forum, S. of the Via Sacra (see Pl. 14). In republican times it appears to have consisted of rooms built round two sides of a small court. It was repeatedly rebuilt and restored in imperial times. In its latest form it was a splendid building of several stories, surrounding an oblong cloistered court.

A'tropos, see *Fates.*

A'tta, TĪTUS QUINTIUS (d. 77 B.C.), writer of *togatae* (q.v.), of whose comedies very little survives. In his 'Aquae Caldae' he depicted life at a Roman watering-place. He is said to have excelled in his female characters.

A'ttalids, the dynasty that in the course of the 3rd c. B.C. acquired Pergamum, in the NW. of Asia Minor, and its surrounding territory, expanded its dominions at the expense of the Seleucids (q.v.), and enjoyed the support of Rome. Attalus I (241–197) was the nephew and adoptive son of Eumenes, who first secured the independence of Pergamum from the Seleucids. By driving back the Galatian barbarians to their Phrygian pastures, Attalus obtained power and prestige, took the royal title, and was able to bring under his control for a time nearly the whole of Seleucid Asia Minor. In 201 the Pergamenes and the Rhodians became embroiled with Philip V of Macedonia (q.v., § 3) and took the momentous step of soliciting the support of Rome. This gave Rome the pretext for the Second Macedonian War and for intervention in Greek affairs. As the ally of Rome against Antiochus III at the great victory of Magnesia (190 B.C., see *Seleucids*), Pergamum established its position as the leading State in Asia Minor, receiving the bulk of the dominions ceded by Antiochus. In 172 Eumenes II of Pergamum again stimulated Rome against Macedonia and provided the pretext on which war was declared against Perseus in 171. The dynasty of the Attalids came to an end in 133 B.C., when Attalus III bequeathed his dominions to Rome. The government of the Attalids was efficient, and it was successful in accumulating wealth, partly from slave labour in the royal factories which produced parchment and textiles. Under them, the treatment of the population and subject cities appears to have been more arbitrary than that of the Seleucids, who were regarded as the champions of Hellenism. This, and the relations of the Attalids with Rome, made Greek feeling hostile to them. On the other hand they provided a bulwark against the Galatians. With their wealth they made Pergamum into a splendid city, adorned with sculptures. Those commemorating the victory of Attalus I over the Gallic invaders included a bronze representation of the 'Dying Gaul' of which a marble reproduction survives in the Capitoline museum. Eumenes II erected a great altar to Zeus with a frieze, some 400 feet long, showing the battle of the Gods and the Giants. Under the same king, Pergamum became an important centre of literary studies, and a great library was built, the rival of that of Alexandria. It was at Pergamum that the use of parchment (a word derived from Pergamum) was first developed on a large scale (see *Books, Ancient*, § 5). The Pergamene kings sent sculptures to Athens

and erected two colonnades there (see *Stoa*).

A'tthis (meaning 'Attic'), a name given to chronicles of early events in Attica. The first of such chronicles was made by Hellanicus in the 5th c. B.C. (see *Logographi*), and the best-known by Philochorus in the 3rd c. B.C. Only fragments of their chronicles survive.

Attic dialect, see *Migrations and Dialects.*

Attic Nights, see *Gellius.*

A'ttica (*Attikē*), a mountainous and in great part arid country, forming the SE. promontory of central Greece, about 1,000 square miles in extent, or a little larger than Derbyshire. Its city was Athens (q.v.). See Pl. 8.

A'tticus, TĬTUS POMPŌNĬUS (109–32 B.C.), the intimate friend of Cicero, was born at Rome of an equestrian family. He withdrew in 88 from the turbulence and bloodshed of Rome to Athens, where he lived for many years (whence his cognomen Atticus). He took no active part in the politics of the ensuing troubled period, but maintained an attitude of neutrality and friendship with all parties. He helped Marians and Pompeians in their hours of difficulty: he protected Cicero's wife Terentia when Cicero went into exile, and Antony's wife Fulvia and his lieutenant Volumnius at the time of Mutina. In consequence he was spared by Antony in the proscriptions. He became the friend of Augustus, and his daughter married Agrippa, the minister of the latter. Their daughter Vipsānia married Tiberius and was mother of the younger Drusus (see *Julio-Claudian Family* and *Germanicus and Drusus*, B. 1). Pompōnia, sister of Atticus, married Cicero's brother Quintus. The series of Cicero's letters to Atticus begins in 68, and their friendship, which had its origin when they were fellow students in youth, continued until Cicero's death. Cicero constantly turned to him for sympathy in distress and difficulty, and for advice, both in connexion with public and private affairs. Atticus had inherited a considerable fortune, with which he bought land in Epirus, and which he gradually increased by judicious investment. He became very wealthy and had strong literary tastes; he kept a large staff of slaves trained in copying and binding manuscripts. He acted as Cicero's publisher. His works, which have not survived, included a 'Liber Annalis', an epitome of Roman history in one book, dealing with laws, wars, and political events from the earliest times to his own day; and a genealogical treatise on certain

Roman families and the magistracies they had held. He also helped to establish the date of the founding of Rome (see *Calendar*.) We have a life of him by Nepos (q.v.).

A'ttis, a Phrygian deity associated with the myth of Cybele (q.v.) or Agdistis. Attis was the son of Nana, daughter of the river-god Sangarius (a river in Asia Minor). She conceived him after gathering the blossom of an almond-tree sprung from the blood of Agdistis. When Attis wished to marry, Agdistis, who loved him and was jealous, drove him mad, so that he castrated himself and died. At the prayer of the repentant goddess, Zeus allowed his spirit to pass into a pine-tree, while violets sprang from his blood. This myth (like that of Adonis) symbolizes the death and revival of plant life. See also *Catullus*.

A'ttius La'beo, a translator of Homer (q.v., *ad fin.*).

Au'fidus, a river in Āpūlia (S. Italy), on which stood Venusia, the birthplace of Horace, who refers in his poems to its swift and roaring current ('longe sonantem natus ad Aufidum'). It was on the banks of this river that Hannibal defeated the Romans in 216 B.C. at the battle of Cannae.

Augē'as (*Augeiās*), see *Heracles* (*Labours of*) and *Trophonius*.

Augury and **Auspices.** Auspices (*auspicia*) were the means by which the Romans sought to ascertain whether the gods were favourable to an undertaking, and the augurs were a priestly college whose members had the knowledge necessary for taking the auspices and interpreting them. In the household nothing of importance was undertaken, Cicero tells us, except with the sanction of the auspices. But of the details of domestic augury we know hardly anything. The auspices were taken by the master of the house, with the assistance, if necessary, of a professional augur. We know also that there were agricultural auguries in spring and at midsummer. The college of augurs was second in importance only to the *pontifices* (q.v.); they were the repositories of tradition about augury and were consulted in cases of doubt, public or private. They alone had the right of public augury, exercised on all occasions when the approval of the gods for public action (e.g. a meeting of the Assembly) was required. The auspices, originally 'signs from birds' (*avis-spicere*) were taken as follows. The augur marked off a *templum*, a rectangular space in which the auspices were to be sought. There, after offering a prescribed prayer for a sign, he sat looking southward. (In certain places, e.g. in the Arx on the Capitoline hill, there were permanent *templa*; the view from these might not be obstructed by new buildings.) Signs on the E. side (the augur's left) were regarded as propitious, on the W. as unfavourable. Hence, in general, signs on the left side were of good omen. (There was also authority for the augur adopting an eastward-facing position.) The signs were either the flight or song of birds, thunder and lightning, or the movement of animals. Later, auspices were taken, especially during military operations, from the manner of feeding (eager or the reverse) of chickens. The gods, moreover, might spontaneously send a sign, such as thunder, upon which the augur advised; and in later republican times public business was frequently obstructed by the observation of pretended signs and similar devices. The college, until the *lex Ogulnia* of 300 B.C., consisted of patricians. The augurs received a salary; their official dress was the *trabea*, a mantle with a purple border, and they were further distinguished by the *lituus* or curved staff without knots, which they used for marking off the *templa*. Much light is thrown on Roman augury by the 'De Divinatione' (q.v.) of Cicero. The classical example of the supposed danger of neglecting the warnings of the auspices was that of the consul C. Flaminius, who, on the morning of the battle of Lake Trasimene (217 B.C.), insisted on marching against the enemy in defiance of the obvious indications of the omens, which he ridiculed. Within three hours the consul lay dead on the field and his army was destroyed. Similarly on the occasion of the great sea-fight off Drepanum in 249 B.C. between the Roman and Carthaginian fleets, it was reported to the Roman admiral that the sacred chickens would not eat. 'Then let them drink', he replied and had them thrown overboard. The utter defeat of the Roman fleet followed.

For omens drawn by the Romans from inspection of the entrails of sacrificial victims, see *Haruspices*.

Augustā'lēs. There were during the Roman empire several priesthoods or dignities bearing this title. (1) On the death of Augustus (A.D. 14) Tiberius instituted the college of *Sodālēs Augustales* to look after the cult of the gens Julia. Its members belonged to the imperial family or were important personages in the State. (2) The *Sēviri Augustales* were members of similar colleges instituted by Tiberius in the provinces for the commemoration of Augustus. They were freedmen, who thus acquired in Rome the social standing they desired. Trimalchio, in the novel of Petronius Arbiter (q.v.), prides himself on being a *sevir Augustalis*, an honour all the greater because he was chosen in absence without having to stand for election. (3) During his lifetime, Augustus had associated his 'genius' (see *Religion*, § 5) for purposes of worship with the Lares Compitales, the Lares of the cross-roads. He instituted the *Magistri Vīcorum* to attend to the worship. These Augustales also were freedmen. The connexion and difference between *Seviri Augustales, Seviri et Augustales, Magistri Augustales*, and *Augustales* (in the provinces), is still far from clear.

Augustā'lia, *Ludi*, § 2 *ad fin.*

Augustan Age of Roman literature, a term applied to the period which followed the Ciceronian Age (q.v.), and of which the empire of Augustus was the chief historical feature; it is generally regarded as covering the years from the death of Julius Caesar (44 B.C.) to the death of Ovid in A.D. 17. The great authors of this period were Virgil, Horace, Tibullus, Propertius, Ovid, and Livy. The period covers a variety of political conditions, for the old republican system did not end until after the battle of Actium in 31 B.C., and even then continued nominally.

The most prominent characteristic of this period was the restoration of tranquillity and order after nearly a century of revolution, civil turmoil, and massacre. Political activity came to an end with the institution of the empire; freedom of political and historical inquiry and expression was limited; hence the disappearance of oratory and the scantiness of prose literature in general during this age. Poetry is frequently under the influence of patrons such as the emperor himself and other men in high official positions, like Maecenas and Messalla; it is addressed to a polished society, and is concerned with patriotic themes (pride in Rome and its imperial destiny), or with the passion of love, or with the beauty of nature. It is a mature literature, the product of study and training, showing less originality and spontaneity than the literature of the preceding age.

Augu'stine, ST. (*Aurēlius Augustīnus*) (A.D. 354–430), was born at Thagastē in Numidia. His father was a pagan; his mother, Monica, was a devout Christian and greatly influenced her son. He taught rhetoric successively at Thagaste, Carthage, Rome (383), and Milan. At Milan he came under the influence of Bishop Ambrose (q.v.), and in 387, after a long intellectual and moral struggle, in which he states that he was influenced by the 'Hortensius' of Cicero, received Christian baptism. He then returned to Africa (Monica dying at Ostia on the way) and became a priest, and in 395 bishop of Hippo, which office he occupied till his death. He was a man of wide erudition, with a bent for philosophy, of strong practical sense, combined with intense sensibility and an ardent religious faith. Many of his writings, especially his earliest works, have a philosophic cast: the 'Contra Acadēmicos', 'De Vīta Beāta', and 'De Ordine' are a criticism, from the religious standpoint, of ancient philosophy. His treatises 'De Immortālitāte Animi' (in which he adopts the Platonic arguments for a future life) and 'De Libero Arbitrio' (in which he discusses the vexed question of free will and divine foreknowledge) are other examples of his philosophical attitude. After his appointment to his bishopric his writings assume a more purely religious character—polemical treatises against the Manichaean and Pelagian heretics and the Donatist schismatics, letters of advice, encouragement, instruction, or direction, and numerous practical treatises. His methods as a teacher of Christianity are set forth in two works, 'De Catēchīzandis Rudibus' ('On the Art of Catechizing') and 'De Doctrina Christiāna' on a scheme of Christian education, including the interpretation of the Scriptures and Christian eloquence. His two most famous works are his 'Confessions', the moving story of his own spiritual struggles, written for the edification of others, with deep psychological insight; and his 'De Civītāte Dei' (q.v.), 'The City of God', the longest (it contains twenty-two books) and the latest of his writings; he worked on it for nearly fourteen years. Augustine's early practice of rhetoric left its mark not only in his wide knowledge of profane literature, but in an easy, supple style and a fondness for rhetorical devices and conceits.

Augu'stus, an honorary title conferred in 27 B.C. on C. Julius Caesar Octavianus, the first Roman emperor. See *Octavian* and *Rome*, §§ 7 and 9. He received this title because it had no monarchical ring and yet designated him as something greater than an ordinary citizen.

The title Augustus was assumed by the succeeding emperors at the request of the Senate and gradually became their official designation. The title *Augusta* was conferred on Livia after the death of Augustus and was afterwards borne by various ladies of the imperial family, not always consorts of the emperor.

Aululā'ria ('The pot of gold'), a comedy by Plautus, probably adapted from a play by Menander. The prologue is spoken by the Lar Familiaris (q.v.).

Euclio, an old curmudgeon, has found a pot full of treasure buried in his house. He hides it away, continues to pretend poverty, and is in terror that the treasure may be taken from him. His daughter Phaedria has been ravished by a young man, Lycōnidēs, at a feast of Ceres. Lyconides is repentant and wishes to marry her. But meanwhile his uncle Megadōrus proposes to Euclio for the girl's hand. Euclio thinks that Megadorus has designs on the treasure, takes it away from his house, and hides it in one place after another. He is seen by a slave of Lyconides. The latter gets possession of the treasure, and restores it to Euclio, who, overjoyed at its recovery, apparently (the end of the play is lost) bestows his daughter on Lyconides.

The play is noteworthy especially for the character of the old miser, on whom the Harpagon of Molière's 'L'Avare' is closely modelled. The incident of the cock that scrapes the earth near Euclio's treasure, and is killed by him for its manifest thievish intention, is also famous. The 'Aulularia' was performed at Cambridge in 1564 before Queen Elizabeth.

Au'lus Ge'llius, see *Gellius*.

Aurō'ra, see *Eos*.

Auso'nia, a poetic name for Italy, from *Ausones*, an ancient, perhaps Greek, name for the inhabitants of middle and southern Italy.

Auso'nius, DECIMUS MAGNUS (c. A.D. 310–c. 395), the son of a physician of Bordeaux, was educated there and at Toulouse, and after teaching rhetoric for thirty years at Bordeaux was appointed tutor to Valentinian's son, Grātian. With his pupil he accompanied Valentinian's expedition of 368–9 against the Germans, and under Gratian received rapid official advancement, becoming prefect of the Gallic provinces, then of Italy, Illyria, and Africa jointly with the emperor's son, and finally consul in 379. He then returned to his family estate at Bordeaux, where he appears to have spent most of the remainder of his life, though he was at Trèves at the time of the usurpation of Maximus. He was nominally at least a Christian, but without any depth of religious feeling: he tried to dissuade his pupil Paulinus from abandoning the world for a life of religion.

He wrote a great deal of verse in a great variety of metres, showing rather the technical ability of a professor of rhetoric than poetic inspiration. He seems to have versified any theme that presented itself, such as the names of the days and months, or the properties of the number three. He particularly delighted in verse catalogues: thus he catalogued in the 'Parentalia' his relatives and ancestors, assigning a few lines of pious praise to each; in other poems the professors of Bordeaux, the famous cities of the world, the twelve Caesars, the Seven Sages, even the Roman consuls (but this work is lost). He delighted also in such feats of skill as the composition of a prayer in 42 rhopalic (q.v.) hexameters beginning 'Spes deus aeternae stationis conciliator', and of nearly two hundred hexameters (the *Technopaegnion*) each ending in a monosyllable.

His more important and interesting poems are, (1) the *Ephēmeris*, or description of a normal day in his life (the date and place represented are uncertain), his awakening, talk with his servant, his cook, his secretary, &c.; and (2) the *Mosella*. This is a long poem on a visit to the Moselle, artificial in its arrangement: his journey through Gaul, apostrophe to the river, list of its fishes, description of its vineyards, the reflections in its water, aquatic sports, the luxurious villas on its banks, its tributaries, ending with its junction with the Rhine and a final tribute of praise. Ausonius possesses neither depth, insight, nor passion; but he shows affection for his country and feeling for natural beauties, and his verse (which includes, besides the pieces named above, Epistles, Epigrams, &c.) throws light, here and there, on middle-class life in the provinces in his day. His prose writing includes a long *Grātiarum actio* or thanksgiving for his consulship, addressed to Gratian.

Auspices, see *Augury*.

Au'ster, the south wind (Gk. *Notos*).

Auto'lycus (*Autolukos*), in Greek mythology, a son of Hermes and a master of trickery and thieving. He received from his father the gift of making himself and his stolen goods invisible, or of changing the appearance of the latter so as to escape detection. But he was outwitted by Sisyphus (q.v.). He was the father of Anticlea, the mother of Odysseus.

Auto'medon (*Automedōn*), in the 'Iliad', the charioteer of Achilles (q.v.).

A'ventine, the most southerly of the seven hills of Rome (see Pl. 14). According to the traditional view, the Aventine, though within the wall of Servius Tullius (see *Rome*, § 1), remained outside the *pōmoerium* or city boundary for religious reasons until the time of Claudius. Another theory is that it was not included within any wall until the rebuilding of the Servian Wall in the 4th c. B.C. It was the scene of the story of Hercules and Cacus (q.v.), whose cave Evander showed to Aeneas (Aen. viii. 184 et seq.). In later times it was a quarter occupied by the poorer classes, and was crowned by a temple of Diana.

Ave'rnus, a lake near Cumae and Naples. Close to it was the cave by which Aeneas descended to the nether world (Aen. vi). The name was sometimes used for the nether world itself. It was generally written in Greek *Ἄορνος*, which was supposed to mean 'without birds', and the lake was in consequence thought to be birdless, a feature which is often referred to.

Avĕs, see *Birds*.

Aviĕ'nus, RŪFIUS FESTUS (4th c. A.D.), who tells us that he was a native of Volsinii and twice proconsul, was author of an extant translation of Aratus (q.v.) into Latin hexameters. Of two other verse translations by him (of Greek poems on geographical subjects) the whole of one and part of the other survive.

B

Ba'brius, VALĒRIUS (?) (c. A.D. 100 ?) of whom nothing is known, author of 123 Aesopic fables (see *Aesop*) in Greek choliambic verse (see *Metre*, § 5), pleasantly told and probably based on some prose collection of these. The fables of Babrius are extant.

Ba'cchae, a tragedy by Euripides, produced in 405 B.C. by his son after his death, probably written after Euripides had gone to Macedon to the court of Archelaus; the last of the great Greek tragedies.

Dionysus, the young god, son of Zeus and the Theban princess Semele (q.v.), travelling through the world to make himself known as god to man, comes to Thebes, where his worship has been rejected, even by Agāvĕ, sister of Semele and mother of Penthĕus, king of Thebes. Dionysus has maddened the recalcitrant women, and sent them to adore him on the mountain. Pentheus, bitterly hostile to the new religion in spite of the remonstrances of his grandfather Cadmus and of Tiresias (qq.v.), insults and tries to

imprison Dionysus (it is usually supposed that the poet intended to represent Dionysus himself in the captive; but in the tragedy itself the captive proclaims himself merely a votary of the god). By him Pentheus is induced to spy on the women's mystic worship, is discovered by them, and torn in pieces. Agave, in her frenzy, bears his head triumphantly to Thebes. It is only when she recovers that she finds she has killed her son. Dionysus proclaims the doom of the house of Cadmus, and Cadmus himself and Agave go their ways into exile.

Pentheus exemplifies the limitations of ordinary human reason, closed to the mysteries beyond the material world. But while Euripides shows sympathy with the mystic side of the Dionysiac religion, he appears to condemn its extravagances.

Bacchanā'lia (*Bacchānālia*), orgies of Dionysus (q.v.) or Bacchus. They spread in Italy early in the 2nd c. B.C., led to excesses, and had to be suppressed in 186 B.C. The decree of the Senate forbidding these rites survives in an inscription.

Bacchi, see *Dionysus*.

Ba'cchiac or **Ba'cchius**, see *Metre*, § 1.

Ba'cchidēs, a comedy by Plautus, adapted probably from a lost play (*Δὶς ἐξαπατῶν*) of Menander.

A young man is searching on behalf of an absent friend for the courtesan Bacchis of Samos; he finds her, but falls under the charm of her sister Bacchis of Athens. His conduct arouses suspicion in his friend's mind until it comes out that there are two courtesans of the same name. The slave Chrȳsalus is the pivot of the play. In contrast to the pedagogue Lȳdus, he aids his young master in his love affair, lying unblushingly and resourcefully. By a bold and ingenious trick he extracts from the young man's father the money required for the affair, and likens himself to a conqueror of Troy. Finally the sisters beguile the fathers of the two young men into forgiveness and all ends merrily.

Ba'cchus (*Bakchos*), see *Dionysus*.

Bacchy'lidēs (*Bakchulidēs*) (c. 505–c. 450 B.C.), born like his uncle Simonides (q.v.) in the island of Cĕōs, a Greek lyric poet. He appears to have visited the tyrant Hieron I of Syracuse (q.v., § 1), whom he celebrated in three odes. He wrote choral lyrics of all the principal kinds. Thanks to a discovery among the Oxyrhynchus papyri (see *Papyri, Discoveries of*), we possess nineteen of his poems (more or less mutilated), including thirteen *epinicia* (q.v.) and five other poems classed as dithyrambs. In the former he celebrated persons from all parts of the Greek world. The dithyrambs treat detached scenes taken from heroic legend. One of them, entitled 'Theseus', is of special interest as being in the form of a dialogue between Aegeus (see *Theseus*) and the chorus. Bacchylides was a poet of great elegance and imagination, of more natural magic than Pindar, but without the latter's grandeur, gravity, and power. He makes ample use of myths; some of them are new to us. But they are less aptly connected with his theme than those of Pindar. There was an edition of Bacchylides by R. C. Jebb in 1905.

Ba′cis (*Bakis*), an old Boeotian prophet, whose name became a common designation for male soothsayers, as Sibyl for prophetesses.

Bacon, ROGER, see *Texts and Studies*, § 8.

Ba′lbus, QUINTUS LŪCĪLIUS, one of the interlocutors in Cicero's 'De Natura Deorum' (q.v.), a learned Stoic, known only from Cicero's dialogue.

Bandu′sia, a fountain celebrated by Horace in the beautiful Ode (III. xiii) 'O fons Bandusiae, splendidior vitro'. It may have been on his Sabine farm, or near his birthplace Venusia.

Basi′lica, from the Gk. word meaning 'royal' sc. house, a roofed hall sometimes divided into aisles by rows of columns, used for judicial or other public business, or as a bazaar. The earliest is said to have been built by M. Porcius Cato in 184 B.C. There were five or six *basilicae* about the Forum at the end of the republican period, among them the Basilica Julia, built by Caesar, and used for judicial proceedings.

A form of *basilica*, with aisles flanking a nave and terminating in an apse, became the prototype of the Christian church.

Ba′ssarids (*Bassarides*), votaries of Dionysus (q.v.); a word perhaps meaning 'wearers of fox-skins'.

Bathos, in rhetoric, a drop from the lofty or sublime to the mean or ridiculous (the Gk. word βάθος, 'depth', was not used in this metaphorical sense). There is an example of it in a line by the bombastic epic poet Furius Bibāculus:

Juppiter hibernas cana nive conspuit Alpes,

'Jupiter spits the bleak Alps over with white snow.' This line is parodied by Horace, Sat. II. v. 39–41.

Baths, ROMAN (*balneae*). For those in private houses see *Houses*. Public baths played an important part in the daily life of the Romans, particularly in late republican and imperial times. They included rooms heated to different degrees (the *frīgidārium*, *tepidārium*, and *caldārium*), provided with hot water for washing and a cold plunge-bath. Women sometimes had separate accommodation or had particular hours allotted to them, though promiscuous bathing was not uncommon under the empire. The vast and luxurious structures built under the emperors (notably Caracalla and Diocletian), of which there are considerable remains, had in addition halls, lecture rooms, and places for exercise, running, wrestling, ball-playing (for it was usual to take exercise before the bath). Rhetoricians used the baths for recitations, and authors read their new works there. Excavations have shown that they were highly ornamented; and beautiful statues have been found in their ruins, such as the Farnese Hercules and the Farnese Bull (from the Baths of Caracalla, and now at Naples). The usual charge for admission to the baths was a *quadrans* (a small copper coin, one-fourth of an *as*).

Bathy′llus (*Bathullos*), see *Pantomime*.

Ba′trachomyoma′chiă, or *Battle of the Frogs and Mice*, a parody of an epic poem, attributed in antiquity to Homer, but probably of much later date.

A mouse named Psicharpax is invited by a frog, Physignathos, son of Peleus, to ride on his back and visit his watery kingdom. Unfortunately, at the sight of a water-snake (or perhaps otter), the frog dives and the mouse is drowned. But the incident has been seen by another mouse, and a great war ensues between the mice and the frogs, in which the mice seem to be winning. At the request of Athena Zeus intervenes, and, having failed with thunderbolts, sends crabs to quell the strife.

Ba′ttus, the founder of Cyrene, see *Colonization*, § 4.

Ba′vius and **Mae′vius**, poetasters sarcastically alluded to in Virgil's Third Eclogue. Maevius is also attacked in Horace's Tenth Epode. In English literature they supplied the titles of Gifford's satires on the Della Cruscan school of poets, 'The Baviad' and 'The Maeviad' (1794–5).

Bē′driacum, between Cremona and Verona, where in A.D. 69 Otho's forces were defeated by the Vitellians, and where the Vitellians later were defeated by the supporters of Vespasian.

Bekker, IMMANUEL, see *Texts and Studies*, § 11.

Belisā′rius, see *Justinian.*

Belle′rophon (*Bellerophŏn* or *Bellero-phontĕs*), in Greek mythology, son of Glaucus (q.v. (3)), the son of Sisyphus (q.v.). He spent some time at the court of Proetus, king of Argos, where Anteia (or Stheneboea), wife of Proetus, fell in love with him. As he slighted her passion, Anteia accused him to her husband. Proetus, unwilling to violate the laws of hospitality by killing Bellerophon under his own roof, sent him to his father-in-law Iobates bearing a letter requesting him to put Bellerophon to death (whence the expression *Bellerophontis litterae.* Homer says σήματα λυγρά; it has been disputed whether this was a letter.). Iobates accordingly sent Bellerophon against the Chimaera (q.v.); but Bellerophon, with the aid of the winged horse Pegasus (q.v.); destroyed it. He then defeated the fierce tribe of the Solymi, and the Amazons, with whom he was sent to fight, and overcame the warriors placed in an ambush to await him on his return. Thereafter Iobates, despairing of killing him, gave him his daughter to wife, by whom he was father of Laodamia, mother of Sarpedon (qq.v.), and of Hippolochus, father of the Glaucus (q.v. (4)), who at the siege of Troy exchanged armour with Diomedes. But he came to be hated of the gods; two of his children perished, and he is last heard of 'wandering alone, eating his heart out, avoiding the paths of men' (Il. vi. 201–2). Later legend relates that he attempted to fly to heaven on Pegasus, but that Zeus by a gadfly caused the horse to throw its rider.

Bello Cīvīli, Commentarii de, see *Commentaries.*

Bello Gallico, Commentarii de, see *Commentaries.*

Bellō′na (in the old form of the name, *Duellōna*), the Roman goddess of war. The first temple to her appears to have been built by Appius Claudius Caecus (q.v.) in the Campus Martius. (In Pliny's 'Natural History' we are told that in 495 B.C. Appius Claudius Regillus consecrated at Rome the images of his ancestors in a temple dedicated to Bellona. Wissowa believes this to be an additional explanation and that the temple of Appius Claudius Caecus is referred to.) The temple, being outside the walls, was used for meetings of the Senate to receive foreign ambassadors and Roman generals returning from active service (see *Triumph*). Here took place, after the battle of the Colline Gate, the meeting between Sulla and the Senate, when the proceedings were interrupted by the shrieks of Sulla's enemies who were being massacred by his orders. Near the temple stood the little column over which the Fetialis (q.v.) symbolically threw his spear on a declaration of war.

The moon-goddess of Asia was introduced at Rome after the Mithridatic Wars. A temple was erected to her, and she seems to have become identified with the Italian Bellona, whose Greek equivalent was recognized to be Enyo (q.v.).

Bellum Catilī′nae, see *Sallust.*

Bellum Cīvīle, see *Pharsalia.*

Bellum Jugurthī′num, see *Sallust.*

Bellum Pū′nicum, see *Naevius.*

Be′ndis, a Thracian goddess of the moon, who was identified at Athens with Artemis and whose cult became popular there in the 5th c. B.C. She had a temple at the Piraeus and her festival was celebrated with a torch-race.

Bentley, RICHARD, see *Texts and Studies*, § 10.

Berenī′cē, see article below and *Titus.*

Berent′cē, The Lock of (*Berenīkēs Plokamos*), the title of a poem in Greek elegiacs by Callimachus, of which only fragments survive. It was translated by Catullus (Poem 66).

This Berenice was the wife of Ptolemy III. Another Berenice, sister of Ptolemy III, had been married to Antiochus II of Syria; but on the death of Antiochus in 247 B.C. his widow had been displaced and killed by Lāodicē, an earlier divorced wife of Antiochus; and Laodice's son, Seleucus II, had been proclaimed his successor. Ptolemy III set out in 246 to vindicate the claims of his sister's son. On his departure, Berenice his wife dedicated to the gods a lock of her hair as an offering for his safe return. This lock mysteriously disappeared. Conōn, the court astronomer, pretended to discover it, transformed into a constellation thereafter known as *Coma Berenices.*

In Pope's 'Rape of the Lock', the lock of Belinda's hair which had been snipped off is finally wafted, as a new star, to adorn the skies.

Bērō′sus (*Bērŏssos*), a priest at Babylon, of the 3rd c. B.C., who wrote in Greek a work on the chronology of Chaldaea.

Bī′as (*Bĭās*), see *Melampus.*

Bī′on (*Bĭōn*) (c. 100 B.C.?), born at Smyrna, a Greek poet, imitator of Theocritus. Of the half-dozen short poems attributed to him that have come down to us, the most remarkable is the 'Lament for Adonis', probably intended for recitation at one of the festivals of Adonis, such as that described by Theocritus in his 'Adoniazusae' (Idyll xv). The others have love for their subject, or the charms of the various seasons. Bion is generally coupled with Moschus (q.v.). It appears from the beautiful dirge in which some friend or pupil, perhaps Moschus, lamented the death of Bion, that the latter was poisoned.

Birds (*Ornithes*, L. *Avēs*), a comedy by Aristophanes, produced at the Great Dionysia of 414 B.C. It won the second prize. The Athenian fleet had set out on the Sicilian Expedition in the previous year. Before it started, the city had been profoundly disturbed by the mysterious and sacrilegious mutilation of the Hermae (q.v.). Mēlos had been cruelly and unjustly destroyed in 416–415. Aristophanes hated the war and its consequences, and turned from political themes to construct an Utopia.

Peithetairos and Euelpidēs, sick of life in Athens with its worries and anxieties, seek out King Tereus (see *Philomela*), who had married an Athenian princess and been turned into a hoopoe, to consult him as to the best place to live in. Tereus suggests various countries, but there are objections to them all. Peithetairos now has a brilliant idea. Let the birds all unite and build a great walled city in the air. From this they will rule both mankind and the gods, for they will control the food supply of both. They can devour the seed in the earth, and intercept the steam of the sacrifices on which the gods are nourished. The chorus of birds, at first hostile, are won over to the proposal, and they quickly set about building the city under the direction of Peithetairos and Euelpides, who grow wings to suit their new condition. Then various unwelcome visitors arrive: a needy poet with a hymn in honour of the new city, an oracle-monger, Metōn (the famous astronomer) to lay out the streets, and an inspector of ceremonies. They are all appropriately dealt with. The new city (Nephelococcygia, 'Cloud-cuckoo-land') is now finished, and the guard come in with a trespasser whom they have caught, Iris, the messenger of Zeus, on her way to discover why the sacrifices have stopped on earth. She is asked for her passport and generally bullied, and finally goes off in tears to complain to her father. Meanwhile mankind has become bird-mad and wants wings. Further visitors arrive: a father-beater, because young cocks fight

their fathers (he is reminded that young storks must also feed their fathers); Cinesias, the lyric poet, because he wants to soar on airy pinions; an informer, who would find wings useful for serving writs; and Prometheus, who hides from Zeus under an umbrella while he tells of the food shortage among the gods, and advises Peithetairos to make hard terms with them, and insist on having Basileia (sovereignty), daughter of Zeus, to wife. Then come ambassadors from the gods, Poseidon, Heracles, and a god of the barbarous Triballians. Thanks to the greediness of Heracles, Peithetairos gets the sceptre and Basileia, is hailed as the highest of the gods, and preparations are made for his wedding.

Birthplaces of Greek authors. These, where of sufficient importance or interest, are dealt with under their several names. The table on p. 72, in which the principal Greek men of letters are summarily grouped according to their birth-places and their periods, brings out,

(1) the predominance of Ionia and the islands of the Aegean as the centre of literary activity in the earliest period;

(2) the shifting of this centre to Attica in the 5th and 4th cc.;

(3) the cessation of literary production at Athens after the end of the 4th c.;

(4) the dispersion of literary talent over all parts of the Greek-speaking world in the period of decadence. This would have appeared even more strikingly if the table had included critics, grammarians, writers on science, and authors generally of minor merit;

(5) the small share in literary production which falls to the States of Greece proper other than Athens. Only ten names are included in this category, and four of them belong to Boeotia. Magna Graecia likewise contributed very little.

Birthplaces of Latin authors. In the table on p. 73 the principal Latin authors of the republican period and the early empire are roughly grouped according to their birthplaces. Some important authors, such as Tibullus and Tacitus, are excluded, because their birthplaces are unknown. It is remarkable how few of the authors of the first rank are thought to have been born in Rome itself. The increased literary importance in imperial times of Spain and other Roman territories outside Italy is the natural consequence of the spread of Roman culture.

Bī'tōn, see *Cleobis.*

Boadicē'a (*Boudicca*), queen of the Icēni in East Anglia, whose rising against the

BIRTHPLACES OF GREEK AUTHORS

Period	Ionia and the Islands		Greece proper				Sicily	Other Greek colonies, &c.
	Poets	Philosophers and Historians	Attica			Other States		
			Poets	Philosophers and Historians	Orators			
9th to 6th centuries	Homer Alcman* Archilochus Mimnermus Alcaeus Sappho Anacreon	Thales Anaximander Anaximenes Pythagoras Xenophanes Cadmus Hecataeus	Solon Thespis (?)			Hesiod (Boeotia) Tyrtaeus (Sparta?) Theognis (Megara)	Stesichorus	Ibycus (Rhegium)
5th and 4th centuries	Simonides Bacchylides Timotheus	Heraclitus Anaxagoras† Theophrastus Theopompus Hippocrates	Phrynichus Aeschylus Sophocles Cratinus Euripides Aristophanes Eupolis Choerilus	Socrates Thucydides Plato Xenophon	Antiphon Andocides Isocrates Demosthenes Aeschines Lycurgus Lysias Hyperides	Pindar Corinna (Boeotia) Isaeus (Euboea) Dinarchus (Corinth) Pratinas (Phlius)	Epicharmus Gorgias Empedocles Timaeus	Herodotus (Halicarnassus) Parmenides (Elea) Zeno the Eleatic (Elea) Democritus (Abdera) Protagoras (Abdera) Aristotle (Stagira) Diogenes (Sinope) Ephorus (Cyme)
Hellenistic, Roman, and Byzantine Ages	Bion		Menander	Epicurus‡	Demetrius of Phalerum	Polybius (Arcadia) Plutarch (Boeotia)	Philemon Archimedes Theocritus (?) Herodas Moschus Diodorus	Diphilus (Sinope) Zeno the Stoic (Cyprus) Callimachus (Cyrene) Carneades (Cyrene) Aratus (Cilicia) Apollonius Rh. (Alexandria) Meleager (Gadara) Menippus (Gadara) Posidonius (Apamea) Pausanias (Lydia) Lucian (Samosata) Strabo (Amasia in Pontus) Galen (Pergamum) Plotinus (Egypt) Epictetus (Phrygia) Appian (Bithynia) Arrian (Alexandria) Athenaeus (Naucratis)

* Lived at Sparta.   † Lived at Athens.   ‡ Born in Samos of Athenian parents.

BIRTHPLACES OF LATIN AUTHORS

	Rome	Rest of Central Italy*	Northern Italy	Southern Italy	Spain	Transalpine Gaul	Africa	Dalmatia, Thrace, and Asia
Republican period	Naevius (?) Cato the Censor (?) Lucretius (?) Julius Caesar (?)	Plautus (Umbria) Accius (Umbria) Lucilius (Latium) Sallust (Sabine country) Cicero (Arpinum) Varro (Reate)	Caecilius (Insubrian Gaul) Catullus (Verona) Nepos (Insubrian Gaul)	Ennius (Calabria) Pacuvius (Calabria)		C. Cornelius Gallus	Terence	Publilius Syrus (Antioch?)
Period of the empire	Suetonius (?)	Propertius (Umbria) Ovid (Sulmo) Juvenal (Aquinum?) Persius (Volaterrae) Valerius Flaccus (Campania?) Statius (Naples)	Virgil (Mantua) Livy (Patavium) Silius Italicus (Patavium?) Pliny the Elder (Como) Pliny the Younger (Como)	Horace (Apulia)	Pomponius Mela Seneca the Elder Seneca the Younger Lucan Martial Columella Quintilian Orosius	Trogus Pompeius Ausonius	Fronto Apuleius Tertullian St. Augustine Nonius Claudian	Phaedrus (Thrace) St. Jerome (Dalmatia) Ammianus Marcellinus (Antioch)

* Latium, Etruria, Umbria, Sabine territory, Campania.

Romans and its suppression by Suētōnius Paulīnus are described by Tacitus (Ann. xiv). Boadicea took her own life after the defeat. (See *Britain*, § 2).

Boccaccio, see *Texts and Studies*, § 9.

Boeō′tia (*Boiōtiā*), the country adjoining Attica on the NW (see Pl. 8). It was occupied in the Migrations (q.v.) by Aeolians from Epirus, who mingled with such of the older inhabitants as remained; but some of these, Cadmeians (see *Cadmus*) of Thebes, Minyans (q.v.) of Orchomenus, &c., migrated to Ionian settlements overseas. The languages of the invaders and the older population coalesced in a special Boeotian dialect of Greek. The cities of the new Boeotia showed a high degree of the usual Greek spirit of independence, and although Thebes was foremost among them, she was unable to impose her rule upon them. A Boeotian Confederacy was formed, from which Orchomenus held aloof until about 600 B.C. The organization of the Confederacy was peculiar. Each of the cities was governed by four councils (*boulai*), membership of which depended on property qualification. Each council sat for three months in the year, dealing with the preliminary consideration of business, but decisions were taken by the four councils sitting jointly. Above these municipal bodies was the federal government. The eleven districts of Boeotia each named one Boeotarch and sixty councillors. Executive power rested with the Boeotarchs under the control of the 660 councillors. Each district was required to furnish an equal contingent to the army. But some of the cities were unwilling members, in particular Plataea, which entered into relations with Athens to protect her independence. Boeotia played an equivocal part, if she was not actively disloyal to the cause of Greece, in the Persian Wars. She was subdued (with the exception of Thebes) by Athens in 457 as a result of the victory of Oenophyta, and was held in subjection until 447. The Boeotian Confederacy assumed its greatest importance in the 4th c., when, under the leadership of Pelopidas and Epaminondas, Thebes (q.v.) reduced Sparta from her position of leadership in Greece.

Boeotia was a rich centre of early legend, as shown by the Hesiodic poems, and the many religious and oracular sites. The origin of writing was associated with the legend of Cadmus (q.v.). Boeotia became proverbial for the stupidity of its inhabitants, though it was the birthplace of Pindar, of the poetess Corinna, and of Plutarch (qq.v.).

Boë′thius, ANICIUS MANLIUS SEVĔRĪNUS

(c. A.D. 480–524), belonged to the *gens* of the Anicii, of which many members had held high office under the empire in the 4th and 5th cc. He entered the service of Theodoric and became consul in 510, but having undertaken the defence of a senator who was accused of secret correspondence with the Emperor of the East, he was charged with high treason, imprisoned, and died under torture.

Boethius was a Christian and has left several treatises on Christian doctrine ('De Trinitate', 'Contra Eutychen et Nestorium', &c.). He also undertook, after learning Greek at Athens, the arduous task of translating the whole of Plato and Aristotle, commenting on them, and showing their essential agreement in philosophical doctrine. This task he was unable to accomplish, but he translated the logical treatises of Aristotle, and also translated and commented on some of the logical treatises of Porphyry. Incidentally, by his discussion, in his commentary on Porphyry, of the question whether genera and species have real existence apart from the sensible objects composing them, he initiated the great dispute which was to separate Nominalists and Realists among the Schoolmen.

But the most famous work of Boethius was the 'Consolatio Philosophiae' which he wrote in prison. It consists of five books in prose interspersed with verse (there are 39 short poems, of great beauty, in 13 different metres). It opens with some melancholy lines 'dictated by the afflicted Muses'. The Muses are ousted by Philosophy, who comes to console the prisoner. She reminds him of the sufferings of other thinkers such as Socrates, and invites him to lay bare his troubles. Boethius sets forth the ingratitude with which his integrity has been met, and laments the triumph of injustice. Philosophy reminds him of the caprices of Fortune, and of the vanity of those things, riches, honours, power, which the world esteems good. The only real good is God. But how, asks Boethius, under a beneficent God can evil exist or pass unpunished (Bk. IV)? Philosophy in reply enters upon the mystery of good and evil. The gist of her exposition is that evil is in fact nothing, and that evil men in the true sense are not; and if they can persecute the good and go unpunished, they suffer all the more for their wickedness. Philosophy passes to the question of the true nature of Providence and Chance, and the reconciliation of free will with the foreknowledge possessed by God.

The 'Consolation' is written from a philosophic, not a Christian, standpoint, and Christ is not mentioned in it. But the wording shows the Christian influence. The work exercised immense influence in the succeeding ages. That it was very widely read is shown by the fact that we possess some four hundred manuscripts of it. It was translated, among others, by King Alfred, by Chaucer, and by Queen Elizabeth. It is frequently quoted by Dante, whose famous lines, 'Nessun maggior dolore. . . .' (Inf. v. 121) were suggested by Boethius, II. iv. 4 'in omni adversitate fortunae infelicissimum . . .'.

Bŏē'thus, see *Toreutic Art*.

Bona Dea, in Roman religion, a goddess of unknown name, probably an earth-spirit protective of women; she was sometimes identified with Maia, Fauna, or Ops. Rites in her honour were celebrated annually in December in the house of a magistrate with *imperium* (i.e. a consul, or sometimes a praetor), and were attended only by women; it was these rites which Clodius (q.v.) profaned by his presence.

Books, ANCIENT.

§ 1. *The earliest texts*

There is evidence that the art of writing goes back, in Egypt to the third millennium B.C., in Mesopotamia even earlier, in the Hittite Empire to the second millennium, and in Crete at least to 2000 B.C. There need, therefore, be no hesitation in admitting the possibility that Homer (q.v.) wrote down his poems, for his own convenience if not to be read by others. In the 7th and 6th c. a further stage must have been reached, for it would seem that poems such as those of Archilochus and Sappho must have passed from hand to hand in manuscript. Later, when tragedies were performed, copies must have been available for the actors to learn their parts. In Plato and Xenophon we have references to the actual reading of the works of philosophers and evidence that books were not expensive.

§ 2. *The papyrus roll*

The chief materials used for writing in the earliest times—apart from inscriptions on stone or metal—were clay tablets in Mesopotamia, Syria, and Crete, and papyrus in Egypt. In Greece the material used at least from the 6th c. appears to have been papyrus (also known as *bublos*, whence *biblion*, a book). According to the descriptions given by Theophrastus (H.P. iv. 8. 3) and Pliny (N.H. xiii. 11–12), the triangular stem of the papyrus, which grew, principally in the Nile, to the height of 15 feet and the thickness of a man's wrist, was sliced length-wise into thin strips. These were placed in two layers, so that the fibres in one layer were at right angles to those in the other. The layers were moistened with water and glue and pressed together, then dried and polished. The sheets thus produced, with a maximum height of about 15 inches and maximum breadth of about 9 inches, were glued together side by side so as to form a continuous roll (generally 20–30 ft. long in Greek rolls). They were called *kollēmata*, and the first sheet *prōtokollon* (on which among the Romans was inscribed the date and place where the roll was made), a word which has survived in our 'protocol'. On this roll, in successive columns across the direction of its length, the manuscript was written with a reed pen. There was a margin between the columns, and a broader margin above and below. The width of the column of writing (governed in the case of poetry by the length of the line of verse) varied generally from 2 to 5 inches. There was no division or space between the words, and little to help the reader in the way of signs or punctuation. A short stroke (*paragraphos*) under the line often indicated the point where there was a pause in the sense, or a change of speaker in dramatic texts (but the name of the speaker was hardly ever given). Titles of books, if given at all, appeared at the end, and might be added on a label (*sillubos*) of parchment projecting from the end of the roll. A roller (*omphalos, umbilicus*) might be attached to the end of the papyrus, ornamented with projecting knobs (*cornua*). The writing on a roll was generally on one side only, the *recto*, on which the fibres ran horizontally; if on both, the roll was known as an *opistho-graph*. An ordinary roll would contain a book of Thucydides or two or three books of the 'Iliad'. The rolls comprising a long work or the complete works of an author might be kept together in a cupboard (L. *armārium*) or bucket (L. *capsa*). A reader would unfold the roll with his right hand, and roll it up, as he proceeded, with his left. Obviously this form of book was extremely inconvenient. It was impossible to index and difficult to consult; it lent itself to errors in copying, especially by uneducated scribes, and the text frequently became corrupted.

§ 3. *Development of book production*

It appears that at the end of the 5th c. and in the early 4th c. books existed at Athens in considerable numbers, and a trade in books, with its centre at Athens, began; but the practice of reading (as distinct from oral instruction) did not become firmly established until the time of Aristotle. It was he who formed the first large collection of manuscripts. (To this period belongs one of the earliest of illustrated books, a work on 'Dissections' with diagrams, to which Aristotle makes frequent reference in his treatises on zoology.) With the organization of the production of papyrus and later of vellum (see below, § 5) by the Hellenistic kings, and the employment of educated slaves as copyists, the output of books greatly increased in the 3rd and subsequent centuries. The price of the roll of papyrus in Greece from 408 to about 333 appears to have been about two drachmas. In 296 the price had fallen to about two obols, presumably in consequence of the throwing open of the Egyptian market by Alexander's conquest. But from 279 the price had risen again to two drachmas. This rise may be attributed to the organization by the Ptolemies (q.v.) of their monopoly of papyrus.

The type of book described above was introduced at Rome with Greek literature in the 3rd and 2nd cc. B.C. As literature becomes more established there in the 1st c. B.C. and the 1st c. A.D., references to books and their appearance occur more frequently, particularly in Catullus and Martial (the first book of Martial's epigrams sold for five denarii a copy; the thirteenth for one denarius). We know that Atticus (q.v.), who had copyists and craftsmen among his slaves, acted as publisher to Cicero. The Sosii are mentioned by Horace (Ep. I. xx. 2) as booksellers. An early illustrated Roman book was the 'Hebdomades' or 'Imaginum libri XV' of M. Terentius Varro (q.v.), a collection of portraits of celebrated Greeks and Romans, with an epigram attached to each. Martial (xiv. 186) refers to a copy of Virgil containing a portrait of the poet at the beginning.

§ 4. *The codex*

The next stage in the evolution of the book was the gradual substitution of the codex, or book made up of quires of folded sheets, for the roll, and of vellum for papyrus. Discoveries in Egypt tend to show that the earliest books in codex form were made of sheets of papyrus, that the papyrus codex was first used for Christian as distinct from pagan manuscripts (the Bible could only be consulted conveniently in this form), and that it was thereafter used principally for manuscripts of this class. The codex took the form either of a large number of quires each consisting of a single sheet folded once and sewn together, or of a single quire of as many as fifty sheets folded once, or of a number of

quires each of several sheets. This last form ultimately prevailed. The codex appears to have come into use in the 2nd c. A.D. The primitive codex was of various sizes, generally about 11×7 inches or 12×8. The manuscript was generally written in one column on a page, sometimes in two. The chief advantages of the codex over the roll was that a far greater amount of manuscript could be contained in a book of codex form, and that the latter was much easier than the roll to handle. Mention should here be made of the note-books (*tabellae*) in use at Rome, consisting of sheets of wood or other material, coated with wax, or whitened, which were fastened together and written on with a *stilus*, the coating being easily renewed. These may have suggested the codex form of book; a folded set of tablets was called a *caudex* or *cōdex*. The British Museum possesses parts of a set of tablets of this description; also *stili*, reed and bronze pens (with split nibs), and Roman inkpots.

§ 5. *Vellum*

Vellum is a material prepared from skins, especially of calves, lambs, and kids. According to Pliny, its discovery was due to the rivalry of Ptolemy (probably Epiphanes) with Eumenes (probably Eumenes II) of Pergamum (q.v.) over their libraries, which led Ptolemy to prohibit the export of papyrus from Egypt. This gave rise to the employment of vellum or parchment (the word 'parchment' is derived from Pergamum) for the manufacture of books at Pergamum. But there is evidence that Eumenes did not discover vellum, but only extended its use.

Vellum did not come into general use for book production till much later, though it had a marked advantage over papyrus in its greater durability; moreover it was better suited than papyrus for writing on both sides. It was not until the 4th c. A.D. that it began to take the place of papyrus in the manufacture of the best books, and the works considered worth preserving were gradually transferred from papyrus roll to vellum codex. It is in this century that the great vellum codices of the Greek Bible (the Vaticanus and the Sinaiticus) were prepared; and the earliest extant vellum manuscripts of pagan works date probably from the same century. For sumptuous books the vellum was sometimes stained purple. But the use of papyrus did not cease then, and papyrus manuscripts have been found of the 4th, 5th, and 6th cc. The roll form was retained for public documents through the Middle Ages to our own times. The use of paper was introduced from China by the Arabs in the 8th c., but was not generalized till much later. See F. W. Hall, 'Companion to Classical Texts', Oxford, 1913, and F. G. Kenyon, 'Books and Readers in Ancient Greece and Rome', Oxford, 1932, on which the above article is mainly based.

Boö'tēs, see *Arcturus*.

Bo'reas, (*Boreās*), the north wind, L. *Aquilo*. In Greek mythology, he was the husband of Oreithyīa, daughter of Erechtheus, and thus specially connected with the Athenians (see under *Winds*); by her he was father of Zētēs and Calāis, who figure among the Argonauts.

Bo'sporus (Gk. *Bosporos*), 'ox-ford', a name applied especially to (*a*) the Thracian Bosporus (now generally known as the Bosphorus), the channel connecting the Sea of Marmora with the Black Sea; the name was sometimes associated with the myth of Io (q.v.); (*b*) the Cimmerian Bosporus, connecting the Black Sea with the Sea of Azov.

Bou'dicca, in Anglicized form *Boadicea* (q.v., and see *Britain*, § 2).

Bou'lē, the Council or Senate in Greek city-states. It existed at Athens (q.v., § 2) from primitive times and was reorganized by Solon and Cleisthenes (qq.v.). At Sparta (q.v.) it was known as the *Gerousia*. The Boule at Athens had general charge of foreign policy (subject to reference to the Ecclesia in grave cases), exercised a general supervision over the administration, notably the finances, prepared legislation for the Ecclesia, and had certain limited judicial functions. It tried officials charged with misconduct, and occasionally persons charged with offences against the safety or interests of the State. For the *Prytany* or executive committee of the Boule, see *Cleisthenes*.

Boustrophē'don, see *Epigraphy*, § 2.

Bra'nchidae, a family that had charge of the temple of Apollo near Miletus. They were accused of betraying the treasure of the temple to Xerxes, and their lives were threatened by the Milesians. Xerxes transported them to Sogdiāna, where they were safe from pursuit. Many generations later Alexander the Great (q.v.) came upon their town when pursuing Bessus. The story goes that Alexander caused their town to be demolished and the inhabitants to be massacred, in punishment for their ancestors' crime.

Bra'sidas (*Brasidās*), a Spartan general in the Peloponnesian War, an energetic and successful commander. His principal achievement was the capture of Amphi-

polis (424 B.C.). See under *Thucydides*. He was one of the most zealous supporters of the war, and his death in the defence of Amphipolis (422) against Cleon (q.v.), and the death of Cleon in the same engagement, rendered possible the Peace of Nicias.

Braurō'nia, see *Artemis*. Also the name of a festival held at Braurōn in Attica in honour of Artemis.

Bre'nnus (1) the leader of the Gauls who defeated the Romans at the Allia and occupied Rome in 390 B.C., but failed to capture the Capitol. For the legend of the Capitol geese, see *Manlius*. Legend also relates that when the gold which the Gauls accepted as the ransom of Rome was being weighed, and the Romans complained of false weights, he threw his sword into the scales, to add even more to the quantity, exclaiming 'Vae victis'.

(2) The leader of the Gauls or Galatians who in 280–279 B.C. invaded Paeōnia and Macedonia and thence Greece (see *Macedonia*, § 3). He was opposed by a force of Athenians and others at Thermopylae and defeated at Delphi. He died of wounds in 278, and the Gauls retreated with great loss.

Bria'reōs (L. *Briareūs*), see *Giants* (*Hundred-handed*).

Brīsē'is, see *Iliad*.

Britain (*Britannia*).

§ 1. *Britain before the Roman conquest*

The ancients had some knowledge of Britain from the time of Alexander the Great, when it was visited and described by Pytheas (q.v.), but the Romans first became interested in it owing to the conquests of Julius Caesar. Early geographers called the British Isles the Pretanic Isles, from a Celtic name which survives in the old Welsh 'Priten' and the Irish 'Cruithin', and which means 'painted' or 'tattooed'; translated into Latin it became *Picti*, the Picts. In the time of Julius Caesar the Celtic tongue was spoken over the greater part, if not the whole, of Britain; but the inhabitants of different regions had not reached the same stage of civilization. Archaeological evidence shows that from perhaps as early as the 6th c. B.C. successive invasions of people of one or other type of Iron Age civilization had penetrated to various parts of the island, where in general a Late Bronze Age culture still prevailed. Julius Caesar found East Kent and parts of Herts and Essex occupied by vigorous Belgic settlers, who had established themselves only about a generation earlier. They had brought with them the use of coinage (see below, § 3) and of the heavy wheeled plough, suited for the cultivation of the stronger soils. Beyond this Belgic area lay a more backward zone, combining elements of Bronze and Iron Age civilizations. Its inhabitants were primitive agriculturists, living in hut villages. The Trinovantes, Iceni, and Regni (see Pl. 12) were its most prominent tribes. To the west of these, in the Cotswolds, Somerset, and Dorset, lived a wealthier and more advanced population, superior to the Belgae in artistic culture, though their inferiors in agricultural skill. To the NE., in Lincolnshire and Yorkshire, a warrior race of a similar civilization were establishing their dominion over a Bronze Age population and founding the kingdom of the Brigantes. A sketch of the state of Britain at this time is contained in R. G. Collingwood, 'Roman Britain' (Oxford, 1936), on which the present article is based.

It is probable that Caesar intended to conquer the island. Britain, to which the power of certain Gaulish chiefs extended, was a refuge for disaffected Gauls and a centre of fanatical Druidism (see under *Gaul*, § 2). His first expedition, in 55 B.C., was in the nature of a reconnaissance, and his ships suffered severely from a storm when at anchor or beached at some point NE. of Dover. The invasion of the following year was a more serious affair. A fleet of 28 warships and 540 transports conveyed the Roman force (including five legions) to a point between Dover and Sandwich. In the operations that followed, Caesar crossed the Thames to attack the Belgic chief Cassivellaunus (who had assumed command of the British forces), captured his principal stronghold at Wheathampstead, and forced him to make terms. Trouble in Gaul obliged Caesar to forgo further operations, and he returned across the Channel. His fleet had again suffered heavy losses from a gale.

§ 2. *The conquest and occupation of Britain*

During the period which followed Caesar's invasion a second migration of Belgic tribes to Britain took place. It was led by Commius, a Gaulish chief who had served Caesar during his invasion, but had since supported the insurrection of Vercingetorix. His followers landed in the neighbourhood of Southampton and spread over central southern England. The energetic king Cunobelinus (Cymbeline), who had inherited the realm of Cassivellaunus and ruled c. A.D. 5–40, extended his dominions over Herts., Kent, Essex, Beds., Bucks., and part of Surrey, and became the most important ruler in south-eastern England. His capital was Camulodunum (Colchester). No further attempt to conquer Britain was made by the Romans until the reign of Claudius, though Augustus was thought by his contemporaries to have intended it and Gaius (Caligula) planned an invasion. In A.D. 43 a force consisting of four legions (the Second, Ninth, Fourteenth, and Twentieth) and auxiliaries, under Aulus Plautius, landed at Rutupiae (Richborough) and addressed itself to the subdual of the realm of Cunobelinus, which had lately passed to his sons. The Romans won a decisive victory on the Medway. Claudius himself subsequently arrived with reinforcements, advanced to Colchester, and received the submission of many tribes. Carātacus, the more energetic of the sons of Cunobelinus, escaped to foment resistance to Rome among the Silures of Wales. The territory of Cunobelinus was made a Roman province, with Colchester as its capital. At least three client kingdoms, of the Iceni to the north of the province, of the Brigantes further north, and of the Regni in W. Sussex, were established. Plautius was left as governor, with orders to subdue the rest of the country. This he set about doing by means of three columns moving respectively N., NW., and W., with their base and supply depot at London. P. Ostōrius Scapula, the successor of Plautius in 47, drew a frontier line across the country, from Seaton in Devonshire, through Bath, Cirencester, High Cross (where it met Watling Street), Leicester, Newark, and Lincoln. This line was the road known as the Fosse, and it was fortified and patrolled to check raids from beyond. Ostorius then established a fortress probably at Gloucester to control concentrations of the Silures; also a *colonia* of veterans at Colchester. In 51 he advanced into central Wales against Caratacus and defeated him. Caratacus fled to Cartimandua, queen of the Brigantes; but Cartimandua had submitted to Rome and surrendered him to the victors, who kept him in honourable captivity. (Caratacus figures as Caratach in Beaumont and Fletcher's 'Bonduca'.) The Silures, though defeated, were not reduced, and although Cartimandua had made her submission, there was a strong anti-Roman faction among her subjects.

In 59 C. Suētōnius Paulīnus, a distinguished military commander, became governor of Britain. He penetrated into N. Wales and reached Anglesey (61), where he was confronted by a body of Druids and their fanatical supporters, whom he put to the sword. But Paulinus was now recalled by grave news. On the death of Prasutagus, king of the Iceni,

Nero decided to abolish his client kingdom and to incorporate the territory in the Roman province. The measure was carried out by the emperor's procurator with great cruelty, and the late king's widow, Boudicca (Boadicea), and her daughters were subjected to gross outrage. A revolt of the Iceni was led by Boudicca and spread to the Trinovantes. Colchester was destroyed. The Ninth Legion under Q. Petillius Ceriālis came to the rescue, but was almost annihilated. London and Verulam were burnt and their inhabitants massacred. It is said that 70,000 perished. Suetonius had hurried back from Wales with his cavalry, but had been unable to save the cities. He rejoined his infantry in the midlands, and with 10,000 men met the far more numerous but unwieldy force of Boudicca and utterly destroyed it. The queen took poison. Ruthless vengeance on the British followed, until the new imperial procurator, Julius Classiciānus, appealed to Nero to replace Suetonius by a more humane governor and to adopt a policy of conciliation; and this was done. The tomb of Classicianus, this benefactor of the British, was found in London and is in the British Museum.

In 71 Q. Petillius Cerialis, the military commander above mentioned, was made governor of Britain. He had fought with distinction, not only against Boudicca but also in quelling the rebellion of Civilis in Gaul. He conquered the greater part of the Brigantian territory and established the Ninth Legion at Eburācum (York), which became the chief Roman military centre in northern England. His successor in 74, Sextus Julius Frontinus (q.v.), subdued the Silures and built a new fortress at Caerleon-on-Usk. Cn. Julius Agricola (q.v.), the father-in-law of Tacitus, who succeeded him in 78, completed his work in Wales, built a fortress at Dēva (Chester), overran the whole of Brigantia, and invaded the lowlands of Scotland, reaching the line of the Forth and the Clyde in 81. In 83 he moved farther north and overcame in 84 the assembled Caledonian forces at the unidentified site of Mount Graupius, probably near Forfar or Brechin. But the military efforts of Rome were required on the Rhine and Danube, Agricola was recalled by Domitian, and at or soon after the end of the 1st c. Scotland was abandoned.

Under Trajan it appears that the frontier was drawn on a line across Britain between the Solway and the Tyne. This policy took its definite form under Hadrian. The frontier or *līmēs*, as fully developed under this emperor, consisted of a military road defended by a rampart and 30-ft. ditch, with seventeen forts at intervals along it, and mile-castles (as they are now called) and signal towers between the forts. The rampart, 73 miles long, was formed by a stone wall eight to ten feet thick and twenty feet high. This gigantic work was built by legionaries, being parcelled out in lengths of 31 to 50 yards to individual 'centuries', as we learn from inscriptions on the Wall. Three legions were employed on it. Part of the western end was built by men of the fleet. The work was designed as an obstacle to raiders from the north, rather than as an actual fortification to resist attack. It was garrisoned by auxiliary regiments in the forts and a patrolling force in addition. Altogether, including its supporting stations, it absorbed two-thirds of the auxiliary troops in Britain.

In 140–2, under Antoninus Pius, the governor, Q. Lollius Urbicus, advanced once more to the line of the Forth and Clyde and built across the peninsula a wall and ditch, 37 miles long, of much less elaborate construction. The wall was of turf and clay, with forts two miles apart, but without intermediate towers. Together with a transplantation of natives, it formed part of a scheme for holding the Lowlands in subjection. About the year 180, under the emperor Commodus, tribes from the north swept over it and destroyed a Roman force. The rising was suppressed in 184, but before the end of the century the Antonine Wall, having proved useless, was abandoned. In the last years of the century the governor, Clōdius Albīnus, declared himself emperor, and, taking troops from Britain, crossed to Gaul, where he was defeated by Septimius Sevērus in 197 and committed suicide. His withdrawal of troops from Hadrian's Wall gave the barbarian tribes their opportunity: great stretches of the Wall were systematically wrecked by them, and the destruction of Roman fortresses extended to York and Chester. The Wall and fortresses were repaired by Severus, a lengthy process which lasted from 197 to 208; and Severus then in person conducted a punitive expedition into Scotland, almost reaching, it is said, its northern extremity. He died at York, worn out with his labours, in 211. For the greater part of a century after this Roman Britain enjoyed security and nothing of moment occurred.

Early in the reign of Diocletian (284–305) Saxon and Frankish pirates became troublesome in the Channel Seas. Carausius, a native of the Low Countries, was appointed to the command of the fleet, the *Classis Britannica*, which had been maintained in the Channel since the 1st c.

He dealt successfully with the pirates, but improperly retained the booty. His arrest and execution were ordered. Thereupon he crossed to Britain and declared himself emperor, with Britain and part of Gaul as an independent empire (286 or 287). Maximian, the colleague of Diocletian, attacked him, but was defeated at sea, and Carausius was recognized as one of the emperors. His government of Britain was efficient and successful. But his recognition had been a measure dictated only by expediency. In 296 Constantius, who had been appointed Caesar by Diocletian, moved against Allectus, the murderer and successor of Carausius, defeated, and slew him. Constantius repaired Hadrian's Wall, which the northern tribes had taken advantage of this struggle again partially to destroy. He also erected forts on the 'Saxon Shore' (from the Wash to Portsmouth) as a protection against raiders, and also on the west coast (against incursions of the Scots of Ireland). In the course of a successful punitive war against the tribes of Scotland, Constantius died at York in 306 and was succeeded as Caesar by his son Constantine (q.v.), who was with him in Britain. From the time of the reign of Constans, who succeeded Constantine in 337, trouble with Picts, Scots, Saxons, and Franks became increasingly serious. In 368 Britain was attacked on three sides (the Wall, the W. coast, and the SE.), and the country was overrun by barbarians. The emperor, Valentinian, sent a strong force to Britain under Theodosius, a Spaniard and a capable military commander. Theodosius drove out the invaders and once more repaired the Wall. It was under his administration that the name of Augusta was given to London; but this official name never became current among the people. In 383, when Gratian had succeeded his father Valentinian, Magnus Maximus, a Spaniard holding high command in Britain, claimed the empire of the west, and crossed to Gaul, taking with him the best troops from Britain. Hadrian's Wall now finally succumbed to the northern tribes and was never restored. Its remains to-day are an impressive witness to the thoroughness and resolution of the Romans. In 395 the emperor Theodosius, son of the Theodosius above referred to, declared his son Honorius emperor of the west, and left his general, Stilicho, as regent of Britain. If we may trust the laudatory poems of Claudian, Stilicho had by the end of the century freed Britain from the invasions of Picts, Scots, and Saxons; but it is probable that the Roman hold of the country north of

the Vale of York was never recovered. In 401 or 402 Stilicho withdrew troops from Britain for the Gothic war. The remaining garrison was inadequate, but Rome itself was in danger from Alaric, and Honorius was unable to send help; he left the tribal authorities to do the best they could for themselves against invaders. The rest of the story is obscure. There may have been a temporary re-occupation by Rome, but Roman government appears in any case to have come to an end before 429. The traces of it are chiefly seen to-day in Hadrian's Wall, the Roman roads, and the cities that the Romans founded.

§ 3. *Britain under the Romans*

One of the most prominent features of the Roman occupation is that under it properly planned cities, an essential element of Roman civilization, were built in a country where previously there had been nothing better than shapeless clusters of huts. The process was a gradual one, but by the end of the 1st c. there were a number of such cities, tribal capitals such as Venta Belgarum (Winchester), Noviomagus (Chichester), Corinium (Cirencester), Durnovaria (Dorchester), or *coloniae* such as Camulodunum (Colchester), Glēvum (Gloucester), Lindum (Lincoln), and Eburācum (York). According to their general plan, these cities had their streets laid out at right angles, a forum (q.v.) in the centre, a basilica or town hall, and public baths. The cities were (then or later) surrounded with walls, and an amphitheatre outside the walls provided for the amusement of the citizens. Aquae Sulis (Bath) was a luxurious health-resort, and Londinium, which became the capital at an unknown date before the time of the Antonines, was from the first important as a commercial centre and military depot.

The occupation of the bulk of the people was agriculture. Those engaged in it lived in villages or villas. The latter were isolated farm-houses, romanized in architecture and arrangements. They were occupied by wealthy landowners or well-to-do farmers, and they included quarters for the labourers of the farm. They appear to have flourished and increased in numbers till the middle of the 4th c., when their defenceless condition exposed them to the inroads of the barbarians. Traces of some 500 of them have been found.

While the delicate Celtic art of the pre-Roman period was ousted by the coarser art of the Roman empire, industry developed under the occupation, and produced to an increasing extent pottery, ironmongery, and in general everything needed for everyday romanized life. Mineral deposits, especially lead and iron, were actively worked. The production of woollen cloth was developed. By the end of the 2nd c. little was imported except wine and oil. Exports included cattle, iron, hides, and slaves. Whether there was a surplus of wheat for export is uncertain.

Roman roads in Britain were at first built for military purposes during the conquest. The system (so far as it has been traced) ultimately extended to some 5,000 miles of metalled roads. It radiated from London and was apparently designed to meet military and official requirements, that is rapid communication between fortresses, *coloniae*, and tribal capitals. It was supplemented by roads of less solid construction to meet the needs of local traffic. See also *Roads*.

Coinage had been introduced by Belgic immigrants. After their settlement coins began to be struck in the island. The coins were imitations of those of Belgic tribes of northern Gaul, which in turn were debased imitations of the gold stater of Philip II of Macedon. By the time of Cunobelinus a tendency had set in to imitate contemporary Roman models; and this became the prevailing style of coinage in SE. Britain before the Roman conquest. Subsequently Roman coins were introduced, and also imitated. In the late 3rd c., when the coinage of the empire was in disorder, Carausius, and later Constantine I, opened an official mint in Britain.

The Roman occupation did not deeply affect religion in Britain. The conquest put an end to the Druids (see under *Gaul*, § 2), whose fanatical nationalistic organization was a source of danger to the Romans. But the remaining religious system of the Britons, an easy polytheism, consisting generally of local cults, met with no hostility from the conquerors, who required in addition only official participation in the imperial cult. Indeed this polytheism harmonized and to some extent blended with that of the Romans; and there was some identification of Roman gods (especially Mars) with Celtic deities. Gradually the latter became predominant in Roman Britain. Eastern religions, such as the worship of Mithras (who had his temples on the Wall), Isis, and Serapis, were introduced, but their devotees belonged principally to the army. The date of the introduction of Christianity in the island is uncertain; it may be placed with probability in the 2nd c., and it became prominent early in the 4th c., when Alban of Verulam suffered martyrdom, and British bishops attended the Council of Arles.

There is a vivid reconstruction of life in Britain towards the end of the Roman occupation in some of the chapters of Kipling's 'Puck of Pook's Hill'.

Britoma′rtis (said by the epitomizer Sōlinus to be a Cretan word, meaning 'sweet maid'), a Cretan goddess, probably of fertility, sometimes identified with the Greek Artemis (q.v.). Like her she bore the name Dictynna (perhaps from δίκτυον, a fishing net), a title explained by the legend that Minos (q.v.) loved her, and that running away from him she leapt over a cliff into the sea, was caught in fishermen's nets, and rescued by Artemis. According to another story she fled to Aegina, where, still pursued by Minos, she escaped under the protection of Artemis, and came to be worshipped under the name of Aphaia, the patron goddess of the island. Dictynna may be from Dicte (q.v.)

Bro′mius (*Bromios*), a name of Bacchus (see *Dionysus*), signifying 'noisy', 'boisterous', from βρέμειν, to roar.

Bro′ntēs, see *Cyclopes.*

Brundi′sium or BRUNDU′SIUM, a harbour on the Adriatic coast of Italy (the modern Brindisi), of importance as the starting-point for the crossing to Greece, Epirus, and other eastern countries. The Via Appia (q.v.) connected it with Rome. The Via Egnatia, starting from Dyrrhachium on the opposite coast of the Adriatic, led to Byzantium. It was from Brundisium that Cicero and Ovid set out on their respective exiles, and it is a journey to Brundisium that Horace describes in Satire I. v. Lucan in the 'Pharsalia' (q.v.) relates Pompey's departure from the same port, and Tacitus (Ann. iii. 1), the arrival there of Agrippina bringing home the ashes of Germanicus.

Brū′tus, or *De Clāris Ōrātōribus,* a treatise by Cicero on eminent orators, written about 45 B.C.

It purports to record a recent conversation between Cicero, M. Junius Brutus, and Atticus (qq.v.), in which Cicero, after a short discourse on Greek eloquence, reviews the long series of Roman orators from Brutus the liberator, but more particularly from Cethēgus, consul in 204 B.C., 'the marrow of persuasion' according to Ennius, to his own times, giving a brief notice of each. A few of the most eminent orators, especially Crassus, Antonius, Q. Scaevola, and Hortensius (qq.v.), are discussed at greater length; and Cicero adds some interesting information about himself, his early life and training as an orator, and gradual rise to the highest position.

Brū'tus, LŪCIUS JŪNIUS, according to Roman tradition, the nephew of Tarquinius Superbus, king of Rome (see *Rome*, § 2). He assumed the disguise of idiocy to escape the fate of his brother, who had been put to death by their uncle. On the occasion of the outrage on Lucretia (q.v.), he led the rising against the Tarquins and liberated the city. He was one of the first two Roman consuls. He is said to have put to death his own sons, who attempted to restore the Tarquins.

Brū'tus, MARCUS JŪNIUS (78?–42 B.C.), son of a half-sister of Cato of Utica (q.v.), an ardent supporter of republican principles, and an idealist rather than a practical statesman. He married Porcia, daughter of Cato. In the Civil War of 49 he joined the Pompeians, but was pardoned after Pharsālus by Caesar, who made him governor of Cisalpine Gaul in 46 and praetor in 44. Nevertheless, from honest and unselfish conviction, Brutus joined the conspiracy for the assassination of Caesar. It is related that Caesar gave up the struggle against his murderers when he saw Brutus among them, exclaiming 'καὶ σύ, τέκνον!' or 'Et tu, Brute!' After the assassination Brutus went to the East, seized Macedonia, and with Cassius prepared to resist the triumvirs. Antony and Octavian marched against them and confronted them at Philippi (q.v.). Cassius took his own life after the first (inconclusive) engagement; Brutus killed himself after his defeat a fortnight later in the second engagement (42). The tragedy of Brutus is vividly depicted in Shakespeare's 'Julius Caesar'.

Another side of Brutus's character, known to us from Cicero's correspondence, is brought out in his financial dealings with the people of Salamis in Cyprus. He lent money to the town at 48 per cent. interest, and was prepared to go to any length to recover the debt. On one occasion his agents shut several prominent Salaminians in the senate-house and kept them there without food, until some died. When Cicero, as governor of Cilicia, refused material aid for the recovery of the debt, Brutus was much aggrieved.

Būce'phalus (*Boukephalos*), the horse of Alexander the Great. Plutarch relates that when first offered to Philip of Macedon for sale, it was found so wild and unmanageable that Philip ordered it to be sent back. But Alexander, observing that it shied at its own shadow, turned its head to the sun, then caressed and soothed it, and finally mounted and mastered it. When he dismounted his father said, kissing him, 'O son, thou must needs have a

realm that is meet for thee, for Macedon will not hold thee'. Bucephalus carried Alexander in his eastern campaigns and a strong mutual affection grew up between horse and rider. Bucephalus died in India, when thirty years old, and Alexander founded the city of Bucephala in northern India in his horse's honour.

Bucolic or PASTORAL poetry, that is to say poetry concerned with the life and loves of herdsmen, had its origin in Sicily, where it was a national type of song, and was said to have been created by the legendary Daphnis (q.v.). It was developed by Theocritus (q.v.), and practised after him by Bion and Moschus, and later by Virgil (qq.v.).

Budaeus, see *Texts and Studies*, § 10.

Bulla, see *Clothing*, § 6.

Burial and Cremation. The method of disposal of the dead varied among the Greeks at different times. In the prehistoric age known as Mycenaean, it was the custom to bury the bodies. In the Homeric poems, the bodies are burnt on a pyre. In historical times it appears that both methods were practised. There are references to burial in the Greek dramatic poets. On the other hand urns survive containing the calcined remains of the dead. It was customary to place a coin in the dead person's mouth as a fee to Charon for his service as ferryman. Greek tombs were usually placed on the sides of roads leading from the city. The funeral monument was usually a slab (*stēlē*) or column, or simply a mound, with an inscription for identifying the dead. At a later period it became the custom to add laudatory verses.

At Rome also both methods of disposal were practised, as appears from the Twelve Tables (q.v.); but cremation gradually became prevalent (except notably with the Cornelian gens, which adhered to burial). The ashes of the more wealthy were generally placed in an urn underneath a monument by the side of one of the great roads leading from Rome. Urns of the poorer classes were placed in a joint tomb, called *columbārium*, containing numerous niches.

Bury, J. B., see *Historians (Modern)*.

Būsi'ris (*Bousiris*), according to Greek mythology a son of Poseidon and king of Egypt. To avert drought it was his custom, on the advice of a seer (by name Phrasios or ⌐hrasios), to sacrifice strangers to Zeus. The seer was his first victim. When Heracles came to Egypt in his quest for the apples of the Hesperides, he allowed himself to be led to the altar, but then broke loose and slew Busiris and his following. See also *Isocrates*.

Byzantine Age of Greek Literature, a term applied to the period from the closing of the Athenian schools by Justinian in A.D. 529 to the fall of Constantinople in 1453. (Sometimes, but less conveniently, it is reckoned as beginning in A.D. 330, the date of the founding of Constantinople.) The period produced few Greek writers of importance. Greek literature had come under various foreign influences, Roman, Eastern, Christian, and had lost much of its original distinctive character. Nevertheless the age rendered an important service in the preservation and transmission of classical works. Its writers, apart from theologians, were much occupied with lexicons and literary commentaries, and with the explanation and emendation of old texts. History continued to be written (see *Anna Comnena*; also legal commentaries. There was much copying of old MSS. The preservation of so much of the old Greek writers as we possess is due to the enlightenment of such eminent ecclesiastics as PHŌTIUS (patriarch 857–886), an industrious lexicographer and good literary critic, and his pupil ARETHAS (archbishop of Caesarea c. 907–32), whose copy of Plato, discovered in a neglected heap of volumes on the floor of the library at Patmos, is now in the Bodleian. See also *Procopius, Suidas, Texts and Studies*, § 4 (for Tzetzes and Eustathius), and *Anthologies*.

Byza'ntium (*Būzantion*), a city on the European shore at the mouth of the Thracian Bosporus (q.v.), the site of the future Constantinople, a position of great importance as commanding the entrance to the Euxine. It was first established by Megarian colonists (c. 657 B.C.). It stood opposite to Chalcedon, which, it is said, was founded first, and the choice of the western position was due to the Delphic oracle, which bade the Megarians place the new city opposite the 'city of the blind men', owing to the superior advantages of the European shore. With the spread of the Persian empire in the 6th c. B.C. it came under the Persian yoke, then alternately under Spartan and Athenian dominion in the 5th and 4th cc., and, after revolting from the second Athenian League in 357, enjoyed a position of independence in the second half of the 4th and in the 3rd c. and became a federate ally of Rome at the time of the Third Macedonian War. It suffered severely from its barbarian neighbours (Thracians, in the mid 3rd c., and Celts, who were particularly aggres-

sive), and paid them huge sums in blackmail, recompensing itself from tolls of the straits, which involved it in a war with Rhodes. It subsequently passed into the Roman empire, and was chosen by Constantine (q.v.) for his new capital (A.D. 330).

C

Cabī'ri (*Kabeiroi*), gods of fertility, worshipped in Asia Minor, and especially at Samothrace; also in parts of northern Greece and in Boeotia. They were also regarded as protectors from dangers, especially those of the sea.

Cā'cus, in Roman legend, a monster or brigand who lived in a cave on the Aventine (see *Rome*, § 1). As Hercules was driving home the cattle of Geryon (see *Heracles*), he rested at the site of the future Rome. Cacus stole some of the cattle and drew them into his cave, tail foremost so as to escape discovery. Hercules departed without perceiving the theft; but the lowing of his other oxen was answered by those in the cave. Hercules then attacked Cacus, slew him, and recovered his cattle. Cacus was probably an ancient Roman deity, perhaps a fire-god.

Cadmē'a (*Kadmeia*), the citadel of Thebes, named after Cadmus (q.v.). It was treacherously seized by Phoebidas the Spartan c. 382 B.C. (see *Sparta*, § 4) and recovered by the bold stroke of Pelopidas (q.v.) with Athenian support.

Ca'dmus (*Kadmos*), (1) in Greek mythology, son of Agenor (king of Tyre), brother of Europa and uncle of Minos (qq.v.), and consequently connected by legend with Phoenicia and Crete. When Zeus carried off Europa, Agenor sent Cadmus to seek her. By the advice of the Delphic oracle Cadmus after a time abandoned the search; he was told to follow a cow which he should meet and found a city where it first lay down. The cow led him to the site of Thebes, where Cadmus founded the Cadmea, the citadel of the future city. Here he sent his companions to fetch water from a spring for sacrifice; a dragon guarding the spring killed the companions and was then destroyed by Cadmus. By Athene's instruction, he sowed the dragon's teeth, and from them armed warriors sprang up. These he set fighting by throwing a stone among them, and they killed each other until only five survived (perhaps the origin of the proverbial 'Cadmean Victory', Hdt. i. 166). These five, the Sparti (*Spartoi*, 'sown men'), helped to build the Cadmea and were the ancestors of the noble families of Thebes. Cadmus married Harmonia, daughter of Ares and Aphrodite, and gave her as wedding present a necklace, the work of Hephaestus, a beautiful but unlucky jewel, which subsequently proved the source of many misfortunes (see *Amphiaraus*, *Alcmaeon*). Their daughters were Ino, Semele (qq.v.), Autonoë (who married Aristaeus and became mother of Actaeon, qq.v.) and Agāvē, the mother of Penthĕūs (see *Bacchae*). Cadmus and Harmonia after a time retired to Illyria, and there were turned into serpents and carried to Elysium. Cadmus is said to have civilized the Boeotians and to have taught them the use of letters. Here the myth is a reflection of historical fact, for the Greek alphabet is largely derived from Phoenician script.

(2) Cadmus of Miletus, see *Logographi* (1).

Caeci′lius Stā′tius (*c.* 219–*c.* 166 B.C.), a Gaul from northern Italy, brought to Rome as a slave and subsequently manumitted. He was a friend of Ennius and the chief comic dramatist of his day; indeed he was ranked first of all Roman comic writers by Sedigitus (see *Comedy*, § 5). He came in point of time and also, it would seem from the little we know of it, in the qualities of his work, between Plautus and Terence. Many of his titles are identical with titles of Menander's plays. Gellius (N.A. II. xxiii) has an elaborate comparison between passages in a play of Menander and in its adaptation by Caecilius. For the anecdote about Caecilius and Terence, see *Terence*.

Cae′lius Rū′fus, MARCUS, son of a banker at Puteoli, was a pupil and friend of Cicero, whose correspondence contains a number of letters from the young man. He was clever, vivacious, unprincipled, and unstable. He joined Catiline for a time, supplanted Catullus as lover of Clodia, was accused by her of an attempt to poison her, and was defended by Cicero. He became a distinguished orator in the courts, and in the Civil War joined the cause of Caesar. As praetor in 48 B.C. he advanced subversive proposals for the abolition of debt and rent, and headed with Milo (q.v.) a rising against Caesar in S. Italy. This was suppressed and Caelius was killed.

Cae′sar, GĀIUS JŪLIUS, was born probably in 102 B.C. (Mommsen's date; the traditional date is 100), and was assassinated on the 15th March 44 B.C. He was, with the possible exception of Lucretius and one or two others (see *Birthplaces*), the only great classical writer actually born in Rome. He belonged to a family claiming royal descent, but his sympathies were not with the aristocratic party. He was nephew (by the marriage of his aunt) of Marius, and husband of Cornēlia, Cinna's daughter, whom he refused to divorce at Sulla's bidding, a refusal that nearly cost him his head. He fled to Bithȳnia, and either then or on a subsequent voyage to Rhodes to study rhetoric, is said to have been taken by pirates, who were amused by his confident bearing and his threat to have them crucified. Having regained his liberty, he manned some ships, captured the pirates, recovered his ransom, and carried out his threat. In the second Mithridatic War (83–81) he first distinguished himself as a soldier at the siege of Mitylene. In 80 he became prominent among those who opposed the Sullan settlement. But it was not till 68 that he became quaestor in Spain. He was aedile in 65 and nearly ruined himself by the gladiatorial shows and public buildings with which he endeavoured to secure popularity. He supported Catiline's candidature for the consulship and was suspected of being privy to his conspiracy. In 63 he was elected praetor for the year 62, and, to the disgust of the aristocrats, *pontifex maximus* (q.v.) as well. His propraetorship in Spain was highly successful and incidentally enabled him to clear off his debts. Returning to Rome in 60 he made a compact with Pompey and Crassus (the 'first triumvirate') by which Caesar was to be consul in 59 and the requirements of the other two were satisfied; Pompey married Caesar's daughter, Julia. From 58 to 49 Caesar was proconsul in Gaul and Illyricum, conducting the wonderful series of campaigns described in his Commentaries (q.v.), by which he not only carried the Roman dominion to the Atlantic and the English Channel, but established his own reputation as a great general and attached to himself a devoted army. The compact with Pompey and Crassus had been renewed at Luca in 56; but the death of Crassus in 53 and the estrangement of Pompey from Caesar following the death of Julia in 54 put an end to the league. The opposition of Pompey and the Senate to Caesar's plans for retaining office, and the intention of his enemies to prosecute him as soon as he relinquished it, brought matters to a head. Early in 49, Caesar at the head of the 13th Legion crossed the Rubicon into Italy to enforce his demands, and launched the first Civil War. His success was rapid. Pompey was outmanœuvred and driven from Italy, and Caesar became master of Rome almost without a blow. He showed a politic clemency to the defeated, in strong contrast with the action of earlier Roman leaders. In the same year (49), by a brief and brilliant campaign he forced the surrender of the Pompeian army in Spain, where it held a strong position at Ilerda. In 48 Caesar followed Pompey to Épirus, finally defeated him at Pharsālus, and pursued him to Egypt, to find he had been murdered. After some months of dalliance with Cleopatra (q.v.), Caesar passed to Syria and Asia Minor, where his easy defeat of Pharnacēs at Zēla in 47 was the occasion of his well-known message to Rome 'Veni, vidi, vici'. After a brief stay in Rome he was called upon to face Cato and the other members of the senatorial party supported by Juba in Africa. These he defeated with great slaughter at Thapsus in 46. His last campaign was in Spain, against the sons of Pompey and the survivors of Thapsus; it was closed by the victory of Munda (45). Less than a year later, in the midst of uncompleted schemes for the reorganization of Rome and the empire, he was assassinated by a band of those whom his measures had offended, led by M. Brutus and C. Cassius whom he had pardoned after Pharsalus. His amazing energy had already done much, in the brief intervals of his campaigns, to found a new régime. Pharsalus had made him an autocrat and he had used his power to re-establish order, to restore the economic situation, to extend the franchise of the provincials, to regulate taxation, and to reform the calendar. He had other projects, such as that of codifying the law and establishing a public library. His measures showed breadth of view and were conceived on a popular basis, but were carried out with a contempt of republican institutions which was in part the cause of his assassination. But Rome had outgrown her ancient constitution, and his murder was a foolish crime, as Dante judged when he placed Brutus and Cassius in the lowest circle of the Inferno

(Canto xxxiv). For Caesar combined pre-eminently the qualities of statesmanship and generalship, discernment, determination, promptitude, and clemency.

His 'Commentaries' (q.v.) on the Gallic War and the unfinished three books on the Civil War are his only extant works. The former, unadorned, straightforward, and detached, are at once military narratives of surpassing interest and a skilfully concealed justification of the author's actions. They were probably written in the winter of 52–51. They contain no argument or comment, but allow events to tell their own tale in his favour, with perhaps an omission here and there where the facts would serve his opponents. The 'Civil War' is rather more of a political pamphlet. The impassive calm and restraint of the narratives are occasionally relieved with a human touch or a flash of sardonic humour.

The Eighth Book of the Gallic War is a continuation by A. Hirtius. Other continuations of the story of his wars are the 'Bellum Africum' on Caesar's conflict with Cato and Juba, and the 'Bellum Alexandrīnum' and 'Bellum Hispāniense' on those campaigns. The authorship of these is uncertain.

Caesar found time for some minor works which have not survived: a treatise on grammar ('De Analogia') written during a journey across the Alps; an astronomical work ('De Astris'); and two books of 'Anticatōnēs' in reply to Cicero's panegyric of Cato. Caesar was an orator of the severe Attic school, simple and restrained in style; Cicero in his 'Brutus' paid a high tribute to the elegance and dignity of his speeches. We have lives of Caesar by Plutarch and Suetonius. According to the tradition recorded by the latter he was tall, pale, with black keen eyes and full lips, and scrupulous about his appearance. He had by Cleopatra a son, Caesarion (q.v.).

Caesar, RELATIONS BY MARRIAGE OF.

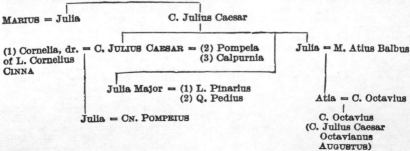

Caesa'rion (*Caesariŏ* or *Caesariŏn*), the son of Julius Caesar and Cleopatra (q.v.). He was put to death by order of Octavian.

Cae'sius Bassus, a friend of Persius, commended by Quintilian as a lyric poet. His works are lost.

Caesū'ra, see *Metre*, § 2.

Ca'lceus, see *Clothing*, § 5.

Ca'lchas (*Kalchās*), a seer who accompanied the Greek host to Troy. See *Iphigenia* and *Iliad*.

Calendar and measure of time.

§ 1. *The Greek Calendar*

The Greek civil year consisted normally of twelve lunar months, alternately of 30 and 29 days, making up a total of 354 days. In certain years, on the basis at first of a cycle of eight years, later of a cycle of 19 years (the cycle devised by the astronomer Metŏn), an additional month was from time to time (not according to any rigid system) intercalated, to maintain correspondence with the solar year. At Athens during the 5th c. two distinct systems of dating were in force concurrently: (1) the civil year, reckoned by lunar months, beginning normally with the first new moon after the summer solstice, but occasionally with the new moon before the summer solstice, and occasionally with the second new moon after the summer solstice, according to the effect of the addition or non-addition of intercalary months. It is found to begin as early as June 20 and as late as August 15 (Meritt, 'The Athenian Calendar', 1928). The names of the months were in general taken from those of festivals held in them, the derivations of the latter being in some cases uncertain; they were as follows:

Hecatombaiŏn (in which the hecatombs were offered), roughly July.

Metageitniŏn, roughly August.

Boēdromiŏn, roughly September.

Pyanepsiŏn, roughly October.

Maimactēriŏn (from the festival of Zeus Maimactēs, 'the boisterous'), roughly November.

Poseideŏn, roughly December.

Gamēliŏn (the time of weddings), roughly January.

Anthestēriŏn (from the 'Festival of Flowers'), roughly February.

Elaphēboliŏn ('deer-hunting', the month known in other parts of Greece as *Artemisiŏn*), roughly March.

Mūnychiŏn (from the festival of the Munychian Artemis), roughly April.

Thargēliŏn, roughly May.

Scirophoriŏn, roughly June.

The intercalary month was generally, but not always, a second Poseideon. The civil year was named for chronological purposes, at Athens after the chief archon, at Sparta after the first ephor. (2) The 'Bouleutic' year, or the year during which the Boule held office. This year under the constitution of Cleisthenes (q.v.) was divided into ten prytanies of 36 or 37 days each, so that over a period of time the senatorial years averaged 365¼ days. This year began about a week after the summer solstice. Most of the dates found in inscriptions of the 5th c. are stated according to this calendar by the number of the prytany, the year being named after the first Secretary of the Boule of that year.

At some date about the end of the 5th c. the 'Bouleutic' year was brought into conformity with the civil year, and thereafter the year is named for all purposes after the chief archon. The historian Timaeus (q.v.) first adopted the practice of dating events with reference to Olympiads (see *Festivals*, § 1), beginning from 776 B.C. But Olympiads were never used for ordinary purposes.

Practically every Greek city had its own calendar. The Macedonian calendar is also of importance, as it came to be universally used in the East (e.g. by Josephus). Years were generally dated in Greek cities after magistrates or priests who held office. In Hellenistic kingdoms regnal years (i.e. the first, second, third, &c. year of such a king) were made use of, or fixed eras. This last was a very important innovation. The most notable of these eras is the Seleucid, from 312 B.C., which is used, e.g., in Maccabees. Many eastern cities also adopted fixed eras, usually dating from their acquisition of freedom.

§ 2. *Greek seasons and divisions of the day*

Some use of the constellations was made for reckoning the seasons. Thus the summer (θέρος) was sometimes regarded as the six months from the morning rising of the Pleiades to their morning setting (May–November); and the morning rising of Arcturus (September) was generally recognized as the beginning of autumn (ἐξ ἦρος εἰς Ἀρκτοῦρον, Soph. O.T. 1137). Sirius (*Seirios*) the Dog-star, setting with the sun in August, marked the period of the greatest heat.

The day from sunrise to sunset, whatever its length, was divided into twelve equal hours. For astronomical purposes the gnomon, a vertical rod on a horizontal plane, was borrowed from the Chaldaeans, and by the length of the shadow it threw enabled mid-day and the various hours to be determined, as also the solstices and the equinoxes. But this was not in general use. The astronomer Meton in the 5th c. was the first to erect one at Athens (on the Pnyx). An instrument of immemorial antiquity for measuring time, the *clepsydra* or water-clock (see below, § 4), was employed in Greece.

§ 3. *The Roman Calendar*

According to tradition, the year under Romulus included ten months, containing a number of days variously stated, but most commonly as 304. It began on 1 March. It is thought probable that this ten-month calendar omitted the period from mid-winter to spring, as being for a primitive agricultural community the dead part of the year, when there was nothing for the husbandman to do but rest and therefore no occasion for a calendar to regulate his labours. Numa Pompilius is said to have added the months of January and February, making a year of twelve months (four of 31 days, seven of 29, February of 28), a total of 355 days; and this was supplemented by intercalary periods to bring it into accord with the solar year. Caesar, on the advice of the mathematician Sōsigenēs, reformed the calendar, making the normal year consist of 365 days (seven months of 31 days, four of 30, one of 28, as in the modern calendar), and adding an intercalary day every fourth year.

In the Roman months (which probably in remote antiquity accorded with the period of the moon) the first day was called the Kalends (*Kalendae*), a name originally indicating the day of the new moon, and connected with the verb *calo* 'to proclaim', since on this day the priest would proclaim the dates for the various special days of the month. The fifteenth day in the four 31-day months of the old calendar (March, May, July, October) and the thirteenth day in all the others was called the Ides (*Īdūs*), a name indicating originally the day of the full moon. The eighth (or according to the Roman method of inclusive reckoning, the ninth) day before the Ides, that is to say the seventh or fifth day of the month, was called the Nones (*Nōnae*). The days in between were denoted by reckoning backwards from the Nones, Ides, or Kalends that next succeeded. But in this reckoning the first and last days of the series were both included: a.d. (*ante diem*) V Kal. Jun. (the fifth, or as we should say the fourth, day before 1 June) was the designation of 28 May. Days were marked in the calendar F, C,

or N, according as they were *fasti*, days on which the court of the praetor urbanus was open for business (*fas est jus dicere*); *comitiālēs*, days on which meetings of the *comitia* might be held (if they were in fact held the praetor's court was closed); *nefasti*, days on which neither was the court open nor might the *comitia* meet, probably because such days were devoted to purification or to worship of the dead and the powers of the nether world. It appears that only 36 days were *fasti* until Caesar increased their number, 184 were *comitiales* and 55 *nefasti*. The calendar further contained certain days marked NP, probably signifying *nefas fēriae publicae*, i.e. that the days were *nefasti* on account of a public festival; EN, for *diēs endotercīsus* or *intercīsus*, days that were partly *fasti* partly *nefasti*. Three exceptional days were marked to indicate that legal business could be carried on after certain religious requirements had been disposed of; these were known as *diēs fīssi*. See also *Nundinae*. There was a tradition that the calendar, showing the days which were *fasti*, was first published in 304 B.C., when Cn. Flavius, a clerk of Appius Claudius the censor (q.v.), posted it up in the Forum. But this tradition was questioned by Cicero (ad Att. VI. i. 8), who pointed out that the XII Tables already showed the calendar, with court days marked for general information. Flavius must therefore have published the calendar, or an account of the principles on which it was constructed, in book form.

The years were denoted by the names of the consuls holding office in each, an inconvenient method which was practically useless for very early dates. At the end of the republican period the date of the founding of the city was finally established by the researches of Varro, Nepos, and Atticus (qq.v), on the basis of certain eclipses, as having occurred in the year corresponding with 753 B.C., and this was adopted as a point of departure for chronology (A.U.C., *ab urbe condita* or *anno urbis conditae*; Livy's work was called 'Ab urbe condita'), but not for practical purposes. Under the empire the consuls continued to be used for dating side by side with the regnal years of emperors and many local eras. The method of reckoning by *indictions* dates from the reign of Constantine and continued to be used through the Middle Ages. The indiction was a fiscal period of fifteen years, at the beginning of which the Roman emperor fixed the valuation on which the property-tax was to be assessed during that period. It was instituted by Constantine in A.D. 313 and reckoned from 1 Sept. 312.

§ 4. *Roman divisions of the day*

In the early republican period there were no means of reckoning time except by sunrise, sunset, and midday. Midday was announced at Rome by an officer of the consuls, when he first spied the sun from the senate house appearing between the Rostra and the Graecostasis (a platform raised above the Comitium). The first sundial, imported from Sicily, was erected at Rome in 263 B.C. A dial corrected for the latitude of Rome was substituted in 164 B.C. The *clepsydra* or water-clock, which was in use in Greece, was introduced by Scipio Nāsica in 158 B.C. It is described by Vitruvius (q.v.) and measured time by the flow of water through a small aperture into a cistern; the water as it rose in this cistern raised a float connected by a rope and counterpoise with a drum, which in turn operated a pointer. Each day from sunrise to sunset, and each night from sunset to sunrise, was divided into twelve *hōrae*; these *horae* consequently varied in length with the season. The Romans when they spoke of 'the first hour' meant as a rule the point of time when the first *hora* from sunrise was completed. The nights were further divided into four *vigiliae* or watches, a term evidently of military origin.

Ca'liga, see *Clothing*, § 5.

Cali'gula, GĀIUS CAESAR, Roman emperor A.D. 37–41, son of Germanicus and Agrippina (see *Julio-Claudian Family*). His true name was Gaius Caesar, but, spending his childhood in the Roman camp and wearing the soldiers' boot (*caliga*), he received from the soldiers the nickname 'Caligula'. See *Rome*, § 10. The story that he proposed to make his favourite horse, 'Incitātus', consul, besides providing it with a retinue of slaves and a luxurious stable, is in Suetonius.

Calli'cratēs (*Kallikratēs*), see *Temples*, § 1, and *Parthenon*.

Calli'machus (*Kallimachos*), born in Cyrene about 310 B.C., a learned critic and poet, who, if he was never head of the Alexandrian Library (as some think that he was), was evidently connected with it and was an industrious bibliographer. For his chief work in this capacity see *Texts and Studies*, § 2. As a poet he wrote in a variety of forms. His 'Hymns' in hexameters and elegiacs, to Zeus, Apollo, Artemis, &c., have survived. He was especially eminent as a writer of epigrams (of which we have sixty-four), some of them epitaphs, others expressions of personal emotion or little sketches of lover's troubles. His beautiful epigram (II) on

his friend Heraclitus of Halicarnassus has been made familiar to us by William Cory's translation 'They told me, Heraclitus, they told me you were dead'. Catullus translated his 'Lock of Berenice' (q.v.), and Ovid drew on him in his 'Ibis' and 'Fasti'. Fragments of his 'Aitia' ('origins' of local religious tradition, in elegiacs) and his 'Iamboi' (in which he assumes the character of Hipponax (q.v.), the satirical poet, restored to life) have been discovered in papyri at Oxyrhynchus. We also have part of his 'Hecale', a short epic on a minor incident in the story of Theseus (q.v.). There was a vigorous literary feud between Callimachus and Apollonius Rhodius (q.v.). In contrast to the latter, he preferred to compose short poems, and his is the proverbial saying, μέγα βιβλίον μέγα κακόν.

Calli'nus (*Kallinos*), of Ephesus, an early Greek elegiac poet, of uncertain date, perhaps of the 7th c. B.C. Only a few fragments of his work survive. He is the first poet known to have written in elegiacs.

Calli'opē (*Kalliopē*), see *Muses*. Orpheus (q.v.) was said to be her son.

Calli'rhŏē (*Kallirhŏē*), see *Alcmaeon*.

Calli'sthenēs (*Kallisthenēs*), a nephew and pupil of Aristotle. He collaborated with his uncle in the preparation of a complete list of victors at the Pythian games from the earliest times. He joined the expedition of Alexander the Great (q.v., § 6) as the historian of his campaigns, and was put to death in 327 B.C. as being privy to a plot against him. To a pseudo-Callisthenes was attributed a fabulous narrative of the exploits of Alexander (see the article under the latter's name, § 10, and also *Julius Valerius*). Landor has an 'Imaginary Conversation' between Callisthenes and Aristotle.

Calli'sto (*Kallistō*), in Greek mythology, a nymph in the train of Artemis (q.v.); she was loved by Zeus and became mother of Arcas, the legendary ancestor of the Arcadians. Artemis (or Hera) in wrath changed her into a she-bear; and in this form she wandered about until her son, now grown up, met her when out hunting and would have killed her with his spear. But Zeus turned both into constellations, Ursa Major (the Great Bear) and Arctophylax (see *Arcturus*). (H. J. Rose, 'Handbook of Greek Literature', remarks that star-myths such as this rarely date from earlier than Alexandrian times.)

Calli'stratus (*Kallistratos*), an eloquent Athenian orator and able statesman of the

4th c. B.C., the organizer of the second Athenian Confederacy (see *Athens*, § 6). He came into popular disfavour when the Thebans took Ōrōpus from Athens in 366, and, although acquitted in this matter, was condemned to death and went into exile after a raid by Alexander of Pherae on the Piraeus (362). Some years later he returned to Athens, but the anger of the Athenians was unabated, and he was put to death.

Calpu′rnius Si′culus, Tītus, a Roman author of eclogues, who probably flourished in the reign of Nero. It is uncertain whether the name 'Siculus' signifies that he was a Sicilian or was given because he imitated the Sicilian pastoral of Theocritus. Of the eleven eclogues attributed to him in the surviving manuscripts, the last four are probably by a later hand (perhaps Nemesiānus, a poet of the later part of the 3rd c. A.D.). The remaining seven are pleasant poems, showing the strong influence of Virgil, and are the only attempt at pastoral in the early post-Augustan empire. Ecl. I, on the dawn of a new Golden Age (the hope of the early days of Nero's reign), resembles Virgil's Fourth Eclogue; Ecl. II is an amoebaean contest between a shepherd and a gardener, resembling Virgil's Seventh Eclogue. In Ecl. III Lycidas tells his remorse for having ill-treated his sweetheart. In Ecl. IV Corydon and Amyntas sing the praises of the young emperor. Their patron Meliboeus (perhaps intended for Seneca) is asked to lay their lines before his majesty, for Corydon (perhaps the author) is poor and humble. Ecl. V is a didactic poem on the rearing of sheep and goats. Ecl. VI is a dispute between two shepherds about the poetic merits of two other swains. In Ecl. VII Corydon, who has been to Rome, describes a display by the emperor of all kinds of wild beasts in the Circus.

Calpurnius helped to carry on the tradition of pastoral writing to the Renaissance. His eclogues were printed at Venice in 1472. See also *Laus Pisonis*.

Ca′lvus, Gāīus Līcinīus (82–47 B.C.), son of the annalist Licinius Macer, was a poet celebrated in his day and an eloquent barrister. He was a friend of Catullus, and the 'salaputtium disertum' of Poem 53. Catullus addressed to him the beautiful lines of consolation (Poem 96) on the death of his wife. His works, none of which survive, included an epyllion on Io (q.v.).

Ca′lydon (*Kaludōn*), a town in Aetōlia, connected with the story of Meleager (q.v.).

Calydō′nian Boar, see *Meleager*.

Caly′pso (*Kalupsō*), in Greek mythology, a goddess, daughter of Atlas (q.v.). See *Odyssey*.

Cambȳ′sēs, see *Persian Wars* and *Egypt*.

Camē′nae, meaning 'foretellers', in the old Italian religion were water-nymphs, who had the power of prophecy. They had a sacred spring outside the Porta Capēna at Rome, dedicated according to tradition by King Numa, from which the Vestals drew the water for their rites. They were identified (first by Livius Andronicus, q.v.) with the Greek Muses.

Cami′lla, in the 'Aeneid', a maiden-warrior, ally of Turnus. When her father Metabus was driven from Privernum, of which he was tyrant, he carried the baby-girl with him. Pursued by the Volscians and stopped by the flooded Amasēnus, he tied the child to his spear, flung it across the river, and then swam across. She was so swift-footed that she could run over a field of corn without bending the blades. For her death see under *Aeneid* (Bk. XI).

Cami′llus, Marcus Fūrius, a great Roman statesman and general, who flourished in the early part of the 4th c. B.C. According to legend he was the conqueror of Veii, went into exile on a charge of having appropriated some of the booty of that city, was recalled and drove the Gauls under Brennus out of Rome, conquered the Volsci and the Aequi, quelled the civil strife at the time of the Licinian Rogations (see *Rome*, § 3), and once more defeated an invasion of Gauls. He was five times dictator, and a reform of the Roman military organization is attributed to him. There is a life of him by Plutarch.

Camp, Roman, see *Castra*.

Campā′nia, a territory in Italy S. of Latium, of exceptional fertility, where many of the wealthy Romans had their villas. It included the towns of Capua, Neapolis (Naples), and Pompeii. See Pl. 10.

Ca′mpus Ma′rtius, at Rome, an open space NW. of the ancient city, the exercise ground of early Roman armies. It was dedicated to Mars. It was also the place of assembly of the citizens in their civil capacity for purposes of election, e.g. the *comitia centuriata* (q.v.). Buildings were gradually erected on it (private houses rarely till the time of the empire), and in 220 B.C. the censor C. Flaminius constructed there the Circus that bore his name. Later, in 55 B.C., Pompey built close to this the first stone theatre of Rome. See Pl. 14.

Candau′lēs, see *Gyges*.

Canē′phorī (*Kanēphoroi*, 'basket-bearers'), maidens of noble families at Athens who carried on their heads at the Panathenaea (see *Festivals*, § 3) baskets containing sacred implements. Their graceful attitude made them a favourite subject for sculptors, and figures representing them were sometimes used as Caryatids (q.v.) to support the entablature of a temple.

Cāni′dia, the witch of Horace's Epodes iii, v, and xvii; and Satires I. viii, II. i, and II. viii.

Cani′nius Re′bilus (quantity of the *e* unknown), GĀIUS, appointed consul by Caesar at noon on the last day of the year 45 B.C. for the remainder of the day (the consul having died whose term of office terminated that evening). His was the consulship in which, according to Cicero's bitter jest, no one breakfasted and the consul never slept.

Ca′nnae, in Āpūlia, the scene of a great defeat of the Romans by Hannibal in 216 B.C. The consul Aemilius Paullus and (it is said) 50,000 Romans were killed in the battle.

Canons (*kanones*), see *Texts and Studies*, § 2.

Ca′ntica, in Roman plays, the portions that were sung or recited to musical accompaniment. See *Comedy*, § 5 *ad fin.* and *Plautus*.

Cantō′res Euphoriō′nis, see *Euphorion*.

Cape′lla, MARTIĀNUS, see *Martianus Capella*.

Ca′pitō, GĀIUS ATĒIUS, an eminent jurist of the time of Augustus and Tiberius. See *Labeo*.

Ca′pitol (*Capitōlium*), the SW. summit of the Capitoline hill at Rome; it stood NW. of the Palatine, overlooking the Forum (see Pl. 14). On this summit was erected the great temple of Jupiter Optimus Maximus (the special guardian of the city) and his companions Juno and Minerva. There sacrifice was offered by magistrates on taking office, and by victorious generals in a triumph (q.v.). On the Capitol also stood the ancient sanctuary of Jupiter Feretrius (see under *Jupiter*). For the other summit of the Capitoline Hill, see *Arx*. For the legend of the saving of the Capitol from the Gauls by the sacred geese, see *Manlius Capitolinus*.

Capitōli′nus, JULIUS, see *Historia Augusta*.

Capitōli′nus, MARCUS MANLIUS, see *Manlius Capitolinus*.

Capti′vī, a comedy of sentiment by Plautus, and one of his most interesting plays. There are no female characters. The prologue is probably by a later hand.

One of the sons of Hēgio has been taken prisoner by the Ēlēans; the other was kidnapped when a child by a slave and has not since been heard of. Some Eleans have now been taken prisoners of war and Hegio has purchased two of these, Philocratēs and his slave Tyndarus, in the hope of recovering by their means his captive son. The slave is to be sent to Elis to negotiate the exchange. From devotion to Philocrates, Tyndarus assumes the name and dress of his master, while Philocrates passes as his slave. Thus it is Philocrates who is released and sent to Elis, while Tyndarus remains in captivity. But the trick is revealed unintentionally by an Elean fellow-prisoner, and Hegio, believing that he has been fooled, and disappointed of his hope of recovering his son, sends Tyndarus, loaded with irons, to work in the quarries. Presently Philocrates returns bringing with him not only the captive son of Hegio, but also the slave who stole his infant boy. From the revelations of the slave it appears that this child had been sold to the father of Philocrates, and by a stroke of dramatic irony is the very Tyndarus whom Hegio has cruelly maltreated.

Ca′pua, the chief city of Campania, famous for its luxury and wealth. It went over to Hannibal after the battle of Cannae, but was recaptured by Rome in 211 and severely punished: its leading citizens were beheaded, the others exiled, and its territory became the property of the Roman State.

Carā′tacus or CARA′CTACUS, see *Britain*, § 2.

Carau′sius, MARCUS AURĒLIUS MAUSAEUS, see *Britain*, § 2.

Cari′stia, see *Parentalia*.

Ca′rmen Saeculā′re, a poem by Horace, written in 17 B.C. by command of Augustus for the celebration of the Secular Games (see *Ludi*, § 2). It is an invocation, in sapphic stanzas (see *Metre*, § 5), of the various gods of the Roman pantheon to grant their blessings to the State. It was sung on the Palatine on June 3, the third day of the celebrations, by 27 girls and 27 boys, whose parents were still alive. An inscription describing the ceremony survives (see *Epigraphy*, § 10). (The number 27, or thrice nine, is repeatedly met with both in Greek and Roman ritual; it was regarded as especially lucky.)

Carme'ntis or CARME'NTA, in Roman religion, a deity possessing the power of prophecy, probably originally a water-spirit, but early associated with child-birth. She was celebrated on the 11th and 15th January. One of the gates of Rome, S. of the Capitol, bore her name (*Porta Carmentālis*). She is sometimes spoken of in the plural, as the *Carmentēs*. In mythology she is the mother of Evander (q.v.), and accompanied him from Arcadia to Italy.

Carnē'a (*Karneia*), see *Festivals*, § 6.

Carne'adēs (*Karneadēs*) of Cyrene (214–129 B.C.), a Greek philosopher of the New Academy (see *Academy*), who held, in opposition to the dogmatism of the Stoics and Epicureans, that certain knowledge was unattainable, but that, in its absence, conclusions of various degrees of proba-bility could be formed, and that these supply a guide to conduct. Cicero was an adherent of his views. For the visit of Carneades to Rome in 155 B.C. see *Philosophy*, § 2.

Ca'rrhae, in the northern part of Meso-potamia, the scene of the defeat of M. Licinius Crassus (q.v.) by the Parthians in 53 B.C.

Carthage (*Carthāgō*, Gk. *Karchēdōn*), a colony founded, perhaps in the 9th c. B.C., by Phoenicians from Tyre, and occupy-ing a strong strategic position on a pen-insula in the centre of the northern coast of Africa, near the modern Tunis. For the legend of its founding see under *Dido*. Byrsa, the name of the citadel of Carthage, signifying 'fortress' in Phoe-nician and 'hide' in Greek, may be the origin of the story of the territory en-closed by strips of oxhide. Carthage gradually took the lead among the inde-pendent Phoenician cities of N. Africa (Utica was her chief rival), founded numer-ous colonies on African soil, and exercised direct rule over the native agricultural population of a considerable region. Her constitution (a controversial subject) ap-pears to have been mainly aristocratic, the government being in the hands of two chief magistrates and a senate. The chief magistrates, originally perhaps judges, held the highest executive functions, and had also frequently, especially in older times, the chief command in war. Hence, because of the similarity of functions, the Greeks called them βασιλεῖς, the Romans *reges*, or more accurately and appropriately *praetores*. The Romanized form of their name was *suffetes*. Though an annual office, this magistracy between 520 and 300 B.C. seems to have been in the power first of the house of Mago, and then of the house of Hanno. But the rule of the aristocracy was not unqualified, and Aris-totle praised the equilibrium of aristo-cratic and democratic elements that he found there. Carthage was pre-eminently a commercial State, carrying on trade all along the coasts of the Mediterranean. Her merchants dealt in Tyrian purple, gold, ivory, slaves, grain, pottery, bronze, perfumes, and textiles. They reached the Cassiterides (q.v.) or Tin Islands, and Guinea on the Atlantic coast of Africa. They founded settlements in Spain, Sar-dinia, and Sicily, and came into conflict at an early date with the Greeks, driving the Phocaeans out of Corsica c. 540 B.C. and carrying on with them in Sicily a struggle that lasted until the Punic Wars (q.v.). With the Roman republic they made commercial treaties, by which Rome was restricted from interfering with Cartha-ginian trade. The earliest of these dated, according to Polybius, from the first year of the Roman republic. These treaties governed the relations of Rome and Car-thage until their great struggle of the 3rd c. B.C. The Carthaginians were essentially a maritime folk, and their powerful navy was manned by their citizens. For their army on the contrary they relied on mer-cenaries, employing Libyans, Ibērians, Ligurians, Sardinians, and Corsicans. Plutarch (De rep. ger., iii. 799) describes them as sour and morose, servile to their rulers, harsh to their subjects, lacking fortitude in danger, ungoverned in anger, obstinate, without elegance or urbanity. Their religion was oriental in its origin, their chief gods being Melkart, Astartē, and Baal-Hammon; but Libyan and Greek deities were gradually introduced. In spite of the Greek influence, their religious rites retained a barbarous charac-ter and included human sacrifices. Agri-culture was highly developed in Cartha-ginian territory. Olive oil, fruit, and to some extent wine, besides corn, were the chief products. A treatise on agriculture by the Carthaginian Magō was translated into Latin by order of the Roman Senate.

For the later history of Carthage, see *Punic Wars*, and *Colonization*, § 7.

Caryă'tids (*Karyātides*), female statues in long drapery used instead of columns to support the entablature of a temple (q.v.). The word means 'maidens of Caryae', a town in Laconia, where, at the annual festival of Artemis, it was customary for bands of girls to perform ritual dances. In these they sometimes took the attitude in which they are represented in the statues. The best-known examples of Caryatids are the six that supported the entablature of the southern portico of the Erechtheum on the Acropolis of Athens. One of these has been removed to the British Museum.

Casaubon, see *Texts and Studies,* § 10.

Ca'sina, a comedy by Plautus, adapted from a play by Diphilus (see *Comedy,* § 4). An old gentleman of Athens and his son have both taken a fancy to Casina, a slave-girl who has been rescued from exposure as a baby and brought up in their household. The father wants to have her married to his bailiff, the son to his own attendant, Chalinus; while the wife of the old man, aware of her husband's scheme, intrigues to defeat it. Recourse to lot favours the father, but at the wedding the bailiff is fobbed off with Chalinus dressed as a bride, and the bailiff and the old man moreover get a good beating. Casina, according to the epilogue, is found to be a free-born Athenian, and is married to the old man's son.

Cassander, see *Macedonia,* § 2.

Cassa'ndra (*Kassandrā* or *Kăsandrā*), daughter of Priam and Hecuba (qq.v.). She was loved by Apollo (q.v.) but resisted him. In consequence, the god rendered useless the gift of prophecy that he had bestowed on her, by causing her prophecies never to be believed. She is a sombre figure in Greek legend, foreseeing the doom of Troy, but foretelling it to deaf ears. When the city fell, she was dragged from the image of Athena where she had taken refuge and violated by Ajax (q.v.), son of Oïleus. To expiate this sacrilege, the Opuntian Locrians, his people, were obliged to send yearly a number of noble maidens to serve as slaves in Athena's temple at Troy. If caught by the inhabitants before reaching the temple, they were executed. (This practice, of which there is evidence in inscriptions, lasted until early in our era.) Cassandra fell to the lot of Agamemnon (q.v.), and was killed with him by Clytemnestra.

Cassiodo'rus (*Flāvius Cassiodŏrus Magnus Aurēlius Senātōr*) (*c.* A.D. 480–575), born at Scylacēum (Squillace) in S. Italy, the son of a praetorian prefect, was himself appointed quaestor to Theodoric, and consul in 514. Under the three successors of Theodoric he was virtually prime minister. He spent the latter part of his long life on his estate in the south, where he founded two monasteries. He wrote a 'History of the Goths' (known to us only in abridgement) and other historical works, and published twelve books of his official writings under the title 'Variae', and a lengthy commentary on the Psalms. His most important work was a treatise

on religious and profane education entitled 'Institūtiōnēs Divīnarum et Saeculārium Litterārum', in two books, of which the first was intended particularly for the guidance of monks. He exhorted them to the careful copying of manuscripts and traced the limits within which corrections were permissible. His 'De Orthographia', written when he was 93, gives them directions on correct spelling and punctuation. (See *Texts and Studies,* § 6).

Cassiopeia (pron. -ē'ia) (*Kassiopeia* or *Kassiepeia*), see *Perseus.*

Cassite'rides, the name given by the Greeks to a group of islands where, according to rumour, tin was found. It appears to be still a matter of dispute whether κασσίτερος (tin) is derived from Cassiterides, or Cassiterides from κασσίτερος. It was known in the Mediterranean that tin came from the Atlantic coast, but owing to the Carthaginian control of the Straits of Gibraltar and the secretiveness of merchants, the precise localities where it was got were unknown. The Cassiterides were thought to be to the north of Galicia or in mid-Atlantic, or were confused with the Canaries, or were located in Belerium (Cornwall). A certain P. Crassus (not definitely identified, perhaps the governor of Further Spain, 96–93 B.C.) was said by Strabo to have found his way there, and the place that he took for the Cassiterides was probably the coast of Cornwall, though this may not have been identical with the Cassiterides of earlier legend, the source whence the Phoenicians and other early traders got the metal, which was perhaps Galicia in Spain. There is evidence that tin was worked in Cornwall from very early times; but it appears to have been undersold in the Mediterranean market during the early Roman empire by cheaper tin from Spain.

Ca'ssius, GAĪus, one of the murderers of Julius Caesar, was an energetic soldier who showed his capacity as one of the lieutenants of Crassus at Carrhae (53 B.C.), where he extricated a division of the Roman army from the disaster. He fought against Caesar at Pharsālus (48), but was pardoned by him after the battle and made praetor. Nevertheless Cassius was one of the leaders of the conspiracy against Caesar. After Caesar's death, Cassius went to Syria, secured the province, and joined Brutus at Smyrna. He met his death at Philippi.

Ca'ssius Di'o (*Dĭō*) **Coccēiā'nus,** generally known as DIO(N) CASSIUS (*c.* A.D. 150–235), of Nicaea in Bīthȳnia, who became consul at Rome and governor of Africa and of Dalmatia, was author of a 'Roman History' in Greek, in eighty books, of which twenty-six survive. It covered the period from the foundation of the city to A.D. 229. Of the surviving books (36–60 and 79) the former deal with the years 68 B.C.–A.D. 54. Dio spent twenty-two years preparing the work. He was a diligent student of earlier historians, whom he treats with discrimination, but does not appear to have carried out independent research. We owe to him the only narrative we possess of the invasion of Britain by Claudius. There is an epitome of Bks. 1–21 by Zonāras (12th c.) and of Bks. 36–end by Xiphilinos (11th c.).

Cassivellau′nus, see *Britain*, § 1.

Castā′lia (*Kastāliā*), in Greek mythology, a nymph who, when pursued by Apollo, threw herself into a spring on Mt. Parnassus. The spring was held sacred to Apollo and the Muses. It is situated a little to the NE. of Delphi, and may still be seen, 'a pool of clear, cold water, lying deep in its rock-cut basin at the foot of the sheer cliff' (Frazer on Pausanias x. viii. 9). The pool is 36 feet long by 10 feet wide, and is fed by subterranean sources.

Ca′stor (*Kastōr*), see *Dioscuri*.

Ca′stra. *Castra*, a Roman camp, was invariably entrenched, and under the republic always of the same form and elaborate arrangement. It was planned out in advance by surveyors (*mensōrēs*), who first marked with a flag the *praetorium* or head-quarters. The camp, as described by Polybius, was a square, each side being about 2,100 feet for a normal army of two legions and auxiliaries (about 12,000 men). It was surrounded by an earthen mound (*agger*) and palisade (*vallum*, a term used also of the mound plus the palisade), for the construction of which each soldier carried stakes in case of necessity. Across the front of the praetorium, which stood midway between the two sides, ran a roadway (*via principālis*) ending in gates on the two sides of the camp and dividing the latter into a larger front portion (*pars antica*), where the legions and their contingents of auxiliaries had their tents, and a smaller portion behind (*pars postica*). In the latter, on either side of the praetorium, were the quarters of the higher officers, those of the *extraordinārii* or picked auxiliary troops, the *forum* or meeting-place and market of the camp, and the *quaestōrium* or paymaster's office. From the front of the praetorium a broad *via praetoria* led to the *porta praetoria* in the front vallum

of the camp. Behind the praetorium another road led to the *porta decumāna* in the back vallum of the camp. There were thus four gates to the camp, one in each of its sides. See Pl. 2c.

In the permanent camps (*castra statīva*), of which many in imperial times were established in conquered territory, the detailed arrangements were different, but the characteristic features remained the same: quadrangular form, division by roads at right angles, four gates, the praetorium midway between the two sides, the forum and quaestorium near it. These camps contained barracks built of permanent materials, and head-quarters sometimes of an imposing appearance, as may be seen in the ruins of the praetorium of Novaesium (Neuss) on the Rhine. The camps of the imperial age are described by Hyginus (q.v.).

Catachrē′sis, the misuse of a term. Quintilian extends it to the adaptation, where a term is wanting, of the term nearest to the meaning, and gives as an example 'equum divina Palladis arte aedificant' (Aen. ii. 16) where 'aedificant' means properly to build a house.

Catale′pton (Gk. 'on a small scale'), sometimes known as CATALECTA, a collection of Latin epigrams and other short poems, perhaps identical with the 'Epigrammata' attributed by Donatus and Servius to Virgil. The author is unknown. A few of the poems may be by Virgil. Among these is an address to Siron's villa, which Virgil occupied for a time.

Catale′xis, CATALE′CTIC. Catalexis is said to take place and a verse or foot is said to be catalectic when a syllable or syllables of the normal rhythm are replaced by a pause of equal duration. For examples see *Metre*, § 2.

Catalogue of Women (*Katalogos Gunaikōn*), a poem in hexameters, of which fragments survive, by Hesiod or an imitator, enumerating the heroines of ancient legend, relating their adventures, and tracing their descendants. The 'Eoeae' (q.v.) is variously thought to be identical with it, or the last part of it.

Ca′taplūs (*Kataplous*), see *Lucian*.

Catēgo′riae, a treatise by Aristotle (q.v., § 3).

Ca′tiline (*Lūcius Sergius Catilīna*), an impoverished patrician, who was praetor in 68 B.C. and in the next year governor of Africa. Dissolute but capable, ruined in reputation as in purse, he saw his only chance in revolution, for which he found supporters among other desperate men.

With these he conspired to effect a general massacre early in 65, but the plot failed. He stood for the consulship in 64 but was defeated. His renewed attempt to secure power in 63 during Cicero's consulship is described under *Cicero*, § 2, where a reference will be found to Cicero's speeches 'In Catilinam'. Catiline fled from Rome in 63, and was defeated and killed near Pistoria in 62. According to Sallust (q.v.) he made a gallant end. Catiline was the subject of a tragedy by Ben Jonson (1611).

Cā'to (*Cătŏ*), MARCUS PORCIUS, 'Cato the Censor' (234–149 B.C.), the son of a farmer of Tusculum, fought in the Second Punic War as private soldier and military tribune under Q. Fabius Maximus (q.v.), and after holding various offices was consul in 195. He had been quaestor in Sicily and Africa, and subsequently praetor in Sardinia; it was probably on the later occasion that he made the acquaintance of Ennius (q.v.). In 184 he held the censorship, the office that made him famous. He applied himself to the reformation of the lax morals of the Roman nobility, and to checking the luxury and extravagance of the wealthy. His ideal was a return to the primitive simplicity of a mainly agricultural State, and he showed a fearless independence and honesty in his attacks on powerful offenders (including the Scipios). He was also strongly opposed to the introduction of Greek culture, and under his influence Greek philosophers and rhetoricians were forbidden to reside at Rome. In his old age, however, he himself studied Greek. Late in life he went as a commissioner to Carthage, and was so impressed by the danger to Rome from her reviving prosperity that he never ceased impressing on the Senate the necessity for her destruction: 'Carthago delenda est'. Jealousy of her agricultural development may have been one of the causes that impelled him. He composed a work on *Origines*, dealing with the rise of the Italian cities (whence the title) and the history of Rome from the time of the kings to 149 B.C., one of the first historical works written in Latin (earlier Roman annalists wrote in Greek), unfortunately lost; also a treatise 'De Agri Cultūra' (q.v.), sometimes known as 'De Re Rustica', which in great part survives. It is the oldest extant literary prose work in the Latin language. Cato was also a successful orator; 150 of his speeches were known to Cicero. The surviving fragments show shrewdness and wit, earnest honesty, and simplicity. To him we owe the phrase 'rem tene verba sequentur'. Cicero makes him the principal interlocutor in his dialogue 'De

Senectūte', There is a life of Cato by Plutarch, who severely censures his meanness, particularly in his practice of selling off his slaves when too old to be remunerative. There is also a short life of Cato attributed to Nepos.

Cā'to (*Cătŏ*), MARCUS PORCIUS 'of Utica' (95–46 B.C.), great-grandson of Cato the Censor (q.v.), a man of unbending character, and absolute integrity, narrow, short-sighted, impervious to reason as to bribery. He was the chief political antagonist of Caesar and the triumvirate, 'the conscience of Rome', 'equally above praise and vituperation' (Livy). We hear of him as voting for the death of Catiline's fellow conspirators when these were arrested by Cicero (q.v.). He was sent on a mission to Cyprus in 58 (at the time when Cicero was banished) in order that he might be got out of the way. In the Civil War he held Sicily in the interest of the Senate and was driven thence by Curio. After the death of Pompey and the battle of Thapsus, he shut himself up in Utica (NW. of Carthage) against the Caesarians, and seeing that his cause was hopeless took his own life. It is said that he spent the last night of his life reading Plato's 'Phaedo'. For Cicero's panegyric on him see *Cicero*, § 4. He is one of the heroes of Lucan's 'Pharsalia' (q.v.). Dante devotes to him a great part of the first canto of his 'Purgatorio'. Cato's last stand and death at Utica form, in part, the subject of Addison's tragedy 'Cato' (1713).

Catō Mājor de Senectūte, see *De Senectute*.

Cats, see *Pets*.

Catu'llus, GĀIUS VALĔRIUS (*c*. 84–*c*. 54 B.C.), was born at Verōna, then a small frontier town, of a well-to-do family, and came about 62 B.C. to Rome. He had access to the refined and profligate society of the day, and became attached to the lady whom he celebrated under the name of Lesbia, Clodia (q.v.), the sister of Cicero's enemy Publius Clodius (q.v.) and wife of Q. Metellus Celer, consul in 60 B.C. His love for her, followed, as a result of her infidelity, by rifts and reconciliations, deepening reproaches, and finally fierce revolt and rupture, inspired some of his most beautiful and of his most bitter poems. After their final separation Catullus in 57 travelled to Asia in the suite of the propraetor C. Memmius, the patron of Lucretius. It was probably in the course of this voyage that he wrote the lament, the famous 'Ave atque vale' poem (101), for his brother buried in the Troad, whose tomb he now visited; the charming poem of spring (46) 'Jam ver egelidos refert tepores'; and on his return (with Helvius Cinna in a yacht which he celebrated in poem 4) the lines to Sirmio (31) expressive of the joy and gratitude of home-coming. The date of his death is not known with certainty, but he died very young, at the age of thirty or thirty-three at most. The melancholy little poem (38) addressed to Cornificius from his sick-bed is perhaps his last work. His poems are mostly short pieces, in hendecasyllables or other lyric forms (iambics, scazons, one in glyconics) or in elegiacs. They are varied in subject and in manner, ranging from graceful trifles on some incident of Roman life, an invitation to dinner on the pilferings of a guest, to expressions of warm attachment and sympathy for friends, genial satires, virulent lampoons, and poems of deepest passion. The best-known of them are the sequence relating to Lesbia, beginning with the first intoxication of love and the tender playfulness of the lines on Lesbia's sparrow, and ending with poignant cries of suffering (such as the lines 'O di, si vestrumst misereri ...' in Poem 76) and venomous insults flung at his unfaithful mistress. The political lampoons of Catullus (especially 29 and 57) reflect, in some measure, the attitude of the aristocratic society of Rome towards Caesar and his associates. Caesar was stung by the attacks, but was reconciled with Catullus in the end. Poem 51, 'Ille mi par esse deo videtur' is a translation of an extant poem by Sappho. All these short poems are strikingly sincere and vivid, and perfect in form. In a different category falls the beautiful short hymn to Diana (Poem 34). The longer poems of Catullus include an epithalamium (61) for the marriage of a friend named Mallius; another wedding-song (62); a strange poem (63) in galliambics on the legend of Attis (a young man is represented as becoming, in a frenzy, an acolyte of the goddess Cybele, undergoing the awful initiation by emasculation; then realizing with vain regrets the loss of his former life); the 'Coma Berenices' (on the legend of the lock of Berenice, q.v.), translated or imitated from Callimachus; and a poem in hexameters on the marriage of Peleus and Thetis (q.v.), in which a digression on the story of Theseus and Ariadne (q.v.) occupies the greater part. Some of these longer poems show the influence on Catullus of the Alexandrian school.

Catullus before his death may have issued a small group of his poems with a dedication to Nepos, but this is a hypothesis over which the authorities are divided. His literary executor appears to have published all his writings indiscriminately, including for instance the invectives against Caesar, in spite of the reconciliation. Our texts all derive from a single manuscript preserved in Verona, the city of his birth.

Catullus not only adapted the hendecasyllable to a great variety of moods and purposes, but also established in Roman literature a new form, the light, witty, elegant poem, to fill a place between tragedy and epic on the one hand, and comedy and satire on the other. He exerted a wide influence on his Roman successors, on the elegiac poets Tibullus, Propertius, and Ovid, on Horace, and on Martial. In English literature his influence may be traced in the Elizabethan wedding-odes and still more in the Caroline lyrics, notably in Herrick. One of his epithalamia was translated by Ben Jonson in his masque 'Hymenaei'. Meredith's 'Phaethon' in galliambics was modelled on Catullus's 'Attis'. Byron translated Poems 3 ('Lugete o Veneres') and 51 ('Ille mi par esse deo videtur'). Tennyson's lines entitled 'Frater Ave atque Vale' are a tribute to the 'tenderest of Roman poets nineteen hundred years ago'.

Ca'tulus, QUINTUS LUTATIUS, consul in 102 B.C., and the colleague of Marius in the defeat of the Cimbri, wrote epigrams and occasional poems in elegiacs (some of which have survived), and developed the use of this metre at Rome. He also wrote a commentary on his part in the Cimbric War, which was distinguished by its purity of style. It seems to have been a source for Plutarch's life of Marius.

An earlier Catulus (GAIUS LUTATIUS CATULUS) was the victor over the Carthaginians at the sea-battle off the Aegatian Islands in 241 B.C.

Cau'dine Forks (*Furculae Caudinae*), the defile of Caudium in Samnium, where the Roman army in 321 B.C. was obliged to surrender to the Samnites (see *Rome*, § 4).

Cavalry Commander, The (*Hipparchikos*), a treatise attributed to Xenophon (q.v.), written at a time when Athens was at peace, probably about 365 B.C.

Xenophon was deeply interested in cavalry and horses, and had probably at one time belonged to the Athenian cavalry corps. This corps was composed, nominally, of one thousand men, of whom each of the ten tribes was required to furnish one hundred. The whole corps was under two commanders. The treatise purports to be addressed to some one about to hold one of these commands. It includes advice on the selection and training of the recruits, the care of the horses, the choice of subordinate officers, the qualities required of a commander, and his duties both in the ceremonial functions of the cavalry and on active service (including tactics, ruses, &c.).

Ce'bēs (*Kēbēs*), of Thebes, a Pythagorean philosopher who figures in the 'Phaedo' of Plato, and in passages of Lucian. A famous allegorical composition on the life of man, known as the 'Pinax' ('Picture') of Cebes, was attributed to him, but is of much later date. It is based on the Stoic philosophy of the time of the Roman empire.

Cē'crops (*Kēkrops*), a legendary ancestor or first king of the Athenians. He is represented as serpent-shaped below the waist (see *Monsters*) and was said to be earth-born. Attica was sometimes called Cecropia after him (see *Athens*, § 2). For the story of the daughters of Cecrops see *Erechtheus*.

Celae'no (*Kelainō*), one of the Pleiades (q.v.); also a Harpy (q.v.).

Ce'lĕus (*Keleos*), see *Demeter*.

Ce'lsus, AULUS CORNĒLIUS, of whom very little is known, lived under Tiberius. He was an encyclopaedist who wrote in Latin on agriculture, medicine, philosophy, and other subjects. Quintilian calls him 'mediocri vir ingenio'. Of his works only eight books on medicine survive. They are largely based on Hippocrates (q.v.) and other Greek medical authors, but also on contemporary practice. They show humanity and good sense, holding the balance between theory and experience, recommending dissection but discouraging vivisection (of criminals), and propounding sound rules for the maintenance of health. The work begins with an historical introduction in which the prevailing tendencies in medical theory and practice in his own day are discussed. The first two books deal with diet and the general principles of the healing art, the third mainly with fevers, the fourth with internal diseases, the fifth and sixth with external ailments (such as wounds and ulcers), and the last two with surgery, showing that difficult and dangerous operations were undertaken in his day. This was the first classical medical work to be printed (Florence, 1478).

Censors, at Rome, two in number, were elected every five years to take the census of the people and carry out the solemn purification (*lustrum*) which accompanied it. Their period of office was eighteen months, but might be extended. They had a general supervision over the conduct of citizens, and in particular the duty of revising the roll of senators (*legere senatum*), removing those who were unworthy and replacing them by others. They had, moreover, the duty of making contracts for public works and for the farming of taxes, and of letting the State lands. The institution dated from about 440 B.C. Its importance was much reduced by the legislation of Sulla. The emperors used censorial powers for revising the composition of the Senate.

Centaurs (*Kentauroi*), a fabulous race of beings shaped like a horse with the body of a man in place of the horse's neck and head (see *Monsters*), said to be descended from Ixion (q.v.) and Nephelē ('Cloud'). They dwelt in Thessaly. When their neighbours the Lapithae were holding a feast for the wedding of their king, Pirithöus, with Hippodamia, the Centaurs, whom they had invited, tried to carry off Hippodamia and other women. A battle resulted, in which the Centaurs were defeated, and were driven from their haunts about Mt. Pelion.

Centu'mviri, at Rome, a board of 105 members (elected annually, three from each of the thirty-five tribes), increased under the empire to at least 180, who formed the jury in trials relating to property and inheritance and other kindred questions. They were divided into four courts, which usually sat separately, but might sit as a single body in important suits. See *Law* (*Roman*), § 2.

Ce'phalas (*Kephalās*), see *Anthologies*.

Ce'phalus (*Kephalos*). (1) In Greek mythology, the husband of Procris, daughter of Erechtheus (q.v.). Eos (q.v.) fell in love with him, causing dissension between husband and wife. Artemis (or Minos) gave Procris a hound called Lailaps ('Storm') which was fated to catch whatever it pursued, and a spear that never missed its mark. These Procris gave to Cephalus and a reconciliation followed. (A difficulty seemed likely to arise when the marvellous hound was set to hunt an uncatchable fox which was devastating Theban territory; but Zeus evaded it by turning both into stone.) Procris was still jealous and, hidden in a bush, watched her husband when he was hunting. Cephalus, thinking that he heard an animal stir in the bush, hurled his spear and killed Procris. There is a reference to this legend in the 'Shafalus' and 'Procrus' of Pyramus and Thisbe (Shakespeare, 'Midsummer Night's Dream', v. i). Milton refers to Cephalus as 'the Attic boy' in 'Il Penseroso'.

(2) The old man in Bk. i of Plato's 'Republic', the father of Lysias (q.v.).

Cěphi'sus or CĚPHI'SSUS (*Kēphīsos* or *Kēphīssos*), (1) the chief river in the Athenian plain, rising in Mt. Parnēs, and flowing past Athens a mile to the west. It is usually dry or nearly so in summer. (2) The chief river of Phōcis and Boeotia.

Cerami'cus (*Kerameikos*), probably meaning the Potters' Quarter, at Athens, a region NW. of the Acropolis, partly within partly without the city wall. The portion outside the walls was used as a burial ground. The Agora (q.v.) was included in the inner portion. See Pl. 13a.

Ce'rberus (*Kerberos*), in Greek mythology, a monstrous dog with three (or fifty) heads, offspring of Typhon and Echidna (qq.v.), the watchdog of Hades. See *Monsters* and *Heracles* (*Labours of*).

Ce'rcidas (*Kerkidās*), a Greek poet of uncertain date (probably *c.* 250 B.C.), of whose works only fragments survive. He professed the Cynic philosophy and wrote in lyric metres on ethical subjects in a simple and popular style.

Cercō'pēs (*Kerkōpes*), in Greek mythology, a monkey-like race of men, who tried to steal the weapons of Heracles and for their pains were slung upside down on a pole carried by Heracles across his shoulders. Whereupon their jokes at his hairiness so amused the hero that he let them go. The tale afforded matter for comic treatment in literature and art.

Cereā'lia, see *Ceres*.

Cě'rēs (*Cěrēs*), probably originally an Italian deity representing the generative power of nature. Her first temple at Rome was traditionally founded in consequence of a famine in 496 B.C., and dedicated in 493. Here the cult had a Greek character and the goddess was identified with Demeter (q.v.). The temple was at the foot of the Aventine and was connected closely with the plebs. The *Cereālia* were held in honour of Ceres on April 12–19. At this festival, connected with the growth of the corn, it was the practice to tie burning brands to the tails of foxes and let them loose in the Circus Maximus. Ovid (*Fast.* iv. 681 et seq.) has a tale to account for this curious rite, of which modern scholars offer various explanations. Virgil describes a festval of Ceres in 'Georgics' i. 338–50. Ceres had also an other aspect, as a deity of the earth: after a death, the house of the deceased was purified by means of sacrifice to her.

Cě'tō (*Kētō*), in Greek mythology, daughter of Pontus and Ge and mother of the Graiae and the Gorgons (qq.v.).

Cě'yx (*Kēux*), see *Alcyone*.

Chae'reas (*Chaireās*) **and Calli'rrhŏě** (*Kallirrhoē*), see *Novel*.

Chaeronē'a (*Chairōneia*), in Boeotia, the scene of the defeat of the Thebans and Athenians by Philip (q.v.) of Macedon in 338 B.C. (this was the battle 'fatal to liberty' referred to in Milton's sonnet 'To the Lady Margaret Ley'); also of the defeat of Mithridates by Sulla in 86 B.C. Chaeronea was the birthplace of Plutarch.

Chalcě'don (*Chalkēdōn*), on the Asiatic shore of the Bosporus, see *Colonization*, § 2, and *Byzantium*. Later the capital of the Roman province of Bithȳnia.

Chalci'dic League, formed early in the 4th c. B.C. by the city Olynthus, of towns on the promontory of Chalcidice (q.v.), on the basis of common laws and common citizenship. It spread to other towns in the neighbourhood. The attempt of the Chalcidians to impose membership on certain Greek towns led to the intervention of Sparta and the dissolution of the League (379). What might have been a check on the growth of Macedonian power was thus suppressed. In 364–2 Timotheus (q.v. (2)) acquired some of the Chalcidic towns for Athens, in order to weaken Olynthus, the chief support of Amphipolis. The latter was originally an Athenian colony, lost in the Peloponnesian War, which Athens constantly desired to recover. Chalcidice was finally reduced by Philip of Macedon, and incorporated in his dominions. Olynthus, the last city to hold out, was captured in 348, an Athenian force sent to its relief arriving too late.

Chalci'dicē (*Chalkidikē*), a promontory in Macedonia between the Thermaic and Strymonic Gulfs terminating in three smaller peninsulas. See *Colonization*, § 2, and *Philip of Macedon*, § 2.

Cha'lcis (*Chalkis*), the chief town in Euboea, on its W. coast, and separated from the mainland only by the narrow strait of the Eurīpus. It was subject to Athens during the greater part of the 5th and 4th cc. B.C. See *Colonization*, § 2.

Cha'os, see *Theogony*.

Charactēres, see *Theophrastus*.

Chara'xus (*Charaxos*), see *Sappho*.

Chariclē'a (*Charikleia*) **and Theā'genēs** (*Theāgenēs*), an alternative title of the 'Aethiopica' of Heliodorus; see *Novel*.

Chariot races were held at the Panhellenic festivals in Greece, especially at the Olympian festival, from early times (see *Festivals*, § 2). The chariots resembled those of the heroic age, which carried the warrior and his charioteer, low and rounded in front, open at the back, on low wheels. They were drawn by two horses, one on each side of the pole, by means of a yoke; where four horses were used, the two additional horses were at the sides of the first two, not in front, and drew by means of traces. The Roman racing chariot was similar, except that the board forming the front was higher. Pausanias (vi. 20) describes the elaborate arrangement for starting the chariot races at Olympia, including a mechanical signal which raised a bronze eagle and lowered a bronze dolphin. He also mentions how horses generally shied at a particular point in the course, called Taraxippus ('Disturber of Horses'). Chariot races (*Circenses*) were held at Rome both in republican and imperial times in the Circus Maximus. The chariots might be two-horsed (*bīgae*) or four-horsed (*quadrīgae*). Four or even six chariots competed in a heat, driving up one side of the Circus (which was divided down the centre by a low wall known as the *spina*) and down the other, rounding the *mētae* or conical pillars at each end of the *spina*; seven rounds of the Circus formed a heat.

In republican times the teams belonged to private owners; under the empire to associations of contractors, who were distinguished by four colours, blue, white, red, and green. Domitian added two new colours, the purple and the gold. It is perhaps from this time that six chariots began to compete in a heat. But the number of chariots so competing is not invariable. The two new factions do not seem to have survived Domitian's reign. There was keen partisanship among the public and betting on the colours. Pliny tells how Caecina of Volaterrae, an owner of chariots, had homing swallows, daubed with paint, to announce his victories. In the later empire, by supporting and cheering the factions that were not favoured by the emperor or his officials, the people frequently expressed their disapproval of the Government. Charioteers earned large sums. Dioclès left a fortune of 35 million sesterces (say £290,000). Caligula gave Eutychus, charioteer of the green, 2 million sesterces.

Cha'rites, see *Graces*.

Cha'riton (*Charitōn*), see *Novel*.

Cha'rmidēs, see *Plato*, § 2.

Chā'ron (*Charōn*), in Greek mythology, the ferryman who conveyed the dead in his boat across the Styx to Hades, represented as an old man of squalid aspect.

He received an obol from each passenger for his pains. To pay his fee the dead were buried with a small coin in their mouths. Charon is unknown to Homer. He figures in the 'Frogs' of Aristophanes and in the VIth Aeneid of Virgil. See also *Lucian*. Charon survives (as Charos or Charontas) in modern Greek folklore, rather in the character of Angel of Death than of the ferryman. But the custom of placing a coin in a dead person's mouth prevailed among some of the Greeks until quite recent times (Rennell Rodd, 'Customs and Lore of Modern Greece').

Chā'ron (*Charōn*) of Lampsacus, see *Logographi* (1).

Chary'bdis (*Charubdis*), in Greek legend, a dangerous whirlpool off the coast of Sicily, opposite Scylla (q.v.). The Argo (see *Argonauts*), according to Apollonius Rhodius, sailed between Scylla and Charybdis; and Homer (Od. xii) has a vivid description of the passage of Odysseus between these two perils.

Chei'ron, see *Chiron*.

Che'rsonese (*Chersonēsos*, 'land-island' or peninsula), *Thracian*, the promontory of Thrace (the peninsula of Gallipoli) that runs along the W. side of the Hellespont. It was acquired by Athens in the time of Pisistratus and further colonized by Pericles. It was threatened by Philip of Macedon and this threat was one of the chief grounds of hostility between Athens and Macedonia. The *Tauric Chersonese* in the Euxine is the modern Crimea.

Chersonese, On the, a political speech by Demosthenes. See *Demosthenes* (2), § 5 (f).

Chia'smus (from the form of the Greek letter *chi*), a figure of speech in which the terms of the second of two parallel phrases reverse the order of the corresponding terms in the first; e.g. 'Odit populus Romanus privatam luxuriam, publicam magnificentiam diligit' (Cic. pro Murena, c. 32).

Chi'lon (*Chīlōn*), a Spartan ephor in the 6th c. B.C., who appears to have had an important influence on the policy of his State (see *Sparta*, § 3). He was included among the Seven Sages (q.v.) of Greece.

Chimae'ra (*Chīmairā*), in Greek mythology, a monster with the head of a lion, the body of a goat, and the tail of a dragon, the offspring of Typhon and Echidna (qq.v.). See *Bellerophon* and *Monsters*. According to Virgil she was 'armed with flame'.

The *Flaming Chimaera* is the name given to a patch of land high up in the

Lycian forest near the sea-coast where an undying fire (apparently burning natural gas), breaks up from vents in the ground. There are the ruins of a church, and the place was probably from ancient times the site of a temple to the Spirit of Fire (see D. G. Hogarth, 'Accidents in an Antiquary's Life').

Chi'os (*Chios*), a large Ionian island off the coast of Asia Minor. It claimed to be the birthplace of Homer. It formed part of the first Athenian Confederacy (see *Athens*, § 4), led the revolt of the allies in 412 B.C., and was laid waste by the Athenians. It formed part also of the second Confederacy and again revolted, recovering its independence in 354. The island was famous for its wine and its figs.

Chi'ron (*Cheirōn*), in Greek mythology, a Centaur (q.v.), son of Cronus (q.v.) and Philyrā, a daughter of Oceanus. It was said that Chiron owed his shape, half-man half-horse, to the fact that Cronus, to escape the jealousy of his wife Rhea, had turned himself into a horse. Chiron was wise and just, and learned in music and medicine. He educated some of the most famous of the Greek heroes, such as Asclepius, Jason, and Achilles. When the Centaurs (q.v.) were driven from Mt. Pelion by the Lapithae, they took up their abode in the Peloponnese. There Heracles, pursuing the Erymanthian Boar in Arcadia, was entertained by one of them, named Pholos. When Pholos set wine before Heracles, the neighbouring Centaurs, attracted by the smell, crowded round and a fierce fight ensued. Heracles drove the Centaurs off and one took refuge with Chiron, who was accidentally wounded in the knee by one of Heracles' poisoned arrows, dipped in the blood of the Hydra. To escape from the pain of the wound, he was glad to surrender his immortality to Prometheus and die.

Chi'tōn, see *Clothing*, § 1.

Chla'mys, see *Clothing*, § 1.

Chŏĕ'phoroe (*Chŏĕphoroi*), see *Oresteia*.

Choe'rilus (*Choirilos*). (1) of Athens, see *Tragedy*, § 4; (2) of Samos, see *Epic*, § 1.

Chōlia'mbic, see *Metre*, § 5.

Choral Lyric, poetry written to be sung in chorus, a development of lyric (q.v.) poetry originating in the song and dance with which, from very early times, the Greeks celebrated important occasions. While at first these celebrations appear to have been of the nature of a public religious duty, they later also took the form of professional entertainments to the order of a patron, and poets were commissioned

to write odes for some private occasion, such as a victory at the Games. The development of the choral lyric was the work at first of Dorians at Sparta and is associated with the names of Thaletas, Terpander, Alcman, and Arion (qq.v.). The later great writers of choral lyrics were Sicilians, Ionians or Boeotians—Stesichorus, Ibycus, Simonides, Bacchylides, and Pindar (qq.v.); but the Dorians had made the choral lyric so much their own that it continued to be written in the Dorian dialect. The principal forms of the choral lyric were the *paean*, the *hyporchema*, the *parthenion*, the *heroic hymn*, the *encomion*, and the *dithyramb* (qq.v.).

Choree', see *Metre*, § 1.

Chorē'giā, see *Liturgy*.

Chorē'gus, see *Chorus*.

Chŏ'riamb, see *Metre*, § 1.

Chorodida'skalos, see *Chorus*.

Chŏrogra'phia, see *Pomponius Mela* and *Varro* '*Atacinus*'.

Chŏ'rus (*Chŏros*), in Greece, a band of men who performed songs and dances at a religious festival, and became an essential part in the drama as this evolved (see *Tragedy*, § 2, and *Comedy*, § 2). This part, at first predominant, later became subordinate to that of the actors. The provision of a chorus was regarded as a public service (see *Liturgy*) and the duty of assembling, paying, and equipping them was borne by some wealthy private citizen selected for the purpose (known as the *choregus*), until with the decline of the prosperity of Athens the duty had to be undertaken by the State. The chorus was trained by the poet himself, who was known in this capacity as *chorodidaskalos*. The leader of the chorus was called the *coryphaeus*. The portions of a drama assigned to the chorus might be written partly in iambics (for dialogue), partly in anapaestic measure (chiefly for the entrance and exit of the chorus), but consisted mainly of lyrics (see *Metre*, §§ 2 and 3). The chorus was frequently divided into two semi-choruses, who sang alternate stanzas; but whether particular lines were sung by the whole chorus, by part of it, or by a single voice, is often, in the absence of stage directions, a matter of more or less probable conjecture. See also *Theatre*.

Chremōnidē'an War, see *Athens*, § 8.

Chronica, see *Nepos, Eusebius, Jerome*.

Chroniclers. (1) GREEK, see *Logographi* (1); (2) ROMAN, see under *Annales*.

Chrȳsā'ōr (*Chrūsāōr*, 'Golden Sword'), see *Gorgons*.

Chrȳsē'is (*Chrūsēis*), see *Iliad.*

Chrȳsi'ppus (*Chrūsippos*), see *Stoics.*

Chrȳsolo'ras, MANUEL, see *Texts and Studies,* § 9.

Ci'cerō, MARCUS TULLIUS (106–43 B.C.), a great Roman orator and statesman.

§ 1. *Early life, 106–65* B.C.

Cicero was born at Arpinum in the Volscian mountains (the birthplace likewise of Marius), a city enjoying full Roman citizenship, of a well-to-do family of some local distinction. His father was a Roman knight. Cicero records the influence exerted on him in his youth by the Greek poet Archias, who was then living in Rome. In 89 he saw military service in the Social War. At Rome he studied rhetoric, philosophy under Philō the Academic and Diodotus the Stoic, and law under the Scaevolae (q.v.). In 81, towards the end of the period of disorder caused by the partisans of Marius and Sulla (qq.v.), he made his first extant speech in the law-courts, 'Pro Quinctio' (q.v.), having as his opponent the greatest advocate of the day, Hortensius. In the next year (80), in his speech 'Pro Roscio Amerino' (q.v.), Cicero first showed not only his ability as a pleader but his anti-Sullan sympathies and his courage, for he did not shrink from attacking Sulla's powerful freedman Chrȳsogonus. After this Cicero travelled to Athens and Asia Minor, to improve his health and pursue his study of rhetoric. At Rhodes he received instruction from Molō the rhetorician, who checked his tendency to exuberance, and from Posidonius (q.v.). He married Terentia, a lady of good family, apparently somewhat domineering, perhaps before leaving for Greece in 79. He returned to Rome in 76 and became, with Hortensius and Cotta, one of the three leading Roman advocates. To this period may belong the speech 'Pro Roscio Comoedo' (q.v.; some authorities place it later, in 68), on behalf of his friend the actor Roscius (q.v.) In 75 he was quaestor in Sicily, a magistracy which carried admission to the Senate. In 72 he delivered the speech 'Pro Tullio' on behalf of a certain M. Tullius who was involved in a dispute about property with a neighbour, one of Sulla's veterans. He was retained in 70 by the Sicilians to prosecute C. Verres, who during his governorship of the island had shown appalling rapacity and cruelty. Cicero's first 'Verrine' ('Actio prima in Verrem', preceded by a 'Divinatio in Q. Caecilium', to prevent a collusive action), in which he formulated the charges he intended to prove, was sufficient to force Verres to throw up the case and retire into exile. Cicero then published the five further orations of the 'Actio secunda' against Verres, designed to bring home to the public the evils of the existing predatory system of provincial administration. This year (70) was that of the consulship of Pompey and Crassus, during which they effected the repeal of the Sullan constitution. Cicero, with his liberal sympathies, supported Pompey, and thereafter looked up to him as his political leader. He was now recognized and courted as the chief advocate of the day, for Hortensius (who had been the advocate of Verres) for a time effaced himself. In 66 Cicero was praetor and delivered in public assembly his first political oration, the 'De Lēge Mānīlia' (or 'De Imperio Cn. Pompeii'). In this he defended the proposal of the tribune Manilius to grant Pompey (q.v.) the command against Mithridates. Under the year 69 we have the (incomplete) speech 'Pro Fonteio', in which Cicero defended M. Fonteius on a charge of extortion as governor of Gaul; and the 'Pro A. Caecina', in a case involving subtle legal points connected with inheritance of land.

§ 2. *64–63* B.C. *Cicero's consulship*

In 64 Cicero stood for the consulship. As a *novus homo*, i.e. without dignity of ancestry, he was at a disadvantage, but he was helped by the revelation of the revolutionary inclinations of Catiline (q.v.), one of his rivals in the contest. Cicero was elected with C. Antonius, an associate of Catiline; he won over his colleague by ceding to him the rich province of Macedonia. As consul in 63 he delivered the speeches 'Contra Rullum' or 'De Lēge Agrāria' (q.v.), combating an agrarian proposal designed to give the popular party a manœuvring ground against Pompey (then absent in the East); Cicero's condemnation of it was endorsed by the people and the proposal was rejected. The 'Pro Rabirio' (q.v.) of the same year was in defence of an aged knight charged by the popular party with having killed, thirty-seven years before, the tribune Saturninus. It will be seen that Cicero now takes up the position of a moderate, in opposition to the popular party and Caesar.

In the second half of Cicero's consulship came to light the anarchic conspiracy of the desperate and unscrupulous Catiline and his band of associates. Cicero by his promptitude and firmness defeated the plot. Catiline's renewed candidature for the consulship was rejected, and when the conspirators prepared for military insurrection, Cicero obtained the 'Senatus consultum ultimum', empowering the consuls to take all measures for the protection of the State (Oct. 22). He frustrated Catiline's projected massacre, drove him from the city by his first speech 'In Catilinam' (Nov. 8), exposed the situation to the people in his second speech (Nov. 9), and secured the detection of five leading conspirators in treasonable correspondence with envoys of the Allobroges, and their arrest (Dec. 2–3). In a third oration Cicero explained the new developments to the people. The fourth was delivered in the Senate (Dec. 5) on the question of the punishment of the prisoners. Silănus had proposed the death penalty; Caesar, it appears, perpetual imprisonment in chains. Cicero recommended the former course as more merciful, and Cato also advocated the death penalty. This was voted by the Senate, and Cicero at once had the sentence carried out. The army of Catiline now began to disperse, and the remainder, with their leader, were cut to pieces a month later. The suppression of this anarchist conspiracy was the first of Cicero's two great feats of political leadership; the second, twenty years later, was his supreme attack on Mark Antony. In the midst of the crisis Cicero found himself called upon to defend the consul-elect, L. Mŭrēna, on an ill-timed charge of bribery brought against him by Cato (see Pro Murena).

§ 3. From 62 B.C. to Cicero's banishment in 58

Cicero's defeat of the conspiracy of Catiline made him unduly jubilant. He had rendered a great service to the State, but he injudiciously referred to it on every occasion. The legality of the executions was questioned by the popular party, and it was significant that the tribune Metellus Nĕpos, a lieutenant of Pompey's, refused to allow Cicero to address the people on laying down his office. But Cato saluted him as 'father of his country' (pater patriae), and Cicero, in spite of the coldness of Pompey, tried to secure the latter as leader of his ideal coalition of Senate and equestrian order as constitutional governors of the empire. At the end of 62 Publius Clodius (q.v.) was detected in disguise at the mysteries of the Bona Dea; his attempt to set up an alibi was defeated by the evidence of Cicero, who thereby incurred Clodius's deadly hatred (though in the actual trial the latter was, thanks to bribery, acquitted). Pompey returned to Italy at the end of 62. The jealousy and hostility of the Senate threw him into the arms of Caesar, who returned from Spain in June 60; the 'First Trium-

virate' was formed, and Caesar became consul in 59. During the period immediately preceding this Cicero had made only two speeches that have survived, one on behalf of Publius Sulla ('Pro Sulla', q.v.) and the other on behalf of the poet Archias ('Pro Archia', q.v.), famous for its eloquent disquisition on the glories and benefits of literature.

It appears that Caesar made advances to Cicero with a view to attaching him to the triumvirate. But Cicero could not reconcile himself to Caesar's unconstitutional attitude and stood aloof. He did more; in a speech for C. Antonius (accused of misconduct in his province), Cicero in 59 made some complaint of the evil state of the times. It was immediately after this that Cicero's bitter enemy Clodius was adopted into a plebeian family to qualify him for a tribunate, with a view to keeping Cicero in check. This was Caesar's reaction to Cicero's attitude, for the adoption of Clodius required the consent of the pontifex maximus, viz. Caesar. That Cicero felt the peril of his position is shown by his only surviving speech of this year, 'Pro Flacco', in which he defended Flaccus, one of the praetors in 63 who had effected the arrest of the Catilinarians, on a charge of extortion in his province. In this speech he takes the opportunity to appeal to popular sentiment in his own favour. Caesar, still anxious to give Cicero a means of escape, offered him a commissionership for executing his agrarian law or a position under himself in Gaul. These offers Cicero declined. Thereupon Clodius was allowed to bring in a Bill exiling any one who had put Romans to death without right of appeal—a measure directed against Cicero's execution of the Catilinarians. Cicero had behind him the support of the Senate, the knights, and the country people; but Clodius controlled Rome by gangs of roughs, and behind him stood Caesar with his army. Pompey, in spite of Cicero's fidelity, refused to help him. Cicero bowed to the storm and left Italy (58). Clodius now carried a decree against him by name; his property was confiscated and his magnificent house on the Palatine was destroyed. Cicero first went to Thessalonica, where he was kindly received by Plancius the quaestor. He was utterly crushed and unmanned by his misfortune. But his exile was not prolonged. Clodius became so reckless that he even attacked Pompey and was met with his own weapons, gangs organized by Milo.

§ 4. 57–45 B.C.

Cicero returned with Caesar's consent in 57 and was enthusiastically received. His speeches during the ensuing period arise out of his return, the continued vexations to which he was subjected by Clodius, and the turbulence of the times. In the two speeches 'Post Reditum' (q.v.) he thanked the Senate and the people for his recall; the 'De Doma Sua' and 'De Haruspicum Responso' (qq.v.) dealt with questions relating to the restoration of his house. In 56 he defended P. Sestius ('Pro Sestio'), a tribune who had exerted himself in his behalf, against a charge of rioting brought by Clodius. The speech, largely occupied with Cicero's own services and an attempt to rally the aristocratic party against the triumvirs, contains some of the orator's finest passages. The speech 'In Vatinium' was an attack on a creature of Caesar's who had been a witness against Sestius in the preceding prosecution. The 'Pro Caelio' was a defence of M. Caelius Rufus on a charge of attempted poisoning brought against him by the notorious Clodia, sister of Clodius and the 'Lesbia' of Catullus. The speech contains a fierce attack on Clodia herself. Cicero now showed signs of assailing, with Pompey's support, Caesar's agrarian law of 59. To check this inconvenient alliance, Caesar met the other triumvirs at Luca in 56 and renewed his understanding with them. Cicero was forced to submission, and his humiliation may be seen in his speech of recantation, 'De Prōvinciis Consulāribus' (56), in favour of the prolongation of Caesar's command in Gaul, and in his 'Pro Balbo', in defence of the right of citizenship of a friend of Caesar and Pompey. The 'In Pisōnem' of 55 was a reply to an angry speech by L. Calpurnius Piso when recalled from the governorship of Macedonia at Cicero's instance. In 54 Cicero defended his friend Plancius (referred to above in connexion with Cicero's exile) on a charge of electoral corruption ('Pro Plancio'), and Rabīrius, a partisan of Caesar, on a charge of extortion ('Pro Rabirio Postumo'); also M. Aemilius Scaurus, ex-governor of Sardinia on a charge of extortion (of this speech we have only fragments). The 'Pro Milone' is a written elaboration of the speech which Cicero attempted to deliver in defence of Milo (q.v.) on the charge of killing Clodius in a faction fight in Jan. 52. The death of Clodius gave rise to great turbulence, in the midst of which the trial was held. Cicero's nerve gave way, his speech was a failure, and Milo was found guilty. The amended version, a splendid defence, was sent by Cicero to Milo in his exile. Milo is said to have congratulated himself that it was not delivered, else he would never have known the excellent red mullets of Massilia. In 53 Cicero was

elected to the College of Augurs, and was much gratified by the honour. In 51, owing to the new law regarding provincial governorships, he was reluctantly obliged to accept that of Cilicia. He disliked leaving Rome; b˄t he carried out his new duties honestly and efficiently. He hoped for a triumph in recognition of his success in a small campaign. He returned to find Rome on the brink of the Civil War. He left the city with many of the Senatorial party when Caesar crossed the Rubicon. The withdrawal of Pompey to Epirus left him in the deepest trouble and perplexity. He decided to remain in Italy, and followed Pompey only at a later stage. After Pharsālus (at which he was not present) he returned to Italy. A period of anxious suspense was ended in 47, when Caesar came to Italy and was completely reconciled with Cicero. The latter was impressed by Caesar's clemency and had hopes that he would restore liberty. But Cicero, during the rest of Caesar's life, exerted no political influence. In 46 he delivered the 'Pro Marcello', a speech of effusive thanks to Caesar for his clemency to an exiled Pompeian; in 45 the 'Pro Ligārio' in defence of Q. Ligarius, tried as an enemy of Caesar, a speech whose eloquence is said so to have moved Caesar that he acquitted the accused; and in the same year the 'Pro Rege Dēiotaro', defending the tetrarch of Galatia on a charge of attempted murder of Caesar. Shortly after Cato's death at Utica in 46, Cicero delivered a panegyric (laudātio) on him, which is not extant. It displeased Caesar, who replied to it in a work called Anticato. In 46 Cicero divorced his wife Terentia, and soon after married Publilia, who had been his ward. In 45 his beloved daughter Tullia (q.v.) died, and Cicero was overwhelmed with grief. Publilia offended Cicero by her lack of sympathy, and this second marriage also was ended by divorce.

§ 5. *Philosophical and literary writings*

This is the period of Cicero's devotion to philosophy and literary work. The humiliation which followed the conference of Luca had already turned him in this direction, and he had then (in 55) written the 'De Ōrātōre' (a treatise on rhetoric designed to replace his crude early work on the same subject, 'De Inventiōne', written before he was 25 years old), and the 'De Re Publica' (qq.v.). It appears from certain passages in the 'De Legibus' (q.v.) that he was engaged on this work in 52; he seems then to have discontinued it and returned to it in 46 and the following year. It had not been published before the 'De Divīnātiōne' (q.v.) was written in 44. There is no evidence whether Cicero ever finished the work or published it during his lifetime. Probably in 53 he had written for his son's instruction a little catechism on rhetoric, called 'Partitiōnēs Ōrātōriae'. Between 46 and 44 he wrote the 'Brutus' (q.v.), a history of Roman oratory, the 'Orator' (q.v.), a picture of the accomplished speaker, and other works on rhetoric (an abstract of the 'Topica' of Aristotle, and 'De Optimo Genere Ōrātōrum', a preface to lost translations of the speeches of Aeschines and Demosthenes, 'On the Crown'). In 45 he wrote the 'Consōlātiō' on the deaths of great men, a work (of which fragments survive) occasioned by the death of Tullia; the 'Hortensius' (not extant) in praise of philosophy; the 'Acadēmica' (q.v.) on the evolution of the philosophical doctrines of the Academy; and the 'De Fīnibus Bonorum et Malorum' (q.v.) on the different conceptions of the Chief Good. After these he wrote during 45–44 the five Books of the 'Tusculan Disputations' (q.v.) on the conditions of happiness; the 'De Nātūra Deorum' (q.v.) on the various theological doctrines; the De Fāto (q.v.); the charming essays 'De Senectūte' and 'De Amīcitia' (qq.v.); the 'De Divīnātiōne' (q.v.); and the 'De Officiis' (q.v., 'On Duty') for the edification of his son. Altogether a wonderful output for two or three years.

As a philosopher Cicero claimed to be a follower of the New Academy of Carneades (q.v.), which held that certain knowledge was impossible, and that practical conviction based on probability was the most that could be attained. But while his general attitude was that of the New Academy, he was an eclectic, that is to say he was not dominated by any one school, but picked from among the doctrines of the various Greek schools those which commended themselves to his reason; and in questions of morality he was inclined (e.g. in the 'Tusculan Disputations' and the 'De Officiis') to accept the positive Stoic teaching. He believed in the existence of God, and stood for the freedom of the will against the doctrine of fatalism. His philosophical works have little claim to present original thought. He drew on Greek sources 'supplying little but the words'; but he rendered a great service in the creation of a Latin philosophical vocabulary, in popularizing Greek thought and keeping it alive for the Middle Ages.

§ 6. 44–43 B.C. The Philippics and Cicero's death

After the assassination of Caesar, Cicero came once more into political prominence.

He had hated the tyrant in Caesar if he had liked and admired the man, and he exulted in the retribution. He soon saw the course of duty clear before him and pursued it with energy. Oblivion for the past and restoration of the commonwealth were his aim. It was no longer a contest of factions but a fight for liberty against Antony. The 'Philippics', delivered or published after the first few months of confusion and perplexity, and when the alinement of the forces was becoming clear, are the expression of his policy. The 'First Philippic' (2 Sept. 44 in the Senate), while attacking the policy of Antony, is conciliatory and in favour of peace. The 'Second Philippic' was not a spoken oration, but a pamphlet published in December 44 when Antony was besieging Decimus Brutus in Mutina; it is a fierce invective against the man who had tried to make Caesar king. The 'Third Philippic' (20 Dec.) is an exposition to the Senate of his policy—support of Decimus Brutus and Octavian against Antony. The 'Fifth' (1 Jan. 43) proposed the grant of the powers of propraetor to Octavian. The 'Fourth' and 'Sixth' (19 Dec. 44 and 4 Jan. 43) were addressed to the people in the Forum. Cicero thus took the position of leader of the State, stimulating the consuls to action, and guiding policy. The series of these great speeches continues till the 'Fourteenth Philippic', celebrating the defeat of Antony at Mutina. But the rejoicing was premature. The armies of Lepidus and Pollio declared for Antony, the Second Triumvirate was formed, and the Commonwealth overpowered. Cicero, whose death was reluctantly consented to by Octavian, was murdered by Antony's agents on 7 Dec. 43, and his head and hands were displayed on the rostra (q.v.). Repeatedly faced during his life by the perplexities of the political situation, he died, in fact, for his loyalty to his ideal of liberty. Plutarch relates how Augustus, many years after, finding a work by Cicero in the hands of one of his grand-nephews, observed, after a long perusal of it, 'An eloquent man, my child, and a lover of his country'.

§ 7. Cicero's Letters and his character

The character and life of Cicero are known to us with exceptional clearness through the letters to which with complete candour he committed the record of his moods and actions. Four collections of these have survived: 'Ad Atticum' (68–44 B.C.) edited by Atticus (q.v.), his intimate friend, himself; 'Ad Familiārēs' (62–43) 'to his Friends', probably edited by Cicero's freedman Tiro; 'Ad Quintum

Fratrem', 'to his brother Quintus' (q.v., 60–54), and 'ad Brutum' to Marcus Brutus (q.v.). The genuineness of the correspondence with Brutus (all of it that survives is subsequent to the murder of Caesar) has been questioned, but is now generally admitted as regards most of the letters. Of the total number of 864 letters in the four collections, 774 are by Cicero, 90 are addressed to him. There are no letters for the year of Cicero's consulship or the preceding year. The bulk of the letters relate to the last years of his life. They are addressed to correspondents of the most diverse political views and social position, to Cato and Dolabella, to Caesar, Pompey, and Antony, to Metellus and Tiro. Their subjects are no less varied, from philosophy, literature, and politics, to household affairs; while their tone ranges from familiar chat to outbursts of passion and despair. The first letter to his brother Quintus is almost a treatise on the duties of a provincial governor. Some are political manifestos intended for circulation. The celebrated letter of December 54 to Lentulus (Ad Fam. I. 9) is a lengthy apologia for Cicero's submission to the triumvirate after Luca. But the most interesting are the intimate letters to Atticus, which throw a vivid light on Cicero's own character. They show him to have been a man of mercurial temper, impressionable, irresolute, and vain; but fundamentally honest, intelligent, affectionate, and amiable. In politics he was what we should call a liberal, opposed alike to reaction and to revolution. In the days of Sulla he appears a democrat; when Caesar and the mob rule of Clodius threatened the constitution, he appears a conservative. His weakest period is that of submission to the triumvirate after the conference of Luca in 56.

There is a life of Cicero by Plutarch. The lives of him by Nepos and Tiro are lost.

§ 8. *Cicero's influence on literature and thought*

Cicero's contribution to literature was as important as it was varied: political and forensic speeches showing every form of rhetorical art, from fierce indignation to tender pity (his oratorical style was intermediate between the severe Attic and the florid Asian); treatises on rhetoric, political science, and philosophy; and charming letters. Cicero was also accounted a good poet in his day, though his poems were later derided by Juvenal (Sat. x. 122 et seq.). Of his verse translation of the works of Aratus (q.v.), the greater part of the 'Phaenonema' survives. He also wrote poems, in his youth on Marius, and later on his consulship and on his times (from which there are quotations in his 'De Divinatione'); and he included verse translations of passages of Homer and the Greek dramatists in his treatises. These show him as a poet at his best; the notorious line 'O fortunatam natam me consule Romam', at his worst. (He wrote an account of the consulship also in Greek prose, and talked of writing one in Latin prose; it is not known whether he did so.) But his principal service to literature was in his development of Latin prose to its perfection, whereby it became the basis of literary expression in the languages of modern Europe. Its chief features are the use of the period (in which subordinate clauses and balanced antitheses form part of the structure of the sentence), and of rhythm and cadence (see *Clausula*). There was a revulsion against his style in the Silver Age, when the tendency was to write in concise epigrammatic sentences (as seen in Seneca and Tacitus). But Quintilian regarded Cicero as the greatest of Roman writers.

Cicero's influence on later thought was immense. It is seen in such writers as Minucius Felix, St. Jerome (who was an ardent if reluctant Ciceronian, see the anecdote under his name), St. Ambrose (whose manual of ethics 'De Officiis Ministrorum' was modelled on Cicero's 'De Officiis'), and St. Augustine (who was first moved by Cicero's 'Hortensius' to abandon frivolity for the search of wisdom). On the other side, the Pelagians, whom Augustine condemned, drew largely on Cicero. Petrarch, the earliest of the humanists, was devoted to Cicero and searched eagerly for manuscripts of his works. We may imagine the delight with which he read Cicero's tribute to literature in the 'Pro Archia', of which he discovered a manuscript at Liége in 1333. He found a manuscript of the 'Letters to Atticus' at Verona in 1345. His sentiments on reading them are expressed in two letters of affectionate reproach addressed by him to the spirit of Cicero (Ad Viros Illustres, i, ii). The admiration of the Renaissance for Cicero's works gave rise to a tendency among writers to imitate his style, and this to a controversy in which Erasmus and the elder Scaliger were ranged on opposite sides. Cicero was highly esteemed in England at an early date. He was a favourite of John of Salisbury and Roger Bacon; Queen Elizabeth when sixteen had read nearly all his works with her tutor Ascham. His influence is seen later in the works of Lord Herbert of Cherbury and the other Deists; in the speeches of the 18th-c. orators; and in the prose of such writers as Johnson and Gibbon.

Ci'cerō, QUINTUS TULLIUS (c. 102–43 B.C.) younger brother of M. Cicero (q.v.), was educated at Rome and in Greece, and was praetor in 62 and governor of Asia from 61 to 58. He served as legate under Pompey in Sardinia in 56, and under Caesar in Gaul in 54 (where he underwent a perilous siege, see *Commentaries*, Gallic War, Book V). In 51–50 he served under his brother in Cilicia. In the Civil War he joined Pompey, but after the latter's defeat was pardoned by Caesar. Like his brother he was killed in Antony's proscriptions.

Q. Cicero wrote some tragedies, which have not survived; also an extant letter to his brother on the art of canvassing, known as 'Commentāriolum petitiōnis consulātus'. We have a collection of letters to him from his brother, of which the first gives elaborate advice on the methods of provincial government.

Ciceronian Age of Roman literature, a term sometimes used to signify the period, centring in Cicero (q.v.), when that literature first reached its zenith. See *Rome*, § 8. A time of civil strife contrasting with the Augustan age which followed it.

Cimme'rians (*Kimmerioi*), (1) a fabulous people, whose land according to Homer was on the limits of the world, in the stream Oceanus. It was shrouded in mist and cloud and the sun never shone on it. It was there that Odysseus had access to the spirits of the dead. (2) In Herodotus the Cimmerians are an historical people, living originally to the N. of the Euxine Sea. In the 8th and 7th cc. B.C. pressure from nomadic tribes from Central Asia compelled them to invade Assyria and Asia Minor. In Assyria they were defeated by Sargon (705). In Asia Minor they twice captured Sardis. The invasion, however, seems to have left no very permanent traces, though a number of Greek colonies on the north coast of the Euxine (e.g. Sinope and Trapezus), founded in the 8th c., had to be refounded in the next.

Ci'mon (*Kimōn*), son of Miltiades (q.v.) and a Thracian princess, a distinguished Athenian commander, and a bold and ambitious aristocrat. He was elected strategus in 479 B.C., and after the ostracism of his rival Themistocles and the death of Aristides (qq.v.) became all-powerful at Athens. His principal naval achievement was the defeat of the Persian fleet at the mouth of the Eurymedōn in 468 (?), but he also did much to consolidate Athenian power in the Aegaean, founding colonies, putting down pirates, and bringing Naxos into subjection, 'the first allied city to be enslaved' remarks Thucydides, a precedent of importance in the later history of the Athenian empire. His policy favoured an understanding with Sparta and concentration of efforts against the Persians, whereas Themistocles saw in the Delian Confederacy an instrument for humbling Sparta. Later, Cimon's policy brought him into antagonism with Pericles. Cimon was ostracized in 461, owing to the failure of his pro-Spartan policy, probably did not return until his ten years of ostracism ran out, and died in Cyprus in 449 in the course of operations against the Persians. There are lives of Cimon by Plutarch and Nepos.

Cincinnā'tus, LUCIUS QUINCTIUS, according to tradition a Roman who lived in the first half of the 5th c. B.C. He was called from the plough in 458 to save the Roman army, which was blockaded by the Aequi on Mt. Algidus. He was made dictator, defeated the enemy, and returned to his farm. He is often referred to as a type of the old-fashioned Roman simplicity and frugality.

Cinē'sias (*Kinēsiās*), an Athenian dithyrambic poet, who flourished in the latter part of the 5th c. B.C. Not only his poetry, but also his irreligion and his personal appearance made him the butt of his contemporaries. Aristophanes ridicules him in the 'Birds' and perhaps in the 'Lysistrata' (qq.v.). He was condemned by Plato ('Gorgias') as a poet who aimed at producing pleasure, not good.

Ci'nna, GAIUS HELVIUS (d. 44 B.C.), a Roman poet, author of a poem on Zmyrna (q.v.) or Myrrha, mother of Adonis, and of a 'Propempticon', a guide-book to Greece in verse. Neither work is extant. But we know that the 'Zmyrna' showed the learning and obscurity of the Alexandrian influence at its worst. He was a friend of Catullus (q.v.) and accompanied him to Bithỹnia. He was murdered by the mob at Caesar's obsequies (see Shakespeare, 'Julius Caesar', III. iii), probably owing to his being mistaken for Cornēlius Cinna, one of the conspirators.

Ci'nyras (*Kinurās*), a name derived from the Phoenician *kinnor*, meaning a harp, the legendary first king of Cyprus and priest of the Paphian Aphrodite. He was regarded as the earliest singer and musician. He became the father of Adonis (q.v.) by his own daughter, Myrrha.

Ci'rcē (*Kirkē*), in Greek mythology, a daughter of Helios (q.v.) and sister of

Aeëtës, king of Colchis (see *Argonauts*). For the story of Circe and Odysseus see *Odyssey*. By Odysseus she was mother of Telegonus (q.v.). There was a legend in Italy that she had her home on a promontory of Latium, Circĕii (see Aen. vii. 10–24), famous for its oysters (Hor. Sat. ii. iv. 33). Milton in his 'Comus' makes the magician Comus the son of Circe and Bacchus.

Circe'nsēs, at Rome, contests and other displays in the Circus, including chariot-races (q.v.). 'Panem et circenses' were, according to Juvenal (x. 78–81), the only things that the degenerate Roman populace cared about.

Ci'rcus Ma'ximus, in republican times and under the early empire the chief place of amusement of the Roman people, a circus lying between the Palatine and Aventine hills, where races and public spectacles were held (see Pl. 14). At first and probably down to some time in the 4th c. B.C. there was no permanent structure; after this, permanent buildings were gradually added. The circus was reconstructed by Julius Caesar, with three tiers of seats, the lowest of masonry, the others of wood. The wooden portion was repeatedly destroyed by fire, notably in the great fire of A.D. 64, and restored. The circus reached its greatest size and splendour in the reconstruction of Trajan. The main structure was then of masonry, covered both on the inside and on the outside with marble, profusely decorated. The exterior consisted of three tiers of arches, like the Colosseum. The arena was about 600 yards long by 100 yards wide. Externally the building was about 700 yards long and, if the additions made in imperial times on the slopes of the adjoining hills are included, about 200 yards wide. The east end was semi-circular, the west end, where stood the *carceres* from which the chariots issued, was curved. The arena was divided along its length by the *spina* (see *Chariot-races*), on which stood shrines and statues. The seating capacity has been much discussed. The circus is stated in the 4th c. to have contained 385,000 *loca*, which has been variously interpreted; it probably means 385,000 running feet of seats, or room for about 200,000 spectators.

Ci'ris, a poem in hexameters doubtfully attributed to Virgil (q.v.). It contains lines which appear also in the 'Eclogues' and 'Georgics'. It may have been written by one of the poets, such as Gallus (q.v.), of the circle to which Virgil belonged, and Virgil may have contributed to it verses which he subsequently introduced into his own poems.

The subject is the infatuation of Scylla, daughter of Nīsus king of Megara, for Minos of Crete, who is besieging her father's city. Nisus is safe so long as a purple lock among his white hair remains intact. To gain her object Scylla treacherously cuts off the lock. Megara is taken and Scylla is dragged through the sea suspended from the ship of Minos. She is turned into a sea-bird (*ciris*), ever pursued with hatred by her father, who is turned into a sea-eagle.

Cistellā'ria ('The Casket'), a comedy by Plautus, probably adapted from a play by Menander. The plot turns on the discovery by means of a casket of the true parentage of a foundling girl, Selēnium, who has passed into the care of a courtesan, and has become the mistress of a young man, Alcesimarchus. She is found to be the daughter of a citizen, Dēmiphō, and is thereupon married to her lover.

Cithae'ron (*Kithairōn*), a mountain range between Attica and Boeotia, on which Pentheus, according to legend, met his death at the hands of the Bacchanals. See *Bacchae*.

Ci'thara, see *Music*, § 1.

City of God, see *Augustine*.

Classic, a word, from Lat. *classicus*, meaning 'of the highest class'. Aulus Gellius has 'classicus . . . scriptor, non proletarius', where the word means 'high-class', as opposed to 'low'. Littré, however, takes the Fr. word *classique* as meaning 'used in or belonging to the classes of colleges and schools', and it is probable that this notion has influenced the word in its extension from the standard authors to the ancient authors generally, together with the associated languages, literature, &c. The word 'classic' has become synonymous with 'ancient Greek and Roman'. In the narrower sense the classical age of Greek literature is generally regarded as having ended about 325 B.C., when the conquests of Alexander the Great brought the changes described under *Hellenistic Age*. Similarly the classical age of Latin literature may be said to have ended with the close of the reign of Augustus. But it must be remembered that in both languages there were writers of almost the first rank after the classical period, such as Theocritus and Tacitus.

Classiciā'nus, Jūlius, see *Britain*, § 2.

Clau'dia Quinta, see *Cybele*.

Clau'dian (*Claudius Claudiānus*), the last great poet of the heathen world, a pagan at heart though perhaps nominally a

Christian. He was a Greek, spent his childhood at Alexandria, was at Rome from about A.D. 395 to 404, and wrote in Latin a number of official poems in hexameters, some in praise of the young emperor Honōrius, of his ministers, and especially of the great general Stilichō (see Gibbon, 'Decline and Fall', c. **xxix**); others in abuse of their enemies, in particular of Rūfinus (the guardian at Constantinople of Arcădius, brother of Honorius), and of the eunuch Eutrōpius, the successor of Rufinus in the favour of Arcadius. He also wrote epics on the wars against the Goths and against the usurper Gildo in Africa; these are in effect eulogiums of Stilicho. These poems show sincere enthusiasm for the Roman empire, great technical and rhetorical skill, and a vigour at times reaching high eloquence, though both his panegyric and his invective are extravagant. He makes abundant use of allegory and mythological episode and allusion. He was honoured for his work with a bronze statue erected in the Forum of Trajan. In addition to the above political poems, Claudian wrote an 'Epithalamium' on the marriage of Honorius, an unfinished mythological poem 'De Raptu Proserpinae' (which contains picturesque descriptive passages), and a number of short pieces, idylls and epigrams, mostly in elegiacs, on a great variety of subjects—the Nile, the Phoenix, a porcupine, a lobster, a statue, a landscape, &c. The best-known is the idyll on the 'Old Man of Verona', imitated from Virgil's description of the old gardener of Tarentum (Georg. iv. 125 et seq.). It was translated by Cowley.

Clau′dius (*Tĭbĕrius Claudius Drūsus Nĕrō Germānicus*), Roman emperor A.D. 41–54, the nephew of Tiberius and younger brother of Germanicus (see *Julio-Claudian Family*, and *Rome*, § 10). He wrote an autobiography, which is not extant, more elegant in style than sensible, according to Suetonius. He was an antiquarian and historian of no mean authority. He wrote a history of the reign of Octavian from 27 B.C. to A.D. 14, and a shorter history from the death of Julius Caesar; and in Greek twenty books of 'Tyrrhēnica' (a history of the Etruscans) and eight books of 'Carchēdonica' (a history of Carthage). None of these works has survived. His learning, combined with a certain ungainliness and dullness of wit, has caused him to be compared to James I.

Clau′sula, in Latin rhetoric, the closing words of a period. The rhythm of the *clausulae* of Cicero's speeches has been carefully studied, and it has been found that the majority of his *clausulae* conform to a definite type, in which a cretic (–∪–) or sometimes a molossus (–––) is followed by two or more syllables trochaic or cretic in their rhythm. Thus:

Non haberemus –∪–|–∪
Cessit audaciae –∪–|–∪
(In)commodo civitatis –∪–|–∪∪

Quintilian (x. 2. 18) says that an orator thinks it a capital imitation of the style of Cicero to close a period with 'esse videatur'. This is a variety of the above, in which two short syllables are substituted for the second long of the cretic, –∪∪∪|–∪.

Clea′nthēs (*Kleanthēs*), of Assos in the Troad (c. 330–c. 231 B.C.), the successor of Zeno as head of the Stoic (q.v.) school. He was author of a noble hymn to Zeus, which survives. The thought is pantheistic, and in the poem Zeus is not the god of mythology but the spirit that permeates and rules the universe. Cleanthes emphasized the religious side of the Stoic doctrine.

Clei′sthenēs (*Kleisthenēs*), (1) the founder of Athenian democracy, son of Megacles the Alcmaeonid (q.v.), who married Agariste the daughter of Cleisthenes, tyrant of Sicyon (see (2) below). After the fall of the tyrant Hippias (510) there was an oligarchic movement in Athens headed by Isagoras and supported by Sparta. Cleisthenes put himself forward as the champion of democracy and overthrew the aristocrats. He completely reorganized the State on a democratic basis. He broke up what remained of the old organization based on family groups and substituted a new system based on topography. He divided the territory of Attica into demes (*dēmoi*) or parishes, of which the city of Athens comprised five (he may have taken existing demes as the basis). All citizens were inscribed on the register of one or other of the demes, and many metics (q.v.) and freedmen were admitted to the citizenship. Each deme had its own finances and its demarch, elected by its assembly (*agora*), which dealt with local affairs. Cleisthenes further divided the population of Attica into ten tribes (*phŭlai*), distributed over the demes so that no tribe had a continuous territory, or represented a local interest: on the contrary, in each tribe were comprised areas in the districts of the city, the shore, and the interior. The tribes were named after Attic heroes (with whom they had in fact no special connexion) and were thus given a fictitious blood-relationship. The *phratriai* (q.v.)

survived in the constitution of Cleisthenes as a kind of religious community for carrying out certain cults, but were re-organized so that no citizen could be excluded from them. Each tribe furnished annually fifty members to the Council of State (*Boulē*), taken from the demes of the tribe by lot proportionately to their popu-lation. These groups of fifty exercised in turn the Prytany (*prutaneia*) or function of executive committee of the Boule, each group holding office for one tenth of the year. Each tribe furnished its military contingent of a regiment of hoplites and a squadron of cavalry.

Cleisthenes subordinated the Boule and the Areopagus (q.v.) to the supreme authority of the *Ecclesia* or assembly of all the citizens, which met regularly at least once in the period of each prytany, and might deal with any important State question. In one respect Cleisthenes was conservative: the existing magistracies were retained, and the archons could be chosen only from the two wealthiest classes of the population. The Eupatrids (q.v.) retained the priestly offices. See also *Strategus*.

Cleisthenes sought to safeguard his con-stitution by the institution of ostracism (q.v.).

(2) Of Sicyon, tyrant in the early 6th c. His policy was consistently anti-Dorian and in particular anti-Argive. In this he was only carrying on the policy of earlier Orthagoridae (descendants of Ortha-gorās, reputed founder of the dynasty). He would not allow rhapsodes to recite Homeric poems (because of their frequent references to Argives) and attempted to expel the worship of the Argive hero Adrastus (q.v.). This, together with his abandoning of the Dorian tribe-names at Sicyon, seems to have led up to open war with Argos, in which the latter State had the better. Earlier, Cleisthenes had taken part in the Sacred War (q.v.) of *c.* 590. His reign is said to have lasted 31 years. For the story of the wooing of his daughter Agaristē, see under *Hippocleides*.

(3) A character ridiculed by Aristo-phanes in his 'Birds', 'Knights', 'Clouds', and 'Thesmophoriazusae'. We know from Lysias (xxv. 25) that he was a professional informer.

Clei'tus (*Kleitos*), brother of the foster-mother of Alexander the Great and one of his cavalry commanders. He saved Alexander's life at the Granicus, and was subsequently killed by him in a drunken brawl (see *Alexander the Great*, § 6).

Clement of Alexandria (*c.* A.D. 160–*c.* 215) was not only one of the early Greek

Fathers, but also conspicuous for his wide knowledge of Greek literature, especially of Greek philosophy. His writings abound in quotations and anecdotes, and contain passages of interest to Greek scholarship; he has preserved many details concerning the Orphic and Eleusinian Mysteries. He was probably born at Athens, and studied and taught at Alexandria. His principal works were 'Protreptikos' or an 'Exhorta-tion' to the Greeks (an attack on pagan religion and philosophy), 'Paidagōgos' (a course of religious instruction), and 'Strō-mateis' or 'Miscellanies' (in which he aims at reconciling Christian faith with reason and philosophy).

Cle'obis and **Bi'tōn**, two Argives who, according to a story placed by Herodotus in the mouth of Solon, drew their mother in a chariot a distance of 45 stadia to the Heraeum (q.v.) to attend a festival of Hera. The men of Argos, who stood near, commended the strength of the youths, and the women blessed their mother. But the mother herself prayed the goddess to grant her sons the greatest blessing that man could receive. Thereafter the youths fell asleep in the temple of the goddess and died as they slept; the goddess thus showing that it is better for a man to die than to live. An inscription on a statue of Cleobis and Biton has been discovered at Delphi.

Cleo'menēs (*Kleomenēs*). (1) Cleomenes I, King of Sparta (*c.* 520–*c.* 490 B.C.). He freed Athens (q.v.) from the tyranny of Hippias. He subsequently supported the aristo-cratic reaction in that city headed by Isagoras against Cleisthenes, and was besieged in the Acropolis with Isagoras and obliged to capitulate. When, before the Persian War, Aegina was suspected of favouring the Persians, he forced the Aeginetans to give hostages for their good conduct to Athens.

(2) Cleomenes III, the last great king of Sparta (236–222 B.C.). Following his pre-decessor Agis IV, he attempted to restore Spartan power by a series of reforms designed to rehabilitate the constitution of Lycurgus. He proposed to abolish the ephorate, extend the powers of the kings, free helots, and make a new distribution of the land. This was in 226–5. Before that, Cleomenes had built up a strong position in the State by his successful wars against the Achaean League (q.v.). The reforms were in part carried out; but in 222 (or 223) Cleomenes was defeated at Sellasia by the Achaeans under Aratus of Sicyon and fled to Egypt, where he was put to death soon afterwards. His ideas (and those of Agis) may have influenced

the Gracchi (q.v.) at Rome. There is a life of Cleomenes by Plutarch. For an imaginative modern reconstruction, see Mrs. Mitchison's 'Corn King and Spring Queen'.

Clĕ′on (*Klĕŏn*) (d. 422 B.C.), an Athenian demagogue prominent at the time of the Peloponnesian War, by trade a tanner, violent and dominating by character, determined to win power by his ascendancy over the people. It must be remembered that he is known to us chiefly through the writings of his enemies (notably Aristophanes, q.v.). He was not a coward, as Aristophanes suggests, but he may have been venal. He was in favour of an imperialist policy, and of a ruthless conduct of the war, by sea and land, until complete victory was obtained, at whatever cost, for it would pay the Athenians in the end. In 427 it was he who proposed, after the suppression of the revolt of Mytilene, the execution or enslavement of the inhabitants. He attacked unsuccessful generals, and his complaints of the slowness of the operations against Sphacteria led Nicias to propose to hand over charge of them to Cleon. By luck and shrewdness Cleon was able to make good his promise to take Sphacteria and bring home the prisoners within twenty days. This achievement made him all-powerful at Athens. But the vigorous operations that followed proved unfortunate; among other disasters Amphipolis and other towns in Chalcidice fell into the hands of Brasidas (q.v.). Cleon was elected strategus, and commanded the expedition for their reconquest. He met with some successes, but was repulsed from Amphipolis and killed (422). His death and that of Brasidas, mortally wounded in the same engagement, removed the principal obstacles to the Peace of Nicias. See also *Aristophanes* and *Knights*.

Cleopa′tra VII (68–30 B.C.), daughter of Ptolemy Aulētēs, king of Egypt (d. 51 B.C.), appointed by him as his successor jointly with her younger brother. She was famous for her beauty and charm, which she exercised on Julius Caesar (who restored her to her throne in 47 B.C. after her expulsion by Pothinus, and had by her a son named Caesarion), and later on Mark Antony (q.v.) whose evil genius, according to the generally accepted view, she became. (For the political aspect of their relations, see under *Antony*.) She took her own life when Antony's cause became desperate in 30 B.C. The true character of Cleopatra, behind the romantic tales about her, we do not know, except that she had personal courage and was

feared by the Romans; there may have been something of the true patriot in her. It is the romantic portrait, based on Plutarch, which Shakespeare presents in his 'Antony and Cleopatra'. See C. A. H., vol. x, for an interesting reconstruction.

Cleopatra was a very ancient Greek name, in Homer (Il. ix. 556) that of the wife of Meleager, and in the legend of the Argonauts that of the wife of Phineus. Cleopatra VII was by descent a Macedonian; it is a mistake to think of her as an Egyptian.

Cle′ophon (*Kleophŏn*), an Athenian demagogue prominent in the latter part of the Peloponnesian War and in the restoration of democratic rule after the battle of Cȳzicus (see *Athens*, § 5). He was tried and put to death in 404 by the oligarchs.

Cle′psydra (*Klepsŭdrā*), see *Calendar*, § 4.

Clĕ′ruch (*Klĕrouchos*), an Athenian citizen who held an allotment of land (*klĕros*) in a foreign country. A cleruchy (*klĕrouchiā*) or group of such cleruchs differed from a colony in that the cleruchs retained their rights of Athenian citizenship, and did not necessarily reside in their allotments. The system was introduced in the last years of the 6th c. B.C., but was much developed in the 5th c. when it became an important feature in the Athenian imperial system, by providing a sort of permanent garrisons in foreign lands and in the countries of the subject-allies. It was also a means of making provision for the poorer and landless citizens of Athens, whose economic position was a constant problem. The leader of a cleruchy was known as the oecist (*oikistēs*). Important cleruchies were founded by Cimon and Pericles (qq.v.), notably in the Thracian Chersonese, Lemnos, Euboea, and Aegina.

Client, at Rome, in republican times, signified a dependant on a patrician, or more generally on a powerful or wealthy patron, to whom he rendered services and from whom he received protection. The relation of client to patron resembled that of vassal to chief, dignified by mutual loyalty. Under the empire the relation became degraded. The clients were then merely hungry hangers-on of some rich patron, attending his receptions, walking behind him about the city, running his errands, in return for a scanty dole of food or money. This relation is especially illustrated by Martial's poems.

Cli′max (Gk. for 'ladder', L. *gradātiō*), a rhetorical figure in which successive notions are arranged in order of increasing impressiveness. Quintilian quotes as an example (from the 'Ad Herennium') 'Africano virtutem industria, virtus gloriam, gloria aemulos comparavit'.

An *anticlimax* (a word apparently first found in Pope's 'Art of Sinking', 1727) is the opposite of a climax; the addition of a particular which, instead of heightening the effect, lowers it or makes it ludicrous. Cf. *Bathos*.

Cli'o (*Kleiō*), see *Muses*.

Cloā'ca Ma'xima, a great sewer at Rome, ascribed to the Tarquins, but probably dating from early republican times, and reconstructed under Augustus. Starting from the valley of Subura it drained the marshy ground at the foot of the Capitol and so made possible its use as the Roman Forum. It was vaulted and paved, and where it emptied into the Tiber it was about 10 ft. wide and 12 ft. high. The system of sewers of which it formed part was regarded, with the aqueducts and roads, as among the most wonderful constructions of ancient Rome. The Cloaca Maxima still forms part of the drainage system of the modern city. See Pl. 14.

Cloa'nthus, in the 'Aeneid', a companion of Aeneas. He figures in the boat-race (Bk. V).

Clō'dia, the sister of P. Clodius (q.v.) and wife of the consul Q. Metellus Celer, a woman notorious for her profligacy. Among her lovers was Catullus (q.v.), who celebrated her as 'Lesbia'. She was the bitter enemy of Cicero (q.v.), who fiercely attacked her in his speech 'Pro Caelio'.

Clō'dius Albi'nus, DECIMUS, see *Britain*, § 2.

Clō'dius Pulcher, PUBLIUS, a patrician of the Claudian *gens*, notorious for his violence and profligacy and as the enemy of Cicero. His profanation of the mysteries of the Bona Dea in 62 B.C., the defeat by Cicero's evidence of his attempt to prove an alibi (though in fact Clodius was acquitted at the trial), the vengeance he took as tribune in 58 by driving Cicero into exile, his feud with Milo carried on by street fights between gangs of ruffians, and his death in 52 in one of these riots, are related under *Cicero*, §§ 3 and 4. He was brother of Clodia (q.v.).

Cloe'lia, according to legend, a Roman maiden who was one of the hostages given to the Etruscan king Porsena in the course of his war with the newly founded Roman republic. She escaped, and swimming the Tiber returned to Rome. She was again surrendered to Porsena, who in admiration of her courage released her together with some of her companions.

Clothing and Toilet.

§ 1. *Greek clothing*

The dress of the Athenians of the 5th and 4th cc. consisted normally of two garments, each composed of an oblong piece of woollen or linen cloth: (*a*) the CHITŌN or tunic, worn next to the skin, doubled round the body, pinned over each shoulder, and held in by a girdle at the waist, leaving the arms free. This was worn by men falling to the knee, by women longer. (*b*) The HĪMATION or cloak, worn by men; it was laid from behind on the two shoulders, and the right end thrown over the left shoulder, but so as to leave the right hand exposed. It could be drawn over the head. Workmen, who could not afford the *himation* (it cost 16–20 drachmas), wore a single garment, known as the EXŌMIS, of coarse stuff made at Megara, with a goat-skin for cold weather. The outer garment of women was the ample PEPLOS, pinned over the shoulders, and variously draped according to the fashion. Horsemen wore a short mantle known as the CHLAMYS. It was usual for men to strip entirely for exercise or sport. The prevailing colour of Greek men's dress was white; but workmen wore dark stuffs, and women gay-coloured materials. Hats were not generally worn, except when travelling or hunting; the PETASOS was a broad-brimmed felt hat, said to have been introduced from Thessaly with the *chlamys*; the PĪLOS was a round felt cap, with little or no brim, chiefly worn by workmen. Sandals and shoes were worn out of doors; tanning and shoemaking were active industries at Athens, and women's shoes were often luxurious and highly decorated.

§ 2. *Greek ornaments and toilet*

Bracelets, rings, and ear-rings were worn. The British Museum has a silver armlet, in the form of a coiled snake, of the 4th or 3rd c. B.C., inscribed with the name of its owner, Cletis. Cosmetics were used, as we know from Xenophon's 'Oeconomicus'. Greek men usually wore beards, but razors are mentioned in Homer. There were public baths attached to the gymnasia, but they were not of the elaborate character found at Rome; bathing scenes represented on vases show men standing about a large vessel, into which an attendant may be pouring water. The oil-flask (*lēcythus*) for anointing was an essential requisite for a bath.

§ 3. *Roman clothes*

Men's dress in republican times consisted of an inner garment, the *tunica*, and an outer the *toga*. The TUNICA was first introduced at Rome as a form of dress for the poorer classes. It was then adopted as an under-dress, first of all by patricians. It was a shirt-like garment, usually with short sleeves, reaching to about the knee. The TOGA was a white woollen garment, roughly semicircular, sometimes about 6 yards long by 2 at its greatest width, but of which the size does not seem to have been definitely fixed. Various passages show that it was worn large or small according as one wanted to be ostentatious or not. One end of it nearly reached the ground in front, while the other was thrown over the left shoulder, brought under the right arm, and again thrown over the left shoulder. It was worn by citizens only and was the obligatory dress on official occasions, even in imperial times when more convenient garments had come into use. The *toga virilis*, that worn by the ordinary citizen, was entirely white. The *toga praetexta*, worn by certain priests and magistrates and also by free-born boys until they reached manhood, was bordered with a purple stripe. Women at first wore the toga, later the STOLA, a garment with slits on either side for the arms, gathered up below the breast by a girdle. They wore also the PALLA, a mantle, over the *stola*. The LACERNA was a man's rough outer cloak worn on journeys against the weather; also later a more elegant outer garment worn in Rome at the games and other outdoor functions (it was prohibited by Augustus in the Forum and Circus). The TRABEA was a cloak worn by the equestrian order, by the consul at certain ceremonials, and by augurs and various orders of priests. Suetonius gives three kinds of *trabea*: (*a*) entirely of purple, (*b*) purple and white, (*c*) purple and saffron. Wool was dyed from an early date with saffron, indigo, kermes, and the purple dye of the murex shell-fish. At first it was prepared by the women of the family, but, with the growth of the proletariate, guilds of fullers, &c. sprang up. The use of linen, cotton, and silk came in later, with the development of trade and increase of wealth.

§ 4. *Roman head-covering*

In lieu of hats the Romans wore a hood (CUCULLUS) or drew their outer garment over the head. In the country or on journeys, and also during the Saturnalia (q.v.), they wore a round felt cap, with little or no brim, known as the PILLEUS.

§ 5. *Roman shoes and boots*

The CALCEUS was the leather shoe worn in the city, the PERO a high boot worn in the country. The *calceus* differed in pattern according to the rank of the wearer;

e.g. patrician magistrates wore a red high-soled *calceus*, senators a black *calceus*, both with a small crescent of ivory. Women wore it white or coloured. Under the empire great splendour was shown in the colour and adornment of shoes. The CALIGA was a hob-nailed boot worn by soldiers and peasants. Sandals (SOLEAE) were worn indoors, but were taken off when guests reclined at dinner. To ask for one's sandals (*poscere soleas*) was the signal that one was going away.

§ 6. *Roman toilet, rings, &c.*

Roman men at first wore long hair and beards. Hair-cutting and shaving were introduced from Sicily about 300 B.C. Scipio Aemilianus (q.v.) is said to have been the first to shave daily. The custom of shaving or wearing the beard short continued under the empire. Roman razors were made of iron and, since they were liable to rust, very few survive (there is one in the British Museum). The head-dress of Roman women was at first simple, but became very elaborate under the empire; false hair was used, and decorated ivory hairpins, besides cosmetics. Combs were of ivory, bone, or wood. Mirrors were generally of silver-plated bronze. Wigs and false hair were in use in Ovid's day. Martial refers to the use of false teeth, and the use of gold in dental operations is mentioned in an old law quoted by Cicero (De leg. ii. 24, 60). Senators and other eminent persons wore a gold signet-ring; others a ring of iron. The use of the gold ring came to be a sign of free birth, and was granted even to freedmen and later to soldiers irrespective of their rank in the army. Betrothal rings were used (there is a gold one in the British Museum). The BULLA was a small box containing an amulet worn by free-born Roman children round the neck; it was of gold, bronze, or leather according to the wealth of the parents. It was worn by boys till they assumed the *toga virilis*, by girls probably till they married. See also under *Baths*; in this connexion mention may be made of the STRIGIL, a curved scraper, generally of bronze, used for scraping the body after exercise, or in the bath, or after anointing.

Clŏ'thō, see *Fates*.

Clouds, *The* (*Nephelai*, L. *Nūbēs*), a comedy by Aristophanes on the subject of Socrates and the New Learning, produced in its original form at the Great Dionysia of 423 B.C. It was unsuccessful, being perhaps considered too subtle or too favourable to Socrates and was rewritten by Aristophanes in the form in which we have it; we know that he substituted two scenes in which hostility to the new school is manifested. In the second edition the play was not produced at either of the great festivals.

Strepsiadēs ('Twister'), an elderly dishonest farmer, has been ruined by his fashionable wife and horse-loving son Pheidippidēs. He has heard of Socrates, a man who can make the Worse Cause appear the Better, and hopes by his teaching to be able to defraud his creditors. As his son refuses to enter Socrates' school (the Phrontisterion, or 'Thinking-shop'), Strepsiades decides to go himself. He is told that he must resign himself to hard work and simple living, and is introduced to the Clouds, who (and not Zeus, as had been believed) are the deities who produce thunder and rain. But Strepsiades is too stupid and too much concerned with his debts to learn anything, and Pheidippides has to become the pupil instead of him. Socrates hands Pheidippides over to be instructed by the Just Plea and the Unjust Plea in person. A contest between these two (one of the substituted scenes) follows, in which the Unjust Plea is victorious. By the help of what Pheidippides has learnt, Strepsiades is able to confute his creditors. But the tables are turned on him when, as a result of the same learning, Pheidippides starts to beat his father (and threatens to beat his mother too) and proves that he is justified in doing so. Strepsiades, disgusted with the New Learning, sets fire to Socrates' school.

Clubs, see *Guilds*.

Cly′menē (*Klumenē*), in Greek mythology, (1) daughter of Minyas (q.v.). She was beloved of the Sun, and to him bore Phaethon (q.v.). (2) Daughter of Oceanus and Tethys, wife of Iapetus, and mother of Atlas, Prometheus, and Epimetheus (qq.v.).

Clytemne′stra (*Klutaim(n)ēstrā*), in Greek mythology, daughter of Tyndareus, (*Tundareōs*) king of Sparta, and Leda (q.v.), and wife of Agamemnon. See *Pelops, Oresteia, Orestes, Electra*.

Cno′ssus (*Knōsos* or *Knōssos*), see *Crete* and *Minoan*.

Cock, The, see *Lucian*.

Co′clēs, PUBLIUS HORĀTIUS, a legendary Roman, said to have defended, with two companions, Sp. Larcius and T. Herminius, the bridge-head leading to Rome against the whole Etruscan army under Porsena (q.v.), while the bridge behind him was being destroyed. Then he sent back his two companions and held the

position single-handed, finally jumping into the river and swimming back to the city. The exploit is the subject of one of Macaulay's 'Lays of Ancient Rome'.

Cocy′tus (*Kōkūtos*), in Greek mythology one of the rivers of Hades (q.v.). It was the name of a tributary of the Acheron in Epirus.

Cō′dex, (1) see *Books, Ancient*, § 4; (2) see *Justinian*.

Cō′drus (*Kōdros*), the last of the legendary kings of Athens. He is said to have sacrificed himself for his country when it was threatened by an invasion from the Peloponnese.

Coinage, see *Money*.

Co′lchis, a country at the E. end of the Euxine or Black Sea, bounded on the N. by the Caucasus, famous in Greek legend as the destination of the Argonauts (q.v.) and the home of Medea.

Collē′gia, see *Guilds*.

Colline Gate, at Rome, on the NE. side of the city (see Pl. 14), the scene of a fierce battle in 82 B.C., in which Sulla (q.v.), after his return from the E., finally overcame the Samnite and Lucanian army, and made himself master of Italy.

Colō′ni, farmers who tilled, as tenants, the land of Roman proprietors. They degenerated into serfs, tied to the soil. See *Agriculture*, § 2, and *Latifundia*.

Colonization.

GREEK COLONIZATION

§ 1. *General character*

The great age of the expansion of Greece beyond Greece proper and the eastern shores of the Aegean lasted from the middle of the 8th to the early part of the 6th c. B.C. This expansion by means of colonies may be regarded as a continuation of the movement which took Greek settlers in the period of the migrations (q.v.) across the Aegean to the shores of Asia Minor and the adjoining islands. Its causes are to be found first in the adventurous spirit of the Greeks, which we see reflected in such myths as that of the Argonauts (q.v.); then in the social and political conditions which prevailed at this time in Greek lands. The area of cultivable land in Greece was very limited, while the land system tended to exclude a portion of the inhabitants from a share in the soil and converted them into needy adventurers. The aristocratic form of government in many States was harsh and bred discontent, so that men were encouraged to seek happier conditions elsewhere.

As regards the Greek cities on the coast of Asia Minor, the pressure of the powerful peoples of the interior checked the natural course of expansion towards the inner territories and favoured oversea migration. Here and elsewhere trade no doubt assisted, and Greek merchants who observed favourable sites on their voyages would recommend them to intending emigrants. The colonies in turn were a stimulus to Greek trade and industry. The colonists demanded the industrial products of the metropolis and exported in exchange food and raw materials. The settlements were at first private ventures, but later were organized by the States. The emigrants about to found a colony took with them fire from the sacred hearth of their State (see *Religion*, § 2), and the State appointed an official oecist (*oikistēs*) as head of the venture. A Greek colony was normally a sovereign State, not politically dependent on its mother-city; but the relations between colony and mother-State remained as a rule friendly and intimate. The Delphic (q.v.) oracle was often consulted on questions of colonial policy.

§ 2. *Greek colonization in the north-east*

The chief founders of colonies in this direction were Euboeans from Chalcis and Eretria, Megarians, Corinthians, and inhabitants of the islands and cities of Asia Minor, notably Miletus. The Chalcidians of Euboea in the late 8th and early 7th cc. founded so many cities on the three-tongued promontory south of Macedonia that it gained the name Chalcidice. Here also Corinth founded a century later the important town of Potidaea. A little to the E. of the Chalcidic peninsula, on the Strymon, Athens founded in the days of Pericles the city of Amphipolis, which she was destined soon to lose. Along the coast of Macedonia and Thrace, from the Euboean towns of Pydna and Methōnē eastwards, colonizing enterprise extended to the Hellespont, where the Lesbians founded Sestos and the Milesians Abȳdos early in the 7th c. On the Propontis the latter established Cȳzicus. In the same century the Megarians gained the keys of the Bosporus by founding Chalcēdōn and Byzantium (q.v.). In the time of Pisistratus Athens acquired the Thracian Chersonese and sent settlers there. The history of the early colonization of the Euxine is obscure. The first Greek settlements on its shores appear to have been swept away about the end of the 8th c. by a wave of Cimmerian invasion. In the middle of the 7th c. colonization was resumed, principally by Milesians, who founded Sinōpē and its daughter city Trapezus (Trebizond) on the southern shore, and, among other settlements on the western shore, the important town of Olbia. In the 6th c. Greek colonists went farther, reaching the Tauric Chersonese and occupying Panticapaeum, which became the commercial centre of the region. The Megarians of Byzantium founded Heraclēa on the Chersonese. The Greek colonies on the Euxine had great economic importance as centres of trade, for they exported large quantities of corn grown on the fertile Scythian plains, besides dried or salted fish, cattle and horses, slaves, and gold; they imported wine and oil, and articles needed for civilized life in general. They worshipped in common a sea-god, Achilles, sometimes identified with the hero of the Trojan War, supposed to be living immortal on the island Leukē in the Euxine.

§ 3. *Greek colonization in the west*

In this direction also Euboeans were the pioneers. They were probably the first settlers in Corcyra (where they were later dispossessed by Corinthians), and they had the distinction of founding (together with Aeolians of Cyme) at a very early date the most distant outpost of Greek civilization on the western coast of Italy, at Cumae (q.v.), on the promontory just N. of the Bay of Naples. Farther north they could not go because of the strong Etruscan power. From there they exercised a civilizing influence on the neighbouring Italian peoples, perhaps introducing the Greek alphabet and a knowledge of Greek religion. Cumae became an important centre of trade not only with the inhabitants of the Italian peninsula but also with the barbarians beyond the Alps. It was Euboeans, together with Ionians from Naxos, who made the first Greek settlement in Sicily, on a little tongue of lava jutting into the sea NE. of Etna; this settlement took the name of Naxos. Other Euboean colonies on the E. coast of Sicily soon followed, including Zanclē, which Messenians later transformed into Messāna or Messēnē (Messina). All these settlements may be assigned to the 8th c. The Corinthians, besides ousting the Eretrians from Corcyra (which subsequently proved a most rebellious colony) and establishing settlements on the neighbouring mainland, founded in Sicily about 734 B.C. the colony of Syracuse (q.v.), destined to be the most brilliant and populous city of the island. Other important Dorian colonies in Sicily were the Megarian Hyblaea and Selinus, and the Rhodian Gela (q.v.) and Acragas (Agrigentum, q.v.). Acragas and Selinus were the most westerly points in Sicily reached by Greek colonization. Beyond these the island was in Phoenician hands. All the above colonies had been founded by the end of the 7th c. Meanwhile Achaeans from the Peloponnese settled on the E. side of the extreme promontory or toe of Italy. Sybaris and its rival Croton (qq.v.), their principal foundations, became extremely wealthy, owing to their fertile territories. Moreover, when the Sicilian straits were in the power of Euboean settlers and these prevented the passage of merchants from Miletus, the latter diverted their commerce to Sybaris, which commanded the short overland journey across the peninsula to the Tyrrhenian sea; and the prosperity of Sybaris was thereby increased. Taras (Tarentum) at the head of the gulf which bears its name, between the toe and the heel of Italy, appears to have been founded by pre-Dorian inhabitants of the Peloponnese; but it was subsequently occupied by Dorians from Sparta (the only foreign settlement of that State). To Tarentum and the other Greek cities on the Tarentine gulf and their dependencies across the peninsula on the Tyrrhenian Sea was given the name of Magna Graecia. See also *Thurii.* One important venture in the extreme west remains to be mentioned. The Ionians of Phocaea, bold mariners, founded in the 7th c. Massalia, in Latin Massilia, the future Marseilles; and the people of Massalia in turn established settlements in many directions, inland at the future Arles, along the Riviera (Agathe = Agde, Antipolis = Antibes, Nicaea = Nice), westward at Pўrēnē (whence the name of the Pyrenees), and at the future Malaga on the coast of Spain.

§ 4. *Greek colonization in the south*

Under the rule of Psammētichus and his successors (from the middle of the 7th c. B.C.), Egypt was thrown open to Greek commerce and to Greek settlers. The Milesians founded Naucratis (q.v.) on the western or Canōpic channel of the Nile, and this was made the centre for all Greek traders in Egypt, who appear later to have been subjected to restrictions. In the latter part of the 7th c. Minyans from the island of Thēra, complying with an oracle, founded a colony which was named Cyrene (q.v.) on the coast of Africa, due S. of the Peloponnese. The leader of the settlers became their king and took the name of Battus, and his son that of Arcesilaus. Under his grandson, Battus II, there was a large influx of new settlers from Crete and the Peloponnese, and the colony became prosperous and important.

§ 5. *Result of Greek colonization.*
Hellenistic colonization

As a result of these various enterprises, the 6th c. saw Greek colonies scattered along most of the shores of the Mediterranean and the Euxine, 'like frogs round a pond' (Plat. Phaed. 109 b), not united under any central control, but at liberty to work out their own destinies, with important consequences for the history of civilization. They were the means of extending the influence of Greek culture to many peoples; and by their very independence, by their contact with a variety of nations, they developed that culture itself, by giving it variety and favouring originality. This is seen in Greek literature, philosophy, and art.

Under Alexander and his successors, Greek colonization took a new form. Alexander himself founded a large number of colonies in the territories he had conquered, designed to hold the natives in subjection, to spread Greek civilization, and to foster trade; and his successors followed his policy. Whence the numerous Alexandrias, Antiochs, Seleucias, &c., found in the East. They were for the most part situated in Asia Minor, Syria, and Egypt, but some in more distant regions, such as Iran and India.

See also *Cleruch.*

ROMAN COLONIZATION

§ 6. *Early Roman colonies*

The early colonies of Rome, unlike those of Greece, were founded by the State, not by private initiative, and during the first centuries of the republic were generally designed for military defence and limited to Italy only (they occasionally served to provide land and occupation for needy members of the Roman proletariate, e.g. Antium, founded in 338 B.C.). They were fortified towns, endowed with a certain area of the public land (acquired by conquest). Parma, Mutina, Pisaurum are examples. The citizens of *Roman colonies* proper (*Colōniae civium Rōmānorum*) were enrolled in some Roman tribe and retained their full civil rights, though owing to distance they might not be able to exercise them. The so-called *Latin colonies* (*colōniae Latinae*), originally colonies composed half of Romans and half of Latins (e.g. Ardea), but after the subjugation of Latium composed of Romans only (e.g. Venusia, q.v.), had a different constitution. Their members surrendered their Roman citizenship, but had rights of trade under the protection of the Roman courts and of intermarriage with Rome, while the colonies enjoyed an independence limited only by Rome's control of their foreign affairs and by their obligation to supply contingents to the Roman army. See *Rome*, § 4.

§ 7. *Roman colonies in later republican and imperial times*

From about the 2nd c. B.C. the character of Roman colonization underwent a change and colonies (some of them overseas) began to be founded more frequently for economic reasons. Thus Gracchus's abortive colonies, e.g. at Carthage, and Caesar's successful colonies, notably at Corinth, were mostly designed to relieve pressure at Rome and redevelop derelict areas. Caesar also revived Gracchus's plan for the restoration of Carthage. Other colonies (e.g. Sulla's and those of the triumviral period) were founded to supply land for veterans. Among the notable colonies of later republican times may be mentioned Corduba (Cordova) in Spain, and Narbō (Narbonne), Aquae Sextiae (Aix), and Arelāte (Arles) in Gaul. Africa became an important area of Roman colonization. Marius settled many of his veterans there, and numbers of Italians went to Cirta and other African cities as merchants and moneylenders.

The process of colonization in outlying parts of the empire was continued under the principate, largely for the purpose of providing land for veterans, and many cities were founded or enlarged. The imposing ruins of some of these, such as Thamugadi (Timgad) in Africa, remain to this day. In other cases, colonies were the outcome of the military system of stationing legions in permanent fortresses on the frontiers. Semi-civilian settlements grew up near these fortresses and were the origins of large modern cities, such as Colōnia Agrippina (Cologne), Lindum (Lincoln), and Eburācum (York).

Colō′nus (*Kolōnos*), a deme of Attica, about a mile NW. of the Dipylon gate of Athens, the legendary scene of the death of Oedipus (q.v.), and the birthplace of Sophocles.

Colosse′um, see *Amphitheatre.*

Colume′lla, LŪCIUS JŪNIUS MODERĀTUS, who wrote c. A.D. 65, was born at Gādēs (Cadiz) in Spain, and served in Syria in Legio V Ferrāta. His treatise 'De Re Rustica', in twelve books, which has survived, deals with the various aspects of a farmer's life and work, the choice of a farm, its cultivation, live-stock, fish-ponds, bees, and gardens, while the last two books expound the duties of the bailiff and his wife. Book X, which treats of gardens, is in hexameters (the others in

prose), and in this book the author takes up the task left by Virgil to posterity—Georg. iv. 147, where, referring to horticulture, he wrote,

praetereo atque aliis post me memoranda relinquo.

Columella's work shows a pleasant modesty and simplicity, a deep respect for agriculture and hard work, and admiration for Virgil, whom he frequently quotes. His prose is simple and dignified, recalling that of the Augustan period, in contrast to the new Latinity of many of his contemporaries. Columella also wrote a shorter manual of agriculture, of which one book, 'De arboribus', is extant.

Comedy.

GREEK COMEDY

§ 1. *The origin of Greek comedy*

Aristotle in his 'Poetics' says, substantially, that the Megarians, both of Sicily and of the Isthmus, claim to have originated comedy; that the word 'comedy' is derived from *kōmē* (village), because the comedians, being despised in the towns, wandered about the villages; that comedy came from 'the leaders of the phallic songs' which still survive as institutions in many cities; that the stages of its development are obscure; that plot-making (as distinct from lampoons) in comedy originally came from Sicily [see *Epicharmus*]; and that the archon first granted a chorus for comedy at a late date (probably 486 B.C.). As regards the derivation of the word there is now general agreement that Aristotle was wrong, and that it is to be found in *kōmos*, not *kōmē*. The word *komos* means revel; there were several kinds of *komoi* and they took place on festivals, particularly of Dionysus, and consisted of or wound up with a procession of revellers, singing, dancing, and bantering the onlookers; there is a part of the Aristophanic comedy which appears to represent a regularized form of *komos*. In other respects Aristotle's statements appear to have some foundation. Comedy in Attica seems to have originated in the villages; it retained for a time a phallic (see *Phallus*) character, being associated with the worship of Dionysus; and its development may have been influenced by the independent comedy of Megara, though more probably by other Dorian mimetic performances.

§ 2. *The Old or Aristophanic Comedy*

Comedies were performed at Athens at the festivals of Dionysus, the great Dionysia and the Lenaea. Five poets competed on each occasion, each producing one play. The normal type of the Old or

Aristophanic Comedy contained the following parts (it must be remembered that comedy was less bound by rules than tragedy, that its form constantly varied and rapidly developed):

(a) a Prologue (*prologos*) or exposition;

(b) a *parodos* or entry of the chorus;

(c) an *agōn* or dispute between two adversaries, the main subject of the play;

(d) a *parabasis*, in which the chorus addressed the audience on behalf of the poet. The *parabasis* consisted of an anapaestic passage followed by a long sentence to be uttered in one breath (*pnigos*); and then of an *ōdē* or invocation to a god, followed by an *epirrhēma* or satiric speech on current affairs, and by an *antōdē* and *antepirrhēma*.

It is probable that in the *parodos*, *agon*, and *parabasis* we have an adaptation of some kind of *komos* in which a contest arose, and which ended in an address to the onlookers.

(e) A number of episodes (*epeisodia*, in iambics) slightly separated by songs of the chorus, sometimes carrying on the main plot, but as a rule only illustrating the conclusion arrived at in the *agon*;

(f) the *exodos* or final scene, in which the predominant note is rejoicing, generally leading up to a feast or wedding.

The subject was some simple story or fable, imaginary, novel, amusing, and at the same time satirical, involving a dispute on some subject of current interest, as a result of which the poet's opinion was made known. The role of the chorus was to excite rather than to pacify and conciliate (as in Tragedy) the disputants, and finally to side with the victor. The characters, whether they were taken from real life or were the personification of abstract ideas (such as Peace or the People), were mere caricatures or symbols, not morally responsible human beings. The parts, both male and female, were taken by men. Their dress was that of ordinary life and they wore masks of certain easily recognized types, but more grotesque than those of the tragic actors; they were also extravagantly padded.

The comic chorus numbered probably twenty-four and were often divided into two half-choruses, e.g. of men and women. They wore masks and grotesque dresses to suit their parts (e.g. as birds or wasps), but took off their outer cloaks for the purpose of their dances. Dances, notably the Cordax (see *Dances*), were an important feature in the performance. Altogether the Old Comedy was a curious blend of religious ceremony, serious satire and criticism (political, social, and literary), wit, and buffoonery.

§ 3. *Authors of the Old Comedy*

Of the authors of the Old Comedy, other than Aristophanes (q.v.), we know little. CRATĪNUS (c. 520–c. 423) was the most successful. He wrote twenty-one comedies (frequently attacking Pericles) and won the prize nine times. He was a drunkard, and Aristophanes in the 'Knights' mocked him in his decline. Cratinus the following year (423) wittily defended himself in 'The Bottle' (*Pūtinē*) and won the prize against Aristophanes' 'Clouds'. CRATĒS won his first victory in 450 and was the first to substitute in comedy themes of a general character for lampoons on individuals. PHERECRATĒS was an imitator of Crates; he is known to have twice won the prize (once in 437). EUPOLIS (c. 446–c. 411) was the contemporary of Aristophanes and for a time his friend and collaborator (afterwards his adversary), and one of the most brilliant writers of the Old Comedy. He won the prize seven times. His witty satire and power of invention were especially praised by the ancients.

§ 4. *The Middle and the New Comedy*

The Old Comedy was followed about 400 B.C. by what is known as the Middle Comedy, in which scurrility gives place to parody, ridicule of myths, and criticism of literature and philosophy. ANTIPHANES and ALEXIS were its principal representatives, and the 'Plutus' of Aristophanes is an example of it. The New Comedy began to prevail about 336; its characteristic features are the representation of contemporary life by means of imaginary persons drawn from it, the development of plot and character, the substitution of humour for wit, and the introduction of romantic love as a theme. It resembles the tragedy of Euripides (the 'Ion' for example) more than the comedy of Aristophanes. Of the chorus no more remains than a band of musicians and dancers whose performances punctuate intervals in the play. The New Comedy is in fact an obvious progenitor of the modern drama. But its moral standard is surprisingly low. It holds up no finer quality than good nature to approval, while it condones such things as rape and seduction. Most of it was written at a time of political and moral disillusionment, when Athens had ceased to be a free State and had come under Macedonian dominion, with a Macedonian garrison at Munychia. PHILĒMŌN and MENANDER were the chief poets of the New Comedy. The former (c. 361–263) was a native of Soli in Cilicia or of Syracuse, but came young to Athens. Some of his plays, none of which have survived, were utilized by Plautus. For Menander, see under his name. DĪPHILUS of Sinŏpĕ was another great comic poet of this period; of his hundred comedies we have only the titles of some sixty; Plautus modelled several of his comedies on him, Terence part of his 'Adelphoe'.

ROMAN COMEDY

§ 5. *Evolution and character*

Roman comedy had its distant origin, according to LIVY (VII. ii) in the dances, accompanied by the flute, of players brought from Etruria on the occasion of a pestilence to propitiate the gods. The young Romans imitated these dances, adding a dialogue of rude improvised verses, like the Fescennine (q.v.). This rude dialogue presently gave place to a somewhat more developed but still plotless dramatic performance, the *satura* or medley (see *Satire*), with appropriate musical accompaniment. Livius Andronicus (q.v.), the historian continues, was the first to abandon the *satura* and compose a play with a plot. When this more serious and artistic form of drama became established, the young Romans left it to professionals, and returned to the improvisation of comic verses and the acting of Atellan (q.v.) farces. Whether this be a correct account or not (and Pauly-Wissowa regard such theories with suspicion; see under *Fescennine Verses*), we may conclude that several elements probably went to the development of Roman comedy: from the north, Etrurian mimetic dances and perhaps Fescennine dialogue; from the south, at a later period, Atellan farce; and the medley or *satura*. Alongside of the Atellan play mention should be made of the Mime (q.v.), probably adopted from Magna Graecia. In a soil prepared by these primitive dramatic forms, Greek comedy, first introduced by Livius Andronicus, gained a temporary hold. This found, in the 3rd c. B.C., its first important Roman exponent in Naevius (q.v.), who appears to have imitated the Attic Old Comedy in his criticisms of political personages. He was followed by Plautus, Caecilius Statius, and Terence (qq.v.), professed imitators of the Attic New Comedy; their plays were known in consequence as *fabulae palliatae* (q.v.). Plautus, in broad strokes of humour, caricature, and farce, wrote for the Roman crowd. Terence, with a more delicate art and refined wit, wrote for a more cultivated audience. But Greek themes made no permanent appeal to the Romans. The *fabulae togatae* (q.v.), in which characters and scenes were Italian though the structure was that of the Attic New Comedy, were rather more popular (see *Afranius*). A frequent feature

in them was ridicule of the 'country cousin', the inhabitant of the country towns. But the *fabula togata* degenerated into farce, and Roman comedy, which had never established itself in public favour, practically ceased to be written in the 1st c. B.C. Volcatius Sedigitus (*fl. c.* 100 B.C.) wrote in verse a short 'canon' (see *Texts and Studies*, § 2) of the Roman comic writers, placing Caecilius first in order of merit, Plautus second, Naevius third, and Terence sixth. Varro (q.v.) placed Caecilius first for plots, and Plautus for dialogue. Horace in Ep. II. i. 50 et seq. has a passage on the contemporary estimation of Roman comic writers.

Roman comedies comprised spoken dialogue and portions that were declaimed and sung. The scenes written in iambic senarii (see *Metre*) were called *diverbium*, designated by DV in the margin. This was the spoken dialogue. All other portions are usually called *cantica*, designated by C and including (*a*) trochaic and iambic septenarii, forming melodramatic recitals, *declaimed* by the actor or actors to a musical accompaniment, (*b*) the lyric or supposedly lyric parts, *sung* by the actor or a concealed substitute, with a flute accompaniment, either as a song or as a recitative. The chorus has practically disappeared in Roman comedy (there is a chorus of fishermen in the 'Rudens' of Plautus and pieces for the whole company at the end of the 'Asinaria' and the 'Cistellaria'). The cantica might be declaimed or sung by a single actor, or by two or more actors in dialogue. For the metre of Roman comedy, see *Metre*, § 4.

See also *Drama, Theatre, Pantomime.*

Comi'tia Centuriā'ta, the assembly of the Roman people in 'hundreds', military divisions attributed to Servius Tullius (see *Rome*, § 2). This assembly was organized so as to give the preponderance of power to the wealthy classes. It elected the chief magistrates in the republic, had the power of legislation, and heard appeals in capital cases.

As a legislative body it could only give assent or dissent to measures proposed by magistrates who were at first patrician; and these measures had to receive the sanction of the Senate. In 339 a measure was passed by Publilius Philō that the sanction of the Senate had to be given before a proposal was put before the comitia. This sanction later became a mere formality.

Comi'tia Cūriā'ta, the assembly of the *cūriae* or wards at Rome, the primitive assembly of the Roman people. It elected the kings and is said (though this is doubted) to have voted on questions of war and peace. In early times it had the function of confirming wills. During the republic it ratified, by the formal *lex curiata de imperio*, the conferment of power (*imperium*) on the newly appointed chief magistrates. It also dealt with cases of adoption, and of the transference of a patrician to a plebeian family, election to certain priesthoods, and other religious matters. In late republican times meetings of the Comitia Curiata were purely formal: an assembly of thirty lictors was a sufficient quorum.

Comi'tia Tribū'ta, the assembly of the Roman people, voting by tribes; it had legislative powers and elected the minor magistrates. It could receive appeals in cases of lesser gravity. It was summoned by the consuls or praetors. See also *Concilium plebis*.

Comi'tium, 'meeting-place', at Rome, a paved area about 80 yards square on the NW. side of the Roman Forum. It was a *templum* or inaugurated area (see *Temples*, § 2) and here in early republican times took place the assemblies of the Roman people for purposes other than elections (see *Campus Martius*). On the N. side of it stood the Curia, on the S. stood the Rostra (qq.v.) and see Pl. 14.

Commentaries on the Gallic War and on the Civil War ('Commentārii de bello Gallico' and 'Commentārii de bello civīli'), memoirs by C. Julius Caesar (q.v.) concerned respectively with his campaigns from 58 to 52 B.C., and with the Civil War which culminated in the battle of Pharsālus (48).

§ 1. *The Gallic War*

In the 'Gallic War', Caesar, after a brief geographical description of Gaul, plunges at once into an account of the migration of the Helvetii into Gaul, of their pursuit and repulse by the Romans, and of their resettlement in their old homes. *Book I* then relates the increasing invasion of Gaul by Germans, Caesar's decision to put an end to it, the fruitless negotiations with their king Ariovistus, and the great battle NE. of Vesontio (Besançon) in which the Germans were routed (58 B.C.). See Pl. 11.

Book II. The Belgic tribes, threatened by the Roman advance and incited by discontented Gauls, combine for war against Rome. The prompt movement of Caesar against them disconcerts their plans, and a series of engagements culminates in a critical battle against the Nervii on the Sambre and their virtual extermination. An expeditionary force under P. Crassus meanwhile subdues the tribes on the

Atlantic seaboard, and the whole of Gaul is temporarily reduced to quiet (57 B.C.).

Book III. Some predatory Alpine tribes are subdued by Servius Galba. Certain Armorican tribes led by the Veneti revolt, and in spite of Roman inexperience of their kind of naval warfare are defeated by the improvised fleet and novel tactics of the Romans. Their allies are dealt with in subsidiary campaigns (56).

Book IV. The Usipetēs and Tenctēri, German tribes, invade Gaul, and are crushed by Caesar near the Meuse. Caesar follows up this success by crossing the Rhine as a demonstration. He makes his first expedition to Britain, which had supported Gaul against the Romans. A small force lands in Kent in face of fierce opposition. Caesar's fleet at anchor suffers severely from a storm, and the British manner of chariot-fighting is disconcerting to his troops. He withdraws his force from Britain in September (55).

Book V. The second invasion of Britain with a larger force. After its landing, a storm again destroys many of the transports. Caesar reaches and fords the Thames, captures the stronghold of the chief Cassivellaunus, and obtains his surrender. Caesar takes hostages, fixes the tribute payable by Britain, and withdraws to the continent. The Book includes a geographical description of Britain. During the winter the Gauls take advantage of the dispersion of the legions to revolt. The Eburōnēs under Ambiorix annihilate the Roman garrison of Aduatuca (Tongres (?)) and then, with their confederates, subject the camp of Q. Cicero (q.v.) in the territory of the Nervii to a determined siege. Cicero is rescued from a most perilous position only by the rapid advance of Caesar himself with two legions from Amiens. The winter passes amid symptoms of further revolt. Indutiomārus, leader of the insubordinate Treveri, is killed in a surprise attack (54).

Book VI. Various punitive expeditions in the NE., the chief of them directed against Ambiorix (the Eburonian leader in the capture of Aduatuca). His kingdom is ravaged, but he himself escapes. A body of German horsemen cross the Rhine to share in the plunder of his territory, but, at the suggestion of a Gaul, attack instead Aduatuca, where the baggage of the Roman army is stored. They nearly succeed in carrying the fort by their surprise attack, but are driven off. The Book contains an account of the customs of the Gauls and Druids, and of the Germans (53).

Book VII. The disturbed state of Italy (Clodius was murdered early in 52) encourages the Gauls to a general revolt, begun by the Carnūtēs, who massacre the Roman residents in Gēnabum (Orleans). A coalition of the principal tribes is formed under Vercingetorix the Arvernian (Auvergne) and threatens the frontier of the Roman province. Caesar hastens back from Italy, makes the province secure, and crosses the Cevennes in mid-winter, drawing Vercingetorix south to the defence of Auvergne. Leaving D. Brutus to keep him occupied, Caesar himself rapidly travels to the legions at Langres and effects a concentration of the Roman army. He recaptures Orleans and besieges Avāricum (Bourges), capital of the Bitūrigēs. In spite of the attempts of Vercingetorix to relieve the place, and much suffering from cold and scarcity of supplies, the town is carried and the inhabitants are indiscriminately butchered. Caesar moves to the attack of Gergōvia, capital of the Arverni. During the siege of this very difficult position, the rashness of some of the Roman troops in the course of a carefully planned attack on an outwork leads to heavy loss. This and news of the defection of the Aedui, hitherto faithful to the Roman cause, induce Caesar to abandon the siege. Unmolested by Vercingetorix he moves to rejoin Labiēnus in the north. That officer had been sent against the Senŏnes (Sens) and the Parisii, but a rising of the Bellovaci, following news of the retreat of Caesar from Gergovia, had imperilled his position. He extricates his force by a skilful manœuvre and joins Caesar at Sens. The united army moves against Vercingetorix, who is again threatening the Roman province, follows him to his stronghold Alēsia (Auxois in the Côte d'Or), invests the place, and in spite of the efforts of a great army of Gauls to relieve it, captures it and Vercingetorix after desperate fighting.

Book VIII, a continuation of the above, was written by A. Hirtius (q.v.). Caesar's work was published in 51 B.C.

§ 2. 'The Civil War'

Book I narrates the opening of the war, after Caesar had crossed the Rubicon; his rapid advance, under pressure of which Pompey retires to Brundisium and withdraws to Epirus before Caesar's works for closing the entrance of the harbour are completed. Caesar passes to Massilia (Marseilles), of which he starts the siege, and thence to Spain, where his strategy in the neighbourhood of Ilerda (Lerida) secures the surrender of Afrānius and Petrēius, the Pompeian leaders.

Book II relates the continuation of the siege of Massilia and its capitulation; the subjugation of Western Spain; and the disastrous campaign of Caesar's lieutenant, C. Curio, in North Africa, where his rashness brings about the annihilation of his force by King Juba. All the above events belong to the year 49 B.C.

Book III relates the operations of Caesar in 48 against Pompey in Epirus, the unsuccessful attempt to blockade the latter in the neighbourhood of Dyrrhachium, Caesar's withdrawal to Thessaly, the battle of Pharsālus (a simple, lucid account), and Pompey's flight to Egypt, where he is murdered. The work ends with an account of the political situation in Egypt, Caesar's proceedings there, and the grave peril to which he and his force are exposed.

Commerce, see *Athens*, § 10, and *Rome*, § 13.

Cō′mos (*Kōmos*)*,* see *Comedy*, § 1*.*

Companions of the King, in the political system of early Greece, retainers attached to the king by personal ties of service. The institution survived in the Macedonian monarchy, and the 'Companions' of Philip of Macedon and Alexander the Great follow them in their campaigns.

Compitā′lia, at Rome, the festival of the Lares (q.v.) of the cross-roads (*compita*). The festival was a movable one, its date being announced by the praetor. Cakes were offered by every family, and woollen effigies of men and women and woollen balls (representing slaves) were hung up at the cross-roads, or at the doors of private houses, in the hope that the spirits would spare the living and be content with the effigies (Frazer on Ov. Fast. ii. 615). Slaves exceptionally had a share in the festival and were allowed much licence (as at the Saturnalia, q.v.). The festival was said to have been instituted by king Servius Tullius, himself the son, according to legend, of a slave-woman by the Lar Familiaris.

Concepti′vae, *Fēriae*, see *Festivals*, § 7.

Conci′lium plēbis, at Rome, the assembly of the plebeians alone, summoned by the tribunes. Voting by tribes it elected the plebeian magistrates (tribunes, aediles); and its decisions (*plēbi scita*) had full legislative authority if approved by the Senate, and after the *lex Hortensia* of 287 B.C. even without this approval. Some authorities do not admit any distinction between the *Concilium plebis* and the *Comitia tributa* (q.v.). The actual composition of the two bodies must have been very similar.

Concord, TEMPLE OF. The original Temple of Concord at Rome was vowed by M. Furius Camillus (q.v.) in 367 B.C. to celebrate the end of civil strife on the passing of the Licinian Rogations (q.v.). The second temple, perhaps a restoration of the first, was built after the death of C. Gracchus (q.v.). The temple was rebuilt by Tiberius (before his accession) from the spoils of his German campaigns. It stood in an elevated position at the west end of the Forum. The Senate often met there and some of Cicero's great political speeches were delivered there. It was there too that Sejanus was condemned to death.

Confarreā'tio, at Rome, the most solemn form of marriage. Servius the commentator states in a note on Virgil that bride and bridegroom sat on two chairs which were covered with the skin of a sheep which had been sacrificed. At this ceremony the sacred spelt-cake (*panis farreus* as it was usually called) was offered to Jupiter Farreus. The ceremony was performed in the presence of the Pontifex Maximus, the Flamen Dialis (qq.v.), and other witnesses. It was in fact a State ceremony. See *Women* (*Position of*), § 2.

Confessions, see *Augustine*.

Cō'non (*Kŏnōn*), one of the Athenian commanders at Aegospotami (405 B.C., see *Peloponnesian War*), whence he escaped with eight ships. He was subsequently appointed with Pharnabāzus to command the Persian fleet against Sparta, and in 394 defeated Peisander at Cnidus, destroying the naval power of Sparta, and avenging the defeat of Aegospotami. He returned to Athens, and with the help of the Persian fleet completed the rebuilding of the Long Walls. There is a life of him by Nepos.

Consōlā'tiō ad Līviam, a poem in Latin elegiacs, incorrectly attributed to Ovid, probably written in the last years of the 1st c. B.C. It is addressed to the empress Livia on the death of her son, the elder Drusus.

Consōlā'tiō ad Marciam, ad Helviam, ad Polybium, see *Seneca* (the Philosopher).

Constantine the Great (*Flāvius Valĕrius Constantīnus Augustus*) (c. A.D. 274–337), son of the Roman emperor Constantius, caused himself to be proclaimed Caesar by his troops at Eburācum (York) on the death of his father in A.D. 306. This was the period when, under an arrangement made by Diocletian about A.D. 293, the Roman empire was governed by four rulers, two Augusti and two Caesars, their subordinates. In 308 Constantine was raised by the troops to the dignity of Augustus.

A complicated struggle followed between rival claimants for imperial power. In 312 Constantine marched boldly against Maxentius, who held an apparently impregnable position in Rome, and completely defeated him near the Milvian Bridge, thus establishing his position as Augustus in the West. The precise relations of Constantine with Christianity have been the subject of much controversy, due in part to doubts as to the genuineness of the various documents, including Constantine's own letters and edicts, which have come down to us. The following brief summary is based on the view of a recent authority (see N. H. Baynes, 'Constantine the Great and the Christian Church', Raleigh Lecture for 1929). In 303 Galerius had forced upon Diocletian the policy of persecuting the Christians and had continued it, as Augustus in the East, nearly until his death in 311. Constantius in the West had refused to follow his eastern colleague's policy, and under him the West had continued to enjoy religious peace. In Rome, Maxentius, when Constantine marched against him, was supported by the leaders of the pagan religion. According to the statement of Eusebius (q.v.), Constantine told Eusebius, years later, that in the course of this march on Rome he had seen a vision of the cross athwart the sun, and beneath it the words 'In this conquer'. Before the walls of Rome Constantine saw a further vision, bidding him place the Christian monogram on the shields of his soldiers. This was done, and the troops were victorious. Shortly afterward an edict of toleration of the Christians was issued by Constantine, and various instructions were sent for the relief of the Christians in Africa. Licinius was now emperor in the East. In 313 Constantine and Licinius met at Milan and a policy of complete religious freedom was agreed upon. But in 314 and again in 323 war broke out between them. In 324 Licinius surrendered, and Constantine became sole master of the Roman empire. He had already exerted himself in vain to secure a settlement of the conflict between the Catholics and the Donatists. In the East he found the Church rent by the Arian controversy. Once more he strove to secure unity. His efforts were in great measure rewarded at the Council of Nicaea (325), over which he presided, and Arius himself was before long converted to the Catholic doctrine. But Athanasius, patriarch of Alexandria, refused to receive Arius back into the Church and remained obdurate in face of the emperor's threat of deprivation. He was finally banished by Constantine to Gaul, where he remained until the emperor's death. In 330 Constantine transferred the seat of government to Byzantium, which was renamed Constantinople; and died in 337, having been, according to Eusebius, baptized a Christian shortly before his death. But he had long before this identified himself with the Christian Church and creed. It appears from his acts and letters that he believed himself entrusted with a personal mission by the Christian God, and that he thought the prosperity of the Roman State bound up with the cause of unity in the Catholic Church. He was probably familiar with, and impressed by, the 'De Mortibus Persecutorum' of Lactantius (q.v.), whom he appointed tutor to his son.

Constitution of the Athenians (*Athēnaiōn Politeiā*), (1) see *Aristotle*, §§ 2 and 3.

(2) A short pamphlet (often referred to as 'De Re Publica Athēniensium') attributed to Xenophon but almost certainly written by an Athenian oligarch about 425 B.C. Beneath an apparent admiration for the Athenian constitution is concealed a bitter criticism of the democracy and all its works, and in particular of the Athenian empire. The work, which is sometimes ascribed to an 'Old Oligarch', is extremely valuable as expressing a contemporary opinion.

Constitution of the Lacedaemonians (*Lakedaimoniōn Politeiā*), a minor work of Xenophon.

Xenophon attributes the power of Sparta to the institutions of Lycurgus, which he describes: the marriage system, the physical training of both sexes, the strange education of the young, the public messes, the discouragement of private property, the preference of an honourable death to a disgraceful life, the army system, the position and functions of the kings. In one chapter (xiv) he interrupts the description to lament the falling away of the Spartans from these institutions. Of the Lacedaemonian constitution, in spite of the title, he tells very little.

Consuā'lia, see *Consus*.

Consul suffe'ctus, see *Consuls*.

Consuls (*Consules*), at Rome, originally called Praetors, were two in number and elected annually by the people. On the expulsion of the kings the consuls received the *imperium*, the military and judicial authority formerly wielded by the kings (but not their religious authority, which passed to the *Rex Sacrorum* and *Pontifex Maximus*, qq.v.). This power was in course of time reduced by the creation of new magistracies, notably the Censorship

(see *Censors*). The chief functions retained by the consuls were those of military command. Later they received as *proconsuls* an extension of their authority after the termination of their year of office, to enable them to carry on a military command or govern a province. In dating, the year was expressed by naming the consuls.

Under the empire the consulate became more and more a mainly honorary office; consuls were appointed as a rule for only six months or for an even shorter period. They retained some judicial functions and introduced cases before the Senate. The consuls appointed to succeed those who had held office during the early months of the year were called *consules suffecti*. See also *Cursus honorum*.

Co'nsus, in Roman religion, an ancient god, of uncertain attributes, perhaps an agricultural deity who was originally a god of the underworld; sometimes identified in antiquity with Poseidon (q.v.) on account of the connexion of each with horses. Consus was celebrated on 21 August in a harvest ceremony, by an offering made by the Flamen (q.v.) Quirinālis and the Vestals, at an underground altar in the Circus Maximus. It was at this festival, the *Consuālia*, that the Rape of the Sabines (q.v.) took place. Consus was also associated with horses; there were chariot-races at the Consualia, and horses had a holiday on that day and were crowned with flowers. There was another festival of Consus on 15 December.

Contra Rullum, see *De Lege Agraria*.

Contro̅ve'rsiae, see *Seneca the Elder* and *Novel*.

Cō'pa, a short poem in elegiacs, doubtfully attributed to Virgil, describing the hostess of a tavern, who dances to castanets to entertain her customers.

Co'rax (*Korax*), a Sicilian rhetorician of the 5th c. B.C. See *Oratory*, § 1.

Co'rdax (*Kordax*), a licentious dance, associated with drunkenness, of frequent occurrence in Attic comedies, though Aristophanes claims to have excluded it from his plays. It appears to have originated in the Peloponnese, where it was danced in honour of Artemis.

Co'rē (*Korē*), see *Persephone*.

Cori'nna (*Korinna*), (1) of Tanagra or Thebes in Boeotia, a lyric poetess of the 6th c. B.C., of whose work few fragments survive. She wrote in the Boeotian dialect, in a simple style, poems on the legends of her native country. Tradition relates that she instructed Pindar (q.v.) in poetical composition. According to an anecdote she criticized the absence of myths from one of his early poems; when Pindar thereupon went to the other extreme, she remarked that one should 'sow by hand-fuls, not with the whole sack', an expression that became proverbial.

(2) See *Amores*.

Corinth (*Korinthos*), mentioned as Ephyrē in the 'Iliad', a city connected in mythology with the legend of Sisyphus (q.v.), and according to tradition occupied by the Dorians at the time of the Dorian invasion (see *Migrations*). Although its territory was particularly unfertile, its position on the isthmus commanding the land-route between Central Greece and the Peloponnese, and giving access to two seas, offered great advantages (see Pl. 8). It was pre-eminent in Greece as an industrial centre, and shipbuilding was one of its chief trades. Ameinoclēs, the first shipbuilder known to history, lived there, and the first triremes were designed at Corinth. For long it was the chief commercial town in Europe. Both Homer and Pindar speak of 'wealthy Corinth'. Its position also gave it a cosmopolitan character. Cypselus and Periander (qq.v.) were famous tyrants of Corinth from c. 655 to 585 B.C. It was at the Isthmus of Corinth that in 481 a congress of representatives of Greek States met to concert measures against the Persian invasion. The chief colonies founded by Corinth were Potidaea, Corcyra, and Syracuse. All three figured prominently in the Peloponnesian War: the first revolted from the Delian Confederacy just before the war; the assistance given by Athens to Corcyra against Corinth was one of the immediate causes of the war; and Syracuse was the objective of the Sicilian Expedition. In this war, Corinth was one of the most active and persistent of the opponents of Athens. But later, Corinth joined Athens, Thebes, and Argos to throw off the Spartan supremacy (the 'Corinthian War', 394–387). Her position at the base of the Isthmus made her hostility a source of grave danger to Sparta, and the struggle centred round Corinth, which endeavoured to close the Isthmus passage against Sparta. The war terminated in 387 in the Peace of Antal-cidas, dictated by the Persian king at the instance of Sparta. In the war against Macedon, Corinth joined Athens in the cause of Hellenic freedom. After the defeat of Chaeronea (338) it was at Corinth that Philip summoned a congress of Greek States to form a confederacy under Macedonian supremacy. Later, Corinth became one of the principal strongholds of the Achaean League (q.v.)

and was destroyed by Mummius in 146 B.C. and its territory confiscated. It was refounded by Julius Caesar under the name of Laus Julii, and Augustus made it the capital of the Roman province of Achaia. Hadrian visited it and constructed baths there, and an aqueduct to bring water from Lake Stymphālus.

Corinth is connected with the early history of Greek literature through Arion (q.v.). Its pottery was especially famous from about 650 to 550 B.C.; and Corinth gave its name to one of the three Grecian orders of architecture (q.v., § 2). It also gave its name to 'Corinthian bronze', an alloy, it is said, of gold, silver, and copper, employed in costly ornaments. Corinth became notorious for luxury and profligacy, and the word 'Corinthian' is used frequently in English literature with allusion to this.

Corinth, ISTHMUS OF. The Isthmus of Corinth is about 3½ miles wide at its narrowest. Ships used to be dragged across this, if it was desired to avoid the long voyage round the Peloponnese. We hear of this being done in the Peloponnesian War (Thuc. viii. 7), and it was done with the fleet of Octavian when he pursued Antony and Cleopatra after Actium. Nero undertook the work of cutting a canal through the Isthmus (the project had occurred to others before him) and actually started it with his own hands and a golden pickaxe; but it was discontinued after a considerable amount of excavation had been done.

Corinthian War, see *Corinth*.

Coriolā′nus, GĀIUS MARCIUS, according to tradition, a Roman patrician and a gallant general of the first half of the 5th c. B.C., who earned the name Coriolanus for the capture of Corioli from the Volscians. He was prosecuted by the tribunes on the charge of aspiring to become tyrant, and exiled; whereupon he betook himself to his old enemies the Volscians, led them against Rome, occupied a number of towns in Latium, and approached within five miles of the city. But yielding to the entreaties of his mother, Veturia, and his wife Volumnia, he drew off his army and returned to Antium, where he was put to death by the Volscians. The story is told by Plutarch and is the subject of one of Shakespeare's Roman plays.

Corn Supply. (1) AT ATHENS. Great care was taken to maintain the supply of this essential foodstuff. At the beginning of each prytany (see *Cleisthenes*) a report on the stock-in-hand was made to the Assembly. In war-time special attention was paid to the security of the imports from the Euxine. The transactions of merchants, millers, and bakers were rigorously controlled by law and supervised by *sitophulakes* to prevent irregularities. But no maximum price was ever fixed. For prices of wheat, see *Athens*, § 10. The principal sources of the foreign supply were the Euxine, Egypt, and (in the 4th c.) Sicily.

(2) AT ROME, see *Annona*.

Cornē'lia, MOTHER OF THE GRACCHI, see *Gracchi*.

Cornē'lius Ga'llus, see *Gallus*.

Cornē'lius Sevē'rus, see *Epic*, § 2.

Cornū'tus, LŪCIUS ANNAEUS, a Stoic philosopher; see *Lucan* and *Persius*.

Corōnē'a (*Korōneia*) in Boeotia, the scene (1) of the battle in 447 B.C. in which the Athenians under Tolmidēs were defeated by the Boeotians; (2) of the battle in 394 B.C. in which the Spartans under Agesilaus (q.v.) defeated the Athenians and Boeotians.

Corō'nis (*Korōnis*), see *Asclepius*.

Corpus Jūris Cīvīlis, see *Justinian*.

Cortese, GIACOMO, Italian scholar, in 1884 described a page of a palimpsest fragment which he had found in the binding of Ovid's 'Metamorphoses'. He gave a reproduction of the page, and attributed the fragment to Cornelius Nepos. The attribution and date were actively discussed by scholars, and the piece, which contained a reference to Ennius, passed into the histories of Latin literature as 'Anonymus Cortesianus'. In 1904 L. Traube showed that Cortese (by this time professor of classical philology at Rome) had invented the text and fabricated the reproduction by taking all the letters from Angelo Mai's plate of a palimpsest of a part of Cicero's 'de Republica', published in 1822.

Coryba'ntes (*Koruhantes*), the companions of the goddess Cybele (q.v.), who followed her with wild dances and music. Also the eunuch priests of the goddess. But some ancient authorities associate them with the Curetes (q.v.) in the ritual of Zeus.

Cōry'cian Cave (*Kōrukion antron*), a cavern on Mt. Parnassus above Delphi, sacred to Pan and the Nymphs.

Cōry'cius sē'nex, the old gardener, a charming description of whom is given by Virgil in Georg. iv. 125 et seq.

Coryphāē'us (*Koruphāīos*), see *Chorus*.

Cos (*Kōs*), one of the Sporades islands, opposite Halicarnassus. In the Hellenistic Age it was a favourite place of abode of men of letters. Philitas (q.v.) was born there, perhaps Ptolemy II, and perhaps also Theocritus, who appears to have spent part of his life there. It was also the birthplace of Hippocrates (q.v.), and the centre of the medical school of the Asclepiadae, who claimed descent from Asclepius (q.v.). 'Coan vestments' (*Cōae vestes*) were light transparent garments for the manufacture of which Cos was famous in the days of the Roman empire.

Cost of Living, see *Athens*, § 10, and *Rome*, § 13.

Cothu'rnus (*Kothornos*), the thick-soled boot worn by the Greek tragic actor (see *Tragedy*, § 2).

Co'tta, GAĪUS AURĒLIUS, consul in 75 B.C. and subsequently proconsul in Gaul, a distinguished orator; one of the interlocutors in Cicero's 'De Natura Deorum'. He figures also in his 'De Oratore'.

Co'ttabus (*Kottabos*), a game popular at Greek banquets, in which the player, reclining on a couch, threw a little wine from his cup at a mark, a small saucer with an image of Hermes above it.

Co'ttus (*Kottos*), see *Giants* (*Hundred-handed*).

Coty'tto (*Kotut(t)ō*), a Thracian goddess, whose cult spread over Greece and Italy. She was associated with the Phrygian Great Mother or Cybele (q.v.), and was worshipped with licentious orgies.

Crā'sis ('mixing'), the running together of the vowel or diphthong at the end of a word with the vowel or diphthong at the beginning of the word immediately following, e.g. καλοκαγαθία, from καλὸς κἀγαθός for καὶ ἀγαθός. The first syllable of κἀγαθός, it should be noted, is long, instead of short as it would be if the diphthong of καί could be elided.

Cra'ssus, LŪCIUS LICINIUS (140–91 B.C.), one of the great Roman orators of his day (see *Oratory*, § 2), a strong supporter of the aristocracy. He is one of the principal interlocutors in the 'De Oratore' (q.v.) of Cicero.

Cra'ssus, MARCUS, praetor in 105 B.C., grandfather of the triumvir, known as ἀγέλαστος because he never laughed. He is said, however, to have laughed on one occasion, on hearing some one say, at the sight of an ass eating thistles, 'Similem habent labra lactucam', 'like lips, like lettuce'.

Cra'ssus, MARCUS LĬCĬNIUS (d. 53 B.C.), one of Sulla's lieutenants, and a man of great wealth, who as praetor in 71 B.C. defeated the insurrection of Spartacus (q.v.). He was consul with Pompey in 70, and combined with him in abolishing Sulla's constitution and diminishing the power of the Senate. During Pompey's absence in the East he joined Caesar in the lead of the popular party, and in 60 with Caesar and Pompey formed the coalition known as the 'first triumvirate'. He chose the province of Syria in 54, as an easy way of acquiring wealth and glory, but was defeated by the Parthians at Carrhae in 53 and subsequently murdered by them. There is a life of him by Plutarch, who relates that he owned silver mines, purchased confiscated estates during Sulla's proscriptions, and also made a practice of buying houses in Rome when they were on fire and consequently cheap, thus coming to own a large part of the city. He made himself popular by his general affability and his good offices to all.

Crā'tēs (*Krătēs*), (1) a comic poet, see *Comedy*, § 3; (2) a Cynic philosopher (*fl. c.* 325 B.C.), author of parodies (including one in Homeric style on the 'Beggar's Wallet' (*Pērā*) which Cynics carried), elegiacs, and plays, of which fragments survive, containing many Cynic maxims. He was the teacher of Zeno the Stoic, and gave up much wealth to take up the life of a preacher and beggar. One of his pupils, Hipparchia, married him and shared his life. (3) A Greek philosopher (*fl.* 270 B.C.), the last leader of the Old Academy (q.v.). (4) Of Mallos in Cilicia, the head of the Pergamene library (see *Pergamum*) under Eumenes II (2nd c. B.C.), and a commentator on Homer. He was sent as an envoy to Rome, where, having been detained through breaking his leg, he gave lectures and aroused an interest in literary study (see *Texts and Studies*, § 5).

Crati'nus (*Kratinos*), see *Comedy*, § 3.

Cra'tylus (*Kratulos*), a dialogue by Plato on the origin of language. Cratylus was a philosopher of the school of Heraclitus (q.v.) and a friend or teacher of Plato. According to the views put into the mouths of Cratylus and Socrates, language is natural, in the sense that words are imitations of things; but there are also in it elements of chance, of design, and of convention; and foreign speech also has an influence on its development. The etymologies given in the dialogue are childish.

Cremation, see *Burial*.

Cremū'tius Co'rdus, AULUS, a Roman

historian of the Civil Wars, put to death by Tiberius because, it is said, he called Cassius the last of the Romans. His history has not survived.

Crē'on (*Krĕōn*), (1) legendary king of Thebes, see *Oedipus*; (2) legendary king of Corinth, see *Argonauts*.

Crepidā'ta, FĬBULA, a term applied to Roman tragedies on Greek themes, such as the tragedies of Pacuvius and Accius (qq.v.); from *crepida*, the cothurnus or tragic buskin.

Crete. The researches of archaeologists have shown that there existed in various places in and around the Aegean a brilliant civilization before the advent of the Greeks into those parts (see *Migrations and Dialects*). The centre of that civilization has been proved to be Crete. For its chronology see *Minoan*. It is impossible to say to what race the early inhabitants of Crete belonged, but there is evidence that they were neither Indo-Europeans nor Semites. The island attained to great prosperity and a dominating position in the Aegean from the period known as the Middle Minoan III to the Late Minoan II (1700–1400 B.C.). This position was based partly on the geographical situation of the island, which was highly favourable for commerce and also for the exercise of seapower, and partly on the industry and craftsmanship of its inhabitants, who excelled in the working of bronze and the manufacture of pottery. The products of these industries were carried by their commerce to Greece, Egypt, Cyprus, Syria, Sicily, and the Cyclades. The early Cretans were a highly artistic people and produced works of great beauty and originality, especially in wall-painting, the decoration of vases, and the sculpture of statuettes. Not only did the Cretans carry on an active commerce with other countries, but they appear in Middle and Late Minoan times to have exerted so powerful an influence at certain places in Greece, of which Mycenae, Tiryns, and Thebes are the most important, as to cause them to adopt a civilization, known as Mycenaean, which was substantially the same, though with local modifications, as that of Crete. In the view of some authorities, these places were actual Cretan settlements. It was this Mycenaean civilization that the Dorian invaders overthrew when at a later period they came to the Peloponnese (see *Migrations and Dialects*). A number of considerable cities had grown up in Crete itself, of which Cnossus and Phaestus were the most important. At some time about the 17th c. B.C., a great catastrophe occurred, perhaps an earthquake, or a foreign invasion, or an internal revolution, and the palaces of these cities were destroyed. But prosperity returned to Crete and reached its height in the 16th and 15th cc. Cnossus became the leading city and its king was ruler of the whole island. There are several mentions of Minos of Crete in Greek legend. There was the Minos who from being a just king became a judge in Hades, Minos the son of Europa, Minos the grandfather of Idomeneus, Minos the husband of Pasiphae, the besieger of Megara in the legend of Scylla (q.v.), the pursuer of Britomartis (q.v.). The name may have been that of several Cretan kings, or a title. In any case, the end of Cnossus and its kings appears to have come about 1400, when a sudden destruction came upon the palace of Cnossus, probably as the result of an invasion from Greece. Attica, in its legend of Theseus and the Minotaur, claims the honour of this victory. It may have been in consequence of it that the Cadmeans left Crete and occupied part of Boeotia. Other Cretans migrated to Asia Minor, Syria, or Egypt. The island under its new rulers never recovered its former prosperity, and Cretan art after 1400 shows degeneration. About 1200 came the further invasion of the Dorians (see *Migrations*), which destroyed any extant monuments of the Minoan civilization.

For the association of Crete with the worship of Zeus, see *Zeus*, *Dicte*, and *Ida* (2).

Cre′tic, see *Metre*, § 1.

Crĕŭ′sa (*Kreousa*), (1) in Greek mythology, daughter of Erechtheus and mother of Ion; (2) wife of Aeneas and mother of Ascanius (qq.v.).

Crimi′sus, a river in the W. of Sicily, near which Timoleon defeated the Carthaginians in 339 B.C. (see *Syracuse*, § 3).

Crina′goras (*Krinagorās*) of Mytilene (*fl. c.* 20 B.C.), a Greek writer of elegiac poetry, of which specimens are preserved in the Palatine Anthology (q.v.).

Crisae′an (or **Crissae′an**) **Plain**, sometimes called the 'Cirrhaean Plain', see *Sacred Wars*.

Cri′tias (*Kritiās*) (c. 460–403 B.C.), an oligarchical politician at Athens, the master spirit among the Thirty (see *Athens*, § 5). He led the extreme section of the tyrants against Theramenes (q.v.) and caused him to be put to death. Critias was killed at Munychia in the civil war that brought about the downfall of the Thirty. He associated at one time with Socrates and figures in Plato's dialogues, 'Prota-

goras', 'Timaeus' (qq.v.), and 'Critias' (see *Plato*, § 2.)

Critias, a dialogue by Plato (q.v., § 2).

Cri′tŏ (*Kritōn*), a dialogue by Plato.

Socrates is in prison, awaiting the hour, now near, when he is to take the poison. His friend Crito comes to him and proposes a means of escape, urging his duty to his children. Socrates replies that the only question is whether an attempt at escape would be a just act; evil must not be done in return for evil suffered. Suppose the laws of Athens should remonstrate with him and ask why he, who was born and has lived under them, should now try to overturn them. Moreover, how will he be a gainer by a life of exile? The laws exhort him to justice first, and afterwards to think of life and children. That is what the divine voice is murmuring to him.

Critolā′us (*Kritolāos*), see *Philosophy*, § 2.

Croe′sus (*Kroisos*), the last king of Lydia (q.v.) (560–546 B.C.). He subdued the Greek cities of Aeolia and Ionia (except Miletus) and the Dorian States of Caria. His wealth became proverbial, and he sent rich offerings to the sanctuaries of Greece, especially to Delphi. Misled by an ambiguous oracle, he crossed the Halys, the boundary of his empire, in an expedition against the Persian king, Cyrus, who had driven Astyagēs (brother-in-law of Croesus) from the throne of Media. Croesus was utterly defeated, and his capital Sardis taken. His life was spared by Cyrus. According to the story of Herodotus (which is chronologically impossible), Croesus had been visited by Solon and had asked him whom he thought the happiest of men. Solon had named some humble Greeks who had ended their lives happily, and when Croesus showed vexation at their being preferred before him, Solon had warned him of the uncertainty of life and the jealousy of the gods. When Croesus was about to be burned alive by Cyrus, he called thrice on the name of Solon, remembering his warning. Cyrus enquired on whom he was calling, and when he heard the story, reflected on the possibilities of his own fate and set Croesus free (Hdt. i. 29 et seq. and 86–7). See also *Ephesus*.

Crŏ′nus (*Kronos*), according to Hesiod one of the Titans (q.v.); Uranus (q.v.) his father had confined his children in Tartarus, the nether world, immediately after their birth. Cronus, at his mother's instigation, rose against Uranus and castrated him (a widely diffused cosmogonic myth; see A. Lang, 'Custom and Myth'). According to one legend the period of the rule of Cronus, when he had overthrown Uranus, was a Golden Age on earth. According to another, he had been warned that one of his children would overthrow him. He therefore swallowed them when they were born. Zeus, the youngest child (eldest in Homer), was saved by a wile of his mother Rhea, and, with the aid of the Cyclopes and the Hundred-handed Giants (qq.v.), waged from Mt. Olympus a long war against Cronus supported by the other Titans (except Themis and her son Prometheus, q.v.). Zeus finally defeated them with his thunderbolts and the stones hurled by the giants, and imprisoned them in Tartarus. According to Pindar and Aeschylus, Zeus afterwards released the Titans. The children of Cronus and Rhea were Zeus, Hestia, Demeter, Hera, Poseidon, and Hades. Cronus was also father of Chiron (q.v.).

Cronus is probably a pre-Hellenic deity, and the myth points to the supersession of the religion of an earlier population by the Olympian cult of the invading Greeks, with perhaps some reference to earthquakes and volcanic eruptions. The Romans identified Cronus with Saturn (q.v.).

Cro'ton (*Krŏtōn*, L. *Crŏtōna* or *Cortōna*), a Greek settlement on the W. coast of the Gulf of Tarentum in S. Italy, somewhat south of its rival Sybaris (q.v.). It was founded by Achaeans about 700 B.C. It was a prosperous place and derived celebrity from Pythagoras, who settled there at the end of the 6th c. and founded his school. The Pythagoreans became involved in local politics on the aristocratic and conservative side, and were overthrown in a democratic movement about 450 B.C. Croton was also famous as the home of the great athlete Milo (q.v.). He is said to have led the army of Croton at the Crăthis when it defeated the Sybarites and destroyed Sybaris about 510 B.C. Croton was conquered by Dionysius I (see *Syracuse*, § 2), and suffered severely in the Roman wars with Pyrrhus and Hannibal. It was re-colonized by the Romans in 194 B.C.

Crown, On the, a speech by Demosthenes in reply to Aeschines' general indictment of his policy. See *Demosthenes* (2), § 5 (*h*).

Cte'sias (*Ktēsiās*), of Cnidos in Asia Minor, a Greek physician of the early part of the 4th c. B.C., who lived for a number of years at the Persian court. He wrote 'Persica', a history of Persia in 23 books, of which we have an abstract, and 'Indica', of which only fragments survive.

Cucu'llus, see *Clothing*, § 4.

Cu'lex ('The Gnat'), a poem in hexa-

meters doubtfully attributed to Virgil. It is known that Virgil wrote a poem of this name, probably about 44 B.C., but questionable, on internal evidence, whether the poem we have was that which he wrote.

The story, told with abundance of mythological allusion, is that of a shepherd who, menaced in his sleep by the approach of a serpent, is awakened by the sting of a gnat. The shepherd crushes the gnat and kills the serpent. The following night the ghost of the gnat visits the shepherd and reproaches him for his ingratitude. Thereafter the shepherd raises a rustic memorial to the gnat.

Cū'mae (Gk. *Kūmē*), on a promontory in Campania, the earliest Greek colony (founded about the middle of the 8th c. B.C.), and the farthest Greek outpost, in Italy (see *Colonization*, § 3). It was named after the Aeolian city of Cyme in Asia Minor, from which (and also from Chalcis and Eretria in Euboea) the original colonists had come. Here was the grotto of the Cumaean Sibyl (q.v.), the 'antrum immane' described by Virgil, which has recently been excavated. Cumae was taken by the Romans in 338 B.C.

Cunobeli'nus, see *Britain*, § 2.

Cu'pid (*Cupīdo*), in Roman religion, the boy-god of love, son of Venus; an adaptation from the Greek Eros (q.v.), of no great importance in the Roman pantheon. In literature his most important appearance is in the first book of the 'Aeneid', where Venus sends him to take the place of Ascanius and to excite the love of Dido for Aeneas.

Cupid and Psyche, see *Psyche*.

Curcu'liō ('The Weevil'), a comedy by Plautus. Phaedromus is in love with Planesium, a slave-girl, but has not the means of buying her. Curculio, a parasite of Phaedromus, steals a ring from the braggart soldier Thērapontigonus, who has deposited with a banker the money wherewith he intends to buy Planesium for himself. By means of a letter sealed with this ring, Curculio secures the girl for Phaedromus. Therapontigonus is furious at the fraud, but the ring reveals the fact that Planesium is his sister, and so all ends well.

Cūrētes (*Kourētes*), according to Hesiod, demigods, 'lovers of sport and dancers'. They are associated with the Cretan Zeus (q.v.) and the myth relates that the infant Zeus was entrusted to them by Rhea for protection against Cronus (q.v.); to conceal the child, they drowned its cries with the clashing of their weapons. The word κοῦρος means a youth, and the Curetes may have been Cretan youths who celebrated the worship of the boy-Zeus. An inscription has been found at Palaiokastro in Crete containing the Hymn of the Curetes in honour of Zeus Kouros.

Cū'ria, at Rome, the Senate-house. It stood in the centre of the N. side of the Comitium (q.v.), which itself was on the NW. side of the Forum (See Pl. 14). Its erection was attributed to Tullus Hostilius and it was known as *Curia Hostilia*. A new curia (known as *Curia Julia*) was built by Julius Caesar close to the old one, which was burnt at the funeral of Clodius.

Cū'rius (*Cŭrius*) **Dentā'tus**, MĀNIUS, famous as a type of ancient Roman virtue and frugality, lived in the early part of the 3rd c. B.C. As consul in 290, 275, and 274, he defeated the Samnites (who had in vain tried to bribe him with gold), and brought the Samnite War to a close, defeated Pyrrhus at Beneventum, and once again defeated the Samnites. He then retired to his farm, having rejected all share of booty.

Cursus honorum, at Rome, the order in which the various political offices could be held and the period that must elapse between successive offices. It was determined by custom at an early date, and was fixed by law in 180 B.C. The quaestorship was the first office to be held. It was preceded, according to Polybius, by ten years' military service and therefore could not be held before the age of twenty-eight. It was followed at intervals of two years between the tenures by the curule aedileship, praetorship, and consulship. Men sometimes passed from the quaestorship to the praetorship, but not earlier than they would have done had they held an aedileship between the two. The consulship was held about a man's fortieth year (about the forty-third after Sulla had raised the minimum age for the holding of the quaestorship to thirty). The holding of the offices of aedile and tribune of the plebs does not appear to have been similarly regulated. By a law of 342 the same office might not be held twice within a space of ten years. But this and other conditions were often relaxed in times of emergency, as during the Hannibalic War.

Cu'rtius, LACUS, in the Forum at Rome. The name is variously explained by three stories: (a) Mettius Curtius, hard pressed when checking the Sabines single-handed in a battle, urged his horse into the lake which afterwards bore his name and succeeded in reaching the farther shore; (b) a soldier, Marcus Curtius, leaped, armed and

on his horse, into a chasm which had opened in the Forum (the soothsayers had declared that the chief strength of Rome must be sacrificed before the chasm would close, meaning, in the opinion of Curtius, arms and valour); (c) C. Curtius Chilō (his name is uncertain, variants are P. Curatius and T. Curatius), consul in 445, consecrated a spot which had been struck by lightning and which was afterwards known by his name (this does not explain *lacus*).

Cu'rtius Rū'fus, QUINTUS, wrote, probably under Claudius or Vespasian, in Latin, a history of Alexander the Great in ten books, of which the first two are lost. The extant books start with Alexander's march through Phrygia and the cutting of the Gordian knot. The author is an excellent story-teller and makes the most of many thrilling or picturesque incidents in the Asiatic expedition; but he shows little critical sense or grasp of Alexander's place in the history of civilization. It is with the romantic side of his career that he is concerned.

Curule magistracies, in Rome, those whose holders were entitled to use the *sella curūlis*, an ivory folding chair, something like a camp-stool. The magistrates in question were consuls, praetors, censors, and curule aediles; the dictator, if there was one, and his master of the horse; also the Flamen Dialis (q.v.).

Cy'belē (*Kubelē* or *Kubēbē*), an Asiatic goddess, the 'Great Mother', a goddess of the powers of nature, identified by the Greeks with Rhea (q.v.). The centre of her cult was Pessīnus in Phrygia, where she was worshipped under the guise of a block of stone. Her worship was introduced at Athens about 430 B.C., when a temple (the *Metroum*, q.v.) was built to atone for the murder of one of her priests and so that the great plague which was thought to be the consequence might be stayed. Her cult and the sacred stone above referred to were introduced into Rome in 204 B.C. in the stress of the Punic War. The stone was fetched from Pergamum by a mission of distinguished Romans in a squadron of five quinqueremes. It was related that when the ship that bore it stuck in the Tiber, a noble Roman lady, Claudia Quinta, was able to tow the ship with her girdle. The temple built for the goddess's reception stood on the Palatine. The cult never became thoroughly Roman. Citizens were forbidden to take part in the rites of the Phrygian goddess or wear the Phrygian dress, but processions of the priests of Cybele were allowed in Rome (they are described by Lucretius, ii. 600 et seq.), and the festival of the *Megalēsia* or *Megalensia* was held in her honour on the 4th April. The priests of Cybele were eunuchs and were called Galli or Corybantes. See also *Attis.*

Cy'clades (*Kúklades*), a group of islands in the southern part of the Aegean Sea. They were so called because they formed roughly a circle (*kuklos*). Their inhabitants spoke the Ionian dialect. They included Delos, Ceos, Naxos, Paros, Andros, and Tenos (see Pl. 8).

Cyclic Poems, see *Epic Cycle.*

Cyclo'pes (*Kúklōpes*), one-eyed giants according to Homer, dwelling in an island afterwards identified with Sicily (see *Monsters*). According to Hesiod they were the sons of Uranus and Ge (qq.v.), three in number, Brontës, Steropës, and Argës (Pyracmōn in Virgil), and made thunderbolts for Zeus. See also *Asclepius, Polyphemus,* and *Cyclops.*

Cy'clops (*Kuklōps*), a satyric (q.v.) drama by Euripides, of uncertain date, the only extant example of this type of play.

Dionysus (q.v.) having been captured by pirates, Silenus has set out in pursuit, accompanied by his Satyrs, and has fallen into the power of the Cyclops Polyphemus. Odysseus and his crew arrive, and bargain with Silenus for food in exchange for wine. Polyphemus returns and makes prisoners of Odysseus and his men. The blinding of Cyclops and escape of Odysseus are told much as in the 'Odyssey' (q.v.). The whole subject is dealt with humorously.

Cy'cnus (*Kuknos*), see *Heracles* (ad fin.), and *Shield of Heracles.*

Cy'lon (*Kúlōn*), see *Alcmaeonidae.*

Cy'mē (*Kúmē*), see *Cumae.* See also *Hesiod.*

Cynēge'tica, see *Oppian* and *Grattius.*

Cynēge'ticus (*Kunēgetikos*), 'Hunting', a treatise attributed to Xenophon, but it is doubtful whether he wrote it, at any rate in the form in which we have it.

After an exordium, exceptional in Xenophon's works, tracing game and hounds to Apollo and Artemis, who gave the invention to Chiron (q.v.), the author urges all young men to take up hunting—i.e. hunting hares and deer on foot. He begins to describe the necessary outfit, the nets, the hounds and their points, but wanders off to the question of scent and the habits of the hare. He then returns to the trappings of the hounds, the proper way to fix the nets, and the actual hunt, where the author shows his enthusiasm. A passage follows on the breeding, training, and naming of hounds. The author

next describes the hunting of deer (for which hounds and snares were used) and of boars (with hounds, nets, javelins, and spears); and gives a short chapter to the hunting of big game in foreign countries. He then enumerates the benefits of hunting, in respect of health, military service, and moral education. The treatise winds up with an attack on sophists, whom he regards as a set of useless humbugs. See also *Arrian.*

Cynic school of philosophy, founded at Athens by Antisthenes (b. *c.* 440 B.C.), a pupil and friend of Socrates. Antisthenes was interested principally in the practical side of morality and regarded virtue as the sole basis of happiness, to be sought in freedom from wants and desires. He held up Heracles, an example of sturdy endurance, as a model. He established his school in the gymnasium of Cynosarges (q.v.), whence its name 'Cynic'; but this alternatively may be derived from *kuōn* (a dog), a nickname given to Diogenes (q.v.), the chief representative of the school at a later date, when its doctrine had been exaggerated into a general contempt of knowledge and of current morality.

Cynosa'rges (*Kunosargēs*), a place outside the walls of Athens on the east, containing a sanctuary of Heracles and a gymnasium. In the latter was founded the Cynic (q.v.) school of philosophy.

Cynosce'phalae in Thessaly, the scene of the defeat in 197 B.C. of Philip V of Macedon by Q. Flamininus (see *Macedonia,* § 3). See also *Alexander of Pherae.*

Cy'nthia, Cy'nthius, names given to Artemis (Diana) and Apollo, derived from Cynthus, a mountain in their native Delos.

Cy'pria (*Kupria*), a lost poem of the Epic Cycle (q.v.), which dealt with the events leading up to the siege of Troy and some early incidents of the war. The reason for the name of the work ('Poem of Cyprus') is not known.

Cyprian, ST. (*Thascius Caecilius Cyprianus*) (c. A.D. 200–258), bishop of Carthage, an African by birth, of pagan family, the first of the Latin Christian writers to hold high official position in the Church. He escaped from the persecution of Decius by hiding himself, but in 257 under Valerian was summoned for examination and exiled, and in 258 put to death. In strong contrast to Tertullian (q.v.) his writings show him gentle, charitable, a lover of peace; yet firm and wise, an earnest worker for the unity of the Church, and a skilful diplomatist. He was not a man of great erudition, and he lacked the intellectual force and eloquence of Tertullian. He wrote many exhortations and theses, dogmatic and moral, animated by earnest conviction and abundantly illustrated by quotations from the Scriptures. A body of 81 letters survives, some by, some to Cyprian, valuable as sources for ecclesiastical history.

Cy′prus (L. *Cyprus*, Gk. *Kupros*), a large island in the NE. of the Mediterranean, which in the Bronze Age supplied copper in large quantities, whence Lat. *cuprum*, copper. Later it was occupied by Greek settlers from the Peloponnese (perhaps as a result of the Dorian invasion, see *Migrations*) and also by Phoenicians. These two races intermingled and influenced the resulting civilization. They found there a mode of writing in which signs were used to represent syllables, and this was adopted for writing Cypriot Greek. The worship of Aphrodite (q.v.) became especially prevalent there, so that the goddess is frequently referred to as the Cyprian Aphrodite or the Paphian, in allusion to a legend that she landed at Páphos in Cyprus when she emerged from the sea (cf. *Cythera*). Cyprus became part of the Roman province of Cilicia in 58 B.C.

Cy′pselus (*Kupselos*), the founder of the Cypselid dynasty of tyrants at Corinth. He overthrew the oligarchy of the Bacchiadae and ruled Corinth from *c.* 655 to *c.* 625 B.C., when he was succeeded by his son Periander (q.v.). He established Corinth as the chief power in Greece at the time, maintaining peace at home (where his methods do not seem to have been very tyrannical) and carrying out successful colonizations in the NW. It was in his reign that the silver mines at Damastium were first exploited, and towards the close of it Corcyra, long rebellious, was subdued and brought under the control of the mother-city.

The origin of the name Cypselus was explained by a legend, suggested by the similarity of the name to *κυψέλη*, a vessel or chest. Éétion, father of Cypselus, a man of humble station, had married Labda, one of the Bacchiadae, who being lame had been obliged to wed beneath her. A Delphic oracle foretold that their son would oust the Bacchiadae from power, and the Bacchiadae consequently endeavoured to have the child killed. From this fate his mother saved him by hiding him in a chest. (A magnificent sculptured chest purporting to be that in which Cypselus was hidden was dedicated by the Corinthians at Olympia (q.v.), and was there seen many centuries later by Pausanias.)

Cyrēna′ic school of philosophy, see *Aristippus.*

Cyrē′nē (*Kūrēnē*), a city a few miles inland from the coast of what is now Libya, originally founded by Greek colonists (see *Colonization,* § 4). It stood on a high plateau within sight of the sea, occupying a large area, supplied with water from the Fountain of Apollo and other springs breaking from the cliffs, the 'place among waters' indicated by the oracle which led to its foundation. The colony attained great prosperity, both as a centre for trade with the Libyan natives, and by reason of the Cyrenae′an export of silphium, a plant possessing medicinal properties and growing abundantly in the region. Between about 630 B.C. and 450 B.C. eight kings of Cyrene bore alternately the names of Battus (the founder of the colony) and Arcesilaus. Cyrene was the birthplace of Aristippus, Callimachus, and Carneades (qq.v.).

Cy′ropaedi′a (*Kūrou Paideia*, 'Education of Cyrus'), a narrative by Xenophon, in eight books, of the career of Cyrus the Great (q.v.), in which characters and historical facts are modified to suit the author's didactic purpose, viz. an exposition of the ideal ruler and form of government. The work is in fact a historical novel with a moral purpose. Cyrus himself is an idealized character, the perfect statesman, ruler, and general, drawn partly from the younger Cyrus of the 'Anabasis' (q.v.). The constitution of Persia and the method of education similarly represent Xenophon's ideals (based in part on the institutions of Sparta). The military precepts, the tactics described, are Xenophon's own. There are a number of minor characters, kings, soldiers, councillors, among them the Indian tutor of Tigranes, unjustly put to death—a portrait of Socrates. The tedium of the work (for most modern readers) is somewhat relieved by the romantic episode of the farewell of Abradatas (who is about to die in battle) and his wife Panthea. After the conclusion of Cyrus's military campaigns by the capture of Sardis and Babylon, the work ends with a description of the organization of the Persian empire and the death of Cyrus. The 'Cyropaedia' was translated into English by Philemon Holland (1632).

Cy′rus (*Kūros*) THE GREAT, of the Persian family of the Achaemenids (q.v.), the founder of the Persian empire. He drove Astyagēs from the throne of Media and by 547 B.C. had extended the Persian realm to the Halys. He then overthrew and captured Croesus (q.v.), king of Lydia, subdued the Greek cities of Asia Minor, and conquered the Babylonians, capturing Babylon. He died in 529.

Cyrus THE YOUNGER was the second son of Darius II, king of Persia. As satrap of the western part of Asia Minor he in 407–5 B.C. rendered active help to the Peloponnesians in their war with Athens. His attempt, after the death of his father, to oust his elder brother Artaxerxēs from the throne, and his own death at the battle of Cūnaxa (401), are related by Xenophon in his 'Anabasis' (q.v.).

Cythēra (*Kuthēra*), an island off the S. coast of Laconia. According to one legend, Aphrodite (q.v.) was said to have landed on it after her birth in the sea; hence her frequent title 'Cythere'an'.

D

Da'ctyl (*Daktulos*). (1) See *Metre*, § 1. (2) The *Daktuloi Idaioi*, or Dactyls of Mt. Ida in Crete, were legendary beings to whom the infant Zeus was said to have been entrusted; perhaps the same as the Curetes (q.v.).

Da'ctylo-e'pitrīte (-eit), see *Metre*, § 3.

Dae'dala (*Daidala*), see *Hera*.

Dae'dalus (*Daidalos* 'cunning worker'), a legendary Athenian craftsman of great skill, son of Mētiōn and descended from Hephaestus (q.v.). It was said that his statues could move themselves. Being afraid that his nephew and pupil, Talus, would outdo him in ingenuity (for he invented the saw and the potter's wheel), Daedalus threw him down from the Acropolis (his grave at Athens was shown in the time of Pausanias) or into the sea, whereupon Talus was changed into a partridge (Perdix, by which name Talus is also known). Daedalus was condemned for his crime by the Areopagus and fled to Crete, where he constructed the Labyrinth for Minos (q.v.). To prevent him from leaving Crete, or because he had given Theseus (q.v.) the clue to the maze, Daedalus was himself confined in the maze, together with his son Īcarus. Thereupon with wax and feathers he made wings for himself and his son, and they flew away. But Icarus flew too near the sun, so that the wax of his wings melted and he fell into the sea and was drowned (hence the name Icarian Sea given to the part of the Aegean Sea near Crete). Daedalus escaped to Sicily, where Minos pursuing him met with a violent death.

Dai'mones, powers or spirits which, in an early stage of Greek religion, were thought to people the world, occupying trees, rivers, springs, mountains, giving rise to everything that affects man. Cf. *Numen*. In Homer *daimōn* is divine power generalized, not individualized in a particular deity. Later, the sense of the word changes, and it is generally used for a man's fate, the spirit that guides him in life, something intermediate between gods and men. (*To daimonion* was the name by which Socrates called his genius or the spirit within him.) Or a man is sometimes thought to have a good and an evil *daimon*; his good *daimon* becomes his protecting spirit and in Stoic philosophy is held equivalent to the divine spark in his nature. The subject of *daimones* was discussed by Plutarch (q.v., § 3) in one of his *Moralia*.

Damas'tēs, see *Procrustes*.

Da'moclēs (*Dāmoklēs*), a flatterer who pronounced Dionysius I, tyrant of Syracuse, the happiest of men. Thereupon Dionysius invited him to experience the happiness of a monarch. He placed him at a banquet where presently Damocles observed a naked sword hanging over his head by a single hair.

Da'naē, in Greek mythology, daughter of Acrisius, king of Argos and brother of Proetus (see *Bellerophon*). An oracle foretold that Acrisius would be killed by his daughter's son, and he therefore confined Danae in a brazen tower, so that no one might approach her. But Zeus loved her, and visited her in a shower of gold. Their son was Perseus (q.v.). Acrisius placed Danae and the child in a chest and cast them adrift in the sea. (A portion of a beautiful poem by Simonides on this incident is preserved by Dionysius of Halicarnassus.) They were borne to the island of Serīphos, where they received shelter from Dictys, brother of Polydectēs, king of the island. For their further story see *Perseus*.

Da'naids (*Danāides*), daughters of Danaus (q.v.).

Da'naus (*Danaos*), in Greek mythology, a descendant, with his brother Aegyptus, of Io (q.v.). Aegyptus had fifty sons, Danaus fifty daughters. Aegyptus and Danaus quarrelled, and Danaus and his daughters fled from their home in Egypt to Argos, of which Danaus became king and of which the inhabitants were called, it was said, *Danaoi* after him. The sons of Aegyptus pursued the daughters of Danaus to Argos to marry them. Danaus was forced to consent, but ordered his daughters to stab their husbands on the wedding night. This they all did, except Hypermnestra, who spared her husband Lynceûs. Another daughter, Amymone (q.v.), was loved by Poseidon and became mother of Nauplius, legendary founder of Nauplia. Those who had killed their husbands were condemned in Hades, for their bloody deed, to try for ever to fill with water a jar with holes in the bottom. The story of the daughters of Danaus is the subject of the 'Suppliants' (q.v.) of Aeschylus. Pindar (Pyth. ix. 193 et seq.) tells how Danaus, in order to select other husbands for his daughters, set these at the end of a race-course and let their suitors run for them.

Dancing, both among the Greeks and Romans, was largely ceremonial and associated with religion, as for instance in the dances of the Greek dramatic choruses, and in those of the Roman Salii or priests of Mars (see also *Cordax*; *Tragedy*, § 2, for *Emmeleia*; and *Satyric Drama* for *Sikinnis*). Plato thought that all dancing should have this religious character. Private dancing, among the Greeks, was in general a performance by professionals hired for the entertainment of guests, and dancing girls were trained for the purpose. In so far as practised by private persons it was regarded chiefly as an exercise to develop grace and beauty. Grown-up men and women did not dance together, but there were dances such as the *Hormos* or chain-dance, performed by strings of youths and maidens holding hands. The Romans had a low opinion of dancing for other than religious purposes, and Cicero in one of his speeches observes that no one except a madman dances when sober. This explains the disgust felt by decent Romans at Nero's partiality for dancing. Ancient statuettes show that gesture and the management of the drapery played an important part in dancing; Ovid in the 'Ars Amatoria' (i. 595) remarks:

Si vox est, canta; si mollia brachia, salta.

Da'phne (*Daphnē*), in Greek mythology, a nymph, daughter of a river (the Pēnēus or the Ladon), who was loved by Apollo and the mortal Leucippus. The latter followed her disguised as a woman, but was discovered and slain by the nymphs. Apollo still pursued her, and she, at her own entreaty, was changed into a bay-tree, which became sacred to Apollo.

Da'phnis, a legendary Sicilian shepherd, son of Hermes and a nymph. He was loved by a Sicilian nymph, and because he did not return her love or was unfaithful, was blinded by her. He thereafter spent his life composing mournful songs on his unhappy fate, the supposed origin of pastoral poetry. According to the first

Idyll of Theocritus the story is different; Daphnis refused to love, and was punished by Aphrodite with a longing for some one unattainable, whereof he pined and died.

Daphnis and Chlo'ē, see *Novel.*

Da'rdanus (*Dardanos*), in Greek mythology, son of Zeus and Electra, daughter of Atlas (q.v.). He was the ancestor of the kings of Troy (see genealogy under *Troy*) and the fact of their descent from a rival of Hera was in part the origin of the latter goddess's hatred of the Trojans.

Da'rēs in the Aeneid, a companion of Aeneas; he figures in the boxing-match (Bk. v).

Da'rēs Phry'gius, in Homer's 'Iliad' the priest of Hephaestus in Troy, was supposed to have written a poem on the siege of Troy. A Latin work of the 5th c. A.D., 'Darētis Phrygii de Excidio Trōiae Historia', purported to be a translation of it. It was fathered on Cornelius Nepos because it is prefaced by a forged letter of Nepos to Sallust, explaining how he had discovered the work at Athens. Medieval writers on the story of Troy made much use of this ridiculous work, and of the companion piece attributed to Dictys Cretensis (q.v.). There was an English translation by Thomas Paynell in 1553.

Dari'us (*Dāreios*) I, an Achaemenid (q.v.), the son of Hystaspēs. With six conspirators he overthrew in 521 B.C. the usurper (Pseudo-Smerdis) who had passed himself off as the son of Cyrus, and obtained the Persian throne. See *Persian Wars.*

Darius III (*Codomānus*) was the king of Persia whom Alexander the Great (q.v.) overthrew.

Dā'vus, the cunning slave in Terence's 'Andria' (q.v.). Davus is also the slave who lectures Horace in Sat. II. vii.

De Agri Cultū'ra or *De Re Rustica*, a treatise by M. Porcius Cato the Censor (q.v.) on agriculture. It is a concise practical handbook, without literary adornment. It deals with the purchase of a farm; the duties of owner, overseer, housekeeper, and slaves; the tilling of the soil; the care of live stock, and a few minor matters, such as a prescription for treating a sick ox, and recipes for curing hams and making cheese-cakes. It is written in a curt, abrupt style, and constantly enjoins a harsh economy.

De Amici'tia, also known as *Laelius*, a dialogue by Cicero (q.v.), composed in 44 B.C. and addressed to Atticus (q.v.). The dialogue is supposed to take place in 129 B.C., shortly after the death of

Scipio Aemilianus (q.v.). The interlocutors are Laelius (q.v.), the intimate friend of Scipio, and his two sons-in-law, one of whom is the augur Quintus Mucius Scaevola. Cicero in his youth had sat at the feet of Scaevola and had heard him, he tells us, repeat the conversation.

Laelius in his discourse discusses the nature of friendship and the principles by which it should be governed. The conclusion is that friendship is founded on, and preserved by, virtue; for it owes to virtue the harmony, permanence, and loyalty that are its essential features. This is one of the most admired of Cicero's dialogues for its dignity and calm and for the melodious quality of its prose. It was one of the two books in which Dante found consolation for the death of Beatrice.

De Architectū'ra, see *Vitruvius*.

De Bello Civi'li and *De Bello Ga'llico*, see *Commentaries*.

De Benefi'ciis, a treatise in seven books by Seneca the Philosopher, addressed to Aebūtius Līberālis, issued, the first four books about A.D. 54, and the rest later. The work deals with the nature of benefit, gratitude and ingratitude, and various problems connected with the conferring and receiving of benefits, and shows insight into human conduct. Some interesting examples are given of heroic self-sacrifice.

De Brevitā'te Vitae ('On the Shortness of Life'), a dialogue by Seneca the Philosopher addressed to Paulinus, an official, probably written about A.D. 49. It urges the value of time, and the need for the wise and thrifty use of it on self-improvement, philosophy, communion with the great thinkers of old, not on luxury and vice. One of the best of Seneca's essays.

De Causis Planta'rum, see *Theophrastus*.

De Clāris Ōrātō'ribus, see *Brutus*.

De Civitā'te Dei ('The City of God'), a religious treatise by St. Augustine (q.v.) in twenty-two books, written in the last years of his life.

The decadence of Roman institutions, ending in the deep humiliation of the capture of Rome by Alaric in A.D. 410, was attributed by many to the influence of Christianity. Augustine in this treatise set about the refutation of the charge. But the work developed into something far greater, a complete theory of the spiritual evolution of humanity. In a survey of the history of the ancient world he shows the vanity of human glory and ambition. He then attacks with ridicule the remains of the old Roman religion;

and criticizes the doctrines of the best of the pagan philosophies, the Stoic, Platonic, and Neoplatonic schools, as incapable of yielding complete happiness, for lack of the promise of eternal life. Finally he sets forth the allegory of two cities or communities, a heavenly city comprising the righteous on earth and the saints in heaven, living in accordance with God's will; and an earthly city, guided by worldly and selfish principles. He traces their evolution on earth in the history of the Jews, through the Christian revelation, to the final Judgement and the future life.

De Clēme'ntia, a treatise by Seneca the Philosopher in three books, of which the first and part of the second survive, on the need of clemency in a ruler. Its theme was suggested by an exclamation of Nero's when unwillingly signing a death warrant in his early days, 'would that I had never learnt to write'. The praise of Nero that it contains must be judged in connexion with the comparative mildness of his rule in the first years. The work was probably written about A.D. 55–6.

De Compendiō'sa Doctri'na, see *Nonius Marcellus*.

De Consōlātiō'ne ad Marciam, ad Polybium, ad Helviam, see *Seneca* (the Philosopher), § 2.

De Consta'ntia Sapie'ntis, see *Seneca* (the Philosopher), § 2.

De Corō'na, see *Demosthenes* (2), § 5 (h).

De Divīnātiō'ne, 'concerning Divination', a dialogue by Cicero composed as supplement to his 'De Natura Deorum'. Its date is probably 44 B.C., when the work was revised and published after Caesar's death.

The dialogue takes place at Cicero's villa at Tusculum, and the interlocutors are his brother Quintus and himself. Quintus expounds, with a wealth of illustration and quotations from the Stoics (and also from Cicero's own writings) his reasons for believing in certain forms of divination. Marcus explodes the belief in divination in general by this dilemma: future events are either at the mercy of chance or are foreordained by fate. If the former, no one, even a god, can have foreknowledge of them; if the latter, there is no room for divination (an investigation of the future in order to avoid unpleasant events), for what is foreordained cannot be avoided. He thinks that divination by augury should be maintained for reasons of public expediency, but proceeds with a good deal of humour to show its absurdity, quoting incidentally the saying of old

Cato that he wondered that a soothsayer did not laugh when he met another soothsayer. Cicero recognizes an art of augury, but denies a science of divination. He similarly demolishes other methods of prediction, by dreams, portents, astrology, and vaticination.

De Domo Sua, a speech delivered by Cicero in 57 B.C. before the College of Pontiffs. Its genuineness has been contested, but is now generally accepted.

When Cicero was exiled, Clodius (q.v.) had destroyed his house, consecrated the site, and erected thereon a monument to Liberty. Cicero asks the College of Pontiffs to annul the consecration on the grounds that Clodius's tribunate was irregular, that his law banishing Cicero was unconstitutional, and that the dedication was unjust and impious. The College decided in Cicero's favour.

De Falsa Lēgātiō'ne, see *Demosthenes* (2), § 5 (c).

De Fāto, a treatise by Cicero, written in 44 B.C., in which at the request of Hirtius (consul in 43) he discusses whether our actions are determined by fate. Only part of the work has survived.

De Fī'nibus Bono'rum et Malo'rum, 'On [the different conceptions of] the Chief Good and Evil', a treatise by Cicero in five books, addressed to M. Brutus (q.v.), in which he sets forth and criticizes the ethical systems of the Epicurean and Stoic schools, and of the Old Academy. It was written in 45 B.C.

The treatise takes the form of three dialogues, each dealing with one of the above systems. In the first the Epicurean view is put forward by L. Manlius Torquatus (q.v.), the scene being Cicero's villa near Cumae in 50 B.C. In the second, M. Cato of Utica (q.v.) puts forward the Stoic view, and the scene is Cicero's villa near Tusculum in 52 B.C. In the third the view of the Old Academy is expounded by M. Pūpius Pīsō Calpurniānus, and the scene is Athens in 79 B.C., when Cicero was studying philosophy there. In each case the criticism is supplied by Cicero who, it must be remembered, detested the Epicureans and accepted in a large measure the ethical doctrines of the Old Academy and Stoics.

Book I opens with a defence by Cicero of the task he has undertaken of reproducing Greek philosophical thought in Latin dress. Manlius Torquatus expounds and defends the view that the chief good is pleasure in the sense of absence of pain. This Cicero demolishes in Book II. In Book III Cato defends the view that the

chief good consists in living in agreement with nature, that is to say, substantially in virtue and wisdom. In Book IV Cicero criticizes this as not sufficiently taking into account the lower faculties of man. Book V opens with a remarkable description of the Athenian scene with its historical and literary associations. The opinion of the Old Academy (as revived by the philosopher Antiochus) is set forth, that the chief good is the perfection of the whole self, and that virtue alone gives happiness, a view largely coincident with that of the Stoics. It is criticized by Cicero on the ground that virtue alone cannot give happiness; for the virtuous man is not always happy, if pain, as is admitted, is an evil. But the last word is left with Piso, who holds that the virtuous man, if not supremely happy (owing to pain), is yet on balance happy; for virtue outweighs everything else.

De Gente Po'pulī Rōmā'nī, see *Varro* (M.T.).

De Gramma'ticis, see *Suetonius*.

De Haru'spicum Respo'nsō ('Concerning the answers of the Soothsayers'), a speech delivered by Cicero before the Senate in 56 B.C.

The soothsayers had attributed some mysterious noises heard near Rome to the anger of the gods, aroused by certain impieties, among others the profanation of consecrated sites. Clodius (q.v.) had interpreted this as applying to the rebuilding of Cicero's house on the site which Clodius had consecrated. Cicero now retorts against Clodius, claiming that the impieties referred to were all of them acts of Clodius.

De Histo'ria Conscrībe'nda, see *Lucian*.

De Impe'rio Cn. Pompeiī, see *Pro Lege Manilia*.

De Interpretātiō'ne, see *Aristotle*, § 3.

De Inventiō'ne, see *Cicero*, § 5.

De Īra, a treatise in dialogue form on Anger, by Seneca the Philosopher, addressed to his brother Novātus. Of the three books, the first two were perhaps written in A.D. 41, just before Seneca's banishment, and the last at a later date. The work deals with the nature of anger, shows that it can be controlled, discusses the means of restraining it, and refers to instances of Caligula's furies and cruelties. The plan of the work is defective.

De Īra Dei, see *Lactantius*.

De Laude Pīsō'nis, a poem in 261 hexameters by an unknown author (perhaps Calpurnius Siculus, q.v.) in praise of a

Piso, probably the Calpurnius Piso who headed the conspiracy against Nero.

De Lēge Agrā'ria or *Contra Rullum*, three speeches delivered by Cicero in the first days of his consulship (63 B.C.), the first to the Senate, the second and third before the people, against the proposed agrarian law of the tribune P. Servilius Rullus. Cicero appears to have delivered a fourth speech, which is lost, on the same subject.

Rullus proposed the appointment of ten commissioners (*decemviri*) authorized to sell all the property of the Roman People acquired outside Italy since 88, and also the remaining property of the People in Italy, and to acquire land in Italy for distribution and the foundation of colonies. Cicero attacks the proposal as giving the commissioners what were in effect unlimited powers; as being directed against Pompey; as being cruelly unfair to the foreign peoples and allies concerned; and as likely to bring no benefit to the Roman public. The Bill, of which the real author was probably Caesar, was defeated.

De Lē'gibus ('On Laws'), a dialogue by Cicero, a sequel to the 'De Re Publica' (q.v.), probably begun about 52 B.C. The date of its completion (if it ever was completed) and publication is unknown. The first three books survive in great part; it is doubtful of how many books the work consisted.

The interlocutors are Cicero, his brother Quintus, and Atticus (q.v.); the scene is Cicero's estate at Arpinum. The First Book is a discussion of the origin and nature of Justice and Law, the latter being defined as right reason in ordering and forbidding. In the Second Book Cicero sets forth and explains the religious laws of an ideal commonwealth, that is to say those dealing with the worship of the gods, priests and augurs, sacrifices, sacrilege, and the rites to the dead. In the Third Book he similarly sets forth and discusses laws relating to the constitution of the commonwealth, and the appointment and functions of the magistrates.

De Lingua Latī'na, see *Varro (M.T.)*.

De Mercē'de Conductis, see *Lucian*.

De Mo'rtibus Persecūto'rum, see *Lactantius*.

De Nātū'ra Deorum, a philosophical dialogue in three books by Cicero, written in 45 B.C. after the death of his daughter, in which he sets out the theological tenets of the three principal Greek schools of philosophy of his day, the Epicurean, Stoic, and Academic. The work is addressed to M. Brutus.

The scene is laid at Rome about 76 B.C. and the interlocutors are C. Vellēius the Epicurean, Q. Lūcilius Balbus the Stoic, and C. Aurēlius Cotta (q.v.) the Academic. The first two are known only from Cicero's writings. Velleius, after attacking the cosmogonies and theologies of the ancient philosophers from Thales to Plato, expounds the Epicurean notion of the gods, anthropomorphic beings living a life of blissful inactivity. Cotta replies, ridiculing this conception and criticizing the arguments in support of it. Next Balbus sets forth in the Second Book the Stoic view of a world governed by a divine active and intelligent providence, a universe which in the last resort is God. Cotta in turn criticizes this doctrine, maintaining the Academic attitude of suspended judgement. See also *De Divinatione*.

De Offi'ciis, a treatise 'on Duties' by Cicero, his last work, written in 44 B.C., in the form of a letter to his son Marcus, then studying philosophy at Athens. It consists of three books, the first two of which are based, as he states, largely on the teaching of Panaetius (q.v.); the third on that of Posidonius (q.v.) and others.

The First Book deals with the four cardinal virtues, Wisdom, Justice, Fortitude, and Temperance, develops the various duties that emanate from these, and passes to their application in the case of individuals, who vary in endowments, age, position, &c. The Second and Third Books treat of the application of the above principles to the pursuit of success in life—the reconciliation of expediency with virtue. The two are shown to be in reality identical, even in cases of apparent conflict; for material gain cannot compensate for the loss of the sense of honour and justice. Cicero's doctrine is illustrated throughout with a wealth of illustrations from Greek and Roman history. Noteworthy are the highly practical character of his precepts, his condemnation of abstention from public activities (in opposition to the Stoics), his insistence on the social character of man and the duty of humanity to one's fellow beings, something beyond patriotism. The work received high praise in later ages from very various quarters, from St. Ambrose and Petrarch, from Erasmus and Frederick the Great. H. E. P. Platt ('Byways in the Classics') describes it as 'the source in great measure of European notions of what becomes a gentleman'.

De O'ptimo Ge'nere Ōrātō'rum, see *Cicer⁻, § 5*.

De Opifi'cio Dei, see *Lactanvius*.

De Ōrātō're, a didactic treatise on oratory in three books by Cicero, written in 55 B.C. and addressed to his brother Quintus. The dialogues of which it is composed are supposed to take place in 91 B.C. and the chief interlocutors are the eminent orators L. Licinius Crassus and M. Antonius (qq.v.); Q. Mūcius Scaevola, the great lawyer, is also present; and after the first dialogue, Q. Catulus the colleague of Marius, and C. Julius Caesar Strabo the orator. The scene of the dialogues is the villa of Crassus at Tusculum.

In Book I Crassus discusses the qualifications of the good orator; these include, in his opinion, a wide knowledge of the sciences and philosophy, and especially of civil law. Antonius disagrees, narrowing the orator's requirements to the faculty of pleasing and persuading, without special knowledge. In Book II he develops in detail the methods of conciliating, instructing, and moving the judges; Caesar is induced to give a dissertation on the use of wit and humour (of which he was regarded as a master) with many illustrations (including the well-known anecdote of Ennius calling on Scipio Nāsīca, II. 68). In Book III Crassus discusses styles, adornments, and delivery.

De Ō'tio, see *Seneca* (the Philosopher), § 2.

De Philoso'phia, see *Varro (M.T.)*.

De Prŏvide'ntia, a dialogue by Seneca the Philosopher, addressed to his friend Lucilius (q.v.), in which he discusses the question why good men meet with misfortune when there exists a Providence. The answer is that misfortune serves a useful purpose: it is a school of virtue. The theme was perhaps suggested by Seneca's own exile. The date of composition is uncertain.

De Prŏvi'nciis Consulā'ribus, see *Cicero*, § 4.

De Re Eque'stri, see *Horsemanship*.

De Re Pu'blica, a dialogue in six books on political science, by Cicero, begun in 54 B.C. and published about 51. We possess the greater part of the first three books, and fragments of the others, including the 'Somnium Scipionis' (q.v., chiefly preserved in a commentary by Macrobius, q.v.) which formed the conclusion of the work.

The dialogue is modelled to some extent on Plato's 'Republic' (q.v.). It is supposed to take place during three days, in the garden of Scipio Aemilianus (q.v.), and the principal interlocutors are Scipio and Laelius (q.v.). Cicero declares that he had a report of the conversation from P. Rutilius Rūfus (who had served under Scipio). After a preface by Cicero, in defence of patriotic statesmanship, the dialogue begins with a conversation on astronomy. At the request of those present Scipio then sets forth the three typical forms of government, monarchy, aristocracy, and democracy, with their degenerate counterparts, and the ideal form, which is a combination of all three. The Roman Republic is an instance of the latter, and serves throughout the rest of the discussion to illustrate his doctrine. The Second Book relates the evolution of the Roman State from earliest times to its contemporary form, and passes to the necessity for justice and harmony in the State. The Third Book opens with a preface by Cicero of which much is lost. Philus, one of the interlocutors, takes upon himself to present the arguments of the philosopher Carneades (q.v.) for the necessity of injustice. Laelius and Scipio on the contrary maintain that the commonwealth cannot exist without justice. Only fragments survive of Books IV, V, and VI. Book VI was evidently concerned with the duties and rewards of the statesman in this life, and closed, after the manner of Plato's 'Republic' (the story of Er the son of Armenius), with an exposition, through the Dream of Scipio, of the life of the soul after death (see *Somnium Scipionis*). The whole work is thought by some to have had real influence on the theory and practice of the early principate.

De Re Publica Atheniensium, see *Constitution of the Athenians* (2).

De Re Ru'stica, (1) of M. Porcius Cato, see *De Agri Cultura*; (2) of Varro, a treatise on farming, written by M. Terentius Varro (q.v.) when his eightieth year admonished him 'that he must be packing his baggage to depart this life'. The treatise is in three books, addressed to different people (the first to his wife Fundānia), and takes the form of conversations, to some extent in a dramatic setting, for the first conversation is interrupted by news of a murder, and the third by incidents in an election. The author quotes in the introduction a large number of previous writers on the subject of agriculture. Book I deals with the farm itself, its buildings, and equipment, and the agricultural operations appropriate to various seasons of the year. Book II deals with live stock; Book III with Roman villas, aviaries, poultry, game preserves, and fish-ponds. The work is written in a more literary form than that of Cato, and is animated by a more kindly and liberal spirit. (3) Of Columella, see *Columella*.

De Rerum Nātū'ra, see *Lucretius*.

De Rhēto'ribus, see *Suetonius*.

De Senectū'te, a dialogue on old age by Cicero, whose title for it was CATO MĀJŎR, written in 45 or 44 B.C. The work is dedicated to Atticus (q.v.). The conversation is supposed to take place in 150 B.C., when M. Porcius Cato the Censor (q.v.) was in his eighty-fourth year. At the request of his young friends Scipio Aemilianus and Laelius (qq.v.), Cato expounds how the burden of old age may best be borne, describes its compensations and consolations, drawing illustrations from his own experience, from reminiscences of old men he has known, and from his reading (notably of Plato and Xenophon). He concludes with a reasoned statement of his belief in the immortality of the soul. The early part of the dialogue is imitated from the conversation of Socrates and Cephalus in Plato's 'Republic'.

De Situ Orbis, see *Pomponius Mela*.

De Sophi'sticis Ele'nchis, see *Aristotle*, § 3.

De Tranquillitā'te A'nimi, see *Seneca* (the Philosopher), § 2.

De Verbo'rum Significā'tu, see *Verrius Flaccus*.

De Viris Illu'stribus, see *Suetonius*.

De Vī'ta Beā'ta, a dialogue by Seneca the Philosopher, addressed to his brother Novātus (now named Gallio by adoption), in which the author discusses in what happiness consists and how to attain it. He finds the answer in the Stoic doctrine that happiness lies in living according to nature, virtuously, with a just estimate of the true value of things, thus acquiring peace and harmony of spirit. There is a justification of the possession of wealth if wisely used, which suggests that the essay was written at a comparatively late date, perhaps A.D. 58 or 59. The work as we have it is incomplete.

De Vī'ta Cae'sarum, see *Suetonius*.

De Vī'ta Po'puli Rōmā'ni, see *Varro* (*M.T.*).

Dea Dīa, see *Arval Priests*.

Decelē'a (*Dekeleia*), an Attic deme on the slopes of Parnes, NW. of Athens, famous as having been occupied and fortified in the Peloponnesian War (q.v.), at the suggestion of Alcibiades, by the Spartans, giving them a stranglehold on Athens. For the origin of the name see *Dioscuri*.

Dece'mviri stli'tibus (an old form of *lītibus*) **jūdica'ndis**, at Rome, a board of ten who (under the later republic) acted as jury in cases relating to freedom and citizenship. See *Law* (*Roman*), § 2.

Dē'cius (*Dĕcius*) **Mūs, PUBLIUS**, one of the Roman consuls at the time of the Latin War of 340 B.C. According to legend he gained the victory for his side by solemnly devoting himself and the enemy to destruction in battle, and rushing on death.

His son, of the same name, played a similar part at the battle of Sentinum (295 B.C.) against the Samnites. The legend about the earlier battle is probably based on the later act of self-sacrifice.

Dēclāmātiŏ'nēs, see *Quintilian*.

Dē'cuma, see *Fates*.

Dēfi'xiō, see *Magic*.

Dei Conse'ntēs, see *Di Consentes*.

Dē'iani'ra (*Dēianeira*), the wife of Heracles (q.v.).

Dē'idami'a (*Dēidamēia*), the mother of Neoptolemus by Achilles (q.v.).

Deina'rchus, see *Dinarchus*.

Dēi'phobē, the name of the Cumaean Sibyl (Virg. Aen. vi. 36); see *Sibyls*.

Dei'pnosophi'stai, see *Athenaeus*.

Dē'lia, see *Tibullus*.

De'lian Confederacy, see *Delos*.

Dē'los, a small island in the Aegean, in the midst of the Cyclades, according to myth the birthplace of Artemis and Apollo (see *Leto*). It became an important centre of the worship of Apollo and the seat of an oracle of the god. For the great festivals at Delos in honour of Apollo and Artemis see *Festivals*, § 6. When Theseus (q.v.) set out for Crete to slay the Minotaur, the Athenians vowed that if he was successful they would send annually a sacred embassy to Delos, and they observed their vow. During the absence of the ship on this mission Athens was kept in a state of ceremonial purity, and no criminal might be executed. It was this which delayed the execution of Socrates (q.v.). Delos was chosen as the centre of the maritime alliance, founded in 478 B.C. and known as the *Delian Confederacy*, originally directed against the Persians under the leadership of Athens. The allies, consisting of the Ionian islands of the Aegean, the cities of Euboea, and a few Ionian and Aeolian cities of Asia Minor, while retaining their autonomy, paid contributions (a few at first supplied ships) for the common purpose (see *Aristides*); the treasure of the Confederacy was kept, and its assemblies held, in the island of Delos. A series of tribute-lists, more or less mutilated, survive in inscriptions from 454 to 415. They show at first about 265 tributaries. The original assessment gave a total of 460 talents, but the amount received in the earlier period appears to have fallen short of 400 talents. When the alliance, after the danger from Persia had come to an end, was converted into an Athenian empire (see *Athens*, § 4), most of the allies lost their independence and the treasure was transferred to Athens. The assessment to tribute was then very greatly raised, probably to about 1,000 talents, perhaps to nearly 1,500. The number of tributaries appears to have been about 300. The inhabitants of Delos were removed in 422 as a measure of purification, but allowed to return in 421 by direction of the Delphic oracle. Delos had always had commercial importance owing to the business transacted there during the festival of Apollo. In the 3rd c. B.C., with the development of Asia, this importance grew and Delos became a great corn-market. It was adorned with porticoes by Hellenistic kings. It attained great prosperity after 166 B.C., when, in order to oust Rhodes from its position as the chief centre of transit trade in the Mediterranean, Rome made Delos a free port (i.e. abolished all duties there on the movement of goods) under Athenian rule. Many Italians settled in the island, and there were contingents there of traders from most peoples of the East. The growing demand for slaves for the great estates of Italy was met at Delos, where, we are told, as many as 10,000 slaves might be sold in a day. The slaves were provided by pirates. This golden age of Delos soon came to an end. The island was sacked in 86 by Mithridates' admiral, and finally devastated by corsairs in 69 B.C. Its place as the chief centre of Italian trade with the East was taken by Puteoli.

De'lphi (*Delphoi*), a very ancient oracular shrine and precinct of Apollo, situated in a deep rocky cleft on the SW. spur of Mt. Parnassus in Phocis (see Pl. 8). The temple and the numerous subsidiary buildings occupied steep semi-circular terraces, forming a sort of natural theatre, at the foot of a tremendous cliff, a scene of gloomy grandeur in strong contrast to the smiling plain of Olympia, the other great Greek religious centre. Pausanias refers to the steepness and difficulty of the highway to Delphi; it was on this road that Oedipus was supposed to have killed his father. Delphi was originally known as Pȳthŏ and in pre-Hellenic times appears to have been a shrine of Mother Earth, guarded by a dragon or serpent (*Pȳthŏn*). Apollo (q.v.), according to legend, slew the Python, ousted the deity, and established at Delphi his famous oracle (see *Delphic Oracle*). This obtained a very wide

reputation and became extremely wealthy as a result of the gifts presented to it. The ancient temple of Apollo (attributed to the legendary architects Trophonius (q.v.) and his brother) was burnt down in 548 B.C., and reconstructed with great magnificence out of subscriptions collected in many lands. The work was carried out by the Alcmaeonids (q.v.). It was destroyed again early in the 4th c., and sacked by the barbarian allies of Mithridates in the First Mithridatic War (88–84 B.C.). It stood on one of the higher terraces of the precinct, with the theatre and the stadium above it. On it were inscribed some of the maxims of the Seven Sages (q.v.), such as 'Know thyself', 'Nothing in excess'. In its inner shrine (*adytum*) was the chasm or underground chamber in which the oracles of the god were uttered. In (or near) the temple stood the Omphalos, a conical block of stone, regarded as the central point of the earth; its sacred character dated perhaps from pre-Hellenic times. In the temple enclosure the various Greek States erected 'treasuries', buildings resembling small temples, often decorated with beautiful sculptures, in which votive offerings, relics, and trophies were displayed. The Athenian treasury was erected shortly after 490 to commemorate the victory of Marathon. There were also many thank-offerings set up by the various Greek States, some of them for victories over one another, for instance the Spartan portico with statues of Lysander and his captains, commemorating the victory of Aegospotami. Another famous memorial was a golden tripod erected, out of the booty of Plataea, on a bronze column formed of three serpents intertwined. The column, 17 ft. high, was removed by Constantine to the Hippodrome of his new capital Constantinople, where it may still be seen. Among the inscriptions that have been found in the precinct of the temple are those on the pedestal of Gelon's offering for his great victory at Himera over the Carthaginians (see *Syracuse*, § 1), and on that of Aemilius Paullus for his victory over Perseus of Macedonia. Above the temple on the mountain side was the Leschē or club-room of the Cnidians, which Plutarch made the scene of one of his dialogues ('De defectu oraculorum'). It was adorned with famous paintings by Polygnotus (q.v.). Delphi was a centre of the cult of Dionysus as well as of Apollo. The ecstatic worship of Dionysus had been regulated by Delphi and he was supposed to be buried there. Of the two peaks of the neighbouring Parnassus, one was held sacred to Dionysus. Neoptolemus (q.v.) also was believed to be buried at Delphi.

What purpose took him there is variously stated; but there he was killed by the contrivance of Orestes, because he had robbed Orestes of Hermione (see *Andromache*, Euripides' play). Near Delphi, at a point not identified with certainty but probably to the SW. of the precinct, was the Pylaea or meeting-place of the Amphictyonic Council, where Aeschines (q.v.) stirred his hearers against the people of Amphissa, with ultimate consequences fatal to the liberty of Greece (see *Sacred Wars*).

Delphic Oracle, the oracular shrine of Apollo in his temple at Delphi (q.v.). Here the priestess of the god, called the Pythia, seated on a tripod over a fissure in the rock, uttered in a divine ecstasy incoherent words in reply to the questions of the suppliants. These words were interpreted by a priest in the form of verses (usually hexameters, sometimes containing errors of metre and diction, which, as emanating from Apollo, the ancients found puzzling). The Delphic Oracle was primarily concerned with questions of religion, how in particular circumstances men were to be reconciled with the gods, and evil averted. In such matters this oracle was the supreme authority in Greece. It regulated the rites of purification and expiation, and its influence, being on the side of law and order and respect for human life, was a beneficent one. On questions of morality likewise its answers were sometimes guided by high ethical principles, notably in the case of the Spartan Glaucus who inquired of the oracle whether he might by perjury acquire certain property and received a fulminating reply (Hdt. vi. 86). The oracle was said by some to have revealed to Lycurgus the laws of Sparta, and Plato in his 'Laws' shows the importance traditionally attached to it as a legislator. In more worldly matters its pronouncements were a curious mixture of wisdom, charlatanry, and triviality. So far as they dealt with the future, they were often obscure and equivocal, capable of being interpreted in accordance with the event. Their political sentiment was generally aristocratic and pro-Dorian. They frequently exerted an influence on the policy of colonization, on which the priests of Delphi were specially competent to advise, thanks to the information gathered from inhabitants of all parts of the Greek world and of other neighbouring countries who visited the shrine. The oracle was often consulted on other political questions also by Greek States, and even by foreigners, especially before the Persian Wars. By the end of the 5th c. B.C. its authority and reputation had much declined, but a response is recorded as late as the time of the Emperor Julian, A.D.353-63.

Delphin Classics, see *Editions*.

Dēmē'ter (*Dēmētēr*), according to Hesiod a daughter of Cronus and Rhea (qq.v.), and sister of Zeus, goddess of the corn and patroness of agriculture in general, identified by the Romans with Ceres (q.v.). She was the mother of Persephone (q.v.). When the latter was carried off by Hades, Demeter sought her all over the world, lighting her torches at the fires of Etna as she pursued her search; and the earth became barren because of her neglect. In her wanderings she came to Eleusis, where, in the guise of an old woman, she was hospitably received by Celěus, king of the place, and Metaneira his wife, and tended their new-born child Dēmoph(o)ŏn (according to some authorities Triptolemus). She was interrupted while holding the child in the fire to purge away its mortality and make it immortal. She explained her action by revealing her divinity, and ordered that rites, known thereafter as the Eleusinian Mysteries (see *Mysteries*), should be instituted at Eleusis in her honour. She also sent Triptolemus, who may have been the child above referred to, or another son of Celeus and Metaneira, or at least an Eleusinian, about the world in her dragon-drawn chariot, teaching the art of agriculture. See also *Plutus*. The worship of Demeter, goddess of agriculture (her name may mean 'earth-mother' or 'corn-mother'), perhaps inherited from a pre-Hellenic people, became general among the Greeks. Only the initiated were admitted to her mysteries, but any Greek, even slaves, might be initiated. Demeter is the subject and title of a poem by Robert Bridges (1905).

Dēmē'trius of Phalerum (*c.* 354–*c.* 283 B.C.), a pupil of Theophrastus (q.v.) and a man eminent in literature and politics. Besides many political and oratorical works, he wrote on Homer, made a collection of Aesop's fables, and compiled a list of Athenian archons. From 317 to 307 he governed Athens as viceroy for Cassander (see *Macedonia*, § 2), and proved an enlightened ruler. When the city fell to Demetrius Poliorcětēs in 307 he went into exile and later joined the court of Ptolemy I at Alexandria, where he exercised great influence and perhaps suggested the foundation of the Museum (q.v.) at Alexandria. He is thus a link between Athens and Alexandria as successive centres of Greek culture. There is a life of him by Diogenes Laertius.

Dēmē'trius Poliorcě'tēs, see *Macedonia*, § 2, *Athens*, § 7, and *Rhodes*.

Dēmiu'rgus (*Dēmiourgos*), a name, in the Platonic philosophy, for the Creator of the world. See *Demogorgon*.

Dēmo'critus (*Dēmokritos*), a Greek philosopher, born at Abdēra about 460 B.C. He travelled in Egypt and Asia and lived to a great age. He wrote, in an early but well-developed prose, praised by Cicero and Plutarch, on natural philosophy, mathematics, morals, and music. Only short fragments of his works survive, but his philosophical doctrine was analysed by Aristotle.

He adopted and developed the atomistic doctrine of Leucippus (see *Philosophy*, § 1) and was opposed to the school of Heraclitus and the Eleatic school of Parmenides (qq.v.). He held that the atoms of which the universe is composed, similar in quality but differing in volume and form, move about in space and are variously grouped into bodies; and that whereas the latter decay and perish, the atoms themselves are eternal. The soul is a subtle form of fire (itself composed of the most subtle atoms) animating the human body. In some respects his doctrine approaches to modern scientific notions. In ethics he held that happiness is to be sought in moderation of desire and in recognizing the superiority of the soul over the body. Juvenal (x. 33) speaks of him as ever laughing at the follies of mankind, 'perpetuo risu pulmonem agitare solebat', and he is sometimes known as the 'laughing philosopher' in opposition to the melancholy Heraclitus.

Dēmo'docus (*Dēmodokos*), in the 'Odyssey', a minstrel at the court of Alcinous; in the 'Aeneid' (x. 413) a companion of Aeneas.

Dē'mogo'rgon. Statius in his 'Thebais' refers to *triplicis mundi summum, quem scire nefastum*, 'the Most High of the triple universe, whom it is unlawful to know'. To this the scholiast (Lactantius ?) added the note that 'Demogorgon' is meant. This is the first known mention of 'Demogorgon', which is perhaps a mistake for Dēmiurgus, the Creator. Demogorgon is described in Boccaccio's 'Genealogia Deorum' as the primeval god of ancient mythology, and this appears to be the sense of the word in modern literature (Spenser, Milton, Shelley, &c.). In Shelley's 'Prometheus Unbound', Demogorgon is an eternal principle or power which ousts the gods of a false theology. The Countess of Saldar's 'Demogorgon' (in Meredith's 'Evan Harrington') is tailordom.

Dēmō'nax, a Stoic philosopher; see *Lucian*.

Dēmo'sthenēs (1), a prominent Athenian general at the time of the Peloponnesian War. It was he who conducted the operations at Pylos in 425 B.C. which terminated in the surrender of the Spartan force in Sphactēria (see *Cleon*). He was sent with reinforcements to Nicias at Syracuse in 413, but was unable to persuade that general to take the decisive course necessary to save the Athenian forces. He commanded the rear of the army in the retreat, was forced to surrender, and probably was put to death.

Dēmo'sthenēs (2) (383–322 B.C.), a great Athenian orator and statesman.

§ 1. *Biography*

He was the son of a wealthy manufacturer of arms of the same name. He was born at Athens, of the deme Paeânia. His father died when he was seven, appointing by his will three guardians for his son. These misappropriated the property left in their charge. Demosthenes, when he reached the age of 18, sought during three years to obtain restitution. In 363, having meanwhile studied under Isaeus (q.v.), he brought an action against them, and won it, though he probably recovered little. According to tradition, his first appearance as a speaker in the Assembly proved unsuccessful (it is said that he could not pronounce the letter ρ); he thereupon made strenuous efforts to improve his delivery, and studied literature and the orators. He also wrote speeches for litigants in civil and political cases and had pupils. In 355 or 354 he appeared in person in the case against Leptines (see below, § 3). His first political speeches followed, but it was not till 351 that he became prominent as a politician, on the side of the opposition. Philip of Macedon (q.v.) had been extending his power over the cities of the N. coast of the Aegean. He had sought to interfere in the sacred war against Phocis and had been stopped at Thermopylae, but had resumed his threatening movements in Thrace. It was at this moment that Demosthenes appears in the First Philippic as the advocate of a vigorous policy of resistance. But the peace party, led by Eubūlus, was in power at Athens, and such efforts as it made to check Philip proved ultimately unavailing. It was during this period of Philip's growing power that Demosthenes' three Olynthiacs (see below) were delivered. Peace became necessary and Demosthenes was one of the negotiators; but the improvidence of his colleagues and the astute delays of Philip made the terms of the 'Peace of Philocrates' more onerous than had been expected, and the Assembly was disposed to reject them. The s,eech of Demosthenes On the Peace' (345) convinced it that it would be prudent to give way. But the aggressions of Philip were renewed and by 341 he was threatening the Chersonese. The Second and Third Philippics and the speech 'On the Chersonese' belong to this period. From 340 to 338 the party of Demosthenes was in power, and during these years his political speeches cease. Shortly after Chaeronea (338), Ctesiphon carried a motion in the Council that Demosthenes should be honoured with a golden crown for his services to the State. Aeschines thereupon laid an accusation against Ctesiphon alleging the illegality of the proposal. The matter remained in abeyance until 330, when it came to trial. Aeschines in his speech reviewed the career of Demosthenes and laid to his charge all the recent misfortunes of Athens. The reply of Demosthenes 'On the Crown' secured an overwhelming vote in his favour. The latter part of Demosthenes' career was clouded by the discreditable affair of Harpalus, the fugitive treasurer of Alexander the Great (q.v., § 8). He had come to the coast of Attica with thirty ships, mercenaries, and 5,000 talents, to stir up revolt against Alexander, but the Athenians had refused to receive him. Leaving his ships and men at Cape Taenarum, he came again to Athens, bringing 700 talents. On the advice of Demosthenes he was arrested and the money impounded. Harpalus presently escaped, and it was discovered that of the money, deposited in the Acropolis under charge of commissioners of whom Demosthenes was one, one half had disappeared. What had happened remains obscure. Demosthenes, if guilty of nothing more serious, had at least been grossly negligent. As the result of an inquiry held at his own request he was condemned to pay fifty talents. He was imprisoned, but escaped into exile. After the death of Alexander he returned to Athens. The defeat at Crannon (322, see *Athens*, § 7) led to the demand for the surrender to Antipater of the chief agitators against Macedon. Demosthenes fled to the island of Calaureia off the coast of Argolis. He was pursued by the agents of Antipater and took poison.

§ 2. *Orations of Demosthenes. The first speeches*

Sixty-one speeches have come down to us under the name of Demosthenes, but the authenticity of some of these, particularly in the category of civil cases, has been contested. Among those generally accepted as authentic, the following are the most important. The first were de-livered against his fraudulent guardian Aphobus (363). By these Demosthenes obtained an ineffectual verdict, and they were followed by speeches against Onetor, brother-in-law of Aphobus, in further fruitless proceedings to obtain the recovery of his property.

§ 3. *Speeches in public prosecutions*

(a) 'Against Androtion' (355), (b) 'Against Timocrates' (353-2), (c) 'Against Aristocrates' (352), all three composed for various prosecutors on charges of illegal proposals; (d) 'Against Leptines' (354), spoken by Demosthenes himself. Leptines had proposed to abolish, in view of the financial difficulties of the State, all exemptions from taxation granted, in the past and in the future, as a reward for public services. Demosthenes argues that the proposal is contrary to good policy and that the resulting economy will be negligible. (e) 'Against Meidias' (347). This speech was never delivered. Meidias, a wealthy and arrogant political opponent, had assaulted Demosthenes in public. The proceedings taken by the latter were delayed through the influence of Meidias, and finally dropped, perhaps owing to the party truce which resulted in the embassy of 346 (see below).

§ 4. *Other speeches on public policy*

(a) 'On the Naval Boards' (*Summoriai*) (354). The duty of equipping triremes had been laid in 357 on the 1,200 richest citizens, divided into twenty Boards, the members of which paid the same share of the cost, whatever the property of each might be. This system worked unfairly and Demosthenes proposes its reform. At the same time he opposes a demand, put forward at that moment by a party at Athens, for war with Persia, as inexpedient in the circumstances. (b) 'For the Megalopolitans' (353). Thebes at this time was hampered by her 'Sacred War' (q.v.) with the Phocians, and Sparta had taken the opportunity to put forward a proposal whose object was to enable her to recover control of the Arcadians and Megalopolis their centre. The Megalopolitans had appealed to Athens for support. Part of the Assembly, actuated by hostility to Thebes, was averse to any action unfavourable to Sparta. Demosthenes takes the opposite view, and urges the maintenance of a balance of power between Thebes and Sparta. If Sparta reduces Arcadia, she will become too strong. (c) 'For the Rhodians' (352 or 351). Rhodes, at the instigation of Mausolus (q.v.) of Caria, had revolted from the Athenian Confederacy. A Carian garrison had been placed in the island, and the democratic party had been driven into exile. These now asked Athens to assist in their restoration and the liberation of Rhodes. Demosthenes urges that in spite of the grievance that Athens has against Rhodes, and in spite of possible complications with Artemisia (successor of Mausolus) and the Persians, Athens should follow her traditional role of liberator.

§ 5. *The Philippics and other speeches on the Macedonian question*

(a) 'First Philippic' (351). Philip's aggressive policy had reached the point of invading the territory of Olynthus and of menacing the Athenian hold on the Chersonese. Demosthenes urges the Athenians to awake from their slothful apathy, and details the measures they ought to take: the immediate dispatch of a small expedition, and the preparation of a larger permanent force to meet the sudden thrusts of Philip in any direction. Moreover the citizens themselves must form part of the force, and they must not rely entirely on mercenaries. (b) The three 'Olynthiacs' (349). Philip had resumed his threat to Olynthus, and had captured some towns of the Olynthian League, but his attack on Olynthus itself was delayed until 348. The Olynthians appealed to Athens, and the latter entered into alliance with them. In the first speech Demosthenes urges the immediate dispatch of assistance and energetic opposition to Philip while he is still far from Attica; also the formation of a citizen-army. The second is a speech of encouragement and enforcement of the same theme. The third contains a proposal to revoke the laws relating to the Theoric (q.v.) or Festival Fund, so as to make it available for military purposes. He contrasts the public spirit that animated the State in former days with the indolence induced by the policy of doles distributed without regard to public service. (c) 'On the Peace' (346). The Peace of Philocrates had been adopted, but for reasons explained below (see 'On the Embassy'), Philip had extended his conquests in Thrace, advanced into Greece, subdued the Phocians, and secured a place on the Amphictyonic Council. The Assembly, feeling itself outwitted, was indignant. Demosthenes had done what he could to avert these misfortunes, but he thought that resistance at the moment was impossible, and in this speech he counsels a pacific policy. (d) 'Second Philippic' (344). After an interval Philip had resumed his interference in Greece, strengthening himself in Thessaly, and supporting the Argives and Messenians

against Sparta. Athens had sent envoys to the Peloponnese to counteract the latter measures and Philip had protested. This speech is the reply of Demosthenes to Philip's protests. He exposes Philip's imperial designs and proposes a reply to him (the text has not survived). (e) 'On the Embassy' (' De Falsa Lēgātiōne ') (343). There had been grave dissensions between Demosthenes and his fellow ambassadors at the time of the conclusion of the Peace of Philocrates. The terms agreed upon were that Athens and Macedon should each retain the territories in their possession at the time the peace was concluded. As Philip was constantly engaged on fresh conquests, it was urgent, when once Athens had accepted the terms, that the second embassy, which was to receive Philip's oath to observe them, should proceed with all speed. In spite of the remonstrances of Demosthenes, the ambassadors delayed, and Philip delayed further, and when the Peace was ratified Thrace had been subdued by Macedon. Moreover, on the return of the embassy to Athens, Aeschines gave so flattering an account of the intentions of Philip in regard to Athenian interests, that the Assembly voted the extension of the treaty to Philip's descendants, allowed Philip to occupy Thermopylae, and abandoned the Phocians to their fate. In 343, when feeling at Athens had been roused by the continuance of Philip's aggressive policy, Demosthenes impeached Aeschines on the ground of the injury done to Athens as a consequence of his delay on the embassy, and of his false reports, and suggested that bribery was the cause of his pro-Macedonian policy. The reply of Aeschines (which we possess) secured a decision in his favour by thirty votes, in a jury of probably 1,501 members. (f) 'On the Chersonese' (341). Philip was in Thrace, in dangerous proximity to the Chersonese and projecting an attack on Byzantium. Athens had, after the Peace of Philocrates, sent settlers to the Chersonese under Diopeithēs. The town of Cardia refused them admission, and Philip sent an expedition for its protection. Diopeithes, ill-provided with funds from Athens, made piratical raids in various directions, among others into Philip's Thracian territory, and Philip sent a protest to Athens. In this speech Demosthenes urges that Diopeithes should be vigorously supported. Philip, though pretending to be at peace, is in fact at war with Athens, and all his operations and intrigues are designed ultimately to compass her destruction. The longer his proceedings are tolerated, the more difficult he will be to overcome. The speech is remarkable both for its statesmanlike substance and for the variety with which the orator's passion is expressed. (g) 'Third Philippic' (341, a few months after the previous speech). The threat to the Chersonese and Byzantium was closer. Demosthenes proposes to unite the Greek States against Philip, and urges the immediate dispatch of reinforcements. He tries to arouse the Athenians to the imminence of their danger. This is one of the finest of the speeches of Demosthenes, marked by a tone of gravity and deep anxiety. There is a remarkable passage where he contrasts the ancient spirit of Athens with the present state of corruption. (h) 'On the Crown' ('De Corona') (330), 'the greatest oration of the greatest of orators' (Lord Brougham). The policy recommended in the Third Philippic was adopted in its main lines and met with some temporary success. War between Athens and Philip was declared in 340 and ended in the defeat of Chaeronea. The circumstances in which this speech was delivered have been stated above (§ 1). On the technical point as to the illegality of Ctesiphon's proposal, Aeschines was probably right; but the case really turned on Aeschines' general indictment of the policy of Demosthenes, and this, from the Peace of Philocrates to Chaeronea, Demosthenes defends in detail, maintaining that the counsel he has given has been in accord with the honourable tradition of Athens, which has never 'preferred an inglorious security to the hazardous vindication of a noble cause'. He interposes a virulent attack on Aeschines, ridiculing (perhaps without strict regard to the truth of the gossip he repeats) his humble parentage and early circumstances, and endeavouring to prove from the facts of his career that he was a traitor to his country, bought by the gold of Philip. Two passages are especially famous: the description of the confusion at Athens on receipt of the news that Philip had occupied Elateia (169 et seq.), and the invocation of the men who had fought at Marathon, Salamis, and Plataea (208).

§ 6. The oratory of Demosthenes

Demosthenes is generally regarded as the greatest of Greek orators, combining nobility of thought and diction with simplicity of language. His speeches are marked by a passionate earnestness, expressed in a great variety of tones, anger, irony, sarcasm, invective; pathos and humour rarely appear. The development of his argument and arrangement of his topics, though often intricate, show great rhetorical skill. A striking feature of his eloquence is that

it is at once elevated and practical.. there is no fine speaking for its own sake; all is directed to the persuasion of his hearers, and in a form calculated to appeal to a popular audience. He uses a pure Attic speech, bold metaphors, and vivid examples: the Athenians in their warfare with Philip are like barbarians boxing, 'Hit one of them, and he hugs the place; hit him on the other side, and there go his hands; but as for guarding, or looking his opponent in the face, he neither can nor will do it' (Phil. i. 40, Transl. Pickard-Cambridge). The principal criticisms on his oratory relate to a certain artificiality in his speeches—they were certainly carefully prepared—and to the sophistical character of some of the arguments.

The method of Demosthenes has been studied by subsequent orators of all ages. He exercised a great influence on Cicero. Quintilian regarded him as by far the greatest of Greek orators and thought that his speeches should not only be examined but learnt by heart by students of rhetoric (Inst. Or. x. i. 105). In modern times traces of his influence may be found in the speeches of Chatham, Burke, Fox, and Pitt (see Sandys, 'Demosthenes'). He received high praise from Lord Brougham ('The Eloquence of the Ancients'). Milton refers to him in the lines,

Thence to the famous Orators repair,
Those ancient whose resistless eloquence
... fulmined over Greece
To Macedon and Artaxerxes' throne.

P.R. iv. 267-71.

There is a fine statue of Demosthenes in the Vatican, believed to be a copy, with variations of detail, of the statue by Polyeuctus which stood in the Agora at Athens.

Dentā'tus, MĀNIUS CŪRIUS, see *Curius Dentatus*.

Deorum Conci'lium, see *Lucian*.

Deorum Dia'logi, see *Lucian*.

Deuca'lion (*Deukaliōn*), in Greek mythology, son of Prometheus (q.v.). Zeus, being angered with the crimes of men, decided to destroy them by a flood. Deucalion, warned by Prometheus, built a boat for himself and his wife Pyrrha, in which they escaped the flood; when the waters fell they landed on Mt. Parnassus. They were advised by an oracle to throw over their shoulders 'the bones of their mother'. Understanding by this the stones of Mother Earth they did as they were directed, and from the stones thrown by Deucalion there sprang up men, and from those thrown by Pyrrha women. The eldest son of Deucalion and Pyrrha was

Hellen, the legendary ancestor of the Hellenic race and father of Dorus, Xuthus, and Aeolus, the legendary progenitors of the Dorian, Ionian, and Aeolian Greeks (see *Migrations*).

Dēvō'tiō see *Magic.*

Di Conse'ntēs, in Roman religion, the twelve great gods, six male and six female; according to two lines of Ennius:

Juno, Vesta, Minerva, Ceres, Diana, Venus, Mars,
Mercurius, Jovi', Neptunus, Volcanus, Apollo.

Di Mānēs, Pare'ntēs, see *Manes, Parentalia.*

Diae'resis ('taking asunder'), the pronunciation of two successive vowels as separate sounds, not as a diphthong; indicated in modern printing by ¨ over one of the vowels.

Dia'dochi (*Diadochoi*), a name given to the rulers who succeeded to various parts of the empire of Alexander the Great (q.v.). See *Macedonia*, § 3 (for Antigonids), *Attalids, Ptolemies, Seleucids.*

Dia'goras (*Diagorās*), a famous boxer of Rhodes; see *Pindar* (under Ol. vii).

Dia'krioi, see *Athens*, § 3.

Dialects, GREEK, see *Migrations.*

Dialogue, a form of literature in which the author seeks to convey information, or inculcate some lesson, under the semblance of a viva-voce discussion. The earliest examples of the form are the dialogues of Plato, followed by those of Xenophon, and later by those of Aristotle (qq.v.). Many other dialogues, some of them only known to us by their titles or by references, were written in Greek during the subsequent centuries, on philosophical and other subjects. One of the longest examples of the form is the 'Deipnosophistai' of Athenaeus (q.v.), but the principal writer of dialogues of the later period of Greek literature is Lucian (q.v.), who made them a vehicle of satire.

In Roman literature the chief examples of the dialogue are to be found in Cicero's political, rhetorical, and philosophical treatises, and the 'Dialogus de Oratoribus' of Tacitus.

Dialogues of the Dead, of the Gods, of the Sea-Gods, see *Lucian.*

Dia'logus de Ōrātō'ribus, a dialogue on the causes of the decline of oratory, attributed to Tacitus and now generally accepted as his work, in spite of differences of the style from that of his later writings. The discussion is supposed to have taken place about A.D. 75 and appears to have

been written about A.D. 81, before Domitian's reign. It is thus the earliest work of Tacitus that we have.

The scene is laid in the house of Curiātius Māternus, a poet, and the other interlocutors are Marcus Aper, a distinguished advocate, of Gallic birth; Jūlius Secundus, a historian; and Vipstānus Messalla, a Roman noble. The first twenty-seven chapters are introductory. Aper, a practical utilitarian lawyer, maintains the superiority of oratory over poetry, for the rewards it brings. Maternus, a meditative idealist, disdains wealth and power, and prefers the quiet life and the companionship of the Muses. Aper admits no decline in oratory. Messalla, a champion of the ancients, criticizes the modern speakers. At the request of Maternus he passes (c. 28) to the causes of the alleged decline, which for the purposes of the discussion is to be assumed. These causes Messalla finds in the lax education of the young, contrasted with the careful methods of former days; and in the defective training given to orators by the so-called rhetoricians. After a lacuna in the manuscript some one else (probably Maternus) is speaking. He urges that the decline in oratory is due to the changed conditions of public life. Oratory throve in the stirring days of the republic, in times of disorder and revolution, when orators were inflamed by party enthusiasm. The calm of the empire has removed these incentives, but has brought compensations.

It will be seen that in this dialogue oratory is discussed from a point of view different from that of Quintilian, who is concerned rather with its technical and literary aspects. Poggio heard of the existence of a manuscript of the 'Dialogus' in 1425; but the monk who offered it failed to produce it. It was recovered in 1451.

Diă'na (*Diăna*), a Latin goddess who had from very early times a temple at Rome on the Aventine, where she was associated with the plebeian class and with slaves; the construction of the temple was ascribed to Servius Tullius. Diana was supposed to promote the union of communities. There appear to have been Greek elements in her primitive cult, and she was identified with the Greek Artemis (q.v.) at an early date. She was especially worshipped by women. She was perhaps originally a spirit of the woods and of wild nature, brought into friendly relation with the Italian farmer and his family. For a short account of her functions see Catullus's hymn to Diana, poem 34.

Her most famous cult, as *Diana Nemorensis* ('of the grove'), was at Aricia in the Alban hills where her shrine stood in a grove and where she was worshipped jointly with a male god of the forest named Virbius, later identified with Hippolytus (q.v.). It was the custom for the priesthood of this shrine to be given to a runaway slave after he had plucked a branch from a certain tree in the grove and killed in single combat the priest who previously occupied the office. The implications of this strange custom have been explained in Sir J. Frazer's 'Golden Bough'. Compare Aen. vi. 136 et seq., where Aeneas plucks the Golden Bough before descending to the nether world. It is the sight of this bough that constrains Charon to ferry Aeneas across Acheron.

From her association with Artemis, Diana took over the character of a moongoddess; and, since Hecate was sometimes identified with Artemis, of an earthgoddess. She had the cult-title *Trivia* from being worshipped, like Hecate, at the crossways.

Dicaea'rchus (*Dikaiarchos*) of Messēnē, a pupil of Aristotle, a geographer and historian whose works are lost. He wrote in particular a treatise on life in Greece ('Bios Hellados'). Some lively and interesting fragments of a topographical description of Greece, which are extant, have been attributed to him, but these are probably by a writer of later date.

Di'casts, see *Judicial Procedure*, § 1.

Dicta'tor, at Rome, a magistrate who in grave emergencies might be elected for a period of six months, on the nomination of the consuls. He had supreme military and judicial authority, and could not be called to account for his actions. He appointed as his assistant a Master of the Horse (*magister equitum*). The dictatorship was introduced at Rome about 430 B.C., probably in imitation of the practice of the Latins, among whom an office of this name already existed. Among famous early dictators were Cincinnatus, M. Furius Camillus, and Q. Fabius Maximus Cunctator (qq.v.). The office ceased to be held towards the end of the 3rd c. B.C., but was revived by Sulla, who was, however, appointed dictator *rei publicae constituendae*, i.e. for an indefinite period. Similarly Julius Caesar was appointed dictator (i) in 49 for the specific purpose of holding the elections for 48; (ii) in 48, perhaps indefinitely, or perhaps for one year; (iii) in 46 for ten years; and (iv) in 44, perpetually. The dictatorship was formally abolished after Caesar's murder and Augustus refused to revive it.

Di'ctē (*Diktē*), a mountain in the E. part of Crete, in a cave on which, according to Hesiod, Zeus was born. D. G. Hogarth in his 'Accidents of an Antiquary's Life' relates how he excavated in 1900 a great grotto on Mt. Lasithi in Crete, a mountain over 6,000 ft. high, now identified with Dicte, and found, in the numerous votive offerings discovered there, proof that it was the cave traditionally associated with the above legend. To Dicte also, according to Lucian, Zeus led the maiden Europa (q.v.), whom he had carried off.

Dictionaries, GREEK AND LATIN. The first to prepare a work of this description appears to have been Aristophanes of Byzantium (q.v.), who compiled a list of unusual Greek words with their meanings. Only a fragment of this survives. Other early scholars such as Pamphilus of Alexandria (of the 1st c. A.D.) followed in his footsteps, and the practice was extended in the 2nd c. A.D. owing to the prevailing tendency to imitate the great Attic writers. Thus Aelius Dionȳsius prepared a lexicon of Attic words with examples of their use (known to us through Eustathius). Notable examples of work of this kind in later centuries are the lexicons of Hesychius of Alexandria (q.v., known to us in an abridged form) and of Hesychius of Miletus (6th c., known through Suidas, q.v.). Both these works are valuable for the light they throw on Greek texts and on the meaning of rare words (e.g. $\dot{\alpha}\chi\eta\nu\acute{\iota}\alpha$ in Aesch. Ag. 419) by the excerpts which they quote. In the 9th c. three lexicons appear to have been prepared under the direction of the patriarch Photius (see *Byzantine Age*), in two of which (known as the 'Etymologicum genuinum' and the 'Etymologicum parvum') attention was paid to the etymology of words. In the 10th c. came the great lexicon or encyclopaedia entitled Suidas (q.v.).

Among the lexicographers of the Renaissance mention must be made of Robert Estienne (Stephanus), a French publisher, author of a 'Thēsaurus Linguae Latīnae', the best Latin dictionary of the time, 1532; and of his son Henri, author of a 'Thesaurus Graecae Linguae' (1572).

In modern times the Greek dictionary of Liddell and Scott first appeared in 1843 (8th ed., 1897, revised edition 1925–40). The authors were H. G. Liddell (1811–98), headmaster of Westminster and Dean of Christ Church, and Robert Scott (1811–87), Master of Balliol and Dean of Rochester. The dictionary had its origin in the German work of F. Passow. There are also some important special lexicons dealing with particular authors, such as that of Bonitz on Aristotle.

Among modern Latin dictionaries are those of R. Ainsworth (Latin-English) 1736; J. M. Gesner (Latin) 1749, undertaken as a new edition of Stephanus, but in effect a new work; E. Forcellini (Latin-Italian) 1771, translated by J. Bailey 1828, revised (in Latin) by V. De-Vit 1858–75; I. J. G. Scheller (Latin-German) 1783–4, translated by J. E. Riddle 1835; W. Freund (Latin-German) 1834–40, translated by E. A. Andrews 1852, revised (in English) by White and Riddle 1862, and again by Lewis and Short 1879. W. Smith based his dictionary (Latin-English, 1855, &c.) on Forcellini and Freund. Of the 'Thesaurus Linguae Latinae', a larger work than any of the above, produced by the five German Universities, the first part was published in 1900, and the work is now proceeding.

Dicty′nna (*Diktunna*), see *Britomartis*.

Di′ctys Crēte′nsis, said to have accompanied Idomeneus (q.v.) to the Trojan War, and to have written a diary of the events thereof. It was said further that this was transliterated from Phoenician into Greek characters in the days of Nero. In the 4th c. A.D. a certain Quintus Septimius put out an 'Ephēmeris Belli Trōiāni' by Dictys Cretensis which was a Latin translation of this Greek version. This fantastic work, with that attributed to Dares (q.v.), provided the principal materials for medieval writers on the story of Troy.

Didactic poetry, poetry designed to give instruction. Before writing came into general use, instruction was conveniently expressed in verse, as thus more easily remembered; poets, moreover, regarded themselves to some extent as teachers, and were so regarded by others. The 'Works and Days' of Hesiod and the lost poem of Empedocles on Nature are early examples of didactic poetry. This form of composition ceased during the great Athenian literary period, but was revived in the Hellenistic Age, for instance in the astronomical and meteorological poem of Aratus (q.v.), which was translated into Latin by Cicero and (part of it) by Germanicus and Avienus; also in Callimachus's poem on 'Origins'. Didactic poetry was a favourite form with the Romans, and we find examples of it as early as the aphorisms of Appius Claudius Caecus and the 'Epicharmus' of Ennius. Later we have the great poem of Lucretius, the 'Georgics' of Virgil, the 'Fasti' of Ovid, the 'Astronomica' of Manilius, and the 'Aetna' of an unknown author (qq.v.).

Didasca′lia (*Didaskaliā*), a Greek word

(from διδάσκω, I teach) meaning the rehearsal or performance of a drama, and later a record of a dramatic performance with the name of the poet and *choregus* (see *Chorus*). From such records Aristotle drew up a collection of 'Didascaliae' (now lost except for fragments), on which similar works by Callimachus and Aristophanes of Byzantium (qq.v.) were based. The information contained in them was sometimes included in the Arguments prefixed to plays by the Scholiasts and has come down to us.

Di′dō, originally the name of a Phoenician goddess; later the name borne by Elissa, the legendary daughter of the Tyrian king Matgēnos or Bēlus. She was married to her uncle Sўchaeus, a man of great wealth. Her brother Pygmalion, coveting his riches, murdered Sychaeus. Dido, the story goes, after the death of her husband fled to Africa, and obtained from Iarbas, king of Mauretania, the grant of so much land as might be covered by an ox-hide. By the device of cutting the hide into narrow strips, she secured space to found the city of Carthage (q.v.). To escape marriage with Iarbas she took her life on a funeral-pyre. For Virgil's adaptation of her story, see *Aeneid*.

Di′dymus (*Didumos*) (c. 65 B.C.–A.D. 10) of Alexandria, nicknamed Chalkenteros ('Brazen-guts') on account of his enormous industry, was the author of a commentary on Homer embodying the opinions of Aristarchus, Zenodotus, and Aristophanes of Byzantium. Extracts from an epitome of this survive in the Codex Venetus of Homer and are the chief source of our knowledge of the work of the Alexandrian commentators. Part of a commentary on Demosthenes by Didymus has survived.

Diga′mma, the late Greek name for the Greek consonant *F*, which survives in inscriptions and must have formed part of certain words when the Homeric poems were composed, for the metre requires it. Similarly it must have occurred in the poems of Hesiod. There is evidence for its occurrence also in certain passages of Sappho and Alcaeus, and it came to be regarded as a peculiarly 'Aeolic' letter. The letter subsequently fell into disuse. It was called 'digamma' because its form was that of two capital gammas combined. Its sound was probably similar to that of our W. It is preserved in languages cognate to Greek, e.g. Latin *vinum* beside Greek (*F*)οῖνος; English *work* beside (*F*)έργον; English *sweet* beside (σ*F*)ηδύς. Bentley (see *Texts and Studies*, § 10) first noticed that it must have been in use when the Homeric poems were composed.

Di'gest (*Dīgesta*), see *Justinian*.

Di'meter, a verse of two units; see *Metre*, § 1.

Dīna'rchus (*Deinarchos*) (b. *c.* 360 B.C.), a distinguished Attic orator, born at Corinth, was a writer of speeches for the courts. Three of these survive, against Demosthenes, Aristogeitōn, and Philoclēs, charged with receiving bribes from Harpalus. See *Demosthenes* (2), § 1.

Dindorf, KARL WILHELM and LUDWIG, see *Editions*.

Dindymē'nē (*Dindumēnē*), a name of the goddess Cybele (q.v.), from Mt. Dindymon in Phrygia, where stood one of her early shrines.

Dio, see *Dion*.

Diodō'rus Si'culus (*c.* 40 B.C.), a Sicilian contemporary of Julius Caesar, wrote in Greek ' Bibliothēkē Historikē ', a history of the world, with Rome for centre, from mythical times to Caesar's conquest of Gaul. Of the forty books of which it consisted fifteen survive (including those dealing with the important period 480–323 B.C.). It is an uncritical compilation from the works of previous writers. Diodorus is one of the sources of our knowledge of the legends of mythology. He traces to Egypt the origin of many of the mythological gods. In others he sees mortals who have attained immortality by discovering the arts and benefits of civilization, e.g. Apollo the inventor of music, Poseidon of ships, Dionysus the discoverer of wine. Cf. *Euhemerus*.

Dio'genēs of Oenoanda, see *Epicurus*.

Dio'genēs of Sinōpē on the Euxine (4th c. B.C.), the principal representative of the Cynic (q.v.) school of philosophy. He lived at Athens and Corinth, and his extravagantly simple mode of life and repudiation of civilized customs made him the subject of many anecdotes. He is said to have lived in a large earthenware tub in the Mētrōum or Sanctuary of the Mother of the Gods at Athens. His tomb was shown at Corinth. See also *Alexander the Great*, § 1. Landor has an ' Imaginary Conversation' between Diogenes and Plato.

Dio'genēs Lāe'rtius (*c.* A.D. 200–250), of Laertē in Cilicia, about whose life nothing is known, was the author of ' Lives and opinions of eminent philosophers ' in Greek, the date of which from internal evidence may conjecturally be placed within the above period. The work, in ten books, purports to give an account of the principal

Greek thinkers (including in the term such men as Solon and Periander), eighty-two in number, from Thales to Epicurus. The author was an industrious, though not always accurate, compiler from the works of earlier biographers and epitomizers of philosophical doctrines. His ' Lives ' are largely taken up with anecdotes, some good, some trivial, designed to bring out the character of the philosopher concerned. Occasionally they have historical importance by reason of the authorities whom he quotes. Some of his portraits are excellent, and there is much that is interesting (e.g. the wills of some of the philosophers) and entertaining in the work. But the chief service he rendered to posterity was the preservation of three epistles and the ' Sovran Maxims ' of Epicurus (q.v.). He also preserved the beautiful epigram of Callimachus (q.v.) on Heraclitus. Diogenes was himself a poetaster and had produced a collection of epigrams on famous men; some of these indifferent verses he introduces in the ' Lives '.

Diomē'dēs, in Greek mythology, son of Tȳdeūs, and leader of the men of Argos and Tiryns in the Trojan expedition; an impetuous, fiery, and chivalrous captain, one of the principal warriors in the ' Iliad ' (q.v.), where many of his exploits are recounted. Among these was the wounding of Ares and Aphrodite. Owing to the resentment of the latter, Diomedes on his return home found that his wife Aigialeia had been unfaithful to him. He left his home and wandered to Italy, where he was reputed to have founded various towns in Āpūlia, and to have been buried in the Islands of Diomedes, near the Apulian coast. In Aen. xi. 225 et seq., Diomedes refuses to join in the resistance to Aeneas. See also *Epigoni, Glaucus* (4), *Palladium*. For the Horses of Diomedes (a different person, king of the Bistones in Thrace) see under *Heracles* (*Labours of*).

Di'on (*Dīōn*), see *Syracuse*, § 2.

Dio(n) Cassius, see *Cassius*.

Di'on (*Dīōn*) **Chry'sostom** (*Chrūsostomos*, ' golden-mouthed ') (1st c. A.D.), born at Prūsa in Bithȳnia, was a philosopher and an orator. He lived at Rome under Domitian, but showed himself an opponent of that emperor's tyrannical rule and of the tendency of the Flavians to make the empire dynastic, that is to say the property of a particular family. In this he shared a view common to the Stoics and Cynics of his day. He was in consequence banished from Rome and from his native Bithynia, and travelled widely. He was held in high esteem by Nerva and Trajan. He has left a collection of discourses in Greek on political, philosophical, and literary subjects. His political discourses, in which he rallies his audiences with a pleasant irony, were directed to remedy the defects of the particular city where each was delivered. Among his other speeches is the 'Olympic' oration, in which Phidias (q.v.) is represented expounding the principles on which his statue of the Olympian Zeus was designed.

Diŏ'nē, whose name is the feminine of Zeus (q.v.), appears in some poets (not Hesiod) as a consort of Zeus and mother of Aphrodite (q.v.).

Diony'sia (*Dionūsia*), see *Festivals*, § 4.

Diony'sius (*Dionūsios*) I and II, tyrants of Syracuse; see *Syracuse*, §§ 2 and 3.

Diony'sius (*Dionūsios*) **of Halicarnassus** (*fl. c.* 25 B.C.), a Greek writer who lived in Rome in the days of Augustus. He was both a literary critic of good judgement and wide knowledge, and a historian. In the former capacity he wrote in Greek a number of treatises, 'On the arrangement of words', 'On the Ancient Orators', 'On the Eloquence of Demosthenes', 'On Dinarchus', 'On Thucydides', &c. which have survived, and which contributed to the temporary revival at Rome of good Attic prose. To the first of these treatises we owe the preservation of Sappho's 'Ode to Aphrodite', and the 'Danae' of Simonides. Dionysius also wrote 'Rōmǎĭkē Archaiologia' or 'Early History of Rome' in twenty books (of which ten and parts of others survive), designed to be an introduction to Polybius; it is mainly a painstaking compilation from the Roman annalists, and is valuable for the evidences of Roman tradition that it has preserved. It contains the observation (i. 3), which has since been repeated, that the style is the man (εἰκόνας εἶναι τῆς ἑκάστου ψυχῆς τοὺς λόγους. The well-known words of Buffon were, 'Le style, c'est l'homme même').

Diony'sius the Thracian (*Dionūsios Thrax*) (b. *c.* 166 B.C.), a pupil of Aristarchus (q.v.) of Samothrace, wrote in Greek a short 'Technē Grammatikē', still extant, which appears to have been the first systematic Greek Grammar, and remained a standard work for many centuries. In it we find the verb τύπτω used to exemplify voices, numbers, and persons; but the full paradigm, with all the possible moods and tenses, was introduced later.

Diony'sus (*Dionūsos*), in Greek mythology, son of Zeus and Semelē, the daughter of Cadmus son of Agēnōr, king of Tyre. Semele was loved by Zeus,

and at the instigation of the jealous Hera prayed Zeus to visit her in all the splendour of a god. This he did and she was consumed by his lightning. But Zeus rescued her unborn child from the ashes and placed him in his thigh, from which in due time he was born. He was entrusted to Ino, sister of Semele and wife of Athamas (q.v.); but Hera, pursuing her vengeance, drove them mad, so that Athamas killed his son Learchus, and Ino leapt into the sea with her other child Melicertes (q.v.). Ino was transformed into a sea-goddess Leucothea, and Melicertes became the sea-god Palaemon. Dionysus was now handed over to the nymphs of Nȳsa, a mountain whose locality is variously stated. When he grew up he was persecuted by those who refused to recognize his divinity, but overcame them and extended his conquests far into Asia. The most famous of these persecutions was that of Penthēus, king of Thebes, which forms the subject of the 'Bacchae' (q.v.) of Euripides. The daughters of Proetus (see *Bellerophon*), king of Argos, also opposed him, and were driven mad, destroying their own children. Their madness was cured by the intervention of the seer Melampus (q.v.). For another similar legend, see *Minyas*. Dionysus is represented as accompanied on his conquests by a rout of votaries, male and female, Satyrs, Sileni, Maenads, Bassarids (qq.v.), dancing about him, tearing animals to pieces, intoxicated or possessed. They were known generally as Bacchi (*Bakchoi*, fem. *Bacchae*, *Bakchai*), from Bacchus, one of the names of the god. The Seventh Homeric Hymn relates that he was seized and bound by Tyrrhenian pirates; but the bonds fell off him, a vine grew about the mast, and the captive turned into a lion. The pirates in terror jumped into the sea and were transformed into dolphins. Other legends concerning Dionysus will be found under *Ariadne* and *Icarius*.

Dionysus was probably in origin a Thracian deity. He is of little importance in Homer, who does not include him among the Olympian gods. Later he appears as a god of vegetation, a suffering god, who dies and comes to life again, particularly as a god of wine, who loosens care (Lyaeus, *Luaios*) and inspires to music and poetry. Hence his connexion with the dithyramb, tragedy, and comedy (qq.v.). With him were introduced into Greek religion the elements of ecstasy and mysticism that are found in his cult (see also *Dionysus Zagreus*, *Orphism*). Dionysus is frequently represented as a youth of rather effeminate expression, with luxuriant hair, reposing with grapes or a wine-cup in his hand, or holding the *thyrsus*, a rod encircled with vines or ivy. The Greeks identified him with the Egyptian god Osiris (q.v.); and the Romans with their wine-god Liber, also called Bacchus. Goats were sacrificed to Dionysus, either because the goat nibbled vine-shoots and injured the vine, or perhaps sacramentally, the god being sometimes conceived as a goat. See also *Iacchos*. For the festivals of Dionysus, see *Festivals*, § 3.

Dionysus, THEATRE OF. The theatre at Athens stood within the sanctuary of Dionysus, and so was known as the theatre of that god. The sanctuary was at the SE. foot of the Acropolis. The first permanent theatre there is said to have been built at the beginning of the 5th c. in consequence of an accident in which spectators were hurt by the collapse of a temporary scaffolding. It was reconstructed, or a new theatre built, in the middle of the 4th c., the work being completed about 330 B.C. The seats of the auditorium were hewn out of the rock of the Acropolis, or were built of stone, the front row consisting of marble chairs reserved for magistrates and priests, the central chair for the priest of Dionysus. There was accommodation, it has been calculated, for some 27,000 spectators. The orchestra, circular in shape, was 78 ft. wide. At first, and probably until Roman times, there was no permanent stage, but a long building with two wings appears to have faced the auditorium beyond the orchestra; the scenery was set up between these wings, a space of 66 ft. The theatre was adorned with statues of poets, among them the three great tragedians and Menander (alone among the great comic dramatists), also of Themistocles and Miltiades. The theatre was used not only for dramatic representations, but for ceremonies of many kinds and even for meetings of the Assembly (it was in the theatre, for example, that Phocion, q.v., according to Plutarch, was sentenced to death).

Dionysus Za'greūs. According to an Orphic (see *Orphism*) form of the legend of Dionysus, Zagreus was the son of Zeus and Persephone (q.v.). At the instigation of the jealous Hera, the Titans destroyed and devoured him, but Athene saved his heart and took it to Zeus, who burnt up the Titans with his lightning. From their ashes sprang the race of men, who therefore have in them some portion of the divine nature. Zeus swallowed the heart of Zagreus, and out of it was later born a new Dionysus Zagreus, son of Semele (q.v.). The legend played an important part in the Orphic ritual (see *Mysteries*). Zagreus is a barbarian name, perhaps Phrygian or Thracian, signifying 'torn in pieces'.

Dio'scūri (Διὸς κοῦροι, 'sons of Zeus'), in Greek mythology, Castor and Polydeuces (Lat. *Pollux*), twin sons of Zeus and Leda (q.v.), regarded as mortals in epic poetry, but also worshipped as deities, protectors of seamen, to whom they appeared in storms in the form of the electrical phenomenon now known as St. Elmo's fire. They were also famous for their bravery and skill in fighting. When their sister Helen was carried off as a child by Theseus (q.v.), they rescued her, her place of concealment having been revealed by Academus, who was honoured as a hero in consequence, or by Decelus, the eponymous hero of Decelea. They took part in the expedition of the Argonauts (q.v., and see *Amycus*). They carried off the two daughters of a certain Leucippus, Hilaeīra and Phoebe, who were betrothed to their cousins Īdās and Lynceūs. In the fight which arose in consequence of this (or of a cattle raid), Castor was killed. Polydeuces, who was immortal and was devoted to his brother, asked to be allowed to die also. Zeus granted that they should together spend alternate days in Hades and in Heaven (or that they should take turns to go to Hades). It may be noticed that Homer (Il. iii. 243–4) speaks of them both as mortal. In later legend they were identified with the constellation *Gemini* (the Twins).

In Roman religion Castor and Pollux were introduced perhaps from Tusculum; Castor seems to have been introduced before Pollux and was always the more popular. Their temple at Rome (nearly always known as the temple of Castor) was vowed by the dictator Aulus Postumius at the battle of Lake Regillus (496 B.C.). Legend related that they fought at the head of the Roman army and after it brought the news of the victory to Rome; they were seen watering their steeds at the Lacus Jūturnae, of which the remains exist to this day beside the Temple of Vesta. (They also announced the capture of Perseus (168 B.C.), on the day that he was taken, to one Publius Vatinius, who reported it to the Senate and was thrown into prison for a liar, until his statement was confirmed by the dispatches.) The temple was rebuilt by Tiberius in A.D. 6, and it is of this reconstruction that remains are still to be seen. The mad Caligula made it a portico of his palace, opening a door to it between the figures of the gods and making them, he remarked, his doorkeepers. The temple was a place where weights and measures were tested, as many inscriptions on these show. The oaths *mecastor* and *edepol* are evidence of the popularity of these gods. Aulus Gellius (XI. vi) states that in very ancient times oaths by Castor or Pollux were used only by women, but that by degrees men began to use the oath *edepol*.

Dioscū'ridēs (*Dioskouridēs*), less correctly *Dioscorides*, a Greek physician who served as a doctor in the Roman army and was author in the reign of Nero of a *Māteria Medica* (*Peri Hūlēs Iatrikēs*) in Greek, in five books, in which he described some six hundred plants and their medical properties. This work survived, and at the time of the revival of learning was regarded as the chief source of the science of pharmacy.

Di'philus (*Diphilos*), see *Comedy*, § 4.

Diplo'mata milita'ria, see *Epigraphy*, § 9.

Di'pylon (*Dipulon*, 'Double Gate'), the principal gate of Athens, on the NW. of the city. See *Athens*, § 1 and Pl. 13a.

Di'rae or FU'RIAE, the Roman counterparts of the Greek Erinyes or Eumenides (see *Furies*).

Dirae ('Furies'), a poem in hexameters attributed to Donatus and Servius to Virgil (q.v.), but probably by another hand. Its subject suggested Virgil as the author. The singer imprecates curses on the soldiers who have dispossessed him of his farm, and bids farewell to his fields.

Di'rcē (*Dirkē*), see *Antiope*.

Dis (*Dis*), in Roman religion, the male god of the underworld, the equivalent of the Greek Pluto, of whose name Dis (*Divēs*) is perhaps a translation. The cult of Dis and Proserpine was founded in 249 B.C. (during the second Punic War) by order of the Sibylline Books. In later literature both Dis and Orcus (his synonym) tend to fade into mere symbols of the lower world.

Disciplī'nae, see *Varro* (*M.T.*).

Di'thyramb (*Dithurambos*), a Greek choral lyric (q.v.) originally connected with the worship of Dionysus, sung by a 'circular choir' (κύκλιος χορός) probably of fifty singers. That the chorus were dressed as satyrs, as is sometimes supposed, is not established. The name, of uncertain origin, is perhaps connected with *thriambos*, the Lat. *triumphus*. Or *dithurambos* may have been a non-Hellenic ritual epithet of Dionysus used as a refrain, becoming the name of the song itself (J. M. Edmunds).

The dithyramb was probably in its origin a revel song led off by the leader (ἔξαρχος) of a band of revellers either in traditional or improvised words, and answered by the others in a traditional refrain. It is thought to have originated in Phrygia and to have come to Greece with the cult of Dionysus. It appears to have been converted to a literary composition by Arion (q.v.) at Corinth, who first instituted the stationary circular chorus, perhaps round an altar, and made them sing a regular poem with a definite subject. This was accompanied on the flute. The dithyramb, it further appears, was first cultivated in Dorian lands, but attained its full development at Athens under Pisistratus and his sons in connexion with Dionysiac festivals. It was also adopted at festivals of other gods, especially Apollo. The earliest dithyrambic contests appear to have taken place at Athens about 509 B.C., perhaps promoted by Lāsus of Hermione (q.v). The successful *choregus* (see *Chorus*) was allowed to erect a commemorative tripod. Apart from one poem by Bacchylides (q.v.), which is in dramatic form, the dithyramb appears to have taken the narrative form. Down to this stage, the names of poets chiefly connected with the dithyramb are Arion, Lasus, Simonides of Ceos, Bacchylides, and Pindar (qq.v.). The Pindaric dithyramb was an antistrophic (see *Strophe*) composition dealing with some mythological theme, but also celebrating Dionysus.

The chief features in the later history of the dithyramb were the growth of greater metrical freedom and the abandonment of the antistrophic arrangement so as to depict emotion more realistically, and the elaboration of the music, which came to predominate over the verse and to assume a tumultuous character. The verse of the dithyramb became proverbial for lack of sense. The names chiefly associated with these changes are those of MELANIPPIDES the elder of Mēlos (*fl. c.* 480), who introduced lyric solos; PHILOXENUS of Cythēra (*c.* 436–380), who introduced in his 'Cyclops' a solo to the lyre; CINESIAS (q.v.) of Athens; and TIMOTHEUS (q.v.) of Miletus.

Dīus Fī'dius, the 'god of faith', perhaps an old Italian religious conception of the sanctity of contracts and human relations. He was identified with Hercules, perhaps because the oaths *medius fidius* and *mehercle* were interchangeable. There was a temple to this god on the Quirinal, dedicated by Spūrius Postūmius in 466 B.C.

Dīver'bium, see *Comedy*, § 5.

Divination, the gift or art of discovering the future, was called by the Greeks *mantikē.* It took various forms. It might be based on direct inspiration by a deity, either through dreams or through a state of ecstasy, such as that in which the Pythian priestess delivered the oracles of the god. Or it might consist in the interpretation of prophetic signs of various kinds (see *Omens*), or of unusual phenomena such as eclipses and meteors. Divination by throw of dice was practised at the temple of Heracles near Būra in Achaia; and other forms of the art are referred to, e.g. chiromancy or palmistry. The Greeks had skilled interpreters of omens, especially of those connected with sacrifices. There also grew up a science of the interpretation of dreams, on which a certain Artemidorus of Daldis in Lȳdia wrote a treatise in five books, entitled *Onīrocritica*, in the 2nd c. A.D. It is stated by Plutarch that a grandson of Aristides (q.v.) made a living by interpreting dreams.

For divination at Rome, see *Augury* and *Haruspices*; also *Sortes Virgilianae.*

Do′chmius or **Do′chmiac,** see *Metre,* § 1.

Dōdō′na, see *Oracles.*

Dogs.

§ 1. *In Greece*

Dogs were kept by the Greeks for hunting, to guard houses and herds, and as companions. The Greek fondness for dogs is attested as early as the time of Homer by the touching incident of Argos, the dog of Odysseus, who recognizes his master after twenty years′ absence, wags his tail, but has not strength to draw near him. See also the reference to Icarius′s dog Maera under *Icarius.* Xenophon, in his treatise on 'Hunting', has much to say on the points, training, and even the names of hounds. They were used for hunting hares, deer, and wild boars (this was done generally on foot). There are frequent references in Greek literature to house-dogs. For instance there is in Aristophanes′ 'Wasps' the amusing description of the trial of the dog Labēs, suspected of stealing some cheese. Plutarch relates that Alcibiades (q.v.) had an uncommonly large and beautiful dog, whose principal ornament was his tail. Yet he caused the tail to be cut off, that the Athenians should talk of this piece of eccentricity rather than find something worse to say of him. The memory has been handed down of the dog of Xanthippus (father of Pericles) which swam by his master's galley to Salamis when the Athenians were obliged to abandon their city, and was buried by his master on a promontory known as Cynossēma (Dog's Grave). Alexander is said to have founded a city called Peritas in

memory of a favourite dog of that name. The Greek anthology contains several touching epitaphs on dogs, showing the affection with which they were often regarded. One even is attributed to the great Simonides, on a Thessalian hound, beginning, 'Surely even as thou liest dead in this tomb I deem the wild beasts yet fear thy white bones, huntress Lycas'. It may be mentioned that greyhounds figure on certain Sicilian coins. Sacred dogs were kept in the sanctuary of Asclepius at Epidaurus, which, like the sacred serpents, were supposed to heal patients by licking them; and Asclepius was sometimes represented as attended by a dog.

§ 2. *At Rome*

The Romans valued the dog as a protector; the figure of a dog stood between the images of the *Lares* (q.v.) *Praestites* of the State. The Romans had Laconian hounds and Molossians, the latter resembling mastiffs. Pliny refers to a small white 'Melitaean' terrier or lap-dog, perhaps from Malta or the Dalmatian island of Melita. His 'Natural History' has many anecdotes of the fidelity of the dog as companion and protector; one resembling the story of the dog of Montargis, which brought to justice the murderer of its master. He also lays stress on its use as a pointer. There is in the British Museum the tombstone of a hunting dog named Margarita, which was much loved by its master and mistress. Columella (q.v.) believed that shortening a dog's tail was a preventive of rabies. This disease, according to Pliny (xxv. 77), could be cured by the root of the dog-rose (*cynorrhodon*, so named, it is said, for this reason). Ovid in the 3rd Bk. of the 'Metamorphoses' gives appropriate names to thirty-seven hounds of Actaeon. British dogs were famous and were exported during the empire; an Irish wolf-hound (*canis Scōticus*) was used in the Circus against wild beasts.

Dokima′sia, see *Athens,* § 9.

Dō′lon (*Dŏlōn*), in the 'Iliad' and the 'Rhesus' (q.v.), a Trojan spy, slain by Odysseus and Diomedes.

Domidū′ca, in Roman religion, the spirit (*numen*) that conducted the bride to the bridegroom's house.

Domi′tian (*Tĭtus Flăvius Domĭtiănus*), Roman emperor A.D. 81–96, younger son of Vespasian, and the last of the Flavian emperors. See *Rome,* § 11.

Domus Au′rea of Nero, see *Golden House.*

Domus Pu′blica, see *Pontifex Maximus.*

Donā'tus, AELIUS, a Latin grammarian and rhetorician of the middle of the 4th c. A.D., author of an 'Ars Grammatica' or Latin grammar which remained in use throughout the Middle Ages. (The word 'Donat' is used in Middle English writings to signify a text-book.) Donatus also wrote a commentary on Terence which appears, combined with the notes of other commentators, in the extant scholia on that author; and a commentary on Virgil from which there are quotations in the commentary of Servius (q.v.).

There was another grammarian of the name of Donatus, TIBERIUS CLAUDIUS DONATUS, who about the end of the 4th c. wrote 'Interpretātiōnēs' of the 'Aeneid'.

Dō'rians, see *Migrations and Dialects* and *Hellenes*.

Dō'richa, see *Sappho*.

Dō'rus (*Dōros*), the legendary progenitor of the Dorians; see *Hellenes* and *Deucalion*.

Drā'co (*Drākōn*), an Athenian legislator, who received in 621 B.C. special authority to codify and promulgate the laws. While basing himself on existing laws, he systematized and amended them according to his views and the need of the period. His principal object was to replace private vengeance for crime by strictly public justice; hence the proverbial severity of his code, a severity which was probably exaggerated in later accounts. He entrusted trials for murder to the Areopagus (q.v.) and instituted other tribunals for lesser crimes. All his laws, except that dealing with homicide (a reformulation of which, published in 409 B.C., survives: see Tod, 'Gk. Historical Inscriptions', I) were abolished by Solon. The constitution attributed to Draco by Aristotle in the Ath. Pol. ch. 4, providing for the franchise for all who bore arms, elective magistrates, and a council, is rejected by most modern scholars as a later compilation.

Dragons, see *Monsters*.

Drama, see the articles on *Theatre*, *Tragedy*, *Comedy*, *Mime*, and *Pantomime*. For the musical accompaniment of plays, see *Music*. For Roman dramatic performances see also *Ludi Scaenici* under *Ludi*, § 1.

Dra'ncēs, in the 'Aeneid' (xi. 336 et seq.), the Italian chief who taunts Turnus. Virgil is said to have modelled him on Cicero.

Dreams (Gk. *Oneiroi*), according to Hesiod daughters of Night. Later poets gave the god of dreams a name, Morpheus, (whence our word 'morphia'); also Icelus or Phobētōr ('the Terrifier'). According to Homer (Od. xix. 562) there were two *Gates of Dreams*, one of ivory, the other of horn, through which false and true dreams respectively issue. There is a reference to this in Aen. vi. 894 et seq. See also *Divination*.

Dress, see *Clothing*.

Druids, see *Gaul*, § 2, and *Britain*, §§ 2 and 3.

Drū'sus. For the various members of the Julio-Claudian family who bore this name see *Germanicus and Drusus*. See also below for *Drusus Caesar* and *Drusus* (*Nero Claudius*).

Drūsus Caesar (15 B.C.–A.D. 23), son of Tiberius and Vipsānia Agrippīna (see *Julio-Claudian Family* and *Germanicus and Drusus*, B 1). His original name before the adoption of his father by Augustus is not known. After the death of Germanicus in A.D. 19 he became the principal collaborator of his father Tiberius and appears to have been designated to succeed him; but his early death in A.D. 23 (attributed by Tacitus to Sejanus) defeated the project.

Drūsus, MARCUS LĪVIUS, (1) tribune of the plebs in 122 B.C., a supporter of the aristocracy against C. Gracchus (q.v.); (2) his son, tribune of the plebs in 91, who proposed, besides various democratic measures, to give the franchise to the Italian allies. The failure of this proposal was the occasion of the Social or Marsian War (see *Rome*, § 6).

Drūsus, NĒRŌ CLAUDIUS (38–9 B.C.), younger son of Ti. Claudius Nero and Livia (and consequently step-son of Augustus), younger brother of Tiberius (see *Julio-Claudian Family* and *Germanicus and Drusus*, A 1). He married Antonia Minor (daughter of Mark Antony and Octavia), and was father of Germanicus and of the emperor Claudius. He carried on a series of brilliant campaigns against Germany during the years 12–9 B.C., and died in the latter year from injuries due to a fall from his horse.

Drȳ'ads (*Drŭades*) or HAMADRȲ'ADS, nymphs (q.v.) of trees; the life of each was associated with that of her own tree, and ceased when the tree died.

E

Ecclē'sia (*Ekklēsiā*), at Athens, the assembly of all the people, summoned for political and occasionally for judicial purposes (see *Solon* and *Cleisthenes*). It decided questions of peace and war, named the strategi (q.v.), and determined the forces to be mobilized. It elected such magistrates as were not chosen by lot, and was the master of all of them, however appointed. It was the legislative body in the State, passing decrees after receiving the report upon them (*probouleuma*) of the Boulē (q.v.). It exercised judicial functions in cases of grave crimes threatening the safety of the State (see also *Ostracism*). At first citizens were not paid for their attendance at the Ecclesia. About 390 B.C. a fee of 3 obols for each day of attendance was introduced, subsequently raised to 1 drachma and for some meetings to 9 obols. The meetings were held at the Pnyx (q.v.) soon after dawn, and were begun by prayers and a sacrifice. They took place, at first once, later four times, in the period of each prytany (see *Cleisthenes*), and were presided over by the prytany and a chairman chosen by lot for the day.

Ecclē'siazū'sae (*Ekklēsiazousai*,' Women at the Assembly'), a comedy by Aristophanes, produced about 392 B.C. A new century, and with it a new social era, had come since Aristophanes wrote the 'Lysistrata'. There is a good deal in the play that shows its late date. There is no parabasis, the role of the chorus is much reduced, the boisterous attacks on statesmen have gone, and there is a new style of quiet witty dialogue of the kind found later in the New Comedy. The philosophic ideas advanced suggest that the author was aware of the views on communism and women's rights subsequently published in Plato's 'Republic'. He makes fun of them after his fashion.

As the result of a conspiracy of women led by Praxagorā, she and her fellow conspirators, disguised as men, take their places at the Assembly, and carry by a large majority a motion by which the affairs of the State are to be entrusted to the women. Praxagora, having been appointed head of the new Government, returns to her husband, who has been put to great inconvenience by her having borrowed his clothes. She explains the new social system that is to be introduced, community of property, community of women and children; and goes off to the Agora to arrange for the reception of all private property and the feasting in common. The simpleton hastens to hand in his property; the sceptic waits to see what will come of the new system. A young man arrives to find his sweetheart, but three old hags assert their prior rights to him, and one succeeds in carrying him off. The chorus hurry away to a communal dinner, where one of the dishes has a name seven lines long-

Echi'dna, in Greek mythology, a monster, half woman half serpent, daughter of Chrysaor (see *Gorgons*). She dwelt in the nether world and was mother by Typhon (q.v.) of the dogs Orthrus and Cerberus, the Chimaera, the Theban Sphinx (qq.v.), the Lernaean Hydra, and the Nemean lion (see *Heracles, Labours of*). The double forms and many members attributed to some of these creatures (see *Monsters*), suggest an oriental, non-Greek origin of the myth. Compare the representations of Hindu deities, and the monsters of Assyrian art.

Echo (*Ēchō*), see *Narcissus* and *Pan*.

Eclogue (*eklogē*), a 'selected' poem, taken out of a larger collection; a term used under the Roman empire for an idyll or satire, and especially applied to the pastoral poems of Virgil. In the 'General Argument' to Spenser's 'Shepheards Calender' the word eclogue is wrongly derived from αἰγῶν or αἰγονόμων λόγοι, i.e. goatherds' tales.

Eclogues (*Eclogae, Būcolica*) of Virgil, the earliest of the poet's published works, a collection of ten short unconnected poems in hexameters. They were composed between 42 and 37 B.C. and published in the latter year. Eclogues ii, iii, v, and perhaps vii, appear to be the first in date of composition. These are all imitations of the Idylls of Theocritus; even the scenery described appears to be that of Sicily—at any rate not that of the Lombard plain. In the Second Eclogue the shepherd Corydon laments his unrequited love for Alexis; the Third, in dialogue, contains the banter and musical contests of shepherds, and a sarcastic reference to the bad poets Bavius (q.v.); and Maevius in the Fifth two shepherds celebrate the death and deification of Daphnis, perhaps symbolizing Julius Caesar, whose birthday was first observed with religious rites in 42 B.C.; the Seventh is a poetical contest between two shepherds. These poems, telling of peaceful pastoral scenes, are in strange contrast with the violent political drama that was being enacted when they were composed, if they are rightly assigned to the year of Philippi. They are highly artificial and conventional in character, for the life of Italian shepherds at this time can have had little resemblance to that depicted.

Eclogues i and ix are thought from internal evidence to belong to the year 41. The usual interpretation of them is that they refer to the confiscation of Virgil's farm; the territory of Cremōna, assigned to grants of land for soldiers of the Triumvirs, had proved insufficient, and had been supplemented by Mantuan territory ('Mantua vae miserae nimium vicina Cremonae'); the dialogue of the shepherds depicts the misery of the dispossessed inhabitants. The lines 7–9 in Eclogue ix may be a description of the scenery of Virgil's farm, and the dialogue appears to take place on the road between the farm and Mantua. Eclogue i contains the line, 'formosam resonare doces Amaryllida silvas', of which Johnson said that all the modern languages cannot furnish one so melodious.

Virgil, expelled from his old home, where he had composed his earlier Eclogues, took refuge at the villa of his teacher Siron, and the Sixth Eclogue was probably written there. It consists mainly of a song of Silenus, who tells of the creation of the world, his account being partly mythological, partly in accord with the doctrine of Lucretius. The Fourth Eclogue was written in 40 B.C., the year of the consulship of Asinius Pollio (q.v.), and shows no imitation of Theocritus. The poet addresses Pollio and predicts the return, under his guidance, of a golden age; a new-born child shall rule a pacified world with the virtues of his father. Early Christian writers supposed that Virgil, under divine inspiration, was referring to the Christian era. The child referred to has been variously thought to be either the expected child of Octavian and Scribonia, or a child of Antony and Octavia, or the son of Pollio, Asinius Gallus, born in this year, and destined to a part of some importance in the reign of Tiberius. The Eighth Eclogue, likewise addressed to Pollio, was written in 39; it contains the songs of two shepherds, of which the first is a lament for the faithlessness of the shepherd's mistress, the second, in imitation of the Second Idyll of Theocritus, represents the incantations by which a country wife seeks to recover her truant husband from the town. This Eclogue contains the exquisite lines beginning (l. 37):

Saepibus in nostris parvam te roscida mala.

The Tenth Eclogue, probably written in 37, has for its subject Virgil's active and ambitious friend, the soldier-poet, C. Cornelius Gallus (q.v.), whom he represents as dying for unrequited love of Lycŏris (the Cythĕris of Gallus's own poems) and mourned by the woods and rocks. The opening was imitated by Milton in his *Lycidas*.

The 'Eclogues' of Virgil, with the 'Idylls' of Theocritus, have been the principal models of pastoral poetry and the inspirers of pastoral romance and pastoral drama in later ages. We see the influence first in the Latin Eclogues of Petrarch and the Italian Eclogues of Boccaccio, and later in the Latin Eclogues of Mantuan (1448–1516). We find it in a different form in the pastoral romances of Boccaccio and Sannazarro, and in the pastoral drama, such as Tasso's 'Aminta' and Guarini's 'Il Pastor Fido'. Through these, or directly, the influence reached English literature, and is seen for instance in Spenser's 'Shepheards Calender', in Sidney's 'Arcadia', in Lodge's 'Rosalynde', in Shakespeare's 'As You Like It', in the 'Faithfull Shepheardesse' of Fletcher, and the 'Sad Shepherd' of Ben Jonson.

Economic Conditions in Athens and Rome, see *Athens*, § 10, *Rome*, § 13.

Editions of Collections of the Classics, FAMOUS. Aldus Manŭtius (Aldo Manuzio, 1449–1515), who gave his name to the ALDINE edition, was the first to print (between 1494 and 1504) a series of the works of Greek authors. His press was at Venice. In 1501 he started the small octavo edition of the Greek and Latin authors, which, by replacing the cumbrous folio, did a great deal to popularize the classics. In this edition was first adopted the sloping type, known as Italic, based on the handwriting of Petrarch. Henri ESTIENNE (Stephanus, 1531–98), the French printer, is famous for the editions of the classics that he issued, but his texts have been condemned as uncritical. The ELZEVIERS (Louis Elzevier, 1540–1617, and his sons and grandson) were famous printers at Leyden and subsequently at Amsterdam, who issued beautiful editions of classical authors from 1595 to 1681. The DELPHIN Classics, *in usum Delphini*, were prepared about 1670–80 under the direction of Pierre Daniel Huet for the education of the Grand Dauphin, son of Louis XIV. They included some sixty volumes by thirty-nine editors. Benedict Gotthelf TEUBNER (1784–1856) was the founder of a publishing and bookselling business in Leipzig, famous for the 'Bibliotheca Scriptorum Graecorum et Romanorum Teubneriana', begun in 1849, which attained high renown as containing the best available texts of the classics. Much of the editing of the Greek texts of this edition was done by the scholars Karl Wilhelm Dindorf (1802–83) and his brother Ludwig. Another important collection is that known as the OXFORD CLASSICAL TEXTS, published by the Oxford University Press from 1898 onwards with many distinguished editors including J. Burnet, I. Bywater, A. C. Clark, W. M. Lindsay, Gilbert Murray, A. C. Pearson, J. P. Postgate, and U. v. Wilamowitz-Moellendorff.

Among other recent collections of classical texts is that known as the BUDÉ edition, in course of publication in France; its name commemorates Guillaume Budé (Budaeus, 1467–1540) one of the chief French humanists of his time. The LOEB Classical Library of Greek and Latin authors, now in course of issue, gives the original text and the translation on opposite pages; it was founded in 1912 by James Loeb (1867–1933), an American banker.

Education.

§ 1. *In Greece*

The early introduction of schools in Greek lands is shown by the statement of Herodotus that at the beginning of the 5th c. B.C. one hundred and nineteen children were killed at Chios by the collapse of a school building. There were probably schools at Athens even in the 6th c. B.C., for Aeschines (c. Tim. 6–12) attributes to Draco and Solon laws regulating such matters as school hours. It is evident that the institution of ostracism (q.v.) could hardly have been established if the great majority of the citizens had not been literate; the man who could not write the name of Aristides (q.v.) must have been exceptional. But schoolmasters and parents were left free as to the character of the education. School fees were low and schoolmasters held a humble situation. Elementary schooling began at the age of six and included, besides reading and writing, the learning to recite passages of Homer and the other poets. In Xenophon's 'Symposium', one of the guests could recite the whole of the 'Iliad' and 'Odyssey'. Simple arithmetic was probably also taught, with the help of the abacus or counting-board. (The British Museum has a Greek schoolboy's wax tablet, with the multiplication table up to $3 \times 10 = 30$ written on one half of it, and a spelling exercise on the other half.) Children were taken to school by their *paedagogus*, a slave charged to see that they got into no mischief. The education of the poor did not extend beyond this primary stage, and probably ceased at about the age of 10–14. The children of the wealthy continued their schooling until 18, the age of military service. For them, music (playing on the lyre and singing) and gymnastics were considered an essential part of education, and instruction in them was given in separate schools (see *Palaestra* and *Gymnasium*). With the development of civilization in the 5th c. came the demand for knowledge of a wider kind, and geometry, geography, and drawing were added to the school curriculum.

A further extension of education, especially for adults, was provided by the sophists (q.v.), who coming from all parts of the Greek world gave for a fee courses of higher instruction in the arts of reasoning and speaking and in social and political questions, designed to fit men for their duties as citizens of a democratic State. For education at Sparta, see under *Sparta*.

There was some advance in education in the Greek cities of the Hellenistic Age (q.v.). It was supervised by a magistrate known as the gymnasiarch. The gymnasium came to hold the same kind of position in Greek life that the public schools hold in England. Some of the gymnasia possessed libraries, but the teaching in them does not appear to have gone beyond grammar, poetry, and some rhetoric. Higher education, in science or philosophy, had to be sought from some special teacher.

§ 2. *At Rome*

Education at Rome in the earlier republican times was very limited in extent, and chiefly given in the home. There was a good training in religious cults, duty to the State, modesty of demeanour, and physical activity; an education calculated to produce frugal, hardy, patriotic, industrious citizens, but intellectually narrow. Children were shown the *imagines* or busts of their ancestors and taught to read the inscriptions recounting their exploits. They were taken to hear the encomiums on great Romans who died. They learnt by heart the Twelve Tables (q.v.) of the law. We read that old Cato himself taught his son his letters, the laws of Rome, and bodily exercises. Later, as a result of contact with Hellenic civilization, education was entrusted to a tutor or a school; the teachers were often slaves or freedmen, frequently Greeks, and the pupils were taught, among other things, *sententiae* or moral maxims, besides reading, writing, and calculation. A characteristic figure, introduced under Greek influences, was the *paedagogus*, a slave who attended the boy to school, waited for him there, and brought him home; he taught the boy to speak Greek and looked after his manners and morals. There was also the higher school of the *grammaticus*, where the teaching was literary, in Latin and Greek, language, grammar, metre, style, and the subject-matter of poems. Under Greek influences music and dancing were introduced into education; these, and especially the latter, were not looked upon with favour by conservative Romans. The only physical training that they approved of was such as would fit young men for war. After a Roman youth had assumed the *toga virilis* (see *Clothing*, § 3), he might be attached as a pupil to an advocate or sent to receive training in oratory under a rhetorician. He might also study philosophy at Rome, or go for this purpose to Athens, Rhodes, or some other Greek educational centre; Caesar, Cicero, Octavian, Horace, all went abroad for study. The effect of the rhetorical education of later republican and early imperial times is seen even in Virgil, more in Ovid, and especially in Lucan and Seneca. It may be added that it was not until the middle of the 1st c. A.D. that the State attempted any control of education; Vespasian instituted State professorships at Rome in Greek and Latin rhetoric, and Hadrian founded a chair of Greek rhetoric at Athens. The salary assigned by Vespasian to the professors was 100,000 sesterces (say about £800), equal to the salaries in the second grade of the Roman civil service.

Ege'ria, in Roman religion, a goddess of fountains, and also of childbirth. She had a sacred spring, whence the Vestals drew water for their ritual, near the Porta Capēna. It was at this spring that according to legend Egeria used to meet King Numa by night and aid him with her counsels. According to one account she was Numa's wife.

Egypt (*Aiguptos*, L. *Aegyptus*). The relations between Egypt and the Greek world date from the earliest known times. There is evidence that during the greater part of the 3rd millennium B.C. there was trade between Egypt and Crete; and in the 2nd millennium there was intercourse between Egypt and Mycenae (q.v.). Mycenaean vases found their way to Egypt; Egyptian porcelain and an Egyptian scarab, bearing names of Egyptian rulers, have been discovered in Mycenaean tombs. In Homeric times we have the story of the visit of Menelaus to Egypt (Od. iv. 351 et seq.). Coming to historical times we read that in the 7th c. mail-clad Ionians and Carians helped Psammetichus I of Egypt in his revolt against the Assyrians, and that these were quartered at 'Daphnae' on the Pelusiac or eastern mouth of the Nile. Psammetichus II took Greek mercenaries with him in his expedition to Nubia; of this there is curious evidence in the *graffiti* left by some of these mercenaries on one of the statues of the temple of Abu-Simbel (see *Epigraphy*, § 5). Amāsis, king of Egypt (570–525), subscribed to the rebuilding of the temple of Delphi. He confined Greek traders, now numerous, to the single settlement at Naucratis (q.v.), on the Canopic or western mouth

of the Nile. It was here, no doubt, that Charaxus, brother of Sappho (q.v.), became entangled with the Egyptian courtesan Doricha. Solon, Thales, and Hecataeus are said to have visited Egypt. Herodotus certainly did so, and devoted the second book of his history to a description of the country. Egypt was conquered by the Persian Cambyses in 525, and the Persian rule lasted for two centuries. There were many attempts at revolt. That led by the Libyan Inarōs in 462 was assisted by an Athenian expedition, which came to an inglorious end in 454. In 361 the Spartans under Agēsilāus supported a revolt against Artaxerxēs. All these risings were unsuccessful and the Persian dominion endured until it was overthrown in 332 by Alexander the Great (q.v.), the founder of Alexandria (q.v.). Then followed the rule of Egypt by the Macedonian kings known as the Ptolemies (q.v.), during which Alexandria became an important centre of Greek culture (see *Hellenistic Age*). This rule was in turn brought to an end by the Roman annexation of Egypt in 30 B.C.

In Egypt the ruler had been the owner of the soil, and the tillers had been his tenants (except that under the Ptolemies property in newly reclaimed land was granted to settlers). This position was inherited by Augustus and was a source of great wealth to the emperors. Egypt under the empire, in fact, was looked upon rather as a personal possession of the emperor than as an ordinary province, and was governed for him by a prefect of equestrian rank, not by a proconsul or propraetor. From early times Egypt had exported pottery, alabaster, papyrus, unguents, and ivory and special woods from Central Africa. Under the Roman empire she continued to export these goods, and also linen, and moreover became an important source of corn supply. Egypt was also an intermediary in trade between the empire and India. Though the local administration retained the Greek character it had acquired under the Ptolemies, many large estates on Egyptian territory were held by members of the imperial family, and a middle class of traders, manufacturers, and landowners, most of them attracted to the country from other parts of the empire, developed with the encouragement of the Roman government.

Ehoi'ai, see *Eoeae*.

Eido'thea (*Eidotheā*), in Greek mythology, a nymph, daughter of Proteus (q.v.). When Menelaus (q.v.) was becalmed off the coast of Egypt and nearly starved, she showed him how to secure her father, in spite of his attempts to escape by assuming different forms, and force him to reveal the cause of this misfortune.

Eileithyi'a (*Eileithuia*), according to Hesiod a daughter of Zeus and Hera, was the Greek goddess of childbirth. Homer mentions a cave sacred to her in Crete and also speaks of the daughters of Hera (in the plural) bearing the name. Hera and Artemis were sometimes invoked under it. The Romans identified their Juno (q.v.) Lucina with Eileithyia.

E'lea (L. *Velia*), a town on the W. coast of Lūcănia, founded by Phocaeans *c.* 540 B.C. It was here that Parmenides and his successor Zeno (qq.v.) founded the ELEATIC SCHOOL of philosophy.

Ele'ctra (*Elektrā*), (1) daughter of Agamemnon and Clytemnestra, see *Pelops* and the articles below; (2) daughter of Atlas, see *Dardanus*.

Electra, a tragedy by Sophocles, of uncertain date, probably an early play.

For the legend on which it is based see *Pelops*. Orestes arrives at Mycenae, with Pylades (q.v.) and an aged attendant, to avenge, in obedience to the Pythian oracle, the death of his father. The attendant is sent on to inform Clytemnestra that Orestes has been killed in a chariot race, and Orestes and Pylades prepare to follow disguised, bearing an urn supposed to contain the ashes of Orestes. Meanwhile Clytemnestra, warned by an ominous dream, has sent her daughter Chrÿsothemis to pour libations on the tomb of Agamemnon. Electra, who is living a wretched life, bullied by Clytemnestra and Aegisthus on account of her fidelity to her father, meets Chrysothemis and persuades her to substitute for the offerings of Clytemnestra others more acceptable to their father's tomb. Clytemnestra appears and rails at Electra, but is interrupted by the arrival of the messenger and learns with scarcely concealed joy the death of Orestes. Electra, on the other hand, is plunged in despair. The announcement of Chrysothemis that she has found a lock of hair, probably that of Orestes, on Agamemnon's tomb, seems only to mock her sorrow. She determines, now that the expected help of Orestes is lost, to kill Clytemnestra and Aegisthus herself. The more prudent and pliant Chrysothemis refuses to share in the deed. Orestes and Pylades now approach, and Orestes gradually reveals himself to Electra. He and Pylades enter the palace. The death-shriek of Clytemnestra is heard. Aegisthus then approaches. He is lured into the palace to see what he supposes

to be the corpse of Orestes, but finds to be that of Clytemnestra. He is driven at the sword's point to the room where Agamemnon was slain, and there killed. The chorus of Mycenean women rejoice at the passing of the curse which has rested on the house of Atreus.

Electra, a tragedy by Euripides, produced about 413 B.C.

The theme is the same as that of Sophocles' play of the same name (q.v.), but there are differences of detail. Aegisthus has married Electra to a humble peasant in order that no son of hers may claim the throne. This peasant is a fine character, and respects Electra's royal birth and misfortunes. Electra takes her share with Orestes in the murder of their mother, an act of justice but a fearful sin, and the play is a deep study of the characters of the exiled Orestes and the haunted and down-trodden Electra, which make them capable of such an act.

Ele'ctryon (*Elektruŏn*), see *Amphitryon*.

Elegi'ac, see *Metre*, §§ 2 and 5.

Elegy (*Elegeia*), a word whose ultimate derivation is uncertain, originally the name for a song of mourning, whose characteristic metre consisted of alternate hexameters and pentameters (see *Metre*, § 2). But this elegiac metre was early adopted by poets for the expression of personal sentiments (as distinct from narrative), for exhortations and reflections on a great variety of subjects, grave or gay. Gnomic (q.v.) poetry took the form of elegy. Among the principal early elegiac poets of Greece were Tyrtaeus, Mimnermus, Solon, Phocylides, Callinus, and Theognis (qq.v.). Elegiacs were occasionally written by the great Greek authors of the 5th and 4th cc., and more frequently by the Alexandrians, such as Callimachus. The elegiac was first associated with love poems by Mimnermus, and later by the Alexandrians.

The principal Roman writers of elegiacs were Gallus, Tibullus, Propertius, and Ovid (qq.v.).

Elephants. Alexander the Great was the first European ruler to acquire elephants. There were elephants in the Persian army opposed to him at Gaugamela (q.v.) and he is said to have obtained a number in India. But it is doubtful whether he ever employed elephants except as baggage animals. They were dangerous to use in fighting because if terrified they might do more damage to their owners than to the enemy. Nevertheless, after Alexander's death his successors made frequent use of them in their wars with each other. Seleucus is said, for instance, to have had

480 elephants at the battle of Ipsus (see *Macedonia*, § 2). Some of these Indian elephants came into the possession of Pyrrhus (q.v.), were taken by him to Italy, and were the first of which the Romans had experience. Pyrrhus had twenty in his army at the battle of Heraclea (280 B.C.) and the Romans captured four at Beneventum. When the Romans first saw the elephant in Lūcānia, knowing neither the animal nor its name, they called it the 'Lucanian ox' (*bōs Lūca*). Ptolemy II appears to have been the first to train African elephants for war. He and Ptolemy III organized elephant hunting grounds on the African coast of the Red Sea. The African elephant is distinguishable from the Indian by its huge flapping ears, sometimes as much as 4 ft. across, and convex forehead. The Indian elephant has relatively small ears and a concave forehead. At the battle of Raphia (217 B.C.) Ptolemy IV had 73 African elephants against the 102 Indian elephants of Antiochus the Great, and Polybius (v. 84) describes the fierce fighting of some of the beasts (but most of the African elephants turned tail). In the reign of Antiochus V the Romans ordered the destruction of the Syrian elephants; the sight of the maimed animals so infuriated the people, that a certain Leptinēs murdered the Roman envoy. It was perhaps from the Ptolemies that the Carthaginians adopted the idea of employing elephants for military purposes. They had a hundred elephants in the army which defeated Regulus. Hannibal started from Spain with fifty elephants, but many perished in the Alps. The remainder were useful to him at the Trebia, but were gradually destroyed. At Zama the Romans, imitating Alexander the Great, arranged lanes in their infantry, into which the enemy's elephants were lured; they were then surrounded and dispatched. Carthage was obliged to surrender all her elephants after Zama, to the great grief of the Carthaginians, who went about the streets calling their lost elephants by their names, for they were very fond of them. The Romans occasionally used elephants in their subsequent wars; for instance Aemilius Paullus had some Indian elephants at Pydna. But they never played an important part in the Roman army. On the other hand they were much used, especially under the empire, in processions and in the Games of the Circus and amphitheatre (see *Venationes*). Some of the names given to elephants are recorded, such as Achilles and Patroclus; the bravest elephant in the Carthaginian army was called Surus.

Eleusi′nian Mysteries, see *Mysteries.*

Eleu′sis, a town of Attica, standing close to the sea, about ten miles NW. of Athens. It owed its fame to a great sanctuary of Demeter (q.v.) where the Eleusinian mysteries (see *Mysteries*) were performed. It is mentioned in the Homeric hymn to Demeter. The sanctuary was destroyed by the Persians and rebuilt or re-designed in the age of Pericles. Considerable remains of it are still to be seen, including those of a Propylaea modelled on that of the Acropolis, and of a great Hall of Initiation (as rebuilt probably in Roman times) about 170 ft. square. The roof of this was supported by six rows of columns and round the hall were eight tiers of steps on which the worshippers probably sat watching the performance of the mysteries in the body of the hall.

Eleusis was originally independent of Athens; and it is improbable that she was incorporated in the latter without a struggle. For a mythological reflection of this see *Erechtheus.*

Eleuthe′ria, see *Festivals*, § 6.

Eleven, THE, at Athens, police-magistrates. See *Athens*, § 9.

Elgin Marbles, see *Parthenon.*

É′lis, a State in the NW. of the Peloponnese, whose chief importance lay in its including Olympia (q.v.). In historical times Elis, with a democratic constitution, was a menace to Sparta. She was a member of the Quadruple Alliance against that State from 420 to 417, and after the end of the Peloponnesian War was reduced and subjected to severe conditions by the Spartan King Agis in 399 B.C., when Sparta was at the height of her power. It was at Scillūs in Elean territory that Xenophon (q.v.) lived in exile.

Elision, the 'thrusting out' of a vowel at the end of one word before a vowel at the beginning of the next; in Greek confined chiefly to the short final vowels *a*, *ε*, *o*, in Latin extended to long vowels and to syllables ending in *m*. (Cf. *Crasis*).

Eli′ssa, see *Dido.*

Elpē′nōr, a companion of Odysseus (q.v.) in his wanderings, who fell off the roof of Circe's dwelling and was killed and left unburied. His is the first shade that Odysseus meets in the nether world; he asks for burial and that his oar may be planted on his grave.

Ely′sium (*Ēlusion*), also known as the ISLANDS OF THE BLEST (*makarōn nēsoi*), in Greek mythology the place where those favoured by the gods (in later conception heroes and patriots) enjoy after death a full and pleasant life (cf. *Hades*). Its position is vague, in earlier myth quite distinct from Hades, somewhere in the far West, a meadow by the stream Oceanus (q.v.), or 'Islands of the Blest' in that stream; in later myth part of the nether world. It was ruled over by Rhadamanthus (or Cronus). Virgil's Elysium is in the nether world.

E'lzevirs, properly *Elzeviers*, see *Editions.*

Ema'thia (*Ēmathiā*), the part of Macedonia between the Axius (Vardar) and the Haliacmōn (Vistriza), including Pella. The name is sometimes extended to the whole of Macedonia and the neighbouring lands, and the epithet 'Emathian' is given to Alexander the Great (see, e.g., Milton's eighth Sonnet).

Embassy, *On the* (*De Falsa Lēgātiōne*), a political speech by Demosthenes. See *Demosthenes* (2), § 5 (*e*).

Embo'lima, see *Tragedy,* § 3.

Emmelei'a, see *Tragedy,* § 2.

Empe'doclēs (*Empedoklēs*), a philosopher and scientist of Acragas (Agrigentum) in Sicily, born in the first quarter of the 5th c. B.C. He belonged to a rich and distinguished family, and it is said was offered the kingship of his city but refused it. He was a most versatile genius, interested in biology, medicine, and physics (he discovered that air is a substance, distinct from empty space), the inventor of the art of rhetoric, a mystic and an eccentric, but he is chiefly famous for his philosophical doctrine. He endeavoured to reconcile the perception of changing phenomena with the logical conception of an underlying unchanging existence, and found the solution in four immutable elements, earth, air, fire, and water, whose association and dissociation produce the various changing objects of the world as we know it. This association and dissociation result from the action of two opposing forces, Love and Discord, which eternally construct, destroy, and reconstruct. These views he embodied in a poem in hexameters, and Aristotle thought them of sufficient importance to be combated. He also left a poem on purifications, in which incidentally he approved the doctrines of Pythagoras, especially on transmigration. There is a warm eulogy of his works by Lucretius (q.v.). Some 450 lines of them survive, written in a lucid and picturesque style. His death is variously recounted; according to one story he threw himself into the crater of Mt. Etna (see M. Arnold, 'Empedocles on Etna').

Ence'ladus (*Egkelados*), see *Giants.*

Enco'mium (*Egkōmion*), a Greek choral hymn (see *Choral Lyric*), in celebration, not of a god, but of some man. The word means a song 'at the kōmos' (here the revel at the end of a banquet), and thus suggests a eulogy of the host. From this it was extended to eulogies in general. The name was first applied to certain poems of this character by Simonides of Ceos (q.v.). The *epinicion*, a triumphal ode for a victory at the Games, and the *thrēnos* or funeral dirge, were in fact variations or developments of the *encomion.*

Endy'mion (*Endumiōn*), son of Calycē (a daughter of Aeolus, q.v.) and her husband Aēthlios, or according to another version a shepherd on Mt. Latmos in Caria. He was the most beautiful of men and was loved by Selēnē (the Moon). By her contrivance (or at his own request) he was thrown into a perpetual sleep, and the moon descended every night to embrace him. He was the father (not by Selene) of Aetōlus (*Aitōlos*), the eponymous hero of Aetolia. The legend of Endymion and the Moon forms the basis of Drayton's 'Endimion and Phoebe' (1593) and of Keats's 'Endymion' (1818).

E'nneads, see *Plotinus.*

E'nnius, QUINTUS (239–169 B.C.), one of the greatest and most versatile of the early Roman poets, was born at Rudiae in Calabria, that is to say in territory that was partly Oscan, partly Greek. He spoke Oscan, Greek, and Latin. He served in the Roman army, in Sardinia, as centurion, and Cato, who was praetor in Sardinia in 198, took him to Rome. Later he accompanied M. Fulvius Nōbilior on his Aetolian campaign in 189, and received the honour of Roman citizenship. He lived in modest style on the Aventine, teaching and writing. He was an intimate friend of the elder Scipio; an anecdote told by Cicero (De Oratore, ii. 68) shows that he was acquainted with Scipio Nāsīca. His principal works were his tragedies and his 'Annales'; but he also wrote 'Saturae' or miscellaneous works, epigrams, one or two comedies (for which he seems to have had little gift), and a *fabula praetexta* (q.v.) on the Rape of the Sabines. If a certain portrait in the 'Annales' is, as Gellius states, a portrait of himself, he was a learned, honest, cheerful man, courteous and discreet. His works show him tinged with various Greek philosophies and critical of the traditional Roman beliefs.

We have the titles and fragments of over twenty of his tragedies. They dealt mainly with themes taken from the Trojan cycle, and one at least, the 'Medea', was translated from Euripides. The fragments show his gift for the expression of passion and pathos, and for vigorous and poetic dialogue. The plays exhibited the problems of life and had a civilizing and humanizing influence. They were written in adaptations of the Greek dramatic metres.

The 'Annales', in eighteen books of hexameters, were the work of his later years. They presented the history of Rome from its mythical beginnings, through the kings, down to the wars of his own day (but omitting the First Punic War, it appears, which Naevius had dealt with), and included a series of portraits of the great Romans. It was from Ennius that the Roman schoolboy got his idea of the old heroes. Fragments amounting to some 600 lines of the work have been preserved. It is inspired by patriotic faith in Rome's greatness, and is marked by gravity of style, and forcible, imaginative, and sonorous diction. The versification is rough, and there are prosaic passages and some eccentricities natural to a period of unrefined taste (see under *Tmesis*, *Alliteration*, *Onomatopoeia*). It was the first Roman poem in epic hexameters in the Homeric manner. It contains the famous line on Fabius Maximus Cunctator (q.v.), who refused to be drawn into open battle with Hannibal:

Unus homo nobis cunctando restituit rem.

The 'Saturae' or miscellaneous works included didactic, humorous, and narrative pieces. The 'Epicharmus' (q.v.) was a poem, in anticipation of Lucretius, on the physical constitution of the universe; the 'Euhemerus' adopted the theory of the origin of the gods expounded by the rationalist of that name (q.v.); the 'Hēduphagětica' was a mock-heroic poem on gastronomy.

Ennius was regarded by the Romans as the father of their literature. His importance rests both on his general humanizing influence, and on his introduction into Latin of the quantitative hexameter in place of the Saturnian, and also of the elegiac couplet (see *Metre*, § 5). Lucretius, Virgil, and Ovid borrowed from him; Cicero admired and quoted him. He enjoyed a long, but not quite unbroken, period of esteem among Roman critics of later ages.

Eny'ō (*Enūō*), (1) one of the Graiae (q.v.); (2) a Greek goddess of war, secondary in importance to Ares. The Roman Bellona (q.v.) was identified with her.

Ēoē'ae (*Eoiai* or *Ēhoiai*), an alternative title of the 'Catalogue of Women' (q.v.), or the title of the latter part of it, in

which, after an opening which probably took a form such as 'Many women won the love of the gods, such as . . .', each succeeding section opened with the words ἢ οἵη ('Or such as . . .') from which the title was formed. Fragments of the poem survive. See also *Shield of Heracles*.

Ē'ōs or **Ē'ŏs**, the goddess of dawn, daughter of Hyperion (q.v.) or of Pallas, the Titan or giant. By Tithonus (q.v.) she was mother of Memnon (q.v.), for whose death at the hands of Achilles she was thought to shed tears in the form of dew. See also *Orion* and *Cephalus*. The Romans called her *Aurora*.

Epamino'ndas (*Epameinōndās*), a great Theban commander, born c. 420 B.C., who, with his friend Pelopidas (q.v.), raised Thebes to be for a time the most powerful State in Greece. He commanded the Theban army at the victory of Leuctra (see *Sparta*, § 4), and thereafter carried out four invasions of the Peloponnese, pushing as far as the gates of Sparta itself. He supported Arcadia against Sparta, and founded on the slopes of Mt. Ithome a new Messene to be a stronghold for the Messenians against their Spartan enemies. Epaminondas was killed at the battle of Mantinea (362), and the fact that in spite of the crushing victory won by the Thebans they felt constrained to make peace with Sparta after it, shows the extent to which the unity and strength of Boeotia depended on the genius of the man. He was buried on the battle-field, where Pausanias five centuries later saw his tomb. There are lives of him by Plutarch and Nepos.

The essential feature of the military tactics invented by Epaminondas, which enabled him to defeat a superior Peloponnesian force at Leuctra, and again at Mantinea, was the massing of a solid column, fifty deep, on one flank, which he launched against the enemy, while 'refusing' or holding back the rest of his line. This heavy column broke through the Peloponnesian line, twelve deep, and threw it into confusion.

Epēi'os, see *Trojan Horse*.

Epeiso'dion, see *Tragedy*, § 3, *Comedy*, § 2.

Ephē'bi (*Ephēboi*, a word meaning 'youths'), under an institution introduced at Athens in the last third of the 4th c. B.C. (after the defeat of Chaeronea), were the young citizens of 18–20 enrolled for military training. They were subjected to strict discipline, messed together by tribes, and carried out guard and patrol duties. They wore a broad-brimmed hat and dark mantle, and received four obols a day for subsistence. When about 300 B.C.

compulsory military service was abolished at Athens, the *ephebeia* was remodelled into a school where philosophy and literature were the chief subjects taught.

E'phesus (*Ephesos*), one of the principal Ionian cities on the coast of Asia Minor, near the mouth of the Caÿster. Adjoining the city stood a famous temple of Artemis (q.v.). It was of great antiquity (perhaps originally dedicated to an Eastern goddess whom the Greeks adopted under the name of Artemis) and was more than once reconstructed. In the new temple that was erected during the rule of Croesus (q.v.) over Ionia, Croesus himself dedicated thirty-six sculptured columns. One of these, bearing part of his name, may be seen in the British Museum. D. G. Hogarth, in 'Accidents of an Antiquary's Life', has an interesting account of the discovery in the pedestal of the statue of the goddess of a vast number of jewels, statuettes, &c., the foundation offerings of the temple. Xenophon (q.v.) deposited in the temple the ransom of some captives taken during the retreat of the Ten Thousand. When this was duly restored to him, he built with the money in Elis a small model of the great temple, and placed in it a cypress-wood image of the goddess modelled on the golden image at Ephesus. In 356 B.C. one Herostratus, to make his name immortal, burnt the temple down (it is said, on the day that Alexander the Great was born). Its fame extended to Christian times (Acts xix. 24 et seq.). Ephesus passed at various times under the domination of Croesus, the Persians, the Macedonians, and the Romans. It formed part of the Delian Confederacy (see *Athens*, § 4), and in the Peloponnesian War was an ally first of Athens, and later of Sparta. It was the birthplace of Heraclitus and the painter Parrhasius (qq.v.). In Roman times Ephesus became the chief city of the province of Asia (though Pergamum was the formal capital), and the seat of the governor.

Ephia'ltēs (1) in Greek mythology, see *Otus*. (2) The Malian who at Thermopylae showed the Persians the mountain path by which they turned the Greek position (see *Persian Wars*). (3) An Athenian statesman, the friend of Pericles and opponent of Cimon (qq.v.), chiefly important for the democratic reforms that he introduced in the constitution, notably the reduction of the ancient powers of the Areopagus. He deprived it of all political functions and left it merely jurisdiction in religious crimes, particularly premeditated murder, and the administration of sacred property. Its other powers were transferred to the

Boule, Ecclesia (see *Cleisthenes*), and Heliaea (q.v.). Ephialtes was murdered in the spring of 461.

E'phors, at Sparta (q.v., § 2), a body of five magistrates exercising control over the kings.

E'phorus (*Ephoros*), born about the beginning of the 4th c. B.C. at Cyme in Aeolia, was a pupil of Isocrates, and the author of a history of the ancient world down to the siege of Perinthus by Philip of Macedon (340) in thirty books. Only fragments survive, but it was much utilized by later historians (Diodorus, Strabo), though its scientific value is questionable.

Epic, narrative poetry of exalted style, celebrating heroic adventures, mythical or historical, in poems of considerable length. The characteristic metre of epic poetry is the hexameter (see *Metre*, §§ 2 and 5).

§ 1. *Greek Epic*

Epic poetry is the earliest surviving form of Greek literature. It existed before drama, history, or philosophy, and in some sort represented all three for the early Greeks. It probably had its origin in hymns celebrating the gods, sung at their festivals, composed by primitive poets, among whom we have traces of such legendary names as Orpheus, Musaeus, and Eumolpus. To such hymns dactylic verse was well adapted. Pausanias (x. 7) asserts that the earliest contests held at Delphi were competitions in religious poetry of this kind. Epic poetry, like the hymns from which it was evolved, was in early times chanted by minstrels to the accompaniment of the lyre. It was developed principally in Asia Minor. There must have been a great mass of it, but, apart from the 'Iliad' and the 'Odyssey' (qq.v.), only fragments of it have survived (see *Epic Cycle*). In course of time (probably about the 6th c. B.C.), perhaps owing in part to the exhaustion of the original subject-matter, epic poetry gave place to the greater freedom of lyric poetry (q.v.), though it produced an offshoot in the philosophical epic of Parmenides and Empedocles (qq.v). See also *Hesiodic Poetry*. In the 5th c. PANYAS(S)IS of Halicarnassus, uncle of Herodotus (q.v.), wrote an epic on Heracles, and ANTIMACHUS of Colophōn (*fl.* 410) a long 'Thebaïd'. CHOERILUS of Samos, said to have been a friend of Herodotus and Lysander, is noteworthy as having composed, in his 'Persēïs', an epic on a historical subject, the Persian Wars, instead of a mythological subject. In the Hellenistic Age Apollonius of Rhodes (q.v.) wrote an 'Argonautica'. In the

5th c. A.D. Nonnus (q.v.) wrote an epic on the exploits of Dionysus, and Quintus of Smyrna a 'Posthomerica', a dull work which dealt with the interval between the events of the 'Iliad' and the 'Odyssey'.

§ 2. Roman Epic

Epic was the most enduring form of poetry at Rome. Cato the Elder, according to Cicero, recorded that the deeds of Roman heroes used to be sung at banquets. On this Niebuhr based his theory that there had been a Roman ballad literature, now lost, on which were founded the legends of early Rome. However this may be—and the theory is now generally discredited—epic in more developed form was introduced at Rome by Livius Andronicus in his translation of the 'Odyssey'. It evolved in native shape in Naevius's poem in Saturnians on the Punic Wars. Ennius in his 'Annales' produced a great epic in hexameters on the history of Rome. Epic at Rome reached its highest point in the 'Aeneid' of Virgil, though it may be objected that the poem is an artificial construction, not a spontaneous growth. In the Silver Age Latin epic became rhetorical in character, probably in a measure owing to the prevailing habit of recitation, which encouraged extravagances for the sake of immediate effect. Declamation also made for insincerity and artificiality. The greatest epic of the age was the 'Bellum Civile' or 'Pharsalia' of Lucan. Other epic poets of the empire, of varying degrees of merit, were Silius Italicus, Valerius Flaccus, Statius, Claudian (qq.v.). Among those whose works are lost were Cornelius Severus (praised by Ovid and Quintilian), who wrote historical poems; and Albinovanus Pedo (q.v.), author of a 'Theseid' and a poem on the campaigns of Germanicus.

Epic Cycle, according to Proclus or Proculus (probably of the 5th c. A.D.), author of a Greek handbook of literature of which excerpts survive, was a term applied to the body of legends which had formed the subject of the old Greek epic poems and constituted a sort of legendary history of the world from earliest times. The CYCLIC POEMS were the lays or poems from which this Cycle was built up. Though the term would strictly include the 'Iliad' and the 'Odyssey', it appears to have been applied to the works of epic poets other than Homer. There was a TROJAN CYCLE completing the story of the Trojan War (q.v.) of which the 'Iliad' and 'Odyssey' give only episodes, and a THEBAN CYCLE, including an important poem, the 'Thebaid'. These formed the storehouse from which Greek dramatic and lyric poets drew many

of their subjects. Though many of the Cyclic Poems are attributed by ancient writers to particular poets, e.g. the 'Aethiopis' to Arctinus of Milētus, nothing is known with certainty about the authors.

Epicha'rmus (Epicharmos), a Greek comic poet of Megara in Sicily (perhaps born at Cos), who lived in the 6th and 5th c. B.C. He wrote in Dorian dialect an early form of comedy, which probably had no chorus and in which he dealt with topics of general interest (as distinct from personal satires) and depicted various types of character, such as the parasite and the drunkard. He excelled in amusing descriptions and enumerations, a kind of 'patter'. (Horace, Epp. ii. 1. 57–8, says 'Dicitur ... Plautus ad exemplar Siculi properare Epicharmi'.) It is possible that he influenced the development of Attic Comedy. Theocritus wrote an epigram for his statue. Epicharmus also came to be regarded as a philosopher in consequence of a philosophic poem, probably by another author, published under his name (see Ennius).

Epictē'tus (Epiktētos) (c. A.D. 60–140) of Hierapolis in Phrygia, an eminent Stoic (q.v.) philosopher whose doctrines are known to us by the record of them made by Arrian (q.v.). This record takes the form of practically verbatim notes of his 'Lectures' (Diatribai), and of a short 'Encheiridion' or 'Manual' of his principal doctrines. The latter is a somewhat dry and formal document, but the 'Lectures', which are the comments with which he accompanied the reading of Stoic writings, have a much more human and familiar character. Epictetus was originally a slave, lame from early youth, owned at one time by Epaphroditus the secretary of Nero. After obtaining his freedom he appears to have conducted a school at Nicopolis in Ēpīrus. The record of his lectures shows him to have been a man of gentle and amiable character, earnest and elevated in his doctrine, a firm believer in the government of the world by an all-wise Providence. According to Aulus Gellius (xvii. 19) Epictetus used to say that, in order to be free from wrong-doing and to live a peaceful life, a man should take to heart two words, ἀνέχου and ἀπέχου, endure and abstain. Thereby man could command independence of external circumstances. Less humble in his attitude than Marcus Aurelius (q.v.), with whom it is natural to compare him, he shows a robust faith in the power of will to overcome the cares and sorrows of life.

Epicū'rus (Epikouros) (341–270 B.C.), the founder of the Epicurean school of philosophy, was born in Samos of Athenian parents, and settled in Athens in 306. His school was known as the 'Gardens' (*Kêpoi*), from the gardens where Epicurus taught. He wrote a large number of treatises, of the titles of which Diogenes Laertius (q.v.) gives a list. The same author has preserved three epistles of Epicurus summarizing his system, as also his 'Sovran Maxims' (*κύριαι δόξαι*), a collection of forty of the most important articles in his doctrine. Some fragments of his great work 'On Nature' survive in the Herculaneum papyri. Epicurus held that philosophy consisted in the wise conduct of life, to be attained by reliance on the evidence of the senses, and the elimination of superstition and of the belief in supernatural intervention. On the physical side he accepted in the main the atomistic theory of Democritus (q.v.), and held that every event has a natural cause; his system was subsequently expounded by Lucretius (q.v.). On the ethical side, he held that pleasure (or absence of pain) is the only good, being the only good known to the senses; and that the best pleasure, as being accompanied by no painful want, is a perfect harmony of body and mind, to be sought in plain living, and in virtue. The teaching of the school is concisely summed up in the twelve words which the Epicurean DIOGENES OF OENOANDA in Lycia inscribed in a cloister in that town, together with other fragments of Epicurean doctrine: '*Αφοβον ὁ Θεός. Ἀναίσθητον ὁ Θάνατος. Τὸ ἀγαθὸν εὔκτητον. Τὸ δεινὸν εὐεκκαρτέρητον.* 'Nothing to fear in God. Nothing to feel in Death. Good can be attained. Evil can be endured.' (Transl. Gilbert Murray.)

Epicurus figures in two of Landor's 'Imaginary Conversations'. The modern English sense of the word 'Epicurean', i.e. 'devoted to refined and tasteful sensuous enjoyment' (O.E.D.), misrepresents the teaching of Epicurus (as also does the 'Epicuri de grege porcum' of Horace).

Epidau'rus (*Epidauros*), in Argolis, the chief seat of the worship of Asclepius (q.v.). The sanctuary contained, besides the temple of Asclepius, a remarkable circular building supported by two circular colonnades, and a great outer colonnade where probably the patients slept. Here have been found inscriptions recording a number of cures effected in the sanctuary. About a quarter of a mile from the sanctuary was the theatre, a very beautiful structure still to be seen in good preservation. See Pl. 5a.

Epidei'ctic oratory, the oratory of display, such as panegyrics, funeral orations, speeches for delivery at festivals; as distinguished from forensic oratory (of the law-courts) and deliberative or political oratory.

Epi'dicus, a comedy by Plautus. The complicated plot turns on the roguery of the slave Epidicus. He tricks his old master out of money, first to pay for a harp-girl to whom the old man's son has taken a fancy; then to pay for a captive whom the son, who has gone to the wars and transferred his affections, has bought with borrowed money. The fraud is discovered, but as the captive turns out to be the old man's lost daughter, Epidicus is forgiven and freed.

Epi'goni (*Epigonoi*), in Greek mythology, the descendants of the Seven Champions who marched against Thebes (see *Oedipus*). Under the leadership of the aged Adrastus (q.v.) the Epigoni took and destroyed the city, an event supposed to have occurred shortly before the Trojan War (Hom. Il. iv. 401 et seq.). The legend is perhaps an echo of real events. The names of the Epigoni (given with some variations by the authorities) are Aigialeus (son of Adrastus), Thersandros (son of Polynices), Alcmaeon (q.v.), Diomedes (q.v.), Promachos (son of Parthenopaeus), Sthenelos (son of Capaneus), and Polydorus (son of Hippomedon).

The term *Epigonoi* was also used of the descendants of Alexander the Great's successors (see *Diadochi*).

Epigram, a word meaning originally an inscription. Inscriptions on tombstones and on offerings to the gods were frequently in verse, and the elegiac (see *Elegy*) was adopted (it is said first by Archilochus, q.v.) as the most appropriate form. The most famous composer of such epigrams was Simonides of Ceos (q.v.). The term was extended to cover occasional short poems, embodying a mood or idea of the author, a favourite kind of composition with the Greek poets of the Hellenistic and Roman Ages (qq.v.). With these the epigram took many forms, dedicatory (inscriptions on votive offerings or works of art), amatory, satirical, &c. Among the most famous epigrammatists of these periods were Callimachus, Meleager of Gadara (qq.v.), and Palladas of Alexandria (*c.* A.D. 400). Collections of epigrams were made in the Hellenistic Age and later (see *Anthologies*).

The epigram was widely adopted at Rome, both for inscriptions and for more general purposes, from Ennius onwards. As a literary form it culminated in the works of Martial.

Epigrams, see *Martial.*

Epigraphy.

§ 1. *Meaning of 'epigraphy' and 'inscription'*

Epigraphy is the science of deciphering and interpreting inscriptions; it is also a term used for inscriptions taken collectively. An inscription is anything from the Monumentum Ancyranum (q.v.) to a potter's mark, provided it is traced, cut, scratched, or impressed on stone, metal, shell, clay, wood, or wax, including *graffiti* (casual scribblings on walls, &c.), but excluding coins and anything written on papyrus or skin.

§ 2. *Direction of writing*

The earliest Greek writing appears to have been always, like that of the Phoenicians, from right to left. Then came a period during which the lines were alternately written from right to left and left to right; a method known as *boustrophēdon* 'turning like oxen in ploughing'. It is found in a number of Greek inscriptions, nearly all of them earlier than 500 B.C., after which date Greek writing generally runs from left to right. As regards Latin writing, in the inscription on the Praenestine *fibula* (see below, § 9), probably of the 6th c., and in the 'Duenos' inscription on the outer edge of a trefoil-shaped vase (probably early 4th c. and called 'Duenos' after the name of the maker), the direction is from right to left. The earliest Latin inscription on stone (probably not later than the 5th c.), discovered in 1899 near the Roman Forum, runs in vertical lines alternately, upwards from the base of the pillar on which it is cut, and from the top downwards. Later inscriptions than the above generally run from left to right, but writing from right to left continues to appear spasmodically; sometimes a whole inscription, sometimes a single word or line, is written in this way.

I. GREEK INSCRIPTIONS

§ 3. *Value of Greek inscriptions*

Greek inscriptions have added greatly to our knowledge of ancient history, institutions, and customs. A vast number have been discovered (it is estimated that we now have more than 75,000), and these have been deciphered, and where mutilated, have frequently been to some extent restored, by the patience and ingenuity of scholars. They have a great value as supplementing or correcting the statements of historians; they throw light on such matters as the evolution of Greek writing, the peculiarities of different dialects, public accounts, and the everyday life of the people. Their value lies especially in their being contemporary records of detailed facts, whereas the statements of historians are as a rule not contemporary, and are apt to be affected by faults of memory, the opinion of the writer, and other sources of error.

§ 4. *Collections of Greek inscriptions*

The first collection of known Greek inscriptions ('Corpus Inscriptionum Graecarum') was begun by the Academy of Berlin in 1815, under the direction of August Boeckh, and completed in 1877. It was by then completely inadequate, for great numbers of new inscriptions had in the interval been discovered. The first volume of a new collection ('Inscriptiones Graecae') was published by the Berlin Academy in 1873, and the work is still proceeding.

§ 5. *Examples of Greek inscriptions*

As illustrations of the light which these inscriptions throw on ancient Greece, the following few examples may be taken:

(*a*) On the leg of a colossal statue of Rameses II before the temple of Abu Simbel on the Nile above the First Cataract is scratched an inscription recording the presence there of a number of Greek mercenaries in the service of the Pharaoh Psammetichus II (594–589 B.C.).

(*b*) After the victories over the Persians at Plataea and Mycalē the Spartans, on behalf of themselves and their allies, offered to Apollo at Delphi a golden tripod on a column representing three intertwined serpents. The column was removed by Constantine to Constantinople, where it still stands. An inscription on the column records the names of those who 'warred the war'.

(*c*) Quota-lists of the tribute payable by the various members of the Delian Confederacy for the years 454–415 have been found (much mutilated) on the Acropolis at Athens. They are particularly interesting as showing (what is also known from a separate inscription) the great increase in the assessment from 425.

(*d*) Accounts have been found for certain years relating to the building of the Parthenon and Propylaea, and the construction of Phidias's great statue of Athene.

(*e*) Accounts have also been found of the loans made from the sacred treasuries of Athene and the other gods to the Athenian State during the Peloponnesian War. These incidentally throw light on the Athenian calendar at this period.

(*f*) We have two decrees about the appointment of the priestess of Athene Nīkē, and her remuneration (c. 448 B.C.).

(g) We have (mutilated) decrees relating to the dispatch of the Sicilian Expedition, giving the purpose of the expedition, the number of ships to be sent, and other details.

(h) Two fragments have been found of a sale-list of the confiscated furniture of Alcibiades.

Among other inscriptions are numerous treaties and alliances, casualty lists, inventories of treasures, dedications, records of the manumission of slaves, &c., as well as a certain number of poems not otherwise known, such as a hymn of Isis discovered at Andros. There are epitaphs of many kinds, ranging from a bare indication of the name of the deceased to laudatory poems. Among epitaphs of historical interest which have survived may be mentioned those (in verse attributed to Simonides) on the Corinthians who fell at Salamis and on the Megarians who fell in the Persian War of 480–479; and a mutilated epitaph (originally in the Ceramicus and now in the British Museum) on the Athenians who fell at Potidaea in 432.

We have minor inscriptions on a great variety of objects, such as badges of admission to (or proof of presence at) the Prytany (q.v.), and tickets of dicasts (see *Heliaea*) bearing the owner's name. We have sling-bolts inscribed with the name of the maker, slinger, or general, or a word to the enemy. We have also many records of votive offerings, such as of a slave to the service of a temple of Poseidon, of a set of toilet requisites, &c.; and inventories of such votive offerings in particular temples. A votive offering of exceptional interest is the Etruscan bronze helmet now in the British Museum, with an inscription showing that it was dedicated by Hieron I of Syracuse (q.v., § 1) from the spoils of his victory off Cumae.

See also *Cleobis and Biton, Curetes, Epicurus* (for Diogenes of Oenoanda), *Ephesus* (for the columns of Croesus), *Gortyn, Marmor Parium*.

II. LATIN INSCRIPTIONS

§ 6. *Utility of Latin inscriptions*

Latin inscriptions, particularly in the imperial period, where they are very numerous, are of great value to the historian as a supplement to the limited literary sources. Besides giving precise facts and dates, they throw light on strata of society, occupations, customs, and beliefs which are hardly touched by historians and other writers. They also throw light on such matters as the evolution of the Roman alphabet (q.v.) and on the spelling and ancient forms of Latin. They

sometimes give support to literary evidence: for instance, Tacitus (Ann. xi. 24) records the delivery of a speech by the emperor Claudius in the Senate on the admission of provincials to public offices; the text of this speech has been found engraved on bronze tablets at Lyons.

Latin inscriptions fall roughly into the following groups:

§ 7. *Epitaphs*

Epitaphs were at first confined to the name of the deceased, and were gradually amplified to give more information (his age, distinctions, &c.), sometimes with a few laudatory verses. Salutations by the survivors to the dead (such as 'Ave, sit tibi terra levis') or by the dead to passers-by ('Ave, viator') were frequently added. The inscribed urns that contained the ashes of Clodius and the elder Agrippina survive; and there are extant epitaphs of several of the Scipios, notably of Scipio Barbātus, consul in 298 B.C. Some of the epitaphs on women show the extreme of simplicity; but many contain eulogies of a deceased wife or mother. One, often quoted, ends with the words 'domum servavit, lanam fecit'. In this connexion the long 'laudatio Turiae' (see *Women*) may be referred to.

§ 8. *Dedicatory and honorary inscriptions*

VOTIVE or DEDICATORY INSCRIPTIONS are found on statues, temples, and other objects dedicated to the gods, for instance that of Mummius, after his victory in Greece and destruction of Corinth, on a temple dedicated to Hercules. There are many inscriptions dedicating spoils of war. Sometimes the reason for an offering is given, e.g. in conformity with a vow or by direction of an oracle, or for the restoration of health. There is an inscription found at Juvenal's birthplace, Aquinum, in which a certain Junius Juvenalis dedicates an offering to Ceres. In Britain we have, among others, a dedication by a military commander to the god Silvanus in gratitude for the capture of a fine boar which many before him had tried in vain to catch. Inscriptions of this class throw light on local cults, the spread of oriental cults, and the nature of the rites. Some foreign deities adopted by the Romans are known to us only in this way; e.g. the Celtic god Camulus, who appears to have been identified with Mars, and whose name is seen in Camulodunum (Colchester). Dedications to Mithras are the principal source of our knowledge of the wide extent of the cult of that god. Several extant inscriptions are to an unknown god 'sive deo sive deae' (there are references in Pausanias and other writers to Greek altars to 'Unknown gods', cf. Acts xvii. 23).

HONORARY INSCRIPTIONS were frequently placed on the pedestals of statues erected to distinguished men, or on columns, arches, or other monuments, in their honour, recording their names, offices, and achievements. We have among others of this kind interesting inscriptions (not all of them contemporary) relating to Valerius Maximus, the dictator of 494 B.C., to Q. Fabius Maximus Cunctator, 'the most cautious man of his time', and to Appius Claudius Caecus (qq.v.). Other inscriptions on public buildings (temples, aqueducts, &c.) commemorate the construction and the name of the person responsible for it, sometimes adding other information. Of the same character are the inscriptions on slabs of stone recording the construction of certain roads (see also for milestones under *Roads*), and the inscribed tablets found on the remains of Hadrian's Wall between the Solway and the Tyne (see *Britain*, § 2), giving the length of the work carried out by the several legions or by detachments from them.

§ 9. *Inscriptions on movable objects*

Inscriptions on movable objects are found on, e.g. (*a*) WEIGHTS AND MEASURES, indicating what they represent and sometimes where they have been tested. (*b*) TESSERAE, tickets or tokens, used for different purposes, for instance entitling the holder to a dole of corn (see the example in the British Museum), or admitting him to a public banquet, or signifying that a gladiator has been released from service in the arena, or used as tokens of hospitality between host and guest or as counters in a game. A slave's badge in the British Museum is inscribed 'Hold me lest I escape, and bring me back to my master Viventius on the estate of Callistus'. The *diplōmata mīlitāria*, which may be mentioned here, are documents of considerable interest for the light they throw on Roman military life. A *diploma* was so called because it consisted of two tablets of bronze hinged together with wire so that they could be folded (there are two specimens in the British Museum). They were delivered to Roman soldiers or sailors in imperial times on discharge after long service. They recorded, under the name of the reigning emperor, the grant to certain classes of veterans of Roman citizenship and the right of legal marriage, with the name and nationality of the soldier to whom the particular diploma was delivered, and a certificate that the text had been checked from the bronze tablet on the Capitol. (*c*) ARMS AND SHIELDS, which

sometimes bore the name of the owner inscribed on them, with those of his legion and cohort. The British Museum has a sword the scabbard of which is inscribed 'Felicitas Tiberi. Vic[toria] Aug[usti]' (probably a sword of honour presented to an officer of Germanicus's army). Slingbolts (like those of the Greeks) were variously inscribed, e.g. with imprecations on the enemy. A sling-bolt used in the Social War (90–88 B.C.) has been found at Asculum bearing the name of the praetor. (*d*) GOLD, SILVER, AND BRONZE ornaments and plate. A very ancient gold *fibula* (i.e. safety-pin or brooch) from Praeneste, usually assigned to the 6th c. B.C., has what is generally thought to be the oldest-known Latin inscription, 'Manios med fhefhaked Numasioi' ('Manius made me for Numerius'). Among other objects inscribed with various information, such as the names of the consuls or emperor of the day, of the manufacturer, of the official in charge, are pigs of lead or other metal (some of these found in Britain), blocks of marble, tiles, and lead water-pipes (a pipe stamped with the name Agricola, q.v., has been found at Chester); also wine-jars, on which the name of the wine, the maker or merchant, and the consuls of the year of vintage are given (cf. Hor. Od. iii. 21: 'O nata mecum consule Manlio...', addressed to an amphora). A lamp bears the inscription 'Don't touch. I belong to Marcus, not to you'. Mention may here be made of the maledictions inscribed on tablets of lead, *dēfixiōnēs* (see *Magic*); also of *sortēs*, tablets bearing inscriptions, which were drawn from an urn and were regarded as oracular.

§ 10. *Public documents*

Public documents inscribed on metal or stone include treaties, laws, *senatūs consulta*, imperial edicts, and municipal decrees. Among the numerous documents of this character which have been discovered is the *lex Acilia repetundarum* of 122 B.C., dealing with the corrupt practices of colonial governors, inscribed on a bronze plate, and having the *lex agraria* of 111 B.C. on the back of it. Another is a letter of the consuls of 186 B.C. embodying the terms of the *senatus consultum de Bacchanalibus* (see *Bacchanalia*). A bronze tablet found at Lyons gives the text of a speech by Claudius (Tac. Ann. xi. 24) on the admission of Gallic citizens to the magistracy. Perhaps most famous is the *Monumentum Ancyranum* (q.v.), the record of the public acts of Augustus drawn up by the emperor himself. Among religious documents preserved for us in extant inscriptions may be mentioned the *Acta*

Collēgii Frātrum Arvālium (see *Arval Priests*) recording (with gaps) the proceedings of the revived college from A.D. 14 to 224, and including the text of their ancient hymn. Also the *Acta Sacrorum Saeculārium* of 17 B.C. recording the ceremonies at the celebration of the Secular Games (see *Ludi*, § 2) of that year and the singing of the 'Carmen Saeculare' composed by Horace. This part of the inscription has been restored as follows: 'Sacrificioque perfecto pueri XXVII quibus denuntiatum erat patrimi et matrimi (that is to say, whose fathers and mothers are alive) et puellae totidem carmen cecinerunt eodemque modo in Capitolio; carmen composuit Q. Horatius Flaccus.' We have also fragments of certain *Fasti Consulārēs* inscribed on blocks of marble which probably formed part of the walls of the new Regia (q.v.) built in 36 B.C., records of the names of consuls, censors, dictators, and *magistri equitum*, with mention sometimes of public events. The *Acta Triumphorum* on four pilasters, probably of the same building, are records of the triumphs of Roman commanders from those of Romulus and Ancus Martius; of these also we have fragments. There are also, in fragmentary form, calendars for a number of years according to the Julian system, in which the days are marked with letters A–H to indicate their position in the *nundina* (q.v.) or week of eight days, and with letters showing whether the days are *fasti* or *nefasti*, &c. (see *Calendar*, § 3); and calendars for farmers containing among other information the agricultural work to be done in each month. See also under *Verrius Flaccus* for the *Fasti Praenestini*.

§ 11. *Inscriptions at Pompeii. Graffiti. Forgeries*

Many curious notices have been found painted on the walls of Pompeii, recommending candidates for election, offering buildings to let, announcing gladiatorial shows, and advertising articles lost or found. There are likewise numerous *graffiti* scribbled by passers on the walls of Pompeian buildings, including quotations from Virgil, Ovid, and Propertius (none from Horace), but most of them of a trivial character. Many *graffiti* have also been found elsewhere; one found in Britain may be translated 'Augustalis has been going off on his own every day this fortnight'. Inscriptions have frequently been forged in later times; indeed the long Part V of Vol. VI of the 'Corpus Inscriptionum Latinarum' is occupied with forged inscriptions. Among these are more than one on Cicero's Tullia, and that on 'Julia Alpinula' which deceived Byron and inspired a

stanza in his 'Childe Harold' (iii. 66). She is the supposed daughter of Julius Alpinus, a citizen of Aventicum in Helvetia, executed by Caecina (one of Vitellius's commanders) for fomenting war against the Romans (Tac. Hist. i. 68).

§ 12. *Collections of Latin inscriptions*

The first collection of Latin inscriptions appears to be that made by a pilgrim, probably a monk from Germany, who went to Rome about A.D. 800 and copied eighty texts. A copy of the collection was discovered by Mabillon at Einsiedeln and published by him in 1685. The collector is known as Anonymus Einsiedlensis. Later collectors included the unfortunate Rienzi, 'last of the Tribunes', assassinated in 1354, and the enthusiastic Poggio (see *Texts and Studies*, § 9). J. T. Scaliger (1540–1609) was apparently the first to prepare a plan for a comprehensive *corpus* of Latin inscriptions, and an early work of this description by Janus Gruter was published in 1603. Finally the proposal to prepare a complete 'Corpus Inscriptionum Latinarum' was adopted early in the 19th c. by the Berlin Academy, and a scheme for the purpose prepared by the great Latin scholar Theodor Mommsen (1817–1903) was accepted. The first volume of this work was published in 1863, and more than forty volumes have now appeared. Vol. I contains the republican inscriptions; later volumes follow a geographical arrangement. The inscriptions of Britain are in Vol. VII. The edited selection of Dessau, 'Inscriptiones Latinae Selectae', is much used. New discoveries are reported in the periodical 'L'Année Épigraphique'.

The principal collections of the actual inscribed stones, metal plates, &c., are those of the Vatican and other museums in Rome and Italy, of the Louvre and the museum of Saint-Germain in France, and in Britain of the British Museum and of the museums, e.g., at Bath, Chester, and Colchester.

Epime'nidēs, a semi-legendary prophet and poet, said to have been a Cretan, to have fallen as a boy into a sleep prolonged for 57 years, and to have lived to a great age. It is also said that he visited Athens in the time of Solon to purify the city from the taint of the murder of Cylon (see *Alcmaeonidae*). He would thus have lived in the first half of the 6th c. B.C. A 'Theogony' in hexameters and other works were attributed to him. The quotation in Titus i. 12, Κρῆτες ἀεὶ ψεύσται, &c. ('The Cretians are alway liars, evil beasts, slow bellies') is said to be from his works.

Epimē'theūs ('After-thought'), in Greek mythology, the brother of Prometheus (q.v.).

Epini'cion (Gk. *epinikion*, Lat. *epinicium*), a Greek choral ode in honour of a victor in the Games. The principal authors of this kind of poem were Simonides of Ceos, Bacchylides, and Pindar (qq.v.). The ode in its normal form, written in groups of three stanzas forming triads (q.v.), contained three parts: the first an account of the victory celebrated, the second a mythical development of the subject, the third a eulogy of the victor, frequently accompanied by moral reflections and exhortations. The *epinicion* was sung on the return of the victor to his town, perhaps in a procession to the temple where he consecrated his wreath, or at the door of his home, or at a banquet.

Epirrhē'ma, see *Comedy*, § 2.

Episode (*Epeisodion*), see *Tragedy*, § 3, and *Comedy*, § 2.

Epistle to the Pisōs (*Epistula ad Pisōnes*), see *Ars Poetica*.

Epistles (*Epistulae*), of Horace, two books in hexameters, written when Horace had reached middle life and was living mainly in retirement on his Sabine farm. They resemble the 'Satires' (q.v.) in their subjects and in their conversational character. They reveal the author's qualities of good taste and good sense at their highest, and show, as compared with the 'Satires', greater maturity and an increased interest in books and philosophy. These and the joys of country life, worldly wisdom, and personal independence, are his principal themes. I. iv is interesting as addressed to the poet Tibullus; I. vi is the well-known discourse on the text 'nil admirari', caring for nothing overmuch; I. ix is a model of social tact, introducing a friend to the future emperor Tiberius; I. xvi contains a description of the author's farm. The Book is full of passages and phrases whose wisdom and felicity have made them familiar: the comparison of the man who puts off the hour of right living to the countryman who waits for the river to flow by; the folly of a bustling search for happiness, 'coelum non animum mutant'; the 'fallentis semita vitae'; and many others.

Book II contains two Epistles: in the first, addressed to Augustus, the author reviews and approves the development of Latin poetry from the ruggedness of the old writers to the refinement of his day under the influence of Greek literature. The second, addressed to Jūlius Flōrus (a writer of satires), contains some interesting biographical reminiscences and some literary criticism and doctrine—unsparing self-criticism is especially recommended.

Epī'stulae ex Pontō, see *Ex Ponto*.

Epitaphs. Apart from sepulchral inscriptions actually surviving (which are dealt with under *Epigraphy*, §§ 5 and 7) the Greek Anthology (see *Anthologies*, § 1) has preserved a large number of Greek epitaphs, ranging in character from the famous lines by Simonides on the warriors who fell at Thermopylae to epitaphs on dogs and other pets. Epitaphs on certain famous Romans are known to us from the works of various authors. For instance the epitaph on Scipio Africanus Major ('Hic est ille situs cui nemo civis neque hostis quivit pro factis reddere opis pretium', 'whose deeds neither fellow-citizen nor stranger could requite') has been preserved for us by Cicero and Seneca; that on Ennius by Cicero; and that on Pacuvius by Aulus Gellius. The epitaph on Naevius (see under his name) and that on Plautus, preserved by Gellius, are thought to be epigrams composed in a later age rather than true epitaphs. There was a practice of composing one's own epitaph in one's lifetime; Ovid, Propertius, and Tibullus, for instance, did this, and Trimalchio (see *Petronius*) does the same.

Epitrepo'ntes ('Arbitration'), a comedy by Menander.

Charisius, a young Athenian, has married the girl Pamphila. A few months later he learns that she has secretly given birth to a child. In deep distress he refuses to live with her and betakes himself to the courtesan Habrotonon. Pamphila's father Smicrinēs attempts to effect a divorce. Meanwhile the child has been found by a shepherd Dāvus, and given to a charcoal-burner Syriscus, whose wife has lost her own child; but Davus refuses to hand over the trinkets found with the child. Davus and Syriscus refer the matter to the arbitration of a respectable passer-by, who happens to be Smicrines, Pamphila's father. He decides that the trinkets should be handed over, and this, thanks to the intervention of the kindly Habrotonon, leads to the discovery that Charisius, who is already thoroughly ashamed of his conduct, is the father of the child; for he had violated Pamphila at a night-festival prior to his marriage, neither knowing the other, but Pamphila had kept his ring. The discovery leads to the reconciliation of the couple.

The plot of Terence's 'Hecyra' (q.v.) closely resembles this.

E'pitrite (-eit) (*epitritos*), see *Metre*, § 1.

Epode, from Gk. ἐπῳδός, (1) a lyric metre invented by Archilochus (q.v.), in which a longer line is followed by a shorter. Hence in Roman literature, poems written in that metre. (2) The third stanza in a triad (q.v.) or group of three lyrical stanzas, varying in metrical construction from the first two (the strophe and antistrophe).

Epodes of Horace, see *Odes and Epodes*.

Epo'nymous, 'that gives his name to anything' (O.E.D.), especially used of mythical persons from whose names the names of places or peoples were reputed to be derived; also of the chief archon at Athens, who gave his name to the year.

Epy'llion, a brief or miniature epic, such as the poem of Theocritus (xxiv) on the infant Heracles, and that of Catullus on the marriage of Peleus and Thetis.

Equestrian Order, *Equitēs* or 'Knights', a class of Roman citizens which had its origin in the primitive military organization of the Roman State. In the regal period and the earlier republican times the wealthiest members of the State served in the cavalry, and, in the *comitia centuriata* (q.v.), formed eighteen 'centuries' of *equites*. After the Second Punic War the Equites lost their military functions. In the last period of the republic the term was applied to a class of wealthy citizens outside the senatorial order, because, it is thought, the property qualification for the jurymen (*jūdicēs*) under the legislation of C. Gracchus (q.v., and see *Judicial Procedure*, § 2) was fixed at that of the cavalry in the Roman army (a capital of 400,000 sesterces). This class was engaged especially in banking, money-lending, and the execution of State contracts, in which they frequently became very wealthy. Those who undertook State contracts were known as *publicāni*, and were organized in companies (*societātēs*), for such purposes as farming the taxes of the provinces and the construction of public works. The bankers, money-changers, and assayers, on the other hand, worked independently or in partnership. Their business was conducted in the Forum (q.v.). The bankers provided facilities for the loan and transmission of money such as a modern bank would furnish. The equestrian order, by reason of its wealth and cohesion, was a considerable political force from the time of the Gracchi. Cicero, himself the son of an *eques*, strove hard to reconcile it and the Senate in a 'concordia ordinum'. In the last century of the republic many Romans were in a state of debt, and the equestrian order, by favouring this, and also by their ruthless exploitation (as *publicani*) of the provinces, did much harm to the State. Under the empire they lost their importance as a political force, though they retained their wealth and continued their lucrative occupations, including tax-farming to some extent. The great innovation of the empire, the civil service, had its highest branches largely, though to a varying degree under the different emperors, recruited from the order (see *Rome*, § 12, and *Hadrian*). Members of the order wore the *trabea*, a cloak with purple border.

Equi'ria or EQUIRRIA, see *Mars*.

Erasi'stratus (*Erasistratos*) (3rd c. B.C.), a great anatomist of Antioch. He carried on the discoveries of Herophilus (q.v.), establishing the distinction between the sensory and motor nerves.

Era'smus, see *Texts and Studies*, § 10.

E'ratō, see *Muses*.

Erato'sthenēs, (1) one of the Thirty at Athens (see *Athens*, § 5, and *Lysias*); (2) of Cyrene, of the second half of the 3rd c. B.C., succeeded Zenodotus (q.v.) as head of the Alexandrian Library (*fl. c.* 234 B.C.). He was a great mathematician and geographer, but also wrote poems, and works of philosophy, history, and literary criticism (he was known as 'Pentathlos', see *Pentathlon*). His great achievement was the calculation, with a surprising degree of accuracy, of the circumference of the earth. Having discovered that the sun was vertical at Syēnē (Assouan) at noon on midsummer day, he measured the angular distance of the sun at Alexandria at the same time, and finding this to be $\frac{1}{50}$th of a circle, and the distance from Alexandria to Syene to be 5,000 stadia, he inferred that the circumference of the earth must be 250,000 (subsequently altered to 252,000) stadia (probably equivalent to 24,662 miles or within 200 miles of the correct figure). Eratosthenes drew the first rough system of latitudes and longitudes on the map of the world. In his *Chronographiae* he made the first scientific attempt to fix the dates of Greek history. He also wrote a treatise in twelve books 'On the Ancient Comedy', which, like his other works, is unfortunately lost.

E'rebus (*Erebos*), primeval Darkness, according to Hesiod, sprung from Chaos, and the father, by his sister Night, of Day.

Erechthē'um (*Erechtheion*), see *Acropolis*.

Ere'chtheūs, a legendary king of Athens, son of Pandīōn, who was son of Erichthonius, with whom Erechtheus is often identified. Erichthonius was said to be a son of Hephaestus and the Earth (i.e. aboriginal) and the following tale was told of him. Earth entrusted the child to Athene, who put it into a chest and gave the chest to the three daughters of Cecrops (q.v.) to take care of, forbidding them to open it. But the two eldest (or all three, or only one) disobeyed, and were so terrified at seeing the child, which was serpent-shaped or had snakes for its feet (see *Monsters*), that they went mad and threw themselves down from the Acropolis. Of Erechtheus it is told that waging war against the Eleusinians and the Thracian Eumolpus, he was advised by the Delphic oracle that in order to be victorious he must sacrifice one of his daughters, which he did. The Eleusinians were defeated, but Poseidon in anger destroyed Erechtheus and all his house. It is this legend which forms the subject of Swinburne's tragedy *Erechtheus*. But the connexion between Poseidon and Erechtheus is obscure, for Poseidon was worshipped at Athens as Poseidon Erechtheus. See also *Ion*.

Erga′stula, see *Slavery*, § 2.

Erichtho′nius (*Erichthonios*), (1) see *Erechtheus*; (2) son of Dardanus (see genealogy under *Troy*).

Eri′danus (*Eridanos*), see *Phaethon*. Eridanus was also the name of a small stream which flowed through Athens.

Eri′gonē (*Erigonē*), (see *Icarius*).

Eri′nna (*Erinna*), a Greek poetess of the island of Tēlos near Rhodes, probably of the 4th c. B.C., who died at the age of 19. She celebrated in a simple graceful poem of three hundred hexameters (*Ēlakatē*, the 'Distaff') her friend Baucis, from whom she had been separated by the latter's marriage and death. Fragments of it survive.

Eri′nyes (*Erinues*), see *Furies*.

Eriphȳ′lē, see *Amphiaraus* and *Alcmaeon*.

E′ros (also pronounced in English Ē′ros) (*Erōs*), a Greek god of love, in Hesiod a primeval force, in later literature the son of Aphrodite (q.v.). In Hellenistic times he becomes associated with romantic love, and is represented as a little winged archer, who mischievously shoots his arrows at gods and men. In general he plays a subordinate part. The Romans identified him with Cupid.

Erōtopae′gnia, see *Laevius*.

Eryma′nthus (*Erumanthos*), a lofty mountain in Arcadia, the haunt of the Erymanthian Boar destroyed by Heracles (see *Heracles, Labours of*). Also a river which rises in that mountain and flows into the Alpheus (q.v.).

E′ryx (*Erux*), (1) a mountain in the NW. of Sicily, the seat of an important cult of Aphrodite, whence was derived the title of the Roman Venus Erycina (see *Aphrodite*). (2) The name of a legendary king of the mountain; see *Heracles* (*ad fin.*).

Estienne, HENRI, see *Editions*.

E′teoclēs (*Eteoklēs*), see *Oedipus*.

Etē′sian (i.e. 'yearly') **Winds,** periodic winds such as those which blow strongly from the N. over the Aegean in July, August, and September. It is related that, the Cyclades being once afflicted by a long drought, the inhabitants by direction of Apollo sent for Aristaeus (q.v.), who sacrificed to Zeus and to Sirius (the Dog Star); thereupon the Etesian winds were sent annually to cool the land. The term is used by Herodotus, Strabo, &c. of the monsoons in Egypt, India, and the Indian Ocean.

Ethiopians (*Aithiopes*), a dark-skinned race, according to Homer living far away by the stream Oceanus; generally placed beyond Egypt to the south. They are the companions of Memnon (q.v.), and accompany him to the siege of Troy in support of the Trojans (after the period of the 'Iliad'). The historical Ethiopians lived rather to the north of modern Abyssinia. Wars against them form part of the history of Egypt under the early empire. A vast expedition against them planned by Nero was not carried out.

Etru′sca discipli′na, see *Haruspices*.

Etruscans or TYRRHĒNIANS, a people of whose origin nothing certain is known and who inhabited in early times a portion of NW. Italy. They were said by some of the ancient authorities to have come from Lȳdia, but Varro and Dionysius of Halicarnassus denied this. In the 8th c. B.C. they were a powerful and industrious people, who built fortified towns, worked in metal, exploited the minerals of Sardinia and Corsica, and carried on an extensive commerce. Their empire over Italy appears to have extended at the end of the 7th c. as far S. as Salerno; later the Tiber was their southern frontier. Their civilization was subject to Greek influences, as shown by monuments of the 7th and 6th cc. For their connexion with the early history of Rome, see *Rome*, § 2. For their defeat in a naval battle off Cumae by Hieron I of Syracuse, see *Syracuse*, § 1. By their religious observances, their methods of divination, and their dramatic performances, they exercised a powerful influence on Roman culture (see *Religion*, § 3, *Haruspices, Comedy*, § 5).

Eubū'lus (*Euboulos*), an eminent Athenian statesman and financier of the latter half of the 4th c. B.C., when Philip of Macedon was extending his dominions; an opponent of the policy of Demosthenes. See *Athens*, §§ 7 and 11.

Euclei'des (*Eukleidēs*) of Megara, see *Megarian School*. For Eucleides the mathematician, see *Euclid*.

Euclid (*Eukleidēs*), a Greek mathematician, whose birthplace and date of birth are unknown, flourished at Alexandria about 300 B.C. His principal work was his 'Elements' (*Stoicheia*), dealing with geometry and the theory of numbers. Of this the first six books on plane geometry, summing up and completing the teaching of his predecessors (some of his propositions are attributed to Thales and Pythagoras, qq.v.), retained their authority until the end of the 19th c. Euclid wrote a number of other mathematical works, including a short treatise, which has survived, on musical notes. It was Euclid who told Ptolemy I that there was no 'royal road' to geometry (Proclus, Comment. on Euclid, Prol. G. 20).

Eu'cliō, the old miser in the 'Aulularia' (q.v.) of Plautus.

Eudē'mus (*Eudēmos*), a pupil of Aristotle, and probably the editor of the work known as the 'Eudemian Ethics' of Aristotle.

Euhē'merus (*Euēmeros*) (c. 300 B.C.), a Greek (Sicilian) writer who, in his *Hierā Anagraphē*, advanced the theory (for which he pretended to have found documentary evidence in an imaginary island, Panchaea, in the Indian Ocean) that the gods of mythology had their origin in kings or heroes deified by those whom they had ruled over or benefited. His theory is known as 'Euhemerism'. It was made known to the Romans by Ennius.

Eumae'us (*Eumaios*), in the 'Odyssey' (q.v.), the faithful swineherd of Odysseus.

Eu'menēs, see *Attalids*.

Eume'nides, see *Furies* and (for Aeschylus's play) *Oresteia*.

Eumo'lpus (*Eumolpos*), in Greek mythology, a son of Poseidon (q.v.), said to have been a king of Thrace and an ally of the Eleusinians (see *Erechtheus*). He was the legendary founder of the Eleusinian mysteries (see *Mysteries*) and ancestor of the sacerdotal family of the *Eumolpidae*, who officiated at the mysteries.

Eunū'chus ('The Eunuch'), a comedy by Terence, adapted from a play of the same name by Menander.

Phaedria, a young Athenian, is in love with the courtesan Thäis. Thrasō (q.v.), a braggart captain (who is attended by an amusing parasite called Gnathō), is courting her, and in order to advance his suit has bought for her at Rhodes a young slave-girl. Thais knows that this girl is of Athenian birth, stolen in childhood, and is anxious to obtain her and restore her to her family. She therefore persuades Phaedria to let her make an appearance of yielding to the captain's advances. Meanwhile Phaedria has bought a eunuch as a present for Thais. Chaerea, Phaedria's brother, has seen the slave-girl on her way to the house of Thais and fallen in love with her. In order to get access to her, he exchanges clothes with the eunuch, assumes his character, is delivered in his place to Thais, and takes advantage of the situation to ravish the girl. Her Athenian birth is revealed by Thais, and she is betrothed to Chaerea. Thraso, who has been repudiated by Thais as soon as her object was achieved, tries to carry the girl off; but the braggart is repulsed and a compromise arrived at by which he is to share the favours of Thais with Phaedria.

The prologue contains the well-known line: 'Nullumst iam dictum quod non dictum sit prius.' The play was imitated by Udall in the later scenes of his *Ralph Roister Doister* (c. 1554).

Eupa'tridae (*Eupatridai*), at Athens, the hereditary aristocracy, owners (at least until the reforms of Solon, q.v.) of most of the land. They were the local chiefs of the period before the union of the communities composing Attica (see *Athens*, § 2), and remained the ruling families of the country until Solon's reforms.

Eupho'riōn, (1) the son of Aeschylus (q.v.). (2) Of Chalcis (fl. c. 235 B.C.), an epic poet of the Alexandrian school, who was head of the library at Antioch, and wrote on various mythological subjects. Cicero (Tusc. Disp. III. xix. 45) groups under the term *cantores Euphorionis* the poets of his own time who were influenced by the Alexandrians (see *Alexandrianism*), including such authors as C. Helvius Cinna and P. Terentius Varro Atacinus (qq.v.), and contrasts them with Ennius.

Euphrā'nōr (fl. c. 360 B.C.), a native of Corinth famous both as a sculptor and a painter. He also wrote a treatise on art. Lucian ranks him with Phidias and Apelles. Three of his works, a Cavalry Battle, the Twelve Gods, and a Theseus, decorated the Colonnade of Zeus at Athens.

Eu'polis, see *Comedy*, § 3.

Euri'pidēs (*Euripidēs*) (c. 480–406 B.C.), the third of the three great Attic tragedians, was born in Salamis on the day, it was said, of the great naval battle off that island. He held no magistracies, lived in retirement, and appears to have been of a somewhat morose disposition. His first play ('The Daughters of Pelias') is said to have been produced in 455. He wrote in all some eighty or ninety plays, and won the prize five times (his first victory in 441). After 408 he went to the court of Archelaus, king of Macedonia, where he was honourably received, and where he died (he was said to have been accidentally torn to pieces by the hunting dogs of Archeläus). Eighteen of his tragedies (if we include the 'Rhesus' of doubtful authenticity) and one satyric play survive: 'Alcestis' (438), 'Medea' (431), 'Hippolytus' (428), 'Trojan Women' (415), 'Helen' (412), 'Orestes' (408), 'Iphigenia at Aulis' (405), 'Bacchae' (405); and of uncertain date, 'Andromache', 'Children of Heracles', 'Hecuba', 'Suppliants', 'Electra', 'Madness of Heracles', 'Iphigenia in Tauris', 'Ion', 'Phoenissae', 'Cyclops' (satyric drama), and 'Rhesus'. These are dealt with under their several titles. The 'Hypsipylē' of Euripides was discovered in a fragmentary condition in a papyrus found at Oxyrhynchus in 1908.

Euripides chose for his tragedies, as a rule, situations of violent stress, showing men and women in the grip of passion or torn by conflicting impulses; showing also the play of natural affection. He approached nearer to ordinary life than did Aeschylus and Sophocles. He did not accept unquestioningly the traditional religion and morality, but displayed vigorous independent thought, frequently scandalizing public opinion. Allusions here and there show him a keen critic of contemporary society. His plays are marked by much variety of mood. The occasional bitterness of his reflections on the human lot is mingled with admiration for heroism and love of the beautiful things of nature. He gave great prominence to female characters, and has left us a wonderful gallery of portraits of women, heroines of virtue or crime. He sought dramatic effect in ingenious devices (e.g. 'recognitions', none more curious perhaps than that in his 'Helen'), modifying legend to suit his purpose. He also made much use of the prologue, a sort of introduction in monologue or duologue setting forth the situation, and of the intervention of a god to clear up an embarrassing situation. His lyrics are graceful and charming, and contain much beautiful description of nature, but without grandeur and often without close connexion with the subject of the play. His expression is natural, clear, and familiar, and admirably reproduces the language of passion. His literary methods (but not his personal character) are subjected to lively criticism by Aristophanes in his 'Acharnians' and 'Frogs', and he is good-humouredly chaffed in the 'Thesmophoriazusae' (qq.v.), in which he is one of the principal characters, and several farcical scenes are constructed with tags from his tragedies. The popularity of Euripides in the ancient Greek world is shown by three anecdotes of Plutarch, who states that some of the Athenian prisoners at Syracuse won their liberty by their ability to recite passages of the poet; also that on one occasion a vessel pursued by pirates was not allowed to enter a Sicilian harbour until it was found that some on board could do this; again that when Athens was conquered in 404 and it was proposed that the city should be destroyed, the Spartan generals were moved to mercy by a Phocian singing the first chorus of Euripides' 'Electra'. This is the incident referred to in Milton's eighth sonnet:

> and the repeated air
> Of sad Electra's poet had the power
> To save the Athenian walls from ruin bare.

Though as a matter of fact the walls between Athens and the Piraeus were then demolished.

Famous editions (1797–1801) of four plays ('Hecuba', 'Orestes', 'Phoenissae', 'Medea') of Euripides were published by the great scholar Richard Porson (1759–1808). Ben Jonson is said to have borrowed from Euripides in his *Discoveries*. Robert Browning's admiration of Euripides is shown in 'Balaustion's Adventure' (1871) and 'Aristophanes' Apology' (1875), in the former of which Balaustion wins welcome from the hostile Syracusans by reciting the 'Alcestis'; and in the latter maintains the superiority of tragedy against Aristophanes and reads in illustration the 'Heracles' of Euripides.

Eurī'pus (*Euripos*), a word meaning any strait where the flow of the tide is violent, the name in particular of the strait separating Euboea from Boeotia.

Eurō'pa (*Eurōpē*), in Greek mythology, daughter of Agēnōr, king of Tyre. Zeus fell in love with her, and in order to win her took the form of a beautiful bull, which played about Europa so gently that she climbed on his back. Thereupon he ran off to the sea, and swam away bearing her to Crete (see *Dicte*), where she gave birth to Minos and Rhadamanthus, and, some say, Sarpedon (qq.v.).

Euro'tas (*Eurōtās*), the chief river of Laconia.

Eu'rus (*Euros*), the east or south-east wind.

Eury'alē (*Euruale*), see *Gorgons*.

Eury'alus, see *Nisus*.

Euryclei'a (*Eurukleia*), in the 'Odyssey', the old nurse of Odysseus.

Eury'dice (*Eurudike*), (1) see *Orpheus*; (2) wife of Creon, king of Thebes (see *Antigone*, Sophocles' tragedy).

Eury'medon (*Eurumedōn*), a river in Pamphȳlia, off the mouth of which Cimon (q.v.) in 468 (?) B.C. won a great victory over the fleet of Xerxes, destroying 200 Phoenician ships. The victory placed southern Asia Minor completely in the hands of Athens. The river flowed through the ancient Greek city of Aspendus, where still stands one of the largest and most perfectly preserved of Roman theatres.

Eury'stheus (*Eurustheus*), the taskmaster of Heracles (q.v.). For his death see *Heracles* (*The Children of*). According to another version he was overtaken, after his defeat in Attica, near the Scironian rocks (q.v.) and slain by Hyllus.

Eury'tion (*Eurutiōn*), (1) the herdsman of Geryon, see *Heracles* (*Labours of*); (2) a centaur, whom Heracles slew.

Eu'rytus (*Eurutos*), king of Oechalia and father of Iole; see *Heracles*.

Euse'bius (A.D. 265–340), bishop of Caesarea in Palestine, was author of a 'Chronicle' in Greek containing an epitome of universal history and chronological tables, the foundation of much of our knowledge of the dates of events in Greek and Roman history to A.D. 325. The Greek text of this work survives in fragments only; but we have a Latin version of it by Jerome and an Armenian translation, from which a reconstruction of the original was begun by Joseph Scaliger. Eusebius also wrote an 'Ecclesiastical History' to A.D. 314, a 'Praeparātio Ēvangelica' including a survey of the philosophy and religion of the Greeks, a 'Dēmonstrātio Ēvangelica', a biography of Constantine, and a topography of Palestine.

Eusta'thius, archbishop of Thessalonica in the latter part of the 12th c.; see *Texts and Studies*, § 4.

Eute'rpē, see *Muses*.

Euthyde'mus (*Euthudēmos*), see *Plato*, § 2.

Eu'thyphro (*Euthuphrōn*), a dialogue by Plato.

Euthyphro, a learned soothsayer, is prosecuting his father, who has unintentionally been guilty of homicide, for murder, doing this as an act of piety. Socrates, who is awaiting his own trial for impiety, meets him and thinks he cannot do better than consult him as to the true nature of piety and impiety. But he can only elicit from him an unsatisfactory answer; piety is what is pleasing to the gods. The dialogue brings out the opposition between the old unintelligent religion, based on the mythological tales which Socrates dislikes, and a true spiritual religion.

Eutro'pius, a historian, who lived under the emperor Valens (A.D. 364–378), and wrote, at his request, in Latin a 'Breviārium ab urbe condita', or abstract of Roman history, in ten books, from the time of Romulus to that of Jovian. The work is dry and concise, without literary merit or interest. The reign of Constantine, for instance, is related without mention of his conversion to Christianity.

Eva'dnē (*Euadnē*), in Greek mythology, the wife of Capaneus, one of the seven champions who marched against Thebes (see *Oedipus*). When he was killed in the attack, she threw herself on the pyre that consumed his body.

Eva'goras (*Euagoras*), king of Salamis in Cyprus, a useful ally of the Athenians at the end of the Peloponnesian War and after. See also *Isocrates*.

Eva'nder (Gk. *Euandros*, 'good man'), in Roman legend, an Arcadian, son of Carmentis (q.v.), who founded a colony of his countrymen on the banks of the Tiber at the place where Rome was afterwards to stand, and introduced the festival of the Lupercalia (q.v.) in honour of Pan. The story is probably due to an attempt to connect the Lupercalia with the Arcadian Lycaea, a festival also connected with Pan. Moreover there was an Arcadian hero named Pallas, supposed to be the founder of the Arcadian city called after him Pallanteion, and this was thought to have some connexion with the Palatine. In the 'Aeneid' Evander helps Aeneas to defeat Turnus.

Ex Ponto, Epistulae, elegiac poems, in four books, by Ovid (q.v.), written at Tomis during the latter years of the poet's exile, c. A.D. 12–16. They are similar in character to the 'Tristia' (q.v.), except that the names of the persons to whom they are addressed are given. Among those addressed are the two sons of M. Valerius Messalla (q.v.), Messalinus and Cotta Maximus; also Sextus Pompeius, of the family of Pompey the Great, consul in A.D. 14, a wealthy man who had helped Ovid on his voyage to Tomis; but most of the recipients of letters are otherwise unknown to us. Ovid's hopes of a mitigation of his sentence are now largely based on the genial character of Germanicus, the adopted son of Tiberius, who is addressed or mentioned in various passages. We hear in these letters of Ovid's studies in the Getic tongue, and of the kindness of his barbarian hosts.

Exe'mpla, see *Nepos*.

E'xodos, see *Tragedy*, § 3, and *Comedy*, § 2.

Exōmis, see *Clothing*, § 1.

Expenditure, PUBLIC, see *Athens*, § 11, and *Rome*, § 14.

Exports and Imports, see *Athens*, § 10, and *Rome*, § 13.

F

Fa'bia (*Fābia*), GENS, a noble clan at Rome who, according to tradition, when the State was hard pressed by its enemies, undertook the whole burden of the war with Veii. Livy in a fine passage (ii. 49) describes how they marched out in 477 B.C., 306 strong, and took up a position near the Cremera. After initial successes they were ambushed and all slain. One youth was left from whom the later Fabii were descended. This was the way the historians took of reconciling the tradition of total male annihilation with the famous Gens Fabia of later times. In this Livy is followed by later historians, and Ovid uses the same legend, but it is ridiculed by Dionysius of Halicarnassus, as if 306 men should not have left relations enough of both sexes to continue the family.

Fā'bius (*Fābius*) **Maximus**, QUINTUS, (1) a famous Roman general of the time of the Samnite Wars. As consul for the fifth time in 295 B.C., he with Decius Mus the younger (q.v.) defeated at Sentinum the combined army of Samnites and Gauls. He has the cognomen Rullus or Rullianus, which distinguishes him from the 'Cunctator' (see below). His story has been much affected by incidents in the career of the latter.

(2) 'CUNCTĀTOR', 'the Delayer', was appointed dictator after the Roman defeat at Lake Trasimene (217 B.C., see *Punic Wars*), and by his policy of following and harassing Hannibal's force while refusing an engagement earned the surname of 'Cunctator'. As consul for the fifth time in 209 he recaptured Tarentum from the Carthaginians. There is a life of him by Plutarch.

Fā'bius (*Fābius*) **Pictor**, QUINTUS (b. c. 254 B.C.), a Roman who wrote in Greek a chronicle of Rome from Aeneas to his own times, of which only fragments survive. He is the oldest Roman historian, and he is treated with great respect by ancient authors because of his love of truth. His was one of the chronicles on which Livy drew. It was an earlier Fabius (C. Fabius Pictor) who earned the surname Pictor by decorating with paintings in the year 304 the temple of Salūs at Rome.

Fabri'cius Lu'scinus, GAIUS, who flourished in the early part of the 3rd c. B.C., was a type of the old Roman honesty and frugality. He was one of the ambassadors sent to Pyrrhus in the winter of 280–279, and resisted all Pyrrhus's attempts to corrupt him. In the campaign of 278, it is said that Fabricius, who was then commanding the Roman army, revealed to Pyrrhus the treacherous proposal of the king's doctor to poison him.

Fā'bula Crepidā'ta, Palliā'ta, Praete'xta, Togā'ta, see *Crepidata, Palliata, Praetexta, Togata*.

Fa'scēs, in Rome, bundles of wooden rods, fastened together with a red strap, and enclosing an axe, the symbol originally of the king's authority, and transferred from him to the high magistrates. A consul had twelve *fasces* carried before him by attendants called lictors. The axe was withdrawn while he paraded with this symbol of authority in Rome. In ancient times only the consul who was functioning had the right to the *fasces*; this custom was revived by Julius Caesar. Besides the consuls, several other magistrates and priests (including dictators, proconsuls, and praetors) had the right to have *fasces* (in numbers varying according to the magistrate's importance) carried before them.

Fa'sti (perhaps meaning '[days] on which it is allowed to speak'), originally lists, drawn up by Roman priests, of the days on which praetors might transact legal business (see *Calendar*, § 3). The *fasti* were extended, by the introduction of notes on historical events, sacrifices, games, and astronomical information, into regular calendars for the whole year. Because of the usual connexion of the list of days with the publication of the name of the magistrates after whom the year was called, the word *fasti* also served for the list of eponymous magistrates and priests. Since the *fasti* thus gave a chronological list, the word came, in the poets, to mean 'history'.

The *Fasti Consulārēs* or *Capitōlīni* were

compiled in the reign of Augustus and gave the names of consuls, dictators, *magistri equitum*, and censors. The *Fasti Triumphālēs* (or *Acta Triumphorum*) gave a list of Roman triumphs and of *Lūdi saeculārēs*, terminating with those of Domitian in A.D. 88. For the inscription of these Fasti at Rome see *Epigraphy*, § 10. The fragments of them are preserved in the Capitoline Museum at Rome. For the *Fasti Praenestini*, see *Verrius Flaccus*.

Fasti, a poem by Ovid in six books of elegiacs, one for each of the first six months of the year. The work, which was to have comprised twelve books covering the whole year, was interrupted by the author's banishment and was not completed (a draft of Bks. vii–xii was perhaps written). The poem was originally dedicated to Augustus, but the dedication was transferred to Germanicus, nephew and later adopted son of the future emperor Tiberius. Ovid appears to have continued work on it during his exile. The poem is modelled on the 'Origins' of Callimachus (q.v.), or perhaps more directly on the last book of the elegies of Propertius, which contains a large number of Roman legends.

Ovid's design, as stated in the preface to the poem, is to study the calendar in the light of old annals, and show what events are commemorated on each day and the origins of the various rites. It accordingly records day by day the rising and setting of the constellations (not without mistakes), and explains the origins of the fixed festivals and the rites noted in the calendar, such as the Lupercalia (q.v.) on the 15th February. It also relates the legends connected with particular dates, such as that of the founding of Rome on the 21st April, and that of the expulsion of the Tarquins on the 24th February. The scheme provides opportunity for telling afresh some of the old Greek myths, such as the tale of Proserpine; and for excursions on a multitude of customs and beliefs, such as those connected with New Year's Day, the unluckiness of marriages in May, and the casting of straw men into the Tiber (see *Argei*).

Fate, see *Religion*, §§ 2 and 6.

Fates, THE (*Moirai*, L. *Fāta*, *Parcae*), according to Hesiod daughters of Night, or, in another passage, of Zeus and Themis. They were probably originally birth-spirits, 'Allotters' of a new-born child's portion in life. In Latin the name *Fata* appears to be adapted from *fatum*, that which is spoken, the decree of the gods. The name *Parcae* signifies birth-spirits, from *parere*, to bring forth. The *Moirai* were three in number, Clōthō,

Lachesis, and Atropos, represented as old women spinning; their occupations were varied by the fancy of later poets, e.g. Clotho held the distaff, Lachesis drew off the thread, and Atropos cut it short:

> Comes the blind Fury with the abhorred shears,
> And slits the thin-spun life.
>   Milton, 'Lycidas',

where Milton appears to confuse the Fates with the Furies (q.v.). The Latin names of the Parcae were Nōna, Decuma, and Morta. For the part played by Fate in Greek and Roman religion, see *Religion*, §§ 2 and 6. The Fates are one of the rare survivals in modern Greek folklore from ancient Greek beliefs. Still known as *Moirai*, they are supposed to appear on the third night after a birth to decide upon the course of the child's life, and are propitiated with offerings (Rennell Rodd, 'Customs and Lore of Modern Greece').

Fā'tua, an Italian goddess with attributes similar to those of Faunus (q.v.) and associated with him in Roman worship.

Fā'tuus, see *Faunus*.

Fau'na, an Italian goddess with the attributes of Faunus (q.v.).

Fau'nus, in Roman religion, a woodland deity, endowed with prophetic power and guardian of crops and herds, developed from an earlier conception of a number of Fauni, who were spirits of the countryside. As an oracular god (see *Oracles*, § 2), Faunus was known as *Fātuus*; as the giver of fertility to herds he was called *Inuus*. In legend Faunus was a king of Latium and father of Latinus (q.v.). Virgil in the 7th Aeneid makes him the son of Picus (q.v.). Under Greek influence Faunus was identified with Pan (q.v.). See also *Lupercalia*.

Fausti'na Minor, ANNIA GALĒRIA, daughter of the emperor Antoninus Pius (q.v.) and wife of the emperor Marcus Aurelius (q.v.). Her death was deeply lamented by him. Writers of a later age have gravely impugned her character, probably without good reason. She bore her husband at least thirteen children (Pauly-Wissowa).

Fau'stulus, in Roman legend, the shepherd who found the infant Romulus and Remus in the she-wolf's den, and whose wife Acca Lārentia brought them up.

Favō'nius, the west wind, also known as Zephyrus, and associated with spring-time.

Fayûm or **Fayoum**, an oasis a short distance to the W. of the Nile valley, some fifty miles S. of Cairo. Here was founded by Ptolemy II a Greek settlement of which Arsinoë was the chief town; and here in modern times have been discovered many papyri containing Greek texts.

Feneste'lla, a Roman nistorical writer who died according to Jerome in A.D. 20. The quotations that have come down to us from his *Annales* show that he was regarded as an authority on ancient law, religion, and manners. We do not know his full name.

Ferā'lia, see *Parentalia.*

Fē'riae Concepti'vae, see *Festivals*, § 7.

Fē'riae Lati'nae, the great common festival of the early Latin communities, held on the Alban Mount. A white heifer was sacrificed, the representatives partook of the flesh together, and the alliance between the communities was renewed. Rome at an early date took the presidency of the festival. The temple on the Alban hill was ascribed to the Tarquins, but the festival probably dated back to pastoral times. It belonged to the group of the *feriae conceptivae* (see *Festivals*, § 7) or movable feasts, and was kept as a holiday in Rome.

Fērō'nia, an old Italian goddess, of whom little is known, apparently associated with fertility. She had a celebrated shrine on Mt. Sōractě in Etruria, which was once a year the scene of a fire-walking rite. Virgil (Aen. viii. 563) refers to her as a goddess of childbirth.

Fesce'nnine Verses (*Versūs Fescennīni*), an ancient Italian form of verse, originally it seems in Saturnian (q.v.) metre, said to have been the form in which was cast the banter of rustics celebrating harvest and vintage festivals. Such verses, sung in rivalry, were supposed to have the power of averting misfortune, and continued long to be sung at marriages and triumphs. The specimens that have come down to us are in trochaic metre. Livy names them among the distant origins of Latin drama, and Horace (Ep. II. i. 145–55) traces their evolution. But the origin and influence of this type of verse are far from clear and the theories of Livy and Horace are suspected of being the attempts of learned Italians to transfer the Aristotelian theory of the origin of drama to Italian ground. The name is perhaps derived from Fescennium in Etruria, less probably from *fascinum* (the phallus). It is occasionally used to designate the satiric verses sung at triumphs, e.g. those composed by Augustus for Pollio's triumph, and so it comes to be a name for satiric verse.

Festivals.

§ 1. *Panhellenic Festivals*

The four great panhellenic festivals, which were attended by visitors from all parts of the Greek world, were the Olympian, Pythian, Isthmian, and Nemean.

The OLYMPIAN festival, held at Olympia (q.v.) in Elis, in honour of Zeus, was traditionally of great antiquity and perhaps originally instituted in honour of Pelops (q.v.). It appears to have been reorganized about 776 B.C., from which date a continuous record was kept of the victors in the Games (see below, § 2) which were the chief feature of the festival. At first the games were of only local importance, but after the First Messenian War (late 8th c.) they attracted competitors from all over the Peloponnese. The festival was held at midsummer in every fourth year, from which was reckoned the 'Olympiad' or chronological period of four years used for dating historical events (see *Calendar*, § 1). On the occasion of each festival a sacred truce (*ekecheiriā*) was proclaimed, whereby a safe-conduct was guaranteed to visitors to Olympia. Poets and orators took advantage of the great concourse to make themselves known by reciting their works. Athletes and owners of race-horses came from many Greek States. A great fair was held. Some idea of the numbers who attended the festival may be obtained from the fact that the Stadium at Olympia had seating accommodation for 40,000 spectators.

The PYTHIAN festival was held at Delphi, in August–September of the third year of each Olympiad, to celebrate the victory of Apollo (q.v.) over the serpent Python. An essential part was a contest in nomes (q.v.) accompanied by the lyre, to which was added a contest of flute-players. There were also athletic competitions and horse-races.

The ISTHMIAN festival was celebrated on the Isthmus of Corinth in the spring of every second year. It was said to have had its origin in funeral games in honour of Melicertes (see *Dionysus*). According to other versions it was instituted by Theseus (q.v.) or by Poseidon himself. It included athletic contests and horse-races, and poetical and musical competitions. It was at the Isthmian festival that Quinctius Flamininus (q.v.), after defeating Philip V of Macedon, proclaimed in 196 B.C. the liberty of Greece.

The NEMEAN festival was held, probably every second year, in the valley of Nemea near Cleōnae in Argos, two months after the Isthmian festival. It was said to have been originally instituted as funeral games in honour of Opheltes, killed in the course of the expedition of the Seven against Thebes (see *Hypsipyle*). The contests were of the same character as at the Isthmus.

These festivals were of great importance in various ways: they emphasized the unity of the Greek race; they encouraged the practice of athletics as part of education; they encouraged poetry and music by affording opportunities for hearing the best works; and they encouraged painting and sculpture by the prominence they gave to the physical development of the human body.

§ 2. *Panhellenic Festivals. The Games*

The Games had much the same character at all the festivals; the Olympian came first in importance, the Pythian next. At Olympia the games were gradually increased from a foot-race of a single course of about 200 yards to include first a double course, then a long race, then the pentathlon (q.v.), then boxing. From 680 B.C. chariot racing was added, at first with four-horse chariots, later with two-horse chariots also (see *Chariot Races*). Other contests were included later, such as the pancration (q.v.) and a race for ridden horses; a mule-cart race was introduced, but soon abolished 'as possessing neither antiquity nor dignity'. Official umpires were appointed, who inflicted fines for breaches of the rules, and with the proceeds of the fines bronze statues of Zeus were erected. There are some amusing references in Pausanias (vi. 21) to cases in which fines were inflicted, for instance that of two boxers who were found to have made a private monetary arrangement before contending, and that of another boxer who arrived too late for the contest, put on the gloves, ran at the winner, and began to pummel him, crowned as he was, though he had taken refuge among the umpires. The races were run in heats of four. The prizes consisted of wreaths of wild olive, but the winner received other rewards from his own State, on which his victory was held to confer honour. He was received at home with great rejoicings; he might, if he needed it, be granted free meals for life; a poet sometimes wrote an ode in his honour, or he might be commemorated by a statue. The numerous statues of athletes that Pausanias saw at Olympia are described by him (Bk. vi).

The principal Greek local festivals were as follows.

§ 3. *Athenian festivals: the Panathenaea*

The PANATHĒNAEA, a festival in honour of Athene, was held every year (the Lesser Panathenaea) on the 28th and 29th Hecatombaeon (roughly July), and with special splendour (the Great Panathenaea) in the third year of each Olympiad from the 21st to the 28th Hecatombaeon. The festival included horse-races and musical contests, to which the Pisistratids added poetical recitations by rhapsodes. Pericles extended the musical contests and built a special theatre, the Ōdēum, for them. The prizes at the athletic contests were beautiful vases (some of which are extant) filled with oil; as many as 140 of them were given as the principal prize. The festival culminated on the last day in a magnificent procession, in which the *peplos*, a costly garment woven by Athenian maidens of good family and embroidered with a representation of the struggle between Athene and the Giants, was carried to her temple on the Acropolis. Living personages were sometimes represented in the embroidery and it was a signal honour to be thought 'worthy of the peplos'. The peplos was carried on a great ship on wheels, followed by girls bearing baskets with the implements of sacrifice, by groups of boys bearing pitchers and old men with olive-branches, by chariots, and finally by a cavalcade of young men on spirited horses. The procession is depicted on the frieze of the Parthenon (q.v.). The feast was completed with a hecatomb of oxen. The Panathenaea had (in the 5th c.) not only a civic but a political character, being held in honour of the patroness, not of the city alone, but of the Athenian confederation also; the part taken by the allies in the sacrifices was regulated by decrees.

§ 4. *Athenian festivals in honour of Dionysus*

These were as follows:

(a) The RUSTIC DIONȲSIA, held about December, and celebrated with a burlesque procession in the rural districts and in the larger demes with dramatic performances also.

(b) The LĒNAEA or feast of the wine-vats, celebrated about January with a procession, sacrifice, and, after 450 B.C., with dramatic contests.

(c) The ANTHESTĒRIA, the oldest of the Dionysiac festivals, held during three days about February, when the casks were opened and the new wine tasted. A special feature was the symbolical marriage of the wife of the King Archon with the god Dionysus. The third day had the character of a family celebration, with rites in appeasement of ancestors, a sort of All Souls' Day. No plays were acted.

(d) The GREAT or URBAN DIONȲSIA, celebrated about March with great splendour, and attended by visitors from the neighbouring country and all parts of Greece. The festival included a sumptuous procession in which the statue of the god was carried on a chariot, and the performance on three consecutive days of new tragedies and comedies (see *Tragedy*, § 2, and *Comedy*, § 2).

(*e*) The OSCHOPHORIA or festival of the vintage, celebrated about October, when vine-branches with clusters of grapes were carried by young men in a race.

§ 5. *Other Athenian festivals*

(*a*) The THESMOPHORIA, a festival held at Athens (and in other parts of Greece) about October, in honour of Demeter, attended only by women. Its purpose was to secure the fertility of the fields.

(*b*) The THARGĒLIA, the principal festival of Apollo at Athens (and throughout Ionia), celebrated about May with a procession, the offering of first-fruits, and an expiatory rite in which two persons, condemned to death, were sacrificed (in later times it appears that the sacrifice was only symbolical, the victims being spared from death and banished). The festival was also the occasion of lyrical competitions.

(*c*) The PYANEPSIA or harvest festival, held about October in honour of Apollo. It took its name from the cooked pulse which was offered to the god as first-fruits and partaken of by all the members of the household. An olive-branch (known as *eiresiōnē*) hung with various fruits and small bottles of wine and oil was carried about and set before each house and the temple of the god.

For the APATŪRIA, see *Phratriai*.

§ 6. *Festivals in other Greek States*

At SPARTA, (*a*) the GYMNOPAEDIAE, a great festival held about July, at which there were displays of gymnastics and dancing by boys and men, and festal hymns were sung in honour of Spartan heroes as well as of the gods. (*b*) The CARNĒA, a harvest festival held about August in honour of Apollo Carnēus (protector of flocks). It in part symbolized the military life of Sparta, but it also had a rural character, including a race between boys carrying bunches of grapes (cf. *the Oschophoria*, § 4 above). A musical contest was added, which was attended by poets and musicians from all parts of Greece.

At ARGOS, a festival known as the HĒRAEA in honour of Hera was held every five years, and was celebrated with a procession to the Heraeum (q.v.), a hecatomb, and a contest in throwing the javelin.

At DELOS a great festival in honour of Apollo and Artemis was in early times held each spring, with gymnastic and musical contests; it was attended by visitors from many parts of the Greek world. But the contests and ceremonies fell into disuse until, in 426 B.C., the Athenians organized at Delos a great quadrennial festival, restoring the contests and adding horse-races. This festival had no panhellenic character, but was in the main Athenian.

There were also certain political festivals, such as the ELEUTHERIA instituted at Plataea after the victory over the Persians and held every five years. See also *Lycaeus* and *Mysteries*.

§ 7. *Roman festivals*

For Roman festivals see *Ludi*, and the names of particular festivals such as SATURNALIA, FERIAE LATINAE, or of the deities in whose honour they were kept. The *fēriae conceptivae* were festivals whose dates were not fixed but movable, appointed each year by the magistrates or priests; such were the Compitalia and the Paganalia (qq.v.). The great majority of Roman festivals were held on odd days of the month, as more lucky than even days.

Fe′stus, SEXTUS POMPĒIUS, the abbreviator of Verrius Flaccus (q.v.).

Fētiā′lēs, Roman priests, apparently of Jupiter Feretrius (q.v.), who were charged with the formalities of international relations and played an important part in making treaties and declaring war. From the temple of Jupiter Feretrius they took on these missions a *lapis silex* (flint, perhaps a stone axe) and a *sceptrum*. At the time of the war with Tarentum (282–272 B.C.), a captured soldier from the army of Pyrrhus was forced to buy a piece of land near the Circus Flaminius, which thereafter was hostile ground. On a declaration of war the Fetial threw his spear from the *columna bellica* by the temple of Bellona into this ground.

Finances, see *Athens*, § 11, *Rome*, § 14.

Fi′scus, in Roman imperial times, the special treasury of the emperor, instituted probably by Claudius. Its principal source of income was the revenue from the imperial provinces, to which was added later that from the indirect taxes in the senatorial provinces also, so that the Senate retained only the direct taxes from its provinces. This revenue was supplemented if necessary out of the emperor's privy purse. For the emperors were immensely wealthy, receiving besides the income from vast private estates, the revenue of Egypt (q.v.). The *fiscus* defrayed the cost of the army and navy, of the corn supply (see *Annona*), of amusements for the populace, and of the improvement and embellishment of the city of Rome. No doubt some of the imperial provinces, such as those on the Danube, showed a deficit on their financial administration, and this was met by the emperor. The *fiscus*, it may be mentioned, was probably the largest banker in the empire, and lent out money at interest.

Fla′mens (*flămĭnēs*, 'those who blow [the sacred fire]' or perhaps 'those who burn [offerings]'), at Rome, the special priests of various deities, fifteen in number; prominent among them being the priest of Jupiter (*Flamen Diălis*) and the priests of Mars and Quirinus (these three flamens were always patricians). Only the ancient Roman deities had flamens, not the gods imported later. The performance of daily sacrifices was the principal function of the flamens. They were exempted from military service and taxation, and in general precluded from holding political office (unlike the *pontifices*, q.v.). But there are records of the Flamen Dialis holding certain political positions (for the first time in 200 B.C., as curule aedile). The temples to which the flamens were attached had property in land, and received fees for admission and for the performance of special sacrifices; and their priests were moreover entitled to certain parts of the sacrificed animals. They wore as emblem of office a white leather conical hat. The Flamen Dialis wore, in addition, the *toga praetexta* (see *Clothing*, § 3) and was entitled to a curule (q.v.) chair. He was a person of especial sanctity and subjected to various restrictions, e.g. he was not allowed to touch a corpse or anything unclean, to wear anything resembling a chain, to behold an armed force. If his conical hat fell off during a sacrifice he had to resign.

The Roman emperors who were deified had flamens assigned to them. Julius Caesar had Antony as his flamen during his lifetime. There were also priests of local cults of this name in Italian towns.

Flămini′nus, Tĭtus Quinctius, consul in 198 B.C. and victor the following year over Philip V of Macedon at Cynoscephalae. It was he who proclaimed the freedom of the Greeks at the Isthmian Games of 196 B.C. The gift was illusory (see Wordsworth's sonnet 'A Roman master stands on Grecian ground' and that which follows it), but the announcement was received with such shouts of enthusiasm that the crows flying overhead are

said by Plutarch (in his life of Flamininus) to have dropped into the theatre. Aurelius Victor calls Flamininus the son of C. Flăminius who fell in battle at Lake Trasimene. But this statement arises from a confusion of the *gens* Flaminia with the *family* of the Flaminini.

Flavian Emperors, see *Rome*, § 11.

Flā′vius, Gnaeus, see *Calendar*, § 3.

Flā′vius Vopi′scus, see *Historia Augusta*.

Flō′ra, an old Italian deity of fertility and flowers. She had a temple near the Circus Maximus, and a special flamen (q.v.); and games, *Ludi Florales* or *Floralia* (see *Ludi*, § 1), were held in her honour.

Flō′rus, Lūcius Annaeus, the name of the author of 'Epitomae de Tito Livio Bellorum Omnium Annorum DCC Libri II', as given in one of the manuscripts of that work. Another manuscript gives the name as Jūlius Florus. Both names may be wrong, and it is thought that the author may be identical with Publius Annius Florus, a poet and rhetorician of whom a few fragments survive and who, it has been suggested, may be the author of the 'Pervigilium Veneris' (q.v.). He was an African, was in Rome as a young man under Domitian, then lived in Spain, and was again in Rome under Trajan.

The 'Epitome' is an abridged history of Rome from Romulus to Augustus, based on Livy, as the title indicates, but also on other sources. It is not written from the point of view of an impartial historian, but is a panegyric of Rome, in which the best complexion is put even on defeats and disasters (e.g., the affair of the Caudine Forks), while instances of Roman valour or virtue elicit from the author such exclamations as 'quis crederet?' or 'mirum et incredibile dictu'. It answers its purpose as an effective exposition of the growth of the Roman empire, being written with some literary skill, but is a rhetorical commentary rather than a true historical work. It was nevertheless much used in the ensuing centuries and was popular in the Middle Ages. Florus's division of Roman history (perhaps borrowed from the elder Seneca) into four ages, infancy, youth, maturity, decline (the period after Augustus), is well known.

Flute, see *Music*.

Food and Wine.

§ 1. *In Greece*

The warriors of the Homeric Age feasted liberally on beef, pork, and bread; milk and cheese were also consumed, but fish was disdained. In later times, when the cultivation of the soil had spread and much of the natural pasture had been converted into arable, there came a corresponding change in Greek diet. Butcher's meat became scarce and was seldom eaten except after sacrifices or at public banquets. Fish came into favour. The staple food of the Greeks of the historical period consisted of wheat or barley (either as bread or broth), supplemented by fish (fresh or salt), various sorts of sausage, vegetables, fruit (fresh or dried), olive-oil, and honey. Their wine was strong and syrupy, and was drunk mixed with water. The banquets given by the rich were naturally more elaborate and costly, and included game and delicate wines. In the philosophical schools rules were adopted for feasting and drinking; Aristotle himself drew up such codes for his school. The fare of the Spartans consisted principally of pork, cheese, figs, bread, and wine, and they had a broth which was notorious among the other Greeks for its nastiness. Greek athletes trained on a diet of freshly made cheese, until a certain Dromeus introduced a meat diet.

§ 2. At Rome

The Roman of the earlier republican times was mainly a vegetarian and his diet was frugal. The only meat eaten was pork or bacon (swine were kept near forests of oak and beech). Wheat provided the staple food, and for the trouble taken to secure adequate supplies of it see *Annona*. Pliny says that until 171 B.C. there were no bakers at Rome, bread being made by the women of the household. But the growth of the urban proletariate made bakers a necessity. The bakers were also millers, and donkeys turned their mills. Many kinds of vegetables and fruits were in use. The olive was introduced during republican times; a terra-cotta relief of the 1st c. B.C. in the British Museum shows oil being pressed out of olives in a rude form of press. Honey took the place of sugar and was imported from Attica and Spain. Fish, poultry, and game were luxuries that came into use in the later republican period. Juvenal (Sat. xi) describes an old-fashioned meal as consisting of kid, wild asparagus, eggs and the hens that laid them, grapes, pears, and apples; also dried pork, bacon, fresh meat (if available from a sacrifice), herbs, spelt. For the humble fare of a small cultivator see Virgil's 'Moretum'. In later republican days we read of the wealthy eating peacocks, pheasants, and thrushes. Varro tells of snails and dormice being fattened for the table. (Snails (*cocleae*) were extracted from their shells with a small

utensil, pointed at one end, spoon-shaped at the other, called *cocleare*, whence the French word for a spoon, *cuiller*; cf. Martial, xiv. 121.) Among fishes the mullet was highly esteemed, especially if of great size; also the *mūrēna*, a sea-eel, which was kept alive in salt-water tanks.

Breakfast (*jentāculum*) consisted of bread dipped in wine, or eaten with honey, cheese, or olives. The *prandium* was a light meal taken about noon. The *cēna* or principal meal was taken usually at the ninth hour—say 3 p.m.—and consisted usually of a light preliminary course, a course of substantial dishes, and a dessert of fruit or pastry. For the arrangement of the dining-room for a dinner-party, see *Triclinium*. The dinner might be followed by a *cōmissātiō* or drinking bout, in which certain Greek rules were followed.

Under the empire the variety and luxury of food increased greatly among the wealthy. Juvenal (Sat. v) refers to truffles, *foie gras*, lobster and asparagus, turbot, mullet, guinea-fowl, mushrooms, oysters (from artificial oyster-beds), and venison. British oysters were highly esteemed. A picture of extravagant luxury in Neronian times is given by Petronius Arbiter (q.v.) in his 'Banquet of Trimalchio'.

Wine was drunk, in early days at least, mixed with water. The Italian production of rough wine (such as the Sabine) was very large in later republican times, and its price very low. The grapes were trodden out, and the new wine or must was partly drunk at once, partly placed in large earthenware jars (*dōlia*) for fermentation. The commoner wines were drawn direct from these *dolia*. Choice wines at first were imported from Greece and the Greek islands. But later the wines of particular districts in Italy, such as Falernian, Caecuban, and Massic, from Campania and Latium, were carefully prepared and highly esteemed. Such wines, after fermentation had taken place in the *dolia*, were preserved in *amphorae*, sealed with pitch or other material, labelled to show the year of vintage, and stored in the *apothēca* (see Horace, Od. 1. xx).

Fordici′dia, at Rome, a festival held on 15 April, at which a pregnant cow (*forda*) was sacrificed in each of the thirty wards (*cūriae*). The intention was to promote the fertility of the cattle and fields. The unborn calves were burnt and their ashes subsequently used in a purificatory rite at the festival of the *Parīlia* (see *Pales*).

Fornāca′lia, in Roman religion, a movable feast celebrated in the early part of February in honour of Fornax, goddess of ovens, separately by each of the several *cūriae* or wards of the city. See *Stultorum Feriae.*

Fortū'na, in Roman religion, 'the goddess who brings' (from *ferre*), represented with a cornucopia and a ship's rudder. At Praeneste, the seat of one of the earliest of her cults, where she had an oracular shrine, she was worshipped as *Primigenia.* This means 'first-born daughter'. According to Frazer, other explanations of this title were devised by modern scholars who were puzzled by the fact that at Praeneste Fortuna is described on inscriptions as 'Fortune, child of Jove', while in the same town there was a statue of Fortuna suckling the infant Jupiter and Juno. One of the inscriptions reads 'A gift to Fortune, first-born daughter of Jove, for the sake of a child'. This would accord with the derivation from *ferre*, 'to bear'. It will be observed that her name is used, not in accordance with the normal and popular meaning of the word *fortuna*, i.e. 'luck', 'chance', but in the sense of 'destiny'. As pure chance, the goddess is known as *Fors Fortuna.*

Forty, The, at Athens, see *Judicial Procedure*, § 1.

Fō'rum (*Fŏrum*), originally a marketplace, a constant feature in large Roman towns, the centre of their town-plan. As trade tended to be transferred to shops in other quarters, the forum remained the focus of the town's political and social life, much frequented by the citizens. It was surrounded by the chief civic buildings. For the various *fora* in Rome itself, see below.

The towns in the Roman provinces were planned in the same way. Roman London had a forum near Leadenhall Market with a large basilica (q.v.) adjoining it. The Silchester forum was a rectangle of 310 ft. by 275, surrounded by a portico.

Forum Augu'stum, at Rome, a forum built by Augustus adjoining on the NE. the Forum Julium (q.v., and see Pl. 14). It was about 140 yds. long by 100 wide, surrounded by a massive wall 100 ft. high, a considerable part of which survives. In it stood Augustus's splendid temple of Mars (q.v.) the Avenger, and it was adorned with many statues, including those of distinguished Romans such as Aemilius Paullus, Marius, and Sulla. Two paintings by Apelles were also displayed there.

Forum Boā'rium, at Rome, an open cattle-market with shops, between the Palatine hill and the Tiber (see Pl. 14).

Forum Jū'lium, a forum built by Julius

Caesar to the north of the Forum Romanum (q.v., and see Pl. 14). It was a rectangular court about 125 yds. long by 30 wide, surrounded by a wall and colonnade, in the centre of which stood a temple of Venus Genetrix (see *Venus*).

Forum Rōmā'num, at Rome, an open space (see *Forum* above), some 200 yds. by 70, between the Palatine and Capitoline hills, the centre of the political, commercial, and religious life of the city (see Pl. 14). By the side of it stood the *Comitium* or place of assembly of the people in early republican days, the *Curia* or Senate-house, and the *Rostra* (qq.v.). Near it stood also the Temple or Gate of Janus, the circular Temple of Vesta and House of the Vestals, and the Temple of Saturn (containing the State treasury) (qq.v.). At a later date the Temple of Concord (q.v.) looked down on it from the slope of the Capitol, and many *basilicae* (q.v.) were erected about it for legal or other business. The shops that had been there in primitive times were transferred elsewhere and replaced by the *tabernae* or booths of bankers and money-changers. The Forum thus became the general meeting-place of the citizens of Rome, who frequented it either for business or religious purposes, or to meet friends and acquaintances and hear the news.

Forum Trājā'num, a forum constructed by the emperor Trajan adjoining on the north the Forum Augustum (q.v.). The forum proper was about 130 yards long by 100 yards wide. Abutting on it, on part of the space cleared by Trajan, was the Basilica Ulpia (a law-court) and two libraries for Greek and Latin works. The column of Trajan, commemorating his victories, stood in a small court between the basilica and the libraries. It still stands in very good preservation, showing, in a spiral sculptured frieze, the wars conducted by the emperor.

Freedmen, enfranchised slaves; see *Slavery.*

Frogs (*Batrachoi*, L. *Rănae*), a comedy by Aristophanes, produced in 405 B.C.

Aeschylus and Euripides were dead; Sophocles had just died. No capable tragic poet remained. Dionysus, who has been serving at Arginusae and who masquerades as Heracles, goes to Hades to bring one back. He finds in progress there a contest between Aeschylus and Euripides for the throne of Tragedy, and is called upon by Pluto to decide it. The two tragedians attack each other's plays, and the comedy provides some serious criticism (some is merely jocular) and admirable parody of their methods. The tag ληκύθιον ἀπώλεσε ('lost his oil-flask'), which Aeschylus interjects in each of Euripides' prologues, became proverbial from this play; the point (or a point) of this was Euripides' fondness for 'resolution', i.e. for tribrachs in iambic trimeters. Finally Aeschylus is chosen, because his poetry weighs more. Not that Euripides is in the eyes of Aristophanes a bad poet; on the contrary Aristophanes admires him; but still, Aeschylus is the greater of the two. The title of the play is taken from a secondary chorus of frogs who sing while Charon is ferrying Dionysus over the marsh; the chorus consists of initiates of the Mysteries.

Fronti'nus, SEXTUS JŪLIUS (c. A.D. 40–103), after being consul in A.D. 73 or 74 was sent as governor to Britain (in which post he preceded Agricola, the father-in-law of Tacitus). There he constructed the Roman road through S. Wales of which traces can still be seen. In 97 under Nerva he was appointed superintendent of the aqueducts of Rome, the service of which had become disorganized and unsatisfactory. He was consul again in 98 and 100, and was succeeded as augur by the younger Pliny. Martial refers to him as a friend, Tacitus speaks of him as *vir magnus*, Pliny as *princeps vir*.

He has left us three books of military 'Stratagems' (*Stratēgēmata*, written as a sequel to his lost work on the art of war) in which he illustrates from the military history of Rome and other countries the stratagems used for various purposes, (*a*) before a battle, (*b*) during a battle, (*c*) in connexion with sieges, grouped under such heads as 'on concealing plans', 'on escaping from difficult situations', 'on ambushes'. A fourth book, containing anecdotes on the management of an army, which has come down to us under his name, is perhaps by an imitator.

The second work by Frontinus that has survived is his 'De aquae ductu' (or 'De aquis urbis Romae') in which, when curator of the aqueducts, he collected, for his own instruction and the benefit of his successors, the facts relating to the aqueducts (q.v.) of Rome, their history, length, altitude, and capacity. He sets out the abuses (such as the secret interception of the water) which he discovered, and the reforms introduced under his supervision. The work shows him a zealous and conscientious official.

Fro'ntō, MARCUS CORNĒLIUS, a Numidian of the 2nd c. A.D., who was a successful pleader at Rome under Hadrian, and under Antoninus Pius became tutor to Marcus Aurelius and consul in A.D. 143. He was an ardent advocate of a return to the style and language of the older Romans, Cato, Ennius, Varro, &c. His influence is seen in Aulus Gellius and in Apuleius. Some of his correspondence (partly in Greek) with Marcus Aurelius (q.v.) has survived; his letters deal with literature, oratory, and the study of words. There are interesting judgements on Seneca, Sallust, and Plautus.

Juvenal (i. 12) refers to a Fronto, a rich patron of literature who lends his garden for recitations. He has not been identified with certainty.

Fu'lvia, the first wife of Mark Antony (she had previously been the wife successively of P. Clodius (q.v.) and of C. Scrībōnius Curio). She played an important political part in the struggle which followed the death of Caesar. With Antony's brother Lucius she held Perusia against Octavian (while Antony himself was in the East with Cleopatra), but was obliged to surrender the town and died shortly afterwards in 40 B.C. Her ambitious and masterful character is depicted in Plutarch's life of Antony. She is referred to in Tennyson's 'Dream of Fair Women' (near the end) as an injured wife.

Funeral Oration, see *Thucydides*.

Fu'riae or DĪ'RAE, the Roman counterparts of the Greek *Erinyes* or *Eumenides* (see *Furies*).

Furies, ERĪNYES, known also by the propitiatory names of EUMĔNIDES ('the kindly') and of SEMNAI ('the holy'), according to Hesiod primeval beings born of the blood of the mutilated Uranus, avengers of crime, especially crime against the ties of kinship. They are represented as winged women, sometimes with snakes about them. But Pausanias remarks that there was nothing terrible in their images in the sanctuary of the Furies near the Areopagus. They are especially prominent in the story of Orestes (see *Oresteia*). The origin of the name Erinyes is not known. The names of the Furies appear in later writers (e.g. Virgil) as Allēctō, Megaerā, and Tīsiphonē.

Fu'rius Cami'llus, MARCUS, see *Camillus*.

Furri'na or FURI'NA (the form 'Furrina' is confirmed by the calendar engraved in stone; the spelling in MSS. varies), in Roman religion, a goddess whose nature and function had become in Cicero's time a pure matter of conjecture. Nevertheless her festival, the *Furrinālia*, continued to be observed on 25 July. The name is connected with *furfur* (bran), doubtless for purificatory rites, and by the ancients fancifully with *Furia*. It was in the grove of Furrina that C. Gracchus caused his slave to kill him.

G

Ga'dara, on the SE. of the Sea of Galilee, made famous by the miracle recounted in the Gospels, appears to have been in the Roman Age a place of considerable literary activity. It was the birthplace of Menippus the satirist, and of the poet Meleager (qq.v.).

Gā'dēs, a famous colony of the Phoenicians, on an island close to the SW. coast of Spain, west of the Pillars of Hercules, the modern Cadiz. The Straits of Gibraltar were known as *Fretum Gāditānum*. Gades is referred to by Herodotus (iv. 8) in connexion with the legend of Geryon (q.v.). It surrendered to the Romans in the Second Punic War, and was made a Roman *municipium* (see *Rome*, § 4) by Caesar.

Gae'a (*Gaia*), see *Ge*.

Gai'us (*Gāius*) (c. A.D. 110–c. 180), a famous jurist of the reigns of Antoninus Pius and Marcus Aurelius, probably born in the east, who lectured on law, perhaps at Rome. We do not know the rest of his name. His *Institūtiōnēs*, first published in 161, is an introduction to Roman jurisprudence. It appears from recently recovered fragments that the main text which we possess (discovered by Niebuhr in a palimpsest at Verona in 1816) is one edition of a text-book which, like some of our modern legal works, was from time to time brought up to date. Besides his Institutes, Gaius wrote a treatise on the 'Edictum Prōvinciāle', and another called 'Libri rērum cotīdiānarum', which came to be known as his 'Aurea' or 'Golden Book'. These are lost. Gaius seems to have been little known by his contemporaries, but became famous some centuries later. His Institutes are of great interest as showing the state of Roman law at an intermediate period between the republic and the *Corpus Juris* of Justinian.

Gai'us Cae'sar, see *Caligula*.

Galatē'a (*Galateia*), one of the Nereids (see *Nereus*), with whom, according to Sicilian legend (Theocritus, Id. xi), the Cyclops Polyphemus (q.v.) fell in love. In one version of the story, she loved a youth called Acis and would have nothing to do with Polyphemus. The latter crushed Acis under a rock, and Galatea trans-

formed him into a river, which bore his name. In another version Galatea and Polyphemus were married. The former story is the basis of Gay's libretto to Handel's 'Acis and Galatea' (1732), where the contrast of the dainty sea-nymph and the clumsy giant is pleasantly brought out by the music.

Gala'tians (*Galătae*), see *Macedonia*, § 3. When settled in Asia Minor between Phrygia and Cappadocia, they remained long untouched by Hellenism and retained their own language and customs. Their three tribes were each divided into four divisions, known by the Greeks as tetrarchies. Their power was finally broken by the Attalid (q.v.) Eumenes II. Galatia was made a Roman province in 25 B.C.

Ga'lba, SERVIUS SULPICIUS (3 B.C.–A.D. 69), Roman emperor for about six months, A.D. 68–9, in succession to Nero, having been proclaimed emperor by his troops in Spain. He was honest and just, but severe and mean. He soon became unpopular; a conspiracy against him was formed among the praetorians, and he was murdered and replaced by Otho. For Tacitus's estimate of his character see under *Histories* (Bk. I).

Gā'len (*Gălēnos*) (c. A.D. 129–199), born at Pergamum, one of the most famous physicians of antiquity. He lived for many years at Rome under Marcus Aurelius. He was a friend of the emperor, but excused himself from accompanying him on his German expedition. He left a great mass of medical writings, covering every department of the science, of no literary value, but of great interest in the history of medicine. Over one hundred of these works survive, including a treatise on the order of his own writings. Galen also wrote on philosophy, grammar, and literature, notably on Ancient Comedy, and commentaries on Plato and Aristotle; but these works, except for some fragments, are not extant. Thomas Linacre (1460 ?–1524), physician to Henry VIII, translated six of his works. Chaucer's Doctor, in the 'Canterbury Tales' (Prologue) had read Galen; and there is a reference to him in the Parson's Tale.

Ga'lli (*Galloi*), eunuch priests of Cybele (q.v.), so named from the river Gallos in Phrygia. The ancients thought that they castrated themselves in imitation of Attis (q.v.). See also *Metre*, § 5, with reference to Galliambics.

Gallia'mbic, see *Metre*, § 5.

Ga'llus, GAIUS CORNĒLIUS (69–26 B.C.), born in Narbonese Gaul, soldier and poet, rose from humble origins to high fortune under the Triumvirs (he was one of the commissioners appointed to distribute lands after Philippi and then befriended Virgil), and under Augustus was first prefect of Egypt. He fell into disgrace and took his own life. He won the affection of Virgil, who celebrates his eminence as a poet in Eclogue vi and again refers to him in Eclogue x. See also *Georgics, ad fin.* His principal literary achievement was the establishment of the elegiac as one of the main forms of Latin poetry; this he did by the success of his poems in that metre, in four books, on his love for the actress Cythĕris, to whom he referred under the name Lycōris. These poems have not survived.

Games, PRIVATE.

§ 1. *Children's Games*

Greek and Roman children in antiquity appear to have been much like modern children in their amusements. They had rattles, balls, draw-carts, and whipping-tops. They had dolls, sometimes with movable arms and legs, as may be seen from an example in the British Museum (Xenophon in his Symposium refers to a travelling puppet-show). They had also little figures of animals, and miniature articles of furniture; and they played with knuckle-bones. We know from the Greek Anthology that such toys were sometimes dedicated to a god when the child grew up.

§ 2. *Games of later years*

The Greeks attached a high importance to physical development, and athletic contests were popular even in Homeric times, witness the competitions in running, wrestling, &c., that followed the banquet of Alcinous. In later times athletics formed a prominent part of Greek education, especially at Sparta (q.v.), but there were gymnasiums and wrestling schools (*palaestrae*) also at Athens. There were games like Blind Man's Buff and Prisoners' Base, and a game resembling hockey; and throwing a ball was an accompaniment of dancing, in which not only the feet, but the arms, hands, and whole body were exercised, and which resembled musical drill. Running and the long jump were practised, also javelin-throwing and throwing the discus, a circular quoit of stone or metal—the object being to throw it, not as close as possible to a mark, but as far as possible. Under the empire the Romans adopted this game of throwing the discus, but their gymnastics in republican times were mainly part of their military training.

The game of draughts is said by Herodotus to have been invented by Palamedes during the Trojan War. Curious counters survive for other games like draughts and backgammon. There is in the British Museum a marble board inscribed with three pairs of words each of six letters, each word separated from that opposite it by a flower in a circle:

CIRCVS PLENVS
CLAMOR INGENS
IANVAE TE(nsae?)

This was probably used for a game. Ancient dice resembled modern ones, with six faces, numbered one to six (exceptionally there were dice with more faces; the *talus* or knuckle-bone was marked on four faces). Aeschylus has a reference in the 'Agamemnon' to throwing three sixes. Games of hazard with dice were prohibited in Rome except during the Saturnalia (q.v.). But the prohibition appears to have been largely ignored, especially under the empire. A slave was regarded as of less value if he was an *aleator* or gambler (Cic. Off. iii. 91). The highest throw was known as 'Venus', the lowest as 'Canis'.

Games, PUBLIC, (1) IN GREECE, see *Festivals,* § 2; (2) AT ROME, see *Ludi.*

Ga'nymēde (*Ganumēdēs*), in Greek mythology, a son of Tros (see genealogy under *Troy*). He was carried off by the gods (Il. xx. 234–5), or according to later writers by the eagle of Zeus or by Zeus himself, on account of his beauty, to be cupbearer to Zeus.

Gates of Dreams, see *Dreams.*

Gaugamē'la, in Assyria, the scene of the final victory of Alexander the Great (q.v., § 5) over Darius.

Gaul (*Gallia*).

§ 1. *Cisalpine Gaul*

In the first half of the first millennium B.C. Celtic tribes migrating westwards occupied the greater part of what we know as France; some of them turning south-eastwards passed thence about 400 B.C. into northern Italy and became known to the Romans as Gauls. The tribe of the Insubres occupied Lombardy, with Melpum (the future Milan) as their centre; their territory is sometimes spoken of as Insubrian Gaul. The Boii and the Senones crossed the Po and occupied territory to the S. and SE. By about 350 B.C. these and other Celtic tribes held the whole of Italy north of the Apennines with the exception of Liguria to the W. and Venetia to the E. The entire Italian territory in Gallic occupation was known as Cisalpine Gaul, the portion beyond the Po as Transpadane Gaul, that to the south of the Po

as Cispadane Gaul. From this territory the Gauls made forays southwards from time to time, actually capturing Rome as early as 391, and proving a constant menace to the security of Italy, until in the latter part of the 3rd c. B.C., after a particularly dangerous incursion of a coalition of Gallic tribes, Rome decided to put an end to the danger by conquering Cisalpine Gaul. This was substantially effected by the campaigns of 224–222. But there were Gallic risings after the Second Punic War and the final reduction was not effected until 191 B.C. Cisalpine Gaul was constituted a Roman province by Sulla.

§ 2. Transalpine Gaul

Transalpine Gaul, what is commonly understood by the single word 'Gaul' or modern France, was occupied by a population predominantly Celtic, which had entered it from the E., superimposed upon a race of earlier inhabitants generally designated by the name Ligurian. To the Celts were added, about the 5th or 4th c. B.C., Iberians from Spain in the S., and about the 2nd c. B.C. Belgae (a mixture of Celts and Germans) in the N.E.

The first contact of Gaul with Mediterranean civilization was through the foundation in the 7th c. B.C. of the Phocaean colony of Massalia (the future Marseilles), which became an important trading centre and threw out new settlements both inland and along the Mediterranean coast of Gaul (see *Colonization*, § 3). The adoption of Greek culture by some of the richer natives facilitated their subsequent Romanization; and even then the Greek language was sometimes used and Narbonensis produced a distinguished sophist (Favōrīnus of Arles) in the time of Hadrian. At the time of the Second Punic War Massilia (as it was called by the Romans) was on friendly terms and perhaps in alliance with Rome. In the latter part of the 2nd c. B.C. Rome sent an army to the assistance of Massilia against Ligurian invaders and became embroiled with the Celtic tribes of the Allobroges and the Arverni. The campaigns against them of 124–121 gave the Romans the possession of the Gallic territory between the Alps and the Pyrenees; it was formed into the province later called Gallia Narbōnensis from its capital Narbo (Narbonne), a colony of Roman veterans. Massilia remained nominally independent.

When Julius Caesar in 58 B.C. undertook the conquest of the remainder of Gaul, Gallic civilization was in a fairly advanced stage. Trade was well developed along the course of the great rivers; Greek and (later) Roman coins and local imitations of them were in use; the Gauls were skilful workers of metal. The form of government of the Gallic tribes was aristocratic, the magistrates as well as the military leaders being drawn from the nobility. The Druids were a powerful priestly corporation, possessing a monopoly of learning (writing was known to them alone among the Gauls); they were exempt from military service and taxation. They exercised jurisdiction, executed criminals, and had a formidable power of excommunication. The transmigration of souls was among the doctrines that they taught. They were credited with prophetic powers. Caesar says that Britain was their cradle and school, and their intolerant nationalism led to their destruction by the Romans both in that island (see *Britain*, §§ 2 and 3) and in Gaul. Though the Gallic tribes were numerous, and in spite of rivalries and conflicts between them, there was some approach to national unity, owing to the predominance of certain tribes, such as the Arverni, and to the Druids, who acted as arbitrators in their disputes. The Gallic infantry was ill-organized and undisciplined, their cavalry was better than that of the Romans.

The occasion for Caesar's conquest was provided by the appeal of the Gauls for help against German invaders under Ariovistus. Its history is related in Caesar's Commentaries 'De Bello Gallico' (q.v.). It detracts little from the magnitude of this military achievement that Caesar through the greater part of his campaigns in Gaul was aided by dissensions among the Gallic tribes. The newly-conquered territory was constituted a province as Gallia Comāta. Augustus divided this into three provinces, Aquitania, Lugdūnensis, and Belgica. There were local risings in Gaul under Augustus and Tiberius; and under Nero the governor of Gallia Lugdunensis, C. Julius Vindex, renounced his allegiance to the emperor and collected a large force in his province. But these various risings were suppressed without serious difficulty. Nor did the rebellion of the Batavians under Civilis on the lower Rhine in 69, though supported by the NE. Gauls under Classicus in 70, spread to Gaul at large, where the benefits of Roman protection were by now generally recognized, and loyalty was secured by the gradual extension of Roman citizenship.

Under Roman administration Gaul became a wealthy and highly civilized country. The land was fertile and produced much corn for export. Industries were developed, particularly metal-working and pottery; the products of the latter in time largely eclipsed the wares of Italy. The manufacture of warm woollen garments was also a special Gallic industry. Commerce was active. Roman remains are numerous in France, especially in the south. Among the most striking of these are the amphitheatre and temple at Nîmes, the arch of honour at Orange, the temple at Vienne, the aqueduct near Nîmes known as the Pont du Gard, and the beautiful mausoleum of the Julii near Tarascon. For the principal Latin authors of Gallic birth, see *Birthplaces of Latin authors.*

Gē or GAE'A (*Gaia*), in Greek mythology the personification of the Earth, according to Hesiod sprung from Chaos. She in turn produced Uranus (q.v.), mated with him, and was the mother of Cronus and the Titans, Cyclopes, and Hundred-handed Giants (qq.v.). By Pontus (q.v.) she was the mother of Phorcys and Ceto (qq.v).

Geese, SACRED, see *Manlius Capitolinus.*

Gē'la (*Gēla*), a city on the S. coast of Sicily, founded about 689 B.C. by Rhodians and Cretans, and the parent of Acragas (Agrigentum, q.v.). Gela became one of the most important cities in the island, and the centre of its pottery industry; but about 485 B.C. its tyrant Gelōn deliberately gave the preference to Syracuse (q.v., § 1) and abandoned Gela. Aeschylus (q.v.) ended his days there. In 405 it was utterly destroyed by the Carthaginians under Himilcō.

Ge'llius, AULUS, of whose life little is known, was probably born early in the 2nd c. A.D., was in Rome as a young man, and after studying there and practising law went to Athens for instruction in philosophy. We know that he was in Athens after A.D. 143. There he was on friendly terms with Herodes Atticus (q.v.), visited him at his villa, and made excursions to Aegina and to the Pythian games at Delphi.

While at Athens he began, for the benefit of his children, his collection of brief essays in Latin, which he named 'Attic Nights' (*Noctes Atticae*). There were twenty books of these, which survive with the exception of Bk. VIII; for this we have only the chapter headings. The essays are based on notes jotted down from the Greek and Latin books he read, and from conversations and discourses he heard, and deal with a great variety of curious points of language, grammar, textual criticism, antiquarian knowledge, and philosophy. We find in them, for instance, Julius Caesar's injunction to avoid 'like a rock' the use of an unfamiliar word; anecdotes of famous persons, such as Socrates and Demosthenes; a note on the use of the pipe in battle and in oratory; the comparison of a Roman comedy with its original by Menander; a note on the Roman sumptuary laws; others on 'analogy' and 'anomaly' in grammar; on the authentic plays of Plautus; and many on the origins of Latin words, some of them of special interest in view of their English derivatives, such as *classicus, prōlētārius, botulus.* The work is a valuable source of quotations from lost authors, containing, e.g., Sedigitus's canon of the Roman comic authors (see *Comedy*, § 5.)

Gē'lon (*Gēlōn*), see *Gela* and *Syracuse*, § 1.

Gemō'niae, SCALAE, see *Scalae.*

Gems, see *Art*, § 2.

Gē'nius (*Genius*), in Roman religion, the indwelling spirit (*numen*) of a man, which gave him the power of generation, so that the marriage-bed (*lectus geniālis*) was its sphere. The notion grew somewhat wider, and the *genius* came to denote all the full powers of developed manhood. The household worshipped the *genius* of the house on the master's birthday. Its symbol was the house-snake. Any locality, such as an open space, might have its *genius loci.* We hear also of a *Genius populi Romani*, and a *Genius urbis Romae*, and in later times of the *Genius* of the emperor, the basis of imperial worship. On the meaning of the word see Horace, Ep. ii. 2. 187–9. The corresponding spirit in woman was known as 'Juno'.

The word in classical usage had apparently nothing approaching the usual modern English senses of the word: exalted intellectual power in a person, the person possessing this, the prevalent spirit of a nation, age, language, &c.

Gens, in the Roman social system, a clan or group of families, descended in the male line from a common ancestor, and bearing a common *nomen* or 'gentile' name. Originally the term was confined to groups of patrician families, but later was extended to plebeians. A *gens* had certain common property (including a burial place), held meetings of its members, and performed religious rites in common.

Geogra'phica (*Geōgraphika*), see *Strabo.*

Georgics (*Geōrgica*, 'agricultural poems'), a didactic poem in four books of hexameters by Virgil, on the various forms of rural industry, written between 37 and 30 B.C., in Campānia. It is said that Maecenas (q.v.), to whom the poem is inscribed, suggested its subject to the author. The poem shows the various influences of Hesiod, of such Alexandrians as Aratus and Nicander, and of the great work of Lucretius; but Virgil imbues the didactic element of the 'Georgics' with great poetic charm, by his sense of the struggle between man and the forces of nature, by bringing out the beauty and dignity of the operations of husbandry, by giving a sort of personal life to the processes of nature, by his feeling for animals, and by his mythological and other allusions. He was in strong sympathy with the object of the work (to revive the love of the land, the simple tastes and virtues of an earlier age), by reason of his own deep love for nature and the rural associations of his youth. His agricultural precepts are drawn from peasant lore and from earlier writers; his conception of nature in part from Lucretius, but with a totally different outlook on life. For Virgil accepts the idea of divine force and guidance, and of man's dependence on a spiritual power, which he can propitiate by piety and prayer.

Book I deals with the raising of crops and the signs of the weather; Book II with the growing of trees, chiefly the olive and the vine; Book III with the rearing of cattle, and contains at the end a notable description of the cattle-plague in the Noric Alps; Book IV with bee-keeping. According to a statement by Servius (now discredited) the episode of Aristaeus, with the story of Orpheus and Eurydice, at the end of Book IV, was written later than the rest of the poem, to replace a passage in praise of Cornelius Gallus (q.v.), the poet's friend, who had fallen into disgrace with the emperor.

It is interesting to recall that Book I (ll. 250–1) furnished a quotation which is famous in our parliamentary annals. In 1792 Pitt was speaking in favour of the abolition of the Slave Trade. 'He burst as it were into a prophetic vision of the civilization that shall dawn upon Africa, and recalled the not less than African barbarism of heathen Britain; exclaiming, as the first beams of the morning sun pierced the windows of Parliament, and appeared to suggest the quotation:

Nos . . . primus equis Oriens afflavit anhelis,
Illic sera rubens accendit lumina Vesper.'
Lord Rosebery, 'Pitt', p. 98.

Germā'nia, a treatise on Germany (q.v.) by Tacitus (q.v.), probably published in A.D. 98 (the same year as the 'Agricola'). The treatise describes the geographical and physical characteristics of the country, and the appearance, political and social customs, and dress of the inhabitants; the organization of their army; their religion and land tenure; their sloth alternating with warlike activity; their intemperance and gambling; the exemplary morality of their family life (sarcastically contrasted with the laxity prevailing at Rome). Tacitus then passes to the geographical situation and special characteristics of the several 'German' tribes (including the Swedes and ending with the Finns). His sardonic humour is shown in the remark that in recent times the Germans have afforded more triumphs than victories to Rome.

Germā'nicus (*Germānicus*) **and Drū'sus.** The various members of the Julio-Claudian family who bore these names are enumerated below. 'Germanicus' was at first only a title of honour conferred on generals, and later exclusively on emperors, for victories over the German peoples.

A. *Germanicus*

1. NERO CLAUDIUS DRUSUS (38–9 B.C.), stepson of Augustus, son of Livia, younger brother of the future emperor Tiberius. He was commonly known as 'Drusus the Elder' to distinguish him from Drusus Julius Caesar ('Drusus the Younger', B. 1), son of Tiberius. After his death Drusus the Elder received the title 'Germanicus', which was also conferred on his posterity.

2. NERO CLAUDIUS GERMANICUS (15 B.C.–A.D. 19), son of Drusus the Elder (A. 1), nephew of Tiberius and later adopted by him as his son. He is most commonly known as 'Germanicus' in ancient writers. Hence his father is sometimes called 'Drusus Germanicus' and rarely 'the elder Germanicus'. When adopted by Tiberius (A.D. 4), Germanicus took the name Germanicus Julius Caesar.

3. CLAUDIUS (10 B.C.–A.D. 54), the younger son of the Elder Drusus (A. 1) and the future emperor Claudius, also took the title 'Germanicus'. After his brother was adopted, Claudius took the name Tiberius Claudius Drusus Nero Germanicus.

In the same way the name became hereditary in the offspring of Germanicus (A. 2) and the elder Agrippina. In ancient authors the following bear the title:

4. DRUSUS JULIUS GERMANICUS CAESAR (d. A.D. 33), son of Germanicus (A. 2), grandson of Drusus the Elder (A. 1). He incurred the ill-will of Tiberius and Sejanus and finally was starved to death in prison.

5. GAIUS (JULIUS) CAESAR AUGUSTUS GERMANICUS (A.D. 12–41), the future emperor Caligula, another son of Germanicus (A. 2).

In the family of Claudius (A. 3):

6. BRITANNICUS (A.D. 41–55), son of Claudius. Before the success of the armies

in Britain, he was called Tiberius Claudius Caesar Germanicus.

7. NERO (A.D. 37–68). After his adoption by Claudius, the future emperor Nero was called Nero Claudius Caesar Drusus Germanicus.

8. One of the twin sons of the Younger Drusus (B. 1), son of Tiberius, was called Germanicus. He died when but four years old.

B. *Drusus*

(i) The name was borne as *praenomen* by:

1. The son of Tiberius, DRUSUS CAESAR (15 B.C.–A.D. 23), called 'the Younger Drusus'.

2. The second son (A. 4) of Germanicus.

(ii) The name was borne as *cognomen* by:

3. The ELDER DRUSUS (A. 1).

4. The emperor CLAUDIUS (A. 3).

5. The son of the Emperor Claudius by Plautia Urgulanilla.

4. The emperor NERO (A. 7).

Germa′nicus (*Germānicus*) **Jūlius Caesar**, NĒRO CLAUDIUS (15 B.C.–A.D. 19), commonly known as 'Germanicus', nephew and adopted son of Tiberius (see *Julio-Claudian Genealogy* and *Germanicus and Drusus*, A. 2), famous for his great campaigns against the Germanic tribes. He was author of Latin paraphrases of the 'Phaenomena' and 'Prognostica' of Aratus (q.v.). The whole of the former and fragments of the latter survive. Germanicus was probably poisoned, during a mission to the East, by Cn. Pisō, governor of Syria, and the latter's wife Plancina, with the connivance of Tiberius. Tacitus (Ann. ii. 82) gives a vivid description of the sorrow and consternation caused at Rome by the death of Germanicus, for whom he shows deep admiration.

Germany (*Germānia*) was for the Romans the country that lay E. of the Rhine and N. of the Danube. According to Tacitus it was to a great extent covered with forests and marshes, but it produced corn and cattle, the latter of small size. Germanic tribes first come into prominence in connexion with Roman history when, late in the 2nd c. B.C., the Cimbri and the Teutones in the course of their migrations invaded SE. Gaul and later northern Italy, inspiring great terror at Rome, and were finally destroyed by Roman armies under Marius (q.v.). Early in the 1st c. B.C. the westward pressure of another Germanic tribe, the Suebi, began to be felt from the region between the Main and the Danube. Their inroads into Gaul led Julius Caesar

in 58 B.C., after fruitless endeavours to come to an understanding with their chief, Ariovistus, to drive them back across the Rhine (as related in Caesar's Commentaries 'De Bello Gallico', Bk. I, q.v.), which river thereafter for many years served as a sufficient defence against German incursions. In the reign of Augustus Roman invasions of German territory were systematically undertaken, mainly with a view to the better protection of Gaul against renewed raids of German tribes. From 12 B.C. Drusus, and after his death in 9 B.C. Tiberius, the emperor's stepson, carried on a series of successful campaigns between the Rhine and the Elbe; but the Roman ascendancy in this region was brought to an end in A.D. 9 when the Roman forces under P. Quinctilius Varus were destroyed by the German chieftain Arminius between the Weser and the Ems. After this the Rhine frontier was once more adopted. Under Tiberius attempts were made to reconquer north-western Germany: the emperor's nephew Germanicus for three years (A.D. 14–16) conducted a series of campaigns, attended by much devastation of territory and slaughter of inhabitants, but Arminius held out, and Tiberius was obliged to abandon his forward policy and recall his nephew. The Rhine borderland was then organized in two military districts, Germania Superior and Inferior. The Flavian emperors effected a rectification of the frontier in the angle between the Upper Rhine and the Upper Danube, designed to give greater strength to the defence. Under Marcus Aurelius there occurred a dangerous invasion of German tribes from Bohemia, the Marcomanni and the Quādi, across the Danube. They invaded Pannonia, penetrated into Italy, and reached Aquileia. The emperor met the crisis with vigour, and before his death the invaders had been driven from Roman territory.

According to the succinct description given by Tacitus, the German tribes chose their kings from noble families, and military leaders for their prowess. Important political decisions were taken in assemblies of the tribe; lesser matters were dealt with by the chiefs. The administration of justice was in the hands of a council. The German gods, whom the Romans identified with gods of their pantheon, were those known to us as Thor, Odin, Freia, Nertha. The Germans had no cities, but lived in wooden houses, each isolated from its neighbours. Tacitus praises their strict morality, the high estimation in which courage was held by them, and their simple mode of life. He mentions their addiction to gambling.

Gerou'siā, the name of the senate at Sparta (q.v., § 2).

Ge'ryon (*Gēruŏn, Gēruonēs,* or *Gēruonēus*), in Greek mythology, son of Chrȳsāŏr (see *Gorgons*). He was a three-headed or three-bodied monster, rich in cattle, who lived on an island in the stream Oceanus (q.v.), in the far west, with his herdsman Eurytion and his formidable dog Orthrus. See *Heracles* (*Labours of*).

Giants (*Gigantes*), THE, in Greek mythology, sons of Ge (q.v.), said to have been produced when the blood from the mutilation of Uranus (see *Cronus*) fell upon her. They were monstrous beings, partly human, of vast size, with serpents for feet. They rose against the gods and attacked them, but were defeated and imprisoned in the earth, e.g. Enceladus under Mt. Etna. See also *Monsters, Giants* (*The Hundred-handed*), *Cyclopes,* and *Otus and Ephialtes.* The three attacks on the gods made respectively by the Titans, the Giants, and the Aloads (see *Otus*), are often confused by the poets.

Giants, THE HUNDRED-HANDED (*Hekatoncheires*), Briareos, Cottus, and Gyes, sons of Uranus and Ge (qq.v.). Unlike the other Giants (q.v.) of Greek mythology, they are represented generally as friendly to the gods. See *Monsters.*

Gibbon, EDWARD, see *Historians* (*Modern*).

Gladiators (*Gladiātŏrēs*), at Rome, men who fought with one another at public shows. They were prisoners of war, or condemned criminals, or slaves purchased for the purpose, or volunteers. Displays of gladiators, which perhaps had their origin in funeral sacrifices, were at first given at Rome exclusively by private persons, e.g. candidates for office to increase their popularity; also at funeral games (*lūdi novendiālēs*), on the ninth day after the funeral. In late republican times large numbers of gladiators were retained by private persons and were a danger to peace and order. We know that there were some two hundred in a private school of gladiators at Capua from which Spartacus (q.v.) escaped to carry out his revolt in 73 B.C. Cicero, in a letter to Atticus (vii. 14), speaks of 5,000 gladiators at Capua. The popularity of gladiatorial shows helped to oust the drama from Rome, but it was not until the time of Domitian that they assumed an official character. There were various types of gladiator, differently armed. The *rētiārius* fought with a net, trying to entangle his adversary in it and then dispatch him. The *laqueārius* carried a noose to throw over his adversary. The *myrmillō* had helmet, shield, and sword. Statius mentions women and dwarfs among the combatants. There is also in the British Museum a relief from Halicarnassus showing a gladiatorial combat between two women. A repeatedly successful gladiator might receive by favour of the people a wooden sword (*rudis*), a token of his discharge from service (see also *Epigraphy,* § 9). A wounded gladiator raised his forefinger imploring mercy of the spectators. These signified their decision either by turning the thumb down (*premere pollicem*) to signify mercy, or by turning the thumb upwards or towards the breast (*vertere pollicem*) to signify the continuance of the combat. See also *Venationes.*

Glass was produced in the East, especially in Egypt and Phoenicia, from very early times; the manufacture was introduced in Italy under the empire. Aquileia, at the head of the Adriatic, was an important centre of the industry, and glass ware was exported thence to the Danube regions. Much glass was also made in southern Italy. Glass window-panes have been found at Herculaneum and Pompeii, and great beauty was attained in coloured glass and mosaics, and in cups and other vessels. The most famous example is the Portland Vase, in blue glass with a mythological design in opaque white enamel, found in a sarcophagus near Rome and now in the British Museum.

Glau'cia, GNAEUS SERVĪLIUS, a Roman statesman. Together with Saturninus and Marius (qq.v.) he launched a series of attacks on the conservative party about the year 100 B.C. His methods were frankly terrorist. He was unpopular with the Roman mob because of his support for the Italians. Finally the *senatus consultum ultimum* (q.v.) was passed against the agitators and Glaucia was killed in December, 100 B.C.

Glau'cus (*Glaukos*), (1) in Greek mythology, a god of the sea, originally a Boeotian fisherman who became immortal through eating a marvellous herb. He figured in some versions of the story of the Argonauts. Aeschylus wrote a play about him (*Glaukos Pontios*) of which fragments survive. (2) Glaucus of Potniae in Boeotia, another legendary figure, who was torn to pieces by his own mares. Aeschylus wrote a play (*Glaucus Potniēus*) about him also, of which we have fragments. (3) Son of Sisyphus (q.v.) and father of Bellerophon (q.v.). (4) In the 'Iliad', a grandson of Bellerophon (q.v.), leader (with Sarpedon, q.v.) of the Lycian allies of the Trojans, a gallant soldier. In his simplicity he exchanges with Diomedes (q.v.) his golden armour worth a hundred oxen for the other's bronze, worth nine—ἑκατόμβοι' ἐννεαβοίων. (5) A son of Minos of Crete, who was drowned in a vat of honey, and restored to life by the seer Poly-idos. This story was the subject of lost tragedies by Sophocles and Euripides. (6) The Spartan who tempted the Delphic Oracle (q.v.).

Glyco'nic (*glukōneios*), see *Metre*, §§ 3 and 5.

Gnā'tho (*Gnáthō*), the parasite in the 'Eunuchus' (q.v.) of Terence.

Gnomic Poetry, a form of early Greek poetry, usually written in elegiacs (see *Metre*, § 2), embodying popular wisdom, often satiric. Phocylides (q.v.) is the best-known gnomic writer.

Golden Age, THE, the period, according to Hesiod and other poets, when Cronus or Saturn ruled the world. It was an age of innocent happiness, when men lived without strife or labour or injustice, the earth yielding its fruits in abundance of its own accord.

It was followed by a Silver Age when men were impious and were finally de-stroyed by Zeus. Then a Bronze Age, when all things, such as houses, were made of bronze. The men of this age destroyed one another. After this came the Heroic Age, that of the Theban and Trojan Wars, which was an improvement on its two pre-decessors. Finally came the present Iron Age, the worst of all.

Golden Ass, see *Apuleius.*

Golden Bough, see *Diana.*

Golden Fleece, see *Argonauts.*

Golden House (*Domus aurea*), the palace built by Nero (q.v.) at Rome, amid vast pleasure-grounds, lakes, and colonnades, extending from the Palatine to the heights of the Esquiline. It is described by Suetonius. The site was devoted by later emperors to the construction of public buildings.

Gordian Knot. Gordius, the father of Midas (q.v.), a peasant, became king of Phrygia, according to the legend, in conse-quence of an oracle which told the Phry-gians, in a time of sedition, that their troubles would cease if they appointed king the first man they met approaching the temple of Zeus in a wagon. Gordius was the man thus chosen. He dedicated his wagon to the god. The knot with which the yoke was fastened to the pole was so artful that the legend arose that whoever should unloose it would gain the empire

of Asia. Alexander, it is said (on poor authority), cut the 'Gordian Knot' with his sword, and applied the legend to him-self.

Go'rgias (*Gorgiās*) (*c.* 485–375 B.C.) of Leontini in Sicily, a celebrated sophist, whose teaching of rhetoric was based, not upon any system of dialectic or treatment of the subject-matter, but upon beautiful and effective expression. For this he relied on poetic rhythm (breaking up his sentences into short symmetrical clauses) and orna-ment. He made his pupils learn by heart typical passages of literature and imitate these. His oratory made a great impres-sion at Athens when he headed an em-bassy of the Leontines in 427 B.C. He thereafter travelled about Greece giving lectures, and ended his long life at Larissa. A statue was erected to him at Olympia by his grand-nephew; the pedestal with its inscription survives. Among the set speeches that Gorgias delivered in person was one made at Olympia, urging the union of the Greek States against Persia. Part of a funeral oration is the only con-siderable fragment of his work extant. His influence on Attic prose-writing is seen in the speeches of Thucydides, in Antiphon, and especially in the speeches of Isocrates (q.v.). See also the next article.

Gorgias, a dialogue by Plato in which Socrates discusses with the rhetorician Gorgias (see above), his disciple Pōlus, and Calliclēs, a man of the world, the nature of rhetoric, and brings out that it is an art of flattery, directed to pleasure, in contrast with the higher form of states-manship (which no one practises but Socrates himself) directed to making men good. In the course of the dialogue, Socrates defends the paradoxes that it is better to suffer evil than to do it, and that when one has done evil it is better to be punished than to go unpunished. It is noteworthy that Socrates shows consider-able deference to Gorgias himself in the dialogue.

Gorgons (*Gorgones*). The Gorgon's head is first mentioned in Homer, as a terrifying design on shields. Hesiod tells of three Gorgons, Sthennō ('Mighty'), Euryalē ('Wide-wanderer'), and Medūsa ('Queen'), daughters of Phorcys and Ceto (children of Pontus and Ge, qq.v.), and thus sisters of the Graiae (q.v.). They are represented with hideous faces, glaring eyes, and serpents in their hair and girdles (see *Monsters*). Medusa alone of the three was mortal, and was loved by Poseidon. She was slain by Perseus (q.v.) when with child by Poseidon, and from her blood sprang the horse Pegasus (q.v.) and Chrȳsāōr ('Golden-sword', the father of Geryon, q.v.).

The Gorgon's head turned to stone any-thing that met its gaze. It retained its petrifying power even after the monster's death. The popular belief in this legend led to the representation of the head or *Gorgoneion* as a protective figure on ar-mour and on walls. As an amulet it was also carved on furniture and ornaments, not always with a hideous face, but sometimes beautiful in death.

Go'rtyn (*Gortūn*), an ancient city of Crete, which became especially important after the fall of the old Cretan civilization (see *Crete*). It is famous in connexion with two groups of inscriptions of local laws, dating respectively, it is thought, from the 5th and 4th cc. B.C. Of the latter group the chief inscription consists of twelve columns of laws, known as the Twelve Tables of Gortyn, which were engraved on the interior wall of some sort of court-house. They deal with such questions as debt, succession, marriage, and the rights of slaves, and throw much light on the Cretan institutions of the time.

Gracchi, THE, Tiberius Semprōnius Gracchus (d. 133 B.C.) and Gāius Sem-pronius Gracchus, his brother (d. 121 B.C.). They were the sons of Tiberius Sempronius Gracchus, the distinguished praetor who by his victories, and still more by his fair-ness to the Spaniards, settled in 179 B.C. the troubled question of the Roman dominion in Spain. They were brought up by their mother Cornelia, daughter of Scipio Africanus, famous for her virtue and accomplishments. A statue was erected to her by the Romans, inscribed, 'Cornelia, Mother of the Gracchi'. There is a well-known story that when a lady made a show of her jewels at Cornelia's house, and asked to see Cornelia's, the latter produced her sons, saying, 'These are my jewels'. The elder brother, Tiberius Gracchus, mar-ried the daughter of Appius Claudius (q.v.).

The fame of the Gracchi rests on their attempt to solve the economic crisis which resulted from the failure of the Roman State to administer its land on fair and sound principles. The Senate had allowed the wealthy classes to absorb large tracts of the *ager publicus* (q.v.). This and other causes were bringing about the ruin of small-scale agriculture and the gradual extinction of the peasant cultivators, from whom the legions were recruited. In 133 Tiberius Gracchus, a tribune of the people in that year, took up the matter and pro-posed that no one should be allowed to occupy more than a certain amount of the public land; the rest of the land was to be

redistributed in small lots. The proposal met with fierce opposition from the wealthy, whom it tended to dispossess of the land they occupied. Nevertheless it was carried, and its execution entrusted to a commission. But when Tiberius sought re-election (unconstitutionally) for the ensuing year, he was killed in an elec-tion riot by a group of senators led by Scipio Nāsīca.

In 124 Tiberius's brother Gaius was elected tribune for 123, and resumed the work of his brother, the execution of whose project had been impeded by the opposi-tion of the aristocracy and of the Italians, who also found themselves menaced by it. Gaius Gracchus first set about strengthen-ing his position. By a series of laws he conciliated both the business interests (q.v.) and the proletariate, while meeting so far as possible the prejudices of the Senate. He obtained the support of the first by a law enacting that public con-tracts for the collection of provincial taxes should be let at Rome and by en-trusting them with the collection of the taxes in the new province of Asia (recently bequeathed to Rome by Attalus of Per-gamum), a sure source of abundant profit. He re-enacted his brother's agrarian law. By a military law he forbade the enrol-ment of Roman citizens in the army before the age of seventeen. By a corn law he secured that corn should be sold at Rome at a stable price. The price appears to have been a comparatively high one (see *Annona*) and the measure must have merely controlled the selling price without being a demagogic sop to the poor. Nor was it a blow to the small farmers, who were the object of the special care of his brother and himself. But the ordinary view is that the measure was one of sub-stantial relief to the poor. Gracchus was now re-elected tribune for the ensuing year, and reached the zenith of his power. Under the *lex Calpurnia* of 149 B.C. which set up a permanent *quaestio* (see *Judicial Procedure*) to try cases of oppression by provincial governors, the members of the jury were exclusively senators. By the *lex Acīlia* Gracchus excluded senators from juries, and substituted members of the wealthiest class outside the Senate (see *Equestrian Order*). He now launched his most radical and far-sighted measure, by which probably all the Latins were to receive the Roman franchise, and the allies the former Latin status (i.e. rights of trade and intermarriage with Rome), thus broadening the basis of the Roman State. But already the forces of reaction were beginning to prevail against him. Gracchus had proposed to establish a number of colonies, mainly in Italy, but including one on the site of Carthage. He set out for Africa to supervise the settlement of this, and during his absence the tribune Livius Drūsus managed to turn the mob against him (he was already unpopular with it by reason of his championship of the Italians) by outbidding him in the liberality of his offers. Thus the projected citizenship law was not carried. Gracchus had meantime failed in an attempt to secure re-election for a third year, and early in 121, when the *lex Rubria* authorizing the colony at Carthage was repealed, he and his supporters were attacked, the *senatus consultum ultimum* (q.v.) was passed against them, and many were killed. Opimius, the consul, is said to have rewarded the slaying of the leaders with the weight of their heads in gold. Gracchus, finding himself cut off, ordered a faithful slave to kill him. The chronological order in which his various laws were adopted cannot be affirmed with certainty. But there is little doubt that the control of the price of corn was one of the earliest, and the projected extension of the franchise the latest, of his measures.

There are lives of the Gracchi by Plutarch.

Graces (*Charites*), in Greek mythology, goddesses whose parentage is variously given, generally three in number, the personification of loveliness or grace, perhaps originally goddesses of vegetation. In legend they appear generally in a subordinate position, as attendants on some greater goddess.

Grādī′vus (the first syllable is short in one passage in Ovid), see *Mars*.

Grai′ae (*Graiai*), in Greek mythology, Pemphrēdō, Enȳō, and Deinō, goddesses represented as grey-haired women, the personification of old age, children of Phorcys and Ceto (qq.v.). They had but one eye and one tooth between them, and were the protectresses of their sisters the Gorgons (q.v., and see *Monsters*). Perseus (q.v.) contrived to steal the eye, and so was able to surprise the Gorgons.

Gra′ttius or **Grā′tius**, the author of a Latin poem on hunting ('Cynēgetica'), of which 536 hexameters survive. Very little of him is known except that Ovid (Ex Ponto IV, xvi. 34) refers to him as apparently a contemporary. See *Hunting*.

Greece, a country of which the limits were not accurately defined in antiquity, but which in the classical period may be taken as including the territory S. of a line from the Ambracian Gulf to the mouth of the Pēnēus, that is to say including Thessaly. but excluding Macedonia and Epirus; see Pl. 8. It is broken up by mountain ranges, which made communication between the habitable areas difficult. This physical characteristic had the effect of dividing the population into a number of communities, each autonomous, with its own institutions and dialect (see *Migrations and Dialects*). The course of history, the founding by each community of its own colonies, the naturally independent character of the people, tended further to distribute the Greeks in a large number of distinct cities, without common allegiance to any centre. The history of Greece consequently consists, during the classical period, of the separate histories of these various States, and has been dealt with summarily in this book, so far as necessary for the purpose of understanding Greek literature, under the heads of Athens, Sparta, Thebes, &c.

Nevertheless the Greeks formed, in a certain sense, a single people. They enjoyed one and the same civilization; they spoke the same language (though with great dialectal differences) and were distinguished thereby from the 'barbarians'; there was a broad similarity in their political institutions (government in city-states, normally under either oligarchic or democratic constitutions); they had a common religion and respected the same oracular shrines; they had a common heritage of literature from Homer downwards; their art, in spite of certain diversities, had unity; many of the Greek colonies were founded in common by emigrants from more than one State. Ionia was the first centre of this common civilization; after the defeat of the Persian invasions, the intellectual leadership passed to Athens, which, by the liberal policy of the Pisistratids and Cleisthenes, had welcomed strangers, in particular poets and artists, from all parts of Greece. The social unity of Greece manifested itself in the common festivals and Games; and some degree of political unity was shown in the common resistance to Persia. But the various attempts, such as that of Pericles, to consolidate this unity always collapsed before the jealous spirit of independence of the several States.

The Greeks called their country *Hellas* and themselves *Hellēnes*, the name of a tribe that in the time of the migrations (q.v.) settled in a part of Thessaly. The Latins gave the name *Graii* to the colonists of Cumae, *Graia* being the name of an obscure district in W. Greece, from which some of the settlers perhaps came. *Gracci* is a derivative from *Graii*, and *Graecia* was a name given by the Romans to Hellas.

The Roman province of Greece was, however, called Achāia.

Gregory the Great, POPE, see *Texts and Studies*, § 6.

Griffin or **Gryphon** (Gr. *Grūps*), see *Monsters*.

Grōmā'tici (from *grōma*, a measuring rod), writers on land-surveying. There were several such Latin writers under the empire, including Frontinus and Hyginus (qq.v.), but the former's treatise on surveying is known to us only by extracts.

Grono'vius, see *Texts and Studies*, § 10.

Grosseteste, BISHOP, see *Texts and Studies*, § 8.

Grote, GEORGE, see *Historians (Modern)*.

Guilds (*Collēgia*). *Collegium*, in its most general sense, is an association of people who share the same function (e.g. priests, magistrates), profession, or worship. The *Collegia* at Rome were of three main classes, military, industrial, or purely funeral. The primary object of all three classes of guilds was to provide an honourable burial for their members and to secure observance of the customary funeral rites. After commemorations of the dead, the guild would frequently meet in a common feast. The guild had the further object of securing the common interests of its members. Each guild had its patron deity.

The military guilds were confined to subordinate officers and looked after their professional interests. Guilds of craftsmen were formed at Rome from very early times; according to tradition they were first founded by Numa. They covered a great variety of trades; their head-quarters were on the Aventine. To some extent they were concerned with the interests of the several trades (e.g. in the matter of taxation), but they do not appear to have exercised such functions of a modern trade-union as the control of wages or hours of labour. Their funds were expended on the burials of members, common worship, and various festivities. It does not appear that they were employed for the benefit of the sick and needy.

Guilds are not prominent during most of the republican era, but reappear in the last century as clubs (*collegia sodālicia*) capable of being used for political purposes. Many of them were suppressed in 64 B.C., were revived by Clodius (q.v.), and again suppressed by Julius Caesar. Under the empire the number of guilds greatly increased, especially in the time of the Antonines (each guild was licensed by the emperor). They were formed for a variety of purposes, not only for commemoration of the dead and mutual aid, but also for business purposes, and for religious and purely social objects. (There had been a great expansion of somewhat similar social and religious clubs all over the Greek world since 300 B.C.) They included members of the richer as well as of the humblest classes. The *collegia* of merchants and shipowners became important, and were recognized and favoured by the State, which made use of them in organizing the transport of commodities. In the later empire trades and professions were organized in guilds under the strict supervision of the emperor. A man was not allowed to leave his profession and guild for another, and his son was obliged to follow the same occupation.

Gȳ'as (*Gyās*), in the 'Aeneid', a companion of Aeneas. He figures in the boat-race (Aen. v). Also, at Aeneid x. 318, the name of a Latin slain by Aeneas.

Gȳ'ēs (*Gūēs*), see *Giants (Hundred-handed)*.

Gȳ'gēs (*Gūgēs*), a Lydian of the family of the Mermnadae, who obtained the throne of Lydia (q.v.) about 685 B.C. by usurpation, killing Candaulēs (or Myrsilus as he was called by the Greeks) the previous king, the last of the Heraclid dynasty. For the story of Gyges and the wife of Candaules see Hdt. i. 8–12, and Plato, Rep. ii. 359. According to the latter, Gyges, a shepherd, descended into a chasm in the earth and there found a hollow brazen horse, containing a corpse, from the finger of which he took a golden ring. This ring when he wore it, made him invisible, and with its help he introduced himself to the queen, murdered her husband, and usurped the crown.

Gyges was the first Lydian monarch to make war on the Asiatic Greeks. Towards the end of his reign he entered into alliance with Assurbanipal of Assyria against the invading Cimmerians (q.v.).

Gyli'ppus (*Gulippos*), a Spartan officer sent to assist the Syracusans during the Sicilian Expedition (see *Peloponnesian War*). Under his energetic leadership the Athenian fleet and army were utterly destroyed.

Gy'mnasia'rchia (*Gumnāsiarchiā*), see *Liturgy*.

Gymna'sium (*Gumnāsion*), in Greek cities, the place where boys and men performed their gymnastic exercises, which were an essential part of Greek education. The word means a place for exercising 'naked', as was the custom. A gymnasium generally consisted of a court surrounded by columns, with spaces for running and jumping, covered hall for wrestling, baths, &c. There were three important Gymnasia at Athens, situated outside the city, the Academīa (see *Academy*), the Lyceum (q.v.), and the Cynosarges (q.v.). It was in the gymnasia that the ephebi (q.v.) underwent their military training.

Gymnopae'diae (*Gumnopaidiai*), a festival at Sparta; see *Festivals*, § 6.

H

Habro'comēs (*Habrokomēs*) *and Anthei'a* or *Ephesiaca*, see *Novel*.

Hā'dēs (*Haidēs, Āidēs*, or *Āidōnēus*, 'the Unseen'), also known as PLŪTŌ (*Ploutōn*, 'the Rich'), the Greek god of the nether world, son of Cronus and Rhea (qq.v.), a grim and terrible but just god (not the enemy of mankind—the Greeks had no Satan). As Pluto, he may have been originally a god of the fertility of the earth. The Romans adopted the name Pluto, and translated it as *Dis* (*Dives*) (q.v.). Hades rules over the ghosts of the dead, with his queen Persephone (q.v.), whom he carried off from the upper world.

The name Hades is also applied to his realm, the position of which varied as ideas of geography changed. In the 'Iliad' it is in the far West beyond the river Oceanus, which was thought to encircle the earth. Later it was placed underground and approached by various natural chasms. Details of the description of the realm of Hades also vary. It contains the dreary Plain of Asphodel, where the ghosts of the dead lead a vague, unsubstantial life. A few fortunate ones escape this fate and are taken to Elysium (q.v.), while those who have been enemies of the gods are removed to Tartarus (q.v.) for punishment. Generally the realm of the dead is separated from that of the living by one of the rivers of Hades, Styx or Acheron (qq.v.). Across this the dead, provided they have been duly buried, are ferried by Charon (q.v.). At the entrance of Hades stands the watch-dog Cerberus (q.v.), who prevents any of the dead from going out again. Within sit the judges of the dead, Minos, Rhadamanthus, and Aeacus, who assign to each ghost its appropriate abode. Besides Styx and Acheron, three other rivers intersect Hades, Phlegethon or Pyriphlegethon ('the fiery'), Cocytus (q.v.), and (in Latin poetry) Lethe (q.v.). Milton (P.L. ii. 575–84) speaks of

four infernal rivers that disgorge
Into the burning lake their baleful streams—

Abhorrèd Styx, the flood of deadly hate;
Sad Acheron of sorrow, black and deep;
Cocytus named of lamentation loud
Heard on the rueful stream; fierce Phlegethon
Whose waves of torrent fire inflame with rage.
Far off from these, a slow and silent stream,
Lethe, the river of oblivion, rolls
Her watery labyrinth.

Ha'drian (*Publius Aelius Hādriānus*), Roman emperor A.D. 117–138, of Spanish origin, a man of extraordinary versatility, soldier, traveller, and able administrator, devoted to literature and philosophy, a Hellenist who spoke Greek better than Latin. He organized afresh the great imperial bureaucracy, placing men of the equestrian order in the high posts formerly held by freedmen. He codified the Praetor's Edict (see *Law*, § 2) and made it the fixed law of the whole empire. He travelled in all the provinces, visiting among others Britain, where he built the famous wall from the Solway to the Tyne. In all the provinces he showed himself a benefactor, 'aiding all men by his liberality'. At Rome he built for himself the great mausoleum (finished by Antoninus) known now as the Castle of S. Angelo, and at Tibur a vast villa, in which were reproduced on a smaller scale the finest buildings he had seen on his travels. A patron of learning and architecture, he formed libraries, wrote mediocre verse, and on his death-bed one inspired piece, the famous lines beginning 'Animula, vagula, blandula'. He founded *c.* A.D. 135 the Athenaeum at Rome, an educational institution, where poets and orators recited and professors gave lectures on philosophy, grammar, law, and rhetoric. He was a great benefactor of Athens, where he had been archon under Trajan; he completed there the great temple of Zeus Olympius begun by Pisistratus (see *Olympieum*) and built a splendid stoa or colonnade, a library ('adorned with a gilded roof and alabaster' says Pausanias), and a gymnasium with a hundred columns.

Hae'mon (*Haimōn*), son of Creon, see *Oedipus*.

Halicarna'ssus, the birthplace of Herodotus and Dionysius, was originally founded by Dorians (see *Migrations*). It stood (the modern Budrum) on the SW. coast of Asia Minor, near the island of Cos. The strength and beauty of its position led Mausolus (q.v.), the tyrant of Caria, to make it his capital. The discovery of the ruins of his tomb, the Mausoleum, with its sculptures (some of them now in the British Museum) is recounted in Sir C. Newton's 'Travels and Discoveries in the Levant'.

Halicarnassus was captured after a hard siege by Alexander the Great, and devastated.

Halieu'tica, (1) see *Ovid*; (2) see *Oppian*.

Hamadrȳ'ads (*Hamadrŭades*), see *Dryads*.

Hami'lcar Barca, a great Carthaginian general and statesman of the time of the First Punic War (q.v.). In the last stage of this war he seized a strong position on Mt. Herctē near Panormus, and afterwards the town of Eryx, and thence checked the Roman attempts to capture the Carthaginian strongholds of Lilybaeum and Drepanum, until the Roman naval victory of the Aegātian Islands made his position hopeless. He subsequently suppressed in a terrible war the rebellion of the mercenaries of Carthage; and then set about founding a new Carthaginian empire in Spain, as a step towards obtaining revenge on Rome. Hamilcar was the father of Hannibal (q.v.). He died in 228 B.C. We have a life of him by Nepos.

Ha'nnibal (247–182 B.C.), son of Hamilcar Barca (q.v.) and the great leader of the Carthaginians against Rome in the Second Punic War (q.v.). His father took him to Spain in 236 when a boy, and solemnly pledged him to hatred of Rome. After his father's death and that of Hasdrubal (q.v. (1)), who had succeeded Hamilcar in the Spanish command, Hannibal was elected general by the army in 221, and at once set about the siege of Saguntum as a preliminary to war with Rome. The vicissitudes of the great struggle that followed are briefly given herein under *Punic Wars*. After the Roman victory, Hannibal undertook the reorganization of the corrupt government of his country; but the Romans, dreading his persistent hostility, demanded his surrender, and Hannibal took refuge at the court of Antiochus of Syria (195). There he encouraged the king to hostilities against Rome. After the defeat of Antiochus at Magnēsia in 190, Hannibal fled first to Crete, then to the court of Prūsias, king of Bīthȳnia. The Romans vindictively pursued him there in his old age, 'like a bird that had lost its tail and feathers' (Plutarch), and demanded his surrender. To escape this Hannibal took poison. There is a life of him by Nepos. Livy (xxxv. 14) has an interesting conversation between Hannibal and Scipio at Ephesus concerning famous commanders. The date of Hannibal's death is given as 182 by Polybius, 183 by Livy. The latter date is probably the result of a desire for coincidence, since Scipio, Philopoemen, and Hannibal, the

three greatest generals of their time, would then all have died in the same year.

Harmo'dius (*Harmódios*) and **Aristogī'ton** (*Aristogeitōn*), see *Pisistratus*. They were revered at Athens as champions of liberty, and their descendants enjoyed certain immunities and exemptions from taxation. Their statues were carried off by Xerxes and were found in a later age by Alexander the Great at Susa; he restored them to Athens, where Pausanias saw them in the Agora. See *Scolion*.

Harmo'nia (*Harmoniā*), NECKLACE OF, see *Cadmus, Amphiaraus, Alcmaeon*.

Ha'rmosts (*Harmostai*, 'Regulators'), the name given to the governors sent by Sparta, during the period of her supremacy after the Peloponnesian War, to conquered cities and islands.

Ha'rpalus (*Harpalos*), the treasurer of Alexander the Great (q.v., § 8); and see *Demosthenes* (2), § 1, and *Dinarchus*.

Harpies (*Harpūiai*, 'Snatchers'), in Greek mythology daughters of Thaumās (son of Pontus, the Sea) and Electra (daughter of Oceanus, q.v.). They appear to have been regarded by Homer and Hesiod as personifications of violent winds that can carry people away. Among their names were Āellō ('storm-wind'), Ōcypetē ('swift flying'), Podargē ('swift foot'), and Celaenō ('dark'). But they are also described and represented in sculpture as birds with the faces of women (see *Monsters*), a form in which the souls of the dead are often depicted. The conception of the Harpies may therefore be connected with the widespread belief that the souls of the dead snatch away those of the living (Rose, 'Handbook of Greek Mythology'). In the story of Phineus (q.v.) the Harpies are noisome, ravenous birds, which carry off or defile his food. Virgil makes Aeneas encounter them at the Strophades Islands (Aen. iii. 225 et seq.). The famous Harpy relief in the British Museum is from the frieze of a monument discovered at Xanthus in Lycia.

Harpo'cratēs, the Greek equivalent of the Egyptian *Harpechrat*, i.e. 'Har or Horus the child', Horus (see *Osiris*) in his character of the youthful Sun, represented as a boy with a finger on his mouth. From a misunderstanding of this attitude, he came to be regarded by the Greeks and Romans as a god of Silence.

Haru'spicēs, Etruscan soothsayers, who interpreted the will of the gods as conveyed by prodigies, or lightning, or as shown by the state of the entrails of sacrificial victims. Their lore was known as the

Etrusca disciplina. It defined with great elaboration the methods by which the above signs could be interpreted and an impending misfortune averted. A meaning, for instance, was assigned to every minute deviation from the normal in the entrails of a victim. The sky was parcelled out into divisions, and the lightning assigned to one or other of nine gods according to the division from which it came. *Haruspices* were frequently summoned to Rome to explain prodigies, and a special college of Roman *haruspices* was formed under the empire. *Haruspices* were consulted, after the return of Cicero from exile, on the question whether the site of his house, which had been consecrated, could be restored to him.

Ha'sdrubal, (1) a Carthaginian general, son-in-law of Hamilcar Barca (q.v.), whom he succeeded as commander in Spain on his death in 228 B.C. He extended, with the help of the youthful Hannibal, the Carthaginian empire in Spain, and founded Nova Carthāgŏ there. He was assassinated in 221 and was succeeded in the command by Hannibal.

(2) Son of Hamilcar Barca, and brother of Hannibal. When Hannibal invaded Italy (218) he left Hasdrubal in command in Spain. There, from 218 to 208, Hasdrubal fought against the Scipios. Having evaded the Roman army in Spain, he then marched to Italy to the relief of Hannibal, but he was intercepted on the Metaurus, utterly defeated, and slain (207). There is a famous reference to him in Horace, *Od.* IV. iv. 38 ('Testis Metaurum flumen et Hasdrubal devictus . . .').

Heau'ton Timŏrū'menos ('The Self-tormentor'), a comedy by Terence, adapted from a play of the same name by Menander, and produced in 163 B.C.

The Self-tormentor is an Athenian father, Menedēmus, who imposes hardships on himself in penitence for the harshness which has driven his son Clinia out of the country on account of his love for Antiphila, supposed to be the daughter of a Corinthian woman of small means. His neighbour Chremēs, perplexed by his behaviour, intervenes ('Homo sum: humani nil a me alienum puto', he says in explanation), and somewhat officiously lectures him on a parent's duty of indulgence. Clinia returns to Attica, taking up his abode wᵗᵗʰ his friend Clitipho (son of Chremes) who unknown to his father is spending his money on the courtesan Bacchis. It is arranged that Bacchis shall come to the house of Chremes, in the character of Clinia's friend, bringing with her Antiphila as a companion. By a trick

of the slave Sȳrus, Chremes is cozened out of some £50 for the benefit of his son's extravagant mistress, and when Chremes discovers this and what has been going on in his house, he angrily disinherits the young scapegrace, repudiating his own doctrine of parental duty. His wife intercedes for her son, and Clitipho is let off on condition of a suitable marriage (not, however, with 'the red-headed, cat-eyed girl' first proposed to him). Meanwhile Clinia has been restored to his repentant father, and Antiphila has been discovered to be the daughter of Chremes, who accords her to Clinia.

The drama, 'The Feast of Bacchus', by Robert Bridges is in part based on this comedy.

Hebdo'mades, see *Varro* (*M. T.*).

Hē'bē, in Greek mythology, daughter of Zeus and Hera (qq.v.), the handmaiden of the gods, for whom she pours out nectar, and associated with perpetual youth.

Nods and Becks and wreathèd Smiles, Such as hang on Hebe's cheek.

Milton, *L'Allegro,* 28–9.

She is represented as married to Heracles after his ascent to heaven. The Roman goddess Juventas was identified with her.

He'calē (*Hekalē*), see *Theseus* and *Callimachus.*

Hecatāē'us (*Hekataios*), a Greek chronicler and geographer, who flourished about 500 B.C., a member of a distinguished family of Miletus. He travelled extensively, and was a judicious adviser of the Ionians in their struggle with the Persians. He wrote 'Genealogies' of the great mythical families, giving the fables concerning them (he tells us) that appeared to him most probable (see *Logographi*). He also wrote a 'Circuit of the Earth' (*Periodos Gēs*), based partly on his own voyages, a sort of itinerary, describing countries, their inhabitants and customs, animals and curiosities, and adding local fables. A map was appended (this was said to be the second map made in Greece; see *Anaximander*). The authenticity of this book of Hecataeus, of which numerous brief fragments survive, has been questioned, but appears to be established.

He'catē (*Hekatē*), a Greek goddess unknown to Homer, but according to Hesiod the daughter of the Titan Persēs and Asteria (sister of Leto, q.v.), a great and beneficent deity in many departments of life, war, council, games, horsemanship, farming, &c. She came to be associated with the lower world and with night, and was transformed into a queen of ghosts and magic, haunting cross-roads, attended by hell-hounds. She was the protectress of enchanters and witches (Medea for instance). In statues she was often represented in triple form, perhaps looking down three roads which met where her statue stood. Her image was set up as an averter of evil. She was sometimes identified with Artemis.

Hecatomb, see *Sacrifices*, § 2.

Hecato'mpedon, see *Parthenon*.

Hecatonchei'res, see *Giants* (*Hundred-handed*).

He'ctor (*Hektōr*), son of Priam, husband of Andromache, and father of Astyanax (qq.v.), the leader of the Trojan forces during the siege. Homer represents him as a man of human affections, devoted to wife and child, noble in victory and defeat, in strong contrast to Achilles. For his story see *Iliad*.

He'cuba (*Hekabē*), the wife of Priam (q.v.) and mother of Hector, Paris, and Cassandra (qq.v.) among many children. In the 'Iliad' a pathetic figure, to whom the loss of Hector, after many other sons, means the loss of all. After the fall of Troy she fell to the lot of the hated Odysseus, and her despair at this and at the fate of her daughter Polyxena, slain on the tomb of Achilles (q.v.), is depicted in Euripides' 'Trojan Women'. The Greek fleet, on its return from Troy, touched on the Thracian coast. For her vengeance there on Polymēstōr, king of the place, for the murder of her last remaining son, Polydorus, see the article below. Thereafter she was transformed into a bitch.

Hecuba (*Hekabē*), a tragedy by Euripides, of uncertain date.

Troy has fallen, the women of Troy have been apportioned to the victors, but the return home of the Greek fleet is delayed by contrary winds. The spectre of Achilles has demanded the sacrifice to him of Polyxena, daughter of Hecuba. Odysseus comes to lead her away. He is unmoved by Hecuba's despair and by her reminder that he once owed his life to herself. But Polyxena, a striking figure in her virginal pride, prefers death to slavery, and willingly goes to her doom. As Hecuba prepares for the burial, a further sorrow comes upon her. Her youngest son Polydorus had been sent to the keeping of Polymēstōr, king of the Thracian Chersonese (where the Greek fleet is now detained), with part of the treasure of Priam. When Troy fell, Polymēstōr had murdered the boy, in order to secure the treasure for himself, and had thrown his body into the sea. It has now been washed up and is

brought to Hecuba. She appeals to Agamemnon for vengeance; but he, though sympathetic, is timid. Hecuba thereupon takes vengeance into her own hands. She lures Polymestor and his sons to her tent, her women kill the sons and put out the eyes of Polymestor; and Agamemnon orders the latter to be left on a desert island.

He'cyra ('The Mother-in-law'), a comedy by Terence, adapted from a play by Apollodōrus of Carystus. The plot, moreover, closely resembles that of Menander's 'Epitrepontes' (q.v.). On the first production of the Hecyra in 165 B.C. the performance was interrupted, the minds of the audience being preoccupied with the rival attractions of a rope-dancer. It was again produced in 160 twice, the first time unsuccessfully. The prologue makes an appeal for support to the dramatic art.

Pamphilus has been reluctantly persuaded by his father to give up his mistress, the courtesan Bacchis, and to marry. Soon after the marriage he is sent to Imbros by his father on business. During his absence, his wife leaves her mother-in-law on a pretext and returns to her own mother's house. There she is delivered of a child, not the fruit of the marriage. Before the marriage she had been violated by a man in the darkness, who had taken from her a ring. By means of this ring and with the assistance of the honest Bacchis, to whom it had been given, it is discovered that Pamphilus himself was guilty of the outrage and is father of the child. Thus Pamphilus, who had reluctantly felt that he must separate from his wife, is reconciled to her. The title of the play is based on the carefully drawn characters of the two mothers-in-law.

Heinsius, NICHOLAS, see *Texts and Studies*, § 10.

Helen (*Helenē*), daughter of Zeus and Leda (q.v.), sister of Castor and Pollux and Clytemnestra, and the most beautiful of women. She was carried off as a child by Theseus, but recovered by her brothers. She was wooed by the principal chiefs in Greece, who at the suggestion of Odysseus (q.v.) agreed to abide by her choice and defend her husband. She was married to Menelaus (q.v.), but carried away by Paris (q.v.) to Troy in the absence of her husband (according to Stesichorus she was carried to Egypt and kept there by the king, Proteus, till her husband should claim her; it was her phantom that accompanied Paris to Troy—a version adopted by Euripides in his 'Helen' and 'Electra'). The Greek princes, led by Agamemnon (q.v.), undertook the expedition to Troy (see

Trojan War) to recover her, and after a siege of ten years took the city. Helen was then reconciled with Menelaus and after their return lived with him at Sparta, where they were visited by Telemachus (see *Odyssey*).

There are numerous references to the legend of Helen in English literature. That most frequently quoted is in Sc. xiv of Marlowe's 'Doctor Faustus':

Was this the face that launched a thousand ships
And burnt the topless towers of Ilium?
Sweet Helen, make me immortal with a kiss.

Among Landor's 'Imaginary Conversations' is one between Achilles and Helen on Mt. Ida in the last year of the Trojan War.

Helen (*Helenē*), a drama by Euripides, produced in 412 B.C.

The play is based on the curious legend in the 'Palinodia' of Stesichorus (q.v.) that it was not Helen but her wraith that accompanied Paris to Troy. Helen herself has been carried by Hermes to the court of Prōteūs, king of Egypt, where she awaits the return of Menelaus from Troy. But Proteus is now dead, and his son Theoclymenus is trying to force Helen to marry him. She has taken refuge at the tomb of Proteus. Teucer, the brother of Ajax, arrives and tells her of the fall of Troy seven years since, and of the probable death of Menelaus. While she is lamenting, Menelaus himself appears. He has been shipwrecked on the Egyptian coast, has left the Helen who was accompanying him in a cave, and has come to the palace of Theoclymenus for succour. A curious scene of recognition follows, for Menelaus is perplexed between the two Helens, and is convinced only when he learns that the wraith-Helen has disappeared into the air, after revealing the cheat. Menelaus and Helen now devise their escape from Egypt, a difficult matter; for Theoclymenus not only is determined to marry Helen, but will kill any Greek whom he finds in the land. But with the help of Theonoē, a priestess, sister of the king, Theoclymenus is fooled with a pretence of a funeral ceremony at sea for the dead Menelaus, and Menelaus and Helen escape on the ship provided for the purpose. Castor and Pollux, Helen's deified brothers, appear at the end to avert the king's wrath against Theonoe for her complicity. The chorus consists of captive Greek maidens attendant on Helen.

The poet does not fail to point out the grim humour of the situation: the ten years' siege of Troy has been all for naught; and the lore of seers is not worth much, for Calchas and Helenus (qq.v.) gave no inkling of the deception.

Helen, Encomium on, see *Isocrates*.

He′lenus (*Helenos*), in the 'Iliad', a son of Priam and Hecuba (qq.v.), gifted with prophecy. According to later legend, he was captured by Odysseus and revealed that the Greeks would not take Troy without the help of Philoctetes (q.v.). At the fall of Troy he became the captive of Neoptolemus, and after the latter's death married Andromache and became king of Chāonia (part of Epirus). There Aeneas (q.v.) in the course of his wanderings visited him and received from him advice as to the course he should follow.

Hēliae′a (*Hēliaiā*), a judicial tribunal at Athens, dating probably from the constitution of Solon, and originally a court of appeal drawn from all classes of the people. The course of its evolution is not known, but it reached its full development after the reforms of Ephialtes (q.v.), when it became the principal and supreme judicial body of the democracy (see *Judicial Procedure*, § 1).

He′licon (*Helikōn*), a mountain in Boeotia, regarded as sacred to the Muses (q.v.). On it were the sacred springs of Hippocrēnē and Aganippē.

Hēliodō′rus of Emesa, see *Novel*.

Hē′lios, the Sun, in Greek mythology the son of Hyperion and Thea (see *Titans*), represented generally as a charioteer. In his chariot he climbs the vault of heaven, and, descending in the evening in the west, is carried back to his starting-point in a golden bowl, sailing along the stream Oceanus (q.v.). He has cattle and sheep in the island Thrinacia (see *Odyssey* (Bk. xii) and *Sicily*). In later poetry there is some disposition to identify him with Apollo. Helios was the father of Aeetes, Circe, and Phaethon (qq.v.).

Hellani′cus (*Hellanikos*), see *Logographi* (1).

He′llas, see *Greece*.

He′llē, see *Athamas*.

He′llēn, see *Hellenēs*.

He′llēnes (*Hellēnēs*), see *Migrations and Dialects*. The name, which came to be applied to the whole Greek race, was referred to an eponymous hero, Hellēn, son of Deucalion (q.v.), and father of Dōrus, Xūthus, and Aeolus, the legendary progenitors of the Dorian, Ionian, and Aeolian Greeks. For the origin of the names 'Greece' and 'Greek', see under *Greece*.

Hellē'nica (*Hellēnika*), a history of Greece from 411 to 362 B.C., in seven books, by Xenophon, apparently written in instalments. The events narrated occurred in the historian's lifetime, and he was present (accompanying his friend Agēsilāus, king of Sparta) during several of the campaigns described. The fact that he was an Athenian who had resided in several other States of Greece, knew Asia Minor and the Persians, and was himself a capable military commander, gave him special qualifications for the task. But his affection for Sparta and hatred of Thebes impair in some degree the completeness and impartiality of his narrative. He imitates the method of Thucydides (q.v.), but without his political philosophy and insight.

The work takes up the story of the Peloponnesian War where Thucydides had left it, and concludes it. It describes the rule and overthrow of the Thirty at Athens; the Spartan War against the Persians (399–387); the attempt of various Greek States to check the growing power of Sparta (the Corinthian War, 394–387) ended by the peace of Antalcidas; the rivalry of Sparta and Thebes, and the triumph of the latter at Leuctra (371); and the supremacy of Thebes under the leadership of Epaminondas, ending with his death at the battle of Mantinea (362).

Hellenistic, a term applied to the civilization, language, art, and literature, Greek in its general character, but pervading people not exclusively Greek, current in Asia Minor, Egypt, Syria, and other countries after the time of Alexander the Great. See *Hellenistic Age*.

Hellenistic (sometimes called ALEXANDRIAN) **Age**, THE, of Greek literature, is that which extended, with Alexandria as its chief centre, from the close of the life of Alexander the Great (323 B.C.) to the end of the Ptolemaic dynasty and the complete Roman subjugation of the Mediterranean world in the latter part of the 1st c. B.C.

§ 1. *Features of the Hellenistic Age*

This was the period during which, as a result of Alexander's conquests, Greek civilization spread to distant lands, including Egypt and roughly so much of Asia as lay between the Mediterranean and northern India. The struggle among Alexander's successors is briefly sketched under *Macedonia*, § 2. By 275 B.C. three dynasties had established themselves: the Seleucids (q.v.) in what had been the Persian em-

pire, the Antigonids in Macedonia (q.v., § 3), and the Ptolemies (q.v.) in Egypt. A fourth dynasty, the Attalids (q.v.), emerged later and with the help of Rome absorbed a part of the Seleucid territory. At the end of the 3rd c. began the interference of Rome, and her conquest of the Hellenistic world was completed within the next two centuries. After Alexander's conquests cities more or less Greek were founded in large numbers in Asia, Greek law and the Greek tongue penetrated to many parts of that continent, Greek and Eastern science came into contact, and there was a great mingling of races, customs, and languages. Though many of the old Greek cities retained for a long time a vigorous political life, the idea of the Greek city-state, as an independent and exclusive unit, gave place to that of the *oecūmenē* or inhabited world, inhabited, that is, by men possessing a common civilization. Commerce increased and helped to extinguish the hatred of the stranger. The notion of a brotherhood of man, imperfectly conceived by Alexander and developed by the Stoic (q.v.) philosophy, bore fruit such as is to be seen in the prevalence, in and after the 3rd c., of arbitration in disputes between Greek cities. War itself tended to become more humane (e.g. in the treatment of the conquered) and was subjected to restrictions (immunity of certain cities and places from war or reprisals). The old isolation of Greek cities was broken down and mutual grants of citizenship and other rights became frequent. A common speech, the κοινή, simpler and less subtle than Attic, developed and gradually replaced the local dialects. The practice grew of entrusting the trial or arbitration of cases to commissions of one or more judges from other cities, thus securing greater impartiality than was possible under the old system of the jury courts. As the bond of the city on the individual weakened, there were formed a large number of professional associations, centred in the worship of some god; their membership was generally foreign or mixed, and slaves were sometimes included in it; so that these clubs tended to break down racial and social barriers. (For a fuller discussion of these phenomena see W. W. Tarn, 'Hellenistic Civilisation', on which much of the present article is based.)

The 3rd and 2nd cc. were in most parts of the Greek world (though not in Athens and Sparta) a period of material prosperity for the upper classes. There was a great expansion of trade and increase of luxury. Asia in particular became extremely wealthy, as we know from the vast sums extracted from her territory by the conquering Romans. A great deal of building was done, with some town-planning in new cities and with improved houses and better water-supply. Private wealth was accompanied by much liberality and public spirit, and we constantly find rich men coming forward with gifts and assistance to their cities. On the other hand, if the rich were richer the poor were poorer. There was temporarily a great depreciation of money when the Persian treasures (which were said to amount to 170,000 talents) were put into circulation by Alexander, and a corresponding rise of prices. These fell again during the 3rd c. but did not perhaps reach their old level till about 200 B.C. Meanwhile wages appear to have actually fallen during the first half of the 3rd c. This had its effect on population, for it was difficult for the poor to rear their children, and there is evidence that during the Hellenistic Age infanticide was common. There was social unrest, directed to the abolition of debt and the redistribution of land; of this unrest the revolutions of Agis IV and Cleomenes III at Sparta (q.v., § 5) are the most prominent illustrations.

§ 2. *Literature, Science, and Art in the Hellenistic Age*

Greek literature now shows a change of character, but it would be an error to regard the Hellenistic Age as solely or even mainly a period of decline. The conditions, as has been indicated above, were new. Though the cities of Greece did not lose their independence for a long while, they tended to sink into a secondary position. Authors were no longer addressing a homogeneous circle of their fellow citizens, but a cosmopolitan audience, either small and highly educated, or large and popular. They were also under the influence of the authoritative Museum (q.v.) of Alexandria. Greek literature in consequence lost something of its inspiration, enthusiasm, and creative force. The great tragedians and lyric poets had no successors who could rival them. But the new age was far from sterile, and the new conditions were in many respects favourable to literature. Trade and exploration (e.g. Nearchus in the Persian Gulf, Megasthenës in India, Pÿtheäs in the Atlantic and North Sea) brought the knowledge of new lands and greatly widened the Greek horizon. The production of books on a large scale was developed. Education spread and the number of readers increased. The Hellenistic monarchs founded libraries, notably those of Alexandria and Pergamum, and many of these monarchs were enthu-

siastic patrons of literature. A common dialect, as has been said, spread over the Greek world. Many theatres were erected in the new cities. Associations of Dionysiac artists (all those connected with the theatre, authors, actors, musicians, costumiers) were formed and enjoyed privileges and importance. The Hellenistic kings multiplied the number of festivals furnishing occasions for literary display.

There was a revival in the writing of epics, of which the 'Argonautica' of Apollonius is the chief example. Many tragedies were produced, and a group of seven tragedians acquired sufficient contemporary fame to be known as the Pleiad (q.v.). Comedy retained its vigour in Menander and Philemon. The mime, of which examples by Herodas survive, took various forms and was designed for the amusement of a more popular audience. A number of didactic poems were written on geography, astronomy, and fishing; the 'Phaenomena' of Aratus is the chief example of the class. But the most characteristic poems of the age were the short and highly polished epigrams and idylls, of which Callimachus was the greatest Alexandrian master. The pastoral idyll was created and perfected by Theocritus; none of his subsequent imitators rivalled him. Oratory, on the other hand, (with the exception of a few political speeches) now died; it was replaced by the art of rhetoric, which flourished in Greek Asia and attached an exaggerated importance to form and style. Under history we find a number of famous names, Timaeus, Hieronymus, Polybius, and Posidonius. But perhaps the most important contribution of Hellenistic civilization was in the sphere of philosophy. The old Greek ethical philosophies had been concerned with man as a member of a State; with the decline of the city-state and the loosening of the bond which united its citizens, the need arose for a philosophy that would support man as an individual. To meet this need the Hellenistic Age furnished two new systems, that of Epicurus (q.v.) and that of Zeno and the Stoics (q.v.); the doctrine of the latter exerted an immense influence, not only on the Greek world, but later on Rome, and ultimately on Christianity. The other schools occupied from now onwards a secondary position. After Aristotle's death, the Peripatetics under Theophrastus and his successor Strato continued their pursuit of scientific knowledge, but their importance thereafter came to an end. The Academy (q.v.) likewise was eclipsed, until under Arcesilas and Carneades it resumed some prominence by its adoption of Scepticism. The old religion with its Olympian gods was now discredited; there was a readiness to accept the deities of Asia and Egypt, and a tendency to see in them various forms of a single god.

The Hellenistic Age saw a striking advance in scientific knowledge, especially in the connected spheres of astronomy and mathematics. The great names in these sciences are Aristarchus, Archimedes, Hipparchus, Euclid, Eratosthenes, and Posidonius (qq.v.); and as regards astronomy it should be noted that much of the knowledge acquired by the Babylonians now became available to the Greeks. Eratosthenes was also notable as a geographer. Among the great instances of progress may be mentioned the discovery of the precession of the equinoxes and the calculation, with remarkable approach to accuracy, of the length of the solar year and lunar month and of the circumference of the earth. Aristarchus advanced the view that the earth and the planets revolved round the sun, though the suggestion was abandoned by his successors. In anatomy the most prominent discovery was that of the nervous system by Herophilus and Erasistratus.

Nor was the period at first one of marked decline in the sphere of art, though Hellenistic art showed a change of character from that of the 5th and 4th cc., especially a loss of the old restraint and repose, and a striving for theatrical effect. But the age still yielded such masterpieces as the Aphrodite of Melos (Venus of Milo), the Nikē (Victory) of Samothrace, the Dying Gaul of the Pergamene school, and the paintings of Apelles (known to us only by descriptions). The coins of the period include some of the finest portraiture that Greek art ever produced.

He'llespont, see *Athamas*.

He'lots (*Heilōtes*), a word of uncertain derivation (perhaps from the stem ἑλ-, capture) applied to the serfs at Sparta, probably the original inhabitants of the country who had been reduced to bondage. They were serfs of the community, ceded to particular citizens, who might neither sell, dismiss, nor free them. They cultivated the land of their masters, paying a rent in kind. They had no political rights and were kept in subjection by a system of terrorism. They were occasionally promoted to citizenship as *neodāmōdes* for bravery in war, which they followed as servants of their masters and in emergencies as soldiers.

Helvi'dius Priscus, son-in-law of Paetus Thrasea (q.v.), a member of the Stoic opposition to Nero, and banished by him.

In Vespasian's reign he renewed his opposition to the imperial rule, and was banished and put to death.

He'ndecasy'llable, see *Metre*, § 5.

Hendi'adys (Gk. ἓν διὰ δυοῖν), a figure of speech by which a single complex idea is expressed by two words connected by a conjunction; e.g. 'pateris libamus et auro' (Georg. ii. 192).

Hēphae'stion (*Hēphaistiōn*) (1) a Macedonian, son of Amyntōr, one of Alexander the Great's captains and his intimate friend. He died in 324 B.C. (2) of Alexandria, probably of the middle of the 2nd c. A.D., was author of a Greek treatise on metre in no less than forty-eight books, of which only his own epitome survives.

Hēphae'stus (*Hēphaistos*), the Greek god of fire and of the arts, such as that of the smith, in which fire is employed. In Greek mythology he was the son of Zeus and Hera (q.v.), or (in Hesiod) of Hera alone; but he was probably of Eastern origin. He is represented in Homer as lame from birth, and Hera is said to have thrown him out of heaven from shame at his deformity. Hephaestus revenged himself on her by sending her a golden chair, in which, when she sat down, she found herself imprisoned; none could release her but Hephaestus, and he refused to return to heaven, till Dionysus made him tipsy and brought him back. According to another story, Hephaestus interfered on his mother's side in a quarrel between Zeus and Hera, whereupon Zeus seized him by the foot and hurled him down to earth;

> from morn
> To noon he fell, from noon to dewy eve,
> A summer's day, and with the setting sun
> Dropt from the zenith, like a falling star,
> On Lemnos the Ægæan isle.
> Milton, P.L. i. 742 et seq.

In the poets Hephaestus is a smith, and makes not only thunderbolts, but works of art, the shield of Achilles, the necklace of Harmonia, &c. He is the husband of Aphrodite (q.v.), who is unfaithful to him. At Athens he was the god of smiths and associated with Athene in the protection of handicrafts; near his temple above the Ceramicus (see *Athens*, § 1) were the shops of the smiths and braziers. The Romans identified him with Vulcan (q.v.).

Hē'ra (*Hērā*) with whom Juno (q.v.) was identified by the Romans, in Greek mythology is daughter of Cronus and Rhea (qq.v.), the sister and consort of Zeus (q.v.), and queen of heaven. She is essentially the goddess representative of women, especially as wives, and protectress of marriage. She is depicted as of a stately form and a severe beauty. Her children are Hephaestus, Hebe, Ares, and Eilithyia (qq.v.). The chief feature of the legends regarding her is her jealousy of Zeus and her hatred of his paramours and their offspring. For her contest with Athena and Aphrodite for the prize of beauty, see under *Paris* (*Judgement of*). In Homer she is especially associated with Argos, Mycenae, and Sparta, and her chief temple, the famous Heraeum, stood about three miles SE. of Mycenae. Samos, her legendary birthplace, was another important seat of her cult. Her temple there was the largest that Herodotus had ever seen. In Boeotia a curious festival known as the *Daedala* was celebrated, every sixty years, in her honour. Zeus and Hera, it is said, had quarrelled. Zeus gave out that he was about to marry another wife, and had a wooden image (*Daidalē*, 'cunningly wrought') decked out in bridal attire and carried in procession over Mt. Cithaeron, where Hera was hiding. Hera rushed out to attack her rival, and on discovering the trick was reconciled good-humouredly to her husband, and founded the ceremony in commemoration. (Sir J. G. Frazer, 'Golden Bough', c. 1, § 5, regards the festival as probably representing the marriage of the powers of vegetation, and designed to avert a failure of the crops.)

Heraclei'dae (*Hērakleidai*), the children or the descendants of Heracles (q.v.), who was father by Dēianira of several sons, of whom Hyllus was the eldest, and of one daughter Macaria. For the story of their taking refuge from Eurystheus in Attica, and of the sacrifice of Macaria to secure the victory of the Athenians over the forces of Eurystheus, see *Heracles* (*Children of*), Euripides' tragedy.

The 'Return of the Heracleidae' is a mythological form given to the story of the Dorian invasion (see *Migrations and Dialects*), for the Dorians claimed to be descendants of Heracles. Hyllus, the son of Heracles, wishing to know how he and his brothers should assert their inherited claim to Tiryns (or according to the Dorian extension of the claim, to the whole Peloponnese) consulted the Delphic oracle. He was told to await 'the third fruit'. Misunderstanding this to mean the third harvest, he duly made his attack three years later and was defeated and killed in single combat by Echemos the Tegean. It was then learnt that 'third fruit' meant 'third generation', and when this was reached Tēmenos and the other Heracleidae conquered the Peloponnese. The territory was divided into three portions, Lacedaemōn, Argos, and Messēnē. Proclēs

and Eurysthenēs, sons of Aristodēmus, received Lacedaemon, and founded the two royal houses of Sparta; Temenos was given Argos; and Cresphontēs (see *Merope*) Messene.

Heraclei'tus, see *Heraclitus.*

He'raclēs (*Hēraklēs*, L. *Herculēs*), the most famous of Greek heroes, noted for his strength, courage, endurance, good nature, and compassion; he was also known for good appetite and lust. According to the evidence of a passage in Pindar (Isthm. iii. 70) he was not conceived as a very big man, though prodigiously strong. Pythagoras, on the other hand, inferred that he was exceptionally tall, from the length of the stadium at Olympia (q.v.), which Heracles was said to have measured with his feet and which was 600 of his feet, whereas other Greek stadia of 600 feet were somewhat shorter than that at Olympia (Aul. Gell. I. 1). He was exalted as an ideal of human virtue by the later Stoics and Cynics on account of his fortitude, to the neglect of his other qualities. He perhaps reflects some real person, a lord of Tiryns it may be, famous as a mighty warrior and hunter, vassal of the great king of Mycenae (Rose, 'Handbook of Greek Mythology'). He caught the popular fancy, and legends, some of them transferred from less-known heroes, accumulated about him, including those of the Labours. For the legend of his birth, see *Amphitryon.* In his cradle he strangled two serpents, which Hera had sent to kill him; for her jealous machinations pursued him, as the son of her husband's paramour, throughout his life. He was instructed in the various arts by all the greatest experts, by Eurytus, grandson of Apollo, in the use of the bow; by Autolycus (q.v.) in wrestling; by Polydeuces (see *Dioscuri*) in the use of arms; by Linus (q.v.) in music. When the last tried to correct him, Heracles killed him with his own lute. Amphitryon then sent Heracles to tend his flocks on Mt. Cithaeron, and there, when eighteen, he killed a mighty lion. It was there also that occurred what is known as the 'Choice of Heracles'. As he was meditating on the course of life he should follow, two women, Pleasure and Virtue, appeared before him, one offering a life of enjoyment, the other a life of toil and glory. He chose the latter. On his return to Thebes, he relieved the city of a tribute it had been forced to pay to Orchomenus; and Creon, king of Thebes, in gratitude gave him his daughter Megara to wife. Creon's younger daughter married Iphicles (the half-brother of Heracles) who already had a son Iolāus. The latter became the faithful comrade of Heracles. After some years Hera sent a fit of madness upon Heracles, so that he killed Megara and his children, under the delusion that they were his enemies. After this calamity he went into exile, and sought advice from Delphi as to how he might be purified. He was bidden to go to Tiryns and serve Eurystheūs, king of that city, for twelve years, and win immortality by performing the labours that Eurystheus should impose. The legend of Heracles was built up from many sources, and there are in consequence divergences of detail. Thus Euripides makes the madness occur after the performance of the Labours. The reason why Heracles served Eurystheus is variously stated. According to Hesiod it is Iphicles, not Heracles, who takes service with Eurystheus, and the labours of Heracles are sent from God. Eurystheus himself is sometimes represented as a cowardly fellow, who takes refuge in a bronze tub when Heracles approaches with Cerberus or some other captured monster. For the Labours see the article below. Subsequently Heracles married Dēïanīra, daughter of Oeneūs of Calydon, winning her by defeating the river-god Acheloūs in wrestling. When he and Dēïanira departed, they came to the flooded river Euēnus. A Centaur, Nessus, carried Dēïanira across, and then offered violence to her; whereupon Heracles shot him with a poisoned arrow. The Centaur, as he lay dying, advised her, apparently with friendly intention, to keep some of his blood, which, smeared on a garment, would win back the love of Heracles if he were ever unfaithful to her; and this Dēïanira did.

A large number of campaigns, combats, and miscellaneous undertakings, are attributed to Heracles, but only a few of these need be mentioned. He accompanied the Argonauts (q.v. and see *Hylas*) in the early part of their expedition. He rescued Alcestis, wife of Admetus (q.v.), from Death. He fell in love with Iolē, daughter of Eurytus, king of Oechalia, but her father and brothers would not give her to him. One of these brothers, Īphitus, who had come to Tiryns in search of some lost cattle of his father's, Heracles, in a fit of madness, threw from the walls of the city. For this murder the Delphic oracle bade him go into slavery for a year, and he was sold to Omphalē, queen of Lȳdia. There he was set to woman's work, while Omphale assumed his lion's skin and club. When his period of servitude was over he led an expedition against Laomedon (q.v.), king of Troy. Poseidon at an earlier time had sent a monster against Troy, and

Laomedon had promised Heracles certain marvellous horses if he would kill it; but when the feat was done had refused the stipulated reward. Heracles now gathered an army, which included Telamon (father of Ajax) and Peleus (father of Achilles), attacked the city, and captured it. Heracles gave Hēsionē, daughter of Laomedon, to Telamon, to whom she bore Teucer.

Finally Heracles attacked Oechalia and carried off Iole. Dēïanira, to win him back, followed the advice of Nessus and sent Heracles a robe smeared with the Centaur's blood. But this, poisoned as it had been by the blood of the Hydra (see *Heracles, Labours of*) on Heracles' arrow, clung to his flesh and caused fearful suffering. To escape from it he had himself carried to the summit of Mt. Oeta and placed on a pyre. He gave Iole to his son Hyllus (see *Heracleidae*), and persuaded Poias, father of Philoctetes (q.v.), by the gift of his bow and arrows, to light the pyre. He was carried to heaven, reconciled to Hera, and married to her daughter Hēbē.

Among the numerous formidable persons whom Heracles at one time or another overcame may be mentioned CYCNUS, a son of Ares, who robbed Apollo of the hecatombs destined to be sacrificed to him at Delphi (this is the subject of the poem 'The Shield of Heracles', attributed to Hesiod); BUSIRIS, king of Egypt, who in order to avert drought used to sacrifice the strangers who came to his country, and attempted thus to sacrifice Heracles on his way to the Hesperides (see *Heracles, Labours of*); ERYX, the legendary king of the mountain in Sicily so named, with whom Heracles wrestled successfully on his return from the Geryon Labour. See also *Prometheus, Antaeus, Chiron, Cercopes.*

Heracles, it will be seen from the above legends, was connected by them both with Thebes and Tiryns. For the claim of his descendants to the latter (extended to the whole Peloponnese), see *Heracleidae.*

Heracles, Children of (*Hērakleidai*), a tragedy by Euripides, perhaps produced in the early part of the Peloponnesian War and intended to recall the gratitude due to Athens for saving the children of Heracles from the persecution of Eurystheus. Iolāus, an old man, formerly the friend of Heracles (now dead), and the children of the latter, have taken refuge from the unremitting persecution of Eurystheus (q.v.) at the altar of Zeus at Athens. The herald of Eurystheus demands their surrender, and, on the refusal of Dēmophōn, king of Athens and son of Theseus, declares war. The soothsayers announce that the sacrifice of a noble maiden is necessary to secure the success of the Athenian arms, and Macaria, daughter of Heracles, voluntarily offers herself as the victim. As the army of Eurystheus approaches, Hyllus, a son of Heracles, comes to aid the Athenian host, and Iolaus, miraculously made young again, joins in the fight and captures Eurystheus. The captive is brought before Alcmēnē, mother of Heracles, is reviled by her, and ordered off to death.

Heracles, LABOURS OF. The twelve 'Labours' (ἄθλοι) of Heracles (the exact number was a later invention), imposed on him by Eurystheus, according to the generally accepted list were as follows: (1) The NEMEAN LION, an invulnerable monster, the offspring of Typhon and Echidna (qq.v.). Heracles choked the monster in his arms, and clothed himself with its skin, using the beast's own claws, by which alone the skin was penetrable, to separate it from the body. (2) The HYDRA, also a child of Typhon and Echidna, a poisonous water-snake that lived in the marshes of Lerna, near Argos. It had numerous heads, and when one was cut off, others grew in its place. Moreover Hera sent a huge crab to help it. As it was not fair that Heracles should have to meet two monsters at once (the proverb 'ne Hercules quidem adversus duos' became popular; Erasmus, Ad. I. v. 39), he was helped in this encounter by Iolāus, who, as Heracles cut off the heads, seared the stumps with burning brands. He then dipped his arrows in the Hydra's blood, which made their wounds incurable. There were various elaborations of the legend, as that the Hydra had one immortal head, which Heracles buried under a rock. The crab, which Heracles crushed under his foot, became the constellation Cancer. (3) The ERYMANTHIAN BOAR. Heracles was to catch it alive, so he drove it into a snow-field, tired it out, and caught it in a net. (4) The HIND OF CERYNEIA in Arcadia. This, too, Heracles had to catch alive, and he spent a year in its pursuit before he ran it down. (5) The STYMPHALIAN BIRDS, which infested the woods round Lake Stymphālus in Arcadia. Heracles scared them from their covert with a brass rattle and then shot some and drove the rest away. The reason for their destruction is variously stated, e.g. that they were man-eating monsters. (6) The AUGĒAN STABLES. Augēas, king of Elis, had enormous herds of cattle, and Heracles was required to clear in one day the dirt that had accumulated in their stables. This he did by diverting the river Alphēus, so that it flowed through their yard. (7) The CRETAN

BULL, either the bull of Pāsiphaē (see *Minos*) or that which bore Europa (q.v.) to Crete. Heracles caught it alive, brought it back to Mycenae, and let it go. It wandered over Greece and finally settled down near Marathon (see *Theseus*). (8) The HORSES OF DIOMĒDĒS, a son of Ares, and king of the Bistonians in Thrace. These horses were fed with human flesh. Heracles killed Diomedes and threw his body to the horses to eat. They thereupon became tame, and Heracles brought them to Mycenae. (9) The GIRDLE OF THE AMAZON. The girdle of Hippolytē, queen of the Amazons, was desired by the daughter of Eurystheus, and Heracles was required to secure it. He defeated the Amazons in battle, and obtained the girdle from Hippolyte's dead body, or as the price of her freedom. (10) The OXEN OF GERYON (q.v.). To reach him and secure his cattle Heracles had to go to the extreme west. To do this he drew his bow against Helios (q.v.) and made him give up his golden bowl, and sailed in it along the stream Oceanus. At the end of his journey he set up the Pillars of Hercules (afterwards identified with the mountains on either side of the Straits of Gibraltar). Having reached the abode of Geryon, Heracles killed his dog Orthrus, his herdsman Eurytion, and lastly Geryon himself, and brought away his cattle, either in the golden bowl of the Sun, or by a long overland route, through Spain and France, Italy and Sicily, reaching even the region of the Black Sea, according to various legends of local origin, before he returned home safely. (11) The APPLES OF THE HESPERIDES. Heracles forced Nereus (q.v.) to tell him the way to the garden of the Hesperides, and having slain Ladon, the dragon that guarded it, carried off the apples. According to another version, he induced Atlas to fetch the apples, holding up the sky in his place while he did this. Some say that Atlas then refused to resume his burden, and had to be beguiled into doing so. (12) CERBERUS (q.v.). Heracles, with the help of Hermes and Athene, descended to Hades, captured and bound Cerberus, brought him to Eurystheus and then returned him to Hades. Homer (Il. v. 395) refers to an older story in which Heracles turns his arrow against Hades himself. The myth, even in its later attenuated form, suggests the conquest of Death, the most arduous of the Labours of Heracles.

Heracles, Madness of (*Hēraklēs Mainomenos, Hercules Furens*), a tragedy by Euripides, of uncertain date. It was originally called simply 'Heracles'.

Heracles (q.v.), engaged on the last of his twelve labours, has gone down to Hades to bring up the hound Cerberus (q.v.). Lycus, supported by a faction of Thebans, has during the long absence of Heracles killed Creon, king of Thebes and father of Heracles' wife Megara, and usurped the crown. He threatens with death Megara and the three young sons of Heracles, fearing their vengeance in the future; also old Amphitryon, Heracles' reputed father. They have taken sanctuary at the altar of Zeus, but, under menace of being destroyed there by fire, prepare for death. At this point Heracles returns, rescues his family, and slays Lycus. But his persistent enemy, Hera, sends Madness (*Lyssa*), who reluctantly seizes on Heracles, and drives him to slay his own children (under the impression that they are the children of Eurystheus) and his wife. Heracles, recovering from his madness, is filled with utter despair. Theseus, whom Heracles has brought back from Hades, comes to his aid, restores in a measure his courage, and carries him away to Athens to be purified.

For the 'Hercules Furens' of Seneca, see that title.

He′raclids, see *Heracleidae*, and *Heracles (Children of)*.

Heracli′tus (*Hērakleitos*), (1) of Ephesus, a philosopher who flourished about 500 B.C. He belonged to a noble family, which had certain regal (perhaps religious) privileges; these he surrendered to his brother and devoted himself to study in retirement. His haughty, aristocratic views and melancholy philosophy caused him to be contrasted with the 'laughing philosopher', Democritus (q.v.). He set forth his system in a prose work (he was one of the earliest writers in Greek prose) which the ancients thought obscure. They called him ὁ σκοτεινός ('the obscure one') in consequence. The fragments of it which survive are written in an artless but condensed, incisive style, and reveal greatness of thought. He rejected the view of Thales (q.v.) and his successors that there is a single permanent and imperishable substance behind the changes we see in the material world, and held that all things are in a state of flux (πάντα ῥεῖ) and that matter itself is constantly changing. He attributed to fire, an immaterial substance, the origin of all things.

(2) Heraclitus of Halicarnassus, see *Callimachus*.

Hērae′a, a festival held at Argos; see *Festivals*, § 6.

Hērae′um (*Hēraion*), a famous temple of

Hera (q.v.), three miles SE. of Mycenae. In it was a celebrated colossal statue of Hera, in ivory and gold, by Polyclitus (q.v.).

He′rculēs, in Roman religion, was probably derived from the Greek Heracles, with whom he was early identified and whose myth had been brought to Italy by colonists of Magna Graecia. It is possible that Heracles was engrafted on to and replaced the similar Italian figure, Recaranus, a legendary hero of great strength. Hercules had an altar (see *Ara Maxima*) in the Forum Boarium at Rome, where he was worshipped as the god of victory and of commercial enterprise. Two patrician families, the Potitii and the Pinarii, had for many generations charge of his cult. The poplar was his sacred tree. The myth of Hercules and Cacus (q.v.), which Virgil makes Evander narrate (Aen. viii), is probably of Roman origin, and very likely was invented to explain the presence of the altar of Hercules in the Cattle Market, in proximity to the Palatine, where there were *Scalae Caci*.

Hercules Furens, a tragedy by Seneca the Philosopher, based on Euripides' drama (see *Heracles, Madness of*). There are departures of detail from the Greek version—e.g. in lieu of threatening death to the children of Heracles, Lycus has demanded Heracles' wife in marriage; and Heracles' slaughter of his wife and children forms part of the actual drama.

Hercules Oetae′us, a tragedy by Seneca the Philosopher, based on the 'Trachiniae' (q.v.) of Sophocles. The play is of great length (part of it is thought by some to be spurious) and shows variations from the original, especially in the character of Dēïanīra (represented merely as a jealous virago, whereas Sophocles makes her a gentle and attractive figure, more loving than jealous), and by the addition of the scene of Hercules' death and deification on Mt. Oeta.

Here′nnium, *Rhētorica ad*, see *Rhetorica*. (The quantity of the first syllable of 'Herennius' appears to be doubtful.)

Hermae, quadrangular pillars surmounted by a bust of the god Hermes (q.v.), with a phallus below this, set up at Athens (and in other places) at street-corners, on the high roads, and in front of houses, some of them inscribed with moral precepts. The sacrilegious mutilation of the Hermae at Athens during a night shortly before the departure of the Sicilian Expedition (see *Peloponnesian War*) threw the city into extreme commotion.

Hermann, GOTTFRIED, see *Texts and Studies*, § 11.

Hermaphrodi'tus (*Hermaphrodītos*), in Greek mythology, a son of Hermes and Aphrodite (qq.v.), was beloved by Salmacis, the nymph of the fountain in which he bathed. He rejected her entreaties, but she closely embraced him and prayed the gods to make the twain one body, which they did; whence the word 'hermaphrodite', for a person combining both sexes in one body. The spring Salmacis was near Halicarnassus. The English poem 'Salmacis and Hermaphroditus', published anonymously in 1602, is doubtfully attributed to Francis Beaumont.

He'rmēs, in Greek mythology, son of Zeus and Maia (q.v.). He was born on Mt. Cyllēnē in Arcadia. By noon on the day that he was born he had left his cradle and invented the lyre, killing a tortoise that he met and making the instrument from its shell. The same day he drove off fifty cows belonging to Apollo, making them walk backwards, so that they should not be traced, and then returned to his cradle. When Apollo, informed by an old man who had seen the theft, arrived in a rage, Hermes so delighted him with the gift of the lyre, that Apollo gave him in exchange the cattle Hermes had stolen and various divine powers. The story is amusingly told in the Fourth Homeric Hymn, which has been translated by Shelley ('Hymn to Mercury'). Hermes was the god of luck and wealth, the patron of merchants and also of thieves, and in many parts of Greece a god of fertility. He was the god of roads, and on these the Hermae (q.v.) were erected in his honour. He was the messenger or herald of the gods, and conductor of the souls of the dead to Hades (*psūchopompos*; in this capacity he several times figures in Lucian's 'Dialogues of the Dead'). He was also the god of sleep and dreams. He is represented with wings on his sandals, a broad-brimmed hat (*petasos*) and a staff on which serpents are twined (*kērūkeion*, L. *cādūcěus*). Hermes was identified by the Romans with their god Mercury (q.v.). See also *Pan* and *Hermaphroditus*.

The name *Hermes Trismegistus* ('thrice great') was given by the Neoplatonists (q.v.) and the devotees of mysticism and alchemy to the Egyptian god Thoth, regarded as more or less identical with the Grecian Hermes. From the 3rd c. A.D. the name was applied to the author of various Neoplatonic writings, some of which have survived.

Hermi'onē (*Hermĭonē*), in Greek mythology, daughter of Menelaus and Helen (qq.v.). See *Neoptolemus*.

Hē'rō, see *Leander*.

Herod (*Hērōdēs*). (1) HEROD THE GREAT, an Idumaean, son of Antipater, who had been appointed procurator of Judaea under the Romans. After Antipater's death by poison Herod obtained from the triumvirs the grant of the title of king of Judaea, and in 37 B.C. took Jerusalem and established his authority. He ruled Judaea on the lines of a Hellenistic kingdom, built and adorned cities, and gave peace and prosperity. But he was a cruel and unscrupulous tyrant (he put to death his wife Mariamne and her two sons) and was hated by the Jews, though he rebuilt the Temple with some splendour. His last years became a reign of terror; according to Matt. ii he ordered the slaughter of the children in Bethlehem, in order that the infant Jesus should be destroyed. He died in 4 B.C. (according to Jewish report, of a horrible disease).

(2) The 'Herod' of Acts xii, M. Julius Agrippa, grandson of Herod the Great, a friend of Caligula and Claudius, who was granted by these emperors territories in Palestine which eventually embraced the whole of his uncle's kingdom. He died in A.D. 44. It was before his son, Agrippa II, that Paul was brought (Acts xxv).

Hēro'das or HĒRO'NDAS (*Hērōdās* or *Hērondās*) (c. 300–250 B.C.), a native of Cos or Miletus, a writer of mimes (q.v). Eight of these (one incomplete) were recovered in an Egyptian papyrus in 1891. Herodas wrote in the Ionic dialect and in scazons (see *Metre*, § 2). He presents with vividness and humour scenes of ordinary city-life (frequently its seamy side), women chaffering for shoes at a shoemaker's, or admiring the works of art at the temple of Asclepius, the flogging of a truant schoolboy, the parody of a speech in the law-court.

Hērō'dēs A'tticus (*Vibullus Hipparchos Tĭbĕrius Claudius Atticus Herodes*, A.D. 101–177), born at Marathon, a famous Greek orator, who enjoyed the favour of Hadrian and Antoninus Pius and was the instructor of Marcus Aurelius and Lucius Verus. His father Julius had been a poor man until he found by chance a treasure buried in his garden. The son attained high office and used his great wealth for the benefit of scholars and artists and in the erection of splendid buildings at Athens (one of the first was appropriately a temple to Fortune) and at other places in Greece. For instance he rebuilt in white marble, on twice its original scale, the stadium at Athens; he also built there, in memory of his wife, the great Odēum or Music Hall, the remains of which may still be seen. Aulus Gellius (q.v.) has left an account of pleasant days spent with him at his villa among the woods of Cêphissia, which was a literary centre. None of his writings have survived, except one speech doubtfully attributed to him and an abstract and part-translation of another by Aulus Gellius.

Herō'dian (*Aelius Hērōdiānus*), the son of Apollonius Dyscolus (q.v.), lived at Rome under Marcus Aurelius, and wrote in Greek on a number of grammatical subjects. His principal work was a treatise on Greek accents in twenty-one books, of which only excerpts and a defective epitome survive.

Herō'dian (*Hērōdiānus*) (c. A.D. 165–c. 250), a Syrian, wrote in Greek a history of the Roman emperors from the death of Marcus Aurelius to A.D. 238.

Hero'dotus (*Hērodotos*) (c. 480–c. 425 B.C.), the historian, was born at Halicarnassus (q.v.), the son of Lyxēs, of a distinguished family. He was a nephew of the epic poet Panyasis (q.v.). He went into exile as a young man in consequence of local troubles, and travelled, then or later, in Egypt and in other parts of the Greek world. He visited Athens and knew Pericles. He became a citizen of Thurii (q.v.) in Magna Graecia, and revisited Athens at some date after the building of the Propylaea (431). He is said to have given in 446 a public reading at Athens of part of his history and to have been awarded a grant of ten talents.

Herodotus has been called by Cicero and others 'the father of history'. He was in fact the first to make the events of the past the subject of research and verification (which is what the word ἱστορίη meant). In this he showed a great advance on the *logographi* (q.v.), who dealt uncritically with a remote and mythical past, whereas the main subject of the history of Herodotus is comprised within the previous century. Not only did he seek by comparison of authorities and estimation of probabilities to arrive at the truth, but he was the first to introduce realistic as opposed to poetical accounts of war and politics. He saw that the sequence of events is capable of rational explanation, though unlike his successors, Thucydides and Polybius, he did not grasp the profound political causes that govern it. He fell short of these also in that his object is merely to maintain the memory of the 'great and wonderful deeds' of Greeks and Barbarians of earlier times; whereas Thucydides and Polybius aimed at producing works of political instruction, enabling their readers to draw con-

clusions as to the future from the narrative of the past.

The subject of the 'History' of Herodotus is the struggle between Asia and Greece, substantially from the time of Croesus to that of Xerxes. The work is perhaps unfinished; the division into nine books named after the Muses is not by Herodotus, but was probably made by Alexandrian editors, though Lucian ascribes it to enthusiastic Greeks who heard the history read by Herodotus at Olympia. While the main subject is the single conception indicated above, Herodotus adds to the narrative many digressions, containing a mass of information more or less closely connected with it, mythical, geographical, and political, interspersed with anecdotes. His method is critical, but his criticism is limited by the conditions of an age that was primitive in its religious beliefs and restricted in its general knowledge. He relied, in foreign countries, on what he was told, and his historical errors arose from the untrustworthiness of his sources. His veracity was attacked by Plutarch and Lucian, but is now generally accepted. He wrote in the Ionian dialect, in a simple, clear, and graceful style, and his narrative as a whole, with its many pleasant and entertaining stories, is one of great charm. The following are the principal subjects of the several books:

Book I. The history of Croesus, with a glance at the early history of Lȳdia (including the legend of Gȳgēs and Candaulēs); the story of the relations of Croesus and Solon (chronologically impossible); the conquest of Lydia and the creation of the Persian empire by Cyrus, with an account of Persia (131 et seq.), of Babylon (178 et seq.), and of the Anatolian Greeks (142 et seq.); the war of Cyrus with the Massagetae (201 et seq.).

Book II. A description of Egypt (story of Rhampsinītus, 121).

Book III. The conquest of Egypt by Cambȳsēs, the story of the false Smerdis, and the rise of Darius to power (anecdote of Polycratēs and his seal, 40; of Zōpyrus, 153).

Book IV. The expedition of Darius against the Scythians and against the Libyans (145 et seq.) with an account of both these peoples.

Book V. The operations of Megabazus with a division of the Persian army against the Thracians and an account of the latter; the Ionian revolt (28 et seq.) and the burning of Sardis (101).

Book VI. The subdual of the Ionians; the march of Mardonius to Macedonia and the wreck of the Persian fleet at Mt. Athos

(43 et seq.); the expedition under Dâtis and Artaphernês (94 et seq.; Marathon, 102 et seq.; Pheidippidês, 105); Cleisthenês and Hippoclidês, 126.

Book VII. Death of Darius, preparations of Xerxes, and invasion of Greece; battle of Thermopylae (201 et seq.).

Book VIII. Battles of Artemisium and Salamis (56 et seq.); withdrawal of Xerxes (97 et seq.).

Book IX. Battle of Plataea and retreat of the Persians; battle of Mycalê (98 et seq.). Capture of Sestos (114 et seq.).

Herodotus may have written other works which have perished. He refers to his 'Assyrian Logoi', which appear to have been known to Aristotle. His history was the first masterpiece of Greek prose. Quintilian, expressing the cultivated judgement of the Roman empire, places Herodotus with Thucydides, far above their Greek rivals, and describes him as 'dulcis, et candidus, et fusus', 'pleasant, lucid, diffuse'. Plutarch has a treatise 'On the Malignity of Herodotus' in which, while commending him as an agreeable historian (though inferior to Thucydides), he quotes a number of passages showing in his opinion lack of fairness and charitableness. Plutarch's criticism arises from the unfriendly attitude of Herodotus to the Boeotians, due probably to the historian's having gathered information at Athens at a time when Athens and Thebes were bitter enemies. In modern times George Rawlinson (1812–1902) was author of 'The History of Herodotus' (1858–60), a translation accompanied by valuable historical and ethnological notes.

Heroic Hymn, a Greek choral lyric (q.v.), sung by a stationary choir accompanied on the lyre, celebrating the exploits of one or other of the heroes of epic poetry, though with great liberty of treatment and invention. These hymns are especially associated with Stesichorus (q.v.); they were often of considerable length and must have been sung at public festivals.

Hērŏ'ides or *Hērŏ'idum Epi'stulae,* 'Letters of Heroines', amatory poems in elegiacs by Ovid, in the form of letters purporting to be addressed by heroines of legend to their lovers or husbands (one is from the historical Sappho to the mythical Phaon). Three of the letters are addressed to heroines by their lovers. Of the twenty-one epistles the last six are considered spurious by some critics; these are letters from Paris to Helen, Leander to Hero, Acontius to Cydippe, and the reply to each. The 'Heroides' were among Ovid's earliest works, probably written between the first and second editions of the 'Amores' (q.v.).

He claimed that they constituted a new literary form, invented by him.

The letters of the heroines are studies of love from the woman's standpoint, based on Ovid's own observation and applied to cases drawn from Greek epic and drama, from Virgil (Dido), Catullus (Ariadne), and the Alexandrian poets. The heroines are represented in various situations, betrayed or deserted (Deïanira, Phyllis, Medea, Ariadne, Oenone, Dido), neglected (Briseis), bound in a hateful marriage (Hermione), punished for their love (Hypermnestra, Canace), the victim of unlawful passion (Phaedra), or anxious for their husbands' safety (Penelope, Laodamia). The characters are depicted with care, but the sentiments and morals are those, not of the heroic age, but of contemporary Rome.

Hēro'ndas, see *Herodas.*

Hēro'philê, see *Sibyls.*

Hēro'philus (*Hērophilos*) (4th–3rd c. B.C.), a great anatomist of Alexandria, famous for his discovery of the nervous system. He also ascertained that the arteries carry, not air as had been thought, but blood from the heart. He practised dissection on corpses, and even, it is said, vivisection on criminals. His treatise 'Anatomica' has not survived.

Hē'rŏs, see *Menander.*

Hēro'stratus (*Hērostratos*), see *Ephesus.*

Hē'siod (*Hēsiodos*), an early Greek poet, author of 'Works and Days' (q.v.), to whom were also attributed by ancient writers, with fairly complete unanimity, the 'Theogony' and the 'Catalogue of Women', with the 'Eoeae' (qq.v.). Modern scholars are not in agreement as to the authorship of these further poems. The 'Shield of Heracles' (q.v.), except as regards its first section, is generally held to be by another hand. Little is known with certainty about the poet himself beyond what may be gathered from the 'Works and Days'. He appears to have written after the composition of the Homeric poems, but not much later, perhaps in the 8th c. B.C. His father, a merchant of Cȳmē in Aeolis, was reduced by poverty to migrate to Ascra in Boeotia, where Hesiod was born and lived the life of a farmer. On the father's death the estate was divided between Hesiod and his brother Perses; the latter claimed more than his share and a dispute ensued in which Perses bribed the authorities to favour him. It appears also that Hesiod once took part in a poetic contest at Chalcis and won the prize with his hymn. According to Plutarch and other late writers, Hesiod was murdered at Oenöē in Locris by the brothers of a woman he had seduced, or to whose seduction he had been privy. His tomb was shown at Orchomenus.

The originality of Hesiod lies in the fact that he was the first among Greek poets to seek his subject elsewhere than in the field of myth and fancy. Instead, he embodies in the 'Works and Days' ethical maxims and practical instructions derived from his own experience and adapted to the life of a peasant. Incidentally he gives a realistic picture of primitive rustic life and reveals his own interesting character (see *Works and Days*). Hesiod wrote in a dialect which is in the main the Ionian of Homer with some admixture of Boeotian.

Hesiodic Poetry. Hesiod had imitators and we know of a number of poems in hexameters, either mythological like the 'Theogony', or didactic like the 'Works and Days', which were ascribed to Hesiod himself or to other authors. Such were the 'Shield of Heracles' (q.v.) and an extension of the 'Eoeae' (q.v.) known as the 'Great Eoeae'; also other mythological poems. The 'Precepts of Chiron' contained moral instruction, and a work on 'Astronomy' was produced by this school. These, with the exception of the 'Shield of Heracles', we know only by fragments or by references in later authors.

Hēsi′onē, see *Laomedon* and *Teucer*.

Hespe′ria, the 'Western land', a poetic name for Italy or Spain.

Hespe′rides, THE, 'Daughters of Evening', in Greek mythology, were supposed to live far away in the west, near the Atlas mountains, guarding a tree that produced golden apples, a present given by Ge to Hera when the latter married Zeus. The dragon Lādōn helped them to keep watch. It was one of the Labours of Heracles (q.v.) to get possession of the apples. See also *Atalanta*.

He′sperus (*Hesperos*), the evening star.

He′stia (*Hestiā*), in Greek mythology daughter of Cronos and Rhea (qq.v.), the goddess of the hearth, the symbol of the home and family. There was a hearth consecrated to her not only in every home, but also in the Prytanēum or town hall of each capital city (and at Delphi and Olympia), where a sacred fire was kept burning. From this, fire was taken to a new colony on its foundation. Sacrifices began and ended with libations to Hestia, and she was mentioned in all prayers. The Romans identified her with Vesta (q.v.).

Hestiā′sis, see *Liturgy*.

Hēsy′chius (*Hēsuchios*), the name of a Greek lexicographer, or of two distinct

lexicographers, of Alexandria and Miletus respectively, of the 5th and 6th cc. A.D., on whose work the lexicon known as Suidas (q.v.) was in part based.

Hetae′rae (*Hetairai*), see *Women* (*Position of*).

Hexa′meter, see *Metre*, § 1.

He′xapla, see *Origen*.

Hiā′tus, a 'break' or 'cleft' in a verse when a vowel at the end of one word is not elided (see *Elision*) before a vowel at the beginning of the next, as it would be by normal scansion. The earlier vowel may if long retain its length or be shortened. Hiatus is common in Greek epic verse (e.g. ἀμφίπολος δ᾽ ἄρα οἱ κεδνὴ ἑκάτερθε παρέστη), rare in Latin ('Glauco et Panopeae') in Virg. Georg. i. 437.

Hi′eroclēs (*Hieroklēs*), probably of Alexandria, a Stoic philosopher of the 1st–2nd cc. A.D., author of an 'Elements of Ethics' (*Ēthikē Stoicheiōsis*) of which a large part has survived. He is probably also the author of a number of fragments attributed to a Hierocles by Stobaeus. There was a later Hierocles, a Neoplatonist, in the 5th c. There was also a historian of that name, probably in the 3rd c.; and a writer of *facētiae*, probably in the 4th c.

Hi′eron (*Hierōn*) I and II, see *Syracuse*, §§ 1 and 3.

Hieron, one of the minor works of Xenophon, a dialogue between Hieron I, tyrant of Syracuse (q.v., § 1), and Simonides, in which the lot of the tyrant and that of the private citizen are compared. Hieron points out the disadvantages under which the former labours, while Simonides shows how a tyrant, by ruling well, may make himself popular and so gain happiness.

Hiero′nymus (*Hierōnymus*), see *Jerome*.

Hiero′nymus (*Hierōnymus*) of Cardia (3rd c. B.C.), a historian of the period from the death of Alexander probably to that of Pyrrhus. He served as general and statesman under Eumenes I, Antigonus I, Demetrius, and Antigonus Gonātas, and thus had first-hand knowledge of the events he related. His history is lost, but was used by Arrian, Diodorus, and Plutarch.

Hīma′tion, see *Clothing*, § 1.

Hi′mera (*Himerā*), a town on the N. coast of Sicily, where Gelon defeated the Carthaginians in 480 B.C. (see *Syracuse*, § 1). It was probably the birthplace of Stesichorus (q.v.).

Hippale′ctryon (*Hippalektruōn*), see *Monsters*.

Hippa'rchicus (*Hipparchikos*), see *Cavalry Commander*.

Hippa'rchus (*Hipparchos*), (1) son of Pisistratus (q.v.); (2) (b. *c.* 190 B.C.), one of the great Greek mathematicians of antiquity, who probably worked at Rhodes and Alexandria. He invented trigonometry, developed Eratosthenes' system of latitudes and longitudes, calculated with surprising accuracy the length of the solar year and of the lunar month, and discovered, unless Kidenas the Babylonian had the priority (a moot point), the precession of the equinoxes from accurate observations, made over his own lifetime, of the morning risings of stars. A short work of his survives in which he corrects errors made by the astronomer Eudoxus and incorporated from the latter by Aratus (q.v.) in his poem. His principal work was a catalogue of some 800 fixed stars, with their positions fixed by latitude and longitude in relation to the ecliptic.

Hi'ppeis (knights), see *Athens*, § 2. For Aristophanes' play, see *Knights*.

Hi'ppias (*Hippiās*), (1) son of Pisistratus (q.v.). (2) Of Elis, a sophist (q.v.); he was a contemporary of Socrates, and two of the minor dialogues of Plato are named after him.

Hippias Major and *Minor*, see *Plato*, § 2.

Hi'ppikēs, *Peri*, see *Horsemanship*.

Hippoca'mpus (*Hippokampos*), see *Monsters*.

Hippocli'dēs (*Hippokleidēs*), the subject of an amusing anecdote in Herodotus (vi. 128). Cleisthenēs, tyrant of Sicyon, had invited to his court suitors for the hand of his daughter Agaristē, in order to make trial of their qualities and accomplishments. Hippoclides, son of Tisander of Athens, had proved first favourite. But at the wedding-feast he ordered the flute-player to play a dance, and 'he danced, probably so as to please himself', and wound up by standing on his head and gesticulating with his legs, to the grave displeasure of his intended father-in-law, who remarked, 'Son of Tisander, you have danced away your marriage'. 'Hippoclides doesn't care', was the reply. (Agaristē married Megacles the Alcmaeorid, and their son was Cleisthenes, the reformer of the Athenian constitution.)

Hippo'cratēs (*Hippokratēs*), a great Greek physician, was born in the island of Cos about 460 B.C., and is mentioned by Plato as already famous at the time when the dialogue 'Protagoras' is supposed to take place (latter part of 5th c.).

He is said to have died, when an old man, at Larissa.

Of the seventy-two works on medicine attributed to him, many are certainly by his disciples, some are even older than Hippocrates. Probably half a dozen were written by him, including Books I and III of the treatise on 'Epidemics', the 'Prognostics', and the interesting treatise on 'Air, Earth, and Locality', dealing with the effect of environment on health. They reveal a true scientific spirit, in the insistence on the permanence of the relation of effect to cause, and the necessity of careful observation of medical facts. Hippocrates was regarded by his contemporaries and successors as the perfect type of physician, learned, humane, calm, pure of mind, grave, and reticent. His name survives in the 'Hippocratic oath', in which the physician undertook to be faithful to the best traditions of the profession (for the text, see 'The Legacy of Greece', Oxford, 1922, p. 213); and in the *Hippocratic facies*, a description, in the 'Prognostics', of the signs of approaching death. The 'Aphorisms' attributed to Hippocrates contain the famous dictum 'Life is short, but the art is long, the opportunity fleeting, the experiment perilous, the judgement difficult' (ὁ βίος βραχύς, ἡ δὲ τέχνη μακρή, ὁ δὲ καιρὸς ὀξύς, ἡ δὲ πεῖρα σφαλερή, ἡ δὲ κρίσις χαλεπή).

Hi'ppocrēne (*Hippokrēnē*), a fountain, sacred to the Muses, on Mt. Helicon (see *Pegasus*). It was higher up the mountain than Aganippe (q.v.).

Hippodamī'a (*Hippodameia*), (1) daughter of Oenomāus, see *Pelops*; (2) wife of Pīrithōus, see *Centaurs*.

Hippo'lytē (*Hippolutē*) or **Hippo'lyta**, (1) or *Antiopē*, a queen of the Amazons, see *Heracles* (*Labours of*) and *Theseus*; (2) or *Astydameia*, wife of Acastus, see *Peleus*.

Hippo'lytus (*Hippolutos*), the bastard son of Theseus (q.v.) and the Amazon Hippolyta. He was a man of perfect purity of life, devoted to the chase, and a worshipper of the goddess Artemis (q.v.). Phaedra, daughter of Minos, king of Crete, and wife of Theseus, fell in love with him, but he rejected her advances. From resentment of his scorn Phaedra hanged herself, after writing a letter to Theseus denouncing him as her seducer. Theseus in wrath invoked the vengeance of Poseidon on Hippolytus and banished him. As Hippolytus was driving along the Troezenian shore in his chariot, a monster sent from the sea by Poseidon terrified the horses;

Hippolytus was thrown from the chariot and dragged to death, and Theseus learnt his error too late. In some versions of the tale, Artemis persuades Asclepius (q.v.) to restore him to life, and he appears again in Roman legend. Virgil (Aen. vii) and other authors relate that Hippolytus, when he fell from his chariot, was conveyed away by Diana to the grove of the nymph Egeria, near Aricia in Latium, where under the name of Virbius he lived out his days (see *Diana*). His son, another Virbius, was among the heroes who resisted the settlement of Aeneas in Latium.

Hippo'lytus, a tragedy by Euripides, produced in 429 B.C. For the story see above. Euripides makes Phaedra a pure woman, resisting the passion of which she is a victim, but betrayed to Hippolytus by her nurse. Afraid that he will reveal her secret to Theseus, she involves him in her own destruction. For the play on this subject by Seneca see *Phaedra*. Racine's great tragedy 'Phèdre' was produced in 1677.

Hippo'nax of Ephesus (*fl. c.* 540 B.C.), a satirical poet of a coarse wit, inventor of the *scazon* or halting iambic (see *Metre*, § 2). He is said to have been exiled and to have lived at Clazomenae (near Smyrna). Only fragments of his work have survived. Pliny relates that two artists, Bupalus and Athenis, having exhibited a statue of him ridiculing his ugliness, the poet lashed them with his bitter verses, so that they were driven to hang themselves in despair (cf. Hor. Epod. vi. 14).

Hippo'tades, see *Aeolus* (1).

Hir'tius, AULUS, one of Caesar's lieutenants in Gaul, and consul with Vibius Pansa in 43 B.C. He was killed in that year in the fighting against Antony that followed the assassination of Caesar. Hirtius was the author of the continuation (Book VIII) of Caesar's Commentaries 'de Bello Gallico'.

Hispa'nia (*Hispānia*), see *Spain*.

Histiae'us (*Histiaios*), tyrant of Miletus at the time of the expedition of Darius into Europe. He guarded the bridge of boats when Darius crossed the Danube (see *Persian Wars*), and resisted the proposal to destroy the bridge when the return of Darius was delayed, thus enabling Darius to escape from this adventure. For this service Darius rewarded him with the grant of Myrcinus in Thrace; but he was soon called to Susa and kept there in honourable captivity. He is said to have been connected with the outbreak of the Ionian revolt, but the confidence of Darius in him was such that he was allowed to proceed to the Aegean coast,

nominally to crush the rising. Suspected by both sides he took to piracy, and at one time occupied Byzantium. He was finally crucified by the satrap Artaphernes.

Histo'ria Anīmā'lium, a treatise by Aristotle (q.v.).

Histo'ria Augu'sta, the name commonly given to a collection of biographies, entitled in the principal manuscript 'Vitae diversorum principum et tyrannorum a divo Hadriano usque ad Numerianum a diversis compositae'. The biographies are those of the emperors and certain heirs and claimants to the empire from Hadrian to Numeriānus (A.D. 117–284). They are attributed to six authors: Aelius Spartianus, Julius Capitolinus, Volcatius Gallicanus, Aelius Lampridius (to these four are attributed the lives down to the Maximins), Trebellius Pollio and Flavius Vopiscus (to whom are assigned the lives from Valerian to Numerianus). The biographies, by Pollio, between the Maximins and Valerian are lost. Nothing is known of the authors. The several biographies are distributed among the first four authors, those of successive emperors being in some instances attributed to different hands. Those by the first four authors are addressed, some to Diocletian, some to Constantine, and the whole series appears to have been written in their reigns. They are modelled, in form, on the 'Lives of the Caesars' by Suetonius, and their typical arrangement (sometimes departed from) is to deal successively with the ancestry of the emperor, his early life, the political events of his reign, his personal characteristics and appearance. Much space is occupied with anecdotes and the life of the palace. A great part of the biography of Elagabalus, for instance, is given to an account of his extravagant mode of life. In spite of its many defects, the historical value of the work has always been recognized. It was studied by Petrarch, first printed in 1475, and edited successively by Erasmus (1518), Casaubon (1603), and Salmasius (1620). It has long been a battle-field of ingenuity. The latest and most authoritative discussion of it is that of Prof. Baynes, 'The Historia Augusta, Its Date and Purpose' (Oxford, 1926).

Histo'ria Plantārum, see *Theophrastus*.

Histo'riae Phili'ppicae, see *Trogus*.

Historians, ANCIENT. (1) GREEK, see *Logographi* (1), *Herodotus*, *Thucydides*, *Xenophon*, *Ctesias*, *Theopompus*, *Ephorus*, *Callisthenes*, *Onesicritus*, *Timaeus*, *Apollodorus*, *Eratosthenes*, *Polybius*, *Diodorus*, *Dionysius of Halicarnassus*, *Cassius Dio*,

Josephus, Plutarch, Arrian, Appian, Herodian, Eusebius. (2) ROMAN, see *Annales, Caesar, Sallust, Sisenna, Hirtius, Nepos, Livy, Trogus, Justin, Velleius Paterculus, Valerius Maximus, Cremutius Cordus, Curtius, Tacitus, Suetonius, Florus, Historia Augusta, Eutropius, Festus, Ammianus Marcellinus, Jerome, Orosius.*

Historians of Greece and Rome, MODERN. British historical writing, which entered into a new phase with Hume and Robertson in the second half of the 18th c., reached its highest development in Edward GIBBON (1737–94). He was practically self-educated for his task, for although he entered Magdalen College, Oxford, at 15 years of age, his 'Memoirs' record how he was left by the 'incredible neglect' of his tutors to pursue his own way of study. He became a Roman Catholic, and was sent by his father to Lausanne, to the house of a Calvinist minister, in the hope that he would be re-converted; as he was. There he became engaged for a time to Suzanne Curchod, afterwards the wife of the famous Baron Necker. He subsequently became colonel of the Hampshire Militia, and his interest in military affairs is seen in many passages of his History. After the disbandment of the militia he went to the continent, and a well-known passage in the 'Memoirs' describes how, musing among the ruins of the Capitol, he first conceived the idea of his great work. In 1774 he became a member of Parliament and in 1779 was appointed a commissioner of trade and plantations. The first volume of 'The Decline and Fall of the Roman Empire' appeared in 1776, the remaining five volumes between that date and 1787. From 1783 he had resided at Lausanne. In this work Gibbon showed himself a master of English prose, a lucid, and with comparatively rare exceptions, an accurate historian. He had a strong sense of the continuity of history; he follows out the evolution of the empire from its origins in the Roman republic to its disappearance in a new order of things. His chapters on the growth of Christianity provoked criticisms, and in the light of the greater knowledge now available the work is in some respects incomplete. The tone is often slightly ironic; Gibbon regarded history as 'little more than the register of the crimes, follies, and misfortunes of mankind', and he has been criticized as lacking in sympathy. His History was edited with notes by H. H. Milman in 1838–9, and again with notes by Milman, Guizot, and William Smith in 1854; a standard edition by J. B. Bury appeared in 1909–13. C. Lamb, it may be noted, included Gibbon among the 'biblia a-biblia' ('Detached Thoughts on Books and Reading').

The great 'History of Rome' of Barthold Georg NIEBUHR (1776–1831) appeared in 1811–32. He was the first to treat the subject in a critical and scientific spirit, and threw a new light on the ancient population of Rome and other interesting matters. It was under the influence of his critical methods that Thomas ARNOLD, the famous headmaster of Rugby School, wrote his 'History of Rome'. It was published in 1828–42, and his 'History of the later Roman Commonwealth' in 1845 (posthumously). Charles MERIVALE'S 'History of the Romans under the Empire' appeared in 1850–64. Theodor MOMMSEN (1817–1903), by reason of his great epigraphic knowledge and his study of Roman Law, superseded all previous works on the subject by his 'Roman History', published in 1854–6, and by other works on chronology, &c. Connop THIRLWALL, who with Julius Hare had translated Niebuhr's 'History' in 1828–32, published his 'History of Greece' in 1835–44. It was immediately followed by that of George GROTE (1794–1871), on which he had been intermittently at work since 1823. Grote was a banker, had been M.P. for the City of London since 1832, and had taken an active part in the reform movement, and his political activities had interfered with his work as a historian. His 'History' was published in 1846–56. It is essentially a political history, reflecting his own interest in political institutions and his republican sympathies; it is less concerned with the economic and social conditions of the people and is in that respect incomplete. Among more recent historians may be mentioned EDUARD MEYER (1855–1930), whose knowledge of Semitic and other languages enabled him to write a *Geschichte des Altertums*, and not merely of Greece and (so far as he got) of Rome. JULIUS BELOCH is a historian of Greece and Rome who has reconsidered the materials for himself without regard for authority and with a special interest in population as a subject of economic study. ETTORE PAIS is the most extreme of Niebuhr's followers, and G. DE SANCTIS is the leader of the reaction to critical conservatism in Roman history. M. ROSTOVTZEFF has made valuable contributions especially to our knowledge of the history of the Roman Empire. Among the later histories of Greece may also be mentioned that of J. B. BURY published in 1900.

Histories (*Historiae*), *The*, of Tacitus (q.v.) were published during the period

A.D. 104–109, and were written before the 'Annals' (q.v.). Portions were revised by the younger Pliny, who sometimes furnished Tacitus with material for them, e.g. the account of the eruption of Vesuvius which caused the death of the elder Pliny. They embraced the period A.D. 69–96, from the principate of Galba to that of Domitian; but only the first four books and part of the fifth survive, i.e. to the early years of Vespasian's reign.

Book I opens with an impressive survey of the times that the historian is about to deal with, 'rich in tragedies, terrible with battles, torn by civil strife' when the very Capitol was fired by the hands of citizens. It describes the brief reign of Galba, the adoption of Piso, and the intrigues of Otho with the military which brought about his accession and the murder of Galba and Piso (A.D. 69). The historian's skill in drawing with incisive touches the characters of the leading personages of the empire is here first seen in his portrait of Galba, his mediocre character, 'rather free from vices than endowed with virtues', the stinginess that was his undoing, the high birth and military reputation thanks to which he would have been judged equal to the imperial office but for his having held it, 'capax imperii nisi imperasset'.

The narrative passes to the mutinous conduct of the legions in Germany, their adoption of Vitellius as emperor, the movement of his forces under Valens and Caecina, the negotiations between Otho and Vitellius, the shifting allegiances of provinces and legions, and the outbreak of civil war.

Book II. Tacitus turns to another aspect of the drama—the important role that Vespasian and Titus were playing in the East, where, except for the resistance of Jerusalem, the war against the Jews had been concluded. Vespasian and Titus (governor of Syria) decide to await developments. Tacitus then returns to events in Italy, the fighting about Bēdriacum and the suicide of Otho, as the only honourable course open to him. The reign of Vitellius is described, the emperor's sloth and gluttony, the disorderly conduct of the legions, the wasteful administration, and the threat of the advance of Vespasian's forces under Mucianus.

Book III narrates the operations of the Flavian generals against Vitellius, the siege and the terrible sack and burning of Cremōna, the fighting in Rome between partisans of the opposing forces which leads to the burning of the Capitol, and the final capture of the city and end of Vitellius, discovered wandering forlornly in the deserted palace and put to death

(December 69). The author's gift of sombre colouring is seen perhaps at its highest in this book.

Book IV and the surviving portion of Book V are occupied with the reign of Vespasian, the rising of the Batavians under Cīvilis, and the expedition of Titus against Jerusalem (the account of the siege is lost).

Hŏ′mer (*Hŏmĕros*), the great Greek epic poet who was regarded in antiquity as the author of the 'Iliad' and the 'Odyssey' (qq.v.). There is doubt as to both his date and birthplace, and many authorities in modern times have rejected the original unity of each poem and questioned Homer's very existence as an individual poet. Some hold that each poem contains, as its kernel, certain detached lays, of moderate compass, perhaps the work of a single poet, expanded and connected into a single whole by later additions; that the poems are in fact the result of a process of growth lasting over centuries and subject to many influences. It is stated by several ancient authors that an authorized text of the poems was settled at Athens under Pisistratus. And there was an ordinance of uncertain date, variously attributed to Solon, Pisistratus, and Hipparchus, that the 'Iliad' and the 'Odyssey' should be recited entire at the Panathenaea (q.v.). These would, on the above theory, be important stages in the process of growth referred to. But recent scholarship tends to recur, in spite of the difficulties involved (difficulties of language, inconsistencies in the narrative, &c.), to the view of 'one Homer', who perhaps worked on pre-existing materials (lays such as those sung by Demodocus in the 'Odyssey'), and remodelled them into complete poems, each possessing unity and each inspired by an artistic purpose.

As regards Homer's date, Eratosthenes (q.v.) made him almost contemporary with the events that he relates (placed by Eratosthenes in the 12th c. B.C.); Herodotus, confirmed in a measure by Thucydides, placed him in the 9th c.; some modern critics date him as late as the 7th c. Recent authorities incline to the 9th c. As to his birthplace, his language shows him familiar with the Ionic and Æolic dialects of the coast of Asia Minor (the poems are written in a mixture of the two) and he displays here and there special knowledge of this region. Of the many cities that claimed his birth, Chios and Smyrna have the best traditional claims. It is improbable that Homer composed the poems, other than the 'Iliad' and the 'Odyssey', sometimes attributed to him, e.g. a *Thēbāis* (on the siege of Thebes), *Margites* (q.v.), and *Batrachomyomachia* (q.v.). See also *Homeric Hymns, Homeridae, Cyclic Poems.*

The 'Iliad' and the 'Odyssey' were composed to be recited or chanted, and it is not impossible that a bard's memory should have been capable of retaining the whole of them. But it is also possible that Homer wrote them down, not for the purpose of being read by others, but for his own guidance (see *Books,* § 1). The poems were the subject of much study in the Alexandrian Age (q.v.), notably by Zenodotus, who endeavoured by comparison of many manuscripts to restore the original text, by Aristophanes of Byzantium, and by Aristarchus (see *Texts,* § 2). The text that we possess is derived from a vulgate text that is at least as early as Plato, influenced in its readings, but not to any considerable extent, by Alexandrian editions. It is based mainly on two manuscripts now in Venice, of the 10th and 11th cc. respectively.

The chief characteristics of Homer's poetry have been well stated by Aristotle. He attributes to Homer 'pre-eminence in the serious style of poetry' and 'unequalled diction and thought'. Homer, he further says, has taught poets the true art of illusion, keeping himself in the background and leaving his characters to reveal themselves. Aristotle notices the unity of plot and perfection of structure in the 'Iliad' and 'Odyssey', the many parts in each centring round a single action. He notices also Homer's vividness of expression, by which he gives life and animation even to inanimate things. See also Matthew Arnold's lectures 'On Translating Homer', where the dominant characteristics of Homer are defined as rapidity, plainness in thought and in diction, and nobility. Arnold also says that what Homer has in common with Milton—the noble and profound application of ideas to life—is the most essential part of poetic greatness. We may also notice how Homer beautifies the myths he deals with by touches drawn from life, Hector's leave-taking, Bellerophon eating his heart out in his old age, the devotion of the swineherd Eumaeus.

Homer was the object of deep reverence in ancient Greece; his writings came to be regarded as a source of general wisdom and were constantly quoted. Passages were frequently imitated or translated by Latin poets (e.g. Lucretius and Virgil). The 'Odyssey' was translated into Latin saturnians by Livius Andronicus (q.v.), and both 'Iliad' and 'Odyssey' into Latin hexameters in the 1st c. A.D. by a certain Attius Labeo. Polybius (the freedman of

Claudius to whom Seneca addressed a 'Consolatio') turned Homer into Latin prose. See also *Ilias Latina.* Homer was the first important work printed in Greek. The *editio princeps* appeared at Florence in 1488, prepared by Chalcondylas of Athens, an immigrant scholar who taught Greek in Italy. Among great modern Homeric scholars must be mentioned the German Friedrich Wolf (1759–1824), a professor at Halle and one of the founders of classical philology. In his 'Prolegomena in Homerum' (1795) he advanced the theory that the 'Iliad' and the 'Odyssey' as we have them were not the work of a single author, but the blending of a number of poems, handed down by oral recitation, and unified by subsequent treatment. Famous English verse-translations of Homer were written by George Chapman (1559 ?–1634 ?) and Alexander Pope (1688–1744). It was the former of these which evoked Keats's sonnet beginning, 'Much have I travell'd in the realms of gold'. Pope's 'Odyssey' contains a famous line, 'Welcome the coming, speed the parting guest' (xv. 74). There are excellent modern prose translations of the 'Iliad' by Lang, Leaf, and Myers, and of the 'Odyssey' by Butcher and Lang. There is also a well-known prose translation of the 'Odyssey' by T. E. Lawrence. For medieval legend connected with the 'Iliad', see *Trojan War.*

Homeric Age. The political, social, and economic conditions of a Greek State as depicted in the Homeric poems are briefly as follows. The government is aristocratic, the power resting with certain families that claim descent from a god or demigod. They are presided over by a king, a member of one of them, who leads the people in war. He is liable to be ousted by some one stronger or more successful than himself. The general population includes landowners, tenants of land or serfs, artisans, labourers working for hire, and slaves, a social system arising perhaps from the mingling of conquerors with a subject-people. But the slaves are not numerous, and some of them are recruited by piracy. They form part of the family and their position is generally tolerable. The men tend the cattle or work in the fields, sometimes lending a hand in the house at banquets. The relations between master and slave may be very kindly. The women grind corn or spin and weave. Hired labourers (*thêtes*) are perhaps the least fortunate part of the population. They lack the secure position of the slave and when unemployed revert to the position of beggars. The latter are tolerably treated. Apart from the followers of what may be called the liberal professions (minstrels, diviners, physicians, heralds), Homeric society includes four kinds of artisans, specialists in their trades, viz.: wood-workers, metal-workers, leather-workers, and potters. The population is supported by agriculture and stock-raising; the culture of the vine and olive is beginning (note the description of the gardens of Alcinoüs in Od. vii). There is navigation, but piracy rather than commerce. The ox is the standard of value (the talent of gold is known but is not in current use): a tripod may be worth twelve oxen, a set of armour nine or a hundred, a slave from four to twenty. There is some trade with Phoenicia, Egypt, Cyprus, Lydia, Caria. The precious metals are in use, but the finest pieces of gold and silver work are imported. Silver probably comes from Spain. In peace-time every one works, from the king downwards, Laertes in his garden, Penelope, Helen, and Andromache weaving or embroidering, Nausicaa sometimes washing clothes; Odysseus is skilled at reaping and ploughing, can make furniture or a ship, and has built his own house. There is much feasting, and guests are entertained with the song of minstrels; there are also dances and athletic contests. As to warfare, the gentry fight from chariots, or dismount from them to engage the enemy; little is heard of the common infantry. Weapons are made of bronze, but iron is known and used for implements of peace; this suggests that the manufacture of iron was at an early stage and that iron weapons were not trustworthy. The position of women is far superior to what we find it in a later age (see *Women*).

Homeric Hymns, the name given to a collection of preludes of the kind sung by minstrels as an introduction to their lays. They were invocations to some god whose feast was being celebrated, or to the Muses. The shorter hymns recite the god's titles and some of his achievements. The longer ones develop into epic narratives, some of them of great beauty. They are of various dates and relate to different localities. The authors are not known. Of the extant hymns the most notable are the 'Hymn to the Delian Apollo' (attributed to Homer by Thucydides and Aristophanes), the 'Hymn to the Pythian Apollo' (these two are combined as one in the MSS.), and the 'Hymn to Hermes' (q.v., a lively and amusing account of the god's achievements as a baby, translated by Shelley in his 'Hymn to Mercury'), to Aphrodite (her marriage to Anchises), and to Demeter (the legend of Demeter

and Persephone, and the founding of the Eleusinian rites).

Homē′ridae, a name borne in historical times by a clan (γένος) at Chios who claimed to be descendants of Homer and who, as minstrels, preserved the Homeric tradition. Some authorities attribute to them, not only some of the later Homeric poems, but also the 'Iliad' and the 'Odyssey' in their form of single continuous poems.

Ho′plites (*Hoplitai*), see *Army*, § 1.

Horace (*Quintus Horātius Flaccus*) (65–8 B.C.), was the son of a freedman of Venusia on the Aufidus in S. Italy, a Latin colony which had joined the rebellion of 90 B.C. and had then been granted the citizenship. It has been conjectured that the name Horatius was taken by his father from the Horatian tribe, in which Venusia was included. He was five years younger than Virgil. His father was a *coactor exactiōnum*, a collector of payments at auctions, and had acquired a small estate. He gave his son the best education obtainable, first at Rome under Orbilius (q.v.), and later at Athens. The Civil War broke out while Horace was in Greece; he received a commission as tribune in the army of M. Brutus and fought (and, he says, ran away) at Philippi (42 B.C.). Thereafter he returned to Italy and made his submission. He obtained a clerical post in the civil service (he was one of the *scribae quaestōrii* or quaestor's clerks), but his estate was forfeited and poverty drove him to write verses. About 38 B.C. he was introduced by Virgil and Varius Rufus (q.v.) to Maecenas (q.v.), who after some delay took him under his protection, admitted him to the circle of Augustan poets, and about 33 B.C. gave him the Sabine Farm (near Tibur, in the valley of the Digentia, now the Licenza) which was to be the source of much happiness to Horace and the inspiration of some beautiful passages in his writings. About 35 B.C. he had issued the first Book of his Satires (q.v.). It was followed about 30 B.C., after Actium, by the second Book of the Satires and the Epodes (which include some of his earliest poems; see under *Odes*). The first three Books of the Odes, composed gradually in the course of some ten years and reflecting the political events of 33–23 B.C., were published in 23; the first Book of the Epistles (q.v.) about 20. The 'Carmen Saeculare' (q.v.) appeared in 17, Book IV of the Odes about 15 B.C. There remain three literary essays, two of which form Book II of the 'Epistles', while the third is known as the 'Epistle to the Pisos' or more usually as the 'Ars

Poetica'. These are generally assigned to the last years of the poet's life; but the question of their date is undecided. The second epistle of Book II and the 'Ars Poetica' are placed by some authorities as early as 19 B.C. Horace died in 8 B.C., a few months after Maecenas, with whom he had maintained a friendship of thirty years. He was never married. We have a life of Horace by Suetonius, who describes him as short and stout. Horace speaks of himself as prematurely grey.

Horace's position as one of the greatest of Roman poets rests on the perfection of his form, the sincerity and frankness of his self-portraiture, his patriotism, his urbanity, humour, and good sense. His poems give a vivid picture of the Roman society, high and low, of his day. He has endowed literature with a multitude of happy phrases. If surpassed by Catullus in passion and force and by Lucretius in grandeur, he in turn surpasses both in the breadth of his interests, and Catullus in moral dignity. Quintilian calls him 'felicissime audax', and Petronius refers to his 'curiosa felicitas' or 'studied felicity'.

Horace has been so universally read and admired that his influence on English poetry, both lyrical and satirical, is almost all-pervading. Of direct imitations the most famous and successful are Pope's adaptations of certain of the Satires and Epistles (1733–38). Milton translated his Ode to Pyrrha (I. v). Horace was the first Latin author that Bentley edited (1711), introducing in the text a large number of emendations. The famous edition of Horace by Orelli (q.v.) appeared in 1837–8.

Hō′rae, see *Seasons.*

Horā′tii and Curiā′tii. According to Roman legend, the struggle between Rome and Alba in the reign of Tullus Hostilius (see *Rome,* § 2) was decided by the single combats of three Roman brothers, the Horatii, with three Latin brothers, the Curiatii. The latter were defeated and killed. But the victory was given a tragic turn when one of the Horatii slew his own sister for mourning her dead lover, one of the Curiatii. He was condemned to death, but was spared on appeal to the people.

Horse, THE TROJAN, see *Trojan Horse.*

Horsemanship (Peri hippikēs, L. *De Rĕ Equestri),* a treatise by **Xenophon** (q.v.).

The author, himself a keen and experienced horseman, gives advice to his younger friends on the management of horses, under the following heads: (a) buying a colt, the points, beginning with the feet and working upwards; (b) breaking a colt; (c) buying a horse that has already been ridden, age, mouth, behaviour, &c., of the animal; (d) stable and yard; (e) duties of a groom; (f) instructions to the rider, mounting, seat, exercises, jumping, dismounting; (g) treatment of a spirited horse; (h) bits; (i) horses for parade; (j) armour for man and horse and arms for the rider. See also *Horses.*

Horses.

§ 1. *In Greece*

The horse was much esteemed in Homeric times, and the breeding of horses was practised with care and was a source of wealth. Erichthonius of Dardania, 'the wealthiest of mortals', was a horse-breeder. Andromache herself carries corn and wine to the horses of Hector. Horses were bred in many parts of Greece, notably Thessaly, Boeotia, Euboea, and Ionia. Pausanias remarks that after the Persian War the Spartans were more keenly interested in horse-breeding than all the other Greeks, as appeared from statues of victors in the horse races at Olympia (vi. 2, 1). (Among these was the statue of Cynisca, sister of Agesilaus, king of Sparta, who claimed to be the only woman who had ever won the chariot race.) Riding was a favourite occupation of rich Athenians. Horses were kept at Athens, not only for amusement, but also for the cavalry, for travelling, and for racing. The second class of citizens was known as *Hippeis* ('Knights'), because they were sufficiently wealthy to keep a horse. Horses were not shod, and were ridden bare-backed, or on a cloth, but without saddle or stirrups. According to the author of the treatise on 'Horsemanship' (q.v.) there were two kinds of bit, one mild and one severe. The British Museum has a bit from Achaea, perhaps of the 5th or 4th c. B.C., evidently of the latter class. The author of the treatise on 'Horsemanship' (q.v.) describes the method of mounting, both hands grasping the mane; he also refers to mounting with the help of a spear, and to horses taught to stoop for the purpose. He further describes the proper seat when jumping, &c. The riding of horses in the procession of the Panathenaea may be seen depicted on the frieze of the Parthenon at the British Museum. There were both chariot races and races for ridden horses at the Panhellenic Games (see *Festivals,* § 2, and *Chariot Races*). The Greeks were fond of visiting neighbouring cities: men travelled usually on foot or on horseback; women were drawn in carriages.

In Greek mythology Poseidon was the god especially associated with horses, which he was thought to have created (*Hippios* was one of his titles). Among famous mythological horses were Pegasus, Arion (qq.v.), the horses of Diomedes (see *Heracles, Labours of*), and Xanthus and Balius the immortal horses of Achilles; and among historical horses, Bucephalus the horse of Alexander the Great.

§ 2. *At Rome*

Besides a good breed from Apūlia, the Romans employed horses from many parts of the empire, Asia, Africa, and especially Spain; they were much used for chariot races, and a famous winner might have a monument erected to him. Ponies or cobs from Gaul were used for lighter work. In general one derives the impression that, apart from the races, the Romans took less interest in horses than the Greeks. But the points of the horse are described by Virgil (Georg. iii. 72 et seq.), and there is a good deal about them in Varro (De Re Rust. ii. 7) and in Columella (vi. 29). Among horses specially named in Roman literature may be mentioned: Rhaebus, the horse of Mezentius, whom his master addresses (Aen. x. 860) and whom Aeneas kills; Aethōn, the horse of Pallas, who weeps for his master's death (Aen. xi. 89–90); the horse of Sejus (q.v.); and Incitātus, the favourite horse of Caligula, whom he proposed to make consul.

The Romans rode on a saddle, but without stirrups; they used plain prick-spurs. Horse-shoes are occasionally mentioned, but do not appear to have been in general use. Nero had his mules shod with silver.

Horte′nsia, daughter of Q. Hortensius Hortalus (q.v.), famous as having made in 42 B.C., contrary to custom, a speech in the Forum against a proposal of the Triumvirs to impose special taxation on the property of wealthy women. Her plea was successful.

Horte′nsius, the title of a lost dialogue by Cicero, composed in 45 B.C., an introduction to, and an exhortation to the study of, philosophy, which he defended against Roman prejudices. It was based on the 'Protrepticus' of Aristotle, and St. Augustine attributes to it his own conversion (Confess. iii. 4. 7).

Horte′nsius Ho′rtalus, QUINTUS (114–50 B.C.), generally known as 'Hortensius', consul in 69 B.C., an older contemporary of Cicero and his chief rival in the law-courts. He first pleaded in 95 B.C., on behalf of the province of Africa, which was accusing a Roman governor of malversation. He was eclipsed by Cicero as the leading orator of the day after Cicero's success in the trial of Verres, an eclipse which did not affect the friendly relations of the two. Cicero paid a tribute to the genius of Hortensius after his death in the 'Brutus'; he had also praised him in the 'De Oratore' (qq.v.). Hortensius was remarkable for his voice, gesture, memory, and wealth of language; his oratory was of the Asian flamboyant style.

Hō′rus (*Hōros*), see *Osiris* and *Harpocrates*.

Houses and Furniture. The ancient house, whether Greek or Roman, differed from the modern house in one fundamental respect, that whereas the modern house has doors and windows looking outward, the ancient house looked inward, being built round a courtyard or receiving light and air from an opening in the roof.

§ 1. *Greek houses*

(*a*) The Homeric house consisted of a large room (*megaron*), which served as reception-room, dining-room, and kitchen, with a hearth in the centre (there was no chimney and the smoke escaped with difficulty); of an inner room (*thalamos*) occupied by the women and used also as a store for precious possessions; and sometimes of an upper chamber. The *megaron* opened on an antechamber (*prodromos*) and thence on a courtyard (*aulē*), surrounded by store-rooms and stables, and partly occupied by a manure-heap.

(*b*) The town-house of the 5th and 4th cc. (see Pl. 1) was a modification of the Homeric house. A typical house of a well-to-do Athenian had a porch (*prothuron*) on the street, from which, when the door was opened, one passed into the courtyard (*aulē*). This had a portico at each end, and rooms serving various purposes (kitchen, store-rooms, and rooms for young men and guests) on either side. An altar to Zeus Herkeios stood in the centre. Beyond the inner portico was the main building, containing the reception-room (*andrōn*) with the hearth and the women's quarters beyond or above it. There was some decoration of walls with paintings and tapestry, but little comfort; no heating apparatus (such as the Romans used) beyond a charcoal brazier; no drainage; the floors were of beaten earth, and the furniture simple and austere. We gather from the sale-list of Alcibiades' furniture (see *Epigraphy*, § 5) and from Xenophon's 'Oeconomicus' that it consisted of little beyond chests, beds, couches, tables, earthenware vessels, implements for sacrifice, and cooking and table utensils (Alcibiades had couches of Milesian workmanship).

§ 2. *Roman houses*

The primitive Roman house consisted of a quadrangular chamber known as the *ātrium*, with an opening in the tiled roof which admitted light and rain (the latter flowing into a tank in the ground known as the *impluvium*) and allowed the exit of smoke from the hearth. This primitive dwelling was gradually developed by the addition of side rooms, but the back of the *atrium* was left clear, and in aristocratic houses was decorated with portrait-masks (*imāginēs*) of ancestors. The *atrium* was the living and reception-room, and here sat the mistress of the house with her maids. At the end opposite the entrance was the marriage bed (*lectus geniālis*) of the master and mistress.

In later days, under Greek influence, a garden (*peristȳlium*) with colonnades was added at the back of the *atrium*; this was surrounded with side-buildings, containing dining-rooms, sleeping apartments, living-rooms, kitchen and store-rooms. The *atrium* now served only as the official reception-room. See Pl. 1; see also *Triclinium*.

Upper stories were added to the Roman houses before the end of the republican period. The mass of the population then lived in large lodging-houses called *insulae* (islands) three or four or more stories high (Trajan later limited the height of houses in Rome to 63 ft.), let in single rooms to lodgers. These provided no 'home', in the sense of a centre of domestic religion. Owned by capitalists and speculators such as Crassus (q.v.; Cicero had a share in one), they often collapsed or were destroyed by fire. But there may have been some of a better class, for M. Caelius Rufus had apartments (*aedicula*) in an *insula*.

The houses of the wealthy in imperial times contained statues, vases, imported furniture (such as cedar-wood tables), and carpets from the East. The walls were decorated with marbles or frescoes, and the floors with mosaics. There were skilful arrangements for warming the rooms from a central furnace, and elaborate bath-rooms (Seneca (Ep. Mor. 86) contrasts with these the simpler bathroom of the house of Scipio Africanus). Houses had an abundant supply of water, sometimes even in the upper stories. There are many descriptions (e.g. in Pliny's letters) of the spacious country-houses (see under *Villa*) of the rich Romans of imperial times, by the sea, or on the spurs of the Apennines, designed especially to suit the changing seasons or to command beautiful views. Glass (q.v.) was in use, and windows might be glazed. At first Roman houses were lit at night with torches and candles. Work was in general done in the early hours of the day, and the Romans probably retired early to bed. With the introduction of the olive, oil lamps began to be substituted, and

were common in the 1st c. B.C. They were of clay or bronze, sometimes elegantly decorated, holding one or more wicks, and sometimes adapted for hanging from the ceiling. Or they might be placed on candelabra, of which the surviving specimens are chiefly of bronze; but the candelabra might be made of wood, as we know from Martial's epigram (xiv. 44):

Esse vides lignum; sérves nisi lumina fiet
De candelabro magna lucerna tibi.

The streets, it may be noted, also appear to have been lit in certain cities (an electoral poster at Pompeii, for instance, has the addition 'lanternari, tene scalam').

Hunting. For the treatise on this subject attributed to Xenophon, see *Cynegeticus*, a work which sufficiently shows how developed this form of sport was among the Greeks. There are, moreover, dedications and epigrams which indicate the large part played by hunting in their life. See also *Arrian*.

The Romans appear not to have been greatly addicted to it. Republican Rome probably despised hunting (Sallust refers to it as 'servile officium'). Scipio Aemilianus (q.v.) was trained in hunting by Polybius. This was one of the many examples of his fondness for Greek customs. Trajan and Hadrian were keen hunters, but they were Spaniards. The younger Pliny hunted, but he took his writing materials with him when he did so. The frequency of hunting incidents in the elegiac poets and Virgil is due to Greek sources or Greek influence. The Roman writers on hunting, Grattius and Nemesianus (qq.v.), are largely influenced by the poetical tradition, and give no true picture of Roman conditions.

Hyacin'thus (*Huakinthos*), in Greek mythology, a beautiful youth of Amyclae near Sparta, who was loved both by Apollo and Zephyrus (qq.v.). Hyacinthus returned Apollo's love, and Zephyrus, from jealousy, blew a quoit thrown by Apollo, as he played with his favourite, so that it struck and killed Hyacinthus. From his blood sprang a flower marked with the letters *AI*, meaning 'alas', 'that sanguine flower inscribed with woe' referred to by Milton. The hyacinth, as we know it, does not answer to this description; but the flower in question may be a small purple iris with markings capable of being taken for these letters.

Hy'ades (*Huades*, the 'raining ones'), in Greek mythology daughters of Atlas (q.v.). They were the nymphs who supplied moisture to the earth, and were said by later legend to have nursed the infant

Dionysus. They were placed by Zeus as stars in the sky and their rising at the same time as the sun was thought to portend rainy weather.

Hy'dra (*Hudrā*), see *Heracles* (*Labours of*).

Hygie'a (*Hugieia*), the Greek goddess of health, daughter of Asclepius (q.v.).

Hygi'nus, GĀIUS JŪLIUS (*c.* 64 B.C.–A.D. 17), a Spanish freedman of Augustus, and a friend of Ovid. He was one of the greatest scholars of his time, and was appointed by Augustus head of his newly founded library. He wrote on the *Urbēs Ītaliae* (a work quoted by Servius but otherwise lost) and on various other subjects; also an important commentary on Virgil, parts of which are preserved by later writers. Under his name we possess only two works, 'Fābulae' (a collection of myths) and a 'De Astronomia' (also in part mythological); but it is very doubtful whether they are in fact by Hyginus. In later times certain writers on land-surveying and the laying out of camps (such writers were known as *gromatici*, q.v.) bore the name Hyginus. According to the Index to the 'Thesaurus Linguae Latinae' these were:

1. Hyginus Gromaticus, in the time of Trajan.
2. Hyginus Gromaticus, in the 2nd c. A.D., probably younger than (1).
3. Hyginus (author of 'De Munitionibus Castrorum'), in the 3rd c.

Hy'las (*Hūlās*), in Greek mythology, a favourite page of Heracles and his companion on the expedition of the Argonauts (q.v.). When the ship touched at Cios on the coast of Mȳsia (Heracles having broken his oar), Hylas was sent for water. But the water-nymphs, enamoured of his beauty, drew him into the spring and he was lost. The Argonauts went on their way, but Heracles remained seeking him, and the Mysians continued to sacrifice to Hylas annually at the spring, in obedience to the orders of Heracles.

Hy'llus (*Hullos*), see *Heracles* and *Heracleidae*.

Hyme'ttus (*Humēttos*), a mountain overlooking Athens on the E., famous for its honey and its marble. The honey is mentioned by Strabo and Pausanias; the marble is of a bluish-grey colour. The beautiful purple glow sometimes to be seen towards sunset on Hymettus is perhaps the origin of the epithet 'violet-crowned' applied to Athens by Pindar and Aristophanes. It was when the glow appeared on Hymettus that Socrates drank the hemlock.

Hypā'tia (*Hūpátiā*), see *Neoplatonism*.

Hyper'baton, a rhetorical figure, the violent transposition of words from their natural order for purposes of emphasis, e.g.

'Per ego has lacrimas dextramque tuam te ... Oro.'

(Virg. Aen. iv. 314.)

Hyper'bolē (*Huperbolē*, 'throwing beyond', 'exaggeration'), a figure of speech consisting in an exaggerated or extravagant statement, used to express strong feeling or to produce a strong impression, and not intended to be understood literally; e.g. 'Nisus emicat, et ventis et fulminis ocior alis' (Aen. v. 318).

Hyperbo'reans (*Huperbore(i)oi*), 'dwellers beyond Boreas (the north wind)', a legendary people, supposed by the Greeks to have their abode in the distant north, where the sun rose and set only once a year, and where they lived in peace and happiness. They were said to be especially worshippers of Apollo.

Hyperi'dēs (*Hupereidēs*) (b. 389 B.C.), a distinguished Attic orator, was a pupil of Isocrates (q.v.), but resembled Lysias in the simplicity, suavity, and persuasiveness of his oratory. His character as an epicure and gamester was the subject of contemporary jests recorded by Athenaeus. He began his career as a writer of forensic speeches, but soon mingled in politics and appeared as an accuser of men of eminence. He supported Demosthenes in act and speech in the struggle against Philip of Macedon, but later, at the time of the affair of Harpalus (see *Demosthenes* (2), § 1), Hyperides appeared as the prosecutor of Demosthenes. He was one of the principal promoters of the war of revolt against Macedonia in 323 (see *Athens*, § 7), and after the defeat of Athens was put to death by Antipater. Of the six more or less fragmentary speeches of his that survive, the best-known is the Funeral Oration over Leōsthenēs and the others who fell in the Lamian War. His speech in a private suit against Athēnogenēs (a speech praised in the treatise 'Longinus on the Sublime', q.v.) is a model of urbanity. Among his lost speeches was one in defence of the famous courtesan Phrȳnē, on a charge of impiety. In this speech he appealed to the sentiment of the jury by throwing open her dress and showing the beauty of her bosom.

Hype'rion (*Hūperiōn*), in Greek mythology, one of the Titans (q.v.), the father of the Sun, or the Sun itself. See *Helios*.

Keats wrote in 1818–19 two versions of a fragment of a poem on Hyperion. It deals with the passing of the reign of Saturn, and the fate of Hyperion, the last of the Titans, who is dethroned by Apollo.

Hyperm(n)e'stra (*Huperm(n)ēstrā*), see *Danaus*.

Hyporchē'ma, a Greek choral lyric (q.v.), originally in honour of Apollo or Artemis, invariably accompanied by a dance (the word means 'a dance to music'), differing in this respect and in its less solemn character from the *paean* (q.v.). Like the *paean* it is said to have originated in Crete, where the Curetes (q.v.), according to myth, danced it before the infant Zeus.

Hypsi'pylē (*Hupsipulē*), in Greek mythology, daughter of Thoäs, son of Dionysus and legendary king of Lemnos. The women of Lemnos, from jealousy, decided to kill all the men of the island; but Hypsipyle saved her father and aided his escape. When the Argonauts (q.v.) came to Lemnos, they spent a year there and married the women, and Hypsipyle bore twin sons to Jason, Euneös and Thoas. But Hypsipyle was driven away from Lemnos when it was discovered that she had spared her father, was captured by pirates, and sold to Lycurgus, king of Nemea. When the Seven were marching against Thebes (see *Oedipus*) and their army halted near Nemea, Hypsipyle, who was nurse of the king's infant son Opheltēs, laid the child on the ground in order to lead them to a spring. During her absence the child was killed by a dragon. The Seven gave him a splendid funeral and founded the Nemean games in his honour. Hypsipyle was saved from the anger of Lycurgus by the army and finally rescued by her sons who arrived and recognized her.

A tragedy by Euripides on this subject ('Hypsipyle') was discovered in a fragmentary condition at Oxyrhynchus in 1908. The story is also told in the 'Thebaid' (q.v.) of Statius.

I

Ia'cchos, one of the three deities (the others being Demeter and Persephone, qq.v.) who were celebrated at the Eleusinian Mysteries. He was identified with Dionysus (q.v.), but little is known about him. Herodotus recounts that shortly before the battle of Salamis, a great cloud of dust, 'as if occasioned by about 30,000 men', was seen by certain persons coming from the direction of Eleusis, and a voice apparently of the mystic Iacchos was heard proceeding from it. The cloud was borne towards the Greek encampment and was held to portend disaster to the Persians.

I'amb (*Iambos*, L. *Iambus*), **Ia'mbic**, see *Metre*, §§ 1, 2, 4, and 5.

Ia'mbē, see *Iambic Poetry*.

Ia'mbic Poetry, the type of poetry in which the iambic metre (see *Metre*, § 2) prevailed. It appears to have been associated originally with the cult of Demeter (q.v.) and to have had a satirical or mocking character. It was said that when Demeter, mourning the loss of Persephone, entered the house of Celĕus at Eleusis, she was first made to smile by the maiden Iambē's jests. In its early form it was especially developed by Archilochus (q.v.). As being nearest to ordinary speech, the iambic verse came later to be used as the medium of dramatic dialogue.

Ia'mblichus (*Iamblichos*) (d. c. A.D. 330), a Syrian and a mystic, a pupil (in the school of Neoplatonism, q.v.) of Porphyry (q.v.). He was author of a work on the Pythagorean philosophy, part of which survives. There was also a Greek novelist of the name in the 2nd c. A.D.

Ia'petus (*Iapetos*), in Greek mythology, one of the Titans (q.v.), father of Atlas, Prometheus, and Epimetheus (qq.v.).

Ia'sion (*Iasiōn*), see *Plutus*.

Ibē'ria (or **Hibē'ria**), see *Spain*.

I'bis, a poem in elegiacs, an invective against some imaginary personal enemy, attributed to Ovid (but the authorship has been questioned).

I'bycus (*Ibukos*), a native of the Aeolio-Dorian colony of Rhēgium in Magna Graecia, of the latter part of the 6th c. B.C., a lyrical poet who spent part of his life at the court of Polycrates of Samos (q.v.). He wrote choral lyrics which were much praised, but of which little survives. A papyrus recently discovered contains a large part of a poem which is probably the work of Ibycus, addressed to Polycrates, showing the choral lyric (q.v.) in a fairly advanced form.

AVENGERS OF IBYCUS: according to legend Ibycus was attacked and killed by robbers. A flock of cranes was passing overhead and Ibycus exclaimed 'Those cranes will avenge me'. One of the robbers later in a town, seeing a flock of cranes, said to his companion, 'There go the avengers of Ibycus'. This was overheard and the murderers were brought to justice. The story is the subject of a poem by Schiller.

Ica'rius (*Ikarios*), (1) a legendary inhabitant of Attica, who entertained Dionysus kindly, and received from the god the gift of wine. Of this he gave to the country-people, who, becoming intoxicated, killed Icarius. His daughter Ērigonē, with the faithful dog Maera, sought him, and when she found his body hanged herself from grief. Maera is one of various legendary dogs associated with the Dog-star. (2) Of Sparta, father of Penelope (q.v.).

I'caromeni'ppus (*Ikaromenippos*), see *Lucian*.

I'carus (*Ikaros*), see *Daedalus*.

I'celus (*Ikelos*), see *Dreams*.

Ichneu'tae, see *Sophocles*.

Ictīnus (*Iktinos*), see *Temples*, § 1, and *Parthenon*.

I'da (*Idē*), (1) a range of mountains in southern Phrygia, the southern boundary of the Troad. It was there that Paris (q.v.) was said to have been exposed and brought up by shepherds and to have fallen in love with Oenone (it is the 'Mother Ida, many-fountained Ida' of Tennyson's poem 'Œnone'). From its summit Zeus watched the Trojan War. (2) A mountain in the centre of Crete. In a cave on this mountain (or on Mt. Dictē) Zeus (q.v.) is said to have been born.

I'das (*Idās*), see *Lynceus* and *Marpessa*.

Ido'menēus, in Greek mythology, grandson of Minos (q.v.), and leader of the Cretans at the siege of Troy. In a storm on his way home he vowed to sacrifice the first thing that met him, if he returned safe. This proved to be his son. He fulfilled, or tried to fulfil, his vow, and in consequence a plague broke out, and Idomeneus was driven into exile by the Cretans.

I'dyll, from the Gk. *eidullion*, 'a little picture', a short poem descriptive of a scene, generally of a pastoral character. See *Theocritus*.

Ileithyi'a, see *Eileithyia*.

I'lia or RHEA SILVIA, according to Roman legend, the daughter of Numitor, a Vestal Virgin who became by Mars mother of Romulus and Remus (see *Rome*, § 2), and was thrown into the Tiber by order of her uncle Amūlius. The river-god took her to wife (Hor. Od. i. 2. 17–20).

I'liad (*Ilias*), *The*, an epic poem by Homer, in twenty-four books. This division is said to have been made by Aristarchus (q.v.) in the 2nd c. B.C.; it may have originated in the distribution of the manuscript over twenty-four papyrus-rolls (see *Books, Ancient*). The title is derived from Īlion, another name of Troy, which was so called from Ilus, its legendary founder (see *Troy*). The subject is the Wrath of Achilles

(q.v.), arising from an indignity put upon him by Agamemnon (q.v.), leader of the Greek host at the siege of Troy (see *Trojan War*), and the tragic consequences of his wrath. This is an episode in the story of the siege, a short part of which, in its tenth year, forms the more general subject of the work. The gods in Olympus are divided in their sympathies and intervene on one side or the other, and even fight among themselves. A plague has broken out in the Greek camp, and the seer Calchas declares that it can be stayed only by the surrender of Agamemnon's prize, the maiden Chrȳsēis, to her father, a priest of Apollo. Agamemnon reluctantly consents to the surrender, but takes in her place Brisēis, a slave-girl belonging to Achilles. The latter, incensed at this high-handed act, retires to his tents with his Myrmidons (q.v.) and his friend Patroclus, and refuses to take further part in the fighting. The Greek army, deprived of his powerful support, suffers grievously and is driven to its camp (Bks. i–viii). Recognizing under stress of adversity the wrong that he has done, Agamemnon sends an embassy to Achilles offering to make handsome amends if he will cease from his wrath. But Achilles has been nursing his grievance, is now disgusted with thankless war, rejects Agamemnon's offers, and announces that he will sail home on the morrow (Bk. ix). Nevertheless he stays on to see the Achaeans further abased. His friend Patroclus is stung to shame and regret by their reverses, and obtains Achilles' permission, when the Trojans are actually setting fire to the Greek ships, to join, together with the Myrmidons, in the fight. Moreover, Achilles lends his armour to Patroclus. The Trojans are driven back, but Patroclus is killed by Hector (q.v.), and retribution thus comes on Achilles for his selfish wrath (Bk. xvi). Achilles, maddened with grief, is reconciled with Agamemnon and goes out to fight, in new armour forged by Hephaestus (q.v.), to revenge on Hector the death of his friend. He kills Hector and, forgetting his chivalry, treats the dead body with gross outrage (Bk. xxii). Priam (q.v.), the aged king of Troy, comes to Achilles to beg the body of his son and save it from the threatened fate of being thrown to the dogs. Achilles' passion has now spent itself: he feels pity for the old man and returns the body (Bk. xxiv).

Side by side with this tragedy we have a picture of the life in Troy, under the shadow of its impending calamity: Priam and Hecuba (q.v.) bereaved of many of their sons and finally mourning their dearest, Hector; Hector talking with his

Iliad 221 *Index Rerum a se Gestarum*

wife Andromache (q.v.) and playing with his little son; Helen (q.v.), a pathetic figure, conscious of her guilt and the trouble she has brought on Troy, and weary of Paris (q.v.), whom she despises.

A host of other warriors and statesmen are presented, some of them sharply characterized (see *Æneas, Ajax, Diomedes, Menelaus, Odysseus, Nestor, Sarpedon, Glaucus*), while the poem throws much light on the manners, religion, and art of the age that Homer is depicting.

Notable passages in the course of the work are the following: the Catalogue of Greek Ships, ii. 484–785; the Catalogue of Trojan forces, ii. 786–877; the τειχοσκοπία (Helen and Priam viewing the Achaean chiefs from the walls of Troy), and the duel of Menelaus and Paris, Bk. iii; the ἐπιπώλησις (Agamemnon's review of his forces), iv. 223–421; the exploits of Diomēdēs, iv. 422 et seq. and Bk. v; the meeting and recognition of Diomedes and Glaucus, vi. 119–236; Hector's farewell to Andromache, vi. 370–529; the Δολώνεια (night expedition of Odysseus and Diomedes, the slaying of the spy Dolōn and of the Thracian Rhesus, q.v., and the capture of the latter's horses), Bk. x; the Διὸς ἀπάτη (beguilement of Zeus by Hera), xiv. 153–362; the forging of the arms of Achilles, xviii. 468–617; the fight of Achilles with the River, xxi. 211–382; the Funeral Games for Patroclus, xxiii. 257–897. The principal events, from the beginning of the fighting to the death of Hector, occupy four days.

For English translations, see under *Homer*. For medieval legend connected with the story of Troy, see *Trojan War*.

Iliad, Little, the title of a lost poem of the Epic Cycle (q.v.), of unknown authorship, a sequel to Homer's 'Iliad'.

Īlias Latīna, a paraphrase in some 1,000 Latin hexameters, by an unknown author, of Homer's 'Iliad'. The initial letters of the first and last eight lines appear intended to read 'Italicus scripsit'.

Īli'ssus (*Īlissos*), a stream which has its source in springs on Mt. Hymettus and descends through the stony plain of Attica past Athens on the SE. and S. In the neighbourhood of the city the river-bed is generally dry. There are some pleasant lines in Ovid (Ars Am. iii. 687–94) describing the source.

Ī'lium (*Īlion*), see *Troy*.

Ī'liŭpe'rsis (*Īliou persis*, 'Sack of Troy'), (1) a poem of the Epic Cycle (q.v.), ascribed to Arctīnus of Miletus, a sequel to the 'Iliad'; (2) see *Stesichorus*.

Īlus (*Īlos*), see *Troy*.

Īlȳthī'a, see *Eileithyia*.

Imā'ginēs, wax masks moulded in resemblance of distinguished Romans and set up, with honorific inscriptions, round the hall (*ātrium*) of the families to which they belonged. These masks of ancestors were worn at funerals of their descendants by persons clad in robes such as the ancestors would have worn, e.g. the robes of a consul.

Imagines, a dialogue by Lucian (q.v.).

Ima'ginum Librī XV, see *Varro (M. T.)*.

Imperā'tōr, originally a military title given by acclamation of the troops to their general after a victory. The usual practice under the republic was for the title to be given to a general between this acclamation and the triumph which normally followed it, and this seems to have been followed in the case of Julius Caesar; the statements of Suetonius and Dio that the title was given Caesar as a *praenomen* in 45 are full of difficulty. Octavian, probably in 40 B.C., was the first to avail himself of the *praenomen imperatoris*, being known at this date as 'Imperator Caesar divi filius'. In this practice he was not followed by some of the early emperors, e.g. by Tiberius and Claudius. In the reign of Vespasian, Vespasian himself had the *praenomen imperatoris*, whilst Titus, his son and associate in the government, enjoyed the title as a *cognomen* (see *Names*).

Impe'rium, in the Roman constitution, the 'power to command', possessed by a dictator, consul, praetor, and *magister equitum*; the magistrates, in fact, who might command an army. It was in theory unrestricted outside the *pomoerium* or consecrated boundary of the city of Rome, but restricted in various ways within it. A magistrate possessing pro-consular imperium forfeited it on entering the city. Thus generals awaiting triumphs were compelled to remain outside Rome, and because of this meetings of the Senate were sometimes held outside the walls (e.g. in 61 B.C. after Pompey's return from the East).

Imports and Exports, see *Athens*, § 10, and *Rome*, § 13.

In Pīsō'nem, see *Cicero*, § 4 (under the year 55).

In Vatī'nium, see *Cicero*, § 4 (under the year 56).

I'nachus (*Īnachos*), see *Io*.

Īna'rimē, see *Typhon*.

Index Rērum a se Gestarum, an epitomized account of the deeds of Augustus, by the emperor himself, inscribed on bronze in his mausoleum. Copies were placed in various temples of the empire, and one of these survives, in imperfect form, on the temple of Rome and Augustus at Ancyra (Angora), besides fragments of others; see *Monumentum Ancyranum.*

Indictions, see *Calendar,* § 3.

Indigitāme'nta, in Roman religion, a list, taken from the books of the pontifices (q.v.), of the *numina* (see *Numen*) or deities to be invoked on special occasions of human life, and of the forms of prayer to be addressed to them.

I'nō, in Greek mythology, a daughter of Cadmus (q.v.) and Harmonia, and wife of Athamas (q.v.). See also *Dionysus* for her death and transformation into a sea-goddess. It was she who saved Odysseus (see *Odyssey,* Bk. V) when his raft was wrecked, giving him her scarf to buoy him up.

Inscriptions, see *Epigraphy.*

Institutes, see *Gaius* and *Justinian.*

Institū'tiō Ōrātō'ria ('The Education of an Orator'), a treatise in twelve books by Quintilian (q.v.).

Book I deals with early education of the future orator; the influence of nurses, parents, slaves; the superiority of school education over education at home; the importance of a thorough study of language as a foundation; the need of Greek and various other subjects; the commercial value of the matters taught is not to be considered. The book, by reason of the breadth and wisdom of the author's views, contains much of permanent value.

Book II is on the general method and object of training in rhetoric, on the qualifications of a good teacher and the proper treatment of pupils, on the need in an orator for moral character as well as wide knowledge.

Books III–VII pass on to technicalities, the three kinds of oratory (judicial, deliberative, laudatory), the parts of a speech (exordium, narrative, &c.), the arrangement of matters to be dealt with, all principally in relation to speeches in the courts.

Books VIII–XI deal with style and delivery. Of these Book X contains the famous discussion of authors, Greek and Latin, to be studied, with Quintilian's judgements on them. Of the Greeks he places Homer first, for his sublimity, propriety, and other qualities. Pindar is by far the greatest of the lyric poets; Aristophanes, Eupolis, and Cratinus the greatest of the old, and Menander of the new comic writers. Sophocles and Euripides are the most perfect of the tragedians, for Aeschylus,

in spite of loftiness and dignity, is often uncouth. In history he sets far above the others Thucydides ('densus et brevis et semper instans sibi') and Herodotus ('dulcis et candidus et fusus'). He discusses Demosthenes and his lesser rivals. He praises Plato's acuteness and divine and Homeric gift of style, Xenophon's unaffected style, and Aristotle's knowledge and penetration. Of the Romans he places Virgil first, as most nearly approaching Homer. The style of Lucretius he thinks difficult. Ennius he compares to those ancient sacred groves whose mighty trunks inspire awe rather than admiration. Ovid is too much an admirer of his own genius. Satire is 'all our own'; he places Horace as a satirist before Lucilius, and mentions Persius favourably. Horace is also the only lyric poet worth reading (he mentions Catullus only for his bitterness). He thinks, the (lost) 'Thyestes' of Varius the equal of any Greek tragedy, and commends the (lost) 'Medea' of Ovid, but makes no other high claim for Roman tragedy. Comedy is Rome's weakest point. In history he regards Sallust as equal to Thucydides, Livy to Herodotus. Cicero is a match for any Greek orator; Quintilian compares his style with that of Demosthenes. Caesar might, if he had had the leisure, have equalled him by reason of his vigour, acumen, and elegance of language. Seneca's style is condemned, as spoilt by every kind of error, but his matter is good.

Book XII treats of the moral qualifications and discipline of the finished orator (in the words of Cato 'vir bonus dicendi peritus').

Institūtiō'nēs, see *Gaius* and *Justinian.*

Institūtiō'nēs Dīvī'nae, see *Lactantius.*

Intercessio, at Rome, the veto which an official might impose upon the public acts of a colleague or official of lower rank. Tribunes of the plebs had the right of *intercessio* against any official (except a dictator). This tribunician power was temporarily restricted under Sulla's constitution.

I'nuus, see *Faunus.*

I'ō, in Greek mythology, daughter of Inachus, king of Argos. Zeus fell in love with her, and turned her into a heifer to conceal her from the jealousy of Hera (q.v.). But Hera obtained the heifer from Zeus and set the herdsman Argos, who had eyes all over his body, to guard her. Hermes contrived to kill Argos, whereupon Hera sent a gadfly to persecute Io, and force her to long wanderings, in the course of which she came to Egypt. Here she bore a son Epaphos, and was thereafter worshipped by the Egyptians as Isis. Epaphos was the ancestor of Danaus (q.v.) and Aegyptus.

Io′batēs, see *Bellerophon*.

Ioca′stē, see *Jocasta*.

Iolā′us (*Iolāos*), see *Heracles* and *Heracles (Children of)*.

I′olē (*Iolē*), see *Heracles* and *Trachiniae*.

I′on (*Iōn*), According to Greek legend (as preserved by Euripides, see below), Crĕūsa, daughter of Erechtheus (q.v.), was loved by Apollo and bore him a son, whom for fear of her father's anger she left in a cave. Hermes carried the child to Delphi, where he was reared as a servant of the temple. Creusa afterwards married Xūthus, but as they remained childless they went to Delphi to ask for offspring. At the order of Apollo, Xuthus accepted as his son the first person he met on coming out of the shrine, and this was Ion. Creusa, angered at the adoption of one whom she supposed to be a bastard son of her husband, attempted to kill the boy, but being detected, and in danger of death, took refuge at the altar of Apollo. By the intervention of the priestess, who produced the swaddling clothes in which the infant Ion had been wrapped, Creusa recognized her child, and Athene revealed what had happened. Ion returned to Athens with Xuthus and Creusa, to become, according to Athene's prophecy, the ancestor of the Ionian race.

Ion, a drama by Euripides, of uncertain date. It deals with the story of Ion as set out above. The essential features of the plot—a woman wronged, her child exposed, and the subsequent recognition—became typical of the New Comedy (see *Comedy*, § 4, and *Menander*).

I′on (*Iōn*), a dialogue by Plato (q.v., § 2) called after a rhapsode (q.v.) of that name.

Iō′nia, a portion of the W. coast of Asia Minor, roughly from Smyrna to Miletus, and the adjacent islands, occupied by Ionian Greeks (see *Migrations* and Pl. 8). It was the region in which early Greek literature and philosophy were principally developed. For the legendary origin of the name see *Ion* (first article).

Io′nic Verse, see *Metre*, §§ 3 and 5.

Iphiana′ssa, the name under which Iphigenia (q.v.) figures in Hom. Il. ix. 145.

I′phiclēs (*Iphiklēs*), the half-brother of Heracles (q.v.).

I′phiclus (*Iphiklos*), see *Melampus*.

Iphi′cratēs, see *Army*, § 1.

Iphigeni′a (*Iphigeneia*), in Greek mythology, a daughter of Agamemnon and Clytemnestra (qq.v., and see genealogy under *Pelops*). The Greek fleet, when about to sail to Troy (see *Trojan War*), was weather-bound at Aulis. The seer Calchas declared that Artemis required the sacrifice of Agamemnon's daughter, and Agamemnon sent for Iphigenia on the pretext that she was to be married to Achilles. When she was about to be slain, Artemis took pity on her and carried her off to be her priestess in the land of the Tauri (the Crimea), substituting a deer for her at the altar.

The Tauri had a savage rite by which all strangers coming to their land were sacrificed to Artemis, and Iphigenia was required to consecrate the victims. Orestes, her brother, to expiate his blood-guilt (see *Pelops*), was ordered by Apollo to secure the image of Artemis of the Tauri and bring it to Attica. He had long been separated from Iphigenia, and indeed believed her dead. He and his friend Pylades were captured by the Tauri and ordered to be sacrificed. But Iphigenia recognized her brother, and was persuaded to flee with him from the country, carrying off the image of the goddess.

Iphigenia at Aulis (*Iphigeneia hē en Aulidi*), a tragedy by Euripides, left unfinished at his death, and perhaps completed by his son; produced about 406 B.C. Several passages in it are of doubtful authorship.

The play deals with the legend of the sacrifice of Iphigenia at Aulis (see *Iphigenia*). The poet makes Agamemnon wavering and miserable. After sending for Iphigenia, at the instance of Menelaus, on the pretext of her marriage to Achilles (of which the latter knows nothing), he countermands the summons. But the messenger is stopped by Menelaus. Clytemnestra and Iphigenia arrive. Menelaus repents his cruel device and offers to give up the expedition; in vain, for Agamemnon now dreads the anger of the army. Achilles learns that he has been used as a lure, and boldly decides to defend the innocent girl. But Iphigenia, after pitifully pleading for her life, rises to the height of her role as the saviour of Hellas, and willingly goes to the sacrifice.

The tragedy shows great advance in structure; it is concerned almost exclusively with the interplay of the various characters, and the chorus is reduced nearly to insignificance.

Iphigenia in Tauris (*Iphigeneia hē en Taurois*, i.e. 'among the Tauri'), a drama by Euripides, of unknown date.

The play deals with that part of the legend of Iphigenia (q.v.) which relates to her life in the land of the Tauri as priestess of Artemis. The heroine is represented as a woman who has long brooded over her wrongs, bitter against the Greeks who have sought to murder her, yet longing for home. The coming of Greeks to the Tauric Chersonese for the first time in her priesthood and the discovery that she is required to sacrifice her own brother (see *Iphigenia*) awaken her natural feelings of affection. A plan of escape is concerted; Thoås, king of the Tauri, is fooled; and Iphigenia and Orestes, with Pylades, escape, taking the image of the goddess.

I'phitus (*Iphitos*), see *Heracles*.

Ipsus, BATTLE OF, see *Macedonia*, § 2.

I'ris, in Greek mythology, the goddess of the rainbow. She was the daughter of Thaumås (son of Pontus, the Sea) and Electra (daughter of Oceanus, q.v.), and consequently sister of the Harpies (q.v.). Iris is not only a personification of the rainbow, but also the messenger of the gods, particularly of Hera. In Virgil the rainbow is the path along which she travels. She was the wife of Zephyrus, the west wind.

I'rus (*Iros*), in the 'Odyssey' (q.v., xviii), the beggar with whom Odysseus fights.

Isae'us (*Isaios*), an Athenian orator, of whose life little is known. He is represented as by birth either an Athenian or a Chalcidian, and appears to have been born about 420 B.C. and to have died about 350. He was a pupil of Isocrates (q.v.), and a professional writer of speeches for litigants. He took no part in political life. Of some fifty speeches with which he was credited, eleven and part of a twelfth have survived. The eleven all deal with cases of inheritance and are important as illustrative of Athenian testamentary law. He was considered 'clever in elaborating pleas for the worse part'. He imitated Lysias in plainness and simplicity of language, but was more elaborate in logical proof and more vigorous in controversy. In these latter characteristics he influenced Demosthenes.

Isidore of Seville, see *Texts and Studies*, § 6.

I'sis, a great Egyptian goddess, sister and wife of Osiris (q.v.) and mother of Hôrus. She represented the female productive force of nature, in which capacity her symbol was the cow. She was also, with Osiris, ruler of the lower world. Her worship was adopted in Greece, with mysteries akin to those of Demeter (q.v.), and spread also to Rome. (See *Religion*, § 5.)

Islands of the Blest, in Greek mytho-

logy, islands in the stream Oceanus, far away in the west, extremely fertile, where the blessed among the dead live again in bliss. They were described by Hesiod (W. and D., 170 et seq.), Pindar (Ol. ii. 68 et seq.), and Horace (Epod. xvi. 41 et seq.). The idea perhaps reflects the tales of mariners who had reached islands off the W. coast of Africa. See *Elysium*.

Ismē'nē, see *Oedipus* and *Antigone*.

Iso'cratēs (*Isokratēs*) (436–338 B.C.), a great Athenian orator, son of Theodõrus, a man of some wealth. He came under the influence of Socrates (Plato in the 'Phaedrus' makes Socrates prophesy the young man's future greatness either as an orator or a philosopher), and of the Sophists, especially of Gorgias (q.v.). He was debarred from public life by a weak voice and lack of nerve. He lost his fortune in the latter part of the Peloponnesian War, and appears to have fled from the tyranny of the Thirty to Chios, where he taught rhetoric, and to have returned to Athens on the restoration of democracy. For a period he wrote speeches for litigants. About 392 he opened a school at Athens and also began to write political discourses. The school was distinguished from those of the Sophists by the greater breadth of the education it gave and by the high moral tone of the instruction; also by its method, which relied greatly on the efforts and hard work of the pupils themselves. It became famous, and pupils came to it from all parts of the Greek world; among these were men subsequently distinguished as politicians, orators, and historians. The political writings of Isocrates were chiefly devoted to the cause of the unity of Greece. In his 'Panēgyricus', published in 380, he urged Athens and Sparta to lay aside their rivalry and unite against Persia. When this appeal failed, his pan-Hellenism took another form: he sought for a strong man who should assume the leadership of united Greece in an expedition to Asia, and hoped to find him, first in Dionysius I of Syracuse, then in Archidamus III of Sparta, and finally in Philip of Macedon (herein sharing in a measure the ideas of Aristotle). This conception of the interests of Greece and Athens, the failure to perceive the danger that it involved to the independence of the latter, naturally brings Isocrates into contrast with Demosthenes (q.v.). His political discourses also include other themes of a more limited scope (see below). Isocrates died, at a great age, shortly after Chaeronea (q.v.), it is said by suicide. If this is true, the reason of the act may be, not that Philip had been victorious—thus rendering practicable the chief hope of Isocrates—but that Athens was still determined to resist him.

Isocrates was (apart from Gorgias, q.v.) the first to treat rhetorical prose as a work of art. He adopted a flowing, luxuriant style, with ample periods, marked and sometimes overburdened with antitheses and other artificial figures. His rhetoric was of a literary character rather than practical oratory. Owing to the popularity of his school and the wide range of its pupils, his influence on literature was great. It extended to Cicero and through him to modern prose. It was perhaps greatest in his studied rhythms, which contain the germ of the Ciceronian *clausulae* (q.v.). Isocrates, it may be added, avoided *hiatus* (q.v.) between words, which also was influential. Twenty-one of his discourses and nine letters survive, divided by R. C. Jebb ('Attic Orators' on which this article is largely based) into Scholastic writings (Hortatory Letters, 'Epideictic' or Display pieces, and Essays on Education), Political writings, and Forensic speeches. Of the Displays, the 'Busiris' and the 'Encomium on Helen' are criticisms of the works of other rhetoricians, in which he shows how the themes should have been handled; the 'Evagoras' (q.v.) is an encomium on a king of Salamis in Cyprus who had recently died (374); the 'Panathēnāicus', written when he was 94 years of age, is in the main a laudatory historical review of the deeds and constitution of Athens, probably for publication at the time of the Panathenaic Festival of 342. Of the two Essays on Education, 'Against the Sophists' (391 or 390) and 'On the Antidosis' (*c.* 354), the first is a protest against the narrow and futile instruction given by the Sophists and an exposition of his own principles of teaching; the second, written thirty-six years later, is a defence of himself and of his educational method. Isocrates had been challenged, as a wealthy citizen, by one Megacleidēs to undertake a trierarchy (see *Liturgy*) or accept an exchange of properties (see *Antidosis*). The matter had come to trial and Isocrates had been defeated. This discourse was a subsequent vindication of himself.

The Political Discourses are the most important of his writings. The 'Panegyricus', (meaning 'festival oration') probably published at the time of the Olympic Festival of 380, is his greatest work in structure and expression, and valuable as a historical document. Its theme, a plea for the union of Athens and Sparta against Persia, supported by a historical review, has been mentioned above. The 'Philip-

pus', written in 346 after the conclusion of hostilities between Athens and Philip of Macedon, is an appeal to the latter, as a Hellene and descendant of Heracles, to take up the championship of Hellas against the barbarians. The 'Platăicus', written in 373 after the seizure of Plataea by the Theban Nicoclēs, is a plea for Athenian support spoken by a Plataean before the Ecclesia. 'On the Peace', written shortly before the end (355) of the Social War which terminated the second Athenian Confederacy, urges the advantages of a non-aggressive policy and the surrender of the maritime empire. It is the most vigorous of the discourses of Isocrates and is inspired by strong feeling. The 'Archidamus' (366) purports to be spoken by the Spartan king of that name (Archidămus III) on the Theban proposal, as a condition of peace, that Sparta shall recognize the independence of Messene. In the 'Areopagiticus' Isocrates contrasts the degenerate Athenian democracy of the day with the more primitive democracy of Solon and Cleisthenes, with particular reference to the function, formerly exercised by the Areopagus (q.v.), of censor of public morals. It was probably written in 355. (Milton's 'Areopagitica', 1644, deals with the censorship of the State over publications.)

The Forensic Speeches, referred to at the beginning of this article, are of less importance. They were written for private litigants and include one for the younger Alcibiades. An Athenian citizen alleged that the elder Alcibiades had robbed him of a team of horses and sued his son for their value. The speech is interesting for the defence it contains of the character of the statesman.

Many translations of portions of Isocrates were made in England in the 16th c.; one, entitled 'The Doctrine of Princes' (1534), by Sir Thomas Elyot (1490?–1546). Milton refers to Isocrates in the sonnet 'To the Lady Margaret Ley':

as that dishonest victory
At Chaeronea, fatal to liberty,
Killed with report that old man eloquent.

Isthmian Festival, see *Festivals*, § 1.

Ītaʹlia, a word perhaps meaning 'land of calves' (cf. *vitulus*), appears to have been at first applied to the SW. portion of the Italian peninsula, but there is no trustworthy evidence before the 5th c. In the 3rd c. the name was officially extended to the whole territory S. of the Rubicon and the Macra, see Pl. 10. After the death of Caesar, Gallia Cisalpina became part of Italy. The peninsula as a whole, S. of the Alps, was inhabited by a variety of races, Celts in the N., Etruscans (q.v.) S. of these, Greeks in the S. of the peninsula, and in the centre an agglomeration of kindred tribes, Umbrians, Sabellians, Oscans, and Latins. The physical characteristics of the country are no less varied than were its inhabitants, from the Apennines and other ranges, which produced breeds of hardy, frugal mountaineers, to the warm southern sea-board, where Greeks led an easy and luxurious life, e.g. at Sybaris and Croton. The achievement of Rome during the republican period was to conquer and absorb all the inhabitants of the peninsula, receiving from them in return influences that are clearly seen in her literature. It is, in fact, remarkable how few authors Rome herself produced (see *Birthplaces*). Virgil, Livy, and Catullus, for instance, came from northern, Horace and Ovid from southern Italy.

I'thaca (*Ithakē*), the island-kingdom of Odysseus, in the Ionian Sea, near Zacyn-thus (Zante), 'lying low, furthest up the sea-line toward the darkness', 'a rugged island'. See *Odyssey*.

Ithō'mē, MOUNT, a lofty rock in the centre of Messenia, where in 464 B.C., after the great earthquake of Sparta, the Mes-senian serfs, having revolted against the Spartans, took refuge. There they were blockaded and not reduced until 459 (or 454). On the slopes of Ithome, after the defeat of Sparta at Leuctra, Epaminondas (q.v.) in 370–369 founded a new citadel of Messene, as a stronghold against the Spartans.

Itinerā'ria, the Latin name for lists of stations on the Roman roads and of the distances between them. The most impor-tant of those which have survived is the 'Itinerarium Antonini Augusti', an official list of the roads in the Roman empire, with the distances between stations, prob-ably compiled early in the 3rd c. A.D. and embodying a good deal of information from the 2nd c. Nothing is known of the author. Another example is the 'Iti-nerarium Hierosolymitānum' or Burdi-galense' (the 'Jerusalem Itinerary') of A.D. 333, giving the route of a pilgrimage from Bordeaux to Jerusalem, by Arles, Milan, Constantinople, and Antioch.

For the 'Peutinger Map' see *Maps*.

I'tylus (*Itulos*), see *Aedon*.

I'tys (*Itus*), see *Philomela* and *Aedon*.

Iū'lus or ASCA'NIUS, the son of Aeneas (see *Aeneid*).

Ixī'ōn, in Greek mythology, a Thessalian who married Diā, daughter of Dēïoneūs (or Ēïoneūs). When his father-in-law came to fetch the bridal gifts that had

been promised, Ixion contrived that he should fall into a pit containing burning coals. For this murder he obtained puri-fication from Zeus. Ixion with gross in-gratitude tried to win the love of Hera. Thereupon Zeus formed a cloud, Nephelē, to resemble Hera, and by her Ixion be-came the father of the Centaurs (q.v.). As a punishment for his crimes Ixion in the underworld was bound on a wheel that turned for ever.

J

Jāni'culum, a hill on the right bank of the Tiber opposite Rome, probably occu-pied in the main, during republican times, by tradesmen and their guilds. An ancient outwork of the city, protecting it against attack from the north, stood on the hill: this was thought to have been founded by Janus (Aen. viii. 357). The removal of the flag from the Janiculum was a signal that the enemy were approaching and that the Campus Martius was in danger, and put a stop to public business. It was the removal of this flag by the praetor Q. Metellus Celer that brought to a close the trial (in 63 B.C.) of Rabirius, whom Cicero was defending. (See *Pro Rabirio*). See also *Janus*.

Jā'nus, in Roman religion, was probably *Diānus*, the male counterpart of Diana. He was originally one of the principal Roman gods: the 'god of gods' in the song of the Salii (q.v.), the first to be mentioned in prayer, and the first to receive a portion of the sacrifice. His connexion with the door (*jānua*) has been much discussed. According to Frazer (on Ov. Fast. i. 89) it is probable that *janua* was called after him. The regular Latin word for 'door' is *foris*, and it may have been customary to set up a symbol of Janus at the prin-cipal door of the house, which might be known as *janua foris*. Ovid (Fast. i. 117 et seq.) describes Janus as the custodian of the universe, the opener and fastener of all things, looking inward and outward from the gate. He developed into the god of beginnings, e.g. of the first hour of the day, and of the first month of the year, *Jānuārius*. The temple of the national Janus was a small bronze shrine in the Forum, with doors on its eastern and western sides. The doors stood open in time of war and were closed in time of peace. Livy records that from the time of Numa the shrine had been closed only twice, after the First Punic War and after the victory of Octavian at Actium (31 B.C.). Augustus in the 'Monumentum Ancyra-num' mentions that it had been thrice closed in his reign. There is an impressive description of the opening of the doors in the 'Aeneid' (vii. 607 et seq.). Janus was represented as *bifrons*, with two faces, perhaps suggestive of vigilance, looking both before and behind. Macrobius thought that his two faces indicated his wisdom: he knew the past and foresaw the future. It was a statue of *Janus bifrons* that stood, with that of old Saturnus, in the hall of the palace of Latinus (Aen. vii. 180).

Janus, according to Roman tradition, was an early king of the country, an immigrant, according to some accounts from Greece, who settled on the Janiculum (so named after him).

Jā′son (*Iāsōn*), see *Argonauts.*

Jā′son (*Iāsōn*) OF PHERAE, a tyrant of the Thessalian town of Pherae, who came into short-lived prominence about 371 B.C. He succeeded in uniting the Thessalian towns under his control and aimed at acquiring the hegemony of Greece, and leading a Greek expedition against Persia; he even began to build a fleet. To further his ambition he allied himself with Thebes against Sparta, still at that time the most powerful State in Greece. After the defeat of Sparta at Leuctra (371), he mediated between Thebes and Sparta, not wishing to see Thebes unduly aggrandized. He availed himself of the Spartan defeat to secure the pass of Thermopylae (giving access to the south), which was commanded by the Spartan fort of Heraclêa. He decided to display the strength of his army at the next Pythian festival and to preside at the games, and made preparations to this end; but was assassinated in 370, while sitting to hear petitions, by seven young men who approached him under pretence of laying a dispute before him.

Je′rome, ST. (*Hierŏnymus*) (c. A.D. 340–420), was born at Stridōn near Aquileia in Dalmatia, of a well-to-do Christian family. (He is called in the titles of his works Eusebius Sōphrōnius Hieronymus, but he himself and his contemporaries employ simply the name Hieronymus. The additions are probably due to later writers. His father's name was Eusebius, and Sophronius was the friend who translated several of his works into Greek.) He was educated at Rome (a pupil of Donatus, q.v.), then returned to Aquileia and adopted the practice of asceticism (in reaction from a period of dissipation). After living for some time at Antioch he spent three years, 375–7, in the desert of Chalcis on the frontier of Syria. But interference by the other hermits made life there intolerable to him. He returned to Antioch, visited

Constantinople (where he received instruction from Gregory of Nazianzus) and spent the years 382–5 at Rome. Here he became the friend of Pope Damasus and the spiritual counsellor of a group of noble Roman ladies, ardent Christians, among whom Marcella, Paula, and her daughter Eustochium are famous. His advocacy of asceticism and his unsparing censures of the frivolous aroused hostility, and, accompanied by Paula and Eustochium, he returned to the East. He settled at Bethlehem in 386, where he died in 420. Paula founded a monastery over which Jerome presided, and three convents for women which she herself directed. Jerome's was an ardent, passionate, intensely human nature, and it is reflected in the vivid variety of his letters, in his tender affection for his friends, his hatreds and combativeness, his attacks on hypocrites and heretics, and his condemnation of himself. He had a deep admiration for pagan literature, which asserted itself in spite of his attempts to quell it, and is seen for instance in a quotation of the story of Dido from the 'Aeneid' in support of an argument against remarriage. There are also numerous quotations in his letters from Horace, Persius, Terence, &c. In his 22nd Letter he recounts how, when he separated himself from his home and family, he was unable to separate himself from his library. He would fast, to read Cicero afterwards. In a feverish vision he saw himself borne before the Judgement Seat and asked his condition, and when he replied that he was a Christian, the answer was, 'Mentiris, Ciceronianus es, non Christianus'. At Bethlehem he taught his monks to copy manuscripts.

His principal works were, (1) a series of biographies of early eremites, simple, amusing, and edifying narratives of much charm, combining fact and imagination; (2) the 'Chronica', a translation of the Greek chronicles of Eusebius of Caesarea, with the addition of certain facts of general history, and a continuation down to the end of the reign of Valens; (3) 'De Viris Illustribus', notices of eminent Christian writers, modelled on the work of Suetonius which bears the same title, and following closely the information given by Eusebius so far as the latter had dealt with these writers. He includes certain heretics and even a few profane writers such as Philo Judaeus; (4) the translation of and commentary on the Scriptures. The authoritative text of the O.T. in the Christian world of Jerome's time was the Greek version known as the Septuagint (q.v.). With this Jerome was dissatisfied. He had studied Hebrew in the desert of Chalcis and pursued the study at Bethlehem. He now undertook a complete retranslation of the O.T. into Latin from the Hebrew. He had already made a translation of the N.T. from the Greek, using as a basis earlier Latin translations (Latin versions of the Bible earlier than Jerome are called 'Old Latin'). He also wrote at least sixty-three volumes of commentaries on the text, paying special attention to the prophets. His version of the Scriptures, at first received with hostility, gradually established itself, and became known as the Vulgate (q.v.) or common text, which, as revised by order of Clement VIII, is now the authorized text of the Roman Catholic Church.

Jewelry, see *Toreutic Art.*

Joca'sta (*Iocastē, Epikastē* in Homer), the mother and wife of Oedipus (q.v.).

John of Salisbury, see *Texts and Studies,* § 8.

Jōsē'phus, FLĀVIUS (A.D. 37–c. 100), a Jewish statesman and soldier, the author (in Greek) of an 'Early History of the Jews' (*Ioudaīkē Archaiologiā*) to A.D. 66, and of a 'History of the Jewish Wars' (*Peri tōn Ioudaīkōn polemōn*) from the capture of Jerusalem in 170 B.C. by Antiochus Epiphanēs to its capture (which he witnessed) by Titus in A.D. 70. He earned the esteem of Vespasian and Titus and received Roman citizenship.

Judicial Procedure.

§ 1. *At Athens*

Under the democratic Athenian constitution of the 5th and 4th cc. B.C. the administration of justice was almost entirely in the hands of the popular courts, and the magistrates took a relatively small part in it. The Areopagus (q.v.) retained its ancient jurisdiction in cases of murder, malicious wounding, poisoning, and arson. The Boule and Ecclesia (qq.v.) dealt with misdeeds of officials and grave crimes against the State; and trifling cases, where the amount in dispute did not exceed ten drachmas, were finally disposed of by judges known as 'the Forty' (four drawn by lot from each tribe), a sort of justices of the peace. Most other cases fell within the jurisdiction of the popular tribunals developed from the Heliaea (q.v.). The judges (dicasts) composing these tribunals appear to have numbered 6,000; they were citizens over thirty and not disqualified in any way, distributed into ten sections numbered from A to K, so that each tribe should be represented in each section. From these the courts or juries (*dikasteria*) were selected by lot, in numbers varying

from 201 upwards, according to the importance of the cases to be tried, but again so that each tribe should be represented. The distribution of the courts and cases was carried out by the Thesmothetae (see *Athens,* § 2). Each dicast received a fee of two obols (raised to three in 425) for a day's attendance.

Judicial suits were either public or private. In public suits, where (in most cases) some offence against the State was involved, the charge might be introduced either by some magistrate or by a private citizen. The case came first before one of the Thesmothetae, who prepared it for trial, and subsequently presided over the court where it was heard. The dicasts decided the verdict by vote, a shell or (later) a bronze disk placed in an urn. If the accused was convicted, accuser and accused each proposed a penalty (unless the penalty was fixed by law); and the dicasts decided by vote between the two proposals. The penalty might be death, imprisonment, banishment, disfranchisement, confiscation of property, or a fine. It usually took the last form. The amount varied from a few drachmas to very large sums. Demosthenes, for instance, was once fined twenty talents, Timotheus a hundred (qq.v.). The prosecutor was liable to a fine of 1,000 drachmas if he withdrew before the trial or failed to obtain one-fifth of the votes. The fines (and fees of the litigants) went to supply the fund from which the dicasts were paid.

The majority of private suits (on rights of property, debts, contracts, &c.) came first before the Forty, who, if the matter in dispute exceeded the small amount of ten drachmas, referred the case to arbitration by one of the public arbitrators (*diaitētai*), Athenians in their sixtieth year. Only if this failed did the case come before the courts for trial, on submission by the arbitrator. Accuser and accused were allowed sometimes two speeches each, sometimes only one. The length of the speeches, fixed according to the importance of the matter in dispute, was measured by a water-clock. The parties had to conduct their own cases, though they were normally allowed to call in 'friends' to assist them. Hence there were no barristers in Athens, only speech-writers (see *Logographi* (2)), who composed speeches for the parties to learn and deliver.

This judicial system had both advantages and disadvantages. It gave a considerable measure of security against injustice, for the intimidation or corruption of a large number of jurymen (especially as it was not known beforehand who these would be) was impossible. On the other hand such juries were more susceptible to emotional appeals, more inclined to admit what was not properly evidence, and less familiar with the law than trained judges would have been. Aristophanes, in his 'Wasps' (q.v.), attacks the system on the ground of the ferocity of the juries in time of war and of their liability to influence by irrelevant motives.

§ 2. At Rome

(1) CRIMINAL PROCEDURE. Criminal jurisdiction, originally in the hands of the king, passed in republican times at first to the consuls, whose officers, the quaestors, were charged with the duty of tracing and arresting criminals. It was provided, however, that in capital cases an appeal (*prōvocātio*) might be made to the *comitia centuriata*; appeals in less important cases could come before the *comitia tributa* (qq.v.). In effect this meant that criminal jurisdiction passed from the magistrates to the people. For judicial purposes the centuries were presided over by the praetor, the tribes by a magistrate with *imperium* (q.v.). The magistrate, if satisfied that there was a case for investigation, named a day for the first hearing. There had to be in all four hearings, and twenty-four days had to elapse between the third and final hearing. Any person might act as prosecutor, provided that he was not for some cause incapacitated from public functions. The State encouraged the prosecution of criminals by offering rewards; but an unsuccessful accuser might in turn be prosecuted. Proceedings before the comitia might be stopped by *intercessio* (q.v.); see also under *Janiculum*.

The Senate, moreover, from time to time appointed a special tribunal (*quaestio extraordināria*), whose members were senators, to try grave political cases. In 149 B.C., by the *lex Calpurnia*, was set up the first permanent judicial body, the *quaestio perpetua de repetundis*, to try cases of extortion by provincial governors. The members of this court also were senators, until C. Gracchus transferred the membership to the equestrian order (q.v.). There is no clear evidence of the institution of any further *quaestio* till the early years of the 1st c. (shortly before Sulla), when *quaestiones* were set up to deal with murder cases (*de sīcāriis*) and with treason (*de mājestāte*). Sulla further developed the system of *quaestiones*, increasing their number to eight or nine and regulating the proceedings of each by a law. The importance of the *quaestiones* is that by their institution criminal jurisdiction passed out of the people's hands, the people voting away its rights in enacting

the law establishing each. Sulla once more made the members of these courts senators. By the *lex Aurēlia* of 70 the jurors were drawn from senators, *equites*, and *tribuni aerarii* (q.v.). Both accuser and accused were allowed within certain limits to reject jurors. Voting was secret, by means of tablets placed in an urn, from the 2nd c. B.C. Under Sulla's arrangements the number of praetors was increased to eight, of whom six presided over *quaestiones*; men who had been aediles presided over the remaining courts, being known as *jūdices quaestionis*. There was no public prosecutor. Prosecutions before the *quaestiones*, as before the *comitia*, were undertaken by private persons, or in political cases by tribunes. The accused might have a *patrōnus* or several *patroni* to speak on his behalf; the prosecutor, except in cases of *repetundae* (see above) and where a woman or child was the nominal prosecutor, had to conduct his case in person, but might be supported by *subscriptōrēs*. The length of the speeches, at first unlimited, was later regulated by the water-clock. There was no appeal from the decision of the *quaestiones*.

Under the principate the *quaestiones* (drawn from senators and *equites*) continued to exist, but their importance gradually declined until they disappeared in the 3rd c. The emperor might try any case that he thought fit. The Senate was constituted a criminal court (especially for its own members), and the *praefectus urbi* had criminal jurisdiction in Rome and for 100 miles around. By the 3rd c. the *praefectus praetorio* had criminal jurisdiction in the rest of Italy (both the prefects acting as delegates of the emperor). During both republican and imperial times, it may be added, many minor cases must have been dealt with, as police offences, by magistrates such as the *tresviri capitālēs* (see *Vigintivirate*).

In the latter part of the republican era appeals to the popular assemblies became obsolete. Under the principate they were replaced in a measure by the power possessed by the emperor (unless he renounced it in favour of his delegates) of interfering, in virtue of his *tribūnicia potestas*, with the sentence of any court. During the 1st c., moreover, the criminal jurisdiction of provincial governors was limited by the right of Roman citizens to appeal to a Roman court or to the emperor. Thus St. Paul's claim to 'appeal to Caesar' from the procurator of Judaea was allowed.

As regards punishments, the death penalty might, in republican times, be pronounced by the *comitia centuriata*, but in practice it was rarely inflicted and was

replaced by exile from Roman territory.
This penalty as inflicted by the *quaestiones*
took the form of *aquae et ignis interdictio*,
the equivalent of exile, which *eo nomine*
was never inflicted by a republican court.
Such executions as took place were generally the result of exceptional circumstances, e.g. a *senatus consultum ultimum*
(q.v.). The death penalty was more frequent under the empire. Fines, or some
diminution of civil status (such as *infâmia*,
'disgrace'), were the most common penalties under the republic. In later times
punishment became more varied and
severe, including deportation to some
desolate island, confiscation of property,
penal servitude (e.g. in the mines), and
even scourging.

(2) CIVIL PROCEDURE. The civil jurisdiction, like the criminal, passed from the
king to the consuls, until in early republican times a special judicial magistracy,
the praetorship, was instituted. About
240 B.C. a second praetor, the *praetor peregrinus* (as distinguished from the original
praetor urbânus) was appointed to deal with
suits in which foreigners were concerned.
For the judicial functions of the praetors
and for the development of Roman civil
law under them, see *Law (Roman)*. See
also *Decemviri* and *Centumviri*.

Jugu'rtha, an illegitimate grandson of
Masinissa (q.v.), king of Numidia. As a
young man he served, at the head of a
Numidian contingent, under the younger
Scipio in the war against Numantia (134
B.C.) and earned Scipio's approval by his
soldierly qualities. He was also ambitious
and unscrupulous and learnt in Spain the
venality of many of the Romans. After
the death in 118 of Micipsa (who had succeeded Masinissa in 149), he put to death
first one then the other of his cousins,
Hiempsal and Adherbal, and made himself master of Numidia. In spite (according to Sallust) of Jugurtha's lavish use
of bribery, the Roman people decided to
crush him, and after two unsuccessful
campaigns (111–110) sent the capable
Q. Caecilius Metellus against him. Metellus
repeatedly defeated Jugurtha, but found
it impossible to subdue him. Finally, after
Marius (q.v.) had replaced Metellus in the
command and Jugurtha had taken refuge
with Bocchus, king of Mauretania, Sulla,
Marius's quaestor, persuaded Bocchus to
betray the fugitive. Jugurtha was taken
to Rome and put to death in 104.

The story of the war against him, with
its many exciting incidents, is vividly told
in the 'Bellum Jugurthinum' of Sallust.

Jū'lia. Among the numerous Roman
ladies who bore this name, the following

are the most important. (1) Aunt of
Julius Caesar and wife of Marius. (2) Sister
of Julius Caesar and mother of Atia, the
mother of Augustus. (3) Daughter of
Julius Caesar and wife of Pompey; she
died in 54 B.C. (4) Daughter of Augustus
and Scribōnia, and the wife first of
Agrippa (q.v.), then of Tiberius the future
emperor. She was banished by Augustus
for her profligate conduct. (5) Livia (q.v.),
the wife of Ti. Claudius Nero and afterwards of Augustus; she was known later
as Julia Augusta. See genealogies on pp.
85 and 231.

Jū'lia Domna, of Emesa in Syria, the
second wife of the emperor Sevêrus and
mother of Caracalla, a woman of great
intelligence and character, 'the patroness
of every art, and the friend of every man
of genius' (Gibbon, c. vi).

Jū'lia, GENS, a distinguished patrician
gens (or clan) at Rome, which claimed
descent from Iulus (Ascanius) the son of
Aeneas, and through them from Venus.
To this *gens* belonged Julius Caesar, and
Augustus through his adoption by Caesar.

Ju'lian (*Flâvius Claudius Jūliânus*),
Roman emperor A.D. 361–3, surnamed by
Christian writers 'The Apostate'. He was
the son of a half-brother of Constantine
(q.v.). He was educated in the doctrines
of Christianity (which he disliked) under
the harsh and suspicious control of his
cousin Constantius, but his affection was
for the Greek classics, and he reluctantly
gave up his studies at Athens for the cares
of State. When he ascended the throne he
revealed himself as a pagan, and did what
he could for the conservation of Hellenism
and the restoration of the ancient religion.
He tried to bring about a religious revival
at Antioch and made himself very unpopular there; he avenged himself by writing
a satire on that city entitled 'Misopōgōn'
('Beard-hater', perhaps in allusion to the
luxurious and effeminate Syrians). He also
wrote a satirical treatise 'Against the
Christians' (known to us only by the refutation of Cyril) and other works. He was
a man of religious and moral tendencies,
but bitter and aggressive. He was killed
in the third year of his reign in an expedition against the Persians. He founded a
secular library at Constantinople, which
was destroyed by fire in 491. The story
that he was murdered by a Christian and
died exclaiming 'Vicisti, Galilaee' ('Thou
hast conquered, Galilean') is unfounded.
It is referred to in English literature, e.g.
by Swinburne in the 'Hymn to Proserpine'
(*Poems and Ballads*, First Series, 1866).

Julio-Claudian Family, GENEALOGY OF

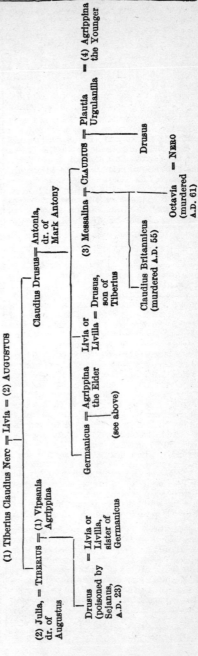
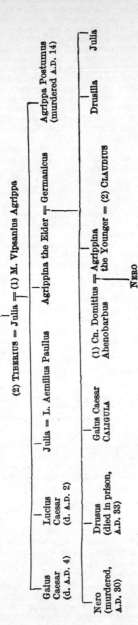
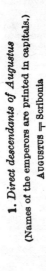

Jū'lius Capitōli'nus, see *Historia Augusta*.

Jū'lius Po'llux (*fl.* A.D. 180), a Greek of Naucratis and teacher of the emperor Commodus, was a lexicographer and author of an extant 'Onomasticon', a valuable list of Attic words and technical terms, with explanations and quotations. The work contains much useful information on the Greek theatre, on Athenian administration, on coins, &c.

Jū'lius Vale'rius (who may have had the additional names ALEXANDER POLEMIUS) (*fl.* A.D. 300), translated from the Greek of the Pseudo-Callisthenes (see *Callisthenes*) the romantic history of Alexander the Great: 'Res Gestae Alexandri Macedonis', in three books, I Birth, II Acts, III Death. This work is important in connection with the transmission of the Alexander story in the Middle Ages.

Jū'no, in Roman religion, the female counterpart of Jupiter (q.v.), later identified with the Greek Hera (q.v.). She was sometimes associated with the moon, but was primarily the goddess of women. She had many distinctive names indicating her various attributes, e.g. LŪCĪNA, 'the goddess who brings to light', as presiding over child-birth; MONĒTA, the giver of counsel. In the temple of Juno Moneta on the northern summit of the Capitoline hill was established the Roman mint, and hence is derived our word 'money'. There was another temple to Juno in the Campus Martius, and another on the Aventine. The latter was dedicated in 392 B.C. by M. Furius Camillus, the conqueror of Veii, who placed in the temple a wooden statue of Juno brought from the captured city. The festival of Juno, confined to women, was the Matronalia (q.v.). There was also a festival of women on 7 July to *Juno Caprōtina*, when a goat was sacrificed to her. See also under *Genius*. Ovid relates that being annoyed at the birth of Athena (q.v.) without a mother, she determined to produce a similar miracle. She was made pregnant by a magic flower given her by Flora and gave birth to Mars (q.v.).

Jū'piter or JUPPITER (from *Jovis-pater*, where *Jovis* = *Djovis*, a word akin to *dies*, signifying 'the bright heaven'), in Roman religion originally a sky-spirit (*numen*), connected with the grape-harvest (see *Vinalia*) and also propitiated before the sowing. In the Song of the Salii (q.v.) he figures as a State deity and is addressed as *Lūcetius*, the god of light. He is also associated with the lightning and thunderbolt. Later the worship of *Jupiter Feretrius* (q.v.) became prominent as the bond

of union of the community, and Jupiter appears as the protector in battle, the stayer of rout (*Jupiter Stator*, q.v.), and the giver of victory. In peace again he becomes associated with public morality and justice; he is the god of oaths. The oak is his special tree, the eagle his special bird. Before the introduction of Greek elements in his character and his identification with Zeus, he becomes the chief of the Roman gods, Jupiter Optimus Maximus, 'Jupiter the best and greatest', with his temple on the Capitol. Here the magistrates do sacrifice on entering on their year of office, and the general brings his spoils after a victorious campaign. His origin as a sky-spirit is recalled by the use of his name as a synonym for the sky, e.g. 'manet sub Jove frigido venator' (Horace).

Jūpiter Capitōli'nus, 'Jupiter of the Capitol'. The great temple of Jupiter on the Capitol, referred to in the preceding article, was said to have been founded by Tarquinius Superbus. It contained three shrines, that of Jupiter in the middle, while the other two were sacred to Juno and Minerva.

Jūpiter Fere'trius (derivation uncertain, according to Livy from *fero*), Jupiter (q.v.) as associated with a sacred oak on the Capitol, on which Romulus was said to have hung his *spolia opima* (q.v.); perhaps originally the spirit supposed to inhabit the tree. The temple of Jupiter Feretrius was reputed the oldest in Rome.

Jūpiter Sta'tor (*Statōr*), 'Jupiter the stayer' of rout. Tradition related that Romulus vowed a temple to him in the midst of a battle in which the Romans were being driven back by the Sabines. The temple, which stood near the highest point of the Via Sacra, appears not to have been built till much later (294 B.C.). In it was held the meeting of the Senate at which Cicero delivered his first oration against Catiline.

Jūs trium libero'rum. Augustus granted certain privileges, known compendiously by this name, to fathers of three children. The privileges included exemption from certain taxes and preference among candidates for office. Later we hear of the grant being made, as a favour, to persons not qualified, e.g. to Martial.

Justin (*Marcus Jūniānus Justīnus*), of uncertain date (2nd or 3rd c. A.D.), wrote in Latin an abridgement of the universal history of Trogus Pompeius (q.v.). It is for the greater part colourless and tedious; but the style is good and the history contains a few striking passages, such as the description of the multitude of Athenians pouring out to see Alcibiades on his return from exile (v. 4), and of Brennus and his army at Delphi (xxiv).

Justi'nian (*Justiniānus*), Roman emperor at Constantinople A.D. 527–65. He was born on the borders of Thrace and Illyricum, and raised to power by his uncle Justin, who himself had risen from obscurity and attained the empire through the favour of the soldiery. The importance of his reign lies partly in the conquests of his great general Belisārius, who recovered Africa from the Vandals, occupied Rome, and overthrew the Gothic kingdom in Italy; but even more in his reorganization of Roman law, in which he was assisted by Tribōnian, quaestor of the palace. The 'Corpus Juris' of Justinian consists of four parts: (1) the 'Institutes' (*Institutiones*), (2) the 'Digest' or 'Pandects' (*Digesta seu Pandectae*), (3) the 'Code' (*Codex*), and (4) the 'Novels' (*Novellae*). The 'Institutes' is a short manual of the whole law, intended as a text-book for students, prepared by a commission of three, and published in 533. It is based largely on the 'Institutes' of Gaius (q.v.). The 'Digest' is a much longer work consisting of extracts from the writings of jurists of authority, grouped under subjects. It was prepared by a commission and published in 533 shortly after the 'Institutes'. The 'Code' first appeared in 529, but a revised edition was published in 534. It is a collection of the enactments of the emperors, and their 'rescripts' or answers to legal questions submitted to them. The 'Novels' are a supplementary work, consisting of the laws made by Justinian after the issue of the Code.

Justinian was the builder of the great church of St. Sophia at Constantinople. It was by Justinian's order that the schools of philosophy at Athens were closed in 529.

Jūtu'rna, an Italian goddess of fountains. It was at her spring, near the Forum, that Castor and Pollux were said to have watered their horses after the battle of Lake Regillus. The temple of Juturna at Rome was vowed to her by C. Lutatius Catulus during the sea-battle off the Aegatian Islands in 241 B.C. Virgil, in the 'Aeneid' (q.v., Bk. xii), gives her name to the sister of Turnus.

Ju'venal (*Decimus Jūnius Juvenālis*), a great Roman satirist, of whose life little is known with certainty. His birth may be conjecturally placed about A.D. 60–70. He was probably born at Aquīnum, but an inscription found there, referring to a

Junius Juvenalis who was tribune in a Dalmatian cohort and held two local offices, may refer to another member of the same family. The various lives of Juvenal which survive are of late date and contradict each other in some respects. They mostly agree in referring to a period of banishment, in consequence of an offence given to the actor Paris, a favourite of Domitian; and the best of the lives states that he practised declamation till middle age (Martial, who was a friend of Juvenal, speaks of him as *facundus*). From internal evidence of the dates at which the Satires were written or published, the period of Juvenal's literary activity appears to have been the thirty years A.D. 98–128, i.e. in the reigns of Trajan and Hadrian. From similar evidence it appears also that Juvenal was at one time poor, but later acquired a farm at Tibur and could offer hospitality in his house at Rome; and that he visited Egypt.

The Satires of Juvenal are sixteen in number, divided by ancient editors into five books. They are fierce attacks on the vices, abuses, and follies of Roman life. They profess to be directed not at his contemporaries, but at their predecessors, now dead. But it is evident that he regards the evils of their day as still persisting. The Satires are notable for their bitter ironical humour, power of invective, grim epigram, sympathy with the poor, and a narrow pessimism which sees only the seamy side of life. Juvenal claims Lucilius and Horace as his masters; but of the latter at least he has none of the kindly humour. His extravagant hatred of the rich, the exaggeration of his censures, his unsparing condemnation of the whole female sex, suggest that he was a man soured by experience. The picture he gives of Roman life is in strong contrast with that given by his contemporary, the younger Pliny. What is perhaps most remarkable in his writing is his power of evoking by a few graphic strokes a scene of Roman life (see in particular Satire III).

Juvenal found many admirers among English satirists. Chaucer in 'Troylus and Cryseyde' (iv. 197) appeals to his authority on the subject of wise objects of prayer (Sat. x), and in the Wife of Bath's Tale paraphrases the 'cantabit vacuus'. Juvenal was a favourite of Skelton's, and influenced Hall and Donne. Dryden had a high regard for him, translated the Satires, and prefixed to them a pleasant essay on the Roman satirists (1693). Juvenal also influenced Pope. Johnson's poem 'London' is an imitation of his Third Satire; his 'Vanity of Human Wishes' an imitation of the Tenth. But

Swift's satire, with its *saeva indignatio*, is perhaps closest to the spirit of Juvenal.

For the subjects of the various Satires see *Satires*.

Juve'ntas, the Roman goddess of youth, identified with Hebe (q.v.).

K

For Greek names beginning with K, see under C.

Knights, at Rome, see *Equestrian Order*.

Knights (*Hippeis*, L. *Equitēs*), a comedy by Aristophanes, produced at the Lenaea in 424 B.C., when Cleon was at the height of his power, after his success at Sphacteria. Demosthenes and Nicias (caricatures of those Athenian generals), slaves of Demos (personification of the Athenian People), are abusing Cleon, the leather-monger, a new favourite of Demos, and a spying flatterer of his master. They learn from a roll of oracles that Cleon is to be ousted from favour by a seller of black-puddings. One of this trade comes along, is told his promised good fortune, and that the knights will support him against Cleon. Cleon enters threateningly, but the chorus of knights arrive, and abuse and buffet him. They urge the Black-pudding man to stand up to him, and a furious quarrel between the two begins. The rest of the play is occupied with the contention of the two demagogues for the favour of Demos, by flattery, bribes, interpretation of oracles, and abuse of each other. The Black-pudding man wins the day. Finally it is revealed that his name is Agorakritos, 'the Choice of the Agora', and that he is to be the reformer and saviour of the State.

L

La'beō, MARCUS ANTISTIUS, an eminent jurist of the time of Augustus. He held to his republican views, and was the founder of a progressive school of lawyers, in distinction from that of Ateius Capito (q.v.), which was conservative.

La'beō, ATTIUS (1st c. A.D.), author of translations of the 'Iliad' and 'Odyssey' into Latin hexameters, which have not survived.

Labe'rius, DECIMUS (c. 105–43 B.C.), a Roman knight and writer of mimes (q.v.). According to Macrobius, his outspoken political criticism brought upon him the humiliation of being required by Caesar in 45 B.C. to appear on the stage and act in his own mimes, in competition with Publilius Syrus (q.v.). 'Necesse est multos timeat quem multi timent' was one of his thrusts at Caesar; it is said that when the line was spoken, the eyes of every one in the theatre turned towards Caesar.

Labyrinth (*Laburinthos*), the name given to the maze in Crete, said to have been devised by Daedalus (q.v.), where the Minotaur (see *Minos*) was kept. The word 'labyrinth' is of uncertain origin, perhaps from λάβρυς, a Lydian or Carian word meaning double-headed axe, a symbol of religious signification, found frequently incised on stones and pillars in Cretan remains of the Minoan period. The idea of a maze may have been derived from the intricate plan of the great Minoan (q.v.) palace at Cnossus.

Lacedae'mon (*Lakedaimōn*), see *Sparta*.

Lacedaemo'nians, *Constitution of the*, a work by Xenophon, see *Constitution of the Lacedaemonians*.

Lace'rna, see *Clothing*, § 3.

La'chēs, see *Plato*, § 2.

La'chesis, see *Fates*.

Lachmann, KARL, see *Texts and Studies*, § 11.

Lacō'nia or **Lacō'nica** (*Lakōnikē*), a territory in the S. of the Peloponnese, bounded on the W. by Mt. Tāygetus, on the S. and E. by the sea. It included a fertile plain through which flowed the Eurōtās, and its capital was Sparta (q.v.).

Lacta'ntius, CAECILIUS (or CAELIUS) FIRMIĀNUS, was probably an African, born about A.D. 250, a pagan who became professor of rhetoric at Nicomēdia in Bīthȳnia and was there converted to Christianity. In his old age he was appointed by Constantine tutor to his son Crispus. Among his chief (Latin) writings on the Christian faith are his 'De Opificio Dei', a defence of the doctrine of Providence based on the evidence of design in the human organism; 'De Ira Dei', refuting the pagan notion that God is impassive and incapable of wrath; and the 'Institūtiōnes Dīvīnae'. This last is a work of wide scope, a defence of Christian doctrine as a harmonious and logical system; it is addressed to cultivated pagan readers and appeals not to the Scriptures but to the testimony of pagan writers themselves. It begins with a criticism of polytheism and of pagan philosophies, and passes to an exposition of the Christian faith, of the Christian idea of justice and morality, of the purpose of creation, and of immortality. Though Lactantius has been criticized as unorthodox, he shows grasp of the essential principles of the Christian religion. He writes in an oratorical Ciceronian prose (he has been called the Christian Cicero), in a persuasive rather than polemical tone, seeking to reconcile faith with reason. An exception to this manner is the 'De Mortibus Persecutorum' (whose attribution to Lactantius has been questioned), in which, shortly after the triumph of Christianity, he celebrates with a passionate exultation the successive downfalls of the emperors who persecuted the Christians.

Lā'das (*Ládās*), a runner employed by Alexander the Great, famous for his swiftness. Ladas was the name of Lord Rosebery's Derby winner in 1894.

Lā'dŏn, (1) a river of Arcadia, tributary of the Alpheus (q.v.); (2) a river of Thessaly, tributary of the Peneus (q.v.); (3) the dragon that guarded the Apples of the Hesperides (q.v.).

Lae'lius, GĀĬUS (b. *c.* 186 B.C.), consul in 140 B.C. and the intimate friend of Scipio Aemilianus (q.v.). He was a good soldier and performed heroic exploits as an officer under Scipio in the Third Punic War. He was also an eminent orator and surnamed 'Sapiens' ('the Wise') for his wide learning and philosophical attainments. It was said that the plays of Terence, who also belonged to Scipio's circle, owed much to Laelius. He is made by Cicero the principal speaker in his dialogue 'De Amicitia' (q.v.). He is also an interlocutor in Cicero's 'De Senectute' and 'De Re Publica'. Cicero (De Or. ii. 6. 22) has a pleasant anecdote that Laelius and Scipio liked going for a holiday to the seaside, 'where they became incredibly childish and used to collect shells and pebbles on the beach'.

Laelius, de Amicitiā, see *De Amicitia.*

Lāe'rtēs, in the 'Odyssey', the father of Odysseus.

Laestry̆'gonēs (*Laistrūgones*), see *Odyssey* (under Bk. x).

Lae'vius (?MELISSUS) (b. *c.* 129 B.C.), a Roman poet of whom very little is known, except that he was author of *Erōtopaegnia* ('diversions of love'), amatory poems in a great variety of lyric metres. He is important as a pioneer of the Alexandrian influence at Rome (see *Alexandrianism*), as an experimenter in metres, and as a predecessor of Catullus in the lyric. Only fragments of his work survive.

Lā'ĭus (*Láĭos*), a legendary king of Thebes, son of Labdacus (*Labdakos*), and great-grandson of Cadmus (q.v.). See *Antiope* and *Oedipus.*

La'machus (*Lámachos*), an Athenian general of the time of the Peloponnesian War (q.v.). He was killed in 414 B.C. at the siege of Syracuse. He figures in the 'Acharnians' (q.v.) of Aristophanes.

La'mian War, the war (323–322 B.C.) that followed the revolt of Greek States from Macedonia after the death of Alexander the Great (see *Athens,* § 7).

La'mpadēdro'miā, see *Torch-race.*

Lampri'dius, AELIUS, see *Historia Augusta.*

Lānuvi'nus, LUSCIUS, see *Luscius Lanuvinus.*

Lāo'cŏon (*Láokŏōn*), see *Trojan Horse.*

The great German scholar and critic G. E. Lessing (1729–81) made the famous sculptured group of Laocoon and his sons in the coils of the serpents (now in the Vatican) the basis of his work ('Laokoon' 1766) 'on the limits of Poetry and Painting'.

Lā'odamī'a (*Láodameia*), (1) wife of Protesilaus (q.v.); (2) daughter of Bellerophon and mother of Sarpedon (qq.v.).

Lāo'medon (*Láomedōn*), in Greek mythology, king of Troy (see genealogy under *Troy*). He employed Apollo and Poseidon to build the walls of Troy, but when they had finished refused to pay them. Poseidon thereupon sent a sea-monster against Troy. The danger from this could be averted only if Laomedon sacrificed to the monster his daughter Hesione. Heracles undertook to slay the monster if Laomedon would give him his famous horses. But Laomedon defrauded him likewise. Heracles raised an army, captured the city, and gave Hesione to Telamon (q.v.), who had distinguished himself in the attack.

In the 'Aeneid' (iii. 248) the harpy Celaeno taunts Aeneas and his men by calling them 'Laomedontiadae'.

La'pithae (*Lapithai*), see *Centaurs.*

Lā'rēs (*Lárēs*), in Roman religion, spirits (*numina*) whose original character is disputed. In the opinion of Frazer (on Ov. Fast. ii. 615) the *Lares Compitālēs,* who were worshipped at the cross-roads (*compita,* see *Compitalia*), were dangerous spirits, probably spirits of the dead, who had to be propitiated. There was a clear distinction between these and the *Lares Familiārēs,* the spirits who had the special care of the house and household, and were worshipped at the domestic hearth on the Kalends, Nones, and Ides of the month and on occasions of importance to the household, such as a wedding. These Lares, like the Lares Compitales, were, in Frazer's opinion, spirits of ancestors, but were regarded as good and beneficent, so long at least as they were treated with due respect. Other authorities (including Wissowa) regard the Lares as originally rustic spirits, guardians of the farm, who were invoked (in the words of Tibullus) to 'give good crops and wine', and were only at a later time transferred to the house.

The *Lares Familiares* had their counterpart in the *Lares Praestitēs* ('Guardians') of the State. They had a temple at the head of the Via Sacra; the figure of a dog stood between their images, and the images were clad in the skins of dogs (because, according to Ovid, the dog is a faithful guardian, like the Lar). In later times the Lares were identified with the Dioscuri (q.v.).

La'rvae, see *Lemures.*

Lā'sus (*Lāsos*) of Hermione in Argolis (b. c. 548 B.C.), an early Greek lyric poet, who is said to have been connected with the institution of dithyrambic contests at Athens under Hipparchus, and to have developed the form and music of the dithyramb (q.v.). It is said also that he was the teacher of Pindar. It was he who detected the forgeries of Musaeus (q.v).

Latifu'ndia (*Lātifundia*), in Roman territories, large agricultural estates, worked by slave labour under an overseer (*vilicus*), or later by *colōni*, tenants who degenerated practically into serfs. They were especially prevalent in Apūlia and Calabria, and later in Africa. Columella regarded the system as quite uneconomical. Pliny (H.N. xviii. 6 (7), 35) was of opinion that *latifundia* were the ruin of Italy. The smallholder had no chance, especially since so much land was turned into pasture tended by slave herdsmen.

Latī'nus, in Roman legend, son of Faunus and the nymph Marica, and through Faunus and his father Picus, according to Virgil, descended from Saturnus (q.v.). He was king of Latium and father of Lavinia, whom Aeneas married (see *Aeneid*). A Latinos was known to Hesiod, who makes him a son of Circe (q.v.).

Latin Language, see p. 454.

Lātō'na, see *Leto.*

Laudā'tiō Tu'riae, see *Women,* § 2.

Laurentian Library, see *Texts and Studies,* § 9, and *Libraries.*

Lau'rium (*Laurion*), see *Mines* and *Athens,* § 11.

Laus Pīsō'nis, see *De Laude Pisonis.*

Lau'sus, (1) in the 'Aeneid' (q.v.), the son of Mezentius (q.v.). He is killed, while trying to save his father, by Aeneas. (2) The name of a son of Numitor king of Alba Longa, killed by his uncle Amūlius (Ov. Fast. iv. 55).

Lavi'nia (*Lāvīnia*), in the 'Aeneid' (q.v.), daughter of Latinus (q.v.); she is betrothed to Turnus (q.v.), but is given by her father in marriage to Aeneas.

Law, ROMAN.

§ 1. *The Twelve Tables*

The history of Roman Law begins, for practical purposes, with the publication in the middle of the 5th c. B.C. of the 'Twelve Tables' (q.v., and see *Rome,* § 3). These were the codification of the customary law of the period. They remained for centuries the fount of all public and private law at Rome, and were still so regarded by Livy. They were modified to some extent by statute (the criminal law in particular underwent important changes by this method), and under the principate there were modifications by *Senatus consultum,* and some of importance by imperial rescript; but throughout late republican and early imperial times the main development of private law was not by enactment, but (1) by the qualified legislative power of the praetor, and (2) by the interpretative action of the *responsa prudentium.*

§ 2. *The Praetor's Edict*

There were under the republic two principal kinds of civil procedure, the archaic procedure *per lēgis actiōnem* and the procedure *per formulam.* The former probably began to die out in the 3rd or 2nd c., though it may have survived to the end of the republic; our knowledge of it is imperfect. Its characteristic feature was a first stage, in which the judge (the praetor) and the parties observed certain technical rites laid down by law; the slightest mistake in performing the ritual was fatal to the litigant. The procedure *per formulam,* introduced about 150 B.C., was more elastic. It was divided into a first stage before the praetor, who declared the law, and a second stage before a juror (*jūdex*) or the standing courts of the *decemviri* or *centumviri* (qq.v.), who decided the issue on the facts (these courts, it should be observed, existed before the formulary system). Before the praetor the case was said to be *in jūre,* before the *judex* it was said to be *apud judicem.* After discussion before the praetor, the issue was defined by him in a written instruction (the *formula*) to the *judex,* directing him to decide the case according to the answer he should find to the question set out in the *formula*. It was the custom for the praetor on entering office to issue an edict laying down the principles he should follow in granting legal remedies. But as it was obviously impracticable each year to adopt a new set of principles, the praetor appears always to have adopted his predecessor's edict with occasionally such amendments as, on the advice of the jurists of his council, seemed to him to be called for. This traditional edict, known as the *ēdictum perpetuum*, contained the *formulae* of actions, and in the last century of the republic was the main instrument for the development of the law. This process came to an end, and the praetor's edict took its final form, with that issued by Salvius Jūliānus under the emperor Hadrian. It may be noticed that the praetor's importance in the development of Roman Law increased vastly as a result of the formulary system.

§ 3. *The Responsa Prudentium*

The *responsa (juris) prudentium* were the 'answers of the learned in the law' to the questions regarding the interpretation of the law put to them by their clients or the *judices*. These answers were recorded and edited by the pupils of the jurisconsult, and had authority proportionate to his reputation as a lawyer. The *responsa* were a source of power, which Augustus brought to some extent under control by limiting the right of giving *responsa* to certain jurists. Similarly the praetor's edict came under imperial control because the princeps exercised influence over the appointment of the praetors. After it had taken its final shape in the edict of Julianus, jurisprudence was developed mainly by the writings of great jurists, such as Papinian and Ulpian, down to the reign of Alexander Sevērus.

§ 4. *Jus Gentium and Jus Naturale*

Roman Law was originally the *jus civīle*, the law applicable to Roman citizens and to some extent to those allies of Rome to whom the rights of trade and intermarriage had been extended. The question early arose as to the principles on which disputes should be adjudicated where one or both the parties were foreigners, of whom trade and business brought an ever increasing multitude to Rome. The large number of such cases is shown by the appointment from c. 240 B.C. of a special praetor, known as *praetor peregrinus* to deal with them. The most general solution was found in the idea of a *jus gentium*, the universal element to be found in the laws of all

nations. In a practical sense, the *jus gentium* covered little more than the law of contract, and presumably embodied the customs generally observed by the Mediterranean peoples in their commercial intercourse; and this law of contract became in fact incorporated in the Roman Law as applicable between citizens, either as a result of custom or as introduced through the praetor's edict. Under the influence of Greek theory, the *jus gentium* in the last century of the republic became identified for most practical purposes with *jus nātūrāle*, natural law, the law as dictated by reason. Aristotle had divided political justice into τὸ φυσικόν and τὸ νομικόν, the natural and the conventional, and the Stoics, by whom the cultured Roman classes and particularly the lawyers were much influenced, regarded life according to nature as the guiding principle of conduct. This notion provided the later Roman jurists with a philosophical basis for their liberal spirit of equity; the *jus gentium* or *jus naturale* was the element in law which the praetor's edict was supposed to have worked into Roman jurisprudence.

§ 5. *Diffusion of Roman Law*

Alongside of the process of evolution above described came a process of diffusion by which Roman Law spread gradually over a large part of the civilized world. The diffusion was at first by conquest. In the provinces conquered by Rome the system applied varied according to the degree of social organization prevailing among the natives and the development of their own laws and institutions. In the provinces cities were often granted the right, and even more often were allowed in practice, *suis legibus uti*. The edict which the governor of a province, like the praetor at Rome, issued when entering on his office, appears to have included legal regulations for the governor's court in the various categories of disputes, between Roman citizens, between these and aliens, and probably between one alien and another. The experience of the *praetor peregrinus* at Rome supplied a body of rules applicable between parties whose native laws were not the same, and these no doubt would serve as a model for provincial courts. But the natural tendency was to Romanize the law of the province, while Roman Law itself, as we have seen, was becoming permeated with the *jus gentium* So that the two laws approximated, especially as regards property and contract.

A further stage in the process of diffusion was reached when, by the *Constitūtio*

Antoniniána of A.D. 212, Roman citizenship was extended by Caracalla to all subjects of the empire, and Roman Law in consequence became applicable to a great variety of *peregrini*, to some of whom, particularly the peoples of the East with their well-established institutions, it was not suited. As a consequence local law and native customs persisted, and Roman Law was modified to cover them. Roman Law, subjected after the transfer of the real centre of government to Constantinople to further Hellenistic and Christian influences, lost much of its original national character. As expressed in its final form, the 'Corpus Juris' of Justinian (q.v.), it represents in part the effect of non-Roman influences. The main development of law in this period was by imperial constitutions, which were issued in the joint names of the Western and Eastern emperors and were normally valid throughout the empire. The Theodosian Code, issued by Theodosius II in A.D. 438, was a collection of those issued from Constantine onwards.

§ 6. *Diffusion of Roman Law in medieval and modern times*

The later diffusion of Roman Law was effected chiefly by peaceful penetration, radiating from two centres, Italy and Constantinople. After the Dark Ages a great impulse to its extension was given by the revival of legal study at the University of Bologna towards the end of the 11th c. Thence the study of the 'Corpus Juris' of Justinian spread to the universities of France, England, Spain, and Germany. The development of Canon Law for the regulation of ecclesiastical affairs, largely based on Roman Law, was a further stage in its diffusion. By the definite adoption of Roman Law, or by the codification on Roman principles of local customs, this law, more or less modified, prevails to-day in France, Italy, Belgium, Holland, Spain, Portugal, Greece, and in the territories acquired by some of these countries in other continents, such as Quebec, Louisiana, the Dutch East Indies, Ceylon. The law of Scotland is also partly based on Roman Law. In Germany a code, founded in part on Teutonic custom, came into force in 1900, but German law is still very Roman. In England from the time of Henry III, owing to the early development of independent English institutions, English Common Law has been established; but even here the influence of Roman Law has been appreciable. English Common Law prevails not only in England, Wales, and Ireland, but in most of the English dominions and dependencies (i.e. other

than those where earlier settlers had established Roman Law, such as Quebec, S. Africa, Ceylon), and in the United States (except Louisiana). Modern International Law contains legal conceptions taken from Roman Law, notably that of the theoretical equality of all States. The Roman Law of Property also contributed to the part of International Law relating to the acquisition of territory.

§ 7. *Special features of Roman Law*

Among the many important and interesting features of Roman Law may be mentioned the following:

(1) The principle of *patria potestas*, the lifelong authority of the father over the person and property of his descendants, an outcome of the family organization of primitive society. This authority, in the earliest form in which we find it, included power of life and death (and therefore also of chastisement), control of the marriage of son or daughter, and power of transferring them to another family or selling them. These powers over the persons of descendants were in course of time limited (already in the Twelve Tables some restrictions are apparent), and in the later imperial period were reduced to mere vestiges. But the father's control over the son's property remained extremely wide and effective; it was the result of the primitive notion of property as belonging to the family (and not to the individual) and administered by the head of the family. It endured with certain practical modifications (such as the *peculium* or permissive property of sons, slaves, and soldiers) until the time of Justinian.

With the *patria potestas* are connected (a) the Roman conception of *agnatic kinship*, which included all the descendants from a common male ancestor, with the exception of those descended through a female (the reason being that if a woman married, her children came under the *patria potestas* of her husband and were thus lost to her own family); the tendency of the praetorian edict was to substitute the more natural conception of cognatic kinship, including all who can trace descent to a common pair; and (b) *the status of Roman women*. A son became enfranchised on the death of his father owing to his capacity to become thereupon the head of a new family. But a woman had no such capacity and in the earliest times remained under the 'perpetual tutelage' of her nearest male relations or other guardians unless married *in manu* (i.e. so as to come under the *manus* or control of her husband). But this conception became discredited, the control by guardians ceased in practice to be effectively exercised, and the Roman woman obtained during the empire a position of great independence, both personal and in respect of property, whether married or unmarried. For whereas by the older forms of marriage the woman generally passed under the *manus* of her husband, these forms fell into disuse, and a form was adopted under which the woman remained in her own family and retained effective control of her property, while social custom reduced her husband's authority over her person.

(2) *The Will or testamentary disposition.* This had its origin in the Roman conception of 'universal succession', the succession of the heir to the whole of the rights and duties of the deceased man, whose legal personality survived in the heir or co-heirs. When a Roman citizen died intestate, those of his descendants who were enfranchised by his death became his heirs. The will or testament was an instrument for regulating the succession otherwise than if left to the rules of intestate succession. The power of making wills was already recognized by the Twelve Tables. Unlike the modern will, the will in its earliest form was not secret, but was published, either in the *comitia curiata* (the primitive legislative assembly) or, if the testator were on active service, as a battle-field will (*in procinctu*), and it was irrevocable except by the making of a fresh will with the same formality. A citizen at the point of death could not wait for the next meeting of the *comitia* to make his will, and accordingly a procedure was adopted based on the Roman *mancipatio* or conveyance (see below). Under it the will took the form of a conveyance, accompanied by ancient ceremonial, of the testator's family and property to the heir, described as the *emptor familiae*, on the understanding that these should be returned to the testator in the event of his recovery. This form of will was less public and more easily revoked; it was, moreover, developed in time by the ingenuity of lawyers into a genuine will, a conveyance taking effect only after death.

(3) *The distinction between two classes of property*, (a) a higher kind, known as *res mancipi*, things which required for their conveyance (or legal transfer to another person) the full ceremony known as 'mancipation', involving the presence of the seller and the buyer, five witnesses, and a person called the *Libripens* who brought a pair of scales to weigh the uncoined copper that served as money in primitive Rome. These things included land, slaves, oxen, and the instruments of agriculture generally, forms of property,

in fact, that were of especial importance in a simple agricultural community. (b) An inferior order, *res nec mancipi*, which did not require mancipation but could be conveyed by simple delivery. As time went on the *res mancipi* lost some of their relative importance, while that of the *res nec mancipi* increased. By the time of Justinian the difference between the two disappears, and delivery becomes the one prevalent form of conveyance.

(4) *The Roman doctrine of contract.* The word *nexum* appears in primitive times to have been applied to the solemn ceremonial which accompanied important transactions, including both conveyance and contract. Later the special term *mancipātio* was applied to the ceremony of conveyance, and *nexum* was applied to the ceremony of contract. The essence of contract was agreement between the parties by which either or both bound himself or themselves to give or do or refrain from doing something; but Roman Law did not originally enforce agreements unless they were accompanied by certain formalities, or were from the frequency and importance of their subject-matter strictly deserving of consideration. As Roman Law developed, contracts were classified into four kinds, Verbal, Literal, Real, and Consensual. In the Verbal contract the agreement was confirmed by a *stipulātio*, a solemn interrogation summing up the terms of the agreement, and a reply assenting to those terms, thereby adding obligation to the pact. In the Literal contract the obligation was added by an entry in the ledger or book of account of one (or both) of the parties (book-keeping was extremely regular and systematic in ancient Roman times). In the Real contract obligation arose from the delivery of the specific thing to which the agreement related. The Consensual contract included *mandātum* (commission or agency), *societās* (partnership), *emptio venditio* (purchase and sale), *locātio conductio* (letting and hiring), that is to say, the most frequent transactions in a civilized community. In this type of contract no formality was necessary to supplement the pact, and obligation resulted directly from mutual assent. It is the basis of modern conceptions of contract. Most forms of contract were open to foreigners as well as Roman citizens. The order of their evolution is uncertain; sale, hire, *societas*, and *mandatum* were probably developed in that order.

For *Criminal cases* see under *Judicial Procedure*.

Law Courts, see *Judicial Procedure*.

Laws (*Nomoi*), a dialogue by Plato, his last work. It shows decline of vigour and charm, the style is tortuous, the sentences very long, and it was perhaps left in an unfinished state. The interlocutors are an Athenian stranger, Cleinias the Cretan, and Megillus a Spartan. They converse as they walk from Cnossus in Crete to the cave and temple of Zeus. The Athenian does most of the talking. After a criticism by him of the laws of Lycurgus and Minos as directed only to superiority in war, whereas peace not war is the business of the legislator, there is a preliminary discussion of the principles of politics, and it is discovered that Cleinias is about to found a new colony. The Athenian proceeds to lay down for him its general polity, the number of its citizens and their distribution, its organization in respect of magistrates, marriage, property (including slaves), and the material conditions of life generally, education, festivals, and other regulations. The three last books are mainly occupied with criminal offences and their expiation.

Lea′nder (*Leandros*), a youth of Abўdos who according to legend was in love with Hero, the beautiful priestess of Aphrodite at Sestos on the opposite shore of the Hellespont. Leander used at night to swim across to Hero, who directed his course by holding up a lighted torch. One tempestuous night Leander was drowned, and Hero in despair threw herself into the sea. See *Musaeus* (2). Marlowe's 'Hero and Leander', which he left unfinished, was published posthumously in 1598. Lord Byron swam from Abydos to Sestos in 1810, and published 'The Bride of Abydos' in 1813.

Lectiste′rnium, a religious ceremony adopted at Rome, after consultation of the Sibylline Books, in 399 B.C., and repeated later in great emergencies. Images of certain gods were laid on couches and a meal set before them. Cf. *Theoxenia*.

Lē′cythus (*lēkuthos*), see *Clothing*, § 2.

Lē′da (*Lēdā*), in Greek mythology, daughter of Thestios, king of Aetōlia, and wife of Tyndareus (*Tundareōs*), king of Sparta. She was loved by Zeus, who approached her in the form of a swan. Among her children were the twins Castor and Polydeuces (Pollux, see *Dioscuri*), Clytemnestra (see *Agamemnon*), and Helen (q.v.). Of these Castor, Pollux, and Helen are generally said to have been children of Zeus, but the accounts vary.

Legion (*legiō*), see *Army*, § 2.

Le′mnos (*Lēmnos*), a large island in the

N. of the Aegean, where Hephaestus (q.v.) is said to have fallen when thrown out of heaven; it became a centre of his cult. For the story of the Lemnian women and the Argonauts see *Hypsipyle*. Herodotus relates that when the Pelasgians were driven out of Attica they occupied Lemnos, and later carried off a number of Athenian women. The Pelasgians afterwards became suspicious of the children of these women (for they banded together and spoke the Attic language), and therefore murdered them and their mothers; so that 'Lemnian deeds' became proverbial in Greece for atrocious deeds. Lemnos was acquired by Persia under Darius, but was retaken by Miltiades (q.v.) and passed under Athenian dominion.

Le′murēs or LARVAE, in Roman religion, spirits of the dead, regarded as maleficent and supposed to visit the houses of the living on the 9th, 11th, and 13th May, the festival of the *Lemūria*. To exorcise the ghosts, the householder threw black beans to them (to redeem therewith the living members of his family, whom otherwise the ghosts would carry off), and ushered them forth with the words, 'Ghosts of my fathers, go out' (Ov. Fast. v. 419 et seq.). Contrast the *Parentalia*, when the spirits of the dead were regarded as beneficent. Ovid indicates that the Lemuria was the older ceremony. For the superstitions of antiquity about beans, see Frazer on the passage in the Fasti above referred to. Beans were among the things that the Flamen (q.v.) Dialis might not touch.

Lēnāē′a, see *Festivals*, § 4.

Leo′nidas (*Leōnidās*), (1) king of Sparta and commander of the Greeks at Thermopylae (see *Persian Wars*). (2) Of Tarentum, a Greek writer of epigrams (*fl.* 274 B.C.), one of the best poets in the Anthology. His work is characterized by restraint and simplicity.

Leō′sthenēs, the Athenian general in the Lamian War (see *Athens*, § 7). See also *Hyperides*.

Leptinēs, *Against*, a speech in a public prosecution by Demosthenes. See *Demosthenes* (2), § 3 (d).

Lernae′an Hў′dra (*Hudrā*), see *Heracles* (*Labours of*).

Le′sbia, see *Catullus*.

Le′sbos, a large island off the coast of Mўsia in Asia Minor, occupied early by Aeolians (see *Migrations*). Its chief towns were Mitylēnē (or Mytilēnē) and Mēthymna. Terpander, Arion, Sappho, and Alcaeus (qq.v.) were born there. It formed part of the Delian Confederacy (see *Athens*

§ 4) but revolted (except Methymna) from Athens in 428 B.C. during the Peloponnesian War. It was subdued by an Athenian expedition in 427, and under the influence of Cleon (q.v.) the Assembly at Athens voted that the whole people of Mytilene should be put to death or enslaved. But on the following day came remorse: on the proposal of Diodotus the cruel edict was revoked, and a swift trireme was sent to Lesbos to prevent the massacre. It arrived just in time. The leaders of the revolt were alone put to death, and the land of the island (with the exception of Methymna) was distributed among Athenian cleruchs (q.v.).

Lē'thē ('oblivion'), in Latin poets a river in Hades (q.v.); its water was drunk by souls about to be reincarnated, so that they forgot their previous existence. In Aristophanes it is a plain in Hades. The name was borne also by a spring in the cave of Trophonius (q.v.). Virgil has a famous passage (Aen. vi. 703 et seq.) where Aeneas sees the ghosts drinking at the river of Lethe before their reincarnation.

Lē'tō (Lat. *Lātōna*), a Greek goddess, daughter of the Titans (q.v.) Coeus and Phoebe. She was loved by Zeus and conceived twin children. But, owing to fear of Hera's anger, no land would receive her when the time of their birth drew near, until she came to Ortygia (identified later with Delos), then a floating island, but thereafter secured to the bottom of the sea. There she gave birth to Artemis and Apollo (qq.v.).

Leuci'ppē (*Leukippe*) **and Clei'tophon** (*Kleitophōn*), see *Novel*.

Leuci'ppus (*Leukippos*), (1) see *Philosophy*, § 1. (2) In Greek mythology, see *Daphne*.

Leucothe'a (*Leukotheā*), a Greek goddess of the sea, see *Dionysus*.

Leuctra, in Boeotia, the scene of a battle in which the Thebans, under Epaminondas, defeated the Spartans (371 B.C.), thus bringing to an end the period of Spartan hegemony in Greece which had followed the Peloponnesian War. See *Sparta*, § 4.

Lexicons, see *Dictionaries*.

Liba'nius (*Libanios*) (c. A.D. 314–393), of Antioch, a rhetorician who after studying at Athens opened a school of rhetoric at Constantinople, where he enjoyed the favour of the emperor Julian the Apostate. Though an opponent of the Christian faith, he had Christian pupils, among them St. John Chrysostom. His numerous extant writings include a life of Demosthenes and synopses of his orations.

Li'ber, an old Italian deity, probably a general spirit of creativeness, whose characteristics are obscured by Greek ideas subsequently introduced. He became the god of vine-growers, and when the cult of Dionysus spread in Italy became identified with that god or Bacchus. Virgil presents Liber both in the character of the Greek god with his legends and orgiastic rites, and in his more Italian character of the god of the vine. He was celebrated on 17 March at the festival of the *Liberālia*; it was at this festival that Roman youths generally first assumed the *toga virilis* (see *Clothing*, § 3). Liber had a female counterpart, named *Libera*.

Liber Spectāculo'rum, see *Martial*.

Libe'rtus, see under *Slavery*, § 2.

Libiti'na, an Italian goddess of the dead, afterwards identified with Proserpina (q.v.).

Libraries. The first considerable collection of books of which we hear with any certainty in ancient times was that of Aristotle, though Polycrates of Samos was said to have collected books, and tradition ascribed the formation of a public library at Athens to Pisistratus. Euripides is also said to have possessed a collection. The greatest of ancient libraries was that of Alexandria (see *Alexandrian Library*). The kings of Pergamum also formed a great library, said to have contained 200,000 volumes, and to have been given by Mark Antony to Cleopatra. Antiochus the Great had a library at Antioch, of which the poet Euphorion (q.v.) had charge. There is evidence that about the 1st c. B.C. the gymnasia at Athens possessed libraries. The library of the gymnasium known as the Ptolemaion was visited by Cicero and Pausanias.

At Rome we hear of private libraries formed by Aemilius Paullus, Sulla, and Lucullus (qq.v.), who brought to Rome the collections of Greek manuscripts which they captured in their wars in the East. Julius Caesar had the intention of instituting a public library at Rome and of placing Varro (q.v.) in charge of it. In fact, the first public library there was founded by Asinius Pollio (q.v.) under Augustus. It contained Greek and Latin books, was adorned with portraits of authors, and was housed in the Ātrium Lībertātis, the site of which is not known with certainty. Augustus founded two other libraries, the Octavian and the Palatine. The *Bibliotheca Ulpia* of Trajan was the most famous of those instituted at Rome by the later emperors.

Among later and modern libraries

important for their collections of classical manuscripts may be mentioned, besides the British Museum, the Bodleian at Oxford (founded by Sir Thomas Bodley (1545–1613), and opened in 1602), the Ambrosian at Milan (founded in 1609, and named after St. Ambrose, originally the private library of Cardinal Borromeo), the Laurentian or Medicean at Florence (which had its origin in the private collections of Cosimo and Lorenzo de' Medici in the 15th c.), and the Vatican library (built up by various popes, notably Nicolas V and Leo X). Venice is noteworthy for its manuscripts of Homer. Paris also has an important collection, but the bulk of the manuscripts acquired as a result of Napoleon's conquests were repatriated in 1815. Vienna (formerly the Imperial Library there) is also rich in classical texts, as are Munich and Madrid.

Lici'nian Rogations, in Roman history, proposals originally made in 376 B.C., and finally passed in 367, by the tribunes P. Licinius Stolō and L. Sextius Laterānus, with a view to reducing the political inequalities between plebeians and patricians and to remedying the distress among the poor due to debt and the dearth of agricultural land (see *Rome*, § 3). Niebuhr says that their adoption saved Rome from being one of the many oligarchic States that have been buried and forgotten.

Li'ctors, attendants who walked before certain Roman magistrates (consuls, dictators, praetors, and the *Flamen Dialis*) carrying the *fasces* (q.v.).

Liddell and Scott, see *Dictionaries*.

Li'nus (*Linos*), in Greek mythology, a hero whose untimely death (in circumstances that are variously told) was celebrated in a dirge, the 'Song of Linus', sung annually from Homeric days at harvest time. He appears to have had his origin in the word *αἴλινον*, or words *αἶ Λίνου*, in an ancient harvest or vintage song. The myth of Linus is perhaps connected with the celebration of the changing seasons. According to another tale, Linus was the teacher of Heracles, who killed Linus with his own lyre when the latter tried to punish him.

Li'totēs ('frugality'), a rhetorical figure, a form of *meiosis* (q.v.), in which emphasis is produced by substituting for what one means its opposite with a negative; e.g.

> Audire magnos jam videor duces
> non indecoro pulvere sordidos.
> Hor. Od. II. 1. 21–2.

Liturgy (*Leitourgiā*), at Athens, a public service which one of the wealthier citizens was required to perform. Descendants of Harmodius and Aristogiton (q.v.) were exempt; also archons and members of the Boule during their year of office. The principal ordinary or periodic liturgies (of which there were some sixty a year in the city alone, apart from the rest of Attica) were the following. (1) The CHORĒGIĀ or provision of a chorus for one or other of the various lyric and dramatic contests (at the Panathenaea, Thargelia, Dionysia, and Lenaea; see *Festivals*, §§ 2–4, *Tragedy*, § 2, *Comedy*, § 2). This was a very costly service and the *choregi* rivalled one another in lavish expenditure. A client of Lysias spent 15,000 drachmas on eight of these liturgies. (2) The GYMNASIARCHIĀ, the recruiting and training of one of the ten teams that competed in the torch race. Lysias records the cost as reaching 1,200 drachmas. (3) The ARCHITHEŌRIĀ or provision of the cost of a sacred embassy to one of the Panhellenic festivals. (4) The HESTIĀSIS or provision of a banquet for the members of the tribe or deme on the occasion of a festival; this might cost 700 or 800 drachmas.

There were in the 5th c. some 1,200 citizens liable to these charges. They undertook them in rotation, the heavier services being laid on the wealthier citizens. The only method of escaping the charge was that of the *Antidosis* (q.v.).

In addition to the ordinary liturgies, there was also the extraordinary charge of the *Trierarchia*, or equipment of a trireme. This was imposed only or principally in time of war, and only on the wealthiest citizens. The State provided the hull, mast, and sails. The trierarch had to maintain these, supply the remainder of the equipment, provide and train the crew, and command in person (in the 5th c.). The State provided the pay of the crew. The cost of the service came nearly to one talent, and after the Sicilian Expedition it became necessary to allow the expense to be shared by two or three trierarchs. In 358, *summoriai* or companies of sixty citizens were set up to divide the expense; and later again the charge was spread over all but the poorest citizens in proportion to their property (see *Demosthenes* (2), § 4 (*a*)). Service in the cavalry, entailing the provision of a horse and servant, was a lighter form of extraordinary liturgy. After 457 an allowance was granted for the maintenance of the horse.

Litye'rsēs (*Lituersēs*), in Greek legend, son of Midas (q.v.), king of Phrygia. It is said he used to require all comers to help in the harvest, and if they did not surpass him in activity would kill or beat them, until a mightier hero (some say Heracles) arrived and killed him. He is probably, in origin, some sort of harvest divinity. A harvest song was associated with his name. Matthew Arnold, in 'Thyrsis', writes:

For thee the Lityerses-song again
Young Daphnis with his silver voice doth sing.

Li'via, (1) later known as JŪLIA AUGUSTA (b. 58 B.C.), wife, first, of Tiberius Claudius Nero, mother of the emperor Tiberius and of Claudius Drusus the father of the emperor Claudius. After divorce she in 38 B.C. married Octavian and retained his affection till the end of his life (she survived him and died in A.D. 29). There were no children of this marriage. She was a woman of ability and high character, imbued with the spirit of the old Roman aristocracy, and she won the reverence of the Roman people. The title Augusta was conferred on her after the death of Augustus. She was the link between the Julian and the Claudian houses in the Julio-Claudian dynasty (see *Julio-Claudian Family*).

(2) Livia or Livilla, the granddaughter of (1), daughter of Claudius Drusus, sister of Germanicus, and wife of Drusus the son of Tiberius. In league with Sejanus she caused her husband to be poisoned. Sejanus proposed to marry her, but Tiberius put the proposal aside (see *Julio-Claudian Family*).

Li'vius Androni'cus, LŪCIUS (c. 284–204 B.C.), probably a Greek of Tarentum, taken as a captive, after the fall of that city, to Rome in 272. He probably entered the family of the father of M. Livius Salinātor, the conqueror of Hasdrubal, and was manumitted. He translated the 'Odyssey' into Latin Saturnians (see *Metre*, § 4), and gave instruction in Greek and Latin. In 240 he produced a tragedy and a comedy, adapted from the Greek, at the *ludi Romani* (see *Ludi*, § 1) of that year, which were of special magnificence to celebrate the close of the First Punic War. He continued as a playwright, and the titles of at least nine of his tragedies and fragments of three of his comedies survive. The tragedies dealt with mythological, especially Homeric, themes. A national hymn which he composed in 207 to be sung by a choir of maidens (or a later hymn) earned him the position of president of an academy of poets (*collēgium poētarum*) domiciled in the Temple of Minerva on the Aventine. Though his work, of which we have only short fragments, was regarded by Cicero as antiquated and of little interest, the historical importance of Livius as an innovator is

great. He represents the first literary impact of Greece on Rome. For he introduced to Roman literature the epic, the Greek drama, and the lyric. His 'Odyssey' remained a school-book till the time of Augustus, and Horace tells us he used to learn it by heart under the ferule of Orbilius.

Livy (*Titus Livius*) (59 B.C.–A.D. 17), was born at Patavium (Padua) in NE. Italy, probably of a well-to-do family. His city obtained the Roman franchise in 49 B.C. There is no evidence that he came to Rome before reaching full manhood. He won and retained the friendship of Augustus, in spite of the preference for the old republican constitution revealed by passages in his writings. He appears never to have held any public office, but to have devoted his life to literary labours. He had at least two children, a son and a daughter. He began his great history of Rome 'Ab Urbe Condita' between 27 and 25 B.C., and published it in instalments. It at once brought him fame. Livy survived Augustus by three years and is said to have died at Patavium.

The history consisted of 142 books, which were divided by copyists at an early date into 'decads' of ten books. An Epitome of it was written as early as the 1st c., and from this were drawn up *Periochae* or short abstracts of each book, apparently in two versions. Of the original work we possess Books I–X and XXI–XLV (XLI and XLIII are incomplete). The Epitome is lost, but we have the *Periochae* of all the books but CXXXVI and CXXXVII. Books I–V deal with the legendary founding of the city, the period of the kings and the early republic down to its conquest by the Gauls in 390 B.C. Books VI–XV deal with the subjugation of Italy before the conflict with Carthage. Books XVI–XXX recount the first two Punic Wars; XXXI–XLV the Macedonian and other Eastern wars; XLVI–LXX, the succeeding period to the outbreak of the Social War; LXXI–XC, to the death of Sulla; XCI–CVIII, to the Gallic War; CIX–CXVI, the Civil War to the death of Caesar; CXVII–CXXXIII, to the death of Antony; CXXXIV–CXLII, the rule of Augustus down to 9 B.C.; the whole survived to the end of the Roman Age. The books known to the Middle Ages were those we now have.

The work opens with an introduction in which Livy explains his purpose, to commemorate the deeds of the leading nation of the world, to describe the men and mode of life that had raised Rome to greatness, and the decline of morals which brought about the troubles of the 1st c.

B.C., so that his readers may draw therefrom the appropriate lessons. His general purpose is thus an ethical one. His attitude to the early legends which he relates is that he neither affirms nor denies their truth, but regards it as of no great importance; if some of them are not true, yet they resemble the truth. They illustrate, in fact, the old Roman character, which Livy idealizes. In general he appears to have relied upon earlier chroniclers and historians without making the fullest possible use of such original records as were available. He had neither the critical faculty nor the scientific method and insight of such historians as Thucydides and Polybius. He had no special knowledge of military or political affairs. He was not interested in meticulous accuracy. His narrative is in consequence not always historically trustworthy. It throws little light on economic conditions and social life in Rome. But Livy had enthusiasm for his subject, complete honesty (though his patriotism sometimes blinds him to Roman faults and his fairness is affected by his pro-senatorial prejudices), an art of graphic description and a sense of the dramatic that give great vividness to his characters and incidents. His prose is eloquent, clear, orderly, and abundant, developed from that of Cicero. Asinius Pollio (q.v.) saw in it an element of 'Patavinity' or provincialism.

Livy was much praised by his immediate successors, Tacitus, the Senecas, Quintilian, and drawn upon by Plutarch, Lucan, and other writers. He is little heard of in the Middle Ages, but the Renaissance adopted him with enthusiasm. Dante speaks of him as the historian 'who errs not' (Inf. xxviii. 12). The first edition of Livy was printed at Rome *c.* 1469. An English version of the extant books was made by the great Elizabethan translator, Philemon Holland (1552–1637). The important edition by the Danish scholar, J. N. Madvig, appeared in 1861–6.

Among the many famous and interesting narrative-passages in the extant books of Livy's history, the following may be mentioned:

Book I. The story of Romulus and Remus (4–7); the seizure of the Sabine women (9–13); the fight of the Horatii and the Curiatii and the death of Horatia (24–6); the coming of Lucumo (Tarquinius Priscus) to Rome (34); the accession of Lucius Tarquinius and the crimes of Tullia (46–8); the story of Lucretia, Sextus Tarquinius, and Brutus (57–60).

Book II. The execution of the sons of Brutus by their father (5); Horatius Cocles at the bridge (10); Mucius Scaevola's attempt to kill Porsena (12); Cloelia swimming the Tiber (13); Menenius Agrippa and the fable of the belly and the members (32); the meeting of Coriolanus and his mother outside Rome (40); the three hundred and six Fabii marching out against the Veientes (49).

Book III. The summoning of Cincinnatus from the fields to be dictator (26); Appius Claudius and Verginia (44–58).

Book IV. The fight between Cossus and the Etruscan king, in which the former won the *spolia opima* (q.v.) (19).

Book V. The siege of Veii, and the Gauls in Rome.

Book VI. The execution of M. Manlius Capitolinus.

Book VII. M. Curtius leaping into the abyss.

Book VIII. T. Manlius Torquatus ordering the execution of his son who, in defiance of orders, had fought and killed an enemy chief; P. Decius Mus devoting himself to death for the victory of his army; the wrath of Papirius Cursor against his Master of the Horse.

Book IX. The disaster of the Caudine Forks; and the interesting discussion of what would have happened had Alexander the Great encountered the Romans.

Books XXI–XXX, occupied with the narrative of the Hannibalic War, contain a multitude of exciting incidents and vivid descriptions. Only a few can be mentioned.

Book XXI. The character of Hannibal, the siege of Saguntum, Hannibal's crossing of the Alps, the battle of the Trebia.

Book XXII. The battle of Lake Trasimene, the fearful storm that Hannibal encountered on the Apennines, the conflict of Fabius with his impetuous Master of the Horse, the defeat of Cannae. Maharbal's criticism of Hannibal, that he knew how to conquer but not how to use his victory, is in Ch. 51.

Book XXIII. Hannibal at Capua, the enervation of his army, and the turning point of the war.

Book XXIV. The siege of Syracuse by Marcellus and the defensive devices of Archimedes (Ch. 34).

Book XXV. The capture of Syracuse and the death of Archimedes.

Book XXVI. Hannibal's approach within three miles of Rome (the land on which his camp stands is sold in Rome without reduction of price); Scipio Africanus is appointed commander in Spain at the age of 24, and captures Nova Carthago; his generosity and restraint in the treatment of a beautiful Spanish captive.

Book XXVII. The interception and defeat of Hasdrubal.

Book XXX. The romantic story of

Sophonisba (q.v.), Syphax, and Masinissa; the battle of Zama.

Book XXXIII. The defeat of Philip V of Macedon at Cynoscephalae, the notable speech of Flamininus on making peace with a vanquished foe (Ch. 12), the proclamation of Greek freedom at the Isthmian Games (Ch. 32).

Book XXXIV. The repeal of the Oppian sumptuary law.

Book XXXV. The conversation of Scipio and Hannibal at Ephesus about great military commanders.

Book XXXVIII. The proud reminder of Scipio Africanus when tried for embezzlement that the day was the anniversary of Zama (Ch. 51).

Book XXXIX. The discovery and suppression of the Bacchanalian orgies; the character of Cato the Censor (Ch. 40).

Book XLIV. The victory of Pydna.

Logo′graphi (*Logographoi*), (1) early Greek chroniclers (most of them Ionians), predecessors of the true historians such as Herodotus; their writings marked the transition from the verse of the epic poets to prose. Their narratives were bald and uncritical records of local traditions relating to a remote or mythical past, and were generally concerned with the legendary foundations of cities or the genealogies of gods and heroes. They were numerous in the 6th and 5th cc. B.C., but only fragments of the works of a few of them have survived. The first of them that is known is CADMUS of Miletus, who appears to have lived about the middle of the 6th c. He is said to have written a work on the foundation of Miletus. HECATAEUS (q.v.) of Miletus is better known. PHERECȲDES of Leros spent part of his life (probably in the 5th c.) at Athens, and wrote a work in ten books containing a genealogy of the gods, of which we have many fragments. CHARŌN of Lampsacus, XANTHUS (*Xanthos*) of Lydia, and HELLANICUS of Mytilene were a little anterior to, or contemporary with, Herodotus. Of these Hellanicus shows an advance on his predecessors, for among his numerous works was an 'Atthis', a history of Athens down to recent times, which was criticised by Thucydides.

(2) The name given at Athens to persons who wrote speeches for litigants to deliver. Antiphon (q.v.) was the first of these, and Lysias (q.v.) one of the most eminent and successful.

Lo′llius U′rbicus, QUINTUS, see *Britain*, § 2.

Long Walls at Athens. The two Long Walls connecting Athens with the Piraeus and Phalerum were begun about 460 B.C.,

and were completed in a few years. The third or Middle Wall, which ran parallel to the Piraeus Wall at a distance of some 200 yards from it, was built, at the instance of Pericles, after the Thirty Years' Peace of 445. The Phalerum Wall was allowed to fall into decay. The other two were destroyed after the capitulation of Athens in 404, but rebuilt by Conon after his victory at Cnidus in 394. Their subsequent history is obscure, but they were in ruins when Philip V of Macedon attacked Athens in 200 B.C. The ruins have now disappeared, but from the accounts of travellers who saw their remains in the 18th c., they appear to have been 12 ft. thick, built in part at least of large squared blocks. The two Piraeus walls were each about four miles long.

Longi′nus, CASSIUS (*c.* A.D. 220–73), to be distinguished from the supposed author of the treatise 'On the Sublime' (see below), was an eminent Greek writer on rhetoric and philosophy. He was a Neoplatonist (q.v.) and the instructor of Porphyry, and after teaching for thirty years at Athens ended his life as the counsellor of Queen Zenobia at Palmȳra; for his loyal support of her he was put to death by Aurelian. A treatise by him on the 'Art of Rhetoric' survives.

Longi′nus on the Sublime (Διονυσίου (ἢ) Λογγίνου περὶ ὕψους), a Greek work of unknown date and authorship. The manuscripts attribute it to 'Dionysius Longinus' or to 'Dionysius or Longinus'. The work appears to belong to the 1st or 2nd c. A.D.

It is a treatise, addressed to a friend, Postumius Terentiānus, on what constitutes sublimity in literature. By its clearness of expression, by the felicity and interest of its illustrations, by the soundness of its criticism, and by its enthusiasm, it makes a strong appeal to the reader, and it is not surprising that it should have found admirers in modern times in such men as Dryden, Addison, Pope, Goldsmith, and Gibbon. The author analyses the qualities of writing that constitute sublimity, and finds them in grandeur of ideas ('sublimity is the echo of a noble mind', ix. 2) and the capacity for strong emotion, which are generally congenital, supplemented by artistic construction and nobility of phrase ('truly beautiful words are the very light of the spirit', xxx. 1); these qualities give an effect of dignity and elevation, and must have underlying them a natural facility of expression. He discusses the faults to be avoided, such as tumidity, puerility, and frigidity; the part played by imagination and various figures of speech; and illustrates his points by a wealth of quotation. There are interesting comparisons of the 'Iliad' and the 'Odyssey', and of Demosthenes and Cicero. The author finds the chief examples of sublimity of style in Homer, Plato, and Demosthenes, of whom he speaks with enthusiasm; and in one place gives an ode of Sappho, otherwise not preserved, though it was translated by Catullus (Poem 51, 'Ille mi par esse deo videtur'). There is a notable passage in Ch. ix. 9 in which the writer points out, as an instance of grandeur in the representation of divinity, the first verses of the Book of Genesis.

This work evoked the memorable lines in Pope's 'Essay on Criticism',

Thee, bold Longinus! all the Nine inspire,
And bless their critic with a poet's fire.

. . . . . .
Whose own example strengthens all his laws;
And is himself the great sublime he draws.

Lo'ngus, see *Novel*.

Lotus-Eaters (*Lōtophagoi*), in the 'Odyssey' (q.v., ix), a fabulous people whose land Odysseus visits. They eat the lotus-fruit, whose property is to make those who eat it forget their home and desire to remain for ever in Lotus-land. See Tennyson, 'The Lotus-Eaters'.

Lū'can (*Marcus Annaēus Lūcānus*) (A.D. 39–65) was born at Corduba in Spain. He was grandson of Seneca the Rhetorician, and nephew of Seneca the Philosopher (qq.v.) and of the Gallio of Acts xviii. He was educated at Rome, partly under the Stoic Cornūtus, whose tuition he is said to have shared with Persius. He showed precocious brilliancy, was favourably noticed by Nero, and was advanced at an early age to the quaestorship. But he incurred the jealousy of the emperor over literary matters (Nero himself was a poet), is said to have been forbidden to write further poetry or to plead in the courts, and from indignation joined the conspiracy of Piso against the emperor. When this was discovered, Lucan, in spite of confessions and abject pleas, was commanded to take his own life. There is a biography of him by Suetonius.

Lucan wrote a number of minor works which are lost, among them an address to his wife, Polla Argentāria. His one surviving poem is the 'Pharsalia' (q.v.), the greatest Latin epic after the 'Aeneid'. Lucan's brilliance won the admiration of his contemporaries. Quintilian, while recognizing his qualities, adds 'magis oratoribus quam poetis imitandus'. Dante placed him as a poet with Homer, Horace,

Ovid, Virgil, and himself (Inf. iv. 88–90). Chaucer set him on a column in the House of Fame.

Lu'cian (*Lūciānus, Loukiānos*) (c. A.D. 115–c. 200), born at Samosāta on the Euphrates, was apprenticed to a statuary, but soon abandoned this profession, and became a rhetorician. He travelled in Greece, Italy, and southern Gaul, earning his living by declamations. When he was about forty he settled at Athens and devoted himself to philosophy under the Stoic Dēmōnax, and to writing dialogues. But before long he renounced philosophy as a subject of dialogues (except for the exposure of false philosophers), and turned to the development of a new form of literature, the satirical dialogue, for which he is chiefly famous. In later life, under the emperor Commodus, he was appointed to a legal post in Egypt, which he appears to have retained until his death.

Among his writings on literary and quasi-philosophic subjects may be mentioned, (1) THE VISION (*Somnium*), a chapter of his early life, telling how he abandoned sculpture for learning; (2) NIGRINUS, which contains an interesting picture of the simplicity and peace of contemporary Athens contrasted with the turbid and luxurious life of Rome; (3) THE LITERARY PROMETHEUS (*Ad eum qui dixerat, 'Prometheus es in verbis'*), in which he describes the origin of his Satires, viz. a blend of comedy and dialogue; (4) THE WAY TO WRITE HISTORY (*De historia conscrībenda*), an amusing criticism of the eccentricities of contemporary historians, followed by an exposition of the qualities required in a history and its author; (5) The TRUE HISTORY (*Vēra historia*), a parody of the cock-and-bull tales of adventure put forward as true by ancient writers. (6) DĒMŌNAX, an account of the character of the philosopher of that name, Lucian's teacher. (7) IMĀGINĒS (*Eikones*), containing interesting references to the chief works of some of the great Greek artists, such as Phidias, Praxiteles, Polygnotus, and Apelles.

Lucian's satirical dialogues are numerous, and, together with his fantastic tales, are his most characteristic works, showing his humorous questioning spirit and hatred of shams, applied in particular to the myths of the old religion and to philosophy. Among the best-known of these dialogues are: (1) the DIALOGUES OF THE GODS (*Deorum Dialogi*) and OF THE SEA-GODS (*Marinorum Dialogi*), short dialogues making fun of the myths about, e.g. the birth of Athene, Apollo's love affairs, the Judgement of Paris, the story of Poly-

phemus and Galatea. (2) DIALOGUES OF
THE DEAD (*Mortuorum Dialogi*) short
dialogues held in the lower world, the
interlocutors being such characters as
Pluto, Hermes, Charon, Menippus, Diogenes, Heracles, Alexander, Achilles. Death
shows up the vanities and pretences of
living men, and defeats the intrigues of
expectant heirs. The irony is grim, and
tinged with melancholy and resignation.
(3) MENIPPUS (also called *Necyomantia*):
Menippus (q.v.), the Cynic philosopher,
baffled by the contradictions of philosophy,
visits the lower world to consult Tiresias
(q.v.) as to the best life to lead, and is
merely told to do, with smiling face, the
task that lies to his hand. Similar themes
are those of the CHARON, who visits the
upper world (Life seen from the point of
view of Death) and the VOYAGE TO THE
LOWER WORLD (*Cataplūs*). (4) THE COOK,
of Micyllos the tanner, which in a previous
existence was once Pythagoras (at another
time Aspasia), and now instructs its owner
in the advantages of poverty over wealth.
(5) THE SALE OF LIVES (*Vitarum auctio*),
an amusing description of an auction at
which the various philosophic creeds, in the
persons of their exponents, are put up for
sale. (6) ICAROMENIPPUS: Menippus (q.v.),
puzzled by the contradictory opinions of
philosophers about the gods, decides to
investigate the matter for himself, and
visits heaven with the help of an eagle's
wings. On his way he calls at the Moon,
where he finds Empedocles, who has been
carried there by the vapours of Etna. He
is civilly received by the gods, watches
Zeus receiving human prayers through a
trapdoor in the floor of heaven, attends a
banquet, and hears the gods decide to
destroy all the philosophers as useless
drones. (7) ZEUS CONFUTATUS, on the conflict between the doctrine of fate and that
of divine omnipotence. (8) DEORUM CON-
CILIUM, in which Momus protests before
the assembled gods against the admission
among the genuine deities of a number of
foreigners and persons of mixed origin,
from Dionysus and his hangers-on to Apis
and Anubis. (9) DEPENDENT SCHOLARS
(*De Mercēde Conductis*), the sad tale of the
philosopher or man of letters, who, for
a pittance coupled with hardships and
humiliations, sells his liberty to an em-
ployer. (10) PEREGRINE (*De morte Peregrini*), a satirical narrative of the career
of a Cynic, who, in pursuit of notoriety,
caused himself to be burnt alive on a pyre
(he was an historical character); the work
contains a reference to the early Christians.
(11) LUCIUS OR THE ASS, doubtfully attributed to Lucian, perhaps the remodelling
of an earlier work which served also as the

basis of the 'Golden Ass' of Apuleius
(q.v.). See also *Timon* (1).

Lucian adopted, with surprising success,
Attic Greek in his writings. His views on
philosophy and religion are discussed in
one of Landor's 'Imaginary Conversations', 'Lucian and Timotheus'. Some of
his fantastic tales inspired Rabelais and
were the prototype of Swift's 'Gulliver'.
There is a translation of his works by
H. W. and F. G. Fowler.

Lūci′lius (*Lūcīlius*), GAIUS (180–102 B.C.),
born at Suessa Aurunca in Campania,
was a member of the literary circle of Scipio
Aemilianus, and is famous as the creator
of that purely Roman form of literature
which came to be known as the Satire
(q.v.). Lucilius wrote, chiefly in hexameters, thirty books of 'Sermones', as he
called them, informal discourses, mainly
autobiographical, on incidents in the lives of
himself and his friends, travels, banquets,
and literary subjects. In these were included outspoken criticism of authors and
men in public life, and protests against
luxury and gluttony. These 'Sermones',
except for fragments, have perished. They
served as a model for the earlier Satires of
Horace, who refers in Sat. I. iv. 9–10 to the
facility with which Lucilius composed, and
describes in Sat. II. i. 30 et seq. his method:

Ille velut fidis arcana sodalibus olim
Credebat libris . . . quo fit, ut omnis
Votiva pateat veluti descripta tabella
Vita senis.

These words (from 'quo fit') were appropriately prefixed by Boswell to his 'Life
of Johnson'. Lucilius also inspired Persius
and Juvenal.

Lūci′lius (*Lūcīlius*) the Younger, a
friend of Seneca the Philosopher (q.v.), to
whom Seneca addressed the dialogue 'De
Providentia', the series of 'Moral Epistles',
and the 'Quaestiones Naturales'. Lucilius
was procurator of Sicily and a poet, and
it is thought that he may have been the
author of the poem 'Aetna' (q.v.).

Lūci′na, see *Juno*.

Lūcius or the Ass (*Loukios ē Onos*), see
Lucian.

Lucrē′tia, the wife of L. Tarquinius Col-
lātīnus, nephew of Tarquinius Priscus (see
Rome, § 2). According to legend she
suffered outrage at the hands of Sextus,
son of Tarquinius Superbus, and having revealed this to her husband took her own life.
This incident led to the insurrection in which
the Tarquins were expelled from Rome. The
story, in English literature, has been told by
Chaucer in his 'Legend of Good Women',
by Gower in his 'Confessio Amantis', and
by Shakespeare in 'The Rape of Lucrece'.

Lucrē′tius Cārus, Tĭtus (c. 99–c. 55 B.C.), generally known as 'Lucretius', a great Roman philosophical poet, of whose life very little is known. St. Jerome, in his version of the 'Chronica' of Eusebius, states that he was born in 94 B.C., was poisoned by a love-philtre, wrote in the intervals of madness some books which Cicero edited, and took his own life at the age of 44. We have no knowledge how far these statements may be accepted, though Cicero's letters show that he and his brother had both read the poet's work by 54 B.C., and there is independent evidence that he died in 55. His birth in 99 is inferred from a combination of this with the passage in Jerome. Lucretius was a friend of C. Memmius, the propraetor whom Catullus accompanied to Bīthȳnia, and to him he addressed his poem. He lived at a time when the old Roman religion had lost its hold on the educated classes and a general scepticism prevailed; but the gloom and uncertainty of the times no doubt rendered people superstitious and nervous. Lucretius remarks that even those who express contempt for the gods will in time of trouble sacrifice black sheep to them. He was himself a man of a scientific and inquiring turn of mind, and a convinced and ardent believer in the Epicurean system of philosophy. By his great didactic poem 'De Rerum Natura' ('On the Nature of Things'), in six books of hexameters, the fullest exposition we possess of that system, he sought to dispel the superstition and anxiety of his contemporaries.

After an invocation of Venus, the great creative force of nature, he sets forth the atomic theory of Epicurus, which, he holds, satisfactorily explains, and alone explains, the phenomena of the world. The atoms, infinite in number and eternal, endlessly falling through space by their own nature, colliding when they swerve a little from their path, form into masses, from which the universe by chance arrangement is built up. This universe and all that is in it act according to law, and there is no room in it for the gods and their interference. Popular religion and the terrors introduced by it have no foundation. Man is an exception to the general law of causation, for he retains free will, originating in that element of spontaneity in the atoms which causes them occasionally to swerve in their downward path. The soul, material in its nature, though composed of extremely rarefied elements, is mortal and dies with the body. To the proof of its mortality and to the folly of the fear of death Lucretius devotes the greater part of Book III. He proceeds to discuss the

nature of sensation and the various biological processes, ending Book IV with a vigorous denunciation of love. In Books V and VI, after elaborating the explanation of the formation of the world, in which the gods have had no share and in which there is no design, and showing reasons for thinking that the world itself is mortal, Lucretius explains a number of celestial and terrestrial phenomena. Perhaps the most interesting part of the whole work is the section (v. 772–1457) in which he traces the origin of vegetable and human life, and with remarkable insight describes the development of primitive man and the birth of civilization. There is no specific treatment of the subject of moral conduct, but it is clear from various passages that Lucretius accepted the view of Epicurus. Pleasure and pain are the only guides to conduct, but by pleasure he understands the calm that proceeds from absence of pain and desire, and freedom from care and fear. He condemns the luxurious and artificial life of the day and contrasts with it the joys derived from simple tastes and the beauties of nature. There are indications that the work was left not quite completed. The style (unlike that of Catullus) shows the influence of the old Latin poets, Ennius, Naevius, Pacuvius, and Accius; and the author had read Cicero's translation of Aratus. He uses alliteration freely, and constructs new compound words, such as 'terriloquus', 'horrisonus'.

The poem is a piece of earnest controversial writing, designed to instruct and convince rather than please, and much of the matter does not lend itself easily to poetical treatment. But the author's stately manner is in harmony with the magnitude of his theme; and the rapture of his reverential contemplation of nature, the ardour with which he combats what he regards as a debasing superstition, his sense of the beauty of rural scenery and of the pathos of human life, inspire many noble passages, as well as many vivid individual lines and phrases. One of his most striking similes is the comparison of a body at rest and yet composed of atoms in perpetual motion to a flock of sheep or armies engaged in battle, when seen from afar (ii. 308–32).

Lucretius aroused the admiration of Virgil ('Felix qui potuit rerum cognoscere causas'), of Statius (who speaks of the 'docti furor arduus Lucreti'), even of Ovid. But in the Middle Ages he appears to have been completely forgotten, and the preservation of his text seems to have hung at one time upon a single manuscript (see Munro's Introduction in his edition of Lucretius). Poggio obtained a manuscript of Lucretius about 1417, since lost, of which many imperfect copies were made, and the first edition was printed about 1473. The restoration of the text has engaged the labour of many scholars. In England the poem was known in the 16th c. to W. Gilbert, physician to Queen Elizabeth and author of a treatise, 'De Magnete', in which Lucretius is quoted. In the 17th c. John Evelyn translated the first book, and Mrs. Lucy Hutchinson the whole. Milton imitated Lucretius in many passages of the 'Paradise Lost'. Dryden translated portions of the first five books. The great edition of Lucretius by H. A. J. Munro appeared in 1864. Tennyson's fine poem 'Lucretius' presents the sage, his mind deranged by the love-potion administered by his wife, his philosophic doctrine distraught by phantoms of the gods, lamenting his subjugation to some unseen monster, and finally taking his own life.

Lucrē′tius Vespi′liō, QUINTUS, supposed author of the remarkable memorial known as the 'Laudatio Turiae'. See under *Women*, § 2.

Lūcu′llus, LŪCIUS LĪCINIUS (c. 114–57. B.C.), a member of a noble but impoverished family, who showed ability as a general and statesman in Asia under Sulla in 87 B.C., and honesty and humanity as pro-praetor in Africa. He was consul in 74 and carried out a series of brilliant campaigns against Mithridates in the Third Mithridatic War, until his soldiers mutinied, wearied by his energy and ambitious plans. He was superseded by Glabrio in 67, but the *lex Mānīlia* invalidated this appointment, and Pompey was given command in the East in 66. Lucullus thereafter gave himself up to the indulgence of his luxurious tastes, having acquired great wealth in Asia. He was an ardent Hellenist. The books of the Pontic kings remained his private property; but he was always ready to lend them, and his library became a centre for literary Greeks at Rome. He wrote an account of the Marsian War (90–89 B.C.) in Greek. See also *Pro Archia*. He is said to have introduced the cherry into Italy from Cerasus in Pontus. There is a life of him in Plutarch, where his luxury is described.

Lū′di, the public games at Rome. Like the panhellenic games in Greece, they were closely associated with religion. Each *ludus* had its origin in some religious festival, instituted to win the favour or avert the anger of the gods or to comply with some oracular command. They followed an exact ritual, any deviation from which entailed a repetition (*instaurātio*) of the proceedings. Unlike the Greek games they

included no element of athletic contests. This was first introduced in imperial times in what were known as *agōnēs*, such as the *Agōn Nerōniānus* and the *Agon Capitōlinus* (see below, § 2).

§ 1. *Republican period*

The earliest *ludi* appear to have been chariot races held in honour of Mars or Consus. The *Ludi Rōmāni* or *Magni* were also of very early date. They were celebrated in September and are said to have originated in the return of a general with his army after a victorious campaign, when he carried out the vow he had made to give a festival to Jupiter if successful. From being 'votive' these games became annual and their duration was extended from one day to fifteen (4–18 September). They included a great procession to the temple of Jupiter on the Capitol in which images of the great gods were carried. They also included chariot races (*circenses*, see *Chariot Races*) and military evolutions.

Ludi scaenici, consisting in the performance of plays, were added to the *Ludi Romani* in 240 B.C., when Livius Andronicus (q.v.) produced his adaptations from Greek drama. But this was not the occasion of the first public dramatic performances at Rome, for Livy states that in 364 B.C. pantomimic dances by Etruscans were exhibited to appease the divine anger in a time of pestilence (see *Comedy*, § 5). From 240 B.C. *ludi scaenici* regularly formed part of the *Ludi Romani* and later were also included in the *Ludi Plebeii*, *Apollinares*, and *Megalenses* (see below). It is probable that at first only two tragedies and two comedies were produced annually. In the later republican times there were fifty-five days in each year on which *ludi scaenici* took place and the number was further increased under the empire.

The *Ludi Plēbēii*, extended from one to fourteen days (4–17 November), appear to have been a plebeian repetition of the *Ludi Romani*, but little is known about them.

The *Ludi Apollinārēs*, in honour of Apollo, were instituted at a perilous moment in the Second Punic War. They were shortly afterwards made annual on the proposal of the *praetor urbanus* at a time of epidemic. They were extended from one to eight and then to nine days (5–13 July), and consisted mainly of scenic performances, one day only being given to games in the Circus.

The *Ludi Megalensēs* (4–10 April), were established in 204 B.C. to celebrate the arrival from Phrygia of the sacred stone of the goddess Cybele (q.v.). Only one day was occupied with games in the Circus, the others with scenic performances.

The *Ludi Cereālēs* (12–19 April) were a plebeian festival in honour of Ceres (the tutelary goddess of the plebs). One day was given to games in the Circus.

The *Ludi Flōrālēs*, instituted in 238 B.C. and made annual in 173 B.C., were designed as an invocation to the goddess Flora, the protectress of blossom. Men decked themselves with flowers and women put on gay dresses and the period of the festival, 28 April–3 May, was a time of general merriment. The first five days were occupied with scenic performances (chiefly mimes), the last day with *venationes* (q.v.), the hunting of animals in the Circus.

All these games were given by the State, and the displays were supplemented at the cost of the magistrates concerned (aediles, curule or plebeian, except in the case of the *Ludi Apollinares*, which were under the direction of the *praetor urbanus*). The magistrates sought thereby to increase their popularity and chances of election to higher office.

Displays and hunting of large animals, first mentioned as occurring in 186 B.C., became a popular feature of the public games (see *Venationes*; we read in Cicero's letters how M. Caelius Rufus begged Cicero when he was governor of Cilicia to send him panthers). Gladiators (q.v.) were apparently not introduced in the official games till the end of republican times, though their displays, given by private persons, had by then become popular. For *naumachiae*, mimic sea-fights, see under that word.

§ 2. Imperial period

The games above enumerated were continued under the empire and others were added, of which the following are the most important:

The *Ludi Saeculārēs*, though strictly of republican origin, came into prominence only in imperial times. They appear to have been instituted, at an unknown date, in the hope of bringing to an end some period of national danger or distress, from pestilence or other cause. They were supposed to be held at intervals of a *saeculum*, which was commonly interpreted as either a hundred or a hundred and ten years. These games were celebrated by Augustus in 17 B.C. (31 May–2 June) and the ceremonies and performances of plays are recorded in detail in an inscription which survives (see *Epigraphy*, § 10); it was for this occasion that Horace wrote his 'Carmen Saeculare'. The *Ludi Saeculares* were celebrated again by Claudius in A.D. 47 (as the eight hundredth year from the found-

ing of Rome), and by Domitian in A.D. 87 (about a century after the celebration by Augustus). On the latter occasion Tacitus the historian was one of the *quindecimviri* in charge of the ceremonies, and the celebration is referred to by Martial and Statius.

In the reign of Augustus were also founded *Ludi Martiālēs*, in honour of Mars (12 May), and *Augustālēs* (or *Augustalia*, 3–12 October) to celebrate the return of Augustus from the East. There were also birthday games (*nātālicii*) in honour of Augustus and later emperors.

The *Agon Nerōniānus* was instituted by Nero in A.D. 60 in partial imitation of the Olympian Games. It was to be held every five years and to include chariot races, athletic contests, and contests in music and poetry. The *Agon Capitōlinus* was instituted by Domitian in A.D. 86, also in imitation of the Olympian Games. It was held every four years and included athletic and musical contests.

Lūdus Trō'iae, a very old Roman game, which fell into abeyance in the later republic, but was revived by Julius Caesar and by Augustus. The meaning of 'Troiae' is obscure. The word is found on an Etruscan vase bearing the picture of two armed horsemen. Virgil (Aen. v. 596 et seq.) connects the *Ludus Troiae* with the games celebrated at the tomb of Anchises.

Lupercā'lia, a very ancient festival at Rome, held on 15 February, probably in honour of Faunus (q.v.), worshipped under the name Lupercus. Its purpose was to secure fertility for the fields, the flocks, and the people. The worshippers gathered at the Lupercal, a cave on the Palatine, where Romulus and Remus were supposed to have been suckled by the wolf. Goats and a dog were sacrificed. Two youths belonging to the colleges known as the *Luperci* (chosen from particular families), were smeared with the blood of the sacrifice, clad themselves in the skins of the slain goats, and ran a purificatory course round the Palatine (the ancient *Rōma Quadrāta*, see *Rome*, § 1), with strips of goat's hide in their hands. Women placed themselves on their course to receive blows from these thongs, which were believed to procure fertility. The thongs were called *februa*, that is 'means of purification', and the month in which the ceremony took place was called *februārius* (our February), the month of purification. Cf. Shakespeare, 'Julius Caesar', I. ii., which presents the famous occasion in 44 B.C. when Antony ran as a Lupercus, and in his course mounted the Rostra and offered Caesar the crown. The ceremony survived into

Christian times and was finally suppressed in A.D. 494. The etymology of the name, and the precise significance of the Lupercalia are still matters of dispute. The festival was thought by the Romans, who connected it with the Greek *Lycaea* (see *Lycaeus*), to have been imported from Arcadia; they identified Faunus with Pan, who was especially worshipped in Arcadia.

Lu'scius Lānuvi'nus, a writer of Latin comedies, contemporary with Caecilius (q.v.). He was the 'malevolus vetus poeta' whose criticisms Terence rebuts in many of his prologues. His works have not survived.

Lustrā'tiō, in Roman religion, a ceremony designed to effect purification and protection from evil influences. It consisted in a solemn procession round the thing to be purified, whether city, fields, army, or flocks, and the offering or prayer and sacrifice at certain points. A lustration, after the funeral rites for Mīsēnus, is described by Virgil (Aen. vi. 229).

Lyae'us (*Luaios*), see *Dionysus*.

Lycae'us (*Lukaios*), the name of a mountain in Arcadia, and an epithet of Zeus, who according to one account was born on the mountain. The name appears, like Lycaon (q.v.), to be connected with the word for 'wolf'. A festival, the *Lycaea*, was held on Mt. Lycaeus in honour of Zeus Lycaeus. At this festival a man was supposed to undergo transformation into a wolf and he was believed to retain that form for nine years. This perhaps is an echo of human sacrifices primitively included in the ritual of Zeus Lycaeus. On Mt. Lycaeus there was also a sanctuary of Pan. There was probably something in common between the Lycaea and the Roman Lupercalia (q.v.), a festival which was thought in antiquity to have been imported from Arcadia; but the subject is obscure.

Lycā'on (*Lukāōn*), a legendary king of Arcadia who, as the host of Zeus, offered him human flesh to eat, in order to try his divinity. He was killed by lightning or turned into a wolf (see *Lycaeus*).

Lycei'us (*Lukeios*), an epithet of Apollo (q.v.).

Lȳcē'um (*Lūkeion*), a grove and gymnasium near Athens, sacred to Apollo Lyceius, where Aristotle taught. The name is sometimes used to signify the philosophic school of Aristotle. The Lyceum lay to the E. of the city near the Ilissus.

Ly'cophron (*Lūkophrōn*), (1) younger son of Periander (q.v.), tyrant of Corinth, exiled by his father to Corcyra (then under direct Corinthian control) on account of his bitter hostility. In his later years

Periander proposed to hand over his kingdom to Lycophron, and to go himself to Corcyra; but the Corcyreans, to prevent Periander from coming to their country, put Lycophron to death. For this Periander took vengeance on the Corcyreans. (For the whole story, see Hdt iii 50-3). (2) Of Chalcis (b. *c.* 325 B.C.), a Greek poet of the Hellenistic Age (q.v.), to whom is doubtfully attributed the extant poem 'Alexandra', a dramatic monologue in 1474 iambic trimeters, in which Cassandra prophesies, in an obscurely allusive style, the fall of Troy, the fate of the heroes of the Trojan War, and other events down to the rise of the Roman power. Lycophron was also a writer of tragedies, which have not survived; and the author of a treatise on Comedy, of which we have only fragments.

Lȳcu'rgus (*Lūkourgos*), (1) a legendary king of the Ēdōnes, a Thracian people; he persecuted Dionysus (q.v.) and for his impiety was struck blind, or driven mad, so that he killed his own son Dryas. (2) The legendary legislator of Sparta (q.v.). Herodotus refers to him (i. 65, 66), Xenophon praises his institutions, and Plutarch later wrote an account of him and his legislation, but admits that nothing certain is known about him or when he is supposed to have lived. The reforms generally ascribed to Lycurgus are now dated, mainly on archaeological evidence, about 600 B.C. (3) A distinguished Attic orator, a member of the illustrious family of the Eteobūtadae (hereditary priests of Poseidon Erechtheus), a man of noble character, an eminent financial administrator, and an advocate of the old social discipline. He was a pupil of Isocrates (q.v.). Of his fifteen speeches one survives, the indictment for treason of one Lēōcratēs, for having fled from Athens on the receipt of the news of Chaeronea. Lycurgus was in charge of the finances of Athens during the period 338-326 B.C., and carried out some important public works. He rebuilt the gymnasium of the Lyceum and reconstructed in marble the theatre of Dionysus. He also carried a decree that official copies should be prepared and preserved of the works of the three great tragedians. After his death, a deficit in the treasury was laid to his charge, and his children, in spite of a defence by Hyperides (q.v.), were imprisoned. See *Athens*, § 11 *ad fin.*

Lȳ'cus (*Lūkos*), see *Antiope*.

Ly'dia (*Lūdiā*), a country occupying the centre of the western part of Asia Minor, between Mysia on the N. and Caria on the S.; the river Hermus and its tributaries flowed through it, and its capital was Sardis. Under the dynasty of the Mermnadae, which was founded by Gyges and ended with Croesus (q.v.) and reigned from the beginning of the 7th c. to the middle of the 6th c. B.C., a Lydian empire was formed. Its exact limits are not known, but it extended northwards to the Troad and pressed against the territories of the Greek cities on the coast. This empire was brought to an end by the Persian Cyrus (q.v.). To the Lydians is ascribed the invention of coinage. For the influence of its civilization on the Greeks see *Asia Minor*. Maeonia (whence *Maeonides*, q.v.) was an ancient name of Lydia, probably derived from Maeonian conquerors of Phrygian origin. See Pl. 8.

Ly'dia (*Lȳdia*), a Latin poem, probably incomplete, of which we have eighty hexameters. Owing to the fact that 'Lydia' is also mentioned in the 'Dirae' (q.v.) it was at one time associated with that poem and ascribed to Virgil. The author is unknown. It is a lament by a lover for the loss of his mistress.

Ly'gdamus, see *Tibullus*.

Ly'ncēus (*Lugkeus*), in Greek mythology, (1) son of Apharēus, and one of the Argonauts, whose eyesight was so keen that he could see through the earth. In a fight with Castor and Polydeuces (see *Dioscuri*), he and his brother Idas (an inseparable pair like their adversaries) were killed, as also was Castor. (2) A son of Aegyptus, and husband of Hypermnestra (see *Danaus*).

Lyre, see *Music*, § 1.

Lyric Poetry.

§ 1. *Greek Lyric Poetry*

Lyric poetry, meaning 'poetry sung to the lyre', is a term applied originally to songs accompanied by music; at first to *Scolia* (q.v.) or drinking songs, and to light songs of love; but always to songs as expressing the untrammelled and personal sentiments of the poets, as distinguished from epic and dramatic poetry. Lyric poetry had its origin in the Aeolian island of Lesbos, with Terpander, Sappho, and Alcaeus (qq.v.), and in Ionia with Anacreon (q.v.). It was accompanied at first on some kind of lyre. It employed a great variety of metres, of which the most characteristic were combinations of dactyls and trochees (see *Metre*, § 3). It was chiefly developed among the Dorians, where Terpander, who migrated to Sparta, is said to have established it. It there took the more solemn and elaborate form of the *Choral Lyric* (q.v.), accompanied by the flute as well as the lyre. This reached its greatest perfection with Pindar. The age of the great lyric poets ended about 452 B.C., when Pindar and Bacchylides wrote their last known odes. But by this time lyric poetry had found a new field in the choruses of the Greek drama. Greek tragedy was at first essentially lyric in character. The early tragedian Phrynichus was famous for the sweetness of his lyrics; and although as tragedy developed the chorus was more and more relegated to a subordinate position, the lyrical element continued a source of delight to the end of the period of the great tragedians. Lyrics are an important feature likewise in the comedy of Aristophanes, and there is often in his choruses 'a rush of real feeling and beauty, quickly apologized for and turned off with a laugh' (Murray). For the lyric metres of Greek drama, see *Metre*, §§ 2 and 3. For *Elegiac Poetry*, sometimes included under lyric poetry, see *Elegy*.

§ 2. *Roman Lyric Poetry*

The adoption in Latin of the Greek lyric metres presented great difficulty, especially with the restrictions that the Romans introduced, and the number of great Roman lyric poets is small. Livius Andronicus (q.v.) composed a national hymn to be sung by a choir of maidens; and Laevius (q.v.) was another early writer of lyrics, but only fragments of his work have survived. The two chief Roman lyric poets were Catullus and Horace, and they had no important successors (except perhaps Statius). Seneca used a variety of lyric metres in the choruses of his tragedies, Sapphics, Glyconics, Asclepiads; but without the metrical skill of the great Greek tragedians and without the variety of the strophic arrangement (see *Strophe*). See *Metre*, § 5.

Lȳsan'der (*Lūsandros*) (d. 395 B.C.), a Spartan naval commander in the latter part of the Peloponnesian War (q.v.), the victor of Aegospotami, a man of great courage and ability, but cruel and unscrupulous. He became very powerful in Greece after the defeat of Athens and established in that city the Thirty Tyrants (see *Athens*, § 5). He even received divine honours in Greek cities. But he was deposed by the Spartan ephors in consequence of his misgovernment and insubordination. He fell at the siege of the Boeotian city of Haliartus (395). We have lives of him by Nepos and Plutarch.

Ly'sias (*Lūsiās*), a great Attic orator, son of Cephalus (*Kephalos*), a wealthy Syracusan, who settled as a metic at Athens on the invitation of Pericles. There Lysias was born about the middle of the 5th c.

B.C. (according to tradition in 458). Lysias had two brothers, Polemarchus and Euthydēmus. Cephalus and his sons figure in the 'Republic' of Plato, the scene of which is laid at their house in the Piraeus. At the age of fifteen Lysias, with one or both his brothers, went to Thurii and is said to have studied rhetoric under Tisias of Syracuse, himself a pupil of Corax (see *Orators*, § 1). The defeat of the Athenian expedition to Sicily led to the expulsion of Lysias and his brother from Thurii in 412, and they returned to Athens, where the family lived prosperously (owning a shield factory) until the tyranny of the Thirty (404). These, to procure funds, arrested wealthy persons, among them Lysias and Polemarchus, and seized their property. Lysias escaped, but Polemarchus was put to death. After the deposition of the Thirty, Lysias returned to Athens, and being now in straitened circumstances, became a professional writer of forensic speeches. But he first brought an action against Eratosthenes, one of the Thirty and the man principally responsible for the death of his brother. His speech in this case is the most important of his extant orations (to be distinguished from the speech 'On the murder of Eratosthenes', a different person). Lysias wrote a large number of speeches (over 200) for litigants in all kinds of cases, of which 34 have survived. His originality lay in his power of putting himself in his client's place and preparing for him a speech such as he and not a professional advocate would have made. The rhetorical devices for convincing a jury are concealed under a language simple and natural, in general without ornamental figures, varied according to the client's circumstances and case. The speeches are harmonious and agreeable in form, clear and vivid, and orderly in arrangement (preface, narrative, proof, conclusion). They contain occasional touches of humour, as where (in a fragment preserved by Athenaeus) he describes how Aeschines, having borrowed money to start a scent shop, had so many creditors hanging about it that people thought it must be a funeral. He is rarely passionate, and pathos is not his strong point. Among the most interesting of the speeches are: 'For Mantitheus' (a young man accused of having served in the cavalry under the Thirty); 'For the invalid' (the claim of an infirm person not to be deprived of public relief); 'Against Alcibiades' (the younger, for dereliction of military duty); and 'On the murder of Eratosthenes' (by the husband of a woman whom he had seduced). Of the epideictic ('display') speeches of Lysias, we have a fragment of his 'Olym-

piacus', made at the Olympic festival of 388, in which he urges the Greeks to put an end to civil strife and unite against the two great enemies, the Persian king and Dionysius, tyrant of Syracuse. It is said that he wrote a defence for Socrates to speak at his trial, but that Socrates refused it. After Socrates' death, at some date later than 392, the sophist Polycrates published an 'Accusation of Socrates'. It may be that the speech of Lysias above referred to was in fact a 'Defence of Socrates' in reply to this. The 'Phaedrus' of Plato contains an extract from, or parody of, a disquisition by Lysias on Love.

Lȳsi′machus (*Lŭsimachos*), see *Macedonia*, § 2, and *Seleucids*. Also the name of the father of Aristides (q.v.).

Lȳsi′ppus (*Lŭsippos*) of Sicyon, a famous and prolific sculptor, a contemporary of Alexander the Great. His statues were of bronze, and he was noted for his skill in rendering, in particular, the harmony of the male human body; also for his numerous portraits. He was the favourite sculptor of Alexander. There is in the Vatican a good copy in marble of his statue of an athlete scraping himself with a strigil, known as the 'Apoxyomenos'.

Lȳ′sis (*Lŭsis*), see *Plato*, § 2.

Lȳsis′trata (*Lŭsistratē*), a comedy by Aristophanes, produced in the spring of 411 B.C. The Sicilian Expedition had ended in disaster, and Sparta had made an alliance with the Persian satrap Tissaphernes; the situation of Athens appeared desperate. Aristophanes made in this play a last appeal, half farcical half serious, for peace. The play contains no parabasis (see *Comedy*, § 2), the beginning of a change in the form of the Old Comedy.

The men having failed to bring the war to an end, it occurs to Lysistrata ('Dismisser of Armies') that the women should take over the control and force a peace, firstly by obliging the men to continence so long as the war lasts, secondly by getting possession of the Acropolis and the treasure in the Parthenon. She gets the women together, including Lampito from Sparta and women from other enemy States. After some hesitation they fall in with her scheme and swear to carry it out. The Acropolis is seized. The chorus of old men try to recapture it, but are driven off by the chorus of old women with pails of water. The Scythian police are also overcome, and the magistrate defeated in argument and forced to retire. Cinesias (q.v.) comes to recover his wife, is tantalized and pressed to vote for peace, and left disappointed outside the Acropolis.

A herald, talking broad Doric, comes from Sparta, a peace conference follows, Lysistrata scolds both sides and urges reconciliation, peace is made, and all ends in a banquet and a procession of Athenians and Spartans, each man with his wife.

M

Mabillon, JEAN, see *Texts and Studies*, § 11.

Maca'ria (*Makariā*), see *Heracles* (*Children of*).

Maccabees, see *Seleucids*.

Macedonia and the Macedonian Empire.

§ 1. *Early history to Alexander the Great*

Macedonia, in the times of the early Macedonian monarchy, was the country bordering the W. and N. shores of the Thermaic Gulf, from Mt. Olympus to the Strymon; but its territory was much enlarged by Philip II in the 4th c. B.C. Its inhabitants in historical times were of Greek stock, a military people, who held in varying degrees of subjugation the Illyric tribes of the hilly country to the W. and N. The Macedonian monarchy retained primitive characteristics. On the death of the king, his successor was appointed by the army, the free citizens in arms. The king had his 'Companions', retainers bound to him by personal ties of allegiance. The Macedonian kings claimed to be in origin Argives, and a good deal of early Greek chronology was falsified by later Greek historians in trying to make this claim plausible.

At the time of the invasion of Xerxes (see *Persian Wars*), the Macedonian king, Alexander I, played an ambiguous part, nominally allied with the Persians, but showing sympathy with the Greek cause. Perdiccas II (d. 413 B.C.) played an equally shifty part, as between Athens and Sparta, at the time of the Peloponnesian War. Archelaus, who succeeded him (413–399), is notable for his sympathy with Greek culture: he invited to his court at Pella Euripides, Agathon, Choerilus of Samos, the musician Timotheus, and the painter Zeuxis (qq.v.). But the importance of Macedonia in Greek history begins with the accession to power of Philip II and culminates in the reign of his son, Alexander the Great. For this phase see *Philip* and *Alexander*

§ 2. *The struggle for Alexander's succession* (323–280 B.C.)

The death of Alexander in 323 left no competent successor in his family. Philip

Arrhidaeus, his half-brother, was illegitimate and mentally unfit; he was executed by Olympias in 317. Alexander, son of Roxana, was not born until after his father's death; he fell into the power of Cassander (see below) in 316 and was ultimately put to death. It was decided by the Macedonian army at Babylon that Antipater, Alexander's representative in Europe, should be confirmed in his position as ruler of Macedon; Perdiccas was appointed regent of the empire, and the satrapies allotted to various generals, Egypt to Ptolemy, Great Phrygia to Antigonus, Thrace to Lysimachus, Cappadocia to Eumenes, &c. There followed during nearly half a century a complicated struggle for the fragments of Alexander's empire. Perdiccas was overthrown by a coalition of satraps (he was murdered while attacking Egypt). A new settlement was adopted at Triparadisos (320) by which Antipater was made regent of the empire and satrapies were redistributed (Seleucus received Babylonia). Antipater died the next year and Antigonus becomes the leading figure, aspiring to rule all the empire. He proclaimed himself and his son, Demetrius, kings in 306, and Ptolemy, Seleucus, Lysimachus, and Cassander (the son of Antipater) also took the royal title. This marks the dissolution of Alexander's empire. Antigonus was defeated and killed at Ipsus in Phrygia in 301, and his territories were divided between the victors, Seleucus and Lysimachus. His place in the struggle was taken by his son Demetrius Poliorcêtês ('the Besieger'), who after Cassander's death became king of Macedon and master of nearly all Greece. Already in his father's time, in 307, he had captured Athens and ousted Demetrius of Phalerum (q.v.), Cassander's viceroy. He received his surname Poliorcetes in consequence of a prolonged siege of Rhodes (304), which he failed to take. His career ended in an unsuccessful invasion of Asia. There is a life of him by Plutarch. Ptolemy, Seleucus, and Lysimachus remained. The division of Asia Minor after Ipsus between Seleucus and Lysimachus had left the seeds of future quarrels. In 282 Seleucus attacked his rival and defeated him at Corupedium (near Magnesia in Lydia); Lysimachus died on the field. Seleucus himself was assassinated in 280 by Ptolemy Ceraunus (*Keraunos*, a son of Ptolemy I), who became king of Macedonia. With the death of Seleucus the possibility of the reunion of Alexander's empire under one ruler came to an end. He was the last survivor of Alexander's marshals, for Ptolemy I had died in 283. For the later *Diadochi*, or successors to the empire of Alexander the Great, see under *Attalids. Ptolemies, Seleucids.*

§ 3. *The Antigonids and the struggle with Rome*

In 279 Macedonia was invaded by a Celtic people known as Galatians (or Gauls). They broke into several parties: one swept over Greece and reached Delphi, but was driven back; another stayed in Thrace; a third passed into Asia Minor. In resisting this invasion Ceraunus was killed. He was succeeded by Antigonus Gonātas, son of Demetrius Poliorcetes, named Gonatas, it seems, because born at Gonnos or Gonnoi in Thessaly. Gonatas was interested in philosophy and history and drew literary men to his court. He proved a vigorous and successful ruler (277–39) and established the *Antigonid* dynasty in Macedonia. This dynasty maintained a partial control over Greece, varying in extent from time to time as a result of such incidents as the Chremonidean War (see *Athens*, § 8), the interventions of the Ptolemies and of Pyrrhus (qq.v.), and the activities of the Aetolian and Achaean Leagues (qq.v.). The control was exercised in some States by means of Macedonian garrisons; in others Gonatas established his own supporters as tyrants. After Gonatas, the most prominent of the Antigonids was his grandson Philip V (221–179), a man of remarkable energy and misplaced ambition, largely responsible for bringing Greece under Roman domination. The operations undertaken by Rome against Illyrian pirates in 229 and 219, in which she had the support of the Greek cities of Apollōnia and Epidamnus, brought nearer the prospect of a collision between Rome and Macedonia. In 216, when Rome was in the crisis of the Second Punic War, Philip entered upon a naval adventure in the Adriatic within the Roman sphere of influence, and in the following year offered an alliance to Hannibal. By this embroilment with Rome, coupled with his ruthless piratical expeditions against Greek States of the Aegean, he brought about the successive Macedonian Wars (First Macedonian War, 215–205; Second Macedonian War, 200–197), as a result of which Rome assumed the position of arbiter in the affairs of Greece. The first war was inconclusive. In the second Philip was defeated by Q. Flamininus at Cynoscephalae in 197, and his rule thereafter was limited to Macedonia proper. In the course of the Third Macedonian War, when Philip had been succeeded by his son Perseus, the Macedonian army was practically annihilated at the battle of Pydna (168) by the consul Aemilius Paullus (q.v.); and

this was followed by the dethronement of the Antigonids, and the break-up of the Macedonian realm into four federal republics. The end came twenty years later, when an attempt by a pretender to reunite Macedon was defeated by Caecilius Metellus, and the country was constituted a Roman province.

§ 4. *The Macedonian Princesses*

No sketch of Macedonian history would be complete without some reference to the great Macedonian princesses, women of ability and character, who played a large part in affairs. Outstanding among them was Arsinoe II Philadelphus (see *Arsinoe* (2)), who as the wife of her brother Ptolemy II was the true ruler of Egypt and brought her country triumphantly out of an unpromising war with Antiochus I. She was deified in her lifetime and her head appears with her husband's on the coinage. Cleopatra Thea, daughter of Ptolemy Philometor and wife of Demetrius II, was a powerful Seleucid queen, who coined in her own name. Berenice, wife of Ptolemy III, was another important queen, whom Callimachus celebrated in a poem. Finally came Cleopatra VII, the last of her line, famous for her beauty, her lack of moral scruple, the part she played in Roman history, and her tragic end.

Macedonian Wars of Rome, see *Macedonia*, § 3.

Ma'cer, AEMILIUS (d. 16 B.C.), of Verona, was the author of Latin didactic poems, 'Ornīthogonia' on birds, and 'Thēriaca' on snake bites, which have not survived. He was a friend of Virgil (the 'Mopsus' of the 5th Eclogue) and of Ovid.

Ma'cer, GĀIUS LICINIUS (d. 66 B.C.), orator and annalist, the father of the poet Calvus (q.v.). He claimed to have consulted, for the purpose of his annals, certain *libri lintei* or ancient chronicles. His annals have not survived.

Machā'ōn and **Podalei'rios**, in the 'Iliad', sons of Asclepius (q.v.), and surgeons of the Greek host.

Macrō'bius (*Macrŏbius*) **Theodo'sius**, generally known as 'Macrobius'; a distinguished Roman writer and philosopher who flourished about A.D. 400. He was not, according to his own statement, of Roman birth. He makes no direct reference to Christianity in his works, and the prominence that he gives in his 'Saturnalia' to the eminent pagans Praetextatus and Symmachus (see below) shows that he belonged to the pagan party. His 'Saturnalia' in seven books dedicated to his son is a dialogue supposed to take place, on the occasion of the festival of that name, among a number of eminent Romans at the house of Vettius Praetextatus, at one time Praetorian Prefect and learned in the ancient cults of Rome. Among the interlocutors are the orator and administrator Symmachus (q.v.), the Virgilian commentator Servius (q.v.), and a certain Euangelus, a sceptic and bitter scoffer, who even speaks disrespectfully of Virgil and Cicero. The discussion covers a multitude of subjects, but is chiefly devoted to the works of Virgil. Book I is occupied with the subject of ancient religion, and Praetextatus expounds the theory of the solar origin of mythology, all the gods being ultimately identified with the sun under one or other of its aspects. Book II contains a number of anecdotes on the religious and political changes at Rome, notably that of Laberius (q.v.) compelled to act his own mime and taunting Caesar. Books III–VI discuss Virgil from various points of view, his knowledge of ritual, his power of expressing emotion, his debt to Homer and other Greek authors, his debt to Ennius and other ancient Romans. Book VII passes to a discussion of various physical, physiological, and psychological questions and shows incidentally a great advance in the understanding of the mental processes.

The second work of Macrobius is a commentary, also dedicated to his son, on the 'Somnium Scipionis' (q.v.) from the sixth book of Cicero's 'De Republica'. The successive passages of Cicero's narrative are set out (and have thus been preserved for us), and Macrobius, taking them as his text, examines the enigma of the soul and its destiny in the light of the Neoplatonic doctrines of Plotinus and Porphyry, and of the astronomical and mathematical sciences of the day. The general tendency is to reinforce the doctrine put forward in the 'Somnium' of the immortality and divine quality of the soul, and thus to purify and strengthen the old pagan religion.

Chaucer, at the opening of his 'Parliament of Fowls', describes how he had been reading the 'Somnium Scipionis' with 'Macrobye's' commentary. Readers of Boswell's 'Johnson' will remember the description (under the year 1728) of Johnson's first evening as an undergraduate at Oxford; how he behaved modestly and sat silent while his father talked with the head of Pembroke College, until, upon something which occurred in the course of the conversation, he suddenly struck in and quoted Macrobius.

Maecē'nas, Gᴀıus [Cılnıus], born between 74 and 64 B.C. of a distinguished Etruscan family, is famous as the trusted counsellor of Augustus, and as the enlightened patron of a literary circle which included Virgil and Horace, Propertius and Varius (qq.v.). He is said to have suggested to Virgil the subject of the 'Georgics'; Horace owed his independence to him; and both poets address him in terms of admiration and gratitude. He died in 8 B.C. He wrote a 'Prometheus', probably a tragedy, and a Dialogue, probably in the style of the Menippean satires (see *Menippus*). His prose-works were numerous and miscellaneous. Only a few fragments survive. Seneca regards him as typical of the adage that the style is the man; it was turgid and capricious, a sort of poetical prose. His official name was Gaius Maecenas, as appears from inscriptions. Tacitus calls him 'Cilnius Maecenas', but Cilnius was not his gentile name. It was perhaps the name of his mother's family (Pauly-Wissowa).

Mae'nads (*Mainades*), a word meaning 'mad women', votaries of Dionysus (q.v.).

Mae'nalus (τὸ Μαίναλον), a mountain in Arcadia. See *Pan*.

Maeo'nidēs, a name sometimes applied to Homer, either because Maeonia was an ancient name for Lydia (q.v.) where Homer was supposed to have been born, or because he was said to be the son of one Maeōn. Milton (P.L. iii. 35) refers to 'blind Thamyris and blind Mæonides'.

Mae'ra (*Maira*), the dog of Icarius (q.v.).

Mae'vius, see *Bavius*.

Magic, the pretended art of influencing the natural course of events by incantations, spells, and other rites, was universal among primitive peoples. It had its origin in a misunderstanding of physical laws, and the difficulty of accounting, in the early stages of knowledge, for abnormal phenomena. It was encouraged and developed by the widespread belief in the existence of spirits, who permeated the universe and intervened in natural processes, and whom it was hoped to influence by appropriate ritual. This belief brought magic into relation with religion, with which for a long period it was closely connected, so that the line between religious and magical practices in early times is not always easy to draw. The belief in magic was gradually ousted by increased knowledge of physical laws and the growth of the scientific spirit; magical elements were eliminated from science, and medicine, for instance, discarded incantations and charms.

The Greeks and Romans were no exception to the general rule. The word 'magic' (μαγεία, magīa) means the science of the Magi, the priests of the Zoroastrian religion, for the Greeks drew some of their later magical practices from Persia. The Greek word for native sorcery was goēteia (from γόης, one who howls incantations). Magical practices are referred to in early Greek literature. When Odysseus is wounded by a boar, the flow of blood is stayed with a song of healing (ἐπαοιδή, Od. xix. 457). Circe (Od. x. 276), an enchantress 'knowing many drugs and charms' (πολυφάρμακος), works transformations with a wand, aided by drugs (φάρμακα, a word used both of healing and of baneful drugs). In the myth of the Argonauts (which was known to Homer, Od. xii. 69), Circe's niece, Medea, is an enchantress, by whose magic powers Jason is enabled to perform impossible tasks and the aged Aeson is restored to youth. Later myth made her a priestess of Hecate, who came to be regarded as the divine patroness of witches and was invoked by magicians (Theoc. Id. ii. 12). Thessaly was from early times regarded as the especial home of witches. Jason and Medea were supposed to have lived there for a time, and Medea was said to have lost there her box of wonder-working plants, which sprang up again in Thessalian soil. Thessalian witches had a reputation for brewing poisons and working wonders, such as bringing the moon down from the sky (Arist. Nub. 749 and cf. Canidia's words in Hor. Epod. xvii. 77 'polo deripere Lunam vocibus possim meis'; a lost play by Menander alluded to this power). In a later age Thessalian witches figure largely in the 'Metamorphoses' of Apuleius.

In the historical times of Greece and Rome a distinction must be drawn between the survival of magical practices in official religion and the popular uses of magic. Official religion on the whole repudiated magic, but magical rites had passed over into the ritual of the appropriate gods, weather-magic into the ritual of Zeus, rites designed to produce fertility into that of Demeter, &c. There are traces of magic also in the Greek rites of purification. The pollution of guilt was regarded as something which could be washed away with water or the blood of sacrificial victims or burned away with fire; in Athens the object which had caused a person's death was removed beyond the borders of the country. At certain Greek festivals the hair might not be tied into a knot and rings might not be worn, on account of the supposed magical hampering effect of knots and rings. Similarly at Rome, the Flamen Dialis (q.v.) was not allowed to wear knots or rings. In Rome again, at the Lupercalia (q.v.), the mere touch of the Lupercus's thong was believed to remove sterility (a belief alluded to in Shakespeare's 'Julius Caesar', i. ii). On the border-line between the religious and the popular uses of magic were the practices designed to affect weather. In countries where drought was frequent and might entail famine, to control weather was a natural aspiration. We probably see an early attempt at this reflected in the legend of Salmoneus (q.v.). Like was thought to produce like, and that king's imitations of thunder and lightning may have been thought capable of inducing that kind of weather. Rain-making was practised at Crannon by means of an amphora full of water which was drawn about in a cart; probably the water splashed about simulating rain. In Arcadia, when there was a drought, the priest of Zeus went to a certain well on Mt. Lycaeus and stirred the water with a twig. The bathing of the image of the Great Mother in the brook Almo (a tributary of the Tiber), described by Ovid (Fast. iv. 337 et seq.), may have been a charm designed to procure rain. There was a certain stone (known as the *Lapis mānālis*) outside the walls of Rome which was drawn into the city when rain was desired.

Among the purely popular uses of magic may be mentioned (1) *Medical charms, love philtres, &c.* Magic and medicine were in antiquity closely interwoven. Pindar (Pyth. iii. 91) represents Chiron as treating his patients either with soothing incantations (μαλακαῖς ἐπαοιδαῖς) or with potions. The poems of Nicander (q.v.) and the works of Dioscurides (q.v.) illustrate the connexion. Plutarch refers to the amulet hung about Pericles' neck when he was sick of the plague (though Pericles himself thought it nonsense). Incantations were among the remedies recommended by Cato (' De Re Rustica ') in certain cases. The use of these, and of philtres by lovers, is illustrated in Theocritus (Id. ii), Virgil (Ecl. viii), and Horace (Epod. V). There is some further information on magical concoctions in Apuleius (Apol. chs. 30–31 and 42). The *fascinum*, a phallic emblem, was employed as an amulet to protect children from witchcraft. The strange use of the wryneck (ἴυγξ) in charms is referred to by Pindar and Theocritus. Fastened on a wheel and turned, it was thought capable of turning the hearts of men. (The wryneck was a sacred bird in Egypt and Assyria; it was credited with magical powers perhaps in consequence of its curious colouring, odd attitudes, distinctive voice, and the habit attributed to it of hissing like a snake and feigning death when held in the hand.)

(2) *The magical treatment of images, names, &c.* It was a doctrine of magic that an effect could be produced on a person by corresponding action on something having an analogy or relation to that person, such as his image. Both in Greece and Rome recourse was had to waxen images of a person whose sickness or death was to be procured, or whose love was desired; if the image was pierced by a needle, the person represented was thought to suffer correspondingly; if the image was melted, the person would be consumed with love. There are references to this belief, e.g. in Plato (Laws, 933 B), Theocritus (Id. ii), and Ovid (Her. vi. 91–2). At Rome the practice was known as *devotio*. Not only the image, but the mere name of a person, as being in some sort identical with him, might be used for similar purposes. The name would be inscribed on a leaden tablet and a nail driven through it, with or without an accompanying indication of the result desired. The process was known as κατάδεσις or *defixio*, 'binding' or 'nailing down'. Sometimes an appeal to a god was added, which would give a semi-religious character to the rite. Many such tablets have been discovered in modern times. They were sometimes used, with appropriate inscriptions, for other purposes, such as the recovery of lost or stolen property or an errant lover, or the 'binding' of chariots in races.

(3) *Evocation of spirits (necyomantia).* The earliest example we have of this is the story of Odysseus summoning the ghosts, in 'Odyssey' xi. That it was practised in Greece in historical times is shown not only by the story of Periander in Herodotus (v. 92), but also by the statement in Plutarch ('Cimon') that there was a temple at Heraclea in Elis where it was customary to consult the spirits of the dead. There was a class of magicians called ψυχαγωγοί or necromancers. There are several references in Cicero to necromancy as practised in his time, and Nero and Caracalla are said to have had recourse to it. Horace's Canidia says 'possim crematos excitare mortuos' (Epod. xvii. 79), and there are references to this form of sorcery in Ovid (Metam. vii. 206, and Rem. Am. 253). Lucan (Phars. vi. 569 et seq.) has a scene where a Thessalian witch revives a dead body in order to learn the future course of the war.

The use of magic by private persons, for the purpose of harming their enemies, damaging crops, &c., was repressed by law both in Greece and Rome. Demosthenes in one of his speeches refers to a law condemning sorcerers to death, and a witch named Lamia was (according to Pausanias) actually executed in Demosthenes' day. In Rome the Twelve Tables (q.v.) provided for the punishment of the man 'qui malum carmen incantassit', and there were later penal laws against sorcery. The attempts to suppress it were due, not to disbelief in the genuineness and efficacy of magical power, but on the contrary to the fear of its pernicious consequences. Magic received a considerable impulse under the Roman empire from the speculations of the Neoplatonists (q.v.), especially in the direction of rites to conciliate or exorcise the good and evil spirits supposed by them to people the universe. On the other hand the practice of magic was energetically condemned·by the early Christian Fathers, not as a delusion, but as impious. The authors, such as Juvenal and Lucian, who showed a sceptical spirit towards it, were very few.

See also *Astrology, Augury, Haruspices*.

Magi′ster E′quitum, or Master of the Horse, at Rome, the assistant of a dictator (q.v.).

Magna Graecia (*Megalē Hellas*), a term applied to the Greek cities on the shores of the Tarentine Gulf in the S. of Italy, notably the Achaean colonies of Sybaris and Croton, and Tarentum, including also their dependencies across the peninsula on the coast of the Tyrrhenian Sea. The term is sometimes used more loosely to include also the more northerly Greek cities of Neapolis and Cumae.

Magna Mäter, the goddess Cybele (q.v.).

Mai′a, (1) in Greek mythology, daughter of Atlas (q.v.) and mother of Hermes; (2) an old Italian goddess, associated with Vulcan (q.v.); she was thought by some to be an earth-goddess, and is hardly distinguishable from Fauna, Ops, &c. Sacrifices were offered to her in the month of May, the name of which is perhaps ultimately derived from her.

Mu′mertines (*Mämertini*), Samnite mercenaries engaged by Agathocles of Syracuse (q.v., § 3) for his operations in Sicily. See *Punic Wars*.

Mämu′rra, Caesar's chief engineer in Gaul, where he acquired much wealth. He was the first to face with marble his palace at Rome. He is prominent in Catullus's invectives against Caesar. Horace refers satirically to Formiae as Mamurrarum urbs' (Mamurra was born at Formiae).

Mä′nës, in Roman thought, were primarily the spirits of the dead, taken collectively, regarded as hostile, and euphemistically thus named the 'kindly ones'. From a sense of their supernatural power they were collectively worshipped as the *Di Manes*. When the practice of the family tomb was introduced, the *Di Manes* were individualized, and identified with the *Di Parentes*, the dead of the family. The individual tomb led to the conception of the spirit of the dead individual, and the word *manes* (which has no singular) came to be used of a single spirit. By a different process of development the *Di Manes* became identified with the *Di Inferi*, the rulers of the lower world, Dis (or Orcus), Proserpina, and Hecate (qq.v.). It was the custom in Italian cities to dig a pit, known as a *mundus*, symbolizing their abode, and closed with a stone which was removed thrice a year on their festivals, when these deities were supposed to come forth. It is a question whether there was a Roman cult of the dead as distinct from a cult of the gods of the nether world. There were offerings to the dead, but it is doubtful whether there were prayer and worship.

Ma'nethō, a priest of Heliopolis in Egypt, of the 3rd c. B.C., who wrote in Greek a work on the chronology of Egypt, portions of which have been preserved by later writers such as Eusebius, and have been of great service to Egyptology.

Māni'lius (or *Manlius* or *Mallius*), MARCUS, author of a Latin didactic poem in hexameters in five books, entitled 'Astronomica', dealing with astrology and written probably about the end of the reign of Augustus. The poem was probably left unfinished. In contrast to Lucretius the author sees design and 'heavenly reason' in the organization of the universe. Though much of it is prosaic, the work contains fine passages and shows technical skill in versification, power of thought, and lucid expression. It has been the subject of commentaries by Scaliger, Bentley, and A. E. Housman.

Man'lius Capitōli'nus, MARCUS, the Roman who, when the Gauls occupied Rome in 390 B.C., held the Capitol against them. It is said that, awakened by the cries of the geese, he repulsed a night attack on the Capitol and drove back the Gauls in confusion. (Thereafter the feeding of the sacred geese, contracted for by the censors, was a charge on the State treasury, and a goose gorgeously arrayed was borne annually in procession.) Later Manlius intervened on behalf of the poorer class of Romans, who were suffering under the stringent law of debt. He was accused of attempting to make himself tyrant, and was thrown down from the Tarpeian Rock.

The name 'Capitolinus' occurs in the family both before and after the time of this man, and is a name in other *gentes* also. It is derived from the district in which the family lived.

Man'lius Torquā'tus (whose full name was *Titus Manlius Imperiōsus Torquātus*), a Roman who, according to tradition, in resisting an invasion of the Gauls in 361 B.C., gained the name Torquatus by defeating in single combat a gigantic Gaul and taking from him his ornamental neckchain (*torquis*). In the Latin War of 340 B.C. the consuls, of whom Torquatus was one, forbade single combats with the enemy. The son of Torquatus nevertheless engaged and defeated a Latin champion, and was executed for his disobedience.

The L. Manlius Torquatus of Cicero's 'De Finibus' was one of Pompey's supporters who after Pharsālus went to Africa and was slain in the hostilities there.

Mantinē'a (*Mantineia*), in Arcadia, the scene, (1) of a battle in 418 B.C. between the Spartans on the one hand and the Athenians and Argives on the other (see *Peloponnesian War*); (2) of the battle in 362 B.C. between Sparta and Thebes in which Epaminondas was killed (see *Sparta*, § 4). Gryllus, the son of Xenophon, was killed in a cavalry engagement at Mantinea shortly before the main battle.

The State of Mantinea entered into alliance with Athens, Argos, and Elis in 419 B.C. (during the Peloponnesian War), but previously, though often showing democratic tendencies, had been friendly to Sparta (she did not, e.g., take part in the war of the Arcadians against Sparta of c. 470 B.C., and she rendered the Spartans great help in the Helot revolt). In the 4th c., however, Mantinea was attacked by Sparta and broken up into villages (386–5). After the battle of Leuctra (q.v.), the city was rebuilt (370) and took part in the pan-Arcadian confederacy founded at this time.

Ma'ntō, see *Mopsus*.

Ma'ntua, on the river Mincius in Cisalpine Gaul, a town famous as the birthplace of Virgil (who was in fact born in the adjoining village of Andes).

Maps. The earliest map was made by Anaximander (q.v., 6th c. B.C.). A map was brought to Sparta by Aristagoras of Miletus (Hdt. v. 49) in 499 B.C. Aristophanes mentions maps in the 'Clouds'. Dicaearchus (q.v.), a pupil of Aristotle, was a map-maker, and Eratosthenes and Hipparchus (qq.v.), great geographers of the Hellenistic Age, worked at the improvement of the map of the world. There were certainly maps at Alexandria in that age, and Crates (q.v. (4)) of Mallos made a terrestrial globe.

The maps so far referred to were probably general maps of the known world; but Varro refers to a map of Italy painted on a wall of the Temple of Tellus at Rome, to be seen in his day. In imperial times maps were in wide use at Rome; they are mentioned in Propertius (IV. iii. 37), Pliny, Seneca, Suetonius, and Vitruvius. An official map of the known world was prepared in the reign of Augustus under the orders of Agrippa (q.v.), who wrote a commentary on it; it was displayed in the Porticus Vipsania at Rome. Geographical knowledge was by this time widespread, and maps must have been in use in schools, yet no fragment of any of these has so far been found. The earliest European world-map that survives is in a seventh-century codex of Isidore of Seville (c. A.D. 570–636). The *Tabula Peutingeriana* (so called from the name of the 16th-c. scholar who published it) is a strip 21 ft. by 1 ft., showing the course of Roman roads in a distorted form.

Ma'rathon (*Marathōn*), PLAIN OF, a crescent-shaped plain between the spurs of Pentelicus and Parnes and the sea, some twenty-two miles NE. of Athens; the scene of the defeat of the invading Persians by Miltiades in 490 B.C. (see *Persian Wars* and Pl. 8; see also *Phidippides*). The mound erected over the Athenian dead at Marathon is still to be seen.

Marce'llus, MARCUS CLAUDIUS, (1) a famous Roman general of the 3rd c. B.C. In the campaign against the Gauls of 222 he won the *spolia opima* (q.v.) by slaying with his own hand the Gallic king. He showed promptitude and determination in the trying period that followed the disaster of Cannae (see *Punic Wars*), and it was he who captured Syracuse after a long siege in 212. He was killed in an ambush by Carthaginian forces when consul for the fifth time in 208.

(2) Son of C. Marcellus and Octavia the sister of Augustus. He was born in 43 B.C., was adopted by Augustus in 25 B.C., and was married to the latter's daughter Julia. He was probably intended to succeed his adoptive father in the principate but died two years later. He was a youth of much promise, and his death was regarded as a national loss and was lamented by Virgil in a famous passage of the 'Aeneid' (vi. 861–87), the reading of which so affected Octavia, the mother of Marcellus, that she fainted.

Marcus Aurē'lius Antōni'nus, Roman emperor, A.D. 161–80. His original name

was M. Annius Vērus; he was adopted, at the desire of the emperor Hadrian, by Antoninus Pius, and married the latter's daughter Faustina (q.v.). Marcus Aurelius has left a collection of 'Meditations', in twelve books, private devotional memoranda written in Greek. They show him a disillusioned and somewhat despondent man, seeking in self-communion and the Stoic philosophy fortitude against the fear of death, the cares of this world, and the misdeeds and injustices of others. It is not known by what happy chance the work came to be preserved and published. Through many translations, Marcus Aurelius has influenced thousands who could not read his Greek. Part of the correspondence between Marcus Aurelius and his tutor Fronto (q.v.) has survived. It shows the deep affection that united them, and some of the letters give a pleasant picture of the activities and domestic life of Aurelius.

Margī'tes, a famous lost poem of antiquity, a satirical epic having a fool (*margos*) as its hero; ranked by Aristotle as bearing the same relation to comedy that the 'Iliad' and 'Odyssey' bore to tragedy. Iambics were here and there intermixed in it with hexameters. The author and date of the poem are unknown; the authorship of Homer was accepted by Aristotle and Zeno.

Mā'rius (*Marius*), GĀIUS (157–86 B.C.), born at Arpinum (the birthplace also of Cicero), served under Scipio Aemilianus (q.v.) against Numantia, became tribune of the plebs, and married Julia, the aunt of Julius Caesar. He came into prominence in the war against Jugurtha: in 107 he became consul and by popular vote supplanted Metellus in command of the Roman army. Thanks to the diplomacy of his quaestor Sulla (q.v.), he was able to capture Jugurtha himself and bring the war to an end. But his greatest achievement was the overthrow in 102 and 101, at Aquae Sextiae and Vercellae, of the Teutones and Cimbri, Germanic tribes who were invading Gaul and Italy, and had inflicted severe defeats on Roman armies. Marius won these victories with a reorganized army (see *Army*, § 2), having converted the old citizen militia, recruited on a property basis, to a professional army of volunteers recruited from all classes, dependent on their general for their reward. He thus paved the way for the domination of successful generals, and ultimately for the empire. From 104 to 100 Marius, though a member of a family which had never before held high office, was every year consul. In 100 he entered into close relations with the demagogue Saturninus (q.v.), who, as tribune in that year, brought forward various measures on Marius's behalf. But when Saturninus in the same year had resort to political assassination, Marius broke with his ally, surrounded him with an improvised force, and caused his surrender. In 89, after the Social War, he came into conflict with Sulla, who like himself had taken a prominent part in that war, and as a leader of the aristocratic party had been given by the Senate the command against Mithridates. This was an appointment that Marius desired for himself, and by a popular resolution the command was transferred to Marius. But Sulla appealed to his legions and marched on Rome, and Marius, after perilous adventures (in the course of which he was captured while hiding in the marshes of Minturnae), escaped to Africa. There the governor sent him an order to leave the country; his reply to the messenger is said to have been, 'Tell the praetor you have seen Gaius Marius sitting, a fugitive, amid the ruins of Carthage'. After Sulla's departure for the East in 88, Marius returned to Italy, joined the democratic leader Cinna, occupied Rome, and was consul in 86 for the seventh time, thus fulfilling what it is said had been predicted, that Marius should be seven times consul. He now began to take vengeance on his enemies by cruel massacres, but shortly died, probably insane. There is a life of him by Plutarch.

Ma′rmor Pa′rium, one of the Arundel Marbles, which were secured in Asia Minor by an agent of Lord Arundel about 1627 and sent to England. This particular marble was originally found in the island of Páros. On it is an inscription of a chronological table running from Cecrops (q.v.) to 354 B.C. Among the events connected with Greek literature that it records is the flight of Sappho from Mitylene to Sicily. A later part of the table, ending with 263, is lost. It was first deciphered by John Selden (1584–1654). The marbles were subsequently neglected, some, including part of the Marmor Parium, were used to repair Arundel House, until attention was drawn to them by John Evelyn (1620–1706). They were then presented to Oxford University, and what remains of them is in the Ashmolean.

Mā′ro (*Mărō*), the cognomen of Virgil (q.v.), by which he is referred to by Martial and frequently in the Middle Ages, e.g. in the goliardic lines of the Archpoet (12th c.) in reply to an invitation to celebrate the deeds of the Emperor Frederic:

vis et infra circulum parve septimane
bella scribam forcia breviter et nane,
que vix in quinquennio scriberes, Lucane,
vel tu, vatum maxime, Maro Mantuane.

Also in the medieval lines (quoted under *Virgil*) connecting him with St. Paul. Also occasionally in English literature, e.g. in Cowper's 'The Task':

Those golden times
And those Arcadian scenes that Maro sings.

Marpe′ssa (*Marpěssa*), in Greek mythology, daughter of the river-god Euênos, was loved by Idas (see under *Lynceus*) and carried off by him in a winged chariot given him by Poseidon. They were pursued by Apollo, who also loved the maiden; whereupon Idas prepared to fight with him. Zeus interposed and left the choice to Marpessa, who chose Idas, fearing that Apollo would desert her.

Marriage, see *Women (Position of)*.

Mars, in early Roman religion, appears to have been regarded as a spirit (*numen*) of vegetation (see *Ambarvalia*). Cato has preserved the farmer's prayer to him at the lustration of the fields. But in the religion of the State he was primarily associated with war. The wolf, a predatory animal, was sacred to him. His sacred shields (*ancilia*, q.v.) were carried by his priests, the Salii (q.v.), round the city during his month of March. His altar was in the Campus Martius. A great two-horse chariot race, held on the Ides of October, was connected with his cult, for the right-hand horse of the winning team was sacrificed to him. Other chariot races (*equiria*) in his honour were held in February and March. There were also purifications of arms and of war-trumpets associated with him. At the quinquennial purification that accompanied the census, the people were drawn up round his altar in the Campus Martius, and the sacrifice of the *suovetaurīlia* (ox, sheep, and pig) was offered to him to secure military success. He was later identified with the Greek Ares, and consequently regarded as the son of Juno (Hera). The name *Grādivus*, often applied to him, probably signifies 'he who marches forth' to war. A temple of Mars, probably dedicated during the Gallic War of 390 B.C., stood on the Appian Way outside the city. Here was celebrated annually the victory of Lake Regillus. In the Forum Augustum (q.v.), at a later period, was erected the temple of Mars Ultor ('the Avenger'), which Augustus, before he attained the empire, had vowed to build if he should succeed in avenging the murder of his adoptive father Julius Caesar. It was dedicated in 2 B.C. and was one of the most magnificent temples in Rome. Here were laid the standards lost by Crassus and by Antony, and recovered by Augustus from the Parthians.

Marsian War, see *Rome*, § 6.

Ma'rsyas (*Marsŭas*), in Greek mythology, a satyr (god of the river Marsyas near Celaenae in Phrygia), who picked up the flute that Athene (q.v.) had invented, but had thrown away (because, some authors say, it distorted the face of the person playing on it). He became so proficient a player that he challenged Apollo to a contest, it being agreed that the victor should treat the vanquished as he wished. The victory was adjudged to Apollo by the Muses, whereupon he tied Marsyas to a tree and flayed him alive, or had him cut up by a Scythian. There are several extant sculptures dealing with the story, and according to Herodotus the skin of Marsyas was exhibited at Celaenae in Phrygia. The origin of the legend lies perhaps in the opposition between the music of Apollo's instrument, the lyre, and that of the Phrygian flute.

Ma'rtial (*Marcus Valĕrius Martiālis*) (c. A.D. 40–104), named 'Martialis' because he was born on the 1st March, was a native of Bilbilis in Spain and claimed Iberian and Celtic descent. He came to Rome in A.D. 64, where he was protected by his fellow Spaniards, Seneca and Lucan. He was poor and lived in a third-floor lodging, but later he had a farm at Nomentum and a small house in Rome. He wrote poetry for his living, depending on the favour of rich patrons and the sale of his books. He was granted the rank of *tribunus* and *eques*, and the *jus trium liberorum* (q.v.), but took no part in public affairs. His first-known work was a *Liber Spectaculorum* to celebrate the opening in A.D. 80 of the Colosseum; of this work thirty-three poems survive, interesting for what they tell us of the spectacles displayed on this occasion. About 84 were published the collections of elegiac couplets which appear as Books XIII and XIV of the 'Epigrams'. These are mottoes appropriate to gifts sent to friends (*Xenia*) or taken home from banquets (*Apophorēta*) at the festival of the Saturnalia. The gifts are the most varied kinds, stationery, clothing, furniture, playthings, works of art, food, pets, even slaves.

Martial's more important work, the first twelve books of the 'Epigrams', began to appear in 86. Between that year and 98 eleven of these books were issued. In 98, apparently disgusted with Roman life, he returned to Bilbilis, to a quiet country life

on a farm given him by a patroness. From there he issued the twelfth book of his Epigrams in 102. The Younger Pliny, in a letter of 104, mentions his death. Among Martial's friends, besides Pliny (who speaks of him as talented, acute, vigorous, witty, and sincere), were Juvenal, Quintilian, and Silius Italicus. Martial makes no mention of his contemporary Statius, but refers unfavourably to mythological poems such as the latter wrote.

Martial's 'Epigrams', short poems expressing concisely and pointedly some single idea, are for the most part written in elegiacs; about one-sixth are in hendecasyllables, a few in choliambics, two in hexameters. Many consist of a single couplet; they rarely exceed a score of lines. Several of the books are preceded by a preface in prose defending the author's work against criticism, actual or anticipated. The epigrams are for the most part addressed to some individual, real or imaginary (Martial does not give the real names of the persons he satirizes—'parcere personis, dicere de vitiis' is his aim), and in them he depicts with realistic detail the most diverse characters of contemporary Rome, fortune-hunters, gluttons, topers, debauchees, poetasters, hypocrites of various kinds; he includes a few devoted wives, faithful friends, true poets, and honest critics. Many of the pieces are complaints of the stinginess of patrons, or requests for gifts or loans. Some are invitations to a simple hospitality, or take leave of a departing friend or greet his return. Some give vivid glimpses of a Roman scene, the vendor of hot sausages on his round, the Gaul who has sprained his ankle in the street and gets a lift home on a pauper's bier, the imperfect guest who arrives too late for breakfast and too early for lunch (viii. 67). Those addressed to the emperor (Domitian) are marked by a servile adulation, perhaps inevitable in the author's circumstances. A large proportion are spiced with gross obscenity (which he attempts to defend in the preface to Book I and in I. 35) and he shows as a rule amusement rather than indignation at the degrading vices he reveals (Book V, addressed to 'matronae puerique virginesque', and Book VIII are free from this taint). His role of mendicant for patrons' favours does not appear to have struck him as humiliating. As against these less attractive aspects of his work may be set his pride in his Spanish fatherland, his admiration for republican heroism, his delight in country life, his affection for his friends. There are among the 'Epigrams' some touching epitaphs and laments, including three for Lucan, and notably that for the young girl Erōtion, on whom he bids the earth press lightly, 'for she pressed light on thee'; lines that in a later age were parodied in the mock epitaph on Vanbrugh, the architect of Blenheim Palace,

> Lie heavy on him, earth! for he
> Laid many heavy loads on thee.

Martial writes as a rule in a natural straightforward style, without rhetoric and with little mythological allusion. He shows a sense of humour, e.g. in the picture of the barber who could not shave fast enough to keep pace with the growth of Lupercus's beard, or of the man who boasts he never dines at home, because he does not dine at all unless asked out. Some of his lines have become well known, such as that frequently seen on sundials, 'soles . . . qui nobis pereunt et imputantur'. One couplet (I. 32) has acquired in its English translation a wide currency:

> Non amo te, Sabidi, nec possum dicere quare;
> hoc tantum possum dicere, non amo te.

> I do not love thee, Dr. Fell,
> The reason why I cannot tell, &c.

Dr. John Fell (1625–86) was an eminent dean of Christ Church, Oxford; the translator was an undergraduate of his college. Martial does not claim to produce high literature and he admits the inequality of his work. But he was widely read, and known, he says, even in Britain.

Martiā'nus Cape'lla, an African, who early in the 5th c. A.D. wrote under the title 'De nuptiis Mercurii et Philologiae' an elaborate allegory in nine books of the marriage of Mercury and Philologia. The work is in Latin prose interspersed with verse. Mercury, having decided to marry, consults Apollo, who commends to him the learned virgin Philologia. The bride is carried off to heaven, accompanied by a song from each of the Muses. The last seven books describe the persons of the seven bridesmaids, Grammar, Logic, Rhetoric, Geometry, Arithmetic, Astronomy, and Music, and these expound their several principles. The work thus forms an encyclopaedia, in which pedantry and fantasy are mingled, of the seven liberal arts. It is largely founded on the 'Disciplinae' of Varro.

Masini'ssa, see *Sophonisba*.

Massi'lia (Gk. *Massalia*), now Marseilles, see *Phocaea* and *Colonization*, § 3. In the civil war between Caesar and Pompey, after a resolute stand in favour of the latter, it surrendered to Caesar in 49 B.C.

Master of the Horse, see *Dictator*.

Mātrā'lia, the matrons' festival at Rome,

celebrated on 11 June, centered in the goddess Matuta (q.v.).

Mātrōnā'lia, in Roman religion, the festival of Juno (q.v.) on 1 March, when prayers were offered to her and her son Mars. It was a sort of Saturnalia (q.v.) of women. March 1st was old New Year's Day. The women served food to their slaves, and married ladies received presents from married men.

Mātū'ta, in Roman religion, perhaps a dawn-spirit (connected with *mane*, 'morning', and *mātūtinus*), a female counterpart of Janus (q.v.). She developed into a protectress of childbirth, and was worshipped at the *Matralia* (q.v.). Later she was identified with the Greek goddess Leucothea (q.v.).

Mausō'lus (*Maussōllos*), a native of Cāria (SW. of Asia Minor) who in 377 B.C. succeeded his father Hecatomnus as dynast or ruler of that country, recognized by the king of Persia as his satrap. He extended his rule over the Greek cities of the coast and over Lycia, and plotted to get control of the neighbouring islands. For this purpose he fomented the revolt of Rhodes, Cos, and Chios from the Athenian Confederacy in 357 (see *Athens*, § 6) in order to bring them under his control. In this he was successful; but he died in 353 and was succeeded by his widow Artemisia. His statue and some sculptures from his spendid tomb (the *Mausolēum*) at Halicarnassus (q.v.) are in the British Museum.

Measures, see *Weights and Measures*.

Mēdē'a (*Mēdēia*), in Greek mythology, daughter of Aeētēs, king of Colchis, and like her aunt Circe (q.v.) an enchantress. See *Argonauts* and the article below; also *Magic*.

Medea, (1) a tragedy by Euripides, produced in 431 B.C. It deals with the later portion of the story of Jason and Medea (see *Argonauts*). They have fled to Corinth after Medea has, for Jason's sake, murdered his uncle Pelias. Jason, ambitious and weary of his barbarian princess, has arranged to marry the daughter of Creon, king of Corinth. The desertion and ingratitude of the man she loves rouse the savage in Medea, and her rage is outspoken. Creon, fearing her vengeance on himself and his daughter, pronounces instant banishment on Medea and her two children. By dissimulation Medea obtains one day's respite, and contrives the deaths of Jason's bride and of her father. Then she kills her own children, partly to make Jason childless, partly because, since they now must surely die, it is better they should perish by her hand than by her enemies'. Finally, taunting Jason in his despair, she escapes to Athens, where she has secured an asylum from King Aegĕus.

(2) A tragedy by Seneca the Philosopher, based on the play of Euripides above, with variations of detail. Medea's children are not sentenced to banishment; she asks that they should accompany her in exile, but Jason's love for them forbids. Medea thus learns where Jason is vulnerable, and kills them to revenge herself on him. The play contains Seneca's famous prophecy of the discovery of a New World (ll. 374 et seq.):

> Venient annis
> saecula seris quibus Oceanus
> vincula rerum laxet, et ingens
> pateat tellus Tethysque novos
> detegat orbes, nec sit terris
> ultima Thule.

(3) A tragedy by Ovid, of which only two lines have survived. It was praised by Quintilian.

Medicāmina faciēi fēminĕae, a poem in elegiacs by Ovid, containing recipes for the care of the complexion. The text, as we have it, is incomplete.

Medū'sa (*Medousa*), see *Gorgons*.

Me'gaclēs (*Megaklēs*), see *Alcmaeonidae*.

Megae'ra (*Megaira*), see *Furies*.

Megalē'sia or MEGALE'NSIA, the festival at Rome of the Phrygian *Magna Mater*, Cybele (q.v.), introduced in 204 B.C., and held on 4 April.

Megalo'polis, a city in Arcadia founded (about 370 B.C.) after the battle of Leuctra (q.v.), with the encouragement of Epaminondas, as a capital for the Arcadian confederacy. It joined the Achaean League in 234, and was subdued, and its inhabitants expelled, by Sparta under Cleomenes III. The city was restored by Philopoemen after the battle of Sellasia (222). It was the birthplace of Polybius and Philopoemen.

Megalopo'litans, For the, a political speech by Demosthenes. See *Demosthenes* (2), § 4 (*b*).

Me'gara (τὰ Μέγαρα, 'The Temples'), a Dorian city, originally known as Nisa (a name preserved in that of the adjoining port of Nisaea), near the base of the Isthmus of Corinth overlooking Salamis. It showed colonizing enterprise by founding Chalcedon, Byzantium, and other settlements in the NE. in the 7th c. B.C., also a new Megara in Sicily. A period of tyranny which prevailed at Megara in the 7th c. was followed by political struggles, reflected in the poems of the Megarian poet Theognis (q.v.). A war with Athens in the latter part of the 7th c. led to the loss of

Salamis and the decline of Megara as a power in Greece. After the Persian War Megara, in consequence of a dispute with Corinth, placed herself under Athenian protection and was occupied by an Athenian force (459). A revolt from Athens and massacre of the Athenian garrison followed the Athenian defeat at Coronea in 447. Megara suffered severely at the hands of Athens in the Peloponnesian war, and the city only escaped capture owing to the prompt succour brought by Brasidas. See also the article below.

Mega'rian School of philosophy, founded by Eucleides of Megara (*fl. c.* 390 B.C.), a disciple of Socrates. Its metaphysical doctrines resembled those of Parmenides (q.v.), except that Eucleides identified the universal principle of the Eleatics with moral good. The school was much addicted to dialectical controversy.

Mĕi'dias, *Against*, a speech prepared by Demosthenes, but not delivered. See *Demosthenes* (2), § 3 (*e*).

Meiō'sis (Gk. 'lessening'), a rhetorical figure, in which the words express less than they import; an understatement used to enhance the impression on the hearer. The idea is made out to be less than it deserves, so that, in consequence of the feeling of contradiction thereby produced, the idea becomes prominent. In the amusing letter (ad Fam. v. xii) in which Cicero asks Lucceius to write his life, he gives as his reason

> 'ut . . . nosmetipsi vivi gloriola nostra perfruamur';

'gloriola' was no doubt intended as a meiosis. See also *Litotes*. Quintilian uses the term *Meiosis* to indicate a fault of style, 'when something is wanting to an expression, so that it is not sufficiently full'.

Mē'la (*Mēla*), POMPŌNIUS, see *Pomponius Mela*.

Mela'mpus (*Melampous*), in Greek mythology, a famous seer, son of Amythāŏn (a grandson of Aeolus, q.v.). He took care of some young serpents whose parents had been killed by his servants, and these one day licked his ears as he was sleeping. Thereafter he understood the language of birds and could predict the future. His brother Bias sought the hand of Pērŏ, daughter of Neleus (q.v.), but the latter demanded as bride-price the cattle of Iphiclus. Melampus undertook to get them for his brother, but was caught and imprisoned. However, Iphiclus later gave the cattle to Melampus in return for the services rendered him through the seer's prophetic powers. And so Bias married

Pero. Among the descendants of Melampus were Amphiaraus (q.v.) and Theoclymenus (see *Odyssey* under Book XX). See also *Dionysus*.

Melani'ppidēs, see *Dithyramb* (*ad fin.*).

Meleā'ger (*Meleagros*), in Greek mythology, son of Oeneūs, king of Calydon, and his wife Althaea. The Fates appeared at his birth and declared that he should live so long as a brand that was on the fire was not consumed. Althaea snatched the brand from the fire and carefully preserved it. Later, when Meleager was a young man, Oeneus omitted to sacrifice to A. temis, and the goddess in wrath sent a great boar to ravage Calydon. Meleager collected a band of heroes to attack the creature and they succeeded in destroying it, the virgin huntress Atalanta (q.v.) being the first to wound it. Meleager, who loved Atalanta, gave her the head of the boar. His mother's brothers, angered at this partiality, tried to take it from her, and thereupon Meleager killed them. When Althaea learnt that he had killed her brothers, she threw into the fire the fatal brand, and as soon as it was consumed Meleager died. The women who mourned for him were changed into guineafowls (*meleagrides*).

For a beautiful modern treatment of the myth of Atalanta and Meleager, see Swinburne's 'Atalanta in Calydon' (1865).

Meleā'ger of Gadara (*fl. c.* 60 B.C.), a Greek poet of exquisite ability within his limited sphere (short elegiacs on love and death). He was also the compiler of an early anthology of epigrams (see *Anthologies*), entitled 'Stephanos' ('the Garland'). Many of his own epigrams are included in the Greek Anthology.

Melēsi'genēs, a name sometimes applied to Homer, in allusion to his traditional birthplace Smyrna, on the river Melēs.

Blind Melesigenes, thence Homer called,
Whose poem Phoebus challenged for his
   own.
           Milton, P.R. iv. 259.

Mēlian Dialogue, in Thuc. v. 84 et seq., the discussion between Athenian envoys and the magistrates of Mēlos, an island occupied by Dorians and friendly to Sparta, which had refused to surrender to Athens, and which the Athenians were proposing to subdue (416 B.C.). It is an exposition of the ruthless imperial policy of Athens at the time of the Peloponnesian War. Melos was taken by the Athenians shortly afterwards and the inhabitants put to death or enslaved.

Melice'rtēs (*Melikertēs*), see *Dionysus*. The body of the drowned Melicertes (who was deified as *Palaemon*) was washed up

on the Isthmus of Corinth, where the Isthmian Games (see *Festivals*, § 1) were founded in his honour. There was a temple of Palaemon at Corinth.

Melpo'menē, see *Muses*.

Me'mmius, Gaius, poetaster and patron of poets, praetor in 58 B.C., propraetor in 57 of Bithynia, where he was accompanied by Catullus and Helvius Cinna. Lucretius addressed his great poem to him.

Me'mnon (*Memnōn*), in Greek mythology, son of Tithonus and Eos (qq.v.), and leader of the Ethiopians who fought on the Trojan side at the siege of Troy. He was killed by Achilles. A tradition arose that a colossal statue near Egyptian Thebes (in reality representing King Amenōphis of the 18th dynasty) was a statue of this Memnon. The musical sound which, before the statue's partial destruction by an earthquake, it gave forth when struck by the rays of the morning sun, was regarded as Memnon's greeting to his mother, the Dawn.

Memorābi'lia (*Apomnēmoneumata*), reminiscences of Socrates by Xenophon, describing his character and some of his opinions, chiefly by means of more or less imaginary conversations between Socrates and various persons (one of the conversations is with Xenophon himself).

The first part is a refutation of the particular charges on which Socrates was tried and sentenced to death, as developed after his death in a literary exercise by one Polycrates. Xenophon then proceeds to illustrate the character and opinions of Socrates, his helpfulness to his friends, his piety, his views on education and various philosophical questions, probably derived in part from Xenophon's own recollections of Socrates, in part from other sources. The opinions attributed to Socrates (e.g. on the Good and the Beautiful) do not always accord with those attributed to him by Plato. The work winds up with a noble peroration in which the author sums up the virtues of Socrates. There is some confusion in the arrangement of the work, perhaps due to the existence of more than one edition, unskilfully blended at a later date.

Menae'chmi, a comedy by Plautus.

A merchant of Syracuse had twin sons so much alike as to be indistinguishable. One of these, Menaechmus, was stolen when seven years old. The other, Sōsiclēs, had his name changed to Menaechmus in memory of his lost brother. When grown up, Sosicles-Menaechmus sets out in search of his brother, and finally arrives at Epidamnus where that brother is living. Comical situations arise when Sosicles-Menaechmus successively encounters the mistress, the wife, and the father-in-law of his brother, and is mistaken by them for his twin. The wife and father-in-law come to the conclusion that he is insane, but owing to a further confusion it is the original Menaechmus whom they attempt to lock up. Finally the twins are confronted, and the puzzle cleared up.

This play, directly or indirectly, furnished the main ideas for Shakespeare's 'Comedy of Errors'. It may be of interest to recall that the 'Menaechmi' was performed before Pope Alexander VI and the Cardinals on the occasion of the marriage of Lucrezia Borgia to Alfonso d'Este.

Mena′nder (*Menandros*) (c. 342–29? B.C.), an Attic poet, the most famous writer of the New Comedy (see *Comedy*, § 4). He was a nephew of the comic poet Alexis (see *Comedy*, § 4), a pupil of Theophrastus (q.v.), and a companion in military service (σνέφηβος) of Epicurus. He was drowned, it is said, in the harbour of Piraeus. He wrote about one hundred plays. Substantial fragments of four of them were found in an Egyptian papyrus in 1905 (*Epitrepontes, Samia, Perikeiromenē, Hērōs*), and we possess shorter fragments of many others. Menander presents the life of contemporary Athens in its serious and pathetic, as well as in its more amusing aspects, though it may be questioned how far the kind of life that he depicts was representative. The reflections that occur here and there in his plays show him to have been a man of gentle character and wide sympathy, tolerant, with a tinge of melancholy. He was not very successful in his life-time, winning the first prize only eight times (Martial, v. 10, has the line 'rara coronato plausere theatra Menandro'), but became famous soon after his death. His plots have all much the same general character, with a love entanglement as the central feature. A typical theme is the seduction or violation of a girl, the abandonment of her child, its later recognition by means of some trinket, and the reconciliation and marriage of the parents. The subsidiary characters, if of a somewhat conventional order—the angry father, the cunning slave, the good-hearted courtesan—are treated with much variety and resource.

In the 'Epitrepontes' (q.v., 'Arbitration'), which is the most complete of the surviving comedies, the theme is as stated above. In the 'Samia' ('The Girl from Samos') the plot again turns on the question of the paternity of the child of an irregular union. The 'Perikeiromene' ('The Shorn Girl') is Glycera, the mistress of the soldier Polemōn. He sees her kissing Moschion, and in a passion shears off her hair.

It turns out that Moschion is her brother, and that she is the free-born daughter of the wealthy Pataecus. The play ends in reconciliation and marriage. In the 'Heros' the theme is again that of a girl who marries her seducer.

Quintilian regarded Menander as supreme among the writers of the New Comedy, and warmly recommends the study of his plays by students of rhetoric (Inst. Or. x. i. 69 et seq.). The exclamation of Aristophanes the Grammarian deserves mention: 'O Menander and Life, which of you imitated the other?' (ὦ Μένανδρε καὶ βίε, πότερος ἄρ' ὑμῶν πότερον ἀπεμιμήσατο;).

Menander is the source of many quotations (such as 'evil communications corrupt good manners', 1 Cor. xv. 33; 'whom the gods love die young'). Through Plautus and Terence (qq.v.) he deeply influenced modern comedy, notably in Molière, the Restoration dramatists, and Sheridan.

Menelā′us (*Menelāos, Meneleōs*), in Greek mythology, king of Sparta, son of Atreus, brother of Agamemnon, and husband of Helen (qq.v.), whom Paris (q.v.) carried off to Troy, thus bringing about the expedition of the Greek chiefs to recover her. In the 'Iliad' he is represented as unfortunate both in war and in love, and is overshadowed by Agamemnon, leader of the host. He reappears in the 'Odyssey' (q.v.) living at Sparta reconciled with Helen, and visited by Telemachus. He had returned to Sparta when Orestes had just killed Clytemnestra and Aegisthus (see *Pelops*). See also genealogy under *Pelops*; also Sophocles' *Ajax* and Euripides' *Helen*, *Andromache*, and *Trojan Women*.

Menē′nius Agri′ppa, consul at Rome in 503 B.C., is said to have induced the plebeians who had seceded from Rome to return to the city (see *Rome*, § 3) by relating to them the fable of the belly and the members.

Mene′xenus (*Menexenos*), see *Plato*, § 2.

Meni′ppus (*Menippos*) of Gadara, by birth a slave, who lived in the 3rd c. B.C., was a Cynic (q.v.) philosopher, who satirized the follies of men and philosophers in a mixture of prose and verse. His writings are lost, but they were imitated by Varro (q.v.) in his 'Saturae Menippeae' and by Lucian (q.v.) in his dialogues. Menippus himself figures frequently in the latter's 'Dialogues of the Dead', and one of Lucian's satires bears his name.

Mĕ′no (*Mĕnōn*), a dialogue by Plato on the question whether virtue can be taught. The origin of knowledge is discussed, and it is indicated that knowledge is latent in the soul, which is immortal; that knowledge is in fact reminiscence, and that teaching consists in eliciting it. There is no knowledge of virtue, but at most a right opinion, such as statesmen have, and this they cannot impart.

The historical Meno was a Thessalian general in the expedition of the Ten Thousand, whose treacherous conduct is related by Xenophon (Anab. ii. 5. 28).

Me'ntōr, (1) in the 'Odyssey', a companion of Odysseus, to whom Odysseus, when he departed for Troy, gave charge of his house. He acts as an adviser of Telemachus. (2) A famous Greek master of the art of working and adorning metal (the toreutic art, q.v.).

Mercā'tor ('The Merchant'), a comedy by Plautus, adapted from a play by Philemon (q.v.). A young man, sent abroad on a trading venture by his father, falls in love with a girl at Rhodes and brings her back to Athens, pretending that she is a present for his mother. His father discovers her, and himself falls in love with her, with consequent complications.

Mercury (*Mercurius*), in Roman religion, a god of trade (*merx*), particularly of the corn-trade, and early identified with the Greek or Graeco-Etruscan Hermes (q.v.).

Merivale, CHARLES, see *Historians (Modern)*.

Me'ropē, in Greek mythology, wife of Cresphontes (see *Heracleidae*). Cresphontes, king of Messene, was killed by Polyphontēs (another Heraclid), as were also two of his sons. A third son, Aepytus, was saved by Merope, and sent out of the country. Merope was forced to marry Polyphontes. Aepytus, when he reached manhood, killed Polyphontes and recovered the throne. This story is the subject of M. Arnold's drama 'Merope'.

There were others of the name: one was a daughter of Atlas and a Pleiad (q.v.); another the wife of Sisyphus (q.v.); a third, known also as Polyboea, the wife of Polybus, king of Corinth, who brought up Oedipus (q.v.).

Messali'na (*Messālina*), VALĒRIA, great-granddaughter of Octavia (sister of Augustus) and wife of the emperor Claudius, a woman with a reputation for profligacy which has become proverbial, though there are grounds for thinking that her misconduct was much exaggerated by contemporary scandal. In A.D. 48, though still apparently married to Claudius, she went through a solemn form of marriage with the senator Silius. To explain this strange action, it has been suggested that she had in fact been divorced by Claudius,

and that the new marriage was part of a plot to oust Claudius from the throne. In any case Claudius took alarm, and Messalina and Silius were put to death or forced to commit suicide. Messalina was the mother by Claudius of Britannicus and Octavia (the wife of Nero).

Messa'lla Corvi'nus, MARCUS VALĒRIUS, a member of the old Roman aristocracy, held an important command on the republican side at Philippi, and subsequently, though loyally accepting the new regime, kept somewhat aloof from the imperial court. He was a distinguished orator and author, and the patron of a literary circle which included Tibullus.

Metamorphō'seōn libri XI, see *Apuleius*.

Metamorphō'sēs, a series of mythological tales in fifteen books of hexameters by Ovid, his longest work. It purports to tell of miraculous transformations, but the transformation is sometimes of minor importance in the story, and the work is in fact a collection of the principal myths and legends of Greece and Rome. It begins with the transformation of Chaos into the ordered universe, and after a succession of tales drawn from Greek mythology passes to Aeneas and Dido, Numa and Egeria, the doctrines of Pythagoras, and recent times, ending with the death and deification of Julius Caesar. Ovid goes beyond the range of Graeco-Roman legend in the tale of Pyramus and Thisbe, the lovers of Babylon. The episodes are scantily connected; there is no guiding thought, no moral or religious lesson.

The poem shows Ovid at his best as a story-teller. Among the pleasantest of the narratives may be mentioned:

Book II, Phaethon driving the chariot of the Sun; Book III, Echo and Narcissus; Book IV, Pyramus and Thisbe, Perseus and Andromeda; Book V, the rape of Proserpine; Book VI, Pallas, Athene and Arachne; Book VII, Jason and Medea, Cephalus and Procris; Book VIII, the flight of Daedalus, Philemon and Baucis; Book X, Orpheus and Eurydice, Venus and Adonis; Book XI, Midas, Ceyx and Halcyone; Book XIII, Polyphemus and Galatea (qq.v.).

Metanei'ra, see *Demeter*.

Meta'phora (a Gk. word meaning 'transferring'), the transfer of a name, action, or descriptive term to an object different from, but analogous to, that to which it is properly applicable, e.g. where Catullus speaks of 'Minacis Hadriatici litus' (Poem 4); or Virgil's 'classique inmittit habenas' (Aen. vi. 1).

Metaphysics, a group of treatises by Aristotle (q.v., § 3) on the nature of existence.

Me'tic (*metoikos*), at Athens, a resident alien, who bore the ordinary burdens of citizenship, but exercised no political rights, and was not allowed to own land. The metics served in the army or navy, and took an important part in the industry and commerce of the city. They included the chief capitalists of Athens, and some of them carried on important businesses as bankers, shipowners, importers, and contractors. Others shone in the intellectual professions, as physicians, philosophers, sophists, orators (e.g. Aristotle, Protagoras, Lysias), or as Comic poets (e.g. Antiphanes and Philemon).

Mē'tis ('Counsel'), in Greek mythology, the first wife of Zeus, whom he devoured, fearing that her son would be stronger than himself. See *Athena*.

Mē'ton (*Mĕtōn*), an Athenian astronomer of the 5th c. B.C., who devised a calendar (q.v., § 1) designed to reconcile the solar and lunar years.

Meto'nymy, a rhetorical figure in which an attributive or other suggestive word is substituted for the name of the thing meant; e.g. 'jam proximus ardet Ucalegon' (Aen. ii. 311), where Ucalegon is substituted for his house.

Metre.

I. GREEK

§ 1. *Varieties of feet and metres*

The rhythm of Greek verse depended on 'quantity', that is to say on certain arrangements of syllables according to the length of time each took to pronounce. Syllables were regarded as either long or short, and a long syllable as having twice the length of a short syllable. The metre varied with the arrangement of long and short syllables in groups, each of which was called a 'foot' (πούς); and a verse (στίχος) consisted of a number of such 'feet'. Accent played no part in the construction of Greek metre.

The principal 'feet' were the following:

(1) Dactyl ('finger'): – ∪ ∪
(2) Spondee (from a word meaning 'libation'; a metre suitable for solemn ceremonies): – –
(3) Anapaest ('reversed', a reversed dactyl): ∪ ∪ –
(4) Iamb (from a verb meaning 'I assail'; see *Iambic Poetry*): ∪ –
(5) Trochee ('running') or Choree (*Chorĕus*): – ∪ (for a Latin author – ∪ is a *choreus*; by *trochaeus* he normally means ∪ ∪ ∪).
(6) Tribrach ('three short'): ∪ ∪ ∪

(7) Cretic ('Cretan') – ∪ –
(8) Paeon (from 'Paean', q.v.): – ∪ ∪ ∪ or ∪ ∪ ∪ – } 'paeonic' feet
(9) Bacchius or Bacchiac (from 'Bacchus'): ∪ – –
(10) Choriamb (Choree or trochee+iamb): – ∪ ∪ –
(11) Epitrite ('divided in the ratio of 4 : 3'): – ∪ – –
(12) Dochmius or Dochmiac ('a hand's breadth'): ∪ – – ∪ – (typical form, but each long syllable may be resolved into two shorts).

Feet were classified according to the proportion which the length of one part of the foot bore to that of the other. Thus in feet (1) to (3) above the proportion was equal (ἴσον), one long syllable being equivalent to two short. In feet (4) to (6) the proportion was double (διπλάσιον). In feet (7) to (9) the proportion was as 3 to 2 or 2 to 3 (ἡμιόλιον). Feet (10) to (12) were compound.

In practice the substitution of one foot for another, subject to certain rules, was frequent, but generally on the basis that the time was preserved, e.g. that a dactyl was replaced by its equivalent in time, the spondee. In the case of iambs, trochees, and anapaests, the Greeks regarded the unit (μέτρον) as consisting of two feet, a dipody; in the case of dactyls and spondees as consisting of one foot. An iambic trimeter accordingly consists of six iambs, an iambic tetrameter of eight iambs, a dactylic hexameter of six dactyls.

Greek metres appear to have been originally sung or chanted. But a distinction arose: while the simpler metres, such as those used in epic poems, were merely chanted, and before long were recited and divorced from music, another class of metres, more complicated, the lyric and the choric, retained its connexion with song and dance.

§ 2. *Dactylic, elegiac, iambic, trochaic, and anapaestic metres*

Of the former class of metres the principal example is the DACTYLIC HEXAMETER, the oldest known form of Greek verse, the metre of the epic poems and in particular of Homer. It consists of six feet, dactyls or their equivalent spondees. A spondee might replace a dactyl in any foot, though this was rare in the fifth foot, while the sixth foot was necessarily a spondee, of which the last syllable was common, that is to say ambiguous (*anceps*) in length, the pause at the end of the verse making good the deficiency if the syllable was naturally short. (Another view is that the sixth foot is a catalectic dactyl, i.e. one in which the last syllable is replaced by a pause.) There was generally a *caesura*, or break of the line into unequal parts (κῶλα), in the third foot or less frequently in the fourth foot, to enable the reciter to take breath. (The hexameters of Theocritus often have a break at the end of the fourth foot, known as the *bucolic caesura*.) There might be other subordinate pauses, arising from the sense, especially in the second foot, or after the fourth. The following lines offer examples of the main caesura in the third and fourth foot respectively; there is also a subordinate pause after ἄειδε in the first line:

(1) μῆνιν ἄειδε, Θεά, | Πηληιάδεω Ἀχιλῆος.
(2) Διογενὲς Λαερτιάδη | πολυμήχαν' Ὀδυσσεῦ.

The following line is an example of a 'weak' or trochaic caesura in the third foot:

ὑμῖν μὲν Θεοὶ δοῖεν | Ὀλύμπια δώματ' ἔχοντες.

The ELEGIAC COUPLET, which is first found in the 7th c. B.C. (see *Callinus*), consists of a dactylic hexameter followed by a dactylic pentameter constructed as follows:

$$- \overline{\cup\cup} | - \overline{\cup\cup} | - \| - \cup\cup | - \cup\cup | \underline{\cup}$$

that is to say of two equal parts each of 2½ feet, the end of a word marking the caesura between them. In the second half, spondees might not be substituted for dactyls. The pentameter does not roll on confidently, like the hexameter, to its close; the double pause of half a foot (*catalexis*, q.v.) makes it appropriate for the expression of grief or other emotions. (The term 'pentameter' for the second verse of the elegiac couplet is in fact a misnomer: the verse is really a hexameter of which the third and sixth feet are catalectic.) The following is an example of the elegiac couplet:

ἥλιον ἐν λέσχῃ κατεδύσαμεν· ἀλλὰ σὺ μέν που,
ξεῖν' Ἁλικαρνησεῦ, τετράπαλαι σποδιή.
(Callimachus.)

The IAMBIC TRIMETER or SENARIUS of six iambs, first written in exact form by Archilochus in the 7th c., is pre-eminently the metre of Greek tragic dialogue. The first syllable of each pair of feet or dipody might be either short or long:

$$\underline{\cup} - \cup - | \underline{\cup} - \cup - | \underline{\cup} - \cup -$$

A caesura was introduced normally after the fifth syllable. Long syllables in the second part of the foot, subject to certain limitations, might be resolved into two short ones. An anapaest might be substituted in the first foot. If the line ended in a word forming a cretic (− ∪ −), the preceding syllable had to be short or to be a word of one syllable closely

connected with that which followed (Porson's Law), e.g.

ὡς τοῖσιν ἐμπείροισι καὶ τὰς συμφοράς.

In comedy there was great freedom in the construction of iambic verse; in particular, anapaests were admitted in any foot except the last. It should be noticed that an iambic line can be regarded as trochaic with *anacrusis* (the addition of a syllable at the beginning of a verse before the normal rhythm) and a pause in the place of the last syllable, and this method of scansion is adopted by some:

$$\underline{\cup} | - \cup - \underline{\cup} | - \cup - \underline{\cup} | - \cup - \wedge$$

For the SCAZON, CHOLIAMBIC, or 'limping' iambic, invented by Hipponax (q.v.), and for 'pure' iambics, see below, § 5.

The TROCHAIC TETRAMETER also occurs in Greek tragedy. It consists of four trochaic dipodies, of which the first three may end with a long syllable, and of which the last is catalectic (i.e. has its last syllable cut off and a pause substituted); there is a break after the second dipody:

$$- \cup - \underline{\cup} | - \cup - \underline{\cup} \| - \cup - \underline{\cup} | - \cup - \wedge$$

Tribrachs were substituted freely, and anapaests (with the stress on the first syllable) were admitted in the second, fourth, and sixth feet.

περιβαλὼν πολλὴν κέλευθον ἤνυσεν πολλῷ στρατῷ.
(Aeschylus, Pers.)

ANAPAESTIC metres, originally no doubt warlike or march-rhythms (the short syllables coinciding with the raising of the foot, the long with setting it down), occur in the drama principally in the *parodos* or entrance-song of the chorus, in the form of groups of anapaestic dimeters closing with a catalectic line:

μαλακαῖς ἁδόλοισι παρηγορίαις,
πελάνῳ μυχόθεν βασιλείῳ.
(Aesch. Ag.)

Anapaestic dimeters of greater freedom, with a great preponderance of spondees, were sometimes used in laments and other emotional passages. Aristophanes also uses a form of anapaestic tetrameter (catalectic):

ἐντειναμένους τὴν ἁρμονίαν, ἣν οἱ πατέρες παρέδωκαν.
(Ar. Nub.)

The ANAPAESTIC DIMETER CATALECTIC or PAROEMIAC

$$\overline{\cup\cup} - | \cup\cup - | \cup\cup - | \underline{\cup}$$

is found frequently in proverbs (μελέτη δέ τοι ἔργον ὀφέλλει, or καιρὸς δ' ἐπὶ πᾶσιν ἄριστος). It has been regarded as the basis of the hexameter.

§ 3. *Lyric and Choric Metres*

Coming now to the purely *lyric and choric* metres (the anapaestic metres are on the border line), we find a broad distinction between those which are constructed uniformly from feet of the same type and those which are built up from different types of feet. Among the former we have various kinds of lyric verse used in the choruses of Greek drama and elsewhere, based respectively on (1) the trochee, (2) the dactyl, (3) the paeon or cretic, and (4) the dochmius. The following are examples of the four types:

(1) $-\cup-\cup-\cup-$

ἅτ᾽ ἐγὼ κατεύχομαι
θεσπίσασα πρευμενῶς.
(Aesch. Eum.)

(2) $-\cup\cup-\cup\cup-\cup\cup-\cup\cup$

ὦ πολύμοχθος᾽ Ἄρης, τί ποθ᾽ αἵματι
καὶ θανάτῳ κατέχει Βρομίου παρά-
μουσος ἑορταῖς;
(Eurip. Phoen.)

(3) $-\cup-|-\cup-$

φρόντισον καὶ γενοῦ
πανδίκως εὐσεβὴς
πρόξενος· τὰν φυγάδα μὴ προδῷς.
(Aesch. Suppl.)

(4) $\cup--\cup-|\cup\underline{\cup\cup}-\cup-$

μεθεῖται στρατός· στρατόπεδον λιπών
(Aesch. Sept. c. Theb.)

Lyrical iambics (sometimes analysed as trochaic with anacrusis) are a conspicuous feature of the choruses of Aeschylus, who uses the metre with frequent syncope or protraction of a long syllable ($\backsim$), so that it is equivalent to $1\frac{1}{2}$ long syllables; e.g.

πνοαὶ δ᾽ἀπὸ Στρυμόνος μολοῦσαι.
(Aesch. Ag.)

IONIC VERSE, either *a majore* (falling) ($--\cup\cup--\cup\cup$) or *a minore* (rising) ($\cup\cup--\cup\cup--$), sometimes used by Sappho and Alcaeus, occurs in Aeschylus, e.g. in his description of the advance of Xerxes (Pers. 65 et seq.)

πεπέρακεν μὲν ὁ περσέπτολις ἤδη
βασίλειος στρατὸς εἰς ἀν-
τίπορον γείτονα χώραν.

This metre was modified by Anacreon into the metre known as ANACREONTIC,
$\cup\cup-\cup-\cup-$:

φέρ᾽ ὕδωρ, φέρ᾽ οἶνον, ὦ παῖ.

In the metres in which different types of feet are combined a distinction may be drawn between the verse of Sappho and Alcaeus, where the range of variation is limited, and the choric odes of Pindar and Bacchylides, where it is unlimited. Among

the principal metres of the former class were:

(1) the SAPPHIC stanza, consisting of the Sapphic verse

$-\cup|-\underline{\cup}|-\cup\cup|-\cup|-\underline{\cup}$

three times repeated and followed by an Adonic

$-\cup\cup|-\underline{\cup}$

(2) the ALCAIC stanza, consisting of

$\underline{\cup}|-\cup|-\underline{\cup}|-\cup\cup|-\cup|-$

twice repeated, followed by

$\underline{\cup}|-\cup|-\cup|-\cup|-\underline{\cup}$
$-\cup\cup|-\cup\cup|-\cup|-\underline{\cup}$

The first three lines of the Alcaic stanza afford an example of *anacrusis* (the addition of a syllable at the beginning before the normal rhythm). The Sapphic and Alcaic stanzas are familiar to most readers (in a slightly modified form, see below § 5) from the Odes of Horace.

(3) the GLYCONIC stanza, formed on the basis of the glyconic verse,

$\underline{\cup\cup}-\cup\cup--$

ξανθὴ παῖ Διὸς ἀγρίων.

Anacreon repeated this verse three times and added a PHERECRATEAN line

$\underline{\cup\cup}-\cup\cup--$

δέσποιν᾽ Ἄρτεμι θηρῶν.

(The name Pherecratean is derived from Pherecrates, see *Comedy*, § 3.) Sappho modified the glyconic basis by inserting a dactyl or prefixing a cretic, and Alcaeus by inserting one or more choriambs, thus forming the ASCLEPIADEAN metres (the name is derived from Asclepiades, q.v.):

(*a*) $\underline{\cup\cup}-\cup\cup--\cup\cup-\cup-$

ἦλθες ἐκ περάτων γᾶς ἐλεφαντίναν.

(*b*) $\underline{\cup\cup}-\cup\cup--\cup\cup--\cup\cup-\cup-$

μηδὲν ἄλλο φυτεύσῃς πρότερον δένδριον ἀμπέλω.

Glyconics with various modifications are also found in tragic choruses.

The combinations found in the PINDARIC odes are extremely varied, but can usually be resolved into simple elements. One feature noticeable in them is the frequent use of epitrites ($-\cup--$) in combination with dactyls (the *dactylo-epitrite*):

$-\cup--|-\cup\cup--$

σάμερον μὲν χρή σε παρ᾽ ἀνδρὶ φίλῳ Λ
στᾶμεν εὐίππου βασιλῆι Κυράνας.

II. LATIN METRE

§ 4. *Saturnian and Plautine verse*

The primitive Latin verse of native origin was called by later poets SATURNIAN, to suggest its connexion with a remote past. It was based, unlike the Greek, not on quantity but on accent; that is to say its rhythm depended on the arrangement of accented syllables. What this arrangement was is not known with certainty, but it may have been as follows:

immortális mortális | sí forét fas fiére fierent dívae Caménae | Naévióm poétam
(from the epitaph ascribed to Naevius).

Alliteration, it should be added, played an important part in Saturnian verse. Verse of this kind was used in religious hymns, such as those of the Arval and Salian priests (qq.v.), in prayers, incantations, and maxims. Livius Andronicus and Naevius (qq.v.) wrote in Saturnians (besides using Greek metres in drama). Ennius was the first Latin poet who definitely adopted the Greek quantitative scansion. The plays of Plautus and Terence show a compromise between accent and quantity, accent (as in popular pronunciation) on the whole prevailing. The dialogue of their plays was usually written in iambic *senarii* or iambic or trochaic *septenarii*, that is to say in lines consisting of six iambs or seven and a half iambs or trochees (or equivalents), words being frequently admitted as trochees or iambs according to accent by the shortening of long syllables.

The following are examples of (1) trochaic and (2) iambic *septenarii*:

(1) Pró Cyrénensés populáres, véstram ego imploró fidem

(2) necéssitáte quídquid ést domi id sat ést habéndum.

The songs (*cantica*) of Plautus included a great variety of lyric metres; the following are examples (1) of Bacchiacs and (2) Cretics:

(1) recordatu' multum et diu cogitavi

(2) nempe equo ligneo per vias caerulas.

§ 5. *The later Latin metres*

The principal Latin metres, apart from the above, were the following:

The DACTYLIC HEXAMETER, introduced by Ennius, and perfected by Virgil and Ovid, similar to the Greek hexameter (see above, § 2), with variations from it in practice in the matter of the *caesura* and the close of the verse which make Virgil's rhythm utterly different from Homer's. In particular the true weak caesura, i.e. the trochaic break in the third foot without fourth-foot caesura, common in Homer, is rare in Virgil, e.g.:

Luna premit, suadentque ₎ cadentia sidera somnos.

The ELEGIAC COUPLET, also similar to the Greek prototype, introduced by Ennius and perfected by Tibullus, Propertius, and Ovid, but with restrictions as to the end of the verse in the practice of the three later

poets, viz. that the pentameter must end with a disyllable or a word of five syllables.

Among *lyric* metres:

The SAPPHIC stanza, similar to the Greek, but with restrictions imposed by Horace as to the position of divisions of words, e.g. there must be a division in the first three lines after the fifth or after the sixth syllable and the fourth syllable must be long. This is the metre of Horace's 'Odes' i. 2, 10, 12, 20, and many others.

Mercuri, facunde nepos Atlantis,
Qui feros cultus hominum recentum
Voce formasti catus et decorae
More palaestrae.

The ALCAIC stanza, similar to the Greek alcaic, with various restrictions in Horace's practice, e.g. the first syllable practically always long and the second complete foot of the first three lines always a spondee. This is the metre of many of Horace's 'Odes', e.g. i. 9, 16, 17, 26, &c.

O matre pulchra filia pulchrior,
Quem criminosis cunque voles modum
Pones iambis, sive flamma
Sive mari libet Hadriano.

Various ASCLEPIADEAN metres (see § 3 above), of which the basic form is

$$— — \,|\, — ∪ ∪ — \,\|\, — ∪ ∪ — \,|\, ∪ \,\underset{\smile}{}$$

Maecenas atavis edite regibus.

It is found in various 'Odes' of Horace (i. 1, 3, 11, &c.), sometimes followed by a GLYCONIC — — | — ∪ ∪ — | ∪ ∪ (e.g. i. 6), or by a PHERECRATEAN — — | — ∪ ∪ — | ∪ and a Glyconic (e.g. i. 5). (Catullus allows − ∪ as well as − in the first two syllables.)

Various IAMBIC metres, found chiefly in the 'Epodes' of Horace, e.g.

Beatus ille, qui procul negotiis,
Ut prisca gens mortalium,

sometimes in combination with dactylic lines (e.g. Epod. 13, 15, 16):

Nox erat, et caelo fulgebat Luna sereno
Inter minora sidera.

The Iambic trimeter (see above, § 2) was the ordinary metre used in the dialogues of Roman, as of Greek, tragedies.

The HENDECASYLLABLE (line of eleven syllables), originally a Greek metre, generally in Catullus and invariably in Martial in the form

$$— — — ∪ ∪ — ∪ — ∪ — —$$

Vivamus mea Lesbia atque amemus
(Catullus.)

The SCAZON or CHOLIAMBIC, also adopted from the Greek by Catullus and Martial, a 'limping' iambic verse in which the last foot reverses the natural rhythm:

$$\underset{\smile}{} — | ∪ — | \underset{\smile}{} — | ∪ — | ∪ — | — \underset{\smile}{}$$

It lends itself also to trochaic scansion, thus:

$\smile | - \smile | - \smile | - \smile | - \smile | - \smile | - \smile$

Miser Catulle, desinas ineptire. (Catullus.)
'Pure' iambics (i.e. without admission of spondees) are occasionally used, e.g. by Catullus in:

Phaselus ille quem videtis hospites.

The IONIC metre (see § 3 above) *a minore* is used by Horace in Od. iii. 12:

$\smile \smile - - - - \smile \smile - - - \smile \smile$

Miserarum est neque amori dare ludum neque dulci.

One other metre has a certain importance, the GALLIAMBIC, a variety of the above, and the metre in which the 'Attis' of Catullus is written. It reproduced the peculiar rhythm of the chants used in the worship of Cybele (whence its name, see *Galli*). The normal line is

$\smile \smile - \smile - \smile - - - \smile \smile \smile \smile$

Super alta vectus Attis celeri rate maria.

Catullus doubtless heard the chants of the Galli in Asia Minor; there was, moreover, a temple of Cybele on the Palatine at Rome, near the house of Clodia.

Metrō'um (*Mĕtrŏon*), at Athens, the sanctuary of the 'Great Mother' (Cybele, q.v.). It stood in the Ceramicus (see *Athens*, § 1) and served as the Record Office of the Athenians. It was in the precinct of the Metroum that the large earthenware tub stood in which Diogenes is said to have taken up his abode.

Mĕze'ntius, in the 'Aeneid' (q.v.), a cruel tyrant who has been expelled by his people and joins Turnus (q.v.) in opposing the Trojan settlement in Italy. He and his son Lausus are killed by Aeneas. He has a gallant horse called Rhaebus.

Mī'das (*Mĭdās*), a semi-legendary king of Phrygia, who, having hospitably entertained Silenus (q.v.), the companion of Dionysus, when he had lost his way, was given a wish, and wished that all he touched might become gold. But when he found that the very meat he attempted to eat became gold in his mouth, he asked to be relieved of the gift. He was ordered to wash in the river Pactolus, whose sands thereafter contained gold. For another legend of Midas and Silenus, see *Silenus*. On another occasion when Pan and Apollo had a contest in flute-playing, Midas had the indiscretion to declare Pan the superior player, whereupon Apollo changed his ears to those of an ass, to indicate his stupidity. This Midas attempted to conceal; but his barber saw the deformity, and, unable to keep the secret but afraid to reveal it, whispered the news in a hole which he had dug in the ground and then filled up the hole again; but the reeds that grew above the place, whenever stirred by the wind, repeated to the world that Midas had the ears of an ass.

Historically, 'Midas' was a title of all the kings of Phrygia, like 'Pharaoh' of the kings of Egypt. A Midas perhaps of the 7th c. B.C. dedicated a throne to the god of Delphi.

Migrations and Dialects, GREEK. Archaeologists have not arrived at agreement in their efforts to throw light upon the prehistoric Greek migrations, but the following general outlines represent the view perhaps most widely held. The tribes that introduced Indo-European speech into Greece appear to have come from the N. either at the end of the 3rd millennium B.C. or the beginning of the 2nd millennium, dispersing the earlier inhabitants, who are vaguely described as Pelasgians ('sea-people', also probably the name of a definite nation). Some of the earliest new-comers seem to have settled near the head of the Maliac gulf and may have been the first to call themselves Hellenes (q.v.). The invaders as a whole, known probably as Achaeans (q.v.), gradually overspread the greater part of Greece, reaching and conquering the Cretan settlements in Argolis, notably Mycenae, and thus coming into contact with Cretan civilization (see *Crete*). The more southerly bodies of invaders came to speak the Ionic dialect, the more northerly (in Thessaly and Boeotia) the Æolic. Whether the Ionians and Æolians were distinct tribes is uncertain, but they formed part of the Achaean confederacy, as it is represented in the 'Iliad'. Achaean tribes from the W. of Greece crossed the Corinthian Gulf and occupied the greater and more westerly part of the Peloponnese, where they introduced the Arcadian dialect, perhaps the original Achaean speech.

Early in the 12th c. B.C., after the capture of Troy by the Achaeans (see *Trojan War*), a fresh body of invaders (how connected with the Achaeans is uncertain), known as Dorians, who according to tradition had settled in Epirus, were driven from their home by pressure from the north. They are supposed to have invaded Thessaly and Boeotia, some of them remaining in the small district between Mount Oeta and Mount Parnassus which was named Doris. Others appear to have crossed the Corinthian Gulf, via Naupactus, to the Peloponnese. Here they occupied Argos, overthrew the Achaean kingdoms, destroyed Mycenae and Tiryns, and brought to an end the period of Mycenaean civilization (see *Mycenae*) in Greece. Corinth is, by tradition, one of the latest of Dorian conquests. This movement, which is known as the *Dorian Invasion*, ended probably in the 11th c.

Some of the Ionian and Aeolian-speaking peoples subdued by the Dorians, unwilling to remain under their rule, migrated across the Aegean. Aeolians had already settled in Lesbos and the Troad. They now established cities in the northern portion of the coast of Asia Minor, extending as far S. as Smyrna (which subsequently became Ionian); while the Ionians occupied the more northerly islands of the Cyclades, and the coast from Smyrna as far S. as Miletus, their influence extending to the great islands of Chios and Samos.

The Dorians themselves followed this example of oversea migration. They occupied the island of Cythera and the southerly belt of Cyclades, completed in Crete the destruction of the relics of Minoan (q.v.) civilization, seized Cos and Carpathos, and established themselves at Halicarnassus on the coast of Asia Minor and also at Rhodes. See *Asia Minor (Greek cities of)*.

As a result of these and other minor movements, the Aeolian dialect was spoken from Thessaly and Boeotia to Aeolis in the N. of Asia Minor; the Ionian from Attica and Euboea (Attic was a special form of Ionian) across the Aegean to Ionia; the Dorian in the greater part of the Peloponnese, Megara, and in the southern islands of the Aegean; at Halicarnassus it was displaced by Ionian. The Arcadian dialect survived in Arcadia, and in Cyprus and Pamphylia, where settlements of Achaeans appear to have been placed by Atreus (q.v.). See Pl. 8.

As time went on the use of distinct dialects, at least for literary purposes, tended to decline. The Athenian empire had a unifying influence on the language of Athens and her allies. The conquest of Greece by Macedon had a still more powerful effect in levelling the barriers that had existed between the small Greek States, and in promoting the adoption of a single dialect, based on Attic and known as the κοινὴ διάλεκτος, common to all Greek-speaking peoples. This is the dialect in which Polybius and most subsequent Greek authors wrote their works, though there was a revival of Attic under the Roman empire; of this revival Lucian is the best example. The κοινή or common dialect above referred to was a literary language; alongside of it was a less formal, spoken idiom, showing greater differences from Attic. This was the idiom in which the New Testament was written.

Mi′lēs Glōriō′sus ('The Braggart Soldier'), a comedy by Plautus. It is uncertain from what Greek original it is adapted.

The braggart captain Pyrgopolynicēs (a name combining the ideas of 'fortress' and 'much strife' and recalling the mythological Polynices), carries off the girl Philocōmasium from Athens to Ephesus, while her lover Pleusiclēs is absent at Naupactus. Pleusicles' slave sets off to inform his master, but is captured by pirates and given to Pyrgopolynices at Ephesus. The slave thereupon writes a letter to Pleusicles, who arrives and takes up his residence next door to the soldier. By the ingenuity of the slave and the help of Pleusicles' accommodating old host, Pleusicles and Philocomasium meet by means of a hole made in the wall between the two houses. It is given out that the girl's twin sister has arrived, and this explains Philocomasium's appearance now in one house, now in the other. Then Pyrgopolynices is fooled into believing that Pleusicles' host has a young wife who is dying for love of the soldier, is induced to dismiss Philocomasium in order to pursue this new amour, and is lured into the neighbouring house, where he is well beaten as an adulterer, while Pleusicles and his mistress sail off to Athens.

The *miles gloriosus* was a stock character in Roman comedy (see the prologue to Plautus's 'Captivi'); he is the prototype of Ralph Roister Doister and of Bobadil and other braggarts of the Elizabethan stage.

Milē′sian Tales, of Aristīdēs of Miletus, a writer of the 2nd c. B.C., were probably short stories of love and adventure; the type may be seen in the tale of the Ephesian Matron, in the 'Satyricon' of Petronius Arbiter (q.v.). They were translated into Latin by L. Cornelius Sisenna (q.v.). Their generally licentious character may be inferred from the fact that a copy found among the spoils of Carrhae aroused the disgust of the Persian Vizier. They were forerunners of such medieval collections of tales as the 'Gesta Romanorum', the 'Decameron' of Boccaccio, and the 'Heptameron' of Marguerite of Navarre.

Milestones, see *Roads*.

Milē′tus, an Ionian city with a splendid harbour on the coast of Asia Minor, near the mouth of the Maeander; it attained a brilliant position under the tyrant Thrasybulus about 610 B.C. Its chief importance in early Greek history was as a colonizing state: it took the chief part in founding settlements in the region of the Hellespont and the Black Sea (see *Colonization*, § 2). It was the birthplace of the early philosophers Thales, Anaximander, and Anaximenes, and later of Hecataeus the historian and Phocylides the poet (qq.v.). Miletus took a leading part in the Ionian revolt against Persia (see *Persian Wars*), and was besieged and captured by the Persians in 494 and its inhabitants carried off to Susa. It was refounded in 479, entered the Delian Confederacy (see *Athens*, § 4), and revolted against Athens in 412. It became independent, but was torn by struggles between the oligarchic and democratic parties. It was conquered by Alexander the Great in 334. Miletus was a manufacturing town and the centre of the wool industry; her wool was regarded as the finest in the world.

Miliā′rium au′reum, the 'Golden Milestone', was erected in Rome by Augustus, as the point from which roads radiated to various parts of Italy. It was probably a column inscribed with names of places and their distances.

Mi′lō (*Mīlōn*), a famous athlete of Croton (q.v.) in Magna Graecia, who is said to have lived in the latter part of the 6th c. B.C., and to have led the army of Croton against Sybaris in 510 B.C. He gained six victories in wrestling at Olympia, and Pausanias (vi. 14) relates some of his remarkable feats of strength. He could, for instance, hold a pomegranate in his hand so firmly that none could wrest it from him, yet so lightly that he did not crush it. He fell a prey to wolves in the end, his hands caught in the trunk of a tree that he was trying to split open.

Mi′lō (*Tītus Annius Mīlō Pāpiniānus*), famous as the rival, on the aristocratic side, of Clodius (q.v.) in the struggle of the period 57–52 B.C. He fought Clodius with his own weapons, organizing bands of ruffians for street fighting. He was active, as tribune of the plebs in 57, in getting Cicero recalled from exile. In 52 Milo and Clodius met on the Appian Way; a conflict followed in which Clodius was killed. Milo was tried, and was defended by Cicero. The latter was intimidated by the presence of the soldiers with whom Pompey, to preserve order, had lined the Forum, and failed in his speech (see *Cicero*, § 4). Milo was condemned and went into exile. He returned to Italy during the troubles of the year 48, and was killed at the head of a band of criminals and slaves.

Milti′adēs (*Miltiadēs*), an Athenian of noble family, prominent at the end of the 6th and beginning of the 5th cc. B.C. His uncle, Miltiades son of Cypselus, had been selected, in the days of Pisistratus, as leader of an Athenian colony to the shores of the Hellespont, and had ruled the peninsula as tyrant. Miltiades the younger was tyrant of the Chersonese at the time of the Persian invasion of Thrace

(c. 512 B.C.; see *Persian Wars*). He was present at the bridge over the Ister (Danube) by which Darius crossed on his expedition against the Scythians, and is said to have advised the destruction of the bridge when Darius's return was delayed. When the Ionian revolt failed, Miltiades for safety returned to Athens; he was not implicated in the revolt, but generally suspect to the Persians. He commanded as strategus (under the polemarch Callimachus) the Athenian force at Marathon (see *Persian Wars*). An unsuccessful attack on the island of Paros in 489, for which the Athenians had entrusted him with 70 ships, led to his being impeached and fined. He died of wounds received in the attack. His son was Cimon (q.v.). There is a life of Miltiades by Nepos.

Mime (*Mimos*, L. *mīmus*).

§ 1. *In Greece*

Originally meaning a mimic, the term came to be applied to a kind of dramatic sketch, representing a scene in everyday life. Mimes appear to have had their origin among the Dorians of Sicily. We have fragments of the mimes of Sophron (a Syracusan of the 5th c. B.C.) and eight mimes, and fragments of others, by Herodas (q.v.).

§ 2. *At Rome*

The name was applied to a kind of dramatic performance which appears to have been introduced at Rome from Magna Graecia. It was at first probably an intermezzo, a dance with flute accompaniment. It gradually ousted the Atellan Farce (q.v.) as an after-piece to tragedies. It developed into a licentious farce, without dialogue at first, and accompanied by music. The husband, the faithless wife, her lover, and the maid, were stock characters. The female parts were played by women. The mime took a literary form in the 1st c. B.C. The principal writers of mimes in that century were D. Laberius and Publilius Syrus (qq.v.), who made them the vehicle of social and political criticism. Mimes continued to be written and acted under the empire, and helped to drive comedy from the stage.

In modern use the sense of the word 'mime' is different; it signifies a play in which the parts are played with mimic gesture and action, and usually without words. Cf. *Pantomime*.

Mimne′rmus (*Mimnermos*), of Colophōn in Ionia, flourished in the second half of the 7th c. B.C. He wrote chiefly elegiac (see *Elegy*) love poems, and reflections on the short-lived pleasantness of youth, somewhat melancholy in character, which were collected under the title 'Nanno', the name of the flute-player who accompanied the poet and was loved by him. Only fragments of his work survive. William Cory in 'Mimnermus in Church' (*Ionica*, 1905) has put into the mouth of the old Greek poet his own preference for 'this human life', 'this warm kind world', over the less substantial joys of a hereafter.

Mine′rva, probably an old Italian goddess of artificers and trade guilds, introduced into Roman religion from Etruscan sources, to form one of the great State triad, Jupiter, Juno, Minerva. Her festival was the *Quinquatrus* (q.v.). She was later identified with Pallas Athene (q.v.) and took over the martial characteristics of Athene Promachos. Virgil presents her both as goddess of handicrafts and as a goddess of war.

Mines. Among the mines famous in antiquity were (1) the silver-mines of Laurium in Attica, which were leased by the State to contractors and worked by slave labour. They were the source of great wealth to Athens in the 5th c. B.C., but their importance declined from the time of the Spartan occupation of Decelea. Activity was resumed later, and they probably came under Roman control in the 2nd c. B.C. They were practically exhausted by the time of the Roman empire, and Spain was then the chief source of the supply of silver. The Laurium mines, however, are still worked, chiefly for their lead, at the present day. (2) The gold- and silver-mines of Mt. Pangaeus in Macedonia. They were seized by Philip of Macedon and provided him with funds for his conquests. The Romans closed them after the subjection of Macedonia in 167 B.C., to avoid oppression of the provincials and consequent discontent. The mines appear to have been reopened in 158 B.C. but were abandoned after a time. (3) The copper-mines of Cyprus, from which much of the bronze of antiquity was derived (the tin for this alloy being drawn probably from Spain or Cornwall). (4) The mines of Spain, especially of the Sierra Morena, which furnished gold, silver, and copper from very early times, and were the most important source of metals (including also tin, lead, and iron) in the 1st c. B.C. and the 1st c. A.D. The Romans derived great wealth from them.

The conditions under which mines were worked in Greek and Hellenistic times are a grave reproach to Greek civilization. There was fearful mortality among the unfortunate slaves who worked in the silver-mines of Laurium and the quicksilver-mines of Cappadocia; and the famous account given by Agatharchidēs (a historian and geographer of the 2nd c. B.C.)

of the working of the Nubian gold-mines under the Ptolemies shows the inhuman treatment to which slaves, criminals, and even prisoners of war, were there exposed.

In Italy itself the principal mining district was Etruria, which furnished copper, iron, tin, and argentiferous lead. In the later republican times the State endeavoured to check the development of mining in Italy, by limiting the number of workmen allowed in the mines, probably from fear that the concentration of large numbers of slaves might facilitate revolt. Elba was an important source of iron, Sardinia of argentiferous lead. The Romans worked mines in most of their provinces, notably the iron of Nōricum, besides those mentioned above. In Britain there were important tin-mines in Cornwall (see *Cassiterides*) and argentiferous lead-mines in the Mendips. The Romans probably worked a gold-mine in Wales.

There appears to have been no legal monopoly of mining of any kind in the Roman empire, but in point of fact most mines came sooner or later, either having been royal on annexation or by confiscation, into the hands of the State. For instance, the copper-mines of Cyprus were royal under the Ptolemies and passed directly to the Roman government; some silver-mines in Spain, on the other hand, were still in private ownership under Tiberius and were confiscated by him. Mines might be leased to large companies or leased shaft by shaft to small contractors (both are called *conductōrēs*). Government officials (*prōcūrātōrēs*) might supervise the *conductores* or exploit the mines directly. The Romans frequently used slaves or criminals for mining; fetters and stone blocks with rings have been found in ancient workings, and there is other evidence of harsh treatment.

Minō′an, the name given by Sir Arthur Evans to the civilization revealed by his excavations at the Palace of Minos at Cnossus in Crete. Of this civilization he has recognized three main phases, Early Middle, and Late Minoan, and he has subdivided each phase into three sub periods, of advance, acme, and decline, I, II, and III. The earliest Minoan dates from the last part of the Neolithic Age. It has been found possible to relate the phases of this civilization to the history of Egypt, Early Minoan being roughly synchronous with the first ten Egyptian dynasties (3400–2100 B.C.), Middle Minoan with the 11th–17th Egyptian dynasties (2100–1600 B.C.), and Late Minoan with the 18th and 19th Egyptian dynasties (1600–1200 B.C.). There are numerous inscriptions in Minoan script, which have not as yet been deciphered. See also *Crete.*

Mi'nos (*Mĭnōs*), in Greek legend, a great king of Crete in ancient times. What historical facts the legends about him may reflect it is impossible to say (see *Crete*). Minos may have been the name of one or more Cretan kings, or the name of a dynasty, or a title like Pharaoh. He was generally regarded as having been a just ruler, who was promoted to be judge of the dead in Hades. Attic legend on the other hand represented him as a cruel tyrant who imposed on Athens a yearly tribute of seven youths and seven maidens (see *Theseus*). He was said to be a son of Zeus and Europa (q.v.). He married Pasiphae daughter of the Sun and had by her two daughters, Ariadne and Phaedra (qq.v.) and two sons. He refused to sacrifice to Poseidon, as he had promised, a beautiful bull that the god had sent him. To punish him Poseidon caused Pasiphae to become enamoured of the bull, and she gave birth to a monster, part bull and part man, known as the *Minotaur* (see *Monsters*). Daedalus (q.v.), who had fled or been exiled from Athens and was then in Crete, devised a maze, called the Labyrinth (q.v.), in the centre of which the Minotaur was kept. Here it consumed the youths and maidens sent by Athens as a tribute, until Theseus destroyed it. It is noteworthy in connexion with the legend of the Minotaur that representations of a sport of bull-leaping or -baiting (perhaps ritual or ceremonial) are numerous in Cretan art of the Minoan period. Herodotus states (vii. 170) that Minos, pursuing Daedalus to Sicily when the latter escaped from Crete, there met with a violent death. According to Homer (Od. xix. 178) Minos was grandfather of Idomeneus (q.v.). He appears again in the legends of Britomartis and of Scylla (qq.v.).

Mi'nos, Rhadama'nthus, and Ae'acus (qq.v.), judges of the dead, appointed to this position in consequence of their just lives on earth. Rhadamanthus was also ruler of Elysium (q.v.). Plato includes Triptolemus (q.v.) among the judges of the dead. Virgil mentions Minos and Rhadamanthus alone in his description of the nether world (Aen. vi).

Mi'notaur (*Mĭnōtauros*), see *Minos* and *Labyrinth*.

Minū'cius (*Mĭnŭcius*) **Fēlix**, MARCUS, an early Latin Christian apologist, was probably of African origin, and a contemporary of Tertullian, i.e. he probably lived in the 2nd–3rd c. He was an advocate at Rome, and author of the dialogue *Octavius*. The setting is imitated from Cicero:

three interlocutors, Caecilius Nātālis a pagan, Octāvius Jānuārius a Christian, and the author, are walking by the sea at Ostia; Caecilius is taken to task because he salutes an image of Serapis, and a discussion on Christianity results. Caecilius criticises the Christians (*a*) for their dogmatism, seeing that the human intelligence is incapable of grasping the mystery of the universe, (*b*) for their rejection of the ancient religion of Rome, (*c*) for their immoral life. Octavius replies, establishing the existence of God and Providence by the testimony of the pagan writers themselves, attacking the Roman mythology, and repudiating the charges brought against the manner of life of the Christians, of which he depicts the virtue and heroism. Caecilius declares himself convinced, and the friends separate. Christ is referred to only indirectly in the dialogue, and the defence is rather of the moral and philosophic side of the Christian religion than of its specific dogma. It is addressed in fact to the cultivated Roman pagan and is intended to dissipate his prejudices. The work is written with much literary art and persuasiveness. The tone of the interlocutors is urbane, and the whole presents a strong contrast to the imperious vehemence of Tertullian.

Mi'nyans (*Minuai*), a legendary people, perhaps among the earliest invaders of Greece, whose centre was Orchomenus in Boeotia. Their name is associated with a special type of primitive glazed pottery.

Mi'nyas (*Minuās*), the legendary ancestor of the Minyans (q.v.) of Orchomenus. He was also father of Clymene (q.v.), and of other daughters. Of the latter it is told that they resisted the cult of Dionysus, were driven mad, and tore in pieces Hippasos, the son of Leucippē, one of themselves. They were turned into bats.

Misē'nus, in 'Aeneid' vi. 162 et seq., the trumpeter who challenged the gods to a contest in music, and was dragged into the sea and drowned by Triton.

Mi'thras (*Mithrās*), see *Religion*, § 5.

Mithridā'tēs (or *Mithra-*) **VI, Eu'patōr**, king of Pontus, an indefatigable enemy of Rome. He was of a Hellenized Persian family, and ascended the throne, jointly with his brother Chrestus (whom he subsequently removed), at an uncertain date about 115 B.C. He extended his dominions by invading Paphlagonia, Colchis, and Armenia Minor, and on a request for help from the Greek cities of the Crimea against their Scythian and Sarmatian neighbours conquered the whole N. coast of the Black Sea. His great increase of power involved a threat to Rome, but Rome was then occupied with the menace of the Cimbri and Teutones, and the Senate temporized and negotiated. Mithridates then seized Cappadocia, was expelled in 92, reoccupied it in 90, and dispossessed the king of Bīthȳnia. In 88, when Rome was engaged in the Social War, Mithridates after elaborate preparations declared war against her and invaded Greece and Macedonia. He is said to have caused 80,000 Italian citizens to be put to death in the various cities of Asia. He was aided by the hatred felt in Asia for Rome and for the *publicani* (see *Equestrian Order*) and was supported by some of the Greek States, including Athens, which stoutly resisted the Roman army under Sulla but was taken in 86. Mithridates was driven out of Europe by Sulla, who came to terms with him by the treaty of Dardanus. Mithridates renewed the war in 74 by invading Bithynia, was defeated and driven out of his conquests first by Lucullus, then by Pompey, and took refuge in Tauris. Thence he conceived a plan for the invasion of Italy; but his son Pharnacēs revolted against him. Mithridates preferred death to captivity. He had fortified himself by antidotes against poison so strongly that he could not poison himself and had to get a slave to stab him (63).

Mi′tylēnē (*Mitulēnē*) or **MY′TILĒNĒ** (*Mutilēnē*), see *Lesbos*.

Mnēmo′synē (*Mnēmosunē*), in Greek mythology, a Titaness (see *Titans*), a personification of Memory; mother of the Muses (q.v.).

Mnē′siclēs (*Mnēsiklēs*), see *Temples*, § 1, and *Propylaea*.

Moe′rae (*Moirai*), see *Fates*.

Mola Salsa, in Roman religious practice, a cake, or more probably loose meal, of spelt (a particular kind of wheat) gathered, roasted, and ground by the Vestal Virgins (q.v.), and mixed with salt. It was used for sacrificial purposes.

Mommsen, THEODOR, see *Historians* (*Modern*).

Mō′mus (*Mōmos*), according to Hesiod, a son of primeval Night; in Greek mythology the personification of criticism and fault-finding.

Monē′ta, see *Juno*.

Montfaucon, BERNARD DE, see *Texts and Studies*, § 11.

Money and Coins

§ 1. *In Greece*

The Greek measures of value in post-Homeric times were the talent (*talanton*), the mina (*mnā*), and the drachma, that is to say certain weights of silver. These weights varied in the systems of different States. The principal systems were the Euboïc (adopted by Athens and Corinth) and the Aeginetan. The talent, originally a Persian measure of weight, in the Euboïc and Attic coin system was equivalent to about 58 lb., and that quantity of silver would be worth about £200. (It may be noticed here that the Homeric talent was probably much smaller than the Attic talent; one of Aristotle's 'Homeric Problems' was 'why are two talents of gold given as the *fourth* prize in a chariot race?' Il. xxiii. 269.) The mina was the sixtieth part of a talent, and the drachma the hundredth part of a mina. The obol (*obolos*) was the sixth part of a drachma. (The origin of the words 'obol' and 'drachma' is said to have been this: when in primitive times weights often served as a medium of exchange, iron spits (*oboloi*) were used to represent small amounts, and six of these formed a 'handful' or drachma.) 'Drachma' was the name not only of a weight but also of a corresponding silver coin. Under the system which prevailed from the time of Pisistratus it weighed about 66 grs. and was worth about 8d. The principal silver coin was the tetradrachm of four drachmas. The talent in the Aeginetan system (which had a wide currency) weighed about 83 lb., and the Aeginetan drachma was worth about 1s. 1d. Gold was little used for coinage in Greece. The Persian relation between the value of gold and silver (1:13½) was originally adopted, but the ratio fell, with the increase in the supply of gold, to 1:10 in the 4th c. There was a *statēr* of 20 drachmas, but the gold coin chiefly current in Greece was the Persian daric (*dareikos*). Copper was used for a coin, the eighth of an obol. The earliest Greek coins were struck in Asia Minor, where coinage had probably been invented by the Lydian kings (electrum, a natural alloy of gold and silver, was the first metal used for the purpose). In the course of the 7th c. the practice of coinage spread to many Greek cities, each of which had its own emblem. In the 6th c. the art had already reached a high degree of beauty; it was at its best in the 5th and 4th c., when coins of remarkable design and execution were produced not only in Greece itself, but in Greek colonies so widely separated as Lampsacus (on the Sea of Marmora) or Panticapaeum (on the Euxine) and the cities of Sicily, where some of the most beautiful coins of all time were minted. The Athenian coins retained an archaic design, on the obverse a head of Athene, on the reverse an owl, a crescent, a sprig of olive, and the inscription $A\Theta E$. These were notable for their reliable character in point of weight and fineness and were widely used throughout the Mediterranean; Athens in her darkest days never debased her currency. The drachma of Alexander the Great was identical with that of Athens, and this standard was adopted in many parts of the Hellenistic world (not in Egypt). Greek coins of the Hellenistic period continued to show admirable technique, but the design tended to become less simple and dignified. Alexander and the Hellenistic kings issued an abundant currency. The gold Philippus had a very wide circulation: some of the Gallic and British coinage before the Roman conquest was copied from it. Alexander and his successors introduced portraits of themselves (some of them very fine) on their coins.

§ 2. *At Rome*

The original unit of currency was a bar of bronze weighing one Roman pound and known as an *as*; this had subdivisions. From a certain time these bars were stamped, as a guarantee, with figures of animals (the word *pecunia* is probably derived from the use of cattle, *pecus*, as units of exchange). The first Roman coined money was of bronze (*aes grave*), the series consisting of the *as*, *semis* (half), *triens* (third) of four ounces, *quadrans* (quarter) of three ounces, *sextans* (sixth) of two ounces, and the *uncia* or ounce. The dates of the introduction and early changes in Roman currency are still matters of discussion (see H. Mattingly in the 'Journal of Roman Studies', vol. xix, and H. Mattingly and E. S. G. Robinson in 'Proceedings of the British Academy', vol. xviii). Bronze money was probably first issued *c.* 289 B.C. In the financial stress resulting from the Punic Wars the *as* was reduced first to six ounces (probably *c.* 235 B.C.), then to four ounces, then to two ounces (the 'sextantal *as*', probably in 187 B.C.), and finally to one ounce (the 'uncial *as*'). Bronze coins bore the heads of a god or goddess on one side, and on the other the prow of a ship. This device, which perhaps commemorated the conquest of Antium in 338 B.C. when the *rostra* were brought to Rome, or indicated Roman interest in naval affairs during the First Punic War, remained on the reverse of Roman bronze money throughout republican times, and Macrobius tells us that when boys tossed a coin, the call was 'heads or ships'. Silver was first coined for Roman use, according to Livy and Pliny, in 269 or 268 B.C. It then probably took the form of what is known

as the Romano-Campanian didrachm, minted at Capua. Reasons have been advanced (in the above-mentioned articles) for thinking that the *denarius*, notwithstanding the statements of Roman writers, was not issued until the early part of the 2nd c. B.C., probably in 187. It was equivalent to 10 sextantal *asses* (later to 16 uncial *asses*), the *quinarius* was equivalent to 5 *asses*, and the *sestertius* to 2½ *asses* (later to 4 *asses*). *Sestertius* is *semistertius* = 2½; it was written in abbreviated form HS, that is $II + S(emis)$. The denarius weighed 70 grs. (it was later reduced to 60 grs.), and was roughly equivalent to the Attic drachma. It may be taken for purposes of very rough calculation as equivalent to about 8*d.*, and the sesterce to 2*d.* Roman coins were minted in the Temple of Juno (q.v.) Moneta at Rome, and also at Capua. In republican times the supervision of the mint in the Temple of Juno was entrusted to a commission known as the *Tresviri Monetales*.

Gold was first used by the Romans for currency in the Second Punic War. Sulla, Pompey, and Caesar struck *aurei* of various weights, and gold pieces (*aurei* or *solidi*) continued to be struck under the empire. The minting of gold and silver was then monopolized by the emperor. Bronze (or copper) was struck by the Senate at Rome, and nearly all eastern cities struck their own bronze (or copper) coins (down to the mid-3rd c. A.D.). In Nero's reign there was a debasement of the gold and silver currency; both the aureus and the denarius were lightened and the silver of the denarius was alloyed with base metal. There was further tampering with the currency during the 3rd c., till a state of great confusion was reached, which Aurelian and Diocletian attempted to remedy. Finally a sound currency was re-established by Constantine. The currency was all of it imperial from Aurelian's time.

The early silver coins (3rd c. B.C.) sometimes bear the name or other indication of the magistrate who struck them. Julius Caesar was the first to have his own head represented on coins, and we have a series of portraits of the emperors on their coins. On the reverse side of Roman gold and silver coins appeared symbols of Rome, such as Janus, four-horse or two-horse chariots, and Castor and Pollux.

While the coinage of the Roman republic was uniform throughout the Roman territories, the independent Italian communities in early times had their own coinage. Their coins reached Rome in course of trade, as did at a later date the currencies of the East. Hence arose the need for the services of *argentarii* or money-changers, to whom there are frequent references in Roman literature. For Roman and other coins in Britain see under *Britain, ad fin.*

Monsters. The Greeks were fond of introducing monsters of various kinds, many of them derived from eastern sources, into their myths. These monsters, of various degrees of strangeness, can be classified according as they take the form of (1) human beings of merely exaggerated size; (2) human beings with some extraordinary feature, such as excess or deficiency of the normal limbs and organs; (3) creatures combining human and animal shapes; (4) creatures combining the shapes of two or more animals.

Class 1 consists of the Giants (q.v.) as primitively conceived, creatures of human form so huge that after the defeat of their attack on the gods they were buried under islands, Enceladus for instance under Sicily, and Polybōtēs under Cos; while Tityus in Hades covered nine roods of ground. But in course of time, to differentiate them from gods and heroes, their attributes became more terrific and they passed into classes 2 and 3. Giants, in the traditions of various races, were the personification of violent forces of nature, such as volcanoes.

Class 2 includes such monsters as the Hecatoncheires (the Hundred-handed Giants, q.v.); the three Graiae (q.v.), having only one eye and one tooth between them; the Cyclopes (q.v.), with a single eye apiece; the Medusa (q.v.) with her huge and hideous head and petrifying eyes; Argus (q.v. (3)) with eyes all over his body.

Class 3 embraces a very large number of monsters: the Giants, as later represented, with their legs terminating in serpents; Cecrops and Erechtheus (qq.v.), whose bodies also terminated in serpents; Typhōēūs (q.v.), a particularly terrible creature, with a hundred serpents' heads; Echidna (q.v.), with the head and bust of a young woman, the rest a serpent; the Arcadian Satyrs (q.v.), goat-footed with horns and tail, and the Anatolian Satyrs, with the ears, feet, and tail of a horse. The Sphinx (q.v.) of the dramatic poets was a winged woman with the body of a dog or lion; she was derived probably, not from Egypt, but from Chaldaea. Scylla (q.v.), a marine monster, had, according to Homer, twelve dangling feet, six long necks and a hideous head on each, with three rows of teeth, the body lying concealed in a cavern. The idea was perhaps derived from some kind of squid. Later she was given a more human form: Virgil describes her as having the body of a young woman, the tail of a dolphin, and

a girdle of dogs' heads. The Tritons (q.v.) were monsters combining a human body with a fish's tail. The Centaurs (q.v.) had a human body rising from the body and legs of a horse; in primitive representations the front legs are those of a man. The Minotaur (see *Minos*) had a human body with the head of a bull; it is noteworthy that the Phoenicians had a god, Baal Moloch, of this form. Two types of monster, the Sirens and the Harpies (qq.v.), joined a woman's head to the body of a bird, a widespread fancy found in fables in all parts of the world. The Harpies were primitively represented as women with birds' wings, later as birds with women's heads.

In Class 4 may be included the Dragons, though the dragon (Gk. *drakōn*, L. *draco*) is not properly a monster at all, but merely a large serpent. It figured frequently as the guardian of shrines (e.g. the Python at Delphi slain by Apollo), as an attribute of Asclepius, or as *genius loci* (see *Genius*). But dragons were sometimes given monstrous peculiarities, such as wings or additional heads. Winged dragons drew the cars of Triptolemus and Medea. Fire-breathing dragons are especially a product of Christian art. In the same class we have such monsters as Cerberus (q.v.), with his three heads and hair composed of snakes; the Chimaera (q.v.), combining the head of a lion, the body of a goat, and a tail ending in a serpent's head; and the Griffins, part eagle and part lion (see Tenniel's illustrations of the Gryphon in 'Alice in Wonderland'). The Griffins were first referred to, we are told, by Hesiod (in a lost passage); according to Herodotus they guarded the gold in Scythia. One of the strangest monsters is the Hippalectryon: it had the head and forelegs of a horse, and behind these the legs, tail, and body of a cock. There are extant representations of it on two vases by Nicosthenes, and it is mentioned by Aristophanes (Ran. 937–8), from whom we learn that it (as also the Tragelaphus or goat-stag) was copied from Persian sources. It is not surprising that so inelegant a conception disappeared before long from Greek art and finds no place in Greek myth. The Hippocampus was a horse with fish-like tail, on which gods of the sea are often represented riding.

Monsters made little appeal to the Romans. In the comparatively rare cases where monsters figure in their literature (e.g. Scylla in the 'Aeneid'), it is generally in imitation of Greek models.

Monume'ntum Ancȳrā'num, an inscription in Latin (with Greek translation) found at Ancȳra (Angora), the Latin text being a copy of the record of the principal events of the reign of Augustus (*index rerum a se gestarum*) which, in accordance with his wish, was after his death engraved on bronze tablets at Rome. It is sometimes referred to as 'Res Gestae divi Augusti'. The inscription sets out the offices Augustus held and the honours he received, including the title of 'pater patriae'; his victories and conquests (and his clemency to the conquered); his political measures and incidentally his attempt to revive the ancient Roman virtues; the closing thrice in his reign of the Temple of Janus and the celebration of the Secular Games (qq.v.); his benefactions and his grants to veterans; the public buildings he erected or restored; the games and spectacles he provided.

The text was inscribed on the walls of a temple of Rome and Augustus, and is still extant. Fragments of two other copies have been found at Apollonia in Galatia and at Antioch in Pisidia, and it is probable that copies were set up in all the provinces. Its existence was not known until after the Renaissance, and a number of attempts from 1555 onwards were made to obtain complete copies of it. It was not until 1882 that casts of the whole of the Latin and Greek versions were obtained by an expedition under the auspices of the Academy of Berlin.

Mo'psus (*Mopsos*), in Greek mythology, a seer, son of Mantō, who was herself a prophetess, daughter of Tiresias (q.v.). He encountered Calchas (q.v.) and showed himself superior to him in prophetic skill. There was also a seer of the name of Mopsus who accompanied the Argonauts (q.v.). Mopsus is also the name of a shepherd in Virgil's 5th and 8th Eclogues.

Mōrā'lia, see *Plutarch*.

Morē'tum ('The Salad'), a poem of 123 hexameters, doubtfully attributed to Virgil. It vividly describes a peasant rising early on a winter morning, lighting his fire, grinding his corn in a handmill, collecting herbs from his garden for his salad, and preparing his meal with the help of his old negress servant; then starting off for his day's work at the plough.

Mo'rpheūs, the Greek god of dreams (q.v.).

Mo'rta, see *Fates*.

Mortuo'rum Dia'logi, see *Lucian*.

Mo'schus (*Moschos*) (c. 150 B.C.), a poet of Syracuse, whose extant poems include, besides short pastoral pieces, an idyll on the story of Europa (q.v.), and a dialogue

in which Megara and Alcmene, wife and mother of Heracles, bewail their misfortunes. The beautiful 'Lament for Bion', doubtfully attributed to Moschus, is a dirge for the author's friend and teacher. There is an echo of it in Milton's Latin 'Epitaphium Damonis', on his friend Charles Diodati, as well as in his 'Lycidas'; also in Shelley's 'Adonais' and in Matthew Arnold's 'Thyrsis'.

Mostellā'ria ('The Ghost'), a comedy by Plautus, probably adapted from a play by Philemon (see *Comedy*, § 4).

The plot rests on the effrontery and resourceful lying of the slave Trāniō. Philolachēs, during his father's absence abroad, purchases and frees a girl whom he loves, borrowing money for the purpose from a usurer, and brings her to live in his father's house. The father unexpectedly returns. Tranio, to prevent him from entering the house and discovering what is going on, pretends that the house is haunted by the ghost of a murdered man and has consequently been vacated. But the usurer appears and demands his money. Tranio tells the father that Philolaches has borrowed it to buy the house of their neighbour Simō, and Simo is induced by further lies to allow it to be inspected. At last Tranio's roguery is exposed, but the father's anger is appeased.

This play was imitated by T. Heywood in the by-plot of his 'The English Traveller' (1623).

Mu'lciber, a name of Vulcan (q.v.), meaning 'the smelter' of metals.

Mu'ndus, see *Manes*.

Mūny'chia (*Mounuchia*), the Acropolis of the Piraeus (q.v.) and a small harbour adjoining it. See Pl. 13 *b*.

Mūsāe'us (*Mousaios*), (1) a legendary pre-Homeric Greek poet, said to have come from Thrace and to have been a pupil of Orpheus (q.v.). A collection of oracles, and poems connected with Orphism (q.v.), were attributed to him, and Plato speaks with respect of his poetry. See also *Onomacritus*. (2) A Greek poet of the 4th or 5th c. A.D. who wrote a poem on Hero and Leander, which survives, and a translation of which provided the groundwork for Marlowe's 'Hero and Leander'. Nothing is known about the poet.

Muses (*Mousai*), in Greek mythology, daughters of Mnemosyne (q.v.), goddesses of literature and the arts. The original seats of their worship were Pieria near the Thessalian Olympus, and Mt. Helicon in Boeotia, whence they are often spoken of as Pierian or Heliconian. They were nine in number and in later legend were severally associated with the different arts, variously stated, e.g. Calliopē (epic poetry), Cliō (history), Euterpē (flute-playing), Melpomenē (tragedy), Terpsichorē (dancing), Eratō (the lyre), Polyhymnia (sacred song), Ūraniā (astronomy), Thaliā (comedy). Though the Muses are often spoken of as 'Pīerides' (see *Pieria*), the Pierides, according to one form of their legend, were nine daughters of Pīerus, king of Ēmathiā in Macedonia. These challenged the Muses in song, and for their presumption were changed into magpies. See also *Thamyris*.

Musē'um (*Mouseion*), at Alexandria, a literary academy, founded by Ptolemy II (q.v.), perhaps under the impulse of Demetrius of Phalerum (q.v.). It included a common hall where the members had their meals, and an arcade with recesses and seats. It possessed endowments for the maintenance of the scholars, and in fact somewhat resembled a modern university college, though we have no evidence that there was any provision for teaching. A satirical poet of the 3rd c. B.C. described it as a 'bird-coop of the Muses'. It appears to have continued in existence for many centuries, for Theōn the mathematician (4th c. A.D.), the father of Hypatia (q.v.), is mentioned as a member of it.

Museums, MODERN. In Great Britain the important museums of Greek and Roman antiquities are the British Museum, the Ashmolean at Oxford, and the Fitzwilliam at Cambridge. There are in various places excellent collections of Roman antiquities found in Britain, e.g. at the Guildhall Museum and the London Museum in London; at the Bath Institute and the Baths Museum at Bath; at the Museum of the York Institute at York; at the Cardiff Museum of Antiquities; at the Black Gate Museum, Newcastle-on-Tyne; and at the National Museum of Scotland, Edinburgh. The Acropolis and National Museums at Athens, and the Capitoline and National Museums at Rome contain many notable antiquities. In France, the museum of Saint-Germain near Paris is well known for its collection of Gallo-Roman antiquities; the Louvre has many beautiful examples of sculpture and Greek vases. In Germany the Glyptothek at Munich and the Berlin Museum are important. In America the most famous collections are those of the Metropolitan Museum in New York and the Boston Museum of Fine Arts. The Athenian National Museum, the Munich Glyptothek, and the British Museum contain the most representative collections of Greek vases.

Music (*Mousikē*, 'art of the Muses').

§ 1. *In Greece*

Music included, for the Greeks, not only music in our sense of the word, but literature and the other parts of a higher intellectual and artistic education. Their principal musical instruments were the lyre (a stringed instrument of the harp kind) and the flute. Both these instruments were in use in Crete in pre-Hellenic times, and the flute was also a Phrygian instrument. There were two kinds of lyre, the *cithara* and the lyre proper. The cithara had a large wooden sounding-board and straight arms; it was as a rule used by professional musicians. The lyre proper was the more popular instrument; it had a sounding-board of tortoise-shell and curved arms. Flutes were, it appears, generally played in pairs (thus covering an octave), and were sometimes joined together by a mouth-band. Flute-playing was condemned by Plato and Aristotle, but, as we know from a vase-painting in the British Museum, was taught at Athens.

The primitive lyre had four strings. Terpander (q.v.) is said to have introduced the seven-stringed lyre, but it was certainly known before his day; he appears to have in fact increased the compass of the instrument to a full octave. The four-stringed lyre was the basis of the several forms of Greek music, which varied with the intervals between the tones of the four strings. In the *diatonic* genus the intervals were semi-tone, tone, tone; in the *chromatic*, semi-tone, semi-tone, tone and a half; in the *enharmonic*, quarter-tone, quarter-tone, and two tones. The *modes*, or types of scale or octave, differed according to the order in which the various intervals followed one another. The principal modes were the Dorian (a national Greek mode), and the Phrygian and Lydian (foreign modes); for down to the middle of the 5th c. Dorian Sparta and Dorian Asia Minor were the chief centres of Greek music. The Dorian mode was virile and grave, especially adapted to choral music; the Phrygian stirring and emotional; the Lydian plaintive and pathetic. There is a passage in the Masque of the Judgement of Paris in the 10th Book of the 'Metamorphoses' of Apuleius (q.v.) which describes the soft, lingering character of the Lydian mode, and the passionate energy of the Phrygian. In the course of the 5th c. these modes were added to and diversified, and more strings were added to the seven of the lyre. Instrumental music, which at first was used mainly as an accompaniment to the recitation or singing of poetry, became more and more independent of it. There had been, at the Pythian games, contests of solo flute-players since 590, and of solo lyre-players since 558. We hear of concerts of lyre-players and duets on lyre and flute at Sicyon in the 5th c. At Athens music was principally vocal with instrumental accompaniment (e.g. the songs of the dramatic choruses). Pericles built a special theatre, the Odeum (q.v.), for the musical contests of the Panathenaic festival. At the Dionysia and Thargelia the ten tribes competed, each with a choir of fifty voices. They sang chiefly nomes (q.v.). But in the 4th c. the words of the poem tended to become subordinate to the musical effect, and the music itself became elaborate, imitative, and full of contrasts and discords, a change vigorously condemned by the more conservative Athenians, including Plato. Similarly in tragedy (q.v.) the songs of the chorus gave place to mere musical interludes. See also under *Education*.

§ 2. *At Rome*

The *tibia*, a pipe, single, or double with a connecting mouthpiece, a sort of oboe, was the principal native Italian musical instrument. The *tuba*, perhaps of Etruscan origin, was a long straight tube of brass with bell mouth, used for ceremonial purposes. The *tubae* were purified at the annual festival of the *Tubilustria* on 24 March. Music for the sung portions (*cantica*) of dramas was played on the *tibia*, and specially composed. We know, for instance, the names of some of the composers for the plays of Plautus and Terence. The music of the flute accompanied prayers, sacrifices, triumphal marches to the Capitol, processions to the Circus Maximus, and funeral processions. The number of flute-players at a funeral was limited to ten by the Twelve Tables (q.v.). It is recorded by Livy (ix. 39) that in 311 B.C. the flute-players of Rome went on strike and retired to Tibur, whence they were brought back by a stratagem and pacified by a concession. Stringed instruments were introduced from Greece, and under Greek influence musical contests were occasionally held at Rome in later republican times and were continued under Augustus and developed by Nero in the *Agon Neronianus* (see *Ludi*, § 2). Domitian built an *Odeum* (Music Hall) for the musical contests held at the *Agon Capitolinus* (see *Ludi*, § 2). Under the empire there was, moreover, a development of music as an accompaniment of the pantomime (q.v.); orchestral concerts were also given in the theatre, and music became a regular feature of the dinner-party.

Mūsō′nius Rūfus, GĀIUS, a Stoic philosopher of the 1st c. A.D., banished by Nero as being concerned in the conspiracy of Piso (A.D. 65), but subsequently recalled. Some notes of his philosophical lectures, taken by a listener, survive.

My′calē (*Mukalē*), a promontory in Asia Minor, the scene of the last great battle of the Persian Wars (q.v.), where the Greeks destroyed the Persian army and fleet (479 B.C.).

Mȳcē′nae (*Mūkēnai*), a city on the NE. side of the plain of Argos (see Pl. 8), dating perhaps from pre-Hellenic times, which became in the latter part of the second millennium B.C. one of the chief centres of the Aegean world. It was perhaps a Cretan settlement in origin; at any rate it was so influenced by intercourse with Crete as to adopt a modified form of the Minoan (q.v.) civilization, which has received the distinctive name of Mycenaean, and which spread to many parts of Greece. Among the principal features of this culture are the city walls, built of large roughly hewn blocks (known as Cyclopē′an masonry), and the great tombs, shaped like beehives, the largest 50 ft. high, found at Mycenae and other places.

Mycenae, according to Greek mythology, was founded by Perseus (q.v.) and is associated in tradition with the story of Atreus and Agamemnon. In the 'Iliad', Agamemnon, king of Mycenae, is represented as the most powerful of Greek rulers and as exercising some sort of overlordship over the other Achaean chiefs. Tiryns, which stood nine miles away, resembled Mycenae in the character of its massive walls. It may have been the older town, ousted by the growing importance of Mycenae. Both cities lost their importance after their conquest by the Dorians (see *Migrations and Dialects*). Mycenae sent a contingent to Plataea but was destroyed by Argos in 468 B.C. Impressive remains of the walls of its citadel are still to be seen. Over the principal gateway through these walls, the famous Lions' Gate, is a triangular slab of limestone on which are sculptured two lionesses facing each other on either side of a column, with their forepaws on a raised pedestal. Within the citadel Schliemann discovered in 1876 a number of graves containing a vast quantity of jewelry, gold masks, and other objects, besides human remains, clearly indicating that these were the graves of the royal family of Mycenae. They may be the graves which were pointed out to Pausanias as those of Atreus, Agamemnon, and his companions; but the view that they were in fact their graves is not now accepted.

The beehive tombs are in the lower part of the city, below the citadel.

My'rmidons (*Murmidones*), see *Aeacus*.

My'ron (*Mŭrōn*), of Eleutherae in Attica, one of the most celebrated sculptors of ancient Greece, an older contemporary of Phidias and Polyclitus (qq.v.). He flourished 460–40 B.C. Among his most famous statues were those of Ladas (q.v.) represented running; of the Discobolus ('quoit-thrower'); and of the group of Athene and Marsyas. Of the last two we possess copies. His 'Cow in the market-place of Athens' was celebrated in several extant epigrams.

Myrrha or SMYRNA, see *Adonis*; see also *Zmyrna*.

My'rtilus (*Murtilos*), the charioteer of Oenomaus; see *Pelops*.

Mȳs (*Mūs*), see *Toreutic Art*.

Mysteries, in Greece, secret forms of worship, involving religious doctrines revealed only to the initiated, and probably connected with the life beyond the tomb. The principal mysteries were the 'Eleusinian Mysteries' of Demeter, and the 'Orphic Mysteries'. The former were celebrated at Eleusis in Attica in honour of Demeter and Persephone, with whom was soon associated Dionysus, worshipped here under the name Iacchos (qq.v.). They arose from an agrarian festival, peculiar to certain families of Eleusis (see *Eumolpus*), and appear to have been originally a feast of purification and fertility having reference to the autumn sowing of the corn. With this came to be connected the idea of the gods of the lower world, the descent into Hades, and the future life. The mysteries culminated in a rite carried out in a darkened hall, where the worshippers were shown visions in flashes of light. The nature of these visions is not known. They were probably mythological scenes with some bearing on the doctrine of life after death. The 'Orphic Mysteries' were those of the Orphic sect (see *Orphism*) and were based on the legend of Dionysus Zagreus (q.v.).

Mythology.

§ 1. *Greek Mythology*

The legends of Greek mythology may be divided into three classes: (*a*) myths proper, 'the result of the working of a naïve imagination upon the facts of experience' (H. J. Rose, 'Handbook of Greek Mythology'), seeking to explain natural phenomena (such as thunder), the origins of various animals or their peculiarities (such as the song of the nightingale), or customs and religious practices; the Greek imagina-

tion is here frequently anthropomorphic, that is to say it explains the forces of processes of nature in terms of human life; (*b*) tales or *sagas* containing an historical element, such as the legends about wars or heroes, gradually altered in transmission by the addition of picturesque, and omission of prosaic, details; (*c*) stories of adventure pure and simple, designed solely for amusement, and dealing with natural or supernatural matters. A legend may contain elements from more than one of the above classes, e.g. that of Cadmus. Greek myths were not all of Greek origin; some were imported from Asia or Thrace (see e.g. *Echidna*). It is noteworthy that many of the principal myths are connected with Mycenaean (q.v.) centres, e.g. the stories of Perseus and Atreus with Mycenae itself, that of Oedipus with Thebes, that of Heracles with Thebes and Tiryns. Many of them are evidently pre-Homeric, and Homer seems to be conscious of their absurdities. The sources of our knowledge of Greek mythology are in the first place Homer and Hesiod, then the later Greek poets (notably Pindar and the dramatists). Further material is provided by the Alexandrian poets (such as Callimachus) and by compilers (such as Diodorus and the author of the 'Biblothēkē' attributed to Apollodorus); also by the Roman poets, notably Ovid. Finally the scholiasts, in their explanations of passages in early authors, frequently furnish mythological information. The stories drawn from these various sources do not always agree, as is natural: different versions of a legend may have been current, where the subject allowed scope to the fancy of the narrator. The diversity of local legends may explain one feature of Greek mythology, the frequent alliances of gods and heroes with their close relations, an idea repugnant to Greek custom: this may be due to the blending together of varying stories representing a god and goddess either as husband and wife, or as brother and sister.

The principal myths are dealt with in this book under the name of the god or hero principally concerned, but it will be convenient to state here some of the underlying conceptions. The earth was regarded by the early Greeks as a more or less flat plain, encircled by the stream Oceanus (q.v.), overarched by the solid dome of the sky (of bronze or iron according to Homer) rising from its limits, and with Tartarus, a place of punishment for the wicked, sometimes conceived as below it. The gods inhabit at times the sky, at times Mt. Olympus, a kind of acropolis or stronghold. The cosmogony, or creation of the universe, is imagined in the form of a series of marriages and births, e.g. the marriage of Uranus and Ge, whose offspring is Oceanus, who in turn is father of the rivers and lakes.

§ 2. *Mythology at Rome*

A Roman mythology can hardly be said to exist. The old Italian gods (see *Religion*, § 3) are vague personalities, hardly anthropomorphic; they are not actuated by human motives, they do not marry or fight, or enter into personal relations with mortals. The myths that the Roman writers attached to them were borrowed from Greece (e.g. by the process of identifying Roman deities with Greek deities), or invented largely under Greek influence. Such native Italian traditions as there were have either been lost, or, where they survive, contain few elements of popular fancy. Imagination comes into play in them only to explain some old custom, ritual, or name.

My'tilēnē (*Mutilēnē*) or MITYLENE (*Mitulēnē*), see *Lesbos*.

N

Nae'niae or NĒNIAE, funeral poems sung in primitive times at Rome by the female relatives of the deceased, or by hired singers. They gave place in later times to funeral orations.

Nae'vius, GNAEUS (*c.* 270–*c.* 199 B.C.), an early Roman poet, probably of Roman birth and a plebeian, author of tragedies, comedies, and an epic in Saturnian (q v.) verse. His outspoken criticism of men in high places led to his imprisonment, from which he was released on the intervention of the tribunes. His equivocal comment on the Metelli,

Fato Metelli Romae fiunt consules,

drew from Metellus (consul in 206) the threatening rejoinder,

Dabunt malum Metelli Naevio poetae.

Finally Naevius was exiled and died at Utica. His epitaph in Saturnians, said to have been composed by himself, ran:

Immortalis mortalis si foret fas fiere,
Flerent divae Camenae Naeviom poetam:
Itaque postquam est Orci traditus thensauro,
Oblitei sunt Romai loquier lingua Latina.

He wrote tragedies on Trojan themes, and dramas on the legend of Romulus and Remus and on contemporary events (thus founding the *fabula praetexta*, q.v.). We have the titles of thirty-four of his comedies on the Greek model (*palliatae*), which gave scope for his mordant criticism. But his most important work, from the point of view of his influence on Latin literature, was his epic poem in Saturnians on the First Punic War ('Bellum Punicum'), the work of his old age. In this, by way of introduction, he traced the legendary origins of Rome and Carthage, and made Romulus the grandson of Aeneas, perhaps also introducing Dido into the story. Only fragments of the various works of Naevius have come down to us. From these and the notices of later authors he appears to have been a man of originality and independence; his epitaph shows that he prided himself on the idiomatic purity of his Latin, a claim which Cicero implicitly acknowledges. There is an interesting comparison of Naevius and Ennius in Cicero's 'Brutus', xix. 75.

Nai'ads (*Nāïades*), nymphs (q.v.) of springs, rivers, and lakes.

Names of persons. (1) The GREEKS had no family names, and as a rule bore only one name chosen at the discretion of the family. A boy was usually given his grandfather's name, or sometimes that of his father. To his own name was generally added that of his father, to distinguish him, e.g. 'Demosthenes son of Demosthenes', 'Thucydides son of Olorus'. Cleisthenes (q.v.), the Athenian lawgiver, made an attempt to have the name of a man's deme, rather than that of his father, added to his own name, in this way making matters easy for the new citizens he had enrolled. This attempt was at first only partially successful, as the practice of Herodotus and Thucydides shows (as well as the above examples); but in Aristophanes' comedies characters always introduce themselves by their demes, and in 4th-c. speeches men are most often referred to in this way.

(2) The ROMANS generally bore three names, the *praenomen*, corresponding to our Christian name; the *nōmen*, the name of the *gens* (q.v.) or clan; the *cognōmen*, the name of the family. But many members of ignoble families possessed only two names, e.g. Gaius Marius. The *praenomen* was often written in an abbreviated form:

A. for Aulus	P. for Publius
C. for Gāius	Q. for Quintus
Cn. for Gnaeus	Ser. for Servius
D. for Decimus	Sex. for Sextus
L. for Lūcius	Sp. for Spurius
M. for Marcus	T. for Titus
M'. for Mānius	Ti. for Tībērius

The *nomen* was such as Claudius or Cornēlius, indicating that the bearer of it belonged to the *Gens Claudia* or *Cornēlia*. It always ended in *-ius*.

The *cognomen* was such a name as

Scipio, indicating that the bearer belonged to the family of the Scipiōnēs, itself forming part of the *Gens Cornēlia*. The *cognomina* generally had reference to some personal characteristic, such as Rūfus, Nāso.

A fourth name was sometimes added, the *agnōmen*, being that of a particular branch of the family, e.g. Scipio *Nāsica*, or commemorating some exploit, e.g. Scipio *Africānus*, or recording an adoption. e.g. Scipio *Aemiliānus*.

Women at first bore only one name, the feminine form of the *nomen* of the father, e.g. Tullia. Sometimes after marriage they also bore the feminine form of the husband's *praenomen*. Under the empire they habitually had two names, the feminine forms of the *nomen* and *cognomen* of the father, e.g. Sōsia Galla, or the *nomina* of father and mother.

Freedmen bore the *nomen*, or both *praenomen* and *nomen*, of the man who had freed them, retaining their slave-name as *cognomen*; e.g. M. Tullius Tīro (the freedman of Cicero).

Na'nnō, see *Mimnermus*.

Narci'ssus (*Narkissos*), in Greek mythology, a beautiful youth, son of the river-god Cephisus (q.v.) and the nymph Leiriopē. The nymph Echo fell in love with him, but was repulsed. Aphrodite punished him for his cruelty by making him enamoured of his own image in a fountain. His fruitless attempts to approach this beautiful object led to his despair and death. He was changed into the flower that bears his name.

Nā'sō, the cognomen of Ovid (q.v.), by which he always refers to himself. It is derived from *nasus*, 'nose', and Holofernes in Shakespeare's 'Love's Labour's Lost' (IV. ii) remarks, 'and why, indeed, Naso, but for smelling out the odoriferous flowers of fancy, the jerks of invention?'

Nātūrā'lēs Quaestiō'nēs, see *Seneca* (the philosopher), § 3.

Nātūrā'lis Histo'ria, see *Pliny the Elder*.

Naucrā'riai, see *Athens*, § 2.

Nau'cratis, a town in the Delta of Egypt, founded *c.* 675 B.C. on the Canōpic (western) branch of the Nile by the Milesians. Amasis, a Pharaoh of the 26th dynasty (570–526 B.C.), restricted the Greeks of Egypt to Naucratis as their commercial and industrial centre. The town contained separate quarters occupied by Milesians, Samians, and Aeginetans respectively, while other Greeks had an enclosure in common. It became a very important trading settlement, and was the birthplace of Athenaeus and Julius Pollux (qq.v.).

Nauma'chiae, mimic sea-fights, held as a popular spectacle in the flooded arena of an amphitheatre (q.v.). They were also shown in specially constructed basins (Augustus built one, called the Naumachia, on the right bank of the Tiber). The first display of this kind was given by Julius Caesar and simulated a sea-battle between Tyrians and Egyptians. Claudius gave a famous *naumachia* on the *Lacus Fūcinus*, in which two fleets, each of twelve triremes, representing Sicilians and Rhodians, were engaged. The combatants in *naumachiae* were prisoners or criminals, and fought to the death, unless spared by the emperor.

Nau'plius (*Nauplios*), the father of Palamedes (q.v.). The town of Nauplia was named after another Nauplius, son of Poseidon and Amymone (q.v.).

Nausi'căa or **Nausicā'a** (*Nausikāā*), in the 'Odyssey', the daughter of the Phaeacian king, Alcinous. The shipwrecked Odysseus approaches her, as she is playing at ball with her maidens on the shore after washing the household linen. She receives him kindly and conducts him to the house of her father. She is perhaps the most charming of Homer's characters, uniting courage and dignity with maidenly grace, kindness, and discretion. Samuel Butler believed that she represents the authoress of the 'Odyssey' (q.v. at end).

Naval Boards (*Summoriai*), *On the*, a political speech by Demosthenes. See *Liturgy* and *Demosthenes* (2), § 4 (*a*).

Navy, see *Ships*.

Nea'rchus (*Nearchos*), see *Alexander the Great*, §§ 7 and 8. Nearchus wrote an account of his voyage from the Indian Ocean to the Euphrates, of which only fragments are extant.

Necyomanti'a (*Nekuomanteia*), see *Lucian*.

Nē'lēus, in Greek mythology, a son of Poseidon and Tyro (q.v.), and king of Pylos. Heracles (q.v.), after he had killed Iphitus, sought purification from Neleus, who refused it. Thereupon Heracles killed him and all his sons except Nestor (q.v.).

Nē'mēan Festival, see *Festivals*, § 1, and *Hypsipyle*.

Nē'mēan Lion, see *Heracles* (*Labours of*).

Ne'mesis, according to Hesiod a child of Night, was in early Greek thought a personification of the gods' resentment at, and consequent punishment of, insolence (*hubris*) towards themselves.

Nē'niae, see *Naeniae*.

Neopla'tonism, a school of philosophy

which arose at Alexandria in the 3rd c. A.D. and revived and developed the metaphysical and mystical sides of the Platonic teaching. Its chief exponents were Plotinus, Porphyry, and Iamblichus (qq.v.). See also *Longinus* (*Cassius*). One of the most famous members of the school in later times was HYPATIA (daughter of Theōn the mathematician), murdered by the Alexandrian mob in A.D. 415, whose noble figure and death are depicted in C. Kingsley's novel bearing her name (1851). She commented upon Plato and Aristotle, and also taught astronomy. Among her pupils was SYNESIUS of Cyrene (c. A.D. 370–413), a most versatile man, country gentleman and learned author, Neoplatonist and eventually Christian bishop of Ptolemāĭs, who has left a discourse entitled 'Diōn' and a collection of letters and hymns (one is translated in 'Hymns, Ancient and Modern'). The last considerable writer of the Neoplatonic school was PROCLUS of Byzantium (c. A.D. 411–85), who produced a vast and consistent system, embracing the philosophical traditions of antiquity, in support of paganism against Christianity. Many of the later Neoplatonists had carried metaphysical speculations to fantastic lengths, with a mingling of magic and eastern superstitions. Demonology in particular was highly developed by them, and a complete hierarchy of good and evil demons was devised, who were thought to people the universe and were the object of semi-religious semi-magic rites. The Neoplatonic school at Athens was closed by Justinian in 529, but survived at Alexandria till the end of the 6th c.

The leading doctrines of the Neoplatonic school are briefly stated under *Plotinus*; they exercised a considerable influence on medieval philosophy through such thinkers as Johannes Scotus Erigena (*fl.* 850), and later on the Cambridge Platonists of the 17th c.

Neopto′lemus (*Neoptolemos*), also named Pyrrhus ('yellow-haired'), son of Achilles (q.v.) and Dēidamīa. He was summoned to the siege of Troy after the death of his father; he went with Odysseus to bring Philoctetes (q.v.) to the siege; and it was he who killed Priam. Andromache (q.v.) fell to his lot after the capture of Troy, and accompanied him to his kingdom in Epīrus. According to a legend preserved in the 'Andromache' (q.v.) of Euripides, he married Hermione, daughter of Menelaus and Helen, but Orestes (q.v.) murdered him and carried off Hermione.

Nē′pos (*Nĕpōs*), CORNĒLIUS (c. 100–c. 25 B.C.), whose praenomen is unknown, was probably a native of Ticīnum in Insubrian Gaul. He spent much of his life at Rome, where he was a friend of Catullus (who dedicated to Nepos a book of his poems and praised the lost 'Chronica') and of Atticus. He was acquainted with Cicero, but there seems to have been little sympathy between them. Nepos took no part in the public life of Rome and devoted himself to literary work. His writings included a history of the world ('Chronica'), a collection of extracts from Roman history ('Exempla'), lives of Cato and Cicero, a treatise on geography, and some love poems. All these are lost. Of his books (sixteen at least) 'De Viris Illustribus', we possess twenty-four lives. They are biographical sketches designed to bring out the characters of their heroes rather than the historical events of their lives. Indeed, from an historical point of view they are marked by many inaccuracies and omissions and by lack of proportion (the battle of Leuctra, for instance, is barely mentioned in the biography of Epaminondas). They show no dramatic sense or large historical views, but they do justice to the merits of the great men of foreign nations. Nineteen of the extant biographies are those of Greeks (including some Sicilians); there are also lives of Datamēs the Persian, Hamilcar and Hannibal, a short life of the elder Cato, a longer one of Atticus, and a brief sketch of notable kings. Of the Greek lives the best is that of Alcibiades, of whose character Nepos gives a good description. But the most interesting of the surviving works is the biography of Atticus, drawn from personal knowledge, and giving a clear account of the man, his political attitude, and literary interests.

Ne′ptune (*Neptūnus*), an old Italian deity, of whom in his original form hardly anything is known. He was worshipped at the *Neptūnālia* on 23 July, in the heat of the summer, when booths of foliage were put up to protect worshippers from the sun, and appears to have been associated with water. When we first find him in Roman history, he is a sea-god with the attributes of Poseidon (q.v.). Owing to Poseidon's connexion with horses, and because horse races were celebrated in honour of Consus (q.v.), Neptune was popularly associated with the latter god.

Nē′reīds (*Nērēĭdes*), see *Nereus*.

Nē′reūs, according to Homer, the 'Old Man' of the sea, a wise and kindly deity, the father of the Nēreīds or sea-maidens, beautiful, benevolent, but ill-defined creatures, of whom two were famed in mythology, Thetis (see *Peleus*) and Galatea (q.v.).

Like Proteus (q.v.), he has the power of transforming himself into various shapes.

Nē′rō (*Nĕrō*), Roman emperor A.D. 54–68, son of Cn. Domitius Ahenobarbus (q.v.) and Agrippina, daughter of Germanicus. He was originally named Lūcius Domitius Ahenobarbus, and assumed the name of Nero on adoption into the Claudian family. See *Julio-Claudian Family* and for the chief events of his reign *Rome*, § 10. See also *Suetonius* (under the sub-head 'Lives of the Caesars'). He appears to have been a man of considerable talents; he drew, painted, modelled, and composed verses. His patronage of the arts and encouragement of musical and dramatic contests (in which he himself sometimes performed) scandalized the senatorial classes, and were responsible for much of his unpopularity. There is no trustworthy basis for the rumour that he caused the fire of Rome (though it may be true that he sang as he watched it burn). His own house was destroyed, and he showed zeal in endeavours to mitigate the disaster to the city. But he was of a cruel and unrestrained brutality, with a passion for self-advertisement, especially by spectacular display. The remark attributed to him when he was about to die is famous: 'Qualis artifex pereo!', 'What an artist dies in me!' Suetonius describes him as having pleasant features but a spotty complexion, yellow hair, spindle shanks, and a prominent belly, and as being careless of his appearance. Robert Bridges' drama 'Nero' contains good history.

Ne′ssus (*Nessos*), see *Heracles*.

Ne′stōr, in Homeric legend, son of Neleus (q.v.) and king of Pylos. He plays an important part, as an aged statesman, in the 'Iliad'. He is presented as a wise and indulgent prince, garrulous and reminiscent, counselling moderation in the quarrel of the leaders.

He reappears in the 'Odyssey' (q.v.), at home in Pylos, where Telemachus visits him and is kindly received.

Nica′nder (*Nikandros*) of Colophōn, a Greek didactic poet of the 2nd c. B.C., of whose numerous works there survive 'Thēriaca' and 'Alexipharmaca', poems in hexameters on the bites of venomous animals and on antidotes to poison.

Ni′cias (*Nīkiās*) (d. 413 B.C.), an honest but mediocre Athenian statesman of the time of the Peloponnesian War (q.v.), a leader of the peace party and an opponent of Cleon (q.v.). It was he who negotiated the peace that bears his name, concluded in 421, by which the war was for a short time suspended. It was a calamity for Athens that he was appointed one of the commanders of the Athenian forces in the Sicilian Expedition (after the departure of Alcibiades and the death of Lamachus he was in sole command), for he was opposed to the whole undertaking, he was incurably ill, and his irresolution and fear of responsibility were the principal cause of its disastrous failure. He was captured when the Athenian army surrendered, and was put to death.

Nico′machus (*Nikomachos*), the son of Aristotle (q.v.); he perhaps edited the 'Nicomachean Ethics' of the latter.

Niebuhr, BARTHOLD GEORG, see *Historians* (*Modern*).

Nigrī′nus, see *Lucian*.

Ni′kē, the Greek personification of victory, generally regarded rather as an attribute of Athene (q.v.) than as a separate goddess.

Ni′obē (*Niobē*), in Greek mythology, daughter of Tantalus (q.v.) and mother of seven sons and seven daughters. She boasted of her superiority to Leto, who had only two children. Apollo and Artemis then killed her sons and daughters with their arrows. Niobe wept for them until turned into a column of stone (on Mt. Sipylus in Lȳdia), from which her tears continued to flow.

Ni′sus, king of Megara, see *Ciris*.

Ni′sus and Eury′alus, in the 'Aeneid', companions of Aeneas and faithful friends, who figure in the foot-race in Book V. They are killed in a sortie from the Trojan camp in Italy.

Nō′bilēs, at Rome, those families, whether patrician or plebeian, members of which had held curule (q.v.) office. They were allowed to have images (*imāginēs*) of their ancestors. In the unusual event of a man attaining curule office who did not belong to one of these families, he was known as a *novus homo*. By 133 B.C. it was only with the greatest difficulty that any could attain to office save members of families already 'ennobled', who regarded an official career as their birthright; though Marius and Cicero were among those who did.

No′ctēs A′tticae, see *Gellius*.

Nome (*Nomos*), the name applied to a type of very ancient Greek liturgical hymn, sung as a solo to the lyre, and later also to the flute, and addressed to a god, especially, it seems, to Apollo. Nomes appear to have been composed in various metres, generally of a spondaic and solemn character, but only scanty fragments of them survive. See *Terpander*. In the 5th and 4th cc. the nome was transformed, owing to the growing predominance and elaboration of the musical element. The name of PHRYNIS (*fl. c.* 412 B.C.), of whom little is known, is associated with the change. In his hands and those of Timotheus (q.v.), the nome approximated in character to the dithyramb, owing to the inclusion of choral passages.

Nō'men, Praenō'men, &c., see *Names.*

Nōmen Lati'num, a term including, in Roman republican times, Latin cities that remained unincorporated in the Roman State (such as Tibur and Praeneste) and *Latin* colonies (see *Colonization*, § 6). They were in alliance with Rome, but were distinguished from the other *socii* by possessing certain privileges, *commercium* (the right of conducting law-suits at Rome on the same footing as Roman citizens) and *cōnūbium* (the right of intermarriage with Romans). These Latins, moreover, had a right of voting if individually present at Rome, and of becoming full Roman citizens on migration to Rome. But they were permitted to migrate only if they left a son behind to carry on the family in the original town. See *Rome*, § 4.

Nōme'ntum, a town on the edge of the Sabine hills some fifteen miles NE. of Rome, with which it was connected by the *Via Nōmentāna*. There Atticus had a farm, Seneca a country-house, and Martial a cottage. Martial told a friend he went there because sleep in Rome was impossible for the noise.

Nō'na, see *Fates.*

Nō'nius Marce'llus, a Numidian of the first half of the 4th c. A.D. who wrote under Constantine an encyclopaedia for his son, entitled 'De Compendiōsa Doctrīna', in twenty books (of which Book XVI is lost). It is occupied in part with the diction and grammar of the older Latin writers, in part with their subject-matter. Though a poor compilation, it is a useful source of quotations from such authors as Lucilius and Varro.

No'nnus (*Nonnos*) (*fl. c.* A.D. 400) of Panopolis in Egypt, was author of a Greek epic in forty-eight books on the adventures of the god Dionysus, in which he assembled all the legends relating to the god, and dealt especially with his expedition against the Indians. This has survived, and apart from its vast fund of mythological lore, is chiefly interesting for metrical peculiarities which appear to be the prelude of the accentual versification of a later age.

No'stoi ('Returns'), a lost poem of the Epic Cycle (q.v.), dealing with the adven-

tures of various heroes on their return from the Trojan War.

No'tus (*Notos*, L. *Auster*), the south wind.

Novel or Prose Romance, THE. The elements that went to the production of the prose romance as a late literary form in Greek and Roman literature are found in other combinations in many writers: in Homer (who in the 'Odyssey', a romantic epic, mingled pathos with adventure), in Euripides (who introduced a sentimental element in Tragedy), in Xenophon (who combined imagination with history in the 'Cyropaedia'), in Menander, in the character-sketches of Theophrastus, in the travellers' tales stimulated by the exploits of Alexander the Great, in pastoral poetry, and in the stories collected and versified by the Alexandrian elegists and by Ovid. The rudiments of the novel may be seen in the 'Milesian Tales' (q.v.) which scandalized the Persians after Carrhae. An impetus to its development may have been given by the rhetorical schools, where *Suasoriae* and *Controversiae* (exercises such as those collected by the elder Seneca or the 'Declamations' attributed to Quintilian) provided as themes for discussion imaginary situations well suited for elaboration as romances; for we find in them young lovers, harsh fathers, pirates, seductions, shipwrecks, and so forth.

In Greek the novel finally took shape in the 2nd and 3rd cc. A.D. in the work of the writers known as *Erōtici Graeci*: CHARITON (author of 'Chaereas and Callirhoe'), ACHILLĒS TATIUS ('Leucippe and Cleitophon'), XENOPHŌN of Ephesus ('Habrocomes and Antheia'), LONGUS ('Daphnis and Chloe'), and HĒLIODŌRUS of Emesa ('Aethiopica' or 'Theagenes and Chariclea'). The story of 'Apollonius of Tyre' by an unknown Greek author, the ultimate source of Shakespeare's 'Pericles', survives only in a late Latin translation. The typical characteristics of these novels are the separation of two lovers, hairbreadth escapes from a series of appalling perils and adversities, and final reunion and a happy ending. The best-known of the above tales is the 'Daphnis and Chloe' of Longus (about whom nothing is known), a charming pastoral romance in which narrative of adventure for the first time gives place to description of sentiments and scenery. The 'Aethiopica' of Heliodorus is the story of Chariclea, a priestess of Delphi, with whom Theagenes, a Thessalian, falls in love. He carries her off to Egypt. In Ethiopia Chariclea is on the point of being immolated when she is discovered to be the daughter of the king of the country. In Roman literature the novel first appears, in a very different form, in the 'Satyricon' of Petronius Arbiter (q.v.); and the second great work of the kind is the 'Metamorphoses' or 'Golden Ass' of Apuleius (q.v.).

Novels (*Nove'llae*), see *Justinian*.

No'vius, see *Atellan Farces*.

Nŭ'bēs, see *Clouds*.

Nŭ'ma (*Nŭma*) **Pompi'lius,** in legendary Roman history, successor of Romulus as king of Rome. He had, according to tradition, a long and peaceful reign, regarded in later times as a sort of Golden Age, and to him the Romans attributed many of their religious institutions: festivals, sacrifices, and other rites, the *pontifices*, the Vestal Virgins, and the Salii (qq.v.). He is said to have constructed the *Regia* (q.v.) or royal palace near the Forum, the Temple of Vesta, and other temples; also to have reformed the calendar (q.v.), adding January and February to the ten months of the earlier calendar. See also *Ancilia*. Legend says that he was aided by the counsels of the goddess Egeria (q.v.), who loved him. It was also believed that he wrote a number of books on sacred law and that these were discovered, many centuries later, in his tomb on the Janiculum. There is a life of him by Plutarch.

Nŭ'men, in ancient Roman religion, the power or spirit dwelling in each natural object—a tree, a fountain, the earth—and also in each man, controlling the phenomena of nature and the actions of man. See *Religion*, § 3. The word is probably derived from *nuere*, to nod (as a signification of the will); hence arises the meaning of will, of power, and of the spirit that has the power.

Nu'mitōr, see *Rome*, § 2.

Nu'ndinae, the first (or according to Macrobius the last) day in the Roman week of eight days (*nundinum*, a 'nine-day period' according to the Roman method of reckoning). The days of this week were marked in the calendar with the letters A–H, the origin of the 'dominical' letters given in our Prayer-book, and *Nundinae* had A assigned to it. The *Nundinae* was a day of rest from agricultural labour, and was a market-day, on which countrymen came into Rome.

Ny'ctēus (*Nuktēus*), see *Antiope*.

Nymphs (*Numphai*), in Greek mythology, female personifications of various natural objects, rivers, trees, mountains; vague beings, represented as young and beautiful, fond of music and dancing, long-lived but not immortal, usually gentle, occasionally formidable. They possessed some divine gifts, such as that of prophecy; in fact they resembled fairies. The nymphs of trees were called Dryads (or Hamadryads); those of springs, rivers, and lakes, Naiads; those of mountains, Oreads.

O

Ōce'anus (*Ōkeanos*), in early Greek cosmology, the river supposed to encircle the plain of the earth. Also personified as one of the Titans (q.v.), and with his consort Tethys, as the progenitor of the gods (Il. xiv. 201 et seq.), and as parent of the rivers of the world and of the ocean nymphs (*Ōkeanides*, in Virgil *Ōceanītides*).

Octa'via, (1) the sister of Octavian (Augustus) and wife of Mark Antony (q.v.). One of her daughters by Antony was the grandmother of Nero; the other was the mother of Claudius. (2) The daughter of Claudius and wife of Nero. See *Julio-Claudian Family*.

Octa'via, a Roman tragedy, included in the manuscripts with the tragedies of Seneca the Philosopher (q.v.), but probably written by an imitator of later date.

Octavia, daughter of Claudius and the wife of Nero, laments her lot and the crimes of her mother Messalina and her stepmother Agrippina. Nero has decided to take a new consort, the profligate Poppaea. Seneca appears and protests in vain against Nero's misdeeds and the desertion of Octavia; and the ghost of Nero's mother foretells the emperor's doom. A revolt of Octavia's sympathizers rouses Nero to fury, and Octavia is haled off to execution. A tedious play, with an excess of lamentation and mythological display. But it is the only Roman historical drama (*praetexta*) we have in complete form.

Octa'vian (*Gāius Octāvius*, 63 B.C.–A.D. 14), grandnephew of Julius Caesar (see *Caesar, Relations by Marriage*), named C. Julius Caesar Octāviānus after his adoption by Caesar, and later known as Augustus (q.v.) the first of the Roman emperors. See *Rome*, §§ 7 and 9, and *Julio-Claudian Family*.

Octavian was a patron of learning and himself an author. He wrote an autobiography in thirteen books, which is unfortunately lost, and other minor works (see also *Monumentum Ancyranum*). We owe to him the saying 'to pay on the Greek kalends', i.e. never.

Octā'vius, a dialogue by Minucius Felix (q.v.).

Odes* and *Epodes of Horace, short poems in various lyric metres. For the dates when they were written and issued see under *Horace*. The 'Epodes' were Horace's first attempts in the form of the Greek lyric, some of them, notably xvi (a lament over civil strife), on political themes, some of them lampoons on personal enemies, some of them on love and miscellaneous subjects. Epode ix is thought by some to consist of two parts, one written immediately before, the other immediately after the battle of Actium. The prevailing metre in the 'Epodes' is the iambic couplet (the metre of Archilochus, q.v.), in which a longer line is followed by a shorter, the latter being known in Greek as an *epôdos* or 'after-song', whence the title of these poems; in some of them the iambic verses are combined with dactylic.

Horace's lyrics reach perfection, within their range of emotion and thought, in the four books of the 'Odes'. It is on these that the author based his claim to immortality. Thirty-seven of them are in the Alcaic metre (see *Metre*, § 5), twenty-five in the Sapphic, a considerable number in various Asclepiadean metres, a few, experiments as it were, in divers others. They include a series of splendid political poems (those in Book IV were written at the request of Augustus), reflecting the transition of Roman feeling from anxiety for the safety of the State to security and triumph under the guidance of Augustus, whom Horace sincerely admired. They established the author's position as a great national poet. These patriotic lyrics were inspired by the model of Pindar; Horace's admiration of the Greek poet is expressed in Od. IV. ii, 'Pindarum quisquis studet aemulari . . .'.

Other odes deal with incidents in his own life or those of his friends, their departures on voyages or happy returns, their love affairs and his own, the changing seasons, the joys of country and wine, or, on the other hand, the brevity and melancholy of life ('pulvis et umbra'). They show Horace, if not so religious in spirit as Virgil, yet a firm believer in the value of piety. Their good sense, the moderation and avoidance of excess which they inculcate ('aurea mediocritas'), urbanely and happily expressed, have commended and endeared them to the generality of men.

Ŏdē′um (*Odeion*), the Greek name for a theatre built for musical performances, and, unlike other Greek theatres, provided with a roof. An Odeum was built by Pericles for the musical contests of the Panathenaea. It was a circular building, in imitation, it is said, of the tent of Xerxes, with a conical roof. Later Music Halls were built at Athens by Agrippa and by Herodes Atticus (qq.v.). The latter building, of which the remains are well preserved, was in the form of a Roman theatre; it stood at the SW. foot of the Acropolis. For the Odeum at Rome see *Music*, § 2.

Ody′sseus (*Odusseus*), or, according to his Latin name, *Ulixēs* or *Ulyssēs*, in Greek mythology, the son of Laertes, king of Ithaca (q.v.), and Anticlea, daughter of Autolycus (q.v.). He was one of the suitors for the hand of Helen (q.v.), but despairing of success married Penelope (q.v.). It was by his advice that Tyndareus, step-father of Helen, bound the suitors by an oath to unite in protecting her from violence. When she was carried off to Troy, Odysseus joined the other Greek princes in the expedition to recover her, after having failed to escape his obligation by feigning madness (see *Palamedes*). He figures prominently in the 'Iliad', notably in the embassy to Achilles and the night expedition with Diomedes. After the death of Achilles, a contention arose between Odysseus and Ajax (q.v.) for the arms of the hero; they were awarded to Odysseus. It was Odysseus who with Neoptolemus brought Philoctetes (q.v.) to Troy from Lemnos. For his adventures on his way home to Ithaca from Troy, as related by Homer, see *Odyssey*. After his return, and the destruction of the suitors of Penelope, he appeased his enemy Poseidon, founding a shrine in his honour so far inland that an inhabitant mistook the oar he was carrying for a winnowing fan. Odysseus met his death at the hands of Telegonus, his son by Circe, who had come to Ithaca to make himself known to his father and slew him unwittingly. See also *Palladium* and *Trojan Horse*.

In the 'Iliad' Odysseus is represented as good in counsel no less than in battle, cool, tactful, energetic, and at times cunning. In the 'Odyssey' his chief characteristics are his longing for his home, his endurance of suffering in order to reach it, and the self-control he shows until the moment is ripe for the destruction of the suitors. He is less favourably depicted in some of the tragedies. Euripides in particular makes him heartless and unscrupulous. In Latin literature too he is rather unfavourably represented (see especially Hor. Sat. II. v).

Tennyson, in a dramatic monologue 'Ulysses', presents him setting out in his last years 'to sail beyond the sunset', 'to follow knowledge like a sinking star'. The episode is not in classical literature, but in Dante, 'Inferno', xxvi.

O'dyssey (Odusseia), The, an epic poem by Homer in twenty-four books (this division, like that of the 'Iliad' is said to be the work of Aristarchus of Samothrace (q.v.), but may represent a stage in the history of the manuscript when it occupied twenty-four papyrus rolls). It is the story of the return of Odysseus (q.v.) from Troy, and of the vengeance he took on the suitors of his wife Penelope. Various internal indications—such as the more complex structure of the poem—suggest that the 'Odyssey' is a later work than the 'Iliad', but the language shows that the two poems belong to the same general period. The gods are not, as in the 'Iliad', divided into factions, though Poseidon and Helios exact punishment for offences done to them personally; while Athene, hostile to the returning Greeks in the early stage of the story, later protects Odysseus and takes an active part in promoting his return. The actual events of the poem occupy six weeks.

When the story opens, ten years have nearly elapsed since the fall of Troy. All the Greek chiefs have returned to their homes, or are dead, except Odysseus, who is in the isle Ogygia, where the goddess Calypso has detained him seven years. Penelope has put off the choice among her many suitors, island princes, by pretending she must first finish a winding-sheet for Laertes (the father of Odysseus), unravelling each night what she has woven during the day. But the trick has been discovered, and she must come to a decision. Meanwhile the suitors are wasting the substance of Odysseus, of whom no news has reached Ithaca. Telemachus the son of Odysseus, visits Nestor (q.v.) at Pylos, and Menelaus and Helen (qq.v.) at Sparta, to seek tidings of his father. The suitors lay an ambush for Telemachus against his return (Bks i–iv). Calypso is ordered by Zeus to release Odysseus. The latter builds a raft and sails on it for seventeen days till within sight of Scheria, the land of the Phaeacians. Poseidon, who hates Odysseus because the latter has blinded Poseidon's son Polyphemus (q.v.), raises a storm and destroys the raft. Odysseus, after two days in the sea, buoyed up by a scarf given him by the sea-goddess Ino, is cast ashore on the coast of Scheria (Bk. v). He is found by Nausicaa, daughter of the Phaeacian king, Alcinous, and by her help is hospitably received in the palace (Bks. vi and vii). Odysseus is entertained with the lays of the minstrel Demodocus (about the quarrel of Odysseus and Achilles, viii. 75–82; love of Ares and Aphrodite, 266–366; the Trojan Horse 499–520) and with the games of the Phae-

acians (Bk. viii). He reveals his name and tells of his adventures since leaving Troy, first of his piratical raid on the Cicones at Ismarus, then of his visit to the land of the Lotus-Eaters (q.v.), and afterwards to that of the Cyclōpes, where he encounters Polyphemus (q.v.) (Bk. ix). Next of his entertainment by Aeolus (q.v.) and the gift of the bag containing the adverse winds (which his company release), of his adventure with the Laestrȳgones, cannibal giants who destroy eleven of his twelve ships, and of his coming to the island Aeaea, where the enchantress Circe turns his companions into swine; but he himself is protected by the herb moly, given him by Hermes, and obtains the restoration of his companions. After a year Circe releases him and directs him to consult Tiresias (q.v.) in Hades (Bk. x). Odysseus recounts his visit to Hades, where he sees the ghosts of many dead heroes, their wives and daughters, and converses with some of them, including his mother Anticlea; and where Tiresias prophesies to him the manner of his return (Bk. xi). He then tells of his passage by the Sirens and by Scylla and Charybdis (qq.v.), and of his coming to Thrinacia where, in spite of warning, his company kill the cattle of Helios (q.v.). This sacrilege brings about the destruction by a thunderbolt of his ship and of his company. Odysseus alone is borne on the wreckage to Ogygia, where Calypso receives him kindly (Bk. xii). After finishing his tale Odysseus is carried in a ship of the Phaeacians to Ithaca; this ship on its return Poseidon turns into a rock. Athene disguises Odysseus as an old beggarman (Bk. xiii). He learns of the insolence and riotous living of the suitors from his faithful swineherd Eumaeus. He reveals himself to Telemachus, who returns from Sparta, escaping the ambush; and they concert the destruction of the suitors (Bks. xiv–xvi). Odysseus now goes to his house, where he is recognized by his old dog Argus, is smitten and reviled by the goatherd Melanthius, and the suitors Antinous and Eurymachus, and fights with the beggar Irus (Bks. xvii and xviii). Odysseus is recognized by his nurse Eurycleia. Penelope tells her purpose of marrying the man who shall next day string the bow of Odysseus and shoot an arrow through twelve axe-heads (Bk. xix). The seer Theoclymenus has a vision of the doom of the suitors (Bk. xx). Odysseus alone bends the bow and shoots the arrow through the axes. He then shoots down Antinous, and aided by Telemachus, Eumaeus, and another faithful thrall kills the rest of the suitors. The women, paramours of the suitors, are hanged. Penelope is at last·

convinced, by the hero's knowledge of the peculiar construction of the bedstead, that he is her husband (Bks. xxi–xxiii). Odysseus makes himself known to his father Laertes. The relatives of the suitors attempt revenge, but are repulsed, and Athene stops the blood-feud (Bk. xxiv).

For Latin and English translations see under *Homer*. Samuel Butler (1835–1902) held that the 'Odyssey' was written by a woman and had its origin at Trapani in Sicily. See his 'The Authoress of the Odyssey' (1897).

Oecono′micus (*Oikonomikos*), a treatise by Xenophon on the management of a household and estate, in the form chiefly of a dialogue between Socrates and a certain Ischomachus; but the opinions and reflections are clearly those of Xenophon himself. It throws an interesting light on Xenophon's tastes and pursuits and on the agricultural science of his day, also on the relations which he thought should prevail between a man and his wife; and there is an agreeable picture of the young lady, wife of Ischomachus, no doubt Xenophon's own wife, who is given lessons in household management and good taste.

Oe′dipus (*Oidipous*, 'swell-foot'), in Greek mythology, the son of Laïus (q.v.), king of Thebes. When Amphion and Zethus (see *Antiope*) gained possession of Thebes, Laïus had taken refuge with Pelops (q.v.), but had ill requited his kindness by kidnapping his son Chrȳsippus, thereby bringing a curse on his own family. Laïus recovered his kingdom after the death of Amphion and Zethus, and married Jocasta, but was warned by Apollo that their son would kill him. Accordingly, when Oedipus was born, a spike was driven through his feet and he was exposed on Mt. Cithaeron. There a shepherd found him, and he was taken to Polybus, king of Corinth, and Merope his queen, who brought him up as their own son. Later, being taunted with being no true son of Polybus, he enquired of the Delphic Oracle concerning his parentage, but was only told that he should slay his father and wed his mother. Thinking this referred to Polybus and Merope, he determined never to see Corinth again. At a place where three roads met, he encountered Laïus (whom he did not know), and was ordered to make way. A quarrel followed, in which Oedipus slew Laïus. He went on to Thebes, which was at that time plagued by the Sphinx, a monster that asked people riddles and killed those who could not answer them. Creon, brother of Jocasta and regent of Thebes, offered the kingdom and Jocasta's hand to whoever should rid the country of this pest. Oedipus solved the riddle of the Sphinx (q.v., which thereupon killed itself), became king of Thebes, and married Jocasta. They had two sons, Eteocles and Polynices, and two daughters, Ismene and Antigone. At last, in a time of dearth and pestilence, the oracle announced that these disasters could be averted only if the slayer of Laïus were expelled from the city. Oedipus thereupon set about discovering who had killed Laïus. The result was to establish that he himself was Laïus's son and his murderer. On this discovery Jocasta hanged herself and Oedipus blinded himself. (According to the variant in Euripides' 'Phoenissae' and in Statius, Jocasta killed herself, not at this stage, but over the dead bodies of her sons, Eteocles and Polynices; see below.) Oedipus was deposed and banished, and wandered, attended by Antigone, to Colonus in Attica, where he was protected by Theseus (q.v.) and died (see *Oedipus at Colonus*). According to another version he remained shut up in Thebes. His sons having given him cause for displeasure, he set on them a curse that they should die by each other's hand. When they succeeded to the throne on the deposition of Oedipus, they agreed to divide the inheritance, ruling in alternate years. But Eteocles, who ruled first, when his year of kingship had elapsed, refused to make way for Polynices. The latter had spent his year of absence from Thebes at the court of Adrastus, king of Argos, and had married his daughter. Adrastus now gathered an army to support the claims of his son-in-law, headed by seven champions, the famous Seven against Thebes. These were (the list is not uniformly given) Adrastus himself and Polynices, Tȳdeus of Calydōn in Aetōlia (the other son-in-law of Adrastus), Capaneūs, Hippomedōn, Parthenopaeus (son of Atalanta, q.v.), and Amphiaraus (q.v.). To each of the seven champions was allotted one of the gates of Thebes to attack, and Eteocles similarly assigned a Theban defender to each. The Argive army was routed. Eteocles had set himself against Polynices, and each killed the other. Creon, now king of Thebes, ordered that the bodies of the enemy and particularly that of Polynices should be refused burial (a grievous injury, for unless put underground, the dead could not enter Hades). What followed is variously told. One version is that given by Euripides in the 'Suppliants' (q.v.). Another, the more common version, is that Antigone, rebelling against Creon's decree, contrived secretly to perform the rite of interment over her brother. For this she was placed alive by Creon's order in a sepulchre, though she was betrothed to his son Haemon, and there she took her own life. Haemon stabbed himself beside her body. This is the version in the 'Antigone' (q.v.) of Sophocles. According to yet another version, perhaps invented by Euripides (we have only fragments of his 'Antigone'), Antigone, detected burning her brother's body by night, was handed over by Creon to Haemon to be killed. But Haemon hid her in a shepherd's hut and pretended that he had killed her. Later their son, having come to Thebes for a festival, was recognized by a birthmark common to all his family. To escape from Creon's vengeance, Haemon and Antigone killed themselves or were saved by divine intervention. See also *Epigoni*.

Oedipus, a tragedy by Seneca the Philosopher, based on Sophocles' play 'Oedipus Tyrannus' (q.v.), but marred by long descriptions of the pestilence at Thebes, and of necromantic and sacrificial rites. Jocasta's suicide takes place on the stage.

Oedipus at Colō′nus (*Oidipous epi Kolōnōi*, L. *Oedipus Colōnēus*), a tragedy by Sophocles, one of his most beautiful plays, produced in 401 B.C., after his death, by his grandson, Sophocles the Younger.

Oedipus (q.v.), blind and banished, has wandered, attended by his daughter Antigone, to Colonus, a deme of Attica. He is warned by the inhabitants to depart, but having learnt from an oracle that this is the spot where he is to die, refuses to go. Theseus, king of Athens, is appealed to, and assures Oedipus of his protection and of a burial-place on Attic soil; thereby his spirit will be a protection to Athens. Ismene joins Oedipus and tells him of the strife of Eteocles and Polynices for the throne of Thebes, awakening his anger against his callous sons. Creon arrives to seize Oedipus; his guard carry off Ismene and Antigone, and Creon is about to lay hands on Oedipus himself when Theseus intervenes, and rescues him and the maidens. Meanwhile Polynices has arrived, and with professions of repentance asks for his father's favour in his struggle with Eteocles. Oedipus upbraids him, and invokes on his sons the curse that they may die by each other's hand. Peals of thunder warn Oedipus that his hour is at hand. He blesses his daughters, withdraws to a lonely spot, and, in the presence of Theseus alone, is borne away to the gods.

Oedipus Tyrannus (*Oidipous Turannos*, L. *Oedipus Rex*), a tragedy by Sophocles, of unknown date, regarded by many as his masterpiece, and particularly admired by Aristotle in the 'Poetics'; but the group of plays to which it belonged did not win the prize.

It deals with that portion of the story of Oedipus (q.v.) in which he is king of Thebes and husband of Jocasta, when the discovery that he is the son and murderer of Laïus and son of Jocasta leads him to blind himself, and Jocasta to take her own life. It illustrates the Greek conception of human impotence in the presence of destiny, which may hurl a man, for no fault of his own, from the height of prosperity to appalling misery. A striking feature in the play is the eagerness with which Oedipus himself pursues the enquiry that is to be his undoing. He learns from Delphi that a plague which has fallen on the city is due to the presence there of the slayers of King Laïus. He calls upon all who have any knowledge of the matter to come forward. Tiresias, the blind seer, is first summoned. He knows the dreadful truth, but at first refuses to divulge it. Accused by Oedipus of plotting with Creon against him, he in part reveals the facts: it is Oedipus himself who murdered Laïus. Still utterly unsuspicious of his own guilt, Oedipus next turns against Creon, whom he charges with trying to oust him from the kingship. He is deeply disturbed by Jocasta's description of the scene of Laïus's death and of the retinue he then had with him, which accord with the circumstances of an affray in which Oedipus had once killed a man. On one point light now comes to him: he is not as he supposed the son of Polybus, king of Corinth. For a messenger comes from Corinth to announce the death of Polybus and the election of Oedipus to succeed him, and Oedipus, dreading the oracle that he is to wed his mother, shrinks from returning to Corinth; but the messenger reveals that he himself brought the infant Oedipus, given him by a shepherd on Mt. Cithaeron, to Polybus and Merope. Whose son then is he? An old herd who has been sent for, as the only survivor present at the death of Laïus, now completes the disclosure. It was he who had carried the infant Oedipus, son of Laïus and Jocasta, to Cithaeron and had from pity given him to the Corinthian. Oedipus rushes into the palace, to find that Jocasta has hanged herself, and blinds himself with her brooch.

Oe′neus (*Oineūs*), see *Meleager*.

Oeno′mäus (*Oinomaos*), in Greek mythology, king of Elis and father of Hippodamia; see *Pelops*.

Oenō′nē (*Oinōnē*), in Greek mythology, a nymph of Mt. Ida, who was loved by Paris (q.v.) before his adventure with Helen. He deserted her; but afterwards, when wounded by the poisoned arrow of Philoctetes (q.v.), sought her help, too late. Tennyson's 'Œnone' is the lament of the nymph for the lover who has deserted her.

Ogy′gia (*Ōgygiā*), in the 'Odyssey', the island of Calypso. It is represented as being far away to the westward, beyond Scheria, the land of the Phaeacians.

Oly′mpia (*Olumpiā*), a small plain on the N. bank of the Alphēus, in Elis (see Pl. 8), in a fertile region and among gentle hills, in strong contrast to the sombre grandeur of Delphi. This was the second of the two great religious centres of Greece and here were held every fourth year the Olympian Games (see *Festivals*, §§ 1 and 2), said to have been founded by Heracles, but whether by the famous Heracles or one of the Dactyls (q.v.) of Mt. Ida who bore that name, opinions were divided. The sacred precinct at Olympia, known as the *Altis* and surrounded by a wall, contained, besides a multitude of altars and statues, two famous temples, of Zeus and Hera respectively. The first was a large temple about 90 ft. wide by 220 long and 68 high, of the Doric order, with a colonnade of huge columns 7 ft. in diameter. In it was the colossal statue of Zeus, wrought in ivory and gold over a core of wood, by Phidias (q.v.), the most famous statue of antiquity. The god was represented sitting, but the statue according to Strabo was out of proportion to the temple, giving the impression that if the god were to rise he would lift the roof off. Oil was applied to the statue, or, perhaps injected into the wooden core, to prevent the ivory from cracking. The statue deeply impressed the Roman general Aemilius Paullus, and Dion Chrysostom spoke of it with enthusiasm. Caligula thought of conveying it to Rome, and substituting his own head for that of the god; but the impious design was frustrated, for the ship built to carry it was struck by lightning. The ultimate fate of the statue is not known; it probably perished in a fire. The temple of Hera was smaller (about 60 ft. wide by 165 long) and very ancient, dating perhaps from 700 B.C. or a little earlier. Its columns appear to have been originally of wood (some of these wooden columns were still standing in the days of Pausanias) and to have been replaced from time to time by columns of stone as the wood decayed. The walls are thought to have been originally in part of sun-dried bricks. In it was found in 1877 the famous statue by Praxiteles (q.v.) of Hermes holding on his arm the infant

Dionysus. Here also, according to Pausanias, was a magnificent carved cedar-wood chest, said to be that in which Cypselus (q.v.) had been hidden by his mother. Besides the very numerous statues of athletes and horse-breeders who had been successful at the games (erected by themselves or their friends) there were in the Altis statues of other distinguished men, among them Aristotle and Gorgias, Lysander, Philip of Macedon, Alexander the Great, Pyrrhus of Epirus, Hieron of Syracuse, and Mummius the conqueror of Corinth. Certain States had treasuries at Olympia like those referred to under *Delphi*. The stadium or racecourse stood outside the Altis; it was supposed to be 600 ft. long; but the Olympic foot was longer than the ordinary Greek foot, because, it was said, Heracles measured the Olympic stadium with his own feet, which were larger than ordinary feet.

Oly′mpiacus, see *Lysias*.

Oly′mpiad, see *Festivals*, § 1, *Calendar*, § 1.

Oly′mpian Festival, see *Festivals*, §§ 1 and 2.

Olympias, see *Philip of Macedon* and *Alexander the Great*.

Olympiē′um (*Olumpieion*), the sanctuary of Zeus Olympius at Athens, situated SE. of the Acropolis. It was a massive artificial platform about 225 yds. by 140, on which stood a temple to the god, begun by Pisistratus but left unfinished. Antiochus Epiphanes undertook, about 174 B.C., to rebuild it at his own expense, but it again remained unfinished. Sulla removed some of the columns to Rome. It was finally completed by Hadrian. It was one of the largest of Greek temples, 354 ft. long by 135 wide. It was surrounded by one hundred Corinthian columns, each 56 ft. high. Fifteen of these remain. See Pl. 13*a*.

Oly′mpus (*Olumpos*), (1) the mountain at the eastern extremity of the chain which forms the northern boundary of Thessaly and Greece proper, overlooking the Vale of Tempe. In Greek mythology its summit was regarded as the residence of the gods. (2) Mysian Olympus, the eastern extremity of a chain of mountains extending across the north-west of Asia Minor.

Oly′nthiacs, three political speeches by Demosthenes. See *Demosthenes* (2), § 5.

Oly′nthus (*Olunthos*), see *Chalcidic League*.

Omens. An omen, in Greek and Roman thought, was a phenomenon or circumstance foreboding good or evil. Omens were seen notably in the flight and song of birds, and in lightning or thunder, according to the direction in which these were seen or heard. As early as the time of Homer we know that the Greeks paid attention to such signs: vultures seen on the left were an unlucky omen; the cry of a heron, or lightning, on the right was lucky. The Greeks drew omens from the reluctance or willingness of the sacrificial victim to approach the altar, and from the condition of its entrails when slaughtered. Aristophanes rallies his countrymen on their practice of calling many things, such as a sneeze or a chance meeting, an ὄρνις in the sense of an omen (Av. 719 et seq.). For the Greek art of interpreting omens see under *Divination*.

The Romans, besides drawing omens from birds, lightning, and sacrificial victims, attached importance (as did also the Greeks) to a noticeable word or phrase casually spoken. For instance L. Aemilius Paullus, hearing his little daughter say that their dog Persa was dead, drew from this a good omen as regards his campaign against King Perseus. The Romans, differing herein from the Greeks, regarded signs on the left as generally favourable, on the right as unfavourable. But there were, under Greek influence, exceptions to this view. For the Roman art of interpreting omens see *Augury, Haruspices*.

O'mphalē, see *Heracles*.

O'mphalos, see *Delphi*.

Onēsi'critus (*Onēsikritos*), a Greek historian who accompanied Alexander the Great (q.v., § 7) on his expedition, and with Nearchus examined the sea-route from India to the Persian Gulf. The longest surviving fragment of his narrative of Alexander's Indian campaign describes an interview between the author and some Indian fakirs.

Onē'tōr, see *Demosthenes* (2), § 2.

Onoma'critus (*Onomakritos*), an Athenian who lived at the court of Pisistratus (q.v.) and his sons. He was employed to collect and edit the oracles of Musaeus (q.v.) and is said to have been detected by Lasus of Hermione (q.v.) falsifying them. This appears to have given rise to an idea that he concocted the Orphic poems (see *Orphism*). There is also a late statement that he was employed by Pisistratus to edit the Homeric poems.

Ono'matopoē'ïa, the forming of a word to resemble that which it signifies. A good example is in Ennius's line,

At tuba terribili sonitu *taratantara* dixit.

The word is used also, in a wider sense, of the formation of sentences or phrases suggestive in sound of what they describe, as in Homer's line about the stone of Sisyphus:

αὖτις ἔπειτα πέδονδε κυλίνδετο λᾶας ἀναιδής,

in Virgil's

Quadrupedante putrem sonitu quatit un- gula campum,

and in Valerius Flaccus's description of a cave shaken by the sound of the sea:

Infelix domus et sonitu tremibunda pro- fundi.

Opeconsi'va or OPICONSI'VIA, see *Ops*.

Opi'sthograph, see *Books*, § 2.

O'ppian (*Oppiānos*) of Cilicia, author in the time of Caracalla (A.D. 211–217) of a Greek didactic poem in five books of hexameters, entitled 'Halieutica', on fish and fishing. Another didactic poem, in four books, on hunting ('Cynegetica'), is often attributed to him, but appears to be by an author of the same name and period, but a native of Apamēa in Syria. The two works are extant.

Ops, in Roman religion, the goddess of the wealth of the harvest, celebrated at the *Opeconsiva* (or *Opiconsivia*) on 25 August. This was a harvest ceremony in the shrine of the *Regia* or ancient royal palace, attended only by the *Pontifex Maximus* and the Vestals, symbolizing the storage of the State crops by the king and his daughters. Ops was later identified with Rhea (q.v.).

Optimā'tēs, see under *Populares*.

Oracles.

§ 1. *In Greece*

An oracle (*manteion*) was the answer given by particular deities, usually through a priest or priestess, to the enquiries of those who consulted them. The word is also used of a shrine where such answers were imparted. The most famous of these shrines were those of Zeus at Dōdōna in Ēpirus, and of Apollo at Delphi. The oracles of the former date from very ancient times, and are mentioned in the 'Iliad' and the 'Odyssey'. They were interpreted by priests from the sound made by a spring gushing from the roots of a sacred oak, or from the rustling of the leaves of the oak-trees about the shrine (later by the sound of a brazen gong). Few traces of these have survived. For the Delphic Oracles, which were interpreted from the ecstatic cries of the Pythian priestess, see *Delphic Oracle*.

There were many other oracular shrines, in Greece and Asia Minor, of less importance. At Epidaurus, for instance, Asclepius (q.v.) sometimes revealed to patients sleeping in his temple, by means of dreams, how they might be cured. Oracles were also given by dreams at the cave of Trophonius (q.v.) in Boeotia and at the shrine of Amphiaraus (q.v.) at Ōrōpus. In the temple of Heracles at Būra in Achaea oracles were delivered by lots or dice. Among foreign oracles, that of Jupiter Ammon in the Libyan desert had a high reputation among the Greeks.

§ 2. At Rome

Oracles, apart from the Sibylline Books (q.v.), were not held in much repute at Rome in republican times, and the State did not resort to them to ascertain the will of the gods. Under the empire the use of oracular predictions grew in favour with the populace, especially in connexion with the worship of the Greek and oriental divinities. The collection of oracles must have begun fairly early. In 213 B.C. the Senate made the praetor Acilius seize several collections. Augustus had two thousand books of prophecies burnt. There were no oracular shrines in Italy comparable in importance with those in Greece; but at Cumae under the Temple of Apollo was the Sibyl's cave (see *Sibyls*), and at Praeneste there was an ancient and famous temple of Fortune (see *Fortuna*), where oracles known as *sortes* were uttered, by means of tablets bearing some oracular inscription, shuffled and drawn by a child. Faunus was regarded as a prophetic god, and Carmentis had a similar power. Both are referred to by Virgil. At the temple of Faunus at Tibur *incubātiō* or the obtaining of oracles by dream was practised (Ov. Fast. iii. 291); a sheep was slain and the person seeking an oracle then slept in its skin. The haphazard choice of a line of Virgil, by opening his works at random (*Sortēs Virgiliānae*), became at a later period a popular method of trying to discover the future (see *Virgil*).

Ōrātōr, a treatise by Cicero (q.v.), written in 46 B.C. and dedicated to M. Brutus, in which he describes the ideal orator and outlines a scheme for his education. He must be master of the three styles, the plain, the grand, and the intermediate (Demosthenes was a perfect example of all three). The qualifications of the orator in technical respects (invention, elocution, style, &c.) are set forth; his functions (to teach, to please, to persuade); and the branches of knowledge which he must have mastered (philosophy, physics, &c.). The treatise ends with a disquisition on euphony and rhythm. There are interesting references to works of art, taken as illustrations; e.g. the Venus of Apelles, the Zeus of Phidias, the chryselephantine statue of Athene.

Oratory.

§ 1. Greek Oratory

Rhetoric, the art of speaking, in the age of the great Greek orators (5th–4th c. B.C.) was regarded as an accomplishment for which preparation was made by careful training in composition and delivery. The accomplishment was of great practical importance, for at Athens a man's life and property might depend on the power of persuading the judges in a lawsuit, while successful eloquence in the Ecclesia opened the path to ambition. Attic oratory, in its period of splendour, differed from modern oratory in two main respects: speeches made no pretence to be extemporary, and, being addressed to popular audiences, the part played in them by purely logical argument was less, and that played by appeal to the feelings was greater, than it is to-day. Moreover the Greek audiences, being used to listen to poetical recitations, would be keen critics of the verbal form of the speeches addressed to them. The speeches might be political, or they might be forensic (i.e. delivered in a court of law), or they might be epideictic (funeral orations, panegyrics, &c.). Owing to the care spent on their composition, they were an important factor in the formation of Greek prose. Treatises on the science of rhetoric were written by Aristotle and his successor Theophrastus (q.v.).

The development of Attic oratory was influenced by two external forces: the rhetoric of Sicily, and the teaching in dialectic and the use of language given by the Sophists (q.v.). The art of rhetoric originated in Sicily, in the middle of the 5th c. B.C., when the rule of tyrants gave place to democracy; the lawsuits which followed this change are said to have given the Sicilian Corax the idea of systematizing and writing down the rules of forensic speaking. According to Aristotle, Empedocles (q.v.) had some part in their development. Gorgias (q.v.) of Leontini in Sicily made artistic expression the basis of oratory, adopting in particular a poetic rhythm (for his style see the speeches in Thucydides). His influence on Attic oratory is especially seen in Antiphon and Isocrates.

We have no authentic record of the form of the speeches of Pericles, though Thucydides may give a generally accurate record of their substance. The earliest of the Attic orators whose speeches in part survive is Antiphon (q.v., c. 480–411 B.C.), who was followed by Andocides (q.v.), and the great orators Lysias, Isocrates, Isaeus, Demosthenes, and Aeschines (qq.v.). Of the remaining Attic orators the most important were Lycurgus, Hyperides, and Dinarchus (qq.v.). After the end of the 4th c. B.C. the study of oratory was pursued chiefly among the Greeks of Asia Minor, and showed a tendency to become turgid and declamatory. This tendency has been given the name of Asianism. But this tendency was not universal, and the Hellenistic school of Greek oratory became important, for all the great Roman orators were trained by Greek masters.

§ 2. *Roman Oratory*

At Rome, as in Greece, oratory was from early times recognized as an art. Even in the 4th c. B.C. Appius Claudius (q.v.) the Censor had a high reputation as an orator. In the survey that Cicero gives in his 'Brutus' (q.v.) of the great Roman speakers, the principal names are those of Cato the Censor (q.v.), the Gracchi (especially Gaius, described by Cicero as wise, lofty, and weighty, but lacking the final polish), M. Antonius (grandfather of the triumvir), L. Licinius Crassus (consul in 95 B.C., whose speeches were deliberately built up in accordance with the rules of Greek oratory), Julius Caesar, C. Licinius Calvus (q.v., an exponent of the pure Attic style), and Hortensius (q.v., noted, on the contrary, for his luxuriant Asianism). For the oratory of Cicero see under his name. For the decline of oratory under the empire see *Rome*, § 9.

Oratory, among the Romans as among the Greeks, was extraordinarily popular. It formed an important element in education, and exercised in consequence a strong influence on all forms of literature. Higher education under the Roman empire and so long as ancient civilization lasted was practically equivalent to rhetorical training. Augustine, Ausonius, for instance, were among the teachers of rhetoric in the West; Dion Chrysostom, Aelius Aristides, in the East. Chairs of rhetoric were endowed in every important city of the empire.

Orbi'lius Pūpi'lius (*c.* 112—*c.* 17 B.C.) of Beneventum, a grammarian, famous as the schoolmaster of Horace, who speaks feelingly of the raps he received from him. There is an account of him in Suetonius.

O'rcus (*Horkos*), meaning 'oath', in Greek mythology an infernal deity who punishes perjury. In Roman religion Orcus is apparently a synonym of Dis (q.v.), the god of the underworld. It is uncertain whether the Roman Orcus was originally a deity of Italian folklore, or whether his name is merely transliterated from the Greek.

O'rěads (Gk. *Oreiades*, L. *Orēades*), nymphs (q.v.) of the mountains.

Orelli, JOHANN KASPAR (1787–1849), Swiss scholar, famous as a commentator on Horace, Cicero, and Tacitus.

Orestei'a, a trilogy by Aeschylus on the story of Agamemnon, Clytemnestra, and Orestes (see *Agamemnon*), produced in 458 B.C., when it won the prize. It is the only connected Greek trilogy that survives. It comprises 'Agamemnon', 'Choëphoroe' ('libation bearers'), and 'Eumenides' ('the Gracious Ones', a euphemism for the Furies). It was Aeschylus's last and greatest work.

AGAMEMNON. The watchman on the roof of Agamemnon's palace in Argos is looking out for the signal beacon that is to announce the fall of Troy. He suddenly beholds it, and the news is presently confirmed by a herald, and finally by the arrival of Agamemnon himself with his captive, Cassandra. But the chorus of Argive Elders, while celebrating in their song the fall of Troy, are gloomy and hint at trouble—the sacrifice, unforgiven by Clytemnestra, of her daughter Iphigenia, and its consequences. Clytemnestra treacherously welcomes Agamemnon and leads him into the palace. Cassandra, filled with prophetic frenzy, foresees his murder and her own, and utters a lament. She follows him into the palace, ready for death. The cry of the dying Agamemnon is heard. Clytemnestra reappears, with the two bodies, glorying in her deed of vengeance. Aegisthus, her paramour, appears, also rejoicing, and meets with threats the indignant reproaches of the chorus.

CHŒPHOROE. Orestes, the son of Agamemnon, who has been living in exile, comes with his friend Pylades to his father's tomb, and dedicates on it a lock of his hair. Electra, Agamemnon's daughter, and the chorus of Argive women approach to pour libations on the tomb, by order of Clytemnestra, who has been disturbed by ominous dreams. Electra recognizes the lock of her brother's hair and is presently reunited with him. (In Euripides' 'Electra' there is an implied criticism on this recognition. An old servant has seen Orestes' footprints and a lock of his hair by the tomb; but Electra rejects these proofs of identity.) Brother and sister decide on immediate vengeance, which Apollo has ordered Orestes to execute, and invoke the aid of their father. Orestes and Pylades, in the guise of travellers bearing news of the death of Orestes, enter the palace. Aegisthus is summoned, and on his arrival slain by Orestes. Clytemnestra pleads with her son for her life, while he holds her under the threat of his sword. He drags her into the palace and kills her. As Orestes is justifying his action, the Furies appear, threatening the murderer, who flies from them.

EUMENIDES. Orestes is at the shrine of Apollo in Delphi. The Furies, forming the chorus, are asleep around him. Apollo promises him protection and bids him go to Athens to seek justice from Pallas Athene. Orestes goes. The ghost of Clytemnestra stirs up the Furies. The scene changes to the temple of Athene at Athens. Athene, having heard the pleas of the Furies and of Orestes, refers the suit to a tribunal of Athenian judges (the Areopagus, q.v., of which this was the legendary foundation). The votes for and against are equal, and Orestes is acquitted by the casting-vote of Athene. The Furies are indignant, but are conciliated by Athene's promise of a permanent abode and honour in her land.

Ore'stēs, in Greek mythology, son of Agamemnon (q.v.) and Clytemnestra, and brother of Iphigenia and Electra. See *Pelops*, and the articles on the tragedies *Oresteia, Orestes, Electra, Iphigenia in Tauris*. For his marriage with Hermione see *Neoptolemus*.

Orestes, a drama by Euripides, produced in 408 B.C.

Orestes (see above) is presented, after the murder of his mother, maddened by the avenging Furies, and tenderly nursed by his sister Electra. The Argive democracy is about to pass judgement on them for their crime, and a sentence of death is expected. Menelaus (q.v.) appears, having returned with Helen from Troy. Orestes appeals to him for protection, on the ground that he has avenged the murder of Agamemnon, the brother of Menelaus. But the latter shows himself a craven. The expected sentence is passed. Orestes and Electra, stimulated by Pylades (q.v.), now plot to kill Helen, the source of all their troubles; but she mysteriously disappears. They then try to gain the support of Menelaus under threat of the death of his daughter Hermione. The confused situation that results is solved by the appearance of Apollo, who dictates a general pacification, and explains that Helen has been carried off to heaven.

O'rganon, see *Aristotle*, § 3.

O'rigen (*Órigenēs*) (A.D. 185–254), the successor of Clement as head of the Christian school of Alexandria, and the first great scholar among the Greek Fathers. Apart from many theological works he is chiefly famous for his 'Hexapla', an edition of the Old Testament containing in six parallel columns the Hebrew text, four Greek translations, and a revised text of the Septuagint. We have only fragments of the work.

Ori'on (*Órīōn*), in Greek mythology, a giant and hunter of Boeotia, the subject of various legends, according to which he was deprived of sight by Dionysus, or killed by Artemis (either from jealousy because he was loved by Eos, the Dawn, or because he challenged her to throw the discus against him), or stung to death by a scorpion, by the same goddess's design, while ridding the earth of wild beasts. Another story is that he pursued the Pleiades (q.v.) and both he and they were turned into constellations. For the curious story of his birth, see Ovid, 'Fasti', v. 495 et seq., a story based on the false derivation of the name Orion from the Greek *ouron* (urine).

Orō'pus (*Órōpos*), a town on the borders of Attica and Boeotia, near the sea; for a long time a subject of contention between the two States. For the oracular shrine there see *Amphiaraus*.

Oro'sius, a Christian ecclesiastic of Tarragona, of the 5th c. A.D., friend of St. Augustine, and author at the latter's request of a history of the world to 417 A.D. Its principal sources were Justin and Jerome–Eusebius (qq.v.), and it was designed to promote the Christian faith.

O'rpheūs, a legendary pre-Homeric poet, a Thracian, a follower of Dionysus (q.v.), a son of Calliope or some other muse, and so marvellous a player on the lyre that the wild beasts were spellbound by his music. He is said to have taken part in the expedition of the Argonauts (q.v.), and by his song helped them to resist the lure of the Sirens (q.v.). He married Eurydice, a Dryad (q.v.). Eurydice, while running away from Aristaeus (q.v.), who was forcing his attentions upon her, trod on a snake, was bitten, and died. Orpheus went down to Hades to recover her and by his music induced Persephone to let her go, but on condition that Orpheus should not look back at her as she followed him. When they approached the world of the living, Orpheus forgot the condition and looked back, and Eurydice immediately vanished for ever. Later, Orpheus was torn to pieces by Thracian Maenads (q.v.), either for interfering with their worship, or because of his hatred for women since he had lost Eurydice. His head, floating down the Hebrus, and in some versions still speaking, reached the island of Lesbos (q.v.), where it was buried (see the lines, 58–63, in Milton's 'Lycidas', ending, 'Down the swift Hebrus to the Lesbian shore.'). Orpheus was regarded as the founder of the Mysteries (see *Orphism*) which took his name. The story of Orpheus and Eurydice —of the man who goes down to the lower world to recover his wife or sister—is found in the folk-lore of widely distant countries. The tearing in pieces of Orpheus may be connected with the ritual of Dionysus (cf. the legends of Pentheus and Minyas). There is an echo of the story of Orpheus in the fine lines in Milton's 'Paradise Lost' (vii. 30 et seq.) and in 'L'Allegro' (145 et seq.). The myth of Orpheus and Eurydice is the subject of an opera ('Orfeo', 1762) by Gluck.

Orphism, a mystic Greek cult, connected with Orpheus (q.v.) as the legendary source of the sacred poems whence the Orphic doctrines were derived (see *Musaeus* and *Onomacritus*). Orphism explained the mixture of good and evil in human nature by the myth of Dionysus Zagreus (q.v.). It departed from the primitive Greek religion in making the guilt and punishment of the individual the centre of its doctrine. It taught the transmigration of souls and inculcated ritual and moral purity as giving the soul its final release to the life of the blessed. Hades the Orphics conceived as a Hell, a place of retribution for the unrighteous. In their asceticism the Orphics approximated to the Pythagoreans (q.v.), with whose doctrines their own had much in common. The Orphics celebrated mysteries in which purification and initiation played an important part. The tearing to pieces and devouring of the god personified in an animal appears to have been among their rites. Orphism was prominent in the 6th c. B.C. Later it sank to the position of a despised popular superstition, though Pindar and Plato were attracted by its doctrines. There was a revival of it under the Roman empire.

Orthrus, in Greek mythology, the dog of Geryon (q.v.). It was the offspring of Typhon and Echidna (qq.v.). See *Heracles (Labours of)* and *Sphinx*.

Ortygia (*Ortugia*), see *Leto* and *Syracuse*, § 1.

Oscans, an Italian race akin to the Umbrians, Sabellians, and Latins, speaking a dialect related to theirs. They established themselves S. of Latium, principally in Campānia, also in Lūcānia and Apūlia. The Samnites were the principal Oscan-speaking people. The Oscan dialect probably once had its literature and was the original language of the Atellan plays

(q.v.). Oscan certainly influenced Latin and survived alongside of it till the 1st c. B.C.

Oschopho'ria, see *Festivals*, § 4.

Osi'ris, the most widely worshipped of the gods of the Egyptians, representing the male productive principle in nature, incarnated in the bull Apis. Myth related that as a king of Egypt he had civilized and educated his people, but had been murdered and his body cut in pieces by his brother Set (identified with the Greek Typhon, q.v.). Isis (q.v.), his sister and wife, collected and buried his mangled remains, and with her son Horus took revenge on Set, the author of all evil. Thereafter Osiris was regarded as the god of the dead, but the source, through Horus (the Sun), of renewed life. The Greeks identified him with Dionysus (q.v.). See also *Serapis* and *Harpocrates*.

Ostō'rius Sca'pula, Publius, see *Britain*, § 2.

O'straca (Gk. *ostraka*, potsherds), broken fragments of pottery used as writing material. This was a very common practice in ancient Egypt; ostraca were also used in Greece, but apparently to a less extent than in Egypt. For the use of ostraca at Athens in voting for the banishment of certain persons, see *Ostracism*.

Ostraca vary very widely in size and shape; usually the writing is in ink; the letters are occasionally carved with a knife. The term is sometimes extended to limestone fragments, which were also used as writing material in Egypt, though only rarely in the period, after Alexander's conquest, when Greek was the national language of Egypt. Ostraca inscribed in Greek make their appearance in Egypt in the 3rd c. B.C. They are most common in the reigns of the emperors Hadrian (A.D. 116–138) and Antoninus (138–161). Most of them come from Thebes or its neighbourhood in Upper Egypt (probably because papyrus was less plentiful in Upper Egypt than in Lower); large numbers have also been found in the Fayoum. In general ostraca were used for documents of minor importance, such as receipts for the payment of taxes or for the delivery of corn into the public granaries, or for private payments. There are also many lists of names, accounts, and memoranda of various kinds. Occasionally school exercises were written on ostraca, sometimes the alphabet, sometimes verses from the Bible or lines from Homer, Euripides, Menander, &c.

The importance of Greek ostraca consists chiefly in their value as evidence for the economic history of Graeco-Roman

Egypt, but they are also of some interest for the study of ancient writing, for the topography of the districts from which they come, and for the history of the art of pottery. The largest collections of ostraca are those of the Bodleian Library at Oxford, the British Museum, the Louvre, and the Berlin Museum.

O'stracism, an institution introduced at Athens by Cleisthenes (q.v.), designed to prevent any attempt against the established order. Each year the Ecclesia considered the question 'whether it was expedient to apply ostracism'. In the event of an affirmative vote each citizen inscribed on a potsherd (*ostrakon*, see *Ostraca*) the name of the person whose withdrawal from the State seemed to him necessary to the public safety. Any person so designated by a certain number of votes (6,000 had to be cast in all) was to leave Athens for ten years, without loss of his property. Not more than ten citizens in all (among them Aristides, q.v.) ever suffered ostracism, and ostracism was discontinued by the end of the 5th c. B.C.

A considerable number of ostraca bearing votes of this kind have been found at Athens, the most remarkable discovery being that of twelve ostraca in 1932 on the site of the Agora. Four of these bear the name of Aristides, two of Themistocles, three of Megacles (uncle of Pericles, ostracized in 486), and one of Hipparchus (cousin of the tyrant, ostracized in 487).

O'thō, *Marcus Salvius*, Roman emperor in A.D. 69, a former boon companion of Nero (and see *Poppaea*). He took his own life after defeat by the army of Vitellius.

Ō'tus (*Ōtos*) and **Ephia'ltēs**, in Greek mythology, giant sons of Alōëus (whence called *Alōïdae*), or of Poseidon and the wife of Aloeus. They attacked the gods and tried to pile Ossa on Olympus, and Pelion on Ossa, in order to climb to heaven. They were destroyed by Zeus. A passage in the 'Iliad' tells how they imprisoned Ares, the god of war, in a bronze jar, for thirteen months; he would have perished there, had not Hermes released him. A different tradition makes them beneficent heroes who founded cities and the worship of the Muses. They may be survivors from an older religion.

Ephialtes was also the name of the demon of nightmare among the Greeks.

Ovā'tio, see *Triumph*.

O'vid (*Publius Ovidius Nāsō*) (43 B.C.–A.D. 18), born the year after the death of Julius Caesar, at Sulmo, in a valley of the Apennines, Paelignian territory east of Rome. His family was of equestrian rank.

He was educated at Rome and by his father's wish studied rhetoric with a view to the practice of law, but his taste for poetry asserted itself. According to the Elder Pliny he had applied himself to the emotional rather than the argumentative side of rhetoric. He travelled, studied also at Athens, and visited Asia and Sicily. For a time he held some minor official posts at Rome. Horace and Propertius were among his friends; he mourns the death of Tibullus; Virgil he only saw. His poetry soon brought him popularity in idle, fashionable Roman circles. He was three times married; his first two marriages were of short duration; his third wife remained devoted to him and loyal during his exile. He had a daughter (or perhaps stepdaughter, though he calls her *nata*). In A.D. 8 the course of his life at Rome was interrupted by the overwhelming blow of an imperial edict banishing him to Tōmis (or Tōmi) on the W. shore of the Black Sea. According to Ovid the grounds of this sentence were a poem (no doubt the immoral 'Ars Amatoria') and an error. What this last was remains unknown; something, it may be supposed, which directly offended the emperor's personal susceptibilities. His name was connected with that of Julia, the emperor's profligate daughter. Ovid has described in his 'Tristia' the last sad night at Rome, the hardships of his voyage to Tomi, and the tedious years of boredom and deprivation in his bleak land of exile. His hopes of some mitigation of his punishment were disappointed, and he died at Tomi after ten years of banishment. He seems to have become reconciled to its inhabitants; they were kind and considerate and won his esteem. He learnt the Getic language, and wrote in it a poem (not extant) in honour of Augustus and Tiberius.

The approximate order in which his works were written appears to be as follows, but cross-references in them from one to another make their sequence uncertain: 'Amores', 'Heroides', 'Medicamina faciei femineae', 'Ars Amatoria', 'Remedia Amoris', 'Medea', 'Metamorphoses', 'Fasti', 'Tristia', 'Epistulae ex Ponto'. These, with the exception of 'Medea', a tragedy (praised by Quintilian) of which only two lines have survived, are dealt with under their several titles. Works doubtfully attributed to Ovid are the 'Halieutica' (of which we have only a fragment) on the marine creatures of the Black Sea, and the 'Ibis', a satirical poem imitated from Callimachus and directed against some enemy. 'Nux', a complaint by a nut-tree, and 'Consōlātiō ad Līviam' (or 'Epicēdion Drūsi') on the death of Drusus Nero, at one time attributed to Ovid, are spurious. Ovid's writings, with the exception of the 'Metamorphoses' and 'Halieutica' (in hexameters) are in elegiacs (see *Metre*). Ovid is a fluent, superficial, witty, and ingenious writer, neat in verse and phrase, a vivid and lucid story-teller, with many charming plays of fancy and picturesque descriptions. In him the poetic art has lost the serious character which it had with Virgil and Horace, nor is it (except in the 'Tristia' and 'Epistulae') the expression of strong personal feeling (as sometimes with Catullus). Its purpose is to amuse. His amorous poetry is artificial; his Corinna had no single living counterpart. The 'Metamorphoses' contains passages of more solid merit, tender and simple episodes such as those of Ceyx and Halcyone, Philemon and Baucis. The elder Seneca has preserved a pleasant story illustrating Ovid's fondness for verbal extravagances. He was once asked by his friends that they might choose three lines to be erased from his works. He agreed, provided he might also choose three lines on no account to be sacrificed. The lines chosen on each side turned out to be the same. One of them was, 'semibovemque virum semivirumque bovem'.

It is as a story-teller and a guide to Greek mythology and Roman legend that Ovid chiefly exerted influence on later Roman writers, who freely imitated and borrowed from him. He was read, quoted, and adapted during the Middle Ages; and he was the favourite Latin poet of the Renaissance (first printed at Rome in 1471). There were many translations of parts of his works into English in the 16th c., notably those of Caxton (1480), Golding, Turberville, and Churchyard. Parts again were translated or paraphrased by Dryden in 'Fables, Ancient and Modern'. The translation of the 'Metamorphoses' published in 1626 by George Sandys (1578–1644) was an important work.

Chaucer drew largely on him in the 'Book of the Duchess', 'House of Fame', and 'Legend of Good Women'; to a less extent in the 'Canterbury Tales' (for instance in the 'Manciple's Tale' of the crow). Gower's 'Confessio Amantis' has a multitude of Ovidian tales. The 'Faerie Queene' contains many allusions to him. Marlowe's Faustus in his last speech quotes the 'Amores' ('O lente, lente, currite noctis equi'). Shakespeare knew the 'Metamorphoses' in Golding's translation, but appears also to have known the Latin text, from which he took the name 'Titania', and from that of the 'Fasti' the story of the

Rape of Lucrece. Francis Meres, the critic, in his 'Palladis Tamia' (1598), made the well-known observation that 'the sweet witty soul of Ovid lives in mellifluous and honey-tongued Shakespeare, witness his "Venus and Adonis", his "Lucrece", his sugared sonnets among his private friends'. 'As You Like It' (III. iii. 9) has a reference to Ovid's exile 'among the Goths'. The line in 'Romeo and Juliet', 'At lovers' perjuries they say, Jove laughs' (II. ii), is a translation from the 'Ars Amatoria'. The 'Taming of the Shrew' (III. i) gives two lines from the 'Heroides'. (See also under *Naso*.) Ben Jonson in his 'Poetaster' introduces the incident of Ovid's banishment by Augustus. Shirley in his 'Contention of Ajax and Ulysses' for the arms of Achilles (chiefly known for the great dirge at the end, 'The glories of our blood and state') adapts Ovid's account in the 13th Book of the 'Metamorphoses' of the debate between the heroes.

Oxymo'ron (from Gk. ὀξύς, 'sharp', μωρός, 'dull'), a rhetorical figure by which two incongruous or contradictory terms are combined in an expression so as to give it point, e.g. 'splendide mendax' (Hor. Od. III. xi. 35).

Oxyrhy'nchus, a place (*Behnesa*) in Upper Egypt, S. of the Fayoum, where many ancient manuscripts on papyrus have been found in the last decade of the 19th and in the 20th c. These include (besides important Biblical fragments) texts of parts of the works of Homer, Bacchylides, Pindar, Aristotle, and Callimachus (qq.v.).

P

Pacto'lus (*Pactōlos*), a river in Lydia, whose sands contained gold. See *Midas*.

Pacu'vius (*Pācŭvius*), MARCUS (c. 220–c. 130 B.C.), a nephew and pupil of Ennius, born at Brundisium. He came to Rome, formed part there of the circle of Laelius (q.v.), and besides being a painter became a celebrated tragedian. We have the titles and fragments of twelve of his tragedies and of one national drama (*praetexta*) on Paullus (probably L. Aemilius Paullus, q.v.). The titles show the Greek sources of his tragedies, one at least, the 'Antiope' (his most famous work), being an imitation of Euripides, and the 'Niptra' probably of Sophocles. Some peculiarities of diction incurred the ridicule of Lucilius and Persius, but his work showed command of pathos and passion, and impressive character drawing. He was known as 'doctus', probably on account of his Hellenism, i.e. his research into and treatment of unfamiliar Greek saga-cycles. The term was regarded as high praise. Cicero looked upon him as the greatest of Roman tragedians, and in his ʻDe Amicitiaʼ testifies to the popular enthusiasm with which a scene in his ʻOrestesʼ was received.

Paeʹan (*Paiān*), a Greek choral lyric (q.v.), probably of Cretan origin, deriving its name from the invocation ʻIē Paiōnʼ addressed to Apollo, which formed a refrain. The song was sometimes, but not always, accompanied by a dance. It might be either an invocation or a thanksgiving (perhaps originally a song of healing or incantation) at first addressed to Apollo, later to other gods also. It was much in vogue at Sparta, at the feasts of Apollo. A paean is said to have been composed by Sophocles to Asclepius, and one by Socrates to Apollo. Some fragmentary paeans by Pindar survive.

Paedagōʹgus (Gk. *Paidagōgos*), see *Education*, §§ 1 and 2.

Paeliʹgni, inhabitants of lofty valleys of the Apennines, E. of Rome. In Paelignian territory lay Sulmo, the birthplace of Ovid, who speaks of Sulmo ʻgelidis uberrimus undisʼ. Horace refers to ʻPaeligna frigoraʼ, (Od. III. xix. 8).

Paeʹon, see *Metre*, § 1.

Paeʹstum, the Roman name of Poseidōnia, a colony founded by Sybaris (q.v.) on the coast of Lūcānia about 600 B.C. It is famous for its Greek temples, of which the fine ruins still remain. It was conquered by Rome in 273 B.C. Virgil speaks of its roses flowering twice a year.

Paeʹtus, see *Arria*.

Pāgānāʹlia, at Rome, the celebration in the *pāgi* (divisions of rural areas) of the sowing, a festival associated with the earth-goddesses Ceres and Tellus, who according to Ovid were then invoked to protect the seed. The feast was a movable one.

Painting. (1) GREEK. We do not know very much about Greek methods of painting, and are mainly dependent on the statements of Pliny, Pausanias, and Lucian. The Greeks appear to have used fresco (painting on wet plaster), tempera (the use of some sticky medium), and the encaustic method (the nature of which is not certainly known, but which appears to have involved the use of melted wax as a medium). Some idea of the skill of the Greek painters may be derived from the beautiful examples that we possess of the kindred art of vase (q.v.) decora-

tion. Apart from the wall-paintings of Mycenae and Tiryns, and the beautiful frescoes of Cnossus in Crete, Greek painting may be divided into three main periods: (*a*) that of Polygnotus (q.v.), the first half of the 5th c. B.C., when the artist's object is to give a simple, dignified representation of some mythological scene; (*b*) the period of Zeuxis and Parrhasius (qq.v.), the latter part of the 5th c., in which, though the subjects are still in the main mythological, the object is to extract from the scene the elements of beauty that it contains; (*c*) the period of Apelles (q.v.), the 4th c., when technical skill was developed in various directions in a number of different schools, at Athens, Sicyon, and in Ionia. The school at Sicyon was famous. Apelles himself is said to have studied there, but it appears to have been notable rather for formal and technical excellence than for feeling and imagination. After the 4th c. the Greek art of painting declined. There is much interesting information about Zeuxis, Parrhasius, and Apelles in Pliny (N.H. xxxv. 36).

(2) ROMAN, see *Art, Roman*.

Palaeʹmon (*Palaimōn*), see *Dionysus* and *Melicertes*.

Palaeʹmon, QUINTUS REMMIUS, a famous grammarian and teacher at Rome under Tiberius and Caligula, referred to by Juvenal. Persius was his pupil, and Quintilian is also said to have had him for instructor. There is a curious account of him in Suetonius, ʻDe Grammaticisʼ.

Palaeography, see *Texts and Studies*, § 11.

Palaeʹstra (*Palaistrā*), ʻwrestling-schoolʼ, in Greek cities, the place where boys were instructed in wrestling and gymnastics.

Palamēʹdēs, in Greek mythology, one of the Greek heroes of the Trojan War, an ingenious man who is said to have invented some of the letters of the alphabet and the game of draughts. When Odysseus (q.v.) tried to avoid his obligation to join in the expedition to Troy by feigning madness, Palamedes exposed his deceit. Thereafter Odysseus, to avenge himself, forged a letter purporting to come from Priam (q.v.) offering gold to Palamedes to induce him to betray the Greeks; and the gold, by the contrivance of Odysseus, was found in Palamedes' tent. Palamedes was consequently stoned to death. His father Nauplius avenged him. When the Greek fleet was returning home from Troy, he lured it, by false beacons, on the rocks of Euboea.

Paʹlatine, THE (*Palātīnus Mons*), the hill on which the first Roman settlement was made (see *Rome*, § 1, and Pl. 14). It was here that Aeneas was shown by Evander the cave of Lupercal (Aen. viii). In later times the residences of many important Romans were situated there, e.g. Cicero, Hortensius, Crassus, Antony, Clodius, Clodia and her husband. The house of Augustus on the Palatine was enlarged to form the first of the imperial palaces, to be followed by others on the same hill. The name is perhaps derived from Pales (q.v.). The derivation from *palus*, 'marsh', has also been suggested; there was marshy ground between the hill and the Tiber.

Palatine Anthology, see *Anthologies*.

Pā′lēs (*Pálēs*), in Roman religion, a rustic spirit (*numen*), male according to Varro and others, female according to Virgil and Ovid. The latter describes her as silvan (*silvicola*). The *Parilia*, or festival of Pales, was a ritual purification of shepherds and flocks (which were driven through the flames of blazing straw), and an invocation of prosperity in the coming season. At the urban celebration of the festival the ashes of the calves burnt at the *Fordicidia* (q.v.) were sprinkled on the fire. The festival took place on 21 April, and similar ceremonies have been performed, at about the same time of the year, in various parts of eastern Europe down to recent times. Ovid believed, no doubt rightly, that the festival was of older date than Rome itself.

Palimpsest, a manuscript in which the text is written over an effaced earlier text. The practice of writing on the renovated surface of an old manuscript was frequent among the monks of the Middle Ages. Attempts have been made in modern times to recover the ancient writing by means of chemical reagents, sometimes successfully.

Palinō′diā, see *Stesichorus*.

Palinū′rus, in the 'Aeneid' (q.v., Bks. V and VI), the pilot of the ship of Aeneas. He falls into the sea off the coast of Italy, is borne to land, and murdered by the inhabitants. Aeneas finds his ghost in the nether world; it had not crossed the Styx, because his body remained unburied. A headland on the W. coast of Lucania is said to derive its modern name from Palinurus. He has been further immortalized by modern scientists, who have given his name to the sea-crayfish or langouste (*Palinurus vulgaris*).

Pa′lla, see *Clothing*, § 3.

Pa′lladas (*Palladās*), a Greek writer of epigrams who lived at Alexandria in the early 5th c. A.D. He may be said to have been the last Greek poet of any real distinction, for his work, unlike that of later

elegists, is characterized by a fierceness and vigour which arise out of real feeling. A pagan, he saw the ancient world crumbling about him, and he had no hope for the future.

Palla′dius (*Pallādius*), PUBLIUS RUTILIUS TAURUS AEMILIĀNUS, author in the 4th c. A.D. of a Latin treatise on agriculture in fourteen books, compiled from the works of earlier writers. The first book contains general directions on the choice of a site, on farm buildings, the management of poultry, and agricultural implements. The next twelve books deal with the work to be done on the farm in each month. These books are in prose. The last book, on the cultivation of trees, is in elegiacs. The work was rather well known in later times and a translation was made into Middle English.

Palla′dium (*Pallādium*), in Greek and Roman belief, an image of immemorial antiquity on which the safety of a city was thought to depend. It was said to be the image of Pallas (q.v.), whom the Greeks identified with Athene and the Romans with Minerva, and to have fallen from heaven in answer to the prayer of Ilus the founder of Troy. Since Troy could not be captured while it contained this image, Diomedes and Odysseus (or Diomedes alone) carried it off. According to various versions it found its way to Athens, or Argos, or Sparta, or Rome. To this last city it was either brought by Aeneas (Diomedes having only succeeded in stealing an imitation) or surrendered by Diomedes. It was kept there in the Temple of Vesta.

Pa′llās (gen. *Pallados*, to be distinguished from *Pallās*, gen. *Pallantos*), part of the title of the goddess Pallas Athene (see *Athene*). The meaning of the name is unknown. It was explained by various stories, such as that Athene killed a giant, or a maiden, of that name. It was perhaps the name of a goddess of some other religion with whom the Greeks identified Athene. See *Palladium*.

Pa′llās, in Greek mythology, the name of a Titan, a giant, and of an Attic hero, none of them of particular importance. There was also an Arcadian hero of the name, founder of the city Pallanteion. He was the grandfather of Euandros (Evander, q.v.) who figures in the story of the founding of Rome. In Roman legend (see *Aeneid*, Bk. X) another Pallas is the son of Evander. He accompanies Aeneas to the war against the Italians and is killed by Turnus.

Palliā′ta, FĀBULA, in Latin literature, a

term applied to comedies adapted or imitated from Greek comedies, for instance the plays of Plautus and Terence. The name is derived from *pallium*, a Greek cloak.

Palmy'ra, see *Zenobia*.

Pān, the Greek god of flocks and shepherds, variously described as the son of Hermes, or of Zeus, or of some other deity, and represented as partly goat-like in form. He was originally an Arcadian deity, and Mt. Maenalus in Arcadia (where, according to Pausanias, the inhabitants thought they could still hear Pan piping) was sacred to him. He invented the musical pipe of seven reeds, which he named *Syrinx* in honour of the nymph of that name whom he loved and who was changed into a reed in order that she might escape him. Pan also loved the nymphs Pitys and Echo, who when they fled from him were changed respectively into a pine tree and a voice that can only repeat the last words spoken to her. Pan was reputed to be the cause of sudden and groundless fear, especially that felt by travellers in remote and desolate places, known in consequence as Panic fear. It is said (Hdt. vi. 105) that when Phidippides, before the battle of Marathon (see *Persian Wars*), was sent to ask help from Sparta, Pan appeared to him and promised to help the Athenians in battle. In consequence of this, his worship was introduced at Athens after Marathon. By the Romans he was identified with Faunus (q.v.). Plutarch relates that in the reign of Tiberius a ship with passengers was driven near the coast of the isles of Paxi. A loud voice was heard calling to one Thamous that the great god Pan was dead. The emperor ordered an enquiry, but no satisfactory explanation was found. The incident in Christian legend is associated with the birth of Christ. According to S. Reinach, the explanation may be found in the lament of the worshippers of the oriental god Thamuz (see *Adonis*), 'Θαμμοὒζ ὁ πάμμεγας τέθνηκε', overheard and misunderstood by the passengers of a ship while his annual obsequies were being celebrated.

Shelley's 'Hymn of Pan' is an echo of a story that Pan once engaged in a musical contest with Apollo (see *Midas*).

Panae'tius (*Panaitios*) (*c.* 180–*c.* 110 B.C.), of Rhodes, a Greek Stoic philosopher, who came to Rome, was admitted to the friendship of Scipio Aemilianus (q.v.), and accompanied him on a mission to Egypt and Asia. He powerfully influenced the circle of Scipio and through them Roman thought. He returned to Athens, where he directed the Stoic school, and there he

died. He was author of a treatise 'On Duties' (which has not survived), on which Cicero modelled his 'De Officiis'.

Panathēnāē'a (*Panathenaia*), see *Festivals*, § 3.

Panathēnā'icus, see *Isocrates*.

Pancra'tion (*Pagkration*), in Greece, a form of contest combining wrestling with boxing. It was a brutal form of sport, in which almost any method of vanquishing the opponent was allowed. The Pancration was introduced into the Olympian Games (see *Festivals*, § 2) from 648 B.C. It was also included in the Nemean and Isthmian Games.

Pa'ndarus (*Pandaros*), in Greek mythology, son of Lycaon (q.v.) and leader in the Trojan War of the Trojans who lived about the foot of Mt. Ida. It is he who, in 'Iliad' iv, breaks the truce and wounds Menelaus with an arrow. In 'Iliad' v he is slain by Diomedes. The story of his relations with Troilus and Cressida as told by Chaucer and Shakespeare was developed by Chaucer from an episode in the 'Roman de Troie' of Benoît de Sainte-Maure, whose poem is based on Dictys Cretensis and Dares Phrygius (qq.v.).

Pa'ndects (*Pandectae*), see *Justinian*.

Pandi'on (*Pandiōn*), a legendary king of Athens, sometimes described as grandson of Erechtheus (q.v.). He was father of Philomela and Procne (qq.v.).

Pandō'ra (*Pandōrā*), see *Prometheus*.

Panēgy'rici. (1) For the 'Panegyricus' of Isocrates, see under his name. (2) For the Panegyric on Trajan by Pliny see *Pliny the Younger*. (3) A collection of Latin complimentary speeches by rhetoricians of the late 3rd and the 4th cc. A.D. in honour of the emperors of their time, chiefly Maximian, Constantius, Constantine I and II, Julian, and Theodosius. The collection contains also Pliny's panegyric (see (2) above) on which the later speeches were modelled. These are eleven in number and range in date from A.D. 289 to 389. They were composed in the rhetorical schools of Gaul. They are artificial declamations of little literary merit.

Panthe'on or **Pa'ntheon** (L. *Panthēon* or *Panthēum*), at Rome, a splendid building erected by M. Vipsanius Agrippa (q.v.) in 27 B.C., for what purpose is uncertain. The internal niches were decorated with statues of various gods. The walls and arches survive. It was dedicated as a Christian church by Pope Boniface IV in A.D. 609.

Pantomime, a form of dramatic entertainment at Rome of which the name is a purely Roman creation. The themes chosen were almost entirely mythological; the words were sung, while the actor silently danced or acted the roles. The Greek actor Pylades, *c.* 20 B.C., introduced a large choir or orchestra in lieu of a single singer. There was scenery and only one actor (male), who took many parts, wearing the appropriate mask for each. Bathyllus was so popular in this form of drama that his name came to be used for any pantomime actor (cf. Juvenal, vi. 63, where Bathyllus dances Leda). Pantomime became popular at Rome and contributed to the decline of tragedy.

Panya'ssis (*Panuasis* or *Panuassis*) of Halicarnassus, uncle of Herodotus (q.v.) and an epic poet (see *Epic,* § 1). He was put to death about 454 B.C. by the tyrant Lygdamis.

Pā'phos (*Păphos*), see *Cyprus.*

Papi'nian (*Aemilius Păpiniānus*), a famous Roman jurist under Marcus Aurēlius and Septimius Sevērus, probably of African origin. He accompanied Severus to Britain. Imperial tribunals sat at York, and Papinian was on the bench there. He was Prefect of Praetorians from A.D. 205. It is said that when, after the death of Severus, Caracalla murdered his brother Geta, and asked Papinian to defend his action before the Senate, Papinian replied, 'Parricide is not so easy to defend as to commit'. Caracalla had Papinian put to death.

Papinian wrote 37 books of *Quaestiōnēs* and 19 books of *Responsa;* there are many excerpts from them in the 'Digest' of Justinian (q.v.).

Papȳ'ri, DISCOVERIES OF. It was not until the 19th c. that it became known that the dry sands of Egypt had preserved large numbers of papyrus rolls (see *Books,* § 2). Some fifty rolls had been found in 1778, but all except one were carelessly destroyed, and that one of no literary importance. But a great number were discovered in the course of the last century, some in tombs, designedly buried with their owners, others in rubbish heaps where they had been thrown away. Many of these rolls contained only domestic documents, others contained classical texts, some of these written on the reverse side of a papyrus whose face had been used for farm accounts or some such private purpose. The first considerable find in the century was in 1820; these were domestic documents, but they aroused the hope of more valuable discoveries. This was encouraged in 1821 when the 'Bankes Homer' containing the greater part of Book xxiv of the 'Iliad' (now in the

British Museum) was bought by William Bankes at Elephantinē (near Assouan). Several papyri containing portions of Homer have since been secured, including the 'Harris Homer' (a large part of Il. xviii) found in 1849–50 in the Fayoum, and a manuscript in large uncials of part of Il. ii recovered by Flinders Petrie at Hawara in 1889. Three orations of Hyperides (q.v.) were acquired in 1847, and, somewhat later (1856), his funeral oration on Leosthenes. In 1889–90 Flinders Petrie discovered that some cartonnage coffins from a necropolis in the Fayoum were composed of layers of papyri pasted together. These when separated were found to contain documents of the 3rd c. B.C., including fragments of Plato's 'Phaedo', and of the lost play 'Antiope' of Euripides. In 1890 the learned world was startled by the discovery of a manuscript of the lost treatise of Aristotle on the 'Constitution of Athens' (acquired by the British Museum). It was written on the back of a set of farm accounts of a bailiff in the district of Hermopolis in the reign of Vespasian, in four different hands, probably a copy made for the private use of the owner. Another important discovery was that of the Mimes of Herodas (q.v.) in 1891. In 1896–7 a vast collection of thousands of papyri was found at Behnesa (the ancient Oxyrhynchus) by Messrs. Grenfell and Hunt. These included the *Logia* or 'Sayings of Our Lord' and fragments of classical authors. Further finds at the same place in 1902–3 and 1906 brought to light many fragments of lost Greek classics, among them the 'Paeans' of Pindar. In 1896 were acquired papyri containing a large part of the odes of Bacchylides (q.v.), now in the British Museum, and in 1902 of the 'Persae' of Timotheus (q.v.), a manuscript assigned to the 4th c. B.C., perhaps the oldest Greek literary manuscript in existence (now in Berlin). Other discoveries have revealed to us previously unknown fragments of Sappho, Corinna, and Menander.

A vast number of papyri have been recovered containing private letters and accounts, legal documents, and administrative documents; these have thrown a flood of light on the social and economic life of Ptolemaic, Roman, and Byzantine Egypt, on Hellenistic and Roman Law, and on the administrative system. Among the important papyri of this class may be mentioned that containing the Letter of Claudius in reply to the congratulations which Alexandria had sent him on his accession in A.D. 41 and to the apologies of the same city for disturbances that had arisen with the Jewish inhabitants.

Another contains the *Constitutio Antōnini-dna*, an edict of the emperor Caracalla of 212, conferring Roman citizenship on all *peregrini* in the Roman empire with certain exceptions.

Papyri have also been found at Herculaneum, but in too charred a condition to be of much value. This recalls the wish expressed by Wordsworth in 1819 :

> O ye who patiently explore
> The wreck of Herculanean lore,
> What rapture! could ye seize
> Some Theban fragment, or unrol
> One precious, tender-hearted scroll
> Of pure Simonides.

Papy'rus, see *Books*, § 2. For the price of papyrus, see *Books*, § 3.

Para'basis, see *Comedy*, § 2.

Pa'raloi, see *Athens*, § 3.

Pa'ralos, the name of one of the two warships kept by the Athenians for ceremonial and exceptional purposes.

Pa'rcae, see *Fates*.

Parentā'lia, at Rome, the days of sacrifice in connexion with the dead, beginning on 13 Feb., and reaching their climax in the *Feralia* on 21 Feb. During this period magistrates laid aside the insignia of their office, temples were closed, marriages forbidden, and each family carried out rites at the tombs of its dead members. The concluding ceremony, on 22 Feb., was a family reunion and worship of the *Lar Familiāris* (see *Lares*), an acknowledgement of the subsisting relation between the dead and living members of the family (contrast *Lemures*); it was called the *Caristia*.

Pare'nthesis, the insertion of a clause or sentence into a passage where it is not grammatically essential, e.g.

> Haud procul inde citae Mettum in diversa
>   quadrigae
> distulerant (at tu dictis, Albane, maneres!),
> raptabatque viri mendacis viscera Tullus
> per silvam.   .
>   Virg. Aen. viii. 642–5.

Parian Chronicle, see *Marmor Parium.*

Pari'lia, see *Pales.*

Pa'ris, (1) in Greek mythology, a son of Priam and Hecuba (qq.v.), called *Alexandros* for his valour. He was exposed when a child because of a prophecy that he should bring destruction on Troy, but was brought up by shepherds. He fell in love with the nymph Oenone, but deserted her, and carried off Helen (q.v.), the wife of Menelaus, thus bringing about the Trojan

War (q.v.). In the course of this he was wounded with a poisoned arrow by Philoctetes (q.v.), sought the aid of Oenone, but died before she could give it. See also *Paris (Judgement of)*. (2) The name of two popular pantomimic dancers, one of whom was executed under Nero (A.D. 67), the other under Domitian (A.D. 87). For one of them Statius (q.v.) wrote his libretto 'Agave'.

Paris, JUDGEMENT OF, the subject of a Greek myth. At the marriage-feast of Peleus and Thetis (qq.v.), Eris (Strife) threw down a golden apple, inscribed 'For the fairest'. Hera, Athene, and Aphrodite (qq.v.) all claimed it, and the contention was referred to Paris (q.v.), the handsomest of mortal men. Hera offered him greatness, Athena success in war, Aphrodite the loveliest woman for his wife. Paris awarded the apple to Aphrodite, and with her help carried off Helen (q.v.). It was thus the Judgement of Paris that originated the Trojan War, but this myth appears to be unknown to Homer.

Parme'nidēs of Elea, a philosopher born probably about 510 B.C. He was a man of rank and is said to have given laws to his city. According to tradition he was a pupil of Xenophanes (q.v.) and is said by Plato to have conversed late in life with Socrates (see under *Plato*, § 2, for the dialogue 'Parmenides', in which he is one of the chief interlocutors). He was the founder of the Eleatic school of philosophy and expounded his doctrine in a poem composed of a prologue and two books of hexameters, the first dealing with the reality, the second with illusion. The real universe is a single, indivisible, eternal, unchanging whole, and the only object of knowledge; what is mutable and perishable, and phenomena such as motion, are illusions, and about them we can only have conjectures. Only fragments of this work survive. They display the philosophical enthusiasm of the author and his recourse to argument in support of his opinions, in lieu of the bare assertions of the earlier philosophers.

Parmenides, a dialogue by Plato (q.v., § 2).

Parna'ssus (*Parnassos*), a lofty mountain, whose summit, a few miles north of Delphi, rises to about 8,000 ft. On it were the Corycian Cave and the Castalian spring (qq.v.) and the mountain was associated with the worship of Apollo and the Muses. It was often referred to as having two summits, one sacred to Apollo, the other to Dionysus. The name is sometimes used allusively in modern English with reference to literature, or as the title of a collection of poems.

Pa′rodos, see *Tragedy*, § 3, and *Comedy*, § 2.

Paroe′miac, see *Metre*, § 2 (*ad fin.*).

Paronoma′siā, a play on words. Quintilian gives as an example, 'Amari jucundum est, si curetur ne quid insit amari'.

Parrha′sius (*Parrhasios*), of Ephesus, a famous Greek painter, who flourished about 400 B.C. He is said by Pliny to have been especially skilful in depicting character by the face. The story of his contest with Zeuxis (q.v.) in producing illusion is well known. Zeuxis painted some grapes so perfectly that birds came to peck at them and the victory seemed to be his. He then called upon Parrhasius to draw back the curtain which concealed the latter's picture. But the curtain itself turned out to be painted by Parrhasius. Whereupon Zeuxis confessed himself defeated. Zeuxis had deceived the birds, but Parrhasius had deceived Zeuxis.

Parthe′nion or PARTHENEI′ON, a Greek *choral lyric* (q.v.), a processional hymn sung by a choir of maidens (whence the name). It was semi-religious, semi-profane, and of a less solemn character than the *paean* and *hyporchema* (qq.v.). Parthenia were composed by Alcman, Simonides of Ceos, Bacchylides, and Pindar (qq.v.). We possess a considerable part of a *parthenion* by Alcman; in this, after the singing of a mythological tale about Heracles, the members of the chorus fall to bantering one another.

Pa′rthenon (*Parthenōn*, 'Temple of the Maiden'), the temple of Athene Parthenos ('the maiden') on the Acropolis at Athens, erected under the administration of Pericles between 447 and 438 B.C. The architects were Ictinus and Callicratēs, and the work was supervised by Phidias (q.v.). It was built of marble from Pentelicus (q.v.) and was surrounded by a colonnade of forty-six Doric columns, about 35 ft. high. Slight curves in the main lines of the structure skilfully prevented an appearance of monotony. The platform of the temple was 225 Attic feet long by 100 Attic feet wide. The cella (see *Temples*, § 1) was about 100 feet in length and was known as the *Hecatompedon*, the name of the earlier temple which the Parthenon had replaced (the title 'Parthenon' applied strictly only to the chamber west of the cella, the *opisthodomos*, see *Temples*, § 1). The cella faced eastward and contained the great statue, in gold and ivory, of the goddess by Phidias. The further adornment of the temple with sculptures under the direc-

tion of Phidias continued until 432. These consisted of ninety-two metopes (square panels along the architrave) representing in high relief the battles of the gods and the giants, the victory of the Athenians over the Amazons, the struggle of the Centaurs and the Lapithae, and the Trojan War. The eastern and western pediments (the triangular spaces forming the gables) represented the birth of the goddess and her struggle with Poseidon for the possession of Attica. Round the outside of the walls of the cella ran a frieze, 524 ft. long, representing in low relief the Panathenaic procession (see *Festivals*, § 2). This frieze and some of the metopes are now in the British Museum. They were acquired by Lord Elgin when envoy to the Porte in 1799–1803 and sold to the British Government.

We have in inscriptions fragmentary accounts for the building of the Parthenon and the making of Phidias's statue. Thus the accounts for the former for 434 show a receipt of 25,000 drachmas from the Treasurers of the goddess, and 2677 drachmas for sale of surplus gold and ivory. The accounts for the latter for a year (about 440) show 100 talents received, 87 talents paid for gold, and 2 talents for ivory. Some 700 talents were spent in nine years on the building of the Parthenon, and 900 talents on the gold and ivory in seven years.

In the *opisthodomos* (see *Temples*, § 1) of the Parthenon was kept not only the treasure of Athena, but also the public treasure of Athens, and the treasure of the Delian Confederacy (see *Athens*, § 11).

The temple remained standing, converted first into a church, then into a mosque, until 1687 when, in the course of a siege of the Acropolis by a Venetian force, it was partially destroyed by the explosion of the gunpowder stored there by the Turkish garrison.

Parthe′nopē, see *Sirens*. Parthenope was the name of a Greek settlement from Cumae on the site where Naples now stands.

Partitiō′nēs Ōrātō′riae, see *Cicero*, § 5.

Pāsi′phaē, see *Minos*.

Pastoral poetry, see *Bucolic.*

Patri′cians, members of certain distinguished families at Rome, a privileged class, as distinguished from the *Plebeians* (q.v.). The relationship between patricians and plebeians is still matter of dispute. These are the three principal views on the subject:

(1) The patricians were originally the only citizens of Rome and they alone had *gentes* and *curiae* (see *Rome*, § 2). As Rome grew in power a large number of free men collected in the city who were outside the

original system. Some were attached to the patrician *gentes* as clients (q.v.). Others came under the protection of the king. They became an important body known as the *plebs*, and they grew in number.

(2) The distinction was originally one of race. Patricians represent an aristocracy of invaders (Sabines). The *plebs* represent the mass of the old population.

(3) The patricians were an aristocracy created by selection by the kings and afterwards by co-optation into the Senate. It was originally an aristocracy of office, but it was closed at some period and converted into one of birth.

For the struggle of the plebeians to win social and political equality with the patricians, see *Rome*, §§ 3 and 6.

Patro'clus (*Patroklos* or *Patroklês*), in the 'Iliad', son of Menoetius, and the favourite companion of Achilles. For his story, see *Iliad*.

Paul the Silen'tiary (*Paulus Silentiārius*), an officer of the imperial household of Justinian) (*fl. c.* A.D. 540) was the author of a Greek poem on the church of St. Sophia at Constantinople, of some architectural interest; also of some hundred epigrams in the Greek Anthology (q.v.).

Pauly-Wissowa. The great German classical encyclopaedia, known as the 'Real-Encyclopädie' of Pauly-Wissowa had its origin in a work by Pauly (d. 1845) published in 1839–66. A new edition, edited by G. Wissowa (d. 1931), W. Kroll, and others, was begun in 1894 and is still incomplete. The work endeavours to cover the whole of classical antiquity in the widest sense (geography and topography, history and biography, history of literature, mythology and worship, archaeology and history of art). The articles (some of them veritable treatises) are by various contributors, nearly all of them German.

Pausa'nias (*Pausāniās*), (1) regent of Sparta from 479 B.C., in command of the Greek forces at Plataea (see *Persian Wars*). In subsequent operations against the Persians he captured Byzantium, and became notorious for his arrogance and misuse of authority. He was also suspected of entering into secret relations with Xerxes. The Spartans recalled him in 477. He was tried, but not convicted of anything very serious and returned to Byzantium, whence he was driven by Cimon (q.v.), and lived at Colōnae in the Troad. Reports that he was intriguing there led to his being once more recalled to Sparta, but it was difficult to find evidence against him until a messenger to whom Pausanias had entrusted a letter for the Persian Artabazus showed it to the Ephors. Pausanias was walled up in the sanctuary where he had taken refuge. We have a life of him by Nepos.

(2) The author of an extant 'Description of Hellas' (*Hellados Periēgēsis*), who appears from passages in it to have been a native of the region about Mt. Sipylus in Lȳdia, and to have written in the second half of the 2nd c. A.D. His work is a guidebook written for tourists, in which, taking in succession various parts of Greece, he enumerates the objects in them most worthy to be seen, especially statues, pictures, tombs, and sanctuaries, with their legends, derivations of names, anecdotes, and historical digressions. He mentions villages, rivers, and roads met with on the way, records curious customs and superstitions, and occasionally refers to the scenery and natural products of the regions that he describes. He notices, for instance, the honey of Hymettus, the bustards seen about the Phōcian Cēphīsus, the white blackbirds of Mt. Cyllēnē, and the oaks, cork-trees, and great tortoises of Arcadia. But in general he is not interested in the economic aspects of the country or in its inhabitants. What he tells us is mostly based on his own travels; his historical information appears to be in the main reliable and his general accuracy is frequently attested by the remains of the monuments he describes. He is frank about reputed marvels, such as the trout of the Aroanius, which he admits he did not hear sing like thrushes (which they were said to do) though he waited by the river till sundown. He applies some degree of criticism to the stories he relates. Of the two about the acquisition of the body of a Triton preserved at Tanagra, he rejects the tale that the monster had been killed in single combat by Dionysus, in favour of the less pretentious explanation that it had been lured ashore by a bowl of wine, and decapitated as it lay drunk on the beach. He tells some interesting things about the paintings of Polygnotus and the statues of Myron and Phidias, but has little to say of Praxiteles and the later sculptors. He rises to a restrained enthusiasm about the Propylaea, the theatre of Epidaurus, and the temple of Bassae, the ruins of which enable us to approve his judgement. His work is simple, unpretentious, and uninspired. It is in ten books, dealing with (1) Attica and Megara; (2) Corinth and Argolis; (3) Lacōnia; (4) Messēnia; (5 and 6) Ēlis; (7) Achaia; (8) Arcadia; (9) Boeōtia; (10) Phōcis.

Peace (*Eirēnē*, L. *Pax*), a comedy by Aristophanes, produced at the Great Dionysia in 421 B.C. It gained the second prize.

Cleon and Brasidas (qq.v.) had recently died, and negotiations for the Peace of Nicias were nearly complete. Aristophanes anticipates their success. Trygaios, an Athenian vine-grower, who with his family is suffering from the food-shortage, decides to imitate Bellerophon on Pegasus, and ride to heaven on a gigantic beetle from Mt. Etna, in search of rolls for supper. The voyage is successfully accomplished, and he finds Hermes at the door and the War-god (*Polemos*) in charge, for Zeus and the other gods have left Olympus in utter disgust with the Greeks. The War-god has buried Peace in a well and is preparing to bray up all the Greek States in a mortar. While he is looking for a pestle, Trygaios and the Greeks whom he has summoned (particularly the farmers), having bribed Hermes, draw Peace out of the well and return with her to Greece. General jubilation follows (except on the part of manufacturers of armaments), and preparations are made for the wedding of Trygaios and Peace.

Peace, On the, the title of speeches by (1) Isocrates (q.v.); (2) Demosthenes (see *Demosthenes* (2), § 5 (c)).

Peace of Nicias, see *Nicias* and *Peloponnesian War*.

Pe'diakoi, see *Athens*, § 3.

Pĕ'gasus (*Pēgasos*), in Greek mythology, a winged horse sprung from the blood of Medusa when Perseus cut off her head (see *Gorgons*). The fountain Hippocrene, on Mt. Helicon in Boeotia, sacred to the Muses, was said to have been produced by a stamp of the hoof of Pegasus. It was with the aid of this horse that Bellerophon (q.v.) destroyed the Chimaera and attempted to fly to heaven.

Peiraeus, see *Piraeus*.

Peiri'thous (*Peirithoos*), see *Centaurs* and *Theseus*.

Peisistratus, see *Pisistratus*.

Pelasgians, see *Migrations and Dialects*.

Pĕ'leūs, in Greek mythology, son of Aeacus (q.v.) and king of Phthiā. Legend thus connected him both with Aegina and with Thessaly; his name appears to mean 'man of Pelion'. He went to Phthia, being guilty of some murder, and there Acastus, the king, purified him. Hippolyte, wife of Acastus, fell in love with Peleus, and being repulsed by him, denounced him to her husband. Acastus contrived to abandon Peleus asleep on Mt. Pelion, having first removed a wonderful knife which Hephaestus had given him. But Chiron restored the knife and Peleus was able to overcome the wild beasts that threatened his life.

He was married to the goddess Thetis (see *Nereus*) in the following circumstances. It was fated that Thetis should have a son more powerful than his father. Zeus, who loved Thetis, knew that he would be in danger from one of his sons, but did not know from which. The secret was known to Prometheus (q.v.), who refused to reveal it until released from his captivity. Thetis was then married to Peleus a mortal, so that her son might not be immortal. This son was Achilles (q.v.).

Pe'lias (*Peliās*), see *Tyro* and *Argonauts*.

Pĕ'lion, a wooded mountain near the coast of Thessaly. Otus (q.v.), and Ephialtes, according to Greek mythology, heaped it on Ossa, and Ossa on Olympus, in their attempt to overthrow the gods. About it lived the Centaurs.

Pe'lla, the capital of the Macedonian kings. It stood near the modern town of Yenidje, near the lower course of the Vardar. Except for a few fragments of marble it has utterly disappeared, though a fountain in the neighbourhood is said still to bear the name of Pel.

Pelo'pia (*Pelopiā*), daughter of Thyestes and mother of Aegisthus. See *Pelops*.

Pelo'pidas (*Pelopidās*), a great Theban commander, who first came into prominence when in the winter of 379–378 B.C. he restored democratic rule at Thebes. With six confederates dressed up as women he slew the pro-Spartan polemarchs who with the support of a Spartan garrison were tyrannizing over Thebes, and drove out the Spartans. He was one of the commanders at the Theban victory of Leuctra (see *Sparta*, § 4) and subsequently extended Theban influence in the N. of Greece by three expeditions to Thessaly, where he brought Larissa and the N. of Thessaly under the Theban protectorate, settled the struggle of pretenders to the throne of Macedon, and sent the young Philip of Macedon to Thebes as a hostage. In 364, in an expedition against Alexander of Pherae (q.v.), an ally at that time of Athens, he was, though victorious, killed at the battle of Cynoscephalae. He was the friend and colleague of Epaminondas (q.v.), and together they brought Thebes to the zenith of her power. There is a life of Pelopidas by Nepos.

Pe'loponnese (*Peloponnēsos*), 'island of Pelops', perhaps deriving its name from the mythical Pelops (q.v.), was the southern part of Greece, connected with Central Greece by the Isthmus of Corinth. Its chief political divisions were Argos, Laconia, Messēnia, Ēlis, Achāia, and Arcadia.

Peloponne'sian War, THE (431–404 B.C.),

was in its more prominent features a struggle between Athens, a democratic State and a sea-power, which had converted the Delian Confederacy (designed to resist the Persians) into an empire under her own rule, and most of the States of the Peloponnese together with Boeotia and headed by Sparta, an oligarchical and conservative power, whose land army was the most efficient military force of the day. The truest explanation of the conflict, according to Thucydides, was the rise of Athens to greatness, which caused the Spartans to become afraid of them. A deeper cause, according to modern theory, lay in the commercial rivalry of Athens and Corinth. The first ten years of the war (known as the Archidāmian War, after the Spartan king who led the invasions of Attica) were indecisive, the Spartan forces merely ravaging Attica, while Athens, conforming to the policy of Pericles (q.v.), risked no land engagement and confined herself to naval operations. A great plague in 430 intensified her ordeal. Her chief success was the defeat of the Spartans at Pylos (425) and the destruction or capture of 420 Spartan hoplites on Sphactēria (the island that almost blocks the bay of Pylos, famous in later days as the scene of the battle of Navarino). In 424 Athens moreover captured Nisaea and Pēgae, the ports of Megara. Important operations also took place, first in Boeotia, where an Athenian attempt to win over the country was defeated at Dēlium (424) in the biggest battle of the Archidamian War; second in Thrace and Chalcidice, where Potidaea, which had revolted from the Athenians, submitted to them after a costly siege in 430. The energy of the Spartan commander Brasidas secured the adhesion to the Peloponnesian cause of a number of Thracian cities, including Amphipolis; the historian Thucydides, then in command of an Athenian squadron, arrived too late to retain it (424). In 422 Cleon led an expedition for its recapture. He was defeated and killed, but Brasidas also fell in the battle; and thus were removed the two chief opponents of peace. The Peace of Nicias was concluded in 421. Its terms were unsatisfactory to Corinth, Megara, and Boeotia, and it was only partially observed. Under the influence of Alcibiades (q.v.) Athens entered into alliances with Argos (which had taken no part in the Archidamian War, having a treaty of neutrality with Sparta which ran out in 421), Elis, and Mantinea; the allies attacked Epidaurus and advanced on Tegea, and Sparta moved against them. A great battle was fought at Mantinea in 418, in which the Spartans were victorious.

Argos abandoned the Athenian alliance and Athens was left once more isolated. In 415 Athens undertook, again under the influence of Alcibiades, the great Sicilian Expedition, designed to curb the growing power of Syracuse (q.v.), to win a footing in Sicily, and to obtain complete control of the sea. While the expedition was being prepared the Athenians were thrown into painful excitement by the discovery one morning that nearly all the Hermae (q.v.) in the city had been mutilated. The sacrilege was regarded as ominous for the expedition, and Alcibiades was brought under suspicion. Nevertheless it was decided that the expedition should sail and that his trial should be postponed. Thucydides has described in a striking passage (VI. xxx) the mingled feelings of hope and apprehension with which the Athenians went down to the Piraeus at dawn to see the departure of the fleet; but their courage revived at the sight of its strength, and the galleys raced to Aegina when they reached the open sea. The Athenians made the mistake of appointing, along with Alcibiades and Lamachus, Nicias to command the expedition, a man of cautious and irresolute temper, who was opposed to the whole adventure. The operations were not conducted with the promptitude and vigour that such a case demanded, and when the Syracusans obtained the assistance of Gylippus, an energetic Spartan general, the chances of success turned definitely against Athens. Despite the arrival of a relieving force under Demosthenes, the expedition ended in 413 in the destruction of the Athenian fleet and army, and the exhaustion of the Athenian finances. Most of the Athenian allies in the Aegean (led by Chios) shortly afterwards (412) revolted from her. But Athens built a new fleet, and the war continued for another eight years, in consequence of the incapacity of the Spartan commanders and the extraordinary energy of Athens, especially under the leadership of Alcibiades, who played (on both sides) a part of great importance in the war (see *Alcibiades*). Sparta had occupied Decelea (q.v.) in 413, thereby inflicting great suffering on the Athenians. She also obtained the assistance of Persia, even agreeing to surrender the Greek cities of Asia Minor to Persian rule. The NE. of the Aegean became the chief theatre of war, the Spartans hoping to deprive Athens of the main source of her food-supplies. Athenian naval victories at Cynossēma (411) and Cȳzicus (410) for a time prevented the Spartans from attaining this end. But in 407 Cyrus the younger (q.v.) was appointed Persian satrap of Asia Minor and threw his whole weight on the Spartan side, co-operating with the regent Lysander, who this year commanded the Spartan fleet. The Athenian fleet was defeated at Notium, and Alcibiades, who had been appointed strategus with full responsibility for the war, retired to exile. Even so, the Athenians won one more victory next year (when Lysander was no longer in command) at Arginūsae. But the end came with the Athenian defeat at Aegospotami (405). In 404, after a siege, left without ships, money, or allies, Athens was obliged to accept Sparta's terms, and become virtually the subject-ally of the victor. See *Demosthenes* (1), *Nicias, Cleon, Alcibiades, Lysander*; also the article on *Athens*, § 5. The principal authority for the greater part of the Peloponnesian War (including the Sicilian Expedition) is the history of Thucydides; for the latter years of the war, Xenophon ('Hellenica').

For what is sometimes known as the 'First Peloponnesian War' (459–446) see *Athens*, § 4.

Pe'lops, in Greek mythology, son of Tantalus (q.v.). When he was a child, his father killed him and served his flesh to the gods at a banquet, to see if they could tell it from that of some animal. Demeter (q.v.), absorbed in her grief, ate part of the shoulder, but the other gods detected the nature of the dish. Pelops was restored to life, the missing shoulder was replaced by one of ivory, and Tantalus was punished in Hades. Pelops, when grown to manhood, presented himself as suitor for Hippodamía, daughter of Oenomáus, king of Elis. The condition of winning her was that he should outdistance Oenomaus in a chariot race. If he was caught, Oenomaus would spear him. Pelops bribed

Myrtilus, the king's driver, to take out the linch-pin of his master's chariot, and so won the race and the bride. But he refused to give Myrtilus the promised reward, and threw him into the sea. This murder was the origin of the curse that fell upon the house of Pelops. The sons of Pelops were Atreus and Thyestes, in whom the curse was manifested. Atreus was king of Mycenae. Thyestes seduced Aërope his wife. Thereupon Atreus banished Thyestes, but later recalled him and set before him a dish containing the flesh of Thyestes' own children. Thyestes fled in horror, invoking a curse on the house of Atreus. He now, by his own daughter Pelopia, became father of Aegisthus, who carried on the feud. Aegisthus was exposed at birth by his mother, but brought up by shepherds and adopted by Atreus, the father of Agamemnon and Menelaus (qq.v.). Atreus sent Aegisthus to kill Thyestes, but Thyestes recognized him as his own son, and the two contrived the death of Atreus. When Agamemnon led the Greek expedition to Troy and left the kingdom of Mycenae in the care of his wife Clytemnestra, Aegisthus seduced her, and joined with her in murdering Agamemnon on his return. Later, Orestes, with the help of his sister Electra, avenged their father Agamemnon by slaying Aegisthus and Clytemnestra (see the articles on the tragedies *Oresteia, Orestes,* and *Electra*).

The above legend (except the murder of Agamemnon) is not known to Homer and Hesiod. According to the former, the kingdom passes naturally from Pelops to Atreus, from Atreus to Thyestes, and from Thyestes to Agamemnon. According to the more elaborate legend the genealogy of the house of Pelops is as follows:

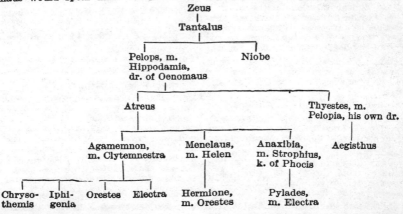

Pe′ltasts (*Peltastai*), see *Army*, § 1.

Penā′tēs, in Roman religion, the spirits (*numina*) of the store-cupboard (*penus*), who had their place in the *atrium* of every early Roman house (see *Houses*), and were regarded, together with the Lares (q.v.), as protectors of the house. There were also State Penates, protectors of the Roman commonwealth, to whom (with Jupiter) the Roman magistrates took oath. According to Virgil, Aeneas had brought these to Italy from Troy. Indeed Virgil conceives not only Rome and Troy as having their Penates, but also Carthage and other cities. He even speaks of the bees, alone among animals, having their Penates, or fixed abode (Georg. iv. 155). The Penates of the household, at first vague spirits, came to be identified with various gods of the State religion, Jupiter, Juno, Ceres. The worship of the domestic Penates and Lares centered in the family meal. A portion was then set aside and thrown on the flames of the hearth for the gods. Sometimes statuettes representing them would be brought from the shrine (*larārium*) and placed on the table in token of their presence at the meal. There was a shrine of the national Penates by the side of the Via Sacra near the Forum. Augustus gave them an altar in his own palace. The Palatine thus became the centre of a national cult. Moreover the hearth-gods of the Julian gens (descended from Aeneas who had introduced them) were thus identified with the gods of the State.

Pēne′lopē (also *Pēnelopeiā*), in the 'Odyssey', daughter of Icarius of Sparta, and wife of Odysseus. She is represented as a faithful wife, prudent and resourceful in the difficult position in which she is placed by her husband's long absence, but showing lack of decision: she 'neither refused the hated bridal [with one of the suitors] nor had a heart to make an end'.

Pēnē′us (*Pēneios*), the principal river in Thessaly; it flows through the beautiful vale of Tempe between Mts. Olympus and Ossa.

Pentakosiomedi′mnoi, see *Athens*, § 2.

Penta′meter, a verse of five units (*metra*); see *Metre*, §§ 1 and 2. In practice the term is applied only to the elegiac pentameter.

Pentā′thlon, in the Greek games, a contest including five events, wrestling, long jump, running, throwing the discus, and throwing the javelin. The winner of most events was the victor.

Pentēcontaë′tia, a term applied to the fifty years of Greek history between the Persian and Peloponnesian Wars (480–430 B.C.), the period of the growth of the maritime empire of Athens and of her greatest literary and artistic eminence. This was the age of Pericles, of the great tragedians, of Anaxagoras, Zeno, Protagoras; of Polygnotus and Phidias and the building of the Parthenon. It was in various parts of Greece the age of Pindar, Herodotus, Hippocrates, Polyclitus, Empedocles, and Democritus. Socrates, Thucydides, and Aristophanes grew to manhood during this period.

Despite all this, it is not easy to reconstruct the detailed history of these years, owing to the lack of contemporary literary sources. Apart from a few chapters of Thucydides, some scattered references in Herodotus, and what can be gathered from works like the 'Oresteia' and fragments of the early comedians, we are entirely dependent on later writers for literary records. The archaeological and numismatic study of the period is, however, both flourishing and fruitful. The best collection of material is still that by G. F. Hill, 'Sources'; cf. also M. N. Tod, 'Greek Historical Inscriptions', vol. i.

Pente′licus (*Pentelikos*), a mountain about 3,600 ft. high, which closes the Athenian plain on its NE. side, some ten miles from Athens. It was famous for its quarries of marble. This is of a close-grained milky whiteness, in contrast to the more sparkling marble of Paros (q.v.). It weathers to the beautiful golden brown now to be seen on the columns of the Parthenon. It was largely used for sculpture and architecture in the earlier times, but from the 4th c. Parian was preferred.

Penthesilē′a (*Penthesilēia*), see *Achilles*.

Pe′nthēus, a legendary king of Thebes, grandson of Cadmus (q.v.); see *Bacchae*.

Pe′plos, see *Clothing*, § 1 and *Festivals*, § 3.

Perdiccas, see *Macedonia*, § 3.

Pe′rdix, see *Daedalus*.

Pe′regrine (*Peregrinus*), see *Lucian*.

Pe′rgamum (*Pergamon*), originally a hill-fortress above the valley of the Cäicus in the NW. of Asia Minor. In the 3rd c. it became the capital of the Attalids (q.v.) and was transformed by them into a splendid and picturesque city. For its importance as a literary centre and as the place where parchment was first used extensively for books, see *Books, Ancient*, § 5.

Peri Hi′ppikēs, see *Horsemanship*.

Peri Hu′psous, see *Longinus on the Sublime*.

Peria'nder (*Periandros*), a famous tyrant of Corinth, who succeeded his father Cypselus (q.v.) and ruled *c.* 625–*c.* 585 B.C. According to Herodotus (v. 92), Periander having consulted Thrasybulus, tyrant of Miletus, how he might rule securely, the latter by way of answer took the messenger into a field of corn, and cut off the ears of corn that were taller than the rest. Though Periander may have been a stern ruler, he acquired a reputation for justice and experience, and was included among the Seven Sages (q.v.) of Greece. He is said to have encouraged music and poetry, and Arion (q.v.) was received at his court.

Historically, there can be no doubt that Periander was a very important person, with a reputation that was virtually international. He was called on to mediate between Lydia and Miletus, and again between Athens and Mitylene. He subdued Corinth's rebellious colony Corcyra, sending his son Lycophron (q.v.) as its viceroy, and made Corinth's hold over north-western Greece secure. It was in his reign that Potidaea was planted in Chalcidice, and Sollidamnus on the Epirote coast north of Corcyra. These two towns marked either end of the trade route along which the Romans were later to build the Via Egnatia. Corinthian trade in general owed very much of its importance about the year 600 to the efforts of its tyrant, not the least of whose works was the opening up of the silver mines at Demastium in the NW. Periander became more of a real tyrant than his father had been, but there can be little doubt of the great benefits he conferred on the city he ruled.

Pe'ricles (*Periklēs*) (*c.* 500–429 B.C.), the great Athenian statesman, was an Alcmaeonid (q.v.), the son of Xanthippus (q.v.), and a man of powerful character, sober, incorruptible, and reserved. He was elected strategus, it appears continuously, from 443 to 429; but long before this, from about 460, he dominated Athens by his persuasive oratory, by his character, and by his policy, which commended itself to the majority of the citizens. So great was his authority that the period of his power came to be known as the Age of Pericles, and Thucydides says that under him Athens, though nominally a democracy, was in fact ruled by its first citizen. He was influenced by the doctrines of Anaxagoras (q.v.) and the political theorist Damon of Oa. He associated with men of culture (Protagoras, Phidias, Sophocles, Herodotus) and took for his lifelong companion the celebrated *hetaera* or courtesan Aspasia of Miletus, a very accomplished woman. His political object was to make Athens an ideal democracy in which there should be equilibrium between the interests of the State and of the individual citizens, and which should be the leader and the school of Greece. He appears to have sought to draw all Greece together in some measure of political union, but the attempt was checked by the conservatism and jealousy of Sparta and the spirit of independence of the Greek States generally. This having failed, Athens under the guidance of Pericles adopted an imperialistic policy, and the Delian Confederacy, created to oppose the Persian inroads, was converted into an Athenian empire (see *Athens*, § 3). Pericles extended its influence to the Euxine (see *Cleruchs*), and himself penetrated to the Cimmerian Bosporus in 437, after having in 439 subdued the insurrection of Samos. To what extent Pericles was responsible for the policy that involved Athens in war with Sparta, Corinth, Aegina, and Boeotia during the period 459–446 is not known. When the inevitable revolt of the Greek States against Athenian domination broke out in 431 (see *Peloponnesian War*), Pericles dictated a policy for Athens calculated to meet the Spartan superiority on land, but involving grave sufferings for the population of Attica. His adversaries, fortified by the resentment that these sufferings caused, brought against him a charge of malversation of public funds, and Pericles was condemned (430) to a fine of fifty talents. None the less he was re-elected strategus, but died the following year, a grievous loss to Athens at a moment when his sound judgement was needed for the successful conduct of the war.

Pericles is also famous for the great public works constructed at Athens under his direction, notably the Parthenon and Propylaea (qq.v.), and the additional 'Long Wall' between Athens and the Piraeus. These had the economic advantage that they provided a great deal of much-needed employment for the poorer citizens.

The chief opponents of Pericles, during his career, were Cimon (q.v.), who favoured a policy of good relations with Sparta, and Thucydides the son of Melesias. The latter in 443 brought against Pericles a charge of misappropriating the money of the Delian Confederacy to the construction of splendid buildings in Athens. The Athenians decided in favour of Pericles against both his opponents by ostracizing them.

There is a life of Pericles by Plutarch. There are also references of some interest in contemporary comedians; see Pickard-Cambridge, 'Comic Fragments'.

The famous 'Funeral Oration' of Pericles delivered at the celebration of the Athenians who fell in the first year of the Peloponnesian War, is given by Thucydides (ii. 35–46); but to what extent this reproduces the actual words of Pericles we do not know. In English literature he figures prominently in the 'Pericles and Aspasia' of W. S. Landor (1836), a collection of imaginary letters relating to the period of the union of Pericles and Aspasia. There is also among Landor's 'Imaginary Conversations' one between Pericles and Sophocles.

In deference to Pericles, his son by Aspasia, the younger Pericles, though of illegitimate birth, was granted citizenship in the last year of his father's life. He was strategus in 406, and was executed after Arginusae (q.v.).

Perikeiro'menē, see *Menander*.

Pe'riochae, see *Livy*.

Perioe'ci (*Perioikoi*, 'dwellers round'), in Laconia, were free inhabitants, citizens of their own cities, but not of Sparta (q.v.). They managed their own local affairs, but their cities were forbidden to federate. They paid tribute to Sparta, and were required to give military service. They carried on the trades and businesses from which Spartans were precluded.

Peripatetic School, see *Aristotle*. The successor of Aristotle as head of the school was Theophrastus (q.v.). Under him and his successor, Stratō of Lampsacus, the school devoted itself chiefly to physical research, and thereafter made little advance on its founder's doctrine.

Peripetei'a, see *Tragedy*, § 3.

Peri'phrasis ('roundabout speaking'), a figure of speech in which the meaning of a single word or phrase is expressed by several words or many, e.g. 'Dardanius senex' for Priam (Ovid).

Pe'riplous, see *Arrian* and *Scylax*.

Pe'riplus Maris Erythrae'i, a description in Greek, by an unknown Greek-speaking merchant of the 1st c. A.D., of the coasts of the Red Sea and the Gulf of Aden. It shows knowledge of part of India, and of E. Africa as far as Zanzibar.

Pē'rō, daughter of Neleus, see *Melampus*.

Pē'rō, the Roman boot, see *Clothing*, § 5.

Pe'rsa ('The Persian'), a comedy by Plautus. The subject is the fooling of a pimp. A Persian sells him a pretended Arabian captive. The Persian is in reality the parasite Saturiō, and the captive is his daughter; and he has lent himself to the deceit for the sake of a good meal.

Persae of Aeschylus, see *Persians*.

Perse'phonē (corrupted by the Romans to *Prōserpina*), also known as *Korē* ('The Maiden'), in Greek mythology, the daughter of Zeus and Demeter (q.v.), a beautiful goddess who, as she was picking flowers in the meadows of Enna in Sicily, was carried off by Hades (q.v.) in his chariot and made his queen in the lower world. (Enna lay on a high plateau in the centre of Sicily, watered by springs. Cicero in his Verrines tells of his visit to the place and of his finding the priestesses and inhabitants plunged in grief owing to the theft by Verres of their statue of Demeter.) For the mother's search for Persephone over the earth, see *Demeter*. Though Zeus yielded at length to Demeter's lamentations, Persephone could not be entirely released from the lower world, for she had eaten some pomegranate seeds there (as was revealed by Ascalaphus, son of Acheron, who was turned into an owl for his betrayal). But it was arranged that she should spend eight (or six) months of the year on earth and the remainder with Hades. The myth is probably symbolical of the burying of the seed in the ground and the growth of the corn. It is told in the Homeric Hymn to Demeter, by Ovid in his 'Fasti' (iv. 417 et seq.) and 'Metamorphoses' (v. 391 et seq.), and by Claudian (De Rapt. Pros.). It has been treated by Tennyson in his 'Demeter and Persephone' and by Robert Bridges in his masque 'Demeter'. There is an allusion to the myth in Milton (P.L. iv. 268–72):

Not that fair field
Of Enna, where Proserpin gathering flowers,
Herself a fairer flower, by gloomy Dis
Was gathered—which cost Ceres all that pain
To seek her through the world.

Pe'rseūs, in Greek mythology, the son of Zeus and Danae (q.v.). Under her name is given the story of his birth, of the prophecy that he would kill Acrisius, his grandfather, and of the casting away of mother and child and their arrival in the land of Seriphos, where Polydectēs was king. Polydectes fell in love with Danae, but his love was not returned. Perseus was now a young man, and Polydectes, finding him an obstacle to his designs on Danae, persuaded him to undertake a dangerous adventure, the obtaining of the head of the Medusa (see *Gorgons*), thinking that he would be destroyed. But the gods favoured Perseus. Pluto lent him a helmet that would make him invisible, Hermes lent him wings for his feet, and Athene a resplendent mirror (so that he need not look directly at the Medusa). He was thus enabled to escape being turned into stone, and to cut off her head. Pursuing his flight, Perseus discovered Andromeda chained to a rock. She was the daughter of Cêphêûs, king of the Ethiopians, and of his wife Cassiopeia, who had offended the Nereids (q.v.) by boasting herself more beautiful than they. Thereupon Poseidon had sent a sea-monster to ravage the country, and this monster could be placated only by the sacrifice of Cassiopeia's daughter. Perseus changed the monster to a rock by showing it the Gorgon's head, and married Andromeda, but only after defeating another suitor, Phinêûs, who attempted to carry off the bride, and was, with his attendants, changed to stone by the Medusa's head. It is also said that Perseus, by the same means, turned Atlas (q.v.) into a mountain, because Atlas had received him inhospitably on his travels. Perseus then returned to Seriphos, just in time to save Danae from the violence of Polydectes, whom he likewise destroyed. Placing Dictys (see *Danae*) on the throne, Perseus now went to his native Argos, but found that Acrisius his grandfather had gone to Larissa in Thessaly. There Perseus, taking part in some games, accidentally killed him with a discus that he was throwing, thus fulfilling the prophecy. He refused to ascend the throne of Argos to which by this calamity he became heir, but withdrew to Asia, where his son Persês became ruler of the Persians, who were supposed to be named after him; or according to another version, took Tiryns in exchange for Argos, and founded Mycenae.

The legend of Perseus and Andromeda is the subject of a poem by C. Kingsley, 'Andromeda'.

Persian Wars, THE. The Assyrian empire had collapsed with the fall of Nineveh in 606 B.C., and had been followed by the Median empire under Cyaxarês and Astyagês. This in turn had fallen before Cyrus (q.v.) the Persian in 550. Cyrus extended his dominion over vast territories. He conquered Lŷdia (of which Croesus was then king) and the Greek cities of Asia Minor, and carried his rule far eastwards. His son Cambyses (529–522) conquered Egypt. The Persian empire thus encircled the eastern Mediterranean. Darius (q.v., 521–486) succeeded Cambyses, consolidated the empire (as recorded in the famous *Behistun Inscription*), and established a beneficent despotism over its provinces. He next sought to make his northern frontier secure by an expedition (? 512) through Thrace into Scythia. This almost ended in disaster; but

Darius had obtained a footing in Europe. His further operations in this direction were delayed by a revolt of the Ionian cities of Asia Minor (499), in which Miletus took the leading part. Aristagoras of Miletus sought help in Greece; he failed at Sparta, but obtained support at Athens and Eretria. An Ionian force, with a body of Athenian hoplites, reached Sardis, which was burnt (498). Despite further rebel successes in Caria and Cyprus, the vengeance of Darius was complete. A large Greek fleet was utterly defeated at Ladê in 494, and Miletus fell to the Persian siege-engines in the same year (see *Phrynichus*). The Persian king, not forgetting the part played by Athens and Eretria in the revolt, now turned his attention to Greece. He set about his preparations methodically. Thrace and the island of Thasos were reduced, and Macedonia submitted, but it was not until 490 that the Persian host under Dâtis and Artaphernês landed in Euboea, destroyed Eretria, and guided by the renegade Hippias (q.v.) crossed to Marathon. Here (according to the traditional account, which is not accepted by modern scholarship) the Athenians, on the advice of Miltiades (q.v.), decided to encounter it. A speedy runner, Phidippides, had been sent to Sparta to summon the promised reinforcements (see also in this connexion *Pan*); but the Spartans, whether from religious scruples or for some other reason, refused to start before the full moon. Thus it fell to some 10,000 Athenians under Miltiades (with Callimachus as polemarch in chief command), aided by 1,000 Plataeans, to face the Persians. The latter were expecting a signal from a disaffected party in Athens that the moment was ripe for an advance on the city, and after some days prepared to attack it. Part of their troops were embarked on the ships. Miltiades, whose force was stationed on the heights overlooking the narrow plain of Marathon, now fell upon the remainder, who were utterly routed. The Athenian force then hastened back to their city. The signal, a shield gleaming in the sun on Mt. Pentelicus, had been given by the traitors. Miltiades arrived in time, and Datis and Artaphernes, disinclined to meet the Athenian hoplites again, abandoned the enterprise. Thus ended the First Persian War, a minor affair, aimed only at Athens and Eretria.

Darius, infuriated by the check, at once set about measures for a new invasion. But a revolt broke out in Egypt, and before this was subdued Darius died (485), and was succeeded by Xerxes, his son by Atossa. Xerxes devoted three years to vast and methodical preparations, both diplomatic and military. Negotiations were entered into with various Greek States—Thessaly, Boeotia, Argos. It was probably arranged that Carthage should invade Sicily and Magna Graecia at this time. A canal was cut across the promontory of Mt. Athos, to save the Persian fleet a dangerous piece of navigation; a bridge was built across the Strȳmon; and a bridge of ships across the Hellespont (when this was destroyed by a storm, two other bridges were constructed in its place, and Xerxes had fetters thrown into the sea, a futile symbol of his mastery). An enormous army was assembled, and provisions for it collected. In 480 the host, after defiling at Abȳdos before Xerxes, crossed over to Europe. The Persian fleet set out at the same time. The numbers given by Herodotus for the enemy strength are fantastic. The real numbers are largely a matter of conjecture, but it is improbable that the land force exceeded 400,000 men, if so many, and the fleet 800 ships. AtAthens Themistocles (q.v.) had come to power: under his guidance the city had devoted its efforts to strengthening itself at sea. Sparta, though jealous, co-operated with Athens to resist the threatened invasion. A congress of Greek States was convoked at Corinth to concert measures of defence; but there were defections, and the Delphic oracle showed doubtful patriotism. Athens yielded the command of the joint fleet to Eurybiadēs, and that of the army to Leōnidās, both Spartans. An attempt to resist the Persian advance in Thessaly having been abandoned, a Greek force (some 6,000 men) took up its position in the defile of Thermopylae on the Maliac Gulf, with the Greek fleet near it, close to the headland of Artemisium at the northern end of Euboea. During two days Leonidas held back the Persians at Thermopylae and inflicted heavy losses on them. Then Ephialtēs, a Malian, showed the Persians a mountain path by which they could turn the Greek position. Leonidas with his Spartans and the Thespian and Theban contingents held his ground, while the remainder of the Greek force was perhaps detached to meet the Persians as they descended from the mountain. Leonidas, attacked in front and in the rear, was overwhelmed. It is said that the Thebans surrendered. Leonidas himself was killed. (A famous epitaph on those who fell was written by Simonides.) Meanwhile the Persian fleet had suffered heavy losses from storms and had had a series of indecisive engagements with the Greek fleet. The latter, on receiving the news of Thermopylae, retired to Salamis. Xerxes, reinforced by the Boeotian cavalry, im-

mediately advanced against Attica, and ravaged it. Athens was evacuated; the Acropolis, held by a few defenders, was captured and the buildings on it burnt. The Peloponnesian force meanwhile was engaged in building defences across the Isthmus of Corinth. By the persuasion of Themistocles, Eurybiades and the Greek fleet were induced to await the onset of the Persian fleet in the narrow waters between Salamis and the mainland; and by a ruse, Themistocles brought about the Persian attack before the Greek commanders could change their mind. The Persians, secure of victory and fighting under the eyes of Xerxes, were utterly routed; a force which they had landed on the little island of Psyttaleia to dispatch any shipwrecked Greeks, was massacred. Xerxes at once returned to Persia, leaving Mardonius with a picked force in Thessaly. In the following year (479) Mardonius, after a fruitless attempt at negotiations with Athens, returned to the attack. The opposing forces met near Plataea, the Greeks being under the command of the Spartan Pausanias, and the Athenian contingent under that of Aristides (q.v.). The Greeks won a complete victory, thanks to the valour of their hoplites, and Mardonius was killed. The Persians retreated to their entrenched camp, but this was carried by assault and the defenders massacred. At about the same time the Greek fleet under Leōtychidās attacked the Persians, who had withdrawn to Mycalē (on the Ionian coast opposite Samos) and drawn up their ships on the shore. Near by a large Persian army was encamped. The Greeks landed, captured the Persian camp and destroyed their ships. The Ionian troops included in the Persian army deserted and helped to make the Greek victory complete. The Peloponnesians now returned home, but the Athenian squadron under Xanthippus (q.v.) proceeded to the Hellespont and there captured Sestos. With this success the 'Persian Wars' were ended. The struggle between Greeks and Persians continued for a long time, but henceforward the Greeks were the aggressors.

Our knowledge of the history of these wars is derived mainly from Herodotus. Of contemporary evidence we have only some verses of Simonides and a tragedy of Aeschylus. The Persian side of the story is unknown to us.

Persians (*Persai*, L. *Persae*), a tragedy by Aeschylus, produced in 472 B.C.

The chorus of Persian elders give voice to their anxiety for the fate of Xerxes' expedition against Greece (see *Persian Wars*), and Atossa, mother of Xerxes, tells of ominous dreams and portents. A messenger arrives and announces the disaster of Salamis, giving a vivid account of the battle and the destruction of the Persian fleet. The chorus call up the ghost of Darius, who sees in the catastrophe the accomplishment of oracles and the punishment by the gods of the overweening pride of Xerxes. He foretells the future defeat at Plataea. Xerxes himself arrives and the play ends in general lamentations. The work displays a certain compassion for the vanquished, mingled with the author's pride in the great victory of the Greeks.

Pe′rsius Flaccus, AULUS (A.D. 34–62), known generally as 'Persius', was born at Volaterrae in Etruria; he belonged to an equestrian family and was a relative of the famous Arria (q.v.), wife of Paetus. He was educated at Rome in literature and rhetoric, but showed no liking for the latter. He also attended (with Lucan for fellow pupil) the school of the Stoic Cornūtus, and the influence of the latter's philosophy may be seen in his satires. The Fifth Satire is addressed to Cornutus, and to him Persius bequeathed his books and part of his large fortune; the philosopher accepted the books but not the money. Persius is said to have been a man of modest bearing and gentle character. He took no part in public affairs, died young, and left only a small amount of literary work, six Satires, some 650 hexameters in all, and a prologue in scazon iambics (see *Metre*, § 5). Except the First Satire, these poems are homilies rather than satires in the strict sense. They were inspired by the satires of Lucilius (q.v.). They inculcate the Stoic moral doctrine in private life, and only incidentally touch on politics. Their style is involved and obscure, but they are marked by an elevated moral tone, with occasional passages of genial humour, and forcible graphic expression, showing the poet's keen observation of life within his limited range. He quotes and imitates Horace, but in character and uncompromising stoicism is utterly unlike him.

The First Satire is a criticism of the poetasters and the debased literary taste of the day, as significant of the corruption of Roman virtue and loss of manhood. Satire II is concerned with the prayers and sacrifices that are acceptable to the gods. Satire III is directed against sloth, and urges serious pursuits and self-control. Satire IV demands virtue and self-knowledge in public men. Satire V is addressed to Cornutus, and contains a beautiful passage describing the poet's simple and

studious mode of life in company with the philosopher; its subject is the rarity of true freedom—we are all the slaves of our passions or our superstitions. Satire VI is addressed to Caesius Bassus (a lyric poet commended by Quintilian) who edited Persius's satires after his death, and is said to have perished in the eruption of Vesuvius; it is a defence of the poet's right to spend his income on reasonable enjoyment without regard to the complaints of his prospective heir.

There is a life of Persius by Suetonius. He is among the Latin poets translated by Dryden.

Pervigi′lium Ve′neris, a Latin poem of 93 lines in trochaic tetrameters (see *Metre*, § 2), of unknown authorship and date, preserved in the Latin Anthology. It dates perhaps from the time of Hadrian and is possibly the work of Florus (q.v.); or it may have been written as late as the 4th c. It is a song in celebration of the spring festival of Venus Genetrix, and is remarkable not only for its exquisite melody and romantic evocation of spring-time and its associations, but also as an experiment in a new form of poetry, making large use of assonance, recurrence of words and phrases, and even occasionally of rhyme, in anticipation of the accentual Latin poetry of a later age. The refrain 'Cras amet qui nunquam amavit, quique amavit cras amet', occurring irregularly in the imperfect text, may have been intended to recur after every fourth line.

W. Pater in 'Marius the Epicurean' has fancifully reconstructed the composition of the poem, in the reign of Marcus Aurelius, by a young scholar, who had caught 'something of the rhyming cadence, the sonorous organ-music of the medieval Latin, and therewithal something of its unction and mysticity of spirit'.

Pe′tasos, see *Clothing*, § 1; also *Hermes*.

Peti′llius Ceri′ālis, QUINTUS, see *Britain*, § 2.

Petrarch, see *Texts and Studies*, § 9.

Petrō′nius A′rbiter, GAIUS (?) (d. A.D. 65), according to Tacitus was at one time consul and governor of Bithȳnia, and subsequently was admitted by Nero to the inner circle of his intimates and chosen by him as his arbiter of taste (*elegantiae arbiter*). Tigellinus, Prefect of the Praetorians, whose jealousy he aroused, falsely accused him to the emperor, and an ominous order from Nero to remain at Cumae caused Petronius to take his own life. Tacitus describes him as a man of polished luxury, indolent in his ordinary life, but capable of energy in public affairs, vicious or aping vice. An idealized portrait of him is given by Sienkewicz in his 'Quo Vadis'. Petronius is probably the author of the satirical picaresque Latin novel known as the 'Satyricon', a comparatively small portion of which survives. Like the Menippean (q.v.) Satires it is in prose interspersed with verse, and describes the disreputable adventures of two rogues Encolpius and Ascyltus, and their servingboy Giton, as they wander about the semi-Greek cities of southern Italy. Stories, such as the famous one of the Widow of Ephesus (see below), form digressions from the main thread. The principal episode in the surviving portion of the work is the 'Banquet of Trimalchio' (the manuscript of this episode was not recovered until the 17th c.). Trimalchio is a vulgar, wealthy parvenu, simple and good-natured, and the adventurers obtain admission to a banquet given by him. Petronius describes the ostentatious display of wealth in the decoration of the house and in the profusion of fantastic dishes set before the guests, the grotesque incidents of the banquet, the comical conversation of the guests and absurd conduct of Trimalchio as he becomes more and more drunk, finally reaching a maudlin stage in which he describes the provisions of his will and expresses his wishes regarding his funeral monument. He has a ridiculously confused notion of mythology, supposes that Hannibal was present at the siege of Troy, that Daedalus confined Niobe in the Trojan Horse, and that Cassandra killed her children. In the course of the banquet come two good stories, one of a werewolf, and another about witches substituting a straw changeling for a boy. The whole is told with astonishing vivacity and rollicking humour.

A further character in the remaining incidents is a disreputable old poet named Eumolpus, with whom the adventurers travel to Crotona to advance their fortunes by fraud. There are some lively scenes in the course of the sea-journey which ends in shipwreck, and the extant portion of the work ends with various amorous adventures and misfortunes. In the course of these Eumolpus propounds his views on epic poetry (§ 118) and recites in illustration sixty iambics on the fall of Troy and some three hundred hexameters on the Civil War of 49 B.C. He criticizes the rhetorical extravagances of contemporary poetry. It is in his remarks that occurs the well-known phrase 'Horatii curiosa felicitas', the 'studied felicity' of Horace. It is Eumolpus who at an earlier stage (§ 111) relates the story of the 'Ephesian Matron', who, watching incon-

solably in the vault where her recently dead husband has been laid, is induced by a kindly soldier to take food, and presently to accept him as her lover.

The whole work gives an extraordinarily dramatic picture of Italian life in Nero's time, and reproduces in the conversation of some of the characters the actual speech of the lower classes, with amusing bits of slang (such as 'olim oliorum', 'ages ago'). There are passages of gross indecency, but the spirit of the whole is the humorous satire of writers such as Rabelais.

Pets. Apart from dogs (q.v.), the Greeks do not appear to have had many pets, though they kept cicadas for their chirping. The Romans kept nightingales for their song, parrots (whose loquacity they found was increased by wine), and other talking birds such as magpies. Lesbia's 'sparrow' (see *Catullus*) is famous; it was probably the blue thrush often seen at the present day in Italian bird-cages. Cocks were reared for cock-fighting both in Greek and in Roman times, quails also for fighting by the Romans. We read in Statius of a tame lion; and of monkeys' tricks in Juvenal. The Romans also kept squirrels. They bred peacocks, pheasants, and pigeons, and used the last as carriers. Rather strangely, there is little mention of cats either in Greek or Latin literature, and it is doubtful to what extent the cat was domesticated in Greece and Italy in classical times. Herodotus describes the interest taken in these animals by the Egyptians. The cat referred to by Aristophanes ('Acharnians', 879) is probably of the wild species. But there is what appears to be a tame cat behind the master's chair in the picture of a music lesson on a Greek vase in the British Museum. The Romans used weasels and snakes to kill mice. The cat represented in a mosaic at Pompeii is perhaps a wild cat, as also the cat in one of Phaedrus's fables; but Pliny refers to the common cat more than once as a well-known animal, and on a Roman lamp in the British Museum a representation of performing animals includes a cat climbing a ladder.

Peutinger Map, see *Maps*.

Phaeā'cians (*Phaiākes*), in the 'Odyssey', a sea-faring folk, inhabitants of the land of Scheria, on which Odysseus was cast ashore.

Phae'do (*Phaidōn*), a dialogue by Plato, in which Phaedo of Elis, a disciple of Socrates, narrates the discussion that took place between Socrates and his friends during the last hour of his life, and the manner of his dying. This discussion deals with the nature of death and the question of the immortality of the soul. The arguments for and against its immortality are considered, notably the theory of reminiscence (see *Meno*), and the theory of the existence of eternal ideas in which the soul is a partaker. Socrates goes on to expound the fate of the soul after death, the judgement and retribution that await it. He is not confident of the literal truth of what he describes, but he is sure that something of the kind must be.

This is the work in which Cato of Utica (q.v.) is said to have sought fortitude on the night before his death.

Phae′dra (*Phaidrā, Phaedrā* in Ovid and Seneca), see *Hippolytus*.

Phae′dra, a tragedy by Seneca the Philosopher, based on the 'Hippolytus' (q.v.) of Euripides, with certain variations. It is Phaedra herself (not the nurse) who avows her love to her stepson; she then in person slanders him to Theseus; and finally it is she herself (not the goddess Artemis, as in Euripides) who discloses her guilt before she dies.

Phae′drus (*Phaidros*), a dialogue by Plato, in which Socrates discusses with his young friend Phaedrus, in a pleasant spot on the bank of the Ilissus, the subject of rhetoric, distinguishing the conventional rhetoric designed to deceive from the true rhetoric based on dialectic and truth. This is illustrated by speeches on the subject of love composed in either style. In the course of the discussion occurs the well-known simile of the soul to a charioteer driving two steeds, one representing the spiritual, the other the sensual element in man, which the charioteer (reason) has to restrain. The previous existence of the soul in association with the gods is indicated.

Phae′drus or PHAEDER, GĀIUS JŪLIUS, a Thracian slave who came to Rome and became a freedman in the household of Augustus, was the author of a collection of Fables, in five books containing some hundred pieces, published probably under Tiberius and Caligula. There is also an 'appendix' of thirty-two fables, probably likewise by Phaedrus. The collection includes fables proper, and also a number of stories or anecdotes (some of them about Aesop, Socrates, Menander, &c.) and defences of the author against detractors. The fables are based on those of Aesop (q.v.) and on beast-stories from other sources which had come to be attributed to Aesop. They are written in iambic senarii (see *Metre*, § 4), and their object is twofold, advice and entertain-

ment. They are generally serious or satirical, dealing with the injustices of life, and social and political evils, but occasionally light and amusing. They in general express the attitude of the humble and oppressed under Tiberius and Caligula, and inculcate the lesson of resignation. Their references, intentional or imagined, to political personages got Phaedrus into trouble; proceedings were taken against him by Sejanus, and he was probably imprisoned. Many of the fables are well known to us, having been handed on (probably through the Greek collection of Babrius) to medieval and our own times. They include such favourites as 'The Wolf and the Lamb', 'The Fox and the Sour Grapes', 'King Log and King Watersnake', and many others. One book is dedicated to Eutychus, the celebrated chariot-driver of the Greens in the reign of Caligula.

The author falls short of La Fontaine in dramatic sense and lacks his touch of genius, so that his apologues appear a little dry and lifeless beside those of the great French fabulist. His style is clear and his phrases neat. He is the source of the expression 'adding insult to injury' ('injuriae qui addideris contumeliam', v. iii. 5).

Pha′ethon (*Phăĕthōn*), in Greek mythology, son of Helios (the Sun) and Clymene (q.v.). When he grew up he sought out his father who recognized him and offered him what gift he chose to ask. Phaethon asked to be allowed to drive his father's chariot for one day. In spite of the warning of Helios, he attempted this, but soon proved unequal to guiding the horses of the Sun. These bolted from their course, and the earth was in danger of being burnt up, when Zeus intervened and hurled a thunderbolt at Phaethon, who fell into the river Ēridanus. His sisters wept for him till they were turned into poplars; their tears, oozing from the trees, are hardened into amber. The Eridanus was variously identified by the ancients with one of the rivers which flowed into the northern ocean and at the mouth of which amber was found, or with the Po in Italy. G. Meredith wrote, in English galliambics (see *Metre*, § 5), a poem 'Phaethon' on this myth.

Pha′lanx, the Macedonian military formation, based on that of Epaminondas (q.v.), and developed by Philip of Macedon (q.v.). It consisted of sixteen ranks of infantry soldiers, armed with long spears, 13 to perhaps 18 ft. in length, so that it presented an impenetrable thicket of shafts. The phalanx had little flexibility, and prevailed by sheer weight and perfect drill. It was dangerously open to flank attack and needed strong guards on its flanks, such as Alexander the Great provided with his cavalry and light infantry. At the end of his career he tried the experiment of transforming it by substituting for twelve of the ranks of pikemen, from the fourth to the fifteenth, an equal number of ranks of light-armed Persians, carrying bows and javelins. The inferiority of the phalanx as a formation to the Roman maniple was shown at Cynoscephalae and Pydna, but the phalanx had once more grown rigid and inflexible.

Pha'laris, a tyrant of Acragas in Sicily, probably in the first half of the 6th c. B.C. He is said to have been a cruel ruler, who roasted his victims in a brazen bull, invented by one Perillus. The inventor was the first to be thus put to death. The 'Epistles' attributed to Phalaris were proved by R. Bentley (see *Texts and Studies*, § 10) to be forgeries. Bentley showed that certain towns mentioned in them were not founded, and that the names of Tauromenium and Messana were not in use till long after the time of Phalaris; and that the letters were written in Attic not Dorian Greek.

Phalē'rum (*Phalēron*), the modern PHA'-LERON, the principal harbour of Athens in the days before the Persian Wars and the development and fortification of the Piraeus (q.v.), E. of which it lies. It is an open roadstead, offering little protection to ships. For the Long Wall connecting it with Athens, see *Long Walls*.

Pha'llus (*Phallos*), the male organ of generation, adopted by many primitive peoples as the symbol of fertility, and figuring in religious ceremonies designed to stimulate the fruitfulness of the earth, the flocks, and the people, and so to avert the weakening of the tribe. In Greece the phallus was especially associated with the worship of Dionysus, the god of fertility (whence its connexion with comedy; the Athenian actor of the Old Comedy commonly, though not always, wore the phallic emblem); of Hermes, the god of pastures, crops, and herds; and of Pan, the protector of flocks; also with the worship of Demeter, the earth-goddess.

Phā'on (*Phāōn*), a legendary boatman of Mitylene, to whom Aphrodite gave youth and beauty, because he had carried her (in the guise of an old woman) across the sea without taking payment. See *Sappho*.

Pha'ros, see *Alexandria*.

Pharsā'lia or PHARSA'LUS in Thessaly, the scene of the decisive defeat of Pompey by Caesar in the summer of 48 B.C. (See *Rome*, § 7.) Pharsalus was the name of the town, Pharsalia of its territory.

Pharsā'lia, an epic poem by Lucan, in ten books of hexameters, on the war between Caesar and Pompey (the title in the MSS. is 'De Bello Civili'). The poem was not completed and ends abruptly with Caesar at war in Egypt. It is unknown how far the author intended to carry the narrative. The poem, written in strong sympathy with the cause of Pompey, first touches on the sources of the war and gives a vivid sketch of the characters of the two leaders; then proceeds to Caesar's crossing of the Rubicon. A striking passage shows him confronted by the Spirit of Italy, which challenges his right to advance. The dismay at Rome is described, and the flight of citizens and senators.

Book II continues the relation of events in Italy (with a long digression on the massacres of Marius and Sulla), the resolution of Cato and Brutus to resist Caesar, the episode of the defence of Corfinium by Domitius, Pompey's withdrawal to Brundisium and escape to Epirus.

Book III treats of the occupation of Rome by Caesar and of the fighting on land and sea about Massilia (there is a notable description of the Druid grove in the neighbourhood of the town).

The first part of Book IV deals with Caesar's campaign in Spain. The narrative then passes to Illyria and includes the stirring incident of the attempted escape of some Caesarian soldiers on three rafts; one of these is stopped and the soldiers on board slay each other rather than surrender. Curio's expedition to Africa follows, and his death; with a digression on the legend of Hercules and Antaeus.

The most interesting portions of Book V describe the Delphic Oracle, which Appius, a Pompeian, goes to consult; and Caesar's attempt to cross the Adriatic in a small boat on a stormy night.

Book VI is occupied with the fighting about Dyrrhachium and Caesar's withdrawal to Thessaly. Sextus Pompeius consults the Thessalian witch Erichtho, who employs necromancy to foretell the destiny of the Pompeians.

Book VII. Pompey's dream before the battle of Pharsalia and a description of the battle, and the ensuing scenes.

Book VIII. Pompey's flight first to Lesbos and then to Egypt, and his murder there by the order of Pothīnus.

Book IX. Pompey's spirit is borne to heaven, and Cato pronounces a splendid panegyric on the dead leader. Cato resolves to continue the war and marches with his troops to Maurētānia. Confident in his Stoic faith and in the rightness of the course that he has chosen, he refuses to consult the oracle of Ammon. The book is in large measure a laudation of Cato. There is a strange digression on Egyptian serpents, their legendary origin in the blood of Medusa, and their varieties. Pompey's head is presented to Caesar, who hypocritically laments his fate.

Book X. Caesar's doings in Egypt, and his dalliance with Cleopatra. He is besieged by the troops of Pothinus and Achillas. The poem ends abruptly.

The work is marred by rhetorical extravagances, irrelevant divagations, and errors of taste (e.g. the realistic description of the wild beasts devouring the dead after the battle of Pharsalia), and it contains historical inaccuracies. But it is carried through with great vigour and brilliance; and there are many passages of power and pathos, such as that describing Pompey's farewell to Italy, and others that have been indicated above. The author's gift for fine epigram is repeatedly shown, e.g. in the famous line 'Victrix causa deis placuit sed victa Catoni' (i. 128), that about Caesar 'Nil actum credens cum quid superesset agendum', and the well-known 'Victurosque dei celant, ut vivere durent, felix esse mori'. The most astonishing thing about the poem, apart from the youth of its author (he was 26 when he died), is the audacity of the theme. For to write, under such an emperor as Nero, a poem in praise of Pompey and Cato, the opponents of autocratic rule, was to incur the utmost risk. (The audacity, it is true, is tempered by fulsome adulation of Nero in a passage in Book I.) There is also originality in the treatment of the theme; for Lucan, breaking with epic tradition, spares his readers the outworn machinery of the intervention of the gods in human affairs. Although the place of this element is to some extent taken by the supernatural, in the form of prodigies, omens, oracles, and witchcraft, the author is in the main content to rely for the success of his poem on the dramatic interest of the struggle and the greatness of the protagonists.

Phē'geūs, see *Alcmaeon*.

Pheidias, see *Phidias*.

Pheidi'ppidēs, see *Phidippides*.

Pherecratē'an, see *Metre*, §§ 3 and 5.

Phere'cratēs (*Pherekratēs*), see *Comedy*, § 3.

Pherecȳ'dēs (*Pherekūdēs*), see *Logographi* (1).

Phi'dias (*Pheidias*) (b. c. 500 B.C.), son of Charmidēs, was one of the greatest of Athenian artists, famous especially as a sculptor, but also as an architect and painter. He contributed, under his friend Pericles (q.v.), to the adornment of Athens, where his principal works were three statues of Athene on the Acropolis, one of them wrought in ivory and gold. He perhaps designed and certainly supervised the construction of the frieze of the Parthenon. Another of his foremost works was the colossal statue, also wrought in ivory and gold, of Zeus at Olympia (q.v.). In 432 enemies of Pericles accused Phidias of having stolen some of the gold from the statue of Athene. This he was able to disprove; but he was further accused of impiety and died in prison.

Phidi'ppidēs (*Pheidippidēs*) or PHILI'P-PIDES, the Athenian runner who, according to Herodotus (vi. 105–6), was sent to request help from Sparta before the battle of Marathon (see *Persian Wars*, also *Pan*). He is said to have covered the distance between Athens and Sparta, 150 miles, in two days.

Philē'bus (*Philēbos*), see *Plato*, § 2₁

Philē'mōn, see *Comedy*, § 4.

Philē'mōn and Bau'cis (*Baukis*), in Greek mythology, a poor old couple who entertained Zeus and Hermes hospitably, when they visited the earth in disguise and were repulsed by the rich. For this Philemon and Baucis were saved from a deluge that overwhelmed the land where they lived, and their dwelling was transformed into a temple, of which they were made the priest and priestess. They were also granted their request to die at the same time, and were changed into trees, whose boughs intertwined.

Philē'tās, see *Philitas*.

Philip (*Philippos*) **of Macedon** (c. 382–336 B.C.), Philip II, younger son of Amyntas, king of Macedonia (390–369).

§ 1. *Early years*

Philip was, as a boy, sent to Thebes by Pelopidas (q.v.) as security for the maintenance of Theban influence in Macedonia. At Thebes he was brought up in the military school of Epaminondas (q.v.). He returned to Macedonia in 364, and in 359, after the death of his elder brother Perdiccas, he assumed the government of the country as regent for his nephew Amyntas. He devoted the first years of his rule to consolidating his position, reorganizing the Macedonian army on the basis of the phalanx (q.v.), decisively defeating the Paeonians and Illyrians (a constant menace to the peace of Macedonia), extending his territory eastward to include the rich gold-mines of Mt. Pangaeus, and, by tricking the Athenians, securing Amphipolis on the Strȳmōn, which commanded the road to the mines. More than this, he gradually ousted the Athenians from all their positions on the Thermaic Gulf. In these various operations he first showed his consummate ability both as a military commander and as a diplomatist. The control of the gold-mines, it may be added, enabled Philip to supplement his diplomacy with bribery on a large scale. He now set his nephew aside and assumed the royal title. He married Olympias, an Epirot princess; their son, Alexander the Great, was born in 356.

§ 2. *Interference in Greece, 353-346*

Before long Philip found in the Sacred War (q.v.) against Phocis an opportunity for pushing Macedonian supremacy southwards into Greece. In 353 the Thessalian League invited his assistance against Lycophrōn of Pherae and his allies the Phocians, and Philip readily accorded it. By the prompt action of Athens he was prevented from capturing Thermopylae, but he secured Pagasae on the Thessalian coast, began to build a fleet, and with this harassed the trade of Athens. Returning N. he marched against Thrace and forced its three kings, one by one, to accept his overlordship. The Chersonese was saved from capture only by his falling ill. His dominion over the sea-coast of the Aegean now extended from the neighbourhood of Thermopylae to the Propontis, with the exception of the Chersonese and Chalcidicē. The interests of Athens were gravely threatened, and Demosthenes (q.v., § 5), in his First Philippic, called upon the Athenians to gird themselves to oppose the enemy. But the Athenian policy was at this time directed by Eubulus (q.v.), a cautious statesman and an advocate of peace (though it was he who had checked Philip at Thermopylae). In 349 Philip attacked Chalcidice, and Olynthus sought and obtained an alliance with Athens. But a revolt of Euboea, fomented by Philip, divided the efforts of Athens; Olynthus fell, Chalcidice was incorporated in Macedonia, and Athens had to recognize the independence of Euboea. The exhaustion of the Athenian treasury, coupled with the news that Philip, at the request of Thebes, was about to undertake the subjugation of the Phocians, brought home to Athens the necessity for peace with Philip, and this, known as the Peace of Philocrates (one of the Athenian negotiators), was

concluded in 346, on the basis that Athens and Macedonia should retain the territories of which each was then in possession. Athens thus retained the Chersonese, but surrendered her long-standing claim to Amphipolis. Philip appears to have been prepared to go further and negotiate a general understanding for friendly co-operation, but any such idea (though not unwelcome to Eubulus) was vehemently opposed by Demosthenes (q.v., § 5 (e)), and nothing came of it. In effect Athens abandoned the Phocians to their fate. Philip now advanced south, Thermopylae was surrendered to him by its Phocian garrison, the Phocians were ousted from Delphi, and Macedonia replaced Phocis on the Amphictyonic Council. Philip signalized his new position by presiding over the Pythian festival in the same year (346).

§ 3. *Philip's further conquests and death (345-336)*

In 342 Philip completed the subjugation of Thrace, made it a tributary province of Macedonia, and founded there among other cities Philippopolis, which still celebrates his name. This extension of his dominions to the immediate neighbourhood of the Chersonese was a fresh threat to Athenian interests, and Demosthenes in the Third Philippic enforced the necessity of military preparations. Various acts of hostility in 341 developed into open war in 340; Philip's attack on Byzantium (which had revolted from the Macedonian alliance) was checked by the Athenian fleet, and he was forced to retreat into Thrace. He decided to meet Athens, where she was most vulnerable, on land. A pretext was furnished by the Amphictyonic Council. It decided to proceed against the people of Amphissa for sacrilege and invited Philip to lead once more a Sacred War (338). The latter at once advanced through Thermopylae. Though it is uncertain whether he had any real intention of invading Attica, the threat that he would do so brought Athens and Thebes, in spite of their inveterate hostility, into alliance against him; for the subjugation of Athens by Philip involved a menace to Thebes itself. The decisive battle of Chaeronea, 'fatal to liberty', was fought in the same year (338) and the armies of Thebes and Athens were completely defeated. The hegemony of Greece had definitely passed to Macedonia. Philip broke up the Boeotian League and established a Macedonian garrison in Thebes; but he showed leniency to Athens, whose sea-power rendered her still formidable. He summoned a Hellenic congress at

Corinth and announced his intention of making war on Persia and releasing the Greek cities of Asia Minor from the Persian yoke. But though he made preparations for the invasion, and his general Parmeniō secured a footing in Asia Minor, he was not destined to carry out his project. Philip had taken a new consort (Cleopatra, niece of his general Attalus) and thereby aroused the fierce jealousy of Olympias and the anger of Alexander. In 336 Philip was assassinated at the instigation of Olympias, and it may be that Alexander was privy to the plot.

Various pithy sayings are attributed to Philip by Plutarch ('Apoph. Reg.'), among them one that has become proverbial. When the traitors who had delivered up Olynthus to him complained of the opprobrious name by which they were called at Philip's court, he replied that the Macedonians were a rude and clownish people, and called a spade a spade (σκαφήν, literally 'a tub').

Philip V of Macedonia, see *Macedonia*, § 3.

Phi'lippi, a town in Macedonia, E. of the river Strȳmōn, the scene of the defeat in 42 B.C. of the forces of Brutus and Cassius by those of Antony and Octavian, and of the death of the two former. See *Rome*, § 7. Brutus and Cassius held a strong position and were kept well supplied by sea. It was to their advantage to avoid a decisive battle with a force larger than theirs, but whose supplies were precarious. Antony did what he could to provoke an engagement. At last Cassius and Brutus made a sortie, and an inconclusive conflict followed in which Cassius, when his wing was repulsed, killed himself. A fortnight later Brutus was persuaded by his impatient officers to renew the battle, was defeated, and took his own life. The campaign of Philippi forms the subject of Act V of Shakespeare's 'Julius Caesar'.

Phili'ppics, three political speeches by Demosthenes (2) (q.v., § 5). The title was adopted by Cicero (q.v., § 6) for the speeches that he delivered against Antony.

Phili'ppus, the title of a discourse by Isocrates (q.v.).

Phili'tas (or *Philētas*) of Cos (c. 300 B.C.), a Greek grammarian and poet of the Alexandrian Age, said to have been the teacher of Ptolemy II and Theocritus. He was a writer of amatory poems, imitated by Ovid and praised by Propertius. Only fragments of his work survive. Athenaeus relates that he was so slender that he was obliged to ballast himself with leaden balls on his shoes, to prevent the wind upsetting him!

Phi'lō Jūdae'us (*fl.* A.D. 39), a Graeco-Judaic philosopher of Alexandria, who wrote a large number of works, including principally commentaries on the Old Testament. This he interpreted allegorically, finding in it the source of the main doctrines of Plato, Aristotle, and other Greek philosophers. A considerable portion of his writings survives. In A.D. 40 he visited Rome as a representative of the Jews of Alexandria in an embassy they sent to Caligula.

Philo'chorus, see *Atthis.*

Philo'cratēs, PEACE OF, see *Philip of Macedon*, § 2, *Demosthenes* (2), § 5, *Aeschines.*

Philoctē'tēs (*Philoktētēs*), in Greek mythology, son of Poïās, whom Heracles (q.v.) had persuaded to light the pyre on which he was consumed alive, by the gift of his bow and arrows. These descended to Philoctetes. In the expedition to Troy Philoctetes showed the Greeks the way to the island containing the shrine of the goddess Chrȳsē, that they might sacrifice to her. There he was bitten in the foot by a serpent, and this produced so fetid a wound and his cries during his paroxysms were so terrible that the Greeks landed him on the uninhabited island of Lemnos. After many years the Trojan seer Helenos, captured by Odysseus, revealed that Troy could be taken only by the bow and arrow of Heracles. Odysseus and Neoptolemus (or Diomedes) accordingly went to Lemnos and brought Philoctetes back with them. Machaon (q.v.) healed his wound, and Philoctetes, by shooting Paris, helped to conquer Troy. He is mentioned in the 'Iliad' (ii. 718) and is the subject of a play by Sophocles (see below).

Philoctetes, a tragedy by Sophocles, produced in 409 B.C.

Philoctetes (q.v.) is living wretchedly on Lemnos, suffering from his wound, supporting himself by shooting birds with his beloved bow of Heracles. Odysseus and Neoptolemus arrive to carry him to the siege of Troy. Odysseus reveals to Neoptolemus his plan : Neoptolemus is to pretend that he has quarrelled with the leaders of the Greek host and is on his way home; he is to heap abuse on Odysseus, and to try to possess himself of the bow. Neoptolemus, though at first unwilling to lend himself to the deceit, consents. He meets Philoctetes and tells his story. Philoctetes makes a piteous appeal to him to take him to Greece, and Neoptolemus agrees. But Philoctetes is seized with a paroxysm of pain, after which he is wont to fall asleep. He entrusts his bow to Neoptolemus.

When he awakens, Neoptolemus, stung with remorse, confesses the plot. He is on the point of returning the bow when Odysseus intervenes. Odysseus and Neoptolemus depart to the ships, carrying off the bow. Philoctetes is left lamenting his loss, while the chorus of sailors try to persuade him to join them. They are about to leave him, when Neoptolemus returns, determined to give back the bow, but pursued by Odysseus. Philoctetes, having regained the bow, seeks to shoot Odysseus, but is prevented by Neoptolemus, who again tries to persuade Philoctetes to accompany him to Troy. He fails, and reluctantly decides to abide by his promise and carry him home. At this point Heracles appears in a vision; he bids Philoctetes go to Troy, and Philoctetes yields to the voice of one whom he cannot disobey.

Philomē'la (Gk. *-lă*, L. *-lă*) and **Pro'cnē** (*Proknē*), in Greek mythology, daughters of Pandīōn, a legendary king of Athens. Procne was married to Tērēūs, king of Thrace. The latter became enamoured of Philomela, and after having seduced or outraged her, cut out her tongue and hid her in a lonely place, that she might not reveal his ill-usage. But Philomela managed to depict her misfortunes on a piece of needlework and send it to Procne. Procne sought out her sister and, to revenge her, killed her own son Itys and served up his flesh to her husband. Tereus drew his sword to slay the sisters, but was changed into a hoopoe, Philomela into a swallow, and Procne into a nightingale (or, according to Latin authors, Philomela into a nightingale and Procne into a swallow).

Philopoe'men (*Phlopoimēn*) (c. 250–183 B.C.) of Megalopolis in Arcadia, the bold and vigorous general of the Achaean League (q.v.) and one of the last great men produced by Greece in the period of her decline. He first distinguished himself at the battle of Sellasia in 221 (?), where the Spartans under Cleomenēs were defeated. He was subsequently eight times elected general of the League, in which post he reorganized its army and repeatedly defeated the Spartans. It is recorded that after one of his victories, Philopoemen was present at the Nemean games when Pyladēs, the most famous minstrel of his day, was singing an air from 'The Persians' of Timotheus (q.v.). At the words 'The glorious crown of freedom who giveth to Greece', the people rose and gave an ovation to Philopoemen. In 183, when he was seventy years of age, he took part in an expedition against Messēnē, which had revolted from the League. He was taken

prisoner by the Messenians, thrown into a dungeon, and forced to drink poison. His remains were brought back to Megalopolis, his urn being carried by the historian Polybius. There is a life of him by Plutarch.

Philosophy (*Philosophiā*).

§ 1. *Greek Philosophy*

In the restricted sense in which the term came to be used in Greece in the latter part of the 5th c., philosophy meant the endeavour to understand and to teach how to live well and wisely, which involved the holding of right opinions about God, the world, man, and virtue. It combined religion, morals, and metaphysics. The first use of the word in this sense is ascribed to Pythagoras (q.v.), and this is the sense in which it was probably used by Socrates and certainly by Plato. An earlier Greek philosophy had its origin in the 6th c. B.C. among the Ionians of Asia Minor. It was then chiefly occupied with speculation as to the cause of the universe as we know it. The first of the schools of philosophy was that of Miletus, founded by Thales (q.v.), whose chief successors were Anaximander and Anaximenes (qq.v.). These sought the basis of the universe in some single uncreated and imperishable substance (such as they thought air or water to be) undergoing various modifications. Heraclitus (q.v.) of Ephesus, standing apart from this school and rejecting the notion of a permanent substance underlying the modifications of matter (though he attributed to fire the origin of the universe), saw all things in a state of flux, and matter itself constantly changing. Pythagoras (q.v.), an Ionian of Samos, migrating to Crotona, founded at the other end of the Greek world the second school of philosophy, which saw in numbers and their relations the basis of the universe. The third school was that of Elea also in Magna Graecia, founded by Parmenides and carried on by Zeno (qq.v.). This school distinguished between the single, eternal, and unchangeable reality, and the unreal phenomena of change and motion. Empedocles (q.v.) of Acragas in Sicily, Anaxagoras (q.v.) of Clazomenae in Ionia, and Leucippus, evolved fresh hypotheses of the physical basis of the universe, assuming not a single but plural constituents of matter. Anaxagoras, moreover, introduced the important conception of spirit or intelligence (*Noūs*) as a principle of force and order distinct from matter. Leucippus, of whom practically nothing is known, was said to be the originator of the school of atomistic philosophy, which rested on the doctrine that the universe is composed of a vast number of atoms, mechanically combined. This doctrine was developed by Democritus (q.v.), and found its most eloquent exponent in a later age at Rome, in Lucretius. Greek philosophy culminated in Socrates, Plato, and Aristotle (qq.v.) from whom it received a great extension, particularly on the moral side. But the conquests of Alexander the Great swept away the basis of their moral teaching, man as member of an independent city-state; and the later philosophies, those in particular of the Stoics (q.v.) and Epicureans (see *Epicurus*), reveal a change of outlook. They show that interest has shifted from the theoretical problems of metaphysics and epistemology to the practical problems of everyday behaviour. They are philosophies of resignation rather than of hope; they seek a road to peace and happiness in the state of mind of the individual, by making him independent of outward circumstance. See also *Sceptics, Cynics, Megarian School, Aristippus* (founder of the Cyrenaic School), *Theophrastus* (the successor of Aristotle), and *Neoplatonists*.

§ 2. *Roman Philosophy*

The attention of the Romans was first drawn to the Greek schools of philosophy by the visit in 155 B.C. of an embassy from Athens composed of the three philosophers Carneadēs, Diogenēs, and Critolāus, the heads respectively of the Academic, Stoic, and Peripatetic schools. Somewhat later Scipio Aemilianus (q.v.) received into his household the Stoic philosopher Panaetius (q.v.) of Rhodes; and in the early part of the 1st c. B.C. a successor of the latter, Posidonius (q.v.), became the friend and teacher of Varro, Pompey, and Cicero. The Romans were not much interested in theories as to the constitution of the universe, nor in elucidating the processes of thought and knowledge; and they produced no great original speculative philosophers or metaphysicians. Lucretius alone, in his poem, expounded with enthusiasm the atomic explanation of the universe put forward by Leucippus and Democritus. The attention of the Romans was chiefly concentrated on ethical principles, and here they were mainly divided between Epicureans (see *Epicurus*) and Stoics (q.v.), the latter prevailing. Cicero, who did much to make Greek philosophical thought known to his countrymen, was himself a follower of the New Academy (see *Academy*), with leanings to the Stoic school; he was in fact an eclectic, that is to say he did not accept wholly the teaching of any one school, but picked out from their various doctrines those which commended themselves to him. Seneca (q.v.) was the principal Roman Stoic author, and his writings had considerable influence on Christian ethics. The most famous of the later Roman Stoics were Marcus Aurelius and Epictetus (qq.v.). Persius, under the influence of his teacher, the Stoic Cornūtus, and Lucan were followers of the same school. The general tendency of Stoicism as developed by Seneca and his successors was to become more practical and more human. The tranquillity which the earlier Greek Stoics thought the exclusive possession of the sage living in detachment from the world, was now seen to be attainable by fortitude and self-control.

Philo'stratus (*Philostratos*), the name borne by four members of a family belonging, according to Suidas, to Lemnos, who appear to have lived in the 2nd–3rd c. A.D. The more important works (in Greek) that have come down under the name are the following: (1) 'Lives of the Sophists', that is to say of the orators and rhetoricians from Protagoras (q.v.) to the author's own times. (2) A life of the wandering Pythagorean mystic Apollonius of Tyana (rendered notorious by a religious controversy between Christians and pagans that sprang up with regard to it). (3) 'Eikones', two sets of descriptions in prose of pictures which the author purports to have seen. (4) 'Hērōicus', a dialogue in which the ghosts of heroes of the Trojan War appear. (5) A collection of 'Letters' (sophistical exercises) chiefly noteworthy as containing the source of Ben Jonson's 'Drink to me only with thine eyes' (ἐμοὶ δὲ μόνοις πρόπινε τοῖς ὄμμασιν, in Ep. 33, &c.) and of Herrick's 'To Anthea'. (1) and (2) above are generally assigned to Philostratus III, known as 'the Athenian', *fl. c.* A.D. 210. The authorship of the bulk of the Letters is doubtful.

Philo'xenus (*Philoxenos*), see *Dithyramb* (*ad fin.*).

Phi'neūs (1) a legendary king of Salmydessus on the Euxine, blinded by Zeus for reasons variously given. According to one version, Phineus had had two children by his first wife, Cleopatra, daughter of Boreas; his second wife prevailed upon him to blind them. Whereupon Zeus gave him the choice of death or blindness. He chose the latter. At this Helios (the Sun) was so offended that he sent the Harpies (q.v.) to steal or defile the food of Phineus, so that he almost died of hunger. According to another version, the double punishment was for his misuse of his prophetic power. In this miserable state the Argonauts (q.v.) found him. They rid him of the Harpies, and he in return told them the route they should pursue and in particular how to escape from the Symplegades (q.v.). (2) See *Perseus*.

Phle'gethon (*Phlegethōn*) or PYRIPHLE'-GETHON, see *Hades*.

Phobē'tōr, see *Dreams*.

Phōcae'a (*Phōkaia*) (to be distinguished from Phocis, q.v.), the most northerly of the Ionian settlements on the coast of Asia Minor (see *Migrations*). It became an important maritime centre. When Ionia was conquered by Cyrus in the 6th c. B.C. the Phocaeans migrated to their own colony of Alalia in Corsica, though some of them returned later, and one of these, Dionysius, commanded the Greek forces at Ladē (494 B.C.). The Phocaeans were also founders of Elea (q.v.) and Massalia, the future Marseilles.

Phō'cion (*Phōkiōn*), an Athenian general and statesman of the time of Philip and Alexander of Macedon (see *Athens*, § 7). He belonged to the party of Eubulus, and although a soldier was an advocate of peace, being convinced that the days of Athens' military efficiency were passed. He was a concise and effective orator and was forty-five times elected polemarch. He was sentenced to death on a charge of treason in 318 B.C. There are lives of him by Nepos and Plutarch. Landor in his 'Imaginary Conversations' includes one between Phocion and Aeschines.

Phō'cis (*Phōkis*), in northern Greece, the country adjoining Boeotia on the west, important in Greek history as including Delphi. In consequence, it became involved in the Sacred Wars (q.v.). In the third of these it was subdued by Philip of Macedon.

Phōcy'lides (*Phōkulidēs*), of Miletus, probably of the 6th c. B.C., chiefly famous for the gnomic couplets in elegiacs and hexameters in which he embodied moral observations and precepts; a few of these survive. In each he introduced his own name.

Phoe'be (*Phoibē*, 'the bright one'), according to Hesiod a Titaness (see *Titans*). In later mythology she was associated with the moon, perhaps through confusion with Artemis, who was daughter of Leto the daughter of Phoebe.

Phoebus Apollo, see *Apollo*.

Phoeni'cia (*Phoinīkē*), a country forming a narrow strip along the coast of Syria and including the towns of Tyre and Sidon. Its inhabitants were important from early times as pioneers of navigation and trade,

and as artistic workmen. The Greek alphabet was based on their letters, and the Phoenicians were in consequence regarded as the inventors of letters. They carried their trade and their settlements throughout the Mediterranean and beyond the Straits of Gibraltar, and to the Euxine. Their most important colony was Carthage (q.v.). A prominent element in their trade was the purple (q.v.) dye.

Phoeni'ssae (*Phoinissai*, 'The Phoenician Maidens'), a tragedy by Euripides, produced after 413 B.C. The play derives its name from the chorus of Phoenician maidens, dedicated by the Tyrians to the temple of Apollo at Delphi, who happen to be at Thebes on their way to Delphi. The subject is the same as that of Aeschylus's 'Seven against Thebes' (q.v.).

The drama takes up the legend of Oedipus (q.v.) at the point where Polynices, having been refused by his brother Eteocles his alternate share of the rule of Thebes, has come with Adrastus, king of Argos, and the army of the seven chiefs, to enforce his rights. Jocasta, wife of Oedipus, endeavours to conciliate the two brothers, but her efforts fail and the attack on Thebes becomes inevitable. Tiresias (q.v.) predicts the victory of the Theban arms if a son of Creon (brother of Jocasta and friend of Eteocles) is sacrificed. Accordingly Menoikeūs, Creon's younger son, gives his life heroically for his city, in spite of his father's resistance. The Argives are driven back in the first onset, and it is arranged that the quarrel shall be settled by a single combat between the brothers. In this each slays the other, and Jocasta in despair takes her own life. Creon, who inherits the kingdom of Thebes, drives the blind Oedipus, with Antigone his daughter, into exile.

A paraphrase of this play (from a Latin translation), entitled 'Jocasta', by George Gascoigne and Francis Kinwelmersh, was produced at Gray's Inn in 1566.

Phoenissae, a tragedy by Seneca the Philosopher, which survives in an imperfect condition. It appears to combine material from the 'Oedipus at Colonus' of Sophocles (the blind Oedipus wandering under the guidance of Antigone), with a situation derived from other sources (Antigone is at Thebes with Jocasta, who tries in vain to reconcile her two sons). Perhaps we have here fragments of two distinct plays.

Phoe'nix (*Phoinix*), in Greek mythology, son of Amyntor. Having left his home owing to a violent quarrel with his father, he was kindly received by Peleus (q.v.) and made king of the Dolopians. He reared Achilles (q.v.) from childhood, and as an old man took part in the embassy sent, during the Trojan War, to try to reconcile Achilles and Agamemnon (Il. ix. 432 et seq.).

Pho′rcys (*Phorkus*), a Greek sea-god, son of Pontus and father of the Graiae and the Gorgons (qq.v.), and of Scylla (q.v.).

Pho′rmiō, a comedy by Terence (q.v.), based on a play by Apollodōrus of Carystus, and produced in 161 B.C.

Antiphō, a young Athenian, while his father Dēmiphō is out of the country, has fallen in love with a girl whom he has found, alone in the world, and weeping for her dead mother. Phormiō, a resourceful parasite, taking advantage of the law that orphans must be married to their next of kin, has obtained, in collusion with Antipho, an order of the court that Antipho is to marry the girl; and the marriage has taken place. Antipho's cousin Phaedria is desperately in love with a music-girl, but lacks the money required to obtain her from the slave-dealer; his father, Chremēs, has been away at Lemnos. The two fathers now return. Demipho is furious and determines to break his son's marriage. Phormio, again resourceful, undertakes for a sum of money to take her away and marry her himself. Having got the money, he hands it to Phaedria, who thus secures his music-girl. Meanwhile it is discovered that the girl whom Antipho has married is the daughter of Chremes, who has secretly had a love affair in Lemnos. To avoid further trouble the two fathers decide to recognize Antipho's marriage. But their attempt to recover the money that has been paid to Phormio leads to the exposure of Chremes to his wife.

It is in this play that first appears the proverbial expression 'to have a wolf by the ears' (l. 506).

Phō′tius, see *Byzantine Age*, *Texts and Studies*, § 4, and *Dictionaries*.

Phrā′triā ('brotherhood'), at Athens, in primitive times, a clan, consisting of a noble family and its dependants, who shared in the family cult. Later the *phratriai* were religious organizations which carried out certain cults and kept lists of the citizens. Their great festival was the *Apatūria* held in the month Pyanepsion (October) and celebrated with sacrifices. The children born during the preceding year were then presented to the *phratria*, and admission into this conferred on the child civic rights. See *Athens*, § 2, and *Cleisthenes*.

Phri′xus (*Phrixos*), see *Athamas*.

Phrȳ′nē, a famous Greek courtesan of the 4th c. B.C., said to have been the model for the Aphrodite of Apelles and for that of Praxiteles. See *Hyperides*. There was a golden or gilded statue of her at Delphi, dedicated by herself (according to Pausanias) or by her admirers (according to other authorities).

Phrȳ′nichus (*Phrūnichos*), (1) of Athens, an early tragedian, of whose plays only scanty fragments survive. He flourished from about 512 to 476 B.C. His tragedies appear to have contained little action or development of character, dealing with a single pathetic situation. His 'Capture of Miletus' so painfully moved the Athenians that he was fined. His 'Phoenissae', celebrating the Greek victories over the Persians in 480–479, with a chorus composed of the wives of the enemy's Phoenician sailors, was another famous play.

(2) One of the extreme oligarchical party at Athens at the time of the Four Hundred (see *Athens*, § 5). He was assassinated, perhaps by Thrasybulus (q.v.).

Phrȳ′nis (*Phrūnis*), see *Nome*.

Phy′sica (*Phusikē akroāsis*), a treatise by Aristotle (q.v., § 3).

Pico della Mirandola, see *Texts and Studies*, § 9.

Picu′mnus and **Pīlu′mnus**, in Roman religion, deities of uncertain attributes, probably gods of agriculture, regarded also as protectors of women in childbed. Pilumnus was thought to be the inventor of the pestle (*pilum*) for grinding corn; Virgil makes him the ancestor of Turnus.

Pī′cus, an Italian god of agriculture, sometimes described as a son of Saturn and as the first king of Italy, possessed of prophetic powers. He also appears in legend as a warlike hero, and is associated with the woodpecker, the Latin for which is *picus*. The woodpecker was venerated as sacred to Mars and was of great importance in augury; omens were drawn from the sight of it and from its note. It was said to have helped to feed Romulus and Remus. There was a story that Picus spurned the love of Circe, who turned him into a woodpecker. Virgil makes Picus the father of Faunus and grandfather of Latinus (qq.v.).

Pie′ria (*Pieriā*), a district on the northern slopes of Mt. Olympus (q.v.), whence tradition says that a colony migrated to Mt. Helicon (q.v.) in prehistoric times. The cult of the Muses (q.v.) was said to have been brought from Pieria to Helicon. Hence the Muses are sometimes described as Pierian (*Pierides*).

Pie'rides, see *Muses* and *Pieria*.

Pi'etas, see *Religion*, § 6.

Pi'llĕus, see *Clothing*, § 4.

Pī'los, see *Clothing*, § 1.

Pīlu'mnus, see *Picumnus*.

Pi'nakes, see *Texts and Studies*, § 2.

Pinā'rii and Poti'tii, see *Hercules*.

Pi'nax, see *Cebes*.

Pi'ndar (*Pindaros*), a great Greek lyric poet.

§ 1. *Biography*

Pindar was born in 522 or 518 B.C. at a village near Thebes. He belonged, according to his own statement (Pyth. v), to the noble Spartan family of the Aegeidae, and his poems reveal an aristocratic and pro-Dorian temper. Legend relates that he received instruction in poetical composition from the Boeotian poetess Corinna (q.v.). He went early in life to Athens, which thanks to Pisistratus and his sons now held an important place in Greek intellectual life. There he probably became acquainted with Aeschylus (q.v.). He appears to have had some special connexion with Delphi, perhaps as a member of the Aegeidae family (Pyth. v. 74–80), and to have retained a peculiar devotion to the shrine of Apollo (Paean vi). He also shows a special affection for the island of Aegina (see below), which he evidently visited. His early reputation as a poet is shown by the fact that in 498, when he was some twenty years old, he was commissioned by the great Thessalian family of the Aleuadae to compose an ode (Pyth. x) in honour of the victory in the double foot-race of a boy of their family. His attitude in the Persian invasion of 480–79, in the difficult situation in which he was placed by the pro-Persian policy of Thebes, is uncertain; his later admiration, at any rate, for Athens is shown in his poems. It is said that he was fined by his countrymen for his praises of her, but that the Athenians paid him the amount of the fine twice over; they also erected a statue of him (which Pausanias saw) but probably long after his death. In 476, at the invitation of Hieron I of Syracuse (q.v., § 1), he went to Sicily and stayed there probably two years. He is said to have been eighty when he died at Argos. He attained great fame in his lifetime, and was soon quoted as a classic (e.g. by Herodotus and Plato). In the destruction of Thebes (335) Alexander the Great ordered Pindar's house to be spared.

§ 2. *General character of his work*

Pindar wrote in the literary Dorian dialect. His numerous poems, which in-clude all the chief forms of *choral lyrics* (q.v.), were grouped by the Alexandrians into seventeen books according to their types; paeans, dithyrambs, epinicia, &c. Of his work about a quarter survives, chiefly epinicia (q.v.). The latter are usually constructed, after the model of Stesichorus and Simonides, on the basis of triads (q.v.). He used a variety of metres, chiefly the dactylo-epitrite (see *Metre*, § 3). His poetry is marked by elevation of thought and grandeur of style, and the constant use of bold metaphors and a highly coloured language. He skilfully interweaves myths into his odes, so as to produce great poems on the monotonous and unpromising themes of athletic victories. Mythology he treats with great freedom, modifying or even perhaps inventing myths to suit his conception of the dignity of the gods. He was evidently acquainted with the mystic Orphic teaching, and one of his odes (Olymp. ii) expounds the doctrine of life after death and reincarnation. His view of life held the mean between optimism and pessimism; there is an occasional strain of melancholy in the midst of his buoyant enthusiasm. In his exhortations and counsels he praises virtue, courage, strength, the just and moderate use of power, and the glory that these bring. But he is a poet of beauty rather than a moralist.

Nearly all Pindar's poems that have been preserved, in whole or in part, contain points of interest, and are marked by his peculiar genius. The epinicia are divided into four groups according as their occasion was a victory in the Olympian, the Pythian, the Nemean, or the Isthmian Games (see *Festivals*, § 1). Among the most notable of these odes are the following:

§ 3. *Olympian Odes*

Olympian I, to Hieron tyrant of Syracuse (q.v.), celebrating the victory of his horse Pherenikos ('victory-bringer') probably in 476. The Olympian odes were placed first by the Alexandrian editors because of the pre-eminence of the Olympian Games among Greek festivals, and this ode first among Olympians perhaps because of the powerful position of Hieron among Sicilian tyrants or because of the high estimation in which this particular poem was held. The scheme of the ode is that common, with slight variations, to nearly all the epinicia. It begins with praise of Hieron and his horse; passes to the myth of Tantalus, his son Pelops (q.v.), and the latter's winning of Hippodamia for his bride by defeating Oenomaus in a chariot race; then returns to praise of

Hieron, and a hope that he will win a greater triumph in the chariot race, a victory which Pindar will worthily celebrate.

Ol. II, to Theron, tyrant of Acragas, on his victory in 476 in the chariot race, important not only as one of Pindar's greatest works, but also for the doctrine it sets out (referred to above) of life after death, and retribution.

Ol. III, to Theron, on the same victory as Ol. II. It contains a curious myth, perhaps invented by Pindar, of Heracles bringing the wild olive to Greece from the Danube, the country of the Hyperboreans.

Ol. VI, to Agēsias of Syracuse, victor in the mule-race. Some lines (93–6) of this ode, bidding men remember Syracuse and Ortygia, realm of the wise Hieron, have been found stamped on an ancient brick at Syracuse.

Ol. VII, to Diagoras of Rhodes, winner in the boxing-match (464). Statues of Diagoras, his three sons, and two grandsons, all Olympic victors, stood in a group at Olympia. This ode was engraved in letters of gold in the temple of Athene at Lindos in Rhodes.

Ol. XIV, to Asōpichos of Orchomenus, remarkable for its brevity and perfection, and interesting for its invocation of the Charites or Graces, who were worshipped especially at Orchomenus.

§ 4. *Pythian Odes and other poems*

Pythian I, to Hieron of Syracuse, winner in the chariot race, probably in 470. The ode is a glorification of Hieron's new city of Aetna (see under *Syracuse*, § 1) and is of interest for its historical allusions (Dorian invasion, victories of Cumae and Himera, &c.), for its poetical description of the great eruption of Etna (478 and following years), and for its exhortation to righteous conduct as a ruler.

Pyth. III is exceptional, in that it is not so much a triumphal ode, as a poem of sympathy and consolation addressed to Hieron of Syracuse when he was ill. The illness suggests Asclepius and the myth of Coronis, which the poet tells. He reminds Hieron that there must be vicissitudes in the happiest lots, citing the instances of Peleus and Cadmus.

Pyth. IV, to Arcesilāus, king of Cyrene, winner in the chariot race, composed probably about 462. It is the longest of the surviving odes, a glorification of Cyrene (q.v.), tracing its origin, through Battus its first king, back to Euphēmus one of the Argonauts (q.v.). This brings up the story of Jason and Pelias and the golden fleece, most stirringly told. The ode, which has little of the epinician character, ends with a petition, by parable and myth,

for the restoration from exile of Dāmophilos, a Cyrenean noble, a recent guest-friend of Pindar.

Pyth. X, to Hippocleas of Thessaly, the earliest of Pindar's surviving works; see above, § 1.

Nemean I, to Chromios of Aetna, victor in the chariot race, composed about 473. It contains what is apparently the first account in literature of Heracles as a baby strangling the two serpents sent by Hera to destroy him.

Mention should also be made of the numerous odes that display Pindar's affection for Aegina, e.g. Ol. VIII, Pyth. VIII, Nem. III–VIII, Isthm. V, VI, and VIII; his interest in Cyrene, Pyth. IX; and his love of his native Thebes, Isthm. VII. Of the fragments of poems that have been preserved, the most notable are perhaps the 'Hymn to Thebes', famous in antiquity, dealing with the marriage of Zeus and Themis; the Paean for Thebes (IX) giving the impression made on the poet by the solar eclipse of 463; and the Parthenion (q.v.). His *Threnoi* or dirges throw light on his beliefs regarding the soul and future life.

§ 5. *Later estimates and imitations of Pindar*

Horace, in the fine opening stanzas of Od. IV, ii ('Pindarum quisquis studet aemulari'), praises Pindar's unrivalled qualities, his rushing eloquence, his bold originality in metre and diction, and his admirable use of myths. It was in imitation of Pindar that Horace introduced the patriotic lyric. Quintilian, who expresses the cultured judgement of a later period, also thinks him by far the greatest of the Greek lyric poets (Inst. Or. x. i. 61).

The form of the Pindaric ode was imitated, with varying degrees of success, by several English poets. Cowley in his 'Pindarique Odes' endeavoured, not very happily, to reproduce Pindar's 'enthusiastical manner'. Dryden wrote a 'Threnodia Augustalis' on the death of Charles II, not a very hopeful subject. His 'Song for St. Cecilia's Day' (1687) and 'Alexander's Feast' are among the greatest English poems in this form. The other chief writer of Pindaric odes was Thomas Gray ('The Progress of Poesy' and 'The Bard', 1757). Swift's unsuccessful attempt at a Pindaric provoked Dryden's well-known remark, 'Cousin Swift, you will never be a poet'.

Pīraē'us (*Peiraieus*), the chief port of Athens, on a peninsula five miles SW. of the city. It was adopted as the principal port, in preference to Phalerum, and fortified, at the instance of Themistocles, who would have made Piraeus the capital, but could never persuade the Athenians to remove to it. For the Long Walls connecting the Piraeus with Athens, see *Long Walls*. The fortifications, which completely enclosed the peninsula, including the great harbour (*Cantharus*) and the smaller harbours of Zea and Munychia, were finally destroyed by Sulla after he had captured Athens in the Mithridatic War. In the latter part of the 4th c. the Piraeus contained docks, distributed over the three harbours, for 372 ships of the Athenian navy, and an arsenal for the storage of tackle; the remains of the docks, which were about twenty feet wide, in rows like stalls in a stable, may still be seen, and an inscription preserves the directions for the construction of the arsenal. There was a quay where the Council sat to inspect the galleys as they put out to sea on an expedition. There was also a sort of exchange where foreign merchants and Athenian bankers did business; it was here that the Boastful Man in Theophrastus talked big to foreigners about the sums he had at sea, while in fact he kept tenpence at the bank. The remains of Themistocles are said to have been brought home and appropriately buried near this great fortress. Piraeus was the scene of the struggle between Thrasybulus and the Thirty (see *Athens*, § 5). See Pl. 13*b*.

Pīrē'nē (*Peirēnē*), a celebrated fountain at Corinth.

Pīri'thŏus (*Peirithoos*), see *Centaurs* and *Theseus*.

Pīsi'stratus (*Peisistratos*) and the PISI'-STRATIDS or PEISISTRA'TIDAE. Pisistratus, whose father's name was Hippocrates, first came into prominence at Athens in a war with Megara about 570 B.C., when he captured the port of Nisaea from the enemy. He was ambitious, energetic, and resourceful. He took advantage of his popularity to get himself assigned a bodyguard, appearing in the Agora one day, wounded, he said, by his adversaries. He gathered about himself a party of those dissatisfied with the settlement of Solon (q.v.) and professed revolutionary opinions. In 560 he occupied the Acropolis and made himself tyrant. He was twice expelled, and twice returned to power from exile. His tyranny was of a moderate and beneficent kind. He maintained the constitution of Solon in its form, but saw to it that the chief offices were held by his supporters. He settled the agrarian question which had given rise to much trouble in the past, improving the lot of the small cultivators and converting Attica into a country of small and medium properties

(by what precise measures is not known). He reorganized the public finances and provided Attica with good roads and Athens with a water-supply from the Upper Ilyssus; he and his sons beautified the city with new temples and encouraged art and literature. For instance, Simonides (q.v.) of Ceos received a pension and Anacreon (q.v.) was invited to Athens (see also *Homer*). The Panathenaic festival was celebrated with splendour and with contests in athletics, poetry, and music. New religious cults, especially those of Dionysus and Demeter (qq.v.), were encouraged, and the Great Dionysia (see *Festivals*, § 4) was instituted. Pisistratus strengthened himself abroad by a skilful policy of alliances. He recovered Sigēum at the mouth of the Hellespont, and with his approval the Athenian Miltiades became tyrant of the Chersonese; as a consequence access to the Euxine was made easier for Athenian merchants. By his special interest in Delos (q.v.), the religious centre of the Ionians, he laid the foundation of the Athenian leadership of the Ionian race. He was friendly with Sparta, Argos (he married an Argive wife), and Thessaly. Under him the commercial importance of Athens greatly increased. Her wine, oil, and pottery reached all the surrounding countries. Pisistratus died, still holding the tyranny, in 527. Landor has an 'Imaginary Conversation' between Pisistratus and Solon.

His eldest son Hippias succeeded him, and associated his brother, Hipparchus, in the tyranny. They are known as the *Peisistratidae*. Hippias continued the policy of his father, but he incurred unpopularity as a consequence of the following event. Hipparchus, disappointed in his love for a young man named Harmodius, avenged himself by a public insult to the youth's sister. Harmodius, with his friend Aristogīton, conspired to slay the two tyrants at the Panathenaea. The plot miscarried and Hipparchus alone was killed. Harmodius was immediately cut down by the tyrants' guard. Aristogiton was tortured and put to death (514). For the reverence in which they were subsequently held see *Harmodius*. The rule of Hippias became harsher. His fall was brought about chiefly by the exiled Alcmaeonids (q.v.), who, with the assistance of the Delphic oracle (which had been gained to their cause), induced Sparta to invade Attica. Hippias, besieged in the Acropolis, capitulated and retired to Sigeum (510). Here he entered into relations with the Persians in order to secure by their help his restoration.

At Marathon (see *Persian Wars*) he even assisted them by his counsel. He subsequently died at Lemnos.

Pi′ttacus (*Pittakos*), a leader of the democracy in Lesbos in the latter part of 7th c. B.C., a contemporary of Sappho and Alcaeus. He was included among the Seven Sages (q.v.)

Pi′tys (*Pitus*), see *Pan*.

Planu′dēs, see under *Anthologies* and *Aesop*.

Platae′a (*Plataia* or *Plataiai*), in Boeotia on the frontier of Attica, the scene of the great battle in 479 B.C. in which the Greeks under Pausanias defeated the Persian army under Mardonius (see *Persian Wars*).

Plataea, alone of the Boeotian towns, was allied to Athens at an early date (519 or 509 B.C.; the figure depends on a disputed reading in Thucydides). At Marathon the Plataeans were the only Athenian allies to give assistance in the battle. Plataea was bitterly hostile to Thebes, and her loyalty to Athens led Thebes to attack her in what was in fact the first engagement of the Peloponnesian War. Plataea was besieged and after many vicissitudes taken. The town was razed to the ground by the Thebans, and the remaining Plataeans (those captured at the surrender were executed) became Athenian citizens (427). The Plataeans had hoped to escape this fate in virtue of the guarantee of integrity given them by the Greek States after the defeat of Mardonius.

Platā′icus, see *Isocrates*.

Pla′to (*Plătōn*), a famous Greek philosopher, the founder of idealism in philosophy, and one of the greatest of Greek prose-writers.

§ 1. *Biography*

Plato was born about 427 B.C. at Athens, of a noble family which claimed descent from Codrus (q.v.). He at first wrote poetry, but meeting Socrates probably about 407, turned his attention to philosophy. He was ill at the time of Socrates' execution (399) and was not present during his last moments. After Socrates' death he retired to Megara, and is said to have travelled extensively and to have made the acquaintance of the Pythagoreans in Magna Graecia. He visited Syracuse on three occasions, about 389, 367, and 361, in the reigns of Dionysius I and II, at whose courts he had a strong supporter in Dion (see *Syracuse*, § 2). After his first visit he returned to Athens and began teaching philosophy in the Academy (q.v.), whence his school derived its name. According to

his seventh epistle (see below, § 4) he twice made some attempt to enter political life: under the Thirty, and after the restoration of democracy. But he was repelled by the iniquities perpetrated by the former, and by the condemnation of Socrates under the latter. He died in 348.

§ 2. *Philosophical writings*

Plato himself thought that the spoken word was superior to the written; hence the authentic statement of his views was to be found in his lectures, the doctrines of which are unknown to us except from some obscure references in Aristotle. His written works were intended to be of a popular character. They have come down to us complete and in a fairly perfect state, and took the form of dialogues. Their chronological arrangement is a matter of discussion, but differences in their general design, the evolution of doctrine that they present, and changes in points of grammar and style, concur in indicating a broad distribution into three groups. The first, which presents Socrates as the principal figure examining and demolishing the views put forward by his interlocutors, includes the 'Charmides', 'Crito',* 'Euthyphro',* 'Hippias Major' (its authenticity is contested), 'Hippias Minor', 'Ion', 'Laches', 'Lysis' and also the 'Apology'* (not a dialogue, but a reproduction of Socrates' defence at his trial). The second, in which Socrates, still the foremost figure, puts forward positive doctrines which may be regarded as Plato's own, or Plato's interpretation of the views of Socrates, includes the 'Alcibiades', 'Cratylus',* 'Euthydemus', 'Gorgias',* 'Menexenus', 'Meno',* 'Parmenides', 'Phaedo',* 'Phaedrus',* 'Protagoras',* 'Republic',* 'Symposium',* and 'Theaetetus'.* The third group, the work of Plato's later years, includes the 'Critias', 'Philebus', 'Politicus', 'Sophist',* and 'Timaeus';* the 'Laws'* was Plato's last work, left in draft, and published after his death. Of the above, those marked with an asterisk are briefly dealt with herein under their several titles. Of the others, the 'Charmides', 'Laches', and 'Lysis' are concerned with the nature respectively of Temperance, Courage, and Friendship. The 'Hippias Major', in which, with assumed deference, Socrates demolishes the arguments of the Elean sophist of that name, is a discussion of the nature of the beautiful; in the 'Hippias Minor', a discussion with the same sophist, Socrates proves by a sophistical argument that he who does evil intentionally is less blameworthy than he who does it unintentionally. The 'Ion' is the genial mockery of a rhapsodist, who is shown to possess no art of his own. The 'Alcibiades' is concerned with knowledge as a qualification of the statesman. The 'Euthydemus' is a satire, in a broad vein of mirth, on the sophists. The 'Menexenus' is attributed with some hesitation to Plato; in it Socrates recites a funeral oration, after the style of Thucydides, which purports to have been composed by Aspasia (see *Pericles*). The 'Parmenides', in which the great Eleatic philosophers Parmenides and Zeno are introduced, is a difficult dialogue in which a form of the theory of ideas (see below) is severely criticized. The 'Critias' is an unfinished dialogue, a sequel to the 'Timaeus' (q.v.). The 'Philebus' is a discussion of the relations of pleasure and wisdom to the good. In the 'Politicus' ('Statesman'), the character of the true king or statesman is investigated; in the absence of the ideal monarch, the best practical course is for the citizens to frame the laws and make them inviolable.

Much of the charm of Plato's dialogues consists in their dramatic setting, the description of the scenes in which they take place, the amusing and interesting characters that he stages, and the genial irony of Socrates.

§ 3. *Plato's philosophy*

Plato's philosophy contains two principal elements, moral and metaphysical. To the views of Socrates (q.v.) on the nature of virtue, he added certain metaphysical conceptions, on the nature of God (though explicit theology is never very prominent in Plato), the soul, and the relation of God to the world, with which Socrates did not concern himself. In some of his earlier dialogues is found one of his principal contributions to philosophical thought, the Theory of Ideas. The *idea* or *form* of a thing, in this theory, is something of the nature of our abstract conception of that thing, but having a real existence outside the world of sense; it is the unchanging reality behind the changing appearance. The knowledge of these *ideas* is to be attained only by pure reason (νοῦς or διάνοια) unaffected by sensation, and proceeding by dialectic. The supreme *idea* is that of the Good, on which all the others are ultimately founded. With Plato, as with Socrates, virtue is knowledge, knowledge of this supreme *idea*. Plato's later doctrines are more vaguely inferred from the dialogues and from statements by Aristotle: they appear to have included a system of logical categories and a tentative identification of the *ideas* with numbers. His doctrine of the soul, the motive element in the

universe, and its relation to God, is an important feature in the later dialogues. Plato's general conception of the system of the universe is summed up in mythical form in the 'Timaeus'.

For Plato, political science is the science of the soul, and includes moral science. The good of a city depends on the moral value of its citizens, on the prevalence in each and in the whole of justice, and of harmony between the higher and lower elements. His views respecting this are set out in the 'Republic', and in a more practical form in the 'Laws'.

§ 4. *Plato's Epistles*

Thirteen Epistles attributed to Plato have come down to us. They were regarded as genuine by the ancients, and are quoted by Cicero and Plutarch. Three of them are now considered as certainly spurious, and three as certainly authentic; the remainder are generally accepted as probably his work. They all relate to Plato's connexion with Dion and Dionysius and are addressed to correspondents in Sicily. The three most important, which are accepted as genuine, are the third, seventh, and eighth; they were intended for publication and are a defence of the course taken by Plato in his relations with the rulers of Syracuse; they were written probably between 356 and 352. The third is addressed to Dionysius II, while the struggle between him and Dion was still proceeding. The seventh is addressed to the friends of Dion after the murder of the latter (353) and is of great interest for its autobiographical matter, for its defence of Plato's political ideals, and for its passionate lament for his friend Dion. The eighth is a letter of political advice to the friends of Dion.

§ 5. *Plato's influence*

By his idealism, his sense of an invisible eternal world behind the changing unrealities of the world of sense, his conception of God and of the relation of religion to morality, Plato exercised an immense influence on philosophic and religious thought. Cicero had deep veneration for his philosophy. Quintilian speaks with enthusiasm of his acumen and divine style. Manuscripts of his works reached Egypt early: a papyrus ascribed to the 3rd c. B.C., containing part of the 'Phaedo', has been found in the Fayoum. Plato paved the way for Christianity, and, especially through the Neoplatonists (q.v.), helped to shape it. His influence on religion is particularly seen in St. Augustine (e.g. 'De civitate dei'), and in England at a later period, again through the Neoplatonists, in the Cambridge Platonists, Whichcote, More, and Cudworth, of the 17th c. On English literature and philosophy his influence is constantly manifested; there are notable examples of it in Spenser (through the Italian Ficino), Sir Thomas More, Addison (in his myths), Berkeley ('Alciphron' and 'Hylas'), Coleridge, and Shelley. It is seen most strikingly in Wordsworth, in the mood of the poet who feels the eternal behind the beauties of the visible world. Among Landor's 'Imaginary Conversations' is one between Diogenes and Plato, which may be taken as conveying the author's criticisms on the latter. Jowett's famous translation of and introductions to the Dialogues of Plato were published in 1871.

Plau′tus, TĪTUS MACCUS or MACCIUS (c. 254–184 B.C.), the earlier of the two great Roman playwrights whose comedies survive (his period falls between those of Naevius and Ennius), was born in humble circumstances at Sarsina, just within the borders of Umbria. He is said to have supported himself as a stage-carpenter; also to have worked in a flour-mill, writing his plays in the intervals of manual labour, to eke out his wages. Twenty of the one hundred and thirty plays that were attributed to him have survived, all included in the twenty-one named by Varro as unquestionably authentic. They are adapted from Athenian comedies of the 4th and 3rd cc. B.C., such as those of Menander, Diphilus, and Philemon, and they reproduce Greek life, and with humorous exaggeration, Greek character, as presented by those authors. They were consequently known as *palliatae* (q.v.). They contain no satire on public affairs. But while Plautus preserves these Greek features in order to avoid offending Roman taste, e.g. in regard to the conduct of women and slaves as depicted, he introduces elements from Roman life and the Roman environment; and his adaptations are moreover pervaded with his own gift for comedy and his familiarity with the humble and middle classes of Rome. The prologues (some of them, however, by a later hand) contain contemporary allusions and make us acquainted with the sources from which the plays are drawn and with the audiences whom Plautus addressed, the noisy, unlettered crowd that attended the Roman festivals. The extant comedies show a wide variety of manner, the sentimental comedy of the 'Captivi', the domestic comedy of the 'Trinummus', the romantic comedy of the 'Rudens', the burlesque of the 'Amphitruo', and the

farcical comedy of the 'Miles Gloriosus' (qq.v.). But the plots of the majority centre in the knavish tricks of a slave, designed to favour the affairs of a young lover and his mistress, who is often discovered to be of free Athenian birth and is accordingly married to her lover. Besides the cunning slave, the stock characters include fathers gullible or libertine, braggart captains, and greedy pimps. The plays are marked by fertility of intrigue and vivacity of dialogue, and even the stock characters show considerable diversity in details.

The best-known of Plautus's comedies are 'Amphitruo', 'Aulularia', 'Bacchides', 'Captivi', 'Menaechmi', 'Mostellaria', 'Miles Gloriosus', 'Pseudolus', 'Rudens', and 'Trinummus'. The titles of the less important are 'Asinaria', 'Casina', 'Cistellaria', 'Curculio', 'Epidicus', 'Mercator', 'Persa', 'Poenulus', 'Stichus', and 'Truculentus'. They are all briefly dealt with herein under their titles. The twenty-first of the plays named by Varro as undoubtedly authentic is the 'Vidularia' ('Wallet') of which fragments survive in a palimpsest.

In the plays of Plautus the dialogue (*diverbium*) occupied only about one-third, the sung portion (*cantica*) about two-thirds, of each play; they were in fact a sort of musical comedies. The dialogue was written chiefly in iambic senarii (see *Metre*, § 4), but the scansion was far less regular than in later authors, and was based in great part not on the quantity but the accentuation of the syllables, probably in accordance with colloquial pronunciation. The sung portion was written in a variety of lyric metres.

The earliest (but incomplete) manuscript of the extant plays is a palimpsest, in which the Latin version of the Book of Kings was written in the 8th c. over a 4th c. text of the comedies. The influence of Plautus in English literature may be traced in many plays, from the 'Ralph Roister Doister' of Udall (1505–56), the 'Mother Bombie' of Lyly (1554?–1606), the 'Comedy of Errors' of Shakespeare, and many of the comedies of Ben Jonson, to the 'Amphitryon' of Dryden. The stock character of the braggart soldier, e.g. Jonson's Bobadil, is derived from Plautus. The revival of interest in Plautus at the beginning of the 16th c. is shown by the fact that Henry VIII had two of his comedies performed at an entertainment given to the French ambassador in 1526.

Plebs, Plebeians, the Roman burgesses other than the patricians. For the nature of the original distinction between the two classes, see under *Patricians*. The plebeians gradually increased in number as new elements were added to the population, either from the subjugation of the Latin tribes, from the emancipation of slaves, or from the influx of refugees from other cities. At first they were a non-privileged class, but gradually their position improved. See *Rome*, §§ 3 and 6.

Plei'ad, THE, a name given to the seven most eminent Greek tragic poets of the reign of Ptolemy II (see *Ptolemies*). Their names are variously given, but none of their works have survived except the 'Alexandra' of Lycophron (q.v.), and this is not a tragedy. In some lists the names include poets other than tragedians, such as Theocritus and Aratus. The name was derived from the Pleiades (q.v.). The name *La Pléiade* was later given to a group of 16th-c. French poets including Ronsard and du Bellay.

Plēī'ădĕs (or *Plēīades*), in Greek mythology, the seven daughters of Atlas (q.v.) and Plēīonē. Their names were Maia (the mother of Hermes by Zeus), Tăygetĕ, Ēlectrā, Alcyonĕ, Asteropĕ, Celaenō, and Meropĕ. They were pursued by Orion (q.v.), and he and they were turned into constellations. The morning rising of the Pleiades marked the beginning of summer, their morning setting the beginning of winter.

Plēī'ŏnē, the mother of the Pleiades (q.v.).

Ple'onasm, the use of language copious beyond what is necessary; e.g. 'Abiit, excessit, evasit, erupit', said by Cicero of Catiline (in Cat. ii. 1).

Pli'ny the Elder (*Gāius Plīnius Secundus*) (A.D. 23 or 24–79) was born at Cōmum, on the Lake of Como, of an equestrian family, and came early to Rome. He knew and was influenced by Pomponius Secundus (q.v.), whose biography he subsequently wrote, and was perhaps actually trained in literature by him. He pleaded at the bar as a young man, and subsequently saw military service, being at one time the comrade-in-arms of the future emperor Titus, and perhaps serving on his staff in Syria. After A.D. 70 he held a succession of procuratorships in Gaul, Africa, and Spain, which he discharged 'summa integritate' (Suetonius), and when at Rome was in close relations with the emperor Vespasian. He perished in the great eruption of Vesuvius of the year 79. The younger Pliny has described in a letter to Tacitus (vi. 16) how his uncle, being then in command of the fleet at Mīsēnum, had his attention drawn to the column of smoke rising above the nearer

mountains, and hastened in a light vessel to investigate; how he dictated his observations under a hail of stones, and the next day went out on the sea-shore, with a pillow about his head as a protection against the stones, in the darkness and amid violent concussions, and was asphyxiated by the sulphurous fumes.

Pliny was a man of extraordinary industry and thirst for knowledge. He slept little, had books constantly read to him, and took an immense quantity of notes. He wrote works, which are lost, on military science, oratory, grammar, biography, and history (twenty books on the German Wars, and thirty-one books of recent Roman history in continuation of the work of Aufidius Bassus). But his greatest achievement, which has survived, is the 'Naturalis Historia' in thirty-seven books, dedicated to the future emperor Titus in 77, and published for the greater part posthumously.

Book I consists of a table of contents and a formidable list of authorities, Latin and Greek. The question of the extent to which this is reliable and how far Pliny had direct recourse to the Greek and the older Roman authors has been the subject of much controversy. Book II deals with the physics of the universe, and its constituent elements; III–VI are on the geography and ethnology of Europe, Asia, and Africa; VII on the physiology of man; VIII–XI on zoology (land animals, sea animals, birds, insects); XII–XIX on botany; XX–XXVII on the medical properties of plants; XXVIII–XXXII, on medicaments derived from animal sources; XXXIII–XXXVII on minerals and metallurgy, including the use of minerals in medicine and the arts, with a digression on the history of art.

In spite of many vulgar errors, much credulity, superficiality, unscientific arrangement, and the tediousness of dry catalogues, the work is not only remarkable for the vast labour that it represents, but contains much that is interesting and entertaining, and much information about the art, science, and civilization of the author's day that would, but for it, be lost to us. The 'Natural History' is hardly a work that one can read through continuously, but wherever one dips into it, curious passages occur: such as that about the skeleton of the monster to which Andromeda had been exposed, brought from Joppa and exhibited at Rome (ix. 4; Joppa evidently traded on the legend, for the chains with which Andromeda was fastened were also shown there, v. 14); the tricks that elephants were taught (viii. 2–4); the anecdote of Lysander and the funeral of Sophocles (vii. 30): the perils to which sponge-divers were exposed (ix. 70); the coracles of the British (vii. 57); the first introduction of barbers into Italy (vii. 59). Roman life is illustrated by such passages as those about the variety of mattresses and woollen cloths in use (viii. 73 et seq.); about hedgehogs' quills used for carding wool, and the senate's decrees to prevent their being monopolized (viii. 56); the price of a cook (ix. 31); Lollia Paulina's jewels (ix. 58); ostrich feathers worn in military helmets (x. 1); *foie gras* and pillows of goose-feathers (x. 27); wrinkles removed with ass's milk (xxviii. 51). The chapters on the history of painting (xxxv. 36) and of sculpture (xxxvi. 4) are especially interesting, telling us much about Zeuxis, Parrhasius, and Apelles, and about Phidias, Praxiteles, and Scopas (qq.v.), and showing the estimation in which they were held at Rome.

Like Seneca, Pliny is a believer in a beneficent deity, a spirit pervading the world. He is an enthusiastic admirer of nature, and a vigorous critic of contemporary man, his folly, luxury, inhumanity, and ingratitude. He is a sturdy Roman in his dislike of the Greeks and distrust of their influence. A translation of the 'Natural History' was made into English by Philemon Holland (1601).

Pli'ny the Younger (*Gāius Plīnius Caecilius Secundus*, as he was called after adoption under his uncle's will, having previously been named P. Caecilius Secundus) (A.D. 61 or 62–c. 113), was born at Cōmum on the Lake of Como and was nephew of the Elder Pliny (see above). He studied at Rome under Quintilian, whose influence may be seen in the good taste and restraint of the pupil's writing, and under the Stoic philosopher Mūsōnius (who was also the teacher of Epictetus). He was three times married; his letters show that his marriage with Calpurnia, the third wife, was a very happy one. He had no children, but received from Trajan the *jus trium liberorum* (q.v.). He passed through the regular series of magistracies and succeeded by his discretion in avoiding (though he stood in some danger) Domitian's persecution of the Stoic opposition, in spite of his sympathy with their views. Under Trajan he became one of the prefects of the State treasury, *consul suffectus* in A.D. 100, then a curator of the Tiber and its banks (an important office owing to the liability to floods), augur (succeeding Frontinus, q.v.), and was governor of Bithȳnia probably from A.D. 111 till his death about 113. Pliny was very rich, and owned estates in various parts of Italy, which he adminis-

…ered with efficiency. He was notably considerate to his slaves, and munificent. He founded a library at Comum and made many large gifts and charitable bequests.

Pliny practised in the courts and was proud of his oratory. The only speech of his that has survived is a revised edition of the 'Panegyricus' he pronounced on Trajan, when entering on his consulate. It is on the whole a sincere eulogy, an expression of the relief felt under the new reign from the oppression of Domitian, and an important historical document, throwing light on Trajan's reforms. There are some notable phrases in it, such as the description of the previous emperors: 'cum essent civium domini, libertorum erant servi.' Among the other important speeches that Pliny delivered was one impeaching, on behalf of the Africans, Marius Priscus, who had been proconsul of Africa. In this he was associated with Tacitus (A.D. 100).

Pliny's fame rests on his 'Letters'. Of these he published nine books before he left Rome for his Bithynian governorship. A tenth book, containing his official correspondence with Trajan, mainly from his province, was published after his death. The first nine books are a collection of his more carefully composed epistles, written or revised with a view to publication, ranging from short notes asking for news of a friend and notable only for their elegance, to elaborate discussions, for instance, of some point of senatorial procedure. The subjects are very varied, public affairs (especially the prosecutions of officials with which he was concerned), descriptions of his villas or of scenery, a wild-boar hunt (to which Pliny takes his writing materials), reproof of a friend who fails to come to dinner, literary or rhetorical points, interpretation of a dream, ghost stories, the purchase of a statue or an estate, a murder. Several of them are addressed to his friends Tacitus and Suetonius. Among the former is the famous letter (vi. 16) describing the eruption of Vesuvius and his uncle's death. Other interesting letters are those containing eulogies of Silius Italicus and Martial (iii. 7 and 21), and that relating the story of Paetus and Arria (q.v., iii. 16). A bibliography of the works of the Elder Pliny is contained in iii. 5. The style is adapted to the subject, grave or gay, and strikes the mean, in general, between the amplitude of Cicero and the brevity of Seneca; but the Letters, in view of their intended publication, are more artificial, less unstudied, than Cicero's letters to Atticus. They are not dated, and Pliny professes to have arranged them at haphazard.

Apart from the charm communicated to them by the amiable character of the author, they are interesting for the picture they give us of the life of a wealthy Roman noble in a happy period of the empire. They also afford some useful evidence on the history of the times, correcting the unfavourable impression left by the bitter satire of Juvenal and the sombre pessimism which Tacitus retained when writing under Trajan. We see, for instance, the Senate deliberating on matters of importance within its restricted sphere, punishments inflicted on dishonest officials, and family life pursuing its course under normal conditions of loyalty and virtue.

The correspondence with Trajan in the 10th Book, apart from some earlier letters asking for various favours, throws a valuable light on the administration of an imperial province. It displays Pliny as an honest but timid governor, referring to Rome such small matters as the absence of a fire-brigade and water-buckets at Nicomedia. The emperor's replies, though occasionally a little curt when the question is obviously unnecessary, are precise and clear and show him encouraging an extraordinary degree of centralization. The most famous of these letters are Pliny's submission of the question how the Christians should be treated, and the emperor's answer.

Pliny prided himself not only on his oratory but on his poetry, and published a volume of hendecasyllabic poems. Some specimens of his mediocre verse are included in his 'Letters'. His simple vanity in his literary fame appears amusingly where (ix. 23) he tells how a Roman knight, sitting next to Tacitus at the Circus and conversing with him, asked him who he was, and being answered 'You certainly know me from my writings', inquired 'Are you Tacitus or Pliny?

Plōti'nus (*Plōtinos*), born (*c.* A.D. 205) probably at Lycopolis in Egypt, the chief exponent of Neoplatonism (q.v.). He settled in Rome in 244, after having, it is said, accompanied the expedition of Gordian to Mesopotamia, in order to consult the Magi. He was a man of an extremely spiritual and mystical character. 'He seemed ashamed to be in a body' says his biographer, Porphyry. The essence of his philosophy is the desire to escape from the material world. He explains the universe by a hierarchy rising from matter to soul, soul to reason, and reason to God, the final abstraction, without form or matter, pure existence. Reality is the spiritual world contemplated by reason. The phenomenal world is a creation of the

soul and has no real existence, matter being a mere receptacle for forms imposed on it by the soul. In ethics Plotinus enjoined purification by self-discipline, with a view to ascent to the spiritual world and the pursuit, impelled by love and enthusiasm, of the divine. His writings were edited by his pupil Porphyry (q.v.) in six books of nine chapters each, hence called *Enneads*. Plotinus has been elucidated, and his influence on Christianity discussed, by Dean Inge (Gifford Lectures, 1918). The 'Enneads' have been recently translated by the late Stephen McKenna.

Plū'tarch (*Ploutarchos*) (*c.* A.D. 46–*c.* 120), a famous Greek biographer and moral philosopher.

§ 1. *Life and works*

Plutarch was born at Chaerōnēa in Boeotia. We know little of his life. He appears to have visited Rome at least twice and to have lectured there on ethical subjects, to have visited Alexandria and various parts of Italy and Greece, to have been a member of the college of priests at Delphi, and to have held municipal office at Chaeronea in his later years. Many of his treatises are probably the expanded notes of lectures that he gave. He is one of the most attractive of ancient authors, writing with charm, geniality, and tact, so as always to interest the reader. His surviving works consist of (*a*) a series of 'Parallel Lives' (*Bioi parallēloi*), in which he relates the life of some eminent Greek (statesman or soldier) and the life of an eminent Roman offering some points of resemblance, and then adds a short comparison of the two. (*b*) 'Syngrammata ēthika' (*Mōrālia*), a collection of eighty-three treatises on questions of conduct and also on points of physics, archaeology, literature, &c. They reveal the author's moral dignity and throw an interesting light on the conditions of the times. They are an attempt to satisfy the demand for moral guidance in an age of reaction against the decadence of the Roman world, when the faith in the old gods and philosophies was failing.

§ 2. *The Parallel Lives*

There are twenty-three pairs of lives, and also four single lives, making fifty lives in all. They include such interesting personages as Solon, Themistocles, Pericles, Alcibiades, Aristides, Demosthenes, Nicias, Philopoemen, Timoleon, Dion, Alexander, Pyrrhus, Marius, Sulla, Pompey, Antony, Brutus, Julius Caesar, and Cicero. Plutarch's object in each case is to bring out the moral character of his subject, rather than to relate the political events of his time. He therefore gives his attention chiefly to anecdotes calculated to reveal the nature of the man, 'a light occasion, a word, or some sport' which 'makes men's natural dispositions more plain than the famous battles won, wherein are slain ten thousand men'. But he was careful in his choice of historical sources, and dealt with them honestly and intelligently. His treatment shows no unfairness in his comparison of Greek and Roman worthies, no flattery of the dominant race, no vanity in favour of compatriots. The 'Lives' contain, besides curious anecdotes, many memorable historical passages, such as the catastrophe of the Syracusan expedition ('Nicias'), the defeat and murder of Pompey, the death of the younger Cato, and the suicide of Otho. There are also great battle-pictures, the victory of Marius over the Cimbri, Timoleon's victory at the Crimīsus, the siege of Syracuse by Marcellus; and also striking descriptions of a quite different kind, of the happy state of Italy under Numa, of Sicily pacified by Timoleon, and of Cleopatra sailing up the Cydnus to join Antony.

The most famous translation of Plutarch's 'Lives' into English was that of Sir Thomas North (1579). It was made not from the Greek, but from the French version of Amyot. It was closely followed by Shakespeare in his three Roman plays, 'Julius Caesar', 'Antony and Cleopatra', and 'Coriolanus' (particularly in the first). The translation by W. and J. Langhorne (1770) was for more than a century the standard Plutarch. R. Browning appears to have drawn on Plutarch's 'Nicias' in a passage of his 'Balaustion's Adventure'; and Wordsworth's 'Dion', is based on Plutarch's life of that great Sicilian (see *Syracuse*, § 2).

§ 3. *The Moralia*

The subjects of these treatises are extremely various (the treatises are generally known by their Latin titles). There is an ethical group dealing with such questions of conduct as 'Advice to married couples' (*conjugālia praecepta*), 'How to discern between a flatterer and a friend' (*quomodo adūlātōr ab amīco internoscatur*), 'About busybodies' (*de cūriōsitāte*), 'On garrulity' (*de garrulitāte*), 'On the restraint of anger' (*de cohibenda ira*). There is a religious group, in which Plutarch appears as the interpreter and defender of the old theology. It includes the treatise 'On Superstition' (*de superstitiōne*), which he regards as the opposite extreme to atheism, the superstitious regarding the gods as cruel, revengeful, and capricious. Plutarch was a Platonist and was opposed to some of the

doctrines of the Stoics, and still more to the Epicurean school and to its encouragement of withdrawal from the duties of social life (see his treatises, *an recte dictum sit, latenter esse vivendum*, and *praecepta gerendae reipublicae*; also *non posse suaviter vivi secundum Epicurum*). There is an interesting treatise 'On the delays of divine justice' (*de sera nūminis vindicta*), in which he explains the puzzle of the apparent prosperity of the wicked; also treatises 'On the Ē at Delphi' (*de Ē apud Delphos*), i.e. on the explanation of the letter Ē inscribed on the temple of Apollo there; and 'On the cessation of oracles' (*de dēfectu ōrāculorum*), which contains a discussion of demons (see *Daimones*), beings intermediate between gods and men, and refers to the legend of the genii of the British Isles. A different kind of treatise is that 'On the face in the Moon' (*de facie quae in orbe lūnae appāret*), a cosmical speculation. Included in the 'Moralia' are Plutarch's 'Symposiaca' (*Quaestiones conviviāles*), table-talks of wise men (rhetoricians, physicians, &c., some of them historical characters) on a multitude of subjects. It is noteworthy that Plutarch, in spite of his familiarity with Roman society, and Roman history, archaeology, and ritual, completely ignores Roman literature (his knowledge of Latin appears to have been limited). He gives, indeed, in his life of Lucullus, the Greek version of one passage from Horace, but never makes mention of Virgil or Ovid. He wrote some literary criticism, including a comparison of Aristophanes and Menander, and an essay 'On the malignity of Herodotus' (see under *Herodotus, ad fin.*)

Plutarch's 'Moralia' were studied by many later authors, notably Montaigne (who modelled the form of his Essays upon them), Jeremy Taylor, and Francis Bacon. They were translated into English by Philemon Holland in 1603. Wyttenbach's edition appeared in 1795–1830. Southey in 'The Doctor' includes the 'Moralia' among the few books that Daniel Dove has on his bookshelves. A good introduction to them is to be found in Archbishop Trench's lectures on Plutarch (1873).

Plu'to (*Ploutōn*), in Greek mythology, a name of Hades (q.v.), meaning according to Plato the wealth-giver (from πλοῦτος), in the sense that the earth is the source of wealth (cf. *Plutus*).

Plū'tus (*Ploutos*), in Greek mythology, the personification of wealth, the son of Demeter (q.v.) and a certain Iasīon, of whom the ancients gave various accounts and who may be conjectured to be some ancient deity of agriculture. From the fact

that Plutus was the fruit of the above
union, combined with a passage in the
'Odyssey' (v. 125 et seq.), it is evident
that Plutus originally symbolized agricultural wealth, abundant crops.

Plū′tus (*Ploutos*, 'Wealth'), a comedy by
Aristophanes, produced in 388 B.C., the
last of his extant plays. The lyrics that it
contains for the chorus are very scanty,
but provision appears to have been made,
at various places, for choric interludes
having no special connexion with the plot.
There were two versions of the play, of
which we have the second. In it the
author humorously exposes the consequences that would follow from the
equalization of wealth and the abolition
of poverty.

Chremylus is so indignant at seeing
scoundrels on all sides grow rich, while
he himself is honest and poor, that he
consults Apollo whether he would not do
well to bring up his son as a rascal. The
god advises Chremylus to follow the first
person he meets on leaving the shrine and
induce him to enter his house. This person proves to be an old blind man, who
under pressure of threats reveals that he
is Plutus, the god of wealth, whom Zeus
has blinded out of ill-will to men. Chremylus decides that the sight of Plutus must
be restored, so that he may avoid the
wicked and consort only with the virtuous,
which his blindness has prevented him
from doing. Plutus is terrified of the vengeance of Zeus, but is presently persuaded
that he is really more powerful than that
god, and consents to be taken to the
temple of Asclepius to be cured. The
goddess of Poverty intervenes and tries
to deter Chremylus, pointing out the disastrous effects of what he proposes to do,
for it is Poverty, the source of all virtue
and effort, that has made Hellas what she
is. But Chremylus remains unconvinced.
The proceedings in the temple of Asclepius
are amusingly described, and Plutus, with
his sight restored, returns to the house of
Chremylus, who is now rich. Then come
a series of visitors: an honest man who has
long been poor and is now prosperous, who
wishes to dedicate his old, worn-out cloak
and shoes to the god; an informer, indignant at being ruined; an old woman who
has lost the lover who flattered her for
her riches; Hermes, who can now get
nothing to eat in heaven, and wants a job
on earth; and finally the priest of Zeus
himself, who likewise is dying of hunger.

Pni′gos, see *Comedy*, § 2.

Pnyx (*Pnux*), a hill at Athens, about a
quarter of a mile W. of the Acropolis,
where from the time of Cleisthenes to the
latter part of the 4th c. the ecclesia (q.v.)
or assembly of the people held its sittings.
A large amphitheatre had been hewn out
of the side of the hill, capable of holding
some 20,000 citizens. There was a raised
dais for the president, his herald, and
secretary; on it also stood an altar of Zeus
Agoraios ('of the assembly'). See Pl. 13a.

Podali′rius (*Podaleirios*), see *Machaon*.

Poe′nulus ('The Little Carthaginian'),
a comedy by Plautus. The two daughters
of Hanno, a Carthaginian, were stolen from
him in their childhood, and have been
bought by a procurer and taken to Sicyon.
In the same place is living Agorastoclēs,
son of Hanno's cousin; he likewise was
stolen in infancy and has been adopted by
a wealthy citizen of Sicyon. He has fallen
in love with the elder of the sisters, not
knowing of their kinship to himself. He
and his slave devise a plot for ruining the
procurer in order to free the girl. Meanwhile Hanno, who has been searching
every country for his daughters, arrives
at Sicyon, discovers them and his relative
Agorastocles, recovers the girls, and bestows the elder on her lover. Some of
Hanno's speeches appear to be in the
Punic tongue.

Poetics (*Peri Poiētikēs*, Lat. *Poëtica*), a
treatise by Aristotle on Poetry. Poetry,
he points out, like music, dancing, painting, and sculpture, has imitation for its
basis, but differs from them in the means,
objects, and manner of the imitation. In
the portion of the treatise that survives,
Aristotle divides poetry according as it
imitates men above or below the average
level of humanity (tragedy represents
good characters, comedy bad), and according as it is narrative (epic) or dramatic. He
finds the origin of poetry in the instinctive
love of imitation, and traces the special
origins and development of tragedy and
comedy (qq.v.). An analysis of tragedy
follows: its constituent elements (plot,
character, language, thought, spectacle,
song); what it represents (a single action
or experience, of a certain magnitude); its
purpose (to provoke pity and terror and
so give an outlet to these emotions and
thereby produce pleasure); its construction or plot (including the use of 'reversal
of fortune' and 'discovery'); the characters, and the diction. This part includes
the notable saying that poetry is more
'philosophic' than history, because it
rather tells general truths, while history
tells particular facts. Some of Plato's
criticisms of tragedy are referred to and
rejected.

Aristotle proceeds to discuss epic poetry, the rules to which it should conform.

and its metre; and then compares tragedy with epic. Finally he deals with 'problems', i.e. the censures of commentators like Zoïlus (q.v.), and how they may be met. The work attained great fame and exerted much influence in the 17th c. on French classical drama: the doctrine of dramatic unities which dominate the latter was thought to derive from Aristotle, though in fact the necessity of the unity of action alone is insisted on in the 'Poetics'. The work was first printed separately in 1536, after which there were numerous editions and commentaries.

Poggio Bracciolini, see *Texts and Studies*, § 9.

Po'lemarch, at Athens (q.v., § 2), one of the archons, originally the commander-in-chief of the army; but when the chief command was transferred to the strategi (q.v.), the polemarch was reduced to certain judicial and ceremonial functions.

Politian, see *Texts and Studies*, § 9.

Politics (Politika), a treatise on the science of politics by Aristotle (q.v., § 3 (4)).

Poli'ticus (Politikos), see *Plato*, § 2.

Polity of the Athenians, see *Aristotle*, § 3 (4).

Po'llio, GAIUS ASINIUS (76 B.C.–A.D. 5), in his youth an associate of Catullus, a supporter of Caesar in the Civil War and later of Antony, whose legate he was in Transpadane Gaul. He was consul in 40 B.C., and obtained a triumph for his victory over an Illyrian tribe in 39 B.C. It was he who first recognized the genius of Virgil, and came to his assistance when Virgil's farm near Mantua was confiscated after Philippi. The poet celebrated him in his 4th and 8th Eclogues. Horace addressed him with high praise in 'Odes' II. i. Pollio was an orator, a literary patron, and an author. He wrote a 'History of the Civil Wars' from the consulate of Metellus in 60 B.C. to Philippi, which has unfortunately not survived, but was used by Appian and Plutarch; he also wrote tragedies and erotic poems, and may be the author of the 'Bellum Alexandrinum' which continues Caesar's 'Commentaries'. He founded the first public library in Rome, and he is said by the elder Seneca to have introduced the practice of reciting his own works to an audience.

Po'llio, TREBELLIUS, see *Historia Augusta*.

Po'llux, see *Dioscuri*.

Pollux, JULIUS, see *Julius Pollux*.

Polyae'nus *(Poluainos)*, of the 2nd c. A.D., author of *Stratēgēmata*, a collection of ruses in war, written in Greek and dedicated to the emperors Marcus Aurēlius and Vērus. The work is extant.

Poly'bius *(Polubios)* (c. 202–120 B.C.), a great Greek historian, was born at Megalopolis in Arcadia, the son of Lycortās, who was a prominent member of the Achaean League (q.v.) and a friend of Philopoemen (q.v.). Polybius carried the ashes of Philopoemen to burial in 183, went with his father on an embassy to Egypt in 181, and was *hipparchus* (commander of cavalry) of the League in 169/8. He was a supporter of the view that Greece must accept Roman supremacy if it was to retain any sort of autonomy for its cities. But the neutrality of the League in the war between the Romans and Perseus of Macedonia brought its leaders under suspicion at Rome, and Polybius was one of the thousand Achaeans deported to Italy after Pydna (168). He was chosen as tutor to the sons of Aemilius Paullus, the younger of whom became by adoption Publius Scipio (q.v.) Aemilianus. An enduring friendship grew up between Polybius and Scipio. In 150 Polybius was allowed to return to Greece with the other survivors of the deported Achaeans, but he accompanied Scipio to the siege of Carthage in 147–146. He was once more in Greece after the destruction of Corinth by Mummius in 146, and was entrusted with the organization of the details of the administration under the new settlement. In this difficult task he earned the approval of the Romans and the gratitude of the Greek cities. Little is known of the last twenty years of his life, which must have been largely occupied with his literary work. Besides his 'History', he wrote a life of Philopoemen and other works, which have perished.

The 'History' was originally designed to record the rapid and dramatic rise of Roman supremacy in the Mediterranean from the beginning of the Second Punic War to the end of the Third Macedonian War (220–168 B.C.). Polybius subsequently extended his scheme to cover the preliminary period from the beginning of the First Punic War (264), and the succeeding period to the destruction of Carthage and Corinth (146). In this complete form the history consisted of forty books, of which the first five alone survive entire; of the rest we have only excerpts and quotations. Book VI includes a sketch of the Roman constitution in Polybius's day, and a comparison of this with the constitutions of the Greek cities. To the perfection of the former, as a blend of monarchical, aristocratic, and democratic elements, Polybius attributed the greatness of Rome. Polybius was exceptionally qualified for his task, by his personal experience of politics, diplomacy, and war, by his travels (which extended to the Atlantic and to Libya) and his acquaintance with many of the leading Romans, and by his earnest devotion to truth, in pursuit of which he made a painstaking study of documents and records. He had a clear understanding, remarkable in a contemporary, of the position which Rome had achieved in the Mediterranean world. He systematically seeks the causes of events ('nothing, whether probable or improbable, can happen without a cause'), tracing the evolution of nations and their decline. He does not shrink from exposing the sources of the decadence of Greece. His narrative is clear and simple, without rhetorical artifice, written in the common dialect, founded on Attic, which prevailed from 300 B.C., and without the elegance of the Greek prose-writers of the great period. It is somewhat monotonous, but contains stirring passages, for instance the account of the defeat of the Gauls in 225 B.C. (ii. 27 et seq.). There are severe strictures on the methods of other historians. Some of his judgements are interesting, as when he agrees that 'war is a fearful thing, but not so fearful that we should submit to anything in order to avoid it' (iv. 31).

Polycli'tus (*Polukleitos*) or POLYCLETUS, of Argos or Sicyon, who flourished 450–420 B.C., was, after Phidias (q.v.), the most celebrated sculptor of antiquity. He sought to embody in his statues the perfect proportions of the human body, and to give an impression of calm and repose. His most famous statues were the *Doryphorus*, known as 'The Canon' or standard, a powerful youth carrying a spear; and the *Diadūmenus*, a youth tying a band about his head. Replicas of these statues exist. As an exception to his usual practice of working in bronze, he made a colossal statue of Hera in ivory and gold, for the Heraeum (q.v.).

Poly'crates (*Polukratēs*), tyrant of Samos in the second half of the 6th c. B.C. He made Samos a strong naval power, and when Cambyses (see *Persian Wars*) undertook his expedition against Amāsis of Egypt, he supported the Persians, though he had previously defied them and had entered into friendly relations with Amasis. His squadron revolted and sought the help of Sparta against him. Polycrates was beguiled by the Persian satrap Oroetes into his power and crucified (522).

Polycrates constructed great works for the improvement of his capital, and maintained a sumptuous court, where Anacreon and Ibycus (qq. v.) spent part of their lives. Herodotus (iii. 40–3) relates that Amasis, alarmed by the constant good fortune of Polycrates, advised him to throw away something that he valued highly, so as to avert nemesis. Polycrates accordingly threw into the sea a seal-ring of extraordinary beauty. But a few days later the ring was found in the belly of a fish that a fisherman had presented to Polycrates. Amasis, concluding that Polycrates could come to no good end, renounced his friendship. Among Landor's 'Imaginary Conversations' is one between Polycrates and Anacreon.

Polydeu'cēs (*Poludeukēs*, Lat. *Pollux*), see *Dioscuri*.

Polydō'rus (*Poludōros*), (1) the youngest son of Priam and Hecuba, murdered by Polymēstōr, king of the Thracian Chersonese (for the story see *Hecuba*). In Virgil's narrative (Aen. iii. 22 et seq.) Aeneas, landing in Thrace, pulls up some cornel bushes and finds to his horror the roots dripping with blood. He hears groans and a voice from the mound telling him that the murdered Polydorus is there buried. Aeneas performs funeral rites and the spirit of Polydorus then rests in peace. (2) One of the Epigoni (q.v.).

Polygnō'tus (*Polugnōtos*) of Thasos (q.v.), a famous Greek painter, who flourished c. 475–445 B.C. Pausanias describes his celebrated paintings of the 'Capture of Troy' and the 'Descent of Odysseus to Hades', in the Leschē at Delphi (q.v.), large mural pictures containing each about seventy figures. Polygnotus decorated with mural paintings part of the *Stoa Poikile* (see *Stoa*) at Athens; and other works at Athens and in other cities were attributed to him. He painted large compositions, with many figures, and a slight indication of landscape; serious and dignified in character, but showing advance on earlier art by the life and expression of the faces; for this he is praised by Aristotle and Lucian. The subjects he took were chiefly mythological. See *Painting*.

Polyhi'stōr, see *Solinus*. Polyhistor was also the surname of a certain Alexandros of Miletus (1st c. B.C.), a learned man who wrote in Greek treatises on history and geography and on literary subjects. Only fragments of his work survive.

Polyhy'mnia (*Polumniă*), see *Muses*.

Polyni'cēs (*Poluneikēs*), see *Oedipus*.

Polyphē'mus, a Cyclops (see *Cyclopes*), son of Poseidon (q.v.). He is represented in the 'Odyssey' as one of a race of savage one-eyed giants, rearing sheep and goats in an island generally identified as Sicily. Odysseus with twelve of his men enters his cave. Polyphemus, returning with his flocks and closing the mouth of the cave with a huge rock, discovers the intruders and kills and eats two of them. The next evening, Odysseus, who has been kept imprisoned in the cave during the day and has seen four more of his men devoured, intoxicates Polyphemus with wine, and destroys his eye with a pointed stake. He has told Polyphemus that his name is Noman (Οὖτις), and when the other Cyclopes come at the cry of Polyphemus, the latter replies to their enquiries that Noman is killing him. They therefore go away. Next morning Odysseus lashes the rams together in threes, and under each three conceals one of his comrades. When the blinded Polyphemus releases his flocks, they thus escape, Odysseus hiding himself under the shaggy belly of the largest ram. He thereafter taunts Polyphemus, who hurls rocks at the departing ship and nearly destroys it. See also *Cyclops* (Euripides' play).

In Sicilian legend the boorish Polyphemus is represented as falling in love with the nymph Galatea, and either as repulsed by her, or as crushing with a stone her other lover, the young Acis (this is the version adopted by Gay in his libretto to Handel's 'Acis and Galatea'), or as marrying Galatea. His love is the subject of the 12th Idyll of Theocritus.

Poly'xena (*Poluxenē*), a daughter of Priam and Hecuba (qq.v.). See *Achilles*.

Pōmō'na, the Roman goddess of fruit (*pōma*), the wife of Vertumnus (q.v.). For the story of his wooing her under various shapes, see under his name.

Pompē'ius Tro'gus, see *Trogus*.

Pompey 'THE GREAT' (*Pompēius, Gnaeus*) (106–48 B.C.), son of one of the consuls for the year 89 B.C., first came into prominence by raising an army to support Sulla (q.v.) on his return to Italy in 83, and by distinguished service against the Marians in Sicily and Africa. After Sulla's death he held an extraordinary command against Sertorius (q.v.) in Spain. In 70 he and Crassus (q.v.) having sunk their differences obtained the consulship, intending to revoke some of Sulla's outstanding laws. In 67 he was charged with the mission of expelling the pirates from the Mediterranean, which he successfully accomplished; and in the next year was given the command against Mithridates (q.v.) with extraordinary powers. He utterly defeated Mithridates, made provinces of Bithynia-

Pontus and Syria (capturing Jerusalem after a siege), enlarged the province of Cilicia, and effected a general settlement. He was a great founder and restorer of cities in the East. But on his return to Italy in 62 he failed to take advantage of his strength, as leader of a devoted army, to make himself a secure position in the State. Though a good general and a great organizer, he lacked political enterprise and originality. He dismissed his legions and allowed himself to be humiliated by the Senate, which refused to ratify his Eastern settlement and to recompense his troops. The story of his subsequent coalition with Caesar and Crassus, his marriage with Caesar's daughter, followed before long by alienation from Caesar and reconciliation with the Senate, his great struggle with Caesar in the Civil War, his final defeat at Pharsālus and his death in Egypt, will be found briefly told under *Caesar* and *Cicero*. There is a life of Pompey by Plutarch.

Pompō'nius of Bonōnia, see *Atellan Farces*.

Pompō'nius Mē'la (*Mēla*), of Tingentera in Spain, one of the few Roman geographers, wrote his 'Chorographia' or 'De Situ Orbis' in three books about A.D. 43. In this, after a summary account of the earth and the three continents, Europe, Asia, and Africa, he describes in greater detail the countries round the Mediterranean, starting from Mauretania and working round to Spain; then passing to Gaul, Germany, Scythia, the islands (including Britain), India, and the Persian Gulf. He enlivens his account by descriptions of national characteristics and customs, scenery, and natural phenomena, and by references to birthplaces, battle-fields, historical and legendary associations. He offers explanations of the tides (the action of the moon is one of them) and of the midnight sun; he regards the earth as a disk, with flat edges.

Pompō'nius Secu'ndus, a Roman dramatist who became suspect to Tiberius, but attained consular rank and military command in Germany after the latter's death. Pliny the Elder served under him against the Germans and wrote his life. Quintilian regarded him as the best tragic poet of his day. Only the title of one of his plays—'Aeneas'—survives.

Pons Subli'cius ('bridge on piles'), the oldest bridge, and for several centuries the only bridge, at Rome. It was built exclusively of wood and was held sacred. It was in the charge of the *pontifices* (q.v.), and any repairs to it were accompanied by religious rites. See also *Argei*.

Pontic Epistles, see *Ex Ponto*.

Po′ntifex Ma′ximus, the chief representative in religious matters of the ancient kings of Rome. He was the head of the college of *pontifices* (see the following article) and appointed the Vestals, flamens, and *Rex Sacrorum* (qq.v.). He had special supervision over the Vestals, and published the decisions of the college of pontifices. He had his official head-quarters in the Regia (q.v.) and an official residence (the *domus publica*). The position was one of great dignity and importance, though, according to Festus, it ranked in precedence after those of the *Rex Sacrorum* (q.v.) and of the Flamens (q.v.) Diālis, Martiālis, and Quirīnālis. It was held by Julius Caesar and by all the emperors.

Ponti′fices, at Rome, in the regal period, the priests appointed to assist the king in the duties of the state cult, forming his religious council, and acting as depositories of religious tradition. Later they, and especially the *pontifex maximus* (q.v.), became responsible for the organization of the state religion. The pontifices had technical knowledge in the matter of the calendar (q.v.), and determined the dates of festivals and the days that were *fasti* and *nefasti*. They also kept a record of the principal events of each year (see *Annales*). They had no more than a general supervision of private worship; they intervened in the solemn form of marriage known as *confarreatio* (q.v.), for this was regarded as a state ceremony. They were not precluded (like the *flamens*, q.v.) from taking part in public affairs; Julius Caesar, for instance, was *pontifex maximus*. They were originally all patricians; later the office was thrown open to plebeians also. They wore the *toga praetexta* (see *Clothing*, § 3) when officiating, and had certain privileges, such as exemption from taxation and military service. Like the holders of political offices they were unpaid.

The origin of the name is not known with certainty, but the obvious derivation from *pons*, 'bridge', and *facere*, 'to make', has been accepted by most authorities ancient and modern, though Plutarch (Numa, ix. 2) ridiculed it and it has been questioned by some scholars. It is noteworthy that the *pontifices* had charge of the Pons Sublicius (q.v.) at Rome, and that they took part in the rite of the Argei (q.v.).

Pontus (*Pontos*) (1) the Sea; according to Hesiod, son of Ge (q.v.), and father of Nereus and Phorcys (qq.v.). (2) A district in the NE. of Asia Minor situated between Paphlagonia (later Bithȳnia) and Armenia and adjoining the Black Sea (from which it derived its name, as being ἐν Πόντῳ, 'on the Sea'). It was the centre of the empire of Mithridates VI (q.v.). After the Mithridatic Wars Pompey annexed the western part of it to the province of Bithynia, and in A.D. 64 Nero incorporated the eastern portion in the province of Galatia.

Popilius Laenas, C., see *Seleucids*.

Poppae′a Sabi′na, the wife of Nero's boon companion, the future emperor Otho; and subsequently the second wife of Nero himself. For her sake Nero murdered his mother Agrippina, and divorced and caused the death of his first wife Octavia. Poppaea is said to have died (A.D. 65) from a kick given her by Nero.

Populā′rēs, the name adopted at Rome after the time of the Gracchi (q.v.) by the party opposed to the senatorial nobility (who retorted by calling themselves 'Optimātes', 'the best men').

Population, see *Athens*, § 10 and *Rome*, § 13.

Po′rcia, daughter of Cato of Utica (q.v.) and wife, first of Calpurnius Bibulus (consul in 59 B.C.), and secondly after his death of Marcus Brutus (q.v.). She was an ardent supporter of the republican cause, and is said to have inflicted a wound on herself, in order to show that she was worthy to share her husband's counsel at the time of the conspiracy against Julius Caesar. Shakespeare presents her in a famous scene of his 'Julius Caesar'.

Po′rphyry (*Porphurios*, a rendering of his Tyrian name, *Malchus*, 'King') (A.D. 233–c. 301), one of the chief exponents of Neoplatonism (q.v.) and a pupil of Plotinus (q.v.). He wrote, besides the biography of his master, a 'History of Philosophy', including a life of Pythagoras which survives; an introduction to Aristotle's 'Organon' (translated into Latin by Boethius, q.v.); and other works.

Po′rsena or **Porsenna**, LARS (the word 'Lars' is Etruscan, signifying 'lord'), prince of Clūsium at the end of the 6th c. B.C. and head of the united forces of Etruria. According to tradition he marched against Rome in order to restore the Tarquins to the Roman throne. In the campaign that followed occurred the feats of Horatius Cocles, Mucius Scaevola, and Cloelia (qq.v.). Repulsed in his attack, Porsena made peace with Rome. One tradition implied by Tacitus and the elder Pliny seems to have made Porsena at one time master of Rome.

Porson, RICHARD, see *Texts and Studies*, § 11.

Portō'ria, see *Rome*, § 14.

Portū'nus, an ancient Roman god, of harbours (from *portus*), or of gates (from *porta*), or of both; the ancients appear to have been doubtful as to his functions. Virgil (Aen. v. 241–3) makes Portunus give one of the galleys in the boat-race a shove 'into port'. He was represented with a key in his hand. His festival, the *Portūnālia*, was on 17 August, the anniversary of the dedication of his temple. Portunus had a special flamen (q.v.), the *Flamen Portūnālis*.

Pō'rus (*Pōros*), see *Alexander the Great*, § 7.

Posei'don (*Poseidōn*), in Greek mythology, brother of Zeus and lord of the sea; also of earthquakes and horses. The derivation of the name is uncertain, but appears to be connected with a word for water. He is represented as a dignified figure, like Zeus, but more uncouth and without his stately calm, carrying a trident (probably a fish-spear). He may be a blend of the god of the earthquake or the wind (he is generally spoken of as violent and ill-tempered) with a sea-deity of the country that the Greeks came to occupy. The Romans identified him with the water-god Neptune (q.v.). His connexion with horses can only be conjecturally explained, perhaps because he was worshipped in horse-breeding countries such as Thessaly. One of the principal legends about Poseidon relates his contest with Athene for the land of Attica (see *Athens*, § 2). One form of the legend of Theseus (q.v.) makes Theseus the son of Poseidon and Aethra; and Poseidon was worshipped at Athens as Poseidon Erechtheus (see *Erechtheus*). In the Trojan War Poseidon takes an active part against the Trojans because of the refusal of Laomedon (q.v.) to pay for the work done by Poseidon and Apollo in building the walls of Troy. In the 'Odyssey' he persistently seeks the hero's destruction, because Odysseus had blinded Polyphemus, his son by the nymph Thōōsa. His wife is Amphitrite, by whom he has a son, the merman Triton (qq.v.). By Ge he is the father of the giant Antaeus (qq.v.). By Medusa (see *Gorgons*) he is the father of Pegasus (q.v.) and Chrysaor (father of Geryon and Echidna, qq.v.). By Demeter, who to escape him had taken the form of a mare, he is the father of the horse Arion (who passed into the possession of Adrastus, q.v.). The great temple dedicated to him at Mycalē between Ephesus and Miletus was the religious centre of the Ionians of Asia Minor.

Posidō'nius (*Poseidōnios*), of Apamēa in Syria (c. 135–51 B.C.), who spent most of his life at Rhodes and became head of the Stoic school there, was a historian, scientist, and philosopher, 'the last great creative genius in literature and science' of the Greek world (Rostovtzeff). He wrote a continuation of the history of Polybius in fifty-two books. In philosophy he followed with some modifications the Stoic doctrine; it is probable that he sought to reconcile the Stoic principle of a divine spirit animating nature with the Graeco-Roman religion of his day. He was also an eminent geographer, ethnographer, and astronomer, and wrote on tides and volcanoes. He expressed the opinion that a man sailing west from Europe would reach India, a remark which was handed on and ultimately influenced Columbus. Unfortunately his works have not survived. He visited Rome as an envoy from Rhodes in 86 B.C. Varro received instruction from him, and Cicero visited him at Rhodes. Marius and Pompey were also among his friends.

Post Reditum, two speeches probably delivered by Cicero (q.v., § 4; their genuineness has been questioned) after his return from exile in 57 B.C., one addressed to the Senate, the other to the people, thanking them for his recall, reviewing the incidents of the recent years, and attacking his enemies.

Posting-Houses, see *Roads*.

Poti'tii, see *Hercules*.

Pottery. The potter's wheel, as a means of making domestic utensils, is a very ancient invention; it is mentioned in Homer (Il. xviii. 600). In archaic times the manufacture of common pottery was widespread among the Greeks. But about 650 B.C. Corinth took the lead and her pottery was exported not only all over Greece, but also to most of the lands bordering on the Mediterranean, including Etruria, whence it reached the barbarians of the N. and W. From about 550 B.C. the Corinthian ware was in turn ousted by that of Athens. There was good clay near Phalerum, and Attic pottery was in high esteem for its fine material, beautiful shapes, thinness, and careful execution. It was widely exported to lands bordering on the Mediterranean and Euxine seas. See *Vase-painting*.

Though there was a guild of potters at Rome from early times, the finer Roman household ware was at first imported from the Etruscans. In later republican times an industry for its manufacture sprang up at Arrētium (Arezzo). The Samian ware, an imitation of ware originally brought from Samos, a thin reddish-brown, highly glazed pottery, often ornamented with reliefs, was made at Arretium, and in imperial times in Gaul.

Bricks baked in a kiln, and tiles, were first extensively used by the Romans; such bricks, replacing sun-dried bricks, enabled buildings of several stories to be erected. The brick walls were covered with stucco or marble. The Roman bricks were of high quality and are found in many parts of the Roman empire. Earthenware pipes for conveying water, and for sewers, were also made by the Romans. The manufacture of bricks, tiles, and ordinary pottery became an important industry under the empire, often in the hands of rich capitalists, even of members of the imperial family.

Small figures of gods, throughout classical antiquity, used to be made of clay. Then moulded clay figures, painted after baking, became popular, for ornament and for playthings. The high degree of art attained is shown by the 'figurines' discovered at Tanagra in Boeotia in 1874 and subsequently. There are many specimens of these in the British Museum.

Praefec'ti Ca'puam Cūmas, see *Vigintivirate*.

Praefec'tus Annō'nae, at Rome under the empire, an official of equestrian rank responsible for the supply of corn, the regulation of its price, and distributions to the poor. See *Annona*.

Praefec'tus Praetō'riō, at Rome under the Empire, the officer (of equestrian rank) who commanded the praetorian cohorts, the emperor's guard (see *Praetorians*). His authority extended to the army outside Italy and he occupied the position next to the throne. His power was so great that Augustus and certain of his successors sought to lessen it by appointing two *praefecti*. When the praetorian guard was disbanded by Constantine, the four *praefecti praetorio* lost their military authority and became governors of the four divisions of the empire; thus we find that the father of St. Ambrose (q.v.) was Praetorian Prefect of the Gauls.

Praefec'tus Urbi, at Rome under the Empire, the Prefect of the City, responsible for order within its boundaries. He was of senatorial rank and had three urban cohorts under his orders.

Praefec'tus Vi'gilum, at Rome under the Empire, the officer (of equestrian rank) in command of the cohorts of *vigilēs* forming the fire brigade instituted by Augustus.

Praene'stine fi'bula, see *Epigraphy*, § 9.

Praete'xta, FĀBULA, in Roman literature, a drama having its subject in Roman history. The name is derived from the *toga praetexta* (see *Clothing*, § 3), because celebrated Romans were presented in such dramas. Cf. *togata*. The invention of the *fabula praetexta* is attributed to Naevius. We have only one complete *praetexta*, the tragedy 'Octavia' (q.v.), and fragments or traces of eleven others, such as the 'Clastidium' of Naevius (on the exploits of M. Claudius Marcellus, winner of the *spolia optima*, q.v., in 222 B.C.), the 'Rape of the Sabines' of Ennius, the 'Brutus' of Accius, and the 'Aeneas' of Pomponius Secundus (qq.v.).

Prae'tor, at Rome, originally the generic term for the holders of *imperium* or executive authority, and the name of the two magistrates who replaced the king, later called consuls. Subsequently it was the title of the magistrate who administered justice between Roman citizens (*praetor urbānus*) and the magistrate who did the same where foreigners were involved (*praetor peregrīnus*) (see *Law, Roman*, §§ 2 and 4). Later, additional praetors were appointed for the government of certain provinces, and after 150 B.C. it became the usual practice to employ propraetors (who had completed their year of office as praetors), as well as proconsuls, for this purpose. The special courts of law (*quaestiones*, see *Judicial Procedure*) were ordinarily presided over by magistrates of praetorian rank. The praetors were elected annually by the people. From 336 B.C. the office was thrown open to plebeians.

Praetorians. Under the Roman republic it was customary for a general to have a bodyguard of his friends and clients. These were replaced (towards the end of the republican period) by professional soldiers, and generals used to have several such cohorts. Augustus, for the protection of Italy (where no legion was stationed) formed nine cohorts (each one thousand strong) composed of his body-guard and of veterans. These were the famous Praetorians who played so important a part in the history of the Empire at certain moments. They were at first distributed in various parts of Italy, but were concentrated by Sejanus (q.v.) in a camp on the north side of Rome. The Praetorians received 500 denarii a year, raised to 720 by Domitian. Their term of service was 12 (soon raised to 16) years. See also *Praefectus Praetorio*.

Praetō'rium, the head-quarters of a Roman camp, see *Castra*.

Prāti′nās (the second syllable is probably long) of Phlīus in the NE. of the Peloponnese, a poet who flourished about 496 B.C. He is reputed to have invented the satyric drama (q.v.). He also wrote tragedies (in these he was a rival of Aeschylus at Athens), dithyrambs, and *hyporchemata* (q.v.).

Praxi′telēs, one of the most famous of Greek sculptors, born at Athens *c.* 390 B.C. One original work of his survives, Hermes with the infant Dionysus on his arm, found at Olympia in 1877. Other celebrated works of his were the Aphrodite of Cnidus, described by the ancients as a masterpiece of beauty, and statues of Eros and of an Apollo Sauroctonus ('lizard-slayer'). Praxiteles showed, at its best, the tendency of the Greek sculptors of the 4th c. to abandon the more reverent and dignified style of the 5th c. for the expression of softer and finer shades of form and feeling.

Pri′am (*Priamos*), in Greek mythology, son of Laomedon (q.v., and see genealogy under *Troy*), king of Troy at the time of the Trojan War (q.v.), and husband of Hecuba (q.v.). He was the father of fifty sons and many daughters (including Hector, Paris, Polydorus, and Cassandra, qq.v.). He was slain by Neoptolemus (q.v.) at the taking of the city. In the 'Iliad' Priam is a pathetic figure, lamenting the death of many sons and the sufferings of his people, but loyal and kindly to Helen, the cause of these misfortunes. He nerves himself to the perilous undertaking of entering the Greek camp alone to beg from Achilles the dead body of Hector.

Priāpē′a, a collection made in the reign of Augustus of eighty poems addressed to the god Priapus (q.v.). Three *Priapea* attributed by Donatus and Servius to Virgil are among the minor poems included in his collected works.

Priā′pus (*Priāpos*), a god of fertility of gardens and herds, whose cult spread from Asia Minor, especially Lampsacus, to Greece and Italy. He was said to be the son of Aphrodite and Dionysus or some other god. In his statues, often placed in gardens or at the doors of houses, he was represented as a grotesque deformed creature with the phallic symbol. Virgil makes him rather a humble deity, 'little more than a venerable scarecrow' (Bailey), keeping off thieves and birds from the poor man's garden. It was customary to inscribe short humorous poems or epigrams on his statues (see *Priapea*).

Prices and Cost of Living, see *Athens*, § 10, and *Rome*, § 13.

Priests. (1) IN GREECE. Priests and priestesses were appointed to the service of the gods and goddesses, to perform sacrifices and other rites, and to instruct worshippers in the ritual. They had no special sacerdotal authority, nor (except the priests attached to the Mysteries) special religious knowledge. They were appointed for a definite period or for life. They received perquisites from the sacrifices and in some cases a stipend in money. We know from an inscription that the priestess of Athene Nikē was appointed for life and received fifty drachmas a year besides the perquisites. The priests and priestesses of certain deities (e.g. the virgin goddesses Athene and Artemis) were required to be celibate; the priests of Artemis at Ephesus, and those of Cybele (both foreign cults), were eunuchs. Certain priesthoods were confined to particular families, to which the cult had originally belonged. Thus the priestess of Athene Polias on the Acropolis was chosen from the noble family of the Būtadae, and the Mysteries at Eleusis were conducted by certain priestly families of that place. In ceremonies performed in places other than sanctuaries it was a magistrate, e.g. the archon at the Dionysia, or the head of the family at domestic sacrifices, who officiated.

(2) AT ROME. See *Flamens, Pontifices, Vestals*.

Pri′nceps, the title taken by Augustus and adopted by his successors, signifying 'chief' or 'leader'. The title was not official; it was in fact complimentary (compare 'Il Duce' or 'Der Führer'). 'Princeps' did not signify 'princeps senatus'. This rank had always existed, and 'princeps senatus' meant primacy within the senate, but nothing outside it.

Pri′scian (*Prisciānus Caesariensis*), a native of Caesarēa in Mauretānia and a grammarian at Constantinople under the emperor of the East, Anastasius (A.D. 491–518). He wrote in Latin a Grammar in eighteen books, rich in quotations from the classic authors, and founded largely on the work of Apollonius Dyscolus (q.v.). It became famous in the Middle Ages and survives in more than a thousand manuscripts.

Pro A′rchia Poē′ta, a speech by Cicero, delivered in 62 B.C. in defence of the claim of Archias to Roman citizenship.

Archias was a Greek poet attached to the household of the great general L. Licinius Lucullus (q.v.). His claim to Roman citizenship was based on the fact that he had been enrolled a burgess of Heraclēa in Lūcānia, a town which had been granted full Roman civic rights. The claim was impugned on the ground of the absence of documentary evidence of his enrolment. Cicero meets this by producing witnesses of the enrolment. He also appeals to the sentiment of the jury by an eloquent panegyric (since become famous) of literature.

Pro Balbo, see *Cicero,* § 4 (under the year 56).

Pro Cae'cina, see *Cicero,* § 1 (under the year 69).

Pro Cae'lio, see *Cicero.* § 4 (under the year 56).

Pro Clue'ntio, a speech by Cicero, delivered in 66 B.C. in defence of Aulus Cluentius Habitus. Cluentius some years previously had obtained the conviction and exile of Oppiānicus on a charge of attempting to poison him. He was now accused of having himself poisoned Oppianicus in his exile and of having bribed the jury at the trial. and was acquitted. The speech is one of Cicero's best pieces of advocacy in a criminal trial, and throws a curious light on the domestic relations of Roman life.

Pro Flacco, see *Cicero,* § 3 (under the year 59).

Pro Fontē'io, see *Cicero,* § 1 (under the year 69).

Pro Lēge Mānī'lia or **De Imperio Cn. Pompeii,** a speech by Cicero, delivered before the people in 66 B.C., when Cicero was praetor, in support of the proposal to extend Pompey's command in Asia to Bithȳnia, Pontus, and Armenia, to enable him to take over the conduct of the war against Mithridates. This was Cicero's first speech on purely public matters, and was delivered in furtherance of the interests of the equestrian order (which were suffering from the disturbed conditions in Asia) and against the views of the Senate. The proposal was carried.

Pro Ligā'rio, see *Cicero,* § 4 (under the year 45).

Pro Marce'llo, see *Cicero,* § 4 (under the year 46).

Pro Milō'ne, see *Cicero,* § 4 (under the year 52) and *Milo (Titus Annius).*

Pro Mūrē'na, a speech by Cicero, made in 63 B.C., when he was consul. in defence of Lucius Murena, who had been elected consul for the next year, and was accused at the instigation of Cato of bribery in the election. The charge was brought at the height of the crisis due to Catiline's conspiracy; and the upsetting of the election

of Murena, a man of proved courage and military ability, would have been favourable to the cause of Catiline. The speech is an admirable example of persuasive pleading, and is famous for its good-humoured banter of Cato.

Pro Pla'ncio, see *Cicero.* § 4 (under the year 54).

Pro Qui'nctio, the first extant speech of Cicero (q.v.), delivered in 81 B.C. He therein refers to earlier speeches, which have not survived. In it he defends his client, Publius Quinctius, against one Servius Naevius (represented by the great orator Hortensius, q.v.) in an action arising out of their partnership in a farm in Gaul. The result of the action is not known. The contrast of the solemn exordium with the comparative triviality of the matter in dispute was parodied by Racine in 'Les Plaideurs'.

Pro Rabī'rio, a speech by Cicero, delivered in 63 B.C. when he was consul, in support of the appeal of C. Rabirius, a knight, who had been convicted, at the instance of Caesar, of having killed Saturninus (q.v.), a tribune of the people and ally of Marius, in 100 B.C. The demagogic coalition had in that year been overthrown by the Senate, a *senatus consultum ultimum* (q.v.) had been passed, and Saturninus had been killed in a faction fight. The question now at issue was whether the *senatus consultum ultimum* justified the putting to death of a citizen without appeal. The speech was probably delivered in the Comitia Centuriata, and the proceedings were brought to an end and Rabirius in effect discharged by the lowering of the flag on the Janiculum (q.v.). There was something farcical about the whole affair, which was not seriously intended as a trial, but as an advertisement of Caesar and the *populares.* For a discussion of the procedure see E. G. Hardy, 'Some Problems of Roman History'.

Pro Rabī'rio Po'stumo, see *Cicero,* § 4 (under the year 54).

Pro Rēge Dēio'taro, see *Cicero,* § 4 (under the year 45).

Pro Ro'sciō Amerī'nō, a speech by Cicero in defence of Sextus Roscius of Ameria on a charge of murdering his father, delivered in 80 B.C. This was Cicero's first speech in a criminal case, and showed his courage, for it involved an attack on Sulla's freedman Chrȳsogonus at a time when Sulla was all-powerful.

The father of Sextus Roscius had been murdered in Rome on a day when the son was at Ameria. He had left a large property and the prospect of acquiring this had induced Chrysogonus to enter into a conspiracy with two other Roscii of Ameria, who had been at feud with the father. The father's name was put on the proscription list, the property was bought by Chrysogonus for a nominal sum, and Sextus Roscius the son was expelled from it. A movement in favour of the latter sprang up at Ameria and made the conspirators uneasy. They tried to get the young Roscius out of the way, first by attempted murder and then by fabricating a charge against him of murdering his father. Cicero shows the accusation to be baseless, throws suspicion upon one of the associates of Chrysogonus of being the true criminal, and finally attacks Chrysogonus himself, while pretending to dissociate Sulla from any knowledge of his favourite's proceedings. Sextus Roscius was acquitted.

The speech gives incidentally the origin of the expression *cui bono?* If Sextus did not kill his father, says Cicero, who did? He then quotes the frequent saying of an illustrious judge, L. Cassius Longīnus, in trials of this kind, *cui bono?* 'Who has profited?'; and proceeds to show that the accusers of Roscius had themselves profited.

Pro Ro′scio Cŏmoe′dŏ, a speech by Cicero (q.v.) on behalf of the great actor Quintus Roscius (q.v.), of uncertain date, probably c. 67 B.C.

A certain C. Fannius had a slave, Panurgus, of such ability that Roscius entered into a partnership with Fannius by which the slave became their joint property; Roscius was to train him as an actor, and the partners were to share the profits. Panurgus became a promising actor, but was murdered by one Q. Flavius. Flavius agreed to pay certain damages to Roscius, in the shape of a derelict farm. This farm improved in value under the management of Roscius, and now Fannius claimed from Roscius half the value of the farm.

Pro Scauro, see *Cicero*, § 4 (under the year 54).

Pro Se′stiŏ, see *Cicero*, § 4 (under the year 56).

Pro Sullā, a speech by Cicero, delivered in 62 B.C. in defence of P. Cornēlius Sulla (elected consul for 55 B.C., but convicted of bribery, accused of having participated in the conspiracy of Catiline of 65 B.C. The prosecutor had attacked Cicero himself in respect of his proceedings against the conspirators, and the speech of Cicero contains a defence of his actions.

Pro Tu′llio, see *Cicero*, § 1 (under year 72).

Probou′loi, a board of ten commissioners appointed at Athens in 413 B.C. after the destruction of the Sicilian Expedition (see *Peloponnesian War*) to have the general direction of affairs. Sophocles (q.v.) was one of these commissioners.

Prŏ′bus, MARCUS VALERIUS, see *Texts and Studies*. § 5.

Pro′clus (*Proklos*), (1) see *Neoplatonism*. He also wrote a commentary on Euclid. (2) Variously assigned to the 2nd or the 5th c. A.D., author of a *Chrēstomatheia* or handbook of literature of which extracts survive.

Pro′cnē (*Proknē*), see *Philomela*.

Proconsul, see *Consul*.

Procŏ′pius (*Prokópios*), of Caesarea in Palestine, was secretary to Belisārius (the great military commander under the emperor Justinian) from A.D. 523. He wrote in Greek a history of his own times, especially of the wars of Justinian, and 'Anecdota' supplementing the previous work with an account of the scandals of the court which he had been unable to include in his official history.

Pro′cris (*Prokris*), see *Cephalus*.

Procru′stēs or DAMA′STĒS, a legendary brigand of Eleusis, who used to lay travellers on a bed, and if they were too long for it, cut short their limbs; but if the bed was longer, stretch them to make their length equal to it. He was killed by Theseus (q.v.).

Prōcūrā′tŏr, at Rome under the empire, a fiscal agent of the emperor, charged with the supervision of the imperial revenues in the imperial provinces, and also, independently of the governors, in the senatorial provinces. Some of the minor provinces were also governed by officials called procurators. Under Claudius and his successors certain high officials at Rome were known as *procurator a rationibus, ab epistulis*, &c. (see *Rome*, § 12).

Pro′dicus (*Prodikos*), see *Sophist*.

Proe′tus (*Proitos*), see *Bellerophon* and *Dionysus*. Proetus was twin brother of Acrisius (father of Danae, q.v.); he had a life-long feud with him, was banished by him from Argos, and ousted him in turn.

Prolē′psis (1) in a speech, is the forestalling of objections which an opponent may raise; (2) as a figure of speech, is the reference to a person or thing by a name, or the description of a person or thing by an epithet, which, at the time is not yet applicable; e.g. 'submersasque obrue puppes', 'whelm the ships till they sink' (Virg. Aen. i. 69), or 'sublimemque feres ad sidera coeli . . . Aenean' (Aen. i. 259).

Prōlētā'rii, at Rome, the citizens placed in the lowest property-class, who were exempted from compulsory military service and from the *tribūtum* or property-tax, and served the state only with their children (*prōlēs*).

Prologue (*Pro'logos*), see *Tragedy*, § 3 and *Comedy*, § 2.

Promē'theus ('Forethought'), in Greek mythology son of the Titan Iapetus, and of Themis or Clymene (qq.v). He made mankind out of clay, and when Zeus oppressed them and deprived them of fire, stole fire for them from heaven (or from the forge of Hephaestus) and taught them many arts. In the apportionment of sacrifices between men and the gods, he induced Zeus by a trick to choose the less desirable portions of the victim, so that men ate the best part of the meat at the sacrificial banquets. To avenge himself Zeus caused Hephaestus to fashion a woman, Pandora, out of clay; Athene breathed life into her, and the other gods endowed her with every charm (whence her name, 'all gifts'), but Hermes taught her flattery and guile. This woman was sent, not to Prometheus, who foresaw the trouble she would bring, but to his brother Epimetheus ('after-thought'), who readily accepted her. She brought with her a box, from which when opened there issued all the evils and distempers that have since afflicted the human race. Hope alone remained at the bottom of the box to assuage the lot of man. The fable is charmingly turned to the advantage of Epimetheus in C. Kingsley's 'Water Babies'.

Prometheus knew, moreover, the secret concerning the marriage of Thetis (see *Peleus*), but refused to reveal it. To punish him for his rebellious conduct, Zeus had him chained to a lonely rock in the Caucasus, where an eagle daily fed on his liver, which was restored each succeeding night. This torture continued for ages, till Prometheus was either released by Heracles, or, according to another version, submitted and revealed the secret about Thetis.

Prometheus was probably originally a fire-god, superseded in this respect by Hephaestus (it is Hephaestus who chains him to the rock). He was the father of Deucalion (q.v.) by a wife variously named.

There is a poem by Robert Bridges, 'Prometheus, the Firegiver' (1884). For Shelley's 'Prometheus Unbound' see the next article (*ad fin.*).

Promē'theus Vinctus (*Promḗtheus desmṓtēs*, 'Prometheus Bound'), a tragedy by Aeschylus of uncertain date (perhaps written when the poet was in Sicily, for there is in it a reference to the great eruption of Etna in 478), part of a connected trilogy of which 'Prometheus Unbound' (*Prometheus lŭomenos*) and perhaps 'Prometheus the Fire-bearer' (*Prometheus purphoros*) were the sequel.

Prometheus the Titan (perhaps represented by a huge dummy figure behind which the actor spoke), who has aided Zeus to set up his rule over Cronus and the primeval nature-forces, has incurred his wrath by becoming the champion of mankind and giving them fire and the arts. In the opening scene of the play Hephaestus, at the order of Zeus, reluctantly nails Prometheus to a rock in the wilderness of Scythia, to suffer torment during Zeus's pleasure. The chorus of Oceanides, the daughters of the Titan Oceanus (q.v.), come to grieve with him and comfort him. Oceanus himself also comes, and tries to persuade Prometheus to submission. But Prometheus is unyielding, his will and endurance are unconquered, and he knows the secret on which the safety of Zeus and his rule depend (see *Peleus*). Another victim of Zeus's tyranny appears, Io (q.v.), a mortal whom Zeus has loved and Hera's jealousy has turned into a heifer. She is doomed to long wanderings pursued by a gad-fly, and haunted by the ghost of the myriad-eyed Argos. Prometheus foretells to her her future. Hermes is sent by Zeus to demand from Prometheus knowledge of his secret. Prometheus haughtily refuses, and is hurled into the abyss with the Oceanides, who decide to share his fate.

As the other plays of the trilogy are lost, it is impossible to say precisely how Aeschylus devised the reconciliation which must ultimately have followed between Prometheus and Zeus. We know from fragments that the second play opened with Prometheus restored to light after thirty thousand years, and that the chorus was composed of Titans.

The 'Prometheus Bound' suggested to Shelley his 'Prometheus Unbound'. But Shelley would not accept the idea of the submission of Prometheus: in his poem it is Jupiter who succumbs.

Prometheus es in verbis, see *Lucian*.

Prope'rtius, SEXTUS (*c.* 50–*c.* 16 B.C.), a native of Umbria, deprived of his estate when young by the confiscations of 40 B.C., was educated at Rome for the practice of the law, but turned to love and poetry instead. He left four books of elegies (the second is divided by some editors into two, making five in all), of which the first, published about 26 B.C., brought him fame and admission to the circle of Maecenas (q.v.). One of his poems (ii. 34) shows his admiration for Virgil; and he addresses other literary friends. He was acquainted with Ovid but does not mention him. Horace, whom he likewise does not mention, perhaps refers to him with some contempt as aping Callimachus and Mimnermus. Propertius acknowledges his debt to the Alexandrian poets, and claims to be the first to treat Italian subjects in Greek strains.

The principal subject of his poems is his infatuation for 'Cynthia', whose real name according to tradition was Hostia, thought by some to have been a freedwoman and courtesan, by others to have been a lady of good family, probably the grand-daughter of Hostius, an epic poet who wrote on the Illyrian war.

The work of Propertius, in its abuse of mythological ornament and in the laboured and artificial character of some of its passages, shows Alexandrian influence. But it has also strong personal characteristics, the recurrent melancholy, the sense of the picturesque, and the sincerity with which, when he lays aside his erudition, he expresses the ecstasy, torments, and humiliation of his feverish passion. This passion is treated in a great variety of moods, inspired by Cynthia's beauty, or her venality, or her dangerous illness, and by the vicissitudes of his relations with her. His transports are often interrupted by sombre reflections on death. There is on the other hand a grotesquely humorous picture (iv. 8) of a supper-party with disreputable companions, on which Cynthia breaks in, claws her rivals' faces, and belabours the poet. His thraldom lasted five years, after which came separation. But his love persisted after her death. A beautiful elegy (iv. 7) relates how the ghost of Cynthia visited the poet in a dream.

His other poems include addresses to friends, an imaginary epistle from Arethusa to Lycôtas (a fictitious name), a fine poem in which the spirit of Cornelia (perhaps the daughter of Scribonia and step-daughter of Augustus) consoles her widowed husband, a few pieces on public events, and some poems (prototypes of Ovid's 'Fasti') on antiquarian subjects, such as the story of Tarpeia.

Mackail ('Latin Literature') draws attention to the instinct of Propertius for richness of sound and says of the splendid cadence of the opening couplet of the elegies:

> Cynthia prima suis miserum me cepit ocellis
> Contactum nullis ante cupidinibus

that 'nothing like it had ever been written in Latin before: itself and alone it assures a great future to the Latin elegiac'. The self-absorption and self-pity of his early books also mark a new spirit in Latin poetry.

Propylae′a (*Propulaia*), at Athens, the great portal and only entrance of the Acropolis, at its western end. It consisted of a wall running approximately N. and S., through which were pierced five gateways, the central one about 14 ft. wide by 24 ft. high, the others smaller. These could be closed by gates. On either side of the wall were porticoes facing respectively W. and E., about 60 ft. wide, but the western portico deeper than the eastern. The columns at the front of each portico were Doric; at right-angles to these, a row of Ionic columns stood on each side of the roadway under the W. portico. This structure was flanked at its N. and S. ends by halls, one of which (that at the NW. corner) is known as the *Pinakothēkē* or picture-gallery, because Pausanias describes the paintings that were in it when he visited Athens.

This building, of which impressive remains are still standing, was erected under the administration of Pericles. It was begun in 437/6 (i.e. after the completion of the Parthenon) and completed in five years, but the plans of the architect, Mnēsiclês, were never carried out in their entirety. We are told that 2,012 talents (say £400,000) were spent on it, and inscriptions survive relating to the expenditure. The building was partially destroyed about 1656, when some gunpowder, stored there by the Turkish garrison, blew up.

Prose.

§ 1. *Greek Prose*

Prose, as a means of literary expression, was developed in Greece (as in other countries) long after poetry. It seems probable that in primitive times, when writing was in its infancy and literary compositions had to be committed to memory, it was found convenient to couch these in some metrical form, which would make them easier to remember. The earliest writers of Greek prose appear to have been the chroniclers (see *Logographi* (1)) and philosophers of Ionia, of the 6th c. B.C. Already with Heraclitus (*c.* 500 B.C.) prose had taken some measure of literary form. Democritus (*c.* 460–360), to judge from his fragments, was a competent prose-writer, and the works attributed to Hippocrates show at least the capacity for accurate and concise statement. But the first fully developed prose work that has come down entire to us is the history of Herodotus (*c.* 480–*c.* 425). Attic prose reached its zenith in the dialogues of Plato (428–347) and the speeches of Demosthenes (384–322). Isocrates (436–338) exercised through his school a deep influence on later Greek prose, in the direction of greater elaboration and ornament. With the end of the 4th c. came the close of the period of true Attic literature, the dialect of Athens then giving place to a common Greek dialect (κοινή), less subtle, varied, and accurate in expression. Greek prose was moreover corrupted by 'Asianism', the florid style favoured by the rhetoricians of the 3rd c. There was an energetic reaction against this, and an Attic revival, at Rome in the Augustan age; of this, Dionysius of Halicarnassus (q.v.) is the best example. In the 2nd c. A.D. Lucian (q.v.) wrote in a very good imitation of Attic prose.

§ 2. *Latin Prose*

Latin prose was developed, in its characteristic features, out of public speech, though it originated partly in the 'Annales' (q.v.) of the priests and their records of traditional ritual, the forerunners of History. Roman Law (published and often learned by heart) was also one of the formative influences. Latin prose, unlike Latin poetry, owed little to Greek influences, for it already possessed, before the advent of these, the essential qualities of pure diction: clarity, precision, and conciseness. In a community where politics played so great a part as at Rome, these qualities were naturally esteemed in oratory. We hear of Appius Claudius Caecus and Cato the Censor (qq.v) as noted speakers; and oratory was further developed, with a great variety of appeal, by Gaius Gracchus (q.v.). Latin prose reached its highest point in the speeches and writings of Cicero (q.v.). Thereafter it tended to become artificial, epigrammatic, and poetical, under the influence of the prevailing education in rhetoric and the poets, and of the practice of declamation. Seneca's prose is typically epigrammatic; that of Tacitus is marked by its excessive compactness and its poetical quality. The younger Pliny also shows the influence of the rhetorical schools Quintilian opposed the artificiality of his day and wrote in a style free from conceits and studied effects; but although a professed follower of Cicero, he did not recapture the amplitude and symmetry of Cicero's prose.

Pro'serpine (*Prōserpina*), perhaps an original Italian goddess of the earth; or perhaps an altered form of the Gk. *Persephone*. In either case Proserpina in Roman religion was identified with Persephone (q.v.). For her cult at Rome, see *Dis*.

Protagonist, see *Tragedy*, § 2.

Prōta'goras (*Prōtagorās*) of Abdēra, born *c.* 485 B.C., one of the most famous of the professional sophists (q.v.). He came to Athens, was a friend of Pericles, and was known to Socrates. He was prosecuted and expelled on account of atheistical opinions. He is the principal interlocutor in Plato's dialogue 'Protagoras' (see below).

Protagoras, a dialogue by Plato, which stages, besides Socrates, the great sophists Protagoras, Hippias, and Prodicus.

Starting with the question whether political science, the science of life, can be taught, it leads to the conclusion that pleasure, properly measured, is the only real good; that knowledge of the good underlies all virtue, that all virtues reduce themselves to one; and that virtue is in fact knowledge.

Protagoras is presented as frank, honest, and good-tempered, though Plato makes a little fun of him. His arguments are based on common sense; those of Socrates are more paradoxical and abstruse. The dialogue contains a noteworthy declaration by Protagoras that under a rational system a man is punished to deter him from doing wrong again, not as a retribution for his past act.

Prōtesilā'us (*Prōtesilāos*), in Greek mythology, a Thessalian prince who took part in the expedition against Troy. When the Greek fleet reached the Trojan coast, he was the first to spring ashore and was immediately killed. His young wife, Laodamīa, whom he had left at home, was plunged in such deep grief that the gods allowed her husband to return to her for three hours. But when he left her again, she took her own life. See Wordsworth's poem 'Laodamia'.

Prō'teūs, in the 'Odyssey' (iv. 351 et seq.), an 'ancient one of sea', who herds the seals, knows all things, and has the power of assuming different shapes in order to escape being questioned. By the advice of his daughter Eidothea, Menelaus, when becalmed and reduced to extremities at Pharos off the coast of Egypt, consults him as to the reason for his misfortune. According to post-Homeric legend Proteus was an early king of Egypt (see Hdt. ii. 112 and 118; also the *Helen* of Euripides), where in later times he was worshipped as a god.

Provinces, ROMAN. The word *prōvincia*, originally meaning the sphere of a magistrate possessing *imperium* (the right to command), came to mean in later republican times a territory outside Italy, subject to the Roman people, and governed by a resident Roman magistrate. The earliest Roman provinces, acquired from motives of defence, were Sicily (241 B.C.), Sardinia and Corsica (237 B.C.), and the two Spains (206 or 197 B.C.), which comprised at first only a relatively small portion of the peninsula. During the next half-century the policy of Rome refrained from adding to its territories. But this was reversed from 146 B.C., under the influence of the increase of wealth and luxury, which called ever for further expansion. In the next thirty years occurred the acquisition as provinces of Africa (the territory of Carthage) in 146, Macedonia (146), Asia (130), and Gallia Narbonensis (120). In the first half of the first century B.C., Cilicia (c. 100), Bīthȳnia (74; Pompey annexed western Pontus to it in his eastern settlement), Cȳrēnē (74), Crete (67), Syria (64), and Cyprus (58), were added, while Caesar secured Gaul by his campaigns of 58–50. Augustus reorganized the provinces, dividing Gaul into three provinces, separating Achāia from Macedonia and Lusitānia from Hispānia Ulterior and making them distinct provinces. During his reign were added Egypt (30 B.C.), Achaia (27 B.C.), Galatia (25 B.C.), Raetia (15 B.C.), Nōricum (15 B.C.), Moesia (c. A.D. 6), and Pannonia (A.D. 10). The list was increased under later emperors by the addition of Cappadocia in A.D. 17 under Tiberius, and of the two Mauritānias (A.D. 42), Britain (43), Lycia (43), and Thrace (46), under Claudius. Trajan added Arabia (105) and Dācia (107), and Marcus Aurelius Mesopotamia (165). See Pl. 9.

The organization of a province was settled in republican days, probably on the occasion of each annexation, by the edict of the commander who annexed, usually assisted by ten senatorial commissioners. In 227 B.C. two additional praetors were elected to govern, one Sicily, the other Corsica and Sardinia. Two further praetors were later created for the Spains. Under Sulla's arrangements consuls and praetors, when their year of office at Rome was finished, were sent out as *pro consule* or *pro praetore* to govern the provinces; these were assigned, usually by lot, under the direction of the Senate. Under the control of the governor the provincial communities (cities or tribes) enjoyed varying degrees of self-government, and the Romans showed, in theory at least, much regard for local customs and re-

spected even local systems of taxation. But the system of government led, in practice, under the republic to grave abuses. The governor was in fact an autocrat: he did not share his office with a colleague, he was not restrained by tribunes, his capital sentences were not subject to appeal. Moreover he was not experienced in the administration of foreigners, and his tenure was too short to allow him to become so. Finally, he had strong inducement to make his office a source of personal enrichment. As a consequence of this, we hear repeatedly of cases of oppression and extortion. The example best known to us is that of Verres (q.v.). The system of farming out the taxes of the provinces to *publicani* (see *Equestrian Order*) was moreover a source of grave abuses.

Conditions changed under the empire. Augustus divided the provinces into two classes, (1) the more settled and richer provinces, such as Sicily and Africa, where no legions were required. These remained under senatorial administration and were still governed by proconsuls under the old system; (2) the imperial provinces, on the frontiers, where legions were quartered, such as Syria. These were under the direct control of the emperor, who appointed *legati* (senators) to the charge of the more important, *procuratores* (equestrian) of the less important provinces. These men became experts in provincial administration, and won promotion by efficiency.

Other reasons for the improvement of provincial administration under the empire are to be found in the census and the regulation of taxation (the *publicani* virtually disappeared), in the payment of a fixed salary to the governors, improved communications, and the wide extension of Roman citizenship among the provincials. In consequence the provincial administration was generally sound and free from oppression under the early emperors, even the worst. There was considerable centralization, as we see from the correspondence of the younger Pliny with the emperor. Provincial municipalities were administered under a great variety of conditions; in the West they enjoyed self-government, under somewhat aristocratic constitutions, with a *curia* or senate, *duumvirs* (the chief executive officers), aediles, and quaestors.

Pro'xenus (*Proxenos*), in Greece, the official representative of a State, chosen from the citizens of another State, to look after the interests of its citizens residing or sojourning there; a sort of consul (in the modern sense). Pindar at Thebes was *proxenus* of Athens; Demosthenes at Athens was *proxenus* of Thebes. The *proxeni* received privileges and distinctions from the state which they represented.

Pro′xenus (*Proxenos*), the name of the Boeotian friend of Xenophon, at whose invitation he took part in the expedition of Cyrus related in the 'Anabasis'.

Prude′ntius Cle′mens, AURĒLIUS (b. A.D. 348), a Christian Latin poet, native of Spain, known for his hymns and for poems on Christian dogma and tales of martyrs.

Prytane′um (*Prutaneion*), in Greek capital cities, the 'town-hall', consecrated to Hestia (q.v.). The hearth of the State stood in it, and guests of the State were entertained there.

Pry′tany (*Prutaneia*), see *Cleisthenes*.

Pseu′dolus, a comedy by Plautus; the title is taken from a character in the play.

A Macedonian captain has bought a girl, Phoenicium, from a procurer for twenty minae, paying fifteen down. The girl is to be delivered to his messenger when he sends the remaining five minae and a certain token. Calidōrus, a young Athenian, is in love with her. The play deals with the trick by which his father's slave, Pseudolus, having intercepted the captain's letter and token, cheats the procurer and carries off Phoenicium for Calidorus.

Psȳ′chē (*Psūchē*, 'Soul'), in the 'Golden Ass' of Apuleius (q.v.), Bks. iv–vi (in the tale told by an old woman to amuse the girl captured by the robbers), a damsel who was so beautiful that Venus became jealous of her. She sent Cupid to make Psyche fall in love with some unsightly creature, but Cupid himself became her lover. He placed her in a palace, but only visited her in the dark and forbade her to attempt to see him. Her sisters from jealousy told her he was a monster and would devour her. One night she took a lamp and looked at Cupid while he slept. Agitated by the sight of his beauty, she let fall on him a drop of oil from the lamp, and woke him. Whereupon the god left her, angry at her disobedience. Psyche, solitary and remorseful, sought her lover all over the earth, and various superhuman tasks were required of her by Venus. The first of these was to sort out before night an enormous heap of various kinds of grain. But the ants took pity on Psyche, and coming in hosts, did the task for her. So, by one means or another, all the tasks got done, except the last, which was to go down to Hades and fetch a casket of beauty from Persephone. She had almost accomplished this, when she had the curiosity to open the casket. It contained

not beauty, but a deadly sleep, which overcame her. But Jupiter, at Cupid's entreaty, at last consented to her marriage to her lover, and she was brought to heaven.

This fable was the subject of a poem by Shackerley Marmion (1637), and of another by William Morris in his 'Earthly Paradise'; and there are versions of it in Pater's 'Marius the Epicurean', and in the 'Eros and Psyche' of Bridges.

Pto′lemies (*Ptolemaioi*), the dynasty that ruled over Egypt from the death of Alexander the Great until the Roman conquest. For the foundation of the dynasty, see *Macedonia*, § 2. The principal members of the dynasty were Ptolemy I (Sōtēr, son of Lāgus, 323–283 B.C.); his son Ptolemy II (Philadelphus, 285–246), at first joint ruler with his father; and Ptolemy III (Euergetēs, 246–221), who won for a time a large part of Seleucid Asia.

The first Ptolemies constantly endeavoured, with varying success, to extend their dominions over Syria and Asia Minor, and to obtain a footing in Greece itself. They were thus in frequent conflict with the Seleucids (q.v.). They held southern Syria fairly continuously till 200 B.C., and coastal possessions round Asia Minor till a few years later. Cyrene they retained till 98 and Cyprus till 58 B.C. Judaea remained under their sway till 200. The book of *Ecclesiastes*, which dates from the end of that period, reflects the despondency of part of the Jewish aristocracy under the Ptolemaic rule and their preference for the Seleucids; but according to Polybius the common people were favourable to the former. The attempts of the Ptolemies on Greece were defeated by the Antigonids (see *Macedonia*, § 3). The Ptolemies owed the control of their dominions outside Egypt in great part to their naval power; but their fleet lost its supremacy in a severe defeat by Antigonus off Andros in 246 or 245.

Under the later Ptolemies Egypt entered a period of great confusion, owing to domestic strife within the dynasty, civil wars and mob-rule. The last chapter in the history of the Ptolemaic dynasty opened when Ptolemy XI (Aulētēs) in 51 B.C. left his throne to be shared by his daughter Cleopatra VII and his young son Ptolemy XII. During the discord that followed, Julius Caesar made a descent on Egypt in 48. He was for a time besieged in the palace at Alexandria, but finally defeated his assailants, and established Cleopatra in power. Cleopatra followed Caesar to Rome in 46, and lived with him there till his death in 44, when she returned to Alexandria. She bore to Caesar a son who was named Caesarion (q.v.). For her relations with Mark Antony, see under the name of the latter. After the defeat of Actium and Antony's death, Cleopatra, having failed to beguile Octavian, took her own life, and the dynasty of the Ptolemies came to an end.

The Ptolemies claimed the ownership of the entire soil of Egypt (except the lands of Alexandria, Naucratis, and Ptolemâis, a city in Upper Egypt founded by Ptolemy I). Part of it was farmed for them by their own peasants, practically serfs. The use (but not the property) of the rest was granted, on various terms, to different categories of holders. All corn-land paid a tax in corn, which ultimately found its way to the great King's Barn in Alexandria, whence it was sold. Vineyards, orchards, and gardens were also taxed. The king had an important monopoly of oil, protected by a heavy import duty on foreign oil, and monopolies of textiles, papyrus, mines, and quarries. He had shares in certain businesses, and licences had to be purchased to carry on others. In fact practically every business was either owned in part or in whole by the king, monopolized, taxed, or subject to licence. This vast system of exploitation, which offers a striking contrast to the policy of the Seleucids in Asia, was carried on by a highly organized army of officials. The condition of the fellahin (the Egyptian peasants) was miserable. An artisan received 2–3 obols a day, a labourer doing heavy work one obol. Strikes were frequent. The army consisted of mercenaries, and under the first three Ptolemies no native was admitted to it. Ptolemy IV recruited native troops, and it was these who defeated the army of Antiochus III at Raphia in 217. The national consciousness of the Egyptians was awakened by this victory, the position of the Greeks was weakened, and Egyptian influence increased. A mixed Graeco-Egyptian race was gradually formed. Meanwhile grave abuses developed in the Ptolemaic system of administration, which depended on the honesty and efficiency of the officials, and only the energetic reforms of Ptolemy VII (Euergetes II) enabled it to survive till the Roman conquest.

The Ptolemies were immensely enriched by their exploitation of Egypt, and they raised their capital, Alexandria, to great wealth and magnificence. By their patronage of art and literature, and especially by the establishment of the Museum (q.v.), or literary academy of Alexandria, and the Alexandrian Library (q.v.), the first Ptolemies made the city a centre of Hellenistic culture. Ptolemy I himself wrote a narrative of Alexander's campaigns, which was used by the historian Arrian (q.v.). Greek settlers were planted in many parts of Egypt, more extensively in the reclaimed land of the Fayoum. To these settlements we owe numerous papyri (q.v.), discovered in modern times where physical conditions have been suitable for their preservation, containing portions of Greek works.

Pto'lemy (*Claudius Ptolemaeus*), a celebrated astronomer, who lived at Alexandria in the 2nd c. A.D., and who in his 'Mathēmatikē Syntaxis' ('System of Mathematics', translated later into Arabic and known as the 'Almagest', i.e. 'The great work') summed up the astronomical knowledge of the age. In it he developed a theory of the relative movements of the sun, moon, and planets round the earth, which he supposed to be stationary. This theory (with modifications) was accepted until the time of Copernicus and Kepler. Ptolemy also wrote a 'Geōgraphikē Huphēgēsis' or 'Geographical Outline', for long a standard geographical text-book, and a number of other scientific treatises, including one on optics and one on the theory of music. His principal works survive. Ptolemy invented the science of trigonometry, and improved the method of fixing geographical positions by reference to their latitude and longitude; his 'Geography' contains tables of the positions of all the principal places in the world as then known. The work was provided with maps; some of these, which may be contemporary, have survived.

Chaucer's Wife of Bath quotes a proverb from the Almagest of 'the wise astrologe daun Ptholomé'.

Publicā'ni, see *Equestrian Order*.

Publi'lius Sÿ'rus (*Sÿrus*), a writer of Latin Mimes (q.v.) of the 1st c. B.C. He was brought to Rome as a slave, probably from Antioch, and was manumitted. He is known to us by a collection of maxims which purport to have been culled from his plays, and of which these are specimens:

Nimium altercando veritas amittitur.
Heredis fletus sub persona risus est.
Avarus nisi cum moritur nil recte facit.

Another of his maxims, 'Judex damnatur cum nocens absolvitur', was adopted by the 'Edinburgh Review' (1802) to express its stern attitude in literary criticism. The collection was used as a school book.

Punic Wars. Rome, having by 270 B.C. made herself mistress of the Italian peninsula and become a Mediterranean power, found herself confronted across the Straits of Messina by the rival power of Carthage, which now held the greater part of northern Africa, cities on the coast of southern Spain, Sardinia and Corsica, and the north and west of Sicily. To the political rivalry between the two states was added a trade rivalry. The Carthaginians were rapidly closing the western seas to Rome. The conflict between them was precipitated by a trivial incident, the appeal of the Mamertines (originally a band of Italian mercenaries hired by Agathocles of Syracuse (q.v., § 3) for war against Carthage), who had occupied Messina, for protection against the Syracusans. The appeal was addressed first to the Carthaginians and then to the Romans, and led to these becoming embroiled with one another.

The FIRST PUNIC WAR lasted from 264 to 241 B.C. The Romans built a fleet, and won a great naval victory in 260 at Mylae near Messina, largely thanks to the device of the *corvi* (gangways by which the soldiers could board an enemy ship when laid alongside her). They disembarked on the coast of Africa, and after some early successes were there defeated, Regulus (q.v.), one of the consuls, who had been left in command of a diminished army, being taken prisoner (255). They lost the greater part of their fleet in a storm, and after further naval disasters confined their efforts to driving the Carthaginians from Sicily. From 247 they were there confronted by the great general Hamilcar Barca (q.v.), father of Hannibal, and after a succession of adverse campaigns won the war and secured Sicily by the naval victory off the Aegates Insulae (242). Sicily (except the dominion of the faithful Hieron II, see *Syracuse*, § 3) became the first Roman province. Sardinia and Corsica were annexed a few years later (237) during a revolt of the Carthaginian mercenaries which followed the first Punic War.

The SECOND PUNIC WAR, the great ordeal in which the stubborn courage of Rome was seen at its highest, was launched when Hannibal, who had been vowed by his father Hamilcar to undying hatred of Rome, succeeded to the command of the Carthaginian army in Spain, and in spite of Roman protests captured Saguntum, a city in alliance with Rome. Hannibal reached Italy after an arduous passage over the Alps in 218, was joined by the Gauls of northern Italy, and defeated one great Roman army after another, at the Ticinus, the Trebia (218), and Lake Trasimene (217). He moved to the S. to detach Rome's allies from her. The skilful policy adopted by Quintus Fabius the *Cunctator* or delayer, of following the invader and harassing him, while refusing a general

engagement, proved successful; but it caused discontent at Rome, and was abandoned in 216, with the result that Hannibal overwhelmed the Roman army at Cannae. But the spirit of Rome was unsubdued and her allies for the most part remained faithful to her. Steps had already been taken to prevent reinforcements reaching Hannibal from Spain, and similar precautions were taken against his new ally, Philip V of Macedon. The war languished in Italy and Hannibal turned his attention to the conquest of Sicily. The tide turned slowly in favour of Rome. M. Claudius Marcellus captured Syracuse in 212 and weakened the power of Carthage in Sicily. Campania was recovered. The young P. Cornelius Scipio showed his military genius in Spain, and when Hannibal summoned his brother Hasdrubal thence to his aid, the latter was intercepted and his army destroyed at the Metaurus (207). The conquered portions of Spain were formed into two Roman provinces in 206 (or 197). The war was transferred to Africa, where the successes of Scipio, after forcing the withdrawal of Hannibal from Italy (which he had occupied for fifteen years), ended the war with the victory of Zama in 202. Carthage was forced to renounce her conquests, pay an annual tribute, and limit her army. She lost her position as a great Mediterranean power.

She retained however her commercial importance, and continued to compete successfully with Rome in trade. This was a source of uneasiness at Rome. Carthage had undertaken to wage no wars in Africa without the consent of Rome. In 151 the depredations of Masinissa, the ruler of the adjoining Numidian kingdom and the friend of Rome, goaded her into retaliation, and thereupon Rome declared war (the THIRD PUNIC WAR). Rome was now determined on the final extinction of her rival (see *Cato the Censor*). A perfidious attempt was made to gain the city by a stratagem, and when this failed it was regularly besieged. It was captured and demolished by Scipio Aemilianus (q.v.) in 146. The Carthaginian dominions were for the greater part constituted a Roman province (called 'Africa'), and the ancient commercial empire of Carthage came to an end.

Pū′nica, see *Silius Italicus*.

Purple (*purpura*), a dye discovered by the Phoenicians and perhaps known in Homeric times, derived from certain organs of the *mūrex*, a shell-fish found in the Mediterranean. The best kinds of this dye were made by the Tyrians and fetched a high price. It was used for dyeing garments of a distinctive nature such as the mantles of the archons at Athens, and the purple stripes on the togas of Roman magistrates (see *Clothing*, § 3).

Pyane′psia (*Puanepsia* or *Puanopsia*), see *Festivals*, § 5.

Py′dna, in Macedonia on the Thermaic Gulf, the scene of the battle in 168 B.C. in which L. Aemilius Paullus decisively defeated Perseus king of Macedonia (q.v., § 3) and ended the Third Macedonian War.

Pygmā′lion (*Pugmaliōn*), a legendary king of Cyprus, who fell in love with a beautiful statue (according to Ovid made by himself). He prayed to Aphrodite to give him a wife resembling the statue; and she did more than this, for she gave the statue life, and Pygmalion married the woman so created. The story is the basis of Marston's poem 'The Metamorphoses of Pygmalion's Image' (1598); is among the tales told in W. Morris's 'Earthly Paradise' (1868–70); and is the subject of a comedy by W. S. Gilbert, 'Pygmalion and Galatea' (the name Galatea for the transformed statue appears to be a modern invention). 'Pygmalion' is also the title of a play by G. Bernard Shaw.

Pygmies (*Pugmaioi*, from *pugmē*, a measure of length, c. 13 inches), dwarf inhabitants of Africa, with whom the cranes were supposed to carry on war. This belief is frequently referred to by ancient writers, e.g. Homer, Aristotle, Ovid, and Pliny. Dwarf tribes have in modern times been found in Equatorial Africa.

Py′ladēs (*Pŭladēs*), (1) in Greek mythology the constant friend of Orestes (q.v.). He accompanied him to the land of the Tauri (see *Iphigenia*), and later to Mycenae when Orestes took vengeance on Clytemnestra and Aegisthus (see *Electra*, Sophocles' tragedy). (2) An actor at Rome, see *Pantomime*.

Py′los (*Pŭlos*), (1) the legendary kingdom of Neleus and Nestor (qq.v.) in the Peloponnese; (2) a town on the W. coast of the Peloponnese, in Messenia. This and the adjoining Bay of Pylos, and Sphacteria, the island which almost closes the mouth of the bay, were the scene of an important defeat of the Spartans by the Athenians in 425 B.C. (see *Peloponnesian War*). It was here that in later times was fought the battle of Navarino (1827).

Py′ramus (*Pŭramos*), the subject of an Asiatic legend. He was a youth of Babylon, who loved his neighbour Thisbe. The two lovers, whom their parents forbade to marry, exchanged their vows through

a chink in the wall that separated their two houses. They agreed to meet at the tomb of Ninus outside the walls of the city, under a white mulberry tree. Thisbe came first to the appointed place, but being frightened by a lion, fled into a cave, dropping her veil, which the lion worried and covered with blood. Pyramus, arriving, found the bloody veil, and concluding that Thisbe had been devoured, stabbed himself with his sword. Thisbe, coming from the cave, distraught at the sight of the dying Pyramus, fell upon his sword. Their blood flowed to the roots of the mulberry tree, which thereafter bore only red fruit. The story is told by Ovid in the 'Metamorphoses'; it is also the subject of the 'tedious brief scene' played by Nick Bottom and his friends in 'A Midsummer Night's Dream'.

Py′rgopolyni′cēs, the braggart captain in the 'Miles Gloriosus' (q.v.) of Plautus.

Pyriphle′gethon (*Puriphlegethōn*), see *Hades*.

Pyrrhic Dance (*Purrichē*), the Spartan mimic war-dance, perhaps a form of the *hyporchema* (q.v.). It is said to have originated with the Dorians in Crete. It was danced at the Spartan Gymnopaediae and also at the Panathenaea at Athens (see *Festivals*, §§ 5 and 2). The origin of the name is uncertain.

Py′rrhon (*Purrhōn*), see *Sceptics*.

Py′rrhus (*Purrhos*), a name of Neoptolemus (q.v.).

Pyrrhus I (*Purrhos*) (319/8–272 B.C.), king of Epirus from 307, was second cousin of Alexander the Great, for the father of Pyrrhus, and Olympias, mother of Alexander the Great, were the son and daughter respectively of two brothers, Epirot princes. Pyrrhus was ousted from his throne in 302, served under Demetrius Poliorcētēs at Ipsus (see *Macedonia*, § 2), and by Ptolemy's help was restored in 297. He was a skilful commander, a good organizer, and an ambitious military adventurer. He hoped to revive the empire of Alexander the Great, and was at one time (286) the most powerful ruler in the European part of it, having secured Thessaly and a portion of Macedonia; but he was soon driven back to Epirus by Lysimachus. He then turned to the west and accepted the invitation of Tarentum to lead the Italian Greeks against Rome. He won battles in 280 and 279 but was unable to establish himself in Italy. The expression 'Pyrrhic victory', a victory won at too great a cost, alludes to an exclamation attributed to Pyrrhus after the battle of Asculum in 279, where he routed the Romans but lost the flower of his army, 'One more such victory and we are undone'. He then landed in Sicily, and by the end of 277 had driven back the Carthaginians to Lilybaeum. But his Siceliot allies refused to support him in his plan to attack Carthage itself. Whereupon he abandoned his western adventure. He once more invaded Macedonia (274) with some success, but was diverted to an attack on Sparta, which successfully resisted his siege (272). He was killed in the same year in an attempt to seize Argos. There is a life of Pyrrhus by Plutarch, who relates the stories about Pyrrhus and Fabricius referred to herein under *Fabricius*.

Pÿtha'goras (*Pūthagorās*), a celebrated Greek philosopher, born at Samos about 580 B.C. He is said to have travelled in Egypt and the East, and later, when Polycrates (q.v.) became tyrant of Samos, to have migrated to Croton in Magna Graecia, and there founded a school or brotherhood. This was primarily religious and philosophical in character, but it also exercised political influence in favour of oligarchy. Pythagoras may have perished in the democratic revolt at the end of the 6th. c. which destroyed this school. The members of the school were bound by strict vows to their leader, and practised asceticism, particularly in the matter of food. He was said to have derived his moral doctrines from Delphi (his name means 'mouthpiece of Delphi'). He taught the doctrine of the transmigration of souls (found also in Orphism, q.v., and the religions of India) and himself claimed to remember his earlier incarnations. He discovered the numerical relation between the length of strings and the musical notes which they produce when vibrating, and evolved the idea that the explanation of the universe is to be sought, not in matter, but in numbers and their relations, of which the objects of sense are the representations. Nothing survives of his writings. He greatly advanced mathematical, geometrical, and astronomical science. He knew that the earth is a sphere, and is said to have sacrificed a hecatomb when he discovered that the square on the hypotenuse of a right-angled triangle is equal to the sum of the squares on the other two sides.

The Pythagorean doctrines revived later (at Rome in the early times of the Empire) and became fused with Orphism, with which they had affinities.

Py'theas (*Pūtheās*), a Greek of Massilia, contemporary with Alexander the Great, who made a courageous voyage up the W. coast of Europe to Britain, Jutland, and the Orkneys and Shetlands. His narrative is lost, but was used by Strabo, who however (wrongly) distrusted it.

Py'thia (*Pūthiā*), the priestess of Apollo at Delphi (q.v.).

Py'thian Festival (*Pūthia*), see *Festivals*, § 1.

Pÿ'thon (*Pūthōn*), see *Delphi*.

Q

Quaestio, see *Judicial Procedure*, § 2.

Quaestiō'nēs, see *Papinian*.

Quaestiō'nēs Convīviā'lēs, see *Plutarch*, § 3.

Quaestors, at Rome, originally assistants of the consuls in tracing criminals, later received charge of the state treasury (*aerarium*). They collected and recorded revenue, and paid it out on order of a magistrate. They were at first two in number, subsequently four, and more were added as the Roman dominions increased and financial officials were required in the provinces. They were elected annually by the people. Under the legislation of Sulla election to the quaestorship gave admission to the Senate.

Quattuo'rviri viis purga'ndis, see *Vigintivirate*.

Quindeci'mviri sacris faciu'ndis, at Rome, a board of fifteen officials charged with keeping, consulting, and interpreting the Sibylline Books (q.v.). They were required to see to the carrying out of the measures indicated by the Books, and also to supervise the worship of Greek and oriental divinities, such as Cybele (q.v.), introduced at Rome as a result of consulting the Books.

Quinqua'trus, in Roman religion, originally a festival of Mars at which the sacred shields (*ancilia*, q.v.) were purified, held on the fifth day (whence its name) after the Ides of March, i.e. the 19th. On this day the Salii (q.v.) performed a ceremonial dance in the Comitium before the *pontifices* and the officers of cavalry. The same day was regarded as the birthday of Minerva, and it came to be thought that the festival was in honour of that goddess. It was further erroneously supposed (by Ovid, Livy, and others) that *Quinquatrus* signified a festival of five days' duration.

Quinque'nnium Nerō'nis, a phrase applied to the early years of Nero's reign, viewed, in retrospect and in contrast to the later period, as a sort of Golden Age.

Quinti'lian (*Marcus Fābius Quintiliānus*) (*c.* A.D. 35–*c.* 95), of Calagurris in Spain, received part at least of his education at Rome and listened assiduously to the orators of the time. After a return to Spain, from which he was brought back by Galba, he taught rhetoric at Rome, being the first to receive an official salary as a teacher, and became wealthy and famous. The younger Pliny was among his pupils. He also pleaded in the courts. Domitian made him consul and tutor to his grandnephews. After twenty years of teaching he retired, and the last part of his life was given to the composition, at the request of his admirers, of his 'Institutio Oratoria' (q.v.). The introduction to the 6th Book of this refers touchingly to the loss of his surviving son after the deaths of his wife and another son. His earlier work on the Decline of Oratory ('De Causis Corruptae Éloquentiae') is lost. Two collections of 'Dēclāmātiōnēs', rhetorical themes on imaginary problems of conduct in various circumstances or on problems arising out of the conflict of laws, &c., attributed to Quintilian, are probably not by him, though some may represent themes used in his school. For Quintilian's style see *Prose*, § 2.

The 'Institutio' is perhaps chiefly prized to-day for the list of authors to be studied, with Quintilian's judgements on them, contained in the tenth book; but there is much of enduring value in his discussion of education generally, and we come here and there on incidental sayings showing profound insight into human nature and the principles of art. The treatise, after having been loudly acclaimed (Martial calls Quintilian 'the supreme guide of wayward youth'), lost its influence in the Middle Ages. Petrarch had an imperfect copy of it. Poggio discovered a complete manuscript. It was first printed in 1470, and it acquired a great reputation in the Renaissance; for Quintilian's conception of the purpose of education—to produce not a pedant but a man of high character and general culture—was in harmony with that of the humanists of the 16th c. In England Quintilian influenced Sir Thomas Elyot's 'The Governour' (1531) and Thomas Wilson's 'Arte of Rhetorique' (1562); and Ben Jonson drew on him in his 'Timber; or Discoveries'.

Quinti'lius Vā'rus, see *Varus*.

Qui'ntus Cu'rtius, see *Curtius*.

Qui'ntus Smyrnae'us, Quintus of Smyrna, who lived probably in the 4th c. A.D., was author of a Greek epic poem (called Τὰ μεθ' Ὅμηρον) to fill the gap between the 'Iliad' and the 'Odyssey', in fourteen books. The work survives, but is chiefly of antiquarian interest.

Quiri'nus, in Roman religion, originally the local deity (perhaps the war god) of the Sabine community settled on the Quirinal hill. When this community came to be embodied in Rome (see *Rome*, § 2), Quirinus was included among the state gods of the city, with Jupiter and Mars. His festival, the *Quirinālia*, was celebrated on 17 February (see *Stultorum Feriae*), but nothing is known of his ritual. Quirinus was identified with Romulus by the Romans of the late republic. He had his own flamen (q.v.), the *Flamen Quirinālis*.

Quirītēs, a word of uncertain derivation, applied to the oldest inhabitants of Rome, Latin and Sabine, and later to the Roman people in their civil capacity. The term was not applicable to Romans when serving in the army; Caesar on one occasion quelled a mutiny of his soldiers by addressing them as 'Quirites' (Suet. Caes. 70; Tac. Ann. i. 42). *Quiris* is said to be the Sabine for 'lance'. It may therefore have been the title of citizens who had the privilege of bearing arms. Some think that *Quirites* originally signified the inhabitants of the Sabine town of Cūrēs.

R

Ra'mnēs, Tit'iēs, Lŭ'cerēs, the names of the three tribes of which the primitive Roman people is said to have consisted. The origin of the names is obscure. See *Rome*, § 2.

Rā'nae, see *Frogs*.

Rape of the Sabines, see *Rome*, § 2.

Recension, see *Texts and Studies*, § 11.

Recurrent verse, see *Sidonius Apollinaris*.

Rē'gia, in ancient Rome, the royal palace of Numa (q.v.) near the Forum. It adjoined the Temple of Vesta and the House of the Vestals. In republican times the Regia was the official head-quarters (not, it is thought, the residence) of the Pontifex Maximus. The building was several times burnt and restored. In 36 B.C. it was rebuilt of marble, and on its walls were inscribed the *fasti consulārēs* and *fasti triumphālēs* (see *Epigraphy*, § 10).

Rēgifu'gium, a ceremony held at Rome on 24 February, of which all that we know is that after a sacrifice in the Comitium (q.v.), the Rex Sacrorum (q.v.) fled from the Forum. It was thought in antiquity that this symbolized the flight of the last Tarquin king from Rome. But this view is questioned by modern scholars, though they are not in agreement as to the true explanation. It has been pointed out by Frazer (on Ov. Fast. ii. 685) that the intercalary period (see *Calendar*) of eleven days a year was introduced just before 24 February, the date of the Regifugium, and he suggests that the ceremony represented the termination of the rule of a temporary king who held nominal sway during the intercalary period.

Rēgi'llus (the first syllable is presumably long), LAKE, a lake in Latium on the shores of which the Romans in the early days of the republic (*c.* 496 B.C.) defeated the Latins, who were endeavouring to re-establish the Tarquins at Rome. It was said that the gods Castor and Pollux appeared in the battle and bore the news of the victory to Rome.

Re'gulus (*Rēgulus*), MARCUS ATILIUS, consul in 267 and 256 B.C. In the latter year he was one of the commanders of the Roman expedition to Africa in the First Punic War. His colleague was recalled and he was left in sole command with only 15,000 men. From over-confidence he proposed exorbitant terms when the Carthaginians attempted to negotiate peace. Thereupon the enemy in despair placed the Spartan Xanthippus in command of their army, and defeated and captured Regulus. In 250 the Carthaginians, defeated at Panormus (Palermo) in 251, sent him with an embassy to Rome to propose peace, making him swear to return if the negotiations failed. He advised the Romans to continue the war, returned to Carthage, and was put to a cruel death.

Religion.

GREEK RELIGION

§ 1. *Sources of Greek religion*

Greek religion was a highly complex product and there is much in connexion with its origins and development that is still matter of controversy. It appears to have had its source, in part, in the personification by a primitive people of the powers of nature as affecting man, either universal powers (*daimones*, q.v.) such as the earth and its fertility, the sky and its lightning and rain, or the local powers in particular rivers, springs, and trees (see for instance *Naiads, Dryads, Oreads*); in part in primitive ideas of magic, e.g. that by the performance of certain rites desirable results, such as a bountiful crop, can be obtained;

in part in primitive ideas of taboo, that certain things are sacred or accursed, clean or unclean, whence arose the notion of purification. To these ideas was joined the primitive cult of the dead, who were supposed to continue their life in the grave, retaining a power corresponding to that which they had exercised while living. They were propitiated by offerings placed or poured on the grave (not burnt, like the sacrifices to the personified powers of nature). There was an annual festival of the dead, when they were supposed to visit the houses, were welcomed with an offering, and were then requested to depart (see under *Lemures* for a similar Roman custom). From this belief in the survival of the spirits of the dead arose the Greek hero-cult; the hero is the powerful ancestor, not of the single family, but of the whole people, who is honoured and conciliated so that he may protect and avenge his folk. It appears probable that the Greek religion was, moreover, in part a blend of the beliefs of the early Hellenes when they migrated into Greece with those of the earlier inhabitants of that country. Thus Poseidon combines the characters of a northern god of the horse with a southern god of the sea. And Zeus combines attributes that seem to point to a mixed origin. There is strong evidence for a Minoan-Mycenaean (see *Mycenae*) origin for many of the Greek myths, which are connected with centres of Mycenaean culture such as Mycenae itself, Tiryns, and Thebes. Some of the Greek gods, notably Apollo and Dionysus, were later immigrants from foreign regions. Visitors and slaves introduced foreign cults, such as that of the Great Mother from Asia, and these occasionally became popular.

Among the ideas prominent in early Greek religion are those of the *sanctity* of what is devoted to a god (either as a possession or as something accursed, i.e. dedicated to his anger) and withdrawn from profane use, e.g. the Crissaean plain near Delphi, which might not be cultivated; and of *purification*, the removal of impurity, conceived as an infection, arising from contact, e.g., with death. This might be effected by carrying about the infected place or person a human being, a pig, or a cock, which absorbed the impurity and was then destroyed. See also *Sacrifice* and *Magic*. Morality, the ideas of righteousness, guilt, and retribution, formed no part of the archaic religion.

§ 2. *Evolution of Greek religion*

By the time of Homer, Greek religion had assumed an anthropomorphic form; that is to say the powers of nature had been conceived in the semblance of men and women, with the needs, desires, and failings of mankind. In the 'Iliad' they live in a community on Olympus, ruled over by Zeus. They direct the affairs of men, subject however (in an unexplained manner) to the decrees of Fate, a conception which belongs to an earlier stage of religious evolution. The gods are localized, not omnipresent (Poseidon is absent when the homeward journey of Odysseus is sanctioned by the council of the gods), they are not omniscient, and they are not omnipotent. Their rule has no connexion with morality. They govern according to their personal inclinations, and sometimes the inclinations of various gods conflict, and in the last resort Zeus decides. Consequently religious cult is a matter of conciliating the gods and making them favourable to human enterprises by prayer, offerings, and burnt sacrifice.

There soon came a tendency, already visible in the 'Odyssey', and still more marked in Hesiod, to introduce a moral element in the relations of gods and men (the recognition of justice, piety, and law-abidingness as acceptable to the gods). Apollo, who inculcated the need for expiation of crime, and Dionysus, who introduced a mystic element in Greek religion, emerged by the side of Zeus. Under various influences—the speculations of the philosophers and poets, the pronouncements of the Delphic oracle, the development of the city-state, and the work of the great lawgivers—Greek religion developed further. On the one hand, its moral and spiritual elements were strengthened: the notions of crime and guilt, retribution, expiation, and purification became prominent; the idea of the soul coming to judgement after death obtained a certain currency (see *Orphism*); while the anthropomorphic conception of the gods tended among the more cultivated Greeks to be replaced by abstractions such as 'the divine' (see also *Daimones*, *Tyche*). On the other hand, religion assumed a strongly civic side. The State represented in theory a blood relationship, and the religion of the State was an expansion of the religion of the family and the cult of the hero. The king, or the official who replaced him in the republican city, acted as the guardian of religion. There was a State hearth in the Prytaneum (q.v.) of many cities, where Hestia (q.v.) was worshipped as she was in each household. When a colony was founded, fire from this sacred hearth was carried to it. The cult of the hero, the mythological ancestor and patron of the State, acquired great importance. The worship of the gods was regulated by the State and made an

affair in which the whole people was interested. The festivals were given a political side: they were made the occasion for conferring honours on deserving citizens; the allies were summoned to attend them. By this process religion tended to lose its personal and intimate character and to become an outward show. Meanwhile the old myths were being undermined by the criticisms of the sophists, or explained away (e.g. by Euhemerus, q.v.). They were for a time defended by democratic prosecutions of persons accused of atheism (e.g. Protagoras, Socrates), but they finally perished among·the educated classes in the Hellenistic age, with the disappearance of the city-state, though they survived among the peasantry. Among the former the old religion was replaced, so far as it was replaced at all, by philosophic systems, notably the Stoic and Epicurean. Its position had never been very strong. It had evolved from primitive conceptions of man's relation to nature and the dead, under the influence of social, political, and other conditions. It possessed no authoritative theology, no sacred book inculcating immutable dogma and morality, no priestly caste to convey religious teaching (except perhaps in connexion with the mysteries; see *Priests*). Its mythology (which Homer did much to fix) was in large measure the outcome of imagination controlled only by the reasoning faculty, and the interpretation of the myths was open to all alike.

It may be noticed also that king-worship was widespread in the Greek world during the Hellenistic Age. Alexander and his successors were worshipped in various cities; Demetrius I for instance was worshipped in Athens and elsewhere. This was a political religion without true religious spirit, the worship of a king as benefactor and protector, more powerful than the discredited gods of Olympus. Later, the worship of Rome and of Roman governors grew up with the growth of Roman influence in eastern politics.

ROMAN RELIGION

§ 3. *The primitive religion*

The Latin word *religio* is of uncertain derivation. Its primary meaning for the Romans was probably the sense of awe or anxiety felt in a place believed to be the abode of a *numen* (q.v.) or spirit, and therefore holy. The primitive religion of the Romans, originally an agricultural community, was animism, the recognition of the existence of spirits (*numina*) localized in woods, springs, rivers, and the home, who exercised their will therein, and could be propitiated by suitable offerings and ritual. This sense of spiritual presences permeated daily life, especially the life of the home and the fields. Instances of its influence will be found under such headings as *Lares*, *Penates*, *Janus*, *Terminus*. In the city-state some of these *numina* took on a new character: Jupiter, the spirit of the open sky, becomes the deity of actions done under the heavens, the god of justice; Mars from an agricultural spirit becomes the god of war. A great triad of divinities is formed, with their temple on the Capitoline hill, Jupiter, Mars, and Quirinus; later, under Etruscan influence, Jupiter, Juno, and Minerva. This religion, through the necessity of consulting the will of the gods by auspices in relation to all State undertakings, came to govern political activities and was sometimes used unscrupulously for partisan purposes. It was highly ritualistic, and the most scrupulous attention was paid to the minutiae of the traditional ceremonies, which might be invalidated by the squeaking of a rat or the falling off of a priest's hat. More attention was paid to the ritual than to the personality and attributes of the deity: indeed, it sometimes happened that the ritual survived when the deity itself was forgotten (see *Furrina*). The practical and businesslike character of the Roman religion is seen in the very frequent use of vows (*vōta*), public and private. The public *vota* were undertakings given in the name of the State to offer to the gods special sacrifices, games, a share of booty, or a temple, if some peril were averted, some success achieved, or prosperity assured for a certain period. Such vows were recorded in writing and the record retained by the *pontifices* (q.v.). Private vows of offerings were made in similar circumstances, often accompanied by a votive tablet in a temple. Cloanthus vows a white bull if he is successful in the boat-race (Virg. Aen. v. 235); Horace refers to the tablets of mariners escaped from shipwreck (Od. I. v). The person under the obligation of a vow was known as *voti reus*.

The Roman attitude towards the dead is somewhat obscure. It appears to have been thought that the spirits of the dead survived, capable of influencing in some vague way the fortunes of the living. These spirits were at first regarded as hostile (see *Lemures*); later the fear of them gave place to a more friendly feeling, and the sense of the bond between the living and the dead members of the family developed (see *Manes*, *Parentalia*). Moreover the idea of deities of the underworld sprang up, the *Di Inferi* (Dis or Orcus, Proserpina, Hecate, qq.v.) and the *Di*

Manes (see *Manes*); and of other shadowy gods of that region, Vejovis, Acca Larentia, and Tarpeia (qq.v.).

For the cult and festivals (*fēriae*, our word 'fair') of the various *numina* and deities of Roman religion, as they were carried out both in the home and fields by private persons, and in the city by the State, see under the names of those deities and of the festivals. See also *Lustratio*.

§ 4. *Greek influences*

This primitive religion under the influence of contact with Greek thought was deeply modified by the Greek anthropomorphic theology, and the old Roman *numina* were in many cases identified with Greek gods and endowed with their attributes and the myths relating to them. Thus Jupiter was identified with Zeus, Minerva with Athena, and so on. But the primitive faith in the spirits of the home and the countryside survived, especially in rural districts. Religious doubt sprang up in the 3rd C. B.C. Ennius translated the sceptical work of Euhemerus (q.v.); and plays like the 'Amphitruo' (q.v.) of Plautus probably undermined belief. Later came the influence of Greek philosophy. The embassy of the three Greek philosophers in 155 B.C. (see *Philosophy*, § 2 led to the study of the doctrines of the various Greek schools, of which the most important at the time were the Stoic and the Epicurean. The Romans were more interested in the ethical than in the speculative side of philosophy; they also picked and chose among the doctrines of the Greeks those which suited them; and in the main it was a modified Stoicism as taught by Panaetius and Posidonius (qq.v.) which appealed to them, harmonious as it was with their approved qualities of *pietas* and *gravitas*, that is to say the observance of proper relations with gods, family, and State, and self-restraint in prosperity and adversity. The Epicurean ideal, though so ardently put forward by Lucretius, was not widely pursued. Stoicism was in close harmony with religion; it sought to reconcile the popular beliefs with its own monotheism by representing the various gods as diverse forms which the single deity assumes.

§ 5. *Eastern influences. Emperor-worship*

With the two closing centuries of the republic new religious influences came from the East. The cult of the *Magna Mater* (Cybele) was brought from Phrygia to Rome as early as 204 B.C. in the stress of the Punic War. A little later the orgiastic worship of Dionysus spread over

Italy, and was suppressed with difficulty in 186 B.C. The Mithridatic wars brought the worship of Mâ, the sanguinary goddess of Comana in Cappadocia, assimilated to Bellona. The contact with Egypt brought Isis and Osiris. Evidence of the persistence of the primitive religious beliefs at the beginning of the Empire is seen in Virgil (q.v.), in Ovid's 'Fasti', in the poems of Tibullus; also in the shrines of the ancient gods (*sacrāria* and *larāria*) found in the houses of Pompeii. Nevertheless the new foreign cults found a welcome at Rome, a sign of the inadequacy of the old beliefs to meet the religious cravings of a part at least of the population. The worship of Isis was soon popular with the masses, but established itself gradually, in face of vigorous conservative opposition, under the empire. The 'shaven linen-clad' priests of Isis are mentioned by Juvenal, and there is much about her cult in the closing scenes of the 'Metamorphoses' of Apuleius (q.v.), who represents his hero as initiated into the rites of Isis, the supreme deity 'of the thousand names' 'whose godhead under many forms the whole world worships'. In imperial times, in spite of the government's opposition, we also find such deities as the Phrygian Sabazios and the Syrian Atargatis received at Rome, and their worship spreading to the provinces. In particular the cult of the Persian god of light, Mithras, whose religion bears a superficial resemblance to Christianity, found the widest favour in the Roman army and was carried to remote parts of the empire (the remains of a temple of Mithras have been found at Housesteads in Northumberland). Caesar-worship was probably suggested by contact with the East and harmonized with the tendency of the Romans to glorify the heroes of the past. The habit of regarding a person who had conferred great benefits as god-like or a god, was common to both Greeks and Romans (for the Greek king-worship and worship of Rome in the Hellenistic Age, see above § 2 *ad fin.*). Caesar received divine honours after his death; Augustus had difficulty in restraining the people from regarding him as a god in his lifetime. The popular attitude is reflected in Virgil, Horace, and Ovid. This cult of the emperors was the one general test of loyalty to the empire. Subjects might worship any divinity they pleased, but they had also to worship the emperor as a sign of loyalty. Apart from this the cult had no great importance.

The oriental cults had their influence on Stoicism, introducing a more spiritual and personal relation between God and man. The need of reconciling the various creeds also led to a revival of a modified Platonism, of which the monotheistic idea was the vital centre (see *Neoplatonism*). Into this medley of religions and philosophies Christianity came, admitting no compromise with alien faiths, refusing to worship the deified emperor, and demanding an exclusive allegiance. It was this uncompromising spirit that caused the persecution of the Christians, but assured the ultimate triumph of their faith.

§ 6. *Religion, Fate, and Morality*

The relation of fate to the will of the gods in the old Roman as in the Greek religion is somewhat obscure. The original meaning of the word *fatum* was probably the spoken word of the prophet announcing destiny, the ordained future; its later and more common meaning was the expressed divine will. But there are different kinds of destiny, that of individuals or of races, and the overriding destiny of the world. The fate of individuals and races may conflict, or be overruled or thwarted; the world-destiny, as ordained by the *Parcae* is supreme. There are many illustrations of this distinction in Virgil, who inherited Greek ideas on the subject. The ultimate fate, the world-destiny, Virgil, basing himself on Stoic philosophy, seems to have regarded as identical with the will of the gods, or since their wills sometimes conflicted, of God, as represented by Jupiter.

The early Roman religion had hardly any relation with morality. It represented merely a businesslike relation with the unseen powers, whose favour might be obtained on certain terms. None the less, it may be thought to have had an important influence on Roman character. The obligation to the exact fulfilment of religious duties promoted discipline and obedience to the State. There was a sense of divine justice, which served as a sanction to human law. More than all, the religion of the home, the sense of divine presence in the daily round of domestic events, calling for the maintenance of right relations (*pietas*) both with the gods and the other members of the family, strengthened the family tie, the basis of Roman society. Similarly the sense of national solidarity was maintained by the annual State festivals of the various gods, so that religion became, as it has been said, the sanctification of patriotism. For this reason Cicero and Augustus insisted on its value. See also *Augurs, Flamens, Pontifices, Sacrifices*.

Reme'dia Amŏris, a poem in elegiacs by Ovid, of some 800 lines. It professes to give instructions for overcoming unfortunate or misplaced love, by hunting, travel, agricultural occupations, avoidance of wine and of amorous poets, and other less innocuous precepts.

Re′mus (*Rēmus*), see *Romulus*.

Republic (*Politeia*), a dialogue by Plato concerning Justice. The interlocutors are Socrates, an old man named Cephalus (father of Lysias, q.v.) and his son Polemarchus, Thrasymachus a sophist, and Plato's brothers Glaucōn and Adeimantus. The discussion takes place at the house of Cephalus. The definitions of Justice by the poet Simonides and by Thrasymachus having been found unsatisfactory, it is suggested that justice will best be seen in a perfect city-state, and if discovered there, can be found by analogy in man. Accordingly Socrates proceeds to construct the ideal State. This is seen to consist of three classes, guardians or magistrates, auxiliaries or soldiers, and producers. In the first resides the wisdom of the State, in the second its courage. Temperance or restraint must be present in all three classes; while political justice is that which keeps each class to its proper functions. Similarly man is wise in virtue of the rational element in him, courageous in virtue of the spirited element, and temperate when reason governs; while justice is seen to consist in the harmony of all the elements in him. The discussion of the ideal State is continued; Socrates' proposal for the community of women and children is explained, and it is shown that for the efficient working of the constitution the supreme power must be in the hands of philosophers. Socrates expounds the proper education of the guardians (from which the misleading tales of the poets must be excluded) and the nature of true knowledge, which is not of the objects and images of the world of the senses, but of the realities of the intellectual world, apprehended by pure intelligence. The Theory of Ideas or Forms (see *Plato*, § 3) is developed; and the nature of right education is illustrated by the simile of men chained in a subterranean cavern, who see only the shadows of objects behind them thrown by a fire on the wall in front of them, so that they take these shadows for the only realities. Socrates resumes the subject of the various types of political organization and personal character, and traces the process of degeneration from the perfect state and perfect man, viz. aristocracy and the aristocratical man, to the worst, viz. tyranny and the tyrannical man. Finally the rewards of virtue are considered, chief among these being the

rewards that the soul receives in its future life, for the soul is immortal. The nature of this future life is indicated in the tale of Er the son of Armenius, who twelve days after his death returned to life and described what he had seen in the other world.

Respo′nsa, see *Papinian*.

Revenue, PUBLIC, see *Athens*, § 11, *Rome*, § 14.

Revenues (*Poroi ē peri Prosodōn*, L. *de vectigālibus*) one of the minor works of Xenophon, written not before 355 B.C. and probably his last work. The ascription to him has been questioned.

Xenophon discusses various means of increasing the revenue of Athens, notably by encouraging the resident aliens and trade generally, and by acquiring a large number of public slaves to be hired out to the concessionaires of the Laurium silver mines (a transaction from which the author anticipated a return of 33 per cent. on the capital expended).

Rex Sacrō′rum, at Rome after the expulsion of the kings, a priest whose duty it was to perform some of the king's religious functions. He was a patrician, appointed for life, and unlike the *pontifex maximus* (q.v., to whom he was superior in dignity and precedence though inferior in religious authority) disqualified from holding any other office. He and his wife (the *rēgina*, who shared in the priesthood) performed certain state sacrifices, and it was he who, before the publication of the calendar, announced to the people the festivals of each month.

Rhadama′nthus, in Greek mythology, a son of Zeus and Europa (q.v.), who became a judge of the dead and ruler of Elysium (q.v); see *Minos Rhadamanthus and Aeacus*.

Rhampsinī′tus (*Rhampsinitos*), a Pharaoh of Egypt (Rameses III?), of whom Herodotus tells the following story. He had a treasury built, in the wall of which the builder secretly left a movable stone. The builder's sons, by means of this, were able to creep in and steal the treasure. The king, finding the seals unbroken but the treasure diminished, set a man-trap, in which one of the brothers was caught. He immediately called to his brother and bade him cut off his head and take it away to avoid detection, which was done. Cf. the story of *Trophonius*.

Rha′psode or **Rha′psodist** (*Rhapsōdos*), meaning 'one who stitches songs together', sometimes a bard who recited his own poems, but later generally used for one of a class of persons who made a living by reciting the poems of Homer. Plato's 'Ion' is a satire on their pretensions.

Rhē'a (*Rhēā* or *Rheiā*), according to Hesiod one of the Titans (q.v.), hardly distinguishable from Ge (the Earth), and commonly identified with the Asiatic goddess Cybele (q.v.). The Romans identified her with Ops (q.v.). For her children, see *Cronus*.

Rhē'a Si'lvia or ILIA, see *Ilia*.

Rhē'sus (*Rhēsos*), a tragedy doubtfully attributed to Euripides.

It is a dramatization of the 10th Book of the 'Iliad'. The Greeks have been driven back to their ships and Hector sends Dolon by night to spy out their intentions. Rhesus, king of Thrace, arrives with his army to support the Trojans. Hector reproaches him for his delay; Rhesus replies proudly and confidently, and then retires to rest. Ulysses and Diomedes enter the Trojan camp; they have killed Dolon after learning from him the pass-word. Directed by Athene, they fall upon the sleeping Thracians, kill Rhesus, and lead away his horses. His charioteer recounts his death by an unknown hand and charges Hector with his murder. Hector is exculpated by the Muse Terpsichore, mother of Rhesus, who descends from heaven to carry off her son's body.

Rhetoric, the theoretical art of speaking, oratory reduced to a system capable of being taught, first developed among the Sicilians (see *Oratory*, § 1) and further cultivated by the Sophists (q.v.). As a result of contact with Hellenic culture, it was introduced in the 1st c. B.C. at Rome as part of the more advanced education, and exercised an increasing influence on Roman literature during the empire (see *Education*, § 2).

Rhetoric (*Rhētorika*), a treatise by Aristotle (q.v.), § 3 (5), on the art of popular persuasion.

Rhēto'rica ad Here'nnium (q.v.), a treatise on oratory in four books, written about 86–82 B.C., usually attributed to one Cornificius. Cicero made use of it in his early 'De Inventione'. The work is modelled on Greek writers on rhetoric, and is interesting as an early extant example of Latin prose.

Rhodes (*Rhŏdos*), the most easterly of the islands of the Aegean, colonized by Dorians, and itself the founder of Gela in Sicily, Phasēlis in Lycia, and Soli in Cilicia. It contained three separate cities, Lindus, Iālysus, and Camīrus, which amal-

gamated in 408 B.C. By the end of the 4th c. the Rhodian republic also incorporated many other islands and a substantial area on the Carian mainland (Peraea). During the Peloponnesian War Rhodes revolted from the Athenian confederacy. It joined the second Athenian League, but again revolted in 357 (see *Athens*, § 6). During the 3rd c. it was a considerable naval power, standing for freedom of trade and suppressing piracy. In the struggles that succeeded the death of Alexander, it tried to follow a policy of neutrality. But Antigonus I, alarmed at the friendly relations between Rhodes and Ptolemy, sent his son Demetrius Poliorcētēs against it. The capital endured a long and famous siege in 304 at his hands, and Demetrius was finally obliged to come to terms with the Rhodians. It was after this that the celebrated *Colossus* of Rhodes, a huge statue of the Sun-god, was erected at the entrance of the harbour. Rhodes was associated with Pergamum (q.v.) in a policy of friendship to Rome at the time of the Second Macedonian War and the war with Antiochus III. After his defeat it was rewarded with Caria and Lycia, but it soon excited the jealousy of Rome by its independent attitude, especially in the Third Macedonian War, and was deprived of these new possessions. Its trade was also severely hit by the Roman free port of Delos. It sank into insignificance, remaining, however, a free city. Rhodes became a considerable literary centre, and was the birthplace of Panaetius (q.v.) and the seat of the school of his pupil Posidonius (q.v.). Hipparchus the mathematician (q.v.) probably spent part of his life there. It was destroyed by an earthquake in 225 B.C., and again *c.* A.D. 155; as rebuilt, it was described by Aelius Aristides (q.v.) as the most beautiful of Greek cities. Rhodian maritime law was famous, and portions of it may have in later times passed into that of Venice.

Rhodians, For the, a political speech by Demosthenes; see *Demosthenes* (2), § 4 (c).

Rhodŏ'pē or RHODŌ'PIS, a Greek courtesan, said to have been a Thracian and a fellow slave of Aesop, and to have been taken to Naucratis in Egypt. Aelian relates that one day while Rhodope was bathing, an eagle flew away with one of her slippers and dropped it in the lap of the Pharaoh of the day, Psammētichus. The king was struck with the beauty of the slipper, had search made for the owner, and married her—a curious parallel to the story of Cinderella. There was a story (rejected by Herodotus) that she built the third pyramid; to this Tennyson alludes in 'The Princess', ii:

The Rhodope that built the pyramid.

Landor has two 'Imaginary Conversations' between Rhodope and Aesop. Herodotus (ii. 134–5) confuses Rhodopis with the courtesan Doricha (see *Sappho*).

Rhopa'lic Verse (from the Gk. *rhopalos*, a cudgel, thicker towards one end), verse of which each word contains one more syllable than that before it; e.g. 'Lux verbo inducta, peccantibus auxiliatrix'. See *Ausonius*.

Roads. (1) GREEK. The Greeks had a network of roads, levelled but unpaved, many of them perhaps designed primarily to connect various cities with the great religious centres, but serving also purposes of trade. There were a number of roads in Attica, for instance the important road from Athens to the Piraeus, another from Athens to Eleusis and thence on the one hand to Megara on the other to Plataea, and roads to Laurium and to Marathon. There was a road from Corinth to Megara, Plataea, and Thebes, and roads from Thebes to Delphi and to the north. There were roads from Sparta and from Argos in various directions. Several roads centred in Olympia. There were also commercial roads from early times to the Greek cities on the Euxine.

(2) ROMAN. The great network of Roman roads was created for military and political, rather than for economic purposes. It was intended for the maintenance of Roman authority in conquered territories and for the defence of Roman frontiers. According to tradition it was initiated by Appius Claudius the Censor (q.v.), who in 312 B.C. began the construction of the road which bore his name, the *Via Appia*, running in a straight line SE. from Rome to the coast at Terracina, and thence to Capua. But it is probable that the *Via Latina* from Rome to Capua, by the more inland route over Mt. Algidus and the valley of the Liris, is of older date, and had its origin in the Roman conquests of the 5th and early 4th centuries. The *Via Appia* was extended later to Beneventum and Brundisium. The other principal roads of the republican period were as follows (they bore the names of the censors or consuls who constructed them). The *Via Flāminia* was built by the censor C. Flaminius in 220 B.C. across the Apennines to Ariminum (Rimini); it was restored by Augustus, whose triumphal arch may still be seen in the main street of Rimini. It was extended to Placentia under the name of *Via Aemilia*, and the district through which it passed is still named Emilia. The *Via Aurēlia* ran by the coast from Rome

to Genoa. The road to Genoa by the more inland route through Arretium appears to have borne the names both of *Via Clōdia* and *Via Cassia*. Another *Via Aemilia* joined the fortress of Aquileia in the NE. with Bonōnia, and the *Via Popillia* joined Aquileia with Ariminum. The Popillius who built the latter also extended the Appian Way to Rhēgium at the southern extremity of Italy. The *Via Caecilia* connected Rome with the Adriatic by a direct route across the Apennines, but its course is not known. The *Via Domitia* ran from the Rhone to the Pyrenees. The *Via Egnātia*, constructed after the conquest of Macedonia, crossed the Balkans from Dyrrhachium (Durazzo) to Thessalonica.

The road system was greatly extended under the empire, spreading through Byzantium far into Asia, to the Euphrates and the Red Sea. It was particularly developed in Gaul; several roads crossed the Alps. It has left many traces in Britain, in such roads as the Fosse Way, Ermine Street, and Stane Street (see also under *Britain*, §§ 2 and 3).

The best of the Roman roads were generally 2½ to 5 metres wide, running in straight lines where the nature of the ground permitted, well constructed with several layers of substructure (though these may sometimes be due to successive repairs), often paved, and provided with milestones. In and near towns there were often raised side-walks on either side. There were also minor roads less carefully designed and constructed. The milestones gave the distance from some centre and sometimes the name of the constructor of the road and the emperor under whom it was built. Milestones found in many parts of the empire thus often furnish valuable information (see also *Miliarium Aureum*). On the principal roads there were posting-houses, with relays of horses, at short intervals; these might be used by officials and others who had 'diplomas', or permits; there were also inns (*mansiōnēs*) providing night quarters. The principal roads were maintained from 20 B.C. by *cūrātōrēs viarum*, highway commissioners, the expense being borne partly by the *fiscus* (q.v.), partly by the local authorities. Roads of only local importance were maintained by the labour and funds of the district. The Romans built many bridges, some of them still in use, e.g. the great bridge over the Tagus at Alcantara in Spain.

Rōbī'gus or **RŌBĪ'GŌ**, in Roman religion, the spirit (*numen*) of red mildew ('rust'), a pest which attacks corn. It was propitiated and the pest averted by the annual sacrifice of a red dog, at the festival of the *Röbigālia* on 25 April.

Roman Age of Greek Literature, THE,

is generally regarded as extending from the latter part of the 1st c. B.C., when with the fall of the Ptolemaic dynasty the Roman subjugation of the Mediterranean world became complete, to A.D. 529, when Justinian closed the schools of philosophy at Athens and ended the long history of that city as a centre of Greek culture. When the period opened, that culture had become widely diffused over the Hellenistic east. But Greek literature was no longer nourished in the fertile soil of popular sympathy and support. Only a small literary society was interested in it, and that society of a heterogeneous description, consisting largely of Romans, Egyptians, Syrians, &c. Greece herself now played a small part. She had suffered grievous devastation in the Mithridatic and Civil wars. Her philosophy survived, but appealed only to a small intellectual class, whereas Christianity, by its simplicity and definite promise, came in time to have a strong hold on the masses. The first portion of this period (to the death of Augustus) is marked chiefly by the names of a few critics, historians, and philosophers, Diodorus Siculus, Dionysius of Halicarnassus, Strabo, and Posidonius (qq.v.). It is marked also by a revival (seen in Dionysius of Halicarnassus) of good Attic prose, free from the florid extravagances of Asianism. But the rhetoricians soon asserted themselves afresh in declamations, popular lectures, and rhetorical exercises on imaginary themes; their activities are sometimes referred to as the *New Sophistic*. Some revival of serious Greek literary activity occurred under the encouragement of the Antonines in the 2nd c. A.D., especially in the domains of moral philosophy and history. The principal names are those of Plutarch, Epictetus, Marcus Aurelius, Arrian, Appian, Dio Cassius, Galen, the geographers Ptolemy and Pausanias, and the satirist Lucian (qq.v.). Subsequently the decline becomes more marked, and is relieved only by the important philosophical work of Plotinus (q.v.) and his successors, and the growing prominence of Christian writers such as Clement of Alexandria (q.v.). There were a number of graceful writers of elegiac poetry throughout this age, such as Meleager of Gadara, Antipater of Sidon, and Crinagoras of Mytilene (qq.v.). Much of their work is preserved in the Palatine Anthology (q.v.). See also *Novel*. The succeeding period of Greek literature is known as the Byzantine Age.

Roman Law, see *Law (Roman)*.

Romance, see *Novel*.

Rome (*Rōma*).

§ 1. *General topography*

Ancient Rome stood on the left bank of the Tiber, about fourteen miles from its mouth, and near the northern boundary of Latium, adjoining Etruria. The original settlement was on the Palatine, one of a group of hills some 100–150 ft. high standing near the river. This settlement formed what was known as *Rōma Quadrāta*, the fortified city supposed to have been built by Romulus. It was first extended to include the region known as the *Septimontium* (the seven *montes* being the three divisions of the Palatine, three of the Esquiline, and the Caelian), together with the *pomoerium* (sacred enclosure) round it. This in turn was united with a kindred settlement on the opposite hills, the Quirinal and Viminal. Within the boundaries of this combined city were included the Forum or market-place and the Capitol, the central fortress. The city as enclosed within the Servian Wall (that is, the wall attributed to Servius Tullius) included the seven hills of Rome (to be distinguished from the seven *montes* above), viz. the Palatine, Aventine, Capitoline, Caelian, Esquiline, Viminal, and Quirinal. This was the city of republican times, though by the end of that period houses extended beyond the walls (a law of Julius Caesar directed that for a mile outside the gates each resident should maintain the road outside his house). The city grew further in imperial times, and was ultimately enclosed by Aurelian (A.D. 270–275) with a wall which included not only an enlarged area on the left bank, but a portion of the Janiculum on the right bank of the Tiber. The centre of the city was extremely cramped and congested; Julius Caesar improved its communications with the northern part (the Campus Martius) by the creation of the *Forum Julium*, and Augustus continued his work with the *Forum Augustum*. It was completed by the construction of the great *Forum Trajanum* by the emperor Trajan. The streets of Rome, at least until the reconstruction which followed the fire under Nero, were narrow and crowded, so much so that a law of Julius Caesar forbade vehicular traffic in the city during the day time. A plan of the city on marble, of which fragments survive, was affixed to the wall of an edifice north of the *Via Sacra*; it is thought to have been executed under Septimius Severus and

Caracalla, perhaps the copy of an earlier plan of the time of Vespasian. For various important parts of the city see *Aventine, Capitol, Circus Maximus, Forum, Palatine, Subura, Velabrum, Via Sacra,* etc. See also *Aqueducts* and Pl. 14.

§ 2. *Legendary origins and regal period*

The legend that gave the Romans a Trojan ancestry is related under *Aeneas*. To reconcile this legend with the tradition that Rome was a colony of Alba Longa, the head of the Latin League, and to fill the gap between the supposed date of the fall of Troy and that of the foundation of Rome in the 8th c., a series of Alban kings was invented, of whom Ascanius, son of Aeneas, was the first. Amulius, the last of the series, ousted Numitor the rightful king, and made Numitor's daughter, Rhea Silvia, a Vestal Virgin (q.v.), thereby preventing her from marrying. But she became by Mars mother of twin children, Romulus and Remus. Amulius made away with the mother and threw the children into the Tiber. They were washed ashore and suckled by a she-wolf (perhaps the totem of a Latin tribe) until discovered by the royal herdsman Faustulus, who with his wife Acca Larentia brought them up. They were eventually recognized, overthrew Amulius, and restored Numitor. They then decided to found a new settlement where they had been washed ashore. An omen by the flight of birds decided that Romulus should be king of it. Romulus proceeded to build his city on the Palatine Mount, and Remus showed his contempt for it by jumping over the newly built wall. He was thereupon killed by Romulus or one of his companions. To secure wives for his people, Romulus invited the neighbouring Sabines to witness games that he was celebrating, and while these were proceeding the Romans carried off the Sabine women (the 'Rape of the Sabines'). War followed, and the Sabines under Titus Tatius besieged the Capitol, an outpost of the city. Here Tarpeia (q.v.), the daughter of the officer in command, undertook to betray the citadel if the Sabines would give her what they had on their left arms, meaning their golden bracelets. But when the Sabines broke in, they rewarded her treachery by crushing her under their bucklers. (In some, perhaps Sabine, accounts, Tarpeia is presented as a heroine). The Romans, who still held the Palatine, were after further fighting reconciled with the Sabines by the captured women, and the two peoples settled down together. Romulus subsequently disappeared, it was said, in a thunderstorm: but there was a rumour that he had been torn to pieces by his councillors. Rome, according to tradition, was at first ruled by a succession of six further kings, Numa Pompilius, Tullus Hostilius, Ancus Marcius, Tarquinius Priscus, Servius Tullius, and Tarquinius Superbus. Very little credence can be attached to the legends of this period, but the Romans believed them and incorporated them in their literature; some of them appear to be developed out of elements of later Roman religion and ritual, others show Greek influence in their invention. But the last three kings evidently have some historical basis.

According to the official chronology, Rome was founded in 753 B.C. The story of its Trojan origin is a fable, but the tradition that it was a colony founded by the Latins of Alba may be true. It was favoured by its position near the sea and controlled the navigation of the Tiber. There was gradual expansion and perhaps infiltration of other peoples, notably Sabines. The names of the three ancient tribes of Rome, Ramnes, Tities, and Luceres, were thought to represent three original stocks, Latin, Sabine, and Etruscan, and there may be truth in the tradition. The king appears to have been nominated by an *interrex* elected by a Senate or royal council composed of the heads of the *gentes* or clans, into which families with a common ancestor, and their dependents, were grouped; and the election was confirmed by the people in an assembly (*comitia curiata*) of the thirty *curiae* or territorial groups of families into which the population was divided. The noble families were known as patrician (q.v.), the others as plebeian. There appear to have been many wars during the regal period, by which the Roman territory was enlarged. Rome destroyed Alba, according to legend, when Tullus Hostilius was king (see *Horatii and Curiatii*), and under Ancus Marcius founded a colony at Ostia near the mouth of the Tiber. Under Tarquinius Priscus (an adventurer, it is related, half Greek and half Etruscan, who came to try his fortune at Rome and won the throne), and his two successors, Etruscan influence became strong at Rome. The Etruscans, a powerful commercial and industrial people, may have conquered Rome; or the Etruscan cities may have accepted Tarquin as their king. Servius Tullius (q.v.), a man of humble origin, enlarged the city, enclosing it, it is said, in the wall that bears his name. Other important works, the Cloaca Maxima (q.v.), the Temple of Jupiter on the Capitol, etc., are likewise said to have been executed by the later kings of Rome. To Servius Tullius are attributed certain administrative reforms, important for features that endured throughout the republican period. He created the *tribûs*, originally twenty in number, finally raised to thirty-five; these 'tribes' were territorial districts, and the *census* or registration of the citizens and their property, and the *tributum* or wartime tax on property, were closely connected with them. He further divided the people, according to the wealth of each citizen, into five classes, and the classes into *centuriae*, which for most purposes replaced the older *curiae*; the number of the *centuriae* in each class being so arranged as to give the preponderance of voting power in the assembly (*comitia centuriata*, voting by centuries) to the richest class. On the other hand it was this class which bore the heaviest burden of taxation and of military service. These reforms had later a political effect in substituting residence and wealth for birth as qualifications for political rights. Tarquinius Superbus, the last of the kings, is said to have consulted the oracle at Delphi about a proposed colony, an illustration of the early relations between Italy and Greece.

The Tarquins were expelled and the monarchy came to an end in 510, no doubt as the result of a struggle between the kings and the patrician families. The struggle is reflected in the famous legend of the outrage on Lucretia (q.v., see also *Brutus, Lucius Junius*). The period thus terminated, apart from the legends it transmitted to posterity and the indication it gives of the mixed blood of the early inhabitants of Rome, has little bearing on Roman literature. There was little in the early Roman State to suggest its capacity for political and literary greatness.

§ 3. *The Republican period; internal struggles*

The constitution that followed the expulsion of the kings in 510 B.C. was an aristocratic republic. The king was replaced by two magistrates annually elected (praetors, later called consuls), who had to be patricians. The Senate retained its former position of national council. It was the real governing force in the State. The *comitia centuriata*, or popular assembly, was organized, as described in the previous section, so as to give a preponderance of power to the wealthy classes.

The history of the Roman republic consists in the main of the record of two orders of struggles, one internal, the other external. The first were the struggles of the plebeian and poorer classes with the

patricians. The second were the struggles of Rome with external foes, at first mainly defensive but subsequently aggressive, in the course of which Rome became mistress of Italy and of vast territories beyond the seas. The struggle between the privileged and unprivileged classes lasted two centuries. It took the form from time to time of a threat by the plebeians of secession, i.e. of withdrawal to form a separate community. It arose (*a*) from the desire of the mass of the plebeians for personal security against the arbitrary oppression of the patrician magistrates, for land, and for relief from debt; (*b*) from the desire of the wealthier plebeian families for full political equality, especially admission to the consulate. At the outset the plebeians found leaders and spokesmen in their tribunes (q.v.), whose powers were gradually enlarged until they had brought within the control of their veto (*intercessio*) the actions of all the magistrates. In 451 B.C. after a long struggle, the plebeians obtained the appointment of a commission of ten (*decemviri*) who drew up and published the Ten (increased in the next year to Twelve) Tables of the law, the knowledge of which had hitherto been confined to the magistrates who administered it. These Twelve Tables (q.v.), the basis of the future Roman Law, were of immense value, not only by their definition of rights and offences, but also as an instrument of education. The Twelve Tables did not, by their contents, satisfy the plebeians. A secession to the Aventine followed and a more thorough organization of the order. A plebeian parliament was constituted (*concilium plebis tributum*, q.v.), which in course of time obtained recognition as a legislative organ of the State. It elected annually the ten tribunes of the plebs and two aediles (q.v., supervisors of streets and markets, with a general disciplinary supervision). In 445, according to Livy, a *lex Canuleia* sanctioned intermarriage between patricians and plebeians, which had been expressly forbidden by the Twelve Tables. In 433 military tribunates with consular power (*tribûni mîlitâres consulâri potestâte*) were set up to exercise high military command, and these offices were opened to plebeians. Admission to the consulship itself followed in 366, after the tribunes Licinius and Sextius had, about 376, brought forward, in the 'Licinian Rogations' (q.v.), a proposal that plebeians should become eligible for one of the two consular offices, a proposal which was vigorously opposed by the patricians. Meanwhile the quaestors (q.v.) had been increased from four to six and the office thrown open to plebeians in 421; the first plebeian quaestor was elected in 409. Two *curule* (q.v.) aediles had been created in 367 by the patricians, with functions similar to those of the plebeian aediles. To this office also the plebeians gained admission in 366. In 356 a distinguished plebeian soldier (C. Marcius Rutilus) was appointed to the dictatorship; in 351 the same plebeian was elected to the censorship. The first plebeian praetor was elected in 337. The reform begun by the publication of the Twelve Tables was completed when in 304 B.C. the aedile Cn. Flavius published the calendar (q.v.) of *Dies Fasti* and *Nefasti* (the days on which legal procedure might and might not take place) and the *formulae* or rules for pleading. The outcome of the struggle was the formation of a mixed patrician and plebeian oligarchy of *nobiles* who monopolized office, and the dominance of the Senate (now composed of ex-magistrates).

The poorer classes were less successful in their demand for an improvement of their economic situation. The long and frequent wars of the republic wrought havoc among the small yeoman class to which the Roman soldiers practically all belonged. They were called away from the land when their labour was required; some were killed, many more were impoverished, and the rich found many opportunities of buying up small properties and combining them in large estates worked by slaves. Moreover, it was from early times a privilege of the rich to take up on lease large areas of the territory conquered from enemy states, leaving little or nothing for the poor. The resulting clamour of the poor for land, which we find constantly repeated in the history of the republic, found expression about 376 in the proposals, already referred to, known as the 'Licinian Rogations', which were adopted after a long struggle. These provided among other concessions to the plebeians that the extent of public land (*ager publicus*) which a patrician might hold should be limited to 500 *jugera* (about 300 acres) and that the excess should be divided among the poorer citizens. But the fundamental trouble persisted, in spite of steps taken from time to time to correct it. Measures were also taken for the alleviation of debt, widespread among the poorer classes, and for the mitigation of the cruel law under which the insolvent debtor might be reduced to slavery.

§ 4. *Republican period; the conquest of Italy*

In its external relations, the young republic had to face assaults from every side. It was attacked and for a time sub-

dued by Etruria (an episode with which are associated the names of Porsena, Horatius Cocles, Cloelia, and Mucius Scaevola, qq.v.). An attack by the Latins appears to have been defeated in a great battle by Lake Regillus (496). The Roman territory was ravaged by the hill tribes of the Apennines (Volsci and Aequi). It was in the course of these wars that occurred the incidents connected with the names of Coriolanus and Cincinnatus (qq.v.). Having successfully survived these ordeals Rome towards the end of the 5th c. passed from defence to aggression, and attacked the Etruscan town of Veii (twelve miles from Rome), with which it had been intermittently at war for a century, probably with a view to acquiring its valuable land (see *Fabia Gens*). Veii fell after a long siege, captured by the dictator M. Furius Camillus (*c.* 396). The Etruscan defence had been indirectly weakened by invasions of Gauls in northern and central Italy. About 390 a body of Gauls pushed south towards Latium and utterly defeated the Roman army at the Allia, a tributary of the Tiber. The mass of the population fled from Rome. The old men of noble birth remained seated in their halls, and were massacred by the Gauls, who were at first overawed by their silent dignity. The Gauls destroyed the city, except the Capitol, which was bravely held by a small force under M. Manlius Capitolinus (q.v. for the story of the geese saving the Capitol). Finally the Gauls were induced to return to their own country by a payment of gold (see *Brennus*). A great part of the ancient Roman records perished in the destruction of the city, though the extent of the loss has been questioned. After recovering from the inroad of the Gauls Rome entered on a long and arduous period of expansion. Latium was finally reduced (see below) and the great struggle with the Samnites, the warlike mountaineers of the Abruzzi, was begun. In the course of the second Samnite war the Romans suffered the celebrated disaster of the Caudine Forks (321), when the consuls, misled by false information, tried to march through the narrow defile of Caudium, were encircled, and obliged to surrender. The subsequent repudiation by the Senate of the terms of the capitulation was the source of increased bitterness between the opponents. The Samnites were finally conquered in the third Samnite War early in the 3rd c. (see *Decius Mus* and *Curius Dentatus*). The struggle with them had lasted for 70 years and had been of a terrible character. Southern Italy was devastated by it and never recovered. The Samnites themselves, though subdued, remained unreconciled. They rose in support of Hannibal; they revolted in the Social War; they supported Marius in his march to Rome.

Shortly after the conclusion of the Samnite wars a quarrel broke out between Rome and Tarentum, the richest and most powerful of the Greek cities of Southern Italy. Tarentum invited to her assistance Pyrrhus (q.v.) king of Epirus. Pyrrhus landed in Italy with his forces and his elephants in 280, as the champion of Hellenism, bringing the military knowledge he had acquired under Alexander the Great. He won two difficult and inconclusive victories over the Romans, and saw that he was not strong enough to crush them. He thereupon accepted an invitation to help the Sicilians against the Carthaginians, and sought to make peace with Rome. But the war party there, led by the aged Appius Claudius Caecus (q.v.), prevailed, and hostilities continued. The double task Pyrrhus had undertaken was too heavy for his forces. He was defeated by M. Curius Dentatus at Beneventum, abandoned his Italian and Sicilian enterprises, and left Italy (275) to pursue a new scheme for the conquest of Greece. In the following five years (275–270) Rome captured Tarentum and completed the subjugation of Southern Italy. By successful wars (270–266) with the Umbrians, Picentes, and Sallentini she became supreme in the whole peninsula from the Arno and the Rubicon to its southern extremity.

The political relations of Rome with the peoples that she conquered during this period of expansion may be briefly indicated. About 493 Rome entered into a treaty for common defence with the Latin League (the federation of Latin cities which she had defeated at Lake Regillus). But in the next century, after Rome had passed from defence to aggression, she imposed upon the Latins a new treaty (about 360) which in effect converted them from allies into dependants, and assumed military control of the League. The Latins revolted in 340 but were subdued in detail by 338. Some of their cities were incorporated in the Roman state; others were forced to enter into separate conventions with Rome by which they were required to furnish troops when called upon and were subjected to certain restrictions in the matter of trade and intermarriage. Rome followed a policy of securing strategic points by means of colonies (see *Colonization*, § 6) either of Roman citizens (*colōniae Rōmānae*) or of Roman and Latin citizens jointly (*coloniae Latīnae*). As Rome extended her conquests, she dealt with the case of each city as appeared advisable. The nearer communities, in general, were incorporated in the State, with variations in the rights granted: thus some were given the full franchise, others the *cīvitās sine suffrāgio* (without the right to vote). The more distant communities, known as *socii* or allies, were bound to Rome by treaties, which defined their rights and obligations. All were required to render military service to Rome, and were subjected to restrictions on their political and commercial intercourse. Otherwise they were left substantially free, and they might look forward to possible promotion to a higher status in the Roman association.

When about 270 B.C. Rome completed the subjugation of the Italian peninsula south of the Rubicon, her dominions consisted of these elements: (1) the *Ager Romanus* or Roman State proper, which included (*a*) *Roman* colonies and (*b*) *Municipia*, towns which were subject to Roman law, military service, and taxation, and which gradually developed local self-government; (2) the *Nomen Latinum* (q.v., Latin communities that had remained unincorporated into the Roman state) and *Latin* colonies; they were in alliance with Rome, but with special privileges which distinguished them from (3) *Socii*, the Italian allied cities.

Rome retained to the end of this period her primitive austerity and simplicity. She was still pre-eminently an agricultural state. Rectitude and good faith (in spite of occasional lapses, such as the repudiation of the agreement made at the Caudine Forks) predominated in Roman relations with other peoples, and inspired respect. As instances of ancient Roman virtue may be mentioned the stories of the Roman ambassadors, on their return from Alexandria in 273, delivering to the public treasury the gifts they had received from Ptolemy Philadelphus; C. Fabricius, who warned Pyrrhus of the offer of his physician to poison him; and L. Papirius, who reserved for himself only a wooden cup from the rich booty of Tarentum. It was at the end of this period that Rome first came under the influence of Hellenic culture, though no doubt commerce had before this brought some measure of intercourse with the Greeks, and the Romans had adopted the Greek alphabet in very early times. It was a Greek slave, Livius Andronicus (q.v.), taken at the fall of Tarentum, who first introduced Greek drama and epic to the Romans. Greek influence is also seen in the development of the Roman religion (see *Religion*, § 4).

§ 5. *Republican period. Expansion beyond Italy, c.* 270–c. 120 B.C.

Rome was now a Mediterranean power, and confronted across the Straits of Messina by her great rival, Carthage. For the struggle between them, and Rome's triumph, see *Punic Wars.* But this was not the only direction in which Roman activity extended beyond the shores of Italy. The depredations of Illyrian pirates in the Adriatic interfered with Rome's growing trade. In two campaigns (229 and 219) Rome subdued the Illyrians and obtained a foothold on the Balkan peninsula, thus coming into closer relations with the Greeks. These relations became even closer after the second Punic War. Although Philip V of Macedon had done little to help his Carthaginian ally, he had shown ambitious designs, and Rome was reluctantly drawn into two successive wars with him. The second was terminated by the victory of T. Quintius Flamininus (q.v.) at Cynoscephalae in 197. Macedonia was obliged to surrender her conquests, but was allowed for a time to survive as a State dependent on Rome. At the Isthmian Games (see *Festivals*, § 1) of 196, Flamininus, amid great enthusiasm, read a decree declaring free the Greek cities that had been subject to Philip. Rome at this time desired no further conquests; but she desired security (which meant crushing any rival power). She picked a quarrel with Antiochus III of Syria (see *Seleucids*), with whom Hannibal, expelled from Carthage, had taken refuge, and who invaded Thessaly in 192. He was soon driven out by the Romans, and finally routed in 190 near Magnēsia in Lȳdia. Of the Seleucid territory in Asia Minor the bulk was added to the Attalid (q.v.) kingdom; a few cities were declared free, and Rome received a large war indemnity.

Rome had by these various successful wars acquired immense wealth in the form of tributes and booty. Important public works were undertaken, such as the Via Aemilia from Ariminum to Placentia, and the Via Cassia across Etruria. There was a great increase of luxury of all kinds. Greek culture now made progress at Rome. The first Punic War, which lasted twenty-three years, was waged in Sicily, and during this period young Romans quartered in the island must have come into close contact with Hellenic civilization. The work of the poet Naevius was strongly Roman in character; but Plautus, Ennius, and Pacuvius show the Greek influence. Terence was to follow shortly. On the other hand, there was for a time a reactionary movement in favour of the old Roman simplic-

ity, led by Cato the Censor (q.v.). But this proved ineffectual against the opposite tendency, and Cato himself spent much of his last years learning Greek. A fresh point of contact with Greek culture was introduced when in 168, after the victory of L. Aemilius Paullus (q.v.) at Pydna over Perseus of Macedonia, a thousand of the citizens of the Achaean League (q.v.), which had supported Perseus, were transported to Italy, among them the historian Polybius. In 155 an embassy from Athens, headed by the philosophers Carneades, Diogenes (the Stoic), and Critolaus, visited Rome and introduced there the study of the various Greek schools of philosophy. Macedonia was annexed and declared a Roman province in 146. A revolt of the Achaean League in the same year was rapidly subdued, and L. Mummius captured and destroyed Corinth, whose commercial importance had aroused the jealousy of Rome. Central Greece and the Peloponnese were left in independence but were subjected to a temporary tribute. In 146 also Carthage was destroyed; it had recovered its economic importance and Cato became alarmed at its renewed wealth and power. It was taken by Scipio Aemilianus (q.v.) and its territory became a Roman province. A long series of Spanish campaigns, terminated in 133 by the capture of Numantia, resulted in the subjugation of the greater part of Spain. Attalus (see *Attalids*) of Pergamum in 133 bequeathed his dominions to Rome. They were formed into a Roman province named Asia. Gallia Narbonensis was made a province in 120. There was thus an enormous expansion of Roman territory in the 2nd c.

§ 6. *Republican period. The Gracchi, Marius, and Sulla*

The last century of the Roman republic was a period of acute social and political struggle. The tendency towards a more democratic form of government had been arrested, and the Senate, strengthened by the inclusion of some of the richest and ablest of the plebeians, was once more in undisputed possession of power. But this ruling class had become venal and demoralized. Other important factors in the situation were, the rise in influence of a wealthy class outside the Senate (see *Equestrian Order*), the growth of large estates worked by slave labour and the diminution of the small-holder class, and the demand of the allies of Rome for the citizenship. The first attempt to deal with this situation was made by the Gracchi, and is briefly described under their name. The failure of the Gracchi was followed by a conservative reaction, and by foreign wars, notably that against Jugurtha (q.v.) and the far more serious campaigns in which Marius (q.v.) destroyed the invading hordes of the Cimbri and Teutonês in 102 B.C. The internal struggle was revived by the aggressive democratic proposals of Saturninus (q.v.) and led to an armed contest between the Senate and the popular party. Even graver were the consequences of the proposal of M. Livius Drusus (q.v.), tribune of the plebs in 91, to extend the Roman franchise to all the Italians. It may be that Drusus even entered into treasonable correspondence with the Italians. At any rate, the proposal aroused bitter opposition at Rome and Drusus was assassinated. But the disappointment of the hopes he had aroused among the Italians was the occasion of a widespread revolt, and of a war for its suppression known as the Social or Marsian war (from the name of the people who gave the signal for the revolt). This lasted from 90 to 88 and from a military point of view was inconclusive. But judicious concessions brought it gradually to an end; the full citizenship was granted to all the Italians.

In a literary connexion the period is interesting for the development that the stress of politics gave to Roman oratory. Cato the censor had been a notable orator; the fragments of his speeches which survive show him a vigorous patriot and an earnest speaker. Scipio Aemilianus and his friend Laelius were famous orators shortly before the time of the Gracchi. Of the two brothers, Gaius was the more impassioned and effective speaker, remarkable according to Cicero for energy, dignity, and fulness. And Cicero names a number of other orators of this period. This was also the age of Lucilius (q.v.) the satirist.

The Social War was followed by the period of civil war and cruel bloodshed which attended the struggle between Marius and Sulla (qq.v.), the leaders respectively of the democratic and aristocratic factions. It left the party of Sulla and the Senate temporarily triumphant. (For the First Mithridatic War, which intervened, see under *Mithridates*.) It was, not unnaturally, a period of literary eclipse, and no great intellectual achievement is associated with it. Q. Mucius Scaevola, consul in 95, one of the greatest of early Roman jurists, who powerfully influenced the development of Roman law, was murdered in the Marian reign of terror. Sulla wrote his memoirs ('Commentārii Rērum Suarum') before his death, but they have not survived.

§ 7. *The last period of the Republic, 70–30 B.C.*

We now come to the second stage of the civil war, the period of the complicated struggle associated with the names of Pompey, Caesar, Crassus, and Cicero (qq.v.). In this struggle the idea of the common weal gave place to the ambitions of military leaders, who built their own political fortunes on their conquests. Pompey, victorious over Sertorius in Spain, and Crassus, who had suppressed the revolt of Spartacus (q.v.) in Italy, united as consuls against the Senate and repealed much of Sulla's legislation in 70. While Pompey was subduing the East, Caesar and Crassus became leaders of the democratic party. Their intrigues, and the attempt at revolution by Catiline (foiled by Cicero in 63), failed to give the democrats the control of Rome. In 60 was formed the compact between Caesar, Pompey, and Crassus known as the First Triumvirate, by which they secured a commanding position in the State. It endured, while Caesar was conquering Gaul, until Crassus was killed after the defeat at Carrhae (53) and relations between Caesar and Pompey became strained. The Senate, dreading the military prestige acquired by Caesar in Gaul, was thrown into alliance with Pompey. Caesar crossed the Rubicon, and civil war broke out. Pompey was utterly defeated at Pharsālus and murdered in Egypt (48), and Caesar became dictator, to introduce prematurely into the Roman constitution the principle of personal autocracy, and to be assassinated by senatorial conspirators in 44.

During the above period great additions were made to the Roman dominions. Bithȳnia was bequeathed to Rome by its childless king in 74; the attempt of Mithridates (q.v.) to forestall the Roman conversion of it into a province was defeated by Lucullus in 74–3 and Pontus itself was invaded and subdued by 70. In 74 Cyrene was garrisoned and made a province as a measure of protection against the Mediterranean pirates. The province of Syria was formed by Pompey about 64 out of territory taken from the Seleucids and from Judaea. Crete and Cyprus were annexed in 64 and 58 respectively.

The third stage of the civil war followed. The struggle was at first between the republican party, backed by Octavian (Caesar's heir), and Mark Antony (who had been Caesar's ally and his colleague as consul). This phase was terminated, after the battle of Mutina (43), by the compact of the three Caesarian leaders, Antony, Octavian, and Lepidus, the Second

Triumvirate. A conflict followed between the forces of the triumvirs and those of the senatorial party led by Brutus and Cassius, who met their death at Philippi (q.v., 42), and finally between the two principal members of the triumvirate, Antony and Octavian. This ended in Antony's defeat at Actium (q.v.) in 31 and his death at Alexandria in 30, leaving Octavian sole master of the Roman empire and closing the period of republican government at Rome (see *Antony, Brutus*).

§ 8. *The Ciceronian Age*

The last years of the republic, the period sometimes described in its intellectual aspect as the 'Ciceronian Age', beginning about 70 B.C., saw a remarkable outburst of literary activity. It was an age rendered illustrious by the great names of Lucretius and Catullus, Cicero and Varro. Virgil is generally associated with the Augustan Age; but he had written the 'Eclogues' and 'Georgics' by 30 B.C. The most important characteristic of this period is that the long process of the unification of Italy now reached its completion; so that we have a single Italian nation joined in a common civilization and to some extent in an identity of political and commercial interests. This union is at once revealed by the contribution made to Latin literature by men hailing from different regions of Italy, a contribution continued and increased in the succeeding age (see *Birthplaces of Latin authors*). Catullus was from Verona, Varro and Sallust were Sabines, Cicero came from Volscian Arpinum, Virgil from Mantua, Nepos from Cisalpine Gaul.

A second feature of the age is the variety and vigour of this literary activity, stimulated perhaps (as in other similar periods of history) by the political stress, and certainly by the democratic tendency of the times, and by the increasing influence of Greek culture and in particular of the Alexandrian school. This feature is manifested in the great diversity of poetic forms evolved, epic, lyric, didactic, pastoral; in the various styles of oratory, ranging from austere Attic to florid Asian; in the conflict of schools of philosophic thought; in the greater independence and personal quality, sincerity, and vividness, of literary work; in the practice of completing a liberal education in the schools of Athens; and in the interest taken in all kinds of learning, and especially in Roman antiquities (as exemplified in Varro).

§ 9. *The Early Empire. The Augustan Age*

It appears to be generally agreed that the principate was only a disguised monarchy from the beginning. But Octavian did not desire exclusive autocratic power, and had leanings to the old aristocratic republic. He attempted a compromise by which, while retaining sole control of the military forces and foreign policy, and general supervision over the machinery of government, he left a share in administration to the Senate and equestrian order, as reconstituted by himself in virtue of his censorial power. By his first settlement of the constitution (27 B.C.) the government of Rome and Italy and of certain provinces was entrusted to the Senate. It was given judicial as well as legislative functions (see below, § 12, and *Judicial Procedure*, § 2); and Augustus (a name conferred upon him by the Senate in 27) consulted it on questions of policy. The equestrian order retained seats as jurors in the criminal courts. Augustus himself adopted the outward appearance and mode of life of a republican magistrate. He assumed the title of *princeps* (q.v.), i.e. 'chief' or 'leader'. But his real position soon exceeded this. Owing to the inexperience, lethargy, or timidity of the Senate, its functions devolved increasingly on the emperor. By his second settlement of 23 B.C. Augustus resigned the consulate which he had held since 31, assumed the tribunician power, and was granted a *majus imperium* over the senatorial provinces. By the control which he exercised, in virtue of these and other powers, over legislation, criminal jurisdiction, and a large part of the revenues of the State; by the wide patronage in his hands; and above all by his command of the army, Augustus was raised to what was in effect a monarchical position. For the general administration and development of the imperial civil service under the early emperors, see below, § 12; for the reorganization of the finances by Augustus, see below, § 14; for the provincial administration, see *Provinces*.

Augustus made a great effort to restore by legislation the ancient morality of the Roman people, to encourage desirable marriages, and to restrain luxury. The effect of his laws for this purpose were at best only temporary. As regards foreign policy, ambitious plans in the East were abandoned, a policy of peaceful settlement with Parthia adopted, and the efforts of the empire concentrated on the Romanization of Gaul and the acquisition of a strong frontier in the West. The centre of gravity of the empire was definitely fixed in the West, a matter of immense influence on subsequent history.

The change in the political situation

which came about with the establishment of the principate is reflected in the literature of the Augustan age. The political tranquillity of the time has its counterpart in the tranquil spirit which permeates Augustan poetry, notably the 'Aeneid' and the later poems of Horace. New themes and ideals (Rome's imperial mission, the return of the Golden Age) provide inspiration for poets. On the other hand, the daring and freedom which characterized Lucretius and Catullus are gone. Ovid incurs banishment for his licentiousness. Oratory, whether in the Senate or the Forum, finds itself cramped by the new conditions and degenerates into mere rhetoric. Jurisprudence comes under imperial control. History labours under similar disadvantages. Nevertheless the age had in Livy the greatest of Roman historians, who in spite of the admiration he showed for republican heroes, retained the esteem of Augustus.

§ 10. *Tiberius, Caligula, Claudius, Nero*

Tiberius (q.v.), who succeeded Augustus and reigned A.D. 14–37, was animated by the traditions of the aristocratic government of the past. He desired to restore the power of the Senate. But he incurred the increasing hostility of that body, while his austere parsimonious government alienated the populace. In spite of the excellence of his routine administration, the prevalence of order, justice, and economy, the good government of the provinces, and his patient and on the whole successful treatment of the international situation, he was the object of constant suspicion. His difficulties were greatly increased by the feuds within his own family, where Agrippina (q.v.), the widow of Tiberius's nephew Germanicus (q.v.), led a faction violently hostile to the emperor and his mother Livia. Embittered by his unhappy experience, old and weary and increasingly misanthropic, Tiberius retired to Capri and ruled the empire through Sejanus (q.v.), Prefect of the Praetorians, who became practically omnipotent, until his ambition to succeed Tiberius and his intrigues to that end brought about his downfall. The good administration of Tiberius continued to the end, though the hatred with which he was regarded at Rome led to a crop of appalling calumnies on the aged emperor (now over 70) in his solitary life at Capri; while Rome itself suffered from a torrent of delations, prosecutions, vengeances, and suicides, which Tiberius more than once endeavoured to check. He died in A.D. 37. His character has been painted in the blackest colours by Tacitus and Suetonius (qq.v.), and

must remain under some degree of suspicion in spite of the enthusiastic praise of Velleius Paterculus (q.v.).

The reign (A.D. 37–41) of Gaius Caligula (q.v.) was, except for its first few months, that of a cruel, prodigal, and insane tyrant. His successor Claudius (41–54) was a man of learning and shrewdness, rendered ridiculous by an ungainly person, timidity, gluttony, and other defects. His reign was notable for its vigorous foreign policy (the conquest of Britain was begun and other new provinces annexed), for the liberal extension of the Roman franchise, for great public works, and for the development of the imperial civil service, in which freedmen were given a dominating position. It was marred by the evil influence of Messalina (q.v.), the emperor's third wife, who interfered in public affairs and whose scandalous private conduct (perhaps exaggerated by report) led to her death. In his later years Claudius was entirely in the hands of his freedmen and of his fourth wife, Agrippina, daughter of Germanicus.

The reign of Nero (54–68) is remarkable more for the crimes and eccentricities of the emperor and their effect on the society of the capital than for important political events. Begun under the good influence of Seneca, the philosopher, and Burrus (Prefect of Praetorians), it degenerated when the former was driven into retirement and the latter was succeeded by Tigellinus. The height of brutal crime was reached when the emperor caused his mother Agrippina and his wife Octavia to be put to death to facilitate his marriage with Poppaea Sabina. His craze for acting and music, and his public appearances on the stage added to the hatred and contempt with which Nero was regarded by the decent elements of the empire. The burning (probably accidental) of a great part of Rome in A.D. 64 was attributed to the Christians and was followed by the first persecution of the sect. The regulations for the rebuilding of the city were wisely conceived. An important rebellion in Britain in A.D. 61, led by Boadicea (Boudicca), widow of the East Anglian king, after initial successes was put down by the Romans under Suētōnius Paulīnus. The discovery of the conspiracy of C. Calpurnius Piso against the emperor in A.D. 65 (the outcome of his general unpopularity) led to the enforced deaths of Lucan, Seneca, and Petronius Arbiter (qq.v.). Nero's reign was brought to an end by a revolt which broke out in Gaul and rapidly spread. The emperor was at once deserted; he fled from Rome and took his own life.

Rome 374 Rome

The reigns of the four preceding emperors, known as the Julio-Claudian dynasty (from their origin in the families of Julius Caesar and Tiberius Claudius Nero, father of the emperor Tiberius—see *Julio-Claudian Family*) show an abrupt decline in literary activity at Rome. The atmosphere of suspicion and anxiety which prevailed, the arbitrary power of the rulers, and the unrestrained cruelty of some among them, were evidently unfavourable to literature. The only remarkable authors of the period are Lucan, Seneca, Persius, Phaedrus, Petronius, and Columella. Literature, which had been won over by Augustus, now showed an anti-imperial bias.

§ 11. *Galba, Otho, Vitellius, the Flavians, and the Antonines*

The period of internal strife and bloodshed (A.D. 68–9) which accompanied the brief reigns of Galba, Otho, and Vitellius is chiefly important for its revelation that emperors might be made elsewhere than at Rome, by the will of the legions. Galba was proclaimed by the Spanish army, a protest by provincial troops against the degenerate rulers of the dynasty of Augustus, nominees in practice of the praetorians. The praetorians in turn proclaimed Otho, who was expelled by Vitellius, nominee of the German legions, and he by Vespasian, nominee of the Eastern army supported by the legions of the Danube. This period of strife was followed by a phase of recuperation under the wise and efficient rule of the Flavian emperors Vespasian, Titus, and Domitian, a dynasty of humble origin, descended from a tax-collector of Reàte. Vespasian (A.D. 70–79) restored the finances (which had been utterly disorganized by the prodigality of Nero and the civil war), reorganized the army, created a new aristocracy of provincial origin, and by this means as well as his own example checked the luxury and licence that had prevailed in the capital. He undertook great public works, of which the Colosseum at Rome is the most striking example. He, and still more Domitian, gave the principate an increasingly monarchical character, especially by means of the censorship, which gave them control of the composition of the Senate. Domitian (81–96), a lover of literature and the fine arts, appears at first to have pursued the welfare of Rome and the empire very much in the spirit of Augustus, reviving the severity of ancient times and restoring the ancient religious cults. Unfortunately he was faced with the hostility of the Senate, and his assumption of the censorship for life exacerbated their relations. Irritated by the Senate's opposition, Domitian turned into a cruel and suspicious tyrant, and the last seven years of his reign were a period of terror, which ended in his murder.

The stream of literature shrank still further under the Flavians, particularly under the terror of Domitian. The only important names of the period are those of the elder Pliny, Statius, Martial, and Quintilian. The mild and conciliatory reign of Nerva (96–8) and the simple, orderly rule of Trajan (q.v., 98–117) brought intense relief, signalized by the great historical works of Tacitus, the satires of Juvenal, and the letters of the younger Pliny. The beneficent governments of Hadrian (117–138) and the Antonines call for little notice here; Hadrian and Marcus Aurelius have points of special interest and are briefly dealt with under their names. But classical Roman literature, in the widest sense of the term, had by this time come practically to an end; Suetonius, Aulus Gellius, and Apuleius are the principal authors of the period.

§ 12. *Administration*

(a) *In the republican period.* An essential feature of Roman administration was its largely collegiate character; that is to say, authority was in most cases entrusted not to one but to two or more magistrates who shared the same office. A *Dictator* and his *Magister equitum* (qq.v.) were appointed only in grave emergencies. The principal regular magistrates were the Consuls, Praetors, Censors, Quaestors, Tribunes of the Plebs, and Aediles; their functions are described herein under their several names. With the exception of the Censors, they were elected annually by the people. For certain minor functionaries see *Viginti-virate*. For the order in which the various offices might be held and the obligatory periods between holding them, see *Cursus honorum*. For the legislative assemblies see *Senate, Comitia, Concilium Plebis*. For the administration of justice, see *Judicial Procedure*. For the administration of conquered territory, see § 4 above and *Provinces*.

(b) *Under the early emperors.* The legislative and administrative powers of the State were in fact, if not in theory, gradually gathered up in the hands of the *princeps*, although various emperors made a practice of consulting the Senate to a greater or less extent. *Senatus consulta* had the force of law without being ratified by the *comitia*, and the emperor in addition issued edicts. Legislation by the *comitia* became rare. The *comitia* met to elect magistrates (the urban magistracies were retained) until A.D. 14, after which the Senate elected to the magistracies. The emperor had a limited (legal) right of nominating the candidates to these. The *quaestiones* (see *Judicial Procedure*, § 2) continued, but judicial powers were given to the Senate, which became the high court of the empire. Moreover, the emperor, aided by a council (*consilium*) of assessors, took power to deal with any case. For the provincial administration, see *Provinces*. In general, the civil service was appointed and ruled by the emperor. He depended largely on his own household for help in the administration of the empire, and a large staff of secretaries and accountants under his immediate control was developed. Freedmen were among these from the beginning, and the tendency to employ them in important posts increased. Some of these freedmen were extremely able and exercised great authority. Their power reached its climax under Claudius. Under him we find the treasury supervised by a freedman known as *procurator a rationibus*, the equivalent of a minister of finance. The principal private secretary of the emperor, a freedman known as *ab epistulis*, dealt with reports of governors of provinces and the grant of personal privileges. Another, the clerk of petitions, *a libellis*, had important functions as interpreter of the law. All these were in effect ministers of state, and the household civil service of the emperor encroached on the ancient magistracies. Under Hadrian the great posts, *a rationibus*, &c., were entrusted to men of the equestrian order. Other important posts under the empire were the *Praefectus Urbi*, *Praefectus Praetorio*, *Praefectus Annonae*, and *Praefectus Vigilum* (qq.v.). Mention may also be made of the *cūrātōrēs viarum* in charge of the upkeep of the Italian roads, the *curatores operum publicorum*, who looked after the public buildings, and the *curator aquarum* (see *Aqueducts*). For the financial administration, see below § 14.

§ 13. *Economic Conditions*

It is impossible to state the population of ancient Rome with any certainty, and very different results have been arrived at by students of the question. The record in the Monumentum Ancyranum (q.v.) that a gratuity of 60 denarii was made in 5 B.C. to 320,000 persons has led to the estimate that the whole population of the city in the age of Augustus was about 800,000, including 300,000 slaves and foreigners. But the number of slaves was probably far greater, and the total population is likely to have exceeded one million. As

regards the population of Italy, estimates based on the census figure given by the Monumentum Ancyranum again differ greatly; a figure of about ten millions is a mean between the extreme estimates.

The Roman State in its first phase was essentially an agricultural community (see *Agriculture*, § 2), producing mainly corn, though the city itself owed its early importance partly to its position on the chief navigable river on the W. coast of Italy, and to its possession of a bridge facilitating communication between industrial Etruria and the S. of Italy. With Rome's conquest of Italy, the subdual and later the destruction of Carthage, and the acquisition of Sicily, Sardinia, Corsica, and Spain, the character of the Roman economy to some extent changed. Italy itself was not a poor country. Campania and Etruria possessed, besides a prosperous agriculture, manufactures of metal ware and pottery. Vineyards, olive-yards, and orchards were numerous in suitable regions. Southern Italy (at first), Sardinia, and Sicily produced much corn. There were moreover vast areas of pasture land, including mountain grazing for the summer months; Apulia in particular yielded very fine wool. From being almost entirely a community of peasant proprietors (which included even certain aristocratic families), Rome, after the Punic Wars, developed a capitalist class, who were landowners, not farmers, and worked large tracts of land with tenants and slaves, and also conducted industries by means of slaves. Men like Pompey and Domitius Ahenobarbus owned such large areas that they could raise armies from their tenants. The cultivation of the vine and the olive was increased by these landowners. The best wine of Campania came to rival the choicest wines of Greece. We hear of Roman farmers in Gaul and Africa. The Spanish mines (q.v.) were a source of vast profit not only to the State, but to individual speculators. There were under the later republic a sufficient number of Romans with a capital of more than 400,000 sesterces (say £3,500) to form a separate order (the equestrian order) in the State. That Rome's maritime trade was from early times considerable is indicated by two treaties with Carthage (the first of which, according to Polybius, dated from 509 B.C.) limiting the Roman sphere of commercial activity. This trade naturally increased with the expansion of the Roman dominions and the development of new needs among the wealthy Romans. The destruction of Corinth (146 B.C.) and the acquisition of territory in Asia further expanded Italy's trade with the East. Delos (q.v.) became an important Italian emporium. But although commerce increased, the Romans themselves, and particularly the Senate, took comparatively little interest in it during early republican times, and rather despised it (senators were forbidden to engage in trade); and the general carrying trade of the Mediterranean was left to Greeks and Phoenicians. There is little evidence of industrial development at Rome before the empire; the only industries in the city appear to have been such as supplied the simple needs of the agricultural and military community, and to have been carried on largely by the slave or newly enfranchised classes and with few exceptions on a small scale. But Campania was a considerable industrial centre from the 2nd c. B.C.: Capua produced bronze ware, Pompeii textiles, and Puteoli had important iron works, using the ore of Elba and ousting the Etrurian cities from their lead in this industry. Arrētium in Etruria was famous for its pottery, which was widely exported. Both commerce and manufacture increased during the early empire, the former being encouraged by the improved system of roads and the general security. There was a greater use of metals, e.g. for lead water-pipes. The brick-making industry developed at Rome and elsewhere (it was especially stimulated at Rome, in Nero's reign, by the fire which destroyed a large part of the city). The glass industry also became of some importance, which increased after the discovery of the art of glass-blowing.

If Italian industry was comparatively limited in republican times, banking and money business in general reached a high state of development. The Roman Forum in the 1st c. B.C. was a great stock-exchange, where men transacted commercial and financial business extending to the whole ancient world. The rate of interest at Rome itself was normally 4 to 6 per cent. and capital found more profitable employment in the outlying parts of the empire, where property was less secure. There 12 per cent. was regarded as a low rate, and 48 per cent. was sometimes exacted. Apart from members of the equestrian order (q.v.), who undertook banking and large contracts, the trading class consisted to a great extent of manumitted slaves, many of them men of intelligence and enterprise, who acquired wealth and position. The principal commercial port was now Puteoli on the Bay of Naples, which eclipsed Ostia at the mouth of the Tiber. The principal imports at the end of the republican period and under the early empire were (besides slaves) grain, various

metals and marble, linen, papyrus, furs, ivory, amber, and other articles of luxury, including silk from China, sometimes woven and dyed in Syria, and Arabian and Indian wares, which came to Italy via Alexandria. So far as these imports came from provinces of the empire—and the internal trade of the empire was more important than the foreign trade—they did not require exports of the same value to pay for them, for the provinces as a whole were tributary to Rome. The chief articles of export were wine, olive-oil, and manufactured goods, which found active markets in Spain, Gaul, Africa, and even Germany; imports from the East were paid for in part in gold and silver coins. Trade and industry were not interfered with by the State. Trade within the empire was facilitated by the excellent land communications (see *Roads*) and by the moderate level of the harbour dues (see § 14 below). For trade by sea, see *Ships*, § 2. A trading-vessel from Puteoli could reach Alexandria in a very few days in summer, when northerly winds prevailed; though the return voyage was often much longer. Pirates disappeared from the Mediterranean for nearly a century after Pompey's dispersal of them in 66 B.C.; and although there was some revival of piracy in the latter part of the reign of Augustus, the wide distribution of Roman fleets under the succeeding emperors kept it in check.

Thus Rome, from being originally an agricultural community, of which frugality was one of the leading characteristics, became by the end of the republican period the chief centre of wealth and luxury in the ancient world. Under the empire its temples, basilicas, forums, baths, theatres, circuses, and libraries were on a magnificent scale and richly adorned. Life was easy: the poorer citizens, to the number of 200,000 or 300,000, were supported by the State; for the middle classes there were abundant opportunities for trade and employment; the rich had the services of a great army of slaves (see *Slavery*, § 2). Many of them owned vast estates. The literature of the late republic and early empire presents many instances of very large fortunes, such as those of Lucullus, Crassus, Atticus, and Maecenas (qq.v.). The civil troubles, the conquests in Spain and the East, the opportunities of extortion in the provinces, had enriched many individuals. Cicero, though a man of integrity, was able to amass two million sesterces in his one year's governorship of Cilicia. In civil professions we find, for instance, that Roscius, Aesopus, and later actors were extremely rich. Cicero could spend 750,000 denarii (say £25,000) on his house at Rome and own a dozen country villas besides. Tacitus (Dialogus 8) mentions two lawyers, one worth 200 million sesterces (say £1,700,000), the other worth 300 million (say £2,550,000). The famous freedmen, Pallas, Callistus, and Narcissus, under Claudius, were immensely wealthy; their fortunes were derived from the sale of offices and favours. The highest civil officials in the 2nd c. A.D. received salaries of 200,000 sesterces (about £1,700). The ruins of Herculaneum and Pompeii, the traces of fine villas in many parts of the empire, the beautiful monuments of the dead, not only in Rome but also in the provinces, are evidence of the wide distribution of wealth. There was a great development of city life in most of the Roman provinces under the early emperors; there grew up a large number of splendid cities, well paved, drained, abundantly supplied with water, and beautified with public buildings provided by wealthy donors. 'One may say without exaggeration that never in the history of mankind (except during the nineteenth and twentieth centuries in Europe and America) has a larger number of people enjoyed so much comfort as in the first two centuries of the Roman Empire' (Rostovtzeff). But it is to be remembered that these conditions of wealth and ease, whose sources were chiefly industry, trade, and agriculture, to a large extent carried on by capitalists, did not extend to the humbler classes of the city population.

Precise data as to prices, earnings, and cost of living under the republic and early empire are scanty, and in any case their absolute equivalent to-day is very difficult to determine. Rome and many parts of the Roman dominions were dependent, for the staple food of the people, on imported corn. There were great fluctuations in its market price, owing to variations in the harvests and the difficulties of transport. Polybius, in a bumper year, found wheat in Cisalpine Gaul as low as 1½ asses the modius (peck). At the other extreme we find in Cicero (II Verr. iii. 92) mention of a famine price of three to five denarii the modius. C. Gracchus fixed the sale at 6⅓ asses the modius as a moderate price (a modius would supply a man with bread for a week). The price of common Italian wine was very low, but variable. We know from an inscription of early imperial date that the charges at an Italian inn were 1 as for bread and wine, 2 asses for pulmentārium (relish), and 2 asses for a mule's forage. The bare cost of subsistence for a single man, with wheat at a moderate price, may perhaps be taken as about

100 denarii a year. We have no precise information as to the rate of wages, but it appears probable, from such evidence as there is, that at the end of the republican period ordinary unskilled labour received about 1 denarius a day (while employed). The pay of a legionary soldier, inclusive of the cost of rations, under the late republic was 120 denarii a year, until raised by Caesar to 225 denarii. A schoolmaster in Horace's native town received 8 asses a month per pupil; for fifty pupils this would be 400 asses or 25 denarii (of 16 asses) a month, or at the rate of 300 denarii a year. The price of a slave was roughly from 2,000 to 8,000 sesterces (£18–70) according to his skill. The price of volumes of Martial's poems is referred to as from 1 to 5 denarii each.

§ 14. Finances

The only direct tax paid by Roman citizens in republican times was the tribūtum, an assessment levied on property; it was abolished in 167 B.C. owing to the great accession of wealth to the State. Portōria, harbour dues not exceeding 5 per cent., were levied on imports and exports. There was also a tax of 5 per cent. on the value of manumitted slaves. The provinces paid either a fixed yearly sum (stipendium) raised by the officials of the various districts according to their taxable capacity, or a quota (normally a tithe, decumae) of the produce of the soil, which was farmed out to publicāni (see Equestrian Order). The provinces were also subject to harbour dues. There was no centralized effective control of the finances under the republic. The quaestors (q.v.) were financial officers, but the Senate was in general control of the State finances. The censors were important financial magistrates under the republic; they gave contracts for public works and took contracts for the taxes.

Under the empire the emperor was the central financial authority. The aerarium or public treasury remained, nominally at least, in the hands of the Senate and received the taxes from Italy and the senatorial provinces. But alongside of it was the emperor's special treasury (fiscus), which received the revenue from the imperial provinces and bore the bulk of the expenditure, including the maintenance of the army and navy. Augustus and his successors preserved the immunity of Italy from direct taxation. But while retaining the harbour dues and the tax on the manumission of slaves, Augustus introduced new indirect taxes, a tax of 5 per cent. on inheritances of over 100,000 sesterces (payable by Roman citizens both in Italy and in the provinces), a tax of 1 per cent. on sales at auction or by contract, and a tax on the value of slaves sold. In the provinces a general survey and valuation of property was carried out under Augustus (St. Luke ii. 1). On the basis of this, direct taxes were imposed, viz. *tributum soli*, a tax on land, and *tributum capitis*, probably a tax on the capital value of personal (as opposed to real) property. In addition there was a large revenue from imperial domains, which went to the *patrimōnium* or emperor's privy purse. The direct taxes were collected by imperial agents, the indirect continued to be farmed by *publicani*.

In republican times the cost of government was small. The magistrates were unpaid (though a provincial governor received an equipment allowance, *vāsārium*). The chief sources of expenditure were the army (a varying charge according to the number under arms and the rate of pay, see *Army*, § 2); the distributions of cheap corn (see *Annona*); the maintenance of the State religion, including public games; and public works, including the maintenance of roads. Public expenditure increased very much under the empire, both under the above heads, and owing to the establishment of a much larger and adequately remunerated civil service.

See also *Aerarium* and *Fiscus*.

Ro'mulus (*Rŏmulus*) and **Rē'mus** (*Rĕmus*), see *Rome*, § 2.

Ro'scius Gallus, QUINTUS (d. 62 B.C.), a freedman, the most famous comic actor of his day at Rome. He amassed great wealth. See *Pro Roscio Comoedo*. The name of Roscius became prominent in English literature for an actor generally, not merely in comedy.

Ro'stra, in Rome, the platform in the Forum from which orators addressed the people. It was adorned with the bronze prows (*rostra*) of the Latin ships captured at Antium in 338 B.C.

Rostra Jūlia was the name of the platform on which was built the Temple of Julius Caesar (dedicated by Augustus in 29 B.C.). The temple stood on the spot, at the east end of the Forum, where the body of Caesar was burned. The platform was adorned with the prows of the ships captured at Actium (31 B.C.).

Roxa'na (*Rŏxănē*), see *Alexander the Great*, § 6.

Ru'bicon (*Rubicō*), a small Italian river falling into the Adriatic a little north of Ariminum (Rimini). It formed the boundary between republican Italy and the province of Cisalpine Gaul, and Caesar (q.v.) by crossing it at the head of a legion in 49 B.C. declared war on the Senate.

Ru'dens ('The Rope'), a romantic comedy by Plautus, adapted from a play by Diphilus (see *Comedy*, § 4).

This is one of the pleasantest of the author's works. The prologue is spoken by the star Arcturus, and opens with the fine lines,

Qui gentes omnes mariaque et terras
  movet
Ejus sum civis civitate caelitum. . . .

The scene is on the rocky coast of Cyrene, near a temple of Venus and the countryhouse of an old Athenian gentleman, Daemones, whose daughter Palaestra has been stolen from him in her childhood. She has fallen into the hands of a procurer, Labrax of Cyrene; a young Athenian, Plēsidippus, has fallen in love with her, and made part-payment for her purchase. But Labrax has thought to improve his fortunes by secretly carrying the girl off to Sicily. Thereupon Arcturus has raised a storm and wrecked the ship near the scene of the play. Palaestra and another girl reach the land in a boat and are kindly tended by the priestess of Venus. Labrax is also washed ashore; he discovers the girls and tries to carry them off from the temple. They are defended by Daemones, and presently rescued by Plesidippus, who hales Labrax off to justice. A fisherman hauls from the sea in his net a box belonging to Labrax. The fisherman and a slave of Plesidippus quarrel for the box while the fisherman hauls on the rope (*rudens*) of the net, and the quarrel leads to the discovery in the box not only of the gold of Labrax, but also of trinkets belonging to Palaestra, which show her to be the lost daughter of Daemones. Joyful recognition follows, and the betrothal of Palaestra to Plesidippus.

Rūmi'na, in Roman religion, a goddess who protected mothers suckling their children. She had a sanctuary at the foot of the Palatine, where stood the *ficus Ruminālis*, the fig-tree under which Romulus and Remus were supposed to have been suckled by the wolf.

S

Sabā'zios, a Phrygian and Thracian deity, whose worship was connected with that of Cybele (q.v.). The Athenians identified Sabazios with Dionysus, and his cult became popular in the 5th c. B.C. Aristophanes wrote a comedy (not extant) which ended with the expulsion of this foreign deity. The worship of Sabazios was widely spread in Italy under the empire.

Sacred Band (*Hieros Lochos*), at Thebes (q.v.), a company of 300 picked hoplites of the best families, formed at the time of the reorganization of the Theban army under Epaminondas (q.v.), after the recovery of the Cadmea (q.v.) from the Spartans. At the battle of Chaeronea (q.v.), the Sacred Band did not join in the general flight, but fought till they fell; so that Philip, gazing after the battle at the heaps of slain, cursed their detractors.

Sacred Wars, a name given to the wars conducted by the Amphictyonic (q.v.) Council for the protection of the shrine of Delphi and the punishment of sacrilege. The first Sacred War was waged early in the 6th c. B.C. to release Delphi from the inhabitants of Crisa, who claimed control over the shrine and levied dues on pilgrims. The Crisaean plain was thereafter dedicated to Apollo, and it was decreed that it should never be cultivated. A second Sacred War occurred in 448, in consequence of the seizure of Delphi by the Phocians. A third war of considerable importance occurred in the middle of the 4th c., when Thebes, jealous of the independence of her neighbour Phocis, induced the Amphictyonic League to impose heavy fines for sacrilege on a number of Phocians. Thereupon (*c.* 356) the Phocians under Philomēlus seized Delphi and used its treasures to carry on war with Thebes and the Amphictyons. Under Onomarchus, the successor of Philomelus, the power of Phocis was greatly extended, till it reached from the Corinthian Gulf to parts of Thessaly. But the intervention of Philip of Macedon, at the request of the Thessalian League and Thebes, turned the scale against Phocis, though the support given to the latter by Athens delayed the end. In 346, after the Peace of Philocrates, Phocis was subdued, and its place on the Amphictyonic Council taken by Macedonia. In 339 an Amphictyonic war was once more the pretext for an invasion by Philip, this time with momentous results. The Locrians of Amphissa, at the instance of Thebes, brought an accusation against Athens, at the meeting of the Council in the autumn of 340, in connexion with an Athenian inscription offensive to the Thebans. Aeschines (q.v.) the Athenian envoy, turned the tables on

them by pointing to the Crisaean plain which lay below and which the Amphissans were cultivating in spite of the oath taken that it should lie uncultivated for ever. By an impressive speech he persuaded the Amphictyons to punish Amphissa. They marched against it, but were not strong enough to enforce their sentence. In 338 they called on Philip to assist them. He captured Amphissa and then turned on Thebes, now allied with Athens, and won the victory of Chaeronea, which gave him the hegemony of Greece.

Sacrifice.

§ 1. *General character of sacrifices*

Sacrifice, from the Latin *sacrificium* ('making sacred' of something), generally the surrender to the deity of something belonging to the worshipper, was the central act of the ritual of worship among the Greeks and Romans. It was always accompanied by prayer. Sacrifice was usually *tributary*, that is to say of the nature of a gift to the god of something, such as food, for his use. It was sometimes *piacular*, to expiate some offence (by the destruction of the criminal or of a substitute or scapegoat) or to avert the evil portended by some prodigy (at Rome by the offering of *hostiae*, see below). A rarer type of sacrifice was intended to rejuvenate or reinvigorate the god himself, supposed to be incarnate in some person or animal, by the slaying of that person or animal so that its powers might be transferred to a more vigorous successor. Such sacrifices were especially connected with the worship of the powers of vegetation and reproduction.

§ 2. *Tributary sacrifice*

Sacrifices of the first category might be either bloodless offerings or blood offerings. The former consisted of cakes, grain, firstfruits, or other viands laid on the altar or burnt, and libations of wine or milk (the Greeks offered honey especially to the nether gods). Blood offerings consisted of animals of various kinds, slaughtered at the altar with solemn ritual. Cattle and sheep were the most usual victims. A hecatomb (*hecatombē*) in Greece originally meant the sacrifice of a hundred oxen; the term came to be used of any great sacrifice of animals. Besides cattle and sheep, horses were sacrificed to Poseidon, Helios, and (at Rome) to Mars; swine especially to Demeter and Dionysus (otherwise only as a rule in expiatory sacrifices or in the combined sacrifice known at Rome as the *suovetaurilia*, q.v.); dogs to Hecate and Robigus: goats to

Dionysus, Apollo, Artemis, Juno, and at the Lupercalia (q.v.). It was the general custom to sacrifice male animals to male deities, female animals to goddesses; and dark-coloured animals to the nether gods. Only beasts without blemish might be employed, and no sacrifice was regarded as pleasing to the gods unless the entrails on inspection were found to be normal. A large animal was called in Latin a *victima*, a sheep a *hostia*.

§ 3. *Ritual*

In Greek sacrifices the altar and the worshippers were first purified by sprinkling with sanctified water. The victim was decked with garlands, grains of barley were sprinkled on and around it, some of its hair was burnt, it was stunned, and its throat was cut. The blood was caught in a vessel and poured on the altar, or over the worshippers if the sacrifice was piacular. In Roman sacrifices the head of the animal was sprinkled with wine and fragments of sacred cake (*mola salsa*, q.v.), and it was then slain by the priest's assistants. In piacular sacrifices the animal was entirely burnt after having been killed; otherwise, both in Greek and Roman sacrifices, only certain portions were burnt and the rest was consumed by the worshippers. In this common banquet the idea of a communion of the participants and the god is thought to have entered. Whereas the Greek worshipper prayed and offered sacrifice with head uncovered and palms uplifted to heaven, the Roman sacrifice was performed with veiled head, perhaps to prevent the eyes from lighting on some ill-omened object, while the music of a pipe (*tibia*) drowned any ill-omened sounds. See also *Religion*, §§ 1 and 3.

Sa'lamis (*Salamis*), (1) an island separated by a narrow channel from the SW. coast of Attica, near the Piraeus. In legendary times it was the home of Telamon the father of Ajax. It was for long a subject of contention between the Megarians and the Athenians, but was finally conquered by the latter as the result of a stirring appeal by Solon. The adjoining sea was the scene of the great naval battle in 480 B.C., in which the fleet of Xerxes was defeated by the Greeks. It was the birthplace of Euripides. (2) A city in Cyprus, said to have been founded by Teucer, son of Telamon.

Sale of Lives, see *Lucian*.

Sa'lii, or Salian Priests at Rome, an ancient college of twelve (later twenty-four) priests of Mars who annually in the month of March, dressed in a striking uniform and wearing high conical hats, carried the sacred shields (*ancilia*, q.v.) round the city, beating on them with their staves, dancing and chanting ancient hymns, and visiting many places. The proceedings ended, at any rate in later times, with a luxurious banquet. The ritual was probably designed (in the opinion of Sir J. G. Frazer) to drive out demons and to make the corn grow. The traditional hymns they sang (*carmina Saliaria*) in Saturnian (q.v.) verse, were scarcely intelligible to the priests themselves in Quintilian's day. A few fragments of them survive. It appears from Virg. Aen. viii. 285 that the god Hercules also had his Salii.

Sa'llust (*Gaius Sallustius Crispus*) (86–35 B.C.), was born at Amiternum in the Sabine country. At Rome he joined the democratic party and was tribune of the plebs in 52. It is said that the hostility he showed to Milo (q.v.) after the murder of Clodius in that year was increased by the fact that he had been horse-whipped by Milo on account of an intrigue with the latter's wife. He was expelled from the Senate in 50 on account of charges against his character, which political rancour may have exaggerated. Caesar rewarded his adhesion with a quaestorship in 49, and later made him proconsular governor of Numidia. He thereafter retired from public affairs and lived with great splendour, having acquired his wealth, it was said, by extortion in his province. He was the owner of the fine pleasure grounds, *horti Sallustiani*, which became subsequently imperial property. He devoted the remainder of his life to writing historical monographs, the 'Bellum Catilinae', 'Bellum Jugurthinum' (see *Catiline* and *Jugurtha*), and the 'Historiae' of the period 78–67 B.C. (the years following the abdication of Sulla). The first two and fragments of the third have survived. His work shows an advance on that of his Roman predecessors both in the agreeable quality of the narrative and in its more scientific method. Instead of annals he gives a continuous story, and endeavours to explain the causes of political events and the motives of men's actions. He takes Thucydides for his principal model, writing with extreme terseness (Quintilian speaks of his 'famous brevity') and introducing appropriate speeches after the manner of Thucydides, though he has not the Greek historian's detachment and penetration. His narratives are lively and readable, but some of his moral dissertations are out of harmony with his own practice.

Though his histories show a democratic

bias, and he sometimes distorts facts, he is on the whole impartial and can recognize merit in political adversaries and faults on his own side. His characters, notably those of Jugurtha and Catiline, Marius and Sulla, are drawn with great vividness. In selecting as subjects the war with Jugurtha and the conspiracy of Catiline, he was impelled, as he himself states, by the perilous and striking character of these political events. His three monographs are, moreover, connected, as dealing with successive stages in the struggle of democratic power against the insolence of the nobles. For the narrative of the Catilinarian conspiracy he had, besides his own recollection of the events, abundant written records at his command. He had some special qualifications for writing about the Jugurthine war, for besides the literary sources of which he disposed (the memoirs of Sulla and others, and the History of Sisenna), he had himself obtained geographical and ethnological information when in Numidia, and had had Punic documents translated for him.

Sa'lmacis (*Salmakis*), see *Hermaphroditus*.

Salmo'neūs, in Greek mythology, a son of Aeolus (q.v. (2)) and father of Tyro (q.v.), and consequently the ancestor of Pelias and Jason (see *Argonauts*). Post-Homeric legend relates that he emulated Zeus, making a noise like thunder by driving about in a chariot of bronze, and imitating thunderbolts by throwing firebrands. For this impiety he was, according to Virgil, placed in Tartarus. The story probably reflects an attempt at weather-magic (see *Magic*).

Sō'mia (*Sămia*), see *Menander*.

Samian Ware, see *Pottery*.

Samnite Wars, see *Rome*, § 4.

Sā'mos (*Sămos*), an Ionian island off the SW. coast of Asia Minor, between Ephesus and Milētus. It became a strong naval power under Polycrates (q.v.) in the latter half of 6th c. B.C. It formed part of the first Athenian Confederacy (see *Athens*, § 4), revolted in 440, and was reduced by Pericles. At the time of the oligarchic revolution at Athens in 411, the Athenian fleet was stationed at Samos, and the island was the centre of the democratic movement that overthrew the Four Hundred. Alone among the remaining subject-allies of Athens, Samos did not revolt after the defeat of Aegospotami (405). The Samians were in consequence granted Athenian citizenship (as recorded in an inscription still extant). Samos was re-

duced by the Spartan Lysander (q.v.) in 404. Subsequently it fell into the power of Persia; it was recovered for Athens by Timotheus (q.v. (2)), and cleruchs (q.v.) were placed on the lands of exiled Samians. These cleruchs were ousted by Alexander the Great and the exiles restored. Samos was the birthplace of Pythagoras (q.v.).

Samo'sata, the modern village of Samsat, on the Euphrates, the birthplace of Lucian (q.v.), was the capital of the kings of Commagēnē. One of these, Antiochus, a Seleucid (q.v.), opposed for a time the first Roman army that penetrated to the Euphrates. There is a striking description of his tomb on the highest peak of the Nimrud Dagh in D. G. Hogarth's 'A Wandering Scholar in the Levant'. Samosata was the station of a Roman legion.

Sapphic, see *Metre*, §§ 3 and 5.

Sa'pphō (in Aeolian *Psapphō*), a Lesbian poetess, born at Mitylene (or perhaps Eressos) probably about the middle of the 7th c. B.C., of a good family, a contemporary of Alcaeus. Like him, she appears to have left Lesbos in consequence of political troubles in the island; she is said to have gone to Sicily and perhaps died there. She refers to herself as γεραιτέρα, somewhat old, in one of her poems. A statue of her, by Silanion, was set up by the Syracusans in the 4th c., and in a later age was stolen by Verres (q.v.). She appears to have been married and to have had a daughter named Clēis; also brothers, one of whom, Charaxus, she reproached for an entanglement with an Egyptian courtesan named Doricha (Herodotus, who refers to the story (II. 135), confuses Doricha with Rhodopis, q.v.). Sappho, it would seem, gathered round her a group of women, perhaps for the purpose of instruction in music and poetry, or for the worship of Aphrodite. Alcaeus addressed her in an ode of which we have the opening lines, and perhaps the beginning of Sappho's reply. A legend found in the Greek comic poets relates that having fallen in love with one Phaon (q.v.) and been repulsed by him, she threw herself down from the rock of Leucas off the coast of Epirus. But this is mere romance. She wrote nine books of odes, epithalamia, elegies, and hymns, of which only fragments (including one complete ode and four stanzas of a second) survive. She wrote in the Aeolic dialect, and many of the fragments have been preserved by grammarians as illustrations of that dialect.

The principal subject of her poems was

love, expressed always with natural simplicity, sometimes with tenderness, sometimes with passionate fire. She wrote in a great variety of metres, of which one, the Sapphic (see *Metre*, §§ 3 and 5), is especially associated with her name. Her poetry was much admired in antiquity. It was praised by Plato, by many writers in the Greek Anthology, and by Dionysius of Halicarnassus and 'Longinus' in the treatise on the Sublime (who have preserved two of the longer fragments). Her stanzas beginning φαίνεταί μοι κῆνος ἴσος θέοισιν were closely imitated by Catullus in his poem (51) 'Ille mi par esse deo videtur'. Horace has references to her in Odes II. xiii. 24–5 and IV. ix. 11–12 ('Vivuntque commissi calores Aeoliae fidibus puellae'). Ovid wrote in his 'Heroides' an imaginary epistle from Sappho to Phaon (translated by Alex. Pope, 1707). Sappho has also inspired many passages in English poets, including Swinburne (*Anactoria*) and Frederick Tennyson.

Sarpe′don (*Sarpēdōn*), in the 'Iliad' son of Zeus and Laodamia (q.v.), leader (with Glaucus, q.v. (4)) of the Lycians, the best warrior among the allies of the Trojans. He is the friend and comrade in battle of Glaucus. His death by the spear of Patroclus (Il. xvi) is told with deep feeling. According to another version, he was a son of Zeus and Europa (q.v.).

Satire, in Latin *satura*, probably equivalent to *satura lanx*, a dish of mixed ingredients, and so in literature a medley or farrago, of which the variety might lie in the subjects chosen or in the form (dialogue, fable, anecdote, precept, verse or various metres, combination of verse and prose), or in both. The word was early applied to a simple form of drama, somewhat more developed than the Fescennine (q.v.). Livy refers to it in connexion with religious ceremonies to avert plague, as performed by the Etruscans to flute music. It appears to have involved dialogue, but little if any plot. On the one hand it contributed to the evolution of Latin comedy, on the other it developed as a literary form of a mixed and semi-dramatic kind, the 'satire', a commentary. genial or mordant, on current topics social life, literature, and the failings of individual persons. Quintilian claimed satire as a Roman creation ('Satura quidem tota nostra est', Inst. Orat. x. l. 93); but although it was more purely Roman than any other form of literature, it owed something to Greek comedy. Ennius and Pacuvius wrote *saturae*, but the satirical element in them, in the above sense, appears to have been

slight. Lucilius (q.v.) first gave to the satire a definite character of outspoken personal criticism, herein following the Old Attic Comedy. He was followed by M. Terentius Varro (q.v.), who took as a model the satires of Menippus (q.v.), in which prose and verse were intermingled, but wrote in a genial, mildly didactic vein. Lucilius (and also the popular philosophy of the day) inspired Horace's ridicule of folly and bad taste, and in a later age the earnest homilies of Persius (q.v.). Satire again took different forms in the bitter invective of Juvenal and the picaresque novel of Petronius (qq.v.). Most English satire has drawn directly on classical models (see, e.g., under *Horace* and *Juvenal*).

Satires (*Sermōnes*) of Horace, two books of discourses in hexameters, conversational in style, humorous and urbane, modelled (especially the earliest) on Lucilius (q.v.), dealing with a variety of subjects, incidents in the life of the author, the follies and vices of mankind (censuring to an increasing extent as he proceeds the sin rather than the sinner), or the author's poetical methods. For their dates see *Horace*. Among those calling for special mention, Book I. v is a vivid description of a journey to Brundisium in the suite of Maecenas, together with Virgil and Varius Rufus. I. vi is interesting for its autobiographical details, an account of Horace's excellent father and of his own introduction to Maecenas. I. ix ('Ibam forte via Sacra') is an amusing description of an encounter with a bore and the author's efforts to get rid of him. I. viii is in a different class, a ridiculous story of witches put to flight in the midst of their incantations by the sudden cracking of a wooden statue of Priapus. The Second Book shows an advance on the First in literary taste and skill; the poems are less personal and their spirit more mellow and reflective. The author adopts a more dramatic form which gives life and lightness to the discussion of various aspects of Roman life. Special mention may be made of II. v, a parody of epic, in which Odysseus, in continuation of the scene in the Eleventh Odyssey, consults Tiresias as to the recovery of his lost fortune and receives advice in the art of legacy-hunting; and of II. vi, the famous satire on town and country life, containing the fable of the town mouse and the country mouse. Pope's imitation of the latter part of this Satire is perhaps the best known of his 'Imitations of Horace'. Satire I. ix, above referred to, has been a popular model in English; it doubtless suggested, for instance, Donne's satire on the bore.

Satires of Juvenal, see *Juvenal*. The subjects of the several satires are briefly as follows:

I. An introductory poem. Juvenal is driven to write by disgust at the popular poetry of the day, with its outworn mythological themes. He will deal with realities, 'quidquid agunt homines', and expose the scandals of the age. But he will speak only of men now dead. Honesty is praised but left in the cold ('probitas laudatur et alget'). 'Facit indignatio versum', he explains.

II. An attack on those who ape the manners of austere philosophers in public, but are vicious in their private lives.

III. Perhaps Juvenal's best satire, imitated by Johnson in his 'London', a picture of life in Rome. He commends a friend who is fleeing to the country from the thousand perils of the town and 'poets reciting in the month of August'. Umbricius cannot stand the invasion of Greeks (the versatile 'Graeculus esuriens') and Greek fashions. Moreover the honest poor man has no chance in Rome; poverty ('res angusta domi') stands in the way of merit. The city is described: its narrow winding streets, flanked by tall houses with pigeons on the tiles, the mud, porters carrying wine-casks, the noise of wagons, the abuse of cattle-drovers, the slave with a pile of dishes on his head, a house on fire, the upsetting of a builder's wagon. Then the city at night: a great man passing in his scarlet cloak, with torches and a retinue of clients and slaves, the affray with a bully ('si rixa est ubi tu pulsas, ego vapulo tantum'), the burglar.

IV. In lighter vein, a skit on the administration of Domitian. An enormous turbot is presented to the emperor; no dish is large enough to hold it. A council is summoned in hot haste to consider the problem.

V. On the humiliation of poor clients at the tables of their rich patrons.

VI. A denunciation of womanhood in general. The poet professes astonishment that a friend should contemplate marriage when there is so much rope to be had, and then depicts, at great length, the vices of women, their extravagance, tyranny, and quarrelsomeness in the home. The jealous woman, the gossip, the virago are among the offenders, and worst of all the ostentatious pedant. If you chance on a good woman ('rara avis in terris nigroque simillima cygno'), she will be haughty. It is useless to set a guard on one's wife, for 'quis custodiet ipsos custodes?'.

VII. On the decline of the literary professions, especially that of teacher, in the public esteem. Their only hope is in the patronage of the new emperor (probably Hadrian).

VIII. An attack on pride of ancestry. Virtue is the only true nobility. High lineage, if a man is vicious, only makes his vices worse.

IX. Deals with the same vices as II.

X. On the folly of human prayers, whether for wealth (which exposes to dangers, whereas 'cantabit vacuus coram latrone viator'), for power (consider Sejanus), or for eloquence, long life, beauty (all of them sources of trouble). Better leave your fate to the gods, or at most pray for 'mens sana in corpore sano' and a stout heart. The famous expression 'panem et circenses', the only things the populace care for, is found at l. 81. This satire was the model of Johnson's 'The Vanity of Human Wishes'.

XI. Against extravagant expenditure on gluttony. Juvenal invites a friend to a simple and modest repast.

XII. Juvenal offers a sacrifice to celebrate a friend's escape from shipwreck; but from no interested motive. An attack on legacy-hunters.

XIII. Juvenal offers consolation to a friend who has been defrauded of 10,000 sesterces, and warns him against seeking vengeance, the pleasure of a weak and narrow mind. The guilty will be punished by his own conscience. This is the noblest of Juvenal's satires. It includes the notable saying:

Scelus intra se tacitum qui cogitat ullum, facti crimen habet.

XIV. On the influence of parental example in education. The parent's faults will be copied by the children:

Maxima debetur puero reverentia, si quid turpe paras.

XV. The poet narrates a conflict between inhabitants of Ombi and Tentyra in Egypt, in the course of which a Tentyrite is killed and eaten. In contrast with this savagery he praises tenderness of heart, as the quality which distinguishes man from the beasts.

XVI. An unfinished satire on the abusive privileges of the military, which prevent a civilian from getting redress for their misdeeds.

The last three satires show a decline in power. Some of the pithy expressions that have become proverbial are indicated above. There are many others, such as 'crambe repetita' (vii. 154, the monotony of lessons constantly repeated), 'propter vitam vivendi perdere causas' (viii. 84), 'nemo repente fuit turpissimus' (ii 83), and 'dat veniam corvis, vexat censura columbas' (ii. 63, the censor absolves the crow—the man—and condemns the pigeon —the woman).

Sa'turae Meni'ppeae, see *Varro* (*M.T.*).

Sa'turn (*Sāturnus*, 'the sower'), an Italian god of agriculture, later identified with the Gk. Cronus (q.v.). He was thought to have been an early king at Rome, where he introduced agriculture and founded the citadel on the Capitol, and his reign was regarded as the age of gold. His temple stood at the foot of the Capitoline hill and in it was the *aerarium* (q.v.) of the Roman people ; there too were kept the Tables of the Law and the records of decrees of the Senate. His festival was the *Sāturnālia* (q.v.). He was regarded as the husband of Ops and father of Picus (qq.v.).

Saturnā'lia (*Sāturnālia*), in Roman religion, a festival celebrated from the 17th to 19th December (15th to 17th at the end of the republic according to Roscher), in honour of Saturnus (q.v.) and in celebration of the sowing of the crops. It was a period of general festivity, licence for slaves, giving of presents, lighting of candles, the prototype, if not the origin, of our Christmas festivities. It completely lost, probably under Greek influence, its primitive Italian character of an agricultural festival.

Saturnā'lia (*Sāturnālia*), a dialogue by Macrobius (q.v.).

Saturnian, see *Metre*, § 4.

Saturni'nus (*Sāturnīnus*), LŪCIUS AP-PULĒIUS, tribune of the plebs in 103 and 100 B.C., and a supporter of Marius, in whose favour he brought forward several measures. He was an unscrupulous demagogue, and when with his ally Glaucia he had recourse to assassination in order to get rid of a political opponent, Marius dissociated himself from Saturninus. The latter and Glaucia were declared public enemies, were besieged in the Capitol, and killed by the mob, which had turned against them.

Satyric Dramas, in Greece, were plays resembling tragedies in form, but dealing with grotesque portions of ancient legends, or dealing with the legends grotesquely. The chorus in these plays were dressed to represent satyrs (q.v.), whence the name, with horses' tails and ears ; the language and gestures were often obscene. They performed a violent dance known as *Sikinnis*. Heracles frequently figured in these plays as a semi-comic character. Such plays as a rule formed the fourth in the groups of four plays produced at one time by tragic poets in the classical period.

Later, only one satyric play was performed at a tragic contest. Pratinas (q.v.) of Phlius is said to have been the inventor of the form, and at any rate wrote a number of satyric dramas. For the part played in the evolution of tragedy by this kind of play, see *Tragedy*, § 1. Aeschylus, Sophocles, and Euripides all wrote satyric dramas ; the 'Cyclops' of Euripides is the only example of the type that survives, apart from a fragment of the 'Ichneutae' of Sophocles. The satyric drama continued to the Roman period ; rules for it are given by Horace in the 'Ars Poetica'.

Saty'ricon, see *Petronius Arbiter*.

Satyrs (*Saturoi*), in Greek mythology, attendants of Dionysus (q.v.), spirits of the woods and hills, especially connected with the idea of their fertility. They are represented as grotesque creatures, in the main of human form but with some part bestial, e.g. with a horse's tail, or the legs of a goat (see *Monsters*). They are lustful and fond of revelry. The Romans identified them with the Fauni (q.v.). The chorus in Satyric dramas (q.v.) were dressed to represent satyrs.

Scae'vola, GĀIUS MŪCIUS, a legendary Roman, who when Lars Porsena, king of Clūsium, was besieging Rome, made his way to the enemy camp and attempted to kill Porsena. He was taken prisoner and, to show his indifference to the death with which he was threatened, thrust his right hand into the fire. The king was so impressed that he released Mucius, who was thereafter known as Scaevola, 'left handed'.

Scae'vola, QUINTUS MŪCIUS, *Pontifex Maximus*, consul with L. Licinius Crassus the orator in 95 B.C., was himself an orator of distinction, noted according to Cicero for the concise accuracy of his language. He was one of the greatest of early Roman jurists. Cicero in his youth received instruction in the law from him. In his consulship he promoted, with Crassus, a *lex Licinia Mūcia*, which caused many Italians to be expelled from Rome, and was in consequence a cause of the Social War. Cicero remarks on the fact that such an unfortunate measure should be due to such excellent men. He was assassinated by the Marians in 82 in the Temple of Vesta. He is to be distinguished from his relative Q. Mucius Scaevola 'the augur' (q.v.).

Scae'vola, QUINTUS MŪCIUS, 'the augur', consul in 117 B.C., son-in-law of Laelius (q.v.) and father-in-law of L. Licinius Crassus (q.v.) the orator. He died between 88 and 82 B.C. He was a distinguished jurist, and Cicero was among his pupils. Scaevola is one of the interlocutors in Cicero's 'De Oratore', 'De Amicitia', and 'De Re Publica' (qq.v.).

Scā'lae Gemō'niae or 'Stair of Sighs', at Rome, a flight of steps leading to the summit of the Capitoline hill from the Forum, between the Temple of Concord (q.v.) and the Carcer or prison. Criminals were executed in the latter, and their dead bodies were thrown out on these steps, down which they were dragged to the Tiber.

Scā'zon (*Skazōn*), see *Metre*, § 5.

Sceptics, a school of philosophy founded by Pyrrhon of Elis, who lived *c.* 365–275 B.C. and took part in Alexander's expedition. He inferred from the contradictions presented by the evidence of the senses and the operations of the mind that knowledge of the nature of things is unattainable. Hence the proper attitude is one of suspension of judgement, mental quietude, and indifference to outward things. Pyrrhon left no writings, but of Sextus Empiricus (q.v.), one of the later members of his school, we have two works, which contain a full exposition of the Sceptic doctrine. Something is known of it also from the fragments of Timon of Phlius (q.v.), a pupil of Pyrrhon. Scepticism later was taken up by the Academy (q.v.).

Sche'ria (*Scheriē*), the land of the Phaeacians (see *Odyssey*), on the coast of which Odysseus was cast ashore.

Schliemann, HEINRICH (1822–90), the son of a German pastor, acquired sufficient wealth by means of an indigo business at St. Petersburg to devote himself from the age of 36 to archaeology. He excavated the site of Troy (q.v.) in 1870–3, 1878–9, and 1881. He also excavated Mycenae, in 1876, where he discovered the shaft-graves with their wonderful treasures, and Tiryns in 1884.

Scholasticism, see *Texts and Studies*, § 8.

Schō'lium (Gk. *Schŏlion*), a short explanatory note, a commentary on a difficult passage. Scholia were written on manuscripts of Homer, Hesiod, Pindar, the tragedians, &c. by scholars of the Byzantine (q.v.) period, often based on earlier commentaries. For instance a scholium on Il. x. 306 in the Venice MS. of Homer records the readings adopted by the Alexandrian scholars Aristarchus, Zenodotus, and Aristophanes. There are scholia also on Latin authors, e.g. Horace.

Sci'pio (*Scīpiŏ*) **Aemilia'nus**, PUBLIUS CORNĒLIUS, known as SCIPIO AFRICĀNUS MINOR (*c.* 185–129) was the son of L. Aemilius Paullus, the conqueror of Macedonia, and was adopted by P. Scipio the son of Scipio Africanus Major (q.v.). He fought under his father at Pydna (168) and in 148, when the Third Punic War threatened disaster, was elected consul although he was under age and only a candidate for the aedileship. He successfully besieged Carthage and destroyed it in 146. He was consul again in 133 for the purpose of carrying on the war in Spain against the Numantines. He starved Numantia into surrender and ended the war. He died suddenly in 129 in circumstances that suggested murder. In a literary connexion he was famous, not only as a great orator, but also as a patron of Greek and Latin letters, and the centre of a circle which included Polybius, Panaetius, Lucilius, Terence, and Laelius (qq.v.). He was regarded by Cicero as the greatest of the Romans. See also *De Amicitia, Somnium Scipionis*.

Sci'pio (*Scīpiŏ*) **Africā'nus Major**, PUBLIUS CORNĒLIUS (236/5–c. 183 B.C.), son of P. Cornelius Scipio, consul in the first year of the Second Punic War. He saved his father's life when he was wounded at the battle of the Ticinus (218). In 210 when only about 25 years of age he was appointed to the command in Spain. He drove the Carthaginians out of that country, was elected consul for 205, and in 204 crossed over to Africa with his army. There he brought the war to an end by his victory at Zama. In 190 he was associated with his brother Lūcius in the command against Antiochus, and on his return was accused by M. Naevius, a tribune of the plebs, of accepting bribes from Antiochus and misappropriating public moneys. When the matter came for trial, Scipio contented himself with reminding the people that the day was the anniversary of Zama and bidding them follow him to the Capitol to offer thanks to the gods. Public opinion turned in his favour and the charge was not proceeded with. Scipio thereafter retired to his estate at Līternum in Campania, where he died.

Sci'pio (*Scīpiŏ*) **Nāsi'ca**, PUBLIUS CORNĒLIUS, consul in 138 B.C., a member of a distinguished family of Roman nobles, a man of strong aristocratic views, principally known as the leader of the group of senators who attacked and killed Tiberius Gracchus (q.v.).

Sci'ron (*Skeirōn*), a legendary brigand slain by Theseus (q.v.). The *Scirŏnian Rocks*, associated in legend with the above, were on the E. coast of Megaris. The road from Athens to Megara ran along a perilous ledge on these rocks, high above the sea, and had an evil reputation. It had been widened by Hadrian when Pausanias visited it.

Sco'lion, from Gk. *skolios*, 'tortuous', the name given to an early type of Greek drinking-songs, sung at banquets or wine-parties (the reason for the name is uncertain). Tradition makes Terpander (q.v.) the originator of the *scolion*, and *scolia* were composed by such poets as Alcaeus and Pindar (qq.v.). There are examples of *scolia* in Athenaeus (Bk. xv); they deal with some historical incident (such as the attempt of Harmodius and Aristogeiton on the Pisistratids), or some personal sentiment or comment on life.

Sco'pas (*Skopās*) of Paros, an eminent sculptor of the Attic school of the 4th c. (see *Sculpture, Greek*), remarkable for his power of expressing pathos. A group representing Niobe (q.v.) and one of her children, of which a copy is extant, was attributed in antiquity either to him or to Praxiteles.

Sco'tus Eri'gena, JOHANNES, see *Texts and Studies*, § 7.

Sculpture, (1) GREEK, appears to have had its origin in Crete, where as early as the 7th c. B.C. sculptors were working in stone. It developed simultaneously in the Peloponnese and in Ionia. Two Cretan sculptors, Dipoinos and Scyllis, are said by Pliny to have been working in Argos and Sicyon about 550 B.C. An important school grew up there, which is seen in its fullest development in the sculptures of the temple of Aphaia in Aegina (q.v.). It was characterized by a certain austerity and a rigidity of facial expression. The Ionian school was exposed to Oriental influences and is marked by greater elegance, softness, and attention to detail. These two currents united in the Attic school, each correcting the defects of the other. In Attica sculptors were hampered by the material in which they worked, until under the Pisistratids marble came into use, and made it possible to dispense with colours, previously employed to conceal defects in the coarser stone. Sculpture in bronze was also practised, particularly at Sicyon and Argos. The practice of erecting statues of victors in athletic contests tended to free the art from the traditional bonds of religion and to bring it into closer harmony with nature. This development, of which Athens was the chief centre, began in the latter part of the 6th c. and reached its highest point in the 5th. The principal sculptors of this great period were Myron, Polyclitus, and Phidias

(qq.v.). In the 4th c. the 'noble simplicity and calm grandeur' (Winckelmann) that characterized the works of the above artists gave place to a greater play of the emotions and to a softer expression. Of this phase the chief representatives were Praxiteles, Scopas, and Lysippus (qq.v.). After the time of Alexander the Great, Greek sculpture changed its character; the simplicity of the earlier periods gave place to a striving for theatrical effect, a lack of restraint, and a loss of repose; the technical skill remained at its highest. The most productive schools of this period were those of Pergamum and Rhodes. To the former of these we owe the famous statue of the 'Dying Gaul' of the Capitol (popularly known as the 'Dying Gladiator' after Byron, *Childe Harold*, iv. 140) and the group of the Gaul who has killed his wife and is killing himself (also at Rome). The latter produced among its best works the 'Praying Boy' now at Berlin, and in its more theatrical decline the famous groups of the Laocoon (q.v.) and the Farnese Bull, now in Rome. The huge Colossus of Rhodes, one of the wonders of the world, was also the product of this school. Among the greatest surviving works of the Hellenistic period are the Venus of Milo (Melos) and the splendid Victory of Samothrace (a winged figure of Victory alighting on the prow of a ship) now in the Louvre. After the Roman conquest of the Greek world, Greek sculpture lost much of its originality, while retaining its mastery of technique. With a few exceptions, its chief works were imitations of earlier masterpieces. There was an enormous importation of Greek works of art into Italy. Some idea of its extent may be derived from the statement of Livy that at the triumph of M. Fulvius Nōbilior in 187 B.C. 785 bronze statues and 230 marble statues, from the spoils of Ambracia, were carried in procession before him. The taste for Greek statuary developed at Rome, and rich men desired to possess examples. So great did the demand become that an industry in the wholesale production of statues, some of them copies of old works, others original, grew up in Greece. A Roman firm set up branches in Greek cities to deal with the supply. The remains of three wrecked ships, loaded with Greek statues, have been discovered at various points in the Mediterranean.

(2) *Roman.* See *Art*, § 2.

Scȳ'lax (*Skúlax*), a native of Caryanda in Cāria, sent by Darius on a voyage of exploration from the Indus round the coast of Arabia. He may have described this in a work entitled 'Periplous'. A

Periplous' of the civilized world, falsely attributed to Scylax, dates from the 4th c. B.C.

Scy′lla (*Skulla*), in Greek mythology, (1) daughter of Phorcys and Hecate (qq.v.). She was loved by Poseidon. Her rival Amphitrite (q.v.) by magic herbs turned her into a monster (see *Monsters*), which seized and devoured the mariners that sailed near its cave (situated according to tradition in the Straits of Messina, with the whirlpool of Charybdis opposite it). Homer describes the passage of the ship of Odysseus by the cave of Scylla in Od. xii. 85 et seq.

(2) Daughter of Nisus, king of Megara. For her legend, see under *Ciris*. The Latin poets (Virgil, Ovid, Propertius) sometimes confuse the two Scyllas.

Seasons (*Hōrai*), THE, in Greek mythology, daughters of Zeus and Themis (q.v.), generally three in number (spring, summer, winter), attendants on the gods.

Secular Games (*Lūdi saeculārēs*), see *Ludi*, § 2.

Sēdi′gitus, VOLCATIUS, see *Comedy*, § 5.

Seisachthei′a, see *Solon*.

Sējā′nus, LŪCIUS AELIUS, Prefect of Praetorians under the emperor Tiberius (his father, L. Sējus Strabō, had held the same command at the end of the reign of Augustus). He gained the emperor's confidence and was regarded as a rival to Drusus, the emperor's son. He was suspected of the death of Drusus by poison, and hoped to marry Livilla, Drusus's widow, but the emperor put aside his request. When Tiberius withdrew to Capri, Sejanus became all-powerful in the State, and plotted to obtain the imperial throne. But Tiberius grew suspicious of him, and denounced him (in the 'verbosa et grandis epistula' of Juvenal) to the Senate, which sentenced him to death. After his execution his body was torn to pieces by the people, whose hatred he had incurred, and thrown into the Tiber. Ben Jonson wrote a play 'Sejanus' on his career, which was acted in 1603 with Shakespeare in the cast.

Sējus, HORSE OF: according to Aulus Gellius (III. ix), Sejus was a clerk who owned a horse reputed to be of the breed of the Horses of Diomedes (see *Heracles, Labours of*), far superior to all other horses in all points. This horse brought ill-luck to those who owned it, including Sejus himself (who was put to death by Mark Antony), Dolabella, Cassius, and Antony.

Selē′nē, in Greek mythology, the Moon, according to Hesiod the daughter of Hyperion (q.v.) and Theia (a Titaness),

and sister of the Sun; but the genealogy is variously given. She is sometimes identified with Artemis (q.v.). See also *Endymion*.

Seleu′cids, the dynasty to which fell the chief share in the inheritance of Alexander the Great, viz. Asia. The founder of the dynasty was Seleucus I, an officer of Alexander, who on the death of the latter became governor of Babylōnia, and by the end of the 4th c. had consolidated his rule over the eastern provinces of the empire. In 301 the issue between him and his chief rival Antigonus I (see *Macedonia*, § 2) was decided at the great battle of Ipsus, which left Seleucus supreme in Asia, though Lysimachus of Thrace, his ally at Ipsus, received probably the whole of Asia Minor, including the Aegean coast. By 281 Seleucus had won this territory from Lysimachus, who was defeated and killed at Corupedium. Seleucus himself, when crossing the Dardanelles to the Thracian capital, was assassinated by Ptolemy Ceraunus, a son of Ptolemy I. His successors, Antiochus I (281–261), Antiochus II (261–247), Seleucus II (247–226), and Antiochus III (223–187) were largely occupied with a succession of wars with the Ptolemies for the possession of Coele-Syria (i.e. Phoenicia and Palestine); this was finally annexed in 200 B.C. by Antiochus III ('the Great'), a ruler of remarkable energy and enterprise. Succeeding to the throne when only fifteen, he put down the dangerous revolt of several of his eastern governors, and then set about the recovery of the territory lost in various directions by his predecessors. In 209–204 he carried out an expedition to the east in which he finally crossed the Hindu-Kush to the Indus; but this arduous undertaking had no lasting result. At the beginning of the 2nd c. Antiochus III became embroiled with Rome as a result of his conquests in Asia Minor, and inconclusive negotiations proceeded for some years. In 192 at the invitation of the Aetolian League (q.v.) Antiochus invaded Greece, but in the following year was driven out by the Romans. The hostilities thus begun were continued in Asia (Syrian War), and Antiochus was utterly defeated in 190 by Scipio Africanus Major (q.v.) and Eumenēs II of Pergamum at Magnēsia-ad-Sipylum, and forced to evacuate all Asia Minor west of Mt. Taurus. There was some revival of Seleucid importance under Antiochus IV (Epiphanēs, 175–164), whose territories of Cilicia, Syria, Babylonia, and Mēdia constituted a strong and reasonably compact realm. Antiochus Epiphanes was an ardent Hellenist, who encouraged the growth of municipal autonomy and Greek manners in his kingdom. He was eccentric and munificent. It was he who began the rebuilding of the Olympieum (q.v.) at Athens. He invaded Egypt, but was forced by the Roman envoy, Popilius Laenas, in the most humiliating manner, to withdraw. In his desire to unify his people in religion and culture as a means of resisting Rome, he sought to abolish the Jewish religion, and thus provoked the rising of the Maccabees. The book of Daniel, which dates from his time, reflects his persecution of the Jews. After his reign the Seleucid power gradually declined under the attacks of Mithridates I of Parthia and his successors, who conquered Babylonia and Mesopotamia, while the rest of the Seleucid dominions broke up into a multitude of free cities and small kingdoms (e.g. that of the Maccabees). The process was encouraged by the perpetual dynastic wars after the death of Antiochus IV. A final attempt by Antiochus VII to recover the territory lost to the Parthians was defeated in 129 B.C. He was the last real monarch of the Seleucid line. Syria and Cilicia were finally annexed to Rome by Pompey in 65–63 B.C. The importance of the Seleucids lies in their Hellenization of Asia, particularly by founding scores of cities, more or less Greek in character; this was done chiefly by Seleucus I and Antiochus I.

Se'melē, see *Dionysus*.

Sēmō'nidēs (less correctly *Simōnidēs*) of Samos, one of the Samian colonizers of Amorgos, an iambic (q.v.) poet, probably of the 7th c. B.C., of whose work little survives. His satire, differing from that of Archilochus (q.v.), was of an impersonal and philosophic character. Of the extant fragments, one is a satiric poem on women, another a philosophic reflection on the unhappy life of men.

Sēnā'rius, see *Metre*, § 4.

Senate (*Senātus*), THE, at Rome, may have originated in Roma Quadrata, before there was a king of Rome. Later it was the king's council. During republican times, it was at first a purely patrician (q.v.) body, but plebeians were constantly admitted to it during the 4th c. B.C., and it became in practice an assembly of ex-magistrates. Nominations to it, at first made by the consuls, were from the latter part of the 4th c. made by the censors. Owing to its functions and permanence, it was the real head of the State. It prepared legislative proposals to be brought before the people, and its resolutions (*senātūs consulta*) had some measure

of practical if not legal authority; it exercised judicial powers through its right of appointing special courts of enquiry (see *Judicial Procedure*); it administered the finances, assigned magistrates to provinces, and dealt with foreign relations; and it supervised the State religion. Since it was recruited mainly from ex-magistrates, it became a body with a strong control over holders of office. It tended to use them as its tools. Under the empire, although the Senate lost its sovereign power, it was not without important functions, and Augustus endeavoured to share with it the administration of the State. The Senate retained the control of certain provinces (q.v.) and of the *aerarium* or public treasury; *senatus consulta* had force of law without requiring to be ratified by the people; and the judicial functions of the Senate were increased. But, in fact, partly owing to its own inefficiency, its power gradually diminished.

In Sulla's time the Senate numbered only 300 and Sulla had to recruit it. Caesar filled its ranks with his supporters, some of whom were unworthy to serve, bringing its numbers to about 900. Augustus reduced them to 600. They were practically selected by the emperors, and were recruited from the ranks of the imperial bureaucracy and the equestrian order. Gradually the old aristocracy of Rome disappeared and the senatorial class was drawn from new families of Italian or provincial origin.

The Senate met for business in the Curia or Senate-house, which stood in the Forum Romanum (q.v.), or in some other consecrated place. Senators wore special shoes (see *Clothing*, § 5), and had privileges such as front seats in the theatre.

Senātūs consultum ultimum, a resolution by the Senate in a grave emergency authorizing the consuls to use force for the protection of the State, and suspending the right of appeal to the people. The resolution took the form, 'videant consules ne quid respublica detrimenti capiat', sometimes with slight modifications. The first instance of such a resolution was in 122 B.C. when the Senate adopted it against C. Gracchus. It was used against Saturninus in 100 B.C., and against Catiline in 63 B.C. But its legality was always contested by the democrats.

Se'neca, LŪCIUS ANNĀEUS, 'the Elder' or 'the Rhetorician', was born at Corduba in Spain probably not later than 55 B.C., and came as a boy to Rome, where he was educated. He died probably *c.* A.D. 37. He had three sons of his wife Helvia: M. Annaeus Novātus, who took the name of Gallio from his adoptive father and was the proconsul of Achaea before whom the apostle Paul was brought for trial; Lucius Annaeus, the philosopher (see below); and M. Annaeus Mela, the father of the poet Lucan (q.v.). He was a student of rhetoric, and in his old age assembled for his sons a collection of 'Contrōversiae' and 'Suāsōriae', arguments on rhetorical themes used in the schools, the former in the form of debates, the latter of monologues. These have survived in an imperfect form, with the exception of five books of the 'Controversiae' known to us only by excerpts. The 'Controversiae' and 'Suasoriae' were exercises in the oratory of the law-courts and in deliberative oratory respectively. The former dealt with imaginary problems in criminal or civil cases, e.g. whether a soldier who, having lost his weapons, takes those from a hero's tomb, fights bravely with them, and restores them, has committed sacrilege. The 'Suasoriae' dealt with such themes as the deliberations of the 300 Spartans whether they should fight or flee before Xerxes. There are interesting prefaces to the Controversiae', describing and discussing various orators, with many digressions, quotations, and anecdotes. The work is a testimony to Seneca's astonishing memory, which he himself tells us was unrivalled. He could repeat long passages of speeches to which he had listened years before. (See Novel).

Se'neca, LŪCIUS ANNAĒUS, 'the Philosopher' (c. 4 B.C.–A.D. 65).

§ 1. His life

Seneca was the second son of Seneca the Elder (see above) and was born at Corduba in Spain. He was brought as a child to Rome and educated there in rhetoric and philosophy. He was drawn especially to the latter and was deeply influenced by the Stoic doctrine, which he himself later developed. He became quaestor, a speaker at the bar, and a senator, but incurred the jealousy of Caligula and is said to have narrowly escaped being put to death. Under Claudius, Seneca occupied a position at court; he was accused of an intrigue with Julia, daughter of Germanicus, the charge being perhaps trumped up by Messalina (q.v.), and banished to Corsica in 41. There he remained for eight years, until recalled in 49 at the instance of Agrippina (q.v.) to be the tutor of her son Nero, in consequence of his literary reputation (for he had devoted the period of his exile to literature). When Nero succeeded Claudius in 54, the influence of Seneca coupled with that of Burrus, prefect of the guard, for a time kept the young emperor

within bounds and the administration sound and just. Later, after the death of Burrus and the elevation of Tigellinus, Nero's conduct changed for the worse, and Seneca asked permission to withdraw from the court, offering to restore his great wealth to the emperor (62). He thereafter lived in retirement, devoted to literature. But in 65, on a charge of complicity in Piso's conspiracy he was ordered to take his own life. Tacitus records the calm and dignity with which he did this.

Seneca has been severely judged. He was a man of high ethical ideals, but did not live up to them. He condoned the murders of Claudius, Britannicus, and Agrippina, and lived and grew wealthy at a court where his moral principles were utterly repudiated. But his influence there was in favour of humanity, clemency, and belief in a Divine Providence. The history of Nero's reign might have been worse but for him. He probably suffered deeply, and we may see a reflection of this in the humility and tolerance of his philosophic teaching.

§ 2. Seneca's 'Dialogues' and moral treatises

Seneca was a voluminous writer. Besides the works that survive, we have the titles or fragments of treatises on geography, natural history, ethics, and other subjects. His extant prose works include twelve Dialogi: 'De Providentia', 'De Constantia Sapientis', 'De Ira' (in three books), 'De Consolatione ad Marciam', 'De Vita Beata', 'De Otio', 'De Tranquillitate Animi', 'De Brevitate Vitae', 'De Consolatione ad Polybium', 'De Consolatione ad Helviam matrem'. Of these the three 'Consolations' are probably among the earliest of the extant prose works and belong to the period 40–3. They follow an established type of rhetorical and philosophical exercises. The 'Consolatio ad Marciam' is addressed to the daughter of Cremûtius Cordus (a historian, victim of Sejanus), in her mourning for her son. The 'Ad Helviam' is addressed to his mother to console her for the exile of her son (himself), and shows fortitude and dignity. The 'Ad Polybium' is addressed to a freedman at court, and in contrast to the previous work is disagreeably marked by the author's flattery of the emperor in hope of recall from banishment. (This Polybius appears to have translated Homer into Latin prose, and Virgil into Greek.) The 'De Constantia', 'De Tranquillitate', and 'De Otio' were addressed to Annaeus Serēnus, an officer of Nero's night-watchmen. The theme of the first is that 'a wise man can suffer neither wrong nor insult'.

The second is concerned with the pursuit of peace of mind amid the troubles of life, and gives much wise advice on the workaday problems of this world. The third is a defence of leisure and relaxation and of the value of speculation and meditation. For the remainder of the above dialogues, see under their titles.

Outside this collection of essays we have the further moral treatises ' De Clementia' and ' De Beneficiis' (qq.v.), and a collection of 124 *Epistles* to his friend Lucilius (q.v.), which are in effect moral essays on various aspects of life: happiness, the supreme good, the terrors of death, riches, and so forth. They are human and persuasive, not dogmatic, in tone; they furnish interesting personal details about the author himself, and throw much light on contemporary life. They were approved and made use of by early Christian writers. Seneca was thought in the Middle Ages to have been a Christian, and was believed by St. Jerome and others to have corresponded with St. Paul. His treatises were studied by Petrarch and were known to Chaucer.

§ 3. 'Naturales Quaestiones' and 'Apocolocyntosis'

Of a different order are the seven books of Seneca's ' Naturales Quaestiones', dedicated to Lucilius and written about A.D. 62, an examination of natural phenomena, not from a scientific but from a Stoic standpoint, and viewed as a branch of ethics. The phenomena are dealt with according as they are related to one or other of the four elements, earth, air, fire, water; with digressions on special subjects such as the rise of the Nile, and a good deal of moralizing. The work, though of no scientific value, was still used in the Middle Ages as a text-book of natural science.

The 'Apocolocyntosis' (q.v.), a burlesque satire on the death of Claudius, is traditionally attributed to Seneca; the ascription has been questioned, but is accepted by modern authorities.

§ 4. Tragedies

Nine tragedies adapted from the Greek are traditionally attributed to Seneca, and there is no reason to question the ascription. A tenth tragedy on a Roman subject, ' Octavia' (q.v.), is included in the manuscripts with the above, but is thought, from internal evidence, to be by a later hand. The nine tragedies are the following; they are dealt with herein under their titles: ' Hercules Furens', 'Medea', 'Troades', 'Phaedra', 'Agamemnon', 'Oedipus', 'Hercules Oetaeus', 'Phoenis-

sae', 'Thyestes'. The first four may be based on Euripides, the fifth on Aeschylus, the sixth and seventh on Sophocles, the eighth on Sophocles and other sources; the source of the ninth is unknown. These plays show departures in detail from their Greek originals, and are marred by excess of declamation, moral disquisition, mythological lore, and clever argument. (Seneca is much given to 'stichomythia', the brisk interchange, line for line, of repartee between two interlocutors, e.g. Clytemnestra and the nurse, when the former is about to kill Agamemnon). Nor have the plays the peculiar spirit and religious background of the old Greek drama. But there are fine passages of description, much high morality, and some effective epigrams. It is improbable that the plays were intended to be acted; they were rather meant to be recited to a literary audience. The metre of the dialogues is the iambic trimeter (see *Metre*); the choruses are in a variety of lyric metres. The plays had a great influence on modern drama, not only in Italy but also in England. The Tenne Tragedies' were translated into English in 1581, and some had been acted at Cambridge before this. 'Gorboduc', one of the first English tragedies (acted before Queen Elizabeth in 1562), was constructed on their model. Gascoigne's Jocasta' (1566), 'Gismond of Salerne' (1567-8), and 'The Misfortunes of Arthur' (1588) by Thomas Hughes also show their influence, as likewise do Marston and Ben Jonson (notably in his Catiline' and Sejanus'). But Marlowe and Shakespeare changed the character of English drama, though even in their romantic plays we find stock characters probably transmitted from the Greek through Seneca, such as the ghost, the nurse, the barbarous villain.

The 'Anthologia Latina' (q.v.) contains a number of short poems by Seneca, some of them containing references to his own life and family.

Septēnā′rius, see *Metre*, § 4.

Septuagint, THE (commonly designated LXX), the Greek version of the O.T., which derives its name from the story (told in a letter now known to be spurious) that it was made by seventy-two Palestinian Jews at the request of Ptolemy Philadelphus (284-247 B.C.) in seclusion on the island of Pharos, in seventy-two days. The translation is now held to have been made by Egyptian Jews working independently of one another and living at different periods in the Hellenistic Age (the translation of Ecclesiastes exceptionally is thought to be later, c. A.D. 100).

Serā′pis or SARĀPIS, a god invented and

introduced into Egypt by Ptolemy I in order to unite the Greeks and Egyptians in a common worship. He was the Egyptian god Osiris (q.v.) combined with elements taken from Zeus, Hades, and Asclepius, and was regarded as the ruler of the universe. He became the Greek god of Alexandria and was worshipped in the great temple in that city called the Serāpēum; but he was not accepted by the Egyptians. The origin of the name is uncertain, perhaps Osiris-Apis.

Sertō'rius, QUINTUS, a Roman of military genius, one of the champions of the democratic party after the victory of Sulla (q.v.). He was invited in 80 B.C. to be leader of the revolted Lusitanians, and with the support of a few exiles from Rome he organized a Spanish army, and for eight years maintained a struggle against the senatorial generals (including Pompey), until treacherously murdered by his lieutenant Perpenna. There is a life of him by Plutarch.

Se'rvius Ma'rius Honōrā'tus, generally known as 'Servius , a Latin grammarian of the second half of the 4th c. A.D. and early 5th c., author of a commentary on Virgil, which survives in two forms, a longer and a shorter. It is of great value by reason of the author's knowledge of historical, antiquarian, literary, and religious subjects. Servius is one of the interlocutors in the 'Saturnalia' of Macrobius (q.v.).

Se'rvius Tu'llius, a semi-legendary king of Rome, the successor of Tarquinius Priscus, in whose house he had been brought up as a slave. His rule is said to have been mild, and a number of public works and constitutional reforms were attributed to him (see *Rome*, § 2). He is said to have been murdered by the order of Lucius Tarquinius, son of Tarquinius Priscus, instigated by his wife Tullia (q.v.); Lucius Tarquinius succeeded him and is known as Tarquinius Superbus. There was a legend of the miraculous birth of Servius Tullius, who was said to be the son of a slave-woman and the fire-god, Vulcan.

Seven against Thebes (*Hepta epi Thēbas*, L. *Septem contra Thēbas*), a tragedy by Aeschylus, produced in 467 B.C., the third part of a linked tetralogy which included the lost plays 'Lāius', 'Oedipus', and 'Sphinx'.

Polynices has come, aided by the Argive army, to assert his rights to the kingdom of Thebes, unjustly detained by his brother Eteocles (see *Oedipus*). The scene is in the city of Thebes, and the chorus is composed of Theban maidens. A messenger describes the array of the hostile army and enumerates the seven champions preparing to lead the attack on the seven gates. To each of these Eteocles appoints an opponent. The seventh enemy champion is Polynices, and Eteocles, in spite of the dissuasion of the chorus, rushes out to face his brother himself. Their death at each other's hand is announced, and their bodies are borne in, mourned by the chorus. In what is perhaps a scene added by an imitator of Aeschylus, the sisters Ismene and Antigone join in the lamentation. A herald announces the decree that the body of Polynices, as having waged war on his city, shall lie unburied. Antigone at once defies the edict. She will herself bury him.

Seven Sages, THE, a name given in ancient tradition to seven men of practical wisdom, statesmen, law-givers and philosophers, of the period 620–550 B.C. The list of the Sages is variously given by different authorities, but all the lists include Solon, Thales (qq.v.), Pittacus of Mitylene, and Bias of Priene. The tyrants Periander of Corinth and Cleobulus of Rhodes are included in some of the lists. Their teaching, which was handed down in the form of aphorisms such as 'Nothing in excess', 'Know thyself', 'Know thine opportunity', appears to have inculcated moderation and submission to the gods and the State. Some of these maxims were inscribed on the temple of Apollo at Delphi.

Se'xtus Empi'ricus (*Empīricus*) (*fl. c.* A.D. 190), a physician whose writings (in Greek) are our chief source of information on the Sceptical (q.v.) school of philosophy. In his 'Pyrrhonean Sketches' (*Purrhōneioi Hupotupōseis*), in three books, he states the position of the Sceptics and attacks that of the Dogmatists. In his other work, generally known as 'Pros tous mathēmatikous' or 'Adversus Mathēmaticos', he refutes the teachers of the various sciences in succession. Incidentally he gives valuable information about the sciences he attacks.

Shield of Heracles (*Aspis Hērakleōus*), a poem in 480 hexameters by some imitator of Hesiod. The first 56 lines appear to form a section of the 'Eoeae' (q.v.) and tell the story of Alcmena. The poem goes on to relate the slaying of the robber Cycnus, son of Ares, by Heracles, who has put on armour given him by Hephaestus, including a shield of which there is a long description (imitated from that of the shield of Achilles in the 'Iliad').

Ships, GREEK AND ROMAN. These may be divided broadly into two classes, according as they were used for warfare or for commerce. The former class were propelled by oars, with masts and sails as a secondary equipment to be used as occasion served; the latter by sails, with the assistance of a few oars, probably used e.g. to bring the vessel round when changing from one tack to another.

§ 1. Warships

We find in the 'Iliad' mention of ships with crews of twenty, fifty, and (in the Catalogue) one hundred and twenty rowers. These last ships would probably have the oars in two banks (we know from Assyrian sculptures that two-banked ships were in use by the Phoenicians about 700 B.C.). Thucydides states that three-banked ships or triremes were said to have been first built in Hellas at Corinth, and that about 700 B.C. Ameinocles the Corinthian made four ships for the Samians; this was the prevalent type of warship during the great period of Athenian history. The arrangement of the oars in a trireme is not known with certainty. It is thought improbable that the rowers were in three tiers one above the other, and more likely that the oars were grouped in threes, attached to three thole-pins in a single porthole, and pulled by three rowers sitting side by side, but the innermost a little further astern and perhaps slightly higher than the second, and the second than the third. But there are various other theories, and the cast in the British Museum of a relief in Athens appears to show the upper oars passing over the gunwales, and the lower oars passing through portholes. An Athenian trireme carried a crew of 200, of whom 170 appear to have rowed in the three banks, and 30 were supernumeraries, sailors, and fighting-men, who if they rowed did so from the upper deck. The trireme was a long narrow ship, probably about 120 ft. long by 15 ft. beam. It had a main mast and sail which were lowered before an engagement, and might be replaced by a smaller mast and sail. There was no spare room on board and the crew had to cook their meals and sleep on land, for which purpose the triremes were constantly hauled up ashore (they had keels of oak). The oars must have been of moderate length and weight, for Thucydides tells us that a body of Peloponnesians made a forced march from Corinth to Megara each man carrying his oar and other equipment. The best speed of a trireme was at least 7½ knots. Athens had 300 triremes at the beginning of the Peloponnesian War. The crews of these must have numbered 60,000. They were recruited firstly from the Athenian *thētes*, but as there were only some 20,000 of these, a great part had to be made up from other sources, such as the poorer metics and slaves, but principally from mercenaries, drawn from the sea-faring population of the confederate States. The pay was three obols a day. The trierarchs, or commanding officers, were drawn from the richest citizens (see *Liturgies*). Under the trierarch was the helmsman (*kubernētēs*, the chief technical officer on board); a boatswain (*keleustēs*), who received and passed on orders and was assisted by a piper (*triēraulēs*), who set the time for the rowers; and a look-out officer in the bows (*prōreus*), who also directed the handling of the sails. Athenian naval tactics consisted principally in so manœuvring as to be able to ram the enemy vessels beak to broadside. For this the Athenian ships depended on their extreme mobility and on a projecting spur armed with wooden teeth shod in bronze. Old ships, with a reduced number of oars, were used as cavalry transports.

The number of banks of oars was increased in the 4th c. B.C. to four, the innovation being attributed to the Carthaginians by Aristotle, and to Dionysius I of Syracuse by Diodorus, and then to five. During the latter part of the 4th c. and the 3rd c. the number was further increased and we hear of ships of 12, 15, and 16 banks in the Macedonian and Egyptian fleets. Archimedes is said to have built a ship of 20 banks for Hieron of Syracuse, and Ptolemy Philadelphus had ships of 20 and 30 banks. Finally we are told of a monstrous ship of 40 banks constructed for Ptolemy Philopator (222–204 B.C.), carrying 4,000 rowers, with oars 38 cubits long, having a leaden counterpoise at the handle end. What the arrangement of the rowers was in these ships we do not know. Some authorities hold that a quinquereme, for instance, does not mean a ship with five banks of oars, but with one bank, each oar pulled by five rowers.

The Romans had no considerable navy or ships of great size until the time of the Punic Wars. For the purpose of the First Punic war they set about building a large fleet, copying a Carthaginian quinquereme which they captured. They adapted the new ships to the tactics of land warfare, fitting them with grappling-irons and bridges for boarding, and placing a number of soldiers on their bows. With these ships they won the war, though they were evidently less experienced seamen than the Carthaginians. After the Second Punic War the fleet fell into neglect; Pompey was forced to collect ships from the Rhodians and others for his operations against the pirates, and Caesar had to improvise a fleet in the Civil War. Sextus

Pompeius, Antony, and Octavian raised large fleets for their struggles with one another, among which figured *liburnae*, swift ships mostly with one or two banks of oars, so named from the Liburnians of Illyria. There is an admirable relief in the Vatican (from the Temple of Fortune at Praeneste) showing one of these two-banked ships. The Roman ships carried a figure-head or a relief or painting on the bows appropriate to the name of the ship (there is a beautiful bronze figure-head of Minerva in the British Museum, found near Actium; Virgil, no doubt inspired by prevailing practice, in Aeneid V and X gives names to a number of Aeneas's ships, 'Chimaera', 'Scylla', 'Centaur', 'Pristis', 'Tiger', and 'Triton', and refers to the figure-heads). There was a great extension of Roman naval power under the empire; the main fleets were based on Mīsēnum on the W. coast and Ravenna on the E. coast of Italy, and there were in addition subsidiary fleets based on various ports in the provinces, and others adapted to navigate the Rhine and the Danube (*lūsōriae*). The Rhine fleet played a very important part in the operations of Drusus, Tiberius, and Germanicus in Germany. From the time perhaps of Claudius's invasion of Britain there was also a Roman fleet in the Channel, based on Gesoriacum (Boulogne). It circumnavigated Britain, discovered the Orkneys, and its marines helped to build Hadrian's wall.

§ 2. *Merchant ships*

MERCHANT SHIPS were of a quite different character: not only were they normally propelled by sails instead of oars, but they were much wider in proportion to their length than warships, so that they were frequently referred to as round ships, as opposed to the long ships of war. Their bows curved upwards instead of being armed with a ram, but they were sometimes equipped with turrets and wooden walls (παραφράγματα) against pirates. A great merchant ship whose dimensions are recorded by Lucian was 180 ft. long, and her width was about a quarter of her length. Merchantmen could go five knots. Greek merchant ships represented on vases have one mast, a yard, and a square sail. Later, a second and even a third mast were introduced; also a triangular topsail, with its base attached to the yard, and its apex to the top of the mast. The capacity of Greek merchantmen is frequently spoken of as 10,000 talents, say 250 tons displacement, and it increased in Hellenistic times. Under the Roman empire commercial vessels were normally of about 400 tons. Special mention may be made of the great

ships built under Augustus and Caligula respectively to bring to Italy the Flaminian and Vatican obelisks. The latter with its pedestal weighed about 500 tons, and the ship carried in addition some 800 tons (according to Pliny) of lentils as packing.

Various other types of ship were used by the Greeks and Romans, such as despatch boats (κέλητες, *celōcēs*, small vessels built for speed), and passenger boats (φάσηλοι, *phasēli*, *vectōriae*, in use about the 1st cc. B.C. and A.D.; Catullus speaks of the yacht that brought him back from Bithynia as a *phaselus*). The *thalamēgi* of the Ptolemies may also be referred to, great luxurious houseboats for use on the Nile, on one of which Cleopatra may have entertained Antony.

Greek ships had an eye represented on each side of the prow; perhaps suggested by the likeness of the prow and ram in profile to the profile of an animal's head. Eyes are still frequently seen painted on the bows of boats in the Mediterranean.

Sibylline Books, THE, frequently referred to in Roman history, were a collection of oracular utterances in Greek hexameters, assigned to the time of Solon, said to have been brought from Greece to Cumae and thence to Rome. According to legend the Cumaean Sibyl (q.v.) offered nine volumes of these oracles to Tarquinius Superbus, the last king of Rome, at a high price. When he refused to buy them she burnt three and offered the remainder at the same price. The king again refused, and the Sibyl burnt three more. Finally the king bought the last three at the original price. He is said to have charged two patricians with the care of these volumes; the number of these custodians was later increased to ten (half of them plebeians) and in the 1st c. B.C. to fifteen, known as the *quindecimviri sacris faciundis* whose business it was to consult the oracles when directed to do so by the Senate. This consultation took place, not with a view to discovering the future, but in cases of great calamities, such as earthquakes and pestilences, in order to learn how the displeasure of the gods might be averted.

The books were kept in a chest in a stone vault under the Temple of the Capitoline Jupiter. They were consumed in the burning of the Capitol in 83 B.C., after which envoys were sent to various places to make a collection of similar oracular sayings. This collection was placed by Augustus in the temple of Apollo on the Palatine, where it remained until destroyed, it is said, by Stilicho, the great general of Theodosius I and Honōrius, early in the 5th c.

Sibyls (*Sibullai*, L. *Sibyllae*), the name given by the Greeks and Romans to prophetesses inspired by some deity, usually Apollo. The most ancient of the legendary Sibyls was Hērophilē, who uttered prophecies relating to the Trojan War. She was known as the Erythraean Sibyl, because of the red earth of Marpessos in the Troad where she was born (the town of Erythrae in Ionia also claimed to be her birthplace). It was told that when bidden by Apollo to choose a gift, she asked to live as many years as she held grains of sand in her hand, but omitted to ask for continued youth. Neither Homer, Hesiod, nor Herodotus mentions her. Plato speaks of one Sibyl, but as time passed, other Sibyls became famous, the Cumaean (sometimes identified with the Erythraean, who wandered to various countries), the Libyan, &c. Trimalchio, in Petronius (q.v.), had seen with his own eyes, he says, the Sibyl at Cumae, hung up in a jar, and when children asked her, 'Sibyl, what do you wish ?', she used to reply, 'I wish to die.' It would seem that her wish was granted, for in the days of Pausanias an urn was shown at Cumae containing her ashes. Collections of the Sibyls' prophecies were made and were known as the Sibylline Books (q.v.). The surviving Sibylline oracles are late works (the oldest, perhaps, of the 2nd c. B.C.) of Judaeo-Hellenic or Judaeo-Christian origin, sombre warnings and prophecies of catastrophes. What is believed to have been the cave of the Cumaean Sibyl was discovered in 1932 on Monte Cuma, near Naples, the site of the ancient Cumae. It consists of a quadrangular chamber, approached by a corridor in the side of the mountain 125 yds. long and 60 ft. high. For the connexion of the Cumaean Sibyl with the story of Aeneas, see *Aeneid* (Bk. **vi**).

Sicilian Expedition, The, see *Peloponnesian War.*

Sicily (*Sikeliā*, L. *Sicilia*), a large island separated from Italy by the Straits of Messina (see Pl. 10). The *Thrinacia* (from *thrinax*, a trident) of the 'Odyssey' is perhaps to be identified with it. *Trinacria* was a Latin poetical name for the island. Its position in the centre of the Mediterranean made it a meeting-place for settlers from East and West, and from Italy and Africa, and gave it great importance in the history of the Mediterranean world. In prehistoric times it appears to have been occupied mainly by two peoples, named Sicans and Sicels, occupying respectively the western and eastern portions of the island, probably immigrants from Italy. The Phoenicians had settlements on the coast from early times and retained in later days three of these, Panormus, Solūs, and Motya, in the west. In the 8th and 7th cc. B.C. Greeks founded many colonies on the coast of Sicily (see *Colonization,* § 3), driving the original inhabitants inland. In the 5th c. the Carthaginians chose the moment when Xerxes was invading Greece to extend the Phoenician power in Sicily, acting perhaps in concert with the Persians; but their design was foiled by Gelon (see *Syracuse,* § 1), who won a great victory over them at Himera in 480. From this time onwards the history of Sicily is in its main features bound up with that of Syracuse (q.v.), its principal city. During the 5th c. the courts of the Sicilian tyrants were centres of culture and of great wealth, as may be gathered from certain of the odes of Pindar, celebrating their victories at the Panhellenic games. At the end of it occurred the Sicilian Expedition of the Athenians (see *Peloponnesian War*), which ended in utter disaster to them in 413. In 409 began a fresh Carthaginian invasion, which avenged the Carthaginian defeat at Himera by capturing and destroying that city. Acragas also was captured in 406. As the result of a long struggle, Dionysius I of Syracuse was able to drive the invaders back in 392 and make peace with them. A further expedition from Carthage against Sicily in 339 was defeated by Timoleon (see *Syracuse,* § 3) at the Crimīsus, and the Carthaginians were once more confined to the western part of the island. But the struggle was only suspended for a time. The history of Sicily now becomes merged with that of Rome. In 278 B.C., Pyrrhus, foiled by the Romans in Italy, set out to conquer Sicily, on an invitation from Syracuse, which was then beset by a Carthaginian fleet and army. But although he drove the Carthaginians out of all Sicily except Lilybaeum, his scheme of empire failed and the venture ended in 275. Carthage recovered the N. and W. of the island and was brought face to face with the growing power of Rome. The First Punic War (q.v.) was waged in Sicily, and as a result of it the island, with the temporary exception of the dominions of Hieron of Syracuse, became a Roman province. This province was the scene of two serious revolts of slaves in the last years of the 2nd c. B.C. (see *Slavery,* § 2). Sicily was granted the Latin franchise by an act of Julius Caesar (executed after his death).

Sicily produced many Greeks famous in literary history, among them the poet Stesichorus, the sophist Gorgias, the scientists Empedocles and Archimedes, the historian Timaeus, the great pastoral poet Theocritus, and Herodas the writer of mimes (qq.v.). It became one of the principal points of contact between Rome and Hellenic culture. It was famous also as the scene of the depredations of Verres (see *Cicero*, § 1).

Si'dō'nius (*Sīdŏnius*), GĀĬUS SOLLIUS APOLLINĀRIS MODESTUS (A.D. 430–*c.* 483 probably), born at Lyons, of a Christian family; his father and grandfather held important offices and he himself was son-in-law of the Emperor Avītus, who caused a statue of him to be placed in the library of Trajan among literary celebrities. He became bishop of Auvergne and won the affection of his flock by his courage and devotion. He wrote poems in hexameters, elegiacs, and hendecasyllables, tricked out with mythological allusion. The chief of these are panegyrics on three successive emperors (Avitus, Mājōrian, and Anthemius), containing much exaggerated eulogy, but little of interest to the historian or ordinary reader. There are verses also in the Letters of Sidonius, mostly epigrams and other short pieces. One of the letters records the classic example of a 'recurrent' line or palindrome, which reads either forwards or backwards, 'Roma tibi subito motibus ibit amor'. Some of the letters are interesting for the light they throw on the social conditions and state of learning in Gaul at this time; there are long descriptions of villas and of country life, and more than one lament on the declining numbers of those who cared for literature. Sidonius was at one time a captive of the Visigoths and gives an interesting account of the barbarians.

Siki'nnis, see *Satyric dramas*.

Silē'nus (*Seilēnos*), in Greek mythology a Satyr (q.v.), sometimes described as son of Hermes or Pan, and a companion of Dionysus. The poets at times refer to a number of Sileni, not a single Silenus, having the same characteristics as the latter, those of elderly drunken Satyrs. Again, they are sometimes described as tutors of Dionysus, musicians, creatures endowed with a store of wisdom. Midas (q.v.) is said to have caught one, by mixing wine with the waters of a spring and so making him drunk. He told Midas that it was happiest for a man not to be born at all, and failing that to die as soon as possible. (For another legend of Midas and Silenus, see *Midas*. See also *Cyclops* (Euripides' play).

Si'lius (*Sīlius*) Ita'licus, TIBERIUS CATIUS ASCŌNIUS (A.D. 25 or 26–101), whose life is known to us chiefly from a letter of the younger Pliny (iii. 7), was probably born at Patavium (Padua), and was consul in 68, the last year of Nero's reign, during which the reputation of Silius had not been good. He was subsequently an efficient proconsul in Asia, and in his later years lived in retirement in Campania. He was a wealthy man, bought country houses (including a villa of Cicero's), and was an amateur of books and works of art. He had a profound admiration for Virgil, whose tomb was on one of his properties. Finding that he was suffering from an incurable disease, he starved himself to death. He was possibly the author of the 'Ilias Latina' (q.v.), but he is remembered for his long epic, the *Punica*, in seventeen books of hexameters, a narrative of the Second Punic War. It begins with Hannibal's oath, his appointment to the command, and treats of the principal episodes of the war, the crossing of the Alps, the battles of the Ticinus, the Trebia, Lake Trasimene, Cannae, the capture of Syracuse, the battle of the Metaurus, Scipio in Spain and Africa, and the battle of Zama. The poem was highly praised by Martial, but the younger Pliny was nearer the mark when he said that it showed more industry than genius. The matter was no doubt derived from Livy; the form from study of Virgil and Lucan. Following Virgil and in contrast with Lucan, Silius reintroduces the traditional intervention of the gods in the conflict. The catalogues (of Hannibal's allies, of the Roman forces at Cannae, &c.), the funeral games, the description of Hannibal's shield, the Nereids disturbed by the Carthaginian fleet, the altercations of antagonists in the field, are all in accord with epic tradition, but prove wearisome. The greatness of the general theme is lost from lack of sense of proportion, and there is an excess of realistic description of slaughter (perhaps due to Lucan's influence). The work as a whole is dull and lifeless, without Virgil's charm or Lucan's power. But the style is generally simple and straightforward, the verse easy and pleasant, and the shorter episodes are well told. There are some pithy sayings, such as 'rarae fumant felicibus arae', and 'explorant adversa viros'.

Si'lloi, see *Timon* (2). The name was applied generally to Greek satirical poems, and appears to have been given to certain poems of Xenophanes criticizing the mythology of Homer and Hesiod.

Si'lvae (the word *silva* was used to signify an *ex tempore* occasional poem), the title of a collection of poems (most of them short), in five books, by Statius (q.v.), of which the first book was published in A.D. 92, the last perhaps posthumously. The manuscript of the poems, after these had long been forgotten, was recovered by Poggio in 1417–18. The majority of the pieces are in hexameters, but six are in hendecasyllables, alcaics, or sapphics. They are written on a variety of subjects suggested by incidents in the poet's life. We find among them dirges on a friend and on a friend's parrot, descriptions of a villa and of an entertainment given by the emperor, a farewell to a friend going overseas. The most notable among them are an invocation to sleep (v. 4), a lament for the author's father (v. 3), a lament for an adopted son (v. 5), an affectionate address to his wife Claudia (iii. 5), and an epithalamium on the marriage of his friend Arruntius Stella (i. 2). The poems as a whole are spoilt by their artificiality and excess of mythological allusion.

Silvā′nus, in Roman religion, a spirit of the woods. He is mentioned by Virgil in association with Pan and the nymphs, and his cult is attributed to the Pelasgians, i.e. is regarded as very ancient. One of the finest Roman altars discovered in Britain is dedicated to this god (see the reproduction in R. G. Collingwood, 'The Archaeology of Roman Britain').

Silver Age of Latin Literature, a term sometimes applied to the Latin literature of the post-Augustan period. See *Rome*, §§ 10 and 11.

Si′mile, a rhetorical figure by which an object, scene, or action is introduced by way of comparison, for explanatory, illustrative, or merely ornamental purpose; e.g.

Nec meum respectet, ut ante, amorem,
Qui illius culpa cecidit velut prati
Ultimi flos, praeter eunte postquam
   Tactus aratrost.
               Catullus, xi. 21 et seq.
or Virgil's
               Inde, lupi ceu
Raptores atra in nebula, quos improba ventris
Exegit caecos rabies . . .
Vadimus haud dubiam in mortem.
               Aen. ii. 355 et seq.

Simo′nidēs (*Sĭmŏnídēs*) of Ceōs (a small Ionian island off the coast of Attica) (c. 556–c. 468 B.C.), a great Greek lyric poet. Part of his life was spent at the court of Hipparchus (q.v.). He subsequently went to Thessaly, appears to have revisited Athens in the days of Themistocles, and after the Persian wars to have retired to Sicily and died at the court of Hieron of Syracuse or at Acragas. His tomb was shown at Syracuse. He was the uncle of Bacchylides (q.v.), and the friend of the leading men in Greece and of the Sicilian tyrants, over whom he exercised much influence. He wrote a variety of choral lyrics, epinicia, encomia (qq.v.), dirges, &c., of which very little survives. He also wrote elegiac poems dealing with the Persian Wars, including a famous epigram on the warriors who fell at Thermopylae. He was a man of a reflective and philosophical cast, and many of his moral sayings were frequently quoted. His philosophy was of a worldly kind, indulgent and slightly sceptical. He is said to have been the first of the Greek poets to write eulogies to order and for payment. His works contain the first known quotation from Homer, οἵηπερ φύλλων γενεή, τοιήδε καὶ ἀνδρῶν. See also under *Danae*. Xenophon wrote an imaginary conversation between Simonides and Hieron of Syracuse.

Si′mo′nidēs of Samos or Amorgos, see *Semonides*.

Si′nis, a brigand killed by Theseus (q.v.).

Si′non (*Sĭnōn*), see *Trojan Horse*.

Si′rens (*Seirēnes*), fabulous creatures that had the power of drawing men to destruction by their song. They are often represented (but not in Homer) as birds with the heads of women (see *Monsters*). The Argonauts, on their return voyage, passed near them; Orpheus, by playing on his lyre, saved his companions from listening to their song (save one man, who sprang overboard, but was rescued by Aphrodite). To escape their lure, Odysseus, when his ship was about to pass their island, filled the ears of his men with wax, and had himself lashed to the mast. According to later legend, the Sirens drowned themselves from annoyance at the escape of Odysseus. The body of one of them, Parthenope, was washed ashore in the bay of Naples, which originally bore her name.

Si′rius (*Seirĭos*, L. *Sĭrius*), the Dog-star. See *Calendar*, § 2, and *Icarius*. In Homer, Sirius is the dog of Orion, the hunter.

Sir′mio, a promontory on the southern shore of Lacus Bēnăcus (Lago di Garda), on which Catullus (q.v.) had a villa.

Si′ron (*Sīrōn*), see *Virgil*.

Sise′nna, LUCIUS CORNĒLIUS, who held office as praetor in 76 B.C. and was one of the defenders of Verres against Cicero, was author of a Latin history of his own age, which has not survived. He also translated into Latin the Milesian Tales (q.v.).

Si'syphus (*Sisuphos*), a legendary king of Corinth, reputed the most cunning of mankind. When Autolycus (q.v.), another master of roguery, stole his neighbours' cattle and changed their appearance so as to avoid detection, Sisyphus was able to pick out his own, having marked them under their hoofs. It is also related that when Death came to take him, the crafty Sisyphus chained him up; so that nobody died till Ares came and released Death again. For misdeeds on earth, variously related, he was condemned in Hades to roll to the top of a hill a large stone, which when it reached the summit rolled down again, so that his punishment was eternal. In post-Homeric legend Sisyphus was the father of Odysseus.

Slavery.

§ 1. *In Greece*

Slavery existed in the society described in the Homeric poems, but plays no very prominent part in it (see *Homeric Age*). The slave was regarded as part of the family and appears to have been, in general, well treated. Very kindly relations sometimes existed between master and slaves (note in particular the case of Eumaeus, and how Odysseus was received on his return by him and the other slaves).

The institution of slavery appears to have become common in most parts of Greece during the 5th–4th cc. It was justified, even by the most humane and thoughtful of the Greeks, on the ground that it was necessary; for without it the citizens would be unable to devote themselves to the service of the State. It was urged moreover that there existed races of inferior beings who were suited for the purpose. The majority of slaves were captives, either of war or piracy. Some 20,000 for instance were sold after Cimon's victory over the Persians at the Eurymedon in 468. Athens was a centre of the slave trade. Few slaves, children of slave parents, were reared in Greek households. From the time of Solon a citizen could not be enslaved for debt at Athens, though he could in other Greek cities. In general there were few Greeks among the slaves, who were for the most part Thracians, Scythians, and Asiatics; but occasionally the inhabitants of a Greek subject-city which had revolted and been subdued were sold into slavery. In theory the slave had no rights; he was the chattel of his owner. In fact, at Athens, where his condition was relatively favourable, certain rights were conceded to him. He might not be beaten except by his owner. He had a right of action if his honour was outraged. If too miserable, he could claim

to be sold to another owner. On the other hand the evidence of slaves in lawsuits was always taken under torture, to make it more trustworthy.

Slaves at Athens wore no distinctive dress. There were three kinds of slaves. Firstly, those in domestic employment, such as cooks, nurses, pedagogues (who took the children to school). A middle-class family would have from three to nine slaves as a rule. Very few slaves were employed in agriculture. Secondly those employed in industrial, commercial, or other undertakings (e.g. in building, or in workshops or factories). Among these must be mentioned in particular the unfortunate slaves who extracted the silver from the mines at Laurium for the concessionaires of those mines. The conditions under which they worked were wretched, and when the Spartans occupied Decelea in the Peloponnesian war, the Laurium slaves deserted in a body. Private slaves were frequently let out for hire both for domestic and industrial employment. They sometimes rose to positions of responsibility. We learn from a speech of Demosthenes that the merchants Chrysippus and his brother sent a slave to direct their branch on the Bosporus; and the Athenian bankers Pasĭon (d. 370 B.C.) and his successor Phormio were originally slaves.

The third category were the public slaves, the property of the State, employed by it in a variety of ways, on public works or the care of the roads, as clerks or minor officials, or as policemen (the Scythian archers, see *Athens*, § 11). The slaves employed on public works at Eleusis in the 4th c. received the fully sufficient allowance of 180 drs. a year for their food, and their clothing in addition. Some public slaves held important positions in the administration, such as that of custodian of the archives or of assistants to the various treasurers. It was a slave named Nicomachus who, at the time of the Thirty, was charged with the codification of the Athenian laws.

Slaves figure occasionally in the plays of Aristophanes. They play a more prominent part in the Greek life of the third century as depicted by Menander and Plautus. Here they frequently occupy a position of importance in the household and of great intimacy and familiarity with their masters, enjoying opportunities of pleasure and recreation.

The number of slaves at Athens in the 5th–4th cc. is unknown; it has been variously estimated at figures between 150,000 and 400,000. It probably exceeded that of the free population. It appears to have diminished in Greece generally in the Hellenistic Age. Slaves might become free either by purchasing their own freedom or by being released by their owner or by the State for exceptional services. But the number of enfranchisements (until about 200 B.C.) was comparatively small. Not only the interest of the owner, but that of the State was opposed to easy enfranchisement; for the previous conditions under which slaves had lived did not tend to make them good members of a free community. On enfranchisement a slave became a metic (q.v.), and conditions were sometimes attached to his freedom, such as that he should continue to render certain services to the former owner. Enfranchisement in many Greek cities was a solemnity carried out at a temple; at Athens it was attended by simpler formalities, such as a declaration before witnesses.

The price of slaves varied with their qualifications. The average price realized by 16 slaves forming part of the confiscated property of a metic in 414 B.C. was 172½ drachmas for the women, and 167 drachmas for the men (about £6). But skilled artisans would fetch a much higher price: the father of Demosthenes had 32 swordsmiths, who had cost on the average 600 dr. (about £20). According to inscriptions found at Delphi the average cost of the enfranchisement of 678 slaves was about 380 dr. for the women and 430 dr. for the men and boys (Glotz).

For the type of bondage known as serfdom, of which the helots of Sparta were the chief example, see *Helots*.

§ 2. *At Rome*

The institution existed at Rome from early times, but the number of slaves in Roman possession rose to very large numbers only from the 2nd c. B.C. We hear of Aemilius Paullus selling 150,000 slaves after Pydna; of Caesar selling on one occasion 53,000. Delos became a great slave market; it is said that 10,000 might be sold there in one day. In Rome slaves were sold at the Temple of Castor. The principal sources of supply were wars, raids, and piracy.

The Roman slave was in primitive theory a chattel, and in practice during republican times he enjoyed few or no rights. The marriage of slaves was as a rule not recognized. A slave might accumulate savings (his *peculium*) with a view to purchasing his freedom. But if he ran away and was recaptured he might be branded or put to death. Though slaves were allowed certain opportunities for merry-making at the Saturnalia and Compitalia, and there must have been

many instances of kindly relations between master and slave, there is also evidence of callous harshness in their treatment (see under *Cato the Censor*). As in Greece, the judicial examination of slaves was conducted under torture. Slaves might be manumitted, either purchasing their freedom or being granted it for good service; and the manumission might be either formal (before a magistrate, or by will) or informal (e.g. before friends). By formal emancipation the Roman freedman attained, unlike the Greek freedman, the full rights of a Roman citizen, except that he was not eligible for office or (until the 1st c. B.C.) for military service. The freedman (*libertus*) continued to belong to the family of his former master (*patrōnus*), and the two were bound by mutual obligations. The freedman assumed the *nomen* and *praenomen* of his liberator, generally adding (from the 1st c. B.C.) a Greek *cognomen*. Manumissions were very frequent. This was not an unmixed good. Many unworthy slaves were thus enfranchized and the citizen body suffered in consequence, apart from any deterioration due to the immixture of alien blood. Under the early empire attempts were made to limit the number of manumissions. Slaves were frequently employed in faction fights; and there were several important revolts of slaves. In Sicily the slaves under a Syrian named Eunus rose against their masters in 135 B.C. and were not subdued till 132. There was a second revolt in Sicily from 103 to 99 B.C. The rising of slaves under Spartacus (q.v.) took two years to suppress.

The position of slaves gradually improved under the empire. They were allowed to marry, to combine in *collegia*, and to seek redress in case of harsh treatment. But instances of maltreatment are still found. For example Seneca (De Ira, iii. 40. 2, see also Tac. Ann. i. 10) relates that Vēdius Pollio, a wealthy freedman, angry with a slave for breaking a cup during a dinner at which Augustus was present, ordered him to be flung into a pond to be eaten by sea-eels. The slave threw himself at the feet of Augustus, who reproved Pollio for his cruelty.

There is no reliable information as to the number of slaves in Rome, still less in Italy, at various times. Estimates as to the number in the city in the time of Augustus range from 300,000 to 900,000. Slaves were employed by the well-to-do in the towns either in domestic service or as teachers, scribes, or craftsmen (sometimes producing goods for sale). In the country slaves were employed on agricultural work, sometimes highly specialized as vine-dressers, &c., or herded together in large gangs and housed in *ergastula*, barracks, where they might be chained and treated like wild beasts. Others again were trained as gladiators (q.v.). The State owned a large number of slaves (*servi publici*) who were employed on public works. The price of an ordinary slave appears to have been about £20; but very much higher prices were paid for those exceptionally qualified.

As time went on under the empire, particularly under the Antonines, the number of slaves decreased, and manumissions became more frequent. Perhaps slave labour was found unremunerative. On agricultural estates, slaves were replaced by *coloni*, tenants paying rent in produce; in the city, slaves tended to be replaced by free artisans. The influences of the Stoic philosophy and later of Christianity were hostile to the institution.

Slaves famous in literature, see *Aesop, Caecilius Statius, Epictetus, Menippus, Publilius Syrus, Terence,* and among the characters of fiction *Davus.* Tiro (q.v.), the secretary and literary assistant of Cicero, was a freedman.

Sleep (Gk. *Hupnos*, Lat. *Somnus*), personified in Greek mythology as the brother of Death. Homer in the episode of Hera beguiling Zeus with the aid of Sleep (Il. xiv. 225 et seq.) appears to place his home in Lemnos; Ovid places it amid the dark mists of the far north.

Smyrna or MYRRHA, see *Adonis*; also *Zmyrna.*

Social War (1) in Greek history, a name given to the war, 357–354 B.C., between Athens on the one hand and Chios, Cos, Rhodes, and Byzantium on the other, which had revolted from her second Confederacy (see *Athens*, § 6); (2) in Roman history, see *Rome*, § 6.

Sŏ′cratēs (*Sōkratēs*), born at Alōpekē near Athens in 469 B.C., was the son of the sculptor Sōphroniscus and the midwife Phaenaretē. He fought at Potidaea (432–29), where he is said to have saved the life of Alcibiades, and at Dēlium (424), where his firm demeanour amid the rout was noted. He was married to Xanthippē, who had the reputation of a scold, but whose sterling qualities (according to a passage in Xenophon's 'Memorabilia') were recognized by her husband. He was a man of uncouth appearance, humorously described in Xenophon's 'Symposium'. Being entirely free from ambition or wish for wealth, he avoided public offices, but was twice placed in positions where he showed his courage in opposing the political passions of the moment; in 406 after the battle of Arginusae, as president of the Assembly, he resisted the popular clamour for the trial of the generals by an illegal procedure; and under the rule of the Thirty he refused to obey an order to arrest a person whom they had condemned to death. In 399, after a trial described in the 'Apology' of Plato and in that of Xenophon, he was sentenced to death on a charge brought by Melētus, Anytus, and Lycōn of introducing new deities and corrupting youth. He had made enemies by interrogating all who had a reputation for wisdom and refuting them; his novel ideas and his perception of the weak points in democratic government were unpopular with the Athenians, who attributed to his teaching the misdeeds of Alcibiades and his associate Charmidēs, and of Critias (one of the Thirty), all disciples of Socrates. His execution was postponed for a month, for the sacred trireme had just been despatched to Delos (q.v.), and during its absence no execution was allowed to pollute the city; on its return, in a scene described by Plato in the 'Phaedo', he drank, as required, the draught of hemlock.

The difficulty in arriving at a clear idea of his doctrines is that while he himself wrote nothing, of his two interpreters Plato is apt to put his own views into the mouth of his master, and Xenophon, not being a philosopher, may not do justice to those doctrines. It seems clear that, turning aside from the physical speculations of the earlier philosophers, he regarded the most useful science as that which contributes to knowledge of virtue, that which makes a good citizen, moral science in a wide sense. He sought to detect errors in the conventional views, and to arrive at true ideas on the subject by a new method. He analysed the definitions of such things as virtue by particular cases and examples, the resulting contradictions showing the errors of those definitions, while the truth of a definition was proved by the consistency of the results. This analysis was carried on by a system of question and answer, each point in succession being accepted or rejected by the interlocutor, who was gradually led to the conclusion at which Socrates wished to arrive. He pretended to know nothing himself, but to elicit from his friends for his own and their edification the truth which was latent in their minds, making much use of the most simple and trivial examples, of irony, and occasionally of myths to illustrate a doctrine. According to the 'Memorabilia', he discussed a great variety of subjects dealing with many sides of life. Plato and Xenophon agree in representing it as his view that virtue is knowledge; no one is willingly wicked, for happiness lies in virtue. If a man is wicked, it is due to his ignorance. Socrates' concern is therefore to discover what the good is. The question of moral intention is with him secondary. But Xenophon gives us little or nothing of Socrates' views (as reported by Plato) on the soul and its destiny and on the nature of true religion. Socrates (it would appear from Plato) inferred from the harmony of the universe that it is organized and vivified by the Divine Spirit, in the same way that the mind is inferred from the actions of man. Hence pious observances are due to the gods, the popular personifications of the Divine Spirit. He inclined to the view that the soul is immortal and will meet with judgement and retribution hereafter. There was a mystical side to his teaching, later developed by Plato and the Neo-Platonists. He believed that he was himself the recipient of warnings addressed to him on occasion by the Divine Voice. It may be noted that according to Aristotle (Metaph. M 4. 1078b) two things may be placed to Socrates' credit, as his contribution to philosophical knowledge, 'inductive argument and universal definition'.

His chief importance may perhaps be said to consist in the fact that he was the first philosopher to connect the notions of virtue and knowledge. His strange personality and the fact that he died for his faith may account in part for the influence he exercised on all later philosophy. The scantiness of his positive doctrines led to schools of most diverse opinions being founded by his disciples, e.g. by Plato, by Antisthenes the Cynic, by Eucleides of Megara, and by Aristippus the predecessor of Epicurus (qq.v.).

See also *Memorabilia*, *Symposium*, and *Apology* of Xenophon; *Symposium*, *Crito*, *Phaedo*, and *Apology* of Plato; and *Clouds* of Aristophanes.

So′leae, see *Clothing*, § 5.

Sōlī′nus, JŪLIUS, probably of the 3rd c. A.D., was author of 'Collectanea rērum memorābilium,' substantially an epitome (in Latin) of the 'Natural History' of Pliny. The title 'Polyhistor', by which the work of Solinus is sometimes known, may have been a new title given by the author himself to the second edition of his work.

Sō′lon (*Sŏlōn*) (*c*. 640–*c*. 558 B.C.), son of Exēcestidēs, a member of an aristocratic family of Athens, was famous as a statesman and as a poet. When young he was poor and travelled as a merchant to enrich himself. On his return to Athens about 612 he stirred the Athenians to the reconquest of Salamis from the Megarians. The success of this undertaking gave him great influence, and about 594 he was named archon and introduced his celebrated constitution, inspired by a sense of the solidarity of the various classes of the State and of the necessity for the just treatment of all. In particular he effected a *seisachtheia* ('shaking off of the burden') or exoneration of debt, by liberating land which had been mortgaged, and by freeing persons who had been sold as slaves or had gone into exile on account of debt. He appears to have reorganized the primitive *Boule* or Senate, which under his constitution was composed of 400 members, one hundred from each of the four tribes; and to have given to each adult male Athenian a seat in the *Ecclesia* or popular assembly; what precise powers this body had is not known. He instituted the *Heliaea* (q.v.) or popular tribunal, as a final court of appeal. The ancient Council of the Areopagus retained, under his constitution, jurisdiction in cases of religious crimes and premeditated murder. After the promulgation of his laws, he is said to have travelled again and (although chronology makes this impossible) to have met Croesus (q.v.). He lived to see his constitution overthrown and the tyranny of Pisistratus set up.

His economic reforms (apart from the *seisachtheia*) are also important. He encouraged Athenian industry, importing craftsmen from Corinth and elsewhere, and granting them Athenian citizenship. He also introduced certain currency reforms, changing Athenian coinage from the Aeginetan to the Euboic standard, a move which was favourable to Athenian trade. The establishment of Athenian influence at Sīgēum in the Troad about this time is related to the same policy and was perhaps due to Solon.

Solon was also the first Attic poet. He wrote elegiacs and iambics, of which fragments alone survive, some of them exhortations to the Athenians, others reflections on moral, political, and social subjects, while others dealt with love and lighter themes. They include the often quoted line,

$$\Gamma\eta\rho\acute{a}\sigma\kappa\omega\ \delta'\,a\grave{\imath}\epsilon\grave{\imath}\ \pi o\lambda\lambda\grave{a}\ \delta\iota\delta\alpha\sigma\kappa\acute{o}\mu\epsilon\nu o\varsigma.$$

There is a life of Solon by Plutarch. Landor has an 'Imaginary Conversation' between Solon and Pisistratus.

So′mnium, see *Lucian*.

So′mnium Scĭpiōnis ('The Dream of

Scipio'), a surviving portion of the lost sixth book of Cicero's 'De Republica' (q.v.), is a narrative placed in the mouth of Scipio Aemilianus (q.v.). He relates a visit to the court of Masinissa (a Numidian ally of Rome during the Second Punic War; see *Sophonisba*), on which occasion there was much talk of the first great Scipio. When the younger Scipio retired to rest, the shade of the elder appeared to him in a dream, foretold the future of his life, and exhorted him to virtue, patriotism, and the disregard of human fame, as the path leading to reward in a future life, the nature of which is indicated. The narrative incidentally gives Cicero's conception of the universe, borrowed from the Greek philosophers. The story is largely modelled on the fable of Er the son of Arminius, in the tenth book of Plato's 'Republic' (q.v.). A poetical summary of it occurs in Chaucer's 'Parliament of Fowls'. The text of the 'Somnium Scipionis' has been preserved chiefly through the commentary of Macrobius (q.v.).

So'phist (*Sophistēs*), originally meaning one learned in some art or craft, then a wise man generally, in which sense it was applied to the Seven Sages (q.v.). Later from the middle of the 5th c. the term was applied especially to persons who gave lessons for money in rhetoric, politics, and mathematics. They were useful in popularizing knowledge; but as time went on, they gave increasing importance to rhetoric, to the form of expression, rather than to the substance of knowledge. For this they were condemned by Socrates and Plato, and the term came to mean a quibbler. Noted sophists of the time of Plato were Protagoras, Gorgias, Hippias of Elis (qq.v.), and Prodicus of Ceõs (5th c. B.C.). The Sophists were prominent in the university of Athens, under the Roman empire, as teachers of rhetoric (see *New Sophistic* under *Roman Age*).

Sophist (*Sophistēs*), a dialogue by Plato, a sequel to the 'Theaetetus' (q.v.). It is an inquiry into the character of the sophist (see previous article), who is declared to be a charlatan, a hireling, a disputant, no true teacher. In the course of the discussion, in which Socrates takes no part, the difficulty which in the 'Theaetetus' had arrested the inquiry into the nature of knowledge is cleared up, a difficulty which arose from the Eleatic denial of reality to 'not-being', whence it had been inferred that falsehood could have no existence.

Sophistic, NEW, see *Roman Age*.

Sophists, Against the, see *Isocrates*.

So'phoclēs (*Sophoklēs*) (496–406 B.C.), the second of the three great Attic tragedians, was born at Colõnus near Athens. His father Sophillus owned a manufactory of armour. The best part of his life coincided with the age of Cimon and Pericles, the period of Athens' greatest prosperity. He took no active part in politics and had no special military gifts; nevertheless he was twice elected *strategus* (q.v.), and after the Sicilian disaster of 413 he was made one of the *Probouloi* (q.v.) or special commissioners, no doubt by reason of his general fame and popularity. He was a man of great charm, handsome, and well-to-do. Herodotus was one of his friends. Sophocles died, as he had lived, at Athens. Aristophanes sums up his character in the line (Ran. 82) ὁ δ᾿ εὔκολος μὲν ἐνθάδ᾿, εὔκολος δ᾿ ἐκεῖ, 'contented among the living, contented among the dead'. He left two sons; by Nīcostratē Iophōn the tragedian, and by Theōris of Sicyon Agathōn, father of the younger Sophocles, who was also a writer of tragedies. After his death Sophocles was worshipped as a hero. He wrote some 120 plays and was victorious with eighteen tetralogies. His first victory was in 468, when he defeated Aeschylus. Seven of his tragedies are extant; in their probable rough chronological order they are: 'Antigone' (441), 'Oedipus Tyrannus', 'Electra', 'Ajax' (some authorities put the 'Ajax' first), 'Trachiniae', 'Philoctetes' (409), 'Oedipus at Colonus' (401, after his death, produced by the younger Sophocles). These are dealt with under their several titles. A large fragment of his satyric play 'Ichneutae' ('Hunters') has been found in a papyrus at Oxyrhynchus. It dealt with the theft by Hermes, soon after his birth, of Apollo's cattle.

Sophocles was an innovator in tragedy. He introduced the third actor, he introduced or at least greatly developed stage scenery (see *Aeschylus*), he increased the number of the chorus from twelve to fifteen, and he abandoned the practice of connected tetralogies, making each play an artistic whole in itself. In his tragedies man's will plays a greater, that of the gods a lesser part than in those of Aeschylus. The course of his dramas is determined by the characters of the protagonists, the influences they undergo, the penalties they suffer, not by external incidents. Sophocles is no philosopher or speculator on the deeper problems of life; he accepts the conventional religion without criticism. His principal characters, though subject to human defects, are in a general way heroic and actuated by lofty motives. This is perhaps what Sophocles meant when he said (as Aristotle relates) that he portrayed people as they ought to be, Euripides as they are. Mention should be made of his great heroines, Antigone and Electra, in whom he depicts a combination of womanly gentleness and superb courage. His lyrics form a less important element in the plays than do those of Aeschylus; they combine charm with grandeur, without the mystery and terror of Aeschylus, or the 'descriptive embroidery' (Croiset) of Euripides. The dialogue of Sophocles is dignified, appropriate to his idealized characters. The whole is marked by a powerful simplicity. According to his own account of his poetic development, as given by Plutarch, having abandoned 'the magniloquence of Aeschylus', he passed to 'his own harsh and artificial period of style' (as exemplified perhaps in the 'Electra'), and finally reached greater ease and simplicity.

The high estimation in which he was held in antiquity has been shared in modern times, e.g. by Lessing and Racine. M. Arnold describes him as one

Who saw life steadily and saw it whole,
The mellow glory of the Attic stage,
Singer of sweet Colonus and its child.

Shelley had a volume of Sophocles in his pocket when he was drowned. A famous edition (1883–96) of his extant plays is that of Sir R. Jebb. Among Landor's Imaginary Conversations' is one between Sophocles and Pericles.

Sophoni'sba, daughter of Hasdrubal, a Carthaginian general, son of Gisco (or Gisgo). She married Syphax king of Numidia, and her influence drew him away from his alliance with Rome during the Second Punic War. Syphax was captured by Masinissa, a Numidian prince in alliance with Rome, and Sophonisba fell into Masinissa's power. Masinissa became enamoured of her and determined to marry her. But Scipio Africanus, fearing that her influence on Masinissa might be as unfortunate to the Roman cause as her influence on Syphax had been, claimed her as a captive to be sent to Rome. Masinissa, to save her from captivity, sent her poison, which she drank without perturbation. The well-known line 'Oh! Sophonisba, Sophonisba, Oh!' is from the 'Tragedy of Sophonisba' by James Thomson (1730; another line was substituted later). Plays on the subject of her story were also written by John Marston (1606), Nathaniel Lee (1676), and Corneille (1663).

Sō'phrōn, see *Mime*, § 1.

So'rtēs, see *Oracles* and *Virgil*.

So'sii, famous booksellers at Rome, referred to by Horace (Ep. I. xx. 2).

Sō'tadēs of Marōneia in Crete, who lived under the first two Ptolemies (323–247 B.C.), wrote in Greek, in a peculiar metre which bears his name, coarse satires and travesties of mythology. Among the objects of his personal attacks were the kings of Egypt and Macedonia, and it is said that Ptolemy II caused him to be sewn up in a sack and thrown into the sea. Only a few fragments and titles of his works remain.

Spain (*Ibēria* or *Hibēria* or *Hispānia*). Iberia was the name, derived from the river Ibērus (Ebro), applied by the Greeks to the country that we know as Spain. The Romans called it Hispania. Of the original inhabitants little is known; the Basques may be their descendants. Celts migrated into the country from Gaul and Iberians from Africa. At an early date Phoenicians founded settlements, notably Gādes (Cadiz), on the coast. In the 6th c. B.C. Phocaeans from Massalia (Marseilles) also founded colonies, but coming into conflict with Phoenicians from Carthage were driven from most of these. In the later part of the 3rd c. B.C., after the First Punic War, the Carthaginians under Hamilcar, Hasdrubal, and Hannibal greatly extended their dominions in Spain, reaching the Ebro and founding Carthāgo Nova on the Mediterranean coast as their principal centre. They used the conquered territory as a recruiting ground for the army destined to renew the struggle with Rome. In 219 Hannibal's siege and capture of Saguntum, which had been promised Roman protection, precipitated the Second Punic War. Rome sent a force to try to hold Hannibal in Spain, but failed to do so. Operations undertaken there later in the war under the elder Scipios ended in disaster, but served a useful purpose by detaining in Spain Carthaginian troops that would otherwise have been sent to Italy. A new Roman army dispatched to Spain in 210 under the younger Publius Scipio restored the Roman fortunes in that country. Scipio captured Carthago Nova and by 206 finally expelled the Carthaginians.

Two Roman provinces (Hispania Citerior, the eastern sea-board, and Hispania Ulterior, roughly the modern Andalusia) were constituted in 197, but the native inhabitants had not then been effectually subdued, and unrest continued for many years. An important pacification was effected in 179 by Tiberius Sempronius Gracchus (father of 'the Gracchi', q.v.), who by his personal character won the confidence of the Spaniards. But native risings were renewed in 154, and Numantia resisted the Romans for nine years. Its capture by Scipio Aemilianus in 133 brought the Spanish wars to a close, the Romans occupying the whole country except the mountainous region in the north and north-west. No systematic Roman colonization was then attempted, but a few settlements of veterans in the south and east served as centres of Roman civilization.

In the Civil Wars of the 1st c. B.C. Spain was held by the Marian leader Sertorius against the party of Sulla and later against Pompey, until Sertorius was murdered in 72. The military talent of Julius Caesar was first revealed when he was propraetor in Spain in 61. He subsequently waged war there in 49 against the Pompeian generals Afrānius and Petrēius, and in 45 against the sons of Pompey, finally making himself master of the Roman empire by his victory at Munda. Notable among the colonies that he founded in Spain were Hispalis (Seville) and Tarraco (Tarragona). A final pacification of the whole peninsula, including the north and north-west, was effected by Augustus.

Many persons of importance in the history and literature of imperial Rome were of Spanish origin. Trajan was born in Spain, Hadrian and Marcus Aurelius belonged to Spanish families. For the list of eminent writers of Spanish birth see *Birthplaces of Latin authors*. From an economic standpoint Spain was a valuable possession especially for its mineral wealth (see *Mines*). The silver mines in particular were a source of great profit both to the State and to individual Romans. The vine and the olive were also extensively cultivated in the southern and eastern parts of the country.

Of Roman remains in Spain the most striking are perhaps the great bridges at Merida and Alcantara. Many Spanish place-names commemorate their Roman origin, e.g. Merida (*Emerita Augusta*), Saragossa (*Caesaraugusta*).

Sparta (*Spartē*), or LACEDAEMON (*Lakedaimōn*), the capital of Laconia, a State in the SE. of the Peloponnese founded by Dorians (see *Migrations and Dialects*, and Pl. 8.) The town, situated by the river Eurōtās, was little better than a group of villages, without fine buildings, and unfortified until the days of the Macedonian domination of Greece.

§ 1. *Early history to Sixth Century*

We have, apart from some verses of Tyrtaeus (q.v.), little reliable information as to its constitution and customs before the 6th c. B.C. (see *Lycurgus* (2)). Its inhabitants were divided into five tribes. There were two royal families, the Āgids and the Eurypontids, who claimed descent from Heracles, and from each of them was taken one of the two kings who jointly ruled the State. In two wars, probably in the 8th and at the end of the 7th c., Sparta effected the conquest of Messēnia. At some period before the 6th c. the monarchical system was transformed into an oligarchy, though the two nominal kings were retained with curtailed powers. In the 7th c. Sparta was not the closed and self-centred State that she later became, but took a normal part in the life of Greece: her art and industry were highly developed; she was the chief home of the choral lyric (Alcman, Thaletas, Tyrtaeus, qq.v.). Then came a change. Military discipline was introduced into the organization of the State, probably as the result of the Messenian wars; it was necessary to hold down the helots (q.v.), who were mostly the conquered Messenians. Sparta withdrew into herself and forbade strangers to sojourn in the city.

§ 2. *Social and political organization from the Sixth century*

In the 6th c. we find the following social organization. At the summit were the full citizens, the warriors, known as the *Spartiātai*. Each head of a Spartan family held an inalienable portion, descending to his eldest son, in the zone of city lands. He did not live there, but it was cultivated for him by his helots (q.v.) or serfs. Spartans could own and dispose of land other than their lots, but where is unknown. They were forbidden to take part in any business or trade. This was the province of the *perioeci* (q.v.) or members of subject communities, as the cultivation of the soil was that of the helots. The citizens were all nominally equal in the eyes of the State, but were controlled by it in the details of their lives, with the sole object of making them efficient parts of a powerful military machine. Thus marriage was under State direction, weakly children were exposed, and the others subjected to collective education, ascetic discipline, and gymnastic training, with a view to developing their endurance and courage. They were promoted after tests to successive classes, until fully qualified. In this training military exercises played the chief part, intellectual education a very small one. Spartan girls had also to undergo gymnastic training. Spartan men lived in barracks till they were 30, and took their meals at public messes till they were 60.

In this way was formed the most powerful army in Greece. It is evident that a society so organized offered little encouragement to art or literature.

The chief elements in the political constitution were the two hereditary kings, the *gerousia* or senate, the *apella* or assembly, and the ephors. The kings were the religious representatives of the State, and the leaders of the army in war, but they were then accompanied and supervised by two ephors, and their power shows a gradual decline. The *gerousia* was composed of the two kings and twenty-eight members, over sixty years of age, elected for life; it was the supreme court of law. The *apella*, composed of all Spartan citizens of 30 in possession of full rights, was a consultative body, without real authority, but declarations of war had to be ratified by it. The five ephors appear to have been chosen virtually by lot. The office was open to all Spartan citizens and was deemed a democratic element in the constitution. The ephors were the supervisors of the State, wielding great powers which they gradually extended. They controlled the general administration and had certain judicial functions; they could even sentence the kings to fine or imprisonment, they could recall generals, they negotiated foreign treaties. Their first proclamation, when they entered office, was that the people should shave their moustaches and be obedient to the laws (Plut. Cleom. 9).

There was a steady diminution in the number of Spartan citizens, due partly to losses in war, partly to the concentration of the lots in a few hands or in the hands of women, and to the loss in the 4th c. of the Messenian lots (see § 4). This caused a gradual decline in the strength of Sparta. There were 8,000 Spartan citizens in 480 B.C., 2,000 in 371, Aristotle estimates them at 1,000, there are said to have been only 700 in 242.

§ 3. *Foreign relations in the Sixth and Fifth centuries*

As regards foreign relations, Sparta at first followed a policy of conquest and expansion, establishing her predominance in the Peloponnese, and defeating and weakening her principal rival, Argos. Towards the middle of the 6th c., perhaps under the influence of the ephor Chilôn, she abandoned this policy and set about consolidating her position. She formed a league of the Peloponnesian States (except Argos and Achaea, but including Corinth and Megara) under her own leadership. These States remained autonomous, paid no tribute, but supplied a military con-

tingent in war, of which Sparta retained the direction. Declaration of war by the league required the consent of the majority of the States members and of the Spartan *Apella*. The assemblies of the league were held at Sparta. Sparta was now at the height of her power. Her narrow and selfish policy was shown when in 499 she refused to assist the Ionian Greeks in their revolt against Persia. But when Xerxes prepared for war against Greece itself (see *Persian Wars*), Sparta combined with Athens in measures of defence and showed the valour of her soldiers at Thermopylae and Plataea. This co-operation ceased after the defeat of the Persians at Mycale, and Sparta once more turned her attention to the Peloponnese. She had to face an attempted coalition of Peloponnesian States against her, a terrible earthquake which destroyed the city in 464, a serious threat from a revolt of the helots, and a first conflict with the imperialism of Athens. From these ordeals she emerged successfully. Her final struggle with Athens (see *Peloponnesian War*) for the leadership of Greece began in 431.

§ 4. *Foreign relations in the Fourth century*

The defeat of Athens left Sparta supreme in Greece, but her institutions did not fit her for an imperial role. She entered on a period of selfish and arrogant aggrandisement which aroused the hostility of her neighbours and led to the rise of Thebes and her own downfall.

Sparta, in the latter part of the Peloponnesian War (q.v.) had entered into alliance with the Persian satrap Tissaphernês, and later with the satrap Pharnabâzus. But after the war Sparta changed her policy. The successful march of the Ten Thousand (see *Anabasis*) produced in Greece a feeling of contempt for the Persian Empire, and an appeal of the Ionian cities for help against Tissaphernes, coupled with the hope of easy plunder, induced Sparta to undertake a war against Persia. It was successfully conducted in 396 and 395 by Agesilaus (q.v.), and might have had important results if Agesilaus had not been recalled to deal with trouble nearer home. A league of Thebes, Corinth, Argos, and Athens had been formed against Sparta, and in spite of the victory of Agesilaus at Coronea in 394, the so-called 'Corinthian war' dragged on until 387, when the Persian King, whose intervention Sparta had invited, enforced the pacification known as the peace of Antalcidas. This left Sparta free to resume her arrogant policy. The Chalcidian Confederacy (composed of Olynthus and other

Sparta

cities of the Chalcidic promontory) aroused her hostility and she sent an expedition against it. It marched through Boeotia, and on the way wantonly seized without pretext the Cadmea (q.v.), the fortress of Thebes (382). An equally unprovoked raid on the Piraeus brought on a war with Athens in alliance with Thebes (378), which lasted until the peace of Callias reconciled Sparta and Athens. Sparta and Thebes were now left alone in the struggle for supremacy. The issue was in a measure decided by the Theban victory at Leuctra in the same year (371), for thereafter Thebes and not Sparta was the aggressor. Sparta was repeatedly invaded by the great Theban commander Epaminondas, who dealt her a fatal blow by freeing Messenia (370–69). The formation of a league of Arcadian cities after Leuctra also weakened her influence; this too was the work of Thebes. But at the battle of Mantinea (362) Thebes, though victorious, suffered an irremediable disaster in the death of her general. Peace was made in the same year. The success of Thebes during this period was due not only to the military genius of Epaminondas, but also to the declining number of Spartan citizens, already referred to.

§ 5. Sparta after the rise of Macedon

Although Sparta was not actually captured by Philip of Macedon when he invaded the Peloponnese, her territory and power were diminished, and her important role in Greece now came to an end. The most interesting incident in her later history (apart from the brave defence of the city in 272 against an attack by Pyrrhus (q.v.), a defence in which the Spartan women took a prominent part) was the social revolution attempted by Agis IV (242 B.C.) and effected by Cleomenes III (227). There are lives of both in Plutarch. As already stated, the concentration of wealth in a few hands, and the reduction in the number of the Spartiates, had impaired the stability and power of the Spartan State. There was much debt, the institution of public meals was neglected, and the old system of land-allotments was completely disorganized. Agis proposed the cancellation of debts and the redistribution of the Spartan land proper among 4,500 Spartiates, perioeci, and selected aliens, who were to constitute the new citizen roll. The scheme was defeated by the conservative party, and Agis was murdered. It was resumed and carried through, with some modification, by Cleomenes, who, after defeating the Achaean League in 227, left his force of citizens in the field, hurried back to Sparta,

deposed the ephors, and made himself master of the State. He then carried out his reforms, restoring what he conceived to be the institutions of Lycurgus. But in 222 Cleomenes was defeated and driven into exile by the Macedonians in alliance with the Achaean League, Sparta was captured, and a reactionary government established. The quarrels of Sparta with the Achaean League (the city was captured by Philopoemen in 188) played an important part in the final reduction of Greece by the Romans in 146 B.C.

§ 6. Special characteristics of Sparta

Sparta differed from other Greek states not only in her peculiar constitution and in the supreme importance she attached to military efficiency, but in certain other respects. For instance, her arrested development was shown by the fact that she never (until the 3rd c. B.C.) admitted the use of coined money; the currency took the form of 'spits' (obeloi) of iron or copper. On the other hand women enjoyed a position of more equality with men, and greater independence and authority than at Athens. The wife at Sparta was not merely a housekeeper, but an active member of the State, expected to interest herself in the welfare of her country.

Spa'rtacus, a Thracian gladiator, who in 73 B.C. escaped from a school of gladiators at Capua, was joined by a number of slaves and other desperate men, and for two years successfully opposed the Roman armies. He was finally defeated and slain by M. Licinius Crassus (q.v.).

Spa'rti (Spartoi), see Cadmus.

Spartiā'nus, AELIUS, see Historia Augusta.

Spartiā'tai, see Sparta, § 2.

Spectāculō'rum, Liber, see Martial.

Speusi'ppus (Speusippos), nephew of Plato and his successor as head of the Academy (q.v.).

Sphactē'ria, see Peloponnesian War.

Sphinx (meaning 'Strangler'), in Greek mythology, a monster represented generally with a woman's bust on a lion's body (see Monsters). In Hesiod she is called Phix and is the daughter of Chimaera and Orthrus (qq.v.); according to others of Echidna and Typhon (qq.v.). In the story of Oedipus (q.v.) and the Sphinx, the riddle she proposed was, 'What is it that walks on four legs in the morning, on two at noon, on three in the evening?' The answer was 'man', who as an infant crawls on all fours, and in old age walks leaning on a stick.

Spo'lia Opi'ma, the 'spoils of honour', the arms taken by a Roman general from the commander of the enemy after defeating him in single combat on the field of battle. They were won three times in Roman history, (1) by Romulus from Acron, king of the Caeninenses, in the hostilities that followed the Rape of the Sabines, (2) by Aulus Cornēlius Cossus, who in 437 B.C. slew Tolumnius the Etruscan king, (3) by M. Claudius Marcellus, who slew the Gaul Viridomarus in 222 B.C.

Spondee, see *Metre*, § 1.

Stā'dium (*Stădion*), a Greek furlong, 600 Greek feet, probably about 194 yards. Hence used as the name of the Greek foot-race course, which was 600 feet long. The Stadium at Athens was outside the walls, E. of the Olympieum (q.v.), on the left bank of the Ilyssus. It was reconstructed in marble by Herodes Atticus (q.v.). See *Olympia* for the important Stadium at that place.

Stagi'ra (*Stageira* or *Stageiros*), a town on the E. coast of the Chalcidic peninsula, the birthplace of Aristotle (sometimes referred to as 'the Sta'girite'). It was destroyed by Philip of Macedon in 348, but rebuilt by him in honour of Aristotle.

Sta'simon, see *Tragedy*, § 3.

Stati'ra (*Stateira*), see *Alexander the Great*, § 8.

Stā'tius, CAECILIUS, see *Caecilius Statius*.

Stā'tius, PUBLIUS PĀPINIUS (c. A.D. 40–c. 96), born at Naples, was the son of a *grammaticus* or schoolmaster and teacher of literature, himself a poet, who encouraged the literary taste of his son. The young man won a prize for poetry at the Neapolitan competition of the *Augustalia* (see *Ludi*, § 2). He appears then to have gone to Rome, where he recited to large audiences from his poems, won a contest held by Domitian at Alba with a poem on the emperor's exploits, but failed, to his deep disappointment, at the Capitoline contest of 94. About this time he retired to Naples, where he died. He married Claudia, a widow, to whom he was deeply attached. He had no children; his sorrow over the death of an adopted child is expressed in the last poem of the 'Silvae'. His lost works include the libretto for a pantomime 'Agave', on the story of Pentheus, and an epic on the campaigns of Domitian in Germany. His extant works are the miscellany 'Silvae', the epic 'Thebaid', and the epic 'Achilleid' (qq.v.) of which only one book and part of a second were written before his death. On the 'Thebaid' he spent twelve years; its closing passage shows his humble

reverence for Virgil. He appears to have been a man of affectionate disposition, learned, a lover of beauty in nature and art. He associated with men prominent in affairs, including Domitian himself, whom he flattered in his poems. It is noticeable that although he belonged to the same period as Martial, neither poet mentions the other; there was probably little sympathy between them. The poetry of Statius is highly artificial, full of conceits and learned allusions, but shows vigour and power of narrative (e.g. in the threatening speech of Tydeus to Eteocles, Theb. ii. 452 et seq., and in the description of the ambush laid for Tydeus. ii. 527 et seq.). His verse is smooth and easy.

Statius was much admired in the Middle Ages; Chaucer for instance in 'Troylus and Cryseyde' associates him with Homer, Virgil, Ovid, and Lucan. For some unexplained reason he was at that time thought to have been a Christian, and Dante devotes Cantos xxi and xxii of his 'Purgatorio' to a charming account of the meeting of the spirits of Virgil and Statius. The latter explains how he was led to Christianity by certain passages of Virgil's. Dante confusing Statius the poet with a rhetorician of the same name of Toulouse, calls him 'Tolosano'; and Chaucer follows him in the error. Pope and Gray both translated portions of the 'Thebaid'.

Ste'ntōr, a Greek with a voice as loud as fifty men (Il. v. 785).

Ste'phanus, see *Editions*.

Ste'ropēs, see *Cyclopes*.

Stēsi'chorus (*Stēsichoros*, 'Choir-setter') (c. 640–c. 555 B.C.), a Greek lyrical poet probably of Himerā in Sicily, whose original name, it is said, was Teisiās. Legend relates that he was struck with blindness for having censured Helen (q.v.) in one of his poems, and that his sight was restored after he had written his 'Palinodia' or recantation, in which it was not Helen, but her phantom, that accompanied Paris to Troy (see *Helen*, Euripides' tragedy). He is said to have died or been assassinated at Catana in Sicily. He wrote lyric poems of various kinds, but was especially famous as the reputed inventor of the choral *heroic hymn* (q.v.). The subjects of a dozen of his poems are known to us, such as various incidents of the Trojan War, the murder of Agamemnon and the vengeance of Orestes, various adventures of Heracles, the tale of Eriphyle, &c. His 'Iliou Persis' ('Sack of Troy') included, and was perhaps the source of, the legend of the wanderings of Aeneas to Italy. He is described as the most Homeric of lyric poets, and as transferring to lyric poetry the grandeur of the epic. He thus prepared the way for the treatment of epic legend in tragedy. He also made an important innovation in lyric verse by introducing the triad (q.v.), which Pindar adopted as the structure of his odes. Of the considerable body of the works of Stesichorus (some twenty-six books) only about fifty lines survive. He is thus a poet 'whose greatness we can only calculate as astronomers infer the presence of an indiscernible star' (J. S. Phillimore). The ancients refer to him always with respect. Horace speaks of 'Stesichori graves Camenae' (*Od.* IV. ix. 8), and Quintilian gives him high praise.

Stheneboe′a (*Stheneboia*), see *Bellerophon.*

Sthe′nnō, see *Gorgons.*

Stichomy′thia (*Stichomūthiā*), in Greek drama, dialogue in alternate lines of verse, especially in disputes. There are examples of it also in Seneca's tragedies.

Sti′chus, a comedy by Plautus. The title is taken from the name of one of the characters, a slave. The comedy has little plot. The two daughters of Antiphō are married to two brothers. These have gone abroad on a trading venture to retrieve their fortunes; they have been absent three years and no tidings of them have been received. Antipho urges his daughters to marry again, but they insist on remaining faithful to their husbands. The husbands have prospered and now return, and their home-coming is celebrated with rejoicings. Much fun is made of a hungry parasite, and there is a scene depicting slaves merrymaking.

Sti′licho, see *Britain*, § 2.

Sto′a, the Greek word for a colonnade, usually roofed and with a wall on one side, erected near temples or gymnasia or in market-places. The wall was often decorated with paintings or inscriptions. Thus the *Stoa Poikilē* or Painted Colonnade in the market-place at Athens was adorned with frescoes by famous artists, including one by Polygnotus (q.v.) representing the destruction of Troy. It was this Stoa which was frequented by Zeno and his disciples and gave its name to the Stoic school of philosophy. The Stoa of Zeus was decorated with paintings by Euphranor (q.v.). The *Stoa Basileios* or Royal Colonnade, also in the market-place, formed the court where the king archon sat as judge in certain religious matters. Colonnades were also erected in Athens by the Pergamene Kings Attalus II and Eumenes (probably the second).

Stobāē′us, JOHANNES (i.e. John of Stobi in Macedonia) compiled, about A.D. 500, an anthology of excerpts from Greek writers, in four books, whose subjects were respectively, philosophy and physics, rhetoric and poetry, ethics, and politics. These were grouped in the Middle Ages under two titles, 'Eklogia' and 'Anthologion'. The work, which has survived, preserves many valuable fragments otherwise unknown to us.

Sto′ics. The Stoic school of philosophy was founded at Athens c. 315 B.C. by Zeno (q.v.) of Citium in Cyprus. The school took its name from the fact that Zeno taught philosophy in the *Stoa* (q.v.) *Poikilē* at Athens. Zeno, in strong contrast to his contemporary Epicurus (q.v.), regarded the world as an organic whole, animated and directed by intelligence, and consisting of an active principle (God), and of that which is acted upon (matter); two inseparable aspects of reality. The universe, according to the Stoic doctrine, at the end of each of a never-ending series of cycles, is absorbed into the divine fire, and then starts on a fresh course exactly reproducing its predecessor. The conception has been expressed by Shelley at the end of his 'Hellas':

> Worlds on worlds are rolling ever
> From creation to decay,
> Like the bubbles on a river
> Sparkling, bursting, borne away.

In ethics Zeno held that the true end of man is an active life in harmony with nature, that is to say a life of virtue, for virtue is the law of the universe, God's will; and right conduct produces happiness. A notable Stoic doctrine was that of the universal brotherhood of man, without distinction between Greek and barbarian, freeman and slave, and of the consequent duty of universal benevolence and justice. But, in spite of this, Stoicism was in the main a doctrine of detachment from, and independence of, the outer world. The immediate successors of Zeno were Cleanthes (q.v.) and Chrysippus of Soli in Cilicia (c. 280–204 B.C.), who completed and systematized the Stoic doctrine. For Panaetius and Posidonius and their influence on Roman thought, see under their names. Stoicism was congenial to the Roman spirit, and helped to mould Roman Law. It came into prominence again in the writings of Seneca the philosopher, and in the Satires of Persius. But the later government of Nero was hostile to it, and Vespasian and again Domitian banished the philosophers from Italy. A modified and more religious Stoicism revived in the teaching of Epictetus and the self-discipline of Marcus Aurelius (qq.v.).

Sto′la, see *Clothing*, § 3.

Strā′bo (*Străbōn*) (c. 64 B.C.–A.D. 19), of Amasīa in Pontus, a Stoic and a traveller, wrote in Greek 'Geōgraphica' in seventeen books (which survive with a lacuna in one book) describing the physical geography of the chief countries in the Roman world, and giving the broad features of their historical and economic development and an account of anything remarkable in the customs of their inhabitants or in their animal and plant life. Though Strabo relies in great measure on the works of predecessors, not always critically used, the 'Geōgraphica' is for the most part a very readable work, assembling much valuable information and containing many interesting and picturesque passages. He tells us for instance how the Indians capture elephants and long-tailed apes, how the Arabians get fresh water out of the sea, and how the Egyptians feed their sacred crocodile; and about the Hanging Gardens of Babylon, the whales of the Persian Gulf, and the aromatics of the Sabaeans. The work, in an epitomised form, was used as a school-book in the Middle Ages. Strabo also wrote 'Historical Studies', a great work in forty-three books, continuing the history of Polybius down to the foundation of the empire. This is unfortunately lost.

Stratēgē′mata, see *Frontinus* and *Polyaenus.*

Stratē′gus (*Stratēgos*), in Greece, a military commander. At Athens there were from 501 B.C. ten strategi, each commanding the regiment of hoplites of his tribe, under the supreme command of the polemarch (see *Athens*, § 2). But a polemarch chosen by lot (as he was after 487 B.C.) was unsuited for the post of commander-in-chief, and a reform was introduced at an unknown date by which his powers were transferred to the ten strategi, now elected by the whole people, though generally one from each tribe; while the command of the regiments of hoplites was entrusted to taxiarchs (see *Army*, § 1). Each strategus appears to have held command in turn for one day, but this system, hardly conducive to efficiency in war, gave place to an arrangement by which the people, when they decided on a military expedition, named the strategus who was to have supreme command of it. In the 5th c. the board of strategi formed an important administrative council, directing foreign and domestic policy subject to the control of the Ecclesia. In the late 5th c. the institution was modified by the introduction of two kinds of strategi: (1) στρατηγὸς δέκατος αὐτός, a sort of president of the board of

generals, chosen not as the other nine from specific tribes but from all the tribes. The first person definitely known to hold this position was Pericles, though it may have been held by Cimon. (2) στρατηγὸς αὐτοκρατώρ, 'general with full powers', conferred for a specific purpose, but in their widest extent tantamount to possession of the full authority of martial law. Pericles seems to have held this authority in 431 and may have suspended the Ecclesia next year in virtue of it. Alcibiades held the same position along with Lamachus and Nicias in 415 and alone in June 407.

Strigil, see *Clothing*, § 6.

Stro′phē ('turn'), a stanza of a Greek choral song sung as the chorus proceeded in one direction, followed by the *antistrophē*, symmetrically constructed, when they turned and proceeded in the opposite direction. See also *Triad.*

Studies, CLASSICAL, see *Texts and Studies.*

Stultō′rum Fē′riae ('Feast of Fools'), at Rome, a name given to the *Quirinalia* or feast of Quirinus (q.v.), because any one who had forgotten to perform the rites of the *Fornacalia* (q.v.) on the day fixed each year for his own *curia* or ward, might perform them on the day of the Quirinalia instead.

Stymphā′lian Birds, see *Heracles* (*Labours of*).

Stymphā′lus, the name of a lake in a narrow upland valley under lofty Mt. Cyllēnē in northern Arcadia. It is entirely hemmed in by mountains and the waters which it receives by springs escape by underground chasms. Hadrian conducted the water from one of these springs by means of aqueducts to supply the reconstructed city of Corinth.

Styx (*Stux*, 'the abhorrent'), in Greek mythology the principal river of the underworld (see *Hades*). According to Hesiod Styx was one of the river-spirits who were daughters of Oceanus (q.v.). She and her children aided Zeus in his quarrel with the Titans (q.v.), in consequence of which she was greatly honoured, and an oath by Styx was held inviolable by the gods. The name was that of a little river which falls down a very lofty cliff on Mt. Aroanius (modern Chelmos) in northern Arcadia, and joins the Crāthis. Solemn oaths were taken by men on its waters, which were supposed to have some deadly property; according to Herodotus (vi. 74) Cleomenes the banished king of Sparta tried to get the Arcadians to swear an oath by the Styx that they would support him. It was from this Styx, guarded by dragons, that

Psyche in the fable of Cupid and Psyche (see *Psyche*) was set by Venus the task of bringing water.

Suāsō'riae, see *Seneca (the Elder)* and *Novel.*

Subli'cian Bridge, see *Pons Sublicius.*

Sublime, Longinus on the, see *Longinus.*

Subū'ra or **Subu'rra**, at Rome, a densely populated hollow between the Esquiline and Quirinal hills, occupied largely by artisans and shops. See Pl. 14*a*.

Suētō'nius (*Gāĭus Suētōnius Tranquillus*) (*c.* A.D. 70–*c.* 160), son of Suetonius Laetus, who as a tribune in the 13th Legion fought at Bedriacum (q.v.). The son practised in the courts at Rome and was a friend of the younger Pliny, who petitioned Trajan for the grant to Suetonius of the *jus trium liberorum* (q.v.). Suetonius was for a time one of the imperial secretaries under Trajan, in which capacity he would have facilities for consulting the imperial archives. Thereafter he devoted himself to historical and antiquarian study and is said to have lived on to the days of Antoninus Pius.

Of his writings, mostly of an antiquarian character, much is lost. The surviving works consist of the 'Lives of the Caesars' (*De Vita Caesarum*) and of part of his 'De Viris Illustribus', viz. most of the sections 'De Grammaticis' and 'De Rhetoribus', and in addition the lives of Terence, Horace, and Lucan. Lives of Virgil, Juvenal, Persius, and the elder Pliny, sometimes attributed to Suetonius, are not generally accepted as genuine.

The 'De Grammaticis' sets forth what is to be understood by 'grammar', i.e. broadly the study of literature, relates its introduction at Rome by Crates (q.v.), and gives some account of twenty of the principal grammarians.

The 'De Rhetoribus' relates the growth at Rome of the study of rhetoric, which at first was disapproved by the authorities, explains the method of teaching it, and illustrates the themes used in the schools. An account of five of the principal professors of rhetoric follows.

The Lives of the poets contain some interesting information and anecdotes about them, including passages about their personal appearance, stating, for instance, that Horace was short and fat.

The 'Lives of the Caesars', the principal surviving work of Suetonius, contains the biographies of Julius Caesar and the eleven emperors from Augustus to Domitian. They give an account of the ancestry and career of each emperor, but consist chiefly of anecdotes, many of them based on report or gossip. They show little historical grasp or penetration, but include much that is interesting or entertaining. There is for instance the account of Caesar's crossing of the Rubicon, and a detailed narrative of his assassination; the mention of his dark piercing eyes and his attempts to conceal his baldness. Augustus was short but well-proportioned, with an aquiline nose and eyebrows that met, negligent in dress, frugal, and sparing in diet. Suetonius gives an interesting account of the sojourn of Tiberius at Rhodes and reproduces the scandalous and perhaps unfounded stories of his evil life at Capri. There is a vivid picture of the grotesque appearance of Caligula, of his eccentricities and insane cruelties; of the awkward gait, loud guffaw, and halting speech of Claudius, and the mixture of culture and occasional good sense with silliness and excessive timidity in his unbalanced mind. The Life of Nero, after relating the quaint story of how the Ahenobarbi (q.v.) got their red beards (given also by Plutarch in his life of Aemilius Paullus) tells us much about Nero's stage displays and his fondness for horses (he used, even after he became emperor, to play with little ivory horses and chariots on a table); about his elaborate organization of a *claque* to applaud his own productions; about his wanderings incognito at night in the streets of Rome; about his Golden House; and his conduct while Rome burnt. The Life of Titus mentions his notable saying at the end of a day when he had done no good to any one, 'I have lost a day', and his mastery of shorthand and aptitude for imitating the handwriting of others; and that of Domitian records his restoration of the libraries which had been burnt down and his efforts to collect manuscripts. An English version of Suetonius was made by the great Elizabethan translator Philemon Holland (1606).

Suētōnius Paulīnus, GĀĭus, see *Britain*, § 2.

Su'idas (*Souidās*), the name of a great Greek lexicon or encyclopaedia, compiled about the end of the 10th c. and containing many valuable articles on Greek literature and history. It is based partly on earlier lexicons (see *Hesychius*), partly on *scholia* and commentaries on Greek authors, partly on excerpts by later hands from the works of historians, grammarians, and biographers.

Su'lla, LŪCĬUS CORNĒLĬUS (138–78 B.C.), a great leader of the aristocratic party at Rome, first distinguished himself when as quaestor to Marius in Africa he secured by his courage and diplomacy the surrender of Jugurtha (107). He also showed his military ability against the Cimbri and in the Social War. He was consul in 88 and was designated by the Senate for the command against Mithridates. But the appointment of this optimate was disliked by the *populares* (q.v.), and the Eastern command was transferred to Marius. The six legions that Sulla had assembled at Capua thereupon declared for their general and marched with him on Rome. For the first time a consul entered the city at the head of his troops. Marius fled, and Sulla, after devising a temporary political settlement, proceeded to the East, captured Athens, crossed to Asia Minor, and came to terms with Mithridates. In 83 Sulla, with a devoted army and possessed of vast treasure (Mithridates had been required to pay an indemnity of 2,000 talents), landed in Italy, to find Rome in the hands of the *populares*. He was joined by the best elements, including Pompey, Crassus, and Lucullus. A ruthless civil war endured for two years and left Sulla (after the defeat in 82 of the revolted Samnites at the Colline Gate) triumphant. He now adopted in his turn Marius's policy of extermination of his enemies, adding the device of 'proscription', the posting up of lists of victims who might be killed without trial and their property confiscated, while murderers and informers were rewarded. The cities that had fought against Sulla were included in his vengeance and in some cases their confiscated lands were distributed among his soldiers. Sulla took the position of dictator and set about a complete constitutional reform, designed to restore and increase the power of the Senate and to restrict that of the people and their tribunes. The knights lost the judicial powers obtained by them in the time of the Gracchi (q.v.); a number of them were co-opted into the Senate. The powers and careers (see *Cursus Honorum*) of the magistrates were strictly defined. Sulla's most important measure was the full organization of a system of criminal procedure—the *quaestiones perpetuae* (see *Judicial Procedure*, § 2). This was one of the few parts of his work which survived the reaction that followed his death. After completing his reforms, Sulla laid down his office and retired into private life in 79. He died shortly after, having devoted his leisure to composing his memoirs in twenty-two books. These have not survived. There is a life of Sulla by Plutarch.

Sulmo, the birthplace of Ovid, in a valley of the Apennines, E. of Rome.

Sulpi'cia, see *Tibullus.*

Sulpi'cius Rūfus, SERVIUS (105–43 B.C.), a great Roman jurist, contemporary of Cicero, known to us by his correspondence with the latter. He was a candidate for the consulship in 63, and having failed to be elected, devoted himself to the study of law. He helped to make Roman Law a permanent force in the world, by establishing sound principles, interpreting and defining them. He was consul in 51 and joined Caesar in the Civil War. He is the author of a famous letter of consolation to Cicero on the death of his daughter, which was admired and copied by St. Ambrose as worthy of a Christian.

Another Servius Sulpicius Rufus was tribune in 88 B.C. and a supporter of Marius. He proposed that the newly enfranchised Italians should vote in all the tribes, not be confined to a few; also that the command against Mithridates should be transferred from Sulla to Marius. These proposals were carried, but Sulpicius was killed in the disorders which followed the march on Rome of Sulla's army (see *Sulla*).

Sū'nium (*Sounion*), a cape (C. Colonna) forming the southernmost point of Attica. It is mentioned by Homer (Od. iii. 278) as the point off which Apollo slew the pilot of Menelaus on his way to Troy. A temple of Athene was built on the lofty headland, of which eleven columns still remain standing, visible from far away at sea. Byron celebrated 'Sunium's marbled steep' in 'Don Juan' (iii. 86), and refers to it in 'Childe Harold' (ii. 86).

Suovetauri'lia, at Rome, the combined sacrifice of a pig, a sheep, and an ox, the principal animals of the farmer. Such sacrifices were made at certain agricultural festivals, such as the Ambarvalia (q.v.).

Suppliants (*Hiketides*, L. *Supplicēs*), from internal evidence the earliest of the extant plays of Aeschylus.

The 'Suppliants' are the fifty daughters of Danaus (q.v.), who have fled from Egypt to avoid marriage (regarded as incestuous) with their cousins, the fifty sons of the usurping king Aegyptus. They have come with their father Danaus to Argos, with which they claim connexion through their descent from Io (q.v.), to ask protection from their pursuers. The king of Argos hesitates and consults his people. These vote in favour of the Suppliants, and the arrogant demand of the enemy herald for their surrender is rejected.

The play was the first of a trilogy, the second and third of which ('The Egyptians' and 'The Daughters of Danaus') continued the legend. The suppliants (or some of them) form the chorus, and their lyrics occupy more than half the play, an indication of its early date.

Suppliants (*Hiketides*, L. *Supplicēs*), a tragedy by Euripides, probably produced soon after 424 B.C., and perhaps designed to promote an alliance between Athens and Argos.

The Thebans have refused to allow the bodies of the seven chieftains who had unsuccessfully attacked Thebes (see *Oedipus*) to be buried, thus violating the sacred custom of Hellas. The mothers of the chieftains (who form the chorus of Suppliants from whom the play is named) have come with Adrastus king of Argos, leader of the expedition against Thebes, to Eleusis in Attica and made supplication to Aethra, mother of Theseus king of Athens, at the shrine of Demeter. Theseus rejects the arrogant demand of the Theban herald for their surrender; he yields to the prayer of the Suppliants, and recovers by force of arms the bodies for burial. Evadne, wife of Capaneūs, one of the chieftains, throws herself on her husband's pyre.

Supplicā'tiō, at Rome, a solemn rite of humiliation or thanksgiving, on the occasion of some misfortune or success (e.g. a military defeat or victory), when the people in procession visited the temples with singing and prayer.

Su'pplicēs, see *Suppliants*.

Sy'baris (*Subaris*), an Achaean colony on the E. coast of Bruttium in southern Italy, founded about 720 B.C. In the 6th c. it was an important trading centre, and its wealth and luxury became proverbial. It was destroyed about 510 B.C. by its rival Croton (q.v.), after its army had been defeated at the Crāthis. See *Thurii*.

Sylle'psis (*Sullēpsis* 'taking together'), the application of a word to two others in different senses, or to two of which it suits only one grammatically; e.g. 'manus ac supplices voces ad Tiberium tendens' (Tac. Ann. ii. 29. 2), where 'tendens' is applied in different senses to 'manus' and 'voces'. Cf. *Zeugma*.

Sy'mmachus, QUINTUS AURĒLIUS (A.D. 345–405), prefect of Rome in 384, a Roman noble and an eminent administrator and orator, whose eloquence is referred to by Macrobius as 'pingue et floridum' and acknowledged by St. Ambrose. His letters were collected by his son in ten books. The first nine books consist of letters to his friends, trivial and uninteresting, contain-

ing little that bears on the social and political conditions of the time. The tenth book contains the official correspondence of Symmachus and shows him courteous, tolerant, yet firm. His best known work is the 'Relātio' or report which he, as prefect of Rome, addressed to the young emperor Valentinian II in 384, defending the ancient religious institutions against Christian inroads, and urging the restoration to the Senate-house of the Altar of Victory (which Gratian had caused to be removed) as a symbol of the historic greatness of Rome. His recommendation, which has been called 'perhaps the noblest defence of a dying creed that has ever been made' (F. W. Hall), was vigorously and successfully opposed by St. Ambrose (q.v.).

Symmo'riae (*Summoriai*), see *Liturgy* and *Demosthenes* (2), § 4 (*a*).

Symplē'gades, the 'clashing' ones, also called *K'uaneai*, the 'dark-blue' ones, two fabulous rocks that stood in the sea at the N. end of the Bosporus, forming the gate to the Euxine Sea. They were believed to clash together, crushing ships that passed between them. The Argonauts (q.v.) narrowly escaped them. The *Planktai* or 'wandering' rocks, mentioned in the Odyssey' (xii. 61) were similar fabulous rocks in an unspecified place.

Sympo'siaca, see *Plutarch*, § 3.

Sympo'sium (*Sumposion*, 'Banquet'), a dialogue by Plato. Internal evidence suggests that it was written between 384 and 369 B.C.

The dialogue is supposed to have taken place at a banquet held at the house of the poet Agathon (q.v.) and is given as narrated by Aristodēmus (an admirer of Socrates) who was present. Each of the guests utters a discourse in honour of love, Phaedrus from a mythical standpoint, Pausanias from that of a sophist, Agathon from that of a poet. Aristophanes gives a comical turn to his discourse, though with underlying seriousness. Socrates takes the discussion to a higher plane. He has learnt from Diotīmā, the priestess of Mantinea, that love may have a nobler aspect. The need in the human being which is manifested on a lower plane by the love of the sexes, can also take an intellectual form, the desire of the soul to create conceptions of wisdom and beauty, such as poets and legislators produce. Man should proceed from the love of a beautiful form to the perception and love of universal divine beauty. Alcibiades now comes in, slightly drunk, and speaks. He confesses the fascination that Socrates exercises on him, and his hope of receiving lessons of wisdom from him, for he is ashamed of his despicable life. He tells various incidents in the life of Socrates; the latter is like the masks of Silenus which conceal images of gods inside them, and like Marsyas the Satyr, who with his pipe could charm the souls of men.

Sympo'sium, the narrative by Xenophon of a banquet that took place, on the occasion of the Great Panathenaea of 421 B.C., at the house of Callias, at which Socrates was present. Xenophon must have been very young at this time and the speeches attributed to Socrates and others are probably more or less imaginary. The persons present at the banquet are all historical characters except Philip the buffoon and a Syracusan impresario. The narrative gives a vivid and interesting picture of what an Athenian banquet was like, with the entertainment by dancers provided by the Syracusan. The conversation is in a mixed vein of pleasantry and seriousness, and Socrates is presented in a mood of genial relaxation. There are a good many jokes about his personal appearance. He is the central figure, and, amid his raillery, utters a serious discourse on the superiority of spiritual love to carnal love.

Synae'resis ('drawing together'), the making of two separate successive vowel sounds into one; the opposite of *Diaeresis*.

Syne'cdochē (-ki), a figure of speech in which a part is used to signify the whole, or the singular where the plural is meant; as in the phrase frequent in Livy 'Romanus proelio victor'.

Syne'sius (*Sunesios*), see *Neoplatonism*.

Sȳ'phax (*Sỹphax*), see *Sophonisba*.

Sȳ'racuse (*Sŭrākousai*, L. *Sȳrācūsae*), on the SE. coast of Sicily, a colony founded by Corinth in 734 B.C. See Pl. 10.

§ 1. *From earliest times to 467* B.C.

The city was originally confined to the small island of Ortygia closely adjoining the mainland, but was subsequently extended to include the neighbouring regions of Achradina and Epipolae. It was a flourishing place by the end of the 6th c., but was raised to the position of the first city in Sicily by GELŌN, ruler of Gela (q.v.), who was called in about 485 by the aristocrats of Syracuse and became ruler of the city. He destroyed Camarina and brought its inhabitants, and many of the inhabitants of Gela, to Syracuse. He won great glory by completely defeating the Carthaginian invaders of Sicily at the battle of

Himerā (480, on the very day, according to Herodotus, of the battle of Salamis). The inscription on Gelon's thank-offering for this victory has been discovered at Delphi.

Gelon was succeeded by his brother HIERŌN I (478-67), an inferior ruler, but rendered famous by the odes of Pindar (q.v.), and the fact that Aeschylus and Bacchylides (qq.v.) spent some time at his court. Xenophon has an imaginary dialogue between Hieron and Simonides (see *Hieron*). Hieron founded a new city, Aetna, at the foot of Mt. Etna. A bronze helmet dedicated in celebration of his victory over the Etruscans in a naval battle off Cumae (474) has been found at Olympia and is now in the British Museum.

§ 2. *467-353* B.C.

The end of the dynasty of Gelon was succeeded by a period of internal dissension at Syracuse, but also of external aggression against other Sicilian towns, which provided the pretext for the great Sicilian Expedition of Athens (415-413, see *Peloponnesian War*). Its failure was followed by the rise to power of DIONȲSIUS I, a man of low birth, who by demagogic art got himself made sole commander against the Carthaginians, and although an indifferent general, was able to establish and maintain himself as ruler from 405 to 367. He made himself master of half Sicily and extended his conquests to the mainland of Italy. He had a taste for literature and actually won the prize at the Lenaea with a play, the 'Ransom of Hector'. He died from the effects of a drinking-bout in celebration of this victory. His brother-in-law DIŌN, a man of culture and high ideals (see his life in Nepos and in Plutarch), had introduced Plato to him, but the philosopher's teaching met with no success, and there is a legend that when Plato departed after a visit to Syracuse, Dionysius contrived to have him sold into slavery, from which Plato's friends rescued him. It was Dionysius I who built the great wall enclosing Syracuse and the heights of Epipolae.

DIONYSIUS II succeeded his father, and was at first much under the influence of Dion, who again induced Plato to visit Syracuse, but apparently without good results, for Dion was banished from Sicily. The misrule of Dionysius II made him unpopular, and in 357 Dion was able to conquer Syracuse and expel Dionysius, but was himself assassinated in 353, though he had tried to provide Syracuse with a liberal constitution. The relations of Plato with Dion and Dionysius form the subject of several of Plato's Epistles (see *Plato*, § 4). The death of Dion inspired the poem by Wordsworth that bears his name.

§ 3. *353* B.C. *to the Roman conquest in 212* B.C.

Syracuse now relapsed into a wretched condition, and Dionysius II recovered his throne. Thereupon the Syracusans appealed to Corinth for assistance. The mother-city in 344 sent them TIMOLEŌN (q.v.), who showed himself not only a consummate general (he quickly secured Syracuse from Dionysius and defeated the Carthaginians in 339 against tremendous odds at the Crīmīsus) but also a wise and moderate statesman. He restored peace to Sicily, and then retired into private life, remaining at Syracuse till his death (336) as the adviser of the people. There are lives of him by Plutarch and by Nepos.

But party rivalry in Syracuse had not been permanently quelled, and in 317 AGATHOCLĒS, a demagogue, established himself in power, and a few years later attacked other Siceliot towns. These called in the assistance of Carthage. In 311 Syracuse was besieged; whereupon Agathocles took the bold course of slipping out of the harbour with a small force, landing in Africa, and attacking Carthage itself. Though Agathocles failed to capture Carthage, the diversion served its purpose by relieving the pressure on Syracuse, and in 306 the Carthaginians agreed to a peace, by which they returned within their former boundaries in the west of the island.

After the intervention of Pyrrhus (q.v.) and the First Punic War (q.v.), Syracuse was left as the head of a small independent kingdom under HIERON II (269–16), a mild and just ruler, celebrated by Theocritus (q.v.) in Idyll xvi. His reign was the last golden age of Syracuse. He had allied himself with Rome against Carthage in the First Punic War and contributed to her final victory. After his death Syracuse forsook Rome and was besieged and captured by a Roman army under Marcellus in 212; in their defence the Syracusans were aided by the devices of Archimedes (q.v.), who perished when the city was taken.

Syracuse was probably the birthplace of Theocritus (q.v.).

Sȳ′rinx (*Sŭrigx*), see *Pan*.

Sy′rtēs, two wide gulfs on the N. coast of Africa, where the navigation was considered perilous in antiquity. The Greater Syrtis was off the coast of what we now call Tripoli, the Lesser off the coast of Tunis.

T

Ta′bula Ī′liaca, a relief in marble found at Bovillae near Albano in Italy, now in the Capitoline Museum, probably dating from the early Roman empire. It represents scenes from the Trojan War, and indicates the sources from which they are taken, among others the 'Iliou Persis' of Stesichorus (q.v.). The last picture represents Aeneas, with Ascanius and Anchises, leaving Troy, and bears the inscription Αἰνήας σὺν τοῖς ἰδίοις ἀπαίρων εἰς τὴν Ἑσπερίαν. From this it has been inferred that Stesichorus is the first authority for the legend of Aeneas's migration to Italy.

Ta′bula Peutingeriā′na, see *Maps*.

Ta′citus, PUBLIUS (?) CORNĒLIUS, whose praenomen is uncertain and birthplace unknown, was probably born *c.* A.D. 55 of a good Roman family, and probably died about the end of the reign of Trajan (A.D. 117). It is conjectured from the words in which he briefly refers to his career that he was a military tribune (*tribunus militum*, see *Army*, § 3) and held one of the offices of the vigintivirate (q.v.) under Vespasian, was quaestor under Titus, and praetor under Domitian (A.D. 88). In A.D. 78 he married the daughter of Cn. Julius Agricola (q.v.), consul and subsequently a distinguished governor of Britain. His 'Dialogus de Oratoribus' (q.v.) was probably written *c.* A.D. 81, when he was 26. He was employed abroad, probably as governor of some minor province, during A.D. 90–3, so that he and his wife were not present in 93 at his father-in-law's deathbed. On his return he found Rome suffering under Domitian's reign of terror, an experience which profoundly affected his later work as a historian. Early in Trajan's reign he published the 'Agricola' (q.v.), an encomium on his father-in-law, and the 'Germania' (q.v.), an account of the various tribes of the German people. Tacitus had studied rhetoric with zeal as a young man, and he became famous as a speaker. In A.D. 97 he delivered a funeral oration over Verginius Rūfus (a distinguished general whom his legions had tried to raise to the empire, and who was consul when he died), and in A.D. 100 spoke as counsel for the province of Asia against the ex-governor Marius Priscus; Pliny the Younger notes the eloquence and dignity of the latter speech. Tacitus succeeded Verginius Rufus as consul in 97 and was pro-consul of Asia *c.* 112–16.

Of his major works, the 'Histories' (q.v.), dealing with the reigns of the emperors from Galba to Domitian (a period forming part of his own lifetime), were published c. A.D. 104–9. Of these we have only the first four books and part of the fifth, covering the years 69–70. The 'Annals' (q.v.), which deal with the earlier period from the accession of Tiberius to the death of Nero, were composed later, c. 115–17. The surviving books are I–IV and fragments of V and VI (Tiberius), XI–XVI (Claudius and Nero; XVI is incomplete. These works show Tacitus to have been one of the greatest of historians, with a penetrating insight into character and the great issues of the period, and an unrivalled gift of vivid and incisive presentment. The impartiality which he claimed was, however, affected by a strong bias against the oppressiveness of the imperial system; and the emphasis is thrown on its evil, rather than on its good sides. In his portrait of Tiberius in particular, he appears to have treated uncritically the evidence regarding the vices attributed to that emperor.

The work of Tacitus seems to have aroused little admiration in the times that immediately followed, and to have received little notice in the Middle Ages. Boccaccio possessed a partial manuscript of the 'Annals' and 'Histories'. Thereafter Tacitus became a subject of unfailing interest to historians and politicians.

Ta'gēs, the legendary founder of Etruscan augural lore. He is represented as a grandson of Jupiter, who sprang from the ploughed earth in the form of a boy, and taught the Etruscans the interpretation of lightning and other signs.

Tala'ssus (or TALASSIO, or other slightly modified forms), probably the name of an old Italian god of marriage, invoked in the word *Talasse* in the refrain of wedding-hymns. It occurs in Catullus, lxi. 127.

Tā'los (*Tălōs*) in Greek mythology, (1) a bronze monster, made by Hephaestus and given by him to Minos or Europa (qq.v.). He used to guard the shores of Crete, clutching to himself any strangers who landed there and either making himself extremely hot or leaping with them into a fire so that they were destroyed. His one vulnerable spot was a vein or tube of blood, and when he tried to drive away the Argonauts (q.v.) from the shores of Crete, Medea by spells contrived his destruction through this. Cf. the Talus of Spenser's 'Faerie Queene', Bk. V. i. 12.
(2) The nephew of Daedalus (q.v.).

Ta'naquil, the legendary wife of Tarquinius Priscus (see *Rome*, § 2, and *Tarquin*). She is said to have encouraged her husband's ambition, and, when he was murdered, to have played an important part in securing the succession of Servius Tullius, thus defeating the designs of the sons of Ancus Marcius.

Ta'ntalus (*Tantalos*), in Greek mythology, the father of Pelops and Niobe (qq.v.). For his sin (either in serving his son's flesh to the gods, or stealing their nectar, or revealing their secrets, as variously related) he was punished in Hades by being set, thirsty and hungry, in a pool of water which always receded when he tried to drink from it, and under fruit trees whose branches the wind tossed aside when he tried to pick the fruit. Another account of his punishment is that a great stone was suspended over his head, threatening to overwhelm him, so that he was prevented from enjoying the banquet set before him.

Tare'ntum, an important city and harbour on the SW. coast of Calabria (Brundisium lies opposite to it on the NE. coast), in the great gulf that bears its name. It was founded by Lacedaemonians in 708 B.C. and after quarrelling with Rome in 282 B.C. and provoking the war between Rome and Pyrrhus, it was finally conquered by Rome in 272. It played an important part in the Second Punic War, being captured by Hannibal and recaptured by Fabius Cunctator. It lay in very fertile country. Its honey, olives, scallops, wool, and purple dye were sung by Horace, its pine-woods by Propertius.

Tarpē'ia, in Roman religion, probably originally a goddess of the lower world. about whom an explanatory myth subsequently arose. For this see *Rome*, § 2. She may have been the guardian spirit of the Tarpeian Rock at the SW. corner of the Capitoline Hill, from which criminals sentenced to death were hurled; or of the *gens Tarpeia*. According to Varro she was a Vestal, and libations were offered annually to placate her spirit.

Tarquin (*Tarquinius*), the name of two of the semi-legendary kings of Rome, who are thought to have been Etruscans, Tarquinius Priscus ('the Elder', so named by Livy), and Tarquinius Superbus (so named on account of his tyrannical character). See *Rome*, § 2. Tarquinius Priscus is said to have been murdered after a reign of thirty-eight years at the instance of the sons of Ancus Marcius. His wife was named Tanaquil (q.v.). For legends relating to Tarquinius Superbus, see *Lucretia*, *Brutus* (*L. Junius*), and *Sibylline Books*.

Tarquin and the whetstone. According to Livy, Tarquinius Priscus, being opposed in a project by the augur Attus Naevius, asked him, in order to ridicule his art, whether what he (Tarquinius) had in mind could be done or not. The diviner replied that it could. The king thereupon said that what he had in mind was to cut asunder a whetstone with a razor, and bade the augur accordingly do it. This the augur proceeded to do, a feat which redounded greatly to the honour of augury.

Ta'rtarus (*Tartaros*), in Greek mythology, a part of the underworld where the wicked suffer punishment for their misdeeds on earth; especially (in the early poets) those, such as Ixion and Tantalus (qq.v.), who have committed some direct outrage against the gods. See *Hades*.

Taxation, see *Athens*, § 11, *Rome*, § 14.

Tăy'getē (*Tăŭgetĕ*), one of the Pleiades (q.v.).

Tăy'getus (*Tăŭgetos*), a range of mountains on the W. of Laconia, separating it from Messenia.

Tecme'ssa (*Tekmēssa*), see *Ajax* (Sophocles' tragedy).

Teire'sias, see *Tiresias*.

Tei'sias (*Teisiăs*), see *Stesichorus*.

Te'lamon (*Telamōn*), in Greek mythology, king of Salamis, son of Aeacus (king of Aegina), and father of the greater Ajax and of Teucer (qq.v.). See also the reference to him under *Laomedon*.

Tele'gonus (*Tēlegonos*), according to post-Homeric legend the son of Odysseus by Circe (see *Odysseus*), and the slayer unwittingly of his father. According to Italian legend Telegonus founded Tusculum (q.v.) on the Alban Hills.

Tele'machus (*Tēlemachos*), in Greek mythology, the son of Odysseus and Penelope. For his history see 'Odyssey'. Post-Homeric legend made Telemachus marry Circe (q.v.). Homer represents him as diffident, lacking his father's energy and decision.

Te'lephus (*Tēlephos*), in Greek mythology, a son of Heracles (q.v.) and king of the Mysians. The Greeks on their way to Troy having landed in his country, he was wounded in battle by Achilles. To be cured of the wound he went to Troy to seek Achilles, having been told by the Delphic oracle that the wounder should also heal. It was found that the spear was meant, rust from which cured the wound.

'Telephus' was the title of a play of Euripides, not extant, the realism of which was much ridiculed by Aristophanes.

Te'llus, in Roman religion, the divinity of the Earth, associated with agricultural ceremonies such as the *Fordicidia* (q.v.).

Te'menos, in ancient Greece, a piece of land marked off and consecrated to a god, and excluded from profane uses.

Temples.

§ 1. *Greek Temples*

Greek temples were intended as dwelling-places for the god to whom each was dedicated and a shelter for his image (in some cases two or more gods were worshipped in one temple). The temples were at first of small dimensions, and even later seldom reached the colossal proportions of the temples of Egypt and the East. The temples of Artemis at Ephesus and of Hera at Samos (226 ft. and 183 ft. wide respectively) and the temple of the Olympian Zeus at Athens begun by Pisistratus (148 ft. wide) were exceptionally large. The Parthenon is 101 ft. wide. The most important part of a Greek temple was the *nāos* (L. *cella*) or chamber containing the image of the god, which stood on a pedestal and had an altar before it. The cella was as a rule roofed (temples in which the cella was open to the sky were known as 'hypaethral') and received light only through its folding doors. It was sometimes divided into aisles by rows of columns. There was usually an open antichamber or porch (*pronaos*) in front of the cella, and often an inner chamber (*opisthodomos*) behind it in which the treasure of the temple was kept. There was sometimes also an inner sanctuary entered only by the priest, known as the *adyton*. The front of the *pronaos*, sometimes also the rear face of the temple, more frequently in later temples all four sides, were flanked by colonnades supporting the architrave. The columns of these colonnades in archaic temples were made of wood, and in some temples survived to a late age; such were seen for instance by Pausanias (q.v.) at Olympia. They generally gave place to columns composed of stone drums, fluted after being put in position. These terminated in a capital (see *Architecture, Orders of*), on which rested the entablature, consisting of the architrave, frieze, and cornice. The stone architrave replaced the great wooden beams of the archaic temples on which lay the timbers of the roof. The triglyphs and metopes of the frieze in the Dorian Order (see *Architecture*) represent the ends of these timbers and the spaces between them. The front and back faces of the temple were surmounted by gables, the triangular space in which is known as the pediment (*tumpanon, tympanum*). The pediments and metopes (or the continuous frieze in the Ionian order) were frequently decorated with sculptures. A temple completely surrounded by a single row of columns is known as 'peripteral'. Temples are also distinguished by the number of columns on the front and back facades, as 'hexastyle', 'decastyle', &c. The whole temple was placed on a platform, approached by steps. The width of the temple was generally about one half its length, but there was great variety in the proportions, arrangement of columns, and details of design.

The earliest Greek temples, very primitive in construction, appear to date from the latter part of the 9th c. B.C. Religious architecture developed during the next three centuries, not only in Greece proper (especially at Delphi and Olympia), but also in Asia Minor (notably in the temples of Artemis at Ephesus and of Hera at Samos) and in Magna Graecia and Sicily (especially at Selīnus and Acragas). It reached its culminating point in the 5th c. in such temples as those of Aphaia at Aegina, of Bassae in the Peloponnese, and particularly in the group of temples erected on the Acropolis of Athens in the second half of the 5th c., the Parthenon, the Erechtheum, and the temple of Athene Nike (see *Acropolis* and *Parthenon*). The great architects of this period were Callicratēs, Ictīnus, and Mnēsiclēs.

§ 2. *Roman Temples*

The word 'temple' is derived from the Latin *templum*, which signified a quadrangular space marked out by the augurs, either on which to erect the *cella* or shrine of a god, or from which to take the auspices (see *Augurs*), or on which to carry on public business (e.g. the Rostra, q.v., and places where the Senate and popular assemblies met). A *templum* might also be a certain space in the sky, or the tent of an augur. A building consecrated to a deity was a 'templum' only if consecrated by the augur as well as by the pontiff. Otherwise it was merely an *aedes*. In the earliest temples that the Romans erected to the gods, they followed the Etruscan model, a quadrangular *cella* with columns in front of it; such was the early temple on the Capitol containing three *cellae*, for Jupiter, Juno, and Minerva.

Subsequently they imitated the various forms of Greek temple, introducing certain modifications, notably the circular temple (e.g. that of Vesta, perhaps a survival of the prehistoric form of hut, see Frazer on Ov. Fast. vi. 257), and the use of the arch, vault, and dome. A peculiarity of Roman temples is their high podium (or raised platform) with a flight of steps leading up to it at one end only. Pliny (N.H. xxxvi. 4) gives an impressive list of the masterpieces of Greek sculpture and painting that adorned the Roman temples in his day.

Te′rence (*Publius Terentius Āfer*) (195 or 185–159 B.C.), the second of the great Roman comedians whose works survive, was born at Carthage (not necessarily of a Phoenician family; it is more probable that he belonged to some African tribe). He was a slave, and was educated and freed at Rome by his owner, the senator Terentius Lūcānus. He received the patronage of Scipio Aemilianus (q.v.) and his circle, and it was said that they collaborated in his plays. An anecdote, perhaps apocryphal, relates that he appeared before Caecilius (q.v.) by order of the aediles to read his first play to him, when Caecilius was at dinner. Caecilius was soon so impressed that Terence was invited to the dinner.

Terence wrote six plays, 'Andria' (produced 166 B.C.), 'Hecyra' (165 and 160), 'Heauton Timorumenos' (163), 'Eunuchus' (161), 'Phormio' (161), 'Adelphoe' (160). They are dealt with herein under their titles. He then visited Greece, perhaps to gain personal knowledge of the people whom he presented in his dramas. He died in 159, but in what circumstances is unknown; according to one account he was lost at sea. There is a short life of him by Suetonius.

His plays with two exceptions are adapted from Menander, and he follows more closely than did Plautus his Greek originals, though sometimes combining portions of two plays. He thus represents scenes of the same Greek life as did Plautus, but without intermixture of Roman elements. But though the subjects (young men's love entanglements), and the characters are much the same as those found in some of the Plautine comedies, the spirit is different. Portraiture takes the place of caricature; the characters are more natural, less exaggerated, generally serious and sentimental; urbanity and courtesy prevail. There is none of the farcical element and little of the comic force and broad humour found in the plays of Plautus. Popular audiences found the comedies of Terence dull; they were suited for more cultivated circles. Their style is clear, simple, and finished. They contain many telling phrases which have become proverbial, such as 'quot homines, tot sententiae' ('Phormio'). The sung portion (*cantica*) is shorter than in the Plautine plays. There is less variety of metre; most of the verses are iambic or trochaic. The scansion is still mainly accentual. The prologues are for the greater part addressed to Terence's critics.

The works of Terence were much admired in antiquity; he is frequently quoted by Cicero and Horace. Caesar apostrophized him as 'dimidiate Menander' and 'puri sermonis amator'. In the Middle Ages his comedies, in spite of their lax morality, were adapted by Hrothswith, the abbess of the Benedictine convent of Gandersheim, for the use of her convent. Terence was much read in England in the 16th c. and even acted (e.g. the 'Phormio' by the boys of St. Paul's School before Cardinal Wolsey). His influence can be traced in early English comedy, and again in the comedy of manners of the Restoration, notably in Congreve, and later in Steele and Sheridan. Bentley's edition of Terence (1726) first elucidated the character of his metre.

Te′rēus, see *Philomela*.

Te′rminus. *Termini*, in Roman custom, were the boundary stones between properties, and were the object of an annual ritual (the *Termindlia*) on 23 February, when offerings (in early times of cakes and first-fruits only) were made at the stones. These rural *termini* had their State counterpart in the 'great god Terminus', the sacred boundary stone which stood in the great temple of the Capitoline Jupiter.

Terpa′nder (*Terpandros*), a famous musician of Lesbos, who probably flourished in the first half of the 7th c. B.C. He appears to have been adopted as a citizen of Sparta, and was the founder of the Spartan school of music. He is said to have replaced the lyre of four strings by one of seven strings, and to have invented the Aeolian and Boeotian *modes* (see *Music*, § 1), perhaps in fact merely popularizing forms of music peculiar to Lesbos and Boeotia. Terpander composed nomes (q.v.); the titles of some of these have descended to us. He is also said to have written other types of lyrical songs.

Terpsi′chorē, see *Muses*.

Tertu′llian (*Tertulliānus*), born at Carthage *c.* A.D. 150–160, was one of the greatest of the early Christian writers in Latin. He belonged to a pagan family and the circumstances of his conversion are unknown, but he became a Christian priest. He was learned in philosophy, science, and especially in law; and a man of an imperious, intractable character. Of his early works the most interesting is his 'Apologēticus' written in 197, in the form of the speech of an advocate addressed to the governors of Roman provinces, in which, with dignified eloquence, blending passion and irony, he seeks to secure for Christians protection from attacks of the populace and, when brought up for trial, from illegality of procedure. His vigorous protest refutes the charges brought against the Christian

sect, retorts them against their authors, and finally sums up the Christian doctrines as opposed to those of the philosophers. Other treatises are directed to regulating in minute detail the life of Christians in the midst of a pagan society, and show Tertullian's strong ascetic cast. He enjoined rules of life of great rigour, and refused pardon to persons, even though penitent, convicted of grave sin. At some period of his life he was won over to Montanism, the doctrine of a Phrygian sect, followers of Montānus, who was regarded by them as a prophet, and even as an incarnation of the Holy Ghost. The acceptance by Tertullian of the Montanist doctrines brought about a rupture, which apparently was never healed, between him and the Catholic church; and Tertullian's later writings show the influence of Montanism in a greater intolerance. He died in old age. Tertullian wrote with much rhetorical skill, and a rich and varied vocabulary; he created many new words, and helped to develop the form and terminology of theological Latin.

Te′thys (*Tēthūs*), according to Hesiod, a Titaness (see *Titans*), consort of Oceanus (q.v.).

Tetra′meter, see *Metre*, § 1.

Teubner, see *Editions*.

Teu′cer (*Teukros*), in Greek mythology, (1) a legendary king in the region of Troy, whose daughter Dardanus married (see *Troy*). From him the Trojans are sometimes called Teucri. (2) Son of Telamon (q.v.) and Hēsionē, and half-brother of Ajax (q.v.). He was called Teucer (i.e. Trojan) because his mother was daughter of Laomedon (q.v.). He was the greatest archer among the Greeks attacking Troy. On his return from the siege he was banished by his father as responsible for his brother's death. He went to Cyprus, where he founded the town of Salamis. See *Ajax* (Sophocles' tragedy).

Texts and Studies

§ 1. *Greek Texts*

The conditions under which Greek texts were in early times transmitted made it inevitable that errors and corruptions should creep in. The early epics and lyrics were composed, not to be read, but for recitation; the prose works on history or philosophy were similarly at first composed to be delivered orally. Until the end of the 6th c. B.C. the text of such works, depending mainly on oral tradition, must have been very uncertain. The development of Attic tragedy in the 5th c. produced a reading public and an organized book trade. But books were still scarce, and copies must often have been privately made. The form of the 5th c. manuscripts (see *Books*, § 2) written continuously without division of words or punctuation must have made it very difficult for a scribe, unless exceptionally educated, to avoid errors in copying. Bad copies became common. Dramatic works were subject to alteration by actors and producers, and in 330 B.C. Lycurgus, the Athenian statesman, carried a decree that an official copy of the works of the three great tragedians should be preserved in the public archives; there is no assurance that this official copy represented closely the original texts. There was at Athens in the 4th c. no school of criticism or philology to protect or recover their purity. Such a school was developed at Alexandria under the Ptolemies in the 3rd c., and another, at about the same time, at Pergamum (q.v.).

§ 2. *The Alexandrian School*

A large number of manuscripts were collected in the Alexandrian libraries. The first task was to catalogue them, and this was done by Callimachus (b. *c.* 310) in his 'Tables' (*Pinakes*), in which the works, it appears, were arranged in eight classes, Drama, Poetry, Legislation, History, &c. and attributed to their authors after inquiry into their authenticity. The authors whose works had survived in considerable bulk were then published in what were regarded as standard editions, together with separate treatises on the texts. These are probably the authors who were arranged by the critics in 'canons' (*kanones*) or lists, as typical representatives of their class. The principal scholars who carried out this work were Zenodotus (*fl. c.* 285), Aristophanes of Byzantium (*fl. c.* 195), and Aristarchus of Samothrace (*fl. c.* 180) (qq.v.). None of their writings survive except in excerpts found in later *scholia* (q.v.). Their first object was to detect and remove interpolations; in a less degree, and with increasing caution as knowledge increased, to introduce their own conjectures. The essence of their method was to respect the manuscript tradition. Their practice was carried on by their successors (see *Didymus*), though with less originality.

§ 3. *Greek texts in the Roman Age*

In the ensuing (or Roman) period, many of the readers of the ancient works were persons to whom Greek was a foreign tongue; and in consequence the demand was not so much for textual and literary criticism as for popular annotated edi-

tions, grammars and other aids to understanding antiquity. From the 2nd c. A.D., with the gradual extinction under the centralized rule of the Roman Empire of a society capable of understanding the ancient spirit of Greek culture, the texts of Greek literature entered to some extent on a period of decay. The demand for the old authors diminished, and their works in many cases disappeared or survived only in selections. Anthologies came into use and aided the process of disappearance. It must not be supposed that all the lost works which we lament to-day perished during this period. Many texts no longer extant, such as the complete Polybius and the 'Philoctetes' of Aeschylus and of Euripides, were still extant as late as the 10th c. But the old papyrus rolls (see *Books*, § 5) were wearing out and in the 4th c. A.D. began the transfer of their contents to vellum codices. Only those works which were considered valuable were chosen for this purpose. Thus certain plays of Aristophanes and a selection of the plays of the three tragedians, corresponding with those which have survived, were republished at this time. Such editions had a marginal commentary (*scholia*, q.v.), rendered necessary by changes in the Greek language. Treatises on various aspects of classical literature, accentuation, grammar, metre, language, were produced during the Roman period by such writers as Herodian, Julius Pollux, and Hephaestion (qq.v.).

§ 4. *Greek texts in the Byzantine Age*

This work was continued during the Byzantine Age (q.v.), and was far from useless. The lexicons of Hesychius, Suïdas, and Photius, the anthology of Stobaeus (including excerpts from five hundred writers), the poetical anthology of Cephalas (qq.v.), have preserved for us much that would have been lost. It was intelligent exponents of the past such as these, zealous collectors of manuscripts such as Arethas (see *Byzantine Age*), as well as the Greek wanderers and refugees of the 14th and 15th cc., who were the precursors of the Renaissance. Among the more important students of the latter part of this period, mention may be made of TZETZES (*c.* 1110– c. 1180), who wrote a long poem in accentual verse on miscellaneous literary and historical subjects (quoting more than 400 authors), a commentary on the 'Iliad', and other works giving valuable information on literary questions; and EUSTATHIUS, who was archbishop of Thessalonica 1175– c. 1192, wrote an important commentary on Homer, and endeavoured to protect the monastic libraries of his diocese. Although the 2nd to the 12th cc. were on the whole a period of loss (owing principally to the cessation of literary activity from the middle of the 7th to the middle of the 9th cc., and perhaps to the destruction of manuscripts in the fires that attended the capture of Constantinople by the Franks in 1204), they were not a period of serious corruption of ancient Greek literature. The next important stage in its history is the revival of learning at Byzantium in the 13th–15th cc. The scholars of this period wrote new editions of the surviving classics in which they showed themselves rash and incompetent revisers, apt to alter texts to suit their ideas of metre, and the process of corruption that they introduced was only arrested by the fall of Constantinople (1453). Their texts were imported into Italy and were for long accepted as authoritative.

Among our best Greek texts accordingly are those which were edited at Alexandria and subsequently protected from corruption by the scholia (based on the work of the Alexandrines) attached to them in the 2nd c. Our texts of the annotated plays of Aristophanes and Euripides are in consequence of a high quality. Poets in general fared better than prose writers, for the former were more valued and received more attention from scholars. Prose texts, where there was no metre to check the variant readings, have frequently come down to us in a far less perfect state. But by some happy accident the texts of certain prose writers, for instance Herodotus, Plato, Isocrates, and Demosthenes, have fared better. Thanks perhaps to the efforts of scholars at some period to restore their purity, by selection from among variant readings, the manuscripts in which these texts have reached us are, as appears from the evidence of papyri, of a high quality.

§ 5. *Latin texts to the barbarian invasions*

While Greek classics have been preserved for us by the work of the collectors and copyists of Byzantium, we owe the preservation of Latin classics mainly to the monasteries of the West. Until the latter half of the 2nd c. B.C. there was no organized system of transmitting texts at Rome, and early works were liable to be corrupted by the notes and emendations of those who used the manuscripts. The drama in particular was liable to alteration and recasting by theatrical producers. The influence of Crates (q.v.), a Pergamene grammarian who visited Rome about 169 B.C., and of the Alexandrian school, gave rise to a desire for authentic texts,

and a succession of scholars worked in this direction down to the Augustan period. On the other hand a popular revival of interest in the old authors during the Sullan period led to a demand for easy intelligible texts, especially of such authors as Plautus; so that vulgate editions containing variant readings grew up by the side of the authentic texts. This process was extended to later popular writers such as Virgil, and systematic recensions of their works became necessary, and were carried out with sound scholarship on the basis of the best manuscripts available, at least during the first three centuries of our era. The most important scholar associated with this period is M. VALERIUS PROBUS (of Bērȳtus in Syria, latter part of 1st c. A.D.), who revised Lucretius, Virgil, and Horace. The famous commentary on Virgil by Servius (Servius Marius Honoratus, q.v.) belongs to the 4th c. A.D.

§ 6. *Latin texts during the early Christian period*

The barbarian invasions of the 5th and 6th cc. brought about a revival of the waning interest in the classical authors among the educated classes, who were anxious to protect the national culture against this threat to their civilization. But the influence of the Christian Church, which had now become strong, was not wholly favourable to the preservation of the classics. In its view, the works of pagan authors were to be used only so far as necessary for education and in defence of the faith (the story that Pope GREGORY THE GREAT (589–604) did his best to suppress the works of Cicero, and burnt all the books of Livy that he could find, has no foundation). CASSIODORUS (q.v., c. 480–575), who established a monastery at Squillace where manuscripts were copied according to his directions, and ISIDORE OF SEVILLE (c. 570–636) author of 'Originēs', an encyclopaedia of classical learning, were the principal exponents of this attempt to reconcile classical literature with Christianity. From the 7th to the 14th c. classical authors were tolerated by the Church so far as required as a training for theology, or as morally sound or harmless. But a few more enlightened churchmen took a broader view and cultivated literature for its own sake.

In the 7th c. Irish missionaries played an important part in the history of texts. Coming to the continent and into touch with classical literature, they did much, by the monasteries they founded (e.g. that of Bobbio founded by Columban) and by their influence on other centres of learning, to stimulate the scholarly spirit and the copying of manuscripts. Their influence extended to Britain, and Anglo-Saxons in turn became missionaries and scholars. A special variety of Latin handwriting, known as 'Insular', is associated with the early scholarship of the British Isles. At the end of the 8th c. came the short-lived revival of learning in the monasteries organized by Charlemagne (742–814). Of this ALCUIN was the chief promoter. Alcuin (735–804) was born and educated at York, made the acquaintance of Charlemagne at Parma in 781, was placed by him at the head of a school attached to his court, and became abbot of Tours. He taught his monks to copy manuscripts; and France contributed greatly to the transmission of texts in the 9th and 10th cc. German monasteries under Charlemagne's revival also played an important part: many writers, e.g. Tacitus and Lucretius, would have entirely disappeared but for manuscripts preserved in these. Texts were copied with the greatest care by the monks of this period, notably at Bobbio and Monte Cassino, Cluny and Corbie; the work of the scribes was revised by the best scholars of the monasteries and special attention was paid to spelling, punctuation, and the collation of any available manuscripts. A legible script was in Charlemagne's time evolved in France, the 'Caroline minuscule', which is the parent of our modern writing and print. Our soundest texts—apart from the little that is attested by manuscripts of greater age—date from this time.

§ 7. *The Dark Ages*

The period from the 6th to the end of the 11th c. must be regarded, in the west, as a period of intellectual darkness, in spite of the efforts above described to keep alive here and there the flame of classical culture. During part of the period Hungarians were ravaging Germany and northern Italy; Danes were overrunning England; the Normans were established in France. The knowledge of Greek in particular had sunk to a low ebb in these centuries, although encouraged in the revival of Charlemagne. JOHANNES SCOTUS ERIGENA (*fl.* 850), who was a teacher at the court of Charles the Bald, is one of the few learned men of the period who shows some familiarity with the Greek language. The Latin author most frequently quoted and referred to is Virgil. The 'Aeneid and 4th Eclogue were allegorically interpreted, and St. Paul was believed in Italy to have shed tears over Virgil's tomb. Terence was imitated in the moral plays of Hrothswith, abbess of Gandersheim (*fl.* 984). Ovid, as

the poet of Love, was the popular Latin poet of the later Middle Ages. Horace, Lucan, Statius, Juvenal, and Persius were also known. The rhetorical and philosophical works of Cicero were often quoted (the 'Somnium Scipionis' as preserved by Macrobius was especially popular). Caesar, Livy, the elder Pliny, Sallust, the younger Seneca, Suetonius, and Valerius Maximus were also quoted, but less frequently.

§ 8. *Scholasticism*

Scholasticism, which was in essence an attempt to reconcile the doctrines of the Christian Church with Greek philosophical thought (particularly with Aristotle), and which became prominent from the latter part of the 11th c., involved a revival of interest in Greek literature, of a very limited character, that is to say as subservient to the study of logic. At this time and until the latter part of the 12th c. Aristotle was known in the West only in the Latin translations of, and commentaries on, a few of his works, by Boëthius and others. Plato similarly was known only through translations and Latin quotations. A great increase in the knowledge of Aristotle was brought about when the Arabic translations of his works by Avicenna (980–1037) and Averroës (1126–98) became known in Latin versions. Aristotle had long been studied by the Arabs, and Avicenna and Averroës were respectively his chief eastern and western exponents. Averroës, who was born at Cordova, wrote in Arabic abstracts of, and commentaries on, a number of Aristotle's works previously unknown in the west. Latin versions of these were made, chiefly at Toledo, from about 1200, and added greatly to the schoolmen's knowledge of the subject. From the latter part of the 13th c. the translations of Aristotle from the Arabic were superseded by translations made direct from the Greek. But ROGER BACON (*c.* 1214–94) censured the badness of all these Latin translations, and lamented the general ignorance of Greek. He himself wrote a Greek grammar and perhaps a lexicon. JOHN OF SALISBURY (d. 1180) the most learned schoolman of his time, author of the 'Metalogicus', in which the treatises of Aristotle on Logic are analysed, knew practically no Greek. BISHOP GROSSE-TESTE (d. 1253), an eminent promoter of Greek learning, probably himself had little familiarity with the language. THOMAS AQUINAS (*c.* 1225–74) though he cites many Greek authors, does not appear to have had any substantial knowledge of Greek. Latin was a living language for church and school purposes, but it departed increasingly from the classical standard, adopting new constructions and inventing terms for things unknown to the ancients. The scholastic Latin of the 14th c. was often atrocious.

§ 9. *The Italian Renaissance*

Unlike the more northern countries, where education was confined to the monasteries and priesthood, an educated laity had continued to exist in Italy, which in spite of the indifference of the Church to the classics and the invasions and wars of the 6th and following centuries, retained an interest in ancient literature, though it produced no authors or scholars. With the revival of learning in the 14th c. came an eager demand for readable texts at a time when scholarship fell far short of enthusiasm. Manuscripts were scarce and copyists incapable. Hence arose the corruptions which are found in the Latin manuscripts of the 14th–15th cc., known as *Itali*, *recentiores*, or *deteriores*. The Greek manuscripts imported into Italy by the Greek teachers of the period suffered a similar process of corruption. The revival, at this period, of interest in the classics is especially associated with the names of PETRARCH (1304–74) and BOCCACCIO (1313–75), both of them eager collectors of manuscripts; and later of Pope Nicholas V (1397–1455, founder of the Vatican collection) and of POGGIO BRACCIOLINI (1380–1459), also an ardent collector. Cosimo and Lorenzo de' Medici, who ruled over Florence 1434–64 and 1469–92 respectively, built up the famous Laurentian Library. MANUEL CHRYSOLORAS (c. 1350–1415), a Greek immigrant, was the first great teacher of Greek in Italy; and among the chief scholars of the period may be mentioned POLITIAN (Angelo Poliziano, i.e. of Montepulciano, 1454–94) and PICO DELLA MIRANDOLA (1463–94). To this period belongs the famous printer Aldus Manutius (see *Editions*).

§ 10. *Sixteenth to Eighteenth centuries*

In the 16th c. the main stream of classical learning is to be found in France and the Netherlands, and critical work on texts is principally associated with the names of the great scholars ERASMUS (1466–1536), BUDAEUS (1467–1540), JOSEPH SCALIGER (1540–1609), LIPSIUS (1547–1606), and CASAUBON (1559–1614), who ended his life in England and was buried in Westminster Abbey. For Henri Estienne (*Stephanus*), the French printer, see under *Editions*. The 17th and 18th cc. saw a large number of vulgate texts issued to meet the needs of a cultivated public, the chief scholars of the period being GRONOVIUS

of Hamburg (1611–71), NICHOLAS HEINSIUS of Holland (1620–81), and RICHARD BENTLEY (1662–1742). The last was famous for his proof that the epistles attributed to Phalaris (q.v.) were forgeries, for his editions of Horace and Terence, for his discovery of the use of the digamma in the Homeric poems, and generally for his skill in textual emendation.

§ 11. *Textual Recension and Palaeography*

Textual criticism, in the modern sense of the term, consists of two processes, recension and emendation. Recension is the selection, after examination of all available material, of the most trustworthy evidence on which to base a text. Emendation is the attempt to eliminate the errors found even in the best manuscripts. The modern method of textual criticism is based on the science of Palaeography, which originated in connexion with the history of the religious orders. As early as the 15th c. attention had been drawn to the forged Decretals of the popes, and to the legends and falsifications that had crept into Church history. This induced a more critical spirit in dealing with ecclesiastical documents, shown in the work of the body of Protestant divines known as the Magdeburg Centuriators, and in the edition of the 'Acta Sanctorum' begun by the Jesuit scholar John Bolland (1596–1655) of Antwerp. In 1675 the Bollandist Jesuit Papebroch, in his introduction to a volume of the 'Acta Sanctorum', aroused the hostility of the Benedictines by denying the authenticity of documents forming the credentials of certain Benedictine monasteries. The learned Benedictines of St. Maur took up the challenge by founding Palaeography, the classification of manuscripts according to their age, in the light of their handwriting and other indications. The Maurist monk JEAN MABILLON (1632–1707) in his 'De re diplōmatica' (*diplōmata* means 'official documents') laid down the principles of the new science, particularly in regard to Latin manuscripts. It was greatly advanced by LUDWIG TRAUBE (1861–1907). It was extended to Greek texts by BERNARD DE MONTFAUCON (1655–1741) another Benedictine, in his 'Palaeographica Graeca'. The application of critical methods to classical texts was developed principally by the Germans, FRIEDRICH WOLF (1759–1824, see *Homer*), IMMANUEL BEKKER (1785–1871), and KARL LACHMANN (1793–1851). Bekker devoted himself to the preparation of critical editions of Greek texts. The transfer of many manuscripts to public libraries as a result of the upheaval following the French

Revolution gave an opportunity for extensive collation. Bekker availed himself of this. He found that many received texts rested on an unsound foundation and that a mass of earlier material existed. He analysed existing manuscripts of an author, grouped them into families where one derived from another, but made the mistake of thinking that the oldest manuscript was necessarily the best; for a late manuscript may be a copy of a lost original and may be of superior value to its extant rivals though these are of older date than itself. Bekker was the editor of sixty volumes of Greek texts, and definitely improved these; he collated some 400 manuscripts. Lachmann went further than Bekker: he showed how, by comparison of manuscripts, it is possible to draw inferences as to their lost ancestors or archetypes, their condition, and pagination ('archetype' is the term used to signify the common ancestor from which two or more manuscripts have been copied). His most famous work was on Lucretius. He showed that the peculiarities of the three chief manuscripts all derived from a single archetype, containing 302 pages of 26 lines to the page, and enabled various transpositions to be made in the received text. GOTTFRIED HERMANN (1772–1848) should be mentioned for his valuable work on Greek metres and grammar, and for his editions of various Greek poets.

Among the great modern scholars of Greek must also be mentioned RICHARD PORSON (1759–1808), son of the parish clerk of East Ruston in Norfolk, who by the help of various protectors was educated at Eton and Trinity College, Cambridge, and became Regius Professor of Greek at Cambridge. He advanced Greek scholarship by his elucidation of Greek idiom and usage, by his knowledge of Greek prosody, and by his emendation of texts.

For famous editions of collections of the classics, see *Editions*.

Thā′lēs (*Thálēs*) of Miletus (b. c. 624 B.C.), the founder of the first Greek school of philosophy (q.v., § 1), and one of the Seven Sages (q.v.). He is said to have travelled in Egypt, to have advanced geometry and astronomy, and to have predicted a solar eclipse. His explanation of the universe was that all things are modifications of a single eternal and imperishable substance, which he held to be water. Thales left no written works.

Thalē′tās, a semi-legendary Cretan poet, perhaps of the 7th c. B.C., who came to Sparta, in order, it is said, to quell an epidemic, and there composed paeans and hyporchemata (qq.v.) for the festivals. He is of importance as perhaps having introduced Cretan metres into Greek poetry.

Thali′a (*Thal(e)íā*), see *Muses*.

Tha′myris (*Thamuris*), a legendary Thracian or Delphian poet and musician, an early victor in a contest at Delphi, where he sang a hymn in honour of Apollo. According to Homer (Il. ii. 594 et seq.) he met the Muses at a place called Dorion in Messenia and challenged them in song: 'but they in their anger maimed (i.e. perhaps 'blinded') him, moreover they took from him his high gift of song, and made him to forget his harping.' The myth perhaps reflects the early introduction of religious poetry into the Peloponnese. Milton (P.L. iii. 35) refers to

Blind Thamyris and blind Maeonides.

Thargē′lia, see *Festivals*, § 5.

Thā′sos (*Thásos*), a rocky island off the coast of Thrace, first occupied by Phoenicians and later (at the end of the 8th c.) colonized by Parians (see *Archilochus*). It became wealthy from its own gold mines, and from the mines which its inhabitants worked on the neighbouring mainland. It joined the Delian Confederacy (see *Athens*, § 4) but twice revolted. It passed under the dominion of Sparta and then of Philip of Macedon, and was freed by the Romans. It was the birthplace of Polygnotus (q.v.).

Theaete′tus (*Theaitētos*), a dialogue by Plato dealing with the nature of knowledge. In the introductory scene, Theaetetus himself (he was an Athenian mathematician) is reported to have been brought home mortally wounded from the Corinthian War, in which he has shown great gallantry. This recalls a conversation between him, as a young man, and Socrates, and this conversation, which a friend relates, furnishes the substance of the dialogue. Various definitions of knowledge are considered, such as that 'knowledge is sensible perception', but are all found wanting; the problem is left unresolved, and is resumed in the 'Sophist' (q.v.). In the course of the dialogue we have Socrates' famous comparison of himself to a midwife, who brings to birth the thoughts of others.

Thea′genēs (*Theāgenēs*) **and Chariclē′a** (*Charikleia*), an alternative title of the 'Aethiopica' of Heliodorus; see *Novel*.

Theatre.

§ 1. *The Greek Theatre*

The Greek theatre appears to have been originally designed for the performance of dithyrambic choruses in honour of Dionysus. The centre of it was the *orchêstrā* ('dancing-place'), a circular space, in the middle of which stood the *thumelē* or altar of the god. Round more than half of the *orchestra*, forming a kind of horse-shoe, was the *theātron* ('seeing-place') proper, circular tiers of seats, generally cut out of the side of a hill, later made of stone or marble. Behind the orchestra and facing the audience was the *skēnē*, originally a wooden structure, a façade with three doors, through which, when the drama had developed from the dithyrambic chorus, the actors made their entrances. In front of this in course of time was probably added a stage, somewhat raised above the level of the orchestra. A special contrivance (*mēchanē*, machine), perhaps a sort of crane, served for the appearances of gods high above the stage. There was a device by which what was happening behind the scene could be revealed to the spectators (e.g. in Aesch. 'Agamemnon', Clytemnestra standing over the dead bodies of Agamemnon and Cassandra). This (known as the *ekkuklēma*) was probably a platform on wheels which could be rolled out through the central door of the *skene*. By another convention a change of scene (such as occurs in Aesch. 'Eumenides' and a few other tragedies) was indicated by means of large wooden prisms (*periaktoi*) turning on pivots, on each face of which was represented something (such as a tree) typical of a particular kind of scenery. The chorus entered by passages (*eisodoi*) between the *skene* and the *orchestra* on either side, and stood on the *orchestra*; the flute-player who accompanied them probably stood on the steps of the *thumele*. At some later date the wooden structures behind the orchestra were replaced by stone. There was no curtain. The large theatres were open to the sky, but the Odeum (q.v.) for musical performances was a smaller structure with a roof. For the actors and their dress, see under *Comedy*, § 2, *Tragedy*, § 2. See also *Dionysus* (*Theatre of*).

Glimpses of the lighter side of theatre-going may be found in the 'Characters' of Theophrastus: the loquacious man who talked so much that his neighbours could not follow the play; the stingy man who availed himself of a free day to bring his children; the shameless man who took advantage of his foreign guests to get admitted without paying; the stupid man, who fell asleep during the play and was left alone in the theatre when the audience had gone.

§ 2. *The Roman Theatre*

There was no permanent theatre at Rome until Pompey built one in the Campus Martius out of the spoils of the Mithridatic War. This was of stone and could accommodate 40,000 spectators. (It was in the *Curia* or hall adjoining it that Caesar was assassinated). Two other stone theatres were subsequently built in Rome, both in the Campus Martius, that of L. Cornelius Balbus, dedicated in 13 B.C., and that known as the theatre of Marcellus, built by Augustus and named after his adopted son. The plays of Plautus and Terence, Ennius and Pacuvius, were originally performed on temporary stages in the Forum or Circus Maximus, with circles of wooden seats. Indeed, a decree proposed by Scipio Nasica in 154 B.C. even forbade seats. The discomfort in which the audience witnessed performances in the theatre or circus is shown by a passage in Ovid (Ars Amat. i. 141 and 157–8) where he refers to the narrow space allotted to each spectator and to the knees of those behind pressing in the backs of those in front. Pliny in his 'Natural History' (xxxvi. 24) describes the strange wooden revolving theatre of C. Curio, which was in fact an amphitheatre of which the two halves could be turned back to back. Roman theatres had a semicircular auditorium (*cavea*), whereas that of the Greeks was a segment of a circle larger than a semicircle. The Roman stage, moreover, was longer and deeper. There were seats in the orchestra, reserved for senators, priests, and officials. The *equites* (see *Equestrian Order*) sat in the front rows of the *cavea*. The chorus in the tragedies of Ennius, Pacuvius, and Accius, unlike the chorus of the Greek drama (see § 1 above), stood on the stage, and could come and go. This was more realistic, but the functions of the chorus had changed and the great lyrical poetry of the Greek drama had come to an end. Stage scenery was first introduced in 99 B.C. The stage curtain was lowered to reveal the stage, instead of being drawn up, as with us. The players were slaves or freedmen, trained to the profession, and organized in companies (*grex, caterva*) under the direction of a manager (*dominus gregis, actor*). Their remuneration, paid by the magistrate who gave the games, gradually rose, and although actors were originally despised, the examples of Roscius and Aesopus (qq.v.) show that popular actors might rise to positions of wealth and distinction. Female parts (except in mimes and late comedy) were played by men. The type of character was indicated at first by wigs (white for old men, red for slaves, etc.) and later by masks. Tragic actors wore long flowing robes and high buskins (*cothurni*), comic actors wore the ordinary dress and the *soccus* or low-heeled shoe. There was a dearth of actors till well into the 2nd c. B.C. Parts had to be doubled; Plautus had only three to five actors, which accounts for some awkward passages in his plays.

Thē'baid (*Thēbāis*), a Latin epic poem in twelve books of hexameters by Statius (q.v.). The author spent twelve years on the work and published it about A.D. 92.

The subject is the expedition against Thebes in support of the attempt of Polynices to recover the throne from his brother Eteocles (see *Oedipus*). The first three books deal with the preliminaries of the war—the arrival of Polynices and Tydeus at Argos, the embassy of Tydeus to Thebes and the attempt to destroy him in an ambush (one of the best passages in the poem), and the prophecy of Amphiaraus. Books IV, V, and VI include the consultation of the seer Tiresias, the Argive march on Thebes, the episode of Hypsipyle (q.v.), and the funeral games for the child Opheltes. With Book VII the fighting begins, after a vain attempt by Jocasta at mediation. Amphiaraus is swallowed up by the earth. The fighting continues through Books VIII, IX, and X, with many incidents—the death of Ismene's lover Atys, the grim episode of Tydeus and Melanippus, the feats of Hippomedon, the devotion of Menoeceus, the death of Capaneus by a thunderbolt. Book XI contains the fatal combat of Eteocles and Polynices, Creon's refusal of burial to the latter, and Jocasta's suicide. Book XII completes the story with the burial of Polynices by his wife and Antigone, the intervention of Theseus, and the death of Creon. At the end, Statius takes leave of his long task, and with a humble reference to Virgil speculates whether his own work will endure.

Statius follows epic tradition in adopting the machinery of divine interference, and in his catalogues of the forces, funeral games, &c. He imitates Virgil in incidents and language. And there is an excess of mythological lore. The occasional vigorous pieces of narrative hardly carry the reader through the tedium of a long poem.

Thē'bais (Gk. *Thēbāis*, L. *Thēbāis*), see *Epic Cycle* and *Thebaid*.

Thebes (*Thēbai*), (1) the principal city in Boeotia. For its early legendary history see *Cadmus, Antiope,* and *Oedipus*. In historical times Thebes first comes into prominence as supporting the Persian cause in the Persian Wars (q.v.) and supplying a base from which Mardonius acted in the campaign of Plataea. She became the leader of the confederacy of Boeotian towns (for its constitution see under

Boeotia) and the bitter enemy of Athens, which supported Plataea, a Boeotian town, in its refusal to yield its independence. By her seizure of Plataea in 431 Thebes precipitated the Peloponnesian War; in 424, by her victory at Delium, she defeated the plan of Demosthenes for the subdual of Boeotia; and Thebes was one of the States which, on the fall of Athens in 404, urged the destruction of the city. After the Peloponnesian War came the period of rivalry of Thebes and Sparta for the supremacy in Greece, a struggle in which, under the leadership of Pelopidas and Epaminondas (qq.v.), Thebes gained the advantage and a temporary hegemony (see *Sparta*, § 4). Not only did she repress and humiliate Sparta, but she extended her power in the north, bringing parts of Thessaly under her protectorate and establishing her authority at the court of Macedon (see *Pelopidas*). It was at this time (368 B.C.) that Philip, the youngest son of Amyntas, king of Macedon, was sent as a hostage to Thebes and brought up under Epaminondas. The death of the latter at the battle of Mantinea (362, see *Sparta*, § 4) brought the hegemony of Thebes to an end. She promoted the designs of Philip of Macedon (q.v., § 3) on Greece by inviting his interference in the struggle between the Amphictyonic League and Phocis; but at a later stage, when in 338 Philip was threatening Athens, Thebes, dreading the effect on herself which the subjugation of her neighbour would entail, allied herself with Athens and suffered with her the defeat of Chaeronea. Philip dissolved the Boeotian Confederacy and established a Macedonian garrison in the citadel of Thebes. Shortly after the accession of Alexander the Great (q.v., § 1) the Thebans revolted, but Alexander descended swiftly upon them and carried Thebes by assault. By decision of the congress at Corinth the detested city was razed to the ground (335). It was rebuilt by Cassander (see *Macedonia*, § 2) and existed throughout Roman times.

Pindar (q.v.) was born at Thebes; Corinna (q.v.) at Thebes or Tanagra. In the destruction of Thebes, the house of Pindar was spared by Alexander's order. This incident is referred to in Milton's sonnet 'When the assault was intended to the city'.

See also *Cadmea*.

(2) The Greek name of a city of Upper Egypt, on the site of which now stands the village of Luxor. It became the capital at the time of the 12th dynasty (c. 2000 B.C.), supplanting Memphis, the earlier capital, and attained great splendour

under the kings of the 18th–20th dynasties (*c.* 1400–1100 B.C.). Homer calls it 'hundred-gated' and speaks of two hundred warriors with horses and chariots sallying from each gate. It is now famous for the remains of its great temples and its royal tombs.

The′mis, according to Hesiod a Titaness (see *Titans*). In Homer she is an officer of Zeus; she summons the gods to assembly and keeps order at their banquets, and summons and dismisses assemblies of men. Later she is a personification of justice. She is the mother of Prometheus (q.v.) and by Zeus mother of the Seasons (q.v.), and, in one version, of the Fates (q.v.).

Themi′stius (*Themistios*) (*fl. c.* A.D. 360)), a rhetorician of Paphlagonia, who lived at Constantinople under the emperors from Constantius II to Theodosius and enjoyed their favour; he also made a sojourn at Rome. He was for a short time prefect of Constantinople under Theodosius and held other distinguished positions. He was surnamed 'Euphradēs', 'the eloquent'. Thirty-three of his orations survive, many of them panegyrics on the emperors. He wrote commentaries on, and paraphrases of, Aristotle's works, some of which are extant. He was himself a pagan, but advocated toleration of other religious beliefs.

Themi′stoclēs (*Themistoklēs*), a celebrated Athenian statesman and commander, who rose from a humble station to be archon in 493 B.C. and strategus in 490, a bold, resourceful, and eloquent man. He induced the Athenians to concentrate on strengthening their fleet, and to devote the produce of the Laurium silver mines to the purpose. He took a prominent part, as strategus, in the second Persian War (q.v.) and secured for his country the victory of Salamis. He fortified the Piraeus and Athens in spite of the opposition of Sparta, which he artfully defeated; but about 472, having come into conflict with Cimon (q.v.), he was ostracized. He took refuge at Argos, where he stirred up trouble for Sparta. His intrigues with Pausanias (q.v.) were discovered, and he was on the demand of Sparta proscribed at Athens and his property confiscated. He found an asylum, first at the court of Admētus, king of the Molossians, then in Asia Minor, and on the accession of Artaxerxes (464) was loaded with honours by that monarch. It is said, but seems improbable, that Themistocles had offered the king his services against Greece. He died at Magnesia in 459. His remains were brought home, it is said, and buried outside the walls of the Piraeus, the fortress that he had created. Lives of him were

written by Plutarch and by Nepos, and there is a famous sketch of his character in the first book of Thucydides (ch. 138).

Napoleon, in his letter to the Regent formally surrendering himself in 1815 to the British, compares himself to Themistocles at the hearth of Admetus.

Theocly′menus (*Theoklǔmenos*), in Greek mythology (1) a seer, descended from Melampus (q.v.). See *Odyssey* (under Bk. xx). (2) See *Helen* (Euripides' play).

Theo′critus (*Theokritos*) (*fl. c.* 270 B.C.) was born probably at Syracuse and spent part of his life in Cos and at Alexandria under Ptolemy Philadelphus. His extant poems, generically known as Idylls (q.v.), include half a dozen pastoral pieces (i, iii, iv, v, vi, and x in the usual arrangement of his poems; the authenticity of viii and ix is doubted); in these he presents, in the dramatic form of contests or dialogues between rustics, and with charming freshness and vivacity, the old country life of Sicily. The first of them contains a beautiful 'Lament for Daphnis', a dirge imitated in the 'Adonis' of Bion, and in the 'Bion' of Moschus (?), and the prototype in later times of such elegies as Milton's 'Lycidas', Shelley's 'Adonais', and M. Arnold's 'Thyrsis'. Two of the Idylls (xiv and xv) have their scenes laid in towns, and recall the mimes of Herodas; the second of these is the famous 'Adōniazūsae', in which the poet amusingly pictures the incidents of a visit by two women to the festival of Adonis at Alexandria, closing with a hymn which they hear sung in honour of Adonis and Aphrodite. Idyll ii tells the story of the unhappy love of Sīmaetha and her unsuccessful incantations to recover her lover. Other Idylls deal with mythological subjects: the amusing tale of the love of Polyphemus for Galatea (xi), the carrying off of Hylas (xiii), the fight between Pollux and Amycus (xxii), the first exploit of Heracles (xxiv). Two are addresses to Hieron II of Syracuse (xvii) and Ptolemy II (xvi), and one (xxviii) is a pleasant poetical epistle accompanying the present of a distaff to the wife of a friend. In Idyll vii the author under the name of Simichidas sings of the loves of a certain Arātus of Cos (not Arātus of Soli, the poet). A number of epigrams are also attributed to Theocritus. He wrote chiefly in hexameters and generally in the Doric dialect. His pastoral poems are his most characteristic work, and he is regarded in virtue of them as the father of this type of poetry. In it he was never equalled, for he was perfectly natural, and depicted peasants, animals, and the countryside with truth and love.

Theodo'sius, see *Britain*, § 2.

Theo'gnis, of Megara, an elegiac poet, who flourished probably in the second half of the 6th c. B.C., at a time of violent political strife between the aristocracy and the plebeians of his city. Theognis himself was an aristocrat, and the poems attributed to him, of which we possess some 1,400 lines, reflect the vicissitudes of the struggle. The best-known part of his work consisted of 'Elegies to Kyrnos', a young friend. They are moral exhortations enjoining piety and moderation in conduct, philosophical reflections on life and its evils, and expressions of hatred and contempt for the populace, frequently marked by energy and passion. The text that has come down to us is very corrupt.

Theo'gony (*Theogoniā*), a poem in hexameters attributed by many authorities in antiquity and in modern times to Hesiod, while others (in particular Pausanias) think it the work of an imitator.

The poem (which refers in its exordium to Hesiod apparently as an earlier writer) recounts the mythological history and genealogy of the gods, beginning with primordial Chaos, followed by Uranus and Ge (qq.v.) and their children (the Titans, Cyclopes, and other giants), Cronus (q.v.) and his children, the advent of Zeus to power by the defeat of the Titans and of the monster Typhoeus (q.v.), and a list of the offspring of Zeus and various goddesses. The remainder of the poem (from line 929), perhaps consisting of later additions, forms a continuation of divine genealogy, in which are enumerated with less method the children of various unions of gods with goddesses, and of gods and goddesses with mortals. The last two lines (beginning, Νῦν δὲ γυναικῶν φῦλον ἀείσατε) point to the 'Catalogue of Women' (q.v.) as a sequel, but they may be a connecting link added later.

The'ōn of Alexandria (5th c. A.D.), a philosopher and mathematician, the last known member of the Museum (q.v.), and father of Hypatia (see *Neoplatonism*). There were others of the same name, notably a grammarian who flourished under Augustus.

Theophra'stus (*Theophrastos*) (c. 371–c. 287 B.C.), of Eresus in Lesbos, the pupil and friend of Aristotle and his successor as head of the Peripatetic school of philosophy. He was the teacher of Dinarchus and of Demetrius of Phalerum (qq.v.). He wrote in Greek on a great variety of subjects, and we still possess his 'Inquiry into Plants' (*Historia Plantārum*) and 'Growth of Plants' (*De Causis Plantarum*), a short treatise on 'Metaphysics', and numerous fragments from other philosophical and scientific works. His treatise 'On Style' was studied and quoted by Cicero. He is best known by a minor work, his 'Characters' (*Charactēres*, i.e. 'distinctive marks') in thirty chapters, perhaps an abridgement of a larger work, in which he describes with remarkable vivacity and keenness of observation various types of contemporary character. Each 'Character' consists of the definition of some failing, such as tactlessness, followed by a list of the things that the tactless person will do. This has its humorous side, in the absurd results of the various failings, simply stated with restrained and unobtrusive art, as when at bedtime the children of the loquacious man say to him 'Talk to us, daddy, that we may go to sleep.' The 'Characters' delineate in a concise form types that Menander was at about the same time presenting in the New Comedy, and they incidentally throw an amusing light on contemporary life at Athens. They were intended as aids to the study of rhetoric. As a work of literature, they were revived by the Latin translation and commentary of Casaubon (1529). They had a considerable influence on 17th c. English literature and were imitated by various authors, notably by Joseph Hall ('Characters of Virtues and Vices', 1608), Sir Thomas Overbury ('Characters', 1614), John Earle ('Microcosmographie', 1628), and by Samuel Butler (1612–80). In France they were imitated by La Bruyère (1645–96) in his famous 'Caractères'. The will of Theophrastus, making provision for the continuance of the Peripatetic school, is preserved in Diogenes Laertius.

Theopo'mpus (*Theopompos*), of Chios, born in 376 B.C., a pupil of Isocrates, a successful sophist, and the friend of Philip and Alexander of Macedon. In spite of an agitated life (he was exiled from Chios, restored, and re-exiled, and barely escaped death at the order of Ptolemy I) he wrote much, especially a 'Hellenica' (history of Greece, 411–394) and a vast 'Philippica' (history of Philip of Macedon). Only fragments of his work survive.

Theo'ric Fund. The *Theōrikon* was a grant of two obols distributed to the poorer citizens of Athens to enable them to pay for admission to the theatre at the Dionysiac festivals. It was introduced in the time of Pericles, suppressed when Athens was impoverished by the misfortunes of the Peloponnesian War, and revived by the demagogue Agyrrhius in 394 (when the grant was raised to one drachma a head). Under the administration of

Eubulus (q.v.), all surplus of revenues was carried to a Theoric Fund, and a law was passed prohibiting the diversion to military purposes of any part of the Fund. Demosthenes secured the abolition of the system after Chaeronea.

Theoxe′nia, a festival held at Delphi and in other places in Greece, in honour of various gods, who were regarded as guests at the feast. There is in the British Museum a Greek vase of about 480 B.C. in which the Dioscuri (q.v.) are represented descending on horseback to take part in such a feast, which is indicated by a couch set for them to recline on. Cf. *Lectisternium*.

Thēra′menēs (*Thērámenēs*), an Athenian politician of moderate oligarchical views, who came into prominence at the time of the revolution of 411 B.C. (see *Athens*, § 5). His moderation at a time of strife between the extreme oligarchs and democrats gave his policy an appearance of shiftiness, and he was known as 'Cothurnus' (the stage boot which could be worn on either foot). He was the author of the constitution, combining oligarchic and democratic elements, which replaced the Four Hundred. In 406 he was a trierarch at Arginusae and one of those most instrumental in having the Athenian generals at that battle condemned to death. Later he was one of the Thirty tyrants, but his opposition to extreme measures brought him into conflict with Critias (q.v.), and he was put to death in 404. His statesmanship is praised by Aristotle.

Thē′riaca, see *Nicander*.

Thermo′pylae (or *Pylae*), a narrow pass between the spurs of Mt. Oeta and the sea, on the boundary of Thessaly and Locris, the gate of eastern Greece. It was the scene of the great defence of Leonidas at the time of the Persian invasion of 480 B.C. (see *Persian Wars*). It was again successfully held by an Athenian force against Philip of Macedon in 353 B.C., but was surrendered to him by Phalaecus of Phocis in 346. See also *Amphictyony*, and *Jason of Pherae*. The features of the place have now greatly changed : the sea has receded from the foot of the mountains and there is a wide level space instead of the ancient 'pass'.

Thē′ron (*Thērōn*), tyrant of Acragas (see *Agrigentum*) in Sicily from 488 B.C., father-in-law of Gelon (see *Syracuse*, § 1). He took part with the latter in the great defeat of the Carthaginians at Himerā (480), and was celebrated by Pindar in two of his Olympian odes.

Thersī′tēs, in the 'Iliad', the most ill-favoured of the Greeks who formed the Trojan expedition, a rancorous reviler of the leaders. For his death, see under *Achilles*.

Thēsē′um, see *Theseus*.

Thē′seus, in Greek mythology, son of Aegeus (a legendary king of Athens, son of Pandīon), or of Poseidon (q.v.), and of Aethra daughter of Pittheūs king of Troezen. When Aegeus left Aethra at Troezen, he placed his sword and sandals under a great rock, and bade Aethra, when the son whom she should bear was strong enough to move the rock, to send him with those tokens to Athens. Theseus, her son, in due course lifted the rock, took the tokens, and set out for Athens by the land route. On the way he destroyed various brigands and monsters, in particular Sinis who used to tie his victims to two pine trees which he bent to the ground and then allowed to fly up tearing the victim in two, Sciron (q.v.) who used to make passers-by wash his feet and while they did so kicked them into the sea, and Procrustes (q.v.). On his arrival at Athens, Medea (see *Argonauts*), who had taken refuge with Aegeus, tried to poison him, but Aegeus recognized his son in time and saved him. Medea was obliged to fly from Athens, with her son Mēdus, and returned to Colchis. Theseus then destroyed the bull which Heracles had brought from Crete (see *Heracles, Labours of*) and which was devastating Marathon. On this occasion he was hospitably entertained by a poor old woman named Hecale, an incident celebrated by Callimachus in the poem which bears her name. The next adventure of Theseus was more serious. Minos (q.v.) of Crete had imposed on Athens a yearly tribute of seven youths and seven maidens, to be devoured by the Minotaur. Theseus volunteered to accompany these and to deliver his country from the tribute. Ariadne daughter of Minos fell in love with him, and gave him a thread by which he was able to find his way in the Labyrinth, kill the monster, and come out again. He sailed away in safety, carrying Ariadne with him, but in the island of Dia (Naxos) deserted her. There Ariadne was found by Dionysus, who wedded her. Theseus had arranged with his father that if he returned successful, his ship should have white sails ; otherwise the sails would be black. Now he forgot this, and his ship approached Athens with black sails. Aegeus seeing these, and thinking his son dead, drowned himself (cf. a similar incident in the Old French romance of Tristram and Iseult and in Swinburne's 'Tristram of Lyonesse').

Theseus was now king of Athens. He defeated an invasion of the Amazons, and the Amazon queen Hippolyte (or Antiope) became his wife. Their son was Hippolytus. Later Theseus married Phaedra, sister of Ariadne (for the tragic story of her love for Hippolytus, see under the name of the latter). When Creon refused burial to the dead chieftains who had unsuccessfully attacked Thebes (see *Oedipus*), Theseus espoused the cause of Adrastus, marched with an army against Creon, and gave burial to the slain. See also under *Oedipus at Colonus*. Theseus was a friend of Heracles (q.v.) and gave him asylum after he had killed Megara and his children. He is also represented as the friend of Pirithöus (see *Centaurs*), king of the Lapithae; he even descended with him to Hades to help him to carry off Persephone. For this crime he suffered imprisonment in Hades until rescued by Heracles. He is also said to have carried off Helen when she was a child; but she was rescued by her brothers Castor and Pollux (see *Dioscuri*). Theseus was finally driven from Athens by rebellions, took refuge in Scyros, and died or was murdered there. After the Persian Wars, Cimon (q.v.) in obedience to an oracle, brought home from Scyros the bones of a gigantic man, which he believed to be those of Theseus, and buried them at Athens in a sanctuary, the Theseum, which became famous. The name has been given traditionally to a small and well-preserved temple NW. of the Acropolis, on which are sculptured scenes from the life of Theseus; but this temple is thought to have been a shrine of Hephaestus.

Theseus, though probably a purely legendary person, was believed by the Athenians to have been one of their early kings; they attributed to him the 'Synoecism' or union of the scattered Attic communities in a single state. There is a life of him by Plutarch, who brings together the various legends.

Thesmopho'ria, see *Festivals*, § 5.

Thesmophoriazu'sae (*Thesmophoriazousai*, 'The women celebrating the Thesmophoria'), a comedy by Aristophanes, produced in 411 or 410 B.C.

The women are about to celebrate their private festival, the Thesmophoria, from which men were excluded. Euripides has learnt that, angered at his revelations of their characters and misdeeds, they intend to plot his death. He tries to persuade the effeminate poet Agathon to disguise himself as a woman, attend the rites, and plead the cause of Euripides. Agathon refuses. Whereupon Mnesilochus, a comic

elderly relative by marriage of Euripides, gallantly offers himself in his place. He is shaved and suitably accoutred, and goes to the ceremony. Speeches are made against Euripides; Mnesilochus takes up his defence by pointing out how much worse things he might truthfully have said about women. The general indignation he causes is interrupted by the arrival of news that a man has got into the festival in disguise. Search is made and Mnesilochus is discovered and put under guard. Imitating a hero of Euripides, Mnesilochus writes a message on a votive tablet of the temple and throws it out. He assumes the character of Helen, and Euripides appears as Menelaus; there is a recognition scene, all in good Euripidean style, but the guard prevents the reunion of the pair. A Scythian policeman now arrives and ties up Mnesilochus. Euripides appears as Perseus, and Mnesilochus becomes the Andromeda of Euripides' tragedy, tied to her rock; but the policeman stops the attempted rescue. Euripides now proposes terms to the women; he will never again speak ill of them if they will release his relative. They agree. But the Scythian remains to be dealt with. This is accomplished through a pretty dancing-girl, who lures away the policeman from his duty, and Mnesilochus escapes.

Thesmo'thetae (*Thesmothetai*), see *Athens*, § 2 and *Judicial Procedure*, § 1.

The'spis, a semi-legendary Greek poet connected with Icaria in Attica, who flourished about 534 B.C. (when he is recorded as having been victor in a contest). He is said to have introduced an actor into performances which had hitherto been given by a chorus alone, this actor impersonating a legendary or historical character and delivering a previously composed speech. He was generally regarded by authors later than Aristotle as the inventor of tragedy. Horace (A.P. 275–7) records a tradition that Thespis took his plays about on wagons to be acted by persons with their faces smeared with wine-lees. It is also said that he introduced the use of linen masks. Though there may be some truth in the tradition about the wagons, the statement regarding wine-lees may arise from confusion as to the origins of tragedy and comedy (qq.v.). It has been suggested (Pickard-Cambridge) that the name 'Thespis' is an assumed name, suitable for a poet, derived from Od. i. 328–9, Τοῦ δ' ὑπερωιόθεν φρεσὶ σύνθετο θέσπιν ἀοιδὴν | κούρη Ἰκαρίοιο.

Thessaly (*Thessalia*), the largest division of Greece, in the NE. of the country, bounded on the N. by the range of mountains which terminates on the Aegean with Mt. Olympus, on the W. by Mt. Pindus, on the S. by Mt. Othrys. Its chief river was the Pēnĕus, flowing into the Aegean through the beautiful gorge of Tempē, between Mt. Olympus and Mt. Ossa. Mt. Pelion stood S. of Ossa, abutting on the sea. The great Thessalian plain produced cereals, and was a centre of horse-breeding. The inhabitants of Thessaly had a distinct civilization in the prehistoric times before the invasions of 'Pelasgians' (see *Migrations*). By these invasions the early inhabitants were reduced to the condition of serfs or vassals, the rulers and nobility belonging to the conquering race. In historical times we find Thessaly broken up into a number of principalities, organized at times in a league, and at times attempting to push their influence southwards. The Thessalians submitted to Xerxes when the Greeks gave up the defence of Tempe (see *Persian Wars*). See also *Jason* of Pherae. In the reign of Philip of Macedon, Thessaly came under Macedonian control and ultimately was incorporated in the Roman province of Achāia.

In mythology Thessaly was the home of the Centaurs and the Lapithae (see *Centaurs*), and it was from Thessaly that the Argonauts (q.v.) set out, for Pelias and Aeson were rulers of Iolcos in Thessaly. It was regarded as pre-eminently the country of magicians (see *Magic*).

Thĕ'tes, see *Athens*, § 2.

The'tis, see *Nereus* and *Peleus*.

Thirlwall, CONNOP, see *Historians (Modern)*.

Thirty, THE, see *Athens*, § 5 and *Critias*.

Thirty Years' Peace, the peace which, in 446 B.C., terminated the war that had been waged between Athens and the Peloponnesians since 459; it was to be for thirty years but lasted only fifteen (see *Athens*, § 4).

Thi'sbĕ, see *Pyramus*.

Thra'sea, PUBLIUS CLŌDIUS (?) PAETUS, a prominent senator under Nero, leader of the Stoic and republican opposition. He was accused of lack of loyalty and driven to suicide (A.D. 66). His wife was the younger Arria, daughter of the famous Arria (q.v.). See also *Helvidius Priscus*.

Thra'sō, the braggart soldier in Terence's 'Eunuchus' (q.v.). The Elizabethan adjective 'thrasonical' (e.g. 'Caesar's thrasonical brag of "I came, saw, and overcame",' Shakespeare, 'As You Like It', v. ii. 34) is derived from this character.

Thrasybū'lus (*Thrasuboulos*), (1) tyrant of Miletus; see *Miletus* and *Periander*. (2) An Athenian naval commander, who

with Thrasyllus led the reaction in the fleet at Samos in 411 B.C. against the oligarchic rule of the Four Hundred (see *Athens*, § 5) and recalled Alcibiades. With Thrasyllus he defeated the Spartan fleet in the same year at Cynossēma. Thrasybulus was once more leader of the democratic party in 404–403, and successfully led the exiles against the Thirty. Thrasyllus was one of the unfortunate commanders tried and executed after the battle of Arginusae (q.v., 406). There is a life of Thrasybulus by Nepos.

Thrasy'llus (*Thrasullos*), see *Thrasybulus* (2).

Thrasy'machus (*Thrasumachos*) of Chalcēdōn in Bithȳnia, a teacher of rhetoric who flourished in the last quarter of the 5th c. B.C. He rendered service in the development of Attic prose, creating a 'middle' style between the poetical style of Gorgias (q.v.) and the colloquial. He figures in the 'Phaedrus' and 'Republic' of Plato.

Thrina'cia (*Thrīnakiĕ*), the island where Helios (q.v.) kept his herds; see *Odyssey* (Bk. xii) and *Sicily*.

Thŭcy'didēs (*Thoukūdidēs*), (1) the historian, *c.* 460–*c.* 400 B.C., son of Olorus, an Athenian of a family having Thracian connexions. As one of the ten generals he was sent in 424 to the coast of Thrace to operate against Brasidas (q.v.), and having failed to relieve Amphipolis was sent into exile, which lasted for twenty years. He appears to have been recalled in 404. According to tradition he was assassinated. His tomb (perhaps a cenotaph) was shown outside the walls of Athens. He wrote a history of the Peloponnesian War (q.v.), one of the greatest historical works of all time, notable for its condensed, direct, and graphic style, for its fairness and scientific method, for the author's sense of the causal connexion between events, and for its reasoning on political questions. It was written in literary (that is, slightly archaic) Attic. Dionysius laments the obscurity due to the condensation of many passages, remarking on the rarity of those 'who are capable of understanding the whole of Thucydides, and not even these can do so without occasional reference to a grammatical commentary'. Quintilian speaks of the history as 'close in texture, terse, ever eager to press forward'. Thucydides himself describes it (i. 22) as 'a possession for all time'—κτῆμα ἐς ἀιεί—not a prize composition to be heard and forgotten. It sets forth the arguments for and against a particular course of action in the form of speeches representing the substance of what was said by participants in the events (Thucydides' exile gave him opportunities for appreciating the point of view of each of the combatants). The history remained unfinished (it breaks off amid the events of 411). It is preceded by introductory chapters tracing the history of the Hellenic race from earliest times. Among noteworthy passages and sections of the work may be mentioned Pericles' Funeral Oration over the Athenians who had first fallen in the war (ii. 35–46), which includes the noble exhortation to courage —τὸ εὔδαιμον τὸ ἐλεύθερον, τὸ δ' ἐλεύθερον τὸ εὔψυχον κρίναντες, 'judging freedom to be happiness, and courage to be freedom'; the account of the plague at Athens (ii. 47–54); the Melian Dialogue (q.v., v. 85–113); and the Sicilian Expedition (vi and vii).

(2) Son of Melēsias, and son-in-law of Cimon (q.v.), a leader of the oligarchical party at Athens who came into acute conflict with Pericles over the question of the right of Athens to employ the tribute of the Delian confederates for her own purposes. He was ostracized in 443.

Thūrii (*Thourioi*), a Greek colony founded in 443 B.C. in Lūcānia, in the neighbourhood of Sybaris (q.v.), which had been destroyed about 510. The descendants of the Sybarites who had then been driven out asked the assistance of Sparta and Athens to refound their city. Under the direction of Pericles, Athens consented. Pericles decided to give the new colony a Panhellenic character, and invited the other Greek states to take part in its foundation. Citizens from many states that were friendly to Athens joined the expedition, and the new city was elaborately organized. Herodotus was among the colonists, and Protagoras (q.v.) revised its constitution. It became very prosperous and a centre of Athenian culture. Later, during the Peloponnesian War and after it, Thurii showed ingratitude and hostility to Athens.

Thye′stēs (*Thuestēs*), see *Pelops.*

Thyestes, a tragedy by Seneca the Philosopher, dealing with the gruesome revenge of Atreus upon his wicked brother (see *Pelops*). No corresponding Greek play is extant, but the theme had already been dealt with by three Roman writers, Ennius in his 'Thyestes', Accius in his 'Atreus', and Varius in his 'Thyestes' (for this last famous play, see *Varius*).

Ti′ber (*Tiberis*, also *Tibris* and *Tybris*), the chief river of central Italy, rising in the Apennines and flowing in a generally southerly direction between Etruria on the one hand and Umbria, the country of the Sabines, and Latium on the other. The old name of the river was *Albula*. Rome stood on its left bank, about 14 miles from its mouth at Ostia. See *Tiberinus.*

Tiberi′nus, according to Roman tradition an early king of the country, who was drowned in the Tiber, which derived its name from him. Also the name of the river-god of the Tiber. This god was highly honoured on account of the importance of the river to the welfare of the State. He had a shrine on the island in the Tiber opposite ancient Rome. He appears to have been known also under the cult name *Volturnus* ('rolling river') and to have had a festival the *Volturnālia* on 27 August.

Tibē′rius (*Tiberius Claudius Nērō Caesar*), born 42 B.C., Roman emperor A.D. 14–37, son of Tiberius Claudius Nero and Livia, and stepson of Augustus. See *Julio-Claudian Family* and *Rome,* § 10. He married first Vipsānia Agrippīna, and after being obliged by Augustus to divorce her, Jūlia the emperor's daughter (qq.v.).

Tibu′llus, ALBIUS (c. 60–19 B.C.), a Roman elegiac poet who formed part of a group under the patronage of M. Valerius Messalla (q.v.), standing somewhat apart from the court poets of the day. He was a friend of Horace, who addressed to him a charming Epistle (I. iv). Two books of the poems of Tibullus, known in ancient times as 'Dēlia' and 'Nemesis' from the names of the women celebrated therein, were published in his lifetime. They are marked by quiet charm and tenderness and their theme is love, peace, and rural simplicity; one poem, in honour of his patron Messalla, celebrates also the glory and prosperity of the Roman Empire. A third book, published after his death, contains some posthumous pieces and also works by other hands (probably by members of the circle of Messalla), notably elegies by one Lygdamus, possibly Propertius's freedman of that name; and six short pieces by Sulpicia, a niece of Messalla, on her passion for her lover Cērinthus, a significant testimony to the freedom which the young women of the upper classes at Rome enjoyed at this time.

Ti′bur, the modern Tivoli, an ancient Latin town, sixteen miles NE. of Rome. Many rich Romans had villas there, the most famous of which was the great villa of Hadrian (q.v.). Horace writes of Tibur (Od. II. vi. 5):

Tibur Argeo positum colono
Sit meae sedes utinam senectae,

referring to a legend that it was founded by Greeks. Juvenal had a farm there.

Tīmae′us (*Timaios*) (*c.* 346–*c.* 250 B.C.), a Greek historian of Tauromenium (Taormina) in Sicily, who lived for fifty years at Athens and wrote a history of Sicily from the earliest times to 264 B.C. It was severely criticized by Polybius as showing the author's lack of political acumen, but was regarded in antiquity as the chief authority on its subject. Only quotations from the work have come down to us. Timaeus also wrote on the 'Campaigns of Pyrrhus'. He was the first to fix chronology by the Olympiads (see *Calendar*, § 1).

Timaeus (*Timaios*), a dialogue by Plato, in form a sequel to the 'Republic' (q.v.), in which the author places in the mouth of Timaeus, a Pythagorean philosopher, an exposition of the origin and system of the universe.

In the beginning God existed, and, being good, created the universe in as perfect a form as possible, from two substances, the incorporeal substance of ideas, and the material elements. From these, mingled in various proportions, God formed the world, its soul, the lower gods, the stars. The lower gods in turn created man and the animals, according to certain geometrical formulae. The origin of sensations and diseases is then traced, the three kinds of soul that inhabit man described, and the fate of man after death briefly indicated.

In a preliminary myth, Critias recounts the conquest of the empire of Atlantis (a continent west of the Pillars of Hercules now sunk below the sea) by the ancient Athenians; a legend which is continued in the dialogue 'Critias'.

Cicero translated or adapted the 'Timaeus', but most of his work is lost.

Time, MEASUREMENT OF, see *Calendar*.

Tīmo′cratēs, *Against*, a speech in a public prosecution by Demosthenes. See *Demosthenes* (2), § 3 (b).

Tīmō′leon (*Timóleōn*), a high-minded Corinthian who about 365 B.C. joined with some friends in killing his brother Timophanēs when the latter attempted to make himself tyrant. The deed was praised by some and condemned by others, and Timoleon lived under a cloud until selected by his countrymen to be sent to Syracuse in 344 in response to that city's request for help. For his further history see *Syracuse*, § 3. There is a life of Timoleon by Plutarch.

Tī′mon (*Timōn*), (1) an Athenian of the 5th c. B.C. who owing to the ingratitude of his friends became a misanthrope. He is said to have later discovered a buried treasure, and when his friends, attracted by this, sought him once more, drove them away with contumely. Part of the story is told by Plutarch in his life of Antony; the discovery of the treasure is perhaps an invention of Lucian, who presents Timon in the dialogue of that name. There was also a play on Timon by Antiphanes, a writer of the New Comedy. Shakespeare's 'Timon of Athens' is based on the story.

(2) of Phliūs (*fl. c.* 250 B.C.), a sceptic philosopher, author of a poem (of which only fragments survive) entitled 'Silloi' (i.e. 'squint-eyed' pieces) in mock-Homeric hexameters, in which he ridiculed the philosophers of other schools.

Timo′thĕus (*Timotheos*), (1) (447–357 B.C.), a poet and musician of Miletus. He is said to have introduced technical innovations in music, increasing the number of strings in the lyre. He was chiefly famous as a composer of nomes (q.v.), but also wrote dithyrambs, hymns, &c. The characteristic feature of his art seems to have been his endeavour to make his poetry and music imitative and realistic, as in his 'Nauplius', where he tried to represent a storm by the music of the flute, and in his 'Travail of Semele'. The fragment of a nome by Timotheus, entitled 'Persae' was discovered in 1902. It is a lyrical impression of the battle of Salamis, and is referred to by Plutarch in his life of Philopoemen. Timotheus figures in Dryden's 'Alexander's Feast'.

(2) Son of Conon (q.v.) and a pupil of Isocrates (q.v.), an able Athenian commander and diplomatist of the period of the second Athenian Confederacy. He captured Samos from the Persians in 365 B.C., and extended the dominion of Athens in the Thracian Chersonese and Chalcidic peninsula; but in consequence of his failure to support his colleague Charēs in an attack on Chios in 356, he was tried and fined a hundred talents. He died shortly after this, and only one tenth of the enormous fine was exacted from his son. There is a life of him by Nepos.

Tīre′sias (*Teiresiās*), in Greek mythology a Theban, who was transformed for a time into a woman for killing the female of a pair of snakes. Zeus and Hera referred to him the question whether man or woman derives more pleasure from love, and when Tiresias supported the opinion of Zeus, Hera struck him with blindness, but Zeus gave him long life and the gift of prophecy. Another story attributes his blindness to his having seen Athene bathing.

In the 'Odyssey' Odysseus is sent to Hades to consult Tiresias as to the manner of his returning home. Tiresias also figures in the 'Antigone' and 'Oedipus Tyrannus' (qq.v.) of Sophocles, and in the 'Bacchae' and 'Phoenissae' (qq.v.) of Euripides. He is the subject of a dramatic monologue by Tennyson in which he recounts the story of his blinding by Athene:

Henceforth be blind, for thou hast seen too much,
And speak the truth that no man may believe.

Swinburne has a poem 'Tiresias' on the same subject.

Ti'rō, MARCUS TULLIUS, the learned freedman, secretary, and friend of Cicero. He was author of a 'Life of Cicero' which is lost, and editor of some of his speeches and of his letters 'ad Familiares' (which include letters to Tiro himself). He wrote also on grammar, and contributed to the Roman art of short-hand writing, the abbreviations of which derived from him in later times the name of *notae Tirōniānae*.

Ti'ryns (*Tīruns*), a very ancient city in the southern part of the plain of Argos, of which the huge Cyclopean walls, twenty-five feet thick (and in places more), built of great roughly hewn blocks, are still standing. The city is associated in legend with Mycenae (q.v.) and with the story of Heracles (q.v.).

Tisi'phonē, see *Furies*.

Tissaphe'rnēs, the Persian satrap of Sardis with whom Sparta (q.v., § 4) entered into alliance against Athens in 412 B.C., and with whom Alcibiades (q.v.) intrigued. It was Tissaphernes who tried to lure the Ten Thousand Greeks to destruction after the failure of the expedition of Cyrus at Cūnaxa (see *Anabasis*). He was once more ruler of the Aegean coast when Sparta began war with Persia in 400, and Xenophon relates in his 'Hellenica' (q.v.) how he was outwitted by Agesilaus. He was executed by order of the Persian king for his failure.

Ti'tans (*Tītānes*), in Greek mythology, children of the primeval couple Uranus and Ge (qq.v.). According to Hesiod (q.v.) they were twelve in number, six sons and six daughters. They were Ōceanus, Cŏēus (*Koios*), Criūs (*Krios*), Hyperīōn, Īapetus, Cronus, Theiā, Rheā, Themis, Mnēmosynē, Phoebē, Tēthȳs. Some of them probably represent nature-powers, others, as Mnemosyne (Memory), are abstractions. The origin of some of the names is probably not Greek, and the Titans may reflect some old vanquished gods of the country occupied by the immigrating Greeks. The marriage of Heaven and Earth and the birth of gods or spirits as offspring of the marriage is a widespread myth. In Iliad

xiv. 201 et seq. Oceanus and Tethys are spoken of as the progenitors of the gods.

Tithō'nus (*Tithōnos*), in Greek mythology, son of Laomedon and brother of Priam (see genealogy under *Troy*). He was loved by Eos (q.v.), the dawn goddess, and by her was father of Memnon (q.v.). She begged Zeus to make Tithonus immortal, but omitted to obtain eternal youth for him, so that he became an old shrivelled creature, little more than a voice, or was turned into a grasshopper. Tennyson wrote a beautiful poem, 'Tithonus', in which 'this grey shadow, once a man' laments his 'cruel immortality'.

Titi'nius, a contemporary of Terence at Rome, author of *togatae* (q.v.), comedies with Roman plots and characters. Only fifteen titles and some fragments of his plays survive. The subjects of many of them appear to have been family affairs and questions of money.

Ti'tus (*Titus Flāvius Sabīnus Vespāsiānus*), Roman emperor A.D. 79–81, having been previously associated with father Vespasian in the empire. See *Rome*, § 11. He is famous for the capture of Jerusalem in A.D. 70 after a long siege. The *Arch of Titus* commemorating this, erected on the Via Sacra at Rome by Domitian, is still standing (in part restored). Titus, during his campaigns in Judaea, fell in love with Berenicē, daughter of the Jewish king Herod Agrippa I, and she accompanied him on his return to Rome. But the Romans disapproved of the connexion of the son and colleague of the emperor with a Jewess, and Titus dismissed her, as Suetonius says, 'invitus invitam'. The rupture of their relations is the subject of Racine's tragedy 'Bérénice'. See also *Suetonius* (under the sub-head 'Lives of the Caesars').

Titus, ARCH OF, see preceding article.

Ti'tus Tā'tius (*Titus Tātius*), a legendary king of the Sabines, who after the reconciliation between his people and the Romans which followed the Rape of the Sabines (see *Rome*, § 2), ruled jointly with Romulus over the combined peoples.

Ti'tyus (*Tituos*), in Greek mythology, a giant, son of Ge (q.v.), slain by Apollo and Artemis for offering violence to their mother Leto. Odysseus saw him bound in Hades, while two vultures tore at his liver. He covered, as he lay, nine roods of ground.

Tmē'sis, a Greek word meaning 'division', in grammar the division of a word into two parts. The classical examples are Ennius's 'Saxo cere comminuit brum' for 'cerebrum comminuit'; and Virgil's 'Talis Hyperboreo septem subjecta trioni', for 'septemtrioni' (Georg. iii. 381).

Tō'ga (*tŏga*), see *Clothing*, § 3.

Togā'ta, FĀBULA, in Roman literature, comedy, Greek in form, but in which the characters and life presented were Roman. Afranius (q.v.) was the chief author of comedies of this class, which had a brief life in the latter part of the 2nd c. B.C. The name is from *toga*, the characteristic Roman garment. See also *Atta* and *Titinius*.

Tolō'sa (*Toulouse*), a town in the Roman province of Gallia Narbōnensis, which at the time of the Gallic rebellion of 107 B.C. fell into the hands of the insurgents. It was recaptured in 106 by the consul Q. Servīlius Caepiō, who sacked its temples and removed the gold from the sacred deposits. This was regarded as an act of impiety and calculated to bring misfortune. The escort which accompanied the gold is said to have been overwhelmed and the gold lost. Hence the expression *aurum Tolōsānum* for ill-gotten goods.

To'pica, see *Aristotle*, § 3; for Cicero's abstract of the work see *Cicero*, § 5.

Torch-race (*Lampadēdromiā*), a form of contest held at the Panathenea and at certain other Greek festivals, notably those of the fire-gods Prometheus and Hephaestus. It was run, according to Pausanias, from the altar of Prometheus in the Academy (outside the walls of Athens) to a point in the city. The competitors had to carry lighted torches to the goal (any whose torch went out was disqualified). The race was run in one of two ways, either by single competitors, or by teams from each tribe as a relay-race. At the festival of the Thracian goddess Bendis referred to in the opening passage of Plato's 'Republic' there was a torch-race on horseback. The preparations for torch-races were among the public services (see *Liturgy*) borne by the wealthier citizens.

Toreutic Art, the art of embossing or chasing metal. It was practised from very early times, for there are many references to it in Homer as applied to the decoration not only of armour but of objects such as brooches and cups. There are indications in the poems that the best work was then imported from abroad. Gold, silver, and copper are among the metals so worked. Many examples of the art, dating from Mycenean times, have been recovered, notably those found by Dr. Schliemann on the sites of Troy and Mycenae; also the famous Vaphio gold cups, found in a beehive tomb in the neighbourhood of Sparta, with designs representing men hunting bulls. In the great age of Greek art, silver was the metal chiefly employed for work of this kind. Pliny (xxxiii. 154 et seq.) enumerates the artists who were pre-eminent in chasing silver. MENTŌR (whose date is uncertain, but earlier than 356 B.C.) was the most famous of them. Crassus purchased for 100,000 sesterces two cups chased by him; Martial frequently refers to his work; and Propertius (iii. 7) compares it with that of another famous artist, MŸS. It appears from statements by Pausanias and Athenaeus that Mys worked on designs supplied by Parrhasius (q.v.), so that he must have flourished about 400 B.C. He is said by Pausanias to have adorned, with a representation of the Lapithæ and Centaurs, the shield of the great bronze statue of Athene by Phidias on the Acropolis. Cicero in the Verrines mentions a water-jug of consummate workmanship by another jeweller, BŒTHUS. One process employed by the ancient jewellers, by which a sheet of gold is decorated with minute globules of the same metal, remains unknown at the present day.

Torquā'tus, see *Manlius Torquatus*.

Tra'bea, see *Clothing*, § 3.

Trachi'niae (*Trāchiniai*), a tragedy by Sophocles of uncertain date.

Heracles (q.v.) has been absent from his home for fifteen months. He has told Deïanira his wife that at the end of this period the crisis of his life would come, and he would either perish or have rest from his troubles thereafter. Deïanira sends Hyllus, their son, in search of his father. As she reflects over her anxious lot, a messenger announces the arrival of Heracles in Euboea nearby. This is presently confirmed by the report of a herald, who brings with him a train of captive women taken by Heracles when he sacked Oechalia, the city of his enemy Eurytus. Deïanira discovers that to one of these, Iole, daughter of Eurytus, Heracles has transferred his love. The centaur Nessus, when dying, has left her a love-charm. With this she decides to win back the love of Heracles, and smears with it the robe of honour that she sends to him. Too late she discovers, by the smouldering away of the wool which she has used to smear the robe, that the charm is in fact a deadly poison. Hyllus returns, describes the agony of Heracles tortured by the robe, and denounces his mother as a murderess. Deïanira goes out in silence, and presently her old nurse appears to say that she has taken her own life. The dying Heracles is borne home, and bids Hyllus carry him to Mt. Oeta and there burn him on a pyre before the agony returns. Thereafter Hyllus is to wed Iole. Hyllus reluctantly consents, bitterly reproaching the gods for their pitiless treatment of his father.

The scene is at Trāchis (in Phōcis), and the title is taken from the chorus of Trachinian maidens.

Trade, see *Athens,* § 10, and *Rome,* § 13.

Tragedy.

§ 1. *The origin of Greek Tragedy*

The general purport of what Aristotle says in the 'Poetics' (q.v.) on the origin of tragedy is that it was developed out of the improvised speeches of the leader of the dithyramb (q.v.), with the satyric drama (q.v.) as an intermediate stage. This view has been widely accepted, but is contested by some authorities as difficult to reconcile with the evidence of the facts. Aristotle, it is said, may have been theorizing from what he knew of the dithyramb and satyric drama in his own time, and of the primitive dithyramb, whose leader (ἐξάρχων) might well have been transformed into an actor (ὑποκριτής). It is more probable, according to this view, that dithyramb, satyric drama, and tragedy each followed its own line of development, and that the origin of tragedy is to be sought in an elementary choral and rustic form of drama in use in the villages of Attica; that Thespis (q.v.) introduced into this an actor's part, and that it was adopted in the second half of the 6th c. B.C. at the Great Dionysia at Athens. With this rustic drama was probably fused a solemn lyric element from the choral Dionysiac songs, invented it is said by Arion (q.v.) and developed in the Peloponnese, particularly at Sicyon. The subjects of tragedy, as of the dithyramb, were probably at first connected with the story of Dionysus; later their range was extended to include the stories of heroes; they were only rarely drawn from history. We have the record of only one tragedy (by Agathon, q.v.) where plot and characters were entirely imaginary.

The word tragedy (τραγῳδία) appears to be derived from *tragōdoi* (τραγῳδοί) meaning probably a chorus who personated goats, or danced either for a goat (*tragos*) as prize or around a sacrificed goat. The later sense of the words 'tragedy', 'tragic', would result from the sorrowful character of the legends dealt with in plays known as tragedies.

§ 2. *Performance of Greek tragedies*

The representation of tragedies in Attica was an incident of public worship and, until the Alexandrian period, appears to have been confined to the festivals of Dionysus. They were performed, that is, in winter and early spring, 'the season when the world is budding but there is not enough to eat' (Alcman), a period of anxiety in a primitive community, of longing that the spirit of vegetation may duly be reborn, and of consequent intercession. The altar of the god stood in the centre of the *orchestra* (see *Theatre,* § 1). It is important to remember that plays could not, as in present times, be seen on any day of the year. The principal production of new tragedies was at the Great Dionysia (see *Festivals,* § 4), on which occasion, during the 5th and 4th c., three poets were allowed to compete, each poet presenting (until the later part of the 4th c.) three tragedies and one satyric play. These four plays (tetralogies) might be connected by community of subject, but rarely were so. Tragedies were produced also at the Lenaea. The representations were organized by the magistrates and the cost borne by the *choregi* (see *Chorus*). The contests were decided at first by popular acclamation, later by judges (probably five) chosen by lot from an elected list. The poet and *choregus* whose plays were successful were rewarded with a crown. The best actor among the protagonists (see below) also received a prize. Only Athenian citizens were allowed to take part in the chorus, though metics (q.v.) were at a later date admitted to it at the Lenaea.

Greek tragedy, as its history indicates, contained two elements, choral and dramatic. The former was expressed in a variety of lyric metres, arranged in strophes and antistrophes, occasionally with epodes (qq.v.) added; the latter mainly in iambic trimeters (see *Metre,* § 2). The chorus was drawn up in a rectangular form (as distinguished from the 'circular chorus' of the dithyramb) and its movements were based on this arrangement. It was accompanied on the flute. Its principal dance, known as *emmeleia,* was of a dignified character. The number of persons in the chorus appears to have been twelve in most of the plays of Aeschylus (whether the chorus in the 'Suppliants' comprised all the fifty daughters of Danaos is uncertain), and to have been increased to fifteen by Sophocles. Choruses continued to form a part of tragedies through the 5th and part at least of the 4th cc., after choruses in Comedy had been discontinued; but their precise duration is unknown.

To the single actor of Thespis, Aeschylus added a second. From the time of Sophocles, the parts were distributed among three actors, the *protagonist*, *deuteragonist*, and *tritagonist*; to the first was assigned the longest and most difficult part, together with such other parts as could be combined with it. The actors were paid by the State (not by the *choregus*) and distributed to the competing poets. They wore masks (see *Thespis*) appropriate to their parts, a head-dress, and (at least in the time of Aeschylus) a long robe; also buskins (*kothurnoi*) having very thick soles. Female parts were played by men. The actor sang certain lyric passages, e.g. κομμοί, lamentations, either solo or with the chorus; iambic passages throughout the classical period appear to have been declaimed, though perhaps in a more musical and singing style than is usual in ordinary speech. In this respect and also in the action (at first solemn and stiff) tragedy gradually became more realistic (Mynniscos, who had acted for Aeschylus, spoke of Callipidēs, a successful actor of a later period, as 'a monkey'). Euripides, moreover, appears to have made the dress more realistic; he was chaffed by Aristophanes (in the 'Acharnians') about the rags in which he clothed his heroes. In primitive tragedy the lyric part, the songs of the chorus, predominated; action and dialogue were subservient to it. This relation was gradually reversed. The role of the chorus is generally that of spectators, humble in rank (the 'Eumenides' is a notable exception) and respectful, sympathizing with one or other of the chief characters, taking a limited part in the action, commenting on or interpreting the dramatic situation.

§ 3. *Divisions and construction of a Greek tragedy*

A Greek tragedy normally contained the following parts:

(a) the prologue (*prologos*), the part before the entrance of the chorus, in monologue or dialogue, setting forth the subject of the drama and the situation from which it starts. In the earliest tragedies the play begins with the entrance of the chorus, who set forth the subject.

(b) the *parodos*, the song accompanying the entrance of the chorus.

(c) the episodes (*epeisodia*), scenes in which one or more actors took part, with the chorus. The word *epeisodion* probably meant originally the entrance of an actor to announce something to the chorus. The episodes might contain lyrical passages, lamentations, incidental songs by the chorus, &c. They were divided by

(d) *stasima*, songs of the chorus 'in one place', i.e. in the orchestra, as opposed to the *parodos* when the chorus was entering. They were originally reflections or expressions of emotion evoked by the preceding episode. But this connexion was gradually severed, until Agathon (q.v.) finally substituted *embolima*, mere musical interludes between the episodes.

(e) After the last *stasimon* came the *exodos* or final scene.

Greek tragedy had always a religious background, in consonance with its religious character. The choruses in some instances show the survival of magic dances, designed to avert pestilence, bring rain, etc. A tragedy was originally the presentment of a single pathetic situation, with little action. Aeschylus introduced the idea of the divine will shaping the course of events; Sophocles the further element of the human will, less powerful than the divine will, working in harmony with or in opposition to it, more at the mercy of circumstances. Hence developed the *peripeteia*, the moment when the action of the tragedy changes its course, a knot or complication having arisen in the relations of the characters which has to be unloosed. With Euripides the *peripeteia* became more complicated, striking, and abrupt; the *anagnōrisis* or 'recognition' (occasionally used by Sophocles) frequently provided in the tragedies of Euripides the turning point in question.

§ 4. *Principal Greek tragedians*

The principal writers of tragedies before Aeschylus, Sophocles, and Euripides (qq.v.) were Phrynichus, Pratinas (qq.v.), and Choerilus of Athens (*fl.* 482, of whom we know very little). There were a great number of tragedians during the 5th and 4th cc. Most of them are known to us only by their names. The most famous of them (apart from the three great authors) was Agathon (q.v.). Some dozen of them won the prize from time to time. The descendants of Aeschylus and Sophocles included tragedians of some eminence. A younger Euripides, son or nephew of the poet, produced posthumous plays by the elder Euripides and was himself a dramatist. But tragedy tended to become exhausted towards the end of the 4th c., and its last period produced no great poet.

§ 5. *Roman Tragedy*

The distant origins of Roman drama are described under *Comedy*, § 5. A new impulse was given when in 240 B.C. Livius Andronicus (q.v.) first put on the stage rough adaptations of a Greek tragedy and a Greek comedy, to be followed by other adaptations from the Greek. Naevius (q.v.), his younger contemporary, appears to have been the first to compose, besides tragedies on Greek subjects, *fabulae praetextae* (q.v.), dramas whose themes were drawn from Roman history or legend. His successors Ennius, Pacuvius, and Accius (qq.v.) also wrote occasional *praetextae* among tragedies modelled on Greek originals. After them Roman tragedy declined, and there was no important tragedian in the later years of the Republic. Under Augustus, Asinius Pollio (q.v.) wrote tragedies which have perished, as have also the 'Medea' of Ovid and the 'Thyestes' of Varius Rufus, both of them popular plays praised by Quintilian. To the age of Nero belong the highly rhetorical tragedies of Seneca (q.v.); like most of his predecessors he borrowed his subjects from Greek sources, and it is improbable that his tragedies were intended for the stage. The ordinary metre of Roman tragedy was the iambic trimeter (see *Metre*, § 5); this was used in dialogue. The sung portions were in simple lyrical metres adapted from the Greek. The chorus, when there was one, appeared on the stage, not as in Greek tragedy in the *orchestra*, and could take a greater part in the action of the play.

Horace in his 'Ars Poetica' (q.v.) seemed to look forward to a national drama; but the conditions were unfavourable to the development of tragedy. The performance of tragedies was not at Rome, as at Athens, a religious solemnity; there was no great homogeneous audience in sympathy with the poet; Greek themes did not greatly attract the Roman spectator; and tragedies on Roman themes were comparatively few. Tragedy at Rome was moral and didactic in purpose, inculcating energy and fortitude, and was also valued for its displays of oratory, and occasionally as appealing to national or political sentiment. But it does not appear to have produced any great original conceptions or the subtlety and character-drawing of its Greek prototype (though Quintilian rated the lost 'Thyestes' of Varius as equal to any Greek tragedy). The extinction of political life under the empire, by rendering the choice of Roman subjects increasingly difficult and dangerous, was a further influence unfavourable to the growth of Roman tragedy.

See also *Theatre* and *Drama*.

Trage′laphus, (*Tragelaphos*), see *Monsters*.

Trā′jan (*Marcus Ulpius Trājānus*), Roman emperor A.D. 98–117 (see *Rome* § 11), of Spanish birth, a great soldier, simple and unassuming, conqueror of the Dacians, whose territory he constituted a Roman province. He also conquered a large part of the Parthian Empire, capturing Ctesiphon, its capital, and reached the Persian Gulf in the course of his expedition. Among his public works at Rome were the construction of the Forum of Trajan, where the Column of Trajan commemorated his campaigns (see *Forum Trajanum*), and the foundation of the library known as the *Bibliothēca Ulpia*. He showed great care for the welfare of Italy and the provinces. Pliny the Younger (q.v.) delivered a 'Panegyric' on him, and when governor of Bīthȳnia corresponded with him.

Traube, LUDWIG, see *Texts*, § 11.

Trebe′llius Po′lliō, see *Historia Augusta*.

Tre′sviri capitā′lēs and **Tre′sviri Monētā′lēs**, see *Vigintivirate*.

Tri′ad, in Greek poetry, a group of three lyric stanzas, of which the first two, the strophe and antistrophe, are symmetrical (i.e. correspond in metre), the third, or epode, is on a different model. The epodes, in Pindar at least, correspond to one another. This method of writing, which broke the monotony of a series of similar stanzas, was introduced by Stesichorus, and followed by Simonides and Pindar.

Tribōniā′nus, of Sīdē in Pamphylia, a great jurist and quaestor of the palace under Justinian, the compiler of the 'Corpus Juris Civilis'. See *Justinian*.

Tri′brach (-k), see *Metre*, § 1.

Tribunes of the plebs (*Tribūni plēbis*), at Rome, originally two in number, subsequently increased to five and then to ten, were magistrates of free plebeian birth charged with the protection of the people, and for this purpose possessed of the right of veto (*intercessio*) by which they could stop the action of any other magistrate. Their persons were inviolable. They could summon meetings of the plebeians to discuss public affairs and propose changes of the law (see *Concilium plebis*). They were elected annually, but it is uncertain by what body they were elected. Patricians might become tribunes by getting themselves adopted into a plebeian family (see the case of Clodius, under *Cicero*, § 3).

After its early prominence (e.g. at the time of the Licinian Rogations, q.v.), the tribunate lost importance and became a tool of the Senate, till revived by the Gracchi (q.v.), after which it was a source of great anxiety to the ruling class (cf. Saturninus and the younger M. Livius Drusus). Sulla curtailed its powers by restricting the scope of the veto and for-

bidding any one who had held the tribunate to advance to higher office. But these
privileges were restored within ten years
of Sulla's death and tribunes played an
important part in the protection of Julius
Caesar's interests at Rome during his
governorship of Gaul. Under the empire
the emperor was endued with *tribunicia
potestas* and the real tribunes lost all
importance.

Tribū'ni aerā'rii, of whom nothing certain is known, appear to have been originally officials of the tribes who saw to the
collection of the *tribūtum* or tax on property and to the payment of soldiers on
service (when pay had been introduced).
In late republican times this was the name
of an order from which the jurors of the
quaestiones were in part drawn (see *Judicial Procedure*, § 2).

Tribū'ni mī'litum, originally subordinate
military commanders in the Roman army.
From early republican times plebeians
were eligible for these tribunates. From
433 *tribūni mīlitārēs consulāri potestāte*
(three and later six in number) were from
time to time appointed and for these posts
likewise plebeians were eligible. These
appointments were discontinued from 366.
In later republican times the command of
each legion was entrusted to six *tribuni
militum*, who commanded in turn, until
Caesar placed a single *lēgātus* at the head
of each legion.

Tribū'tum, see *Rome*, § 14.

Tricli'nium, couches running round three
sides of a dinner-table, the usual arrangement in a Roman dining-room. The three
couches each accommodated three persons, reclining on their left sides. The
host reclined at the upper end of the couch
(*lectus īmus*) which stood on the left of the
table (as seen from the foot of the table);
the chief guest reclined next to him at the
end of the *lectus medius* (along the top of
the table). The *lectus summus* was set
along the right-hand side of the table.
Triclinium was also the name of the room
containing these couches, the dining-room.

Triēra'rchiā, see *Liturgy*.

Trima'lchio's Banquet, see *Petronius
Arbiter*.

Tri'meter, see *Metre*, § 1.

Trīna'cria, see *Sicily*.

Trinu'mmus ('Three bob'), a comedy by
Plautus, adapted from a play by Philemon
(see *Comedy*, § 4). For the meaning of the
word 'trinummus' see H. Mattingly and
E. S. G. Robinson in *Proceedings of the
British Academy*, vol. 18, 1932.

While Charmidēs, a wealthy Athenian,
is out of the country, his dissolute son
Lesbonicus has wasted his substance and
even put up his house for sale. Charmides,
when starting on his travels, has entrusted
his son and daughter and his interests
generally to his friend Calliclēs, and con-
fided to him in secrecy that a treasure is
concealed in the house. To prevent this
treasure from falling, with the house, into
strange hands, Callicles has bought the
house himself. Lȳsitelēs, a rich friend of
Lesbonicus, wishing to do a kindness to
the latter, proposes to take his sister in
marriage without a dowry. Lesbonicus,
though a spendthrift, retains his pride, and
although he would gladly give his sister
to his friend, will not accept an arrangement discreditable to his own family.
Callicles likewise, though he approves the
match, thinks the girl must have a dowry
out of the concealed treasure. The question is how to arrange this without revealing to Lesbonicus the existence of the
treasure. Callicles contrives this by hiring
'for three bob', a 'sycophant', that is
to say an unscrupulous fellow ready (if
paid) for any piece of deceit, who is to
pretend to come to Lesbonicus bringing a
letter from his father and a thousand gold
pieces to be used as a dowry for the daughter. This money is in fact to be taken from
the treasure concealed in the house. But
Charmides himself now arrives unexpectedly, falls in with the sycophant as
the latter is knocking at Charmides' door,
learns his errand, and exposes him. He
finds that the house is no longer his own
but has been bought by Callicles, and
begins to upbraid the latter. On learning
the facts, he warmly thanks Callicles for
his fidelity, gives his daughter with a
portion to Lysiteles, and pardons the now
penitent Lesbonicus.

Tripto'lemus (*Triptolemos*), see *Demeter*
and *Minos Rhadamanthus and Aeacus*.
There was a temple of Triptolemus at
Eleusis.

Tri'stia, elegiac poems by Ovid in five
books, written during the early years of
the poet's exile A.D. 8–12, most of them
in the form of epistles to his wife and
friends (unnamed, a few to enemies), and
most of them lamenting his lot and praying
that some mitigation of his punishment
may be obtained.

Book I consists of poems written in the
course of his long voyage to Tomi on the
Black Sea, describing the storms and
hardships that he encountered. The third
poem of this book is an account of his last
night in Rome.

Book II is a single poem, a plea that his

punishment is disproportionate to his fault.

The remaining books contain some interesting descriptions of his life at Tomi, the flat, treeless landscape, the rigorous climate, the attacks of barbarians on the town (when Ovid himself is constrained to take up arms for its defence), his loneliness among his Getic hosts. There is a certain monotony in the constant complaints, a sense of lack of dignity and fortitude, of which the poet himself appears to have been conscious (v. i). Book IV. x is a valuable autobiography.

The letters appear to have been sent separately and then collected in groups for publication.

Tri′ton (*Trītōn*), in Greek mythology a merman, son of Poseidon (q.v.) and Amphitrītē. The origin of his name (as also of Amphitrite) is obscure, and may not be Greek. Represented as fish-shaped from the middle down, he is comparable to some oriental gods (e.g. Dagon of the O.T.; see *Monsters*). He is also commonly shown blowing on a conch, and Virgil describes how Misēnus challenged him to a contest on this instrument and was drowned by him. In some forms of the legend there are, not one, but a number of Tritons (see under *Pausanias* (2)).

Tritō′nia, an epithet sometimes used of Pallas Athene (e.g. Virg. Aen. v. 704), because according to a story told by Herodotus (iv. 180) she was the daughter of Poseidon and the Tritonian Lake in Libya.

Triumph, the festal procession with which the success of a Roman general in an important campaign against foreign enemies, was, by the authority of the Senate, celebrated at Rome. The general had to remain outside the city till the triumph was celebrated; otherwise he would become a private citizen. For this reason the Senate met in the Temple of Bellona in the Campus Martius outside the walls to receive him on his return from his campaign. The procession, starting from the Campus Martius, passed along the Via Sacra and ascended to the Capitol (see *Rome*, § 1). It included the magistrates and the Senate, the spoils of the campaign carried on men's shoulders, white bulls for the sacrifice, the captives, and finally the general in a triumphal car, wearing a purple toga decorated with golden stars, and wreathed with bay. A crowd of soldiers followed, who sang triumphal songs and, by ancient licence, made ribald jests about their general. At the Temple of Jupiter on the Capitol, the general surrendered his bays to the god and offered sacrifice.

The *Ovatio* was a lesser form of celebration, granted when a general's exploits were not thought to merit the full triumph. In this the victor entered the city on foot (later on horseback), wearing the *toga praetexta* (see *Clothing*, § 3) and a wreath of myrtle.

Tri′via, see *Diana*.

Trō′ades, see *Trojan Women*.

Trō′chee (-kǐ), **Trōchā′ic**, see *Metre*, §§ 1 and 2.

Troe′zen (*Troizĕn*), a plain at the NE. extremity of the promontory of Argolis, the home of Aethra, mother of Theseus (q.v.), and the scene of the death of Hippolytus (q.v.).

Tro′gus, POMPĒIUS (the quantity of the o in Trogus is uncertain), a native of Gallia Narbonensis, whose father had been a lieutenant of Julius Caesar. He lived in the time of Augustus and wrote in Latin 'Historiae Philippicae', a history of the world in 44 books, centred in the history of Macedonia, and probably founded on Greek sources. We have only an abbreviation of it by Justin (q.v.).

Trō′ilus, in Greek mythology, a younger son of Priam (q.v.) and Hecuba, slain by Achilles. For the post-classical story of Troilus and Cressida, see under *Pandarus*.

Trojan Horse, THE, a device resorted to by the Greeks after the death of Achilles, to capture Troy. Epēos, a skilful craftsman, constructed a huge wooden horse, inside which picked Greek warriors, including Odysseus, were concealed. Then the Greek army withdrew, leaving Sinon behind. He declared himself to the Trojans a deserter, and professed to reveal to them that the horse was an offering to Athene, and that if brought within the city it would render it impregnable. In spite of the warning given to the Trojans by Lāocŏon (a priest of Apollo), who with his two sons was thereupon killed by serpents, and of the warning of Cassandra (q.v.), the horse was dragged into Troy. The Greeks came forth from the horse at night and the city was taken. The story perhaps reflects some tradition of an early siege-engine. It is referred to in the 'Odyssey' (iv. 271; viii. 492; xi. 523) and told at the beginning of the second book of the 'Aeneid'.

Trojan War, THE, the subject of a legend which probably reflects a real war between Achaeans (see *Migrations and Dialects* and inhabitants of the Troad, perhaps due to a quarrel about trade. This real war is believed to have taken place in the first quarter of the 12th c. B.C., and Troy to have fallen somewhere about the traditional date 1184. In the Homeric account it was waged by the Achaeans led by Agamemnon to recover Helen, who had been abducted from Greece by Paris (qq.v.). The first nine years of the war were indecisive. Then followed the events recounted in the 'Iliad' (q.v.). After this, according to post-Homeric legend, occurred the coming of the Amazons under Penthesilēa (see *Achilles*) and of the Ethiopians under Memnon to reinforce the Trojans, the death of Achilles (q.v.), the summoning of Neoptolemus and Philoctetes (qq.v.) to reinforce the Greeks, the incident of the Trojan Horse (q.v.), and the fall of the city.

Medieval legend relating to the Trojan War is mainly based on Latin works which purported to be translations of the narratives of Dares Phrygius and Dictys Cretensis (qq.v.). Dares Phrygius, supposed to have been on the Trojan side, appears to have influenced, more than Dictys Cretensis, the Western nations, some of which claimed a Trojan ancestry. Thus Hector, rather than Achilles, became the ideal of chivalry. In England the most prominent form of the medieval Trojan legend was the story to which Geoffrey of Monmouth (1100?–54) gave currency: that Brutus, great-grandson of Aeneas, collected a remnant of the Trojan race and settled in Britain, then uninhabited 'except for a few giants', and founded Troynovant or New Troy (later known as London). The legend was discussed down to much later times, e.g. by Stow (1525 ?–1605) and Speed (1552 ?–1629); it was accepted by Holinshed (d. 1580 ?), and is reproduced in poetical form by Spenser and Drayton. Lydgate (1370 ?–1451 ?) in his 'Troy-book' told the story of Troy, basing himself on Guido di Colonna, who in turn drew on Dictys Cretensis and Dares Phrygius. It is noteworthy that the first book issued from Caxton's press was his 'Recuyell of the Histories of Troy', translated from a French romance.

Trojan Women (*Trōades*), (1) a tragedy by Euripides, produced in 415 B.C., shortly after the conquest of Melos (q.v.) by the Athenians, and the slaughter of its male inhabitants. It is one of the most poignant of the plays of Euripides, the presentation of a single tragic situation: the condition of the Trojan women when their men-folk have been killed and they are at the mercy of their captors. Grieving and anxious they await their fate. Talthybius, the herald, announces that they are to be distributed among the victors. Hecuba herself is to be the thrall of the hated Odys-

seus; her daughter Cassandra has been allotted to Agamemnon; while it is revealed that her other daughter Polyxena has been slaughtered on the tomb of Achilles. The tragic figure of Cassandra appears; she foretells some of the evils that are to befall the conquerors. Then comes Andromache. She carries her little son Astyanax, and is to be the prize of Neoptolemus. Talthybius returns to carry off Astyanax, whose death has been ordered by the Greeks. The meeting of Menelaus and Helen follows; he is determined on her destruction, and Hecuba stimulates his wrath. But Helen pleads her cause, and when Menelaus and Helen depart, their reconciliation is foreshadowed. Talthybius appears once more with the broken body of Astyanax, and Hecuba prepares the burial. Finally Troy is fired and its towers collapse.

(2) A tragedy by Seneca the Philosopher, based on the above play, and combining with it the sacrifice of Polyxena from the 'Hecuba' of Euripides. This is one of the best of the Senecan tragedies and contains passages of deep passion and pathos.

Trophō′nius (*Trophŏnios*) and **Agamē′dēs**, legendary sons of Ergīnus of Orchomenus. They were architects, and were said to have built the temple of Apollo at Delphi and a treasury for Hyriēus the Boeotian or Augēas, king of Elis. About this treasury a tale is told similar to that of the treasury of Rhampsinitus (q.v.). The two brothers robbed the treasury by means of a movable stone in the wall, and when Agamedes was caught in a trap, Trophonius cut off his head to avoid detection. Trophonius was subsequently swallowed up by the earth at Lebadeia in Boeotia, where in a subterranean chamber he was thereafter consulted as an oracle under the name of Zeus Trophonius. The suppliant always emerged from this *Cave of Trophonius* pale and dejected, and it became proverbial to say of persons of melancholy or serious aspect that they had consulted the oracle of Trophonius.

Trōs, see *Troy.*

Troy (*Trōiā, Trŏiā,* or *Trōiă*), an ancient city near the river Scamander on the Asiatic shore of the Hellespont. Its site has been found at the modern Hissarlik, where Schliemann (q.v.) discovered the remains of nine successive settlements, the earliest dating back to the stone age. It was the sixth of these settlements that forms the subject of the legend of the Trojan War (q.v.). It was then in the possession of Phrygians, immigrants from the Balkans, akin to the Achaeans. Excavations have revealed that it was a small place, rather a fort than a city, roughly circular in shape, not more than 200 yards across (which explains how Achilles could chase Hector three times round its walls). The walls were fifteen feet thick and are still twenty feet high, with gates in it and square towers for its defence. The ground within the walls rose in terraces to the palace in the centre.

The Greek legendary history of the foundation of the city is as follows. Dardanus, son of Zeus, 'established Dardania' (Il. xx. 213), a district NE. of Troy, and married the daughter of the local king Teucer (*Teukros*). He had as descendants Trōs (from whom the district of the Troad and the Trojans were named), and Ilus, who founded the city of Troy, known in consequence as Ilium (*Ilion*). The genealogy of the royal family of Troy according to Homer, supplemented by later writers, is as follows:

ligion, the festival, on 23 March and 23 May, of the purification of the trumpets used on ceremonial occasions.

Tu'cca, *Plōtius*, see *Aeneid, ad fin.*

Tu'llia, (1) in Roman legendary history (see *Rome*, § 2), daughter of king Servius Tullius and wife of Tarquinius Superbus. She stirred her husband to oust her father from the throne, and when the latter had been murdered, drove her chariot over his dead body.

(2) the daughter of Cicero, born in 76 B.C. She was three times married, first to C. Calpurnius Piso Frūgi, then to Fūrius Crassipēs, and thirdly to P. Cornēlius Dolābella, a profligate, alternately a supporter of Caesar and of Brutus, consul in 44 B.C. Her death in 45 threw her father into despair; see under *Cicero*, § 4, and *Sulpicius Rufus*.

Tulliā'num, at Rome, an underground

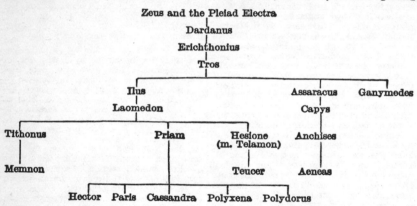

Zeus and the Pleiad Electra
Dardanus
Erichthonius
Tros

Ilus — Assaracus — Ganymedes
Laomedon — Capys

Tithonus — Priam — Hesione (m. Telamon) — Anchises

Memnon — Teucer — Aeneas

Hector Paris Cassandra Polyxena Polydorus

Trucule'ntus ('The Churl'), a comedy by Plautus.

The comedy, which has little plot, is mainly concerned with the doings of a covetous courtesan, who shamelessly exploits her three lovers, a dissolute young Athenian, a braggart captain, and a young man from the country. On one of them, the captain, she palms off a child which she has procured, and pretends that he is its father. The child turns out to be that of the Athenian and a free-born girl, whom in penitence her seducer agrees to marry. The *Truculentus* is the churlish slave of the country bumpkin. He tries to prevent his master wasting his substance on the woman, but himself falls in love with her maid.

Tūbilu'stria (*Tūbilustria*), in Roman re-

prison at the foot of the Capitoline hill, where the Catilinarian conspirators and other notable prisoners were put to death.

Tu'llus Hosti'lius (*Hostilius*), one of the legendary kings of Rome (see *Rome*, § 2). His reign is said to have been a period of constant wars, which included the struggle with Alba (see *Horatii and Curiatii*).

Tully, the name by which Marcus Tullius Cicero (q.v.) was frequently referred to by English scholars and authors down to fairly recent times, e.g. by Scott (through the mouth of Monkbarns in 'The Antiquary'); and by Byron, who wrote ('Childe Harold', iv. 110),

Tully was not so eloquent as thou,
Thou nameless column with a buried base.

Tu'nica, see *Clothing*, § 3.

Tu'riae Laudā'tio, see *Women* (*Position of*).

Tu'rnus, in the 'Aeneid' (q.v.), king of the Rutuli, betrothed to Lavinia (q.v.). He is a fiery warrior, the most spirited character in the poem, and fiercely opposes the invasion of the Trojans and the proposed marriage of Lavinia to Aeneas. He is killed by Aeneas.

Tu'sculan Disputations (*Tusculānae Disputātiōnēs*), a philosophical treatise in five books by Cicero on the conditions of happiness. The work was written in 45 B.C. and addressed to Brutus. It takes the form of conversations between two characters indicated as *M* and *A*. These may signify 'Marcus' and 'Adulescens', or represent *M* and *Δ*, *Μαθητής* and *Διδάσκαλος* ('pupil' and 'teacher'); but these are only conjectures. Cicero's villa at Tusculum was the imaginary scene of the conversations.

After an introduction defending the adoption of philosophy as a subject for treatment in Latin literature, Cicero in Book I deals with the proposition that death is an evil and an impediment to happiness. Death is either a change of place for the soul or annihilation; in neither case is it an evil; 'quod omnibus necesse est, idne miserum esse uni potest ?'

Book II deals with physical suffering, and shows that it is of trifling importance by the side of virtue, that it can be borne with fortitude, and that death is a refuge from it.

Book III discusses mental suffering or distress (*aegritudo*, *λύπη*), whether due to mourning, envy, compassion, vexation, or despondency, and shows that it originates in a mistaken judgement, is an act of will, and can be overcome by reflection, fortitude, and self-restraint.

Book IV. Other mental disorders, excessive delight, lust, and fear, are similarly due to errors of judgement, and can be overcome by philosophy.

Book V discusses whether virtue alone is sufficient to happiness, whether, e.g. the virtuous man can be happy under torture. Cicero adopts the Stoic view that the wise and virtuous man is happy always.

Tu'sculum, an ancient town in the mountains SE. of Rome about ten miles from the city. There Cicero had a favourite villa. For the legendary founder of Tusculum see *Telegonus*.

Twelve Tables, THE, a code of Roman law drawn up by a commission of ten (*decemviri*) and published in 451–450 B.C., on the demand of the plebeians. The tradition that envoys had been sent to Greece to study the laws of certain Greek States is thought improbable; but the Tables certainly incorporated some Greek ideas. Fragments of the code survive in a form which probably represents, not the original text, but the outcome of various revisions. They are couched in a precise succinct language, showing the Roman genius for legal expression. The fragments combine prescriptions of a barbarous harshness with others adapted to a more civilized state of society. The code was taught in Roman schools as late as Cicero's time and influenced Roman thought and Roman literary style. Even by so late an author as Aulus Gellius (2nd c. A.D.) they are referred to with respect, though thought obscure in parts (Noct. Att. xx. 1).

Tỹ'chē (*Túchē*), in Greek religious thought, fortune or chance, the incalculable element in life, which may bring good or evil; a conception which developed as the old belief in the gods declined. The word (from *τυγχάνειν*) means 'that which happens'. Pindar calls Tyche one of the Fates, stronger than her sisters; but she never became fully personified or a subject of mythology.

Tỹ'deūs (*Tūdeūs*), in Greek mythology, son of Oeneūs, king of Calydon. He went into exile for homicide, and at Argos married Dēipylē, daughter of Adrastus (q.v.), while Polynices (q.v.) married her sister Argēiā. He was one of the leaders in the expedition of the 'Seven against Thebes' (see *Oedipus*), and was father of Diomedes (q.v.).

Tynda'ridae, a name sometimes given to Castor and Pollux (see *Dioscuri*), whose mother Leda (q.v.) was wife of Tyndareus (*Tundareōs*) king of Sparta.

Typhō'eūs (*Tuphōeūs*, in Latin *Typhōeūs*) or **Tỹ'phōn** (*Tūphōn*), according to Hesiod son of Tartarus and Ge (qq.v.), a terrible monster with a hundred serpents' heads, fiery eyes, and a tremendous voice, whom Zeus attacked with thunderbolts, set on fire, and flung into Tartarus (see *Monsters*). Virgil's 'Inarime, Iovis imperiis imposta Typhoeo' (Aen. ix. 716), where Inarime is the name of an island off the coast of Campania, appears to be a misunderstanding of Homer's *εἰν Ἀρίμοις* (Il. ii. 783), 'in the land of the Arimi', the resting-place of Typhoeus.

For Typhon, the Egyptian god Set, see *Osiris*.

Tỹ'ro (*Tūrō*), in Greek mythology, daughter of Salmoneus (q.v.). She was loved by Poseidon, who visited her disguised as the Thessalian river Enipeūs and made a great wave curl over and conceal them (Od. xi.

234 et seq.). To Poseidon she bore two sons, Peliãs (see *Argonauts*) and Nēlēus (the father of Nestor, q.v.). By Crētheūs (brother of Salmoneus) she was mother of Aesōn and grandmother of Jāsōn (see *Argonauts*). See also *Melampus*.

Tyrrhē'nians, see *Etruscans*.

Tyrtae'us (*Turtaios*), a poet who lived at Sparta about the middle of the 7th c. B.C., at the time of the second Messenian War. The story that he was of Attic origin and sent by Athens to Sparta in response to a request for assistance in that war may probably be treated as merely a facetious anecdote. He encouraged the Spartans by his war-songs (in anapaests) and also wrote elegies, some of them exhorting the people to political peace and order, others to virtue and bravery. Only fragments of his work survive.

Tze'tzēs, see *Texts and Studies*, § 4.

U

U'lpian (*Domitius Ulpiãnus*), a Tyrian by birth, and a famous Roman jurist under Caracalla (A.D. 211–17). He was a pupil of Papinian (q.v.), became Praetorian Prefect and guardian of the young emperor Alexander Sevērus. He was murdered by soldiers in the imperial palace in 228. He was a voluminous writer of legal commentaries, extracts from which form a large part of the 'Digest' of Justinian (q.v.).

Uly'ssēs or ULI'XĒS, see *Odysseus*.

Ūra'nia (*Ourãniã*), see *Muses*.

Ū'ranus (*Ourãnos*), in Greek mythology the personification of the heavens; according to Hesiod the son of Ge (earth), and as her husband the father of the Titans (including Cronus, the father of Zeus), the Cyclopes, and the Hundred-handed Giants (qq.v.).

V

Vacū'na, a Sabine goddess of uncertain attributes. Horace (Ep. I. x. 49) speaks of himself as dictating the letter (from the Sabine hills) 'behind the mouldering temple of Vacuna'.

Valē'rius (*Valērius*) **Flaccus**, GĀIUS, a Latin poet of whom little is known except that he lived partly in the reign of Vespasian and was perhaps one of the *quindecimviri sacris faciundis* (q.v.). He is described as 'Setinus', and this may mean that he was a native of Setia, but

whether of Sētia in Campania or of Sētia in Spain is unknown. His epic poem, the 'Argonautica', on the quest of the Golden Fleece (see *Argonauts*), appears to have been begun c. A.D. 70. It was left unfinished (eight books were written), and the author appears to have died c. A.D. 90. In this work he followed principally the poem on the same theme by Apollonius Rhodius, but others (including Varro Atacinus, q.v.) had treated the subject, and these he may have consulted. Some of his incidents show the influence of the 'Odyssey' and the 'Aeneid', and he also introduces episodes of his own invention. The best part of the poem is in the 7th and 8th books, where with much art and in a graver and less playful manner than Apollonius he develops the character of Medea, torn between her passion for Jason and her loyalty to her father, and enlists the reader's sympathy for her. Jason he makes weak and irresolute, and leaves him contemplating the betrayal of his bride. The author shows narrative and descriptive power and an interest in psychological analysis. His work was completely forgotten until a manuscript of the first four books was rediscovered by Poggio in 1417.

Valē'rius (*Valērius*) **Maximus**, of whose life very little is known, except that he belonged to the period of Tiberius, was the compiler of an extant collection of anecdotes, 'Facta et Dicta Memorãbilia', in nine books, for the use of orators. The anecdotes are arranged, according to the subjects they illustrate, roughly as follows: Book I, religion, omens, prodigies; Book II, social customs; Books III–VI, virtuous conduct (fortitude, moderation, humanity, etc.); Books VII and VIII, a miscellaneous group including good fortune, military stratagems, famous law-suits, eloquence, and many other items; Book IX, evil conduct. The examples on each topic are grouped separately according as they are drawn from the lives of Roman or foreign worthies. The author's comments show little originality or breadth of view, and he flatters Tiberius. But the work proved useful, and its popularity, which it retained in the Middle Ages, is shown by the fact that two epitomes of it were made. It throws light here and there on the social history of Rome.

Vaphio Cups, see *Toreutic Art*.

Va'rius Rū'fus, LŪCIUS, a friend of Virgil and Horace, and the author of a tragedy on the story of Thyestes (q.v.) and of epics on Julius Caesar and the wars of Augustus. These have not survived. The tragedy 'Thyestes' was performed in 29 B.C. at the games in celebration of the victory of Actium, and the author re-received a million sesterces (say £8,000) for it from Augustus. Quintilian thought it the equal of any Greek tragedy. Varius was one of the editors of the 'Aeneid' after the death of Virgil.

Va'rrō, MARCUS TERENTIUS, *'Reātinus'* (116–27 B.C.), 'the most learned of Romans' according to Quintilian, was born at Reāte in Sabine territory of a well-to-do family. He was opposed to Caesar in politics, and was a Pompeian officer in Spain at the time of the Civil War, but was recon-ciled to Caesar and was to have been the head of the public library whose creation Caesar contemplated. He was a poet, satirist, antiquarian, jurist, geographer, grammarian, and scientist; and his voluminous writings (over 600 volumes) included also works on education and philosophy. Little of all this has survived except his 'De Re Rustica' (q.v.), six books out of the twenty-five of his 'De Lingua Latina', and fragments amounting to some 600 lines of his 'Satirae Menippeae'.

The 'De Lingua Latina' is a systematic treatise on Latin Grammar, dealing suc-cessively with Etymology, Inflexion, and Syntax, a pioneer work showing occasional penetration, but many of his derivations are absurd. Books V–X, which we possess, are dedicated to Cicero.

The 'Satirae Menippeae', satires on the model of Menippus (q.v.), in a mixture of prose and verse, some of them in dia-logue or semi-dramatic form, were critical sketches of Roman life, dealing with a great variety of subjects, and seasoned with jocularity. Many of them were directed, in a spirit of genial wisdom, against the growing luxury of the day, or against the doctrines of some of the Greek schools of philosophy. Only fragments have survived. W. W. Merry in 'Frag-ments of Early Roman Poetry' has at-tempted a reconstruction of a number of the Satires.

Varro's 'Hebdomades' or 'Imaginum libri XV' was a collection of character sketches in prose of celebrated Greeks and Romans, accompanied by portraits of the subjects, to each of which an epigram was appended (one of the earliest illustrated books).

Among his other more important works were the antiquarian treatises, 'Antiqui-tates Rerum Humanarum et Divinarum', 'De Gente Populi Romani', 'De Vita Populi Romani', a treatise 'Disciplinae' on the liberal arts (subsequently utilized by Martianus Capella, q.v.), and a treatise

on philosophy 'De Philosophia'. Varro was highly praised by Cicero (who dedi-cated to him the second edition of his 'Academica') and by Quintilian. The Christian Fathers, and St. Augustine in particular, make frequent reference to his works in connexion with Roman custom and religion. Varro himself was a student of Posidonius (q.v.), and a monotheist who saw in Jupiter the divine spirit animating the universe, and in the other gods differ-ent powers or virtues of that spirit.

Va'rrō, PUBLIUS TERENTIUS, 'Atacīnus' ('of Atax', a river in Gallia Narbōnensis), a Latin poet born in 82 B.C. He died before 36 B.C. He wrote satires on the model of Lucilius and an epic poem on Caesar's exploits in Gaul, called 'Bellum Sēquanicum'. He also wrote a free transla-tion of the 'Argonautica' of Apollonius Rhodius, and a geographical poem called 'Chōrographia'. Only fragments of his work survive.

Vā'rus, QUINTILIUS, (1) a critic, friend of Catullus and Virgil, mentioned by Horace in the 'Ars Poetica'. (2) A Roman general who in A.D. 9, when in command of the Roman armies on the Rhine, was lured by the German chief Arminius (= German *Hermann*) into the Teutoburgian forest, where the three legions that accompanied him were overwhelmed. The scene of the disaster was afterwards visited by Ger-manicus with a Roman army (see Tac. Ann. i. 60–2).

Vase-painting, GREEK. The art of deco-rating pottery was highly developed in Crete under the ancient civilization of that island. It reached its summit in the Middle Minoan (q.v.) period, with designs drawn in a graceful and natural style from flowers, shells, and fishes (especially cuttle-fish), usually in white, red, orange, and black. Some of the pottery was of extreme thinness. The industry declined in the Late Minoan period and ceased with the destruction of the Cretan civilization. The art was revived in various parts of the Greek world after the migrations (q.v.), for at a time when the working of metal was in its infancy, pottery was needed for a multitude of purposes. The decoration was at first of a rude and primitive charac-ter: geometrical designs, and, later, clumsy representation of men and animals. Such pottery was made in many places, Asia Minor, the islands of the Aegean, Corinth, Attica, and other parts of Greece. Athenian potters were able to produce as early as the end of the 9th c. the great vases found in the Dipylon cemetery, on which archaic figures of men and horses, in black on the red pottery, mingle with geometrical ornaments. Ionia, in the same archaic period produced vases on which wild animals, sphinxes and monsters of oriental type, appear in parallel bands, with lotus flowers and other decorations. Rhodes, Melos, and Miletus were among the chief sources. But the finest work of the early Greek period was that of the Corinthian artists, who in the 7th and 6th cc., with an improved technique of colour and more delicate design, decorated vases with friezes of animals, human figures, or representations of mythological scenes.

Attic pottery became prominent early in the 6th c. In this period the designs are in black enamel on a slightly glazed red ground; the faces and arms of the figures are in white. A splendid example, known as the François vase (in the Florence Museum) and made by the potter Ergotimus and the painter Clitias, dates from about 570 B.C. It has five zones of figures, representing various mythological scenes. From the time of Pisistratus date the first Panathenaic amphorae, which, filled with oil, were given as prizes to winners in the Panathenaic games. They have a figure of an armed Athene on one side, and on the other a representation of the contest for which the prize was given. The use of these amphorae as prizes continued to the end of the 4th c. B.C., and the name of the archon of the year was inscribed on them. Among the famous vase-painters of the black-figure period are Nicosthenês and Exêciâs (the artists frequently signed their work).

Beautiful as some of the examples of this period are, the art of vase painting reached its perfection in the next stage, when the background was painted black, and the figures were left in the red of the pottery, picked out with accessory colours. This stage began about 500 B.C. There were also vases of great beauty with a white background, specially intended for religious and funeral ceremonies. The great artists of this period include Euphronius, Euthymidês, Dûris, and Brygos (Andocidês was a painter of the transition). The style was at first severe, and mythological scenes predominated, but gradually gave place to pictures of daily life. A period of decadence, with much ornamentation and less simplicity and dignity, set in from about 400 B.C., and the industry declined and finally ceased about 100 B.C.

The word 'vase' is used in this article for vessels of a great variety of shapes and sizes and designed for many purposes, such as the *crâtér* or mixing-bowl, the *hydriâ* or water-jar, the *cylix*, a wide, shallow saucer, the *pyxis* or perfume box. Vase paintings throw light on many aspects of Greek life, religious observances, funeral ceremonies, industries, implements, and domestic conditions generally, filling in details that would otherwise be unknown to us. It was one of these ancient vases that inspired Keats's ode 'On a Grecian Urn' (1819).

Vāticā′nus, in early Roman religion, the spirit (*numen*, q.v.) that opens the child's mouth to cry. Also the name of the Vatican hill on the west bank of the Tiber opposite the ancient Rome.

Vĕ′diovis or **Vĕ′jovis,** in Roman religion, the 'opposite of Jupiter', probably his counterpart as a deity of the lower world, subsequently identified with the Greek Pluto (q.v.). He was celebrated three times a year; but his attributes were forgotten, and are now uncertain.

Vĕ′dius Po′llio, see under *Slavery*, § 2.

Vege′tius (*Flāvius Vegetius Renātus*), a military writer under the Emperor Theodosius I (A.D. 379–395), author of a Latin 'Epitoma Rei Militāris'. He is of great importance as a source of information on the Roman military system. He also wrote a treatise, which survives, on the diseases of mules and cattle.

Vēlā′brum, at Rome, the valley between the Palatine and the Capitol, a densely populated squalid part of the city. Through it ran the Vicus Tuscus, connecting the Roman Forum with the Forum Boarium; this street had an evil reputation (Hor. Sat. II. iii. 228–9). See Pl. 14 *b*.

Vellē′ius, GĀius, one of the interlocutors in Cicero's 'De Natura Deorum' (q.v.).

Vellē′ius Pate′rculus, GĀius, who lived under Augustus and Tiberius, belonged to a family that had been active in the civil and military service of the state. He himself served as a cavalry officer under Tiberius in Germany in A.D. 4, and later in Pannonia, and again in Germany after the disaster of Varus. He was author of a compendious history of Rome from the earliest times to his own days in two books, the first of which, in its extant form, is incomplete. The history shows partiality for the Caesars and enthusiasm, reaching adulation, in particular for Tiberius. It is not profound or philosophic, but mainly biographical, and is especially valuable for its portraits, e.g. that of Tiberius (which is in strong contrast to that left us by Tacitus) and on a smaller scale those of Caesar, Pompey, and Maecenas. The history is notable also as containing some chapters on the evolution of Latin literature. He discusses the reasons for its decline and suggests that the perfection reached in the Augustan age drove later writers in despair to seek minor fields. The style of the history is artificial and epigrammatic; some of the author's concise sayings show considerable observation and power of thought, e.g. 'difficilis in perfecto mora est', 'non ibi consistunt exempla ubi coeperunt'.

Vellum, see *Books,* § 5.

Vēnātiō′nēs, at Rome, the hunting of wild animals as a public display. We first hear of this form of amusement in 186 B.C., and frequently in the 1st c. B.C., as part of the various public games (see *Ludi,* § 1). Elephants (q.v.) were first shown in 99 B.C. Sulla in 93 exhibited 100 lions. The *venationes* displayed by Pompey lasted for five days, when 500 lions and 18 elephants were shown. They were received with mixed feelings: we are told that compassion was aroused for the animals. Cicero expressed repugnance for such spectacles in one of his letters. Roman spectators became more cruel and bloodthirsty under the empire. We hear for instance that 3,500 elephants were killed in the Circus in the reign of Augustus, and 5,000 wild and 4,000 tame animals were killed at the opening of the Colosseum. The men who fought with the animals were condemned criminals or prisoners of war, or were hired for the purpose.

Vē′nus (*Vĕnus*), in Roman religion, perhaps originally a goddess of gardens, this conception being later modified by ideas introduced from Sicily and Greece, and perhaps Cyprus and the East, till she assumed the form of the goddess of love and was identified with Aphrodite (q.v.). The earliest temple to her in Rome was dedicated in 295 B.C. VENUS GENETRIX was regarded as the mother of the Roman people, and more especially as the protectress of the Julian house, which traced its descent to Iulus (Ascanius) the grandson of Venus. There was a temple to Venus Genetrix in the Forum Julium (q.v.), vowed by Caesar on the battlefield of Pharsālus, and dedicated in 46 B.C. VENUS VERTICORDIA was the goddess, worshipped by Roman matrons, who turns women's hearts to chastity. For VENUS ERYCĪNA see *Aphrodite.*

Venu′sia, a town in Apūlia (S. Italy) close to the borders of Lūcānia, on the river Aufidus, the birthplace of Horace.

Ver Sacrum ('Sacred Spring'), in old Italian religion, the dedication to the gods, in time of great emergency, of the whole of the products of the ensuing spring, including the children born then. In historical times the children were not sacrificed but allowed to grow up and then expelled from the country. There was a *ver sacrum* at Rome in the 2nd Punic War (217 B.C.), by which the produce of the herds of swine, sheep, goats, and oxen during the ensuing spring were devoted to Jupiter (Livy, xxii. 10).

Vē′ra Histo′ria, see *Lucian.*

Vercinge′torix, leader of the Arverni (a Gallic tribe from whose name Auvergne is derived) in 52 B.C. in their war against Caesar. See *Commentaries* ('De Bello Gallico', Book vii).

Ve′rrēs, GĀIUS, propraetor in Sicily 73–71 B.C., where he showed himself a cruel and rapacious governor. He was impeached by Cicero (q.v., § 1) on behalf of the Sicilians in 70, threw up his case, and retired into exile. He kept some of his stolen treasures, and these, twenty-seven years later, attracted the cupidity of Antony. Verres was accordingly included in a proscription list and murdered.

Ve′rrius Flaccus, a freedman of the time of Augustus, a grammarian and teacher. We learn that he instituted competitions among his pupils with some fine ancient book for prize. He was appointed by Augustus tutor to his grandchildren. He wrote various works on antiquities, but is especially famous for his great encyclopaedia, 'De Verborum Significatu', 'on the meaning of words', dealing alphabetically not only with the Latin language, but with Roman antiquities generally. The work is lost, but we have a portion of an abridgement by Sextus Pompeius Festus in the 2nd c., and an epitome of Festus by Paulus Diaconus (8th c.). Verrius was also interested in the calendar, and erected in Praeneste, his native town, an annotated stone calendar, which (or a copy of which) survives in a damaged condition. It is known as the 'Fasti Praenestini'. There is a short account of Verrius Flaccus by Suetonius.

Vertu′mnus, see *Vortumnus.*

Ve′spae, see *Wasps.*

Vespā′sian (*Titus Flāvius Sabīnus Vespāsiānus*), Roman emperor A.D. 70–9, son of a tax-collector of Reāte, the first of the Flavian emperors (see *Rome,* § 11). He was remarkable for the simplicity of his mode of life and the economy and efficiency of his adminstration. Among his public works at Rome were the Colosseum (completed by Titus or Domitian), the reconstruction of the temple of the Capitoline Jupiter, and a temple to Peace, thought by Pliny one of the most beautiful buildings in the world. In it were assembled great numbers of works of art from many distant countries; among them the golden candlestick from the temple at Jerusalem.

Vespi'llō, LUCRĒTIUS, see *Women (Position of).*

Ve'sta, in Roman religion, the goddess of the blazing hearth. She was worshipped in every Roman household, while the sacred fire of the State was kept ever burning (except on 1 March, the start of the new year, when it was ceremonially renewed) in the circular Temple of Vesta, tended by the Vestals (q.v.). This temple stood S. of the Via Sacra, where it approached the Forum (see *Rome,* § 1, and Pl. 14 a), and is thought to have represented the house and hearth of the king, as the Vestals represented his daughters. The circular shape of the temple may be a relic of the shape of the prehistoric Roman house. The worship of Vesta, though she corresponded in name and attributes with the Greek Hestia (q.v.) was never affected by Greek influence.

Vestā'lia, the festival of Vesta. It was held on 9 June, and during the period 7–15 June the 'storehouse' in the temple of Vesta stood open and matrons brought their offerings. After this the temple was cleansed, and public business, which had been suspended during the period, was resumed. On 9 June asses were decked with violets and strings of loaves and given a holiday from the mill.

Vestals, in Roman religion, were virgins who represented the king's daughters of the regal period, and were charged with the preservation of the fire in the Temple of Vesta (q.v.), the State hearth. They also made the salt cake (*mola salsa*) for various festivals and had custody of a number of sacred objects, such as the Palladium and the ashes of the *Fordicidia* (qq.v.). The Vestals, originally drawn from patrician families, were four (later six) in number. They lived in a house near the Forum known as the *Atrium Vestae* (q.v.) and received a salary for their maintenance. If found guilty of unchastity they were buried alive in an underground chamber, in a place known as the *Campus Scelerātus* near the Colline Gate. The dreadful ceremony is described by Plutarch, who may have witnessed it, in his life of Numa (see also Pliny, Epist. iv. 11). After thirty years of service the Vestals returned to private life. Their institution was ascribed to king Numa, but there were Vestals at Alba before the foundation of Rome.

Via A'ppia, the first of the great Roman roads (q.v.), built by Appius Claudius Caecus in his censorship of 312 B.C. It ran from Rome to Capua, issuing from the city by the Porta Capēna. It was by the Appian Way that St. Paul entered Rome (Acts xxviii).

Via Sa'cra, at Rome, on the N. side of the Palatine, the approach to the most sacred parts of the city, the temples of Vesta and of the Penates, the Forum, and the Capitol (see Pl. 14 b). Horace's famous satire on the bore (I. ix) begins 'Ibam forte Via Sacra'.

Vidula'ria ('Wallet'), the title of a play by Plautus. This survives in a palimpsest of which only fragments are legible. The plot appears to have resembled that of the 'Rudens' (q.v.).

Vīginti'virate, originally the *Vigintisexvirate*, at Rome, twenty-six officials forming boards for the performance of minor magisterial duties. They included the *decemviri stlitibus judicandis* (q.v.); *tresviri capitāles,* assistants to the magistrates in criminal cases; *tresviri monētāles,* in charge of the mint; *quattuorviri viis purgandis,* in charge of the cleansing of the streets of the city. The above formed the vigintivirate under the empire. There were in addition under the republic two commissioners for the care of roads outside the city and four *praefecti Capuam Cumas,* who administered justice in certain communities outside Rome. These six posts were suppressed by Augustus. As the quaestors were twenty in number, it was usual under the empire for men elected to the vigintivirate to pass thence straight to the quaestorship.

Villa, a Latin term covering (1) the *villa rustica* or farmhouse attached to an estate, containing besides the actual farm buildings quarters for the use of the owner of the estate when he visited it; (2) the *villa pseudo-urbāna,* or country-house of a wealthy Roman, which served as a retreat from city life. We hear of Scipio Africanus occupying a modest villa of this kind at the end of his life; Cicero and his brother each owned several villas, and they became very numerous and luxurious under the empire, the most magnificent example being the villa of Hadrian at Tibur, of which the vast ruins may still be seen. For Roman villas in Britain see *Britain,* § 3.

Vīnā'lia, festivals held at Rome on 23 April and 19 August, in connexion with the cultivation of the vine. The god associated with the festivals was Jupiter, but their relation to the processes of cultivation is uncertain.

Vi'rgil (*Publius Vergilius Marō*) (70–19 B.C.), was born at Andēs near Mantua in

Virgil

447

Cisalpine Gaul, in the year of Pompey's first consulship. He was thus of Gallic origin, a little older than Horace and Augustus. Many see the Celtic element in him in the romantic spirit that pervades the 'Aeneid' (q.v.). The facts of his life are chiefly known to us from the biography of the commentator Donatus (q.v.), itself probably based on Suetonius. His father was a farmer or a potter; his mother's name was Magia Polla. He was educated at Cremona and Mediolanum (Milan), and later studied philosophy, rhetoric, and other higher subjects at Rome, one of his teachers being the Epicurean philosopher Siron. He then returned to a life of study and meditation on his Mantuan farm, and began the composition of the 'Eclogues' (q.v.) in 43 B.C. The confiscations of land which followed Philippi in 41 drove him from his farm. He was on friendly terms with the commissioners for the distribution of the confiscated lands (Gallus, Varus, and Pollio, qq.v.) and his petition to Octavian appears to have led to his reinstatement; but before long he took refuge in the villa of his teacher Siron, and thereafter lived for a time at Rome but chiefly in Campania, at Naples and Nola, where by the favour of Augustus he had residences. He had been introduced to the emperor by his patron Maecenas (q.v.), and to Maecenas he introduced Horace. Virgil completed and published the 'Eclogues' in 37, in which year we find him accompanying Horace on the journey to Brundisium (Hor. Sat. I. v). He completed the 'Georgics' (q.v.) in 30 B.C. and devoted the remaining eleven years of his life to the composition of the 'Aeneid' (q.v.). In his last year he undertook a voyage to the East to visit some of the scenes that he presented; he fell ill at Megara and returned to Italy, but died in 19 B.C. on reaching Brundisium. He was buried at Naples, where his tomb was revered in later ages. His major works are dealt with herein under their titles. A number of minor poems were attributed to him as the works of his youth, but it is doubtful whether any of these, except a few of the short pieces of the 'Catalepton' (q.v.), are in fact by him (see *Ciris, Culex, Moretum, Copa, Dirae, Lydia, Aetna*).

Virgil is represented by Donatus as tall and dark, with an appearance of rusticity. His health was weak, and in later life he shunned visits to Rome. He was diffident of his own poetic powers, but he became famous during his lifetime. His fame was based primarily on his position as the epic poet who revealed the greatness of the Roman empire; but his poetic eminence rests also on the technical perfection of his verse, on his tenderness and melancholy, and on his love of nature. He is the poet not only of the destiny of Rome, but of the beauty and fertility of Italy, and of Roman religion. Religion, indeed, plays an important part in the works of Virgil, especially in the 'Aeneid', to a less extent in the 'Georgics' and 'Eclogues'. Virgil loves to recall the ancient Roman beliefs, to describe religious rites and festivals. His sympathy is chiefly with the primitive animistic (see *Religion*, § 3) conception of the spirits (*numina*) and deities of the household and the countryside, Lar and the Penates, Vesta and Janus, the Fauni and Silvanus. In the anthropomorphic Graeco-Roman gods, except Jupiter, Juno, and Venus, he is less interested. His use for instance, of Aeolus, Iris, Neptunus, is merely ornamental, not religious. But Juno and Venus represent the workings of the opposed destinies of Greeks and Trojans (see *Religion*, § 5). Jupiter for him is not only bound up with his conception of the sanctity and destiny of Rome, but expresses an underlying monotheistic conception of the divine governance of the world. Of the imported Oriental cults he says hardly anything; even of Cybele he speaks only as a foreign deity. His treatment of the subject of the after-life of the spirits of the dead in Aen. vi is especially full and interesting. In it he blends folklore beliefs about the fate of souls and the punishment of the wicked, with Orphic and Stoic ideas about the purification of souls, and Pythagorean ideas of their transmigration. But the religious character of the poet lies, in a wider sense, in his recognition of the spiritual side of life, in his deep sympathy with suffering humanity, even with those who oppose the destiny of Rome (e.g. Dido, Turnus, Mezentius), and in his sense of the spiritual value of suffering.

Virgil's fame grew after his death into superstitious reverence. A legend that St. Paul wept over his tomb at Naples is preserved in a verse sung in a medieval mass:

Ad Maronis mausoleum
Ductus fudit super eum
Piae rorem lacrimae;
Quem te, inquit, reddidissem
Si te vivum invenissem,
Poetarum maxime!

He came to be regarded as a magician, and miraculous powers were attributed to him. The *Sortes Virgilianae*, attempts to foretell the future by opening a volume of his works at hazard, were from an early date widely practised (even by the emperor Hadrian). In later times it is related (Welwood,

'Memoirs of the most material Transactions') that King Charles I being in the Bodleian during the Civil War, at the suggestion of Lord Falkland made trial of his fortune by this method and lit upon Dido's imprecation on Aeneas, 'At bello audacis populi vexatus et armis . . .' (*Aen.* iv. 615 et seq.). Virgil's works also soon became, as they have remained, one of the most widely used of school-books, and the subject of commentaries by Donatus, Servius (qq.v.), and others. The early Christian writers reveal a conflict in their minds between their admiration of his poetry and their distrust of his paganism. The number and high quality of the manuscripts of Virgil that survive dating from the 3rd–5th c. attest the estimation in which he was then held. In a later age Dante regarded Virgil as a prophet of Christianity and made him his guide to the Gates of Paradise. The first edition of Virgil was printed c. 1469. In England and Scotland Virgil was well known from an early date. The story of the 'Aeneid' is given in part by Gower in his 'Confessio Amantis' and by Chaucer in his 'House of Fame' Caxton's version, 'Eneydos', taken from a French translation, dates from about 1490; that of Gawain Douglas from 1513. The Earl of Surrey (1517–47) translated part of the 'Aeneid' into blank verse, and Dryden the whole of Virgil (1697). The 'Aeneids' of W. Morris appeared in 1875. The famous commentaries and translation of Virgil by J. Conington appeared between 1858 and 1872. Tennyson in his lines 'To Virgil' (1882) for the nineteenth centenary of his death, paid a tribute to the 'wielder of the stateliest measure ever moulded by the lips of man'.

Virgi'nia (*Verginia*), according to Roman tradition, daughter of L. Verginius, a centurion, in the days when the decemvirs had been appointed at Rome to publish a code of laws (see *Twelve Tables*). Appius Claudius, one of the decemvirs, became enamoured of her, and in order to obtain possession of her, had her claimed as a slave by one of his dependants, and himself pronounced judgement in the latter's favour. Thereupon her father plunged a knife into her breast, and carrying the bloody knife rushed to the camp. A rising followed in which the decemvirs were overthrown. The story is told by Livy (iii. 44–58), and has been retold by Petrarch, and by Chaucer in the Doctor's Tale.

Vision, The, see *Lucian.*

Vita'rum Auctiō, see *Lucian.*

Vite'llius, AULUS, Roman Emperor after the defeat and death of Otho in April A.D. 69; noted for his gluttony and prodigality. In December 69 his forces were defeated by those of Vespasian, Rome was captured, and Vitellius murdered.

Vitrū'vius Po'llio, who saw military service (c. 50–26 B.C.) under Julius Caesar and Augustus, wrote a treatise in ten books 'De Architectura'. In this he deals not only with architecture and building in general, sites, materials, the construction of temples, theatres, and dwelling-houses, but also with decoration, water-supply, machines, sun-dials, and water-clocks. The work was illustrated with diagrams. It has no literary merits, but is nevertheless interesting, and is important as having influenced the principles of building at the Renaissance.

Volcā'tius Gallicā'nus, see *Historia Augusta.*

Volcā'tius Sēdi'gitus, see *Comedy,* § 5.

Voltu'rnus, see *Tiberinus.*

Volu'mnia, wife of Coriolanus (q.v.).

Vopi'scus, FLĀVIUS, see *Historia Augusta.*

Vortu'mnus (or less correctly VERTU'MNUS) a Roman god of orchards and fruit, who presided over the changes of the year. He was regarded as the husband of Pomona (q.v.), whom he wooed in a succession of various forms, as a reaper, ploughman, pruner of vines, &c. His name was variously explained, from *vertere* to turn, as the god who changes his shape, as the god of the turning year (autumn, the season of fruits), or as the god who once turned back a flood of the Tiber.

Vō'ta, see *Religion,* § 3.

Voyage to the Lower World, see *Lucian.*

Vu'lcan (*Volcānus*), an early Roman deity, a fire-god, perhaps a god of the smithy, later identified with Hephaestus. His festival on 23 May coincided with the *Tubilustria* (q.v.), and there was another festival in his honour on 23 August.

Vulgate (L. *Vulgāta* (sc. *ēditio* or *lectio*)), (1) a version of the Bible (or portion of this), ordinarily limited to (a) the Old Latin version preceding that of St. Jerome, and (b) particularly to the version of St. Jerome (q.v.); (2) in textual criticism, the ordinary or received text of a work or author.

W

Wasps (*Sphēkes*, L. *Vespae*), a comedy by Aristophanes, produced in 422 B.C. at the Lenaea, where it won the first or the second prize.

The play is a satire on the system of the

Jury Courts (see *Judicial Procedure*, § 1), which at that time provided, through the fee of three obols for a day's attendance, the chief means of support of a large number of Athenian citizens. Philocleôn ('Love-Cleon', see *Cleon*) is crazy with love of judging. His son Bdelycleôn ('Loathe-Cleon') has tried to cure him and has finally imprisoned him in his house. The chorus of old jurymen, dressed as wasps, come along before dawn to take him with them to the court; they assist him to escape. There is a scuffle between the jurymen and Bdelycleon's slaves, and a dispute follows between Philocleon and Bdelycleon as to the merits and evils of the jury system, in which Philocleon defends it on the score of the benefits that he personally derives from it, while Bdelycleon shows that the jurors are really the slaves of the rulers, who divert the bulk of the revenue destined to feed the hungry people. The chorus are converted, and Philocleon is persuaded to try his cases at home, beginning with Labês, the dog of the house, who has stolen a cheese. By a trick of his son's, he is led unintentionally to acquit the prisoner, the first that he has ever let off. Bdelycleon now takes in hand the social education of his father, improves his dress and manners, and takes him out to dinners. The results are unfortunate, for Philocleon gets drunk, insults his fellow guests, and behaves generally in an outrageous manner, finally leading off the chorus in a *Cordax* (q.v.). Racine imitated this play in his 'Les Plaideurs'.

Weights and Measures.

(See also Tables on pages 463–4.)

§ 1. *At Athens*

The principal weights and measures were:

(1) MEASURES OF WEIGHT, the talent (*talanton*), divided into 60 minae and 6,000 drachmae, differed from the money talent (see *Money*), and weighed about 83 lb. But the standard varied at different times and the subject is obscure.

(2) MEASURES OF LENGTH, the *plethron*, 100 Greek feet (the Greek foot was a little shorter than the English); the stadium (*stadion*), equal to six plethra or about 200 yards; the *daktulos*, one-sixteenth of a foot, the *kondulos* two-sixteenths.

(3) MEASURES OF CAPACITY, the *medimnos*, about 1·4 bushels; the *choinix* $\frac{1}{48}$ of a medimnus; the *kotulê* $\frac{1}{4}$ of a choenix.

(4) LIQUID MEASURE, the *metrêtês*, about 8¾ gallons; the *kotulê* $\frac{1}{144}$ of a metretes or about half a pint; the *kuathos* a quarter of

a *kotule*. But measures varied locally. There is for instance in the British Museum a Greek clay cup inscribed ἡμικοτύλιον which contains exactly half-a-pint; the *kotule* therefore, according to this standard, measured a pint.

§ 2. *At Rome*

The principal weights and measures were as follows:

MEASURES OF LENGTH, the foot (*pês* or *ûs*, the *as* probably being originally a bar of copper of a certain thickness a foot long), practically the same as the Attic foot and slightly shorter than the English foot, divided into twelve inches (*unciae*), and also into 16 fingers (*digiti*). Five feet = 1 *passus*, and 1,000 *passus* = 1 Roman mile, about $\frac{11}{12}$ of the English mile.

MEASURES OF WEIGHT, the *as* or *libra* or pound, this being the weight of the bar of copper mentioned above. This was divided into twelve ounces (*unciae*). The libra weighed about ¾ of the English pound.

MEASURES OF CAPACITY, (1) *liquid*, the *cadus* or *amphora* (= about six gallons), divided into eight *congii*; (2) *dry*, the *modius* (= about one peck or two gallons), divided into sixteen *sextārii* (each equivalent to a little less than a pint).

Winds, THE, both among the Greeks and Romans, were regarded as divine beings. In Homer, Boreas and Zephyrus have a specially defined personality. They live in a cavern in Thrace and rule over the other winds. Summoned by Iris, they revive the funeral pyre of Patroclus. Sometimes the winds are regarded by Homer as in the custody of Aeolus, sometimes as independent, invoked by men with prayer and sacrifice, or acting under the orders of Zeus. The horses of Achilles are the offspring of Zephyrus and Podargê (one of the Harpies). Hesiod calls the winds (except the maleficent Eurus) the children of Astraeus and Eos (qq.v.). After Thermopylae, Boreas, who was specially connected with the Athenians (see under *Boreas*), invoked on the advice of Delphi, destroyed the Persian fleet at Cape Sêpias. Thereafter an altar was erected to Boreas by the side of the Ilissus. Zephyrus also was worshipped in Greece in historical times. On the Tower of the Winds (of the 1st c. B.C.) at Athens, the winds are represented in human forms. In Italy Favonius, the favourable west wind, was especially venerated. There are many instances (from the story of Iphigenia onwards) of endeavours to conciliate the winds by offerings or magic practices. There was at Rome a temple to the *Tempestātes* or weather-goddesses, where sacrifices were offered. White animals were sacrificed to the beneficent winds, black animals to the stormy winds. See *Aquilo, Auster, Boreas, Eurus, Favonius, Notus, Zephyrus.*

Wolf, FRIEDRICH, see *Homer* and *Texts and Studies,* § 11.

Women, Position of.

§ 1. *In Greece*

In the heroic times, as depicted by Homer and the tragedians, women had a position of considerable independence. Penelope, Nausicaa, Andromache, Helen, Clytemnestra, Electra act and speak with a freedom unknown to Athenian women in later days. At Sparta also, in historical times, women had independence and authority; but not so in other parts of Greece. Corinna (q.v.) of Boeotia is the only poetess of some importance of whom we hear in Greece proper in the early centuries of its history. The women at Athens had their separate quarters in the house (see *Houses*); in these quarters the young girls would remain, under their mother's eye, so that, according to Xenophon, 'they might see, hear, and inquire as little as possible'. They would appear in public only in religious processions. Marriage was a business affair arranged by the parents, and the girl would have no previous acquaintance with her future husband. There was generally a great difference of age between a married pair: the man would be over 30 when he married, the girl often only 15. The daughter of a man who died without leaving a son was obliged by law to marry his nearest relative, so as to carry on the family. A marriage was celebrated, after the contract had been settled, by a sacrifice and a repast, given by the bride's father, at which both families were present; and the newly married pair might be accompanied to their home by a procession of friends, who threw sandals after them to drive away evil spirits. (There is in the British Museum a vase painting showing a wedded couple driving to the bridegroom's home in a mule-cart, attended by a friend seated behind). On the day following the marriage it was customary for relations and friends to bring presents. Once married, the Athenian woman passed under her husband's tutelage, without independent status. Her business was to look after her husband's house and clothes, the children and the slaves. She seldom went out; when she did so, it was generally to a

women's festival, a sacrifice, or procession, or a dramatic performance, and always accompanied by a slave or other attendant. She did not go to market or associate with her husband's friends. It was her duty 'to be spoken of as little as possible among men, whether for good or ill' (Thuc. ii. 45). In Xenophon's 'Oeconomicus' (q.v.), Ischomachus advises his young wife to improve her complexion by exercise rather than the rouge-pot, but the exercise is all to be taken within doors. The husband might divorce his wife by simple declaration before witnesses. The wife could obtain divorce only by judicial decision for grave causes. But in spite of its narrow limitations the married life of an Athenian woman does not appear to have been an unhappy one, and many epitaphs testify to deep affection, and to sorrow at separation. In the latter part of the 5th c. new ideas sprang up tending to the emancipation of women. We find traces of them in Euripides, and Plato gave them expression in the 'Republic' and the 'Laws'. The 'Ecclesiazusae' (392 B.C.) of Aristophanes shows that these ideas were a subject of general discussion, and although they were not destined to be realized, the comedies of Menander point to some change in the position of Greek women, in the direction of greater freedom. During the Hellenistic Age, the influence of the Macedonian court, where women played an important role, and of Stoicism probably tended to emancipation for those who desired it. Education was now within the reach of women, and we hear of women among the pupils of philosophers, of a woman scholar, of another a painter, and once more of poetesses. Women were granted the citizenship of other cities than their own for services rendered, and in the 1st c. B.C. a woman was the chief magistrate of Priene. But such emancipation was the lot of only a minority.

As the law forbade the marriage of Athenian citizens except with the daughters of other Athenian citizens, a sort of irregular union with foreign women was frequent in the 5th and 4th cc. These women, known as hetaerae (*hetairai*, literally 'companions', and including concubines and courtesans), were often Ionians, whose charm was increased by a high degree of intelligence and education, making them more agreeable companions than the cloistered Athenian women. The most famous of these hetaerae was Aspasia (see *Pericles*).

§ 2. *At Rome*

Women, in Roman society, had a position of greater dignity than in Greece.

The woman, when married, was the true mistress of the house, sitting in the *atrium* (see *Houses*, § 2), and not secluded in the women's apartment. She controlled the female slaves and took her meals with her husband. She could go out, wearing the *stola mātrōnālis* (see *Clothing*, § 3), and was treated with great respect; she might be seen in the theatre or law-courts. Marriage, the *justum mātrimonium*, sanctioned by law and religion, was in early times a solemn ceremony, implying the transfer of the woman from her father's control (*potestas*) to that of her husband (*manus*). It took the form of *confarreātio* (q.v.) or of *coemptio*, a symbolical form of purchase with the consent of the bride. Marriage could also be effected by *usus*, if the woman lived with her husband for a year, without absenting herself for three nights.

A process of emancipation of women began from the 2nd c. B.C. The older forms of marriage were gradually abandoned for one in which the woman remained in the tutelage of her father's family and retained, in practice, control of her property. We find women becoming rich. There are many instances of women of literary culture. The frequency of divorces increased. We have clever, ambitious women like Clodia (q.v.), and Semprōnia (wife of D. Junius Brutus), who took a part in Catiline's conspiracy. Women appear to have occasionally been active in the courts: 'Jūrisperīta' is the title of a *fabula togata* by Titinius, and Valerius Maximus tells of a certain Afrānia in the 1st c. B.C. who was a constant litigant and tired the courts with her clamour (see also *Hortensia*). Marriage under the empire became unpopular, and measures had to be taken to encourage it by penalizing the unmarried (see also *Jus trium liberorum*). As early as 131 B.C. Q. Caecilius Metellus Macedonicus, as censor, had delivered a famous speech, which later earned the approval of Augustus, on the necessity of increasing the birth-rate. He said: 'If we could get on without a wife, Romans, we would all avoid the annoyance, but since nature has ordained that we can neither live very comfortably with them nor at all without them, we must take thought for our lasting well-being rather than for the pleasure of the moment' (Suet. Aug. 89, transl. Loeb ed.). Juvenal's 'Satires' point to the demoralization of a section of female society. On the other hand there is abundant evidence in literature (e.g. in Statius and in Pliny's letters) and in epitaphs that happy marriages were not infrequent. The most striking instance is the encomium preserved in an inscription (C.I.L. vi. 1527), supposed to be that of

a certain Lucretius Vespillo who served under Pompey in 48 B.C. and was consul under Augustus in 19 B.C., on his wife Turia. The encomium records how faithfully and courageously she served him in their romantic and perilous adventures, both when betrothed and during forty-one years of married life.

Works and Days (*Erga kai Hēmerai*), a poem in 828 hexameters by Hesiod.

The chief themes of the poem are the need for justice in a tyrannical age and the need for work. After an invocation to the Muses, the poet addresses his brother Persēs, urging him to a reconciliation of their quarrel (see under *Hesiod*). He relates the fable of the Hawk and the Nightingale, illustrative of tyranny, and the myths of Pandora (q.v.) and of the Five Ages of Mankind (Golden, Silver, Bronze, Heroic, and Iron) to explain man's present toilsome lot. The poem then proceeds to a sort of farmer's calendar, in the main an enumeration of the work to be done at various seasons, with a little technical instruction; some brief advice on mercantile navigation; a collection of gnomic precepts on social and religious conduct; and a calendar of lucky and unlucky days. It has the appearance of a group of detached pieces loosely connected, but united by the single personality of the author; in these later interpolations have perhaps been made. It represents the life-experience of a single close-fis**'**d **ṛ**easant, schooled in adversity, circumspɛct, grumbling but courageous, and is narked by simplicity and a sense of human misery.

The 'Works and Days' is a prototype of Thomas Tusser's 'Pointes of Good Husbandry' (1557–80).

Writing Materials, see *Books*.

Wryneck, used in magic spells; see *Magic*.

X

Xanthi′ppus (*Xanthippos*), (1) father of Pericles (q.v.). He commanded the Athenian fleet after Salamis and at Mycalē (see *Persian Wars*). He had come into conflict with Aristides and had been ostracized in 484, but had been recalled at the time of the invasion of Xerxes. (2) A Spartan who, in the course of the First Punic War, commanded the Carthaginian defence force in Africa, and in 255 defeated and captured Regulus (q.v.)

Xa′nthus (*Xanthos*) of Lydia, see *Logographi* (1).

Xa'nthus and Ba'lius (*Xanthos, Balios*), in Greek mythology, the immortal horses of Achilles (q.v.), offspring of Zephyrus and the Harpy (q.v.) Podargē ('Swift-foot'). Xanthus had the gift of speech and prophesied Achilles' death.

Xeno'crates, see *Academy*.

Xeno'phanes of Colophōn in Ionia, whose long life extended over the greater part of the 6th c. B.C., was a wandering poet who visited many parts of the Greek world. He wrote a philosophical poem on Nature, in hexameters of which a few fragments survive. He attacked the polytheism and anthropomorphism of the traditional Greek religion and asserted that God is single and eternal. From the presence of fossils of fishes in mountains he inferred that land and sea had undergone great changes. He also wrote elegies, the fragments of which reveal his amiable gravity and good sense. The view formerly held that he was the founder of the Eleatic School of philosophy is now discredited. See also *Silloi*.

Xe'nophon (*Xenophōn*), an Athenian, son of Gryllus (*Grullos*), born at an unknown date about 430 B.C. He made the acquaintance of Socrates, and although he had no aptitude for philosophy became an ardent admirer of the sage. It is related that Socrates first met Xenophon, then a boy, in the street, and stopping him asked him where various articles could be got. Xenophon told him. Socrates then asked 'and where can you get gallant and virtuous men ?', and when the boy was perplexed for an answer, said 'Then follow me'. In 401 Xenophon, at the invitation of his Boeotian friend Proxenus, joined the expedition of Cyrus related by him in the 'Anabasis' (q.v.). After having, by his personal courage and military gifts, successfully extricated the Ten Thousand Greeks from this adventure, he in 396 accepted service with the Spartan King Agesilaus against the Persian Pharnabazus, and when Agesilaus was recalled by events in Greece, accompanied him and was present (perhaps as a non-combatant) on the Spartan side at the battle of Coronea (394). His exile from Athens and the confiscation of his property were decreed. The date of this is uncertain, but it appears to have been, in any case, after his return from the Anabasis. The Spartans provided him with an estate at Scillūs in Elis, where he spent the next twenty years of his life, as a country gentleman, hunting, and writing his various works. In 370 he was driven from Scillus by a rising of Eleans and retired to Corinth. The decree of his exile was revoked, probably about 365, but it is doubtful whether he ever returned to Athens. His two sons fought on the Athenian side at Mantinea (362), where one of them, Gryllus, was killed. Xenophon died about 355.

He wrote on numerous subjects, suggested by his varied experience. One group of his writings, 'Memorabilia', 'Apology', and 'Symposium', was inspired by his recollections of Socrates; 'Oeconomicus' by his home life; 'Anabasis' and 'Cyropaedia' by his experiences in Persia; his treatises on 'The Cavalry Commander' and 'Horsemanship' by his military career and devotion to sports; 'Hellenica', 'Agesilaus', 'Constitution of Sparta', 'Hieron', 'Revenues', by his acquaintance with political affairs in various countries. The above works are dealt with herein under their several titles; the authenticity of some of them has been questioned, but is now generally accepted. The treatise on 'Hunting' (*Cynegeticus*, q.v.), at any rate in its present form, though often attributed to Xenophon, is regarded by competent authorities as not by him. For the 'Constitution of the Athenians' preserved among Xenophon's works, but almost certainly not by him, see under that title. His two best works are the 'Anabasis' and the 'Hellenica' or History of Greece. Xenophon's writings reveal him as a lover of the country and of rural sports, a keen soldier, pious to the gods, an easy, lucid, and agreeable writer, sensible but not profound, an enthusiastic amateur rather than a specialist in anything, above all a very natural human being behind the author. Quintilian speaks warmly of his unaffected charm. Landor has an 'Imaginary Conversation' between Xenophon and the younger Cyrus.

Xe'nophon of Ephesus, see *Novel*.

Xe'rxēs, see *Persian Wars*.

Xū'thus (*Xouthos*), (1) see *Hellenes* and *Deucalion*; (2) see *Ion*.

Z

Za'grēus, see *Dionysus Zagreus*.

Zēn'o (*Zēnōn*), (1) of Elea (*fl. c.* 460 B.C.), a follower of Parmenides (q.v.) in the Eleatic school of philosophy. He supported the teaching of his master by pointing out the paradoxical results of the views on space and time held by the supporters of other philosophical doctrines. The best known of these paradoxes is that of 'Achilles and the Tortoise'. He figures in the 'Parmenides' of Plato (q.v.). (2) of Citium in Cyprus (*fl. c.* 300 B.C.), regarded by his contemporaries as a Phoenician, the founder of the Stoic school of philosophy (see *Stoics*). Zeno became the teacher and friend of Antigonus Gonātas (see *Macedonia*, § 3). Among his pupils was Sphaerus, who inspired the revolution of Cleomenes III at Sparta (q.v., § 5). Athens honoured Zeno with a public funeral, as a man who 'had made his life an example to all, for he followed his own teaching'.

Zēno'bia, widow and successor in A.D. 266 or 267 of Odenathus, ruler of Palmȳra, a city state in Syria which from the 2nd c. A.D. had enjoyed the favour and protection of successive Roman emperors. Zenobia was an ambitious woman who invaded Asia Minor and Egypt in open hostility to Rome. She was captured and deposed by Aurelian (272) and Palmyra was utterly destroyed.

Zēno'dotus (*Zēnodotos*) of Ephesus, scholar and critic, the first head of the Alexandrian Library (*fl. c.* 285 B.C.); see *Texts and Studies*, § 2. He was the earliest scientific editor of Homer, basing his text on a comparison of numerous manuscripts. He also produced an edition of Hesiod's 'Theogony'.

Ze'phyrus (*Zephuros*), in Greek mythology, the personification of the West Wind, the father of Achilles' horses Xanthus and Balius (q.v.); sometimes also represented as husband of Iris (q.v.).

Zē'thus (*Zēthos*), see *Antiope*.

Zeugi'tai, see *Athens*, § 2.

Zeu'gma ('yoking'), a figure of speech in which a verb or adjective is used with two nouns to one of which only it is strictly applicable; e.g.

> Κυκλώπων δ' ἐς γαῖαν ἐλεύσσομεν ἐγγὺς
> ἐόντων,
> καπνόντ' αὐτῶν τε φθογγὴν ὀΐων τε καὶ αἰγῶν
> (Hom. Od. ix. 166–7)

where ἐλεύσσομεν is not strictly applicable to φθογγήν. Or

> Audis quo strepitu janua, quo nemus
> inter pulchra satum tecta remugiat
> ventis, et positas ut glaciet nives
> puro numine Jupiter?
> (Hor. Od. III. x. 5–7)

where the verb 'audis' is used with two clauses to the first of which only it is applicable. Cf. *Syllepsis*.

Zēūs, in Greek mythology the youngest (according to Homer the eldest) son of Cronus (q.v.), whom he overthrew and succeeded as the supreme god. The name is apparently from a root meaning 'bright', and Zeus is the god of the sky and the weather, but also associated with most aspects of human life. He was born in Crete, according to what is probably the oldest legend, or in Arcadia and brought to Crete, where he was hidden in a cave on Mt. Dicte (q.v.) or Mt. Ida, and fed by the goat Amalthea (q.v.). The Curetes (q.v.), in order to conceal him, drowned his cries by their noisy ritual. After the overthrow of Cronus, Zeus and his brothers divided the universe by casting lots, Zeus obtaining heaven, Poseidon the sea, and Hades the underworld. The legend in parts points to a Cretan origin; on the other hand Zeus appears to have been the principal deity of the Hellenes when they migrated into Greece.

Zeus is represented in various legends as the consort of a number of goddesses. But the Greeks were monogamous, and the idea finally prevailed that Zeus had but one legitimate spouse, generally Hera, to whom, however, he was unfaithful. His unions with mortal women may be accounted for in some cases by the claim of royal houses to be descended from him. According to Hesiod he was first married to Metis (Wisdom) and their child was Athene (q.v.); the latter was probably a pre-Hellenic goddess, and the myth may be due to a desire to reconcile her existence with the cult of the invaders. His other chief alliances were with Demeter, by whom he had Persephone (qq.v.); with Leto, by whom he had Apollo and Artemis (qq.v.); and with Hera, by whom he had Hebe, Ares, and Eileithyia (qq.v.). From his alliance with Maia, daughter of Atlas, was born Hermes (q.v.). For his alliances with mortal women see *Dionysus* (for Semele), *Amphitryon* (for Alcmene), *Danae*, *Io*, *Europa*, *Antiope*, *Leda*.

Zeus is the dispenser of good and evil in the destinies of men, but principally of good; he is the father and saviour (*Zeus Sōtēr*) of men. He is the giver of the laws that rule the course of events, and he knows the future, and sometimes reveals it to men by portents and oracles. He sees that justice is done and punishes perjury. He is the defender of the house (*Herkeios*), of the hearth (*Ephestios*), of the rights of hospitality (*Xenios*), and of liberty (*Eleutherios*). As *Zeus Ktēsios* he is the guardian of property and his image is set up in the store-room. As *Zeus Chthonios* he is the god of the earth and a giver of fertility. He is supreme among the gods, and limited in his universal power only by the mysterious dictates of Fate. He corresponds to, and was identified with, the Roman Jupiter (q.v.). See also *Lycaeus*.

Zeus is represented in art, notably in the Vatican bust (thought to be an imitation of the statue by Phidias), with a noble bearded face, marked by calm and benignity He is generally shown holding the thunderbolt (an object sometimes conceived as like a dumbell with conical ends) and the aegis (a fringed goatskin or shield), the latter when shaken a source of terror to his enemies, sometimes interpreted as a thunder cloud.

Zeus Confūtā'tus, see *Lucian.*

Zeu'xis, of Heraclea in S. Italy, one of the most famous painters of ancient Greece, who flourished in the latter part of the 5th c. B.C., celebrated for his success in rendering the beauty of female forms. His skill in producing illusion is attested by the story that birds flew down to peck at a bunch of grapes that he had painted (cf. *Parrhasius*). One of his most celebrated paintings was a picture of Helen for the temple of Hera on the Lacinian promontory in Magna Graecia. Another, a picture of a Centauress and her young, is described by Lucian. There is a tale that he died of laughing at a comical picture of an old woman that he had drawn. See also *Painting.*

Zmy'rna, a short epic poem in Latin on the myth of Myrrha and Adonis (q.v.) by C. Helvius Cinna (q.v.). It was worked up by its author for nine years, and was a typical instance of the influence of Alexandrianism (q.v.) on Roman poetry. Catullus predicted immortality for it, but only three lines survive.

Zō'ilus (*Zōilos*) of Amphipolis, rhetorician and critic of the 4th c. B.C. who signalized himself by his strictures on Homer, with which he filled nine books. He criticized him mainly on points of invention (such as the description of the companions of Odysseus as 'weeping' when turned into swine), but also on points of grammar. Tradition relates that the indignant Greeks assembled at a festival threw him down from the Scironian rocks (see *Sciron*). His name has become proverbial for a carping critic.

Zo'simus (*Zōsimos*) (5th c. A.D.) author of an extant history in four books, in Greek, of the Roman Empire to about A.D. 410.

LATIN LANGUAGE

Latin is the language of the City of Rome, which spread with the power of Rome until it became the language of most of western Europe. Italian, French, Spanish, Portuguese, and also Roumanian derive from it.

The local speech of Rome was one of several closely related dialects which formed the ITALIC group in the Indo-European family of languages. Of these dialects the best known, apart from Latin, are OSCAN, spoken in the Samnite territories, and UMBRIAN from the district north-east of Rome; but they are recorded only in inscriptions, proper names, and the writings of early grammarians. Classical Latin has some irregular forms which appear to be borrowed from dialects, e.g. *bos* 'ox', *anser* 'goose', where one would expect **uos*, **hanser.*

In the course of its long history, Latin underwent considerable change; and the development of the literary language was particularly influenced by Greek. The following periods are distinguished: Early Latin up to about 100 B.C.; Classical Latin from 100 B.C. to the death of Augustus, A.D. 14 (the literary activity of Cicero and Caesar gives special importance to the years 81–43 B.C.); 'Silver' Latin is applied to the post-Classical period up to about A.D. 150, to mark a falling-off from the preceding 'golden' age. Late Latin merges into Medieval Latin. In all these stages Latin was a literary language. The uncultivated spoken language which survived in Italian, French. &c.. is called Vulgar Latin.

The best sketch of the history of Latin is A. Meillet's *Esquisse d'une histoire de la langue latine.* Good historical grammars are W. M. Lindsay, *Short Historical Latin Grammar* (elementary); W. Sommer, *Handbuch der lateinischen Laut- und Formenlehre*; F. Stolz, J. H. Schmalz, &c., *Lateinische Grammatik* (complete work of reference). For etymology consult Ernout and Meillet, *Dictionnaire étymologique de la langue latine* and Walde and Hofmann, *Lateinisches etymologisches Wörterbuch.* For the later development of Latin and its influence on English, see H. Bradley in *The Legacy of Rome* (Oxford).

DATE CHART OF CLASSICAL LITERATURE

B.C.	Greek authors	B.C.	Latin authors	B.C.	Contemporary events
	HOMER, date unknown, perhaps 9th c.			1184	Fall of Troy (traditional date).
	HESIOD, perhaps 8th c.			c. 12th c.	Dorian Migration.
	EARLY CYCLIC POETS, 8th c. (?)			776	Series of Olympiads begins.
					Assyrian empire predominant in Asia.
	CALLINUS			753	Foundation of Rome (traditional date).
	TERPANDER				
	ALCMAN } lyric poets			c. 670	Gyges, king of Lydia, sends gifts to Delphi.
	ARCHILOCHUS			655–c. 585	Cypselus and Periander, tyrants of Corinth.
7th c.	SEMONIDES OF SAMOS				
	THALETAS			c. 630–600	Sparta conquers Messenia.
	ARION			c. 621	Draco legislates at Athens.
	TYRTAEUS } elegiac poets			612	Fall of Assyrian empire, rise of Media and Babylonia.
	MIMNERMUS				
600					
fl. c. 600	ALCAEUS			c. 593	Legislation of Solon.
"	SAPPHO			586	Babylonian captivity of Jews begins.
"	STESICHORUS				
" 540	SOLON			c. 570	Phalaris, tyrant of Acragas.
fl. c. 540	HIPPONAX			560–527	Tyranny of Pisistratus.
6th c.	PHOCYLIDES } poets			560–546	Croesus king of Lydia.
"	ANACREON			550	Cyrus overthrows Media and founds Persian empire.
"	IBYCUS				
"	THEOGNIS			546–545	Cyrus conquers Lydia and reduces Asiatic Greeks.
fl. c. 534	THESPIS				
6th c.	CORINNA			538	Cyrus captures Babylon.
"	XENOPHANES, poet and philosopher			c. 535	Polycrates, tyrant of Samos.
"	THALES			525	Persians conquer Egypt.
"	ANAXIMANDER } philosophers			521	Accession of Darius.
" 580	ANAXIMENES			514	Harmodius and Aristogiton murder Hipparchus.
b. c. 580	PYTHAGORAS			512	Scythian expedition of Darius.
fl. c. 500	HERACLITUS			c. 507	Reforms of Cleisthenes.
6th c.	CADMUS OF MILETUS } historians				
fl. c. 500	HECATAEUS				
6th c.	AESOP, fabulist				

B.C.	Greek authors	B.C.	Latin authors	B.C.	Contemporary events
500					
c. 556-468	SIMONIDES OF CEOS ⎫ lyric poets			499-493	Ionian revolt against Persia.
b. c. 548	LASUS OF HERMIONE ⎬			490	Persians defeated at Marathon.
c. 518-443	PINDAR ⎭			480	Expedition of Xerxes. Battles of Thermopylae and Salamis.
c. 505-450	BACCHYLIDES			"	Gelon defeats Carthaginians at Himera.
fl. c. 500	EPICHARMUS			479	Defeat of Persians at Plataea.
" c. 496	PHRYNICHUS			478-477	Confederacy of Delos founded.
	PRATINAS			474	Hieron defeats Etruscans off Cumae.
525-456	AESCHYLUS			468	Persians defeated at the Eurymedon.
495-406	SOPHOCLES ⎫ dramatists			462	Reforms of Ephialtes.
480-406	EURIPIDES ⎬			459-446	Athens at war with Peloponnesian alliance.
c. 520-423	CRATINUS ⎭			454	Athenian expedition to Egypt destroyed.
c. 446-411	EUPOLIS			445	Nehemiah at Jerusalem.
c. 448-380	ARISTOPHANES			442	Pericles at height of his power.
fl. c. 470	PARMENIDES ⎫ philosophers			431	Commencement of Peloponnesian War.
fl. c. 460	ZENO OF ELEA ⎬			429	Death of Pericles.
fl. c. 450	EMPEDOCLES ⎭			425	Capture of Sphacteria.
469-399	SOCRATES			421	Peace of Nicias.
fl. c. 420	DEMOCRITUS			419	Peloponnesian war resumed.
5th c.	HELLANICUS ⎫ historians			415-413	Sicilian expedition.
c. 480-425	HERODOTUS ⎬			412	Revolt of Athenian allies.
c. 460-400	THUCYDIDES ⎭			406	Battle of Arginusae.
c. 485-375	GORGIAS, orator and sophist			405	Battle of Aegospotami.
b. c. 485	PROTAGORAS			404	Surrender of Athens. The Thirty in power.
5th c.	HIPPIAS OF ELIS ⎫ sophists				
	PRODICUS OF CEOS ⎭				
c. 480-411	ANTIPHON ⎫ orators				
b. c. 458	LYSIAS ⎬				
b. c. 440	ANDOCIDES ⎭				
b. c. 460	HIPPOCRATES, physician				

B.C.	Greek authors	B.C.	Latin authors	B.C.	Contemporary events
400					
fl. c. 400	ANTISTHENES			404–371	Sparta supreme in Greece.
4th c. (?)	EUCLIDES OF MEGARA ⎫ philosophers			400–386	Sparta at war with Persia.
	⎬			395–386	Corinthian War.
427–348	PLATO			394	Battle of Coronea.
384–322	ARISTOTLE			386	Peace of Antalcidas.
c. 371–287	THEOPHRASTUS			377	Second Athenian confederacy.
fl. c. 325	CRATES (Cynic)			371	Sparta defeated at Leuctra.
fl. c. 300	ZENO (Stoic)			370	First Invasion of Peloponnese by Epaminondas.
341–270	EPICURUS			362	Victory and death of Epaminondas at Mantinea.
c. 365–275	PYRRHON			359	Accession of Philip II of Macedon.
4th c.	ANTIPHANES			357–355	Social War.
"	ANAXANDRIDES ⎫ comic dramatists			346	Peace of Philocrates.
c. 361–263	PHILEMON ⎬			339	Timoleon defeats Carthaginians at the Crimisus.
848–292	MENANDER			338	Athens and Thebes defeated by Philip at Chaeronea.
4th c.	DIPHILUS			336	Accession of Alexander the Great.
436–338	ISOCRATES			333	Alexander's victory at Issus.
c. 420–350	ISAEUS			331	Foundation of Alexandria.
c. 390–314	AESCHINES ⎫ orators			,,	Alexander's victory at Gaugamela.
383–322	DEMOSTHENES ⎬			327	Alexander invades India.
fl. 350–326	LYCURGUS			323	Death of Alexander.
b. 389	HYPERIDES			,,	The Lamian War.
b. c. 360	DINARCHUS			323–288	Ptolemy I in Egypt.
fl. c. 400	CTESIAS			317–307	Demetrius of Phalerum rules Athens.
c. 430–355	XENOPHON			311–306	War of Agathocles of Syracuse against Carthage.
fl. c. 360–340	EPHORUS ⎫ historians			305–304	Demetrius Poliorcetes besieges Rhodes.
b. 376	THEOPOMPUS ⎬			301	Battle of Ipsus.
fl. c. 300	DICAEARCHUS				
c. 346–250	TIMAEUS				
447–357	TIMOTHEUS, musician				
fl. c. 350	ZOÏLUS, critic				
4th c. (?)	ERINNA, poetess				

B.C.	Greek authors	B.C.	Latin authors	B.C.	Contemporary events
300					
fl. 300	PHILITAS			298-290	Third Samnite War.
b. c. 325	LYCOPHRON } poets			285-247	Ptolemy II in Egypt.
b. c. 315	ARATUS	fl. 312-280	APPIUS CLAUDIUS CAECUS, orator	280	Rome at war with Tarentum and Pyrrhus.
fl. c. 270	THEOCRITUS	c. 284-204	LIVIUS ANDRONICUS } poets		
fl. c. 250	TIMON OF PHLIUS	c. 270-199	NAEVIUS	272	Rome takes Tarentum.
b. c. 310	CALLIMACHUS	c. 254-184	PLAUTUS	266	Rome supreme in Italy.
c. 295-215	APOLLONIUS RHODIUS	239-169	ENNIUS	266-262	Chremonidean war in Greece.
c. 300-250	HERODAS	fl. c. 214	Q. FABIUS PICTOR, historian	264-241	First Punic War.
fl. c. 235	EUPHORION			241-197	Attalus I king of Pergamum.
fl. 270	CRATES (Acad.) } philosophers			240	First Latin play performed at Rome.
c. 315-240	ARCESILAS				
c. 330-231	CLEANTHES			227	Reforms of Cleomenes III at Sparta.
fl. c. 285	ZENODOTUS } scholars			223-187	Antiochus the Great rules Syria.
fl. c. 234	ERATOSTHENES				
3rd c.	PHILOCHORUS } historians			218-202	Second Punic War.
" c. 300	BEROSUS			216	Battle of Cannae.
" c. 320	MANETHO			207	Battle of the Metaurus.
	EUCLID, mathematician			202	Battle of Zama.
fl. c. 300	ARISTARCHUS, astronomer				
b. c. 320	ARCHIMEDES, physicist				
c. 287-212					
200					
2nd c.	MOSCHUS } poets			200-197	Second Macedonian War.
	NICANDER	c. 219-166	CAECILIUS STATIUS	197	Battle of Cynoscephalae.
fl. " 195	ARISTOPHANES OF } scholars	c. 220-130	PACUVIUS	190	Antiochus defeated by Romans at Magnesia.
	BYZANTIUM	185-159	TERENCE } poets		
	ARISTARCHUS	170-c. 86	LUCILIUS	183	Death of Philopoemen.
fl. c. 180	DIONYSIUS THRAX	b. c. 150	ACCIUS	171-168	Third Macedonian War.
b. c. 166	POLYBIUS } historians	c. 185-129	AFRANIUS	168	Battle of Pydna. Polybius brought to Rome.
c. 202-120	APOLLODORUS	fl. 140	SCIPIO AEMILIANUS } orators		
fl. c. 140	CARNEADES } philosophers	d. 133	C. LAELIUS	155	Visit of Critolaus, Carneades, and Diogenes to Rome.
214-129	PANAETIUS	d. 121	TI. GRACCHUS		
c. 180-110	HIPPARCHUS, mathematician		C. GRACCHUS	149-146	Third Punic War.
b. c. 190		234-149	CATO, orator and historian	146	Carthage and Corinth destroyed by Romans.
		2nd c.	VOLCATIUS SEDIGITUS, critic	143-133	Numantine War.
				133	Tribunate of Ti. Gracchus.
				123-122	Tribunates of Gaius Gracchus.
				113-102	Cimbrian War.
				111-106	Jugurthine War.

B.C.	Greek authors	B.C.	Latin authors	B.C.	Contemporary events
100		c. 105–43	LABERIUS	100	Suppression of Saturninus.
fl. c. 100 ?	BION	c. 99–55	LUCRETIUS	90–88	Marsian War.
fl. c. 100	ANTIPATER OF SIDON } poets	c. 84–54	CATULLUS	82	Dictatorship of Sulla.
	MELEAGER	82–c. 37	VARRO ATACINUS	73	Revolt of Spartacus.
fl. c. 60	DIODORUS SICULUS, historian	fl. 43	PUBLILIUS SYRUS } poets	70	First consulship of Pompey.
fl. c. 40	STRABO, geographer	70–26	GALLUS	63	Consulship of Cicero.
c. 64–A.D. 19	DIONYSIUS OF HALICARNASSUS, scholar	70–19	VIRGIL	60	First triumvirate.
c. 25		65–8	HORACE	58–51	Conquest of Gaul.
		c. 60–19	TIBULLUS	49	Caesar crosses the Rubicon.
c. 135–51	POSIDONIUS, philosopher	c. 50–16	PROPERTIUS	48	Battle of Pharsalus.
		43–A.D. 18	OVID	45	Pompeians defeated at Munda.
		fl. 76	SISENNA	44	Death of Caesar.
		d. 66	MACER	43	Second triumvirate.
		102–44	JULIUS CAESAR	42	Battle of Philippi.
		c. 100–25	NEPOS	39	Pollio founds first public library.
		86–35	SALLUST } historians		
		d. 43	A. HIRTIUS	31	Battle of Actium.
		76–A.D. 5	POLLIO	27–A.D. 14	Principate of Augustus.
		50–A.D. 17	LIVY	13–9	Campaigns of Drusus in Germany.
		fl. c. 20	POMPEIUS TROGUS	4	Death of Herod the Great.
		d. A.D. 20	FENESTELLA		
		143–87	M. ANTONIUS		
		114–50	HORTENSIUS } orators		
		106–43	CICERO		
		82–47	CALVUS		
		116–27	VARRO		
		c. 112–17	ORBILIUS } scholars and critics		
		109–32	ATTICUS		
		64–A.D. 17	HYGINUS		
		fl. c. 10	VERRIUS FLACCUS		
		fl. c. 50–26	VITRUVIUS, architectural writer		
		c. 70–8	MAECENAS, patron of literature		
A.D.		**A.D.**		**A.D.**	
37–c. 100	JOSEPHUS } historians	15 B.C.–A.D. 19	GERMANICUS } poets	9	Defeat of Varus.
c. 46–120	PLUTARCH	fl. c. 14	MANLIUS	14	Accession of Tiberius.
fl. c. 80	DION CHRYSOSTOM, orator	fl. c. 30	PHAEDRUS	19	Death of Germanicus.
fl. c. 39	PHILO JUDAEUS, philosopher	34–62	PERSIUS	23–31	Sejanus Prefect of Praetorians.

A.D.	Greek authors	A.D.	Latin authors	A.D.	Contemporary events
1st c.	DIOSCURIDES, botanist	39–65	LUCAN } poets	27	Tiberius retires to Capri.
1st c. (?)	'LONGINUS ON THE SUBLIME', critic	d. c. 90	VALERIUS FLACCUS	37	Accession of Gaius (Caligula).
		c. 40–96	STATIUS	41	Accession of Claudius.
		c. 25–101	SILIUS ITALICUS	43	Conquest of Britain begun.
		c. 40–104	MARTIAL	54	Accession of Nero.
		fl. c. 14	VELLEIUS PATERCULUS } historians	59	Murder of Agrippina.
		fl. c. 15	VALERIUS MAXIMUS	61	Rising under Boadicea.
		1st c.	Q. CURTIUS	64	Fire of Rome.
		c. 55–117	TACITUS	65	Conspiracy of Piso.
		fl. c. 100(?)	FLORUS	68	Accession of Galba.
		c. 55 B.C.–A.D. 37	SENECA THE ELDER } orators and rhetoricians	69	Accession of Otho.
		c. 35–95	QUINTILIAN	"	Accession of Vitellius.
		61–113	PLINY THE YOUNGER	"	Accession of Vespasian.
		fl. c. 37	PALAEMON } scholars	70	Capture of Jerusalem by Titus.
		fl. c. 80	PROBUS		
		23–79	PLINY THE ELDER } other prose writers	79	Accession of Titus.
		fl. c. 14	CELSUS	"	Destruction of Herculaneum and Pompeii.
		fl. c. 43	POMPONIUS MELA	81	Accession of Domitian.
		c. 4 B.C.–A.D. 65	SENECA THE YOUNGER	96	Accession of Nerva.
		d. 65	PETRONIUS	98	Accession of Trajan.
		fl. 65	COLUMELLA		
		c. 40–103	FRONTINUS		
c. 60–140	EPICTETUS } philosophers	c. 65–140	JUVENAL, poet	117	Accession of Hadrian.
121–180	M. AURELIUS	c. 70–160	SUETONIUS } historians	122	Hadrian in Britain.
fl. c. 100	BABRIUS, fabulist	2nd c.	JUSTIN	138	Accession of Antoninus Pius.
c. 95–175	ARRIAN } historians	fl. c. 150	GELLIUS, critic	161	Accession of Marcus Aurelius.
fl. c. 160	APPIAN	c. 110–180	GAIUS, jurist		
c. 200	AELIAN, anecdotist	fl. 143	FRONTO, rhetorician	167	Barbarian invasions of Dacia, &c.
2nd c.	PTOLEMY } geographers	c. 155	APULEIUS, novelist	180	Accession of Commodus.
fl. c. 170	PAUSANIAS	c. 150–230	TERTULLIAN, ecclesiastical writer	193	Accession of Pertinax.
2nd c.	APOLLONIUS DYSCOLUS } grammarians and critics			"	Accession of Julianus.
fl. 180	HERODIAN			"	Accession of Septimius Severus.
fl. c. 200	JULIUS POLLUX				
	ALEXANDER OF APHRODISIAS				
101–177	HERODES ATTICUS, rhetorician				

100

A.D.	Greek authors	A.D.	Latin authors	A.D.	Contemporary events
c. 115–200	LUCIAN				
c. 129–199	GALEN				
fl. c. 190	SEXTUS EMPIRICUS ⎫ other				
fl. c. 200	ALCIPHRON ⎬ prose				
" c. 160–215	ATHENAEUS ⎪ writers				
	CLEMENT OF ALEXANDRIA ⎭				
200					
fl. c. 215	OPPIAN, poet	c. 200–258	CYPRIAN ⎫ ecclesiastical	208	Severus in Britain.
c. 150–235	DIO CASSIUS ⎬ historians	b. c. 250	LACTANTIUS ⎭ writers	211	Severus dies at York, succeeded by Caracalla.
c. 165–250	HERODIAN	fl. c. 205	PAPINIAN ⎫ jurists	251	Invasions of empire by Goths and other barbarians begin.
185–254	ORIGEN, ecclesiastical writer	d. 228	ULPIAN ⎭	271	Barbarian invaders of Italy defeated by Aurelian.
b. c. 205	PLOTINUS	3rd c.?	SOLINUS, epitomizer	272	Aurelian defeats Zenobia and takes Palmyra.
220–278	CASSIUS LONGINUS ⎬ philosophers			284	Accession of Diocletian.
233–c. 301	PORPHYRY			293	Two Caesars appointed under the two Augusti.
3rd c. ?	XENOPHON OF EPHESUS ⎫				
" ?	HELIODORUS ⎬ novelists				
" ?	LONGUS				
fl. c. 210	PHILOSTRATUS III ⎫ other				
c. 200–250	DIOGENES LAERTIUS ⎬ prose writers				
300					
265–340	EUSEBIUS, ecclesiastical historian and chronologer	c. 310–395	AUSONIUS ⎫ poets	305	Abdication of Diocletian.
c. 314–393	LIBANIUS ⎫ rhetoricians	fl. c. 400	CLAUDIAN ⎬	306	Constantius dies at York. Accession of Constantine.
	THEMISTIUS ⎭	b. 348	PRUDENTIUS ⎭	312	Conversion of Constantine to Christianity.
fl. c. 360	IAMBLICHUS, philosopher	4th c. (?)	Authors of the *Historia Augusta*	325	Council of Nicaea.
d. c. 330	Q. SMYRNAEUS ⎫ poets	fl. 364	EUTROPIUS ⎫ historians	330	Constantinople adopted as capital.
fl. c. 400	NONNUS ⎭	c. 330–400	AMMIANUS ⎭	337	Death of Constantine.
		fl. c. 353	AELIUS DONATUS ⎫ scholars	361–3	Reign of Julian the Apostate.
		fl. c. 400	SERVIUS ⎬ and critics	363	Jovian restores the Christian religion.
		"	MACROBIUS ⎭	379	Accession of Theodosius.
		340–397	AMBROSE ⎫ ecclesiastical	383	Maximus ruler in Britain and Gaul.
		c. 340–420	JEROME ⎬ writers		
		354–405	AUGUSTINE ⎭		
		345–405	SYMMACHUS, orator		
		early 4th c.	NONIUS, lexicographer		
		c. 380	VEGETIUS, military writer		

A.D.	Greek authors	A.D.	Latin authors	A.D.	Contemporary events
				388	Maximus defeated and killed.
				390	Theodosius obliged by Ambrose to do penance for massacre at Thessalonica.
				394	Honorius emperor of the west, with Stilicho as general.
				396	Alaric and Goths in Greece.
400					
5th c.	PALLADAS, poet				
" "	ZOSIMUS, historian				
fl. c. 500	HESYCHIUS, lexicographer	fl. c. 470	APOLLINARIS SIDONIUS, poet	403	Alaric defeated by Stilicho in Italy.
	STOBAEUS, excerptor	fl. c. 417	OROSIUS, historian	406	Stilicho defeats Germans under Radagaisus.
c. 370–413	SYNESIUS } philosophers	5th c.	MARTIANUS CAPELLA, encyclopaedist	408	Disgrace and death of Stilicho.
d. 415	HYPATIA			410	Sack of Rome by Alaric.
c. 411–485	PROCLUS			c. 425	Evacuation of Britain.
				451	Aetius defeats Huns under Attila.
				455	Vandals plunder Rome.
				476	End of western empire.
500					
fl. c. 530	PROCOPIUS, historian	c. 480–524	BOETHIUS, Christian writer	527	Accession of Justinian.
		fl. c. 500	PRISCIAN, critic	529	Schools of Athens closed.

TABLE OF WEIGHTS AND MEASURES

(All English equivalents are only approximate)

GREEK

Weights (commercial).

		(Aeginetan and commercial Attic standard)
2 ἡμιώβολα	= 1 ὀβολός	= 0·036 oz.
6 ὀβολοί	= 1 δραχμή	= 0·22 oz.
12 „	= 1 στατήρ	= 0·43 oz.
100 δραχμαί	= 1 μνᾶ	= 1·39 lb.
6,000 „	= 1 τάλαντον	= 83·5 lb.

Distance.

		(Attic standard)
2 δάκτυλοι ('finger's breadths')	= 1 κόνδυλος	= 1·46 in.
16 „	= 1 πούς	= 11·65 in.
20 „	= 1 πυγών	= 1·21 ft.
24 „	= 1 πῆχυς	= 1·46 ft.
2½ πόδες	= 1 βῆμα	= 2 ft. 5 in.
6 „	= 1 ὄργυια	= 5·8 ft.
100 „	= 1 πλέθρον	= 97 ft.
600 „	= 1 στάδιον	= 582 ft.
30 στάδια	= 1 παρασάγγης	= 3·3 miles

Square measure.

The unit is a square πλέθρον	= 9424·5 sq. ft.	= ⅖ acre
50 πλέθρα	= 1 γύης	= 11 acres

Capacity (liquid and dry measures).

The unit is a κύαθος (=0·08 English pint).

	1½ κύαθοι	= 1 ὀξύβαφον	= 0·12 pint
	6 „	= 1 κοτύλη	= 0·48 pint
	12 „	= 1 ξέστης	= 0·96 pint
(dry measures only)	4 κοτύλαι	= 1 χοῖνιξ	= 1·92 pints
	48 χοίνικες	= 1 μέδιμνος	= 11 gallons 4 pints
(liquid measure only)	864 κύαθοι	= 1 ἀμφορεύς (= 1 μετρητής)	= 8 gallons 5 pints

ROMAN

Weights.

3 grana hordei ('barley-corns') = 1 siliqua
144 siliquae   = 1 uncia   = 0·96 oz.
1,728   „   *or* 12 unciae   = 1 as *or* libra   = 0·72 lb.

Distance.

1⅓ digiti	= 1 uncia	= 0·97 in.
12 unciae	= 1 pes	= 0·97 ft.
5 pedes	= 1 passus	= 4 ft. 10 in.
1,000 passus	= 1 Roman mile	= 1,620 yards

Square measure.

1 jugerum = ⅝ acre

Capacity (liquid and dry measures).

The unit is a coclear or ligula (a 'spoonful') = 0·02 pint

4 coclearia	= 1 cyathus	=	0·08 pint
6 „	= 1 acetabulum	=	0·12 pint
2 acetabula	= 1 quartarius	=	0·24 pint
2 quartarii	= 1 hemina	=	0·48 pint
2 heminae	= 1 sextarius	=	0·96 pint

(dry measures only)
8 sextarii	= 1 semimodius	=	7·68 pints
2 semimodii	= 1 modius	=	1 gallon 7 pints

(liquid measures only)
12 heminae *or* 6 sextarii	= 1 congius	=	5·76 pints
8 congii	= 1 cadus *or* amphora	=	5 gallons 6 pints
20 amphorae	= 1 culleus	=	115 gallons

DESCRIPTION OF FIGURES

1. GREEK AND ROMAN HOUSES

(a) General plan of a typical fifth-century Greek house.
- A. πρόθυρον (porch)
- B. ἡ αὔλειος θύρα (main entrance)
- C. αὐλή (a courtyard flanked by a colonnade and sleeping-chambers)
- D. Altar
- E. Sleeping-rooms, store-rooms, &c.
- F. Andronitis (men's quarters)
- G. Gunaikonitis (women's quarters)
- H. ἡ βαλανωτὴ θύρα (a bolted door)
- K. ἡ μέταυλος θύρα
- P. ? παστάς

The exact nature and purpose of K and P are doubtful. The women's quarters were sometimes situated on a second story. From B. C. Rider's *The Greek House*, fig. 40 (Cambridge University Press).

(b) House of the Vettii at Pompeii. Houses like this were common in classical times in places where space was not lacking. The rooms are grouped round the *ātria* and the peristyle, and by this means the house is mainly lighted, the windows overlooking the street being few and small. The entrance is by the *vestibulum* (bottom of plan) through the *fauces* to the main *atrium*; a smaller *atrium* is to be seen to the right. About this are rooms for slaves and a kitchen (B). In early Roman houses family life centred round the *atrium*; but in later times it became a public reception room. A-A indicate *ālae*, rooms in which the *imāgines* of noble families stood. There is no *tablīnum* in this example. C-C-C are dining-rooms. The peristyle, a feature borrowed from Greece, is a courtyard garden. Besides the main peristyle there is a smaller peristyle below the large apartment D. A second story ran along the street front and covered part of the rest of the house. For a reconstruction of the external appearance see A. Mau's *Pompeii, its life and art*, Engl. transl., fig. 158 (Macmillan & Co., Ltd.), from which this figure is taken.

(c, d) The so-called Casa di Diana at Ostia. Houses of this type, which are much closer to modern buildings than (b), have been found in some numbers in the commercial town of Ostia, where lack of space led to vertical rather than horizontal development in building. Light is given by windows overlooking the street, though in this example there is also a courtyard in the centre of the block. The ground floor of buildings like this often consisted of shops or warehouses. One or two sets of stairs gave access to the upper stories, which were divided into sets of apartments varying in size. Note the projecting balcony above the second floor, a common feature in this type at Ostia. The *insulae* or blocks of flats, referred to by Martial and Juvenal, probably resembled these Ostian houses, except that in many cases the sets of apartments must have been smaller and more squalid. From G. Calza's *Ostia: Guido storico monumentale*, figs. 18 and 20 (Fratelli Treves Editori, Milan).

2. ROMAN VILLAS AND ROMAN CAMP

(a) Villa at Spoonley Wood, Glos. A good example of the bipartite corridor type. The nucleus of the house is the SE. side, where a long rectangular building is fronted by a veranda-like corridor. At each end of this block is a deep wing, a very common feature in British villas. The chief living rooms seem to have been in the SE. side; of the wings, that to the SW. contained baths and other well-warmed rooms for winter use; that to the NE. unheated rooms. This wing is cut off from the rest of the house and may have been given over to slaves. Note the depth of the wings and the complete enclosure of the court-yard. The whole measures 170 feet by 190 feet. For types of Roman villas in Britain see R. G. Collingwood's *Archaeology of Roman Britain*, chap. 7 (Methuen & Co., Ltd.), from which this example is taken.

(b) Villa at Mayen near Coblenz. Excavation on this site has revealed eight or possibly nine stages in the construction of the central buildings, and as a result light has been thrown both on the nature of the villa as such and on the development of the corridor house. It is now possible to see the villa system gradually developing out of an earlier native economy of isolated farms. The original building at Mayen is a farmhouse of the La Tène culture. It was an oblong structure, like a barn. This discovery disproves the theory that the corridor in a corridor house was the living room and the rectangular block behind it an open courtyard. In the Mayen villa the corridor was certainly added to the original building. The rooms at the ends of the central hall, one of which was probably a tower, are also later additions, but there is no sign of the development of wings, as at Spoonley. From A. Grenier, *Manuel d'archéologie Gallo-romaine*, vol. vi, pl. ii, fig. 271 (A. Picard, Paris), after Oelmann, *Bonn. Jahrb.*, 1928.

(c) Plan of Roman camp. A legionary camp of the late republican period. From H. Stuart Jones's *Companion to Roman History*, p. 230.

3 *and* 4. GREEK AND ROMAN ARMOUR

3. (a) Greek hoplite. In this drawing the hoplite holds a helmet (κράνος) (normally of bronze, though sometimes of leather) in his right hand; in his left a spear (δόρυ) and leather shield (ἀσπίς), with metal rim and boss. The device painted on the latter is customary: such a device, in the fifth century, often represented the badge of the State to which the man belonged. The main protection of the body is the θώραξ, a cuirass of leather or linen with metal plates. Below it the groin is covered by leather πτέρυγες. On his legs the hoplite wears bronze greaves (κνημῖδες). On his left side, beneath his shield, is a short sword (ξίφος). The dress is completed by a cloak, taken off for battle, and not represented in this drawing, and by a χλανίς or jerkin worn beneath the breast-plate. After P. Gardner and F. B. Jevons, *Manual of Greek Antiquities*, fig. 13.

(b) Greek peltast. In the fourth century B.C. the heavy armour of the hoplite went out of favour and the lighter style of the peltast was introduced. For the hoplite's shield was substituted a light flat shield called a πέλτη, which was not covered with metal. The θώραξ gave way to a linen corslet. The helmet and greaves were maintained. The whole equipment allowed of great mobility whilst permitting a certain amount of hand-to-hand fighting. From Gulick's *Life of the Ancient Greeks*, fig. 183 (Appleton-Century Co.).

4. Roman soldiers:

1. End of first century B.C. (Augustan period). *Foot-soldier*: Attic helmet with Phrygian crest; long plated cuirass, fringed; rectangular shield; Iberian sword.

2. Same period. *Foot-soldier*: Helmet with button top of the Weisenau type; plated cuirass, fringed; rectangular shield; Iberian sword on right side with cross belt and sword belt; *pilum*, reinforced by metal cone; sleeved tunic and breeches (for service in cold climates).

3. Same period. *Cavalryman*: Helmet of the Weisenau type with double mane; coat of mail with half-sleeves; large oval shield; Iberian sword worn on left side with cross belt; *hasta*.

4. Same period. *Marine*: Etrusco-Corinthian helmet; large leather cuirass shaped to the body; large oval shield, no boss; leather leggings, lace-boots; *hasta*.

5. First century A.D. *Cavalryman*: Short plated cuirass, fringed; Attic helmet, with representation of hair; hexagonal shield; Iberian sword with double knob, worn on right side on sword belt; spear.

6. Same period; *Legionary*: Attic-Roman helmet of the Weisenau type; leather coat, probably with a coat of mail underneath it; fringed breeches; Iberian sword, cross belt; *cingulum mīlitiae*; *pilum*, reinforced by metal cone.

Figures and descriptions from P. Couissin's *Les Armes romaines*, pl. 3.

5. GREEK AND ROMAN THEATRES

(a) Theatre at Epidaurus in the Peloponnese, the best preserved of Greek theatres. Built in the fourth century B.C. The plan shows: 1. The orchestra, where the chorus danced (the mark in the centre represents an altar, the θυμέλη). 2. The stage, where the actors usually stood (λογεῖον or προσκήνιον). 3. The σκήνη, the permanent background to the action, originally of wood, later of stone. 4. The πάροδοι, entrances to the theatre for the spectators, to the orchestra for the chorus. 5. The auditorium, divided by radial passages into κερκίδες and horizontally by διαζώματα. (From Haigh's *Attic Theatre*, Ed. 3, p. 104.)

(b) Theatre at Pompeii, probably second century B.C., with alterations later. On the plan are shown: 1. The *postscaenium* or dressing-room. 2. The stage (*scaena*). 3. The orchestra, in Roman theatres usually filled with seats for persons of importance. 4. The *īma cavea*, also reserved for important persons and separated from the *media cavea* (5) by a *praecinctio*. The *media cavea* contained the bulk of the seats, the *summa cavea* (6) being very small. 7. *Tribūnālia*, small rectangular platforms over the vaulted entrances, reserved for the magistrate who gave the play and for priestesses. 8. A tank of saffron water. This theatre is mainly of the Greek type, but illustrates innovations made by the Romans (e.g. seats in the orchestra, covered πάροδοι, &c. And the stage at Pompeii was much lower than that at Epidaurus. From A. Mau's *Pompeii, its life and art*, Engl. transl., fig. 62 (Macmillan & Co., Ltd.).

6. GREEK AND ROMAN TEMPLES

(a) The Parthenon, built 447–438 B.C. The temple proper divides into two parts. To the east was the larger room, the shrine (ναός or *cella*) which contained the statue of the goddess. In front of this was a columned porch, the *pronāos*. The smaller room was the Parthenon proper, and this and the porch behind it (the *opisthodomos*) were used as treasuries. The whole was surrounded by a peristyle of 46 columns. The temple is of the type classified by Vitruvius as peripteral. From *Companion to Greek Studies*, edited by L. Whibley, fig. 27a, 4a (Cambridge University Press).

(b) The Maison Carrée at Nîmes, built by Antoninus Pius (d. 161 A.D.). A simple temple of the pseudo-peripteral type. In front of the *cella* is a portico. The temple stands on a platform (*podium*) 11 feet high and is reached by a flight of 19 steps. From W. J. Anderson, R. Phené Spiers, and T. Ashby, *Architecture of Ancient Rome*, fig. 17 (B. T. Batsford, Ltd.).

(c) Romano-Celtic temple near Harlow, Essex. In this type of building the simple rectangular *cella* of native design is modified by the addition of a verandah or portico, probably due to Roman influence. The portico is not, however, as in classical temples, of equal height with the roof of the *cella*. The latter is carried up some way beyond the portico roof, and light is let into the shrine by clerestory windows. The forebuilding, which may have been a raised platform, is very unusual in Romano-Celtic temples. The site (on a hill-top) is normal. Worship in these temples, which are only found north of the Alps, was usually to native deities, less often to Romanized native deities. Third or fourth century A.D. From an article by R. E. M. Wheeler in *The Antiquaries Journal*, April, 1928 (Society of Antiquaries of London).

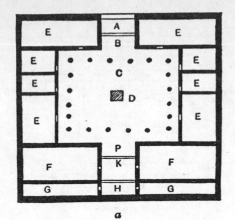

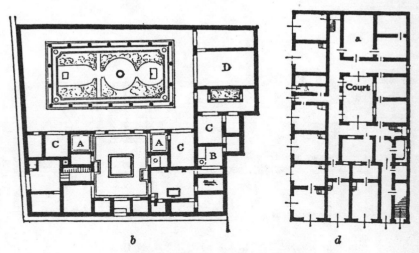

1. GREEK AND ROMAN HOUSES

(For explanation see page 465.)

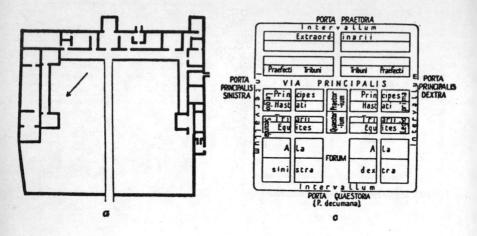

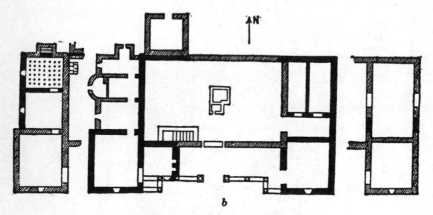

2. ROMAN VILLAS AND ROMAN CAMP
(*For explanation see pages 465–6.*)

3. GREEK ARMOUR

(For explanation see page 466.)

4. ROMAN ARMOUR

(For explanation see pages 486–7.)

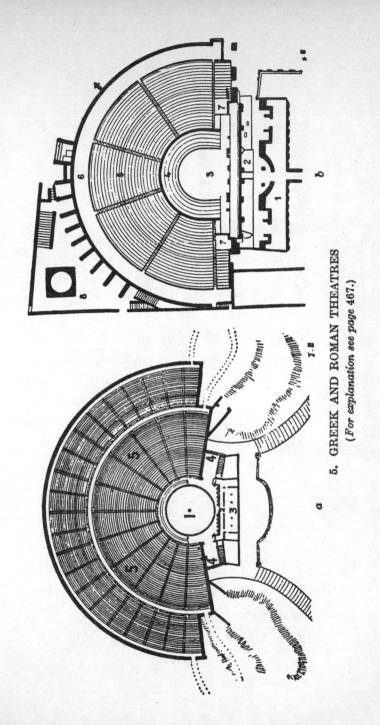

5. GREEK AND ROMAN THEATRES

(*For explanation see page 467.*)

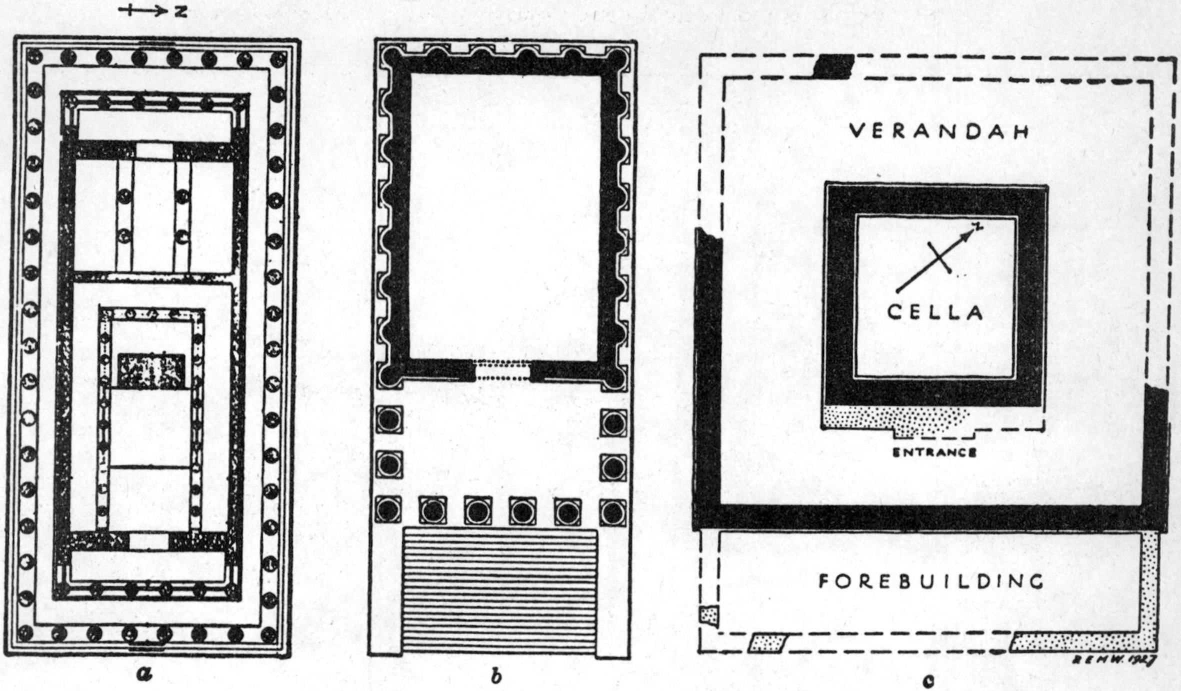

N

VERANDAH

CELLA

ENTRANCE

FOREBUILDING

REAR WALL

c

b

a

N

6. GREEK AND ROMAN TEMPLES

(*For explanation see pages 467–8.*)

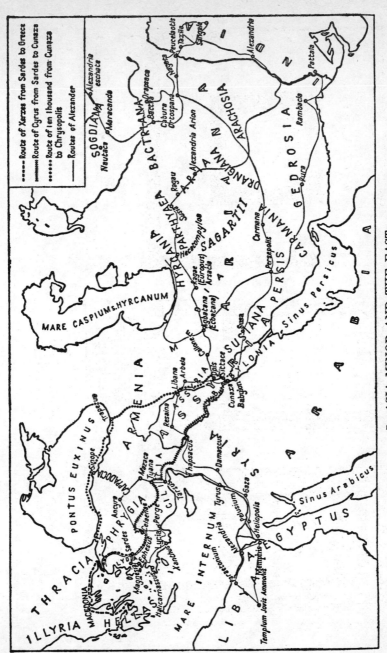

7. ASIA MINOR AND THE EAST

Routes of Xerxes, Cyrus, Alexander, and the March of the Ten Thousand

8. GREECE AND

ASIA MINOR

9. ROMAN

SARMATIA

Tanais

MARE CASPIUM (Hyrcanium)

CIA

PONTUS EUXINUS

IBERIA

Tomi

Sinope

ARMENIA

MEDIA

Philippopolis
Adrianopolis
Byzantium

PONTUS

MEDIA ATROPATENE

MEDIA MAJOR

THRACIA

Nicomedia

BITHYNIA
Niccea

GALATIA

Ancyra

Caesarea

CAPPADOCIA

MESOPOTAMIA

Pharsalus

S I A

Lycaonia

Edessa

Susa

Lesbos

Pergamum

Sardes

Apamea

CILICIA

Ctesiphon

Thebae

Ephesus

PAMPHYL.

Tarsus

Antiochia

BABYLON=I=A

Athenae

LYCIA

S

Palmyra

A CHAIA

Rhodus

Cyprus

Y

Cythera

Xanthus

Berytus

Damascus

Cnossus

Caesarea

R

E

Cyrene

NUM

Pelusium

Cyrene et Cyrenaica

CRETA ET CYRENAICA

Alexandria

Petra

ARABIA

A R A B I A

DESERTA

Memphis

A E G Y P T U S

Thebae

Syene

EMPIRE

10. ITALY

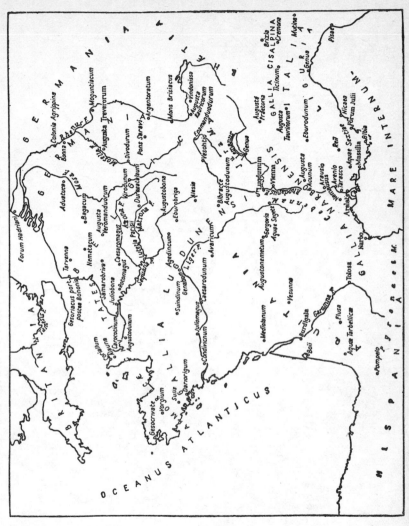

11. GAUL

12. ROMAN BRITAIN

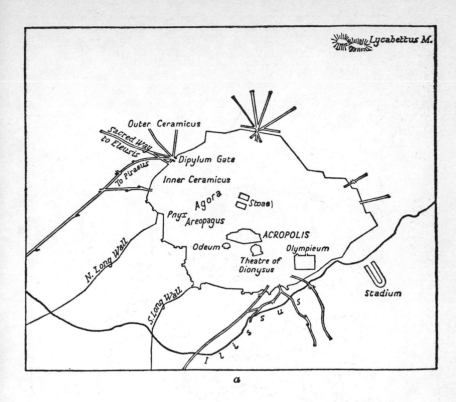

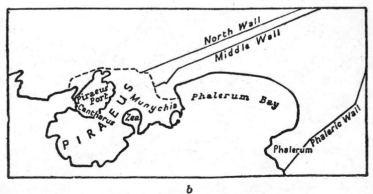

13. *a* ATHENS. *b* PIRAEUS

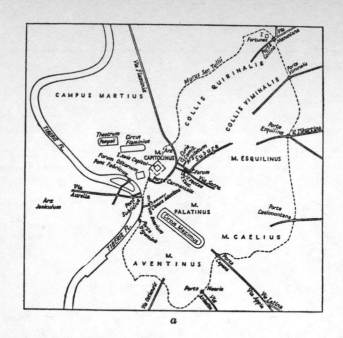

a

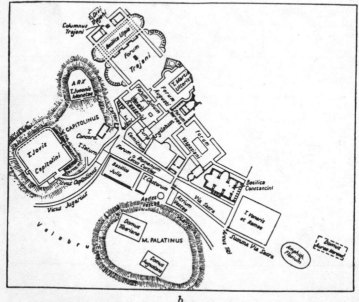

b

14. *a* ROME UNDER THE REPUBLIC
b CENTRE OF ROME UNDER THE EARLY EMPIRE